Turkey

Tom Brosnahan
Pat Yale
Richard Plunkett

LONELY PLANET PUBLICATIONS
Melbourne • Oakland • London • Paris

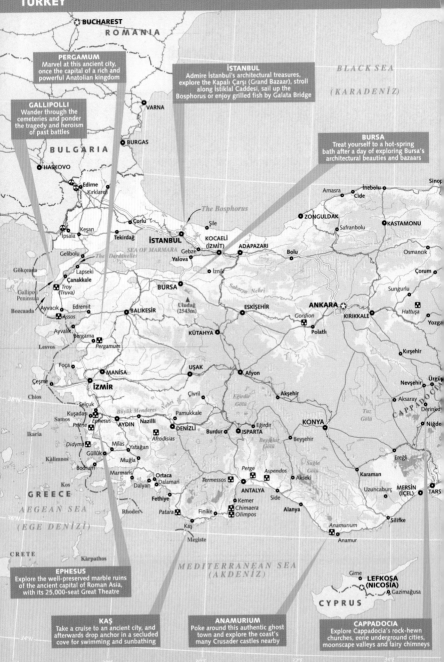

PERGAMUM
Marvel at this ancient city, once the capital of a rich and powerful Anatolian kingdom

İSTANBUL
Admire İstanbul's architectural treasures, explore the Kapalı Çarşı (Grand Bazaar), stroll along İstiklal Caddesi, sail up the Bosphorus or enjoy grilled fish by Galata Bridge

GALLIPOLI
Wander through the cemeteries and ponder the tragedy and heroism of past battles

BURSA
Treat yourself to a hot-spring bath after a day of exploring Bursa's architectural beauties and bazaars

BLACK SEA
(KARADENİZ)

ROMANIA

☆ BUCHAREST

BULGARIA

VARNA

BURGAS

HASKOVO

Edirne
Kırklareli

İpsala

Keşan

Çorlu

Tekirdağ

Gelibolu

Gökçeada

Lapseki

Çanakkale

Gallipoli
Peninsula

Bozcaada

Ayvacık

Assos

Lesvos

Ayvalık

Bergama

Pergamum

Foça

Çeşme

Chios

İZMİR

MANİSA

Selçuk
Kuşadası
Ephesus
Priene
Samos
AYDIN
Nazilli

Ikaria

Didyma

Güllük
Milas
Yatağan

Kalimnos

Bodrum

Kos

Marmaris

GREECE

Ortaca
Dalaman

Dalyan

Fethiye

Rhodes

Patara

Kaş

Megiste

CRETE

Karpathos

Troy
(Truva)

Edremit

BALIKESİR

KÜTAHYA

UŞAK

Çivril

Pamukkale

DENİZLİ

Afrodisias

Muğla

Şile

The Bosphorus

İSTANBUL

The Dardanelles

SEA OF MARMARA

Gebze

Yalova

KOCAELİ
(İZMİT)

ADAPAZARI

İznik

BURSA

Uludağ
(2543m)

ESKİŞEHİR

Afyon

Akşehir

Egirdir
Gölü

Burdur

Eğirdir

ISPARTA

Beyşehir
Gölü

Beyşehir

Termessos

ANTALYA

Perge

Aspendos

Akseki

Side

Alanya

Kemer

Finike

Chimaera
Olimpos

Bolu

Sakarya Nehri

ANKARA ☆

Gordion

Polatlı

Tuz
Gölü

KONYA

Büyük Menderes Nehri

Amasra

Cide

İnebolu

Sinop

ZONGULDAK

Safranbolu

KASTAMONU

Osmancık

Çorum

Sungurlu

KIRIKKALE

Hattuşa

Yozgat

Kırşehir

Nevşehir

Ürgüp

Aksaray

CAPPADOCIA

Derinkuyu

Niğde

Ereğli

Karaman

Uzuncaburç

MERSİN
(İÇEL)

TARS

Silifke

Anamurium

Anamur

Girne

LEFKOŞA
(NICOSIA)

Gazimağusa

CYPRUS

Süğla
Gölü

AEGEAN SEA
(EGE DENİZİ)

MEDITERRANEAN SEA
(AKDENİZ)

EPHESUS
Explore the well-preserved marble ruins of the ancient capital of Roman Asia, with its 25,000-seat Great Theatre

KAŞ
Take a cruise to an ancient city, and afterwards drop anchor in a secluded cove for swimming and sunbathing

ANAMURIUM
Poke around this authentic ghost town and explore the coast's many Crusader castles nearby

CAPPADOCIA
Explore Cappadocia's rock-hewn churches, eerie underground cities, moonscape valleys and fairy chimneys

36°N

34°N

26°E

28°E

30°E

32°E

ELEVATION

3000m
2000m
1500m
1000m
500m
0

SUMELA
Visit this ancient monastery clinging to a sheer cliff, then take a hike into the Kaçkar Mountains beyond

NEMRUT DAĞI
Visit the mighty stone heads on the summit and take in the spectacular views

RUSSIA

GEORGIA

TBILISI

Vladikavkaz

Sokhumi

Kutaisi

Batumi

Hopa

Artvin

VANADZOR

GYUMRI

Ani

YEREVAN
ARMENIA

AZERBAIJAN

Ozero
Sevan

Bafra

SAMSUN

Ünye
Ordu Giresun

TRABZON

Rize

Sumela

Gümüşhane

Bayburt

Kaçkar Dağı
(3937m)

Yusufeli

Göle

Kars

Sarıkamış

Amasya

Niksar

Koyulhisar

Tortum

Pasinler

Horasan

Tuzluca

Iğdır

Turhal

Tokat

Suşehri

Zara

Refahiye

Erzincan

ERZURUM

Ağrı

Mt Ararat
(Ağrı Dağı)
(5137m)

Doğubayazıt

AZERBAIJAN

SİVAS

Tercan

Patnos

Muradiye

IRAN

Divriği

Tunceli

Bingöl

Qzalp

ELAZIĞ

Muş

Tatvan

Van
Gölü

VAN

Kayseri

MALATYA

Bitlis

Cevaş

Gürpınar

Çatak

Darya-che
Orümiye

Göksun

Elbistan

Gölbaşı

Adıyaman

Nemrut Dağı

DİYARBAKIR

Kurtalan

Siirt

Şırnak

Orümiye

Hakkari

Yüksekova

Cilo Dağı
(4168m)

Kahramanmaraş

Siverek

Hilvan

Viranşehir

Mardin

Karatepe

GAZİANTEP

Atatürk
Barajı

ŞANLIURFA

Qamishle

OSMANİYE

Birecik

Kozan

ADANA

İSKENDERUN

Kırıkhan

Mosul

Arbîl

Antakya

Aleppo
(Halab)

Sabhat
al-Gabbûl

Euphrates
River

IRAQ

Kirkûk

Lattakia

SYRIA

Deir ez-Zur

Homs

TRIPOLI

Murkhafad
al-Tharthar

0   75   150km
0   45   90mi

Turkey
7th edition – March 2001
First published – July 1985

Published by
Lonely Planet Publications Pty Ltd ABN 36 005 607 983
90 Maribyrnong St, Footscray, Victoria 3011, Australia

Lonely Planet Offices
Australia Locked Bag 1, Footscray, Victoria 3011
USA 150 Linden St, Oakland, CA 94607
UK 10a Spring Place, London NW5 3BH
France 1 rue du Dahomey, 75011 Paris

Photographs
All of the images in this guide are available for licensing from
Lonely Planet Images.
email: lpi@lonelyplanet.com.au

Front cover photograph
Much of Turkish life revolves around tea, served in tulip-shaped glasses
and advertised here outside a teahouse - Konya, South-Central Anatolia
(Pat Yale)

ISBN 1 86450 213 4

text & maps © Lonely Planet 2001
photos © photographers as indicated 2001

Printed by The Bookmaker International Ltd
Printed in China

All rights reserved. No part of this publication may be reproduced,
stored in a retrieval system or transmitted in any form by any means,
electronic, mechanical, photocopying, recording or otherwise, except
brief extracts for the purpose of review, without the written permission
of the publisher and copyright owner.

LONELY PLANET and the Lonely Planet logo are trademarks of Lonely
Planet Publications Pty Ltd.

Although the authors
and Lonely Planet try
to make the informa-
tion as accurate as
possible, we accept
no responsibility for
any loss, injury or
inconvenience sus-
tained by anyone
using this book.

Contents – Text

THE AUTHORS   7

THIS BOOK   9

FOREWORD   10

INTRODUCTION   13

FACTS ABOUT TURKEY   15

History 15
Geography 27
Climate 27
Ecology & Environment 28
Flora & Fauna 28
Government & Politics 29
Economy 30
Population & People 30
Education 33
Arts 33
Turkish Arts & Crafts 37
Society & Conduct 42
Religion 44
Language 45

FACTS FOR THE VISITOR   46

Suggested Itineraries 46
Planning 47
Responsible Tourism 49
Tourist Offices 49
Visas & Documents 50
Embassies & Consulates 52
Customs 53
Money 54
Post & Communications 57
Internet Resources 59
Books 59
Films 61
Newspapers & Magazines 61
Radio & TV 61
Video Systems 62
Photography & Video 62
Time 62
Electricity 62
Weights & Measures 62
Laundry 63
Toilets 63
Health 63
Women Travellers 72
Gay & Lesbian Travellers 73
Disabled Travellers 73
Senior Travellers 73
Travel with Children 73
Dangers & Annoyances 74
Emergencies 76
Legal Matters 77
Business Hours 77
Public Holidays &
Special Events 77
Activities 79
Courses 80
Work 80
Accommodation 80
Food 81
Drinks 86
Entertainment 87
Spectator Sports 87
Shopping 88

GETTING THERE & AWAY   91

Air 91
Land 96
Sea 100

GETTING AROUND   102

Air 102
Bus 102
Dolmuş 103
Train 104
Car 105
Motorcycle 108
Bicycle 108
Hitching 108
Boat 109
Local Transport 109
Organised Tours 110

İSTANBUL   111

History 113
Orientation 115
Information 124
Old İstanbul 126
Topkapı Palace Museum 127
The Golden Horn 143
Western Districts 144
Beyoğlu 145
Special Events 151
Places to Stay 151
Places to Eat 157
Entertainment 162
Shopping 166
Getting There & Away 167
Getting Around 172
Around İstanbul 175
The Bosphorus 175
The Princes' Islands 184

THRACE 186

Edirne 186
East of Edirne 195
South of Edirne 196
Gallipoli Peninsula 196
Çanakkale 208
Gökçeada 213

NORTH AEGEAN TURKEY 216

Troy 216
Around Troy 220
Bozcaada 221
Assos (Behramkale) 223
Around Behramkale 226
Ayvalık 226
Around Ayvalık 230
Dikili 230
Bergama (Pergamum) 231
Pergamum: Acropolis &
Asclepion 233
Çandarlı 238
Foça 238
Around Foça 240
Manisa 240
İzmir 241
Sardis (Sart) & Salihli 252
Çeşme 253
Around Çeşme 257
Sığacık 258
Akkum 258
Teos 258

SOUTH AEGEAN TURKEY 259

Selçuk 259
Meryemana (Mary's
House) 266
Ephesus (Efes) 266
Ephesus – A Walking Tour 269
Pamucak 274
Şirince 274
Belevi 275
Kuşadası 275
Dilek Peninsula 281
Priene, Miletus & Didyma ..282
Söke 285
Herakleia (Latmos) 285
Milas 286
Around Milas 288
Ören 290
Güllük 290
Bodrum 291
Bodrum Peninsula 300

WESTERN ANATOLIA 305

Yalova 305
Termal 306
İznik 307
Bursa 311
Uludağ 325
Bandırma 326
Kuşcenneti Milli Parkı 326
Balıkesir 326
Eskişehir 327
Kütahya 329
Aizanoi (Çavdarhisar) 333
Midas Şehri 334
Around Midas Şehri 336
Afyon 336
Pamukkale Region 340
Aydın 340
Nyssa 341
Nazilli 341
Around Nazilli 342
Afrodisias 342
Denizli 345
Pamukkale 346
Around Pamukkale 351
Lake District 352
Isparta 352
Sagalassos 353
Eğirdir 354
Around Eğirdir 358
Burdur 359
Beyşehir 359
Yalvaç & Antioch-in-Pisidia 360

WESTERN MEDITERRANEAN TURKEY 361

Muğla 361
Around Muğla 364
Gökova (Akyaka) 364
Marmaris 364
Around Marmaris 371
Reşadiye & Daraçya
Peninsulas 371
Köyceğiz 376
Dalyan 377
Dalaman 382
Göcek 383
Around Göcek 384
Fethiye 384
Ölüdeniz 389
Butterfly Valley 392
Kayaköy (Karmylassos) 393
Tlos 393
Saklıkent Gorge 394
Pınara 394
Sidyma 394
Letoön 395
Xanthos 395
Patara 395
Kalkan 397
Around Kalkan 399
Kaş 400
Üçağız 404
Kaleköy 405
Kyaneai 405
Demre 405
Çağıllı & Gökliman 407
Finike 407
Kumluca to Olimpos 407
Olimpos & the Chimaera ..408
Tekirova 410
Phaselis 411
Kemer 412
Beldibi/Göynük 412
Antalya 412
Around Antalya 422

Contents – Text 3

EASTERN MEDITERRANEAN TURKEY 429

Side 429
Around Side 433
Alanya 434
Around Alanya 440
Anamur 440
Around Anamur 443
Taşucu 443
Silifke 445

Around Silifke 448
Uzuncaburç 449
Uzuncaburç to Konya 450
Kızkalesi 450
Around Kızkalesi 451
Mersin (İçel) 451
Tarsus 454
Adana 455

Around Adana 458
Osmaniye 460
Around Osmaniye 461
İskenderun 462
Around İskenderun 463
Antakya (Hatay) 463
Around Antakya 468

CENTRAL ANATOLIA 469

Ankara 470
Around Ankara 485
North Central Anatolia 487
Safranbolu 487
Around Safranbolu 491
Kastamonu 491
Around Kastamonu 493
Boyabat 493
Boğazkale, Hattuşa &
Yazılıkaya 493
Sungurlu 497
Alacahöyük 497
Yozgat 498
Çorum 498
Amasya 500
Around Amasya 505
Tokat 505
Around Tokat 509
Sivas 510

Around Sivas 515
South Central Anatolia 517
Konya 517
Around Konya 526
Sultanhanı 527
Cappadocia 527
Aksaray 530
Ihlara (Peristrema) 531
Güzelyurt 533
Uzun Yol 534
Nevşehir 534
Uçhisar 535
Göreme 537
Çavuşin 544
Zelve 544
Valley of the Fairy
Chimneys 545
Avanos 545
Around Avanos 547

Ortahisar 548
Ürgüp 548
Ayvalı & Damsa Gölü 552
Mustafapaşa 552
Soğanlı 556
Sultan Marshes
Bird Paradise 556
Niğde 557
Around Niğde 558
Karaman 559
Around Karaman 560
From Nevşehir to Ankara ...560
Gülşehir 560
Hacıbektaş 560
Kırşehir 562
Kayseri 562
Around Kayseri 568

BLACK SEA COAST 570

Amasra 572
Amasra to Sinop 574
Sinop 575
Samsun 578

East to Trabzon 581
Trabzon 585
Around Trabzon 593
Trabzon to Erzurum 594

East from Trabzon 595
Ayder 598
Hopa 600

EASTERN ANATOLIA 601

North-Eastern Anatolia 603
From Sivas to Erzurum 603
Erzurum 604
Around Erzurum 610
Georgian Valleys 611
Yusufeli 612
Around Yusufeli 613
Yusufeli to Kars 614
Artvin 615
Artvin to Kars 617
Erzurum to Kars 617
Kars 618
Ani 623

Kars to İğdir &
Doğubayazıt 626
Doğubayazıt 626
South-Eastern Anatolia 630
Kahramanmaraş 630
Gaziantep (Antep) 634
Around Gaziantep 639
Malatya 639
Elazığ 643
Harput 644
Adıyaman 644
Kahta 645
Nemrut Dağı Milli Parkı 647

Şanlıurfa (Urfa) 652
Harran 660
Around Harran 661
Diyarbakır 662
Mardin 669
Around Mardin 671
Bitlis 673
Tatvan 673
Van Gölü 674
Van 677
Around Van 682
Hakkari 683
North from Van 684

LANGUAGE   685

GLOSSARY   692

ACKNOWLEDGMENTS   695

INDEX   712

Text 711   Boxed Text &
                                        Special Sections 719

MAP LEGEND   back page

METRIC CONVERSION   inside back cover

Contents – Maps

İSTANBUL

Greater İstanbul (Map 1) 112	Karaköy, Eminönu &	Topkapı Palace –
İstanbul (Map 2)...........116-17	Süleymaniye (Map 4) 120-1	Topkapı Sarayı (Map 6) 128
İstiklal Caddesi	Sultanahmet	Aya Sofya (Map 7).............135
(Map 3) 118-19	(Map 5) 122-3	Kapalı Çarşı (Map 8) 141

THRACE

Thrace 187	Gallipoli Peninsula 197	Çanakkale.....................210-11
Edirne 188	Anzac Battlefields...............200	Gökçeada..........................214

NORTH AEGEAN TURKEY

North Aegean Turkey..........217	Bergama 231	Basmane Area 247
Troy 218	Acropolis 233	Çeşme 254
Bozcaada 222	Asclepion 235	
Ayvalık...............................227	İzmir 243	

SOUTH AEGEAN TURKEY

South Aegean Turkey..........260	Kuşadası............................276	Milas 287
Selçuk 262	Priene 282	Bodrum 293
Ephesus 270	Miletus...............................283	Bodrum Peninsula 301

WESTERN ANATOLIA

Western Anatolia 306	Central Bursa 316-17	Hierapolis..........................348
İznik...................................308	Kütahya 330	Pamukkale Town 349
Bursa 313	Afrodisias...........................343	Eğirdir 355

WESTERN MEDITERRANEAN TURKEY

Western Mediterranean	Around Fethiye 390	Kaleiçi...........................416-17
Turkey 362-3	Ölüdeniz & Belcekız..........391	Termessos 423
Marmaris 365	Kalkan 398	Perge 425
Dalyan 378	Kaş 401	
Fethiye 386-7	Antalya 413	

EASTERN MEDITERRANEAN TURKEY

Eastern Mediterranean	Anamur 441	Adana to Antakya 459
Turkey 430-1	Silifke................................446	Antakya (Hatay).................465
Side 432	Mersin (İçel)......................452	
Alanya 435	Adana 456	

CENTRAL ANATOLIA

Central Anatolia.................470	Tokat 506	Avanos...............................546
Ankara...............................472	Sivas 512	Ürgüp 549
Yenişehir 476	Konya 518	Niğde.................................557
Safranbolu-Çarşı 488	Cappadocia (Kapadokya) 529	Kayseri...............................563
Boğazkale 495	Ihlara Valley 531	
Amasya 501	Göreme 538	

BLACK SEA COAST

Black Sea Coast 572-3
Sinop 576
Trabzon 586
Atatürk Alanı 591

EASTERN ANATOLIA

North-Eastern Anatolia 602-3
Erzurum 605
Kars 619
Ani......................................624
Doğubayazıt 627
South-Eastern Anatolia 632-3
Gaziantep (Antep) 635
Malatya 640
Kahta..................................645
Nemrut Dağı Area 648
Şanlıurfa (Urfa) 654
Diyarbakır 664
Van 678

MAP LEGEND – SEE BACK PAGE

The Authors

Tom Brosnahan

Tom Brosnahan was born in Pennsylvania, went to college in Boston, then set out on the road. He first went to Turkey as a US Peace Corps volunteer, teaching English and learning Turkish. He studied Ottoman Turkish history and language for eight years, but abandoned the writing of his PhD dissertation in favour of writing guidebooks.

Since then, he has lived or travelled in Turkey every year or two for three decades, and his 35 guidebooks to various countries have sold nearly three million copies in 12 languages.

Tom is also the author of Lonely Planet's guide to *İstanbul* and has worked on other Lonely Planet titles, including the *Turkish phrasebook, Guatemala, Belize & Yucatán: La Ruta Maya, Mexico, Central America* and *New England*.

Pat Yale

Pat Yale first went to Turkey in 1974 in an old van that didn't look as if it would make it past Dover. After graduating she spent several years selling holidays before throwing away sensible careerdom to head overland from Egypt to Zimbabwe. Returning home, she mixed teaching with extensive travelling in Europe, Asia and Central and South America. A full-time writer now, she has worked on Lonely Planet's *Britain, Ireland, London, Dublin, Middle East* and assorted other titles. She currently lives in an old pasha's house in Göreme in Cappadocia.

Richard Plunkett

Richard grew up near Avenel, in central Victoria, Australia. Before joining Lonely Planet he worked on *The Age* newspaper in Melbourne, helped get the Australian *Big Issue* on its feet, and worked on the family farm during bouts of unemployment. He first visited Turkey in 1994. He has worked on the Lonely Planet's guides to *India, Indian Himalaya, Delhi, Central Asia* and *Bangladesh*. When not travelling he likes to do as little as possible.

FROM THE AUTHORS

Tom Brosnahan My thanks to Mr Selami Karaibrahimgil, director of the Turkish tourism office in New York City; Mr Mustafa Siyahhan of the Turkish Ministry of Tourism in Ankara; Mr Ersan Atsür of Orion-Tour in İstanbul; Mr Süha Ersöz of the Esbelli Evi in Ürgüp; Ms Ann Nevans of the Hotel Empress Zoe in İstanbul; and, as always, the Turkish people (especially the cooks!) who made my research trips so enjoyable.

Pat Yale As ever I have been overwhelmed by the help and hospitality of the Turkish people, but special thanks must go to: Adnan Pirioğlu in Ayder; Memet in Doğubayazıt, Volkan Özkan in Erzurum; Ahmet Baykal in Hattuşa; Roni Askey-Doran and Ken Dakan in İstanbul; Hüseyn Kaplan and Ahmet Bilge in Konya; Özcan Arslan in Şanlıurfa; Suha Ersoz in Ürgüp; and Remzi Bozbay in Van. I might still be battling with the technology required to see this book to the publishers were it not for Mustafa Güney at Göreme's Nese Internet Cafe. In Göreme, too, I'm especially grateful to Maggie Cassidy, Idris Demir, Dawn Köse, Nico Leyssen, Ruth Lockwood, Arif Şehirlioğlu, Kylie Warner, Ali Yavuz and all my lovely neighbours for answering my endless queries, feeding my cat and generally keeping the home fires burning. Finally, for support and encouragement in the last stressful days before the deadline, warm thanks to Paul Harding, Yilmaz Özlük and all the Kiğılı family at the Side Pension in İstanbul, in particular to Mahmut.

Richard Plunkett This list is by no means comprehensive – there are just so many people I should thank. Among those whose names I made a note of, thanks to Kathryn and Franklin Racine-Jones in Silifke for sharing the fare to Uzuncaburç; Father Marco Dondi in Antakya; Abuna Dimitri Yıldırım in Iskenderun; Clare in Olimpos; Halık and the lads in Marmaris; Bronwyn, Jimmy and Jesse in Selçuk; Cem and Diana in Behramkale; the Ünsal family; Kemal Özkurt and Juliette, Kevin O'Connor (where is that bell noise coming from?) and Yalçin in Antalya; Ahmet in Kaş; and TJ, Bee, Billy, Dean, Chantelle, Timon, Bulent, Polat and Yusuf in Eceabat. In Eğirdir thanks to Ahmet for showing me around and Ibrahim for all the trekking advice; thanks also to Lerent Sağdur in Kütahya; Mehmet and Andrew Eather in Afyon; and to Dan Malone and Roger Smith for accompanying me to Aizanoi. Belated thanks to Ted Buehl, who gave me the opportunity to drive unlicensed around Turkey in 1994 in pursuit of migrating waterfowl. Thanks to Pat Yale for her help and for the line about the POW camp, Tom Brosnahan for his experience and sage advice, and to Verity Campbell, Michelle Glynn, Anna Judd and Isabelle Young at LP. Thanks to the guy in the Marmaris bazaar with the sales pitch 'Everything is free! Well, almost free!'

Finally, thanks to my family, and to Scott Thiel, intrepid lawyer, Dardanelles swimmer and Tofaş driver.

This Book

Tom Brosnahan researched and wrote the first five editions of this book, and Pat Yale joined Tom in updating the 5th and 6th editions. For this 7th edition, Tom Brosnahan updated the introductory chapters, İstanbul and parts of the Thrace and Western Anatolia chapters; Pat Yale updated Central Anatolia, Black Sea Coast and Eastern Anatolia; and Richard Plunkett updated parts of Thrace and Western Anatolia, North Aegean Turkey, South Aegean Turkey, Western Mediterranean Turkey and Eastern Mediterranean Turkey.

From the Publisher

This edition of *Turkey* was edited in Lonely Planet's Melbourne office by Isabelle Young, with assistance from Jenny Mullaly, Alan Murphy, Michelle Glynn and Bethune Carmichael. Anna Judd coordinated the design and mapping, with assistance from Heath Comrie, Rodney Zandbergs, Hunor Csutoros, Csanad Csutoros, Sarah Sloane and Leanne Peake. Special thanks to Mick Weldon, Trudi Canavan, Kelli Hamblet and Verity Campbell for the illustrations; Daniel New for the cover design; Birgit Jordan and Hunor Csutoros for the climate charts; and Quentin Frayne for organising the Language chapter.

Last but by no means least, thanks to authors Tom, Pat and Richard for all their hard work.

THANKS
Many thanks to the travellers who used the last edition and wrote to us with helpful hints, advice and interesting anecdotes. Your names appear in the back of this book.

Foreword

ABOUT LONELY PLANET GUIDEBOOKS

The story begins, with a classic travel adventure: Tony and Maureen Wheeler's 1972 journey across Europe and Asia to Australia. Useful information about the overland trail did not exist at that time, so Tony and Maureen published the first Lonely Planet guidebook to meet a growing need.

From a kitchen table, then from a tiny office in Melbourne (Australia), Lonely Planet has become the largest independent travel publisher in the world, an international company with offices in Melbourne, Oakland (USA), London (UK) and Paris (France).

Today Lonely Planet guidebooks cover the globe. There is an ever-growing list of books and there's information in a variety of forms and media. Some things haven't changed. The main aim is still to help make it possible for adventurous travellers to get out there – to explore and better understand the world.

At Lonely Planet we believe travellers can make a positive contribution to the countries they visit – if they respect their host communities and spend their money wisely. Since 1986 a percentage of the income from each book has been donated to aid projects and human rights campaigns.

Updates Lonely Planet thoroughly updates each guidebook as often as possible. This usually means there are around two years between editions, although for more unusual or more stable destinations the gap can be longer. Check the imprint page (following the colour map at the beginning of the book) for publication dates.

Between editions up-to-date information is available in two free newsletters – the paper *Planet Talk* and email *Comet* (to subscribe, contact any Lonely Planet office) – and on our Web site at www.lonelyplanet.com. The *Upgrades* section of the Web site covers a number of important and volatile destinations and is regularly updated by Lonely Planet authors. *Scoop* covers news and current affairs relevant to travellers. And, lastly, the *Thorn Tree* bulletin board and *Postcards* section of the site carry unverified, but fascinating, reports from travellers.

Correspondence The process of creating new editions begins with the letters, postcards and emails received from travellers. This correspondence often includes suggestions, criticisms and comments about the current editions. Interesting excerpts are immediately passed on via newsletters and the Web site, and everything goes to our authors to be verified when they're researching on the road. We're keen to get more feedback from organisations or individuals who represent communities visited by travellers.

> Lonely Planet gathers information for everyone who's curious about the planet – and especially for those who explore it first-hand. Through guidebooks, phrasebooks, activity guides, maps, literature, newsletters, image library, TV series and Web site we act as an information exchange for a worldwide community of travellers.

Research Authors aim to gather sufficient practical information to enable travellers to make informed choices and to make the mechanics of a journey run smoothly. They also research historical and cultural background to help enrich the travel experience and allow travellers to understand and respond appropriately to cultural and environmental issues.

Authors don't stay in every hotel because that would mean spending a couple of months in each medium-sized city and, no, they don't eat at every restaurant because that would mean stretching belts beyond capacity. They do visit hotels and restaurants to check standards and prices, but feedback based on readers' direct experiences can be very helpful.

Many of our authors work undercover, others aren't so secretive. None of them accept freebies in exchange for positive write-ups. And none of our guidebooks contain any advertising.

Production Authors submit their raw manuscripts and maps to offices in Australia, USA, UK or France. Editors and cartographers – all experienced travellers themselves – then begin the process of assembling the pieces. When the book finally hits the shops, some things are already out of date, we start getting feedback from readers and the process begins again …

WARNING & REQUEST

Things change – prices go up, schedules change, good places go bad and bad places go bankrupt – nothing stays the same. So, if you find things better or worse, recently opened or long since closed, please tell us and help make the next edition even more accurate and useful. We genuinely value all the feedback we receive. A well travelled team reads and acknowledges every letter, postcard and email and ensures that every morsel of information finds its way to the appropriate authors, editors and cartographers for verification.

Everyone who writes to us will find their name in the next edition of the appropriate guidebook. They will also receive the latest issue of *Planet Talk*, our quarterly printed newsletter, or *Comet*, our monthly email newsletter. Subscriptions to both newsletters are free. The very best contributions will be rewarded with a free guidebook.

Excerpts from your correspondence may appear in new editions of Lonely Planet guidebooks, the Lonely Planet Web site, *Planet Talk* or *Comet*, so please let us know if you *don't* want your letter published or your name acknowledged.

Send all correspondence to the Lonely Planet office closest to you:

Australia: Locked Bag 1, Footscray, Victoria 3011
USA: 150 Linden St, Oakland, CA 94607
UK: 10A Spring Place, London NW5 3BH
France: 1 rue du Dahomey, 75011 Paris

Or email us at: talk2us@lonelyplanet.com.au

For news, views and updates see our Web site: www.lonelyplanet.com

HOW TO USE A LONELY PLANET GUIDEBOOK

The best way to use a Lonely Planet guidebook is any way you choose. At Lonely Planet we believe the most memorable travel experiences are often those that are unexpected, and the finest discoveries are those you make yourself. Guidebooks are not intended to be used as if they provide a detailed set of infallible instructions!

Contents All Lonely Planet guidebooks follow roughly the same format. The Facts about the Destination chapters or sections give background information ranging from history to weather. Facts for the Visitor gives practical information on issues like visas and health. Getting There & Away gives a brief starting point for researching travel to and from the destination. Getting Around gives an overview of the transport options when you arrive.

The peculiar demands of each destination determine how subsequent chapters are broken up, but some things remain constant. We always start with background, then proceed to sights, places to stay, places to eat, entertainment, getting there and away, and getting around information – in that order.

Heading Hierarchy Lonely Planet headings are used in a strict hierarchical structure that can be visualised as a set of Russian dolls. Each heading (and its following text) is encompassed by any preceding heading that is higher on the hierarchical ladder.

Entry Points We do not assume guidebooks will be read from beginning to end, but that people will dip into them. The traditional entry points are the list of contents and the index. In addition, however, some books have a complete list of maps and an index map illustrating map coverage.

There may also be a colour map that shows highlights. These highlights are dealt with in greater detail in the Facts for the Visitor chapter, along with planning questions and suggested itineraries. Each chapter covering a geographical region usually begins with a locator map and another list of highlights. Once you find something of interest in a list of highlights, turn to the index.

Maps Maps play a crucial role in Lonely Planet guidebooks and include a huge amount of information. A legend is printed on the back page. We seek to have complete consistency between maps and text, and to have every important place in the text captured on a map. Map key numbers usually start in the top left corner.

Although inclusion in a guidebook usually implies a recommendation we cannot list every good place. Exclusion does not necessarily imply criticism. In fact there are a number of reasons why we might exclude a place – sometimes it is simply inappropriate to encourage an influx of travellers.

Introduction

In the minds of some first-time visitors the mention of Turkey conjures up media-generated visions of sultans and harems, oriental splendour and squalor, luxury and decadence, mystery and intrigue.

These inaccurate and outdated stereotypes quickly evaporate once you arrive in the country. The Turkish Republic is rapidly modernising, secular and Western-oriented with a vigorous free enterprise economy. The Turks are friendly to foreign visitors, the cuisine is a savoury surprise, the cities are dotted with majestic old buildings and most of the countryside is as beautiful as a national park. And it's all yours for the lowest travel costs in Europe.

The history of Anatolia, the Turkish homeland, is incredibly long and rich. The world's oldest 'city', dating from 7500 BC, was discovered at Çatal Höyük near Konya. The Hittite Empire, mentioned in the Bible but little known in the West, rivalled that of ancient Egypt and left behind captivating works of art.

Many of the most famous sites from classical Hellenic and Hellenistic culture are not in Greece but in Turkey, including cities such as Troy, Pergamum, Ephesus, Miletus and Halicarnassus. Most modern Turkish cities have a Roman past and a good number are mentioned in the Bible. The Seljuk Turkish Empire which ruled Anatolia in the 13th century could boast of greats such as poet Omar Khayyam and Celaleddin Rumi, the poet and mystic who inspired the whirling dervishes.

The Ottoman Empire ruled the entire eastern Mediterranean, much of Eastern Europe and North Africa for six centuries. The myriad customs, cultures, languages and religions of the sultan's vast domains came together in his capital İstanbul, surely one of the world's most fascinating cities.

Though history and culture abound, there's plenty more to see and do. With over 7000km of coastline, it's an excellent destination for water sports and yacht cruising, especially along the Mediterranean, which

13

enjoys an average of 300 sunny days per year. Its highlands – which include biblical Mt Ararat (5137m) – are scenic and varied, from the pine-clad alpine Kaçkar Mountains (Kaçkar Dağları) of the eastern Black Sea coast to extinct volcanoes such as Mt Argeus (Erciyes Dağı) near Kayseri to the Taurus Mountains along the Mediterranean coast. There are also many opportunities for hiking, white-water rafting, kayaking and skiing.

Turkey is a big country, but transport is usually easy and cheap, especially the marvellous system of comfortable buses.

Hoş geldiniz! (Welcome!) You're in Turkey. Sit down, have a glass of *çay* (tea), listen to the call to prayer from the minaret and get ready for a memorable journey.

Facts about Turkey

HISTORY
The history of civilisation in Turkey is astoundingly long, extending for almost 10,000 years.

Earliest Times
The Mediterranean region was inhabited as early as 7500 BC, during Palaeolithic times. By around 7500 BC a Neolithic city had grown up at what's now called Çatal Höyük, 50km south-east of Konya in central Anatolia. The early Anatolians developed fine wall paintings, statuettes, domestic architecture and pottery. Artefacts from the site, including the wall paintings, are displayed in Ankara's Museum of Anatolian Civilisations.

The Chalcolithic period resulted in the building of a city at Hacılar, near Burdur, in about 5000 BC. The pottery here was of finer quality and copper implements, rather than stone or clay ones, were used.

The Hittite Empire
The Old Bronze Age (2600–1900 BC) was when Anatolians first developed cities of substantial size. An indigenous people known as the Proto-Hittites or Hatti built cities at Kanesh (Kaniş in Turkish; present-day Kültepe, near Kayseri), later rebuilt as Nisa, and Alacahöyük. The first known ruler of Kanesh was King Zipani (circa 2300 BC), according to Akkadian texts. As for Alacahöyük, 36km from Boğazkale (bo-**ahz**-kahleh), it was perhaps the most important pre-Hittite city and may have been the first Hittite capital.

The Hittites, a people who spoke an Indo-European language, overran this area and established themselves as a ruling class over the local people during the Middle Bronze Age (1900–1600 BC). The Hittites took over existing cities and built a magnificent capital at Hattuşa (present-day Boğazkale), 212km east of Ankara near Sungurlu. The early Hittite kingdom (1600–1500 BC) was replaced by the greater Hittite Empire (1450–1200 BC). The Hittites captured Syria from the Egyptians (1380–1316 BC), clashed with the great Rameses II (1298 BC), and meanwhile developed a wonderful culture.

Their graceful pottery, ironwork ornaments and implements, gold jewellery and figurines now fill a large section of the Museum of Anatolian Civilisations in Ankara. The striking site of Hattuşa, set in dramatic countryside, is worth a visit, as is the religious centre of Yazılıkaya nearby. The Hittite religion was based upon worship of a sun goddess and a storm god.

The Hittite Empire was weakened in its final period by the cities of Assuwa (Asia), subject principalities along the Aegean coast, which included Troy. The Trojans were attacked by Achaean Greeks in 1250 BC – the Trojan War – which gave the Hittites a break. But the *coup de grace* came with a massive invasion of 'sea peoples' from various Greek islands and city-states. Driven from their homelands by the invading Dorians, the sea peoples flocked into Anatolia by way of the Aegean coast. The Hittite state survived for a few centuries longer in the south-eastern Taurus Mountains, but the great empire was dead.

Phrygians, Urartians, Lydians & Others
With the Hittite decline, smaller states filled the power vacuum. Around 1200 BC the Phrygians and Mysians, of Indo-European stock, invaded Anatolia from Thrace and settled at Gordion (Yassıhöyük), 106km southwest of Ankara. This Hittite city became the Phrygian capital (circa 800 BC). A huge Hittite cemetery and a royal Phrygian tomb still exist at the site. King Midas (circa 715 BC), he of the golden touch, is Phrygia's most famous son.

At the same time (from 1200 BC onwards), the Aegean coast was populated with a mixture of indigenous peoples and Greek invaders. The area around present-day İzmir became Ionia, with numerous cities. South of Ionia was Caria, between present-day Milas and Fethiye, a mountainous region whose people were great traders. The Carians sided with the Trojans during the Trojan War. When the Dorians arrived they brought Greek culture to Caria, and later, the great Carian king Mausolus developed Caria even further. His tomb, the Mausoleum, was among the Seven Wonders of the Ancient World. Of his capital city, Halicarnassus (present-day Bodrum), little remains.

Further east from Caria were Lycia, a kingdom stretching from Fethiye to Antalya, and Pamphylia, the land east of Antalya.

As the centuries passed, a great city grew up at Sardis, in the Kingdom of Lydia, 60km east of İzmir. Sardis dominated most of Ionia and clashed with Phrygia. Lydia is famous not only for Sardis, but for a great invention: coinage. It's also famous for King Croesus, the world's first great coin collector. Lydia's primacy lasted only from 680 BC to 547 BC, when Persian invaders overran it.

Meanwhile, out east on the shores of salty Lake Van (Van Gölü), yet another kingdom and culture arose. Not much is known about the Urartians who founded the Kingdom of Van (860–612 BC), except that they left interesting ruins and vast, bewildering cuneiform inscriptions in the massive Van Kalesi (Van Castle or the Rock of Van) just outside the present-day town of Van.

The Cimmerians invaded Anatolia from the west, conquered Phrygia and challenged Lydia, then they settled down to take their place among the great jumble of Anatolian peoples. In 547 BC the Persians invaded and jumbled the situation even more. Though the Ionian cities survived the invasion and lived on under Persian rule, the great period of Hellenic culture was winding down. Ionia, centred on Smyrna (İzmir), and with its important cities of Phocaea (Foça, north of İzmir), Teos, Ephesus, Priene, Miletus, and Aeolia, had contributed a great deal to ancient culture, from the graceful scrolled capitals of Ionic columns to the ideas of Thales of Miletus, the first recorded philosopher in the West.

While the city of Athens was relatively unimportant, the Ionian cities were laying the foundations of Hellenic civilisation. It is ironic that the Persian invasion which curtailed Ionia's culture caused that of Athens to flourish. On reaching Athens, the Persians were overextended. By meeting the Persian challenge, Athens grew powerful and influential, taking the lead in the further progress of Hellenic culture.

Cyrus & Alexander

Cyrus, emperor of Persia (550–530 BC), swept into Anatolia from the east, conquering everybody and everything. Though he subjected the cities of the Aegean coast to his rule, this was not easy. The independent-minded citizens gave him and his successors trouble for the next two centuries.

The Persian conquerors were defeated by Alexander the Great, who stormed out of Macedon, crossed the Hellespont (Dardanelles) in 334 BC, and within a few years had conquered the entire Middle East from Greece to India. Alexander, so it is said, was frustrated in attempting to untie the Gordian knot at Gordion, so he cut it with his sword. It seems he did the right thing, as the domination of Asia – which he was supposed to gain by untying the knot – came to be his in record time.

Alexander's effects on Anatolia were profound. He was the first of many rulers to attempt to meld Western and Eastern cultures (the Byzantines and the Ottomans followed suit). Upon his death in 323 BC, in Babylon, Alexander's empire was divided among his generals in a flurry of civil wars. Lysimachus claimed western and central Anatolia after winning the Battle of Ipsus in 301 BC, and he made his mark on the Ionian cities. Many Hellenistic buildings went up on his orders. Ancient Smyrna was abandoned and a brand-new city was built several kilometres away, where the present-day city of İzmir stands.

But the civil wars continued, and Lysimachus was slain by Seleucus, another of Alexander's generals and king of Seleucid lands from 305 to 280 BC, at the Battle of Corupedium in 281 BC. Seleucus was in turn slain by Ptolemy Ceraunus, but the Kingdom of the Seleucids, based in Antioch (Antakya), was to rule a great part of the Middle East for the next century.

MICK WELDON

Alexander the Great's conquest of Anatolia in 334 BC had a profound effect on Turkey's history.

Meanwhile, in 279 BC, the next invaders, the Celts (or Gauls), were storming through Macedonia on their way to Anatolia where they established the Kingdom of Galatia. The Galatians made Ancyra (Ankara) their capital and subjected the Aegean cities to their rule. The foundations of parts of the citadel in Ankara date from Galatian times.

While the Galatians ruled western Anatolia, Mithridates I had become King of Pontus, a state based in Trebizond (Trabzon) on the eastern Black Sea coast. At its height, the Pontic Kingdom extended all the way to Cappadocia in central Anatolia.

Other small kingdoms flourished between 300 and 200 BC. A leader named Prusias founded the Kingdom of Bithynia and gave his name to the chief city: Prusa (Bursa). Nicaea (İznik, near Bursa) was also of great importance.

In south-eastern Anatolia an Armenian kingdom grew, based at Van. The Armenians, a Phrygian tribe, settled around Van Gölü after the decline of Urartian power. Ardvates, who ruled from 317 to 284 BC, was a Persian satrap (provincial governor)

who broke away from the Seleucid Kingdom to found the short-lived Kingdom of Armenia. The Seleucids later regained control, but lost it again as Armenia was split into two kingdoms, Greater and Lesser Armenia. Reunited in 94 BC under Tigranes I, the Kingdom of Armenia became very powerful for a short period (83–69 BC). Armenia finally fell to the Roman legions not long after.

But the most impressive and powerful of Anatolia's many kingdoms at this time was Pergamum. Gaining tremendous power around 250 BC, the Pergamene king picked the right side to be on, siding with Rome early in the game. With Roman help, Pergamum threw off Seleucid rule and went on to challenge King Prusias of Bithynia (186 BC) and also King Pharnaces I of Pontus (183 BC).

The kings of Pergamum were great warriors and governors and enthusiastic patrons of the arts, assembling an enormous library which rivalled that of Alexandria. The Asclepion, or medical centre, at Pergamum flourished at this time and continued to do so for centuries under Roman rule. Greatest of the Pergamene kings was Eumenes II (197–159 BC), who ruled an enormous empire stretching from the Dardanelles to the Taurus Mountains near Syria. He was responsible for building much of what's left on Pergamum's acropolis, including the grand library.

Roman Times

The Romans took Anatolia almost by default. The various Anatolian kings could not refrain from picking away at Roman holdings and causing other sorts of irritation, so finally the legions marched in and took over. Defeating King Antiochus III of Seleucia at Magnesia (Manisa, near İzmir) in 190 BC, the Romans were content for the time being to leave Anatolia in the hands of the kings of Pergamum. But the last king, dying without an heir, bequeathed his kingdom to Rome (133 BC). In 129 BC, the Romans established the province of Asia, with its capital at Ephesus.

An interesting postscript to this period is the story of Commagene. This small and rather unimportant little kingdom in east-central Anatolia, near Adıyaman, left few marks on history. But the one notable reminder of Commagene is very notable indeed: on top of Nemrut Dağı (Mt Nimrod), Antiochus I (68–38 BC) built a mammoth cone-shaped funerary mound, framed by twin temples filled with huge stone statues portraying himself and the gods and goddesses who were his 'peers'. A visit to Nemrut Dağı, from the nearby town of Kahta, is one of the highlights of a visit to Turkey.

Roman rule brought relative peace and prosperity for almost three centuries to Anatolia and provided the perfect conditions for the spread of a new religion.

Early Christianity

Christianity began in Roman Palestine (Judaea), but its foremost proponent, St Paul, came from Tarsus in Cilicia, near present-day Adana in southern Turkey. Paul took advantage of the excellent Roman road system to spread the teachings of Jesus. When the Romans drove the Jews out of Judaea in AD 70, Christian members of this Diaspora may have made their way to the numerous small Christian congregations in the Roman province of Asia.

On his first journey in about AD 47–49, Paul went to Antioch, Seleucia (Silifke) and along the southern coast through Pamphylia (Side, Antalya) and up into the mountains. First stop was Antioch-in-Pisidia, near the present-day town of Yalvaç in western Anatolia. Next he went to Iconium (Konya), the chief city in Galatia. Paul wrote an important Letter to the Galatians which is now the ninth book of the New Testament. From Iconium, Paul tramped to Lystra, 40km south, and to Derbe nearby. Then it was back to Attaleia (Antalya) to catch a boat for Antioch.

His second journey took him to some of the same cities, and later north-west to the district of Mysia where Troy (Truva) is located, and then into Macedonia.

Paul's third trip (AD 53–57) took in Ancyra, Smyrna and Adramyttium (Edremit). On the way back he stopped in Ephesus, capital of Roman Asia and one of the greatest cities of the time. Here he ran into trouble be-cause his teachings were ruining the market for silver effigies of the local favourite goddess, Cybele. The silversmiths led a riot, and Paul's companions were hustled into the great theatre for a sort of kangaroo court. Luckily, the authorities kept order: there was free speech in Ephesus, Paul and his companions had broken no laws and they were permitted to go free. Later on this third journey Paul stopped in Miletus.

Paul got his last glimpses of Anatolia as he was being taken to Rome as a prisoner for trial on charges of inciting a riot in Jerusalem (AD 59–60). He changed ships at Myra (Demre) and was supposed to land at Knidos, at the tip of the peninsula west of Marmaris, but stormy seas prevented this.

Other saints played a role in the life of Roman Asia as well. Tradition has it that St John retired to Ephesus to write the fourth Gospel near the end of his life, and that he brought Jesus' mother Mary with him. John was buried on top of a hill in what is now the town of Selçuk, near Ephesus. The great Basilica of St John, now ruined, marks the site. As for Mary, she is said to have retired to a mountain-top cottage near Ephesus. The small chapel at Meryemana is the site of a mass on 15 August every year to celebrate her Assumption.

The Seven Churches of the Revelation were the Seven Churches of Asia: Ephesus (Efes), Smyrna (İzmir), Pergamum (Bergama), Sardis (Sart, east of İzmir), Philadelphia (Alaşehir), Laodicea (between Denizli and Pamukkale) and Thyatira (Akhisar). At this time, 'Church' meant congregation, so don't go to these sites looking for the ruins of seven buildings.

The New Rome

Christianity was a struggling faith during the centuries of Roman rule. By AD 250, the faith had grown strong enough and Roman rule so unsteady that the Roman emperor Decius decreed a general persecution of Christians. Not only this, but the Roman Empire was falling to pieces. Goths attacked the Aegean cities with fleets and later invaded Anatolia. The Persian Empire again threatened from the east. Diocletian

(AD 284–305) restored the empire somewhat, but continued the persecutions.

When Diocletian abdicated, Constantine battled for the succession, which he won in AD 324. He united the empire, declared equal rights for all religions, and called the first Ecumenical Council to meet in Nicaea in AD 325.

Meanwhile, Constantine was building a great city on the site of Hellenic Byzantium. In AD 330 he dedicated it as New Rome, his capital city; later it came to be called Constantinople. The emperor died seven years later in Nicomedia (İzmit/Kocaeli), east of his capital. On his deathbed he was baptised as a Christian.

Justinian

While the barbarians of Europe were sweeping down on weakened Rome, the eastern capital grew in wealth and strength. Emperor Justinian (AD 527–65) brought the eastern Roman, or Byzantine, Empire to its greatest strength. He reconquered Italy, the Balkans, Anatolia, Egypt and North Africa and further embellished Constantinople with great buildings. His personal triumph was the Church of the Divine Wisdom, or Aya Sofya (Sancta Sophia), which remained the most splendid church in Christendom for almost 1000 years, after which it became the most splendid mosque.

Justinian's successors were generally good, but not good enough, and the empire's conquests couldn't be maintained. Besides, something quite momentous was happening in Arabia.

Birth of Islam

Five years after the death of Justinian, Mohammed was born in Mecca (in present-day Saudi Arabia). In AD 612, while meditating, he heard the voice of God command him to 'recite'. Mohammed was to become the Messenger of God, communicating His holy word to people. The written record of these recitations, collected after Mohammed's death into a book by his family and followers, is the Quran, the holy book of Islam.

The people of Mecca didn't take to Mohammed's preaching all at once. In fact,

they forced him to leave Mecca, which he did in AD 622. The year of his 'flight' *(hejira)* is the starting-point for the Muslim lunar calendar.

Setting up house in Medina, Mohammed organised a religious commonwealth which over 10 years became so powerful that it could challenge and conquer Mecca (AD 624–30). Before Mohammed died two years later, the Muslims had begun the conquest of other Arab tribes.

The story of militant Islam is one of history's most astounding tales. Fifty years after the Prophet's ignominious flight from Mecca, the armies of Islam were threatening the walls of Constantinople, having conquered everything and everybody between it and Mecca, as well as Persia and Egypt. The Arabic Muslim empires that followed these conquests were among the world's greatest political, social and cultural achievements.

Mohammed was succeeded by caliphs whose job was to oversee the welfare of the Muslim commonwealth. His close companions got the job first, then his son-in-law Ali. After that, two great dynasties emerged: the Umayyads (AD 661–750), whose empire was based in Damascus (Syria), and the Abbasids (750–1100), who ruled from Baghdad (Iraq). Both continually challenged the power and status of Byzantium.

But by the beginning of the 11th century, a new people had begun to challenge Byzantium in the east – the Turks.

The Seljuk Empire

The first Turkish state to rule Anatolia was the Great Seljuk Turkish Empire (1037–1109), based in Persia. Coming from Central Asia, the Turks captured Baghdad in 1055. In 1071, Seljuk armies decisively defeated the Byzantines at Manzikert (Malazgirt), taking the Byzantine emperor as a prisoner. The Seljuks then took over most of Anatolia and established a provincial capital at Nicaea. Their domains now included present-day Turkey, Iran and Iraq. Their empire developed a distinctive culture, with especially beautiful architecture and design. The Great Seljuks also produced the Persian poet Omar Khayyam (died 1123). Politically, however, the Great Seljuk Turkish Empire declined quickly, in the style of Alexander the Great's empire, with various pieces being taken by generals.

A remnant of the Seljuk Empire lived on in Anatolia, based in Iconium. Called the Seljuk Sultanate of Rum ('Rome', meaning Roman Asia), it continued to flourish, producing great art and great thinkers, until it was overrun by the Mongol hordes in 1243. Celaleddin Rumi or Mevlâna, founder of the Mevlevi (whirling) dervish order, is perhaps the Sultanate of Rum's most outstanding thinker.

The Crusades

These 'holy wars', launched to save eastern Christendom from the Muslims, proved disastrous for the Byzantine emperors. Although a combined Byzantine and crusader army captured Nicaea from the Seljuks in 1097, the crusaders were mostly an unhelpful, unruly bunch. The Fourth Crusade (1202–4) saw European ragtag armies invade and plunder Christian Constantinople. This was the first and most horrible defeat for the great city, and it was carried out by 'friendly' armies. Having barely recovered from the ravages of the crusades, the Byzantines were greeted with a new and greater threat: the Ottomans.

Founding of the Ottoman Empire

In the late 13th century, Byzantine weakness left a power vacuum that was filled by bands of Turks fleeing west from the Mongols. Warrior bands, each led by a warlord, took over parts of the Aegean and Marmara coasts. The Turks who moved into Bithynia, around Bursa, were followers of a man named Ertuğrul. His son, Osman, founded a principality (circa 1288) which was to grow into the Osmanlı (Ottoman) Empire.

The Ottomans took Bursa in 1326. It served them well as their first capital city. But they were vigorous and ambitious and by 1402 they moved the capital to Adrianople (Edirne) because it was easier to rule their Balkan conquests from there. Constantinople was still in Byzantine hands.

The Turkish advance spread rapidly to both east and west, despite some setbacks. By 1452, under Mehmet the Conqueror (Mehmet Fatih), they were strong enough to think of taking Constantinople, capital of eastern Christendom, which they did in 1453. Mehmet's reign (1451–81) began the great era of Ottoman power.

Süleyman the Magnificent

The height of Ottoman glory was under Sultan Süleyman the Magnificent (1520–66). Called the Lawgiver by the Turks, he beautified İstanbul (as Constantinople was renamed), rebuilt Jerusalem and expanded Ottoman power to the gates of Vienna in 1529. When he died in 1566, the empire covered some 15 million sq km, including all or parts of Hungary, the Balkans, southern Ukraine, Iran, Iraq, Syria, Lebanon, Israel, the Arabian Peninsula, Egypt and the North African coast all the way to Morocco. The Ottoman fleet under Barbaros Hayret-

MICK WELDON

Süleyman the Magnificent, known for his military prowess, legislative and cultural achievements

tin Paşa seemed invincible, but by 1585 the empire had begun its long and celebrated decline. Most of the sultans after Süleyman were incapable of great rule. Luckily for the empire, there were very competent and talented men to serve as grand viziers, ruling the empire in the sultans' stead.

The Later Empire

By 1699, Europeans no longer feared an invasion by the 'terrible Turk'. The empire was still vast and powerful, but it had lost its momentum and was rapidly dropping behind the West in terms of social, military, scientific and material progress. The reasons for this decline were complex, associated with the essentially military organisation of the Ottoman system of government and landholding, and the conservative influence of Islam.

In the 19th century, several sultans undertook important reforms. Selim III, for instance, revised taxation, commerce and the military. But the Janissaries (members of the sultan's personal guard) and other conservative elements resisted the new measures strongly and sometimes violently.

For centuries, the non-Turkish ethnic and religious minorities in the sultan's domains had lived side by side with their Turkish neighbours, governed by their own religious and traditional laws, in what is called by historians the *millet* system. The leader of the millet, or religious community, was responsible to the sultan for the community's loyalty and good behaviour. But in the 19th century, strong currents of ethnic nationalism flowed eastward from Europe. Decline and misrule made nationalism very appealing. The subject peoples of the Ottoman Empire revolted, often with the direct encouragement and assistance of the European powers. After bitter fighting in 1832, the Kingdom of Greece was formed. The Serbs, Bulgarians, Romanians, Albanians, Armenians and Arabs all sought their independence soon after.

As the empire broke up, the European powers (Britain, France, Italy, Germany and Russia) hovered in readiness to colonise or annex the pieces. They used religion as a reason for pressure or control, saying that it was their duty to protect the Catholic, Protestant or Orthodox subjects from misrule and anarchy. The holy places in Palestine were a favourite target and each power tried to obtain a foothold here for later colonisation.

The Russian emperors put pressure on the Turks to grant them powers over all Ottoman Orthodox subjects, whom the Russian emperor would thus 'protect'. The result of this pressure was the Crimean War (1853–56), in which Britain and France fought with the Ottomans against the Russians.

In the midst of imperial dissolution, Western-style reforms were proposed in an attempt to revive the moribund empire and make it compatible with modern Europe. Mithat Paşa, a successful general and powerful grand vizier, brought the young crown prince Abdül Hamit II to the throne along with a constitution in 1876. But the new sultan did away both with Mithat Paşa and the constitution and established his own absolute rule.

Gazi Osman Paşa

Gazi Osman Paşa was born in 1832, to relatively poor parents in Tokat, but grew up to become one of Ottoman Turkey's most famous soldiers, serving in Thessaly, Crete, Bosnia-Hercegovina and Yemen. After a great victory in the Ottoman-Serbian War of 1875–76 he became a *paşa* (general).

During the Russo-Turkish War (1877–78), Russian forces crossed the Danube into Ottoman Bulgaria, headed for Pleven (Plevne). Osman Paşa, ordered to defend the town, surrounded it with earthworks and endured a five-month siege by a Russian force twice the size of his own. Attempting to fight his way out, he was taken captive with serious injuries, and treated as a hero by a Russian tsar astonished at his fortitude.

Equally impressed, Sultan Abdül Hamit II bestowed the title of Gazi (Conqueror) on him. Osman became commander-in-chief and then marshal of the Sultan's household.

Gazi Osman Paşa died in İstanbul in 1900 but there's hardly a Turkish town that doesn't commemorate him in a street name.

Abdül Hamit (1876–1909) modernised without democratising, building telegraph lines and railways, encouraging modern industry, and keeping watch on everything through an extensive spy network. But the empire continued to disintegrate, with nationalist insurrections in Crete, Armenia, Bulgaria and Macedonia.

The younger generation of the Turkish elite watched bitterly as the country fell apart, then organised into secret societies bent on toppling the sultan. The Young Turk movement for Western-style reforms gained enough power by 1908 to force the restoration of the constitution. This provided a brief respite as all Ottoman peoples saw hope of living in harmony. But ethnic rivalries surfaced again quickly as Ottoman Bulgaria declared independence and Austria seized the former Ottoman provinces of Bosnia and Hercegovina. Armenian demonstrations provoked more massacres at Adana in April 1909. Albania and Arabia rose in revolt. War broke out with Italy, Bulgaria, Serbia and Greece. The Ottoman grand vizier was assassinated. The Ottoman Turks felt beleaguered on all sides.

In its last years, although a sultan still sat on the throne, the Ottoman Empire was ruled by three members of the Young Turks' Committee of Union & Progress: Talat, Enver and Jemal. Their rule was vigorous, but harsh and misguided, and it only worsened an already hopeless situation. When WWI broke out, they made the fatal error of siding with Germany.

With the defeat of the Central Powers, the Ottoman Empire collapsed. İstanbul and several other parts of Anatolia were occupied, and the sultan became a pawn in the hands of the victors. The victorious Allies had been planning since the beginning of the war how they would carve up the Ottoman Empire. They even promised certain lands to several different peoples or factions in order to get their support for the war effort. With the end of the war, these promises came due. With more promises than territory, the Allies decided on the dismemberment of Anatolia itself in order to get more land with which to satisfy the ambitions of the victorious countries..The choicest bits of Anatolia were to be given to Christian peoples, with the Muslim Turks relegated to a small landlocked region of semi-barren steppe.

The Turkish Republic

The situation looked very bleak for the Turks as their armies were being disbanded and their country taken under the control of the Allies. But a catastrophe turned things around.

Ever since gaining independence in 1831, the Greeks had entertained the Megali Idea (Great Plan) of a new Greek Empire encompassing all the lands that had once been under Greek influence – in effect, the refounding of the Byzantine Empire. During WWI, the Allies had offered Greece the Ottoman city of Smyrna (present-day İzmir). King Constantine declined for various reasons, although his prime minister, Eleutherios Venizelos, wanted to accept. After the war, however, Alexander became king, Venizelos became prime minister again and Britain encouraged the Greeks to go ahead and take Smyrna. On 15 May 1919, they did.

For the Turks, depressed and hopeless over the occupation of their country and the powerlessness of the sultan, this was the last straw: a former subject people capturing an Ottoman city and pushing inland with great speed and ferocity. Even before the Greek invasion, an Ottoman general named Mustafa Kemal had decided that a new government must take over the destiny of the Turks from the powerless sultan. He began organising resistance on 19 May 1919. The Greek invasion was just the shock needed to galvanise the people and lead them to his way of thinking.

The Turkish War of Independence lasted from 1920 to 1922. In September 1921 the Greeks very nearly reached Ankara, the nationalist headquarters, but in desperate fighting the Turks were successful in holding them off. A year later, the Turks began their counteroffensive and drove the Greek armies back to İzmir by 9 September 1922.

Victory in the bitterly fought war made Mustafa Kemal even more of a national hero. He was now fully in command of the fate of the Turks. The sultanate was soon abolished and, after it, the Ottoman Empire. A Turkish republic was born, based in the region of Anatolia and eastern Thrace. The treaties of WWI, which had left the Turks with almost no country, were renegotiated. By the Treaty of Lausanne (24 June 1923), Turkey relinquished all claims to lands not occupied in the majority by Turks, but recovered Eastern Thrace, the Aegean islands of Bozcaada and Gökçeada, and was confirmed in possession of the territory held by the republican government at the time.

Ethnic Greeks in Turkey and ethnic Turks in Greece were required to leave their ancestral homes and move to their respective ethnic nation-states; Greeks from İzmir moved into the houses of Turks in Salonika, whose owners had moved to İzmir, and so forth. Venizelos even came to terms with Kemal, signing a treaty, the Ankara Treaty of Friendship, in 1930.

Atatürk's Reforms

Mustafa Kemal undertook the job of completely remaking Turkish society. After the republic was declared in 1923, a constitution was adopted (1924); polygamy was abolished and the fez, considered to be a mark of Ottoman backwardness, was prohibited (1925); new, Western-style legal codes were instituted, and civil (not religious) marriage was required (1926); Islam was removed as the state religion and the Arabic alphabet was replaced by a modified Latin one (1928). In 1930, Constantinople officially became İstanbul, and other city names were officially Turkified (Angora to Ankara, Smyrna to İzmir, Adrianople to Edirne etc). Women obtained the right to vote and serve in parliament in 1934.

In 1935, Mustafa Kemal sponsored one of the most curious laws of modern times. Up to this time, Muslims had only one given name. Family names were purely optional. So he decided that all Turks should choose a family name. He himself was proclaimed Atatürk, or 'Father Turk', by the Turkish parliament, and became Kemal Atatürk.

Atatürk lived and directed the country's destiny until 10 November 1938. He saw WWII coming and was anxious that Turkey stay out of it. His friend and successor as president of the republic, İsmet İnönü, succeeded in preserving a precarious neutrality. Ankara became a hotbed of Allied-Axis spying, but the Turks managed to stay neutral.

Post-WWII

In the early years of the republic, Atatürk's Republican Peoples' Party was the only political party allowed. But between 1946 and 1950 true democracy was instituted, and the opposition Democratic Party won the election in 1950.

By 1960 the Democratic Party had acquired so much power that the democratic system was threatened. The army, charged by Atatürk to protect democracy and the constitution, stepped in and brought various party leaders to trial on charges of violating the constitution. The popular Peron-like party leader, Adnan Menderes, was executed, though all other death sentences were commuted. Elections were held in 1961.

In 1970 there was a polite coup d'etat, again because the successor to the Democratic Party had overreached its bounds. High-ranking military officers entered the national broadcasting headquarters and read a short message, and the government fell.

In 1974, all Turks' attention turned to Cyprus, the island nation off Turkey's southern coast where a minority ethnic Turkish population was dominated by a majority of ethnic Greeks. Ethnic strife had been growing for some time, with the minority Turks getting the worst of it. On 15 July, a Greek Cypriot guerrilla named Nikos Sampson, supported by the military junta then ruling in Athens, staged a coup against Cypriot president Archbishop Makarios. Toting twin submachine guns, Sampson proclaimed himself Cyprus' new president. Turkish prime minister Bülent Ecevit, unable to gain support for peace-keeping efforts from London or Washington, ordered Turkish troops to invade northern Cyprus on 20 July. The troops secured a broad beachhead and drove inland, effectively dividing the island into separate Greek and Turkish sectors. It has been divided ever since.

Atatürk

It won't take you long to discover the national hero, Kemal Atatürk. Though he died on 10 November 1938, his image is everywhere in Turkey – his picture is in every schoolroom, office and shop, a bust or statue is in every park, and quotations from his speeches and writings are on every public building. He is virtually synonymous with the Turkish Republic.

Lord Kinross' best-selling biography of Atatürk portrays a man of great intelligence and even greater energy and daring, possessed by the idea of giving his fellow Turks and their homeland a new lease of life. In contrast to many leaders, he had the capability and opportunity to realise his obsession almost single-handedly. His achievement in turning a backward empire into a forward-looking nation-state was extraordinary, and was taken as a model by President Nasser of Egypt, Reza Shah of Iran and other leaders of neighbouring countries.

Early Years

In 1881, a boy named Mustafa was born into the family of a minor Turkish bureaucrat living in Salonika, now the Greek city of Thessaloniki, but at that time a city in Ottoman Macedonia. Mustafa was smart and a hard worker at school. His mathematics teacher was so impressed that he gave him the nickname Kemal (excellence). The name Mustafa Kemal stuck with him as he went through a military academy and Harbiye, the Ottoman war college, and his career as an infantry officer.

Military Career

He served with distinction, particularly in the Tripolitanian War (1911) when Italy seized Ottoman Libya, though he acquired a reputation as something of a hothead. By 1915 he was a promising lieutenant colonel of infantry in command of the 57th Regiment, one of many units posted to the Gallipoli Peninsula. The defence of Gallipoli, which saved Constantinople from British conquest (until the end of the war, at least), was a personal triumph for Mustafa Kemal. His strategic and tactical genius came into full play when circumstances put him at the heart of the battle and he correctly divined the enemy's strategy. He led with utter disregard for his own safety, inspiring his men with his heroism. A superior force of British, Australian, New Zealand and French armies and navies was fought to a standstill and finally forced to withdraw, and Mustafa Kemal became a popular hero.

Under the careful watch of the military, democracy returned and things went well for years, until political infighting and civil unrest brought the country to a virtual halt in 1980. On the left side of the political spectrum, Soviet-bloc countries pumped in arms and money for destabilisation and, it is claimed, supported Armenian terrorist elements who murdered Turkish diplomats and their families abroad. On the right side of the spectrum, fanatical Muslim religious groups and a neo-Nazi party caused havoc. In the centre, the two major political parties were deadlocked so badly in parliament that for months they couldn't even elect a parliamentary president.

The economy was near collapse, inflation was 130% per year, the law-makers were not making laws, and crime in the streets by the fringe elements of left and right was epidemic. The military stepped in again on 12 September 1980, much to the relief of the general population, and restored civil, fiscal and legal order, but at the price of strict control and human rights abuses.

The constitution was rewritten so as to avoid parliamentary impasses. In a controlled plebiscite, it was approved by the voters. The head of the military government, General Kenan Evren, resigned his military commission (as Atatürk had done) and became the country's new president. The old political leaders, seen by the new government to have been responsible for the breakdown of society, were tried (if there was evidence of criminal activity) or

Atatürk

Though he was promoted to the rank of *paşa* (general), the sultan and government were afraid of his brilliance and popularity, and sought to keep this 'dangerous element' in Constantinople under their control. When the war was lost and the empire was on the verge of being dismembered, Mustafa Kemal Paşa had himself posted to Anatolia as Inspector-General of the defeated Ottoman armies – the perfect post from which to begin his revolution.

Founding of the Republic

On 19 May 1919, four days after a Greek army of invasion landed at İzmir, Mustafa Kemal Paşa landed at the port of Samsun. He reorganised the defeated Ottoman armies, and convened congresses to

focus the will and energies of the people. His democratically established revolutionary government at Ankara held off several invading armies (French, Italian and Greek) with very limited resources. Several times the whole tenuous effort neared collapse, and many of his friends and advisers were ready to flee Ankara for their lives. Kemal never flinched, always ready to dare the worst – and he succeeded brilliantly.

Atatürk's Legacy

Many great revolutionary leaders falter or fade when the revolution is won. Atatürk lived 15 years into the republican era, and directed the country's progress with skill and foresight. The forward-looking, Westernised, secular, democratic nation-state you see today is his legacy, and his memory is truly sacred to the majority of Turks.

MICK WELDON

---

excluded from political life for 10 years, though many returned to politics before this time was up.

In 1983, elections under the new constitution were held, and the centre-right Anavatan Partisi (Motherland Party), the one less favoured by the military caretakers, won easily. The new prime minister was Turgut Özal, a former World Bank economist, who instituted economic liberalisation and precipitated a business boom which lasted through the 1980s.

Özal's two terms in office were marked by a resurgence of Kurdish separatist activity, which took a violent turn during the 1980s. Since the collapse of the Ottoman Empire, the Kurds have periodically aspired to their own ethnic nation-state and a mi-

nority have resorted to violence. Kurdistan Workers Party (PKK) guerrillas, based in neighbouring Syria, Iraq and Iran and supported clandestinely by the Palestine Liberation Organisation (PLO), made hundreds of raids into south-eastern Turkey killing thousands of civilians and Turkish troops. The resulting military crackdown embittered many Turkish Kurds, but also brought the matter of Turks and Kurds to the national agenda.

Turkey Today

Özal's untimely death in April 1993 removed a powerful, innovative but controversial force from Turkish politics and left a power vacuum which was partly filled by veteran politician Süleyman Demirel, a

A Future for the Kurds?

After 16 years of fighting and the deaths of around 30,000 people, both Turkish and Kurdish, the year 2000 kicked off more optimistically, with hopes that the long civil war in south-eastern Turkey may at last be at an end.

The root of the problem stems from the fact that Turkey has a large minority population of ethnic Kurds, many of whom, while not necessarily supporting the PKK's early demands for a separate state, want to be able to read newspapers in their own language, to have their children taught in their own language and to watch television in Kurdish which is not beamed in from northern Europe.

Unfortunately, the Kurds were not one of the groups (like the Christians, Jews and Armenians) guaranteed certain rights as minorities under the terms of the Treaty of Lausanne which effectively created modern Turkey. Indeed, until recently the Turkish government refused to even recognise the existence of the Kurds, insisting they be called 'Mountain Turks'. Even today the census form doesn't allow anyone to identify themselves as Kurdish; nor can they be identified as Kurdish on their identity cards. This is in spite of the fact that many people in the east, particularly women, speak the Khirmanca dialect of Kurdish as their first language.

Perhaps surprisingly the best hope for speedy change lies in Turkey's enthusiasm to join the European Union, which champions the rights of cultural and ethnic minorities. There are slight signs of a thawing of attitudes; for example, in 2000 some Kurds were permitted to celebrate Nevroz, the Kurdish New Year (although others were refused permission on the specious grounds that they had spelt the name of the festival in Kurdish rather than Turkish).

Over the years political parties aimed at promoting Kurdish rights have come and gone before the ink on their manifestos had had time to dry. HADEP (the Peoples' Democratic Party) is the latest manifestation of Kurdish political commitment. At the time of writing it held power in several of the big south-eastern towns, including Diyarbakır, and was holding out against the usual calls for its closure.

former prime minister, who was elected president. A series of weak coalition governments followed until December 1995, when the upstart religious-right Welfare Party (Refah Partisi, RP) won 21% of the vote, the largest proportion of any party, and formed a government.

Emboldened by political power, Refah politicians made Islamist statements which alarmed the powerful National Security Council, the most visible symbol of the military establishment's role as the caretaker of secularism. In 1997 the Council announced that Refah had flouted the constitutional ban against religion in politics, and the party was disbanded.

The Kurdish separatist issue continued to be a political problem during the 1990s, when tensions were heightened following the flight of three million Iraqi Kurds into eastern Turkey after the Gulf War of 1991. A virtual civil war raged in eastern and south-eastern Turkey throughout the decade, abating with the capture in Nairobi of the PKK leader, Abdullah Öcalan, by a Turkish commando team in 1999. Tried for treason and murder, Öcalan was condemned to death, but his case is currently on appeal to the European Court of Justice.

In December 1999, Turkey achieved a symbolic victory in its long march toward Europeanisation when it was accepted as a candidate for membership in the European Community. However, no-one – not even the most enthusiastic advocates of Turkish membership – believes that it will become a fully fledged member anytime soon.

The general elections in April 1999 brought veteran social democrat Bülent Ecevit to the prime ministry in an unlikely coalition with the far-right Nationalist Action Party and the right-of-centre Motherland Party. Unlikely as it may seem, the coalition has lasted for over a year.

On 17 August 1999 a major earthquake struck north-western Turkey, destroying most buildings in the cities of İzmit (Kocaeli) and Adapazarı (Sakarya), and doing extensive damage to Yalova. The death toll was in the tens of thousands, and the economic damage, along with a downturn in tourism caused by headlines from the Kurdish fighting, was a serious blow to Turkey's economy. The extent of the damage revealed serious deficiencies in the design and construction of modern buildings and the regulation of builders by government inspectors.

In May 2000, President Demirel stepped down at the end of his term and was succeeded by Ahmet Necdet Sezer, the president of the Constitutional Court. In an unprecedented show of political concord, all of the coalition parties and even the two opposition parties in parliament supported Sezer's candidacy, and he was elected easily in the parliamentary vote. The election of a respected nonpolitical candidate by all parties was an encouraging symbol of Turkey's political maturation.

GEOGRAPHY

Turkey is divided into Asian and European parts by the Dardanelles, the Sea of Marmara and the Bosphorus (the strait connecting the Black Sea and the Sea of Marmara). Eastern Thrace (European Turkey) comprises only 3% of the total 788,695 sq km land area. The remaining 97% is Anatolia, a vast plateau rising eastward towards the Caucasus Mountains. Turkey's coastline is over 7000km long.

Most first-time visitors come to Turkey expecting to find deserts, palm trees and camel caravans. In fact, the country is geographically diverse, with snow-capped mountains, rolling steppes, broad rivers, verdant coasts and rich agricultural valleys.

Turkey is big: the road distance from Edirne on the Bulgarian border to Kars near the Armenian one is more than 1700km. From the Black Sea shore to the Mediterranean coast it's almost 1000km. On flat ground it may take only one very long day to drive 1000km, but Turkey has many mountain ranges which can lengthen travel times considerably.

CLIMATE

Turkey has seven climatic regions. Going from west to east, here's the lay of the land.

The Marmara region (eastern Thrace and İstanbul) is the country's second most

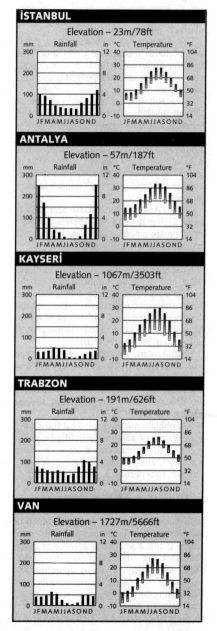

humid, with fertile rolling countryside and relatively moderate temperatures.

The Aegean region has olive, fig and fruit orchards on hillsides, and broad tobacco and sunflower fields in the valleys, with slightly warmer temperatures and a bit less rainfall.

The Mediterranean coast is mountainous without much beach between Fethiye and Antalya, but then opens up into a fertile plain between Antalya and Alanya before turning into mountains again. Temperatures at Antalya are a few degrees warmer than at İzmir. The eastern Mediterranean coast is always very humid, with high rainfall (except summer).

Central Anatolia, the Turkish heartland, is a vast high plateau of rolling steppe broken by mountain ranges. In summer it's hot and dry, in winter it's chilly and often damp.

The Black Sea coast, 1700km long, has two to three times the national rainfall average and moderate temperatures. At the eastern end of the Black Sea coast, the mountains come right down to the sea, and the slopes are covered with tea plantations. All in all, the Black Sea coast is like central Europe, but pleasantly warmer.

South-eastern Anatolia is rolling steppe with outcrops of rock, and is very dry and hot in summer, with maximum temperatures reaching 46.5°C. Minimum temperatures are around -12°C. Average humidity, at 52%, is the lowest in Turkey.

A mountainous and somewhat forbidding zone, eastern Anatolia is a wildly beautiful region with temperature variations between a hot 38°C and a daunting -43.2°C. It's cold out here except from June to September.

ECOLOGY & ENVIRONMENT

Turkey is one of those countries grappling with the environmental dilemma. Much of the country lives in the pre-pollution era of frugal living, home-made goods and dung-cake fuel, but urban dwellers are well into the lifestyle of quickly changing fashion and disposable everything. Village dwellers are just leaving the era when environmental concern was not necessary, and urbanites have recently discovered it as a major problem.

The embryonic environmental movement in Turkey is making slow progress, exemplified by the fact that the government is considering building a new nuclear power station on the Mediterranean coast at Akkuyu Bay, in a known earthquake region. However, it may not be built after all. Pro and con forces both within the government and without are battling over the plan.

A more immediate problem is the danger posed to the metropolis of İstanbul by the constant flow of oil tankers through the Bosphorus. Local authorities warn that it's only a matter of time before there's a disastrous oil spill or explosion, perhaps with enormous property damage and loss of life. Navigation in the strait is governed by international treaty, so the Turkish authorities cannot control it. New pipelines under construction may relieve some of the burden, as may modern navigational aids – if ships can be required to use them.

The gigantic South-East Anatolia Project, known as GAP, is likely to have a major impact on Turkey's ecology. The US$32 billion, 22-dam construction effort harnesses the headwaters of the Tigris and Euphrates Rivers for hydroelectricity and irrigation. Although it promises to turn the poor, arid south-eastern region into an agricultural powerhouse, it has also raised the rates of diseases such as malaria and dysentery in the vicinity of Şanlıurfa, and may have other ecological effects yet unknown.

FLORA & FAUNA

Once cloaked in dense forest, Anatolia is now largely denuded after a thousand years of woodcutting. Although the government encourages conservation and reforestation, the great forests will never return. The Mediterranean coast west of Antalya, the Black Sea area and north-eastern Anatolia still have forests of considerable size. Elsewhere, the great swathes of wild flowers which cover the rolling steppes in spring make fine splashes of colour.

Because of Turkey's temperate climate, plants such as apples, apricots, bananas, cherries, citrus fruit, cotton, dates, grapes, sugar beet, sunflowers and tobacco thrive.

The long roots of deliciously sweet *kavun* melons go deep into the dry soil of the Anatolian plateau to find water. Turkey grows much of the world's supply of hazelnuts, and a large volume of pistachios and walnuts. Of the cash crops, cotton is king, and grains such as wheat and barley are important.

Turkey has similar animal life to that of the Balkans and much of Europe: bears, deer, jackals, lynx, wild boars, wolves and rare leopards. Besides the usual domestic animals such as cattle, horses, donkeys, goats and several varieties of sheep (including the fat-tail), there are camels and water buffalo.

Turkish shepherds are proud of their big, powerful and fierce Kangal sheepdogs which guard the flocks from hungry wolves. The breed is now controlled, and export is only allowed under licence. The same goes for the beautiful Van cats, with pure white fur and different-coloured eyes – one blue, one green.

Birdlife is exceptionally rich, with eagles, vultures and storks. In several parts of the country reserves have been set aside as *kuş cenneti* (bird paradises).

Turkey's coastal waters have rich varieties of fish, shellfish and other sea creatures, though overfishing and pollution are now serious problems. A few nesting sites of the loggerhead turtle remain in Turkey (for example at Dalyan and Olimpos). For more information, contact The Society for the Protection of Sea Turtles (☎ 242-825 7260) in Çıralı.

For more information on Turkey's wildlife, contact Doğal Hayat Koruma Derneği (Foundation for the Protection of Nature; ☎ 212-281 0321, fax 279 5544), PK 18, Bebek, 80810 İstanbul.

GOVERNMENT & POLITICS
Parliament
Turkey is a parliamentary democracy. The Turkish Grand National Assembly (TGNA), elected by all citizens over 19 years of age, is the direct descendant of the congress assembled by Atatürk during the War of Independence to act as the legitimate voice of the Turkish nation in place of the sultan. Of the 550 deputies in recent parliaments, only about 20 have been women, although Turkish women won the right to vote and stand for office in 1934, earlier than women in many other countries.

President & Prime Minister
The president, elected by the TGNA from among its members, serves for one seven-year term and is supposed to be 'above politics' and to symbolise the nation. He or she is the head of state, with important executive powers and responsibilities. The true head of government, who decides its policies and directions, is the prime minister. However, recent presidents have informally expanded the powers of the presidential office.

The prime minister is appointed by the president to form a government, and is customarily the head of the party with the most seats in parliament, or the head of a coalition.

The National Security Council, made up of high-level government and military leaders, meets monthly to advise and influence the government. The judiciary, though theoretically independent, has in many instances been influenced by current government policies.

Political Parties
Though the Turks are firm believers in democracy, the tradition of popular rule and responsibility is relatively short, and is still taking shape. Turkey has had nearly 60 governments since the creation of the republic in 1923. The longest-lived have been those led by strong charismatic leaders, many of whom eventually challenged the pre-eminence of the military establishment and thereby lost their jobs. In recent years there has been a succession of weak, fractious coalition governments, with the heads of the major parties succeeding one another in a game of political musical chairs. Rather than being durable institutions with coherent philosophies and long-term goals, most Turkish political parties are vehicles for the personal ambitions of one or a few top officers, and are formed in their political image.

Tansu Çiller, formerly Turkey's first female prime minister, is the leader of the

True Path Party (DYP), having assumed the mantle of leadership from founder Süleyman Demirel when he was elevated to the presidency (1993–2000). The Motherland Party (AP), founded by former prime minister and president Turgut Özal as his political vehicle, is now headed by Mesut Yılmaz. Though essentially identical in their right-of-centre political programs, these two parties rarely share power because Çiller and Yılmaz can't stand one another.

On the far right, the Islamist Virtue Party (FP) was founded immediately after Professor Necmettin Erbakan's Welfare (Refah) Party (RP) was closed down in 1997. Sharing the right wing with the Islamist Virtue Party is the Nationalist Action Party (MHP). Though founded as a neo-fascist party by the late Alparslan Türkeş, a former general, the MHP has recently moderated its position to that of merely ultra-nationalist.

On the left side of Turkey's political spectrum, current prime minister Bülent Ecevit leads the small Democratic Left Party (DSP) which adheres to the ideals of European social democracy. Though not currently represented in parliament, in recent times Turkey has had a small party advocating Marxism, and another advocating liberalisation in relation to Kurdish cultural and linguistic identity.

ECONOMY

Turkey has a strong agricultural base to its economy, being among the handful of countries that are net exporters of food. Wheat, cotton, sugar beet, sunflowers, hazelnuts, tobacco, fruit and vegetables are abundant. Sheep are the main livestock, and Turkey is the biggest wool producer in Europe.

Manufactured goods now dominate exports and much of the economy. Turkey makes motor vehicles, appliances, pharmaceuticals and consumer goods and exports them throughout the region. Its export growth rate in recent years has been more than 25%, among the highest in the world.

However, the economy is still dragged down by the heavy weight of the 'state economic enterprises' (KITs), government-controlled corporations subject to subsidies,

political influence, payroll-padding and corruption. In 1994, six of the 10 largest corporations were KITs, involved in industries such as refining and selling petroleum products and petrochemicals; generating and distributing electricity; making and selling salt, tobacco products and alcoholic beverages; and refining and marketing sugar. The government is also involved in the marketing of agricultural products including grain, hazelnuts and tea; in coal and steel production; and in transportation, broadcasting and many other industries.

Tourism is now among the most important sectors of the Turkish economy, bringing in billions of dollars in foreign currency earnings. However, it's an insecure 'product' – the headlines about Kurdish separatism and the severe earthquake of 1999 hit Turkish tourism hard. Together, the earthquake damage and lost tourism revenues are estimated to have cost the Turkish economy US$12 billion.

There is still a large Turkish workforce in the industries of Europe, particularly those of Germany, which sends home remittances.

POPULATION & PEOPLE

Turkey has a population of approximately 70 million, the great majority being Sunni Muslim Turks. There is also a significant minority of Muslim Kurds, and small groups of Laz and Hemşin peoples along the Black Sea coast, and Yörüks and Tahtacıs along the eastern Mediterranean coast.

As for Christian Turkish citizens, there are small groups of Armenians and ethnic Greeks, who number fewer than 100,000 and live mostly in İstanbul. Assyrian Orthodox Christians, sometimes called Jacobites, trace their roots to the church founded by Jacob Baradeus, the 6th-century bishop of Edessa (present-day Şanlıurfa). Their small community, threatened in recent years by marginalisation and the Kurdish separatist strife, has its centre south of Diyarbakır, in and around Mardin and the Tür Abdin plateau.

Turks

The Turkic peoples originated in central Asia, where they were a presence to be reck-

Army Days

To the Turks, the army is an honourable institution with a long and glorious history. In a recent public opinion poll, the Turkish populace was asked which national institution they held in the highest regard, and the military won handily over parliament, the courts and the religious establishment.

The Turkish people trace their lineage all the way back to the ancient Turkish states in Dzungaria around 2000 BC, but the earliest great Turkic empire dependent upon military prowess was that of the Huns around 220 BC. During the time of the Göktürks (AD 552–745), the Avars (565–835), the Uygurs (745–940), the Karahanlıs (940–1040), the Ghaznavids (962–1187), the Great Seljuks (1037–1157) and the Ottomans (1281–1922), Turkey's armed forces retained a central role in government and society. In other societies, such as the Arab and Mamluk empires, Turks formed the military caste.

Turkey was neutral during WWII. During the Korean War, the Turkish contingent of the United Nations forces was highly praised for its discipline, courage and tenacity.

To be a Turk is to be a soldier, at least at some point in life. In republican Turkey, every Turkish male, with very few exceptions, is required to spend some months in the army. Despite it being an honourable duty, few Turkish men look forward to it. Conscientious objection is not an option.

Most men do their military service when they are 18. There are several ways in which the moment can be put off. Deferral is allowed, for example, if you are a student or if your brother is already doing his military service. But in practice, a young man over 18 who has not yet done his military service may find it almost impossible to get a job, as no employer wants his new employee to have to run off to the army for months.

Military service serves useful social as well as military purposes. It's not unusual to see army troops doing clean-up or gardening duty at archaeological sites, or planting new forests.

The army has traditionally used compulsory military service as a mechanism for social leavening and cohesion. Young men from the comfortable, developed western provinces are often shipped off to serve in the rugged east, while country boys from poor eastern villages are posted to cosmopolitan İstanbul, İzmir, or the tourist resorts, giving both extremes a close-up view of the 'other' Turkey.

oned with as early as the 4th century AD. The Chinese called them Tu-küe, which is perhaps the root of our word 'Turk'. They were related to the Hiung-nu or Huns.

The normally nomadic Turks ruled several vast empires in Central Asia before being pushed westward by the Mongols. Various tribes of the Oğuz Turkic group settled in Azerbaijan, northern Iran and Anatolia.

At first they were shamanist, but at one time or another these early Turks followed each of the great religions of the region, including Buddhism, Nestorian Christianity, Manichaeism and Judaism. During their western migrations they became more familiar with Islam, and it stuck.

Having begun their history as nomadic shepherds, the Turks used their skills with horses to become excellent soldiers. With the expansion of the Arab empire into Turkish lands, the Turks used their military prowess first to gain influence, and later to gain control. To this day most Turks are proud of their military traditions, while military prowess and courage are widely admired.

Kurds

Turkey has a significant Kurdish minority estimated at 10 million (accurate figures are hard to come by because the Turkish government does not recognise them officially as a separate ethnic group). Some ethnologists believe that the Kurds, who speak an Indo-European language, are closely related to the Persians, and that they migrated here from northern Europe centuries before Christ.

Turkey's sparsely populated eastern and south-eastern regions are home to perhaps six million Kurds and Turkish, Armenian and other minorities. Four million Kurds live elsewhere throughout the country, more or less integrated into greater Turkish society.

Though virtually all of the Kurds living in Turkey are Muslims and look physically similar to the Turks, they proudly maintain their Kurdish language, culture and family traditions. For a discussion of the Kurdish separatist issue, see the History section earlier in this chapter.

Jews

The small Jewish community of about 24,000 people is centred in İstanbul (about 20,000) with smaller communities in Ankara, Bursa, İzmir and other cities. The Turkish Jewish community is the remnant of a great influx which took place in the 16th century when the Jews of Spain (the Sephardim) were forced by the Spanish Inquisition to flee their homes. They were welcomed into the Ottoman Empire and brought with them knowledge of many recent European scientific and economic discoveries and advancements.

Armenians

There are about 70,000 Armenians living in Turkey, mainly in İstanbul and around Lake Van. The Armenians are thought by some to be descended from the Urartians (518–330 BC), but others think they arrived from the Caucasus area after the Urartian state collapsed.

Armenians have lived in eastern Anatolia for a thousand years, almost always as subjects of some greater state such as the Alexandrine empire, or of the Romans, Byzantines, Persians, Seljuks or Ottomans. They lived with their Kurdish and Turkish neighbours in relative peace and harmony under the Ottoman millet system of distinct religious communities. But when this system gave way to modern ethnic nationalism, they suffered one of the greatest tragedies in their history.

Rebellion As ethnic groups on the fringes of the empire rose in rebellion and won their independence, the Armenians followed. Unlike other peoples, however, the Armenians lived in the Muslim heartland, where they were sometimes a plurality but never a majority.

By the 1890s there were frequent protests, rebellions and Armenian terrorist attacks on Ottoman government buildings and personnel, which were inevitably answered with ferocious repression by the police, army and populace. The revolutionaries hoped that if they triggered atrocities, the Christian powers of Europe would be persuaded to come to their aid, opening the way to independence. None of the powers, however, would allow any other to gain an advantage in the dismantling of the Ottoman Empire. Also, the tsar, like the sultan, did not want the creation of an independent Armenian state carved from his territory. The Armenians became the hopeless victims of their own small numbers, European power politics and the Ottomans' alarm at the dissolution of their once-mighty country.

As the terrorist incidents continued, the Armenians' former Turkish and Kurdish neighbours turned against them violently. On 26 August 1896, Armenian revolutionaries seized the Ottoman Bank building in İstanbul, threatening to blow it up. Although they were unsuccessful, the incident provoked widespread massacres in the city and elsewhere in which thousands of innocent Armenians died. The European powers raised their voices in protest, but again put no effective pressure on the sultan to stop the atrocities.

The restoration of the Ottoman constitution in 1908 provided a brief respite as all Ottoman peoples saw hope of living in harmony. However, it wasn't long before ethnic rivalries again came to the surface. Ottoman Bulgaria declared independence and Austria seized the former Ottoman provinces of Bosnia and Hercegovina. In April 1909, Armenian demonstrations at Adana provoked more massacres. War broke out with Italy, Bulgaria, Serbia and Greece, and the Ottoman grand vizier was assassinated.

WWI As WWI approached, a triumvirate of Young Turks named Enver, Talat and Jemal seized power. When war broke out, the Christian Orthodox Armenians of eastern Turkey were seen (with some justification) as being sympathetic to and aiding the advancing Russian army.

On 20 April 1915 the Armenians of Van rose in revolt, massacred the local Muslims, took the *kale* (fortress) and held it until the Russian army arrived. Four days after the beginning of the Van revolt, on 24 April 1915 (now commemorated as Armenian Martyrs' Day) the Ottoman government began the deportation of the Armenian population from the war zone to Syria. Hundreds of thousands of Armenians (mostly men) were massacred in the process, the rest (mostly women and children) were marched to Syria in great privation.

With the Russian victories a short-lived Armenian Republic was proclaimed in north-eastern Anatolia, and the victorious Armenians repaid defeated local Muslims with massacres in kind. But an offensive by the armies of Mustafa Kemal's Turkish nationalist Ankara government reclaimed Kars and Ardahan.

On 3 December 1920, the Ankara government concluded a peace treaty with the Armenian government in Erivan, now a Soviet republic. By the end of the war, the Armenian population of Anatolia had been reduced to a small minority, mostly in the major cities.

The Aftermath The Armenians who survived the cataclysm, and their descendants in the Diaspora, blame both the Ottoman government and the Turkish people as a whole for the tragedy, labelling it genocide. The Turks, while not denying that massacres occurred, deny that there was an official policy of genocide, and claim that many Armenians were indeed traitors, and that many if not most Armenian casualties were the result of civil war, disease and privation rather than massacre. Republican Turks dissociate themselves from the actions of the Ottoman government, pointing out that they themselves (or, more correctly, their parents and grandparents) fought to overthrow it.

Historians and pseudo-historians on both sides trade accusations and recriminations, dispute the actual number of casualties, the authenticity of incriminating historical documents, and the motives and actions of the other side. In the 1970s, Armenian terrorist assassinations of Turkish diplomats, their families, and innocent bystanders raised the level of recrimination and bitterness.

Armenians say they want the Turks to recognise and acknowledge the tragedy, and to provide compensation, perhaps even territory. Turks say they sympathise with the Armenians' loss, but that those who were responsible are long dead and those living today had nothing to do with it and cannot be held responsible, and thus compensation is inappropriate. It is an impasse likely to endure for generations.

EDUCATION

The Turkish Republic provides five years of compulsory *ilkokul* (primary school) and *ortaokul* (middle school) education for all children aged from seven to 12 years. Secondary, *lise* (high school), and vocational or technical education is available free to those who decide to continue. Specialised schools are available for the blind, the deaf, the mentally handicapped, orphans and the very poor. There are also numerous licensed private schools, *kolej* (colleges) and universities that charge tuition fees.

Turkey has 29 government-funded universities to which students are admitted through a central placement system. At Ankara's Middle East Technical University and Bilkent University, and at İstanbul's Boğaziçi (Bosphorus) University, English is the language of instruction.

ARTS
Visual Arts

Ottoman Era Art under the Ottomans was very different from art in the Turkish Republic. Until 1923 and the founding of the republic, all mainstream artistic expression conformed (more or less) to the laws of Islam, which forbid representation of any being with an immortal soul (ie, animal or human). Sculpture and painting as known in the West did not exist – with the notable exception of Turkish miniature painting, which was for the upper classes.

Instead of painting and sculpture, Islamic artists worked at arabesque decoration, faience, filigree, geometric stained glass, gilding, pottery and metalworking, glassblowing, marquetry, repousse work, calligraphy and illumination, textile design (including costumes and carpets), horticulture and landscape gardening. Turks may have invented the art of marbling paper, which is still practised today. Ottoman architecture is outstanding.

In Islamic art the artist's role is to affirm the unity and harmony of Allah's creation by producing beautiful objects; each work of art is a prayer, a tribute to God and a gift to one's fellow humans. Each motif, flower, pattern or Quranic inscription is laden with significance and tradition. Though change and innovation are possible, they are attempted only after deep reflection and in a creative spirit. It is an art of continuity, of community, not of iconoclasm or egotism.

Most of these arts reached their height during the great age of Ottoman power from the early 16th to the late 18th centuries. Turkish museums are full of examples: delicately coloured tiles from İznik, graceful glass vases and pitchers from İstanbul, carved wooden mosque doors, glittering illuminated Qurans, intricate jewellery and sumptuous costumes.

By the late 19th century educated Ottomans were taking up landscape and still-life painting in European styles.

Republican Era Under the republic, Atatürk encouraged European-style artistic expression. The government opened official painting and sculpture academies, encouraging this 'modern' secular art over the religious art of the past.

In the 20th century, Turkish artists have been in touch with European and US trends in the arts. Some have followed slavishly, others have borrowed judiciously, mixing in a good portion of local tradition and inspiration. By the 1970s and '80s, Turkish painting had become vigorous enough to support numerous different local schools of artists whose work is shown by museums, galleries, collectors and patrons.

Music

There are many kinds of Turkish music, almost all of them unfamiliar to foreign ears. Ottoman classical, religious (particularly Mevlevi) and some folk and popular music use a system of *makams*, or modalities, an exotic-sounding series of tones similar in function to Western scales. In addition to the familiar Western whole- and half-tone intervals, much Turkish music uses quarter-tones, unfamiliar to foreign ears and perceived as 'flat' until the ear becomes accustomed to them.

Though Ottoman classical music sounds ponderous and lugubrious to the uninitiated, much Turkish folk music as played in the villages is sprightly and immediately appealing. Türkü music, of which you'll hear lots on the radio, falls somewhere between: traditional folk music as performed by modern singers who live in the city.

The 1000-year-old tradition of Turkish troubadours *(aşık)*, still very much alive as late as the 1960s and '70s, is now dying out in its pure form – killed off by radio, TV, video and CDs. The songs of the great troubadours – Yunus Emre (13th century), Pir Sultan Abdal (16th century) and Aşık Veysel (died 1974) – are still popular, however, and are often performed and recorded.

The *küdüm* (top) and *ud* (bottom) are traditional instruments used in Turkish music.

Top of the Turkish Pops

Turkish rock music has proved astonishingly resilient in the face of the usual onslaught from Western pop music. Once away from the backpacker enclaves of İstanbul, Olimpos and Göreme, you'll hear little other than Turkish music.

Pop music in Turkey is as faddy and ephemeral as anywhere else. The flavour of 2000, for example, was **Kekilli** whose 'Bu Aksam Olurum' blared from turntables countrywide. Kekilli was taking over where teenybop idol **Tarkan** let off. Tarkan rocketed to fame on the back of his *Acayıpsın (You're Weird)* album in 1994 but by 1999 his star was shining so brightly that he preferred to sidestep his military service in favour of taking up the chance to perform to adoring fans in Paris.

Alongside the shooting stars there are also many well-established artists whose back catalogues remain as popular as those of the Stones and Springsteen. Particularly popular was **Barış Manço** whose songs, many of them aimed at children, were so loved that his funeral in 1999 was compared to that of Princess Diana for the emotion it elicited. Queen of 1990s pop was **Sezen Aksu**, a singer-songwriter whose latest contribution to the airwaves is *Deli Veren*.

Another long-established performer is protest singer **Zülfü Livaneli**, a singer and *saz* (Turkish lute) player who is also well known in Turkey as a newspaper columnist with left-wing sympathies who was once narrowly pipped to the post for the position of mayor of İstanbul. Since Livaneli's music often incorporates Western instrumentation, it's fairly accessible to non-Turkish audiences.

More alien to Western ears is the style of music known as *arabesk* which, as its name implies, puts an Arabic spin on home-grown Turkish traditions. The mournful themes (if not the melodies) of this music have led to it being compared to Greek *rembetika* and until the advent of independent radio and TV in the 1990s, the authorities kept arabesk off the airwaves, even conjuring up their own, more cheerful version in an attempt to undermine its power.

Until recently it wasn't at all cool to like a style of music associated, as the *Virgin Guide to World Music* put it, 'with gazinos and the sound systems of taxis'. However, arabesk now attracts a gay following which sits rather oddly alongside its more traditional macho audience.

Playing to arabesk's traditional audience is the hugely successful Kurdish singer **İbrahim Tatlıses** (see the boxed text 'Urfa's Favourite Son' in the Şanlıurfa section), a burly, moustached former construction worker from Şanlıurfa whose life seems positively dull compared to those of arabesk's artier practitioners. In 1980, for example, **Bülent Ersoy's** music was banned following his sex-change operation (male to female). Once the ban was lifted, Ersoy started performing live again – only to be shot at by a member of the reactionary, neo-fascist Grey Wolves militia group for refusing to sing a nationalist anthem.

Faced with music shops packed solid with gaudily packaged cassettes it's hard for a first-time visitor to know what to pick up. If you like your pop frothy you won't got far wrong with anything by **Hakan Peker**, **Sibel Can** or **Mustafa Sandal**. For harder rock, tune into **Haluk Levent**. **Grup Laçin** and **Ayna** are popular with those keener on group sounds while **Zara** or **Yavuz Bingöl** will please those who prefer a touch of folk with their pop. Finally, if you fancy music with a harder-hitting message then **Ferhat Tunç** or **Cem Karaca** could well be your favourites.

Unfortunately, the sorts of Turkish music which are most easily comprehensible to foreign ears are the fairly vapid taverna styles, and the local popular songs based on European and US models. Though this music can be fun, it is also fairly mindless and forgettable. Perhaps the best is Adnan Ergil's series of audio cassettes entitled *Turkish Folk Gitar*.

Though the music of Europe and the USA played a predominant role in Turkish musical life for most of this century, the phenomenal growth and sophisticated development of local Turkish artists and recording studios has recently pushed Western music into a subsidiary role. Many Western soloists and groups are popular in Turkey but you will hear much more Turkish music.

Western classical symphonies, chamber music, opera and ballet have a small but fiercely loyal following in Turkey. Government-funded orchestras, dance groups and opera companies, supported by visiting artists, keep them satisfied.

Literature

Literature before the republic was also bound up with Islam. Treatises on history, geography and science were cast in religious terms. Ottoman poets, borrowing from the great Arabic and Persian traditions, wrote sensual love poems of attraction, longing, fulfilment and ecstasy about the search for union with God.

By the late 19th century some Ottoman writers were adapting to European forms. With the foundation of the republic, the ponderous cadences of Ottoman courtly prose and poetry gave way to use of the ver-nacular. Atatürk decreed that the Turkish language be 'purified' of Arabic and Persian borrowings. This, and the introduction of the new Latin-based Turkish alphabet, brought literacy within the reach of many more citizens. Several Turkish writers, including Nazım Hikmet, Yashar Kemal and Orhan Pamuk, have been translated into other languages and have met with critical and popular acclaim abroad.

The grand old man among Turkish novelists is Yaşar Kemal, who some compare to Nicos Kazantzakis (of *Zorba the Greek* fame). Kemal's novels often take Turkish farming or working-class life as their subject matter, and are full of colourful characters and drama. There are translations in English (by Kemal's wife) of *Memed, My Hawk* and *The Wind from the Plains* and others.

[Continued on page 42]

Nasreddin Hoca, Storyteller Supreme

You won't be long in Turkey before you spot a picture of a bearded man in an outsize turban riding backwards on a donkey. This is Nasreddin Hoca, a medieval joker whose witty moralising stories are as familiar to Turkish children as Aesop's fables are to Europeans.

Strangely enough, almost nothing is known about the man to whom almost 500 stories are attributed. There are even some who claim there was no such living man.

Assuming Hoca is a real character, it seems likely that he was born the son of an imam around 1208 in the village of Hortu in Sivrihisar. As an adult he may have served time as a judge, as an imam, as a university professor and as a dervish. He probably died in 1284 in Akşehir, near Konya. His stories first turned up in a book called *Saltukname*, produced in 1480 and incorporating other folk tales and legends as well.

A typical Nasreddin Hoca story is written in a clipped prose style and concludes with an epigram intended to make people think. Themes are taken from daily life: cooking, riding a donkey, visiting a Turkish bath. Some so-called Nasreddin Hoca stories were clearly written by other people, and new 'Nasreddin Hoca' stories are still produced today.

The following tale is typical.

Hoca went to Bursa market to buy a pair of trousers. Having selected a pair, he was just about to pay when he spotted a robe and decided to take that instead.

As he walked towards the door, the shopkeeper called out that he hadn't paid for the robe. Hoca pointed out that he had returned the pair of trousers.

'But you hadn't paid for those either', he was reminded.

'What a strange man you are,' Hoca said. 'You expect me to pay for a pair of trousers I didn't buy.'

It's also typical of Hoca humour that his tomb in Akşehir has a padlocked gate on one side, although the other three sides are unfenced. What's more, the date inside is written backwards.

Every year in early July an International Nasreddin Hoca Festival is held in Akşehir. The Association of Turkish Caricaturists also runs an annual international Nasreddin Hoca competition.

TURKISH ARTS & CRAFTS

Carpets are only the most famous and visible of Turkey's traditional arts and crafts. Embroidery and lace-making are still practised in rural Turkey, as they have been for centuries. Primitive landscape painters once used horse-drawn wagons and carts as their venue; now it's the wood-panelled sides of trucks.

Turkish artisans also craft decorated wooden spoons, lathe-turned wooden items, lamps and stoves in tinplate, onyx and alabaster carvings, pottery and glass. Almost no-one leaves the country without a blue-and-white *nazar boncuğu* (evil-eye charm), usually of glass but now also of plastic.

Carpets

Turkey is famous for its beautiful carpets and kilims, and wherever you go you'll be spoilt for choice as to what to buy. Unfortunately, the carpet market is very lucrative and the hard-sell antics of some dealers and their shills have tended to bring it into disrepute, putting many visitors off venturing into the shops. Also, with the tourism boom, carpet prices in Turkey have risen so much that it may actually be cheaper to buy your Turkish carpet at home. Indeed, we've heard one story of a man who bought up old kilims in the Paris flea market, had them cleaned, then brought them to Turkey to sell to tourists at high prices – creative recycling!

If you have it in mind to buy a carpet, browse in your local shop before coming to Turkey. This will give you some idea of prices and will acquaint you with the various designs so you can shop more knowledgeably when in Turkey. See Shopping in the Facts for the Visitor chapter for tips on buying a carpet.

Inset: Motifs used in carpet designs are often derived from the natural environment in which weavers lived. This common motif represents a scorpion or spider.

Bottom: Threads in a carpet are knotted row by row. Two types of knots are used in carpet making: the Turkish or double knot and the Persian or single knot. These 'knots' are really more like stitches, and are important in ensuring the carpet is flexible and 'stretchy'. (Illustrations by Verity Campbell)

An Age-old Art Turkish women have been weaving carpets for a very long time. These beautiful, durable, eminently portable floor coverings were a nomadic family's most valuable and practical 'furniture', warming and brightening the clan's oft-moved homes. The oldest-known carpet woven in the Turkish double-knotted Gördes style dates from between the 4th and 1st centuries BC.

It is thought that hand-woven carpet techniques were introduced to Anatolia by the Seljuks in the 12th century. Thus it's not surprising that Konya, the Seljuk capital, was mentioned by Marco Polo as a centre of carpet production in the 13th century.

Carpet Weaving Today Traditionally, village women wove carpets for their own family's use, or for their dowry. Knowing they would be judged on their efforts, the women took great care over their handiwork, hand-spinning and dyeing the wool,

37

Traditional Patterns

The general pattern and colour scheme of old carpets was influenced by local traditions and the availability of certain types of wool and colours of dyes. Patterns were memorised, and women usually worked with no more than 18 inches of the carpet visible. Each artist imbued her work with her own personality, choosing a motif or a colour based on her own artistic preferences, and even events and emotions in her daily life.

In the 19th century, the European rage for Turkish carpets spurred the development of carpet companies. The companies, run by men, would deal with customers, take orders, purchase and dye the wool according to the customers' preferences, and contract local women to produce the finished product. The designs might be left to the women, but more often were provided by the company based on the customers' tastes.

Though well made, these carpets lost some originality and spirit of the older work.

Even carpets and rugs made today often use the same traditional patterns, such as the commonly used 'eye' (above) and 'tree' (right) patterns, and incorporate all sorts of symbols. At a glance two carpets might look identical, but closer examination reveals the subtle differences that give each Turkish carpet its individuality and much of its charm.

and choosing what they judged to be the most interesting and beautiful patterns. These days, many carpets are made not according to local traditions, but to the dictates of the market. Weavers in eastern Turkey might make carpets in popular styles native to western Turkey. Long-settled villagers might duplicate the wilder, hairier and more naive *yörük* (nomad) carpets.

Village women still weave carpets, but most of them work to fixed contracts for specific shops. Usually they work to a pattern and are paid for their final effort rather than for each hour of work. A carpet made to a fixed contract may still be of great value to its purchaser. However, the selling price should be lower than for a one-off piece.

Other carpets are the product of division of labour, with different individuals responsible for dyeing and weaving. What such pieces lose in individuality and rarity is often more than made up for in quality control. Most silk Hereke carpets are mass produced, but to standards that make them some of the most sought-after of all Turkish carpets.

Fearing that old carpet-making methods would be lost, the Ministry of Culture now sponsors a number of projects to revive traditional weaving and dyeing methods in western Turkey. Some carpet shops have stocks of these 'project carpets', which are usually of high quality.

Kilims, Sumaks & Cicims A good carpet shop will have a range of pieces made by a variety of techniques. Besides the traditional pile carpets, they may offer double-sided flat-woven mats such as kilims. Some traditional kilim motifs are similar to patterns found at the prehistoric mound of Çatal Höyük, testifying to the very ancient traditions of flat-woven floor coverings in Anatolia. Older, larger kilims may actually be two narrower pieces of similar but not always identical design stitched together. As this is now rarely done, any such piece is likely to be fairly old.

Other flat-weave techniques include *sumak*, a style originally from Azerbaijan, in which coloured threads are wrapped around the warp. *Cicims* are kilims with small lively patterns embroidered on top of them.

Carpets From Other Countries As well as Turkish carpets, many carpet shops sell pieces from other countries, especially from Iran, Afghanistan and the ex-Soviet Republics of Azerbaijan, Turkmenistan and Uzbekistan. If it matters that yours is actually from Turkey, bear in mind that Iran favours the single knot and Turkey the double knot. Turkish carpets also tend to have a higher pile, more dramatic designs and more varied colours than their Iranian cousins. Some Iranian sumaks are decorated with animal patterns, encouraging shopkeepers to call them 'Noah's Ark carpets' although they have absolutely nothing to do with the Bible story.

Alabaster

A translucent, fine-grained variety of either gypsum or calcite, alabaster is pretty because of its grain and colour, and because light passes through it. You'll see ashtrays, vases, chess sets, bowls, egg cups, even the eggs themselves carved from the stone.

Ceramics

The best Turkish ceramics were made in İznik and Kütahya in the 17th and 18th centuries. These tiles from the great days are now museum-pieces, found in collections throughout the world.

Today, most of the tile-making is done in Kütahya in the Aegean hinterland, which is the place to go for the very best ceramics. Souvenir shops elsewhere also have handmade tiles, plates, cups and bowls. They're not really high-fired so they're vulnerable to breaks and cracks, but they can be attractive and useful even so. The real, old İznik tiles from the 16th and 17th centuries qualify as antiquities and cannot be exported. If you go to İznik, you will find a reviving tile industry on a small scale.

Avanos, in Cappadocia, is a centre for simple but attractive red clay pottery, made from deposits taken from the neighbouring Kızılırmak (Red River).

Copper

Gleaming copper vessels will greet you in every souvenir shop you peep into. Some are old, sometimes several centuries old. Most are handsome, and some are still eminently useful. The new copperware tends to be of lighter gauge; that's one of the ways you tell new from old. But even the new stuff will have been made by hand.

'See that old copper water pipe over there?' my friend Alaettin asked me once. We were sitting in his cluttered, closet-sized shop on İstanbul's Çadırcılar Caddesi, just outside the Kapalı Çarşı. 'It dates from the time of Sultan Ahmet III (1703–30), and was used by the *padişah* (sultan) himself. I just finished making it yesterday.'

Alaettin was a master coppersmith, and had made pieces for many luminaries, including the late Nelson Rockefeller. His pieces might well have graced the sultan's private apartments – except that the sultanate was abolished in 1922. He charged a hefty price for his fine craftwork but not for the story, which was the gift-wrapping, so to speak.

Copper vessels should not be used for cooking in or eating from unless they are tinned inside: that is, washed with molten tin which covers the toxic copper. If you intend to use a copper vessel, make sure the interior layer of tin is intact, or negotiate to have it *kalaylamak* (tinned). If there is a *kalaycı* shop nearby, ask about the price of the tinning in advance, as tin is expensive.

Inlaid Wood

Cigarette boxes, chess and *tavla* (backgammon) boards and other items will be inlaid with different coloured woods, silver or mother-of-pearl. It's not the finest work, but it's pretty good. Make sure there is indeed inlay. These days, alarmingly accurate decals exist. Also, check the silver: is it silver, or aluminium or pewter? Is the mother-of-pearl actually 'daughter-of-polystyrene'?

Jewellery

Turkey is a wonderful place to buy jewellery, especially antique. None of the items sold here may meet your definition of 'chic', but window-shopping is great fun. Jewellers' Row in any market is a dazzling strip of glittering shop windows filled with gold. In İstanbul's Kapalı Çarşı,

---

Antiques

Turkey has a lot of fascinating stuff left over from the empire: vigorous peasant jewellery, water-pipe mouthpieces carved from amber, old Qurans and illuminated manuscripts, Greek and Roman figurines and coins, tacky furniture in the Ottoman Baroque style. However, *it is illegal to buy, sell, possess or export any antiquity*, and you can go to prison for breaking the law. All antiquities must be turned over to a museum immediately upon discovery. See the Customs section in the Facts for the Visitor chapter for more details.

Putting the finishing touches on a carpet is the end of a long process involving many different steps, from the selection and dyeing of fibres, to the choice of a design, weaving and trimming.

DIANA MAYFIELD

EDDIE GERALD

DAVOR PAVICHICH

NEIL WILSON

IZZET KERIBAR

STUART WASSERMAN

Carpet selling is big business in Turkey, and you'll see carpets on display in most towns and villages, however small. Although most carpets are mass-produced, there is still a huge range of designs and colours to choose from. Many designs incorporate traditional motifs and patterns arranged according to age-old traditional rules.

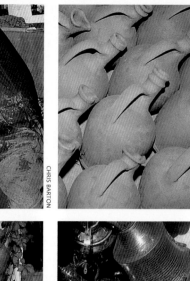

CHRIS BARTON

CHRIS BARTON

GREG ELMS

IZZET KERIBAR

The tourist boom of recent decades has given a new lease of life to Turkish arts and crafts.

Top: This potter, from the village of Avanos in Cappadocia, shows his skill in making the distinctive red pottery the area is famous for.

Middle: Brass and coppersmithing is another age-old traditional craft, and no souvenir shop is complete without a glittering display of copperware.

Bottom: Other souvenir shop regulars are wooden boxes and backgammon sets, inlaid with mother of pearl or different types of wood, and, strictly for the tourists, colourful traditional fezzes and slippers.

DIANA MAYFIELD

JON DAVISON

IZZET KERIBAR

MARTIN MOOS

A riot of colour: intricately decorated tiles (top) make a quintessentially Turkish souvenir; strings of beads (middle) on display in İstanbul's Kapalı Çarşı are reminiscent of Ottoman finery; and gorgeously patterned traditional woollen socks (bottom) are just crying out to be bought.

a blackboard sign hung above Kuyumcular Caddesi (Street of the Jewellers) bears the daily price for unworked gold of so-many carats. Serious gold-buyers should check this price, watch carefully as the jeweller weighs the piece in question, and then calculate what part of the price is for gold and what part for labour.

Silver is another matter. There is sterling silver jewellery (look for the hallmark), but nickel silver and pewter-like alloys are much more common. Serious dealers don't try to pass off alloy as silver.

Leather & Suede

On any given Kurban Bayramı ('Sacrifice' Holiday), more than 2.5 million sheep get the axe in Turkey. Add to that the normal day-to-day needs of a cuisine based on mutton and lamb and you have a huge amount of raw material to be made into leather items.

Shoes, bags, cushions, jackets, skirts, vests, hats, gloves and trousers are all made from soft leather. This is a big industry in Turkey, particularly in and around the Kapalı Çarşı in İstanbul. So much leather clothing is turned out that a good deal of it will be badly cut or carelessly made, but there are lots of fine pieces as well.

The only way to assure yourself of a good piece is to examine it carefully, taking time. Try it on just as carefully; see if the sleeves are full enough, if the buttonholes are positioned well, if the collar rubs. If something is wrong, keep trying others until you find what you want.

Made-to-order garments can be excellent or disappointing, as the same tailor who made the ready-made stuff will make the ordered stuff; and will be making it fast because the shopkeeper has already impressed you by saying 'No problem. I can have it for you tomorrow'. It's better to find something off the rack that fits than to order it, unless you can order without putting down a deposit or committing yourself to buy (this is often possible). Leather items and clothing are standard tourist stuff, found in all major tourist destinations.

Bottom: When carved into a pipe, meerschaum smokes sweet and cool. Over time, it absorbs residues from the tobacco and turns a nut-brown colour.

Meerschaum

The world's largest and finest beds of meerschaum (lületaşı), a soft, white, clay-like material, are found in Turkey, near the city of Eskişehir. This porous but heat-resistant material is used to make pipes, which can be plain or carved in a variety of designs. You'll see pipes portraying turbaned paşas, wizened old men, fair maidens and mythological beasts, as well as many pipes in geometrical designs.

When buying, look for purity and uniformity in the stone. Carving is often used to cover up flaws in a piece of meerschaum. For pipes, check that the bowl walls are uniform in thickness all around, and that the hole at the bottom of the bowl is centred. Prices are very reasonable; you should be able to get the pipe you want for US$10 to US$20, or at least only half of what you'd pay at home.

MICK WELDON

[Continued from page 36]

Orhan Pamuk also has a worldwide following. *The White Tower* and *The Black Book* are his two best-known works translated into English, with *New Life* (1997) gaining recognition.

For a fascinating look into the last years of the Ottoman Empire and the early years of the Turkish Republic, read İrfan Orga's *Portrait of a Turkish Family*. First published in 1950 and recently republished with an afterword by the author's son, it's an absorbing portrait of a family trying to survive the collapse of an old society and the birth of a new one.

Cinema

Cinema appeared in Turkey in 1896, just a year after the Lumière brothers presented their first cinematic show. At first it was only foreigners and non-Muslims who watched movies, but by 1914 there were cinemas run by and for Muslims as well.

The War of Independence inspired actor Muhsin Ertuğrul, Turkey's cinema pioneer, to establish a film company in 1922, making patriotic films. Comedies and documentaries followed. Within a decade Turkish films were winning awards in international competitions, though only 23 films had been made.

Several Turkish directors have won worldwide recognition in recent years. Most prominent is Yılmaz Güney, whose *Yol* (The Road), *Duvar* (The Wall) and *The Herd* have been released with English subtitles. *Yol* (The Road), winner of the best film award at Cannes in 1982, explores the dilemmas of a Kurd from a traditional family integrated into modern, urban Turkish society. Ferzai Özpetek's *Hamam* was a hit in Europe.

Turkey boasts several Turkish-language periodicals dealing with current cinema. For English-language reviews, pick up the *Turkish Daily News*, particularly the Sunday edition, which includes the supplement *Probe*.

SOCIETY & CONDUCT

At first glance, much of Turkish society is highly Europeanised. Men and women march off to jobs in city offices and shops,

Political Headgear

'Put on your hat.' Those were fighting words in Ottoman times, when a hat (defined as headgear with a brim) was seen as a Christian adornment by every self-respecting Muslim Turk. The brim on a hat interfered with Muslim prayer, in which the person performing it must touch the forehead to the ground. A hat was fit only for an infidel.

Indeed, throughout Ottoman Turkey one's headgear was a recognised symbol of one's rank and role in life. Ottoman tombstones were often topped by a stylised headgear that showed the social role of the deceased, and the sultan's Christian and Jewish subjects were required by law to wear certain colours and styles of clothing, and to eschew others.

In early 20th-century Turkey, most Muslim men wore the maroon-coloured felt *tarbuş* (fez) and had done so since this style of headgear had been introduced as a replacement for 'old-fashioned' turbans in 1829.

In 1925, President Mustafa Kemal (Atatürk) pushed through a law requiring all Turkish men to give up the fez, and women the veil, and to wear European-style headgear instead. All religious garb was banned from public places, and could only be worn in places of worship.

This symbolic modernisation – and secularisation – was vigorously resisted in conservative Muslim circles. The wearing of a hat seemed a symbol of apostasy, the highest crime under Islamic law. Men who saw their Muslim identity being ripped from their heads rioted. The government enforced the law vigorously, sentencing men to death in Erzurum, Giresun, Rize and Maraş, and elsewhere to hefty jail sentences.

Headgear is still a sensitive symbol of the struggle between Turkey's European-leaning majority of secularists and its conservative Islamist minority, especially with the upsurge in Islamist political activity. Although the fez is now looked upon as a faintly comical tourist souvenir, Islamist women cling closely to the tradition of the headscarf. Students attempting to attend university classes while wearing headscarves have been expelled, and Merve Kavakçı, an MP from the Islamist Fazilet Partisi, caused a furore in parliament when she stood to take the oath of office in a headscarf.

farmers mount their tractors for a day in the fields, and bureaucrats sit in front of their typewriters and computer keyboards. But Turkish traditions are different from those of Europe, and glimpses of traditional attitudes and behaviour often come through.

Liberal Western attitudes born of Atatürk's reforms are strongest in the urban centres of the west and along the coasts, among the middle and upper classes. These Turks look to Western culture as the ideal, and accept the validity of other religious beliefs alongside their own.

The working and farming classes, particularly in the east, are more conservative, traditional and religious. There is a small but growing segment of 'born again' Muslims, fervent and strict in their religion but otherwise modern. Though always polite, these Turks may give you the feeling that East is East and West is West, and that the last echo of crusaders versus Saracens has not yet died away.

Hospitality is an honoured tradition in Turkey, from the shopkeeper who plies you with tea, coffee or soft drinks to the village family who invite you to share their home and meals for the customary three days. Commercialism has begun to corrupt traditional hospitality in tourist areas, producing the shady carpet merchant who lays on the friendliness with a trowel only to sell you shoddy goods at inflated prices. Don't let the carpet touts make you lose sight of true Turkish hospitality, which is a wonderful thing.

Traditional Culture

Under the Ottoman Empire (from the 14th century AD to 1923), Turkish etiquette was highly organised and very formal. Every encounter between people turned into a mini-ceremony full of the flowery romance of the East.

Though the Turks have adapted to the informality of 20th-century life, you'll still notice vestiges of this courtly state of mind. Were you to learn Turkish, you'd find dozens of polite phrases – actually rigid formulas – to be repeated on cue in many daily situations. Some are listed in the Language chapter at the end of this guide. Use one of these at the proper moment, and the Turks will love it.

Turks are very understanding of foreigners' different customs, but if you want to behave in accordance with local feelings, use all the polite words you can muster, at all times. This can get laborious, and even Turks complain about how one can't even get out the door without five minutes of politenesses. But even the complainers still say them.

Also note these things: don't point your finger directly towards any person. Don't turn the sole of your foot or shoe towards anyone. Don't blow your nose openly in public, especially in a restaurant; instead, turn or leave the room and blow quietly. Don't pick your teeth openly, but cover your mouth with your hand. Don't do a lot of kissing or hugging with a person of the opposite sex in public. All of these actions are considered rude.

Mosque Etiquette

Always remove your shoes before stepping on a mosque's carpets, or on the clean area just in front of the mosque door. This is not a religious law, just a practical one. Worshippers kneel and touch their foreheads to the carpets, and they like to keep them clean. If there are no carpets, as in a saint's tomb, you can leave your shoes on.

Wear modest clothes when visiting mosques, as you would when visiting a church – tatty clothes, shorts (for men or women) or any gear that worshippers might find outlandish are best avoided. Women should have head, arms and shoulders covered, and wear modest dresses or skirts, preferably reaching to the knees. At some of the most visited mosques, attendants will lend you long robes if your clothing doesn't meet a minimum standard. Although the loan of the robe is free, a donation is appreciated.

Visiting Turkish mosques is generally very easy, though there are no hard and fast rules. At most times no-one will give you any trouble, but now and then there may be a stickler for propriety guarding the door, and they will keep you out if your dress or demeanour is not acceptable.

Avoid entering mosques at prayer time (ie, at the call to prayer – dawn, noon, mid-afternoon, dusk and evening, or 20 minutes thereafter). Avoid visiting mosques at all on Fridays, especially morning and noon. Friday is the Muslim holy day.

When you're inside a mosque, even if it is not prayer time, there will usually be several people praying. Don't disturb them in any way, don't take flash photos and don't walk directly in front of them.

Everybody will appreciate it if you drop some money into the donations box; chances are that the money actually will go to the mosque.

Body Language

Turks say 'yes' *(evet)* by nodding forward and down. To say 'no' *(hayır,* **hah**-yuhr), nod your head up and back, lifting your eyebrows at the same time. Or just raise your eyebrows: that's 'no'.

Another way to say 'no' is *yok* : literally, 'It doesn't exist (here)', or 'We don't have any (of it)' – the same head upward, raised eyebrows applies. Remember, when a Turkish person seems to be giving you an arch look, they're only saying 'no'. They may also make the sound 'tsk', which also means 'no'. There are lots of ways to say 'no' in Turkish.

By contrast, wagging your head from side to side doesn't mean 'no' in Turkish; it means 'I don't understand'. So if a Turkish person asks you, 'Are you looking for the bus to Ankara?' and you shake your head, they'll assume you don't understand English and will probably ask you the same question again, this time in German.

There are other signs that can sometimes cause confusion, especially when you are out shopping. For instance, if you want to indicate length ('I want a fish this big'), don't hold your hands apart at the desired length, but hold out your arm and place a flat hand on it, measuring from your fingertips to the hand. Thus, if you want a pretty big fish, you must 'chop' your arm with your other hand at about the elbow.

Height is indicated by holding a hand the desired distance above the floor or some other flat surface such as a counter.

If someone – a shopkeeper or restaurant waiter, for instance – wants to show you the stockroom or the kitchen, they'll signal 'Come on, follow me' by waving a hand downward and towards themselves in a scooping motion. Waggling an upright finger would never occur to them, except perhaps as a vaguely obscene gesture.

RELIGION

The Turkish population is 99% Muslim, mostly of the Sunni creed; there are groups of Shiites in the east and south-east. As non-Muslim groups make up less than 1% of the population, to talk about Turkish religion is to talk about Islam.

Principles of Islam

The basic beliefs of Islam are these: God (Allah) created the world and everything in it pretty much according to the biblical account. In fact, the Bible is a sacred book to Muslims. Adam, Noah, Abraham, Moses and Jesus were prophets. Their teachings and revelations are accepted by Muslims, except for Jesus' divinity and his status as saviour. Jews and Christians are called 'People of the Book', meaning those with a revealed religion that preceded Islam. The Quran prohibits enslavement of any People of the Book. Jewish prophets and wise men, and Christian saints and martyrs, are all accepted as holy in Islam.

However, Islam is the 'perfection' of this earlier tradition. Though Moses and Jesus were great prophets, Mohammed was the greatest and last, *the* Prophet. To him, God communicated his final revelation, and entrusted him to communicate it to the world. Mohammed is not a saviour, nor is he divine. He is God's messenger, deliverer of the final, definitive message.

Muslims do not worship Mohammed, only God. In fact, Muslim in Arabic means, 'one who has submitted to God's will'; Islam is 'submission to God's will'. It's all summed up in the Ezan, the phrase called out from the minaret five times a day and said at the beginning of Muslim prayers: 'God is great! There is no god but God, and Mohammed is His Prophet'.

The Quran

God's revelations to Mohammed are contained in the Kur'an-i Kerim, the Quran. Mohammed recited the suras (verses or chapters) of the Quran in an inspired state. They were written down by followers, and are still regarded as the most beautiful, melodic and poetic work in Arabic literature. The Quran, being sacred, exists in its true form in Arabic only.

Religious Duties & Practices

The Islamic faith is expressed by observance of the five so-called pillars of Islam. Muslims must:

- Say, understand and believe, 'There is no god but God, and Mohammed is his Prophet'.
- Pray five times daily: at dawn, at noon, at mid-afternoon, at dusk and after dark.
- Give alms to the poor.
- Keep the fast of Ramazan, if capable of doing so.
- Make a pilgrimage to Mecca.

Muslim prayers are set rituals. Before praying, Muslims must wash hands and arms, feet and ankles, head and neck in running water; if no water is available, in clean sand; if there's no sand, the motions will suffice. Then they must cover their head, face Mecca and perform a precise series of gestures and genuflections. If they deviate from the pattern, they must begin again.

In daily life, a Muslim must not touch or eat pork, nor drink wine (interpreted as any alcoholic beverage), and must refrain from fraud, usury, slander and gambling. No sort of image of any being with an immortal soul (ie, human or animal) can be revered or worshipped in any way.

Islam has been split into many factions and sects since the time of Mohammed. Islamic theology has become very elaborate and complex. These tenets, however, are still the basic ones shared by all Muslims.

LANGUAGE

The national language of Turkey is Turkish, described in more detail in the Language chapter at the back of this book. Turks don't expect any foreigner to know Turkish, but if you can manage a few words it will always be appreciated. For their part, they'll try whatever foreign words they know, usually English or German.

Facts for the Visitor

SUGGESTED ITINERARIES
You can see a lot of the country in six to eight weeks but if your time is limited, here are some suggestions. These are *minimal* times.

Three to Five Days
Base yourself in İstanbul, and take an overnight trip to İznik and Bursa, or Troy and the Dardanelles. You could also take a day excursion by plane to Ephesus.

One Week
Spend two nights in İstanbul before heading to Bursa (one night), Gallipoli and Troy (one night), Bergama (Pergamum), İzmir and Kuşadası (two nights), with excursions to Ephesus, Priene, Miletus and Didyma. Return to İstanbul (one night).

Two Weeks
To the basic one-week itinerary, add an excursion from Kuşadası to Pamukkale and

---

Highlights of Turkey

There's a lot to see and do in Turkey. Here are some of the highlights to whet your appetite:

Islamic Architecture
The great imperial mosques of İstanbul are perhaps the most famous image of Turkey. If you're at all interested in the art of architecture, Turkey is a treasure-trove. Be sure to see the Süleymaniye, Rüstem Paşa and Blue mosques in İstanbul; the Selimiye and Eski mosques in Edirne; and, way off the beaten track, the great Ulu Cami at Divriği, near Sivas.

Ancient Cities
Turkey's myriad archaeological sites include Ephesus, Afrodisias, Priene, Miletus, Didyma, Hierapolis and Termessos. At the most spectacular sites (such as the ones we've listed), you'll see fine classical buildings, ancient inscriptions, intricate mosaics – and lots of other people. At the more remote sites, you may find yourself alone among picturesque tumbledown marble temples, the only sound being that of the fragrant, soughing pines that surround you.

Water Sports
Turkey's 7000km of coastline means that aquatic activity is a natural. The waters of the Black Sea are pretty chilly, but the Aegean and Mediterranean coasts are excellent from late April to October.

Museums
Every city and town in Turkey has its museum, usually a mundane place with simple displays...but the exhibits may be stone implements from the dawn of human history, Roman sculpture, Hellenic jewellery, Byzantine icons, Ottoman calligraphy or Turkish folklore. A number of Turkish museums are world-class, including İstanbul's Topkapı Palace, archaeological museums and Museum of Turkish & Islamic Arts; Ankara's Museum of Anatolian Civilisations; the Antalya Müzesi; the Antakya Arkeoloji Müzesi for its Roman mosaics; and Bodrum's Museum of Underwater Archaeology.

Hamams
The Turkish bath, or *hamam*, is the direct successor to the Roman steam baths of two millennia ago. If you've never enjoyed a Turkish bath, you must do so in Turkey. You'll never know how clean and refreshed you can feel until you do. All cities and most towns have public baths, often housed in beautiful, historic Ottoman buildings.

Hierapolis via Afrodisias (one to two nights); also take a loop excursion to Ankara, Konya and Cappadocia, and visit the Hittite cities. If you have time left over, spend a day or two on the Turquoise Coast (Kaş, Antalya, Side, Alanya).

Three Weeks

To the basic two-week itinerary, add a yacht cruise or coastal highway excursion from Kuşadası south to Bodrum (Halicarnassus), Marmaris, Fethiye, Kaş, Finike, Kemer and Antalya; or second-best, an excursion along the Black Sea coast. Another option (but not in blazing-hot July and August) is a tour of the south-east – Şanlıurfa, Mardin and Diyarbakır.

Eastern Tour For mid-May to early October only: start in Ankara or Cappadocia, take in Adıyaman and Nemrut Dağı (Mt Nimrod), Diyarbakır, Van, Doğubayazıt and Mt Ararat, Erzurum, Kars, Artvin, Hopa, Rize, Trabzon, Samsun, Amasya and return to Ankara via Boğazkale (Hattuşa).

PLANNING
When to Go

Spring (from April to June) and autumn (from September to October) are best. The

Hiking

Perhaps the best mountain hiking is in the Kaçkar Mountains along the eastern Black Sea coast near Ayder; or on the southern side of the range around Yusufeli. Try the walk from Fethiye to Ölüdeniz via the Ottoman Greek ghost town of Kayaköy, or a hike in the hills above Köprülü Kanyon near Side on the Mediterranean coast. Or try the Lycian Way, a long-distance path which extends along the Mediterranean coast from Ölüdeniz to Antalya . The surreal valleys of Cappadocia make for fine hikes in the morning and evening when there's less heat and more golden light.

Skiing

Turkish ski resorts are simple compared with those in Europe or North America. But if you visit Turkey in winter and simply have to get on a slope, the best facilities are at Uludağ, near Bursa. The slopes of volcanic Erciyes Dağı near Kayseri are convenient to Cappadocia, and new hotels at Palandöken near Erzurum anticipate increased interest in skiing in the mountains of eastern Turkey.

Shopping

İstanbul's Kapalı Çarşı has 4000 shops selling leather apparel and accessories, coloured tiles, brass and copper ware, antiques and fake antiques, old coins, carpets and kilims, meerschaum pipes and ornaments, silk scarves, perfumes and colognes – and much more. Many larger towns also have historic covered markets stuffed with Turkish treasures.

Yacht Cruising

Whether you take a day-long excursion from Fethiye, rent a cabin for a three-day sail from Bodrum, or charter an entire *gulet* (traditional Turkish yacht) for a week-long 'Blue Voyage' out of Marmaris, a journey by boat along the Aegean or Mediterranean coast will be among the most vivid memories of your trip.

Keyf

Keyf is the Turkish art of quiet relaxation. Opportunities for it abound in Turkey. Sitting in the shade of a palm tree, sipping a drink and watching the sun set over the Aegean; enjoying a bracing glass of tea beneath a jasmine branch in the fresh morning air; or stretching out in the warm sun on the deck of a boat headed for the ancient port of Knidos, near Marmaris. That's keyf!

climate is perfect on the Aegean and Mediterranean coasts then, as well as in İstanbul. It's cooler in central Anatolia, but not unpleasantly so. There is usually little rain between May and October, except along the Black Sea coast. If you visit before mid-June or after August, you may avoid the mosquitoes which can be a plague in some areas. The Black Sea coast is best visited between April and September.

High season, when facilities are most crowded and prices highest, is from July to mid-September. Low season, when crowd pressure and prices are low, is from November to March. Most places to stay and restaurants in coastal resorts close from late October to early April, though a few remain open year-round.

The best months for water sports are July and August, but the water is fine in May, June, September and October too.

In the hottest months on the coasts you may have to take a siesta during the heat of the day between noon and 3 pm. Get up early in the morning, clamber around the local ruins, then after lunch and a siesta, come out again for *piyasa vakti* (promenade time) when everyone strolls by the sea, sits in a cafe, and watches the sunset.

The best time for a trip to eastern Turkey is from late June to September. As a general rule, you should not venture into the east before mid-May or after mid-October unless you're prepared, as there may be snow, perhaps even enough to close roads and mountain passes. Unfortunately, a tour of eastern Turkey in high summer usually includes passing through the south-east, which is beastly hot at that time.

Try to avoid travelling during Turkey's most popular public holiday, the Kurban Bayramı; you might also want to take into account when the fasting month of Ramazan falls – for dates and more details of religious festivals and other public holidays, see Public Holidays & Special Events later in this chapter. If you are planning to visit the Gallipoli Peninsula, you're probably better off avoiding Anzac Day (25 April) unless it is important to you to visit at this time.

Maps

Turkish government tourist offices both in Turkey and abroad hand out a useful free *Tourist Map* (1:850,000), which shows highways, railways, ferry routes and points of interest, as well as useful city plans for Adana, Ankara, Antalya, İstanbul and İzmir. Privately produced maps in Turkey often lack detail or contain inaccuracies, so you'd be well advised to bring a good map from home. If you buy a Turkish one, try to get the Turkish Touring & Automobile Association's *East Turkey* and/or *West Turkey* at 1:850,000, for about US$5 each. They divide the country at Kayseri and do not show the railways. Don't trust these maps for back roads, though, particularly in the east.

Of the British maps, the Bartholomew *Euromap Turkey* (two sheets) covers the country at 1:800,000 for about US$10 per sheet. The *AA/ESR Tourist Map Turkey* is also good, covering the entire country at 1:2,000,000, as well as the south-west coast at 1:750,000; and includes street plans of İstanbul, İzmir and several tourist resorts.

Germany produces several good series, including the Reise und Verkehrsverlag's *Euro-Atlas* series that covers the country in two sheets, eastern and western Turkey, at 1:800,000. Kümmerly & Frey has a fairly good sheet that covers the entire country, as does Hallwag.

For İstanbul, Lonely Planet publishes a comprehensive *İstanbul City Map*, which has detailed maps of the city at scales ranging from 1:10,500 to 1:30,000 and a feature map of Topkapı Palace. The useful *İstanbul A-Z Rehber-Atlas* is sold in many foreign-language and tourist-oriented bookshops for about US$10.

What to Bring

In the hottest months from mid-June to mid-September, you'll need light cotton summer clothes, and a light sweater or jacket for the evenings to wear up on the central Anatolian plateau. You won't really need rain gear at all. You would do better to duck between the showers rather than haul rain gear during your entire trip just for a possible day or two of rain on the Black Sea coast.

In spring and autumn, summer clothing is still OK, but the evenings are cooler. If you plan to travel extensively in Central Anatolia (to Ankara, Konya, Cappadocia or Nemrut Dağı) after mid-October or before mid-May, pack a heavier sweater and perhaps a light raincoat.

Winter wear – for December to March – is warm clothes and rain gear. Though it doesn't get really cold along the Mediterranean coast, it does get damp, rainy and chilly in most of the country, including along the southern coast. İstanbul and İzmir get dustings of snow; Ankara gets more. Nemrut Dağı and the eastern region are frigid and covered in snow.

It's worth packing sun block cream and insect repellent, although these are available locally, especially in the tourist resort areas.

RESPONSIBLE TOURISM

Tourism has made a huge economic and social impact on Turkey during the last two decades. While bringing in much-needed money to support local economies and workers, it has also fostered rapid and pervasive social change.

For example, until the 1970s it was frowned upon for a man and woman to show affection in public; even a kiss or holding hands between husband and wife was illegal (though rarely enforced). Today many tourists go topless on Turkey's Mediterranean beaches, are photographed and appear on the front pages of national newspapers. Likewise, public drunkenness used to be almost unheard of; today it is a growing problem.

The shock of this rapid cultural change may have encouraged the growth of Islamic fundamentalism as people seek a firm grounding amid bewildering novelty. As a tourist, you should be sensitive to these currents and to the sensitivities of your Turkish hosts – see Society & Conduct in the Facts about Turkey chapter for more information.

Turkey is one of those countries with treasure-troves of antiquities, some of which are smuggled out of the country and fed into the international contraband art market. The Turkish government takes vigorous measures to defend its patrimony against theft. Antiquity smuggling, like drug smuggling, is a dirty business. Don't do anything that makes you look like you're a part of it – for more details, see the Customs section later in this chapter.

Although Turkey's environmental problems may seem daunting, there is a lot visitors can do to set a good example and encourage local efforts at environmental protection. Despite the insufficient number of rubbish bins, don't litter. Complain to local tourist offices about litter on beaches or sewage near swimming areas. If you are trekking, carry out all your rubbish and bury human waste at least 100m from any watercourse.

TOURIST OFFICES
Local Tourist Offices

Every Turkish town of any size has an official tourist office run by the Ministry of Tourism and marked by the fan-like Hittite sun figure. Tourist Offices are usually open from 8.30 am to noon or 12.30 pm, and 1.30 to 5.30 pm Monday to Friday, longer in summer in popular tourist locations. Some are staffed by helpful people with some knowledge about the area; others are attended by those who see tourists as interruptions in their otherwise somnolent and comfortable daily routine. There may also be an office operated by the city or provincial government, or by a local tourism association (*turizm derneği*). Locations of all are given in the text.

If you need help and can't find an office, ask for the *belediye sarayı* (town hall). They'll rummage around for someone who speaks some English, and will do their best to solve your problem.

Tourist Offices Abroad

Following is a selected list of tourist offices outside Turkey:

Australia (☎ 02-9223 3055, fax 9223 3204, 📧 turkish@ozemail.com.au) Suite 101, 280 George St, Sydney, NSW 2000
Canada (☎ 613-230 8654, fax 230 3683) Constitution Square, 360 Albert St, Suite 801, Ottawa, ON K1R 7X7

UK (☎ 020-7629 7771, fax 491 0773, ⓔ tto@
turkishtourism.demon.co.uk) 1st floor,
170–173 Piccadilly, London, W1V 9DD
USA (☎ 212-687 2194, fax 599 7568) 821 UN
Plaza, New York, NY 10017

VISAS & DOCUMENTS
Passport
Make sure your passport will be valid for at
least three months after you enter the country. If it's just about to expire, you may not
be allowed to enter the country.

Visas
Tourist Visa Nationals of the following
countries can enter Turkey for up to three
months with just a valid passport, no visa is
required: Denmark, Finland, France, Germany, Greece, Iceland, Japan, New Zealand,
Norway, Sweden and Switzerland. Nationals of Austria, Australia, Belgium, Canada,
Holland, Ireland, Israel, Italy, Portugal,
Spain, the UK and the USA must buy a visa
on arrival at the airport or at an overland
border (ie, not at an embassy in advance).

Make sure you obtain your visa before you
join the queue for immigration. How much
you pay for your visa (which is essentially a
tourist tax) depends on your nationality and
changes fairly frequently; at the time of
writing UK citizens paid UK£10 (payable
by bank note only), Australians US$20 and
citizens of the USA a hefty US$45. No
photographs are required.

The standard visa is valid for three
months and, depending on your nationality,
usually allows for multiple entries.

Visa Extensions In theory a visa can be
renewed once after three months, but the
bureaucracy and costs involved mean that
it's much easier to leave the country (usually to one of the Greek islands) and then
come back in again.

Residence Permit If you plan to stay in
Turkey for more than three months, you
might want to apply for an *ikamet tezkeresi*
(residence permit), which is usually valid
for one to two years. Contact a tourist office

Visas for Neighbouring Countries

If you are planning to travel onwards from Turkey, you'll probably need to get a visa in advance.

Bulgaria
A transit visa for Bulgaria (valid for 30 hours) costs US$12 for many nationalities from the Bulgarian
consulate; if you buy it at the border it will cost US$16. Visas for longer stays are more expensive.

Georgia
Visas for Georgia can be obtained from the consulate in Trabzon and cost US$40 for 15 days, US$50
for 30 days, or US$15 for transit (for this you need a visa for the country to which you're heading).

Greece
The list of nationals who can enter Greece without a visa includes Australia, Canada, all EU countries, New Zealand and the USA. The list changes, so contact a Greek embassy to check.

Iran
If you want to visit Iran, you'll need to get a visa in advance. There is an embassy in Ankara and consulates in İstanbul and Erzurum. You must pay a nonrefundable application fee of US$60 and then
wait to hear if your application will be granted. Some people wait a day or so, others weeks. No visas
will be granted to American applicants, and the British aren't too popular either. If you haven't done
this before arriving in Doğubayazıt there are men who will help you organise a visa through the consulate in Erzurum. You will need to travel back to Erzurum but they say that, in most cases, the visa

or tourism police office. You will need to show means of support (savings, a steady income from outside the country) or legal work within the country. Most people staying for a shorter period, or working without a valid permit (as short-term private tutors of English, for example), cross the border into Greece for a day or two every three months rather than bother with the residence permit.

Work Visa It's best to obtain a *çalışma vizesi* (work visa) from the Turkish embassy or consulate in your home country before you leave. Submit in person or by mail the completed visa form, your passport, two photos of yourself, your proof of employment (a contract or letter from your employer) and the required fee. Your passport will be returned with the visa stamped inside; it takes about three weeks.

If you're not at home and you want a work visa, apply for it outside Turkey. The Turkish consulate in Komotini in Greece, a 10-hour overnight bus ride from İstanbul, is

used to such requests. It usually grants the visa within a few hours. If you plan to make a special trip, check to make sure the consulate will be open and issuing work visas when you arrive. Your own consulate or the Greek consulate may be able to tell you.

Once you arrive in Turkey on a work visa, you must obtain a 'pink book', a combined work permit and residence permit, from the *yabancılar polisi* (tourist police). In İstanbul they're in Cağaloğlu behind the İstanbul *valiliği* (local government headquarters) on Ankara Caddesi. Your employer may do this for you. If not, apply with your passport, two more photos, and the US$40 processing fee. They should have your pink book ready in two or three days. The pink book, which takes over from the visa in your passport, is renewable every year, as long as you show proof of continued employment.

If you can't provide proof of employment (ie, if you're working illegally), you may still be able to get a three-month residence permit if you can show bank deposits in Turkey totalling more than about US$200.

Visas for Neighbouring Countries

can be arranged in one hour, allowing you to return to Doğubayazıt the same day. You may also be asked to show a visa for the country you are travelling onto after Iran as well as a bus or airline ticket out of Iran. Contact the Iranian embassy in Ankara for details on current visa requirements.

Northern Cyprus

Visas for Northern Cyprus are available on arrival in Cyprus (so long as you don't have a Greek or Armenian surname). If you're planning to visit Greece or the Greek islands, remember that you will be refused entry to Greece if you have evidence in your passport of having visited Northern Cyprus. If you think this may be a problem, ask the immigration officials to stamp a piece of paper rather than directly in your passport.

Russia

Trabzon's Russian consulate is open for visa applications but, at the time of writing, visas were not being granted to most foreign nationals. However, this could change.

Syria

All foreigners entering Syria need to get a visa in advance. The easiest and safest way to do this is to apply for the visa in your home country, but you can get visas in both Ankara and İstanbul without too much of a problem. However, nonresidents in Turkey need a letter of recommendation from their embassy, for which you may be charged. Visa costs vary from nothing for Australians to a massive US$60 for UK citizens.

You may or may not be able to renew a three-month permit, depending on the whim of the officer.

When all else fails, leave the country for a day or two to Greece, Bulgaria or Cyprus, and get a new three-month tourist visa as you return to Turkey. This may only be possible a few times, however, as the immigration officer will become suspicious of too many recent Turkish stamps in your passport.

For information on the sort of work available in Turkey, see the Work section later in this chapter.

Driving Licence & Permits

Drivers must have a valid driving licence; an International Driving Permit is useful, but not usually required. Your own national driving licence should be sufficient. Third-party insurance, valid for the entire country (not just for Thrace or European Turkey), or a Turkish policy purchased at the border is obligatory.

Student & Youth Cards

Holders of an International Student Identity Card (ISIC) are granted discounts of 25% to 33% on the admission fees at some museums. It's a good idea to show your ISIC card before you show your money.

Holders of ISIC cards also get discounts of 10% on the Turkish State Railways and on Turkish Maritime Lines ships. Turkish Airlines, which used to give very good student discounts to travellers, does not do so any more.

Turkey is part of the Wasteels and Inter-Rail Youth discount schemes for rail, so if you have one of these cards, it will save you money on Turkish train fares.

Seniors Cards

Those over 65 years of age receive free or discounted admission to some archaeological and historical sites and museums. Show your passport to prove that you are of the *altın yaş* (golden age).

Vaccination Certificates

No vaccination certificates are required for entry into Turkey.

EMBASSIES & CONSULATES
Turkish Embassies

Turkish embassies include the following:

Australia (☎ 02-6295 0227, fax 6239 6592, 📧 turkembs@ozemail.com.au) 60 Mugga Way, Red Hill, ACT 2603
Bulgaria (☎ 02-980 2270, fax 981 9358, 📧 turkel@techno-link.com) Blvd Vasil Levski No 80, 1000 Sofia
Canada (☎ 613-789 4044, fax 789 3442, 📧 turkish@magma.ca) 197 Wurtemburg St, Ottawa, Ontario KIN 8L9
Greece (☎ 01-724 5915, fax 722 9597, 📧 turkembgr@hol.gr) Vasilissis Gheorgiou B Street 8, 10674 Athens
UK (☎ 020-7393 0202, fax 393 0066, 📧 info@turkishembassy-london.com) 43 Belgrave Square, London SW1X 8PA
USA (☎ 202-612 6700, fax 612 6744, 📧 info@turkey.org) 2525 Massachusetts Ave NW, Washington, DC, 20008

Embassies & Consulates in Turkey

Foreign embassies and consulates in Turkey include the following:

Australia
  Embassy: (☎ 312-446 1180, fax 446 1188, 📧 ausemank@ibm.net) Nenehatun Caddesi 83, Gaziosmanpaşa, Ankara
  Web site: www.embaustralia.org.tr
  Consulate: (☎ 212-257 7050, fax 257 7054) Tepecik Yolu 58, 80630 Etiler, İstanbul; open from 8.30 am to 12.30 pm Monday to Friday
Bulgaria
  Embassy: (☎ 312-467 1948, fax 467 2574) Atatürk Bulvarı 124, Kavaklıdere, Ankara
  Consulate: (☎ 212-269 0478, 269 2216, fax 264 1011) Zincirlikuyu Caddesi 44, Ulus, Levent, İstanbul; take bus No 210 behind the Sultanahmet tourist office to Beşiktaş, then take bus No 58/L, 58/1 or 58/2 to Zincirlikuyu
  Consulate: (☎/fax 284-225 1069) Talat Paşa Caddesi 31, Edirne
Canada
  Embassy: (☎ 312-436 1275, fax 446 4437) Nenehatun Caddesi 75, 06700 Gaziosmanpaşa, Ankara
  Honorary Consul: (☎ 212-272 5174, fax 272 3437) Büyükdere Caddesi 107/3, Bengün Han, 3rd floor, Gayrettepe, İstanbul
France
  Embassy: (☎ 312-468 1154, fax 467 9434) Paris Caddesi 70, Kavaklıdere, Ankara

Consulate: (☎ 212-292 4810, fax 249 9168)
İstiklal Caddesi 8, Taksim, İstanbul
Georgia
Consulate: (☎ 462-326 2226, fax 326 2296)
Gazipaşa Caddesi 20, Trabzon; open 10 am to
5 or 6 pm
Greece
Embassy: (☎ 312-436 8860, fax 446 3191)
Ziya-ur-Rahman (Karagöz) Caddesi 9–11,
06610 Gaziosmanpaşa, Ankara
Consulate: (☎ 212-245 0596, fax 252 1365)
Turnacıbaşı Sokak 32, Beyoğlu, İstanbul
Consulate: (☎ 284-235 5804, fax 235 5808)
Koca Sinan Mahallesi, 2 Sokak 13, Edirne
Iran
Embassy: (☎ 312-468 2820, fax 468 2823)
Tahran Caddesi 10, Kavaklıdere, Ankara
Consulate: (☎ 212-513 8230, fax 511 5219)
Ankara Caddesi 1, Cağaloğlu, İstanbul
Consulate: (☎ 218 2285, fax 316 1182)
Atatürk Bulvarı, Erzurum; open from 8.30 am
to 12.30 pm and from 2.30 to 4.30 pm daily
except Friday and Sunday afternoon
Netherlands
Embassy: (☎ 312-446 0470, fax 446 3358)
Uğur Mumcu Caddesi 16, Gaziosmanpaşa,
Ankara
Consulate: (☎ 212-251 5030, fax 292 5031,
e nlgovist@domi.net.tr) İstiklal Caddesi 393,
Tünel, 80072 Beyoğlu, İstanbul
New Zealand
Embassy: (☎ 312-467 9054, fax 467 9013,
e newzealand@superonline.com.tr) Level 4,
İran Caddesi 13, Kavaklıdere 06700, Ankara
Consulate: (☎ 212-327 2211, fax 327 2212)
Yeşil Çimen Sokak, Demirel İşhanı 75,
Ihlamur, Beşiktaş, İstanbul
Russian Federation
Consulate: (☎ 326 2600, fax 326 2101) Or-
tahisar Kefik Cesur 6, opposite the Ortahisar
Fatih Büyük Camii, Trabzon
Syria
Embassy: (☎ 312-440 9657, fax 438 5609)
Sedat Simavi Sokak 40, 06680 Çankaya,
Ankara
Consulate: (☎ 212-232 6721, fax 230 2215)
Maçka Caddesi 59, Ralli Apt 3, Teşvikiye,
İstanbul
Turkish Republic of Northern Cyprus
Consulate: (☎ 237 2482) on the corner of
Silifke and Atatürk Caddesis, Mersin; open 8
am to 1 pm, and 2 to 4 pm Monday to Friday
UK
Embassy: (☎ 312-468 6230, fax 468 3214)
Şehit Ersan Caddesi 46/A, Çankaya, Ankara
Consulate: (☎ 212-293 7540, fax 245 4989)
Meşrutiyet Caddesi 34, Tepebaşı, 80072
Beyoğlu, İstanbul
Consulate: (☎ 412 6486, fax 412 5077) Yeşil

Marmaris Travel Agency & Yacht Manage-
ment Bldg, Barbaros Caddesi 249, Marmaris;
open 9.30 am to noon Monday to Friday, and
2.30 to 5 pm Monday to Thursday in summer
USA
Embassy: (☎ 312-468 6110, fax 467 0019)
Atatürk Bulvarı 110, Kavaklıdere, Ankara
Consulate: (☎ 212-251 3602, fax 251 3632)
Meşrutiyet Caddesi 104-108, Tepebaşı, 80050
Beyoğlu, İstanbul

CUSTOMS
Arriving in Turkey
On arrival, customs inspection is often very
cursory for foreign tourists. There may be
spot checks, but you probably won't have to
open your bags. You can bring in up to 1kg
of coffee, 5L of liquor and two cartons (400)
of cigarettes. Things of exceptional value
(jewellery, unusually expensive electronic
or photographic gear etc) are supposed to be
declared and may be entered in your passport to guarantee that you will take the
goods out of the country when you leave.

Cars, minibuses, trailers, towed water-
craft, motorcycles and bicycles can be
brought in for up to three months without a
carnet or special import licence (tryptique).

Departing Turkey
*It is illegal to buy, sell, possess or export
antiquities!* Read on.

You may export valuables (except antiquities) that have been registered in your
passport on entry, or that have been purchased with legally converted money. For
souvenirs, the maximum export limit is
US$1000 of all items combined; if two or
more similar items are exported, a licence
may be required. Also, you may need to
show proof of exchange transactions for at
least these amounts.

Your bags may well be searched when
you leave the country (both for customs and
security reasons) and questions may be
asked about whether or not you are taking
any antiquities with you. Only true antiquities much more than a century old are off
limits, not newer items or the many artful
fakes. If you buy a real Roman coin from a
shepherd boy at an archaeological site, can
you take it home with you? Legally not.

What happens if you get caught trying to smuggle out a significant piece of ancient statuary? Big trouble.

MONEY
Currency
The unit of currency is the Turkish lira, or TL, which was called the Turkish pound (LT) in Ottoman times. A high inflation rate has rendered the single lira nearly worthless in relation to strong currencies. A simple restaurant bill or taxi fare may be in the millions of liras.

The government has announced plans to drop six zeros and revalue the lira at TL1 to US$2 in 2001. If this happens, the new lira will probably be divided into 100 kuruş. There will no doubt be wholesale commercial confusion before new lira coins and notes replace the old.

Under the current system, lira coins are 5000, 10,000, 25,000, 50,000 and 100,000. Notes come as 250,000, 500,000, one million, five million, 10 million, etc. With all those zeros, it's often difficult to make sure you're giving the proper notes – or getting the correct change. Beware of shopkeepers and taxi drivers who may try to give you a 500,000 lira note in place of a five million, or a 100,000 note instead of a one million. Take your time and be sure of amounts.

Exchange Rates
Turkey's inflation rate has hovered around 100% in recent years, though anti-inflation progress is being made, and ambitious government programs aim to bring the rate down to 25%. We'll see. In any case, we haven't provided an exchange rate table as it would certainly be out of date by the time you arrive.

Exchanging Money
Wait until you arrive in Turkey to change your home currency (cash or travellers cheques) into Turkish liras. With the value of the Turkish lira constantly dropping, it's wise to change money every few days rather than all at once.

You will always need your passport when you change travellers cheques in Turkey,

and you may need it when you change cash as well.

Turkish liras are worthless outside the country, so don't take any with you.

Cash US dollars and deutschmarks are the easiest currencies to change, though many banks and exchange offices will change other major currencies such as UK pounds, French francs etc. You may find it difficult to exchange Australian or Canadian currency except at banks and offices in major cities.

It's a good idea to change some money when you enter Turkey – US$25 or US$50 at least. There are currency exchange desks and ATMs at the major entry points to Turkey by road, air and sea. It's a good practice not to change money at the first exchange booth you encounter at an airport or other point of entry, as it may take advantage of its premier position to give a low exchange rate. Also, the clerk may attempt to take advantage of your confusion and jet lag by giving you less than you're supposed to get. Make sure the amount of cash you're given agrees with the amount shown on your exchange receipt.

Travellers Cheques & Eurocheques
Turkish banks, shops and hotels often see it as a burden to change travellers cheques (including Eurocheques) and may try to get you to go elsewhere. You must often press the issue. The more expensive hotels, restaurants and shops will more readily accept cheques, as will car rental agencies and travel agencies, but not at good exchange rates. Generally it's better to change travellers cheques to Turkish liras at a bank.

Some banks charge a fee for changing travellers cheques (though not for changing cash notes). To find out before you begin, ask 'Komisyon alınır mı?' (Is a commission taken?). Sometimes the teller will scribble some figures on the back of the form, then pay out your liras several thousand short, saying this is a commission, but will give no receipt. Don't let them do this. It's your money they're keeping.

Save your currency exchange bordro (receipts). You may need them to change back

Turkish liras at the end of your stay, and to show to the customs officer if you've bought expensive souvenirs such as carpets.

ATMs Automated teller machines (ATMs, cash points etc) are the most convenient way to get money in Turkey. They're common in Turkish cities, towns and resorts. Virtually all offer instructions in English, French, German and Turkish, and will pay out Turkish liras as a cash advance when you insert your credit card (especially Visa). The daily limit on withdrawals is the equivalent of about US$250 per day; the exchange rate at which the transaction is processed is usually fairly good.

Most bank ATMs allow withdrawals only in Turkish liras, but the larger branches of Türkiye İş Bankası will usually allow you to withdraw money via ATMs in US dollars as well, which is useful if you're trying to build up your dollar reserves for travel to another country.

Most machines also accept bank cash (debit) cards. The specific machine you use must be reliably connected to one of the major cash-dispenser networks such as Cirrus, Plus Systems, NYSE etc. Look for stickers with the logos of these services affixed to the machine. If the connection is not reliable, you may get a message saying that the transaction was refused by your bank (which may not be true), and your card will be returned to you. Try another machine.

Credit Cards Big hotels, car rental agencies and the more expensive shops will usually accept major credit cards, but it's always best to check in advance. Turkish Airlines, for instance, accepts only Visa, MasterCard, Access and Eurocard. Turkish State Railways doesn't accept any credit cards, but it may soon do so. A souvenir shop will usually accept most major cards.

International Transfers The Turkish post office (PTT) handles postal money orders, and this is fine for small amounts. For large amounts, you'd do better with a bank.

Banks can wire money in a matter of a day or two (usually), for a fee of US$20 to US$40 per transfer. Sometimes the transfer fee is a percentage of the amount transferred. Have your passport with you when you go to receive your money.

Black Market There is no currency black market as the Turkish lira is fully convertible.

Moneychangers Non-bank currency exchange offices throughout Turkey often provide faster and better service than banks, but may charge a slightly higher commission or fee.

Costs

All costs in this guide are given only in US dollars as prices in Turkish liras (TL) would be hopelessly out of date before the book even emerged from the printer.

Turkey is Europe's low-price leader, and you can travel on as little as US$20 to US$25 (average) per day using buses and trains, staying in pensions and eating one restaurant meal daily. For US$25 to US$40 per person per day you can travel more comfortably by bus and train, staying in one- and two-star hotels and eating most meals in average restaurants. For US$40 to US$80 per day you can move up to three- and four-star hotels, take the occasional airline flight, and eat in restaurants all the time. If you have more than US$100 per person to spend, you can travel in four-star luxury. Costs are highest in İstanbul and lowest in small eastern towns off the tourist track.

To give you an idea: a single/double room without bath in small pension costs US$10 to US$20; a single/double room with bath in a one-star hotel is US$20 to US$40; and a three-course meal in a simple restaurant costs about US$7. Some average costs for basic items are as follows:

Loaf of bread	US$0.40
Bottle of beer (from a shop)	US$1
1L of petrol/gasoline	US$0.90 to US$0.97
100km by express train (1st class)	US$1.80 to US$2.20
100km by bus	US$2.50 to US$3.50
Local telephone call	US$0.10
Turkish Daily News	US$0.80

Price Adjustments Government entities such as Turkish State Railways, Turkish Maritime Lines and the Ministry of Culture (which administers many of the country's museums) may set prices at the beginning of the year, and then adjust them only every three or four months – if at all – throughout the year. Thus a three million TL museum admission ticket might cost you US$5 in January, but only US$4 or even US$3 later in the year. For this reason, many prices in this guide must be looked upon as approximate.

Private enterprises tend to adjust prices more frequently and many in the travel industry, such as Turkish Airlines, Turkish Maritime Lines (international routes), rental car firms and the more expensive hotels, quote prices not in liras but in US dollars or in deutschmarks.

Tipping & Bargaining

In the cheapest restaurants, tipping is not necessary. Some places will automatically add a *servis ücreti* (service charge) of 10% or 15% to your bill, but this does not absolve you from the tip, oddly enough. The service charge goes into the pocket of the patron. Turks will give around 5% to the waiter directly, and perhaps the same amount to the head waiter.

In the cheapest hotels there are few services, and tips are not expected. In most places a porter will carry your luggage and show you to your room. For doing this he'll expect about 2% of the room price.

Turks don't tip taxi drivers, though they often round off the metered fare. A driver of a *dolmuş* (shared taxi) never expects a tip or a fare to be rounded upwards.

Commissions – A Colossal Rip-off

In recent years the practice of paying commissions to anyone who brings in business has got completely out of hand in Turkey. If a taxi driver recommends a hotel and takes you there, he gets a commission. If someone leads you to a carpet shop, they get a commission. If your pension owner books you on a tour, they get a commission.

Commissions, or finder's fees, are a normal part of doing business in most parts of the world. But in Turkey the fee is not 2% or 3% as in many places, or even the 10% common in the travel industry. It's at least 20%, more usually 30% or 35%, and often as high as 50% or more.

This money comes directly out of your pocket, but buys you almost nothing.

Many legitimate businesses despise the rage for commissions as much as travellers do. Pension owners resent freelance touts bringing customers to their door and demanding huge commissions when it's probable that customers would have found their way to the pension in any case. Carpet shops resent having to charge ever higher prices in order to cover the huge commissions demanded by the same importunate types who have badgered you endlessly on the street. Indeed, there have been many ugly incidents between shopkeepers and these types.

The commission rip-off has even become big business. Package tour operators bring planeloads of tourists from Europe at tour prices below the price of the return air fare alone. The groups are put up in hotels which are virtually shopping malls, and every day of bus touring includes a stop of several hours at a shop. The tour company regularly makes far more money from commission markups on purchases than from the tour fee. (If tour participants were to seek out independent shops by themselves, they'd find all prices significantly lower.)

What to do? It's simple: don't go into a shop accompanied by anyone. Make your own reservations for special activities and events. Buy your own tickets. Sign up for a tour at the tour operator's office, not at your pension or hotel. Don't let anyone 'claim' you as their commission bait.

In some situations you needn't worry too much about commissions, for example, when a legitimate travel agency arranges a plane or train ticket for you (the normal 10% commission is included in the ticket price), or when you ask a pension owner to call ahead to a pension in the next town as a favour. Remember, most businesses resent the commission badgers as much as you do.

In hairdressers, pay the fee for the services rendered (which goes to the shop), then about 10% to the person who cut your hair, and smaller tips to the others who provided service, down to the one who brushes stray locks from your clothing as you prepare to leave (5% for that).

In a *hamam* (Turkish bath), there will be fees for the services, and in baths frequented mostly by Turks these will be sufficient. In tourist-oriented baths these prices may be an order of magnitude higher (US$20 instead of US$5), in which case you may assume that service is included.

If staff in a nontourist bath approach you as you are leaving, share out 20% to 30% of the bath fees among them.

For tips on how to haggle for the best bargain, see the Shopping section at the end of this chapter.

Taxes & Refunds

There is a value-added tax (VAT) on most goods and services in Turkey. When leaving the country, tourists can claim the VAT paid on larger purchases. See Value-Added Tax under Shopping later in this chapter for more information.

POST & COMMUNICATIONS
Post Offices

Postal and telegraph services in Turkey are handled by the Posta Telegraf office, usually known as the PTT (peh-teh-**teh**; Posta, Telefon, Telegraf), although the telephone service is now privatised. To find a PTT, look for the distinctive yellow signs with black 'PTT' letters. In post offices, the 'Yurtdışı' slot is for mail to foreign countries, 'Yurtiçi' is for mail to other Turkish cities and 'Şehir-içi' is for mail within the city.

Count your change carefully when buying stamps. Short-changing foreigners is common in some PTTs.

Main post offices in large cities tend to be open every day from 8 am to 8 pm for most services (stamp sales, telephone jeton and card sales, telegrams, fax etc). However, windows may be open only from 8.30 am to noon and 1.30 to 5 or 6 pm for other services such as poste restante and parcel service. Smaller post offices have more limited hours: 8.30 am to 12.30 pm and 1.30 to 5.30 pm, and may be closed part of Saturday and all day Sunday.

Sending Mail

The PTT operates an express mail, courier-type service called *acele posta servisi* or APS, which competes with international express carriers such as DHL, Federal Express and United Parcel Service. If you must have something reach its destination fast, ask for this; it's available during limited hours at major city post offices. Don't confuse this courier service with the traditional *ekspres* (special delivery) service, which is slower.

To mail packages out of the country, or to receive dutiable merchandise, you must have your package opened for customs inspection, and you may have to endure some frustrating red tape. Have paper, box, string, tape and marker pens with you when you go.

If you want to be sure that a parcel will get to its destination intact, send it by APS, an international courier service (DHL, Fedex, UPS) or at least *kayıtlı* (registered mail).

Receiving Mail

Merkez postane means central or main post office, which is where you should go to pick up your mail, passport in hand. The poste restante desk often keeps more limited hours than others, and may close for lunch. Letters should be addressed as follows: [Name], Poste Restante, Merkez Postahane, [District], [Postcode, City, Province], Turkey.

Telephone

Turkey's country code is ☎ 90. Area codes within Turkey are listed below the place name in the relevant sections in this book.

Pay telephones, usually in heavy use, are found in major public buildings and facilities, public squares and transportation termini. Service is provided by Türk Telekom, which still has a monopoly on line service. Although the telephone company is now separate from the postal service (PTT), telephone centres are usually still located in or near post offices. International calls can be made from most pay phones.

You can pay for a call on Türk Telekom's network with a credit card, a Telekart debit card, a Küresel secret-number debit card, or, in a few older phones, a *jeton* (token). Calls are measured in usage units, each of which costs about US$0.10.

Cards Küresel debit cards, sold with an initial value of 100 usage units, have a secret number which you input into the Türk Telekom system to receive calling time. Easier to use are the Telekart telephone debit cards, with a magnetic strip that records your usage. The latter are sold in shops and kiosks near public telephones in values of 30, 60, 100, 120, or 180 telephone usage units.

In general, a 30-unit card is sufficient for local calls; 60 for a short, domestic intercity call; 100 for a domestic intercity call of moderate length or a short international call; and the higher-value cards for longer domestic or international calls. Some newer phones also accept major credit cards.

Kontürlü Telefon Some shops and kiosks have *kontürlü* telephones, that is, a phone with a meter attached. You make your call and the owner reads the meter and charges you accordingly. The cost of the call depends on what the phone's owner charges for each unit (*kontür*) on the meter, so ask *'Bir kontür kaç lira?'* (How many liras does a unit cost?) It can vary from US$0.05 at a kiosk to US$0.15 in a four-star hotel, so it's worth shopping around.

Long-Distance Calls For intercity calls, dial 0 then the area code and the local number. For international calls, dial 00 (the international access code), then the country code, area code and local number. Be patient; it can take as long as one minute for the connection to be made.

Rates for local and intercity domestic calls are moderate, but international calls can be quite expensive: almost UK£1 per minute to the UK, US$3 per minute to the USA, and even higher to Australia. Reduced rates are in effect from midnight to 7 am, and on Sunday. Beware of hotel surcharges, which can be as high as 100%. Perhaps the

best strategy is to make a quick call, give the other person the telephone number and a time at which you can be reached, and have them call you back.

If you make an international call from a Türk Telekom telephone centre, be sure to get a receipt. Fiddling the bills is common as you see no meter and can't tell what a call will cost. Clerks are less willing to fiddle with an official receipt with an amount and their name on it.

Country Direct In theory, you can call one of the numbers below toll-free from Turkey to access your home telephone company, which may have cheaper rates. In practice, the call often doesn't go through.

Australia	☎ 00-800 61 1177
Canada (Teleglobe)	☎ 00-800 1 6677
France (Telecom)	☎ 00-800 33 1177
Germany (PTT)	☎ 00-800 49 1149
Ireland	☎ 00-800 353 1177
Italy	☎ 00-800 39 1177
Japan (IDC Direct)	☎ 00-800 81 0086
Japan (IDC)	☎ 00-800 81 0080
Japan (KDD)	☎ 00-800 81 1177
Netherlands (PTT)	☎ 00-800 31 1177
UK (BTI)	☎ 00-800 44 1177
UK (Mercury)	☎ 00-800 44 2277
USA (AT&T)	☎ 00-800 1 2277
USA (MCI)	☎ 00-800 1 1177
USA (SPRINT)	☎ 00-800 1 4477

Telephone Etiquette Turks answer the phone by saying *'Alo?'*, a word that is defined in Turkish dictionaries as 'Word said when answering the telephone' because it is never used otherwise. Turks may also say *'Efendim?'* (Sir/madam?) or *'Buyurun!'* (At your service!).

Fax
It's quickest and easiest to send and receive faxes at your hotel (for a fee), although you can send a fax from one of the Türk Telekom telephone centres.

Email & Internet Access
Major cities and tourist centres all have Internet cafes. Many hotels, pensions and tour operators have computers with Internet ac-

cess which you can use for a fee to send and receive email. See the individual city sections for addresses and more details.

INTERNET RESOURCES

Lonely Planet's Web site (www.lonelyplanet .com) is a rich resource for travellers. Here you can research your trip, hunt down bargain air fares, book hotels and check on weather conditions. You'll also find succinct summaries on travelling to most places on earth, postcards from other travellers and the Thorn Tree bulletin board, where you can ask questions before you go or dispense advice when you get back. You can also find travel news and updates to many of our most popular guidebooks, and the subWWWay section links you to the most useful travel resources elsewhere on the Web.

There are many other Web sites dealing with Turkey. Many hotels, bus companies and other travel services have their own Web sites, and the Turkish government sponsors many of its own. Most Turkish sites offer glacial download, browser-crashing complexity, mediocre information, and vigorous sales pitches. A few exceptions, all bilingual (Turkish and English), are:

www.beyogluweb.com Good for all sorts of information on İstanbul.
www.infoexchange.com Run by Tom Brosnahan, a co-author of this guide, this site provides updated information on travel in Turkey.
www.neredennereye.com This useful site has detailed public transport information.
www.turkey.org The official site of the Turkish embassy in Washington, DC, and good for visa, passport, consular and economic information, email addresses of Turkish diplomatic missions, and useful links to other sites related to Turkey.
www.turkishdailynews.com The *Turkish Daily News* site has current information, weather and classified ads for rental apartments, jobs as English teachers and translators etc.

BOOKS

Everyone from St Paul to Mark Twain and Agatha Christie has written about Turkey.

Lonely Planet

As well as this guide, Lonely Planet publishes a separate *İstanbul* guide with ex-

panded information on Turkey's largest city, plus many maps and walking tours, while *Middle East* covers Turkey and its neighbours and *İstanbul to Cairo* provides a more adventurous perspective. There's also *World Food Turkey*, which is a good culinary supplement to this guidebook, offering 240 pages of description and photographs of Turkish cuisine.

Lonely Planet's *Turkish phrasebook* is truly a language survival kit, as it contains words and phrases useful to real-life situations. Besides including all the common words and phrases needed during travel, it covers the unmentionable situations in which you need to know the word for tampon or condom.

Guidebooks

Some more specialist guidebooks include John Freely's classic *Strolling Through İstanbul* which, though somewhat dated, is still a valuable walking-tour guide of the Byzantine/Ottoman capital. *Religious Sites in Turkey* (1997), by Anna G Edmonds, provides in-depth coverage of the many Christian, Jewish and Muslim holy places.

Travel

The published diaries and accounts of earlier travellers in Turkey provide fascinating glimpses of Ottoman life. One of the more familiar of these is Mark Twain's *Innocents Abroad*. Twain accompanied a group of wealthy tourists on a chartered boat which sailed the Black Sea and eastern Mediterranean more than a century ago. Many of the things he saw in İstanbul haven't changed much.

For the literary minded, *İstanbul – a traveller's companion* by Laurence Kelly is a delight. The editor has combed through the writings of two millennia relating to Byzantium, Constantinople and İstanbul and collected the choicest bits by the most interesting writers. History, biography, diary and travellers' observations are all included.

A Fez of the Heart by Jeremy Seal is an account of the author's recent journeys throughout Turkey in search of Turks who still wear the fez. Despite its unfortunate title it's a witty, entertaining inquiry into resurgent Islam and what it means to be a 'modern' Turk.

Tim Kelsey's *Dervish* is a more sobering account of a similar journey which grows darker the further east he travels.

In *The Turkish Labyrinth: Atatürk and the New Islam*, journalist James Pettifer examines the pressures on modern Turkey as it struggles to cope with population movements, the Kurdish war and the growth of Islamic fundamentalism.

Neal Ascherson's *Black Sea* is a long essay on that region by the talented *Observer* journalist. *A Traveller's History of Turkey* by Richard Stoneman is also worth a look.

History

Turkey, a Short History by Roderic Davison is a good place to start; or *Turkey – a Modern History* by Erik J Zürcher. *The Ottoman Centuries* by Lord Kinross is longer but not overly dense.

Hugh and Nicole Pope's *Turkey Unveiled: A History of Modern Turkey* is an excellent, entertaining and accessible work.

Professors Stanford and Ezel Kural Shaw's excellent and authoritative *History of the Ottoman Empire & Modern Turkey* comes in two volumes. Volume One is *Empire of the Gazis: The Rise & Decline of the Ottoman Empire 1280–1808*; Volume Two is *Reform, Revolution & Republic: The Rise of Modern Turkey 1808–1975*.

The Emergence of Modern Turkey by Bernard Lewis is a scholarly work covering Turkey's history roughly from 1850 to 1950, with a few chapters on the earlier history of the Turks.

Gallipoli by Alan Moorhead is the fascinating story of the battles for the Dardanelles, which figured so significantly in the careers of Mustafa Kemal (Atatürk) and Winston Churchill, and in the histories of Australia and New Zealand.

The Harvest of Hellenism by FE Peters details Turkey's Hellenic heritage. *Byzantine Style & Civilisation* by Sir Steven Runciman is the standard work on the later Roman Empire.

General

Biography *Atatürk* by Lord Kinross (JPD Balfour) is well written and essential reading for anyone who wants to understand the formation of the Turkish Republic and the reverence in which modern Turks hold Atatürk. A newer alternative is *Atatürk* by Dr Andrew Mango.

Anthropology For a good overview of life during the great days of the empire, look in a library for *Everyday Life in Ottoman Turkey* by Raphaela Lewis.

Archaeology *Ancient Civilisations & Ruins of Turkey* by Ekrem Akurgal is a detailed and scholarly guide to many of Turkey's ruins from prehistoric times to the end of the Roman Empire. The book has 112 pages of photographs and is a good, readable English translation of the original. This is the best handbook for those with a deep interest in classical archaeology.

George Bean (1903–77) was the grand old man of Western travel writers on Turkish antiquities. His four books with maps, diagrams and photos cover the country's great wealth of Greek and Roman sites in depth, but in a very readable style. These four works were written as guidebooks to the ruins. They contain plenty of detail, but not so much that the fascination of exploring an ancient city or temple is taken away.

If you'd like to go deeply into a few sites, just buy Bean's *Aegean Turkey*. It covers İzmir and its vicinity, Pergamum, Aeolis, sites west of İzmir to Sardis, Ephesus, Priene, Miletus, Didyma, Magnesia on the Menderes River and Heracleia. *Lycian Turkey* covers the Turkish coast roughly from Fethiye to Antalya, and its hinterland. *Turkey Beyond the Meander* covers the region south of the Menderes River, excluding Miletus, Didyma and Heracleia (which are covered in *Aegean Turkey*) but including sites near Bodrum, Pamukkale, Afrodisias and Marmaris, and to the western outskirts of Fethiye. *Turkey's Southern Shore* overlaps with *Lycian Turkey* a bit, and covers eastern Lycia, Pisidia and Pamphylia, or roughly the coast from Finike east to Silifke.

As well as these archaeological guides, you'll find shorter, locally produced guides on sale at each site. Most include colour photographs of varying quality. The text, however, is often badly translated, or else doesn't go into much depth. Look closely before you buy.

Food *Eat Smart in Turkey: How to Decipher the Menu, Know the Market Foods & Embark on a Tasting Adventure*, written by Joan & David Peterson, is a delightful in-depth look at the history, practice and enjoyment of Turkish cuisine.

Fiction Everybody knows, or should know, about Agatha Christie's *Murder on the Orient Express*. It has some scenes in Turkey itself, though most of the train's journey was through Europe and the Balkans. In any case, it helps to make vivid the importance of the Ottoman Empire in the late 19th century.

Arts & Crafts *Turkish Traditional Art Today* by Henry Glassie (1993) is a masterful, scholarly and detailed yet superbly entertaining survey of traditional Turkish arts such as calligraphy, carpet-weaving, pottery, metal and woodworking.

Dictionaries Several companies publish Turkish-English pocket dictionaries, including Langenscheidt and McGraw Hill. For a more detailed dictionary, look to *The Concise Oxford Turkish Dictionary*. Similar in scope and easier to find in Turkey is the *Redhouse Küçük Elsözlüğlu* (Small Hand Dictionary). This 702-page work on thin paper was actually intended for Turkish students learning English, but it does the job well when you graduate from a pocket dictionary.

Turkish Grammar by Geoffrey L Lewis is the best general grammar. If a grammar book can be said to read like a novel, this one does.

FILMS

Perhaps the most famous movie about Turkey is *Midnight Express*, a politically motivated, anti-Turkish diatribe in which a convicted drug smuggler is magically transformed into a suffering hero (see the 'Midnight Express' boxed text in the Thrace chapter). Virtually all of the 'Turkish' actors in the movie were of Greek or Armenian extraction. Controversial director Oliver Stone contributed to this visually striking and emotionally chilling story by playing fast and loose with the facts. An entire generation of intelligent cinema-goers never questioned its overt racism.

The classic suspense-comedy *Topkapi*, with Peter Ustinov and Melina Mercouri, is much more fun to watch, as is the James Bond thriller *From Russia With Love*, set in İstanbul.

NEWSPAPERS & MAGAZINES

Local daily newspapers are produced by up-to-date computerised methods in lurid colour. Of prime interest to visitors is the *Turkish Daily News* (US$0.80), an English-language daily newspaper published in Ankara and available in most Turkish cities. It is the cheapest source of English language news in print. On Sunday it comes with a current events and culture supplement called *Probe*, which is worth digesting.

The big international papers such as the *International Herald Tribune, Le Monde, Corriere della Sera, Die Welt* etc are on sale in tourist spots as well, but are much more expensive (eg, US$2 for the *International Herald Tribune*). Check the date on any international paper before you buy it.

Large-circulation magazines including the *Economist, Newsweek, Time, Der Spiegel* and the like are also sold in tourist spots.

If you can't find the foreign publication you want, go to a big hotel's newsstand or check at a foreign-language bookshop.

RADIO & TV

Radio and TV broadcasting is both public and private.

Türkiye Radyo ve Televizyon (TRT) is a quasi-independent government broadcasting service modelled on the BBC. Western classical and popular music, along with Turkish classical, folk, religious and pop music, are played regularly on both AM (medium wave) and FM channels. TRT-TV broadcasts in colour from breakfast time to midnight on four TV channels.

Short news broadcasts in English, French and German are given on national radio each morning and evening. TRT's Tourism (Holiday) Radio broadcasts news and historical, geographical and social information about Turkey in the same three languages from 7.30 am to 12.45 pm and 6.30 to 10 pm in major tourist areas.

A variety of independent commercial broadcast and cable stations provide Turkish musical and variety programs. The familiar Los Angeles-made series and many of the films are dubbed in Turkish. Occasionally you'll catch a film in the original language.

The BBC World Service is often on AM as well as short wave. The rest of the AM band is a wonderful collection of Albanian, Arabic, Bulgarian, Greek, Hebrew, Italian, Persian, Romanian and Russian.

In addition to the Turkish TV channels, many of the more expensive hotels have satellite hook-ups to receive European channels, with programs mostly in German, but often including the European service of CNN, NBC Super-Channel, and/or the BBC.

VIDEO SYSTEMS

Turkey uses the PAL system for TV and video. If your home country uses SECAM (France) or NTSC (North America) and you buy a Turkish video cassette, it will not play properly on your home equipment, even if it is made to be played in a VHS video cassette recorder/ player.

PHOTOGRAPHY & VIDEO

Colour print film costs about US$8, plus developing, for 24 exposures. It's readily available and easily processed in city photo shops, as are slide films such as Ektachrome, Fujichrome and Velvia; however, Kodachrome slide film is rarely found and cannot be developed in Turkey.

Still cameras are subject to an extra fee in most museums; in some they are not allowed at all. For use of flash or tripod, you usually have to obtain written permission from the staff or the appropriate government ministry (not easy). Video fees are usually even

higher, thereby denying Turkey the free publicity which would be provided by thousands of home videos being shown around the world by happy returned travellers.

Do not photograph anything military, whether or not you see signs reading *Foto çekmek yasak(tır)* or *Fotoğraf çekilmez* (No photography).

In areas of the country off the tourist track, it's polite to ask '*Foto çekebilir miyim?*' (May I take a photo?) before taking any close-ups of people, especially women.

TIME

Turkish time is two hours ahead of GMT/UTC, and daylight saving (summer time) is observed, usually from 1 am on the last Sunday in March until 2 am on the last Sunday in September. When it's noon in Turkey, the time elsewhere is:

city	winter	summer
London	10 am	10 am
Paris, Rome	11 am	11 am
Hong Kong	6 pm	5 pm
Sydney	7 pm	11 pm
Auckland	10 pm	9 pm
Los Angeles	2 am	2 am
New York	5 am	5 am

ELECTRICITY

Electricity in Turkey is supplied at 220V, 50 cycles, as in Europe. *Fiş* (plugs) are of the European variety with two round prongs, but there are two sizes in use. Most common is the small-diameter prong. The large-diameter, grounded plug, used in Germany and Austria, is also in use, and you'll find some *priz* (outlets or points) of this type. Plugs for these won't fit the small-diameter outlets. If you have to rig an adaptor, electrical shops have the necessary parts at reasonable prices. Power outages and surges are not uncommon, so it's a good idea to disconnect your appliances from the grid when not in use.

WEIGHTS & MEASURES

Turkey uses the metric system. Basic conversion charts are given on the inside back cover of this book.

LAUNDRY

Ask at the hotel reception desk, or go directly to a housekeeper, to get your *çamaşır* (laundry) done. Agree on a price in advance. The word çamaşır also means 'underwear' in Turkish, frequently causing confusion.

Kuru temizleme (dry cleaners) are found here and there in big cities, usually in the better residential sections or near luxury hotels.

TOILETS

Turkey has two types of toilets, the *klozet* or *alafranga* (the familiar raised-bowl commode) and the *alaturka* (a porcelain or concrete rectangle with two oblong foot-places and a sunken hole). Every toilet is equipped for bottom-washing with a tap and can on the floor nearby or, more conveniently, a copper tube snaking up the back and right to where it's needed.

As washing is the accustomed method of hygiene, toilet paper – used by Turks mostly for drying – is considered a dispensable luxury and may not be provided. Carry your own.

The management may place a wastepaper receptacle next to the toilet for used toilet paper, assuming that the paper will have only been used for drying, and pleading for you not to throw it in the toilet.

Serviceably clean public toilets can be found near major tourist attractions. Most public toilets require payment of a small fee (around US$0.25). Every mosque has a toilet, often smelly and very basic, but it may be better than nothing, depending upon the urgency of nature's call.

HEALTH

In general, Turkey is a pretty healthy country to travel in, although many people will experience the odd day of stomach upset. It's wise to stick with bottled water and to take all the usual precautions over food hygiene, especially in July and August. There's a small but growing risk of contracting malaria in south-eastern Turkey, where the lakes created by the GAP project have made it easier for mosquitoes to breed.

Staying healthy depends on your predeparture preparations, your daily health care while travelling and how you handle any medical problem that does develop.

Predeparture Preparations

Immunisations No vaccinations are required for travel to Turkey but some routine jabs are recommended, especially if you are planning on travelling to remote areas in eastern Turkey. Don't leave your vaccinations until the last minute as some require more than one injection and some can't be given at the same time. Discuss your vaccinations with your doctor, as there are many factors to be taken into account, such as any allergies you have or if you are pregnant. Remember that children and pregnant women are more vulnerable to illness.

Make sure your doctor gives you a record of any vaccinations you have. Vaccinations that may be recommended for this trip include the following:

Diphtheria & Tetanus Vaccinations for these two diseases are usually combined and are recommended for everyone. After an initial course of three injections (usually given in childhood), boosters are necessary every 10 years.

Polio Everyone should keep up to date with this vaccination, which is normally given in childhood. You need a booster every 10 years.

Hepatitis A This vaccine provides long-term immunity (possibly more than 10 years) after an initial injection and a booster at six to 12 months.

Alternatively, an injection of gamma globulin can provide short-term protection against hepatitis A – two to six months, depending on the dose given. It is not a vaccine, but is ready-made antibody collected from blood donations. It is reasonably effective and, unlike the vaccine, it is protective immediately, but because it is a blood product, there are current concerns about its long-term safety.

Hepatitis A vaccine is also available in a combined form with hepatitis B vaccine. Three injections over a six-month period are required, the first two providing substantial protection against hepatitis A.

Typhoid Vaccination against typhoid may be required if you are travelling for more than a few weeks in Turkey. It is now available either as an injection or as capsules to be taken orally.

Hepatitis B Travellers who should consider this vaccination include those on a long trip, as well as those visiting countries where there are high levels of hepatitis B infection, where blood transfusions may not be adequately screened or where sexual contact or needle sharing is a possibility. Vaccination involves three injections, with a booster at 12 months. More rapid courses are available if necessary.

Rabies Vaccination should be considered by those who will spend a month or longer in a country such as Turkey where rabies is common, especially if they are cycling, handling animals, caving or travelling to remote areas, and for children (who may not report a bite). Pretravel rabies vaccination involves having three injections over 21 to 28 days. If someone who has been vaccinated is bitten or scratched by an animal, they will require two booster injections of vaccine; those not vaccinated require more.

Malaria Medication If you are planning to include a trip to south-eastern Turkey in your itinerary, you may need to take antimalarials – see Malaria under Insect-Borne Diseases later in this section, and discuss with your doctor. Antimalarial drugs do not prevent you from being infected but kill the malaria parasites during a stage in their development and significantly reduce the risk of becoming very ill or dying. You need to get expert advice on medication, as there are many factors to consider, including the area to be visited, the risk of exposure to malaria-carrying mosquitoes, the side effects of medication, your medical history and whether you are a child or an adult or pregnant.

Health Insurance Make sure that you have adequate health insurance.

Travel Health Guides There are a number of excellent travel health sites on the Internet. From the Lonely Planet home page there are links at www.lonelyplanet.com/health/health.htm/h-links.htm to the World Health Organization and the US Centers for Disease Control & Prevention.

Lonely Planet's *Travel with Children* by Maureen Wheeler provides comprehensive information about what you can do to prepare yourself and enjoy your trip, wherever you may be travelling.

Other Preparations Make sure you're healthy before you start travelling. If you

---

Medical Kit Check List

Following is a list of items you should consider including in your medical kit – consult your pharmacist for brands of medicines available in your country.

☐ **Aspirin or paracetamol (acetaminophen in the USA)** – for pain or fever

☐ **Antihistamine** – for allergies, eg, hay fever; to ease the itch from insect bites or stings; and to prevent motion sickness

☐ **Cold and flu tablets, throat lozenges and nasal decongestant**

☐ **Antibiotics** – consider including these if you're travelling well off the beaten track; see your doctor, as they must be prescribed, and carry the prescription on you

☐ **Loperamide or diphenoxylate** –'blockers' for diarrhoea

☐ **Prochlorperazine or metaclopramide** – for nausea and vomiting

☐ **Rehydration mixture** – to prevent dehydration, which may occur, for example, during bouts of diarrhoea; particularly important when travelling with children

☐ **Multivitamins** – consider including these if you are a long trip

☐ **Insect repellent, sunscreen, lip balm and eye drops**

☐ **Calamine lotion, sting relief spray or aloe vera** – to ease irritation from sunburn and insect bites or stings

☐ **Antifungal cream or powder** – for fungal skin infections and thrush

☐ **Antiseptic (such as povidone-iodine)** – for cuts and grazes

☐ **Bandages, Band-Aids (plasters) and other wound dressings**

☐ **Water purification tablets or iodine**

☐ **Scissors, tweezers and a thermometer** – note that mercury thermometers are prohibited by airlines

---

are going on a long trip make sure your teeth are OK. If you wear glasses take a spare pair and your prescription.

Though Turkey manufactures most modern prescription medicines, don't risk running out of your medicine. If you take a drug regularly, bring a supply. Take the prescription or better still part of the packaging showing the generic rather than the brand name (which may not be locally available). It is wise to have a legible prescription or letter from your doctor with you to show that you legally use the medication.

Basic Rules

Travellers in Turkey often experience a fair amount of travellers' diarrhoea, known as 'the Sultan's Revenge'. Care in what you eat and drink is the most important health rule.

Food Choose dishes that look freshly prepared and sufficiently hot. You can go into almost any Turkish kitchen (except in the very posh places) for a look at what's cooking. In fact, in most places that's what the staff will suggest, the language barrier being what it is. Except for grilled meats, Turkish dishes tend to be cooked slowly for a long time, just the thing to kill any errant bacteria. But if the dishes don't sell on the day they're cooked, they might be saved.

As for grilled meats, these may be offered to you medium rare. They'll probably be all right, but if they really look pink, send them back for more cooking (no problem in this). The words you'll need are '*biraz daha pişmiş'* (cooked a bit more) and '*iyi pişmiş'* or '*pişkin'* (well done).

Shellfish such as mussels, oysters and clams should be avoided; steaming does not make shellfish safe for eating.

Beware of milk products, and dishes containing milk that have not been properly refrigerated. Electricity is expensive in Turkey, and many places scrimp on refrigeration temperature. If you want a *sütlaç* (rice pudding) or some such dish with milk in it, choose a shop that has lots of them in the window, meaning that a batch has been made recently. In general, choose things from bins, trays, cases, pots etc that are fairly full.

If your food is poor or limited in availability, if you're travelling hard and fast and therefore missing meals or if you simply lose your appetite, you can soon start to lose weight which places your health at risk. Make sure your diet is well balanced. Fruit and vegetables are good sources of vitamins. Eat plenty of grains and bread.

Fluid Balance

In hot climates it's important that you make sure you drink enough – don't rely on feeling thirsty to indicate when you should drink. Not needing to urinate or small amounts of very dark yellow urine is a danger sign. Always carry a water bottle with you on long trips. Excessive sweating can lead to loss of salt and therefore muscle cramping. Salt tablets are not a good idea as a preventative, but in places where salt is not used much, adding salt to food can help.

Water Drink bottled spring water whenever possible – it's widely available. Check the date of manufacture on the bottle, and check that the seal of the bottle hasn't been tampered with. Tap water in Turkey is chlorinated, but it is not certain to be safe, and it rarely tastes good.

A roadside *çeşme* (fountain or spring), may bear the word *içilmez* (not to be drunk), or *içilir* (drinkable), or *içme suyu* (drinking water), or *içilebilir* (can be drunk), but it's probably best to avoid these unless you really know what's upstream from them.

Alternatives to spring water include *maden suyu*, naturally fizzy mineral water, and *maden sodası* (or just *soda*), artificially carbonated mineral water. The latter has bigger bubbles, and more of them, than the former. Both come from mineral springs, and both are truly full of minerals. The taste is not neutral: some people like it, some don't. It's supposed to cleanse your kidneys and be good for you. Packaged *meyva suyu* (fruit juice), soft drinks, beer and wine are usually safe to drink.

Water Purification If you need to, the simplest way of purifying water is to boil it thoroughly. Vigorous boiling should be satisfactory; however, at high altitude water boils at a lower temperature, so germs are less likely to be killed. Boil it for longer in these environments.

Consider purchasing a water filter for a long trip. There are two main kinds of filter. Total filters take out all parasites, bacteria and viruses and make water safe to drink. They are often expensive, but they can be more cost effective than buying bottled water. Simple filters (which can just be a nylon mesh bag) take out dirt and larger foreign bodies from the water so that chemical solutions work much more effectively; if water is dirty, chemical solutions may not work at all. It's very important when buying a filter to read the specifications, so you know exactly what it removes from the water and what it doesn't. Simple filtering will not remove all dangerous organisms, so if you can't boil water it should be treated chemically. Chlorine tablets will kill many pathogens, but not some parasites such as giardia and amoeba. Iodine is more effective in purifying water and is available in tablet form. Follow the directions carefully and remember that too much iodine can be harmful.

Medical Problems & Treatment

For minor problems, it's customary to ask at an *eczane* (edj-zahn-**neh**, pharmacy) for advice. An *eczane* can also dispense many drugs for which you would need a prescription at home. Emergency medical and dental treatment is available at simple *sağlık ocağı* (dispensaries), *klinik* (clinics) and *hastane* (government hospitals). Look for signs with a red crescent or big 'H'. Payment is required, but is usually low.

Everyday Health

Normal body temperature is up to 37°C (98.6°F); more than 2°C (4°F) higher indicates a high fever. The normal adult pulse rate is 60 to 100 per minute (children 80 to 100, babies 100 to 140). As a general rule the pulse increases about 20 beats per minute for each 1°C (2°F) rise in fever.

Respiration (breathing) rate is also an indicator of illness. Count the number of breaths per minute: Between 12 and 20 is normal for adults and older children (up to 30 for younger children, 40 for babies). People with a high fever or serious respiratory illness breathe more quickly than normal. More than 40 shallow breaths a minute may indicate pneumonia.

Your embassy or consulate should be able to recommend a local doctor or dentist, if necessary. Alternatively, in every city and town of any size you will see signs marking the medical offices of doctors and giving their specialities. A *tıbbi doktor*, medical doctor, might specialise in *dahili*, internal medicine; *göz hastalıkları*, eye diseases; *kadın hastalıkları*, gynaecological ailments; or *çocuk hastalıkları*, paediatric (children's) ailments. An *operatör* is a surgeon.

Half of all the physicians in Turkey are women. If a woman visits a male doctor, it's customary to have a companion present during any physical examination or treatment. There is not always a nurse available to serve in this role.

The standard of hygiene and care in Turkey's state hospitals is not high; make sure you have insurance that will cover treatment in a private hospital.

Remember that self-diagnosis and treatment can be risky, so you should always seek medical help. Although we do give drug dosages in this section, they are for information only, and should not be used without a doctor's guidance. Correct diagnosis is essential. In particular, antibiotics should be administered only under medical supervision. Take only the recommended dose at the prescribed intervals and use the whole course, even if symptoms disappear earlier. Stop immediately if there are any serious reactions and don't use the antibiotic at all if you are unsure that you have the correct one.

Environmental Hazards

Sunburn One of the biggest health risks in Turkey is the intensity of the sun. You can get sunburnt surprisingly quickly. Use a sunscreen and take extra care to cover areas that don't normally see the sun; zinc cream or a total sun block is a good idea for your nose and lips. Wear a hat and protect your eyes with good quality sunglasses. Calamine lotion or aloe vera are good for mild sunburn, or you can use the traditional Turkish treatment – smear yogurt on it!

Heat Exhaustion Dehydration and salt deficiency can cause heat exhaustion. Take time to acclimatise to high temperatures, drink sufficient liquids and do not do anything too physically demanding.

Salt deficiency is characterised by fatigue, lethargy, headaches, giddiness and muscle cramps; salt tablets may help, but adding extra salt in your food is better.

Heatstroke This serious, occasionally fatal, condition can occur if the body's heat-regulating mechanism breaks down and the body temperature rises to dangerous levels. Long, continuous periods of exposure to high temperatures and insufficient fluids can leave you vulnerable to heatstroke.

The symptoms are feeling unwell, not sweating very much (or at all) and a high body temperature (39° to 41°C or 102° to 106°F). When sweating has ceased, the skin becomes flushed and red. Severe, throbbing headaches and lack of coordination will also occur, and the sufferer may be confused or aggressive. Eventually the victim will become delirious or convulse. Hospitalisation is essential, but in the interim get victims out of the sun, remove their clothing, cover them with a wet sheet or towel and then fan continually. Give fluids if they are conscious.

Hypothermia Too much cold can be just as dangerous as too much heat. In Turkey, hypothermia can be a risk if you are travelling in central or eastern Anatolia, especially if you are trekking or simply taking a long bus trip over mountains, particularly at night. It is surprisingly easy to progress from very cold to dangerously cold due to a combination of wind, wet clothing, fatigue and hunger. Make sure you are prepared: wear a hat, and dress in layers; silk, wool and some of the new artificial fibres are all good insulating materials. A strong, waterproof outer layer is essential. Carry basic supplies, including food containing simple sugars to generate heat quickly and fluid to drink.

Mild hypothermia (indicated by shivering, numb extremities and exhaustion) should be treated by getting the person out of the wind and/or rain, and replacing wet clothing with dry, warm clothing. Give them hot liquids – not alcohol – and some high-

kilojoule, easily digestible food. Do not rub victims: instead, allow them to slowly warm themselves. This should be enough to treat the early stages of hypothermia. The early recognition and treatment of mild hypothermia is the only way to prevent severe hypothermia, which is a critical condition.

Motion Sickness Eating lightly before and during a trip will reduce the chances of motion sickness. If you are prone to motion sickness try to find a place that minimises movement – near the wing on aircraft, close to midships on boats, near the centre on buses. Fresh air usually helps; reading and cigarette smoke don't. Commercial motion-sickness preparations, which can cause drowsiness, have to be taken before the trip commences. Ginger (available in capsule form) and peppermint (including mint-flavoured sweets) are natural preventatives.

Prickly Heat Prickly heat is an itchy rash caused by excessive perspiration trapped under the skin. It usually strikes people who have just arrived in a hot climate. Keeping cool, bathing often, drying the skin and using a mild talcum or prickly heat powder or resorting to air-conditioning may help.

Infectious Diseases

Diarrhoea Simple things like a change of water, food or climate can all cause a mild bout of diarrhoea, but a few rushed toilet trips with no other symptoms is not indicative of a major problem.

Dehydration is the main danger with any diarrhoea, particularly in children or the elderly, as dehydration can occur quite quickly. Under all circumstances fluid replacement (at least equal to the volume being lost) is the most important thing to remember. Weak black tea with a little sugar, soda water, or soft drinks allowed to go flat and diluted 50% with clean water are all good.

With severe diarrhoea a rehydrating solution is preferable to replace minerals and salts lost. Commercially available oral rehydration salts (ORS) are very useful; add them to boiled or bottled water. In an emergency you can make up a solution of six teaspoons of sugar and a half teaspoon of salt to a litre of boiled or bottled water.

You need to drink at least the same volume of fluid that you are losing in bowel movements and vomiting. Urine is the best guide to the adequacy of replacement – if you have small amounts of concentrated urine, you need to drink more. Keep drinking small amounts often. Stick to a bland diet as you recover.

Drugs such as loperamide or diphenoxylate (various brand names) are widely available and can be used to bring relief from the symptoms, although they do not actually cure the problem. Only use these drugs if you do not have access to toilets, eg, if you *must* travel. For children under 12 years these drugs are not recommended. Do not use these drugs if you have a high fever or are severely dehydrated.

Medical Advice & Treatment In certain situations you may need a course of antibiotics: severe diarrhoea, diarrhoea with blood or mucus (dysentery), any diarrhoea with fever and profuse watery diarrhoea, persistent diarrhoea not improving after 48 hours and severe diarrhoea. These suggest a more serious cause of diarrhoea, and you should seek medical help urgently.

Where medical help is not available, the recommended drugs for bacterial diarrhoea (the most likely cause of severe diarrhoea in travellers) are norfloxacin 400mg twice daily for three days or ciprofloxacin 500mg twice daily for five days. These are not recommended for children or pregnant women. The drug of choice for children would be co-trimoxazole with dosage dependent on weight. A five-day course is given. Ampicillin or amoxycillin may be given in pregnancy, but medical care is necessary.

Persistent Diarrhoea Two causes of persistent diarrhoea in travellers are giardiasis and amoebic dysentery, although these are relatively uncommon in travellers to Turkey.

Symptoms of **giardiasis** include stomach cramps, nausea, a bloated stomach, watery, foul-smelling diarrhoea and frequent gas. Giardiasis can appear several weeks after you have been exposed to the parasite. The symptoms may disappear for a few days and then return; this can go on for several weeks.

Amoebic dysentery is characterised by a gradual onset of low-grade diarrhoea, often with blood and mucus. Cramping abdominal pain and vomiting are less likely than in other types of diarrhoea, and fever may not be present. It will persist until treated and can recur and cause other health problems.

You should seek medical advice if you think you have giardiasis or amoebic dysentery, but where this is not possible, tinidazole or metronidazole are the recommended drugs. Treatment is a 2g single dose of tinidazole or 250mg of metronidazole three times daily for five to 10 days.

Fungal Infections Fungal infections, which occur with greater frequency in hot weather, are usually found on the scalp, between the toes (athlete's foot) or fingers, in the groin and on the body (ringworm). You get ringworm (which is a fungal infection, not a worm) from infected animals or other people. Moisture encourages these infections.

To prevent fungal infections wear loose, comfortable clothes, avoid artificial fibres, wash frequently and dry yourself carefully. If you do get an infection, wash the infected area at least daily with a disinfectant or medicated soap and water, and rinse and dry well. Apply an antifungal cream or powder such as tolnaftate. Try to expose the infected area to air or sunlight as much as possible. Wash all towels and underwear in hot water, let them dry in the sun and change them often.

Hepatitis A This viral infection of the liver is common worldwide, and is transmitted through contaminated food and drinking water. Symptoms include fever, chills, headache and tiredness, followed by loss of appetite, nausea, vomiting, abdominal pain, dark urine, light-coloured faeces, jaundiced (yellow) skin and yellowing of the whites of the eyes. You should seek medical advice, but there is not much you can do apart from resting, drinking lots of fluids, eating lightly and avoiding fatty foods. If you have hepatitis, you should avoid alcohol for some time after the illness, as the liver needs time to recover. Hepatitis E is transmitted in the same way as hepatitis A; it can be particularly serious in pregnant women.

Hepatitis B There are almost 300 million chronic carriers of hepatitis B in the world. This viral infection of the liver causes similar symptoms to hepatitis A, but may be more severe. It is spread through contact with infected blood, blood products or body fluids, for example through sexual contact, unsterilised needles and blood transfusions, or contact with blood via small breaks in the skin. Other risk situations include having a shave, tattoo or body piercing with contaminated equipment. The symptoms of hepatitis B may be more severe than type A and the disease can lead to long-term problems such as chronic liver damage, liver cancer or a long-term carrier state. Hepatitis C and D are spread in the same way as hepatitis B and can also lead to long term complications.

HIV & AIDS Infection with the human immunodeficiency virus (HIV) leads to the acquired immune deficiency syndrome (AIDS), which is a fatal disease. Any exposure to blood, blood products or body fluids may put the individual at risk. The disease is often transmitted through sexual contact or dirty needles – vaccinations, acupuncture, tattooing and body piercing can be potentially as dangerous as intravenous drug use. HIV/AIDS can also be spread through infected blood transfusions; some developing countries cannot afford to screen blood used for transfusions.

The best course is to buy a new *şırınga* (syringe) from a pharmacy and ask the doctor to use it.

Intestinal Worms These parasites are most common in rural, tropical areas and may be a problem in some parts of southeastern Turkey. Different worms have different ways of infecting people. Some (eg, tapeworms) may be ingested via food such as undercooked meat and some (eg, hookworms) enter through your skin. Infestations may not show up for some time, and

although they are generally not serious, if left untreated some can cause severe health problems later. Consider having a stool test when you return home to check for these and determine the appropriate treatment.

Sexually Transmitted Infections HIV/AIDS and hepatitis B can be transmitted through sexual contact – see the relevant sections earlier for more details. Other STIs include gonorrhoea, herpes and syphilis. Sores, blisters or rashes around the genitals and discharges or pain when urinating are common symptoms. In some STIs, such as wart virus or chlamydia, symptoms may be less marked or not observed at all, especially in women. Chlamydia infection can cause infertility in men and women before any symptoms have been noticed. Syphilis symptoms eventually disappear completely but the disease continues and can cause severe problems in later years. While abstinence from sexual contact is the only 100% effective prevention, using condoms is also effective. Gonorrhoea and syphilis are treated with antibiotics. The different sexually transmitted infections each require specific antibiotics.

Typhoid Typhoid fever is a dangerous gut infection transmitted through contaminated water and food. You must get medical help if you think you have this disease.

In its early stages sufferers may feel they have a bad cold or flu on the way, as early symptoms are a headache, body aches and a fever which rises a little each day until it is around 40°C (104°F). The victim's pulse is often slow, relative to the degree of fever present – unlike a normal fever where the pulse increases. There may also be vomiting, abdominal pain, diarrhoea or constipation.

In the second week the high fever and slow pulse continue and a few pink spots may appear on the body; trembling, delirium, weakness, weight loss and dehydration may occur. Complications such as pneumonia, perforated bowel or meningitis may occur.

Insect-Borne Diseases
Malaria Overall, the risk of malaria in Turkey is very small, and most travellers

will not need to take precautions. Officially, malaria is present in south-eastern Anatolia from Mersin on the Mediterranean coast eastward to the Iraqi border, but the highest danger is in the muggy agricultural area called Çukurova north of Adana, and in the newly irrigated areas around Şanlıurfa, where the incidence of malaria has sky-rocketed in the last decade.

If you just pass through these areas, or spend most of your time in cities, the danger is lower; but if you plan to spend lots of time in rural areas and camp out in this region, you're at significant risk and should take appropriate precautions – consult your doctor.

Symptoms range from fever, chills and sweating, headache, diarrhoea and abdominal pains to a vague feeling of ill-health. Seek medical help immediately if malaria is suspected. Without treatment malaria can rapidly become more serious and can be fatal.

If medical care is not available, malaria tablets can be used for treatment. You need to use a malaria tablet which is different from the one you were taking when you contracted malaria. The standard treatment dose of mefloquine is two 250mg tablets and a further two six hours later. For Fansidar, it's a single dose of three tablets. If you were previously taking mefloquine and cannot obtain Fansidar, then other alternatives are Malarone (atovaquone-proguanil; four tablets once daily for three days), halofantrine (three doses of two 250mg tablets every six hours) or quinine sulphate (600mg every six hours). There is a greater risk of side effects with these dosages than in normal use if used with mefloquine, so medical advice is preferable. Be aware also that halofantrine is no longer recommended by the WHO as emergency stand-by treatment because of its side effects, and should only be used if no other drugs are available.

It's important to take precautions to prevent mosquito bites at all times.

- Wear light-coloured clothing.
- Wear long trousers and long-sleeved shirts.
- Use mosquito repellents containing the compound DEET on exposed areas (prolonged overuse of DEET may be harmful, especially to children, but its use is considered preferable to being bitten by disease-transmitting mosquitoes).
- Avoid using perfumes or aftershave.
- Use a mosquito net impregnated with mosquito repellent (permethrin) – it may be worth taking your own.
- Impregnating clothes with permethrin effectively deters mosquitoes and other insects.

Cuts, Bites & Stings

See Less Common Diseases for details of rabies, which is passed through animal bites.

Cuts & Scratches Wash well and treat any cut with an antiseptic such as povidone-iodine. Where possible avoid bandages and Band-Aids, which can keep wounds wet.

Bedbugs & Lice Bedbugs live in various places, but particularly in dirty mattresses and bedding, evidenced by spots of blood on bedclothes or on the wall. Bedbugs leave itchy bites in neat rows. Calamine lotion or a sting relief spray may help.

All lice cause itching and discomfort. They make themselves at home in your hair (head lice), your clothing (body lice) or in your pubic hair (crabs). You catch lice through direct contact with infected people or by sharing combs, clothing and the like. Powder or shampoo treatment will kill the lice and infected clothing should then be washed in very hot, soapy water and left in the sun to dry.

Bites & Stings Bee and wasp stings are usually painful rather than dangerous. However, in people who are allergic to them severe breathing difficulties may occur and require urgent medical care. Calamine lotion or a sting relief spray may help and ice packs will reduce the pain and swelling. There are some spiders with dangerous bites but antivenoms are usually available. Scorpion stings are notoriously painful and sometimes can actually be fatal. Scorpions often shelter in shoes or clothing.

Jellyfish Be wary of jellyfish – although they are not usually lethal in Turkey, their stings can be painful. Dousing in vinegar will deactivate any stingers which have not 'fired'. Calamine lotion, antihistamines and analgesics may reduce the reaction and relieve the pain.

Ticks You should always check all over your body if you have been walking through a potentially tick-infested area as ticks can cause skin infections and other more serious diseases.

If a tick is found attached, press down around the tick's head with tweezers, grab the head and gently pull upwards. Avoid pulling the rear of the body as this may squeeze the tick's gut contents through the attached mouth parts into the skin, increasing the risk of infection and disease. Smearing chemicals on the tick will not make it let go and is not recommended.

Snakes To minimise your chances of being bitten always wear boots, socks and long trousers when walking through undergrowth where snakes may be present. Don't put your hands into holes and crevices, and be careful when collecting firewood.

Snake bites do not cause instantaneous death and antivenoms are usually available. Immediately wrap the bitten limb tightly, as you would for a sprained ankle, and then attach a splint to immobilise it. Keep the victim still and seek medical help, if possible with the dead snake for identification. Don't attempt to catch the snake if there is a possibility of being bitten again. Tourniquets and sucking out the poison are now comprehensively discredited.

Less Common Diseases
The following diseases pose a small risk to travellers in Turkey, and so are only mentioned in passing. Seek medical advice if you think you may have any of these diseases.

Cholera This is the worst of the watery diarrhoeas and medical help should be sought. Outbreaks of cholera are generally widely reported, so you can avoid such problem areas. *Fluid replacement is the most vital treatment* – the risk of dehydration is severe as you may lose up to 20L a day.

Leishmaniasis Leishmaniasis is an insect-borne disease that also occurs in Turkey, but it does not pose a great risk to travellers. This is a group of parasitic diseases transmitted by sandflies, which are found in Turkey as well as other parts of the world. Cutaneous leishmaniasis affects the skin tissue causing ulceration and disfigurement, and visceral leishmaniasis affects the internal organs. Seek medical advice, as laboratory testing is required for diagnosis and correct treatment. Avoiding sandfly bites is the best precaution. Bites are usually painless, itchy and yet another reason to cover up and apply repellent.

Rabies This fatal viral infection is found in many countries, including Turkey. Many animals can be infected (such as dogs, cats, bats and monkeys) and it is their saliva which is infectious. Steer clear of any animal that might bite. Any bite, scratch or even lick from an animal should be cleaned immediately and thoroughly. Scrub with soap and running water, and then apply alcohol or iodine solution. Get medical help promptly so that you can receive a course of injections which will prevent the onset of symptoms and death.

Tetanus This disease is caused by a germ which lives in soil and in the faeces of horses and other animals. It enters the body via breaks in the skin. The first symptom may be discomfort in swallowing, or stiffening of the jaw and neck; this is followed by painful convulsions of the jaw and whole body. The disease can be fatal. It can be prevented by vaccination.

Women's Health
Gynaecological Problems Antibiotic use, synthetic underwear, sweating and contraceptive pills can lead to fungal vaginal infections, especially when travelling in hot climates. Fungal infections are characterised by a rash, itch and discharge and are usually treated with antifungal pessaries or cream, such as nystatin, miconazole or clotrimazole. Alternatively, if no medical treatment is available, they can be treated with a vinegar

or lemon-juice douche, or with yogurt. Maintaining good personal hygiene and wearing loose-fitting clothes and cotton underwear may help prevent these infections.

Sexually transmitted infections are a major cause of vaginal problems. Symptoms include a smelly discharge, painful intercourse and sometimes a burning sensation when urinating. Medical attention should be sought and male sexual partners must also be treated. For more details see the section on Sexually Transmitted Infections earlier. Besides abstinence, the best thing is to practise safer sex using condoms.

Pregnancy When deciding whether to travel, be aware that some vaccinations may not be advisable in pregnancy, and also that some diseases (such as malaria) are much more serious for the mother (and may increase the risk of a stillborn child).

Most miscarriages occur during the first three months of pregnancy. Miscarriage is not uncommon and can occasionally lead to severe bleeding. The last three months should also be spent within reasonable distance of good medical care. A baby born as early as 24 weeks stands a chance of survival, but only in a good modern hospital. Pregnant women should avoid all unnecessary medication, although vaccinations and malarial prophylactics should still be taken where needed. Additional care should be taken to prevent illness and particular attention should be paid to diet and nutrition. Alcohol and nicotine, for example, should be avoided.

WOMEN TRAVELLERS
Attitudes Towards Women

In traditional Turkish society men and women were strictly segregated and rarely socialised together; men gathered in the teahouses, women in each other's homes. Over the last decade or so the situation has changed dramatically in the big towns and along the coast, especially in the west, although in more rural areas and in the east it's still unusual to find men and women mixing.

The result of this gender segregation was that men tended to assume any woman walking alone or talking to unrelated men

was in some way asking for it. That was bad enough, but then to add to the problem came Western films, Western television and above all pornography, all helping to reinforce a widely held belief that Western women were somehow different and leading inevitably to harassment of them.

It's often assumed that female tourists have a harder time of it in less-sophisticated eastern Turkey but in reality taboos against promiscuity remain stronger there and many women have the hardest time warding off unwanted attention in İstanbul and the resorts.

Safety Precautions

It's impossible to explain why some women travel round Turkey almost without problem while others report constant harassment. But it's important to remember that most female tourists are at much greater risk of serious assault in their home countries. Provided you dress and behave sensibly, most men will treat you with great kindness and generosity.

The best way to avoid attracting unwanted attention is to dress and behave discreetly. Wearing a wedding ring and carrying photos of husband and children (whether they exist or not) can be helpful, as can wearing dark glasses to avoid eye contact. At the very least you should cover your torso, legs and upper arms – no shorts or skimpy T-shirts, except perhaps in the resorts. In a society where women rarely drink, getting out of it on alcohol is simply asking for trouble.

Men and unrelated women are not expected to sit beside each other in buses or dolmuşes and lone women are often assigned seats at the front of the bus near the driver. If you're not told where to sit, avoid sitting at the back of the bus since that seems to have 'back-seat-of-the-cinema' connotations in some men's minds. We have also received reports of the *yardımcıs* (conductors) on night buses harassing their female customers. If that happens to you, complain loudly and repeat your complaint on arrival at your destination – you have a right to be treated with respect.

When travelling by taxi avoid getting into the seat beside the driver. Hard though it is for women brought up in the West to believe it, there are even men who manage to mistake a passing smile for flirtation.

When looking for a hotel, you may have to accept that the cheapest fleapits are not necessarily suitable for lone women. It's not that anything will happen to you in them, but it's hard to relax in a place where conversation in the lobby invariably grinds to a halt as soon as you cross the threshold. If men bang on your hotel door late at night, don't open it; in the morning, complain to the manager.

Restaurants that aim to attract women usually set aside a special room (or part of one) for family groups; look for the word *aile* (family) to guide you.

Many Turkish men are extremely charming and countless woman fall in love during their trip. There's nothing wrong with that, of course, though it pays to be a bit careful if the subject of money for visas or tickets out of Turkey comes up. However starry-eyed you may be you should never forget the safe-sex message, especially in the resort areas.

GAY & LESBIAN TRAVELLERS

Although homosexuality is not illegal in Turkey, it is not generally socially acceptable either, so it pays to be a bit careful before engaging in public displays of affection with partners of the same gender. In İstanbul, Bodrum and Kuşadası there are active gay scenes, with a few overtly gay bars and nightclubs; in İstanbul these are mainly around the Taksim Square end of İstiklal Caddesi. Elsewhere, people may be very reluctant to admit their sexual orientation, at least in public. Some hamams, especially in İstanbul, are known as gay meeting places.

DISABLED TRAVELLERS

Turkey has severely limited accessibility for disabled travellers. Though local people will go out of their way to help a disabled traveller get around, with few exceptions the arrangements are ad hoc.

Airlines and the top hotels and resorts have some provisions for wheelchair access, and ramps are beginning to appear (ever so slowly) in a few other places.

A good source of information on accessible travel is the Royal Association for Disability and Rehabilitation or RADAR (☎ 207-250 3222), 12 City Forum, 250 City Road, London EC1V 8AF, UK.

SENIOR TRAVELLERS

Seniors are welcomed and respected in Turkey, and sometimes receive discounts at hotels, museums, other tourist sites, and on some transport fares. Use your passport as proof of age.

TRAVEL WITH CHILDREN

Your *çocuk* (child) or *çocuklar* (children) will be very well received in Turkey. Disposable *bebek bezi* (baby nappies or diapers) are readily available for *bebek* (infants). The best brand is Ultra Prima, sold in pharmacies according to the baby's weight in kilograms. A packet of 24 costs about US$6.

Ultra-pasteurised milk is sold everywhere. Some baby foods in individual jars may also be found, but it's usually better to rely on the willingness and ingenuity of hotel and restaurant staff to make up special dishes for small children. You might also want to carry a small portable food mill, sold in pharmacies and children's products shops at home, to puree vegetables, fruits and meats.

The larger hotels and resorts can arrange for *kreş* (daycare) and baby-sitting services; the seaside resorts often have extensive children's play and activity equipment. Public parks sometimes have basic play equipment.

Child safety seats are available from all large, and many small, car rental companies at a small extra daily charge.

The market for childhood products and services is not as elaborately developed in Turkey as in Europe or the US, but Turks are handy at improvising anything which may be needed for a child's safety, health or enjoyment.

Lonely Planet's *Travel with Children* by Maureen Wheeler has lots of practical information and advice on how to make travel with children as stress-free as possible, for both children and parents.

DANGERS & ANNOYANCES

Turkey is a safe country relative to most of the world; however, if you're travelling to the east, read the boxed text 'Is It Safe?' at the start of the South-Eastern Anatolia section of the Eastern Anatolia chapter.

Beware of urban myths. The sinister but untrue tale that 174 Britons have been murdered for their passports has been circulating inside and outside Turkey for years. When a foreign visitor disappears in Turkey or in any other country, it's usually well publicised.

The Turkish Knockout

There is a small but significant danger of theft by drugging. Thieves befriend travellers, usually single men, and offer them drinks or snacks containing powerful drugs which cause the victims to lose consciousness quickly. The drug is often Nembitol (benzodiazepine), called *sarı bombası* (yellow bomb) in Turkish, a colourless, odourless, tasteless substance that induces sleep. When the victims awake hours later, they have a terrible hangover and have been stripped of everything except their clothes.

The perpetrators of this sort of crime, who are usually not Turkish, often work in pairs or trios. They befriend you and travel with you, perhaps even for a day or two, or more. One report was of foreign (non-Turkish) thieves from another Islamic country befriending a British subject and riding by bus with him across the country to İstanbul. The thieves offered him a soda in Gülhane Parkı. When the victim awoke, his camera, wallet and passport were gone, as was his luggage from the hotel where they were all staying.

Another team – Turks this time – works out of Ankara's otogar. They look for travellers on their way to Cappadocia and start a conversation. They mention that, by coincidence, they're going to Ürgüp as well. They buy their own tickets and join you on the bus. When you arrive at your destination, they break open a container of *ayran* (yogurt drink), each take a sip and then offer it to you. How they get the drugs in after they drink is a mystery, but the effect on the victim is powerful and virtually immediate. One sip knocks you out for half a day.

A variation perpetrated by impatient thieves is to offer you the drink (tea, soda, whatever) on the bus; you 'fall asleep', and they get off at the next town with all your gear. Another variation was described by a female reader who claims that an over-friendly local in the village of Tevfikiye (next to Troy) drugged her husband in the course of a 'friendly' evening of drinking with them, in order to get her alone and pressure her for sex.

This scheme is difficult to defeat, as Turks are generally very hospitable, and it is a Turkish custom to offer visitors drinks. Here are some things you can do to protect yourself:

- If you are a single male traveller, be suspicious of pairs or trios of other males (usually aged 18 to 28 years) who befriend you, whether Turkish or foreign. Be especially suspicious if they ask you where you are going, then travel with you.
- If you are at all suspicious of new-found friends, eat and drink only from your own supplies or those bought fresh in sealed containers from the hand of a waiter or shopkeeper. (It's possible to inject drugs into a sealed container using a syringe through the seal.) True Turkish friends may offer to pay for drinks to satisfy the requirements of traditional hospitality. They needn't deliver the drinks themselves.
- If your new travelling companions insist on staying with you at the same lodging, start thinking of how to get away. Suggest that you want to take their picture as a souvenir, and see how they react. If they've got mischief on their minds, they won't like the idea of photographic evidence.
- If you must, cite 'allergy' *(alerji)* as your reason for not accepting a drink, biscuit or snack. Or 'accidentally' drop and spoil it. And if your new 'friends' accuse you of insulting their generosity, get out of the situation quickly – to the police if necessary. If there is no police station near, try a bank or other location with a security officer.

Police

The blue-clad officers, both men and women, are part of a national force designated by the words 'Polis' or 'Emniyet' (security). If you encounter them, they will judge you partly by your clothes and personal appearance.

Other blue-clad officers with special peaked caps are called *belediye zabıtası*, municipal inspectors or market police.

Soldiers in the standard Turkish army uniforms may be of three types. Without special insignia, they're regular army. With a red armband bearing the word 'Jandarma', they're gendarmes, a paramilitary police force charged with keeping the peace, catching criminals on the run, stopping smuggling etc. In rural areas the jandarma may be the only local police force. If the soldiers have white helmets emblazoned with the letters 'As İz', plus pistols in white holsters connected to lanyards around their necks, they're *askeri inzibat*, or military police.

Theft & Robbery

Theft is not much of a problem, and robbery (mugging) even less, but don't let Turkey's relative safety lull you. Take normal precautions. As is the case in every country, foreign travellers may be targeted by criminals.

Precautions include keeping track of your wallet or other valuables on crowded buses and trains and in markets; not leaving valuables in your hotel room, or at least not in view; and not walking into unknown parts of town when nobody else is around. There are isolated reports of bags being quietly slashed in İstanbul's Kapalı Çarşı, and of 'distract, bump-and-grab' thefts in similar crowded places in the major cities.

Actually, the biggest danger of theft is probably in dormitory rooms and other open accommodation where others can see what sort of camera you have or where you stash your money. Robbery by drugging is not common but is something to be aware of – see the boxed text 'The Turkish Knockout' opposite.

Scams

In İstanbul there's a nightclub shakedown racket aimed at single men. Here's how it works: you're strolling along İstiklal Caddesi or Cumhuriyet Caddesi in the evening. You stop to look in a shop window. A well-dressed man or a couple of men approach and chat about this and that. They offer to buy you a drink in a nightclub nearby. You're given a seat next to some 'girls', and even if you protest at this point, it's too late. They say the girls' drinks are on your bill. If you resist paying an amount which conveniently equals the entire contents of your wallet, you are escorted to the back office and convinced forcibly to pay up. Moral: single men should not accept invitations from unknown Turks in large cities without sizing the situation up very carefully.

We've had some reports of con men with false police identification levying 'fines' on unsuspecting tourists. Don't pay. The real police are very eager to catch the fakes, and will thank you for giving them information on this scam.

Disputes

In general, Turks view foreigners as cultured, educated and wealthy – even if many foreign visitors don't deserve such a view. This means that you will sometimes be given special consideration, jumped to the heads of queues, given the best seat on public transport etc.

In a dispute, if you keep your cool and act dignified, you will generally be given the benefit of the doubt. If it is thought you have powerful friends, you will definitely be given that benefit.

In the case of women travellers in disputes with Turks, you should know that Turkish men are easily offended at any perceived 'insults to their manhood', and will retaliate. Insults to them can include being shouted at or browbeaten by a woman who is not (in their eyes) unquestionably of a higher social status. In general, keep it all formal.

Lese-Majesty

There are laws against insulting, defaming or making light of Atatürk, the Turkish flag, the Turkish people, the Turkish Republic etc. Any difficulty will probably arise from misunderstanding.

At the first sign that you have inadvertently been guilty of lese-majesty, make your apologies, which will be readily accepted.

Natural Hazards

Earthquakes The terrible earthquake of 1999 was a sober reminder that Turkey is, like California, Mexico and Japan, among the most seismically active areas in the world. Whether you experience one is mostly up to Allah.

Undertow & Riptides At some swimming areas, particularly in the Black Sea near İstanbul, this is a real danger. Undertow can kill you by powerfully pulling you beneath the surface, and a riptide does the same by sweeping you out to sea so that you exhaust yourself trying to regain the shore. There may be no signs warning of the danger. Lifeguards may not be present, or may be untrained or not equipped with a boat. Don't trust luck. You can't necessarily see these hazards or predict where they will be.

In either situation, remain calm, as panic can be fatal. Don't exhaust yourself by trying to swim straight back to the beach from a rip, because you'll never make it. Rather, swim to the left or right to escape the rip area, and make for land in that direction. These dangers are usually a problem only on long stretches of open-sea beach with surf. In coves and bays, where waves are broken or diverted by headlands, you probably won't be in danger.

The Imperial Auto

As a pedestrian, give way to cars and trucks in all situations, even if you have to jump out of the way. The sovereignty of the pedestrian is unrecognised in Turkey. If a car hits you, the driver (if not the law courts) will blame you. This does not apply on a recognised crossing controlled by a traffic officer or a traffic signal. If you've got a 'Walk' light, you've got the right of way. Watch out, all the same. Know that every Turkish driver considers you, a pedestrian, as merely an annoyance. A dispute with a driver will get you nowhere and may escalate into an even bigger problem.

Cigarette Smoke

By law, no smoking is allowed on domestic airline flights, or on city or intercity buses (except for the driver, who may smoke!). Trains are supposed to have nonsmoking carriages, but the prohibition is often ignored. Chances are that if you're offended by cigarette smoke, you will have some unpleasant moments in Turkey, but not so many as to ruin your trip.

Noise

Noise can be a source of annoyance in cities and larger towns, so it's worth choosing a hotel room with this in mind. Nightlife noise can be a problem in some places, especially the coastal resorts. When in doubt, ask *'Sakin mi?'* (Is it quiet here?).

Among the most omnipresent noises is the call to prayer, amplified to ear-splitting levels. If there's a minaret right outside your hotel window, you'll know it – something else to bear in mind when choosing a hotel.

Air Pollution

Heating furnaces in Ankara and İstanbul, which used to create severe pollution problems from the burning of lignite (soft coal), have largely been converted to natural gas. However, air pollution can still be a problem, especially in winter. Lignite is still burned in medium-sized and smaller cities, creating moderate pollution. In the big cities, taxis and many buses now run on natural gas, but most vehicles don't. If you find your nose running, your eyes watering and itching, and your head aching, that's the pollution. The heating season lasts from 15 October to 1 April. In summer there is pollution from cars, but it's no worse than in other big cities around the world.

EMERGENCIES

In an emergency, you can phone one of these national emergency numbers (although you're likely to encounter only Turkish-speaking operators):

Police	☎ 155
Jandarma (Gendarmerie)	☎ 156
Ambulance	☎ 112
Fire	☎ 110

LEGAL MATTERS

It's important to remember that when you are in Turkey you are subject to Turkish laws and authorities, not the laws of your home country. Beyond urging the Turkish authorities to treat you fairly, your embassy cannot help you at all. Lese-majesty (see the Dangers & Annoyances section earlier in this chapter), antiquities smuggling (see the Customs section earlier in this chapter) and illegal drugs are the three most likely causes of any legal problems.

Don't import, export, buy, sell or use illegal drugs in Turkey, and don't trust anyone who does.

BUSINESS HOURS

Banks are usually open from 8.30 am to noon and 1.30 to 5 pm Monday to Friday. Government and business offices may open at 8 or 9 am, close for lunch, and reopen around 1.30 pm, remaining open until 4 or 5 pm. During the hot summer months in some cities the working day begins at 7 or 8 am and finishes at 2 pm. Also, during the holy month of Ramazan the working day is shortened.

Grocery shops and markets are usually open from 6 or 7 am to 7 or 8 pm Monday to Saturday. On Sunday most markets close, though one or two grocers stay open in each neighbourhood. İstanbul's Kapalı Çarşı and covered markets in other cities are open from 8 am to 6.30 pm Monday to Saturday. Other shops are open Monday to Saturday from 9 am to noon and 1.30 or 2.30 pm to 6 or 7 pm or even later; many don't close for lunch.

PUBLIC HOLIDAYS & SPECIAL EVENTS
Religious Festivals

The official Turkish calendar is the Western, Gregorian one used in Europe, but religious festivals are celebrated according to the Islamic lunar calendar. As the lunar calendar is about 11 days shorter than the Gregorian, the Islamic festivals arrive 11 days earlier each year.

Actual dates for Islamic religious festivals are proclaimed by Muslim authorities after the appropriate astronomical observations and calculations have been made.

For major religious and public holidays there is a half-day vacation for 'preparation', called *arife*, preceding the start of a festival. Shops and offices close about noon, and the festival begins at sunset.

Friday is the Muslim Sabbath, but it is not a holiday in Turkey. Mosques and baths will be crowded, especially on Friday morning. The day of rest, a secular one, is Sunday.

Only two religious holidays are also public holidays: Şeker Bayramı and Kurban Bayramı.

Ramazan The Holy Month, called Ramadan in other Muslim countries, is similar in some ways to Lent. For the 30 days of Ramazan, a good Muslim lets *nothing* pass the lips during daylight hours: no eating, drinking, smoking, or even licking a postage stamp.

Traditionally, a cannon shot signalled the end of the fast at sunset. The fast is broken with flat *pide* (bread) if possible. Lavish dinners are given and may last far into the night. Before dawn, drummers may circulate through town to awaken the faithful so they can eat before sunrise.

During Ramazan, restaurants may be closed from dawn to nightfall, and in conservative towns it's bad form for anyone – non-Muslims included – to smoke, munch snacks or sip drinks in public view. Business hours may change and be shorter. As non-Muslims, it's understood that you get to eat and drink when you like, and in the big cities you'll find lots of nonfasting Muslims right beside you, but it's best to be discreet and to maintain a polite low visibility.

The 27th day of Ramazan is Kadir Gecesi, the Night of Power, when the Quran was revealed and Mohammed was appointed the Messenger of God.

The fasting of Ramazan is a worthy, sacred act and a blessing to Muslims. Pregnant or nursing women, the infirm and aged, and travellers are excused, according to the Quran, if they feel they cannot keep the fast.

Şeker Bayramı Also called Ramazan Bayramı or İd es-Seğir, this is a three-day festival at the end of Ramadan. *Şeker* means sugar or candy. During this festival children traditionally go door to door asking for sweet treats, Muslims exchange greeting cards and pay social calls, and everybody enjoys drinking lots of tea in broad daylight after fasting for Ramazan. The festival is a national holiday when banks and offices are closed and hotels, buses, trains and planes are heavily booked.

Kurban Bayramı The most important religious and secular holiday of the year, Kurban Bayramı (*kurban* means 'sacrifice') is equivalent in importance to Christmas in Christian countries.

The festival commemorates Abraham's near-sacrifice of Isaac on Mt Moriah (Genesis 22; Quran, Sura 37). In the story, God orders Abraham to take Isaac, the son of his old age, up to Mt Moriah and sacrifice him. Abraham takes Isaac up the mountain and lays him on the altar, but at the last moment God stops Abraham, congratulates him on his faithfulness, and orders him to sacrifice instead a ram tangled in a nearby bush, which Abraham does.

Following the tradition today, 2.5 million rams are sacrificed on Kurban Bayramı in Turkey each year. For days beforehand you'll see herds of sheep being paraded through streets or gathered in markets. Every head of a household who can afford a sheep buys one and takes it home. Right after the early morning prayers on the actual day of Bayramı, the head of the household slits the sheep's throat. It's then flayed and butchered, and family and friends immediately cook up a feast. A sizeable portion of the meat is distributed to the needy, and the skin is often donated to a charity; the charity sells it to a leather products company.

Lots of people take to the road, going home to parents or friends. Everybody exchanges greeting cards. At some point you'll probably be invited to share in the festivities.

Kurban Bayramı is a four- or five-day national holiday which you must plan for. Banks may be closed for a full week, though one or two branches will stay open in the big cities to serve foreigners. Transportation will be packed, and hotel rooms, particularly in resort areas, will be scarce and expensive.

Holidays & Special Events

The following is a month-by-month list of holidays and special events in Turkey.

New Year's Day – 1 January. Decorations in shops, exchanges of gifts and greeting cards, make this public holiday a kind of surrogate Christmas, good for business.

National Sovereignty & Children's Day – 23 April. This national holiday commemorates the initial meeting of the first Grand National Assembly, or republican parliament (1920). It's also Children's Day, an international children's festival, with kids invited from all over the world, held in Ankara and other locations.

Anzac Day – 25 April. The great battle is commemorated with a dawn ceremony at Gallipoli.

Youth & Sports Day – 19 May. A national holiday commemorating Atatürk's birthday (1881), with lots of sports exhibitions.

İstanbul Conquest Day – 29 May. In İstanbul, celebrations remember the capture of the city from the Byzantines in 1453.

Kırkpınar Oiled Wrestling Competition – 2nd week in June. Held at Edirne, this old Ottoman contest always draws huge crowds.

International İstanbul Festival of the Arts – late June to mid-July. This is a world-class festival, with top performers in music and dance, and special exhibitions.

Special Mass for the Virgin Mary – 15 August. Celebrated at the House of the Virgin Mary

Major Islamic Holidays

Islamic year	New Year	Prophet's Birthday	Ramazan begins	Şeker Bayramı	Kurban Bayramı
1422	26 Mar 01	3 Jun 01	16 Nov 01	16 Dec 01	23 Feb 02
1423	15 Mar 02	23 May 02	5 Nov 02	5 Dec 02	12 Feb 03
1424	5 Mar 03	14 May 03	27 Oct 03	27 Nov 03	31 Jan 04
1425	22 Feb 04	2 May 04	15 Oct 04	15 Nov 04	20 Jan 05

(Meryemana) near Ephesus by the Catholic Archbishop of İzmir, it commemorates the Assumption of the Virgin Mary.

İzmir International Fair – 20 August to 9 September. For three weeks İzmir's hotels are packed and transportation is crowded. The fair has amusements, cultural and commercial-industrial displays.

Victory Day – 30 August. This national holiday commemorates the decisive victory at Dumlupınar of the republican armies over the invading Greek army during the War of Independence. Towns and cities celebrate their own Kurtuluş Günü (Day of Liberation) on the appropriate date commemorating when Atatürk's armies drove out the foreign troops during July and August.

Republic Day – 29 October. Commemorates the proclamation of the republic by Atatürk in 1923. It's the biggest civil holiday of the year, with lots of parades and speeches.

Anniversary of Atatürk's Death – 10 November. The most important day of the month, it is the day Atatürk died in 1938. At precisely 9.05 am, the moment of his death, the entire country comes to a screeching halt for a moment of silence.

Mevlâna Festival – approx 10 to 17 December. Honouring Celaleddin Rumi, the great poet and mystic who founded the Mevlevi order of whirling dervishes, this festival is held in Konya.

ACTIVITIES
Water Sports

Water sports are big in Turkey because of the beautiful coasts and beaches. Water-skiing, snorkelling, scuba diving and swimming are all available along the Aegean and Mediterranean coasts, although not along the Black Sea coast. Marmaris and Bodrum are the main diving centres. Because of the many antiquities in the depths off the Turkish coasts, scuba diving is regulated. Diving shops in Marmaris, Bodrum and other coastal towns can provide details. Turkish divers are very safety conscious, so bring your diving credentials.

Yacht Cruising

A journey by boat along the Aegean or Mediterranean coast is on the agenda of most visitors to Turkey. There are endless possibilities, from a day trip out of Antalya to chartering a gulet for a week-long trip out of Marmaris. The main yachting centres are Marmaris, Bodrum and Fethiye. Kuşadası,

Göcek, Antalya and Alanya also have yacht harbours. For more details, see the boxed text 'A Blue Voyage' in the Marmaris section of the Western Mediterranean Turkey chapter.

Trekking

Turkey is a great place for long and short treks. The Kaçkar Mountains offer some of the best mountain hiking, along the eastern Black Sea coast near Ayder or around Yusufeli on the southern side of the range. The valleys of Cappadocia, with their spectacular landscapes, are another excellent area for hiking. Turkey now has its first long-distance waymarked path, the Lycian Way (see the boxed text 'The Lycian Way' near the Tekirova section in the Western Mediterranean Turkey chapter for more details), which extends from Ölüdeniz on the western Mediterranean coast to near Antalya. In theory it takes a month to complete, but there are shorter sections.

Dağcılık (mountain climbing) is practised by a small but enthusiastic number of Turks, and Turkey has plenty of good, high mountains for it. *The Mountains of Turkey* by Karl Smith is a good guide.

Skiing

There is decent skiing at Uludağ, near Bursa, at a few resorts in the Beydağları mountain range near Antalya, on Erciyes Dağı near Kayseri, and at Palandöken on the outskirts of Erzurum. Uludağ and Palandöken have a range of accommodation from moderate to expensive. Ski facilities are rather basic by European or US standards, but the snow can be good and may last well into spring, especially at Palandöken. Lift fees are usually included in your accommodation package.

Cycling

The spectacular scenery, friendly people, easy access to archaeological sites and ready availability of natural camping sites, both official and unofficial, make Turkey a good place for long-distance cycling. The best routes are those along the coasts, particularly the western Mediterranean coast between Marmaris and Antalya. Some of the best routes are the unpaved coastal roads not marked on many maps.

COURSES

Interest in learning Turkish has exploded in recent years. Courses are offered in many cities, particularly in İstanbul and Ankara.

In İstanbul, we can recommend Taksim Dilmer (formerly Taksim Tömer; ☎ 212-292 9696, fax 292 9693, ⓔ info@dilmer.com, info@taksimtomer.com) Tarık Zafer Tunaya Sokak 18, 80090 Taksim, İstanbul, where an intensive course for a month costs US$240. Besides learning some Turkish, it's a great way to make friends. You could also try International House, Nispetiye Caddesi, Güvercin Durağı, Erdolen İşhanı 38/1, 1. Levent, İstanbul (☎ 212-282 9064, fax 282 3218, ⓔ info@ihistanbul.com).

WORK

You can extend your time in Turkey by getting a job. Many people teach English at one of the many private colleges or schools in İstanbul or Ankara. Others work at one of the publication offices such as the *Turkish Daily News*, or find short-term jobs in pensions, travel agencies or restaurants.

ACCOMMODATION
Camping

Using your own equipment and bedding, it is sometimes possible to sleep on the roof of a pension or hotel, or camp in the garden, for a minimal fee of US$3 to US$6 per person, which includes use of the hotel facilities. The fancier camping grounds near seaside resorts and in Cappadocia may have all facilities (showers, shops, swimming pools, gardens) but charge almost as much as cheap hotels.

Camping outside recognised camping grounds by the roadside is often more hassle than it's worth as the police may come and check you out, the landowner may wonder what's up, and curious villagers may decide that they'd rather sit and watch you than the *Dynasty* reruns on TV.

Hostels

As the lowest priced hotels and pensions are already rock-bottom, there is no extensive system of hostels in Turkey. In fact, some cheap hotels call themselves hostels and even boast affiliation with the International Youth Hostel Federation (IYHF), though their prices and facilities differ little from those of other cheap hotels.

In and near Olimpos on the Mediterranean coast south-west of Antalya are groups of 'treehouses', rough-and-ready permanent shelters of minimal comfort in forested settings near the beach. They're cheap and congenial, usually with food and drinks services and an Internet connection, but there have also been some reports of sexual harassment and even occasional danger, as there is little security.

Pensions

Once common and popular, the *ev pansiyonu* (home pension) is now less common, but is still to be found in tourist and resort towns. The classic pension is a relatively modest family home in which several bedrooms are rented by the day or week to guests, who share bathroom and kitchen facilities with the family. Rates are low, but may be comparable to the cheapest class of hotels.

Hotels

Turkey's cheapest hotels (*otels*) are mostly used by working-class Turkish men travelling on business. They usually cost from US$5 per bed in a small town up to US$20 or US$30 for a double room in a large city. Rooms priced less than about US$10 may have a *lavabo* (sink), or no running water at all. Cold-water showers (down the hall) are usually free. Hot-water showers may cost between US$1 and US$2.

Turkey has lots of modern and comfortable hotels rated at one to three stars by the Ministry of Tourism. Facilities in this range include lifts, staff who speak a smattering of German, French and English, and rooms with a private shower or bath and toilet for US$20 to US$90.

Hotels at the top end, rated at four or five stars, are priced from US$90 to US$250 or more for a double room. Turkish hotel chains often provide better value for money than the international names.

Çay (tea), not coffee, is Turkey's national drink, although you will find coffee is available in most places. Gathering round the samovar for a session of çay drinking and talking is a national pastime. If çay doesn't hit the spot, a shot of rakı, the local aniseed-flavoured spirit, should do the trick.

ALL PHOTOS BY GREG ELMS

Turks are passionate about food, and you'll find a great variety on offer. Treat yourself to deliciously fresh seafood, roasted corn on the cob, sesame-sprinkled bread rings, boat-shaped *pide* (Turkish-style pizza) or a kebap straight from the grill.

Sugar, spice and all things nice: Try whole honeycomb dripping with delicately scented honey; some of the huge range of dried fruits and nuts Turkey is so well known for; or, best of all, one of a myriad varieties of Turkish delight (a traditional Ottoman sweet invented in the late 18th century).

ALL PHOTOS BY GREG ELMS

In Turkey, eating is about more than just fuelling up; with every bite you'll learn more about Turkish culture.

In some tourist towns old Ottoman mansions, caravanserais or other historic buildings have been refurbished or even completely rebuilt and equipped with modern conveniences. Charm, atmosphere and history are the attractions here, and they are provided in abundance at prices ranging from US$75 to US$175 for a double room, breakfast included.

Maximum prices should be posted prominently at the reception desk. Unless the hotel or pension is obviously quite full and very busy, you can usually haggle for a lower price.

In some cities, and particularly in summer, water may be cut off for several hours at a time, though many hotels have roof tanks which do away with this problem.

Unmarried couples sharing rooms usually run into no problems, even though the desk clerk sees the obvious when taking down the pertinent information from your passports onto the registration form. The cheaper the hotel, the more traditional and conservative its management tends to be.

FOOD

Turkish cuisine is at the heart of eastern Mediterranean cooking. It demands fresh ingredients and careful preparation. The ingredients are often simple but of high quality. Turkish farmers, herders and fishermen bring forth a wealth of superb produce from this agriculturally rich land and its surrounding seas. Turkey is one of only seven countries on earth that produce a surplus of food.

The variety of dishes found in restaurants is not as great as that found in home kitchens. And when you'd like a change from grilled lamb, you'll rarely find an Indonesian, Mexican, Indian or Japanese restaurant just around the corner. Despite the extent of the Ottoman Empire the Turks did not trade extensively with other nations during the 18th and 19th centuries and never received an influx of foreign populations and cuisines. This is changing, though. Some Chinese restaurants have opened, Japanese ones are sure to follow, and you can now, for better or worse, get authentic Yankee hamburgers and pizza in the larger cities and resorts.

Breakfast

In a hotel or *pastane* (pastry shop), *komple kahvaltı* (breakfast) consists of fresh, delicious *ekmek* (bread) with jam or honey, butter, salty black olives, sliced tomatoes and cucumbers and cheese, as well as *çay* (tea).

You can always order a *yumurta* (egg). Soft-boiled is *üç dakikalık*, hard-boiled is *sert* and fried eggs are *sahanda yumurta*.

Alternatively you can do what many working-class Turks do, and have a bowl of hot soup which, with lots of fresh bread, makes quite a delicious breakfast for a very low price. If that's not for you, try *su böreği*, a many-layered noodle-like pastry with white cheese and parsley among the layers, served warm.

Hot *sıcak süt* (sweetened milk) is also a traditional breakfast drink, replaced in winter by *sahlep*, which is hot, sweetened milk flavoured with tasty *Orchis mascula* (orchid-root) powder and a sprinkle of cinnamon.

Snacks & Main dishes

Meze & Salads A proper Turkish meal consists of a long procession of dishes, starting with meze (hors d'oeuvres), which can include almost anything. You can easily make an entire meal of meze. Often you'll be brought a tray from which you can choose what you want. Salads are primarily served as part of the meze, although simple salads are often served as side dishes to the main course. Meze include:

beyaz peynir white sheep's milk cheese
börek flaky pastry stuffed with white cheese and parsley
cacık yogurt with grated cucumber and mint
domates salatlik tomato and cucumber salad
fasulye beans in tomato sauce
kabak dolması stuffed squash/marrow
patlıcan salatası pureed aubergine salad
patlıcan tava fried aubergine
pilaki beans vinaigrette
turşu pickled vegetables
yaprak dolması stuffed vine leaves
yeşil green salad

Dolma are made of all sorts of vegetables (aubergine, peppers, cabbage or vine leaves) served cold and stuffed with rice, currants and pine nuts, or hot with lamb.

Food & Drinks Glossary

Listed here are some terms you may find helpful if you are shopping for food or ordering in a restaurant.

Basics			mixed grill (lamb)	*karışık ızgara*
bread	*ekmek*		ravioli (Turkish-style)	*mantı*
butter	*tereyağı*		sun-dried, spiced beef	*pastırma*
cheese	*peynir*			
fish	*balık*		**Fish**	
fruit	*meyva, meyve*		crab	*yengeç*
honey	*bal*		lobster	*istakoz*
jam	*reçel*		mussels	*midye*
meat	*et*		sardine	*sardalya*
olives	*zeytin*		shrimp	*karides*
rice	*pirinç*		swordfish	*kılıç*
salads	*salata*		turbot	*kalkan*
salt	*tuz*			
sesame-covered bread ring	*simit*		**Vegetables**	
soup	*çorba*		carrot	*havuç*
sugar, sweets	*şeker*		cauliflower	*karnabahar*
sweet, dessert	*tatlı*		cucumber	*salatalık*
vegetable	*sebze*		green beans	*taze fasulye*
yogurt	*yoğurt*		marrow/squash	*kabak*
			okra	*bamya*
Meat			onion	*soğan*
beef	*sığır*		peas	*bezelye*
chicken	*tavuk, piliç*		peppers	*biber*
lamb stew	*tas kebap*		potato	*patates*
meat & vegetable stew	*güveç*		red beans	*barbunye*
			spinach	*ıspınak*

Turkish sourdough bread *(ekmek)* is fresh, delicious and cheap. Many dishes are served with savoury sauces, and fresh bread is provided with your meal for a nominal charge; dip and sop your bread and enjoy.

Soup This can make a filling main meal, eaten with plenty of fresh bread. Turks eat soup for breakfast, lunch or dinner, and there are endless varieties. Try *balık çorba* (fish soup), *ezo gelin çorbası* (lentil and rice soup), *mercimek çorbası* (lentil soup), *sebze çorbası* (vegetable soup) or *işkembe çorbası* (tripe soup).

Meat Meat *(et)* appears in most main meals in some form, and it is often used to flavour soups, rice and bulgur, and to stuff vegetables. The main ways of cooking meat, each with countless variations, include:

döner kebap meat packed onto a vertical skewer, then roasted and sliced off
güveç meat stewed with vegetables in a clay pot
köfte minced meat made into meatballs and grilled
saç kavurma meat stir-fried in a flat-bottomed pan
şiş kebap cubes of meat grilled *(izgara)* on a skewer *(şiş)*
tandır meat cooked in a woodfired clay oven

In kebap the meat is traditionally lamb, ground or in chunks, although chicken and fish kebaps are also found. Preparation, spices and extras (onions, peppers, bread) make the difference among the kebaps. Some may be ordered *yoğurtlu*, with a side-serving of yogurt. Kebaps are usually eaten with flat bread, a salad and perhaps *ayran*, a drink of yogurt mixed with spring water. There are numerous fancy kebaps, often named for the places where they originated. Best is Bursa

Food & Drinks Glossary

tomato	domates	**Drinks**	
white beans	kuru fasulye	aniseed-flavoured brandy	rakı
		apple tea	elma çay
Sweets		camomile tea	papatya çayı
baked rice pudding (cold)	fırın sütlaç	beer	bira
biscuits	bisküvi	dark	siyah
cake	kek	light	beyaz
cheesecake	peynir tatlısı	draught ('keg')	fıçı bira
flaky pastry, nuts & milk	güllaç	coffee	kahve(si)
ice cream	dondurma	fizzy mineral water	maden sodası
layered filo pastry with	baklava	fruit juice	meyva suyu
honey and nuts		hot milk & orchid root	sahlep
pastry	pasta	instant coffee	neskafe
rice flour & rosewater pudding	muhallebi	lemonade	limonata
rice pudding	sütlaç	milk	süt
Turkish delight	lokum	mineral water	maden suyu
		spring water	menba suyu
Fruit		tea	çay
apple	elma	Turkish coffee	Türk kahvesi
apricot	kayısı	water	su
banana	muz	whisky	viski
cherry	kiraz	wine	şarap
grapes	üzüm	red	kırmızı
orange	portakal	rose	roze
peach	şeftali	sparkling	köpüklü
watermelon	karpuz	white	beyaz
yellow melon	kavun	yogurt drink	ayran

kebap, also called İskender kebap, since it was invented in the city of Bursa by a chef named İskender (Alexander). It comes with a full-flavoured tomato sauce, and is usually served with yogurt. Of the other fancy kebaps, Urfa kebap comes with lots of onions and black pepper; Adana kebap is spicy hot, with red pepper. *Şiş köfte* is *köfte* (meatballs) wrapped around a flat skewer; Adana köfte is the same thing, but spicy hot.

In its wider sense, kebap can mean just about any meat and vegetable dish.

Fish Fish, though generally excellent, is often expensive. A menu is of no use when ordering fish (*balık*). You'll have to ask the waiter what's fresh, and then ask for the approximate price. The fish will then be weighed, and the price computed at the day's per-kg rate. Sometimes you can hag-

gle. Buy fish in season, as fish out of season are very expensive. From March to the end of June is a good time to order *kalkan* (turbot), *uskumru* (mackerel), and *hamsi* (fresh anchovies), but July to mid-August is spawning season for many species, and fishing them is prohibited. In high summer (mid-July to August), the following are the easiest to find in the markets and on restaurant tables: *çinakop* (a small bluefish), *lüfer* (medium-size bluefish), *palamut* (bonito), *tekir* (striped goatfish*)*, *barbunya* (red mullet*)*, and *istavrit* (scad, horse mackerel).

Vegetables Dishes The eggplant (aubergine) is Turkey's number one vegetable. It can be stuffed as a dolma (*patlıcan dolması*), served pureed with lamb (*hünkar beğendi*), stuffed with minced meat (*karnıyarık*) or appear with exotic names like

İskender Kebap

Roast lamb and mutton have been staples of the Turkish diet for millennia, and it does not take an overly fertile imagination to picture nomadic Turkish warriors skewering chunks of mutton on their swords and roasting it over a campfire 1500 years ago. Melted fat would drip into the fire causing flare-ups, smoking and burning of the meat.

Along comes İskender Usta (Chef Alexander), a cook in Bursa. In 1867 he had the idea to build a vertical grill, fill it with hot coals, and put the meat-packed sword on its point next to the grill. This way the fat would baste the meat rather than char it. He sliced the meat off in thin strips as it was cooked.

Like *lokum* (Turkish delight) and the sandwich, this simple innovation was an instant success. Why any of these culinary inventions took centuries to appear is a mystery.

Today döner kebap is Turkey's national dish, served everywhere from street corners to posh dining rooms. Many of the specially made döner grills even continue the symbolism of the sword, with a miniature hilt at the top.

İskender used lamb and mutton from sheep fed on the wild spices (especially thyme) of Uludağ. To compound his fame, he laid the slices of lamb on a bed of flat pide bread, and topped the whole with savoury tomato sauce and browned butter.

The dish's popularity has spread throughout the country and indeed the world, but it's still best in Bursa. The city's most prominent İskender kebapçıs claim direct descent – in both blood and method – from the original İskender Usta.

imam bayıldı – 'the imam fainted' – which means stuffed with ground lamb, tomatoes, onions and garlic.

Pide The best cheap and tasty meal is *pide*, Turkey's version of pizza. To make pide, the dough for flat bread is patted out into an oblong boat shape, dabbed with butter and other toppings, baked in a wood-fired oven, cut into strips and served. It's fresh, delicious and nutritious. As for toppings, say

peynirli for cheese, *yumurtalı* for eggs and *kıymalı* or *etli* for minced lamb. In some parts of Turkey a pide with meat is called *etli ekmek*.

Cheese Although there are some interesting peasant cheeses – such as *tulum peynir* (a salty, dry, crumbly goats' milk cheese cured in a goatskin bag) and a dried cheese which looks just like twine – they rarely make it to the cities and almost never to restaurant tables. What you'll find is the ubiquitous *beyaz peynir*, white sheep's milk cheese. To be really good, it must be full-cream *(tam yağlı)* cheese, not dry and crumbly and not too salty or sour. You may also find *kaşar peynir*, a firm, mild yellow cheese, either fresh *(taze)* or aged *(eski)*.

Sweets & Desserts

Pasta in Turkey is pastry, not noodles, which are usually designated by some Turkicised Italian name such as *makarna or lazanya*. Turkish *pastanes* (pastry shops, patisseries) generally have supplies of *kuru pasta* (dry pastry) such as biscuits of various sorts, and *yaş pasta* (moist pastry) meaning cakes, crumpets, and syrup-soaked baked goods. Soft drinks are served, and tea and coffee are sometimes available.

For dessert, try *fırın sütlaç* (baked rice pudding), *kazandibi* (caramelised pudding), *aşure* (pudding made from up to 40 different ingredients), *baklava* (flaky pastry stuffed with walnuts or pistachios, soaked in honey), or *kadayıf* (shredded wheat with nuts in honey).

Turkish fruits are superb, especially in midsummer when the melon season starts, and early in winter when the first citrus crops start to come in.

Vegetarian

Although Turkish cuisine is very meat-oriented, there are several possibilities for vegetarians. Pide, or Turkish pizza, with a nonmeat topping, is a cheap and delicious option and widely available. Meze are also good as many are vegetable based and, with plenty of fresh bread, can make a filling meal. Vegetable side dishes are an intrinsic part of Turkish meals but they are often made with meat stock. If you don't eat meat, ask '*Etsiz yemek var mı?*' (Have you any meatless dishes?), or say '*Hiç et yiyemem*' (I can't eat any meat). The word *vejeteryan* (vegetarian) is slowly gaining currency. Self-catering is another good option.

Places to Eat

Restaurants *Restoran* or *lokanta* (restaurants) are everywhere, and most are open early in the morning until late at night. Most are inexpensive, and although price is always some determinant of quality, often the difference between a US$6 meal and a US$15 meal is not great, at least as far as flavour is concerned. Service and ambience are fancier at the higher price. Most restaurants serve food continuously from 11 am to 11 pm or later. Many open early (6 or 7 am) for breakfast. The exceptions are a few restaurants in bazaars, business and financial districts that serve office workers primarily and serve only lunch.

Though menus bearing prices have become common in many resorts, they are uncommon in the rest of Turkey, so it's best to ask in advance to avoid any surprises. Prices may be posted on the wall (all in Turkish). The prices of certain items, such as fresh whole fish, may depend upon the daily market, and may be negotiable.

Restaurant waiters are not usually the world's star mathematicians; and widespread tourism has brought with it the sin of bill-fiddling. In resort areas, it's worth redoing the addition, and questioning any items, including obscure *kuver* (cover) and *servis* (service) charges. If you don't get an itemised bill, by all means ask for one.

In any restaurant in Turkey there is a convenient *lavabo* (sink) so that you can wash your hands before eating.

If you're a woman or are travelling with a woman, ask for the *aile salonu* (family dining room, often upstairs) which will be free of the sometimes oppressive all-male atmosphere to be found in many cheap Turkish eateries.

Full service restaurants are the familiar sort with white tablecloths and waiter service. It may be open for three meals a day, and will probably be among the more expensive dining places. They usually serve spirits, wine and beer, and are sometimes called *içkili* (literally, 'serving drinks') because of this.

Hazır yemeki (literally, 'ready food') restaurants are sometimes arranged as *self-servis* cafeterias. Although all restaurants offer some dishes prepared in advance, these places specialise in an assortment of dishes, prepared in advance, kept warm in steam tables. Usually no alcoholic beverages are served, but occasionally, if you order a beer, the waiter will run to a shop nearby and get one for you. Decor may be nonexistent and the letters on the front window may only say 'Lokanta', but the welcome will be warm and the food delicious and cheap.

Kebapçı, Köfteci & Pideci A *kebapçı* is a person who cooks kebap, and a *köfteci* roasts köfte. Pidecis serve pide. Though they may have one or two ready-made dishes, kebapçı and köfteci restaurants specialise in grilled meat, plus soups, salad, yogurt and perhaps dessert. Kebapçıs can be great fun, especially the ones that are *ocakbaşı* (fireside). Patrons sit around the sides of a long rectangular fire pit and the kebapçı sits enthroned in the middle, grilling away. Alcoholic beverages are not usually served in any of these eateries.

Pastanes For pastries, cakes and all manner of good things, try a pastane. Some pastanes serve baklava; others leave this to separate shops called *baklavacıs*. Most serve breakfast, either from their normal stock or as a komple kahvaltı of bread, butter, honey or jam, egg, olives, cheese and coffee or tea. In Kars, out by the Armenian frontier, you can have great gobs of the excellent local honey to mix with butter and spread on fresh bread.

Büfe & Kuru Yemiş Other than restaurants, Turkey has millions of little snack stands and quick-lunch places known as *büfe* (buffet). These serve sandwiches (often grilled), puddings, portions of *börek* (filled pastry), and perhaps *lahmacun*, an Arabic soft pizza made with chopped onion, lamb and tomato sauce.

A *kuru yemiş* place serves dried fruits and nuts and other good things. Prices are displayed in kilograms.

Istanbul's Mısır Çarşısı (Egyptian Bazaar) in Eminönü has several kuru yemiş shops which also sell *pestil*, fruit which has been dried and pressed into flat, flexible sheets (sometimes called 'fruit leather' in English). Odd at first, but tasty, it's a home-made village product made from *kayısı* (apricots), *dut* (mulberries) and other fruits.

DRINKS
Nonalcoholic Drinks

İçki usually refers to alcoholic beverages, *meşrubat* to soft drinks. When waiters ask *İçecek?* or *Ne içeceksiniz?*, they're asking what you'd like to drink. You will find the usual range of soft drinks.

Fresh fruit juice is a favourite refresher in summer, and can be excellent, although there are also numerous watery, sugared fruit-juice imitations.

Water Turks are connoisseurs of good *su* (water) and stories circulate of old people able to tell which spring it came from just by tasting it. Spring water is served everywhere, even on intercity buses. The standard price for a 1.5L bottle of any brand, sold in a grocery, probably chilled, is around US$0.75. If you order it in a restaurant there will be a mark-up of 100% to 300%.

Tap water is supposedly safe to drink because it is treated, but it's not as tasty or as trustworthy as spring water.

Tea & Coffee The national drink is not really Turkish coffee as you might expect, but *çay* (tea). The Turks drank a lot of coffee when they owned Arabia, because the world's first (and best) coffee is said to have come from Yemen. With the collapse of the Ottoman Empire, coffee became an imported commodity. You can get Turkish coffee anywhere in Turkey, but you'll find yourself drinking a lot more çay.

The tea plantations are along the eastern Black Sea coast, centred on the town of Rize. Turkish tea is hearty and full flavoured, traditionally served in little tulip-shaped glasses which you hold by the rim to avoid burning your fingers. (If you need a lot, order a *duble*, which may come in a drinking glass.) Sugar is usually added; milk is often available, though milk in tea is a foreign custom. If you want your tea weaker, ask for it *açık* (clear); for stronger, darker tea, order *koyu or demli* (dark).

For a real tea-drinking and talking session, Turks go to an outdoor tea garden and order a *semaver* (samovar) of tea so they can refill the glasses themselves, without having to call the *çaycı* (tea waiter).

Traditional herbal teas are infusions such as *adaçay* (island tea), made from coastal sage, and *ıhlamur* (linden-flower tea), perfumed and soothing. *Papatya çayı* is camomile tea.

A few years ago a brand-new beverage, *elma çay* (apple tea) was introduced, and it caught on quickly. Tourists love it as much as Turks do, and you may even see street vendors selling packets of it for tourists to take home with them. It's caffeine-free and slightly tart, with a mild apple flavour. There are other, similar fruit-flavoured teas as well. Surprisingly, the list of ingredients yields no mention of fruit, only sugar, citric acid, citrate, food essence and vitamin C.

As for Turkish *kahve* (coffee), you must order it according to sweetness – the sugar is mixed in during the brewing, not afterwards. You can drink it *sade*, without sugar; *az*, if you want just a bit of sugar; *orta*, with a middling amount; *çok* or *şekerli* or even *çok şekerli*, with lots of sugar. Nescafé is readily found throughout Turkey but tends to be expensive, often around US$0.70 per cup.

Alcoholic Drinks

Strictly observant Muslims do not touch alcoholic beverages at all, but in Turkey the strictures of religion are moderated by the 20th-century lifestyle.

In resorts popular with foreigners, virtually every restaurant serves alcohol. In the big cities, restaurants above a certain price range may do so. In mid-sized cities and towns, there is usually at least one restaurant where alcohol is served so that the local movers-and-shakers can get together over long dinners with drinks. In a few religiously conservative cities such as Konya, very few restaurants serve alcoholic beverages, and those that do are so debased as to confirm the opinions of the conservative majority.

Beer A local company with a European brewmaster is Efes Pilsen, which makes light and dark beer claimed by many to be Turkey's best. The light is a good, slightly bitter Pilsener. Tuborg, a Danish company, makes *beyaz* (light or pale) and *siyah* (dark) beer in Turkey under licence. Marmara is another lager, not easily found.

Restaurants and shops usually sign exclusive contracts with beer companies to feature their brand, so you rarely get a choice. Except in the most expensive places, you might as well just order '*bira*' and you'll get whatever they have.

Beer is available in returnable bottles, and also in disposable cans at a higher than average price. You'll save money, get better flavour, and not contribute to the litter problem if you buy bottled beer.

Wine Turkish wines are drinkable and cheap. Doluca and Kavaklıdere are the favoured brands, making good table wines as well as several varietals, such as the Villa Doluca line. Kavaklıdere's serviceable wines include the premium Çankaya (white) and Dikmen (red), and the medium-range wines named Kavak (white and red) and Lal (rose/blush). Tekel, the government alcoholic beverages company, also makes wines.

Strong Liquor The favourite ardent spirit in Turkey is *rakı*, an aniseed-flavoured grape brandy similar to the Greek ouzo, French pastis and Arab arak. Turkish rakı is made by Tekel. The standard is Yeni Rakı. Kulüp Rakısı is somewhat stronger, with a bit more aniseed. Altınbaş is the strongest and most expensive, with the highest aniseed content.

It's customary (but not essential) to mix rakı with cool water, half-and-half, perhaps add ice, and to drink it with a meal, or at least some *çerez* (nibbles, snacks).

Tekel also makes decent *cin* (gin), *votka* and *kanyak* (brandy). When ordering kanyak, always specify the *beş yıldız* or *kaliteli* (five-star or quality) stuff, officially named Truva Kanyak. The regular kanyak is thick and heavy, the five-star much lighter. There is a Tekel *viski* (whisky) named Ankara. You might try it once. Vermouth is *vermut*.

For after-dinner drinks, better restaurants will stock the local sweet fruit brandies, which are nothing special.

Imported spirits are available from shops in the larger cities and resorts. Though they are much more expensive than local drinks, they may not cost much more than what you'd pay at home. Hotels and restaurants usually mark up the prices of imported spirits hugely.

ENTERTAINMENT

İstanbul, Ankara and İzmir have opera, symphony, ballet and theatre. Every Turkish town has at least one cinema and one nightclub with live entertainment.

The seaside resorts throb every warm evening to the sounds of seemingly innumerable clubs and discos.

SPECTATOR SPORTS

Football (soccer), basketball and wrestling are the favoured sports. Every city of any size has a large football stadium which fills up on match days. İstanbul's big three teams – Galatasaray, Fenerbahçe and Beşiktaş – have fanatical national followings, and the aftermath of a victorious match results in cavalcades of flag-waving, horn-blaring fan-stuffed cars racing though city streets.

The famous oiled wrestling matches, where brawny strongmen in leather breeches rub themselves down with olive oil and grapple with equally slippery opponents, take place each June in Edirne (see the 'Oiled Wrestling' boxed text in the Thrace chapter). Another purely Turkish sight is the camel-wrestling matches held in the province of Aydın, south of İzmir, in the winter months. Konya is the traditional location for *cirit*, the javelin-throwing game played on horseback, but in recent years an important competition has been held in Selendi, 60km west of Uşak, on Republic Day (29 October).

SHOPPING

For details on what to buy, see the special section 'Arts & Crafts' in the Facts about Turkey chapter. Most shops and shopping areas close on Sunday. For more details of opening hours, see the Business Hours section earlier in this chapter.

Haggling

For the best buy in terms of price and quality, know the market. Spend some time shopping for similar items in various shops, asking prices. Shopkeepers will give you pointers on what makes a good kilim (flat-woven mat), carpet, meerschaum pipe or alabaster carving. In effect, you're getting a free course in product lore. This is not at all unpleasant, as you will often be invited to have coffee, tea or a soft drink as you talk over the goods and prices.

You can, and should, ask prices if they're not marked, but you should not make a counteroffer unless you are seriously interested in buying. No matter how often the shopkeeper asks you, 'OK, how much will you pay for it?', no matter how many glasses of tea you've drunk at their expense, don't make a counteroffer if you do not plan to buy. If the shopkeeper meets your price, you should buy. It's considered very bad form to haggle over a price, agree, and then not buy.

Some shopkeepers, even in the 'haggle capital of the world' (İstanbul's Kapalı Çarşı), will offer a decent price and say, 'That's my best offer'. Many times they mean it, and they're trying to do you a favour by saving time. How will you know when they are, and when it's just another haggling technique? Only by knowing the market, by having shopped around. Remember, even if they say, 'This is my best offer', you are under no obligation to buy unless you have made a counteroffer, or have said, 'I'll buy it'.

It's perfectly acceptable to say a pleasant goodbye and walk out of the shop, even after all that free tea, if you cannot agree on a price. In fact, walking out is one of the best ways to test the authenticity of the shopkeeper's price. If they know you can surely find the item somewhere else for less, they'll stop you and say, 'OK, you win, it's yours for what you offered'. And if they don't stop you, there's nothing to prevent you from returning in half an hour and buying the item for what they quoted.

If any shopkeeper puts extraordinary pressure on you to buy, walk out of the shop, and consider reporting the shop to the belediye zabıtası (market police).

A Carpet Buyer's Primer

To ensure you get a good buy, you'll have to spend time visiting several shops and compare prices and quality. It's also worth taking a look in the shops at home before you leave. That way, you'll know what's available and for what prices at home.

That said, when deciding whether to buy a particular carpet, it might help to follow some of the guidelines below.

A good-quality, long-lasting carpet should be 100% wool (yüz de yüz yün): check the warp (the lengthwise yarns), weft (the crosswise yarns) and pile (the vertical yarns knotted into the matrix of warp and weft). Is the wool fine and shiny, with signs of the natural oil? More expensive carpets may be of a silk and wool blend. Cheaper carpets may have warp and weft of mercerised cotton. You can tell by checking the fringes at either end. If the fringe is of cotton or 'flosh' (mercerised cotton) you shouldn't pay for wool. Another way to identify the material of the warp and weft is to turn the carpet over and look for the fine, frizzy fibres common to wool, but not to cotton. But bear in mind that just being made of wool doesn't guarantee a carpet's quality. If the dyes and design are ugly, even a 100% woollen carpet can be a bad buy.

Check the closeness of the weave by turning the carpet over and inspecting the back. In general, the tighter the weave and the smaller the knots, the higher the quality and durability of the carpet. The oldest carpets sometimes had thick knots, so consider the number of knots alongside the colours and the quality of the wool.

Compare the colours on the back with those on the front. Spread the nap with your fingers and look at the bottom of the pile. Are the colours brighter there than on the surface? Slight colour variations could occur in older carpets when a new batch of dye was mixed, but richer colour deep in the pile is often an indication that the surface has faded in the sun. Natural dyes don't fade as readily as chemical dyes. There is nothing wrong with chemical dyes, which have a long history of their own, but natural dyes and colours tend to be preferred and therefore fetch higher prices. Don't pay for natural if you're getting chemical.

New carpets can be made to look old, and damaged or worn carpets can be re-woven (good work, but expensive), patched or even painted. There's nothing wrong with a dealer offering you a patched or re-painted carpet provided they point out these defects and price the piece accordingly, but it would be dishonest to offer you cheap goods at an inflated price. But some red Bokhara carpets will continue to give off colour even though they're of better quality than cheap woollen carpets which don't.

Look at the carpet from one end, then from the other. The colours will differ because the pile always leans one way or the other. Take the carpet out into the sunlight and look at it there. Imagine where you might put the carpet at home, and how the light will strike it.

In the end the most important consideration should be whether or not you like the carpet. It's all very well to pluck some fibres and burn them to see if they smell like wool, silk, or nylon or to rub a wet handkerchief over the carpet to see if the colour comes off, but unless you know what you're doing you're unlikely to learn much from the exercise – and you may well end up with a irate carpet seller to deal with!

Pricing & Payment When it comes to buying, there's no substitute for spending time developing an 'eye' for what you really like. You also need to be realistic about your budget. These days carpets are such big business that true bargains are hard to come by unless there's something (like gigantic size) that makes them hard to sell for their true value.

Prices are determined by age, material, quality, condition, demand in the market, the enthusiasm of the buyer, and the debt load of the seller. Bear in mind that if you do your shopping on a tour or when accompanied by a guide, the price will be hiked by up to 35% to cover somebody's commission.

It may be wiser to go for something small but of high quality rather than for a room-sized cheapie. Another way to make the money stretch further is to opt for one of the smaller items made from carpet materials: old camel bags and hanging baby's cradles opened out to make rugs; *sofras* or rugs on which food would be eaten; decorative grain bags; cushion covers; even the bags which once held rock salt for animals.

Some dealers will take personal cheques, but all prefer cash. An increasing number of shops take credit cards but some require you to pay the credit card company's fee and the cost of the phone call to check your creditworthiness. A few dealers will let you pay in instalments.

All this is a lot to remember, but it'll be worth it if you get a carpet you like at a decent price. It will give you pleasure for the rest of your life.

Value-Added Tax

Turkey has a value-added tax (VAT), called *katma değer vergisi* or KDV, added to and hidden in the price of most items and services, from souvenirs to hotel rooms to restaurant meals. Most establishments display a sign saying *'Fiatlarımızda KDV Dahildir'* (VAT is included in our prices). Thus, it is rare that the VAT is added to your bill separately, and you should be suspicious if it is.

There is a scheme where tourists can reclaim the amount paid in VAT on larger purchases such as leather garments, carpets etc. Not all shops participate in the scheme, so you must ask if it is possible to get a *KDV iade özel fatura* (special VAT refund receipt). Ask for this during the haggling rather than after you've bought. The receipt can – in principle – be converted to cash at a bank in the international departures lounge at the airport (if there is a bank open, which there usually isn't), or at your other point of exit from Turkey. Or, if you submit the form to a customs officer as you leave the country, the shop will (hopefully) mail a refund cheque to your home after the government has completed its procedures (don't hold your breath though).

To increase your chances of actually getting the refund, make a photocopy or two of the KDV İade Özel Fatura in advance and, when you're leaving Turkey, take along a stamped envelope addressed to the shop where you bought the goods. Have the KDV form and the photocopy stamped by the customs officer at the airport, then mail the photocopy from the airport to the shop. Enclose a note requesting refund of the tax and giving your address to which the refund cheque should be sent. In some cases it can take as long as four months for the cheque to arrive. Keep the other photocopy for your own records.

Shipping Parcels Home

If practical, carrying your parcels with you is the best idea, as you may escape extra duty payments when you return to your home country; parcels arriving separately may be dutiable. If you decide to ship something home from Turkey, don't close up your parcel before it has been inspected by a customs or postal official, who will check to see if you are shipping antiquities out of the country; take packing and wrapping materials with you to the post office. Wrap it very securely and insure it. Sending it by *kayıtlı* (registered mail) is not a bad idea. Unless you buy from a very posh shop, it's best to ship your own parcels. Several readers have had the sad experience of buying a beautiful kilim and agreeing to have the shopkeeper ship it, only to discover that the kilim shipped was not the one bought, but a much cheaper item.

Getting There & Away

AIR
Airports & Airlines

Turkey's most important international airport as far as foreign travellers are concerned is İstanbul's Atatürk airport. The cheapest fares are almost always to İstanbul, and to reach other Turkish airports, including Ankara, you usually have to transit İstanbul. Other international airports are at Adana, Ankara, Antalya, Bodrum, Dalaman (between Marmaris and Fethiye) and İzmir, all of which are accessible on domestic flights from İstanbul.

Turkey's national carrier is Turkish Airlines (Türk Hava Yolları or THY, symbol TK), which has direct flights from İstanbul to many European cities and New York, as well as destinations in the Middle East, North Africa and Asia. Several smaller Turkish scheduled and charter lines have started to compete with Turkish Airlines.

Buying Tickets

If you are flying to Turkey from outside Europe, your air ticket will probably be the most expensive item in your travel budget, but you can reduce the cost by finding discounted fares. The only people likely to be paying full fare these days are travellers in 1st or business class. Passengers flying in economy can usually get some sort of discount. But unless you buy carefully and flexibly, it is still possible to end up paying too much.

For short-term travel, cheaper fares are available by travelling mid-week, staying away at least one Saturday night or taking advantage of short-lived promotional offers.

When you're looking for bargain air fares, go to a travel agent rather than directly to the airline. From time to time, airlines do have promotional fares and special offers, but generally they only sell fares at the official listed price. One exception is booking on the Internet. Many full-service carriers, and the expanding number of 'no-frills' carriers, offer some excellent fares to Web surfers.

Warning

The information in this chapter is particularly vulnerable to change: Prices for international travel are volatile, routes are introduced and cancelled, schedules change, special deals come and go, and rules and visa requirements are amended. Airlines and governments seem to take a perverse pleasure in making price structures and regulations as complicated as possible. You should check directly with the airline or a travel agent to make sure you understand how a fare (and ticket you may buy) works. In addition, the travel industry is highly competitive and there are many lurks and perks.

The upshot of this is that you should get opinions, quotes and advice from as many airlines and travel agents as possible before you part with your hard-earned cash. The details given in this chapter should be regarded as pointers and are not a substitute for your own careful, up-to-date research.

They may sell seats by auction or simply cut prices to reflect the reduced cost of electronic selling. Many travel agents around the world have Web sites, which can make the Internet a quick and easy way to compare prices. Online ticket sales work well if you are doing a simple one-way or return trip on specified dates. However, online super-fast fare generators are no substitute for a travel agent who knows all about special deals, has strategies for avoiding layovers and can offer advice on everything from which airline has the best vegetarian food to the best travel insurance to bundle with your ticket.

Charter Flights Charter flight tickets are for seats left vacant on flights which have been block-booked by package companies. These tickets can often be much cheaper than a standard flight. Flight-only tickets are usually valid for up to four weeks, and usually have a minimum stay requirement of at least three days. Sometimes it's worth buying a

Air Travel Glossary

Cancellation Penalties If you have to cancel or change a discounted ticket, there are often heavy penalties involved; insurance can sometimes be taken out against these penalties. Some airlines impose penalties on regular tickets as well, particularly against 'no-show' passengers.

Courier Fares Businesses often need to send urgent documents or freight securely and quickly. Courier companies hire people to accompany the package through customs and, in return, offer a discount ticket which is sometimes a phenomenal bargain. However, you may have to surrender all your baggage allowance and take only carry-on luggage.

Full Fares Airlines traditionally offer 1st class (coded F), business class (coded J) and economy class (coded Y) tickets. These days there are so many promotional and discounted fares available that few passengers pay full economy fare.

Lost Tickets If you lose your airline ticket an airline will usually treat it like a travellers cheque and, after inquiries, issue you with another one. Legally, however, an airline is entitled to treat it like cash and if you lose it then it's gone forever. Take good care of your tickets.

Onward Tickets An entry requirement for many countries is that you have a ticket out of the country. If you're unsure of your next move, the easiest solution is to buy the cheapest onward ticket to a neighbouring country or a ticket from a reliable airline which can later be refunded if you do not use it.

Open-Jaw Tickets These are return tickets where you fly out to one place but return from another. If available, this can save you backtracking to your arrival point.

Overbooking Since every flight has some passengers who fail to show up, airlines often book more passengers than they have seats. Usually excess passengers make up for the no-shows, but occasionally somebody gets 'bumped' onto the next available flight. Guess who it is most likely to be? The passengers who check in late.

Promotional Fares These are officially discounted fares, available from travel agencies or direct from the airline.

Reconfirmation If you don't reconfirm your flight at least 72 hours prior to departure, the airline may delete your name from the passenger list. Ring to find out if your airline requires reconfirmation.

Restrictions Discounted tickets often have various restrictions on them – such as needing to be paid for in advance and incurring a penalty to be altered. Others are restrictions on the minimum and maximum period you must be away.

Round-the-World Tickets RTW tickets give you a limited period (usually a year) in which to circumnavigate the globe. You can go anywhere the carrying airlines go, as long as you don't backtrack. The number of stopovers or total number of separate flights is decided before you set off and they usually cost a bit more than a basic return flight.

Transferred Tickets Airline tickets cannot be transferred from one person to another. Travellers sometimes try to sell the return half of their ticket, but officials can ask you to prove that you are the person named on the ticket. On an international flight tickets are compared with passports.

Travel Periods Ticket prices vary with the time of year. There is a low (off-peak) season and a high (peak) season, and often a low-shoulder season and a high-shoulder season as well. Usually the fare depends on your outward flight – if you depart in the high season and return in the low season, you pay the high-season fare.

charter return even if you think you want to stay longer than four weeks. The tickets can be so cheap that you can afford to throw away the return portion. Unlike some countries, such as Greece, Turkey doesn't require you to have an accommodation voucher if you take a charter-flight deal.

Student & Youth Fares Full-time students and people under 26 have access to better deals than other travellers. The better deals may not always be cheaper fares but can include more flexibility to change flights and/or routes. You have to show a document proving your date of birth or a valid International Student Identity Card (ISIC) when buying your ticket and boarding the plane.

Courier Flights Courier flights are a great bargain if you're lucky enough to find one. Air-freight companies expedite delivery of urgent items by sending them with you as your baggage allowance. You are permitted to bring along a carry-on bag, but that's all. In return, you get a steeply discounted ticket.

There are drawbacks: courier tickets are sold for a fixed date and schedule changes can be difficult to make, your time away may be limited and you may be restricted to taking just hand luggage. Be sure to clarify before you fly what restrictions apply.

Courier flights are occasionally advertised in the newspapers, or you could contact air-freight companies listed in the phone book.

Travellers with Special Needs
Most international airlines can cater to travellers with special needs – people with disabilities, travellers with young children, and children travelling alone.

Travellers with special dietary preferences (vegetarian, kosher etc) can request appropriate meals with advance notice. If you are travelling in a wheelchair, most international airports can provide an escort from check-in desk to plane where needed, and ramps, lifts, toilets and phones are generally available.

Airlines usually allow babies up to two years of age to fly for 10% of the adult fare, although a few may allow them free of charge. Reputable international airlines usually provide nappies (diapers), tissues, talcum and all the other paraphernalia needed to keep babies clean, dry and half-happy. For children between the ages of two and 12, the fare on international flights is usually 50% of the regular fare or 67% of a discounted fare.

Departure Tax
Turkey levies a tax of about US$12 on visitors departing by air. The tax is customarily included in the cost of your ticket.

The UK
British Airways and Turkish Airlines, as well as many European airlines, have scheduled flights to İstanbul; British Airways also has flights to Ankara, Antalya, İzmir and Dalaman. To give you some idea, at the time of writing, a return air fare from London to İstanbul in summer (ie, high season) costs around UK£200 to UK£300. The cheapest scheduled flight we found was UK£194, with Air France.

There are lots of charter flights between the UK and Turkey; typical London to Turkey charter fares (return) are UK£149/269 for one/two weeks. These are for advance fares; it's possible to pick up very good last-minute deals. Charter flights to Turkey also go from Birmingham, Cardiff, Luton, Manchester and Newcastle. Contact the Air Travel Advisory Bureau (☎ 020-7636 5000) for information on charter flights, or check out its Web site (www.atab.co.uk) for more details.

London is Europe's major centre for discounted fares. Airline-ticket discounters are known as bucket shops in the UK. Despite the somewhat disreputable name, there is nothing under-the-counter about them. Advertisements for many travel agents appear in the travel pages of the weekend papers, such as the *Independent* on Saturday and the *Sunday Times*. Look out for the free magazines, such as *TNT*, which are widely available in London – start by looking outside the main railway and underground stations.

For students or travellers under 26, popular travel agencies in the UK include STA Travel (☎ 020-7361 6144), which has an office at 86 Old Brompton Rd, London SW7 3LQ, and other offices around the country, or check out its Web site (www.statravel .co.uk). Usit Campus (☎ 0870-240 1010), 52 Grosvenor Gardens, London SW1W 0AG, has branches throughout the UK. Usit's Web address is www.usitcampus .com. Both of these agencies sell tickets to all travellers but cater especially to young people and students.

Other recommended travel agencies include Trailfinders (☎ 020-7938 3939), 194 Kensington High St, London W8 7RG; Bridge the World (☎ 020-7734 7447), 4 Regent Place, London W1R 5FB; and Flightbookers (☎ 020-7757 2000), 177-178 Tottenham Court Rd, London W1P 9LF.

Continental Europe

European airlines such as Aeroflot, Air France, Alitalia, Austrian Airlines, Finnair, KLM, Lufthansa Airlines, Scandinavian Airlines (SAS) and Swissair fly to İstanbul; Lufthansa has flights to Ankara, Antalya, İzmir or Dalaman as well. You'll also find plenty of charter flights from Germany in particular, for example, Condor has charter flights to İzmir, Bodrum, Antalya and Dalaman for around DM700 return; check out their Web site (www.condor.de) for more details.

Although London is the travel discount capital of Europe, there are several other cities in which you will find a range of good deals. Generally, there is not much variation in air-fare prices for departures from the main European cities. All the major airlines are usually offering some sort of deal, and travel agents generally have a number of deals on offer, so shop around.

Across Europe many travel agencies have ties with STA Travel, where cheap tickets can be purchased and STA-issued tickets can be altered (usually for a US$25 fee). Outlets in major cities include Voyages Wasteels (☎ 08 03 88 70 04 – this number can only be dialled from within France – fax 01 43 25 46 25), 11 rue Dupuytren, 756006 Paris; STA Travel (☎ 030-311 0950, fax 313 0948), Goethestrasse 73, 10625 Berlin; Passaggi (☎ 06-474 0923, fax 482 7436), Stazione Termini FS, Galleria Di Tesla, Rome; and ISYTS (☎ 01-322 1267, fax 323 3767), 11 Nikis St, Upper Floor, Syntagma Square, Athens.

France France has a network of student travel agencies that can supply discount tickets to travellers of all ages. OTU Voyages (☎ 01 44 41 38 50) has a central Paris office at 39 Ave Georges Bernanos (5e) and lots of other offices around the country. Their Web address is www.otu.fr. Acceuil des Jeunes en France (☎ 01 42 77 87 80), 119 rue Saint Martin (4e), is another popular discount travel agency.

General travel agencies in Paris that offer some of the best services and deals include Nouvelles Frontières (☎ 08 03 33 33 33), 5 Ave de l'Opéra (1er), Web address www .nouvelles-frontieres.com; and Voyageurs du Monde (☎ 01 42 86 16 00) at 55 rue Sainte Anne (2e).

Belgium In Belgium, Acotra Student Travel Agency (☎ 02-512 86 07) at rue de la Madeline, Brussels, and WATS Reizen (☎ 03-226 16 26) at de Keyserlei 44, Antwerp, are both well-known agencies. In Switzerland, SSR Voyages (☎ 01-297 11 11) specialises in student, youth and budget fares. In Zürich, there is a branch at Leonhardstrasse 10 and there are others in most major Swiss cities. Check their Web site (www.ssr.ch) for more details.

The Netherlands In the Netherlands, NBBS Reizen is the official student travel agency. You can find them in Amsterdam (☎ 020-624 09 89) at Rokin 66 and there are several other agencies around the city. Another recommended travel agent in Amsterdam is Malibu Travel (☎ 020-626 32 30) at Prinsengracht 230.

Greece In Athens, check the many travel agencies in the backstreets between Syntagma and Omonia Squares. For student and nonconcessionary fares, try Magic Bus (☎ 01-323 7471, fax 322 0219).

The USA

In summer, Turkish Airlines flies daily nonstop from New York (Newark) to İstanbul and three times a week from Chicago. Delta flies from various US cities to various European cities and flies from New York to İstanbul via Frankfurt. European airlines also fly one-stop services to/from many North American cities to İstanbul; of these, Lufthansa covers the most cities and has the best connections. Return-trip fares range from US$500 to US$900.

Discount travel agents in the USA are known as consolidators (although you won't see a sign on the door saying 'consolidator'). San Francisco is the ticket-consolidator capital of America, although some good deals can be found in Los Angeles, New York and other big cities. Consolidators can be found through the *Yellow Pages* or the major daily newspapers. The *New York Times*, the *Los Angeles Times,* the *Chicago Tribune* and the *San Francisco Examiner* all produce weekly travel sections in which you will find a number of travel agency ads. Ticket Planet is a leading ticket consolidator in the USA and is recommended. Visit its Web site at www.ticketplanet.com.

Council Travel, America's largest student travel organisation, has around 60 offices in the USA; its head office (☎ 800-226-8624) is at 205 E 42 St, New York, NY 10017. Call it for the office nearest you or visit its Web site at www.ciee.org. STA Travel (☎ 800-777-0112) has offices in Boston, Chicago, Miami, New York, Philadelphia, San Francisco and other major cities. Call the toll-free 800 number for office locations or check its Web site (www.statravel.com) for the latest deals.

Canada

There are no nonstop flights to Turkey from Canada, although there are connections via Chicago or New York. Alternatively, you can connect to İstanbul-bound flights in Europe.

Canadian discount air-ticket sellers are also known as consolidators and their air fares tend to be about 10% higher than those sold in the USA. The *Globe & Mail,* the *Toronto Star,* the *Montreal Gazette* and the *Vancouver Sun* carry travel-agent ads and are a good place to look for cheap fares.

Travel CUTS (☎ 800-667-2887) is Canada's national student travel agency and has offices in all major cities. Its Web address is www.travelcuts.com.

Australia & New Zealand

Direct flights from Australia to İstanbul are offered by Malaysian Airlines (via Kuala Lumpur and Dubai) and Singapore Airlines (via Singapore and Dhahran), with return air fares for about A$1800. Middle Eastern Airlines, Gulf Air and EgyptAir offer cheaper fares of around A$1600. There are also connecting flights via Athens, London, Rome, Amsterdam or Singapore on Thai International, British Airways, Olympic, Alitalia, KLM, Turkish Airlines and Qantas.

Several travel offices specialise in discount air tickets. Some travel agents, particularly smaller ones, advertise cheap air fares in the travel sections of weekend newspapers, such as the *Age* in Melbourne and the *Sydney Morning Herald.*

Two well-known agents for cheap fares are STA Travel and Flight Centre. STA Travel (☎ 03-9349 2411) has its main office at 224 Faraday St, Carlton, VIC 3053, and offices in all major cities and on many university campuses. Call ☎ 131 776 Australia-wide for the location of your nearest branch or visit its Web site at www.statravel.com.au. Flight Centre (☎ 131 600 Australia-wide) has a central office at 82 Elizabeth St, Sydney, and there are dozens of offices throughout Australia. Its Web address is www.flightcentre.com.au.

The *New Zealand Herald* has a travel section in which travel agents advertise fares. Flight Centre (☎ 09-309 6171) has a large central office in Auckland at the National Bank Towers (corner Queen and Darby Sts), and many other branches throughout the country. STA Travel (☎ 09-309 0458) has its main office at 10 High St, Auckland, and has other offices in Auckland as well as in Hamilton, Palmerston North, Wellington, Christchurch and Dunedin. For more information, check its Web site (www.sta.travel.com.au).

Middle East & North Africa

Turkish Airlines has daily flights from İstanbul to Athens (1½ hours), Cairo (2½ hours) and Tel Aviv (two hours), five per week to Amman (2¼ hours), five to Baku in Azerbaijan (2½ hours), two to Beirut (one hour), two to Damascus (2½ hours), three to Dubai in the UAE (6¼ hours), four to Jeddah in Saudi Arabia (5½ hours), two to Riyadh, also in Saudi Arabia (5¾ hours), two to Kuwait (4¼ hours), three to Tehrān (4½ hours) and four to Tunis (two hours). Some sample return fares are US$200 to Athens, US$600 to Cairo and US$475 to Tel Aviv.

Daily nonstop flights on Turkish Airlines and Cyprus Turkish Airlines connect İstanbul, Ankara and Lefkoşa (Nicosia). There are also nonstop flights between Lefkoşa and Adana, Antalya and İzmir several times a week.

LAND

If you are planning to enter Turkey overland, you have plenty of options: Turkey has land borders with seven countries. Bear in mind, however, that Turkey's relationship with most of its neighbours tends to be tense, which can affect the availability of visas and when/where you can cross overland. Always check with the relevant embassy for the most up-to-date information before leaving home.

Border Crossings

Clockwise, from west to east, Turkey has land borders with Greece, Bulgaria, Georgia, Armenia, Iran, Iraq and Syria. Check with the relevant embassy for details on visas for these countries.

Greece Between western Thrace in Greece and eastern Thrace in Turkey, the crossing points are at Kipi, 43km north-east of Alexandroupolis, and at Kastanies, 139km north-east of Alexandroupolis, near the Turkish town of Edirne. For the quickest, easiest border crossing, take one of the four daily buses from Alexandroupolis to the Greek border point at Kipi, then hitch to the İpsala border post. From here you can get a taxi (US$7) to the bus station in İpsala, and

an onward bus to İstanbul. For Edirne or Çanakkale, you may have to change buses in Keşan. The crossing from the village of Kastanies to Edirne takes longer, costs more, and is less convenient. You take a taxi (US$7) from the village of Kastanies to the Greek customs and border posts, then walk across the border (600m) to the Turkish border post of Pazarkule. From here it's a 2km walk to the village of Karaağaç, from where buses take you to the centre of Edirne. These border posts are open only limited hours (9 am to 1 pm weekdays, shorter hours on Sunday).

There's a rail crossing between Uzunköprü and Pythion.

Bulgaria The main border crossing between Bulgaria and Turkey is Kapıkule, 18km west of Edirne in Turkey, on the highway to/from Svilengrad in Bulgaria. This busy border post is open 24 hours daily. You may not be allowed to walk to the border on the Bulgarian side; you may be required to hitch a lift or hire a taxi.

Syria There are at least four border posts between Syria and Turkey. The busiest and most convenient links Antakya in Turkey with Aleppo via the Bab al-Hawa border post. This is the route all cross-border buses take and traffic can get fairly congested here, with waits of up to a couple of hours.

Georgia Most people cross the border at Sarp on the Black Sea coast, near Hopa, but you could also cross from Posof, Near Ardahan. Daily buses run to Batumi and Tbilisi (Tflis) from Trabzon. You need to obtain a Georgian visa in advance at the Georgian consulate in Trabzon.

Armenia The train line from Ankara to Erzurum runs as far as Kars but at the time of writing the Turkish-Armenian border was closed to foreign travellers. The situation was expected to change so it's worth rechecking.

Iran Doğubayazıt is the main crossing point for people heading into Iran. To visit or travel through Iran you must have obtained a visa in advance. If you haven't done this before arriving in Doğubayazıt there are men who will help you organise one through the consulate in Erzurum. You will need to travel back to Erzurum but they say that, in most cases, the visa can be arranged in one hour, allowing you to return to Doğubayazıt the same day. The most unpopular passports tend to be American and British.

Recently the situation in Iran has been easing and although Western women must still be covered from head to toe from the minute they apply for their visa, it is no longer absolutely essential to wear the full *chador* (the all-encompassing black robe favoured by the Revolutionary Guards). These are, however, available in Doğubayazıt's market for about US$18. The situation could always change so ask about before approaching the border to make sure you will be seen as suitably 'modest'.

The Bank Melli branch at the border normally changes cash (dollars or pounds) or travellers cheques into Iranian rials (tomans). Even if this branch refuses Turkish lira, you may be able to change them at banks further into Iran. Note that there is a post office, a tourist office and a reasonable restaurant on the Turkish side of the border despite its off-putting, shades-of-war-torn-Beirut appearance.

Western Europe

It's still fairly easy to get to İstanbul by train or bus. You'll probably find, though, that unless you're travelling from somewhere relatively nearby like Eastern Europe, taking the train works out no cheaper than flying. The advantages are that the train journey is much more pleasant and an experience in itself.

Bus Despite the romantic appeal of train journeys, getting to Turkey overland is usually cheaper and faster by bus. Buses to İstanbul run from many European cities. One of the main operators from Western Europe is Eurolines, which sells tickets through various agencies. Two of the best Turkish companies – Ulusoy and Varan – operate big Mercedes buses on European routes and are also reliable. For details get in touch with the bookings office of any international bus station or any travel agency dealing in bus tickets.

During summer there are regular bus services to İstanbul from the following cities: Bucharest (Romania), Tirana (Albania), Rome and Turin (Italy), Bregenz, Graz, Innsbruck, Salzburg, Vienna and Wiener Neustadt (Austria), several German cities, Paris and Strasbourg (France), Basel and Zürich (Switzerland), Amsterdam, Brussels and London. Sample one-way fares to İstanbul are US$175 from Frankfurt, US$155 from Munich and US$110 from Vienna. Return fares are discounted by about 20%. Ask about student, youth or child discounts.

Train The *İstanbul Express* and *Skopje-İstanbul Express*, which used to connect İstanbul and Munich, no longer run. Apart from the Thessaloniki train, connecting Greece and Turkey, the *Balkan Express* connects İstanbul and Budapest (31 hours) and the *Bosfor Ekspresi* connects İstanbul and Bucharest in Romania (17 hours).

With a change of trains it's possible to get to İstanbul from more European cities. Through tickets can be bought at almost any international railway booking office in Europe, but it's advisable to make inquiries some weeks ahead, especially in summer when demand is greatest.

Car & Motorcycle The E80 highway makes its way through the Balkans to Edirne (see the Edirne section in the Thrace chapter) and İstanbul, then onward to Ankara. Car ferries from Italy and Cyprus can shorten driving time from Western Europe considerably, but at a price. No special car documents are required for visits of up to three months, but be sure to take the car out of Turkey before your three months is up. If you overstay your permit, you may have to pay customs duty equal to the full retail value of the car!

Normally, you cannot rent a car in Europe and include Turkey (or many other Eastern European countries) in your driving plans. If you want to leave your car in Turkey and return to collect it later, the car must be put under a customs seal, which is usually a tedious process.

For stays of longer than three months, or for any other information regarding car travel in Turkey, contact the Türk Turing ve Otomobil Kurumu (Turkish Touring and Automobile Association; ☎ 212-282 8140, fax 282 8042), Oto Sanayi Sitesi Yanı, Seyrantepe, 4. Levent, İstanbul.

Greece

Most people get from Turkey to Greece by boat from the eastern Aegean islands (see Sea later in this chapter for more details).

Bus There are buses daily except Wednesday between Athens and İstanbul operated by Hellenic Railways Organisation. Buses leave from the Peloponnese train station in Athens at 7 pm and travel via Thessaloniki and Alexandroupolis. Varan Turizm (☎ 01-513 5768), Web site www.varan.com.tr, in Athens operates daily buses to İstanbul via Thessaloniki, as does Ulusoy (☎ 01-524 0519, fax 524 3290), also at the Peloponnese train station. The trip takes about 20 hours and costs about US$80 from Athens, US$46 from Thessaloniki, one way. Buses from İstanbul to Athens leave the bus station in Esenler at 10 am daily except Sunday.

Alternatively, you can make your own way to Alexandroupolis and take a service from the intercity bus station to the border town of Kipi (three departures a day, US$2.40). If you're crossing from Turkey into Greece, do so as soon after 9 am as possible in order to catch one of the few trains or buses from Kastanies south to Alexandroupolis, where there are better connections. Alternatively, take a bus from Edirne to Keşan, then to İpsala, and cross to Kipi.

Train There are several daily trains from Sirkeci station in İstanbul to the border near Uzunköprü (US$12/16), where the train wheels are adjusted before it crosses to the Greek side at Pythion (5½ hours). From here, several daily trains run to Alexandroupolis (none connect directly) and there are also di-

rect connections to Thessaloniki. However, trains to the border are relatively few and painfully slow, and most people go by bus.

Car & Motorcycle From Greece, the major road goes to Ferai (Greece) and İpsala (Turkey), then to Keşan and east to İstanbul or south to Gallipoli, Çanakkale and the Aegean coast. The crossing at Kipi is more convenient if you are heading for İstanbul, but the route through Kastanies goes via the fascinating towns of Soufli and Didymotiho in Greece, and Edirne in Turkey.

Bulgaria

If you are planning to enter or leave Turkey via Bulgaria, note that citizens of Australia, the EU and the USA are admitted without a visa for stays of less than 30 days. Travellers of other nationalities need a transit visa, which is issued at the border for US$68.

Bus There are buses from Sofia's international bus station to İstanbul (US$25, 18 hours) daily except Friday. They also pick up in Plovdiv and Svilengrad.

Train The *Maritza Express* leaves Sofia at 8.15 am and arrives in İstanbul at 6.45 pm. The *Balkan Express* runs from Hungary (Budapest) via Bulgaria (Sofia) to İstanbul (US$37, 12 hours). The train leaves Sofia at 8.40 pm. In the reverse direction, it departs İstanbul's Sirkeci station at 10.20 pm. However, we've heard many stories of harassment, especially of women, on crossing this border by train, so it's best to find an alternative way of crossing into/out of Bulgaria. The *Bosfor Ekspresi* between Bucharest and İstanbul passes through Ruse (Bulgaria) at 5.25 pm and arrives in İstanbul at 7.20 pm (US$25 in a sleeper).

A cheaper option is to catch a domestic train to Svilengrad and take a bus or taxi or hitch the 14km from here to Kapitan-Andreevo. After the formalities, you enter the Turkish town of Kapıkule by crossing the Tunca River at the Gazi Mihal Bridge. City bus C-1 runs from Kapıkule to the centre of Edirne; there are *dolmuşes* (shared taxis) on this route as well, but both are infrequent in the early morning and late at night. It's also easy to enter Bulgaria this way, although the Bulgarian taxi drivers will probably want hard currency.

Car & Motorcycle Bulgaria's main road crossing point with Turkey, open 24 hours, is at Kapitan-Andreevo, on the E5 road from Svilengrad; over the fence lies the busy Turkish border post of Kapıkule, 18km west of Edirne. The second is at Malko Târnovo, 92km south of Burgas. Motorists in transit through Bulgaria may only be allowed to cross at Kapitan-Andreevo, depending on the current regulations.

Georgia

To travel to Georgia, you must first obtain a visa from the Georgian consulate in Trabzon. A bus departs from Trabzon's Russian bazaar at 7 pm daily, heading for Batumi, Tflis (Tbilisi, the Georgian capital) and Baku (Azerbaijan). The bus is usually full of Georgian and Azeri traders with bales of goods, which means customs inspection can take forever. Shortly after the bus leaves Trabzon the conductor will come round and collect US$10 from everyone going to Georgia and US$25 from everyone going to Azerbaijan, to pay the assorted 'commissions' along the way. It's pointless to try and resist paying; you'll only delay your arrival.

A cheaper and slightly quicker way to get across the border is to take a minibus to Hopa, then a dolmuş to the border at Sarp. This part of the journey should cost about US$6. At Sarp, walk across the border, ignoring half-hearted demands for dollars from the Georgian customs officials. On the other side of the border, taxis will be waiting to run you the 15km to Batumi for US$12 to US$15.

Leaving Georgia to return to Turkey is more tricky. If you take a taxi back to the border and arrive alone you are at the mercy of the avaricious customs officers. On the other hand if you take the bus for collective protection, the bureaucracy involved can result in a four-hour delay.

Provided you have a 'multiple entry' visa for Turkey and haven't exceeded your three-month stay, you should be able to come back in without further payment.

Minibuses from Hopa, Artvin and Ardahan run up to the Posof border crossing, an alternative way of getting to Tflis (Tbilisi) which is well worth considering, especially given that the endless bus ride from Trabzon is far from enjoyable.

Iran

A dolmuş to the border at Gürbulak, 34km east of Doğubayazıt, should cost about US$1.50. The crossing here may take an hour or more and you may have to pay a bribe on the Iranian side.

From the border you take a shared taxi to Maku, then an Iran Peyma bus from Maku to Tabriz and on to Tehrān.

Armenia

There used to be regular train service between Kars and Yerevan (Armenia), but it was discontinued during the Armenian-Azerbaijani conflict. The border is open to Turks, but not yet to foreigners. Check with a Russian consulate (the Russians handle Armenian diplomatic interests in Turkey).

Syria & Israel

Direct daily buses connect Antakya, at the eastern end of Turkey's Mediterranean coast, with the Syrian cities of Aleppo (Halab, US$12, four hours) and Damascus (US$20, eight hours), and Amman in Jordan (US$28, 10 hours).

You can also buy tickets direct from İstanbul to Aleppo (approximately 24 hours) or Damascus (30 hours). The ticket costs in the vicinity of US$24 to US$30, depending on which company you travel with. Buses leave daily, usually with five or six departures between about 11 am and the early evening.

Some readers have written to suggest there's less delay involved in crossing the border by train. Trains run from Gaziantep, Kahramanmaraş and Osmaniye in Turkey to Aleppo in Syria.

At the moment it's possible to travel between Jerusalem and İstanbul by bus for around US$100, well below the air fare.

SEA

Car ferry services operate between Italian and Greek ports and several Turkish ports, though not to İstanbul.

Italy

Turkish Maritime Lines (TML) runs car ferries from Antalya, Marmaris and İzmir to Venice weekly from May to mid-October. In summer TML also offers ferry services four times a week from Brindisi; fares are often undercut by Med Link Lines. Poseidon Lines also runs summer ferries from Bari (Italy) to İzmir.

TML ferries depart from Venice on Saturday evening, arriving in İzmir midday on Tuesday, and depart İzmir on Wednesday afternoon, arriving in Venice on Saturday before noon.

Per-person one-way Venice to İzmir fares range from US$160 to US$186 for a Pullman seat to US$358 to US$476 for a berth in a luxury cabin; the fare for each of two berths in an air-con B-class cabin with shower and toilet is US$341 in the busy summer months; three meals and port tax are included in these examples. A car costs US$200 one way in high season.

In summer, TML ferries depart Brindisi at noon on Wednesday, Saturday and Sunday, arriving in Çeşme, on Friday, Monday and Thursday; ferries leave Çeşme on Monday, Tuesday and Friday, arriving in Brindisi on Wednesday, Saturday and Sunday.

Per-person one-way Brindisi-Çeşme fares range from US$96 to US$120 for a Pullman seat to US$251 to US$311 for a berth in a luxury cabin; the fare for each of two berths in an air-con B-class cabin with shower and WC is US$220 in the busy summer months; three meals and port tax are included in these examples. A car costs US$174 one way.

For more information, contact TML at the following addresses:

Italy (☎ 831-568 633) Bassani SpA, Corso Garibaldi 19, 72100 Zacmari, Brindisi; (☎ 41-522 9544, fax 520 9211) Bassani SpA, Via 22 Marzo 2414, 30124 Venezia
Turkey (☎ 212-249 9222, fax 251 9025) Türkiye Denizcilik İşletmeleri, Rıhtım Caddesi, Karaköy, İstanbul; (☎ 232-464 8889,

fax 464 7834) Türkiye Denizyolları Acentesi, Yeniliman, 35220 Alsancak, İzmir
UK (☎ 020-7923 3230, fax 7923 3118) Alternative Travel & Holidays Ltd, 146, Kingsland High St, London E8 2NS

Med Link Lines operates two ferries, the *Poseidon* and the *Maria G* on the route Brindisi-Igoumenitsa-Patras-Çeşme from June to September. Fares tend to be lower than on TML, and there are reductions for students travelling in Deck, Pullman or C-class cabins (four to eight beds).

Departures from Brindisi are on Wednesday and Saturday, and from Çeşme on Monday and Friday. You can book online at www.omhros.gr, or contact MLL at:

Brindisi (☎ 831-527 667, fax 564 070) Discovery Shipping Agency, Corso Garibaldi 49, 72100
Çeşme (☎ 232-712 7230, fax 712 8987) Karavan Shipping, Belediye Dükkanları 3, by the harbour
Igoumenitsa (☎ 665-26833, fax 26111) Eleni Pantazi, 8 December St No 27
Patras (☎ 061-62 30 11, fax 62 33 20) George Giannatos, Othonos Amalias St 15

Greece

Private ferries link Turkey's Aegean coast and the Greek islands, which are in turn linked by air or boat to Athens. Greek regulations may require that passengers on trips originating in Greece travel on Greek-flag vessels, which means that you may not be allowed to hop aboard a convenient Turkish vessel for your trip from the Greek Islands to the Turkish mainland. (If you've come over from Turkey for the day, you may return on the Turkish boat.)

Services are usually daily in summer, several times a week in spring and autumn and perhaps just once a week in winter. In summer, expect boats connecting Lesvos-Ayvalık, Lesvos-Dikili, Chios-Çeşme, Samos-Kuşadası, Kos-Bodrum, Rhodes-Marmaris, Rhodes-Bodrum, Rhodes-Fethiye, Rhodes-Antalya and Kastellorizo-Kaş. The cheapest and most frequent ferries are Samos-Kuşadası and Rhodes-Marmaris. The most expensive, and certainly a hassle, is Lesvos-Ayvalık.

The procedure is this: once you've found the ticket office, buy your ticket a day in advance. You may be asked to turn in your passport the night before the trip. You'll get it back just before you board the boat.

Cyprus

There are daily boats and hydrofoils to Turkish Cyprus from Taşucu (near Silifke) and Mersin, on the eastern Mediterranean coast, and from Antalya on the western Mediterranean coast – see Getting There & Away in these sections later in the book for more details.

Bear in mind that relations between the Greek Cypriot-administered Republic of Cyprus and the Turkish Republic of Northern Cyprus (TRNC) are not good. The border between the two regions will probably be closed. Also, if you enter the TRNC and have your passport stamped you may later be denied entry to Greece. The Greeks will reject only a stamp from the Turkish Republic of Northern Cyprus, *not* a stamp from Turkey proper. Have the Turkish Cypriot official stamp a piece of paper instead of your passport.

Russia

Karden Line ferries run between Trabzon and Sochi in Russia, departing from Trabzon on Monday and Thursday at 6 pm and returning from Sochi on Tuesday and Friday at 6 pm. Cabin tickets (US$60) are available in Trabzon from Navi Tour (☎ 462-326 4484), İskele Caddesi Belediye Duükkanları. At the time of writing, most people had to get a visa from a Russian consulate in their home country to use this service, but that may change.

Getting Around

Turks love to travel, a legacy perhaps of all those centuries spent racing across the steppes on fast ponies. Turkey's intercity bus system is a marvel, with big, modern coaches going everywhere, all the time, at reasonable prices. The railway network, though limited and ageing, is useful on a few major routes. Turkish Airlines connects all the major cities and resorts.

AIR

Türk Hava Yolları (THY, Turkish Airlines), the state-owned airline waiting reluctantly for privatisation, has the major route network in Turkey. Fares are reasonable: about US$80 between İstanbul and Ankara.

THY flights serve the following cities and towns: Adana, Ağrı, Ankara, Antalya, Balıkesir, Batman, Bodrum, Dalaman, Denizli, Diyarbakır, Edremit, Elazığ, Erzincan, Erzurum, Eskişehir, Gaziantep, Isparta, İstanbul, İzmir, Kahramanmaraş, Kars, Kayseri, Konya, Malatya, Nevşehir, Samsun, Siirt, Sinop, Sivas, Şanlıurfa, Tokat, Trabzon and Van. Hubs are İstanbul and Ankara; to go from Dalaman to Diyarbakır, for example, you will connect at İstanbul or Ankara.

BUS

The bus and the *dolmuş* (shared taxi or minibus) are the most widespread and popular means of transport in Turkey. Buses go literally everywhere, all the time. Virtually every first-time traveller in Turkey comments on the convenience of the bus system.

The bus service runs the gamut from plain and inexpensive to comfortable and moderately priced. The six-hour, 450km trip between İstanbul and Ankara, for example, costs US$15 to US$24, depending on the bus company.

Though bus fares are open to fierce competition among companies, and even to haggling for a reduction, the cost of bus travel in Turkey usually works out to be around US$2.25 to US$2.75 per 100km – a surprising bargain.

The best companies, offering smooth service at a higher than average price on national routes, are Kamil Koç, Metro, Ulusoy and Varan. Many other regional companies offer varying levels of service, some quite good, others less so.

Bus Station

Most Turkish cities and towns have a central bus station called variously *otogar*, *otobüs garajı, otobüs terminalı* or *şehir garajı* (city garage), depending upon the city. Besides intercity buses, the otogar often handles dolmuşes to outlying districts or villages. Some small towns have a collection of bus company offices rather than a proper station.

Many bus companies (usually the more expensive ones) provide a *şehiriçi servis arabası* (city-centre shuttle bus) to take passengers between the city centre and the otogar, which is often on the outskirts. Ask when buying your ticket whether a servis arabası is available at your destination, and when it leaves (usually from the city-centre ticket office) for the otogar. The availability of shuttle buses depends upon the bus company and the destination. A taxi or city bus is the alternative.

Otogars are often equipped with their own PTT (post office) branches, bank or currency exchange offices, ATMs, telephones with international service, restaurants, snack stands, patisseries, tourist information booths as well as left-luggage offices (*emanet*).

Buying Tickets

Although you can often just walk into an otogar and buy a ticket for the next bus out, it's wise to plan ahead. At the least, locate the companies' offices and note the times for your destination a day in advance. This is especially important along the south-east Mediterranean coast and the east, where long-distance bus traffic is less frequent than in other parts of the country.

Some bus companies will grant you a reduction on the fare if you show your International Student Identity Card (ISIC). This may not be official policy, but just an excuse for a reduction – in any case you win.

The word *yarın* (tomorrow) is handy to know when buying bus tickets a day in advance. Bus departure times will be given using the 24-hour clock, ie, 18.30 instead of 6.30 pm.

When you enter an otogar, touts will invariably approach asking where you're bound for. They work for particular bus companies and will lead you to their company's ticket desk. They will not offer information on competing companies and routes. After you find out about their company, you may want to compare others as well.

Once you've bought a ticket, getting a refund can be difficult, though it's possible. Exchanges for other tickets within the same company are easier.

All seats are reserved, and your ticket will bear a specific seat number. The ticket agent often has a chart of the seats with those already sold crossed off. Look at the chart and indicate your seating preference.

Preferable seats are in the middle of the bus; seats over the wheels are liable to be cramped and will give you a rough ride. You also want to get a seat on the side of the bus which will not get full sun. Turks, it seems, are constitutionally opposed to air draughts of any strength, even (or perhaps especially) on a sweltering hot day. The ventilation or air-con system of the bus may be efficient, but it may not be activated. On a 3½-hour summer afternoon trip from Ankara to Cappadocia, for instance, you'll be too warm if you're on the right-hand (western) side of the bus, while the seats on the left (eastern) side will remain comfortable.

You may want to avoid sitting near the driver as drivers are still allowed to smoke on intercity buses.

The Journey

A bus trip in Turkey is usually a fairly pleasant experience, if it's not too long. Buses are big, modern, comfortable and usually air-conditioned.

Shortly after you head out, the *yardımcı* (assistant, also called the *muavin*) will come through the bus with a bottle of lemon cologne with which to refresh their *sayın yolcular* (honoured passengers). They'll dribble some cologne into your cupped hands, which you then rub on your face and hair, ending with a sniff to clear your nasal passages. You may not be used to the custom, but if you ride buses in Turkey much you will get used to it quickly, and probably love it.

Water is provided at no charge on virtually all buses. Signal to the yardımcı and ask '*Su, lütfen*' (Water, please).

Stops will be made every 1½ hours or so for toilet breaks, snacks or meals and the inevitable *çay* (tea). At some stops children rush onto the bus selling sweets, nuts, sandwiches and the like, or a waiter from the teahouse (buses always stop at a teahouse) may come through to take orders. Most people, however, welcome the chance to stretch their legs.

DOLMUŞ

A dolmuş (**dohl**-moosh) is a shared taxi, which can be a minibus (*minibüs* or *münübüs*), Fiat taxi or huge old US car.

A dolmuş departs as soon as every seat (or nearly every seat) is taken. You can catch one from point to point in a city, or from village to village, and in some cases from town to town.

Though dolmuşes on some routes operate like buses by selling tickets in advance (perhaps even for reserved seats), the true dolmuş does not. Rather, it is parked at the point of departure (a town square, city otogar or beach) and waits for the seats to fill up.

The dolmuş route may be painted on the side of the minibus, or on a sign posted next to the dolmuş, or in its window; or a hawker may call out the destination. When the driver is satisfied with the load, the dolmuş heads off.

Fares are collected en route or at the final stop. Often the fare is posted on the destination sign, whether it's on a signpost or in the vehicle's window. If it's not, watch what other passengers to your destination are paying and pay the same, or ask. Though passengers to intermediate stops sometimes pay a partial fare, on other routes the driver (or the law) may require that you pay the full fare. In either case, prices are low, though slightly more than for a bus on the same route.

If your stop comes before the final destination, you may do some shuffling to ensure that you are sitting right by the door and not way up the back. Also, a woman is expected to sit with other women whenever possible. If this is not possible, choose a side seat, not a middle seat between two men. If a man and a woman passenger get into the front of a car, for instance, the man should get in first and sit by the driver, so that the woman is between 'her' man and the door.

Collection of fares will begin after the car starts off, and the driver will juggle and change money as he drives. If you're still not sure about your fare, hand over a bill large enough to cover the fare but small enough not to anger the driver, who will never have enough change and will not want a large bill. Should there be any doubt about fares or problem in payment (rare), you can always settle up when the car stops for you to get out.

To signal the driver that you want to get out, say '*İnecek var*' (Someone wants to get out) or '*Sağda*' ('On the right', meaning 'Please pull over to the kerb'). Other useful words are *durun* (stop) and *burada* (here).

TRAIN

Turkish State Railways (TC Devlet Demiryolları, TCDD or DDY) runs services to many parts of the country on lines laid out by German companies which were supposedly paid for by the kilometre. Some newer, more direct lines have been laid during the republican era, shortening travel times for the best express trains.

Alas, TCDD trains are the poor cousins in Turkey's transport mix. In the past few decades millions have been poured into highways and airports, but very little into the railway network. Passenger equipment has a distinctly 1960s look to it, with many holes, patches and cigarette burns since then.

It's not a good idea to plan a train trip all the way across Turkey in one stretch as the country is large, and the cross-country trains

are slower than the buses. For example, the *Vangölü Ekspresi* from İstanbul to Lake Van (Tatvan), a 1900km trip, takes almost two full days – and that's an express! The bus takes less than 24 hours, the plane less than two hours. Train travel between Ankara and İstanbul is fast and pleasant, however.

Whenever you take an intercity train in Turkey, you'd do well to take only named *ekspres* (express) trains or a *mavi tren* (blue train). These are fairly fast, comfortable, and comparable in price to the bus. On *yolcu* (passenger) and *posta* (mail) trains, however, you could grow old and die before reaching your destination.

Note that Turkish train schedules indicate stations, not cities; the station name is usually, but not always, the city name. Thus you may not see İstanbul on a schedule, but you will see Haydarpaşa and Sirkeci, the Asian and European stations in İstanbul. For İzmir, the stations are Basmane and Alsancak.

Train Passes

Inter-Rail passes are valid on the Turkish State Railways' entire network. Eurail passes are not valid on any of it.

Classes of Travel

Most of the best trains and the short-haul *mototrens* (motor trains) and rail-buses now have only one class of travel. Coaches on the top trains (such as the *Başkent* and *Fatih Ekspresi*) usually have Pullman reclining seats; the normal expresses usually have European-style compartments with six seats. The very slow trains and those in the east often have 1st- and 2nd-class coaches with compartments.

There are three classes of sleeping accommodation. A couchette *(kuşetli)* wagon has six-person compartments with seats which rearrange into six shelf-like beds at night. *Örtülü kuşetli* means the couchettes have bedding (sheets, pillows and blanket), and there may be only four beds per compartment, so two couples travelling together can get an almost private compartment. A *yataklı* wagon has European-style sleeping compartments capable of sleeping up to three people. Price depends upon the number of occupants: per person cost is lowest when three people share and is highest if you want a compartment all to yourself.

Reservations

Most seats on the best trains, and all sleeping compartments, must be reserved. As the best trains are popular, particularly the sleeping-car trains, you should make your reservation and buy your ticket as far in advance as possible. A few days will usually suffice, except at holiday times (see Public Holidays & Special Events in the Facts for the Visitor chapter for dates of public holidays). Weekend trains, between Friday evening and Monday morning, tend to be the busiest.

If you can't buy in advance, check at the station anyway. There may be cancellations, even at the last minute.

Though Turkish State Railways now has a computerised reservations system, it is usually impossible to book sleeping-car space except in the city from which the train departs. You can buy tickets at the train station, at some post offices in the major cities, and at some travel agencies.

Costs

Full fare is called *tam*. Round-trip (return) fares, called *gidiş-dönüş*, are discounted by 20%. *Öğrenci* or *talebe* (student) fares discounted by 20% to 30% are offered on most routes (show your ISIC). If you are under 26 or over 55, you can buy a Tren-Tur card which allows you one month's unlimited rail travel. Ask at Sirkeci station in İstanbul, or at the Ankara garı. *Aile* (families), meaning a married couple travelling with or without children, are entitled to a 20% to 30% discount; disabled persons get 30% off and press-card holders are entitled to 50% off.

If you decide not to travel and you seek a refund for your train ticket up to 24 hours before the train's departure, you'll pay a cancellation fee of 10% of the ticket price. Within 24 hours of departure the fee is 25%. After the train has departed the fee is 50%.

CAR

Having a car in Turkey, whether owned or rented, gives you unparalleled freedom to enjoy the marvellous countryside and coastline. If you can manage it, car travel in Turkey is rewarding despite the drawbacks.

Road Rules

In theory, Turks drive on the right and yield to traffic approaching them from the right. In practice, Turks drive in the middle and yield to no-one. You must accustom yourself to drivers overtaking you on blind curves. If a car approaches from the opposite direction, all three drivers stand on their brakes and trust to Allah.

The international driving signs are there but are rarely observed. Signs indicating *otoyols* (motorways, expressways) are green. Maximum speed limits, unless otherwise posted, are 50km/h in towns, 90km/h on highways; and 130km/h maximum, 40km/h minimum on otoyols.

Kısmet & Kader

Many local drivers believe in *kısmet* (luck) and *kader* (fate). If Turkish drivers, careering along slippery highways in cars with smooth tyres and accelerator pedals flat to the floor and their minds engaged in heated conversation, swerve to avoid an errant sheep and crash into trees, that's kısmet, and it can't be helped.

Moderating speed, getting better tyres, wearing safety belts or paying attention to the road are considered a waste of time and money, as kader, your fate, is already written in Allah's big book. The Grim Reaper will get you if he's going to, no matter what you do. So why bother?

Whether because of kısmet and kader or not, Turkey's highway accident rate is high: roughly three times higher than that of the European Union, six times higher than the USA, and almost eight times higher than Australia. Almost every family in the country has been touched by the tragedy.

If you drive, be extremely cautious and defensive. When travelling by bus, it's a good idea to give preference to the better companies with newer equipment, better trained and more experienced drivers, and stricter policies regarding vehicular safety.

As there are only a few divided highways and many two-lane roads are serpentine, you must reconcile yourself to spending some hours sniffing the stinky diesel exhaust of slow, seriously overladen trucks. At night you'll encounter cars without lights or with lights missing, vehicles stopped in the middle of the road and oncoming drivers flashing their lights just to announce their approach.

Road Safety

Turkey has one of the highest motor vehicle accident rates in the world, with thousands of fatalities each year, and tens of thousands of injuries. The government, media and non-profit organisations have undertaken a vigorous driver education safety campaign, urging motorists to tame the '*trafik canavarı*' (motoring monster) within them and to drive considerately and at a safe speed, but it may be years before the campaign has a significant effect.

Turkish drivers are not particularly discourteous out on the highway, but they are impatient and incautious. They drive at high speed. They have an irrepressible urge to overtake you. To survive on Turkey's highways, drive cautiously and very defensively, avoid driving at night, and *never* let emotions affect what you do.

That having been said, most foreign visitors travel thousands of kilometres in this beautiful country with nary an incident.

Road Conditions

The quality of Turkish highways is passable. The Türkiye Cumhuriyeti Karayolları (Turkish Republic Highways Department or TCK) undertakes ambitious improvements constantly, but despite its efforts most roads still have only two lanes, perhaps with overtaking lanes on long uphill grades. Otoyols run from the Bulgarian border near Edirne to İstanbul and Ankara, and south from İzmir to Aydın.

In eastern Turkey, with its severe winter, roads are easily destroyed by frost, and potholes are a nuisance year-round.

The expressways are often busy but not impossible; the lesser highways can be busy or pleasantly traffic-free. City streets are usually thronged.

In the cities *düzensizlik* (disorder) is universal. In addition to the customary and very appropriate 'Allah Korusun' (May God Protect Me) emblazoned somewhere on every Turkish car, bus and truck, imagine the additional motto 'Önce Ben' (Me First).

Fuel

Petrol stations are everywhere, operated by international and Turkish companies. Many never close, others stay open long hours, so refuelling is usually no problem. All the same, it's a good idea to have a full tank when you start out in the morning across the vast spaces of central and eastern Anatolia.

Most accept credit cards, though they may not be able to get approval for your charge due to insufficient telephone lines.

Benzin (petrol/gasoline) comes as *normal, süper* and *kurşunsuz* (unleaded). Normal costs about US$0.90 per litre (US$3.41 per US gallon); süper, about US$0.93 per litre (US$3.53 per US gallon); and kurşunsuz, about US$0.97 per litre (US$3.68 per US gallon). *Dizel* (diesel) costs about US$0.65 per litre (US$2.46 per US gallon).

Spares & Repairs

The Türkiye Turing ve Otomobile Kurumu (Turkish Touring & Automobile Association; ☎ 212-282 8140, fax 282 8042), Birinci Oto Sanayi Sitesi Yanı, Seyrantepe, 4. Levent, İstanbul, is useful for driving aids (maps, lists of repair shops, legal necessities) as well as for repairs and advice on repairs.

Spare parts for most cars may be available, if not readily so, outside the big cities. European models (especially Renaults, Fiats and Mercedes-Benz) are preferred, though ingenious Turkish mechanics contrive to keep all manner of huge US models – some half a century old – in daily service.

If you have a model with which Turkish mechanics are familiar, repairs can be swift and very cheap. The little roadside repair shops can often provide excellent, virtually immediate service, though they (or you) may have to go somewhere else to get the parts. The sanayi bölgesi (industrial zone) on the outskirts of every city and town has a row of repair shops.

It's always good to get an estimate of the repair cost in advance. Ask *'Tamirat kaç para?'* (How much will repairs cost?). For tyre repairs find an *oto lastikçi* (tyre repairer). Repair shops are closed on Sunday, but even so, if you go to the repair shop district of town and look around, you may still find someone willing and able to help you.

Traffic Police

Trafik polisi in black-and-white cars (usually Renaults) and blue uniforms set up checkpoints on major highways in order to make sure that vehicle documents are in order, that you are wearing your seatbelt, and that vehicle safety features are in working condition. As they busy themselves mostly with trucks and buses, they'll usually wave you on, but you should slow down and prepare to stop until you get the wave.

If you're stopped, officers may ask for your car registration, insurance certificate and driving licence. They may ask you to turn on your headlights, hoot your horn, switch on the turning signals and windscreen wipers etc, to see that all are working properly. They'll certainly ask your nationality, and try to chat, because one of the reasons you (an 'exotic' foreigner) have been stopped is to break the monotony of checking trucks. If they seem to be requesting money, refuse to understand.

Rental

Minimum age is generally 19 or 21 years for the cheapest cars, 24 for some larger cars, and 27 for the best. You must pay with a major credit card, or you will be required to make a large cash deposit.

Cars may be rented in Adana, Alanya, Ankara, Antalya, Bodrum, Bursa, Çeşme, Dalaman, Fethiye, Gaziantep, İstanbul, İzmir, Kemer, Kuşadası, Marmaris, Mersin, Samsun, Side and Trabzon from the larger international rental firms (Avis, Budget, Dollar, Europcar, Hertz, Inter-Rent, Kemwel and National) or from smaller local ones. Rentals may also be picked up in most other cities by prior arrangement.

Avis has the most extensive and experienced network of agencies and staff, and the highest prices. Some firms will be happy to deliver your car to another place, or arrange for pick-up, at no extra charge; others will charge you.

You might want to consider trying (with caution) one of the small local agencies. Though there is no far-flung network for repairs and people in these places have little fluency in English, they are friendly, helpful and charge from 10% to 20% less than the large firms, particularly if you're willing to haggle a bit.

Costs Rental cars are moderately expensive in Turkey, partly due to huge excise taxes paid when the cars are purchased. Total costs of a rental arranged on the spot in Turkey during the busy summer months, for a week with unlimited kilometres, including full insurance and tax, might be from US$300 to US$600, not including fuel, parking and tolls. Daily rentals may range from US$25 to US$60 and up, depending upon the size and type of car and the rental location. Big cities are more expensive than resort locations. Ask your travel agent to shop around, or to set up a fly-drive arrangement.

Collision damage waiver (CDW) is not a bad thing to have, because a renter is liable not merely for damage, but for rental revenue lost while the damaged car is being repaired or, in the case of a stolen car, until the car is recovered.

Many travellers do not need the personal injury insurance that's offered by the rental company. Your travel insurance or your health insurance from home may cover any medical costs of an accident.

When you look at a rental company's current price list, keep in mind that the daily or weekly rental charge is only a small portion of what you will actually end up paying, unless it includes unlimited kilometres. The charge for kilometres normally ends up being higher, per day, than the daily rental charge. The value-added tax (KDV) should be included in the rental, insurance and kilometres prices quoted to you. It should not be added to your bill as an extra item.

Accidents If your car incurs any accident damage, or if you cause any, do not move the car before finding a police officer and asking for a *kaza raporu* (accident report). The officer may ask you to submit to an alcohol breath-test. Contact your car rental company within 48 hours.

MOTORCYCLE

You can bring your motorcycle to Turkey and have a fine time seeing the country. Spare parts will probably be hard to come by, so bring what you may need, or rely on the boundless ingenuity of Turkish mechanics to find, adapt or make you a part. Or else be prepared to call home, have the part flown in, and endure considerable hassles from customs.

BICYCLE

Though Turks use bicycles primarily as utilitarian vehicles to go short distances, long-distance bicycling for sport is being introduced by foreign cyclers. You can cycle pleasurably through Turkey, though you may want to bring your own bike, as renting and selling good bikes isn't yet widespread.

The pleasures are in the spectacular scenery, the friendly people, the easy access to archaeological sites and the ready availability of natural camping sites both official and unofficial. The best routes are those along the coasts, particularly the western Mediterranean coast between Marmaris and Antalya, and the unpaved coastal roads not marked on many maps.

On the minus side, you must watch out for the occasional inattentive driver; have a rear-view mirror on your bike. Also, maps available in Turkey are sometimes incorrect on such things as grades and altitudes, so search out a suitable map before leaving home (see Maps in the Facts for the Visitor chapter for suggestions).

Cyclists may find relations with Turks somewhat extreme. Along the road, some children not used to cyclists may toss stones. This is often more of an annoyance than a danger, and as cyclists become a more familiar sight it should subside. In hotels and pensions, and on those occasional bus and train rides, you may find people so accommodating and helpful in storing your valuable cycle 'safely' that lights, carriers and reflectors may get damaged unintentionally, so supervise teh operation and say '*yavaş yavaş!*' (slowly!) frequently.

Whenever you stop for a rest or to camp, the rural staring squads of the curious will appear, instantly, as if by magic. You may find, like the royal family, that constant scrutiny, even if friendly, can be wearisome.

You can usually transport your bike by air, bus, train and ferry, sometimes at no extra charge.

You cannot depend upon finding spare parts, so bring whatever you think you may need. Moped and motorcycle repair shops are often helpful, and if they can't do the repairs they will seek out someone who can. High-pressure pumps are not yet available in Turkey; fuel-station pumps may or may not go to 90 psi (high pressure). Inner tubes of 69cm by 3cm are available, but not everywhere; most of the tubes sold are larger, and they won't fit 69cm by 2.5cm rims because of the large valve seat. Be prepared for frequent chain maintenance because of the effects of dust, sand and mud.

HITCHING

Hitching is never entirely safe in any country in the world, and we don't recommend it. Travellers who decide to hitch should understand that they are taking a potentially serious risk.

If you must *otostop* (hitch), Turkish custom requires that you offer to pay for your ride, though these days some drivers pick up foreign hitchers for the curiosity value. The amount is more or less equivalent to the bus fare on the same route. Say '*Borcum kaç?*' (How much do I owe you?) as you prepare to get out. Overcharging hitchers has not been a big problem.

Long-distance hitching, though possible in Turkey, is not all that common. The bus and minibus network is so elaborate and cheap that most people opt for that, figuring that if bus fares must be paid, bus comforts might as well be enjoyed. Private cars are not as plentiful as in Europe, and owners here are not as inclined to pick up hitchers.

Short-distance hitching is somewhat different. As the country is large and vehicles are not plentiful outside towns, short-distance country hops are the norm. If you need to get from the highway to an archaeological site, you hitch a ride with whatever comes along. Again, private cars are the least amenable, but delivery vans, heavy machinery, oil tankers, farm tractors etc are all fair game. You should still offer to pay for the ride; in most cases your offer will be declined (though appreciated), because you are a 'guest' in Turkey.

The signal used in hitching is not an up-turned thumb. In Turkey, you face the traffic, hold your arm out towards the road, and wave your hand and arm up and down as though bouncing a basketball.

BOAT

Türkiye Denizcilik İşletmeleri (Turkish Maritime Administration), also called Turkish Maritime Lines (TML), operates car and passenger ferry services from İstanbul eastwards along the Black Sea coast and southwards along the Aegean coast, as well as passenger services in the Sea of Marmara and shuttle services across the Dardanelles and the Bay of İzmit. There is also a traditional (meaning slow) Bay of İzmit car ferry service every 30 minutes between Gebze (Eskihisar docks), on the coast east of Üsküdar, and Topçular, east of Yalova on the Sea of Marmara's southern shore. A similar car ferry shuttles between Hereke and Karamürsel, further east.

Car and passenger ferries save you days of driving. Even if you have no car, they offer the opportunity to take mini-cruises along the Turkish coasts. Room on these is usually in hot demand, so reserve as far in advance as possible through one of TML's agents, or directly with the İstanbul Karaköy office by fax (212-251 9025).

LOCAL TRANSPORT

Bus

Most municipal *(belediyesi)* buses work on a ticket system, and you must buy a ticket

(otobüs bileti, or simply *bilet)* in advance at a special ticket kiosk. These kiosks are at major bus terminals or transfer points. Some shops may also sell tickets, and scalpers may hang around bus stops selling them for a marked-up price

In some cities, notably İstanbul, private buses called *halk otobüsü* (peoples' bus) operate on the same routes as municipal buses. They're usually older buses. They accept either cash fares or tickets, and follow the same routes as city buses.

Dolmuş

Dolmuşes, which may be either minibuses or sedans, operate in many cities, and are usually faster, more comfortable and only slightly more expensive than the bus (and still very cheap). Intracity dolmuş stops are near major squares, terminals or intersections, and you'll need to ask '[your destination] *dolmuş var mı?'.*

Once you know a few convenient routes, you'll feel confident about picking up a dolmuş at the kerb. In the larger cities, stopping-places are regulated and sometimes marked by signs with a black 'D' on a blue-and-white background reading 'Dolmuş İndirme Bindirme Yeri' (Dolmuş Boarding and Alighting Place).

A true city dolmuş has a solid-colour band, usually yellow or black, painted horizontally around the vehicle just below the windows. Sometimes taxis with a black-and-yellow chequered band operate like the dolmuş. You've got to be careful. If you climb into an empty car, the driver might assume (honestly, or for his own benefit) that you want a taxi, and will charge you the taxi fare. Always ask *'Dolmuş mu?'* (Is this a dolmuş?) when you climb into an empty car.

Taxi

Taxis in most cities have digital meters and routinely use them. If yours doesn't, mention it right away by saying *'Saatiniz'* (Your meter). The starting rate is about US$1. The average taxi ride costs from US$2 to US$4 during the day, 50% more at night.

With the flood of tourists arriving in Turkey, some taxi drivers – and especially

İstanbul's many crooks-on-wheels – have begun to demand flat payment from foreigners. In some cases the driver will actually offer you a decent fare, and will then pocket all the money instead of giving the owners of the cab their share. But most of the time such drivers will offer an exorbitant fare, give you trouble, and refuse to run the meter. Find another cab and, if convenient, make a report to the police.

A woman should not sit in the front seat next to the driver unless there is no other available seat. The driver may misinterpret the gesture as an invitation to greater intimacy.

Ferry & Sea Bus

Public intracity sea transport, mainly in İstanbul, is by *feribot* (ferry) and *deniz otobüsü* ('sea bus' or catamaran).

Traditional ferries steam up, down and across the Bosphorus and the Bay of İzmir, providing city dwellers with cheap, convenient transport, views of open water and (in summer) fresh cool breezes.

Sea bus catamarans are faster enclosed craft which ply certain routes heavily used by commuters.

ORGANISED TOURS

As Turkey's tourist boom continues, the number of companies offering guided tours of cities or regions expands. A travel agency and tour operator of long standing and excellent reputation is Orion-Tour (☎ 212-248 8437, fax 241 2808, ✉ orion@oriontour .com.tr), Halaskargazi Caddesi 284/3, Marmara Ap, 80220 Şişli, İstanbul, about 2km north of Taksim Square. Orion's multilingual staff can arrange almost any sort of travel in Turkey, from flight reservations and airport transfers to guided tours and yacht cruises. Check out Orion's Web site at www.oriontour.com.tr for more details.

In Sultanahmet, you could try Marco Polo, Divan Yolu 54/11 (☎ 212-519 2804).

Along with legitimate operators, the shifty ones are moving in, so you should be extremely careful when choosing a tour company.

The actual tour you get depends greatly on the competence, character and personality of your particular guide, but it's difficult to pick a tour by guide rather than company, so you must go by the reputation of the tour company.

The best course of action is to ask at your hotel for recommendations. Other travellers may be able to give you tips about which companies to use and which to avoid. Watch out for the following rip-offs: a tour bus that spends the first hour or two of your 'tour' circulating through the city to various hotels, picking up tour participants; a tour that includes an extended stop at some particular shop (from which the tour company or guide gets a kickback); a tour that includes a lunch which turns out to be mediocre.

Most of the time, it is a lot cheaper and quicker to see things on your own by bus, dolmuş, or even taxi. Tours can cost from US$20 to US$40 per person; you may be able to hire a taxi and driver for the entire day for less than that, after a bit of haggling.

İstanbul

☎ 212 (European İstanbul), 216 (Asian İstanbul) • pop 12 million

For many centuries İstanbul was the capital of the civilised world. Although in 1922 Ankara became the capital of the newly proclaimed Turkish Republic, İstanbul continued to be the Turkish metropolis. It remains the country's largest city (with about 12 million residents) and port, its business and cultural centre and the first destination for Turkish and foreign tourists alike.

Although İstanbul has yielded some of its pre-eminence to up-and-coming towns such as Ankara, İzmir and Antalya, it remains, without doubt, the heartbeat of the Turkish spirit. The Turks are proud of Ankara, their modern, 20th-century capital, but it is İstanbul, the well-worn but still glorious metropolis, which they love. Its place in the country's history, folklore, commerce and culture is unchallenged.

No matter how you arrive in İstanbul, you'll be impressed. The train skirts the southern coast of the Thracian peninsula, following the city walls until it comes around Seraglio Point (Sarayburnu) and terminates directly below Topkapı Palace (Topkapı Sarayı). Buses come in along an expressway built on the path of the Roman road. Flying in on a clear day may reveal the great mosques and palaces, the wide Bosphorus (Boğaziçi) and the narrower Golden Horn (Haliç), all in a wonderful panorama.

But nothing beats 'sailing to Byzantium' – gliding across the Sea of Marmara (Marmara Denizi) while watching the slender minarets and bulbous mosque domes rise on the horizon. Even Mark Twain, who certainly had control of his emotions, waxed rhapsodic in his *Innocents Abroad* on the beauties of arriving by sea. Today, though fumes from fossil fuels may obscure the view, it's still impressive – and the pollution is much less than it was only a few years ago thanks to the widespread use of natural gas for heating and taxi fuel. If you take the boat-

HIGHLIGHTS

• Gaping at the incredible gems in the Treasury of Topkapı Palace

• Hearing the echoes of centuries in the vastness of Aya Sofya

• Feeling the sacred stillness of the Blue Mosque (Sultan Ahmet Camii)

• Getting lost amid the 4000 shops of the Kapalı Çarşı (Grand Bazaar)

• Seeing the glittering 14th-century Byzantine mosaics in the Chora Church (Kariye Müzesi)

• Cruising up the Bosphorus past Ottoman castles and palaces

BLACK SEA

Map 1 – Greater İstanbul p112
Map 2 – İstanbul p116-17
Map 3 – İstiklal Caddesi p118-19
Map 4 – Karaköy, Eminönü & Süleymaniye p120-1
Map 5 – Sultanahmet p122-3
Map 6 – Topkapı Palace (Topkapı Sarayı) p128
Map 7 – Aya Sofya p135
Map 8 – Kapalı Çarşı (Grand Bazaar) p141

train from İzmir via Bandırma, or the ferry from Yalova, you'll approach the city by sea.

İstanbul has grown ferociously in the past two decades, and now sprawls west beyond the airport (23km from the centre), north halfway to the Black Sea, and east deep into Anatolia. And it is crowded. However, both the Bosphorus, the strait connecting the Black Sea and the Sea of Marmara, and the narrower Golden Horn, a freshwater estuary, help to create a sense of openness and space. More than that, the Bosphorus provides a maritime highway for transport to various sections of the city. For several thousand years before the construction of the Bosphorus Bridge (Boğaziçi Köprüsü) in 1973, the only way to go between the European and Asian parts of the city was by boat. The second Bosphorus bridge, Fatih Bridge (Fatih Köprüsü), north of the first

İSTANBUL

MAP 1 – GREATER İSTANBUL

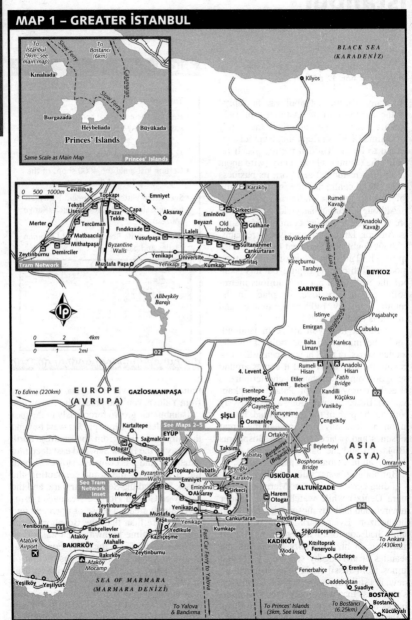

Princes' Islands

To İstanbul (9km, see main map) · Slow Ferry · To Bostancı (6km) · Çatlangav · Slow Ferry

Kınalıada

Burgazada

Heybeliada · Büyükada

Same Scale as Main Map · Princes' Islands

Tram Network

0 500 1000m

Cevizlibağ · Topkapı · Emniyet · Karaköy

Tekstil Lisesi · Pazar Tekke · Çapa · Aksaray · Eminönü · Sirkeci

Merter · Tercüman · Fındıkzade · Beyazıt · Old İstanbul · Gülhane

Matbaacılar · Laleli · Yusufpaşa

Mithatpaşa · Byzantine Walls · Sultanahmet

Zeytinburnu · Demirciler · Yenikapı · Üniversite · Cankurtaran · Çemberlitaş

Mustafa Paşa · Yenikapı · Kumkapı

BLACK SEA (KARADENİZ)

Kilyos

Rumeli Kavağı · Anadolu Kavağı

Sarıyer

Büyükdere

Kireçburnu Tarabya

SARIYER · BEYKOZ

Yeniköy · Paşabahçe

İstinye · Çubuklu

Emirgan

Balta Limanı · Kanlıca

4. Levent · Rumeli Hisarı · Anadolu Hisarı

Etiler · Fatih Bridge

Esentepe · Levent · Bebek

Gayrettepe · Arnavutköy · Kandilli · Küçüksu

Gayrettepe · Kuruçeşme · Vaniköy

ŞİŞLİ · Osmanbey · Çengelköy

Alibeyköy Barajı

To Edirne (220km)

EUROPE (AVRUPA) · GAZİOSMANPAŞA

Kartaltepe

Otogar · Sağmalcılar · EYÜP · Ortaköy · Beylerbeyi

Terazidere · Bayrampaşa · Taksim · Kabataş · ASIA (ASYA)

Davutpaşa · Topkapı-Ulubatlı · Beyoğlu · Bosphorus (Boğazı) · Bosphorus Bridge · Ümraniye

Byzantine Walls · Emniyet · Karaköy · ÜSKÜDAR

Merter · Eminönü · Sirkeci · Harem Otogar · ALTUNİZADE

Zeytinburnu · Aksaray

Bakırköy · Yenikapı · Cankurtaran · Haydarpaşa

Yenibosna · Mustafa Paşa · Yenikapı · Söğütlüçeşme · To Ankara (430km)

Atatürk Airport · Bahçelievler · Yedikule · Kumkapı · KADIKÖY · Kızıltoprak Feneryolu

Ataköy · Yeni Mahalle · Kazlıçeşme · Moda · Göztepe

BAKIRKÖY · Bakırköy · Zeytinburnu

Yeşilköy · Yeşilyurt · Ataköy Mocamp · Fenerbahçe · Erenköy

SEA OF MARMARA (MARMARA DENİZİ) · Caddebostan · Suadiye

BOSTANCI

To Yalova & Bandırma · To Princes' Islands (3km, See Inset) · To Bostancı (6.25km) · Bostancı · Küçükyalı

See Maps 2-5

See Tram Network Inset

Fast Car Ferry to Yalova

A few of İstanbul's many faces: the hustle and bustle of the ferry docks at Karaköy (top left); the 19th-century elegance of İstiklal Caddesi, İstanbul's historic main street (top right); and the serenity of a misty morning over the Golden Horn (bottom)

İstanbul's great imperial mosques are one of the most enduring images of the city. The imposing Blue Mosque (top right and bottom) is instantly recognisable, dominating the skyline. In contrast, the main reason for visiting the Rustem Paşa Camii (top left) is its gorgeously decorated interior.

one at Bebek/Beylerbeyi, was finished in 1988. A third bridge, further north, is planned.

Three days is the minimum time necessary for a meaningful visit to this city; a week is better.

HISTORY
Early Times
The earliest settlement, Semistra, was probably around 1000 BC, a few hundred years after the Trojan War and about the same time that David and Solomon ruled in Jerusalem. It was followed by a fishing village, Lygos, which occupied Seraglio Point where Topkapı Palace stands today. Later, around 700 BC, colonists from Megara (near Corinth) in Greece settled at Chalcedon (now Kadıköy) on the Asian shore of the Bosphorus.

Byzantium
The first settlement to have historic significance was founded by another Megarian colonist, a fellow named Byzas. Before leaving Greece, he asked the oracle at Delphi where he should establish his new colony. The enigmatic answer was, 'Opposite the blind'. When Byzas and his fellow colonists sailed up the Bosphorus, they noticed the colony on the Asian shore at Chalcedon. Looking to their left, they saw the superb natural harbour of the Golden Horn on the European shore. Thinking, as legend has it, 'Those people in Chalcedon must be blind', they settled on the opposite shore, on the site of Lygos, and named their new city Byzantium. This was in 657 BC.

The legend could well be true. İstanbul's location on the waterway linking the Sea of Marmara and the Black Sea, and on the 'land bridge' linking Europe and Asia, is still of tremendous importance today, 2600 years after the oracle spoke.

Byzantium submitted willingly to Rome and fought Rome's battles for centuries, but finally got caught supporting the wrong side in a civil war. The winner, Septimius Severus, razed the city walls and took away its privileges in AD 196. When he relented and rebuilt the city, he named it Augusta Antonina.

Constantinople
Another struggle for control of the Roman Empire determined the city's fate for the next 1000 years. Constantine pursued his rival Licinius to Augusta Antonina, then across the Bosphorus to Chrysopolis (Üsküdar). Defeating his rival in AD 324, Constantine solidified his control and declared this city to be 'New Rome'. He laid out a vast new city to serve as capital of his empire, and inaugurated it with much pomp in AD 330. The place which had been first settled as a fishing village over 1000 years earlier was now the capital of the world, and would remain so for almost another 1000 years.

The Byzantine Empire lasted from the refounding of the city in AD 330 to the Ottoman Turkish conquest in 1453, an impressive 1123 years. Much remains of ancient Constantinople, including churches, palaces, cisterns and the Hippodrome. In fact, there's more of Constantinople left than anyone knows about. Any sort of excavation reveals ancient streets, mosaics, tunnels, water and sewer systems, houses and public buildings.

The Conquest What Westerners refer to as the 'Fall of Constantinople' was to Muslims the 'Conquest of İstanbul'. Though the Byzantine Empire had been moribund for several centuries, the Ottomans were quite content to accept tribute from the weak Byzantine emperor as they progressively captured all the lands surrounding his well-fortified city. By the time of the Conquest, the emperor had control over little more than the city itself and a few territories in Greece.

When Mehmet II, known as Fatih (the Conqueror), came to power in 1451 as a young man, he needed an impressive military victory to solidify his dominance of the powerful noble class. As the Ottomans controlled all of Anatolia and most of the Balkans by this time, it was obvious that the great city should be theirs. Mehmet decided it should be sooner rather than later.

The story of the Conquest is thrilling, full of bold strokes and daring exploits, heroism, treachery and intrigue. Mehmet started with the two great fortresses on the Bosphorus.

Rumeli Hisarı, the larger one, was built in an incredibly short four months on the European side. Anadolu Hisarı, the smaller one on the Asian side built half a century earlier by Yıldırım Beyazıt, was repaired and brought to readiness. Together they controlled the strait's narrowest point.

The Byzantines had closed the mouth of the Golden Horn with a heavy chain to prevent Ottoman boats from sailing in and attacking the city walls on the northern side. In another bold stroke, Mehmet marshalled his boats at a cove (now covered by Dolmabahçe Palace) and had them transported overland on rollers and slides, by night, up the valley (where the Hilton hotel now stands) and down the other side into the Golden Horn at Kasımpaşa. He caught the Byzantine defenders completely by surprise and soon had the Golden Horn under control.

The last great obstacle was the mighty bastion of land walls on the western side. No matter how heavily Mehmet's cannons battered them by day, the Byzantines would rebuild them by night and, come daybreak, the impetuous young sultan would find himself back where he'd started. Then he received a proposal from a Hungarian cannon founder called Urban who had come to offer his services to the Byzantine emperor for the defence of Christendom against the infidels. Finding that the emperor had no money, he went to Mehmet and offered to make the most enormous cannon ever. Mehmet, who had lots of money, accepted the offer, and the cannon was cast and tested in Edirne.

The first shot, which terrified hundreds of peasants, sent a huge ball 1.5km, where it buried itself 2m below ground. The jubilant sultan had his new toy transported to the front lines and started firing. A special crew worked for hours to ready it for each shot, for every firing wrecked the mount, and the gun had to be cooled with buckets of water.

Despite the inevitability of the conquest, the emperor refused surrender terms offered by Mehmet on 23 May 1453, preferring to wait in hope that Christendom would come and save him. On 28 May the final attack began, and by the evening of the 29th Mehmet's troops were in control of every quarter. The emperor, Constantine XI Dragases, died in battle, fighting on the walls.

Mehmet's triumphant entry into the world's greatest city on the evening of 29 May is commemorated every year in İstanbul. Those parts of the city which did not resist his troops were spared, and their churches guaranteed. Those that resisted were sacked for the customary three days, and their churches turned into mosques. As for Sancta Sophia, the greatest church in Christendom (St Peter's in Rome, though larger, was not begun until 1506), it was converted immediately into a mosque.

İstanbul

The Ottoman Centuries Mehmet the Conqueror began at once to rebuild and repopulate the city. He saw himself as the successor to the glories and powers of Constantine, Justinian and the other great emperors who had reigned here. He built a mosque (Fatih Camii) on one of the city's seven hills, repaired the walls and made İstanbul the administrative, commercial and cultural centre of his growing empire.

Süleyman the Magnificent (1520–66) was perhaps İstanbul's greatest builder. His mosque, the Süleymaniye (1550), is İstanbul's largest. Other sultans added more mosques, and in the 19th century numerous palaces were built along the Bosphorus: Çirağan, Dolmabahçe, Yıldız, Beylerbeyi and Küçük Su.

As the Ottoman Empire grew to include all of the Middle East and North Africa as well as half of Eastern Europe, İstanbul became a fabulous melting pot. On its streets and in its bazaars, people spoke Turkish, Greek, Armenian, Ladino (Judaeo-Spanish), Russian, Arabic, Bulgarian, Romanian, Albanian, Italian, French, German, English and Maltese.

However, the most civilised city on earth in the time of Süleyman eventually declined, as did the Ottoman Empire, and by the 19th century it had lost some of its former glory. But it continued to be the 'Paris of the East' and, to reaffirm this, the first great international luxury express train, the famous *Orient Express*, connected İstanbul with Paris.

Republican İstanbul Atatürk's (1881–1938) campaign for national salvation and independence was directed from Ankara. (For more details see The Turkish Republic in the History section of Facts about Turkey.) The founder of the Turkish Republic decided to get away from the imperial memories of İstanbul and to set up the new government in a city that could not easily be threatened by gunboats. Robbed of its importance as the capital of a vast empire, İstanbul lost much of its wealth and glitter. From being the East's most cosmopolitan city, it relaxed into a new role as an important national, rather than international, city.

During the 1980s and '90s İstanbul began to regain something of its former role. Easier to live in than Cairo or Beirut, more attractive than Tel Aviv, more in touch with the Islamic world than Athens, it is fast becoming the capital of the eastern Mediterranean again.

ORIENTATION

İstanbul is divided from north to south by the Bosphorus, the wide strait connecting the Black Sea and the Sea of Marmara, into European and Asian portions. European İstanbul is further divided by the Golden Horn estuary. Governmentally, the İstanbul Metropolitan Municipality (İstanbul Büyükşehir Belediyesi) is divided into 15 smaller municipalities *(belediye)*.

The historic heart of the city on the south shore of the Golden Horn, once called Stamboul by foreigners, is now the belediye of Eminönü. This name also applies to the district centred on the Yeni Cami (New Mosque) at the southern end of the Galata Bridge, which can lead to some confusion. On the north side of the Golden Horn is the belediye of Beyoğlu.

Lonely Planet publishes a comprehensive İstanbul City Map, which has detailed maps of the city at varying scales.

Old İstanbul

Old İstanbul is ancient Byzantium/Constantinople, called Stamboul by 19th-century travellers. It's here, from Seraglio Point jutting into the Bosphorus to the mammoth city walls 7km to the west, that you'll find the great palaces and mosques, the Hippodrome, monumental columns, ancient churches and the Kapalı Çarşı (Grand Bazaar or Covered Market). The best selection of budget and mid-range hotels is also here, with a few top-end places as well. The heart of the old city within the walls is now officially the belediyes of Eminönü and Fatih.

Beyoğlu

North of the Golden Horn is Beyoğlu, the Turkish name for the two ancient cities of Pera and Galata, or roughly all the land from the Golden Horn to Taksim Square. Here you'll find luxury hotels; airline offices and banks; the European consulates and hospitals; and Taksim Square, the hub of European İstanbul.

Under the Byzantines, Galata (now called Karaköy) was a separate city built and inhabited by Genoese traders.

Under the sultans, the non-Muslim European population of Galata spread up the hill and along the ridge, founding Galata's sister city of Pera. In recent times this part of the city has been the fastest growing and has stretched far beyond the limits of old Galata and Pera. Beyoğlu's main street is the pedestrianised İstiklal Caddesi, formerly known as the Grande Rue de Péra.

Old İstanbul and Beyoğlu are connected by the Galata Bridge at the mouth of the Golden Horn. Near the bridge are the docks for Bosphorus ferries.

Asian İstanbul

The Asian part of the city, on the eastern shore of the Bosphorus, is of less interest to tourists, being mostly dormitory suburbs such as Üsküdar (Scutari) and Kadıköy (Chalcedon). One landmark you'll want to know about is Haydarpaşa station, right between Üsküdar and Kadıköy. This is the terminus for Anatolian trains, which means any Turkish train except the one from Europe via Edirne. If you're headed for Ankara, Cappadocia or any point east of İstanbul, you'll board at Haydarpaşa.

[Continued on page 124]

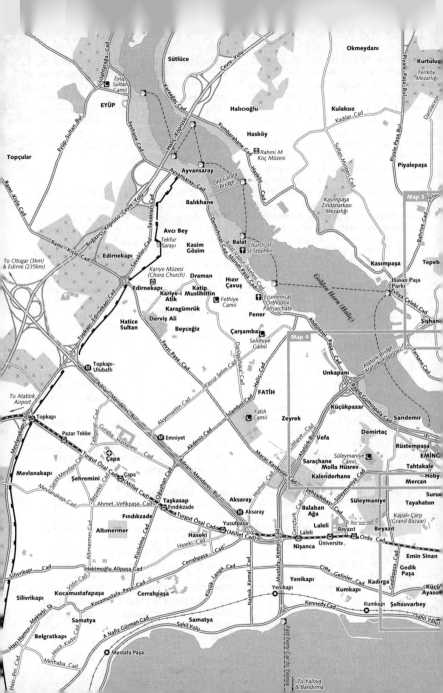

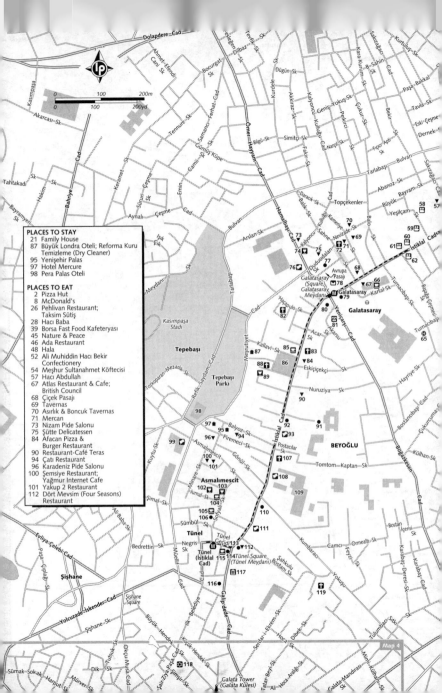

PLACES TO STAY
21 Family House
87 Büyük Londra Oteli; Reforma Kuru
   Temizleme (Dry Cleaner)
95 Yenişehir Palas
97 Hotel Mercure
98 Pera Palas Oteli

PLACES TO EAT
2 Pizza Hut
8 McDonald's
26 Pehlivan Restaurant;
   Taksim Sütiş
28 Hacı Baba
39 Borsa Fast Food Kafeteryası
45 Nature & Peace
46 Ada Restaurant
48 Hala
52 Ali Muhiddin Hacı Bekir
   Confectionery
54 Meşhur Sultanahmet Köftecisi
57 Hacı Abdullah
67 Atlas Restaurant & Cafe;
   British Council
68 Çiçek Pasajı
69 Tavernas
70 Asırlık & Boncuk Tavernas
71 Mercan
73 Nizam Pide Salonu
75 Sütte Delicatessen
84 Afacan Pizza &
   Burger Restaurant
90 Restaurant-Café Teras
94 Çatı Restaurant
96 Karadeniz Pide Salonu
100 Şemsiye Restaurant;
    Yağmur Internet Cafe
101 Yakup 2 Restaurant
112 Dört Mevsim (Four Seasons)
    Restaurant

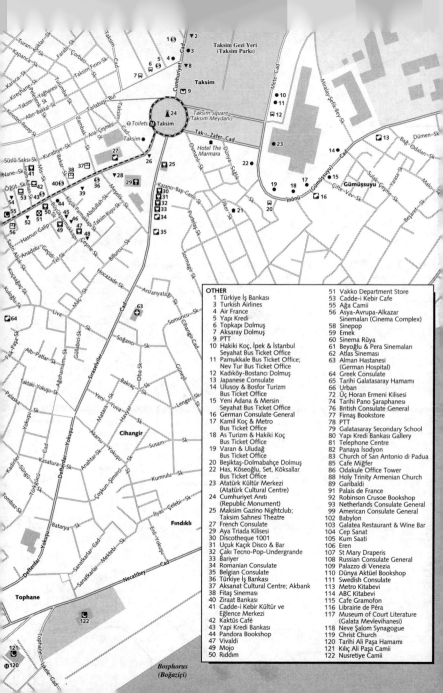

OTHER

1 Türkiye İş Bankası
3 Turkish Airlines
4 Air France
5 Yapı Kredi
6 Topkapı Dolmuş
7 Aksaray Dolmuş
9 PTT
10 Hakiki Koç, İpek & İstanbul
   Seyahat Bus Ticket Office
11 Pamukkale Bus Ticket Office;
   Nev Tur Bus Ticket Office
12 Kadıköy-Bostancı Dolmuş
13 Japanese Consulate
14 Ulusoy & Bosfor Turizm
   Bus Ticket Office
15 Yeni Adana & Mersin
   Seyahat Bus Ticket Office
16 German Consulate General
17 Kamil Koç & Metro
   Bus Ticket Office
18 As Turizm & Hakiki Koç
   Bus Ticket Office
19 Varan & Uludağ
   Bus Ticket Office
20 Beşiktaş-Dolmabahçe Dolmuş
22 Has, Köseoğlu, Set, Köksallar
   Bus Ticket Office
23 Atatürk Kültür Merkezi
   (Atatürk Cultural Centre)
24 Cumhuriyet Anıtı
   (Republic Monument)
25 Maksim Gazino Nightclub;
   Taksim Sahnesi Theatre
27 French Consulate
29 Aya Triada Kilisesi
31 Discotheque 1001
31 Uçuk Kaçık Disco & Bar
32 Çakı Tecno-Pop-Undergrande
33 Bariyer
34 Romanian Consulate
35 Belgian Consulate
36 Türkiye İş Bankası
37 Aksanat Cultural Centre; Akbank
38 Fitaş Sineması
40 Ziraat Bankası
41 Cadde-i Kebir Kültür ve
   Eğlence Merkezi
42 Kaktüs Café
43 Yapi Kredi Bankası
47 Pandora Bookshop
47 Vivaldi
49 Mojo
50 Rıddım

51 Vakko Department Store
53 Cadde-i Kebir Cafe
55 Ağa Camii
56 Asya-Avrupa-Alkazar
   Sinemaları (Cinema Complex)
58 Sinepop
59 Emek
60 Sinema Rüya
61 Beyoğlu & Pera Sinemaleri
62 Atlas Sineması
63 Alman Hastanesi
   (German Hospital)
64 Greek Consulate
65 Tarihi Galatasaray Hamamı
66 Urban
72 Üç Horan Ermeni Kilisesi
74 Tarihi Pano Şaraphanesi
76 British Consulate General
77 Firnaş Bookstore
78 PTT
79 Galatasaray Secondary School
80 Yapı Kredi Bankası Gallery
81 Telephone Centre
82 Panaya İsodyon
83 Church of San Antonio di Padua
85 Cafe Miğfer
86 Odakule Office Tower
88 Holy Trinity Armenian Church
89 Garibaldi
91 Palais de France
92 Robinson Crusoe Bookshop
93 Netherlands Consulate General
99 American Consulate General
102 Babylon
103 Galatea Restaurant & Wine Bar
104 Cep Sanat
105 Kum Saati
106 Eren
107 St Mary Draperis
108 Russian Consulate General
109 Palazzo di Venezia
110 Dünya Aktüel Bookshop
111 Swedish Consulate
113 Metro Kitabevi
114 ABC Kitabevi
115 Cafe Gramofon
116 Librairie de Péra
117 Museum of Court Literature
   (Galata Mevlevihanesi)
118 Neve Şalom Synagogue
119 Christ Church
120 Tarihi Ali Paşa Hamamı
121 Kılıç Ali Paşa Camii
122 Nusretiye Camii

Map 3

Sümak Sk
Dik Sk
Tutsak Sk
Neve Shalom
Synagogue
Büyük Hendek Cad
Küçük Hendek Cad
Serdar-ı Ekrem Sk
Hoca Çeşme Sk
Hoca Ali Sk
Hoca Aralığı Cad
Galata Mandıraları Sk
Nimi Kalhanesi Sk

Harput Sk
Yolkuz Sk
Müneri Sk
Okçu-Musa Cad
Galip-Paşa Laleli
Şair Ziya-Paşa
Yanıkkapı Sk
Şimşir Sk
Çeşme Sk
Galata Kulesi
(Galata Tower)
Galata Kulesi Sk
Tatar-Beyi
Revani Sk
Galata-Hendek Cad
Revani Çelebi Sk
Lüleci-Hendek Cad

Sarı-Zeybek Sk
Deve-Dikeni Sk
Fütühat Sk
Abdül-Selah Sk
Bereketzade Sk
Bankalar Cad
Galata-Mahkemesi Cad
Büyük
Cami-Sk
Midilli-Sk
Alageyik Sk
Kemeraltı Cad
Serçe Sk
Galata Arapoğlan Sk

Bugulu-Sk
Tersane-Cad
Yemeniciler-Sk
Hoca-Tahir Sk
Hediye-Sk
Bakır-Sk
Voyvoda
Cad
Banker Sk
Hacı-Ali-Sk
Yüksek-Kaldırım
Zürafa Sk
Maliye
Hoca
Necatibey
Tahsin Sk
Köleman Sk

Yelkenciler
Sk
Sırmalı-Nafe-Sk
Samur-Sk
Perçemli-Sk
Bereketzade Sk
Billûr-Sk
Söğüt-Sk
Mertebani-Sk
Yolcu Salonu
(International
Maritime Passenger
Terminal)
Kemankeş-Cad

Yüzbaşı-Sabahattin
Ziyalı-Sk
Kalyon-Arap
Zindanı-Han-Sk
Tünel
(Karaköy)
Evren-Cad
Karaköy-Caddesi
Karaköy
Gümrük
Kemankeş-Cad

Fermeneciler
Sk
Karaköy
Meydanı
Rıhtım-Cad

İstanbul Ticaret Odası
(Chamber of Commerce)
Dock for
private ferries
Galata Bridge
(Galata Köprüsü)
To Haydarpaşa &
Kadıköy

Sobacılar-Cad
Zindan
Han
Yağkapanı
Subway
Underpass
To Bosphorus
To Kadıköy

Sobacılar
Kutucular-Cad
Kantarcılar-Cad
City
Buses
Seabus
Boğaz
Bosphorus
Tour
To Üsküdar
To Harem

Rüstem
Paşa-Cami
Rüstempaşa
Hasır-Cılar Sk
Main Entrance to
Mısır Çarşısı &
Pandeli Restaurant
Eminönü
Meydanı
Eminönü
Reşadiye-Cad
Sirkeci
To Prince's Islands
& Yalova

Tahmis-Cad
Balkapanı
Çömlek-Türk
Fındıkçılar
Çiçek-Pazarı-Sk
Yeni Cami
Yenicami-Meydanı
Arpacılar-Caddesi
Hamidiye-Türbesi-Efendi
Yalı
Köşkü
Mimar-Kemalettin-Cad
Harem (Car
Ferry)
Yalova,
Çınarcık
& Adalar
(Princes'
Islands)

Tahtakale
Marpuççular
Sabuncuhan
Mısır Çarşısı
(Egyptian Bazaar)
Tomb of Valide
Sultan Turhan
Hatice
Ali Muhiddin
Hacı Bekir
Confectionery
Köşkü-Sk
Borsa Fast Food
Sirkeci

Gızlıklı-Sk
Uzunçarşı-Sk
Saka-Mehmet-Sk
Yenicami-Cad
Sultan-Hamamı-Sk
Vakıf
Hanı
Hamidiye
EMİNÖNÜ
Mimar-Vedat-Sk
Sirkeci
İstasyon-Cad
Sirkeci Garı

Vasıf-Çınar-Sk
Paşa-Camii-Sk
Nasuhiye-Sk
Sabuncuhan
Şeyhülislam-Cad
Mevlana
Sirkeci
Meydanı
İstasyon Arkası

Mercan
Örücüler-Cad
Aslaahamamı-Sk
Hacı
Küçük-Sk
Fincancılar-Cad
Hocahanı
Aşirefendi
Hanımeli-Sk
Köprücü-Sk
Central
Post Office
Hocapaşa
Hobyar
Muradiye-Cad
Hocapaşa
Restaurants
Nöbethane
Darüssaade-Sk

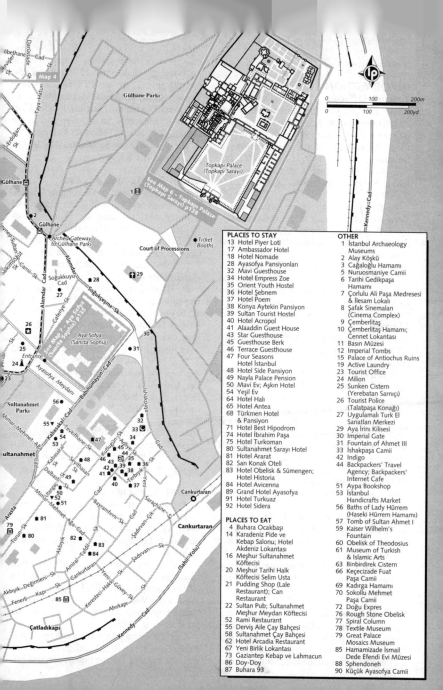

PLACES TO STAY
13 Hotel Piyer Loti
17 Ambassador Hotel
18 Hotel Nomade
28 Ayasofya Pansiyonları
32 Mavi Guesthouse
34 Hotel Empress Zoe
35 Orient Youth Hostel
36 Hotel Şebnem
37 Hotel Poem
38 Konya Aytekin Pansiyon
39 Sultan Tourist Hostel
40 Hotel Acropol
41 Alaaddin Guest House
43 Star Guesthouse
45 Guesthouse Berk
46 Terrace Guesthouse
47 Four Seasons
   Hotel İstanbul
48 Hotel Side Pansiyon
49 Nayla Palace Pension
50 Mavi Ev; Aşkın Hotel
54 Yeşil Ev
64 Hotel Halı
65 Hotel Antea
68 Türkmen Hotel
   & Pansiyon
71 Hotel Best Hipodrom
74 Hotel İbrahim Paşa
75 Hotel Turkoman
80 Sultanahmet Sarayı Hotel
81 Hotel Ararat
82 Sarı Konak Oteli
83 Hotel Obelisk & Sümengen;
   Hotel Historia
84 Hotel Avicenna
89 Grand Hotel Ayasofya
91 Hotel Turkuaz
92 Hotel Sidera

PLACES TO EAT
4 Buhara Ocakbaşı
14 Karadeniz Pide ve
   Kebap Salonu; Hotel
   Akdeniz Lokantası
16 Meşhur Sultanahmet
   Köftecisi
20 Meşhur Tarihi Halk
   Köftecisi Selim Usta
21 Pudding Shop (Lale
   Restaurant); Can
   Restaurant
22 Sultan Pub; Sultanahmet
   Meşhur Meydan Köftecisi
52 Rami Restaurant
55 Derviş Aile Çay Bahçesi
58 Sultanahmet Çay Bahçesi
62 Hotel Arcadia Restaurant
67 Yeni Birlik Lokantası
73 Gaziantep Kebap ve Lahmacun
86 Doy-Doy
87 Buhara 93

OTHER
1 İstanbul Archaeology
   Museums
2 Alay Köşkü
3 Cağaloğlu Hamamı
5 Nuruosmaniye Camii
6 Tarihi Gedikpaşa
   Hamamı
7 Çorlulu Ali Paşa Medresesi
   & İlesam Lokali
8 Şafak Sinemaları
   (Cinema Complex)
9 Çemberlitaş
10 Çemberlitaş Hamamı;
   Cennet Lokantası
11 Basın Müzesi
12 Imperial Tombs
15 Palace of Antiochus Ruins
19 Active Laundry
23 Tourist Office
24 Milion
25 Sunken Cistern
   (Yerebatan Sarnıçı)
26 Tourist Police
   (Talatpaşa Konağı)
27 Uygulamalı Türk El
   Sanatları Merkezi
29 Aya İrini Kilisesi
30 Imperial Gate
31 Fountain of Ahmet III
33 İshakpaşa Camii
42 Indigo
44 Backpackers' Travel
   Agency; Backpackers'
   Internet Cafe
51 Aypa Bookshop
53 İstanbul
   Handicrafts Market
56 Baths of Lady Hürrem
   (Haseki Hürrem Hamamı)
57 Tomb of Sultan Ahmet I
59 Kaiser Wilhelm's
   Fountain
60 Obelisk of Theodosius
61 Museum of Turkish
   & Islamic Arts
63 Binbirdirek Cistern
66 Keçecizade Fuat
   Paşa Camii
69 Kadırga Hamamı
70 Sokollu Mehmet
   Paşa Camii
72 Doğu Expres
76 Rough Stone Obelisk
77 Spiral Column
78 Textile Museum
79 Great Palace
   Mosaics Museum
85 Hamamizade İsmail
   Dede Efendi Evi Müzesi
88 Sphendoneh
90 Küçük Ayasofya Camii

[Continued from page 115]

INFORMATION
Tourist Offices

There are Ministry of Tourism offices at Atatürk airport (☎ 212-663 6363, fax 663 0793) in the international arrivals area, at the north-western end of the Hippodrome in Sultanahmet (Map 5, ☎ 212-518 1802, fax 518 1802), open from 9 am to 5 pm daily, and at Sirkeci train station (Map 4, ☎ 212-511 5888).

In Beyoğlu there is an office at the Karaköy Yolcu Salonu or International Maritime Passenger Terminal (Map 4, ☎ 212-249 5776); another in Elmadağ in the Hilton Hotel arcade (Map 2, ☎ 212-233 0592), just off Cumhuriyet Caddesi, two long blocks north of Taksim Square on the right-hand side of the street as you head north (open from 9 am to 5 pm daily except Sunday).

Money

There are currency exchange booths and ATMs at Atatürk airport's international arrivals area.

Divan Yolu is lined with foreign exchange offices (*döviz bürosu*) and travel agencies offering exchange facilities at fairly good rates. Most exchange offices are open daily from 9 am to 9 pm. Other good areas to look are Sirkeci and around Taksim Square and along İstiklal Caddesi. The rates are worse at offices heavily used by tourists, such as those in Sultanahmet and on İstiklal Caddesi; better rates are offered in Aksaray, the side streets of the Kapalı Çarşı, Eminönü and Şişli.

Most of the banks along İstiklal Caddesi in Taksim have ATMs. There's a handy Yapı Kredi ATM between Aya Sofya and the Blue Mosque in Sultanahmet.

Remember that you can usually change money (preferably cash) at post office branches.

Post & Telephone

İstanbul's main post office is the Sirkeci PTT Merkezi, several blocks west of Sirkeci train station on Mevlana Caddesi. The phone and fax centre is open all the time, although spe-cial services have shorter hours, such as poste restante (8.30 am to 12.30 pm and 1.30 to 5.30 pm). There are PTT branches near Taksim Square at Cumhuriyet Caddesi, Taksim Gezi Dükkanları, just off İstiklal Caddesi in Galatasaray, in Aksaray and in the Kapalı Çarşı near the Havuzlu Lokantası.

The postcode for Sultanahmet is 34400; for Taksim it's 80090.

Email & Internet Access

You can check your email at many hostels, small hotels and cafes in Cankurtaran and Sultanahmet, including the Orient Youth Hostel and the Mavi Guesthouse (Map 5; see Places to Stay). The Sinem Internet Cafe is just off Divan Yolu on Dr Emin Paşa Sokak near the Sultanahmet tram stop, and another one (☎ 212-517 0081) is next to the Hotel Halı on Klodfarer Caddesi. The Beyazıt Internet Cafe (☎ 212-518 4888, ⓔ beyazitcafe@superonline.com), in the Uluçay İşhanı at Yeniçeriler Caddesi 47/1, is across the street from the Grand Bazaar.

In Beyoğlu, try Yağmur Cybercafe (Map 3, ☎ 212-292 3020, ⓔ anu@citlembik.com .tr), near the American consulate general, in the Çitlembik Apartıman building (2nd floor), Şeyh Bender Sokak 18, Asmalı-mescit, Beyoğlu.

Internet Resources

A good source of İstanbul-specific information on the Internet is Beyoğluweb (www .beyogluweb.com).

Travel Agencies

There are lots of travel agents on the northern side of Divan Yolu in Sultanahmet (Map 5), all of them specialising in budget air tickets but also able to arrange bus and train tickets.

Several others are in Cankurtaran, such as Indigo (Map 5, ☎ 212-517 7266, fax 518 5333), Akbıyık Caddesi 24, ⓔ red@indigo -tour.com). We've had complaints about inflated tour prices at some agencies in this area, so shop around.

The fancier travel agencies and major airline offices are in the Elmadağ and Harbiye districts north of Taksim Square along Cumhuriyet Caddesi between the Divan Oteli and İstanbul Hilton Hotel (Map 2).

A travel agent/tour operator with English-speaking staff and a tradition of good service is Orion-Tour (☎ 212-248 8437, fax 241 2808, ℮ orion@oriontour.com.tr), Halaskargazi Caddesi 284/3, Marmara Apartımanı, Şişli, a bit out of the way, about 2km north of Taksim (US$2 by taxi). Orion (pronounced or-yohn in Turkish) can arrange flights, cruises (including private or group yacht charters), transfers to and from the airport, city tours of İstanbul and other major cities, and private or group tours anywhere in Turkey. Check out its Web site (www.orion tour.com) for more information.

Automobile Club
The Türkiye Turing ve Otomobil Kurumu (Turkish Touring & Automobile Association) (☎ 212-282 8140, fax 282 8042), Birinci Oto Sanayi Sitesi Yanı, 4. Levent, about 7km north of Taksim Square, can provide information on car insurance and import permits, and has a breakdown service and repair facilities. The association and its longtime director, Mr Çelik Gülersoy, have been prime movers in efforts at historical restoration and beautification in İstanbul and several other Turkish cities.

Bookshops
In general, the place to find foreign-language books is in Beyoğlu on İstiklal Caddesi, between Galatasaray and Tünel Squares. Prices are often more reasonable than at tourist-epicentre bookshops in Sultanahmet.

Robinson Crusoe (Map 3, ☎ 212-293 6968), İstiklal Caddesi 389, has fiction, general-interest titles and many books (including Lonely Planet) about Turkey in English and, to a lesser extent, in French and German.

Homer Kitabevi (Map 3, ☎ 212-249 5902, fax 251 3962, ℮ homerkitabevi@superon line.com), Yeni Çarşı Caddesi 28/A, just downhill from Galatasaray Square, has lots of books, especially academic titles, in English.

Dünya Aktüel (Map 3, ☎ 212-249 1006), İstiklal Caddesi 469, which also operates shops at the Hilton, Holiday Inn and Swiss-ôtel hotels, has Turkish, French and English books and periodicals.

Metro Kitabevi (☎ 212-249 5827), İstiklal Caddesi 513, sells guidebooks (including Lonely Planet), maps and dictionaries in English, French, German and Turkish. The nearby ABC Kitabevi (☎ 212-293 1629), on Tünel Square, has a few books, but mostly language-learning aids.

Pandora (Map 3, ☎ 212-243 3503, ℮ H.Sonmez@info-ist.comlink.apc.org), Büyükparmakkapı Sokak 3, off the Taksim end of İstiklal Caddesi, has a good collection of books in English on Turkish and Ottoman history and literature.

Firnaş Bookstore (Map 3, ☎ 212-244 5446), at No 5 in the Avrupa Pasajı between Meşrutiyet Caddesi and Sahne Sokak off Galatasaray Square, stocks dictionaries of many languages and some travel guides.

In Sultanahmet, several shops along Divan Yolu facing the Hippodrome carry maps and guides, often at premium prices. Aypa (Map 5, ☎ 212-516 0100), Mimar Mehmet Ağa Caddesi 19, behind the Blue Mosque, has a small selection of guides, maps and magazines in English, French and German.

Karum (☎ 212-241 7988), Akkavak Sokak 19/21/1 Nişantaşı, about 2km north-east of Taksim Square, has a good selection of art books, art prints and posters.

Remzi Kitabevi (☎ 212-234 5475), Rumeli Caddesi 44, Nişantaşı, is a top-quality general English language bookshop with a wide selection on all subjects. Another Remzi shop (☎ 212-282 0245) is in the Akmerkez Shopping Centre in Etiler, about 10km north of Taksim Square.

Libraries
The American Library (Map 3, ☎ 212-251 2675), next to the American consulate general at Meşrutiyet Caddesi 108, Tepebaşı, is open by appointment only.

The British Council Library (Map 3, ☎ 212-252 7474 ext 115, 118 or 119), İstiklal Caddesi 151–253, Beyoğlu, two flights up in the Örs Turistik İş Merkezi building, is open Tuesday to Friday from 10.30 am to at least 5.30 pm (later some nights) and on Saturday from 9.30 am to 2.30 pm.

The Women's Library (☎ 212-534 9550), just east of St Stephen's Church (Map 2) on the south-western side of the Golden Horn, is open from 9 am to 5.30 pm daily except Sunday. The library (Kadın Eserleri Kütüphanesi ve Bilgi Merkezi Vakfı), housed in a historic building, acts as a women's resource centre, with a program of cultural and special events of interest to women.

Cultural Centres

These include the following:

American Library (Map 3, ☎ 212-251 2675) Meşrutiyet Caddesi 108, Tepebaşı. Open by appointment only.

British Council (Map 3, ☎ 212-252 7474 ext 115) Örs İş Merkezı, İstiklal Caddesi 151–253, Beyoğlu. The library is open from 10.30 am to at least 5.30 pm Tuesday to Friday and from 9.30 am to 2.30 pm Saturday.

French Cultural Centre (Map 3, ☎ 212-249 0776) İstiklal Caddesi 8, Beyoğlu

Laundry

If you don't do your own laundry, ask for prices at your hotel. There's also the Active Laundry (Map 5), Dr Emin Paşa Sokak 14, off Divan Yolu beneath Arsenal Youth Hostel.

İstanbul has numerous *kuru temizleme* (dry-cleaning shops), usually open daily except Sunday from 8 am to 7 pm. Bring items in early for same-day service. Two blocks westwards uphill from the southern end of the Hippodrome in Sultanahmet is Doğu Expres (Map 5, ☎ 212-526 0725), Peykhane Sokak 61 (also called Üçler Sokak). In Tepebaşı, try Reforma Kuru Temizleme (Map 3, ☎ 212-243 6862), Meşrutiyet Caddesi 131, near the Büyük Londra Oteli.

Medical Services

İstanbul has several private hospitals which provide good quality care at low government-controlled prices. These include:

Alman Hastanesi (Map 3, ☎ 212-293 2150) Sıraselviler Caddesi 119, Taksim, a few hundred metres south of Taksim on the left-hand side, with German administration

American Hospital (☎ 212-231 4050, fax 234 1432) Güzelbahçe Sokak 20, Nişantaşı, about 2km north-east of Taksim

Florence Nightingale Hospital (☎ 212-231 2021) Abidei Hürriyet Caddesi 290, Çağlayan, Şişli, about 4km north of Taksim

Intermed Check-up Centre (☎ 212-225 0660) Teşvikiye Caddesi, Bayar Apt 143, Nişantaşı, about 2km north of Taksim

International Hospital (☎ 212-663 3000) İstanbul Caddesi 82, Yeşilyurt, west of the centre on the shore near the airport

La Paix Hastanesi (called, simply, Lape) (☎ 212–246 1020) Büyükdere Caddesi 22-24, Şişli, with French administration

Emergency

In case of hassles, stolen or lost documents and the like, you might get some help from the tourist police in the Talatpaşa Konaği (Map 5, ☎ 212-527 4503), Yerebatan Caddesi 2, Sultanahmet, opposite the Sunken Cistern. They have some multilingual staff and experience with foreigners.

If you have a personal crisis – financial, physical, psychological, emotional – and need someone to talk to, dial the İstanbul Blue Line on ☎ 212-638 2626. Multilingual staff will help you to find a solution.

OLD İSTANBUL

In the Old City, Topkapı Palace is right next to Aya Sofya, which is right next to the Blue Mosque, which is right on the Hippodrome, which is right next to the Sunken Cistern, which is only a few steps from the Archaeology Museum complex, which is right next to Topkapı Palace – phew! You can spend at least two days just completing this loop. Start with the palace, which is among the world's great museums.

Aya Sofya (Sancta Sophia) (Map 7)

The Church of the Divine Wisdom (Sancta Sophia in Latin, Hagia Sofia in Greek, Aya Sofya in Turkish) was not named after a saint, but after holy *(sancta, hagia)* wisdom *(sophia)*. Aya Sofya (☎ 212-522 1750) is open 9.30 am to 4.30 pm (later in summer) daily except Monday; the galleries with their mosaics are open from 9.30 am to 4 pm. Admission is US$5.50; no student discount.

[Continued on page 135]

TOPKAPI PALACE MUSEUM

Topkapı Palace (Topkapı Sarayı) was the residence of the sultans for almost four centuries. Mehmet the Conqueror built the first palace shortly after the Conquest in 1453, and lived here until his death in 1481. Many sultans lived the drama of the Ottoman monarchy here until the 19th century. Mahmut II (1808–39), the last emperor to occupy the palace, was succeeded by sultans who preferred living in new European-style palaces, such as Dolmabahçe and Yıldız, which they built on the Bosphorus.

The Seraglio, as it was known in Europe, was romantically portrayed by Mozart in his opera *The Abduction from the Seraglio*, which is performed in the palace every summer from late June to early July during the International İstanbul Music Festival.

Topkapı (☎ 212-512 0480) is open 9 am to 5 pm (later in summer) daily except Tuesday. The Harem is open 9.30 am to 4 pm. Admission to the palace costs US$6, and an additional US$2.50 to visit the Harem.

Seeing Topkapı requires at least half a day, and preferably more. Head straight for the Harem when you enter; tours are every 30 minutes. In summer the crowds are so thick and the tour groups so numerous that individual travellers sometimes are out of luck.

Court of Processions

Topkapı grew and changed with the centuries, but its basic four-courtyard plan remained the same. The Ottomans followed the Byzantine practice of secluding the monarch from the people: the first court was open to all; the second only to people on imperial business; the third only to the imperial family, important personages and palace staff; and the fourth was the 'family quarters'.

As you pass through the great Imperial Gate behind Aya Sofya, you enter the Alay Meydanı, the Court of Processions (or of the Regiments). On your left is the former **Aya İrini Kilisesi**, or Church of Divine Peace (☎ 212-520 6952), Sarayiçi 35, now a concert hall where recitals are given during the International İstanbul Music Festival.

Buy your tickets before entering the Second Court. The ticket booths are on your right as you approach the Middle Gate.

Ortakapı & Second Court

The Ortakapı (Middle Gate, Gate of Greeting or Bab-üs Selâm) led to the palace's Second Court, used for the business of running the empire. Only the sultan and the *valide sultan* (queen mother) were allowed through the Ortakapı on horseback. Everyone else, including the grand vizier, had to dismount. The gate you see was constructed by Süleyman the Magnificent in 1524, utilising architects and workers he had brought back from his conquest of Hungary.

Inset: Detail of the geometric pattern decorating one of the ceilings in the Topkapı Palace. (photo by Davor Pavichich)

The great **palace kitchens**, on the right-hand (eastern) side, now hold a small portion of Topkapı Palace's vast collection of Chinese celadon porcelain. Beyond the celadon are the collections of fine European and Ottoman porcelain and glassware. The last of the

MAP 6 – TOPKAPI PALACE (TOPKAPI SARAYI)

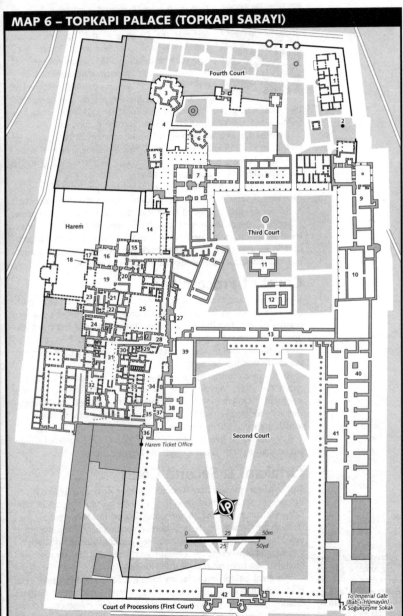

Fourth Court

Third Court

Harem

Second Court

Harem Ticket Office

Court of Processions (First Court)

To Imperial Gate
(Bab-ı Hümayûn)
& Soğukçeşme Sokak

TOPKAPI PALACE (TOPKAPI SARAYI)

SECOND COURT
38 Kubbealtı
   (Divan Salonu)
39 Enderun Hazinesi;
   (Inner Treasury;
   Arms & Armour Display)
40 Helvahane
   (Confectionery Kitchen)
41 Palace Kitchens
   (Porcelain &
   Glass Display)
42 Ortakapı
   (Middle Gate)

THIRD COURT
7 Mukaddes Emanetler
   Dairesi (Sacred
   Safe-keeping Rooms;
   Prophet's Relics)
8 Treasury Barracks
9 Hazine
   (Imperial Treasury)
10 Seferli Koğuşu
11 Library of Ahmet III
12 Arz Odası
   (Audience Chamber)

13 Bab-üs Saade
   (Gate of Felicity)

FOURTH COURT
1 Mecidiye Köşkü;
   Konyalı Restaurant
2 Hayat Balkonu
   (Balcony of Life)
3 Bağdat Köşkü
   (Baghdad Kiosk)
4 Marble Terrace & Pool
5 Sünnet Odası
   (Circumcision Room)
6 Revan Köşkü
   (Erivan Kiosk)

HAREM
14 Favourites' Courtyard
15 Double Kiosk with
   Stained Glass
16 Privy Chamber
   of Murat III
17 Library of Ahmet I
18 Dining Room of Ahmet III
19 Hünkar Sofası
   (Emperor's Chamber)

20 Room with Hearth;
   Room with Fountain
21 Valide Sultan's Hamam
22 Sultan's Hamam
23 Chamber of
   Abdül Hamit I
24 Valide Sultan's Quarters
25 Valide Sultan's Courtyard
26 Altınyol
   (Golden Road)
27 Birdcage Gate
28 Main Gate
29 Chief Black Eunuch's Room
30 Concubines' Corridor
31 Cariye ve Kadınefendi
   Taşlığı (Concubinès' &
   Consorts' Courtyard)
32 Women's Dormitory
33 Black Eunuchs' Dormitory
34 Ağalar Taşlığı
   (Black Eunuchs' Courtyard)
35 Guard Room
36 Carriage Gate
   (Tourist Entrance)
37 Adalet Kulesi
   (Tower of Justice)

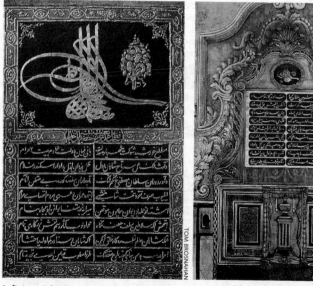

Left: Imperial *tuğra* (signature) on the Middle Gate, leading into the Second Court.
Right: The sound of this water fountain was to prevent people eavesdropping on the sultan.

The Janissaries

The word 'janissary' comes from the Turkish *yeni çeri* (new levies). These soldiers were personal servants of the sultan, 'owned' by him, fed and paid regularly by him, and subject to his will. They were full-time soldiers, an innovation in an age when most soldiers were warriors only in summer.

In a process termed *devşirme*, government agents went out from İstanbul into the towns and villages of the Balkans to round up 10-year-old boys from Christian families for the sultan's personal service. The boy would be instructed in Turkish, converted to Islam, and enrolled in the sultan's service.

The imperial service was a meritocracy. Those of normal intelligence and capabilities went into the Janissary corps, the sultan's imperial guard. The brightest and most capable boys went into the palace service, and many eventually rose to the highest offices, including that of grand vizier. This ensured that the top government posts were always held by personal servants of the sultan.

Topkapı's large Court of Processions, stretching from the church to the Ortakapı, is now a shady park, but in the old days this was where the sultan's elite corps of guards gathered to eat the hearty *pilav* (rice dish) provided by him. When they were dissatisfied with the sultan's rule, they would overturn the great cauldrons of pilav as a symbol of revolt, after which the sultan's hours were numbered.

By the early 19th century, the once-admirable Janissary corps had become unbearably corrupt and self-serving, and a constant threat to the throne. The reforming sultan Mahmut II, risking his life, his throne and his dynasty, readied a new, loyal European-style army; he then provoked a revolt of the Janissaries in the Hippodrome and brought in his new army to wipe them out, ending their 350-year history in 1826.

---

kitchens, the Helvahane in which all the palace sweets were made, is now set up as a kitchen, and you can easily imagine what went on in these rooms as the staff prepared food for the 5000 inhabitants of the palace.

On the left (western) side of the Second Court is the ornate **Kubbealtı** or Imperial Council Chamber, also called the Divan Salonu, beneath the squarish Adalet Kulesi tower which is among the palace's most distinctive architectural features. The Imperial Divan (council) met in the Divan Salonu to discuss matters of state while the sultan eavesdropped through a grill high on the wall.

North of the Kubbealtı in the Guard Room is the *silahlar* (armoury) exhibit of fearsome Ottoman and European weaponry.

Harem

The entrance to the Harem, open by guided tour only, is through the Carriage Gate beneath the Adalet Kulesi (Tower of Justice), the palace's highest point.

Many of the 300-odd rooms in the Harem were constructed during the reign of Süleyman the Magnificent (1520–66), but much more was added or reconstructed over the years. In 1665 a disastrous fire destroyed much of the complex, which was rebuilt by Mehmet IV and later sultans.

Legend vs Reality Fraught with legend and romance, the Harem is usually imagined as a place where the sultan could engage in debauchery at will. In fact, these were the imperial family quarters, and every detail of Harem life was governed by tradition, obligation and ceremony.

Every traditional Muslim household had two distinct parts: the *selamlık* (greeting room) where the master greeted friends, business associates and tradespeople; and the Harem or private apartments, reserved for himself and his family. The Harem, then, was something akin to the private apartments in Buckingham Palace or the White House.

The women of the Harem had to be foreigners, as Islam forbade enslaving Muslims, Christians or Jews (with some exceptions, for example the Janissaries' devşirme). Besides prisoners of war, girls were bought as slaves (often sold by their parents at a good price), or received as gifts from nobles and potentates. A favourite source of girls was Circassia, north of the Caucasus Mountains in Russia, as Circassian women were noted for their beauty, and parents were often glad to give up their 10-year-old girls in exchange for hard cash.

Upon entering the Harem, the girls would be schooled in Islam and Turkish culture and language, the arts of make-up, dress, comportment,

Bottom: The gilded entrance to the Harem, a place steeped in romance and mystery, although the reality was probably a lot more prosaic than many foreigners imagined.

GREG ELMS

Life in the Cage

Imperial princes were brought up in the palace Harem as children, taught and cared for by its women and servants.

In the early centuries of the empire, Ottoman princes were schooled as youths in combat and statecraft by direct experience: they practised soldiering, fought in battles and were given provinces to administer. But as the Ottoman dynasty did not observe primogeniture (succession of the first-born), the death of the sultan regularly resulted in a fratricidal blood bath as his sons battled it out among themselves for the throne. In the case of Beyazıt II, his sons began the battles even before the sultan's death, realising that to lose the battle for succession meant death for themselves. The victorious son, Selim, even forced Beyazıt to abdicate, and may even have had him murdered as he went into retirement.

Fratricide was not practised by Ahmet I, who could not bring himself to murder his mad brother Mustafa. Instead, he kept him imprisoned in the Harem, beginning the tradition of *kafes hayatı* (cage life). This house arrest, adopted in place of fratricide by later sultans, meant that princes were prey to the intrigues of the women and eunuchs who ran the Harem, corrupted by the pleasures of the Harem, ignorant of war and statecraft, and thus usually unfit to rule if and when the occasion arose. Luckily for the empire in this latter period, there were able grand viziers to carry on.

In later centuries the dynasty abandoned kafes hayatı and adopted the practice of having the eldest male in the direct line assume the throne.

music, reading and writing, embroidery and dancing. They then entered a meritocracy, first as ladies-in-waiting to the sultan's concubines and children, then to the sultan's mother and finally, if they were the best, to the sultan himself.

Ruling the Harem was the *valide sultan*, the mother of the reigning sultan. She often owned large estates in her own name and controlled them through black eunuch servants (brought from Africa). She was allowed to give orders directly to the grand vizier. Her influence on the sultan, on the selection of his wives and concubines, and on matters of state, was often profound.

The sultan was allowed by Islamic law to have four legitimate wives, who received the title of *kadın* (wife). If a wife bore him a child, she was called *haseki sultan* if it was a son; *haseki kadın* if it was a daughter. The Ottoman dynasty did not observe primogeniture, so in principle the throne was available to any imperial son. Each lady of the Harem contrived mightily to have her son proclaimed heir to the throne, thus assuring her own role and power as the new valide sultan.

As for concubines, Islam permits as many as a man can support in proper style. The Ottoman sultans had the means to support many, sometimes up to 300, though they were not all in the Harem at the same time.

Touring the Harem Although the Harem is built into a hillside and has six levels, the standard tour takes you through or past only a few dozen rooms on one level, but these are among the most splendid. The tour route may vary from time to time as various rooms are closed for restoration, and others are finished and opened to view.

Most Harem tours are given in Turkish and English, with other languages in summer. Plaques in Turkish and English have been placed here and there in the Harem. They're generally more informative than the guide's brief commentary.

Highlights of the tour include the narrow **Ağalar Taşlığı** (Black Eunuchs' Courtyard), decorated in Kütahya tiles from the 17th century; the **Cariye ve Kadınefendi Taşlığı** (Concubines' & Consorts' Courtyard); the **Valide Sultan's Quarters** and **Courtyard**; and the ornate **Hünkar Sofası** (Emperor's Chamber), among the Harem's largest and most splendid rooms, decorated in Delft tiles. Also don't miss the **Privy Chamber of Murat III** (1578), one of the most sumptuous rooms in the palace. Virtually all of the decoration is original, and is probably the work of Sinan. The **Dining Room of Ahmet III** (1706), with wonderful painted panels of flowers and fruit, was built by Ahmet I's successor. In the **Double Kiosk**, two rooms dating from around 1600, note the painted canvas dome in the first room, and the fine tile panels above the fireplace in the second.

Third Court

If you enter the Third Court through the Harem, and thus by the back door, you should head for the main gate into the court. Get the full effect of entering this holy of holies by going out through the gate, and back in again.

This gate, the **Bab-üs Saade**, or Gate of Felicity, also sometimes called the Akağalar Kapısı (Gate of the White Eunuchs), was the entrance into the sultan's private domain. The sultan preserved the imperial mystique by appearing in public very seldom.

During the great days of the empire, foreign ambassadors were received on days when the Janissaries were to get their pay. Huge sacks of silver coins were brought to the Kubbealtı. High-court officers would dispense the coins to long lines of the tough, impeccably costumed and faultlessly disciplined troops as the ambassadors looked on in admiration.

Arz Odası Just inside the Bab-üs Saade is the Arz Odası, or Audience Chamber, constructed in the 16th century but refurbished in the 18th century. Important officials and foreign ambassadors were brought to this little kiosk to conduct the high business of state. Right behind the Arz Odası is the pretty little **Library of Ahmet III** (1718).

Seferli Koğuşu & Hazine Walk to the right as you leave the Arz Odası, and enter the rooms of the Seferli Koğuşu (Dormitory of the Expeditionary Force), which now house the rich collections of imperial robes, kaftans and uniforms (follow the signs for 'Padişah Elbiseleri') worked in thread of silver and gold.

Next along on the same side are the chambers of the Hazine (Imperial Treasury), packed with an incredible number and variety of objects made from or decorated with gold, silver, rubies, emeralds, jade, pearls and diamonds.

The Kaşıkçının Elması, or Spoonmaker's Diamond, is an 86-carat rock surrounded by several dozen smaller stones. First worn by Mehmet IV at his accession to the throne in 1648, it is the world's fifth-largest diamond. There's also an uncut emerald weighing 3.26kg, and the golden dagger set with three large emeralds which was the object of Peter Ustinov's criminal quest in the movie *Topkapi*.

Also be sure to see the gold throne given by Nadir Shah of Persia to Mahmud I (1730–54). Other thrones are almost as breathtaking.

Mukaddes Emanetler Dairesi Opposite the Treasury is another set of wonders, the holy relics in the Hırka-i Saadet, or Suite of the Felicitous Cloak, now called the Mukaddes Emanetler Dairesi (Sacred Safe-keeping Rooms). These rooms, sumptuously decorated with İznik faience, constitute a holy of holies within the palace. Only the chosen could enter the Third Court, but entry into the Hırka-i Saadet rooms was for the chosen of the chosen, and only on ceremonial occasions.

To the right (north) a room contains the cloak of the Prophet Mohammed and other relics. Sometimes an imam is seated here, chanting passages from the Quran. The 'felicitous cloak' itself resides in a golden casket in a special alcove along with the battle standard. During the empire, this suite of rooms was opened only once a year so that the imperial family could pay homage to the memory of the Prophet on the 15th day of the holy month of Ramazan. Although anyone, prince or commoner, faithful or infidel, can enter the rooms now, remember that it is a sacred place.

Fourth Court

Four imperial pleasure domes occupy the north-easternmost part of the palace, sometimes called the gardens, or Fourth Court. The **Mecidiye Köşkü**, built by Abdül Mecit (1839–61), was designed according to 19th-century European models. Beneath it is the Konyalı Restaurant, which fills up by noon. If you want to dine here, arrive by 11.30 am, or after 2 pm.

Up the stairs at the end of the tulip garden are two of the most enchanting kiosks. Sultan Murat IV (1623–40) built the **Revan Köşkü**, or Erivan Kiosk, in 1635 after reclaiming the city of Yerevan (now in Armenia) from Persia. He also constructed the **Bağdat Köşkü**, or Baghdad Kiosk, in 1638 to commemorate his victory over that city. Notice the İznik tiles, the inlay and woodwork, and the views all around.

[Continued from page 126]

Emperor Justinian (AD 527–65) had the church built as yet another effort to restore the greatness of the Roman Empire. It was constructed on the site of Byzantium's acropolis, which had also been the site of an earlier Sancta Sophia destroyed in 532. Justinian's church was completed in 537 and reigned as the greatest church in Christendom until the conquest of Constantinople in 1453. Aya Sofya remained a mosque until 1935, when Atatürk proclaimed it a museum.

Look up as you enter to see a brilliant mosaic of Christ as Pantocrator (Ruler of All) above the third and largest door (the Imperial Door) in the inner narthex. Once through the Imperial Door the magnificent main dome soars above you. Justinian, on entering his great creation for the first time almost 1500 years ago, exclaimed, 'Glory to God that I have been judged worthy of such a work. Oh Solomon! I have outdone you!'.

The sense of air and space in the nave, the 30 million gold *tesserae* (tiles) that covered the dome's interior, and the apparent lack of support for the dome made the Byzantines gasp in amazement. Indeed, it almost was impossible, because the dome lasted only 11 years before an earthquake brought it down in AD 559. Over the centuries it was necessary for succeeding Byzantine emperors and Ottoman sultans to rebuild the dome several times, to add buttresses and other supports and to steady the foundations.

The dome, a daring attempt at the impossible, is supported by 40 massive ribs constructed of special hollow bricks made in Rhodes from a unique light, porous clay, resting on huge pillars concealed in the interior walls. (Compare the Blue Mosque's four huge free-standing pillars to appreciate the genius of Aya Sofya.)

The curious, elevated kiosk, screened from public view, is the **Hünkar Mahfili** or Sultan's Loge. Ahmet III (1703–30) had it

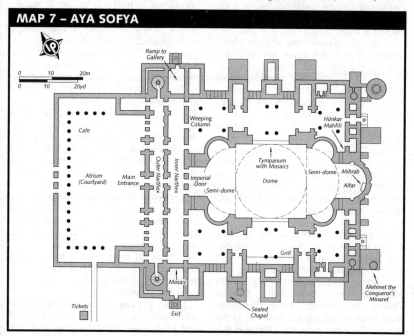

MAP 7 – AYA SOFYA

0 10 20m
0 10 20yd

Ramp to Gallery

Cafe

Weeping Column

Hünkar Mahfili

Atrium (Courtyard)

Main Entrance

Outer Narthex

Inner Narthex

Imperial Door

Tympanum with Mosaics

Semi-dome

Mihrab

Dome

Semi-dome

Altar

Grill

Mosaic

Mehmet the Conqueror's Minaret

Tickets

Exit

Sealed Chapel

built so he could come, pray, and go unseen, preserving the imperial mystique.

In the side aisle to the left of the Imperial Door is the **Weeping Column**, with a copper facing pierced by a hole. Legend has it that those who put their finger in the hole and make a wish will see it come true if the finger emerges moist.

Mosaics Ninth-century mosaic portraits of St Ignatius the Younger (dating from the 800s), St John Chrysostom (around 400) and St Ignatius Theodorus of Antioch are visible high up at the base of the northern tympanum (semicircle) beneath the dome, though obscured by scaffolding at present. Even better mosaics are in the galleries, reached by a switchback ramp at the northern end of the inner narthex.

The striking Deesis (portrayal of Christ between the Virgin Mary and John the Baptist), in the southern gallery (where the best mosaics are found), dates from the early 14th century. Christ is at the centre, with the Virgin Mary on the left, and John the Baptist on the right.

At the eastern (apse) end of the southern gallery is the famous mosaic portrait of the Empress Zoe (1028–50) who had three husbands, and changed this mosaic portrait with each one. The portrait of the third Mr Zoe, Constantine IX Monomachus, remains only because he outlived the empress.

As you leave the narthex and enter the passage to the outside, turn and look up to see the Madonna and Child, one of the church's finest late 10th-century mosaics, above the door. Constantine the Great, on the left, offers Mary the city of Constantinople; Emperor Justinian, on the right, offers her Sancta Sophia.

Baths of Lady Hürrem (Map 5) Every mosque had a *hamam* (public baths) nearby. Aya Sofya's is across the road to the left (east) of Sultanahmet Parkı, the park with the fountain. It's the Baths of Lady Hürrem (Haseki Hürrem Hamamı), built by the great Sinan in 1556 on the site of earlier Byzantine baths, and now fixed up as a government-run carpet gallery and shop, the Turkish Hand-woven Carpets Sale Centre (☎ 212-511 8192). It's open from 9.30 am to 5 pm daily except Tuesday; admission is free.

Designed as a 'double hamam' with identical baths for men and women, the centre wall dividing the two has now been breached by a small doorway. Both sides have the three traditional rooms: first the square frigidarium (cold room) for disrobing (on the men's side, this has a pretty marble fountain and stained-glass windows); then the long tepidarium (warm room) for washing, and finally the octagonal caldarium (hot room) for sweating and massage. In the caldarium, note the four *eyvan* (vaulted halls) and the four semi-private washing rooms. The *göbektaşı* (hot platform) in the men's bath is inlaid with coloured marble.

Blue Mosque (Map 5)

In Byzantine times there was a palace where the Blue Mosque (Sultan Ahmet Camii or Mosque of Sultan Ahmet) now stands. Sultan Ahmet I (1603–17) set out to build a mosque that would rival and even surpass the achievement of Justinian. The Blue Mosque is a triumph of harmony, proportion and elegance, and its architect, Mehmet Ağa, achieves the sort of visual experience on the exterior which Aya Sofya has on the interior.

Go out to the middle of the Hippodrome and approach the mosque from its front. The Blue Mosque is such a popular tourist sight that admission is controlled so as to preserve its sacred atmosphere. Only worshippers are admitted through the main door; tourists enter by the southern door, exit by the northern door, and are not admitted at prayer times .

The layout of the Blue Mosque is classic Ottoman design. The forecourt has an ablutions fountain in its centre. The portico around three sides could be used for prayer, meditation or study during warm weather. The 'blue' of the mosque's name comes from the İznik tiles which line the walls, particularly in the gallery (which is not open to the public).

Inside, you can see immediately why the Blue Mosque, constructed between 1606 and 1616, more than 1000 years after Aya

Sofya, is not as daring as Aya Sofya. Four massive pillars hold up the dome, a less elegant but sturdier solution to the problem.

Note also the imperial box, covered with marble latticework, to the left; the piece of the sacred Black Stone from the Kaaba in Mecca, embedded in the mihrab; the grandfather clock, useful as prayers must be made at exact times; and the high, elaborate *mahfil* (chair) from which the imam, or prayer leader, gives the sermon on Friday. The *mimber*, or pulpit, is the structure with a curtained doorway at floor level, a flight of steps and a small kiosk topped by a spire.

The *türbe* (tomb) of the mosque's great patron, Sultan Ahmet I, is on the northern side facing the fountain park (open daily except Monday and Tuesday from 9.30 am to 4.30 pm). Buried with Ahmet are his brothers, Sultan Osman II, Sultan Murat IV, and other relatives.

Carpet Museum (Map 5) Up the stone ramp on the Blue Mosque's northern side is the Halı Müzesi or Carpet Museum (☎ 212-528 5332), with displays of some of the country's finest. It's open 9 am to 12 noon and 1 to 4 pm Tuesday to Saturday; admission costs US$1.

Great Palace Mosaics Museum (Map 5) When archaeologists from the University of Ankara and St Andrew's University in Scotland dug at the back (east) of the Blue Mosque in the mid-1950s, they uncovered a mosaic pavement dating from early Byzantine times, circa AD 500. The pavement, filled with wonderful hunting and mythological scenes and emperors' portraits, was a triumphal way which led from the Byzantine emperor's Great Palace, which stood where the Blue Mosque now stands, down to the harbour of Boucoleon, south-east of the mosque. The dust and rubble of 1500 years have sunk the pavement considerably below ground level. The pavement is now displayed in the Great Palace Mosaics Museum (Büyüksaray Mozaikleri Müzesi).

Other 5th-century mosaics were saved providentially when Sultan Ahmet had shops built on top of them. The row of

shops, called the **Arasta**, provides rent revenues for the upkeep of the mosque. Now they house numerous souvenir vendors and a small teahouse.

The Great Palace Mosaics Museum, entered from Torun Sokak behind the mosque and the Arasta, is open 9.30 am to 4.30 pm daily except Monday; admission is US$1.50.

The Hippodrome (Map 5)

In front of the Blue Mosque is the Hippodrome (Atmeydanı), where chariot races took place. It was the centre of Byzantium's life for 1000 years and of Ottoman life for another 400, and the scene of countless political and military dramas.

In Byzantine times, the rival chariot teams of 'Greens' and 'Blues' were politically connected. Support for a team was the same as membership in a political party, and a team victory had important effects on policy. A Byzantine emperor might lose his throne as the result of a post-match riot.

Ottoman sultans kept an eye on activities in the Hippodrome. If things were going badly in the empire, a surly crowd gathering here could signal the start of a disturbance, then a riot, then a revolution. In 1826, the slaughter of the debased and unruly Janissary corps was carried out by the reformer sultan, Mahmut II. Almost a century later, in 1909, there were riots here which caused the downfall of Abdül Hamit II and the repromulgation of the Ottoman constitution.

Near the northern end of the Hippodrome, the little gazebo in beautiful stonework is actually **Kaiser Wilhelm's Fountain**. The German emperor paid a state visit to Abdül Hamit II in 1901, and presented this fountain to the sultan and his people as a token of friendship.

The impressive granite obelisk with hieroglyphs is called the **Obelisk of Theodosius**, carved in Egypt around 1500 BC. According to the hieroglyphs, it was erected in Heliopolis in Egypt to commemorate the victories of Thutmose III (1504–1450 BC). The Byzantine emperor, Theodosius, had it brought from Egypt to Constantinople in AD 390.

South of the obelisk is a strange **spiral column** coming up out of a hole in the ground.

İSTANBUL

It was once much taller and was topped by three serpents' heads. Originally cast to commemorate a victory of the Hellenic confederation over the Persians, it stood in front of the temple of Apollo at Delphi from 478 BC until Constantine the Great had it brought to his new capital city around AD 330.

No one is quite sure who built the large **rough-stone obelisk** at the southern end of the Hippodrome. All we know is that it was repaired by Constantine VII Porphyrogenetus (913–59), and that the bronze plates were ripped off during the Fourth Crusade.

Museum of Turkish & Islamic Arts (Map 5)

The Palace of İbrahim Paşa (1524) is on the western side of the Hippodrome. Now housing the Türk ve İslam Eserleri Müzesi, or Museum of Turkish & Islamic Arts (☎ 212-522 1888), it gives you a good glimpse into the opulent life of the Ottoman upper class in the time of Süleyman the Magnificent. İbrahim Paşa was Süleyman's close friend, son-in-law and grand vizier.

The museum is open from 9 am to 5 pm daily except Monday, and admission costs US$2.50. Labels are in Turkish and English.

Highlights among the exhibits, which date from the 8th and 9th centuries up to the 19th century, are the decorated wooden Quran cases from the high Ottoman period; the calligraphy exhibits, including *fermans* (imperial proclamations) with *tuğras* (imperial signatures), Turkish miniatures, and illuminated manuscripts. You'll also want to have a look at the *rahles*, or Quran stands, and the many carpets from all periods. The lower floor of the museum houses ethnographic exhibits.

South of the Hippodrome (Map 5)

Take a detour into the district's back streets for a look at a feat of Byzantine engineering and two exquisite small mosques.

Facing south, with the Blue Mosque on your left, go to the end of the Hippodrome and turn left, then right, onto Aksakal Sokak. Soon you'll see the filled-in arches of the **Sphendoneh**, a feat of Byzantine engineering, on your right. The Sphendoneh supported the southern end of the Hippodrome.

Follow the curve of the street around to the right and onto Kaleci Sokak. The next intersecting street is Şehit Mehmet Paşa Sokak; turn left to the **Küçük Aya Sofya Camii**, or 'Little' Aya Sofya.

Justinian and Theodora built this church sometime between AD 527 and 536. Inside, the layout and decor are typical of an early Byzantine church, though the building was repaired and expanded several times during its life as a mosque after the Conquest.

Go north on Şehit Mehmet Paşa Sokak, back up the hill to the neighbouring **Sokollu Mehmet Paşa Camii**. This was built during the height of Ottoman architectural development in 1571 by the empire's greatest architect, Sinan.

Walk back up the hill on Suterazisi Sokak to return to the Hippodrome.

South-east of the Blue Mosque near the shore is the **Hamamizade İsmail Dede Efendi Evi Müzesi** (☎ 212-516 4314), Akbıyık, Ahırkapı Sokak 17, the restored house of Dede Efendi (1778–1846) a famous Ottoman musical composer of the Mevlevi whirling dervish order. The well-restored house gives you a good idea of living conditions among the Ottoman intelligentsia of the 18th and 19th centuries.

Sunken Cistern (Map 5)

At the northern side of Divan Yolu is a little park with a stone pillar rising from it. The pillar is part of an ancient aqueduct. Beneath the park, entered by a doorway on its northern side (on Yerebatan Caddesi), is the Sunken Cistern (Yerebatan Sarnıçı) or Sunken Palace (☎ 212-522 1259). The cistern is open 9 am to 4.30 pm (5.30 pm in summer) daily and admission costs US$3.50 or US$3 for students. The exit is through a gift shop onto Alemdar Caddesi.

Built in AD 532 the Sunken or Basilica Cistern is the largest surviving Byzantine cistern in İstanbul. In fact it's not a basilica at all, but an enormous water storage tank constructed by Emperor Justinian (527–65), who was incapable of thinking in small terms. Columns, capitals and plinths from ruined buildings were among those used in its construction.

The cistern is 70m wide and 140m long and its roof is supported by 336 columns. Two columns in the north-western corner are supported by two blocks carved into Medusa heads. The cistern was used to support part of the city during lengthy sieges. The water was pumped and delivered through nearly 20km of aqueducts from a reservoir near the Black Sea.

The cistern once held 80,000 cubic metres of water but it became a dumping ground for all sorts of junk, as well as corpses. Since it was built the cistern has undergone a number of facelifts, most notably in the 18th century and then between 1955 and 1960. In the 1980s the cistern was cleaned and renovated by the İstanbul Municipality.

Water still drips through the ceiling and you can see coloured lights, listen to recorded Western classical music (Mozart, Vivaldi), wander along a maze of walkways and spot carp in the water.

Gülhane Parkı & Sublime Porte (Map 5)

Walk downhill from the Sunken Cistern along Alemdar Caddesi with Aya Sofya on your right. Just past a big tree in the middle of the road, the street turns left, but just in front of you is the arched gateway to Gülhane Parkı.

Before entering the park, look to the left. That bulbous little kiosk built into the park walls at the next street corner is the **Alay Köşkü**, or Parade Kiosk, from which the sultan would watch the periodic parades of troops and trade guilds which commemorated great holidays and military victories.

Across the street from the Alay Köşkü (not quite visible right from the Gülhane gate) is a gate leading into the precincts of what was once the grand vizierate, or Ottoman prime ministry, known in the West as the Sublime Porte. Today the buildings beyond the gate hold various offices of the İstanbul *vilayeti* (provincial government).

Gülhane Parkı was once the palace park of Topkapı. The over-urbanised crowds pack it at weekends to enjoy its green shade,

The Sublime Porte

In Islamic societies, and in other societies with strong clan roots, it was customary for the chief or ruler to adjudicate disputes and grant favours. Petitioners wishing justice or favours would appear at the door of the chief's tent, house or palace, and await the chance to protest their claims.

When a Western ambassador arrived at the sultan's door or 'porte' he was looked on as just another petitioner asking favours. In response to an embassy, the sultan would often issue a proclamation which began with the words, 'The ambassador of [country] having come to my sublime porte...' Thus the term 'Sublime Porte' was adopted by European embassies to mean the Ottoman state as personified by the sultan in his palace.

In later centuries, when the grand vizier was the active head of government, ambassadors reported not to the palace but to the grand vizierate, and the term Sublime Porte (or simply 'the Porte') came to mean not the sultan's door but the grand vizierate as functioning head of the Ottoman government.

its small zoo, live music, street food and the musty **Tanzimat Müzesi** (☎ 212-512 6384), open from 9 am to 5 pm daily. 'Tanzimat' (Reorganisation) was the name given to the political and societal reforms planned by Sultan Abdül Mecit in 1839 and carried out through the middle of the 19th century.

İstanbul Archaeology Museums (Map 5)

İstanbul's Archaeology Museums (Arkeoloji Müzeleri, ☎ 212-520 7740), between Gülhane Parkı and Topkapı Palace, can be reached by walking up from Gülhane or down from Topkapı's First Court. Admission to the complex is 9 am to 4.30 pm Tuesday to Sunday for US$4.

The **İstanbul Archaeology Museum** (Arkeoloji Müzesi) houses an extensive collection of Hellenic, Hellenistic and Roman statuary and sarcophagi.

The **Tiled Kiosk** (Çinili Köşk) of Mehmet the Conqueror (Mehmet Fatih) is the oldest surviving nonreligious Turkish building in İstanbul, constructed in 1472 not long after the Conquest. The kiosk, once an imperial residence, now houses an excellent collection of Turkish faience including many good examples of İznik tiles from the 17th and 18th centuries.

The **Museum of the Ancient Orient** (Eski Şark Eserler Müzesi) holds the gates of ancient Babylon in the time of Nebuchadnezzar II (604–562 BC), clay tablets bearing Hammurabi's famous law code (in cuneiform, of course), ancient Egyptian scarabs, and artefacts from the Assyrian and Hittite empires, but it's closed for renovations.

Divan Yolu (Map 5)

Divan Yolu, the Road to the Imperial Council, is the main thoroughfare of the Old City. It was laid out by Roman engineers to connect the city with the Roman roads heading west. The **Milion**, the great marble milestone from which all distances in Byzantium were measured, is on the southern side of the tall shaft of stones which rises above the Sunken Cistern.

Start from Aya Sofya and the Hippodrome and go up the slope on Divan Yolu. The impressive enclosure on the corner of Babıali Caddesi is filled with **tombs** of the Ottoman high and mighty, including several sultans. The tombs are usually open for visits from 10 am to 5 pm daily (donation requested).

Directly across Divan Yolu from the tombs is a small stone **library** built by the prominent Köprülü family in 1659.

On the corner of Türbedar Sokak is the **Basın Müzesi** (Press Museum), Divan Yolu 84, open from 10 am to 5.30 pm Monday to Saturday. Admission is free. The old printing presses will interest some, the lively Müze Café will interest more.

Stroll a bit further along Divan Yolu. On the left, the curious tomb with wrought-iron grille on top is that of Köprülü Mehmet Paşa (1575–1661). Across the street, that strange building with a row of streetfront shops is actually an ancient Turkish bath, the **Çemberlitaş Hamamı** (1584). For admission times and prices, see Hamams under Entertainment later in this chapter.

The derelict, time-worn column rising from a little plaza is one of İstanbul's most ancient and revered monuments. Called **Çemberlitaş** (Banded Stone or Burnt Column), it was erected by Constantine the Great (AD 324–37) to celebrate the dedication of Constantinople as capital of the Roman Empire in 330. This area was the grand Forum of Constantine, and the column was topped by a statue of the great emperor himself.

Beyond Çemberlitaş along Divan Yolu, on the right (northern) side is the cemetery of the Çorlulu Ali Paşa Medresesi. Past the impressive tomb of Grand Vizier Koca Sinan Paşa and to the right is the İlesam Lokalı, a club formed by the enigmatically named Professional Union of Owners of the Works of Science and Literature. Touted as a 'traditional mystic water pipe and tea garden', it almost lives up to its billing. Tables and chairs are set out in the shady cemetery, and there are low benches covered with kilims in the medrese courtyard. Try a nargileh (water pipe, US$1) or a glass of tea or cup of coffee.

Just on the other side of Bileyciler Sokak from İlesam Lokalı is a similar place, Erenler Nargile Salonu, in the courtyard of the Çorlulu Ali Paşa Medresesi and to the right. Most of the other people in this lofty mausoleum-like structure will either be absorbed in studying the racing line-up or watching a horse race on television.

Kapalı Çarşı (Map 8)

İstanbul's Kapalı Çarşı (Grand Bazaar or Covered Market) comprises 4000 shops, mosques, banks, police stations, restaurants and workshops lining kilometres of streets. It's open 8.30 am to 6.30 pm daily except Sunday. Today the main streets are touristy, with touts badgering bus tour groups, but many of the back streets and *hans* (caravanserais) still serve a local clientele as they have for centuries. Guard your bag and wallet here as purse-snatchers and bag- and pocket-slashers are not unknown, especially in the midst of crowds.

Though tourist shops now crowd the bazaar, it is still a place where an İstanbullu, a citizen of İstanbul, may come to buy a few metres of printed cloth, a gold bangle for a daughter's birthday gift, an antique carpet or a fluffy sheepskin.

Turn right off Yeniçeriler Caddesi (the continuation of Divan Yolu) just past the Çemberlitaş and walk down Vezir Hanı Caddesi to the big **Nuruosmaniye Camii** built in Ottoman Baroque style between 1748 and 1755 by Mahmut I and his successor Osman III. Though meant to exhibit the sultans' 'modern' taste, the Nuruosmaniye Camii (Light of Osman Mosque) has surprisingly strong echoes of Aya Sofya.

Out the other side of the courtyard, you're standing in Çarşıkapı Sokak before the Çarşıkapı (Bazaar Gate), its gold-toned Ottoman armorial emblem restored in 1998.

Enter the gate to **Kalpakçılarbaşı Caddesi**, the bazaar's main east-west street.

At the centre of the bazaar is the Cevahir Bedesteni (Jewellery Warehouse; signs read 'Old Bazaar'), the original core of the bazaar dating from the 15th century, which can be closed off with its own set of doors. Shops here hold the best of the bazaar's antiques, old coins and jewellery, and silver new and old. The atmospheric **Zincirli Han**

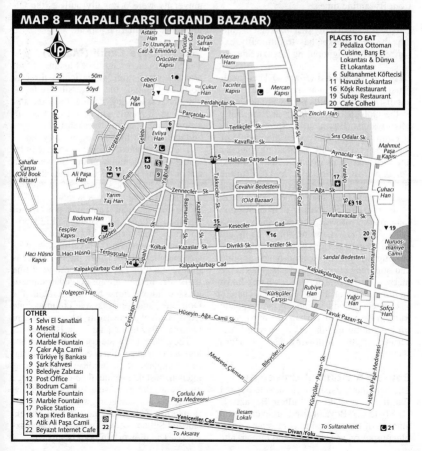

MAP 8 – KAPALI ÇARŞI (GRAND BAZAAR)

PLACES TO EAT
2 Pedaliza Ottoman Cuisine, Barış Et Lokantası & Dünya Et Lokantası
6 Sultanahmet Köftecisi
11 Havuzlu Lokantası
16 Köşk Restaurant
19 Subaşı Restaurant
20 Cafe Colheti

OTHER
1 Selvi El Sanatları
3 Mescit
4 Oriental Kiosk
5 Marble Fountain
7 Çakır Ağa Camii
8 Türkiye İş Bankası
9 Şark Kahvesi
10 Belediye Zabıtası
12 Post Office
13 Bodrum Camii
14 Marble Fountain
15 Marble Fountain
17 Police Station
18 Yapı Kredi Bankası
21 Atik Ali Paşa Camii
22 Beyazıt Internet Cafe

at the far (northern) end of Açiçeşme Sokak, on the right, holds workshops where custom jewellery is made.

Sahaflar Çarşısı (Map 8) Exit the bazaar by walking to the western end of Kalpakçılarbaşı Caddesi. Once outside, turn right onto Çadırcılar Caddesi, then left through a doorway and you'll enter the Sahaflar Çarşısı, or Old Book Bazaar. Go up the steps and along to the shady little courtyard. Actually, the wares in the shops are both new and old; mostly new, though, and mostly in Turkish. The book bazaar dates from Byzantine times.

Out the northern gate of the Sahaflar Çarşısı is a small daily flea market. On Sunday the flea market has traditionally expanded to fill neighbouring Beyazıt Square.

Uzunçarşı Caddesi (Map 4) The Kapalı Çarşı is the southern anchor of a vast market district which spills northward downhill to the Golden Horn, ending at Eminönü's Mısır Çarşısı (Egyptian, or Spice, Bazaar).

From the Şark Kahvesi in the middle of the Kapalı Çarşı, walk north along Yağcılar and Örücüler Kapısı (Gate of the Darners) Sokak, across Çakmakçılar Yokuşu (to the right) and Mercan Caddesi (to the left), and continue on Uzunçarşı Caddesi.

'Longmarket St' lives up to its name: one long market of woodturners' shops, bakeries for *simits* (sesame-sprinkled bread rings), stores selling luggage, guns and hunting equipment, second-hand clothing and hundreds of other products. This is the market district of Tahtakale, where almost anything, legal or illegal, can be purchased.

Uzunçarşı Caddesi ends at the exquisite **Rüstem Paşa Camii**, perhaps the most beautiful small mosque in the city, which is described in the following Golden Horn section.

Beyazıt & İstanbul University

The Sahaflar Çarşısı is right next to **Beyazıt Camii** or Mosque of Sultan Beyazıt II (1481–1512). Beyazıt used an exceptional amount of fine stone in his mosque – marble, porphyry, verd antique and rare granite – which he built in 1501–06. The mihrab is simple except for the rich stone columns framing it.

The main street here, which started out as Divan Yolu, is now called Yeniçeriler Caddesi. It runs past Beyazıt Square, officially called Hürriyet Meydanı (Freedom Square), though everyone knows it simply as Beyazıt. Under the Byzantines, this was the largest of the city's many forums, the **Forum of Theodosius**, built by that emperor in AD 393.

The square is backed by the impressive portal of İstanbul University. The grand gates, main building and tall tower of the university were originally built as the Ottoman War Ministry, which explains their grandiose and martial aspect.

Süleymaniye Camii (Map 4)

The Süleymaniye Camii, or Mosque of Sultan Süleyman the Magnificent, directly north of (behind) the university, is İstanbul's largest mosque. Facing the university portal in Beyazıt, go to the left along Takvimhane Caddesi to reach the mosque and its tombs, which are open every day.

The Süleymaniye Camii crowns one of İstanbul's hills, dominating the Golden Horn and providing a magnificent landmark for the entire city. This, the grandest of all Turkish mosques, was built between 1550 and 1557 by the greatest, richest and most powerful of Ottoman sultans, Süleyman I (1520–66), known as Süleyman the Magnificent.

Inside, the mosque is breathtaking in its size and pleasing in its simplicity. There is little decoration except for some very fine İznik tiles in the mihrab, gorgeous stained-glass windows done by one İbrahim the Drunkard, and four massive columns, one from Baalbek, one from Alexandria and two from Byzantine palaces in İstanbul.

The *külliye* (mosque complex) of the Süleymaniye is particularly elaborate, with the full complement of public services: soup kitchen, hostel, hospital, theological college etc. Near the south-eastern wall of the mosque is the cemetery, with the *türbeler* (tombs) of Süleyman and his wife Haseki Hürrem Sultan (known in the West as Roxelana). The tilework in both is superb.

Bozdoğan Kemeri (Map 4)

Walk along Süleymaniye Caddesi, which goes south-west from the mosque, and turn right onto Şehzadebaşı Caddesi. You can see remnants of the high Bozdoğan Kemeri, or Aqueduct of Valens, on the left side of the street. It's not really certain that the aqueduct was constructed by the Emperor Valens (AD 364–78), though we do know it was repaired in 1019, and in later times by several sultans. After the reign of Süleyman the Magnificent, parts of it collapsed, but restoration work was begun in the late 1980s.

THE GOLDEN HORN

The Golden Horn (Haliç), is İstanbul's historic harbour, shipyard and waterway. Bordered by forests, fields and palaces in the 18th century, by the mid-20th century it had become a poisonous sewer of industrial waste, lined with dilapidated warehouses.

An ambitious program of beautification was carried out during the 1980s, but the waterway still puts out a powerful stench.

Many of the districts along the Golden Horn are heavy with history. Eminönü, with its Mısır Çarşısı, New Mosque and Galata Bridge, was the main customs entry point and market throughout Byzantine and Ottoman times. The view of the Galata Bridge, crowded with ferries and dominated by the Yeni Cami (New Mosque), also called the Pigeon Mosque because of the ever-present flocks of these birds, is a favourite. Fener (Phanar), to the north-west, is the seat of the Ecumenical Orthodox Patriarchate, and was once home to many wealthy and powerful Ottoman Greeks. Balat and Hasköy were once populated heavily by Jews. Between Balat and Fener stands one of the city's most intriguing architectural curiosities: the Bulgarian Church of St Stephen, constructed completely of cast iron.

A limited ferry service (US$0.50) still operates on the Golden Horn between Eminönü and Eyüp stopping at Balat, Fener and Kasımpaşa, and boatmen still ferry passengers from one side to the other as they have done for centuries, but bus and taxi transport has taken much of the trade from these more leisurely forms of transport.

Galata Bridge (Map 4)

In Byzantine times the Golden Horn provided a perfect natural harbour for the city's commerce. Suppliers of fresh vegetables and fruits, grain and staple goods set up shop in the harbour. With the drive to clean up and beautify the Golden Horn, the wholesale markets have been moved to the outskirts of the city.

Still picturesque and interesting is the retail market district which surrounds the Mısır Çarşısı. But before wandering into this maze of market streets, take a look inside the Yeni Cami.

Yeni Cami (Map 4)

Only in İstanbul would a 400-year-old mosque be called 'New'. The Yeni Cami (New Mosque) was begun in 1597, commissioned by Valide Sultan Safiye, mother of Sultan Mehmet III (1595–1603). In plan, the Yeni Cami is much like the Blue Mosque and the Süleymaniye Camii, with a large forecourt and a square sanctuary surmounted by a series of semi-domes crowned by a grand dome. The interior is richly decorated with gold, coloured tiles and carved marble.

Mısır Çarşısı (Map 4)

The Mısır Çarşısı (Egyptian Bazaar) is also called the Spice Bazaar because of its many spice shops. A century or two ago, its merchants sold such things as cinnamon, gunpowder, rabbit fat, pine gum, peach-pit powder, sesame seeds, sarsaparilla root, aloe, saffron, liquorice root, donkey's milk and parsley seeds, all to be used as folk remedies.

The market was constructed in the 1660s as part of the Yeni Cami complex, the rents from the shops going to support the mosque's upkeep and charitable activities. These included a school, baths, hospital and fountains.

The market is open 8.30 am to 6.30 pm Monday to Saturday. Enter the market through the big armoured doors which open onto Eminönü Square.

The number of shops selling tourist trinkets is increasing annually, though there are still some shops that sell *baharat* (spices) and even a few that specialise in the old-time

Maşallah

In İstanbul's Mısır Çarşısı you may see a shop which specialises in the white outfits boys wear on the day (usually Sunday) of their circumcision (sünnet). The white satin suit is supplemented with a spangled hat and red satin sash emblazoned with the word Maşallah (What wonders God has willed!).

Circumcision, or the surgical removal of the foreskin on the penis, is performed on a Turkish Muslim boy when he is between eight and 10 years old, and marks his formal admission into the faith, similar to confirmation in Christianity and Bar Mitzvah in Judaism.

On the day of the operation the boy is dressed in the special suit, visits relatives and friends, and leads a parade – formerly on horseback, now in cars – around his neighbourhood or city attended by musicians and merrymakers. You may come across these lads while visiting the Eyüp Sultan Camii (Map 2), one of Islam's holiest places, where they often stop on the way to their circumcision.

The simple operation, performed in a hospital or clinic in the afternoon, is followed by a celebration with music and feasting. The newly circumcised lad attends, resting in a bed, as his friends and relatives bring him gifts and congratulate him on having entered manhood.

remedies. Some of the hottest items are bee pollen and royal jelly, used to restore virility. You'll also see shops selling nuts, candied fruits, chocolate and other snacks.

When you come to the crossroads within the market, turn right and exit through another set of armoured doors. Go straight along **Hasırcılar Caddesi**, Mat Makers Street, past shops selling fresh fruits, spices, nuts, condiments, cutlery, coffee, tea, cocoa, hardware and similar retail necessities. The colours, smells, sights and sounds make this one of the liveliest and most interesting streets in the city.

Rüstem Paşa Camii (Map 4)

A few short blocks along Hasırcılar Caddesi is the Rüstem Paşa Camii. It's easy to miss as it is not at street level: look for a stone doorway and a flight of steps leading up; there is also a small marble fountain and plaque.

At the top of the steps is a terrace and the mosque's colonnaded porch. You'll notice at once the panels of İznik faience set into the mosque's facade. This beautiful mosque was built by Sinan for Rüstem Paşa, son-in-law and grand vizier of Süleyman the Magnificent. Ottoman power, glory, architecture and tilework were all at their zenith when the mosque was built in 1561.

WESTERN DISTRICTS

There are several points of interest further west, and if you have at least four days to tour İstanbul you should be able to see all the centre's essential sights and still have time for these outlying ones.

Fatih Camii (Map 2)

The Fatih Camii or Mosque of the Conqueror is 750m north-west of the Aqueduct of Valens (Bozdoğan Kemeri), on Fevzi Paşa Caddesi. Catch a dolmuş from Aksaray or Taksim to the city hall (ask for the belediye sarayı) near the aqueduct and walk five blocks; or you can catch any bus or dolmuş to Fatih or Edirnekapı.

The Fatih Camii was the first great imperial mosque to be built in İstanbul following the Conquest. The mosque complex, finished in 1470, was enormous, set in extensive grounds, and including 15 charitable establishments – religious schools, a hospice for travellers, a caravanserai etc. The mosque you see, however, is not the one he built. The present mosque dates from the reign of Abdül Hamit I, and is on a completely different plan.

Chora Church (Map 2)

The Church of the Holy Saviour in the Country was enclosed within the city walls in AD 413, about 80 years after it was built. For four centuries it served as a mosque (Kariye Camii), and is now a museum, the **Kariye Müzesi** (☎ 212-523 3009). It is open from 9 am to 4 pm daily except Wednesday; admission costs US$3. You reach it by taking any Edirnekapı bus along Fevzi Paşa Caddesi.

Beyond the major highlights such as Aya Sofya (bottom left), İstanbul offers a fascinating variety of architectural sights (top left and bottom right) as well as unrivalled opportunities for people watching (top right and middle right).

OLIVIER CIRENDINI

İZZET KERİBAR

CHRIS MELLOR

ANDERS BLOMQVIST

STUART WASSERMAN

Europe ends and Asia begins at the Bosphorus, the narrow strait connecting the Black Sea and the Sea of Marmara. Until 30 years ago crossing it always meant going by boat, except for the occasions when it froze solid. Now there are two bridges, the Bosphorus and Fatih, and a third is planned.

The building you see was built in the late 11th century. Virtually all of the interior decoration – the famous mosaics and the less renowned, but equally striking, mural paintings – dates from about 1320.

The mosaics are breathtaking. The first ones are those of the dedication, to Christ and to the Virgin Mary. Then come the offertory ones: Theodore Metochites, builder of the church, offering it to Christ. The two small domes of the inner narthex have portraits of all Christ's ancestors back to Adam. A series outlines the Virgin Mary's life, and another, Christ's early years. Yet another series concentrates on Christ's ministry. Various saints and martyrs fill the interstices.

In the nave are three mosaics: of Christ, of the Virgin as Teacher, and of the Dormition (Assumption) of the Blessed Virgin.

South of the nave is the parecclesion, a side chapel built to hold the tombs of the church's founder and his relatives, close friends and associates.

Tekfur Sarayı (Map 2)

From Kariye, head west to the city walls, then north again, and you'll soon come to the Palace of Constantine Porphyrogenetus, the Tekfur Sarayı. It's nominally open 9 am to 5 pm Wednesday, Thursday and Sunday, but you can usually just wander in on any day.

Though the building is only a shell these days, it is remarkably well preserved for a Byzantine palace built in the 14th century.

The City Walls (Map 2)

Since being built in the 5th century, the city walls have been breached by hostile forces only twice. The first time was in the 13th century, when Byzantium's 'allies', the armies of the Fourth Crusade, broke through and pillaged the town, deposing the emperor and setting up a king of their own. The second time was in 1453 under Mehmet the Conqueror. Even though Mehmet was ultimately successful, he was continually frustrated during the siege as the walls withstood admirably even the heaviest bombardments by the largest cannon in existence at the time.

Heading north, you can make your way on foot to the Golden Horn at Balat or Ay-

vansaray and then take a bus, dolmuş or ferry to Eyüp. Otherwise, return to the Kariye Müzesi and make your way through the maze of streets to the Fethiye Camii, built as a Byzantine church.

To walk to the **Fethiye Camii** from the Kariye Müzesi (eight to 10 minutes), walk back towards Fevzi Paşa Caddesi, but just past the Kariye Oteli turn left downhill on Neşler Sokak, then left at the bottom of the hill around a little mosque, then straight on along a level street and uphill on Fethiye Caddesi. At the top of the slope most traffic goes right, but you go left towards the mosque, which is visible from this point.

BEYOĞLU (MAP 3)

Beyoğlu is fascinating because it holds the architectural evidence of the Ottoman Empire's frantic attempts to modernise and reform itself, and the evidence of the European powers' attempts to undermine and subvert it.

New ideas walked into Ottoman daily life down the streets of Pera which, with Galata, makes up Beyoğlu. The Europeans, who lived in Pera, brought new fashions, machines, arts and manners, and rules for the diplomatic game. The Old City across the Golden Horn was content to sit tight and continue living in the Middle Ages with its oriental bazaars, great mosques and palaces, narrow streets and traditional values. But Pera was to have telephones, underground trains, tramways, electric light and modern municipal government. The sultans followed Pera's lead. From the reign of Abdül Mecit (1839–61) onwards, no sultan lived in Mehmet the Conqueror's palace at Topkapı. Rather, they built opulent European-style palaces along the shores of the Bosphorus to the north.

The easiest way to tour Beyoğlu is to start from its busy nerve-centre: Taksim Square. You can get a dolmuş directly to Taksim from Aksaray; there are buses from Eminönü as well.

History

Sometimes called the New City, Beyoğlu is 'new' only in a relative sense. There was a settlement on the northern shore of the Golden Horn, near Karaköy Square, before the birth of Jesus. By the time of Theodosius II (AD 408–50), it was large enough to become an official suburb of Constantinople. Theodosius built a fortress here, no doubt to complete the defence system of his great land walls, and called it Galata, as the suburb was then the home of many Galatians.

The word 'new' actually applies more to Pera, the quarter above Galata, running along the crest of the hill from the Galata Tower to Taksim Square. This was built up only in later Ottoman times.

Taksim Square (Map 3)

'Taksim' could mean 'my taxi' in Turkish, but it doesn't; after a look at the square, you may wonder why not. Rather, it is named after the *taksim* (distribution point) in the city's water-conduit system.

The first thing you'll notice in the elongated 'square' is the **Atatürk Kültür Merkezi**, or Atatürk Cultural Centre, the large building at the eastern end. In the summer months, during the International İstanbul Festival, tickets for the various concerts are on sale in the ticket kiosks here.

At the opposite end of the square, at the centre of the İstiklal Caddesi tram's turnaround, is the **Cumhuriyet Anıtı** (Republic Monument), the work of the Italian sculptor Canonica, finished in 1928. Atatürk, his assistant and successor İsmet İnönü, and other revolutionary leaders appear prominently.

To the south of the square is the luxury Hotel The Marmara. To the north is the **Taksim Gezi Yeri**, Taksim Park or Promenade, with the Ceylan Inter-Continental Hotel (Map 2) at its northern end.

North of Taksim (Map 2)

From the roundabout, Cumhuriyet Caddesi (Republic Ave) leads north past streetside cafes and restaurants, banks, travel agencies, airline offices, nightclubs and the Divan and İstanbul Hilton hotels to the districts of Harbiye, Nişantaşı and Şişli.

About 1km north of Taksim, in Harbiye, is the **Askeri Müze** (Military Museum; ☎ 212-248 7115), open 9 am to 5 pm Wednesday to Sunday; admission costs US$1, less for students, US$1.75 for a camera, US$3.50 for a video camera. The daily concert by the Mehter, the medieval Ottoman Military Band, starts at 3 and 4 pm. To reach the museum, walk north out of Taksim Square along the eastern side of Cumhuriyet Caddesi (by Taksim Park) and up past the İstanbul Hilton Hotel. When you come to Harbiye, the point where Valikonağı Caddesi bears right off Cumhuriyet Caddesi, you'll see the gate to the Military Museum on your right.

The new section has fascinating displays of Ottoman tents, imperial pavilions, and a room devoted to Atatürk who was, of course, a famous Ottoman general before he became founder and commander-in-chief of the Turkish republican army, and first president of the Turkish Republic.

The old section is where you really feel the spirit of the Ottoman Empire. It has exhibits of armour (including cavalry), uniforms and field furniture made out of weapons (such as chairs with rifles for legs).

Dolmabahçe Palace (Map 1)

For centuries the *padişah*, the Ottoman sultan, had been the envy of other monarchs. Cultured, urbane, sensitive, courageous; controller of vast territories, great wealth and invincible armies and navies, he was the Grand Turk. The principalities, city-states and kingdoms of Europe, Africa and the Near East stood in fear of a Turkish conquest. Indeed, the Turks conquered all of North Africa, parts of southern Italy, and eastern Europe to the gates of Vienna. The opulent Dolmabahçe Palace might be seen as an apt expression of this Ottoman glory – but it's not.

History Dolmabahçe was built between 1843 and 1856, when the homeland of the once-mighty padişah had become the 'Sick Man of Europe'. His many peoples, aroused by a wave of European-inspired ethnic nationalism, were in revolt; his wealth was mostly mortgaged to, or under the control of, European bankers; his armies, while still considerable, were obsolescent and disorganised. The Western, European, Christian way of life was everywhere ascendant over the Eastern, Asian, Muslim one. Attempting to turn the tide, 19th-century sultans turned to European models, modernising the army and civil service, granting autonomy to subject peoples, and adopting – sometimes wholesale – European ways.

The name Dolmabahçe, 'filled-in garden', dates from the reign of Sultan Ahmet I (1607–17), when a little cove here was filled in and an imperial pleasure kiosk built on it. Other wooden buildings followed, but all burned to the ground in 1814. Sultan Abdül Mecit, whose favourite architects were scions of an Armenian family named Balyan, wanted a 'European-style' marble palace. What he got is partly European, partly oriental, and certainly sumptuous and overdecorated.

Admission & Tours The palace is divided into two *bölüm* (sections), the **Selamlık** (Ceremonial Suites) and the **Harem-Cariyeler** (Harem & Concubines' Quarters). You must take a guided tour, which lasts about an hour, to see either section. Only 1500 people are allowed into each section each day, so it's not a bad idea to reserve your space on a tour in advance. The palace (☎ 212-227 3441) is open from 9 am to 4 pm daily except Monday and Thursday (though the gardens are open for free on those days). Entrance to the Selamlık costs US$8, to the Harem and Cariyeler the same; a ticket good for both sections costs US$14. The charge for a camera is US$8 and US$16 for a video camera. Thus, for a couple with a camera and video to see the entire palace costs a hefty US$52. You may choose to check your camera at the door as the palace interior is dark and difficult to photograph even with fast film, and flash and tripod are not allowed. Rather, take your photos from the small garden near the clock tower, or the park on the southern side of the mosque.

The tourist entrance to the palace is near the ornate clock tower, north of the mosque.

Touring the Palace The tours pass through opulent public and private rooms, into a harem with steel doors, past numerous

Sèvres vases and Bohemian chandeliers, and up a staircase with a crystal balustrade. The magnificent throne room, used in 1877 for the first meeting of the Ottoman Chamber of Deputies, has a chandelier that weighs more than 4000kg.

Don't set your watch by any of the palace clocks, all of which are stopped at 9.05 am, the moment at which Kemal Atatürk died in Dolmabahçe on 10 November 1938. You will be shown the small bedroom which he used during his last days.

When you've finished at the palace, turn right (north) and walk to the suburb of **Beşiktaş**, sometimes called Barbaros Hayrettin Paşa, to visit the Deniz Müzesi.

İstiklal Caddesi (Map 3)

To the south-west of Taksim, two streets meet before entering the square. Sıraselviler Caddesi goes south and İstiklal Caddesi goes south-west. The famous **taksim**, a small octagonal stone building, is to the south-west of the Republic Monument, just to the right of İstiklal Caddesi.

Nestled in the small triangle formed by the two mentioned streets, rising above the shops and restaurants which hide its foundations, is the **Aya Triada Kilisesi**, or Greek Orthodox Church of the Holy Trinity. If it's open, as it is daily for services, you can visit. Walk along İstiklal Caddesi and turn left.

Now head down İstiklal Caddesi for a look at the vestiges of 19th-century Ottoman life. Stretching between Taksim Square and Tünel Square, İstiklal Caddesi (Independence Ave) was formerly the Grande Rue de Péra. It was the street with all the smart shops, several large embassies and churches, many impressive residential buildings and a scattering of tea shops and restaurants. It's now a pedestrian way, which in Turkey means that there are fewer cars, not no cars. The restored turn-of-the-century tram runs from Taksim via Galatasaray to Tünel for US$0.35. It's fun, but sometimes crowded.

Just out of Taksim Square, the first building on the right is the former French plague hospital (1719), for years used as the **French consulate general** in İstanbul. There's a French library here as well.

İstiklal Caddesi is packed with little restaurants and snack shops, bank branches, clothing stores, itinerant pedlars, shoppers and strollers. If you have the time, take a few detours down the narrow side streets. Any one will reveal glimpses of Beyoğlu life. The street names alone are intriguing: Büyükparmakkapı Sokak, 'Gate of the Thumb St'; Sakızağacı Sokak, 'Pine-Gum Tree St'; Kuloğlu Sokak, 'Slave's Son St'.

The **Tarihi Galatasaray Hamamı** (Historic Galatasaray Turkish Bath) is at Turnacıbaşı Sokak 24, off İstiklal Caddesi just north of Galatasaray Square (for prices and opening times, see Hamams in the Entertainment section later in this chapter).

Galatasaray Square Halfway along the length of İstiklal Caddesi is Galatasaray Square, really an intersection, named after the imperial secondary school you can see behind the huge gates on your left. This building once housed the country's most prestigious school, established in its present form by Sultan Abdül Aziz in 1868, who wanted a place where Ottoman youth could hear lectures in both Turkish and French.

Çiçek Pasajı Before coming into Galatasaray Square, turn right into the Çiçek Pasajı (Flower Passage). This is the inner court of the 19th-century Cité de Péra building which symbolised Pera's growth as a 'modern' European-style city. It's home to a collection of taverna-restaurants – see Places to Eat later in this chapter for more details.

Balık Pazar Walk out of the courtyard to neighbouring Sahne Sokak, turn right, then look for a little passage off to the left. This is the Avrupa Pasajı (European Passage), a small gallery with marble paving and shops selling old and new books, prints, antiquities, stamps and coins, and similar goods.

Sahne Sokak is the heart of Beyoğlu's Balık Pazar (Fish Market), actually a general-purpose market with a good number of fish merchants. Small stands sell *midye* (skewered mussels fried in hot oil) and other stands sell grilled *kokoreç* (lamb intestines packed with more lamb intestines).

Further up Sahne Sokak, Duduodaları Sokak leads off to the left and down to the British consulate general. Continuing along Sahne Sokak, near this junction on your right at No 24A is the entrance to the **Üç Horan Ermeni Kilisesi**, the Armenian Church of Three Altars. You can visit if the doors are open.

Past the Armenian church, Sahne Sokak changes name to become Balık Sokak. Leading off to the right from Sahne Sokak is Nevizade Sokak, lined with *meyhanes* (tavernas) where the old-time life of the Çiçek Pasajı continues, untrammelled by the glossy overlays of tourist İstanbul. Feel free to wander in and have a meal and a drink. (See Places to Eat later in this chapter for more details.)

Unless you want to continue down the slope among the fishmongers on Balık Sokak, turn back and then right into Duduodaları Sokak, and stroll down this little street past fancy food shops, butchers', bakers', and greengrocers' shops to the British consulate general.

Meşrutiyet Caddesi At the end of the market street, Duduodaları Sokak, you emerge into the light. Right in front of you is Meşrutiyet Caddesi, and on the corner are the huge gates to the **British consulate general**, an Italian palazzo built in 1845 to plans by Sir Charles Barry, architect of London's Houses of Parliament.

Walk past the British consulate general along Meşrutiyet Caddesi, which makes its way down to the Pera Palas Oteli and the American consulate general. Watch for an iron gate and a small passage on the left, leading into a little courtyard with a derelict lamp post in the centre. Enter the courtyard, turn right up the stairs, and you'll discover the Greek Orthodox church of **Panaya İsodyon**. It's quiet and very tidy, hidden away in the midst of other buildings. The doors are open to visitors most of the day.

When you've seen the church, go down the stairs *behind* it (not the stairs you came up). Turn right, and just past the church property on the right-hand side you will see the entrance to the Yeni Rejans Lokantası, or New Regency Restaurant. Founded, as legend would have it, by three Russian dancing girls who fled the Russian Revolution, the restaurant is still operated by their Russian-speaking descendants.

This area of Beyoğlu was a favourite with Russian emigres after the revolution. The Yeni Rejans, by the look of it, was a cabaret complete with orchestra loft and grand piano. Lunch and dinner are still served except on Sunday.

When you go out of the restaurant door and down the steps, turn right, then left along the narrow alley called Olivia Han, and this will bring you back to İstiklal Caddesi.

Back on İstiklal Caddesi Across İstiklal Caddesi, notice the large Italian church behind a fence. The Franciscan **Church of San Antonio di Padua** was founded here in 1725; the red-brick building dates from 1913.

Cross over to the church, turn right, and head down İstiklal Caddesi once more. After the church you will pass Eskiçiçekçi Sokak on the left, then Nuriziya Sokak. The third street, a little cul-de-sac, ends at the gates of the **Palais de France**, once the French embassy. The grounds are extensive and include the chapel of St Louis of the French, founded here in 1581, though the present chapel building dates from the 1830s.

A few steps along İstiklal Caddesi brings you to the pretty **Netherlands consulate general**, built as the Dutch embassy in 1855 by the Fossati brothers, formerly architects to the Russian tsar. The first embassy building here dated from 1612. Past the consulate, turn left down the hill on Postacılar Sokak.

The narrow street turns right, bringing you face to face with the former Spanish embassy. The little chapel, founded in 1670, is still in use though the embassy is not.

The street then bends left and changes name to become Tomtom Kaptan Sokak. At the foot of the slope, on the right, is the **Palazzo di Venezia**, once the embassy for Venice, now owned by the Italian consulate. Venice was one of the great Mediterranean maritime powers during Renaissance times, and when Venetian and Ottoman fleets were not madly trading with one another, they were locked in ferocious combat.

To the left across the open space is a side gate to the Palais de France. Peek through the gates for another, better view of the old French embassy grounds, then slog back uphill to İstiklal Caddesi.

Continuing along İstiklal Caddesi, the **Church of St Mary Draperis**, built in 1678 and extensively reconstructed in 1789, is behind an iron fence and down a flight of steps.

Past the church, still on the left-hand side, is the grand **Russian consulate general**, once the embassy of the tsars, built in 1837 to designs by the Fossati brothers.

Now take a detour: turn right (north-west) off İstiklal Caddesi along Asmalımescit Caddesi, a narrow, typical Beyoğlu street with some antique shops, food shops, suspect hotels and little eateries. After about 100m the street intersects Meşrutiyet Caddesi. To the left of the intersection is the **American Library & Cultural Center**, once the Constantinople Club. Just beyond it is the Palazzo Corpi (1880), a pretty marble palace built by Genoese shipping magnate Ignazio Corpi and later rented, then sold in 1907, to the USA for use as the American embassy to the Sublime Porte. It is now the **American consulate general**, and heavily fortified.

Pera Palas Oteli The Pera Palas Oteli, opposite the American consulate, was built by Georges Nagelmackers, the Belgian entrepreneur who founded the Compagnie Internationale des Wagons-Lits et Grands Express Européens, in 1868. Nagelmackers, who had succeeded in linking Paris and Constantinople by luxury train, found that once he got his esteemed passengers to the Ottoman imperial capital there was no suitable place for them to stay. So he built the hotel here in the 1890s.

The Pera Palas Oteli is a grand place, with huge public rooms, a pleasant bar, a good but very pricey pastry shop, and a birdcage lift. Atatürk stayed here; his luxurious suite on the 2nd floor (room No 101) is now a museum, preserved as it was when he used it (ask at the reception desk for a visit). Once you've taken a turn through the hotel, and perhaps had a drink in the Orient Express bar (water is US$2) or tea in the pastry shop (not for the budget-minded), walk back up Asmalımescit Caddesi to İstiklal Caddesi.

Just before reaching İstiklal Caddesi, turn right onto Sofyalı Sokak, a typical Beyoğlu backstreet with backgammon and bridge parlours, small eateries, and shops selling a range of goods from antiques to electrical equipment.

Near Tünel Square Back on İstiklal Caddesi, you will notice, on your left, the **Swedish consulate**, once the Swedish embassy. Across İstiklal Caddesi, the large pillared building was the Russian embassy before the larger building on İstiklal was built.

Beside the Swedish consulate, turn left downhill on Şahkulu Bostanı Sokak. At the base of the slope turn left, then right onto Serdar-i Ekrem Sokak to find the Anglican sanctuary of **Christ Church** (☎ 212-244 4828) at No 82. Designed by CE Street (who did London's Law Courts), its cornerstone was laid in 1858 by Lord Stratford de Redcliffe, known as 'The Great Elchi' (*elçi* means ambassador) because of his paramount influence in mid-19th-century Ottoman affairs. The church, dedicated in 1868 as the Crimean Memorial Church, is the largest of the city's Protestant churches. It had fallen into disrepair, but was restored and renamed in the mid-1990s. Ring the bell and with luck the caretaker will admit you for a look around.

Back up on İstiklal Caddesi, the road curves to the right into Tünel Square.

Tünel (Map 3)

İstanbul's short underground railway, the Tünel, was built by French engineers in 1875. It allowed European merchants to get from their offices in Galata to their homes in Pera without hiking up the steep hillside. The Tünel runs between Karaköy and Tünel Square, and the fare is US$0.40. Trains run on the 80-second trip as frequently as necessary during rush hours, about every five or 10 minutes at other times.

Museum of Court Literature (Galata Mevlevihanesi)

Though the main street (İstiklal Caddesi) bears right as you come into Tünel Square, continue walking straight on along Galipdede Caddesi. On the left is the **Museum of Court Literature** (Divan Edebiyatı Müzesi; ☎ 245 4141), originally a meeting place for Mevlevi whirling dervishes and preserved as such.

The museum is open 9 am to 4 pm daily except Tuesday. Admission costs US$1. The dervishes still whirl here on the second and fourth Sundays of each month. Ask for current times and dates, and arrive at least half an hour early as seating is limited.

Dervish orders were banned in the early days of the republic because of their ultra-conservative religious politics, and this hall, once the Galata Whirling Dervish Monastery (Galata Mevlevihanesi), now holds exhibits of *hattat* (Arabic calligraphy) and Divan (Ottoman) poetry.

The whirling dervishes took their name, Mevlevi, from the great Sufi mystic and poet, Celaleddin Rumi (1207–73), called Mevlâna (Our Leader) by his disciples. Sufis seek communion with God through various means. For Mevlâna, it was through a *sema* (ceremony) involving chants, prayers, music and a whirling dance. The whirling induced a trance-like state which made it easier for the mystic to seek spiritual union with God.

The Mevlevi *tarikat* (order), founded in Konya during the 13th century, flourished throughout the Ottoman Empire and survives in Konya today. Like several other orders, the Mevlevis stressed the unity of humankind before God regardless of creed.

This modest frame *tekke*, or dervish meeting hall was restored between 1967 and 1972, but the first building here was erected by a high officer in the court of Sultan Beyazıt II in 1491. Its first *şeyh* (leader) was Muhammed Şemai Sultan Divani, a grandson of the great Mevlâna. Inside the tekke, the central area was for the whirling sema.

Back on Galipdede Caddesi Leaving the mevlevihane, turn left down Galipdede Caddesi, lined with shops selling books, Turkish and European musical instruments, plumbing supplies and cabinetmakers' necessities such as wood veneers. A few minutes' walk along Galipdede Caddesi brings you to Beyoğlu's oldest landmark, the Galata Tower.

Galata Tower (Map 3)

The cylindrical Galata Tower (Galata Kulesi; ☎ 212-245 1160) was the highpoint in the Genoese fortifications of Galata, and has been rebuilt many times. Surrounded by scaffolding at the time of writing, it holds a forgettable restaurant/nightclub as well as a memorable **panorama balcony** open to visitors from 9 am to 7 pm daily, for US$2.75 (US$1.75 on Monday).

During the 19th century, Galata had a large Sephardic Jewish population, but most of this community has now moved to more desirable residential areas. **Neve Shalom Synagogue**, a block north-west of the Galata Tower towards Şişhane Square on Büyük Hendek Sokak, is still used for weddings, funerals and other ceremonies, however.

From the Galata Tower, continue downhill on the street called Yüksek Kaldırım Caddesi to reach Karaköy.

Karaköy (Map 4)

In order to avoid 'contamination' of their way of life, both the later Byzantine emperors and the Ottoman sultans relegated European traders to offices and residences in Galata, now called Karaköy.

As you approach the Galata Bridge from Karaköy, the busy ferry docks and also the docks for Mediterranean cruise ships are to your left. Scattered throughout this neighbourhood are Greek and Armenian churches and schools and the large Ashkenazi Synagogue, reminders of the time when virtually all of the empire's businesspeople were non-Muslims.

At the far end of the square, Karaköy Meydanı from the Galata Bridge, at the lower end of Yüksek Kaldırım Caddesi, Voyvoda Caddesi (also called Bankalar Caddesi) leads up a slope to the right towards Şişhane Square. This street was the banking centre during the days of the empire, and many merchant banks still have their headquarters or branches here. The biggest building was that of the Ottoman Bank, now a branch of the Türkiye Cumhuriyeti Merkez Bankası, the Turkish Republic Central Bank.

Karaköy has busy bus stops, dolmuş queues and the lower station of the Tünel.

To find the Tünel station descend into the hubbub of the Karaköy Meydanı from Yüksek Kaldırım, and turn into the next major street on the right, Yüzbaşı Sabahattin Evren Caddesi. The Tünel station is a few steps along this street, on the right-hand side, in a concrete bunker.

SPECIAL EVENTS

The International İstanbul Music Festival, the most prominent entertainment event in İstanbul, begins in late June and continues to mid-July. World-class performers – soloists and virtuosos, orchestras, dance companies, rock and jazz groups – perform in many concert halls, historic buildings and palaces. The highlight is Mozart's *Abduction from the Seraglio* performed in Topkapı Palace, with the Gate of Felicity as the backdrop. Check at the box offices in the Atatürk Cultural Centre for schedules, ticket prices and availability, or contact the festival office (☎ 212-260 4533, 293 3133, fax 261 8823), İstanbul Kültür ve Sanat Vakfı, Yıldız Kültür ve Sanat Merkezi, 80700 Beşiktaş, İstanbul.

The International İstanbul Theatre Festival, with performances by Turkish and foreign casts, takes place in mid-May. Contact the İstanbul Kültür ve Sanat Vakfı.

The İstanbul International Film Festival is held annually from mid-April to early May. Tickets are sold at the Atatürk Cultural Centre.

PLACES TO STAY

Sultanahmet is the best place to look for a budget or mid-range hotel room, particularly if you favour a restored Ottoman-mansion hotel. Taksim Square has many modern upper mid-range hotels as well as most of the top-end places; Beşiktaş, to the north-west of Taksim, has the rest of the luxury hotels.

PLACES TO STAY – BUDGET
Camping

İstanbul's camping areas are situated along the Sea of Marmara in Florya, Yeşilköy and Ataköy near the airport, about 20km from Sultanahmet. They have good sea-view locations and average prices of US$12 for two people in a tent. All are served by the frequent commuter trains which run between Sirkeci station and the western suburb of Halkalı for less than US$1.

At the *Ataköy Mokamp* (☎ 212-559 6000, fax 559 6007), in the Ataköy Tatil Köyü holiday village complex with bar, restaurant, swimming pools and other services, the best sites are *sahile yakın* – near the shore and away from the highway. Ataköy is accessible by *banliyö tren* (suburban train) from Sirkeci and by bus from Eminönü and Taksim. Coming from the airport, the Havaş bus (see Getting Around later in this chapter) does not stop here; the closest stop is several kilometres further east at Bakırköy, so it's best to take a 10-minute taxi ride from the airport for US$5.

Florya Turistik Tesisleri (☎ 212-574 0000), on the shore road south of the airport and west of Yeşilköy, is over 20km from the city centre, but more pleasant because of it. Transport is by banliyö tren (the station, Florya, is 500m away).

Londra Kamping (☎ 212-560 4200) is on the southern side of the Londra Asfaltı highway between the airport and Topkapı gate, across from the *süt sanayi* (milk factory). On the highway is a truck petrol and service station, but behind it, further off the road, are grassy plots with small trees. You won't escape the noise and pollution completely here, but it's not an impossible location. To reach it, head eastwards from the airport towards Topkapı gate and turn into the *servis yolu* (service road); watch carefully for the sign. About 300m after the turn, the camping ground is on the right-hand side.

Hotels – Sultanahmet & Around (Map 5)

The Blue Mosque (Sultan Ahmet Camii) gives its name to the quarter surrounding it. This is İstanbul's premier sightseeing area, so the hotels here, and in the adjoining neighbourhoods of Cankurtaran and Çatladıkapı to the south and east, are supremely convenient. Cankurtaran is a quiet residential district east of Aya Sofya and the Blue Mosque, and accessible on foot from Sultanahmet or by suburban train from Sirkeci to Cankurtaran station.

Several of the hostels and budget hotels in this area offer sleeping-bag space on the roof for US$5, dormitory beds for US$6 or US$8 per person, and others offer double rooms with private toilet, sink and hot-water shower for as much as US$50. Mostly though, these places have simple but adequate double rooms with a sink or private shower for US$25 to US$40.

Many Sultanahmet hotels, hostels and pensions are run by carpet merchants, who may be tedious in their efforts to get you to buy a rug.

Hotel Side Pansiyon (☎ 212-517 2282, fax 517 6590, ⓔ info@sidehotel.com, Utangaç Sokak 20) has two buildings, an older one (the Side Pension) with singles/doubles/triples for US$20/25/35 with sink, US$30/35/45 with shower; and the newer Side Hotel with quite nice rooms for US$40/50/60 with bath and balcony – as good as rooms costing much more. They also have two small basement apartments with small kitchens – great for families.

Mavi Guesthouse (☎ 212-516 5878, fax 517 7287, Kutlugün Sokak 3), not to be confused with the much more expensive Mavi Ev, charges US$17 for a waterless double room, about half that for dorm beds, even less for roof space, including breakfast – just opposite the US$350-a-night Four Seasons Hotel. An even cheaper option nearby is the *Konya Aytekin Pansiyon* (☎ 212-638 3638, Terbıyık Sokak 15), popular with Japanese travellers, where beds cost US$7, the one double room with bath US$30.

At the other end of Kutlugün Sokak from the Mavi Guesthouse, the *Nayla Palace Pension* (☎ 212-516 3567, fax 516 6306, ⓔ nayla@superonline.com, Kutlugün Sokak 22) has OK rooms with bath and breakfast for US$25 a double.

On Akbıyık Caddesi, the *Orient Youth Hostel* (☎ 212-518 0789, fax 518 3894, ⓔ orienthostel@superonline.com, Akbıyık Caddesi 13) has been renovated and staff improved. Beds cost US$7 per person in waterless eight-bed rooms, a dollar more in quad rooms, US$9 each in a double without bath, or US$35 for two in a double with shower. They sometimes offer rooftop sleeping-bag space for US$5. Services include a travel agency, bar and pool table, email and Internet service, rooftop bar with good views, sun deck and currency exchange. There's a street market on Akbıyık Caddesi on Wednesday.

Across the street, *Star Guesthouse* (☎ 212-638 2302, fax 516 1827, Akbıyık Caddesi 18) has tidy doubles with shower and TV for US$35, including breakfast. The nearby *Alaaddin Guest House* (☎ 212-516 2330, fax 638 6059, Akbıyık Caddesi 32) is similar, if a bit more expensive. The *Sultan Tourist Hostel* (☎ 212-516 9260 or 517 1626, e sultan@feztravel.com, Terbıyık Sokak 3) is cheaper, with waterless rooms for US$20 single or double.

Terrace Guesthouse (☎ 212-638 9733, fax 638 9734, e terrace@escortnet.com, Kutlugün Sokak 39) has only a few rooms, but they're cheerful, with tiny baths, balconies, and sea views, for US$50 a double with breakfast served in the rooftop dining room.

Hotel Şebnem (☎ 212-517 6623, fax 638 1056, e sebnemhotel@superonline.com, Adliye Sokak 1) is clean and fairly quiet with double rooms for US$50 including breakfast.

Just uphill, west of the Hippodrome, is the district of Binbirdirek, named after the Byzantine cistern of that name. *Türkmen Hotel & Pansiyon* (☎ 212-517 1355, fax 638 5546, Dizdariye Çeşmesi Sokak 27) is a modern, nondescript but friendly place on a quiet back street a bit out of the way. Double rooms in the pension have showers, but no toilets, and are priced at US$16; in the hotel, nicer rooms with toilet, sink and shower are US$30 in high summer. Breakfast is included.

At the far south-western corner of the Hippodrome, the *Hotel Best Hipodrom* (☎ 212-516 0902, fax 518 1251, e besthipodrom@ixir.com, Üçler Sokak 9) charges slightly more, US$35, for a double with bath, TV and breakfast in a more convenient location.

Hotels – Around Taksim Square
A few budget options exist amid the banks, airline offices, nightclubs and towering luxury hotels of Taksim Square.

One such place is *Otel Avrupa* (Map 2, ☎ 212-250 9420, fax 250 7399, Topçu Caddesi 32), near the corner of Şehit Muhtarbey Caddesi. It's a converted apartment house with an entrance at street level, a cheerful breakfast room one flight up, and singles/doubles of varying sizes priced at US$36/45 with bath and breakfast.

PLACES TO STAY – MID-RANGE
Mid-range hotels, usually newer buildings constructed during the past two decades, charge around US$50 to US$100 for a double with private shower and/or bath; most include breakfast in the price. Most rooms, though, fall in the range of US$60 to US$75. Reductions are often offered, especially during quiet times, so it's always worth asking.

Sultanahmet & Around (Map 5)
Mid-range hotels are either historic buildings with character or comfortable but characterless modern buildings. There's a cluster of mid-range hotels in the Sultanahmet area, and another selection in the surrounding neighbourhoods of Cankurtaran, Çemberlitaş, Kadırga and Küçük Ayasofya.

Ottoman-Style Hotels The lobby of the small *Hotel Empress Zoe* (☎ 212-518 2504 or 518 4360, fax 518 5699, e emzoe@ibm .net, Akbıyık Caddesi, Adliye Sokak 10) is in a Byzantine cistern next to an old Ottoman hamam. The small rooms above, reached by a narrow staircase, are simply decorated with taste and character. The rooftop bar-lounge-terrace has fine views of the sea and the Blue Mosque, and the pleasant 'secret garden' is a flower-bordered haven. Singles/doubles/triples are US$55/75/90, including breakfast. Run by American expatriate Ann Nevens, it's a fine choice for solo women travellers.

Hotel Poem (☎/fax 212-517 6836, e hotelpoem@superonline.com, Terbıyık Sokak 12–16) is two buildings with a small glass-covered restaurant in between, and rooms (some with sea views and/or terraces) for US$95/110 including breakfast. Sevim Erdoğmuş, the general manager, has placed a poem in each room; this is among the quietest of locations.

Hotel Acropol (☎ 212-638 9021, fax 518 3031, e acropol@acropolhotel.com, Akbıyık Caddesi 25) is among the newer and more comfortable hotels in this quarter, with rooms for US$110/140, and fine views from the penthouse restaurant. They'll pick you up at the airport if you arrange it in advance.

Hotel Ararat (☎ 212-516 0411, fax 518 5241, e ararathotel@rocketmail.com, Torun Sokak 3), facing the Blue Mosque, is newly renovated, with nouveau-Byzantine decor by Athenian designer Nikos Papadakis. Singles/doubles/triples are US$45/60/70.

Aşkın Hotel (☎ 212-638 8674, fax 638 8676, e hotelaskin@hotmail.com, Dalbastı Sokak 16), right next to the prominent Mavi Ev, is a renovated Art Deco (1932) place with 12 tidy rooms for US$60/70 including breakfast. Some rooms have views, TVs and/or Jacuzzis.

For maximum Ottoman ambience, the award goes to *Hotel Turkuaz* (☎ 212-518 1897, fax 517 3380, e hotelturkuaz@yahoo .com, Cinci Meydanı (Işıl) Sokak 36, Kadırga), at the bottom of the hill from the south-western corner of the Hippodrome, somewhat out of the way. The rooms, furnishings, hamam and Turkish folk-art lounge in this period house are the real thing, not modern imitations. When you stay in the 'Sultan's Room', you feel the part. The 14 rooms, all with shower, cost between US$50 and US$80 for a double, including breakfast.

Just around the corner, *Hotel Sidera* (☎ 212-638 3460, fax 518 7262, Dönüş Sokak 14) is the modern version of an Ottoman mansion. It's quiet, with a small garden terrace. Bath-equipped rooms are US$50/70 in summer, less off season.

Go south-west (downhill) from the Hippodrome along Mehmet Paşa Yokuşu and Suterazisi Sokak to find the *Grand Hotel Ayasofya* (☎ 212-516 9446, fax 518 0700, Küçük Ayasofya Caddesi, Demirci Reşit Sokak 28). Another nicely renovated house in a quiet residential area, rooms with shower are US$70/85.

Up the hill a few steps off the Hippodrome, *Hotel Turkoman* (☎ 212-516 2956, fax 516 2957, e info@turkomanhotel.com, Asmalı Çeşme Sokak, Adliye Yanı 2) is a re-

cently renovated 19th-century building with the feeling of a private club. The 12 bath-equipped rooms cost US$80/90/110 a single/double/triple. Most are air-conditioned. Take your breakfast (included in the rates) on the rooftop terrace with fine views of the Hippodrome, Blue Mosque and Museum of Turkish and Islamic Arts, which is right next door.

Behind the Turkoman, the simple, mostly modern *Hotel İbrahim Paşa* (☎ 212-518 0349, fax 518 4457, e pasha@ibm.net) has a lift and 18 small shower-equipped rooms, for similar prices to the Turkoman. The location is quietish and convenient, and the management is friendly and accommodating.

Sarı Konak Oteli (☎ 212-638 6258, fax 517 8635, e sarikonak@superonline.com, Mimar Mehmet Ağa Caddesi 42–46) is a beautifully restored Ottoman town house in a relatively quiet location with singles/doubles for US$70/90, including breakfast.

Hotel Obelisk & Sümengen (☎ 212-517 6869, fax 516 8282, e obelisksumengen@ superonline.com, Amiral Tafdil Sokak 21) is two adjoining hotels built in the style of Ottoman town houses. There's a marble-covered hamam, an airy, light dining room and open-air rooftop terrace with views of the Sea of Marmara. The rooms are small with tiny showers. A few of the rooms have views of the sea but many rooms open only onto corridors. Singles/doubles/triples are US$90/120/110, including breakfast.

Hotel Historia (☎ 212-517 7472, fax 516 8169, Amiral Tafdil Sokak 23), to the right of the Sümengen, is Ottoman on the outside, more modern on the inside, though there is a marble-clad hamam. Rooms with shower or bath are US$70/90/110.

Hotel Avicenna (☎ 212-517 0550, fax 516 6555, e avicenna@superonline.com, Amiral Tafdil Sokak 31–33), to the right of the Historia, is also Ottoman on the outside but modern on the inside, with satellite TV, a rooftop-terrace cafe-bar, and small but pleasant rooms for US$110/130, including breakfast.

Pensions *Guesthouse Berk* (☎ 212-516 9671, fax 517 7715, Kutlugün Sokak 27) is family run and a good choice for solo women travellers, though it is comparatively expensive. The six rooms with bath cost US$40/50 to US$70/90, including breakfast, with reductions for longer stays.

Modern Hotels

The *Ambassador Hotel* (☎ 212-512 0002, fax 512 0005, 📧 reserva tions@hotelambassador.com, Divan Yolu, Ticarethane Sokak 19) has everything: a central but quietish location just off Divan Yolu and the Hippodrome, large-ish rooms with fridge, TV and bath (some with Jacuzzis), a great breakfast terrace on the 5th floor, movies in the basement, and decent prices: US$85/120 a single/double.

Hotel Halı (☎ 212-516 2170, fax 516 2172, 📧 halihotel@halihotel.com, Klodfarer Caddesi 20), in Çemberlitaş, uphill to the north-west of the Hippodrome, is another good modern choice at a lower price: US$55/75, including breakfast. There's a bit more street noise here.

Hotel Piyer Loti (☎ 212-518 5700, fax 516 1886, 📧 ploti@akturk.hotels.com, Piyerloti Caddesi 5), Çemberlitaş, is a modern building with a popular glass-covered sidewalk cafe-restaurant on Divan Yolu two blocks west of the Hippodrome. Simple, modern rooms, single or double, cost US$60 to US$75, a great price for such a convenient location. Half a block south, the three-star *Hotel Antea* (☎ 212-638 1121, fax 517 7949, 📧 antea@istanbulhotels.com, Piyerloti Caddesi 21) is fancier and more expensive with posted prices of US$70/100.

The friendly *Hotel Nomade* (☎ 212-511 1296, fax 513 2404, Divan Yolu, Ticarethane Sokak 15) is just a few steps off busy Divan Yolu. French is spoken here, as well as English, and rooms with shower are US$45/60 including breakfast. It's a good place for solo women travellers.

Taksim (Map 3)

Family House (☎ 212-249 7351, fax 249 9667, Kutlu Sokak 53) has five small four-room apartments for rent in a quiet building. The manager can arrange your transport from the airport for US$25. Apartments have two single beds and one double bed, tele-phone, colour TV, kitchen with fridge, two-burner gas cooker and utensils. In summer it's US$96 per day and US$600 per week for up to four people. To find Family House, walk down İnönü Caddesi from Taksim, turn right at the big red Chinese gate, walk beneath it and down the steps, then down another flight, following the Family House signs. Ask the manager about his guest house in rural Göynük.

The area around Taksim also has over a dozen modern four-star hotels charging US$100 to US$160 for comfortable double rooms with bath, TV, minibar and air-con, including breakfast. All are fairly quiet and have lifts, bars and restaurants, 24-hour room service (of sorts) and English-speaking personnel. You should be granted a discount if you stay for several days; be sure to ask about it. Most customers are here on business or organised tours.

Hotel Lamartine (☎ 212-254 6270, fax 256 2776, Lamartin Caddesi 25) has singles/doubles for US$96.

Riva Otel (☎ 212-256 4420, fax 256 2033, Aydede Caddesi 8) charges US$80/100 and has its own currency exchange office.

Eresin Taksim Hotel (☎ 212-256 0803, fax 253 2247, Topçu Caddesi 34) is older but well maintained, with singles/doubles/triples for US$115/140/160.

The Madison Hotel (☎ 212-238 5460, fax 238 5151, 📧 themadisonhotel@super online.com, Recep Paşa Caddesi 23) is among the newest ones, with rooms for US$120/160. There's a hamam, sauna and small indoor swimming pool.

Tepebaşı (Map 3)

Between Galatasaray Square and Tünel Square, west of İstiklal Caddesi, the district of Tepebaşı was the first luxury hotel district in the city. The main street through Tepebaşı is Meşrutiyet Caddesi.

The four-star *Yenişehir Palas* (☎ 212-252 7160, fax 249 7507, 📧 newcity@comnet .com.tr, Meşrutiyet Caddesi, Oteller Sokak 1–3) is a hotel of eight floors with few views but in a convenient location. The popular lounge-bar features live entertainment. Comfortable rooms with bath, TV and minibar go for US$85/115 to US$110/140, including breakfast.

Büyük Londra Oteli (☎ 212-245 0670, fax 245 0671, Meşrutiyet Caddesi 117) is a bit the worse for wear but it does preserve some of its Victorian-era glory (in the public rooms at least) at a price which includes a significant nostalgia mark-up. A room with shower costs US$60 with one double bed, US$80 with two beds, including breakfast.

PLACES TO STAY – TOP END

The centre of the posh hotel district is certainly Taksim Square, but there are numerous luxury hotels in other parts of the city. Prices range from US$125 to US$300 and higher for a double, but most rooms cost from US$140 to US$200. At the big international hotels, try not to pay the rack rates, which are quite high. Often these hotels offer special packages; ask when you make reservations. The big international chains usually allow children (of any age) to share a double room with their parents at no extra charge or, if two rooms are needed, they charge only the single rate.

Sultanahmet (Map 5)

Türkiye Turing ve Otomobil Kurumu, the Turkish Touring & Automobile Association, has restored historic buildings throughout the city, including several Ottoman mansions next door to Aya Sofya and the Blue Mosque.

Yeşil Ev (☎ 212-517 6785, fax 517 6780, e yesilevhotel@superonline.com, Kabasakal Caddesi 5) is an Ottoman house rebuilt by Turing with 22 rooms furnished with period pieces and antiques; it's the classiest of the restored Ottoman mansion hotels. Behind the hotel is a lovely shaded terrace restaurant. With breakfast, singles/doubles/triples are US$120/160/200, or US$250 for the Pasha's Room with its private hamam.

Mavi Ev (☎ 212-638 9010, fax 638 9017, e bluehouse@bluehouse.com.tr, Dalbastı Sokak 14), meaning 'Blue House', has comfortable rooms, a supremely convenient location, and excellent morning views of the Blue Mosque from its rooftop restaurant for US$110/130/150, including breakfast.

Sultanahmet Sarayı Hotel (☎ 212-458 0460, fax 518 6224, Torun Sokak 19) is a new small luxury hotel just opposite the Blue Mosque. Each of the 36 rooms has its own hamam. There's a good restaurant and terrace gardens, all for US$120/140/150. Visit its Web site (www.sultanahmetpalace .com) for more details.

On the northern side of Aya Sofya against the walls of Topkapı Palace is a row of Ottoman houses, the **Ayasofya Pansiyonları** (☎ 212-513 3660, fax 513 3669, e ayapans@escortnet.com.tr, Soğukçeşme Sokak), which have been rebuilt and refitted by Turing. Rooms with baths are in 19th-century Ottoman style with brass or antique wooden beds, glass lamps, Turkish carpets and period wall hangings. Singles/doubles are from US$80/100 to US$90/120, triples are US$160, including breakfast. The front rooms look directly onto Aya Sofya.

The Four Seasons Hotel İstanbul (☎ 212-638 8200, fax 638 8210, e Hiluer@ fshr.com, Tevkifhane Sokak 1) is İstanbul's top hotel in every respect: location, accommodation, design, furnishings and service. This perfectly restored Ottoman building literally in the shadow of the Blue Mosque and Aya Sofya has only one problem: there aren't enough rooms for everyone who wants one, even at the lofty price of US$360 to US$450, plus 15% tax.

Taksim

Divan Oteli (Map 2, ☎ 212-231 4100, fax 248 8527, Cumhuriyet Caddesi 2), Elmadağ, is a small European-style hotel with excellent cuisine and service by well-trained multilingual staff. Rooms cost US$175 to US$250, tax (but not service) included. As at most luxury hotels, breakfast costs extra.

Two blocks north is the **İstanbul Hilton Hotel** (Map 2, ☎ 212-231 4650, fax 240 4165), set in a 14-acre park overlooking the Bosphorus, with tennis courts, swimming pool, and rooms from US$181 to US$290 and up, plus service.

The **Hyatt Regency İstanbul** (Map 2, ☎ 212-225 7000, fax 225 7007, Taşkışla Caddesi) has the feel of a vast Ottoman mansion – but with a jazz bar, Italian restaurant and swimming pool. Rooms cost US$140 to US$280 and up, plus service charge.

The *Ceylan Inter-Continental İstanbul* (Map 2, ☎ 212-231 2121, fax 231 2180) towers above Taksim Park, with fine views from its upper floors, and even some from the outdoor swimming pool. Rates rise along with the rooms, costing US$220 on the lower floors, US$290 and up on upper floors.

Hotel Mercure (Map 3, ☎ 212-251 4646, fax 249 8033, Meşrutiyet Caddesi) is a modern 22-storey tower across the street from the Pera Palas. All the rooms have satellite TV and minibar; some have great views of the Golden Horn, the Old City and the Bosphorus, for US$120/140, including breakfast.

Across the street, the romantic old *Pera Palas Oteli (Map 3, ☎ 212-251 4560, fax 251 4089, Meşrutiyet Caddesi 98-100)* fills up regularly with individual tourists and groups looking to relive the imperial age of Constantinople. However, indifferent service and a mediocre restaurant are strong reminders that things were better here a century ago. Rooms (of varying quality) with bath cost US$180/220, including breakfast.

The Pera Palas' ingenious promoters claim that Agatha Christie stayed in room 411 when she visited İstanbul, though reliable sources affirm that she stayed at the once prime but now long-gone Tokatlıyan Hotel on İstiklal Caddesi. However, there's no disputing that the great Atatürk preferred room 101, a suite which, kept just as he used it, is now a museum (ask at the reception desk for admission).

Beşiktaş (Map 2)

There are several luxury hotels north-east of Taksim Square, up the Bosphorus in Beşiktaş. However, their out-of-centre location means you'll need to take taxis every time you want to go anywhere. These include:

Çirağan Palace Hotel Kempinski İstanbul
  (☎ 212-258 3377, fax 259 6687) Çirağan Caddesi 84 80700 Beşiktaş
Hotel Conrad İstanbul (☎ 212-227 3000, fax 259 6667) Yıldız Caddesi, 80700 Beşiktaş
Swissôtel İstanbul The Bosphorus (☎ 212-259 0101, fax 259 0105) Bayıldım Caddesi 2, Maçka, 80680 Beşiktaş

PLACES TO EAT

Small *hazır yemek* (ready food) restaurants, *kebapçıs* (kebap joints) and *pidecis* (serving *pide*, Turkish pizza) charge from US$2 to US$3 for a simple main-course lunch to perhaps US$5 or US$6 for a several-course tuck-in. They don't normally serve alcohol.

Mid-range restaurants with white tablecloths, waiters and alcoholic beverages charge from US$8 to US$20 for a three-course meal with wine, beer or *rakı*.

Though meals costing more than US$20 per person used to be rare in İstanbul, this is changing. Chic cafe-restaurants with designer decor and innovative menus are attracting a well-heeled local and foreign clientele willing to pay US$25 to US$35 and higher per person, and the growing scarcity of seafood has also driven up the cost of meals at luxury seafood restaurants.

Sultanahmet (Map 5)

The many restaurants on Divan Yolu offer decent food in pleasant surroundings, but prices are high by Turkish standards.

Köftecis Divan Yolu's *köftecis* were traditionally where the district's workers ate cheap, filling, tasty lunches of *köfte (*meatballs). Order by the *porsyon* (portion): *bir porsyon* (one portion) if you're not overly hungry, *bir buçuk porsyon* (one and a half) if you are, and *duble porsyon* (double) if you're ravenous. An order of köfte, a plate of salad, bread and a glass of *ayran* (yogurt drink) should cost around US$4.

Meşhur Sultanahmet Köftecisi, on Divan Yolu opposite the Firuz Ağa Camii and the tram stop, is about the cheapest. As if the length of its name determined its prices, *Meşhur Tarihi Halk Köftecisi Selim Usta (Divan Yolu 12/A)*, meaning 'Chef Selim, Famous Historic Popular Köfte-maker', is somewhat more expensive, but the most authentic of the lot. *Sultanahmet Meşhur Meydan Köftecisi*, just to the left (west) of the Sultan Pub, is in the middle as far as price is concerned.

Hazır Yemek Restaurants Divan Yolu has many 'ready food' restaurants and grills, but outside the tourist zone you'll find better value places. Most don't serve alcohol.

A longtime favourite is **Doy-Doy** (Fill up! Fill up!). At the south-eastern end of the Hippodrome, walk downhill to Şifa Hamamı Sokak 13. Soup costs US$1, grilled meats about US$2 to US$3. Across the street, **Buhara 93** serves good Turkish pizza, but the cheapest good meal is a bowl of their excellent *mercimek çorbası* (lentil soup) which comes with enormous flats of freshly baked village bread for US$1.

On Divan Yolu, the famous **Pudding Shop**, officially called the Lale Restaurant, is where the drop-out generation of the 1960s kept alive and happy on inexpensive puddings. Now self-conscious and upscale, it trades on its nostalgia, charging US$5 to US$8 for most meals. The neighbouring **Can Restaurant** has better prices.

Going off the beaten track even a block gets you more value for money.

At the south-western end of the Hippodrome, walk up Üçler Sokak to **Yeni Birlik Lokantası** (☎ 212-517 6465) at No 46, a large, light ready-food restaurant favoured by lawyers from the nearby law courts. Meals are available for US$4 to US$6.

Across the street from Yeni Birlik Lokantası, **Gaziantep Kebap ve Lahmacun** will serve you a full meal of roast meat, salad and soft drink for US$5 or US$6, or a snack of *lahmacun* (Arabic-style pizza) for half that.

Karadeniz Pide ve Kebap Salonu, a cheap, simple place on Hacı Tahsin Bey Sokak half a block north of Divan Yolu, does a good business sending out meals to local shopkeepers. Have stuffed cabbage leaves, *pilav* (rice), bread and a drink for less than US$4. The upstairs dining room is nicer than downstairs, and both are open on Sunday. A few steps away, **Hotel Akdeniz Lokantası** is similar.

Cafes At **Derviş Aile Çay Bahçesi** (*Kabasakal Caddesi 2/1*), west of the Yeşil Ev Hotel, stimulants and small sandwiches (US$1) are served in the cool, dark shadows cast by great plane trees. Try *peynirli tost*, a cheese sandwich mashed in a vice-like cooker.

On the other side of the Hippodrome, the **Sultanahmet Çay Bahçesi** is less elaborate, as is the shady little tea garden clinging to the wall of the Blue Mosque.

Restaurants At the Hippodrome end of Divan Yolu, overlooking the small park atop the Sunken Cistern, is **Sultan Pub** (☎ 212-526 6347, Divan Yolu 2). Main courses cost between US$6 and US$10, with full meals for about twice that much. They serve at outdoor tables in fine weather.

Buhara Ocakbaşı (☎ 212-513 7424, Nuruosmaniye Caddesi 7), off Yerebatan Caddesi near the Cağaloğlu Hamamı, is a neighbourhood grill with good mezes, lamb grills and alcoholic beverages. A full dinner with drinks usually costs around US$10 or US$12 per person.

The **Yeşil Ev** hotel's garden restaurant is very pleasant. Full lunches based on meat cost about US$10 to US$20, twice that for fish.

Rami Restaurant (☎ 212-517 6593, Utangaç Sokak 6), in a restored house behind the Blue Mosque, is named after Turkish painter Rami Uluer (1913–88), whose work decorates the dining rooms. Interesting Ottoman specialities such as *hünkar beğendi* (grilled lamb and rich aubergine puree) or *kağıt kebap* (lamb and vegetables cooked in a paper pouch) fill the menu; food and service are of varying quality. With drinks, a meal costs about US$20 to US$30 per person. The rooftop terrace has fine views of the Blue Mosque.

Two hotel restaurants also have good views of the Blue Mosque. Try the one at the **Mavi Ev**, near Rami. The restaurant of the **Hotel Arcadia** has a truly breathtaking view of the Blue Mosque late in the afternoon, and full meals for US$12 to US$25.

Sirkeci & Hocapaşa (Map 4)

Only three short blocks south of Sirkeci train station are good small restaurants in the neighbourhood called Hocapaşa. Exit the train station by the western door (to the tram line), turn left and walk up the slope on Ankara Caddesi, turning into the third little street on the left, İbni Kemal Caddesi, to find the Hoca Paşa Camii and a dozen small restaurants. In good weather, tables are set out in the narrow, shady pedestrian-only street for pleasant dining.

There's variety: **Namlı Rumeli Köftecisi** serves soup for less than US$1, and features köfte (US$1 to US$2) and *piyaz* (white beans vinaigrette), as does **Et-İş Köfte ve Hazır Yemek**. **Tarihi Hocapaşa Pidecisi** serves Turkish pizza, fresh, good and cheap for as little as US$1.50. **Kebapçı Kardeşler** specialises in grills, and several steam-table places, including **Kardeşler Anadolu Lokantası**, feature lots of stews and vegetable dishes as well as some grills priced at US$1 to US$2 per plate. Fresh fruit for dessert is available from sidewalk vendors.

Eminönü (Map 4)

About the cheapest way to enjoy fresh fish is to buy a *fish sandwich* from a boatman. Go to the Eminönü end of the Galata Bridge, and on both sides of the bridge, tied to the quay railing between the ferry docks, are boats bobbing in the water. In each boat, two men cook fish on a grill or griddle. The fried fish, slid into a slit quarter-loaf of bread, costs US$1.

For more upscale fare, try **Borsa Fast Food,** on Yalı Köşkü Caddesi inland from the ferry docks. Turkish classics such as köfte (US$2.50) are served up quickly in modern surroundings.

Pandeli (☎ 212-527 3909), over the main entrance of the Egyptian Bazaar, facing the Galata Bridge, was founded decades ago by a Greek chef, now long dead. Its small dining rooms panelled in faience are beautiful, and its seafood speciality alluring, but readers have complained of high prices and a charge even for hanging up your coat.

Kapalı Çarşı (Map 8)

You will no doubt pass **Şark Kahvesi** (Oriental Cafe), at the end of Fesçiler Caddesi, always filled with locals and tourists. The arched ceilings betray its former existence as part of a bazaar street; some enterprising *kahveci* (coffee-house owner) walled up several sides and turned it into a cafe. On the grimy walls hang paintings of Ottoman

Turkish Delight

For a traditional Ottoman treat, walk through the archway to the left of the Yeni Cami in Eminönü, and turn left onto Hamidiye Caddesi. One short block along, on the right-hand (south) side of the street near the corner with Şeyhülislam Hayri Efendi Caddesi, is the original shop of Ali Muhiddin Hacı Bekir (☎ 212-522 0666), inventor of Turkish delight.

History notes that Ali Muhiddin came to İstanbul from the Black Sea mountain town of Kastamonu and established himself as a confectioner in the Ottoman capital in the late 18th century. Dissatisfaction with traditional, hard sweets led the impetuous Ali Muhiddin to invent a new confection that would be easy to chew and swallow. He called his soft, gummy creation *rahat lokum* (comfortable morsel). Lokum, as it soon came to be called, was an immediate hit with the denizens of the imperial palace, and anything that went well with the palace went well with the populace.

Ali Muhiddin elaborated on his original confection, as did his offspring (the shop is still owned by his descendants), and now you can buy lokum made with various fillings: *cevizli* (walnut), *şam fıstıklı* (pistachio), *portakkallı* (orange-flavoured), or *bademli* (almond). You can also get a *çeşitli* (assortment). Price is according to weight and ingredients. One kilogram of *sade* (plain) costs US$3.75; a kilo of *ekstra fıstıklı* (double pistachio) costs US$12. Ask for a free sample by indicating your choice and saying *'Deneyelim!'* (Let's try it).

During the winter, a cool-weather speciality is added to the list of treats for sale. Helva, a crumbly sweet block of sesame puree, is flavoured with chocolate or pistachio nuts or sold plain. Ali Muhiddin Hacı Bekir has another, more modern shop on İstiklal Caddesi between Taksim Square and Galatasaray next to Vakko.

scenes and framed portraits of sultans and champion Turkish freestyle wrestlers. A cup of Turkish coffee, a soft drink or a glass of tea costs less than US$1; Nescafé is more expensive.

There are small restaurants here and there throughout the bazaar, but three altogether in the Cebeci Han, one of the bazaar's many caravanserais. *Pedaliza Ottoman Cuisine* is the fanciest, serving both stews and grills for about US$5 per person, all in. The *Barış Et Lokantası* and *Dünya Et Lokantası* specialise in grilled meats. Even cheaper places are to be found northwards along Örücüler Kapısı Caddesi outside the Kapalı Çarşı proper.

Though most Kapalı Çarşı eateries are low budget, the prices at *Havuzlu Lokantası* (☎ 212-527 3346, Gani Çelebi Sokak 3) are in the moderate range of US$8 to US$14 for a meal. The food is about the same as at the cheaper places in this area, but you get a lofty dining room made of several bazaar streets walled off for the purpose long ago, and a few tables set out in front of the entrance by a little stone pool (*havuzlu* means 'with pool'), which may have been a deep well centuries ago. Waiter service here is more polite and unhurried, though slow when there are tour groups. To find the Havuzlu, follow the yellow-and-black PTT signs (the PTT is next door).

Outside the bazaar on Divan Yolu at Çemberlitaş, the *Cennet Lokantası*, in the Çemberlitaş Hamamı building, offers country-Ottoman cuisine such as *mantı* (Turkish ravioli) for US$1.50 to US$3 per plate, often with a small band playing traditional Turkish music. Look for the women in the front window smoothing dough with slender rollers.

Topkapı Palace (Map 6)
Konyalı Restaurant (☎ 212-513 9696), beneath the Mecidiye Köşkü in Topkapı Palace, serves decent food at moderate prices (US$12 to US$18 per person for lunch), with views of the Bosphorus, but is impossibly crowded at noon. Go early or late, or snack instead on the cafe terrace beneath the Konyalı.

Süleymaniye (Map 4)
There are several little eateries, serving standard Turkish fare, in the row of souvenir shops outside the mosque enclosure to the south-west, including the *Beydağı* and *Kanaat Lokantası* restaurants.

Darüzziyafe (☎ 212-511 8414, Şifahane Caddesi 6) is an Ottoman-style restaurant in the *imaret* (soup kitchen) opposite the mosque's main portal. Constructed as part of the *külliye* or mosque complex, the building has a courtyard surrounded by porches and centred on a fountain. The court is used for dining in fine weather, and several rooms opening onto it have changing art exhibits. The menu is Ottoman with mid-range prices, such as soup for US$2.50, meze plates for US$3, main courses for US$5 to US$8, and full meals for US$10 to US$18.

Taksim (Map 3)
A few steps down İstiklal Caddesi from Taksim Square is *Pehlivan Restaurant*. This bright, plain place has the standard cafeteria line, steam tables and low prices. Fill up at lunch or dinner for US$4. *Taksim Sütiş*, to the right, specialises in tea, coffee and sweets (US$0.40 to US$1), but serves light meals (US$1.50 to US$4.50) as well.

Otherwise, the Taksim end of İstiklal has the all-too-familiar fast-food places, including McDonald's and Pizza Hut.

More upmarket is *Hacı Baba* (☎ 212-244 1886, İstiklal Caddesi 49) with a pleasant terrace and tables overlooking the courtyard of the Aya Triada Kilisesi next door. The menu is long and varied, the food good, and the service usually competent; some English is spoken. Have a look in the kitchen to help you choose your meal. You'll pay from US$10 to US$20 per person for a full lunch or dinner with wine or beer.

The posh *Boğaziçi Borsa Restaurant* (☎ 212-232 4201), just north of the İstanbul Hilton in the Lütfi Kırdar Kongre ve Sergi Salonu (Convention Centre), serves creatively updated Ottoman specialities and new-wave Turkish cuisine in deluxe surroundings at reasonable prices. A three- or four-course meal with wine need cost only US$15 to US$30 per person.

The dining room at *Divan Oteli* (☎ 212-231 4100) serves Continental and Turkish cuisine in posh surroundings at decent prices, about US$35 to US$50 per person for a fine meal, all in. *Divan Pub*, adjoining, is still fairly fancy but significantly cheaper. The speciality here is excellent *döner kebap* (spit-roasted lamb slices).

İstiklal Caddesi (Map 3)
Borsa Fast Food Kefeteryası (İstiklal Caddesi 89) is modern, bright and popular with Turkish youth – especially the *dondurma* (ice cream) kiosk. Burgers and Turkish grills (US$2 to US$4) are the speciality, and beer is served.

Continuing along İstiklal Caddesi, Büyükparmakkapı Sokak holds many eating and drinking possibilities, including the cheap *Ada Restaurant*, at No 25, where you can fill up for US$3 to US$5. *Nature & Peace*, at No 21, serves vegetarian soups (US$1.50), salads (US$2 to US$3) and main courses (US$3), plus a few chicken dishes, at lunch and dinner (closed Sunday). Around the corner on Çukurlu Çeşmesi Sokak, *Hala* serves mantı and other traditional favourites. Look in the window for the traditionally clad woman rolling out flats of dough.

Behind (north of) the Ağa Camii on Mahyacı Sokak, the untouristy *Meşhur Sultanahmet Köftecisi* serves köfte, lahmacun and pide at prices below those on İstiklal Caddesi.

Hacı Abdullah (☎ 212-293 8561, Sakızağacı Caddesi 17), beside the Ağa Camii, is a Beyoğlu institution, having been in business for a century. Its dining rooms are simple but tasteful, its Turkish and Ottoman cuisine outstanding, with a varied menu of traditional dishes. Service is friendly, and a full meal with soft drink (no alcohol is served) costs US$9 to US$15.

Galatasaray (Map 3)
Atlas Restaurant & Cafe (İstiklal Caddesi 251) in the Örs İş Merkezi directly across from the Çiçek Pasajı, was built by an Armenian architect in 1815. Once the residence of Mr Fethi Okyar, first prime minister of the Turkish Republic (1930s), it's now a favourite lunch place for students at the British Council (in the same building) who come for the good daily three-course set-price lunch for US$3.

Just north of Galatasaray is the Balık Pazar (Fish Market), actually a full food market spread out in two little streets, Sahne Sokak and Duduodaları Sokak, next to the touristy Çiçek Pasajı. The cheapest and simplest is *Mercan*, specialising in *midye tavası* (deep-fried mussels) for about US$0.30, a bit more for *sandviçli* (in bread); the favoured beverage is draught beer.

At İstiklal Caddesi 172 there is an entrance to the Çiçek Pasajı (Flower Passage), a collection of taverna-restaurants open long hours every day in the courtyard of a historic building.

Pick a good place, pull up a stool and order a mug of beer, *beyaz* (pale) or *siyah* (dark). For something stronger, ask for '*Bir kadeh rakı*' (a shot of rakı). As for food, printed menus mean little here. Have a look in the kitchen, point to what you want, and be sure to ask prices. Don't accept unordered items, and be cautious with locals who chat you up and propose outings or nightclubs, which may turn into rip-offs or even, occasionally, robberies.

The locals who used to patronise the Çiçek Pasajı have moved on to the *meyhane* (tavernas) deeper in the market. Walk along Sahne Sokak into the market to the first street on the right, Nevizade Sokak. There are at least eight restaurants here with streetside tables in fine weather charging about US$1.50 to US$2.25 for plates of meze, about twice that for kebaps; ask prices of fish before you order. Alcohol is served enthusiastically. *Çağlar Restaurant* is at No 6 and *Kadri'nin Yeri* nearby. *Asırlı* at No 21 and *Boncuk* at No 19 are currently quite popular, as is *İmroz Restaurant (☎ 212-249 9073, Nevizade Sokak 24)*, down at the end of the row on the right. Run by a Turk and a Greek from the island of Gökçeada (İmroz), it specialises in fish and other island dishes.

The clean, bright *Nizam Pide Salonu (Kalyoncu Kulluk Caddesi 13)* serves great soup with their own freshly baked flat bread, and cheese- or meat-topped pide for US$1.75 to US$3.

Afacan Pizza & Burger Restaurant (İstiklal Caddesi 331), south of the red-brick Church of San Antonio di Padua, is popular for its namesake dishes and low prices: two plates of food and a drink for under US$3.

Self-Catering The Balık Pazar is a prime area for picnic assembly, with greengrocers, şarküteri (charcuterie, delicatessen) shops and bakeries offering cheeses, dried meats such as pastırma (salami), pickled fish, olives, jams and preserves, and several varieties of bread including whole-grain. *Şütte* (☎ 212-244 9292, Duduodaları Sokak 21) is regarded by many as the best of the delis.

Tepebaşı & Tünel (Map 3)

Restaurant-Cafe Teras (İstiklal Caddesi 365/19) in the Beyoğlu İş Merkezi building provides a peaceful terrace dining area overlooking the historic Palais de France. Drinks, snacks, light and more substantial meals are served in good weather at moderate prices. To find it, walk down Nuruziya Sokak half a block, enter on the right and walk straight until you must turn, then turn left.

Near Pera Palas Oteli and the American consulate general, *Şemsiye (☎ 212-292 2046, Şeyhbender Sokak 18)*, meaning 'Umbrella', serves vegetarian meals (US$5 to US$9) at lunch and dinner, with at least one or two meat, fowl or fish dishes as well. It's popular with diplomats and young professionals, who also come for *Yağmur* (Rain), the cybercafe upstairs.

For a light lunch or snack near the Pera Palas Oteli, go to *Karadeniz Pide Salonu* behind and to the left of the Hotel Mercure, where you can get a fresh pide with butter and cheese for little more than US$1.

Popular with the diplomatic set at lunch time is *Dört Mevsim (☎ 212-293 3941, İstiklal Caddesi 509)*, Four Seasons, almost in Tünel Square. Under Turkish-English management, it is well located to draw diners from the US, UK, Dutch, Russian and Swedish consulates. The food is Continental, with concessions to Turkish cuisine; preparation and service are first-rate, and there's a guitar and violin duo most evenings. Lunch is served from noon to 3 pm, dinner from 6 pm to midnight; it's closed on Sunday. If you order the fixed menu at lunch, you might pay US$10, drink and tip included. Ordering from the regular menu at dinner may bring your bill to US$20 or US$22 per person.

Çatı Restaurant (☎ 212-251 0000, İstiklal Caddesi, Orhan Adli Apaydın Sokak 20/7) is on the 7th (top) floor of a building on a small side street which runs between İstiklal and Meşrutiyet Caddesis. Though the view is vestigial at best, the greenhouse-style dining room is pleasant, and the food is quite good and not expensive. Try the *çatı böreği* for an appetiser; it's halfway between a Turkish *börek* (filled pastry) and a turnover, made with cheese. Main courses are mostly Turkish, with a few European specialities. Expect to spend from US$12 to US$18 per person. If you don't like syrupy organ music, come early for dinner.

Yakup 2 Restaurant (☎ 212-249 2925, Asmalımescit Caddesi 35–37) is popular with local artists, musicians, actors and professors. It hasn't been fancied up for tourists, so the decor is minimal but the food is quite good and moderately priced. Full meals with wine, beer or rakı cost about US$8 to US$15. It's open daily for dinner, and for lunch daily except Sunday.

ENTERTAINMENT

For many first-time visitors, the name 'İstanbul' conjures up Hollywood-baroque images of mysterious intrigues in dusky streets, sultry belly dancers undulating in smoky dens, and dangerous liaisons from the sublime to the bestial. As with most aged stereotypes, the reality is entirely different.

Concerts, Dance & Opera

There are symphony, opera and ballet seasons, and tour performances by world-renowned virtuosi. Look for news of performances and concerts in the weekend supplement of the *Turkish Daily News*, and in its Arts & Culture section on Sunday.

İstanbul's major venues for concerts and performances of dance and opera are the *Atatürk Cultural Centre (Map 3, Atatürk Kültür Merkezi, ☎ 212-251 5600, fax 245 3916)* in Taksim Square; the *Cemal Reşit Rey Konser Salonu (Map 3, ☎ 212-240 5012)*, on Gümüş Sokak just north of the İstanbul Hilton and east of the Military Museum; and the former *Aya İrini* church in the Court of Processions at Topkapı Palace.

Outdoor venues for summer performances include the *Açık Hava Tiyatrosu* (Open-Air Theatre) just north of the İstanbul Hilton, and *Rumeli Hisarı*, north of Bebek on the Bosphorus.

Theatre

The Turks are enthusiastic theatre-goers, and as a people they seem to have a special genius for dramatic art, though the language barrier makes their performances relatively inaccessible to foreign visitors. Theatre buffs might well enjoy a performance of a familiar classic. Theatres are concentrated in Beyoğlu along İstiklal Caddesi and near Taksim Square.

Cinema

The *Turkish Daily News'* Friday edition carries current cinema listings. When possible, buy your tickets (US$4 to US$5) a few hours in advance.

The closest cinema complex to Sultanahmet is the *Şafak Sinemaları* in the Fırat Kültür Merkezi (Euphrates Cultural Centre) in Çemberlitaş. Take the tram uphill from Sultanahmet to the Çemberlitaş stop. The Centre is right there at the stop. The seven-screen Şafak shows first-run Turkish and foreign films in the original language with Turkish subtitles. There's an Internet cafe here as well. İstiklal Caddesi (Map 3) between Taksim and Galatasaray is İstanbul's main cinema district.

Aksanat Kültür Merkezi (Aksanat Cultural Centre; ☎ 212-252 3500) İstiklal Caddesi 16–18, in the Akbank building on İstiklal just out of Taksim; movies and films of musical and theatrical performances

Asya-Avrupa-Alkazar Sinemaları (☎ 212-293 2466) İstiklal Caddesi 179; US and international films for US$3.50 to US$6

Atlas Sineması (☎ 212-252 8576) İstiklal Caddesi 209, Kuyumcular Pasajı

Beyoğlu & Pera Sinemaları (☎ 212-251 3240) İstiklal Caddesi 140

Emek (☎ 212-293 8439) İstiklal Caddesi, Yeşilçam Sokak 5

Fitaş Sineması (☎ 212-249 9361) İstiklal Caddesi 24–26, Fitaş Pasajı; four cinemas in one

Sinepop (☎ 212-251 1176) İstiklal Caddesi, Yeşilçam Sokak 22

Cafe-Bars

Many of Sultanahmet's cafe-restaurants such as the *Rumeli Cafe* on Ticarethane Sokak, *Sultan Pub* on Divan Yolu, *Cafeterya Medusa* (all on Map 5) on Yerebatan Caddesi, and the numerous *small places* along Hoca Rüstem Sokak (between Divan Yolu and Yerebatan Caddesi) have cool music, full menus and outdoor tables that are very pleasant in good weather. It's always a good idea to check prices before you order.

Want to try a nargileh? You can at the *Water Pipe Cafe* on İncili Çavuş Sokak just west of the little park atop the Sunken Cistern. Rent a pipe for US$3.50 and puff away.

Real cafe-bars are in Beyoğlu (Map 3). Two of the best are *Kaktüs Café* (☎ 212-249 5979, *İmam Adnan Sokak 4*), half a block north off İstiklal Caddesi, and *Cadde-i Kebir*, directly across the street. Kaktüs is lighter, noisier, more active and with a longer menu. Cadde-i Kebir is quieter; *çerez* (snacks) and light meals (US$5 to US$9) are served. At either place, beer is US$1.75, rakı US$2.50. There are sidewalk tables at both.

Urban (☎ 212-252 1325, *Kartal Sokak 6/A*), just out of Galatasaray Square, is among Beyoğlu's coolest cafes. Classical

Old Pera Wineshops

Tarihi Pano Şaraphanesi, at the corner of Kalyoncu Kulluğu and Hamalbaşı Caddesis just opposite the British consulate general, is a bit of Beyoğlu history come back to life.

The Pano was founded in 1898 by Panayotis Papadopoulos, an Ottoman Greek. In the first half of the 20th century such Greek wineshops were commonplace in Pera (Beyoğlu), but the Cyprus conflict of the 1950s and '60s saw many Turkish Greeks emigrate to Greece. Their wineshops fell on hard times. When the Pano closed in the 1970s, it was a dingy dive patronised by only a few winos.

Now renovated and reopened, it's a hot spot for Turkish Yuppies who come to sip wine, slouch at the stand-up tables, and talk stock prices and dot-coms.

A drink will set you back US$1.50 to US$3 or more, depending on what you order.

music or cool jazz greets you as you enter past a rack of periodicals in six languages. Many and varied caffeine and alcoholic stimulants are served along with a cafe menu of sandwiches and omelettes (US$3), salads (US$4) and a few meat dishes (US$6). The stone-walled rear room was once a Byzantine cistern.

Southern İstiklal Caddesi (Map 3) is an up-and-coming nightlife area, in particular the district of Asmalımescit, centred on the street of the same name.

On İstiklal Caddesi next to the Odakule office tower and a small Armenian church is *Garibaldi* (☎ 212-249 6895), a restaurant-bar with live music (jazz, smooth or Turkish pop) many nights starting around 8.30 pm. The specialities here are the steaks and the extensive salad bar.

Cafe Miğfer (280 İstiklal Caddesi) is an agreeable cafe-bar with live music some nights and a quieter room for conversation upstairs.

Turn right onto Asmalımescit Sokak, then left onto Sofyalı Sokak, a street of small cafes and shops selling antiques, books and art. *Galatea Restaurant and Wine Bar* (Sofyalı Sokak 16) is upscale, but *Kum Saati* (Sofyalı Sokak 28) is a chic cafe for theatre types, with cappuccino for US$2 and fondue for US$6 per person. The cappuccino is a bit cheaper at *Cep Sanat*, at the corner of Sofyalı and Jurnal Sokaks, and the outdoor *tavla* (backgammon) tables are free.

At the end of Sofyalı Sokak continue into the passage to find *K.V.* (☎ 212-251 4338, Tünel Pasajı), pronounced keh-**veh**, opposite the Tünel. It's a posh, arty cafe offering coffees, teas, pastries, light meals and cool recorded music to a sophisticated, well-heeled crowd. A sip and munch here might cost US$5 or US$6, more for something truly filling.

Discos & Rock Clubs
Most of the action is near Taksim Square (Map 3). Walk along Sıraselviler Caddesi past the Hotel Keban to find *Discotheque 1001*, the *Uçuk Kaçık Disco & Bar*, *Çakı Tecno-Pop-Undergrande*, and *Bariyer* (with live music). The types of music found at each place change with the fashions, but the locations remain the same.

The little street with the big name, Büyükparmakkapı Sokak, off of İstiklal Caddesi near Taksim Square, is a good place to look for music. It's probably okay for women before dark, but after dark (8.30 to 9 pm) there are very few single women out alone, so it'd be best to have male accompaniment.

Rıddım (Rhythm) opposite the Pandora bookshop serves up reggae, Latin beat and Afro-pop. Nearby, *Mojo* often has live rock and pop. *Vivaldi*, at the far end of the street from İstiklal, is the longevity king, still rockin' after half a decade. Across the street from it is the equally loud but much newer *Asparagas*.

Cadde-i Kebir Kültür ve Eğlence Merkezi, on İmam Adnan Sokak just down from the Cadde-i Kebir (see Cafe-Bars, earlier) often has bands and special events.

Jazz Bars
Babylon (Map 3, ☎ 212-292 7368, Şeyhbender Sokak 3), off Sofyalı Sokak near Tünel, is one of Beyoğlu's premier jazz venues. Check out its Web site (www.babylon-ist.com) for more details.

Cafe Gramofon (Map 3, ☎ 212-293 0786) in Tünel Square is a restaurant charging about US$14 cover charge when a group is playing. The schedule of groups and performance times is posted by the door.

Kehribar (Map 2, ☎ 212-231 4100) in the Divan Oteli is smooth and luxurious, with excellent music and expensive drinks. Next door in the Hyatt Regency İstanbul, is *Harry's Jazz Bar* (Map 2, ☎ 212-225 7000), with a similar reputation. Or try *Tepe Lounge Bar* (Map 3, ☎ 212-251 4696) at Hotel The Marmara in Taksim, where there's jazz from 10.30 pm to 1 am.

Nightclubs
Nightclubs with entertainment are mostly in Beyoğlu and along the Bosphorus shores. In the Old City there are several Ottoman theme restaurants which offer dinner and an 'Ottoman' show including belly dancers and folk troupes. The larger, more expensive clubs are tame – and hardly authentic –

but safe, as are the clubs in the big hotels. You may get ripped off in smaller clubs.

Kervansaray (Map 2, ☎ 212-247 1630, *Cumhuriyet Caddesi 30, Harbiye)*, on the northern side of the İstanbul Hilton Hotel arcade, is a good if very commercial club of long standing. A full dinner with drinks, tax and the show costs US$75 per person. It's popular with tour groups.

A similar club is *Maksim Gazino Nightclub* (Map 3, ☎ 293 4110, *Sıraselviler Caddesi 37)*, just out of Taksim to the right of the Hotel Savoy. Maksim has a set menu (US$50) which includes dinner and a show (8.30 or 11.30 pm).

Casinos
Many luxury hotels used to have profitable gambling casinos, but when the Islamist Refah Partisi came to power in the mid-1990s laws were passed to close them. Refah is gone, but at the time of writing the law remained the same and it is still illegal to gamble in Turkey.

A traditional Turkish *gazino*, by the way, is not a gambling place, but an open-air nightclub popular during the summer months. A few still survive along the European shore of the Bosphorus, serving up Turkish popular singers, dinner and drinks.

Night Cruises
About the cheapest but most enjoyable night-time activity in İstanbul is to take a ferry from Eminönü to Üsküdar or from Karaköy to Haydarpaşa/Kadıköy. The great, historic buildings are illuminated, and the twinkling city lights, the boats bobbing in the waves, and the powerful searchlights of the ferries sweeping the sea lanes make a lasting impression. The round trip takes about an hour, and costs US$1.

Hamams
A visit to the hamam, or Turkish bath, can be wonderful: cleansing, refreshing, relaxing and sociable.

The tradition of the steam bath was passed from the Romans to the Byzantines, and from them to the Turks, who have fostered it ever since. Islam's emphasis on personal cleanliness resulted in the construction of hundreds of hamams throughout İstanbul. Though modern bath and shower facilities in the home have now cut public bath usage to a fraction of what it was, the tradition of a leisurely steam bath in grand public facilities is alive and well in Turkey.

Traditionally, men and women bathed separately, and bath attendants had to be of the same gender as their clients. Baths were taken frequently – especially on a Friday, the Muslim Sabbath – and prices were low.

Tourism has changed the tradition radically. Some of the finest old baths have raised prices dramatically, meaning that only tourists can afford them. Service has fallen as prices have risen, so you must shop carefully for your Turkish-bath experience. For a description of taking a Turkish bath, see the boxed text 'The Hamam Experience' in the Western Anatolia chapter.

In İstanbul, the price for the entire experience can be US$6 to US$8 in a local bath if you bring your own soap, shampoo and towel, and bathe yourself; from US$8 to US$12 for an assisted bath; from US$16 to US$30 and more at a 'historic' bath, including a perfunctory massage. Tips will be expected all around.

After you're all done, you'll be utterly refreshed, hyper-clean, and almost unable to walk due to the wonderful relaxation of muscles, mind and spirit.

Tourist Baths On Yerebatan Caddesi at Babıali Caddesi, 200m north-west of Aya Sofya, *Cağaloğlu Hamamı* (Map 5, ☎ 212-522 2424) was built over three centuries ago. It boasts (without evidence) that King Edward VIII, Kaiser Wilhelm II, Franz Liszt and Florence Nightingale have all enjoyed its pleasures, no doubt at the same time. Hours are from 7 am to 10 pm (men) or 8 am to 8 pm (women). A self-service bath (wash yourself) costs US$10, the full treatment US$20, the deluxe treatment US$30, plus tips.

Çemberlitaş Hamamı (Map 5, ☎ 212-522 7974, *Vezirhan Caddesi 8)*, off Divan Yolu near the Kapalı Çarşı, is a double hamam (twin baths for men and women) designed by Sinan for Nurbanu Sultan, wife of Sultan Selim II, in 1584. Hours are 6 am to midnight, and prices are similar to those at the Cağaloğlu Hamamı.

Tarihi Galatasaray Hamamı (Map 3, ☎ 212-251 8653, Turnacıbaşı Sokak 24), or Historic Galatasaray Turkish Bath, is off İstiklal Caddesi just north of Galatasaray Square. The men's side, rich in marble decoration, pretty fountains and tip-hungry staff, is open from 5 am to midnight, and charges US$30 for the full treatment – bath, scrub, massage and rest-cubicle use – plus at least 20% more in tips. The women's side, open from 8 am to 8 pm, is not as nice, and charges a few dollars more.

Local Baths If it's just a bath you're interested in, ask at your hotel for directions to a *mahalli hamam* (neighbourhood bath) where locals go. Neighbourhood baths will treat you much better for much less money than the touristy baths, though as more foreigners patronise these local baths they may suffer the same fate. Here are some suggestions:

Tarihi Gedikpaşa Hamamı (Map 5) Downhill (south) from the Kapalı Çarşı along Gedikpaşa Caddesi, this hamam has been here for centuries and looks it, but at least it's cheap.

Kadırga Hamamı (Map 5) The Kadırga Hamamı is on Kadırga Hamamı Sokak, just off the southern end of Piyerloti Caddesi opposite the park. The women's section, or Kadınlar Kısmı, is on the opposite side up the hill on Kadırga Hamamı Sokak. A one-hour bath costs just US$4 or less, a few dollars more with a massage.

Tarihi Ali Paşa Hamamı (Map 3) Off Necatibey Caddesi on Ali Paşa Medresesi Sokak near the Kılıç Ali Paşa Camii, the Tarihi Ali Paşa Hamamı is out of the tourist area, and relatively cheap.

SHOPPING
İstanbul has it all, and prices for craft items are not necessarily higher than at the village source. Leather apparel offers good value, but you must shop around, get to know the market, and inspect your prospective purchase carefully for flaws and bad handiwork.

Carpets
There must be as many carpet shops as there are taxis. The carpet shop touts become ex-

ceedingly tedious very early in your visit, but a Turkish carpet – a good one at a fair price – is a beautiful, durable and useful souvenir.

The carpet shops of longstanding are in and around Kapalı Çarşı (Map 8). Their proprietors and sales personnel are more knowledgeable and less pushy than those at the newly opened shops in Cankurtaran and other hotel areas.

The government-run carpet shop in the Baths of Lady Hürrem (Map 5; Haseki Hürrem Hamamı) between Aya Sofya and the Sultan Ahmet Camii is a safe choice, with guaranteed quality and fixed prices.

If you haggle for a carpet, at least shop around and get to know price levels a bit. Beware of a scam whereby you are befriended by a charming Turk, or perhaps a Turkish-American or Turkish-European couple. They recommend and show you a friend's carpet shop, but there's no pressure on you to buy. Later you go to the shop by yourself and choose a carpet, but the owner urges you to buy a carpet that's more expensive because it's 'old' or 'Persian' or 'rare', or 'makes a good investment'. Beware: you may later find you've paid much more than the carpet is worth or that the carpet that has been shipped to you is not the expensive one you bought.

Make sure that *you* choose the carpet, inspect it carefully, compare prices for similar work at other shops, then buy and, preferably, take it with you or ship it yourself.

One recommended place for fine antique carpets and textiles is Su-De (☎/fax 212-516 5488, ⓔ capas@escortnet.com), İletişim Han 7/2, facing the entrance to the Binbirdirek Cistern (Map 5) a block west of the Hippodrome. Mr Suat Çapas is an expert in this business and fair with his customers.

Leather Apparel
The traditional leather apparel centre is the Kürkçüler Çarşısı section of the Kapalı Çarşı, but today the leather shops fill street after street in the Beyazıt, Laleli and Aksaray districts.

The best way to be assured of quality is to shop around, trying on garments in several shops. Look especially for quality stitching and lining, sufficient fullness of sleeve and leg and care taken in the small things such as attaching buttons and zippers.

Fashions & Silk
İstiklal Caddesi (Map 3) in Beyoğlu, formerly the Grande Rue de Péra, has reclaimed some of its Ottoman chic, and is now lined with shops selling upscale clothing, fashions, leather apparel, furs and silks. For silk scarves, try İpek (☎ 212-249 8207), İstiklal Caddesi 230, just south of Galatasaray.

Handicrafts
Although the Kapalı Çarşı (Map 8) has a great deal of general tourist ware, a few shops specialise in high-quality handicrafts. One such is Selvi El Sanatları (☎ 212-527 0997, fax 527 0226), Yağcılar Caddesi 54, Kapalı Çarşı. The speciality here is Kütahya faience, and not just the *turist işi* (tourist ware) sold in most shops. Many of the tile panels, vases, plates and other items here are fine, artistic Kütahya ware.

İstanbul Handicrafts Market (Map 5; Sanatlar Çarşısı) is in the restored 18th-century Cedid Mehmed Efendi Medresesi on the southern side of the Yeşil Ev hotel on Kabasakal Caddesi, between Aya Sofya and the Blue Mosque. Local artisans ply their traditional Turkish arts and crafts here, and sell their products.

On the west side of Aya Sofya next to the Yücelt Hostel, an old Islamic theological school, the Caferağa Medresesi, is now inhabited by the Uygulamalı Türk El Sanatları Merkezi (Map 5), or Centre for Applied Turkish Handicrafts.

Old Books, Maps & Prints
Librairie de Péra (Map 3, ☎ 212-245 4998), Galipdede Caddesi 22, Tünel, just south of the Galata Mevlevihanesi, is a good antiquarian shop with old books in Turkish, Greek, Armenian, Arabic, French, German, English and more. Eren (Map 3, ☎ 212-251 2858), Sofyalı Sokak 34, Tünel, has old and new history and art books and maps. Ergün Hiçyılmaz, Avrupa Pasajı 17, Galatasaray, has old books, prints and phonograph records.

Sahaflar Çarşısı (Map 8), the used-book bazaar just west of the Kapalı Çarşı across Çadırcılar Caddesi, and in the shadow of the Beyazıt Camii, is best for browsing and not bad for buying. The Üniversiteli Kitabevi (☎ 212-511 3987, fax 216-345 9387), at No 5, is one of the best shops, with a modern outlook and the most up-to-date books published in Turkey. The Zorlu Kitabevi (☎ 212-511 2660, fax 526 0495), at No 22, specialises in books about İstanbul, old documents and maps. Dilmen Kitabevi (☎ 212-527 9934), at No 20, has a good selection of titles on Turkey and Turkish history in English.

GETTING THERE & AWAY
All roads lead to İstanbul. As the country's foremost transportation hub, the question is not so much how to get there but how to negotiate the sprawling urban mass when you arrive. Here is the information you may need on arrival.

Air
Atatürk International Airport in Yeşilköy, 23km west of the city centre, has a new international terminal, right next to the older domestic terminal.

The Ministry of Tourism maintains an information office in the arrivals hall of the international terminal (lower floor). Also in the arrivals hall are ATMs paying out Turkish liras, and various currency exchange offices operated by Turkish banks. If you change money here, count your money carefully and make sure it agrees with the total on the exchange slip. These guys will often short-change you by several percent, relying upon your confusion as a new arrival to get away with it. Also, don't accept an excuse that they 'have no small change'. It's their business to have the proper change.

After landing and before you pass through customs, you might want to check prices on the duty-free goods at the shops in the baggage claim area. It's unusual to be able to buy duty-free goods on your way into (rather than out of) a country.

For details of international flights to and from İstanbul, see the Getting There &

Away chapter earlier in this book; for flights from İstanbul to other Turkish cities, see the Getting Around chapter.

Most of the airline offices are on Cumhuriyet Caddesi (Map 2) between Taksim Square and Harbiye, in the Elmadağ district, but Turkish Airlines has offices around the city. Travel agencies can also sell tickets and make reservations. Contact details of some major airlines include the following:

Air France (Map 3, ☎ 212-254 4356, 254 3196, fax 254 7614) corner of Cumhuriyet Caddesi and Tarlabaşı Bulvarı, Taksim; (☎ 212-663 0600), Atatürk International Airport

British Airways (☎ 212-234 1300, fax 234 1308) Cumhuriyet Caddesi 10, Elmadağ; (☎ 212-663 0574) Atatürk International Airport

Delta Airlines (☎ 212-231 2339, fax 231 2346) in the İstanbul Hilton Hotel arcade; (☎ 212-663 0752) Atatürk International Airport

KLM (☎ 212-230 0311, fax 232 8749) Abdi İpekçi Caddesi 8, Nişantaşı, north-east of Harbiye; (☎ 212-663 0603) Atatürk International Airport

Lufthansa (☎ 212-288 1050, fax 275 6961) Maya Akar Center, B Blok Kat 3, Büyükdere Caddesi 100–102, Esentepe; (☎ 212-663 0594) Atatürk International Airport

Olympic Airways (☎ 212-246 5081, fax 232 2173) Cumhuriyet Caddesi 171-A, Elmadağ; (☎ 212-663 0820) Atatürk International Airport

Qantas Airways (☎ 212-240 5032, fax 241 5552) 4. Gazeteciler Sitesti A-9, 5. Blok, 1. Levent

Turkish Airlines (Map 3, ☎ 212-663 6363, fax 240 2984) reservations; (☎ 212-252 1106) Taksim Square, Cumhuriyet Caddesi, in the Taksim Gezi Yeri shops

Bus

The Uluslararası İstanbul Otogarı (International İstanbul Bus Terminal; Map 1, ☎ 212-658 0505, fax 658 2858), called simply the 'otogar', is in the western district of Esenler, just south of the expressway and about 10km west of Sultanahmet or Taksim. With restaurants, mosques, shops and 168 ticket offices, it is a town in itself, and one of the world's largest bus terminals.

Buses depart the otogar for virtually all cities and towns in Turkey and to neighbouring countries including Azerbaijan, Bulgaria, Greece, Iran, Romania, Saudi Arabia, Syria, and other destinations in Eastern Europe and the Middle East. The top national lines, giving premium service at somewhat higher prices, are As Turizm (*peron* or gate 40), Bosfor Turizm and Ulusoy (peron 127–129), Pamukkale (peron 41–42), Metro (peron 51–52) and Varan (peron 15–16). Other lines are smaller regional or local lines which may have more frequent but less polished service at lower prices.

Except in busy holiday periods, you can usually just come to the otogar, spend 30 minutes shopping for tickets, and be on your way to your destination at a good price within the hour. There is no easy way to find the best bus company and the best fare; you've got to go from one office to another asking for information and looking at the buses parked at the perons at the back.

There is another bus terminal on the Asian shore of the Bosphorus at Harem (Map 2, ☎ 216-333 3763), 2km north-west of Haydarpaşa train station. If you're arriving from the east, get out at Harem and take the car ferry to Sirkeci; it'll save you two hours' crawl through traffic to the main otogar, then the Metro ride back to the centre. If you're heading east you can save some time and hassle by taking the Harem car ferry from Sirkeci and getting the bus there. But the selection of buses, seats, routes and companies is nowhere near as big at Harem as at the main otogar in Esenler.

Bus Ticket Offices Travel agencies on Divan Yolu by the Hippodrome and in Cankurtaran will sell you bus tickets, often at inflated prices.

Some bus companies have ticket offices near Taksim Square on Mete and İnönü Caddesis (Map 3). Pamukkale (☎ 212-249 2791) is at Mete Caddesi 16; Nev Tur (☎ 212-249 7961), with buses to Cappadocia, is nearby. Down the hill along İnönü Caddesi are Varan (☎ 212-249 1903, fax 251 7481), at İnönü Caddesi 29/B, a premium line with routes to major Turkish cities and to several points in Europe (including Athens); Kamil Koç (☎ 212-257 7223), İnönü Caddesi 31; As Turizm and Hakiki Koç lines (☎ 212-245

4244); and Ulusoy (☎ 212-249 4373), İnönü Caddesi 59. You can also buy tickets online from the major companies such as Varan (www.varan.com.tr).

Fares & Travel Times See the table for examples of bus fares and travel times from the otogar in İstanbul to other cities in Turkey. Fares vary among companies, and sometimes can be reduced by haggling or by showing a student or senior card. Departures to major cities and resorts are very frequent.

Train
Sirkeci Garı (Map 4) All trains from Europe terminate at Sirkeci Garı (☎ 212-527

0051), next to Eminönü in the shadow of Topkapı Palace. The station has a small post office and currency exchange booth, as well as a restaurant and cafe, and a tourist office (☎ 212-511 5888).

The northern facade of the building was where passengers entered to board the fabled *Orient Express* to Paris. The new main (western) door is a boring modern structure marked 'TCDD İstanbul Garı', which is confusing as İstanbul has two main train stations, Sirkeci and Haydarpaşa, and Sirkeci is the less active one.

Outside the station's western door is the tram up the hill to Sultanahmet, Beyazıt, Laleli and Aksaray; transfer at Aksaray to

Bus Fares & Travel Times

destination	fare (US$)	time (hr)	distance (km)	offices (perons)
Alanya	23	16	840	63, 90, 111, 155
Ankara	10–23	5–5½	450	many
Antakya	23–28	18	1115	100
Antalya	18–20	12	725	15, 20, 35, 40, 61, 63, 87, 90, 100, 111, 155
Artvin	36–40	24	1352	40, 71, 76
Ayvalık	17–21	8	570	22
Bodrum	22–28	13	830	15, 41, 137, 153
Bursa (ferry & bus)	10	3	230	22, 67, 106, 111, 115, 118, 125, 138, 162
Çanakkale	12	5½	340	138
Denizli (for Pamukkale)	15–20	12	665	41
Edirne (via otoyol)	7	2½	235	26, 106, 110, 115, 140, 164
Erzurum	24–30	16	1275	11, 23, 49, 51, 77, 86, 87, 114, 141, 147, 161, 165
Fethiye	20	12–14	980	41, 137
Gaziantep	18–26	14	1136	75, 83, 91, 163
Göreme	17	11	725	24, 28, 59
İpsala	8.50	4	246	98
İzmir	17–25	8	610	many
Kaş	20–25	12	1090	41
Konya	18	10	660	21, 24, 51, 76, 78
Kuşadası	18	9½	700	41, 137
Marmaris	20–24	13	900	41, 132, 137, 155
Side (via Antalya)	21–24	11	790	see Antalya
Trabzon	24–32	18	1110	22, 40, 58, 63, 64, 71, 96, 115, 117, 127, 149, 158

the Metro for the otogar. On the shore north of the station are car ferries for the Asian otogar at Harem.

Trains leaving Sirkeci Garı include the following:

train	destination	departs
Balkan Ekspresi	Budapest	10.20 pm
Bosfor Ekspresi	Bucharest	9.50 pm
Edirne Ekspresi	Edirne	3.25 pm
Uzunköprü Ekspresi	Uzunköprü	8.20 am

Haydarpaşa Garı This station (Map 2, ☎ 216-336 0475, 348 8020), on the Asian shore of the Bosphorus, is the terminus for trains to and from Anatolia and points east and south. Ignore anyone who suggests that you take a taxi to Haydarpaşa. The ferry is cheap, convenient, pleasant and speedy. Ferries (US$0.70, 20 minutes) run every 15 to 30 minutes between Karaköy (at the northern end of Galata Bridge) and Haydarpaşa. Taxis across the Bosphorus are expensive and slow.

Haydarpaşa has an *emanet* (left luggage room), a restaurant serving alcohol, snack shops, bank ATMs and a small PTT.

Trains leaving from Haydarpaşa include the following:

train	destination	departs
Anadolu Ekspresi	Ankara	10 pm
Ankara Ekspresi	Ankara	10.30 pm
Başarı Ekspresi	Ankara	1.15 pm
Başkent Ekspresi	Ankara	10 am
Boğaziçi Ekspresi	Ankara	1.30 pm
Doğu Ekspresi	Kars	8.35 am
Fatih Ekspresi	Ankara	11.30 pm
Güney-Vangölü Ekspresi	Tatvan or Diyarbakır	8.05 am
Meram Ekspresi	Konya	7.20 pm
Pamukkale Ekspresi	Denizli	5.35 pm
Toros Ekspresi	Gaziantep	8.55 am

The nightly *Anadolu Ekspresi* between Ankara and İstanbul via Eskişehir hauls Pullman (US$6.50), couchette (US$8) and sleeping (US$26 to US$30) cars. It departs İstanbul at 10 pm and arrives in Ankara at 7.15 am. A similar *yataklı* (sleeping-car) train leaves half an hour later.

Private compartments on this nightly all-sleeping-car *Ankara Ekspresi* between İstanbul and Ankara cost US$30/40 a single/double. It departs İstanbul at 10.30 pm and arrives in Ankara at 7.35 am.

The *Başarı Ekspresi* departs İstanbul 1.15 pm and makes the run to Ankara in about 7½ hours, arriving at 8.55 pm. It's an air-conditioned, all-1st-class day train. The fare is US$14, or US$10 for students.

The fastest train to Ankara is the *Başkent Ekspresi* (Capital Express), pride of the Turkish State Railways. It departs İstanbul at 10 am and makes the run to Ankara in 6½ hours. It's an air-conditioned, super-1st-class day train with Pullman seats, video, and meals served at your seat, airline-style. The fare is US$14; US$10 for students. Named after Mehmet the Conqueror (Mehmet Fatih), the *Fatih Ekspresi* is a night train departing İstanbul and Ankara at 11.30 pm, arriving in the opposite city at 7.20 am, otherwise similar to the *Başkent* in comfort, speed and price.

The *Boğaziçi Ekspresi* (Bosphorus Express) is a comfortable, if faded, 1st-class Pullman-car train between İstanbul and Ankara, departing each city at 1.30 pm, and arriving in the other at 10.27 pm. The fare to Ankara is US$10.

The night-time *Pamukkale Ekspresi* departs İstanbul daily at 5.35 pm, via Kütahya, Afyon, Isparta, Burdur and Eğirdir, arriving in Denizli at 8.20 am. İstanbul to Denizli fares are US$9.50; for sleeping compartments, total fares are US$25/40 for singles/doubles.

Though the *Doğu Ekspresi* departs from İstanbul on time at 8.35 am, it is usually late thereafter on its long trip via Ankara, Sivas, Erzincan and Erzurum to Kars near the Armenian border. It is a long, slow trip (about 38 hours) and far from pleasant, but it is certainly cheap, costing only US$14.

The *Güney-Vangölü Ekspresi* leaves İstanbul each evening at 8.05 pm, stopping in Ankara, Kayseri, Sivas and Malatya before arriving at Elazığ Junction. East of the junction, the train continues as the *Vangölü* (Lake Van) *Ekspresi* to Tatvan, or the *Güney* (Southern) *Ekspresi* to Diyarbakır and Kurtalan (east of Diyarbakır), depending upon the day. For the *Vangölü* eastbound, board in İstanbul on Monday, Wednesday or Saturday. For the *Güney*, board in İstanbul on Tuesday, Thursday, Friday or Sunday. At the time of writing, the *Vangölü Ekspresi* was terminating at Elazığ, but this may change.

The *Meram Ekspresi* departs İstanbul daily at 7.20 pm via Kütahya and Afyon, arriving in Konya at 8.50 am. The İstanbul to Konya fare is US$9.50; for sleeping compartments, fares are US$25/40 a single/double.

The *Toros Ekspresi* departs İstanbul on Tuesday, Thursday and Sunday at 8.55 am and heads for the south-east, stopping in Eskişehir (Enveriye), Afyon, Konya, Adana and finally Gaziantep (11.45 am the following day). Fares from İstanbul are US$7 to Konya, US$10 to Adana and US$13 to Gaziantep. A sleeping car berth between İstanbul and Gaziantep costs US$28/25/20 per person, a single/double/triple, total fare.

Car

The E80 Trans-European Motorway from Europe passes north of Atatürk International Airport, then crosses the Bosphorus on the Fatih Bridge. Getting into and out of İstanbul is frustrating. Traffic is chaotic, signs inadequate, and no other driver will give you a break.

Car Rental Avoid driving in İstanbul if possible. It's best to rent your car at the airport, where you can get directly on the motorway, or even in some smaller city.

The well-known international car-rental firms have desks at Atatürk International Airport and in the city centre, mostly near Taksim Square and the Elmadağ district, a few blocks north of it.

Avis (☎ 212-663 0646) Atatürk airport international arrivals hall; (☎ 212-662 0852, fax 663 0724) domestic arrivals hall; (☎ 212-257 7670, fax 263 3918) Reservations Centre; (☎ 212-516 6109, fax 516 6108) Beyazıt office, Ordu Caddesi, Haznedar Sokak 1

Budget (☎ 212-663 0858, fax 663 0724) Atatürk airport international arrivals hall; (☎ 212-296 3196, fax 296 3188) Reservations Centre,

Cumhuriyet Caddesi 12, Seyhan Apartmanı, 4th floor, office 10, just north of Taksim Square; (☎ 212-253 9200, fax 237 2919, e budget@escortnet.com) Cumhuriyet Caddesi 19/A, Gezi Apartmanı

Europcar/Inter-rent (☎ 212-663 0746, fax 663 6830) Atatürk airport international arrivals hall; (☎ 212-254 7788, fax 237 3158) Esin Turizm, Topçu Caddesi, Uygun İş Merkezi 2, 80090 Talimhane, a few short blocks north of Taksim Square and only steps west of Cumhuriyet Caddesi

Hertz (☎ 212-663 0807, fax 663 6797) Atatürk airport; (☎ 212-234 4300, fax 232 9260) Ekin Turizm, Cumhuriyet Caddesi 295, Harbiye

Sun Rent a Car/Sixt (☎ 216-318 9040, fax 321 4014) Kısıklı Caddesi, Nurbaba Sokak 1, 81190 Üsküdar; Auto Europe's representative, a local firm with a good reputation and offices in major cities and resorts, and at Atatürk airport

Boat

For details on ferry routes within greater İstanbul, including cross-Bosphorus ferries, see the Getting Around section, following.

Karaköy (Map 4) Cruise liners dock at Karaköy, near the Yolcu Salonu or International Maritime Passenger Terminal on Rıhtım Caddesi. There's a tourist office (☎ 212-249 5776) in the Yolcu Salonu, near the street doors.

Car ferries operate each week from mid-June to the end of August, departing from İstanbul on Monday at 2 pm, arriving in Samsun on Tuesday at 5 pm and departing at 7 pm, arriving in Trabzon on Wednesday at 8 am, Rize at noon, and back to Trabzon by 7 pm. It leaves Trabzon for İstanbul on Wednesday at 8 pm, arriving in Samsun Thursday morning at 9 am, and İstanbul on Friday at 1 pm.

Per-person fares between İstanbul and Trabzon are US$21 for a Pullman seat, US$44 to US$104 for cabin berths. Meals are US$5 for breakfast and US$12 for lunch or dinner. The fare for a car is US$102, and for a motorcycle it's US$42.

The international dock is next to the Karaköy ferry dock and about 100m east of the Galata Bridge. Bus and dolmuş routes to Taksim pass along Kemeraltı Caddesi, a few short blocks north-west of the Yolcu Salonu.

For destinations in the Old City such as Sultanahmet, go to the western side of Karaköy Square itself, at the end of the Galata Bridge, via the pedestrian underpass; or walk across the bridge and get on the tram at Eminönü.

Seraglio Point (Map 5) Seraglio Point (Sarayburnu), east of Sirkeci, is the dock for the car ferry to İzmir, which operates each weekend throughout the year, departing İstanbul each Friday at 3 pm and arriving in İzmir on Saturday at 9 am. (From mid-July to August, departure from İstanbul is at 5.30 pm, arriving in İzmir at 12.30 pm.)

One-way fares (per person) range from US$23 for Pullman seats to US$155 for deluxe cabin berths; a two-berth B-class cabin would cost US$120 a double. If you want to use your cabin as a hotel room on Saturday night in İzmir, the cost ranges from US$15 a double for the cheapest cabin to US$72 a double for deluxe, with a two-berth, B-class cabin costing US$42.

Meals are extra, at US$5 for breakfast, US$12 for lunch or dinner. The fare for a car is US$60 one way and less than half that for a motorcycle.

Yenikapı (Map 2) Yenikapı, south of Aksaray Square, is the dock for intracity catamarans and for *hızlı feribot* (fast car ferries) on routes across the Sea of Marmara. To Yalova, ferries leave about every two hours and get you to Yalova (for Bursa) in less than an hour for US$28 (car and driver) or US$7 (pedestrian/passenger).

To Bandırma, the voyage is made in less than two hours for US$45 (car and driver), or US$13 (pedestrian/passenger).

Kabataş (Map 3) Ferries run from Kabataş, 3km north of Karaköy on the Bosphorus shore, just south of the Dolmabahçe Palace, to Üsküdar. Catamarans run from here to Bostancı on the Asian shore, with a few to other destinations as well.

GETTING AROUND

Transport by road often creeps. Transport by sea is far more pleasant and speedy, but it serves only a few routes.

To/From the Airport

Airport to City The international and domestic terminals at Atatürk International Airport are next to one another; it's a short walk between them. The fastest way to get into town from the airport is by taxi (from 20 to 30 minutes, US$12 to US$20); the fare depends upon what part of the city you're headed for and whether it's night or day.

A cheaper but slower way is the Havaş airport bus (US$3.50, from 35 to 60 minutes) stopping at Bakırköy, Aksaray and Tepebaşı. Buses leave about every 30 minutes.

For even less, share a taxi (US$6 total; make sure the driver runs the meter) from the airport to the Yeşilköy *banliyö tren istasyonu*, the suburban railway station in the neighbouring town of Yeşilköy. From here, battered trains (US$0.50) run every 30 minutes or less to Sirkeci station. Get off at Yenikapı for Aksaray and Laleli, at Cankurtaran for Sultanahmet hotels, or at Eminönü (end of the line) for Beyoğlu.

City to Airport Several private services run minibuses to the airport, advertising their services at budget hotels in and around Sultanahmet. Fares range from US$4 to US$6 per person. Reserve your seat in advance for pick-up from your hotel. Allow lots of time for the trip: the minibus may spend an hour circulating through the city collecting all the passengers before heading out to the airport (30 to 45 minutes).

If you're staying in Beyoğlu, the cheapest and most convenient way to the airport is the Havaş bus (US$3.50) which departs from Tepebaşı. The trip takes 45 minutes to an hour. There are also dolmuşes to the airport (US$2) from the Yeşilköy-Ataköy-Florya-Hava Limanı dolmuş stand on Şehit Muhtarbey Caddesi at Aydede Caddesi two blocks north of Taksim.

A taxi to the airport costs US$12 to US$20.

Bus

To/From the Otogar If you arrive at the main otogar in Esenler, take the Metro east to Aksaray, then transfer to the Eminönü tram and get out at Sultanahmet.

To get to the Harem bus terminal, take the Harem car ferry (Araba Vapuru) from Sirkeci. An alternative is to take a ferry from Karaköy to Haydarpaşa or Kadıköy, then catch one of the frequent dolmuşes northwards along the shore to Harem. You can also take a ferry from Eminönü, Kabataş or Beşiktaş to Üsküdar, then a dolmuş or bus south 2.5km to Harem.

City Buses Official İETT city buses, which are owned and operated by the city, do not accept cash fares. Similar looking (but older) Özel Halk Otobüsü (Peoples' Buses) are privately owned and operated, and allow you to pay by either city bus ticket or cash.

Buy tickets from kiosks near major stops (look for signs saying 'IETT' and 'bilet'). Fares are US$0.60 per ride, reduced for students, but you may need a Turkish student ID card to get the discount. Hawkers near the major bus stops usually sell tickets for a mark-up of 20% for your convenience. Some longer routes cost two fares.

If you're jammed in the middle of the bus when your stop comes, shout '*İnecek var!*' (een-neh-**jek** vahr, 'Someone needs to get out!').

Dolmuş

İstanbul dolmuşes are minibuses running on defined routes at a set price. Useful routes are mentioned in the text.

Metro

İstanbul's Metro or light railway system will be under construction for a decade

Akbil

If you're staying in İstanbul a few days, consider using Akbil, the electronic transit pass. You buy a metal Akbil 'button' with an initial şarj ('charge') of US$5.50 or more. When you enter the Metro, tram, bus or ferry, you touch the button to the Akbil contact point and the fare is deducted from your button. You recharge your button from Akbil machines at major transit points by inserting money into the machine.

more, but several useful lines are already in service. The fare is US$0.40.

The main Metro line goes from Aksaray north-west along Adnan Menderes Bulvarı (formerly Vatan Caddesi) through the Bayrampaşa and Sağmalcılar districts to the otogar in Esenler, then turns south-west towards the airport, but currently ends at Yenibosna. When construction is finished, it will terminate near Atatürk International Airport.

The 7.8km-long Taksim to 4. Levent metro line has been completed and is now in service, but the planned line between Aksaray and Taksim won't be ready for years.

Train

The Sirkeci-Halkalı suburban train line follows the Sea of Marmara shore south-west from Seraglio Point to the south-western suburbs. The suburban trains are decrepit but serviceable and cheap.

Tram

A shorter, slower tram (US$0.40) line goes from the ferry docks in Eminönü past Sirkeci and uphill to Sultanahmet, then along Divan Yolu/Yeniçeriler Caddesi/Ordu Caddesi past Beyazıt and the Kapalı Çarşı to Laleli and Yusufpaşa (transfer to the Metro here to get to Aksaray); it continues out Turgut Özal Caddesi to the Topkapı (Cannon Gate) and on to the Marmara shore district of Zeytinburnu.

In Beyoğlu, a restored early 20th-century tram runs along İstiklal Caddesi between Taksim and Tünel Squares.

Tünel

İstanbul's little underground train, the Tünel, runs between Karaköy and the southern end of İstiklal Caddesi called Tünel Meydanı (Tünel Square) every five to 10 minutes from 7 am (7.30 am on Sunday) until 9 pm. The 80-second trip costs US$0.40.

Car

It makes no sense to drive in İstanbul. If you have a car, park it in a spot recommended by your hotel and use public transport, except perhaps for excursions up the Bosphorus. If

On Foot

With an overburdened public transport system, walking in İstanbul can often be faster and more rewarding. Watch out for broken pavement, bits of pipe sticking a few centimetres out of the pavement, ankle-breaking holes and all manner of other hazards.

Don't expect any car driver to stop for you, a pedestrian, in any situation. Cars seize the right of way virtually everywhere, and drivers become furiously annoyed with pedestrians who assert ridiculous claims to right of way and safety. The halt, the lame, the infant and the aged flee before the onslaught of the automobile. Swallow your pride and step lively to avoid being maimed.

you plan to rent a car, do so when you're ready to leave İstanbul or, better yet, use public transport to get to your next destination, and rent the car there.

Taxi

Taxis are plentiful, as are honest drivers, though the many dishonest ones seem to congregate in tourist areas.

Most taxis run on nonpolluting natural gas. The fact that some drivers have their blood types painted on the taxi wing/fender should tell you something about their expectations of surviving İstanbul traffic.

All taxis have digital meters, and it is an offence punishable by a large fine to take a passenger but to refuse to run the meter, or to demand a flat fare in place of the metered fare. Still, such practices are common on trips originating from touristy areas. Some drivers also take advantage of the many zeros on Turkish currency to charge you 10 times what the meter reads.

The base rate (drop rate, flag fall) is about US$1.25 during the *gündüz* (daytime); the *gece* (night) rate is 50% higher. A daytime trip between Aksaray and Sultanahmet costs about US$2; between Taksim and Karaköy about US$3; between Taksim and Sultanahmet about US$5, between Sultanahmet and the airport about US$12 to US$15.

Older meters have tiny red lights marked with 'gündüz' and 'gece' to show which rate is being used. Newer meters with LCD displays flash 'gündüz' or 'gece' when they are started.

Ferries

The major ferry docks (Eminönü, Sirkeci and Karaköy) are at the mouth of the Golden Horn. Boats operated by the city authority (white with orange stacks) are docked east of the Galata Bridge; smaller private ferries running some of the same routes dock west of the bridge near the Ticaret Odası (Chamber of Commerce) building. Short ferry rides (less than 30 minutes) cost less than US$1, most longer ones (up to an hour) are US$2.

Buy your token or ticket from the agent in the booth; if you buy them from the men who stand around outside the ferry docks hawking them, you may pay four times the fare.

To Üsküdar City ferries depart for Üsküdar from Eminönü every 15 minutes from 6.15 am and 11.35 pm, every 20 minutes on weekends and holidays. Also, 14 trips a day run between Karaköy and Üsküdar. From Kabataş, just south of Dolmabahçe Palace, ferries run to Üsküdar every hour on the hour from 7 am to 8 pm, with additional boats at 7.30, 8.30 and 9.30 am, and 4.30, 5.30, 6.30 and 7.30 pm. A similar ferry service operates between Beşiktaş and Üsküdar. There are private Eminönü ferries as well.

To Haydarpaşa/Kadıköy To get to the Asian train station at Haydarpaşa, or for a cruise around Seraglio Point and across the Bosphorus (good for photos of Topkapı Palace, Aya Sofya and the Blue Mosque), catch a ferry from Karaköy; they depart every 15 minutes (20 minutes on weekends). Some go only to Kadıköy, 1km south of Haydarpaşa, so check your boat's itinerary. The return trip to Haydarpaşa and/or Kadıköy (US$1.50) takes about an hour. There are both city and private boats.

Ferries also depart the Eminönü docks for Kadıköy every 15 to 20 minutes from 7 am to 8 pm.

Cross-Bosphorus Ferries Passenger ferries run between the European and Asian shores at several points along the Bosphorus, allowing you to cross from one side to the other. You can also hire a boatman to motor you across the Bosphorus for a few dollars.

Southernmost are the routes from Eminönü, Kabataş and Beşiktaş in European İstanbul to Üsküdar in Asian İstanbul.

Another route is from Kanlıca to Anadolu Hisarı and Kandilli on the Asian shore, and across the Bosphorus to Bebek on the European shore, with nine trips daily. The voyage from Kanlıca to Bebek takes 25 minutes and costs US$0.75.

Other ferries run from İstinye on the European side to Beykoz and Paşabahçe on the Asian side. Yet another operates from Sarıyer in European İstanbul to Anadolu Kavağı in Asian İstanbul, with 17 ferries a day (at least one every hour) from 7.15 am to 11 pm, seven of which stop at Rumeli Kavağı as well.

Catamaran (Sea Bus)
Called *deniz otobüsü*, fast catamarans run on commuter routes between the European and Asian shores of İstanbul, and up the Bosphorus. Major docks on the European side are at Yenikapı and Kabataş, with less frequently served docks at Eminönü, Karaköy and several Bosphorus docks such as İstinye and Sarıyer. On the Asian side, major docks are at Bostancı and Kartal, and minor docks at Büyükada and Heybeliada.

Fares for the catamarans are about double those for ferries. Except for the route up the Bosphorus, you may find that you rarely use these commuter-friendly intracity catamarans on touristic excursions.

Around İstanbul

The dense crowding of İstanbul's medieval street pattern is relieved by expanses of water offering fresh breezes and extended views. Take an excursion up the Bosphorus, or to the nearby Princes' Islands in the Sea of Marmara, to fully appreciate the city's renowned natural situation.

THE BOSPHORUS (MAP 1)
The strait that connects the Black Sea and Sea of Marmara, 32km long, from 500m to 3km wide and 50m to 120m (average 60m) deep, has determined the history not only of İstanbul, but of the empires governed from this city.

In Turkish, the strait is the İstanbul Boğazı, from *boğaz*, throat or strait, or Boğaziçi (*iç*, inside or interior: 'within the strait').

The Bosphorus provides a convenient boundary for geographers. As it was a military bottleneck, armies marching from the east tended to stop on the eastern side, and those from the west on the western. So the western side was always more like Europe, the eastern more like Asia. Though the modern Turks think of themselves as Europeans, it is still common to say that Europe ends and Asia begins at the Bosphorus.

Crossing it always meant going by boat – until 1973. Late in that year, the Bosphorus Bridge (Boğaziçi Köprüsü), the fourth-longest in the world, was opened to travellers. Now there is a second bridge, the Fatih Bridge (Fatih Köprüsü; named after Mehmet the Conqueror, Mehmet Fatih), just north of Rumeli Hisarı.

History
Greek legend recounts that Zeus, unfaithful to his wife Hera in an affair with Io, tried to make up for it by turning his former lover into a cow. Hera, for good measure, provided a horsefly to sting Io on the rump and drive her across the strait. In ancient Greek, *bous* is cow, and *poros* is crossing place, giving us Bosphorus: the place where the cow crossed.

From earliest times the Bosphorus has been a maritime road to adventure. It is thought that Ulysses' travels brought him through the Bosphorus. Byzas, founder of Byzantium, explored these waters before the time of Jesus. Mehmet the Conqueror built two mighty fortresses at the strait's narrowest point so as to close it off to allies of the Byzantines. Each spring, enormous Ottoman armies would take several days to cross the Bosphorus on their way to campaigns in Asia. At the end of WWI, the defeated Ottoman capital cowered under the guns of Allied frigates anchored in the strait. When the republic was proclaimed, the last sultan of the Ottoman Empire slunk down to the Bosphorus shore, boarded a launch, and sailed away to exile in a British man-of-war. And when Kemal Atatürk died, his body was taken aboard a man-of-war at Seraglio Point for the first part of its journey to Ankara.

Touring the Bosphorus

The essential feature of any Bosphorus tour is a cruise along the strait, though visits to particular buildings are best done by land, so a trip combining travel by both land and sea is best. Begin your explorations with a ferry cruise for a general view, then visit selected sites by bus and taxi.

Ferry Though tour agencies and luxury hotels offer cruises on the Bosphorus, it's cheaper to go on one of the Bosphorus excursion ferries. The ferry most tourists use is the city-run Eminönü-Kavaklar Boğaziçi Özel Gezi Seferleri (Eminönü-Kavaklar Bosphorus Special Touristic Excursions) on the Bosphorus. These ferries depart from Eminönü daily at 10.35 am and 12.35 and 2.10 pm each weekday, stop at Beşiktaş on the European shore, Kanlıca on the Asian shore, Yeniköy, Sarıyer and Rumeli Kavağı on the European shore, and Anadolu Kavağı on the Asian shore (the turn-around point). Times are subject to change.

The ferries go all the way to Rumeli Kavağı and Anadolu Kavağı (1¾ hours), but you may want to go only as far as Sarıyer, then take a dolmuş or bus back down, stopping at various sights along the way. Arrival at Sarıyer, on the European shore about three quarters of the way up the Bosphorus, is at 11.50 am and 1.50 and 3.30 pm respectively. Departures from Sarıyer for the trip back down the Bosphorus are at 2.20, 3.10 and 5.50 pm on weekdays.

Trips are added on Sunday and holidays, with boats departing from Eminönü at 10 and 11 am, noon, 1.30 and 3 pm.

The weekday round-trip fare is US$5, half price on Saturday and Sunday. Prices are printed on all tickets. Hold on to your ticket; you need to show it to re-board the boat for the return trip. The boats fill up early in summer – on weekends particularly – so buy your ticket and walk aboard at least 30 or 45 minutes prior to departure to get a seat.

Private ferries try to duplicate this tour, but the city boat is bigger, smoother, and offers a better experience.

Bus & Dolmuş If you decide to go north on land rather than by ferry, here's how. Bus No 210 from Sultanahmet (near the tourist office) goes up the European shore of the Bosphorus to Emirgan about every two hours. From Eminönü, buses depart from the ranks just west of the Galata Bridge. Take bus No 22 (to Emirgan), No 22-C (to Bebek), or No 25-E (to Sarıyer) from peron (bus rank) 3.

From Taksim, the downhill walk along İnönü Caddesi to Dolmabahçe is short (about 10 minutes) and pleasant. On the right-hand side of İnönü Caddesi just out of Taksim are dolmuşes going to Beşiktaş, which will drop you at Dolmabahçe if you want to ride. There are also Taksim-Sarıyer buses from opposite Hotel The Marmara, and Taksim-Sarıyer dolmuş minibuses (US$0.75) from Mete Caddesi west of the Hotel Gezi, east of the Ceylan Inter-Continental Hotel.

After seeing Yıldız, you can take a bus or dolmuş north to Bebek and Rumeli Hisarı, or return to Beşiktaş to catch a shuttle ferry over to Üsküdar, on the Asian side, in order to continue your sightseeing. The ferries operate every 15 or 20 minutes in each direction, from 6 am to midnight. There are also boats between Üsküdar and Eminönü. Ferries going to Eminönü may bear the sign 'Köprü' or 'Bridge', meaning the Galata Bridge.

Sights on the European Shore

This section covers the sights to look for as you head north along the Bosphorus from Dolmabahçe. The Dolmabahçe Palace itself is covered earlier in this chapter.

Deniz Müzesi (Map 2) The Deniz Müzesi, or Maritime Museum, is on the Bosphorus shore just south of the flyover in Beşiktaş. It's open from 9 am to 12.30 pm and 1.30 to 5 pm, closed Wednesday and Thursday. Admission is US$1.

Though the Ottoman Empire is most remembered for its conquests on land, its maritime power was equally impressive. During the reign of Süleyman the Magnificent, the eastern Mediterranean was virtually an Ottoman lake. The sultan's navies cut a swathe in the Indian Ocean as well. Sea power was instrumental in the conquests of the Aegean coasts and islands, Egypt and North Africa.

However the navy, like the army and the government, lagged behind the West in modernisation during the later centuries. The great battle which broke the spell of Ottoman naval invincibility was fought in 1571 at Lepanto, in the Gulf of Patras off the Greek coast. (Cervantes, Spanish writer of *Don Quixote* fame, fought on the Christian side and was badly wounded.)

Don't miss the swift imperial barges in which the sultan, avoiding the primitive roads, would speed up and down the Bosphorus from palace to palace. Over 30m in length but only 2m wide, propelled by 13 banks of oars, the barges were obviously the rocket boats of their day. The ones with latticework screens were for the imperial ladies. There's also a war galley with 24 pairs of oars.

You may also be curious to see a replica of the Map of Piri Reis, an early Ottoman map (1513) which purports to show the coasts and continents of the New World. It's assumed that Piri Reis (Captain Piri) got hold of the work of Columbus for his map. The original map is in Topkapı Palace; this one is on the wall above the door as you enter the Bosphorus section. Copies are on sale.

Çirağan Palace (Map 2)
Unsatisfied with the architectural exertions of his predecessor at Dolmabahçe, Sultan Abdül Aziz built his own grand residence at Çirağan on the Bosphorus shore in 1874, only 1km north of Dolmabahçe, replacing an earlier wooden palace. The architect was the self-same Balyan as for Dolmabahçe.

The sultan was deposed, however, and later died in Çirağan under mysterious circumstances. His mentally unstable nephew Murat came to the throne, but was deposed within a year by his brother Abdül Hamit II, who kept Murat a virtual prisoner in Çirağan. Much later (1909) it was the seat of the Ottoman Chamber of Deputies and Senate, but in 1910 it was destroyed by fire, again under suspicious circumstances.

From the Deniz Müzesi and the flyover in Beşiktaş, you can walk north for 10 minutes, or catch a bus or dolmuş heading north along the shore (get out at the Yahya Efendi stop), to reach the entrance to the Çirağan complex. The palace has been restored as part of the luxury Çirağan Palace Hotel Kempinski İstanbul, and is now used for meetings and functions. You can enter the grounds, wander around, admire the view and perhaps have refreshments, although prices are breathtaking, even for a five-star place.

Just a minute's walk north of Çirağan is the entrance, on the left, to Yıldız Park.

Yıldız Palace & Park (Map 2)
Sultan Abdül Hamit II (1876–1909), who succeeded Murat V, also had to build his own palace. He added considerably to the structures built by earlier sultans in Yıldız Park, on the hillside above Çirağan.

The park is open from 9 am to 6 pm every day; admission costs US$1.75 for cars (including taxis); it's free to pedestrians. If you come to the park by taxi, have it take you up the steep slope to the Şale Köşkü. You can visit the other kiosks on the walk down. A taxi from Taksim Square to the top of the hill should cost about US$6.

Pavilion & Malta Kiosks
As you toil up the hill along the road, near the top of the slope to the left you'll see the Çadır Köşkü (Pavilion Kiosk; ☎ 212-258 9020), an ornate kiosk built between 1865 and 1870 as a place for the sultan to enjoy the view, rest from a walk, and have a cup of tea or coffee. It still serves coffee, tea, soft drinks and snacks, and is the prettiest place in the park for refreshments.

To the right (north) as you hike up the road from the gate are two greenhouses, the **Kış Bahçesi** (Winter Garden) and the **Yeşil Sera** (Green Nursery), and the **Malta Köşkü**. The Malta Köşkü (☎ 212-258 9453), restored in 1979, is now a cafe.

Yıldız Şale At the very top of the hill, enclosed by a lofty wall, is the Yıldız Şale (☎ 212-258 3080), a 'guesthouse/chalet' of 64 rooms built in 1882 and expanded in 1898 by Abdül Hamit for use by Kaiser Wilhelm II of Germany during a state visit. You must pay a separate admission fee of US$5 (plus US$8 for a camera or US$16 for a video camera) to see the chalet which is open from 9.30 am to 5 pm, closed Monday and Thursday.

Ortaköy (Map 1) This Bosphorus suburb has an interesting ethnic history in which church, synagogue and mosque coexist peacefully in its narrow streets. Today it is a trendy gathering-place for the young and hip, with art galleries, chic cafe-bars, and boutiques selling antiques, carpets and jewellery. On warm Sundays artisans display their wares in the narrow streets in an impromptu arts-and-crafts show.

At the water's edge by the ornate mosque called the **Ortaköy Camii** are terrace cafes, their open-air tables enjoying views of the Bosphorus and the mosque. Officially called the Büyük Mecidiye Camii, the eclectic-baroque mosque is the work of Nikogos Balyan, architect of Dolmabahçe Palace, who designed it for Sultan Abdül Mecit in 1854. Within the mosque hang several masterful examples of Arabic calligraphy executed by the sultan, who was an accomplished calligrapher.

The **Etz Ahayim Synagogue** has been here since 1660, though the current building dates from 1941, when the old one was destroyed by a disastrous fire. The **Church of Hagios Phocas** (1856) is a short distance north of it.

Arnavutköy, the next town north of Ortaköy, boasts a number of well-preserved Ottoman-era wooden houses, including numerous *yalıs* (waterfront mansions).

Places to Eat Get off the bus or dolmuş at Osmanzade Sokak, near the doorway to the Etz Ahayim Synagogue, and walk east. *The Wall*, on Kaymakçı Sokak against the wall of the synagogue, is a cafe-bar with dancing and beer for US$1.50, local drinks for about US$3. Nearby, *İlhami'nin Yeri* (İlhami's Place) is a full-service restaurant specialising in seafood. Meat, fish and *kalamar* (squid) dishes are usually available for about US$4 to US$9 each.

At the corner of Yelkovan and Ortaköy Değirmen Sokaks is the *Yazarların Evi Restaurant* (Writers' House), an atmospheric place with *ut* (oud or lute) music in the evenings after 9 pm, a three-course lunch menu for US$4.75, and slightly higher a la carte prices in the evening.

The streets near Osmanzade Sokak have more browsing, eating and drinking possibilities. On Yelkovan Sokak, look for *Çardak Café*, which sometimes has live music.

Alaturka (☎ 258 7924, Hazine Sokak 8) is Ortaköy's most popular cafe-restaurant, serving light meals for US$4 to US$6 and full meals for US$8 to US$10.

Fast food follows the crowd, and it has come to Ortaköy in the form of *Burger King*, in a garish yellow building, and *McDonald's*. Next to the McDonald's on Mecidiye Köprüsü Sokak is a row of snack stands selling *kumpir*, big baked potatoes topped with various sauces and condiments; *gözleme* (Turkish pancakes); and midye tavası, fried mussels.

Bebek & Rumeli Hisarı (Map 1) Bebek is a prosperous suburb of İstanbul with a surprising foreign and academic presence because of the Boğaziçi Üniversitesi (Bosphorus University). A ferry service here joins Bebek with Kanlıca and Anadolu Hisarı on the Asian shore.

About 1.5km north of Bebek centre is Rumeli Hisarı, the Fortress of Europe. The fortress is open from 9.30 am to 5 pm daily except Monday. Admission is US$2.50, half-price on Sundays and holidays. Within the walls are park-like grounds, an open-air theatre and the minaret of a ruined mosque. Stairs lead up to the ramparts and towers.

(Check with the tourist office for summer performances here.)

Here at the narrowest part of the Bosphorus, Mehmet the Conqueror had this fortress built in a mere four months during 1452, in preparation for his planned siege of Byzantine Constantinople. To speed its completion in line with his impatience to conquer Constantinople, Mehmet the Conqueror ordered each of his three viziers to take responsibility for one of the three main towers. If the tower's construction was not completed on schedule, the vizier would pay with his life, or so legend has it. Not surprisingly, the work was completed on time, with Mehmet's three generals competing fiercely with one another to finish.

Once completed, Rumeli Hisarı, in concert with Anadolu Hisarı on the Asian shore just opposite, controlled all traffic on the Bosphorus, and cut the city off from re-supply by sea from the north.

On a hilltop above the town of Bebek you'll notice the New England 19th-century-style architecture of **Boğaziçi Üniversitesi** (Bosphorus University). Founded as Robert College in the mid-19th century by the American Board of Foreign Missions, the college had an important influence on the modernisation of political, social, economic and scientific thought in Turkey.

Places to Eat Just north of Rumeli Hisarı on the shore is ***Karaca Fish Restaurant*** (☎ 265 2968, *Yahya Kemal Caddesi 10*), with fine Bosphorus views, excellent fish and squid, and a plethora of mezes; avoid shrimp which are, as everywhere in Turkey, very expensive for what you get. Expect to pay US$12 to US$24 per person with rakı. Cheaper alternatives – snack stands and pastry shops – are nearby.

Getting There & Away From Eminönü, go to the bus lot on the western side of the Yeni Cami, to the 2 Nolu Peron (2nd Bus Rank) and take bus Nos 22 (Emirgan), 22-C (Bebek) or 25-E (Sarıyer). The 22-C goes only as far as Bebek, leaving a 1.5km walk to Rumeli Hisarı, if that's where you're headed.

Tarabya & Büyükdere (Map 1) Originally called Therapeia for its wonderful climate, the little cove of Tarabya has been a favourite summer watering place for İstanbul's well-to-do for centuries. It's now surrounded by restaurants specialising in seafood. North of the village are some of the old summer embassies of foreign powers.

North of Tarabya is its societal continuation, Büyükdere, notable for a number of churches, summer embassies, and the **Sadberk Hanım Müzesi** (☎ 242 3813), Piyasa Caddesi 27–29, on the shore road just north of the Surp Boğos Armenian Catholic Church.

Named after the wife of the late Mr Vehbi Koç, founder of Turkey's foremost commercial empire, the museum is her private collection of Anatolian antiquities and Ottoman heirlooms. It's open from April to September from 10.30 am to 6 pm and in winter from 10 am to 5 pm; closed on Wednesday year-round. Admission costs US$2.50.

Places to Eat More than a dozen seafood restaurants ring the cove at Tarabya. Possibilities include ***Garaj Restaurant*** (☎ 262 0032, *Yeniköy Caddesi 30*), on the southern side of the cove, where the fish is fresh and in vast array. A seafood lunch or dinner here costs from US$18 to US$30 and up per person, wine, tax and tip included.

Going north around the cove you can inspect the ***Aquarius 2***, ***La Mer***, ***Palet 1***, ***Hristo***, ***Filiz***, ***Köşem Bistro*** and ***Sevillanas*** restaurants, all at similar prices to the Garaj.

Sarıyer (Map 1) The villagers of Sarıyer have occupied themselves for most of their history by fishing in the currents of the Bosphorus. Fishing is still a pastime and a livelihood here, and Sarıyer is justly noted for its several good fish restaurants. Turn right as you leave the ferry dock, stay as close to the shore as possible, and you will pass the sea-bus terminal and then the village's historic fish market, the Balıkçılar Çarşısı, and come to several fish restaurants.

Places to Eat By the little harbour where the fishing boats tie up are several small fish restaurants, including *Deniz Kızı* (Mermaid), serving seasonal fish for US$8 to US$12 per plate; and also *Captain's Terrace* and *Aquarius SIT Balık Restaurant* at similar prices. *Dolphin Class* has an upstairs dining room with Bosphorus views.

For cheaper meals, try the kebapçıs just inland from these fish restaurants, such as *A & H Kebapçı*, Yeni Mahalle Caddesi 20, serving kebap, pide and lahmacun.

Getting There & Away The Bosphorus excursion ferries from Eminönü stop at Sarıyer on both the outbound and return voyages. There is a rush-hour sea-bus service to and from the city centre as well.

From 7.15 am to 11 pm, 17 ferries a day cross the Bosphorus (US$0.75) from Sarıyer to Anadolu Kavağı on the Asian side, some stopping at Rumeli Kavağı as well.

Most of Sarıyer's dolmuş and bus stops are near or inland from the small Ali Kethüda mosque. Dolmuş minibuses run to Taksim Square via an inland route, not along the Bosphorus shore, for US$0.75. The stop (Map 2) in Taksim is on Mete Caddesi, east of the Ceylan Inter-Continental hotel.

Heading north, city buses to Kilyos (US$0.40) depart from near the mosque; dolmuşes to Kilyos (US$0.50) depart from a stop 600m inland along Şehit Asteğmen Mithat Yılmaz Caddesi. The trip takes less than half an hour.

Heading south can be difficult. Bus Nos 25-A (Rumelikavağı-Beşiktaş), and 25-E (Sarıyer-Eminönü), are the exceptions, they drive along the shore road via Bebek and Rumeli Hisarı back to the Golden Horn in a few hours. But this shore service is infrequent compared with the inland services, as the narrow shore road, busy with traffic, takes much longer than the inland route.

If you're in doubt as to whether a vehicle follows the shore all the way south, say *'Sahilden mi gidiyor?'* (Does it go along the shore?) to the driver. If he says *'Yukarıdan'* (Via the heights) you'll know it goes inland, not along the shore.

Kilyos (Map 1) İstanbul's coastal resort of Kilyos is a favourite place for a swim in the chilly waters of the Black Sea, or a leisurely meal at any time of year. You can even stay overnight if you like.

Dolmuşes and buses from Sarıyer make the trip over the hills to Kilyos in less than a half hour, passing little impromptu open-air roadside restaurants featuring *kuzu çevirme* (spit-roasted lamb).

Kilyos' best beach is the fenced one in front of the Turban Kilyos Moteli, open daily in warm weather from 8 am to 6 pm for US$3.50 per person. It's very crowded on summer weekends, but not bad during the week. Parking costs US$2, so if you drive, park elsewhere in the village and walk to the beach.

Note that there can be a deadly undertow on Black Sea beaches. Swim only in protected areas or where there is an attentive lifeguard, don't swim alone, and be on guard against undertow and riptide.

Getting There & Away Kilyos is 35km north of the Galata Bridge, and can take several hours to reach in moderately heavy traffic. All public transport comes through Sarıyer.

Sights on the Asian Shore

The Asian shore of the Bosphorus has a number of possibilities for excursions, with the advantage that you will meet far fewer tourists than in European İstanbul.

Crossing the Bosphorus To reach the Asian shore, hop on the Üsküdar ferry from Eminönü, which runs every 15 or 20 minutes between 6 am and midnight, even more frequently during rush hours, for US$0.50. A similarly frequent ferry service operates between Beşiktaş and Üsküdar. From Kabataş, just south of Dolmabahçe Palace, ferries run to Üsküdar every 30 minutes on the hour and half hour from 7 am to 8 pm. There are also city buses and dolmuşes departing from Taksim Square for Üsküdar, but the ferries are faster and more enjoyable.

If you take the ferry to Üsküdar, you'll notice **Leander's Tower** (Map 2), called the Kız Kulesi (Maiden's Tower) in Turkish, to the south just off the Asian mainland. The tower was a toll booth and defence point in ancient times; the Bosphorus could be closed off by means of a chain stretching from here to Seraglio Point. The tower has really nothing to do with Leander, who was no maiden, and who swam not the Bosphorus but the Hellespont (Dardanelles), 340km from here.

The tower is subject to the usual legend: oracle says maiden will die by snake bite; concerned father puts maiden in snake-proof tower; fruit vendor comes by boat, sells basket of fruit (complete with snake) to maiden, who gets hers. There are plans to open a cafe, museum and viewing platform here – check with the tourist office for up-to-date information.

Another landmark is the tall spear of a television tower on Büyük Çamlıca hilltop, a lookout you can visit from Üsküdar.

A landmark especially for travellers is the neoclassical German-style **Haydarpaşa Station** (Map 2), south of Üsküdar, the city's terminus for Asian trains. It was built between 1906 and 1908 by the German Anatolia-Baghdad Corporation, and rests on 1100 21m-long piles driven into the soft soil by steam hammer. In 1917, when it was packed with WWI ammunition, it was blown up, supposedly by sabotage.

You will also notice the large **Selimiye Kışlası** (Selimiye Barracks; Map 2), a square building with towers at the corners. It dates from the early 19th century, when Selim III and Mahmut II reorganised the Ottoman armed forces along the lines of the European armies of the time. Not far away is the **Selimiye Camii** (Map 2) and the storybook Ottoman rest-home for ageing palace ladies, which is now used by Marmara University.

Üsküdar (Map 2) Üsküdar is Turkish for Scutari. Legend has it that the first ancient colonists established themselves at Chalcedon, the modern Kadıköy, south of Üsküdar. Byzas, bearing the oracle's message to found a colony 'opposite the blind', thought the Chalcedonites blind to the advantages of Seraglio Point as a town site, and founded his town on the European shore. Still, people have lived on this, the Asian shore, longer than they've lived on the other.

Florence Nightingale

During the Crimean War (1853–56), when Britain and France fought on the Ottoman side against the Russian Empire, Üsküdar's Selimiye Barracks served as a military hospital. It was here that the English nurse Florence Nightingale, horrified at the conditions suffered by the wounded, established with the assistance of 38 companion nurses the first model military hospital with modern standards of discipline, order, sanitation and care. In effect, her work at the Selimiye Barracks laid down the norms of modern nursing, and turned nursing into a skilled, respected profession.

A small museum (☎ 216-343 7310) in the barracks is dedicated to her work, but it's presently 'closed for renovation' and shows no sign of opening soon.

TRUDI CANAVAN

Today Üsküdar is a busy dormitory suburb for İstanbul, and you may enjoy several hours of browsing through its streets, markets and mosques.

Mosques As you leave the ferry dock in Üsküdar, the **main square**, Demokrasi Meydanı, is right before you. North-east of the square, behind the dolmuş ranks and near the ferry landing, is the **Mihrimah Sultan Camii** (1547), sometimes called the İskele Camii (Dock Mosque), designed by Sinan for Süleyman the Magnificent's daughter. To the south of the square is the **Yeni Valide Camii**, or New Queen Mother's Mosque (1710), built by Sultan Ahmet III for his mother Gülnuş Emetullah. It resembles the Rüstem Paşa Camii near the Mısır Çarşısı in Eminönü. Built late in the period of classical Ottoman architecture, it is not as fine as earlier works.

West of the square, overlooking the harbour, is the delightful **Şemsi Paşa Camii** (1580), also designed by Sinan and built in a fine location. After you have explored downtown Üsküdar a bit, head up to the Çamlıca hilltops.

Büyük Çamlıca This hilltop park, highest point in İstanbul at 261m, has long been enjoyed by İstanbul's nobility, poets and common folk.

To reach the hilltop from Üsküdar's main square, you can take a taxi (US$3) all the way to the summit, or a dolmuş three-quarters of the way. For the latter, walk to the dolmuş ranks in front of the Mihrimah Sultan Camii, take a dolmuş headed for Ümraniye, and ask for Büyük Çamlıca. The dolmuş will pass the entrance to Küçük Çamlıca and drop you off shortly thereafter in a district called Kısıklı. The walk uphill following the signs to the summit takes from 20 to 30 minutes, depending on your speed and stamina.

Neighbouring **Küçük Çamlıca** hilltop, with its tea garden, is not quite as fancy as its loftier sibling, but equally pleasant.

Çinili Cami The Çinili Cami or Tiled Mosque is Üsküdar's jewel, a small and unassuming building harbouring a wealth of brilliant İznik faience on its interior walls.

It's a neighbourhood mosque in the quarter called Tabaklar, up the hillside a way from Üsküdar's main square. It can be tricky to find on your own (a 30-minute walk); a taxi costs less than US$2, and is well worth it. Along the way you'll pass near the prominent **Atik Valide Camii**, the grandest of Sinan's İstanbul mosques except for his Sü-

leymaniye. It was built for Valide Sultan Nurbanu, wife of Selim II and mother of Ahmet III in 1583.

Approaching the Çinili Cami, you first come to the **Çinili Hamam**, the mosque's Turkish bath, which, because it gets virtually no foreign visitors, is cheap (US$4) and friendly.

The **Çinili Cami** uphill from the bath is unprepossessing from the outside: just a shady little neighbourhood mosque with the usual collection of bearded old men sitting around.

Inside, the mosque is brilliant with İznik faience, the bequest of Mahpeyker Kösem (1640), wife of Sultan Ahmet I (1603–17) and mother of Murat IV (1623–40) and İbrahim (1640–48). As it is used heavily by local people for prayer, be properly dressed and on your best behaviour when you visit, and avoid visiting on Friday.

Beylerbeyi Palace (Map 1) Both shores of the Bosphorus have their Ottoman palaces. The grandest on the Asian side is Beylerbeyi, a few kilometres north of Üsküdar. Catch a bus or dolmuş north along the shore road from Üsküdar's main square, the Demokrasi Meydanı, and get out at the Çayırbaşı stop, just north of Beylerbeyi and the Asian pylons of the Bosphorus Bridge.

Beylerbeyi Palace (☎ 216-321 9320) is open from 9.30 am to 5 pm daily, closed Monday and Thursday; admission for the obligatory guided tour costs US$4; a camera permit (no flash or tripod) costs US$8, a video permit is US$16, and is a waste of money.

Every emperor needs some little place to get away to, and 30-room Beylerbeyi Palace was the place for Abdül Aziz (1861–76). Mahmut II had built a wooden palace here, but like so many other wooden palaces it burned down.

Abdül Aziz spent a lot of time here, as did other monarchs and royal guests, for this was, in effect, the sultan's guest quarters. Empress Eugénie of France stayed here on a long visit in 1869. Other royal guests included Nasruddin, Shah of Persia; Nicholas, grand duke of Russia; and Nicholas, king of

Montenegro. The palace's last imperial 'guest' was none other than the former sultan, Abdül Hamit II, who was brought here to spend the remainder of his life (from 1913 to 1918).

Çengelköy (Map 1) The village of Çengelköy, north of Beylerbeyi, is a good place for a break. At its centre, *Tarihi Çengelköy Çınaraltı Çay Bahçesi* (Historic Anchor-Village Tea Garden Beneath the Plane Tree) lives up to its name, clustered around the trunk of a gigantic plane behind a little mosque at the edge of the Bosphorus. Light meals are served as well as tea.

Küçüksu Kasrı (Map 1) The Büyük Göksu Deresi (Great Heavenly Stream) and Küçük Göksu Deresi (Small Heavenly Stream) were two brooks which descended from the Asian hills into the Bosphorus. Between them was a flat, fertile delta, grassy and shady, just perfect for picnics, which the Ottoman upper classes enjoyed here frequently. Foreign residents, referring to the place as 'The Sweet Waters of Asia', would often join them. Sometimes the sultan would be there, and in style. Sultan Abdül Mecit's answer to a simple picnic blanket was the Küçüksu Kasrı (☎ 216- 332 0237), an ornate lodge, actually a tiny palace, built in 1856.

Take a bus or dolmuş along the shore road north from Beylerbeyi to reach Küçüksu Kasrı, open from 9.30 am to 5 pm daily except Monday and Thursday; admission costs US$3.

Anadolu Hisarı (Map 1) North of Küçüksu, in the shadow of the Fatih Bridge is the castle and village of Anadolu Hisarı. This small castle, built by Sultan Beyazıt I in 1391, was repaired and strengthened as the Asian stronghold in Mehmet the Conqueror's stranglehold on Byzantine Constantinople. Anadolu Hisarı is a fraction of the size of its counterpart, Rumeli Hisarı. You're free to wander about the ruined walls.

Kanlıca (Map 1) The Fatih Bridge soars across the Bosphorus just north of Rumeli Hisarı and Anadolu Hisarı. North of the bridge are more small Asian Bosphorus towns, including Kanlıca, famous for its yogurt. The **mosque** in the shady town square dates from 1560.

Hıdiv Kasrı (Map 1) High on a promontory above the town, overlooking the Bosphorus, is the Art-Nouveau villa called the Hıdiv Kasrı or Khedive's Villa (☎ 216-413 9644) built by the khedive of Egypt to be his summer cottage during visits to İstanbul.

The villa is a few minutes by taxi (US$2) uphill from Kanlıca or Çubuklu. To walk, go north from Kanlıca's main square and mosque and turn right at the first street (Kafadar Sokak) which winds up to the villa car park in 15 or 20 minutes.

A much nicer walk is the one up from Çubuklu through the villa's grounds. Take a bus or dolmuş north to the stop marked 'Çubuklu Dalgıç Okulu', which is a naval installation. Just north of the stop is a fire station (look for signs saying 'Dikkat İtfaiye' and 'İstanbul Büyükşehir Belediye Başkanlığı İtfaiye Müdürlüğü Çubuklu Müfrezesi'). Walk in the gate and to the right of the fire station, then up the winding forest road to the villa, a 20- to 30-minute walk.

Paşabahçe & Beykoz (Map 1) North of Çubuklu, the town of Paşabahçe has a large glassware factory whose products you have no doubt already used, perhaps unwittingly.

In Beykoz, legend says that Pollux, son of Leda (she of the swan) and one of Jason's Argonauts, won a boxing match with the local king, Amicus, son of Poseidon.

At Hünkar İskelesi (Emperor's Landing), further north, is a former imperial palace designed by Sarkis Balyan for Sultan Abdül Mecit. There had been imperial kiosks here for centuries. In 1833, the Ottoman and Russian empires signed a historic peace treaty here which took its name, the Treaty of Unkiar Skelessi, from the place. The peace lasted 20 years.

From Beykoz, a road heads eastward towards the Polish village of Polonezköy and the Black Sea beach resort of Şile. Much of the land along the Bosphorus shore north of Beykoz is in a military zone, and you may be denied entry. You can reach the village of Anadolu Kavağı by ferry, either on the Bosphorus cruise from Eminönü or from Sarıyer and Rumeli Kavağı on the European shore.

Anadolu Kavağı (Map 1) Perched above the village are the ruins of Anadolu Kavağı, a medieval castle with seven massive towers in its walls. First built by the Byzantines, it was restored and reinforced by the Genoese in 1350, and later by the Ottomans. As the straits are narrow here, it was a good choice for a defensive site to control traffic. Two more fortresses, put up by Sultan Murat IV, are north of here.

Anadolu Kavağı is the final stop on the special cruise-ferry route, and the land to the north is in a military zone. If you have a picnic lunch, climb up to the fortress, which provides a comfortable picnic location with spectacular views.

THE PRINCES' ISLANDS (MAP 1)

The Turks call the Princes' Islands, which lie about 20km south-east of the city in the Sea of Marmara, the Kızıl Adalar (Red Islands). Most İstanbullus get along with 'Adalar' (The Islands). Of the nine islands in the archipelago, four are inhabited and two – Büyükada and Heybeliada (Heybeli) – are easy to reach by public ferry. The smaller two, Burgazada (Burgaz) and Kınalıada (Kınalı), are harder to reach and of less interest.

In Byzantine times, refractory princes, deposed monarchs and others who had outlived their roles were interned here. A Greek Orthodox monastery and seminary on Heybeliada turned out Orthodox priests until the 1970s.

In the 19th century the Ottoman business community of Greeks, Jews and Armenians favoured the islands as summer resorts. Many of the fine Victorian villas built by these wealthy Ottomans survive, and make the larger islands, Büyükada and Heybeliada, charming places.

Büyükada

Büyükada's splendid Victoriana greets you as you approach by sea, its gingerbread vil-

las climbing up the slopes of the hill and the bulbous twin domes of the Splendid Otel providing an unmistakable landmark.

Only a few minutes after landing, you'll realise Büyükada's surprise: there are no cars! Except for the necessary police, fire and sanitation vehicles, transportation is by bicycle, horse-drawn carriage and foot, as in centuries past.

Walk from the ferry to the clock tower in İskele Meydanı (Dock Square). The market district is to the left along Recep Koç Caddesi. For a stroll up the hill and through the lovely old houses, bear right onto 23 Nisan Caddesi. If you need a goal for your wanderings, head for the Greek Monastery of St George, in the 'saddle' between Büyükada's two highest hills. Several shops have bicycles for rent (*kiralık bisiklet*), and shops on the market street can provide the supplies for picnics, though food is obviously cheaper on the mainland.

Just to the left off the square by the clock tower is the waiting area for horse-drawn *fayton* (carriages). Hire one for a *büyük tur* (long tour) of about an hour for US$16, or a *küçük tur* (short tour) which gives you a look mostly at the town, not the shores or hills, for US$12. Prices are set by the city government, and prominently posted, though you may be able to haggle out of season.

Heybeliada

Called Heybeli for short, this island is home to the Turkish Naval Academy (located to the left of the ferry dock). Within the academy grounds is the grave of Sir Edward Barton, ambassador of Queen Elizabeth I to the Sublime Porte, who died in 1598. Much less touristy than Büyükada, this island is a delightful place for walking in the pine groves and swimming from the tiny, crowded beaches. There's not much accommodation if you don't have your own villa (or an invitation to a friend's), but there are several restaurants with good food and decent prices.

A 50-minute carriage büyük tur of the island costs US$12, the shorter küçük tur US$8. Battered bicycles are for rent at several shops.

Burgazada & Kınalıada

These two smaller islands are also accessible by ferry, but offer less reward for the trouble. They're mostly for the well-to-do İstanbullus who have summer villas here.

Burgaz has a church, a synagogue, and the home of the late writer Sait Faik, now a museum.

Kınalı, flat and fairly featureless except for a forest of cell phone antennas, is even more a collection of summer villas, favoured by Armenian families. If you stop here to eat (there are no hotels), you'll probably be the only foreigner in sight.

Places to Stay

Büyükada Next to the clock tower, *Hotel Princess* (☎ 216-382 1628, fax 382 1949) charges US$60/80 a single/double in summer, breakfast and swimming pool fee included. An extra bed costs US$20.

Splendid Otel (☎ 216-382 6950, fax 382 6775, 23 Nisan Caddesi 71), to the right, 200m up the hill from the clock tower is a perfect if faded Ottoman Victorian period piece, complete with grand dames taking tea on the terrace each afternoon. A room with Victorian-era comforts (the baths have been upgraded, though) costs US$80 per couple, breakfast included.

Heybeliada Prime lodging here is *Merit Halki Palace* (☎ 216-351 8890, fax 351 8483, Refah Şehitleri Caddesi 88), a restored Ottoman Victorian gingerbread villa with 45 rooms, all comforts, and premium prices at US$100 a double per night.

Places to Eat

Büyükada İskele Meydanı is surrounded with restaurants. To the left as you come up from the dock are several small places featuring *kokoreç* (lamb intestines), but *Altın Fıçı* has a much longer menu, and beer from its namesake Golden Barrel as well. *Taş Fırını* (Stone Oven) further into the market along Recep Koç Caddesi serves cheap lahmacun (US$0.50) and pide (US$2) as well as more substantial plates. Up to the right of

the clock tower are even cheaper *büfes* (snack stands). For fancier meals, *Birtat Restaurant* on the waterfront to the east of the ferry docks is a favourite, with meals for US$6 to US$18 and more.

Heybeliada For picnic supplies, turn left from the ferry docks onto the street behind the waterfront restaurants. *Mehtap Pasta ve Unlu Mamülleri* is a bakery selling pastries and French-style bread. Other shops, such as *Gül Market*, can provide other picnic supplies such as preserved meats, cheese, olives, pickles and drinks.

For dining, walk to the right off the ferry dock. *Ada Kebap ve Lahmacun Salonu* has these cheap dishes, and stews as well – seaside dining at bargain prices.

Getting There & Away

At least 10 ferries (US$1.30) run to the islands each day from 7 am to 11.30 pm, departing from Sirkeci's Adalar İskelesi dock, east of the dock for car ferries to Harem. On weekdays there are additional boats for commuters. On summer weekends, board the vessel and seize a seat at least half an hour before departure time unless you want to stand the whole way.

You can also take a fast catamaran from Eminönü or Kabataş to Bostancı, south of Kadıköy, then another from Bostancı to Büyükada, but you save little time, and the cost is much higher.

The ferry leaves from Sirkeci, out of the Golden Horn and around Seraglio Point, offering fine views of Topkapı Palace, Aya Sofya and the Blue Mosque on the right; Üsküdar, Haydarpaşa and Kadıköy to the left. After about 45 minutes, the ferry reaches Kınalıada, the first small island; another 30 minutes brings you to Heybeliada, the second-largest island, and another 15 minutes to Büyükada, the largest (the name translates as Great Island). Some express ferries go directly to Büyükada, from which there are occasional ferries to Heybeliada, and catamarans to Bostancı on the Asian shore.

Thrace

The Roman province of Thrace, to the north of the Aegean and Marmara Seas, today is divided among Turkey, Bulgaria and Greece, with Turkey holding the easternmost part. Turkish Thrace (Trakya) is famous for its vast rolling fields of sunflowers, grown for their seeds and cooking oil, for Edirne, once capital of the Ottoman Empire, and for the battlefields of Gallipoli.

EDİRNE

☎ 284 • pop 115,000

For most of its history, Edirne, once called Adrianople, has been a stopping point on the road to İstanbul. The Trans European Motorway (TEM) has reduced the time needed to travel the 250km from several days on a camel to a 2½-hour ride by bus or car.

Edirne was for a time the capital city of the Ottoman Empire, and an important staging-point for the sultan's annual military campaigns in Europe. As such it was graced with fine mosques, baths and caravanserais, including the serene Selimiye Camii, masterpiece of the great Ottoman architect Mimar Sinan.

Edirne is largely disregarded by tourists, which has helped preserve its Turkish character and appeal. While the towns along the Aegean and Mediterranean coasts are clogged with foreigners and with vast new European-style building projects, Edirne attracts the discerning few who come to enjoy the harmony and history of its mosques, covered bazaars, bridges and caravanserais, and the easy pace of life. If you've just arrived overland from Western Europe, it's the perfect introduction to Turkey and the Turks.

History

The Roman emperor Hadrian founded Edirne in the 2nd century AD as Hadrianopolis. It was soon to become a forward defence post for Constantinople. The town's name was later shortened by Europeans to Adrianople, and later changed by the Turks to Edirne.

HIGHLIGHTS

- Exploring Selimiye Camii in Edirne, the elegant masterpiece that is Mimar Sinan's finest work
- Cheering on the brawny oil-coated wrestlers at Kırkpınar, near Edirne
- Touring the Gallipoli battlefields, with echoes of battles fought nearly a century ago
- Dining along the waterfront in Çanakkale

The Ottoman state, an emirate founded around 1288 in north-western Anatolia, used Bursa as its capital. By the mid-14th century, the Ottoman state had grown substantially in power and size, and was looking for new conquests. The mighty walls of Constantinople were beyond its powers, but not the fertile, rolling country of Thrace. Bent on further conquest, the Ottoman armies crossed the Dardanelles, skirting the great capital. Capturing Adrianople in 1363, they made it their new capital and base of operations for military campaigns in Europe.

For almost 100 years, this was the city from which the Ottoman sultan set out on

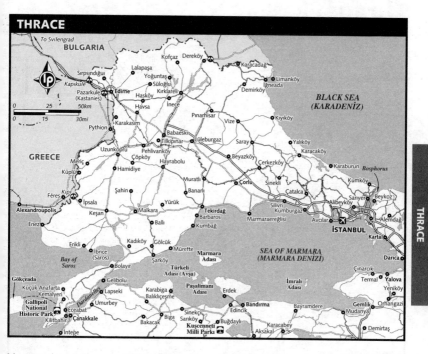

THRACE

his campaigns to Europe and Asia. When at last the time was ripe for the final conquest of the Byzantine Empire, Mehmet the Conqueror (Mehmet Fatih) rode out from Edirne on the Via Ignatia (the ancient road from Rome) to Constantinople.

When the Ottoman Empire disintegrated after WWI, the Allies granted all of Thrace to the Greek kingdom. Constantinople (now İstanbul) was to become an independent, international city. In the summer of 1920, Greek armies occupied Edirne, but several years later Atatürk's republican armies drove them out, and the Treaty of Lausanne left Edirne and Eastern Thrace to the Turks.

Orientation

The centre of town is Hürriyet Meydanı (Freedom Square), at the intersection of the two main streets, Saraçlar/Hükümet Caddesi and Talat Paşa Caddesi. To the north-east of the square is Üçşerefeli Cami. Going east along Talat Paşa Caddesi and north-east

along Mimar Sinan Caddesi will bring you to Edirne's masterpiece, the Selimiye Camii. Down the hill and across Talat Paşa Caddesi is the Eski Cami, Edirne's oldest mosque. South of Hürriyet Meydanı is the Ali Paşa Çarşısı, Edirne's largest covered bazaar.

The new *otogar* (bus station) is 8.5km east of the city centre on the access road to the TEM. The main *dolmuş* (minibus) station, with services to the Greek and Bulgarian border posts, is behind (east of) the Hotel Kervansaray.

Information

The tourist office (☎ 213 9208), Hürriyet Meydanı 17, is just west of the main square, near the bazaar. They can help with accommodation and transport. There are also offices at the İpsala (☎ 284-616 1577) and Kapıkule (☎ 238 2019) border crossings.

Araz Döviz, to the right of the tourist office on Hürriyet Meydanı, changes money, as do other exchange offices and banks nearby

THRACE

EDIRNE

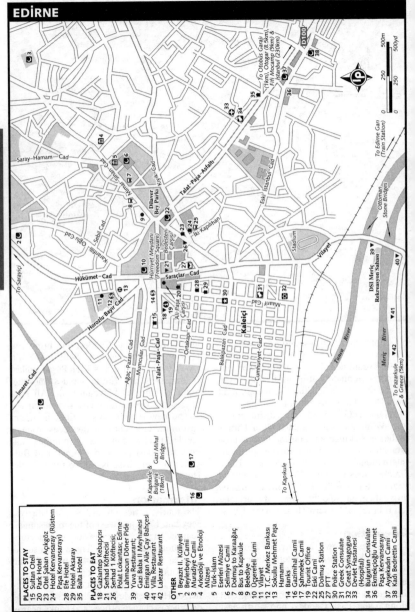

PLACES TO STAY
15 Sultan Oteli
20 Park Hotel
23 Otel Şaban Açıkgöz
24 Hotel Kervansaray (Rüstem Paşa Kervansarayı)
28 Efe Hotel
29 Hotel Aksaray
35 Balta Hotel

PLACES TO EAT
18 Gaziantep Kebapçısı
21 Serhad Köftecisi
26 Serhad 1 Köftecisi;
   Polat Lokantası; Edirne
   Lahmacun Döner Pide
39 Yuva Restaurant;
   Gazi Baba II Meyhanesi
40 Emirgan Aile Çay Bahçesi
41 Villa Restaurant
42 Lalezar Restaurant

OTHER
1 Beyazıt II. Külliyesi
2 Beylerbeyi Camii
3 Muradiye Camii
4 Arkeoloji ve Etnoloji Müzesi
5 Türk-İslam Eserleri Müzesi
6 Selimiye Camii
7 Dolmuş to Karaağaç
8 Bus to Kapıkule
9 Belediye
10 Üçşerefeli Camii
11 Vilayet
12 T.C. Merkez Bankası
13 Sokullu Mehmet Paşa Hamamı
14 Banks
16 Gazimihal Camii
17 Şahmelek Camii
19 Tourist Office
22 Eski Cami
25 Dolmuş Station
27 PTT
30 Police Station
31 Greek Consulate
32 Great Synagogue
33 Devlet Hastanesi (Hospital)
34 Bulgarian Consulate
36 Ekmekçioğlu Ahmet Paşa Kervansarayı
37 Ayşekadın Camii
38 Kadı Bedrettin Camii

and around the corner on Saraçlar Caddesi. Most ATMs are in the same locations.

Üçşerefeli Cami

The Üçşerefeli Cami, with its four strikingly different minarets built at different times, dominates Hürriyet Meydanı. The name means 'mosque with three galleries', a reference to the three galleries or balconies (an innovation at the time) on the tallest of the minarets.

Construction of the mosque was begun in 1440 and finished by 1447. Its design shows the transition from the Seljuk Turkish style mosques of Konya and Bursa to a truly Ottoman style, which would be perfected later in İstanbul. In the Seljuk style, smaller domes are mounted on square rooms. At the Üçşerefeli, the wide (24m) dome is mounted on a hexagonal drum and supported by two walls and two pillars, representing a transitional style.

The courtyard, with its central şadırvan (ablutions fountain), was an innovation in mosque architecture which came to be standard in the great Ottoman mosques. The architect's genius is best appreciated if you enter the mosque across the courtyard from the west, but the courtyard is presently closed for restoration, and the mosque itself will continue to be filled with scaffolding for years to come.

Across the street from the mosque is the **Sokollu Mehmet Paşa Hamamı** built in the late 16th century and still in use. Designed by the great Mimar Sinan for Grand Vizier Sokollu Mehmet Paşa, it is a çifte hamam (twin baths) with identical but separate sections for men (erkekler kısmı) and women (kadınlar kısmı). The opening hours of this hamam are from 6 am to 10 pm. Simple admission costs US$2; washing by an attendant US$3; and a massage US$4.

Ruined fireplaces clinging to the baths' exterior wall facing the street are evidence that a medrese (theological seminary) was once attached to the baths.

Eski Cami

From Hürriyet Meydanı, walk east on Talat Paşa Asfaltı to the Eski Cami (Old Mosque) On your way you will pass the bedesten (covered market) across the park on your right. Dating from 1418, it is now known as the **Bedesten Çarşısı** or Bedesten Bazaar, and is still filled with shops. Behind it to the east is the Rüstem Paşa Hanı, a grand caravanserai built 100 years after the bedesten.

The Eski Cami (1414) exemplifies one of two principal mosque styles used by the Ottomans in their earlier capital, Bursa. Like Bursa's great Ulu Cami, the Eski Cami has rows of arches and pillars supporting a series of small domes. Inside, there is a marvellous mihrab (niche indicating the direction of Mecca) and huge calligraphic inscriptions on the walls. The columns at the front of the mosque were lifted from a Roman building, a common practice over the centuries.

Selimiye Camii

Up the hill to the north-east past the Eski Cami stands the Selimiye mosque (1569–75), the finest work of the great Ottoman architect Mimar Sinan – or so the architect himself believed. Constructed for Sultan Selim II (1566–74) and finished just after the sultan's death, it is smaller than Sinan's earlier (1557), tremendous Süleymaniye Camii in İstanbul, but more elegant and harmonious. Crowning its small hill, it was meant to dominate the town and be easily visible from all approaches across the rolling Thracian landscape.

To fully appreciate its excellence you should enter it from the west as the architect intended. Walk up the street and through the courtyard rather than through the park and the arasta (row of shops), a financially necessary but obtrusive later addition built during the reign of Murat III.

The harmony and serenity of this most symmetrical of mosques surrounds you as you enter. The broad, lofty dome – at 31.5m, wider than that of İstanbul's Aya Sofya by a few centimetres – is supported unobtrusively by eight pillars, arches and external buttresses. This was done so well that the interior is surprisingly spacious and the walls, because they bear only a portion of the dome's weight, can be filled with windows, thus admitting plentiful light to the wide, airy central space.

Centred beneath the main dome is the *kürsü*, or prayer-reader's platform, and centred beneath that is a small fountain which gives the soothing sound of running water to the quiet interior.

As you might expect, the interior furnishings of the Selimiye are exquisite, from the delicately carved marble *mimber* (pulpit) to the outstanding İznik faience in and around the mihrab.

In contrast to its many 'twinnings' (pairs of windows, columns etc), the northern side of the mosque (near the Türk-İslam Eserleri Müzesi) has playful groupings of threes – arches, domes, niches etc – and even triads of pairs (windows).

Part of the Selimiye's excellent effect comes from its four slender, very tall (71m) minarets, fluted to emphasise their height. You'll notice that each is *üçşerefeli*, or built with three balconies – Sinan's respectful acknowledgment, perhaps, to his predecessor, the architect of the Üçşerefeli Cami.

The Selimiye had its share of supporting buildings. The medrese now houses the **Türk-İslam Eserleri Müzesi** (Turkish & Islamic Arts Museum), open 8 am to noon and 1 to 5 pm daily except Monday, for US$1. Collections, labelled in Turkish only, are eclectic, from weapons and chain mail through dervish arts and crafts to artefacts from the Balkan Wars, plus locally made stockings and kitchen utensils. The badly ruined **Sultan Selim Saray Hamamı**, across the street to the north of the mosque, is scheduled for restoration.

Archaeological Museum

The town's main museum, the Arkeoloji ve Etnoloji Müzesi or Archaeological Museum – across the street from the Selimiye Camii and a few steps north-east of the Türk-İslam Eserleri Müzesi – is open 8 am to noon and 1 to 5 pm daily, for US$1.

In front of the museum are several dolmens and menhirs (standing stones), as well as replicas of wattle-and-daub huts such as may have been used by the region's Stone Age inhabitants. The huge marble *aile lâhdi*

(family sarcophagus) to the right of the entrance dates from the 3rd century AD.

The museum, though small, has an interesting and varied collection: prehistoric, Roman and Byzantine artefacts; textiles, including embroidery and weaving; farm implements; dioramas; and even a carriage from Ottoman times.

Muradiye Camii

A short walk (10 to 15 minutes) north-east of the Selimiye along Mimar Sinan Caddesi brings you to the Muradiye Camii, a mosque built on the orders of Sultan Murat II. Finished in 1436, it was once the centre of a Mevlevi whirling dervish lodge. The small cupola atop the main dome is unusual. The mosque's T-shaped plan with twin *eyvans* (vaulted halls) is reminiscent of the Yeşil Cami in Bursa, and its fine İznik tiles, especially in the mihrab, remind one that Bursa (near İznik) was the first Ottoman capital and Edirne, the second. Turkish mosque architecture would change dramatically after the Turks conquered Constantinople (1453) and studied Aya Sofya.

In the small cemetery is the tombstone of Şeyhülislâm Musa Kâzım Efendi, the empire's chief Islamic judge, who fled the British occupation of İstanbul after WWI, and died here in 1920.

The mosque is usually locked except at prayer times; listen for the call to prayer and walk to the mosque to arrive after most worshippers have left but before the door is locked.

From the front of the Muradiye, the famous green lowland meadow of Sarayiçi is visible.

II. Beyazıt Külliyesi & Sarayiçi

Sarayiçi, on the outskirts of Edirne, is the site of the annual Kırkpınar oiled wrestling matches and about 1km from it is the stately, but somewhat forlorn, mosque complex of Sultan Beyazıt II. A morning's pleasant 5km-excursion on foot takes you to both sites.

If you're a mosque enthusiast, start by following the directions to the Muradiye Camii (see that section), then continue to the grassy lowland swathe of Sarayiçi, clearly visible from the Muradiye's hilltop perch, and onward to the Beyazıt II complex. If not, walk along Hükümet Caddesi from Hürriyet Meydanı past the Üçşerefeli Cami (on your right), and turn left immediately after its Turkish baths. Walk one block and bear right at the ornate little fountain. This street is Horozlu Bayır Caddesi; it changes name later to İmaret Caddesi, and takes you to the Ottoman bridge (1488) across the Tunca River to the Beyazıt II complex, Edirne's last great imperial mosque, built for Sultan Beyazıt II (1481–1512).

II. Beyazıt Külliyesi Building mosque complexes was the way the Ottomans populated and expanded their cities. A site would be chosen on the outskirts of a populated area and workers employed for construction. Many of the workers and their families would settle near the mosque construction, thereby attracting necessary services (grocers, cookshops, tailors etc) on which they would spend their pay. The scheme seems not to have worked for the Beyazıt complex (the İkinci Beyazıt Külliyesi), built from 1484 to 1488, as it remains on Edirne's outskirts, unpopulated and little used after 500 years.

The architect of the complex, one Hayrettin, did a creditable job, though he was obviously no Sinan. The mosque's style is between that of the Üçşerefeli and the Selimiye, moving back a bit rather than advancing: its large prayer hall has one large dome, similar to Bursa's mosques, but it has a courtyard and fountain (şadırvan) like the Üçşerefeli Cami's. Though of a high standard, Hayrettin's work can't compare with the Selimiye, built less than a century later.

The mosque's külliye is extensive and includes a *tabhane* (hostel for travellers), medrese, bakery, *imaret* (soup kitchen), *tımarhane* (insane asylum) and *darüşşifa* (hospital). These buildings were fully restored in the late 1970s, though time has obviously been at work since then.

Eski Saray A pleasant 1km walk upriver (east) from the II. Beyazıt Külliyesi are the

ruins of the Eski Saray (Old Palace). The shortest and most scenic route is to walk along the raised flood-control embankment; cars follow a curving (and longer) paved road.

Begun by Sultan Beyazıt II in 1450, this palace once rivalled İstanbul's Topkapı Palace in luxury and size. Today, little is left but a few ruins: a kitchen, a hamam etc, some of which are off limits in a military zone.

Sarayiçi East of Eski Saray, across a branch of the Tunca, is Sarayiçi. This scrub-covered island was once the sultans' private hunting preserve, and today is the site of the famous annual Kırkpınar oiled wrestling matches or Tarihi Kırkpınar Yağlı Güreş Festival.

Next to the rather drab modern stadium is a stone tower with a pointed roof, the **Kasr-i Adalet** (Justice Hall, 1561), dating from the time of Süleyman the Magnificent, with two stones in front of it. On one stone, the Seng-i Hürmet (Stone of Respect), petitioners would put their petitions to the sultan to be collected by his staff. On the other, the Seng-i İbret (Stone of Warning), would be displayed the heads of high court officers who had lost the sultan's confidence in a major way.

If you've made it all the way to Sarayiçi, look for the bridge, Kanuni Köprüsü, to get back to the south bank of the Tunca. Bear right coming off the bridge; the road leads to Hükümet Caddesi, and eventually to Hürriyet Meydanı.

Kaleiçi

The Old Town, called Kaleiçi, was the original medieval town with streets laid out on a grid plan. Saraçlar Caddesi is its eastern boundary, with Talat Paşa Caddesi on the north and the railway line on the south.

Walk south along Maarif Caddesi past the Park and Efe hotels. Look out for the fine, if fragile, old Ottoman wooden houses designed in an ornate style known as Edirnekâri, abandoned churches and, at the southern end of Maarif Caddesi, Edirne's **Great Synagogue**. Though presently a sad

Oiled Wrestling

The origins of *yağlı güreş* (oiled wrestling) are lost in legend, but it's thought that matches have been held near Edirne for at least six centuries.

According to the best-known version of the tale, Süleyman Paşa, son of Orhan Gazi, the second Ottoman sultan, crossed the Dardanelles in the mid-14th century bent on conquest. His vanguard consisted of 40 enthusiastic warriors who wrestled at rest stops to break the monotony of the march through Thrace. At a meadow in Ahırköy, near Edirne, they wrestled until only two remained standing. These two, unwilling to yield, wrestled long into the night and finally died of exhaustion. They were buried where they fell. The next day a spring of clear, cold water sprang up at the spot and was named Kırkpınar, or Forty Springs, for the 40 warriors.

MICK WELDON

A Wrestlers' Lodge was soon thriving in Edirne. Matches were held indoors in winter, and outdoors in summer in the Kırkpınar meadow, which today is just across the border in Greece. The highpoint of the year was the three-day series of matches held during the traditional spring festival of Hıdrellez.

These days hundreds of amateur wrestlers from all over Turkey gather in early June at Sarayiçi. Clad only in shorts of goat or calf leather, they cover themselves with olive oil, and utter a traditional chant.

After this the *cazgır*, or master of ceremonies, offers a prayer, and introduces the matches. Then the *davul* (folk bass drum) and *zurna* (Turkish double-reed instrument) begin the frenetic music which will play throughout the festival. The wrestlers go through *peşrev* (the traditional warm-up routine) consisting of a series of exaggerated arm-swinging steps and gestures.

Wrestlers are organised into 11 classes, from *teşvik* (encouragement) to *baş güreşler* (head wrestlers), with the winner in each class being designated a *başpehlivan*, or master wrestler. On the last day of the festival, the başpehlivans wrestle for the supreme honour. Finally only two are left, and these compete for the top prize, the coveted gold belt, and a small cash prize. With victory comes fame, honour, and the opportunity to earn money endorsing commercial products.

Folk-dancing exhibitions, musical performances and crafts displays are organised as part of the festivities, and these begin on Tuesday. The wrestling begins on Friday, with the winning başpehlivan chosen on Sunday. For exact dates and ticket information, contact the tourist offices in Edirne.

---

ruin of vanished grandeur, this synagogue is scheduled for restoration by Thracian University. Some other fine old houses are along Cumhuriyet Caddesi, which crosses Maarif Caddesi north of the synagogue.

The covered market called the **Ali Paşa Çarşısı**, east of Maarif Caddesi near Saraçlar Caddesi, was designed by Mimar Sinan, built in 1569, restored in 1805, 1867 and 1947, destroyed by fire in 1992 and again restored in 1994–97. There is an entrance off Hürriyet Meydanı to the left of the tourist office.

River Walks

Follow Saraçlar Caddesi south and out of town, under the railway line and across the Tunca Köprüsü, an Ottoman stone humpback bridge spanning the Tunca River. The Meriç Köprüsü, a longer Ottoman bridge, crosses the Meriç to the south. In between the two bridges are several restaurants, tea gardens and bars good for an outdoor drink or a meal in warm weather (see Places to Eat).

The DSI Meriç Rekreasyon Sahası (Meriç Riverbank Recreation Area) is on the northern bank of the Meriç. It lies upriver from the army club which occupies the prime riverbank spot at the northern side of the Meriç Köprüsü. The Recreation Area is a shady park with a children's playground, riverview benches, and paths for strolling.

On the southern side of the Meriç Köprüsü are more restaurants and tea gardens such as the Emirgan, opposite the restored Ottoman çeşme (fountain) of Hacı Adil Bey, with welcome shade and fine sunset views of the river and bridge.

Places to Stay

Fifi Mocamp (☎ 225 1554, Demirkapı Mevkii) is 9km east of Edirne on the old İstanbul road (D100, the eastward continuation of Talat Paşa Asfaltı). It has motel rooms open year-round, as well as hook-ups and services for tents and caravans from April to October.

Hotel Aksaray (☎ 212 6035, Alipaşa, Ortakapı Caddesi), only one long block from the tourist office, is an old Edirnekâri house, dusty but clean, run by an efficient lady who charges US$15 for a double room with shower.

Otel Şaban Açıkgöz (☎ 213 1404, fax 213 4516, Tahmis Meydanı Çilingirler Caddesi 9) is near the park next to the Eski Cami. Clean, fairly quiet singles/doubles with shower and TV are US$16/23, including breakfast, which is good value for money.

A block south of Hürriyet Meydanı, the *Park Hotel* (☎ 225 4610, fax 225 4635, Maarif Caddesi 7) is drab, but still charges US$22/30 for rooms with bath, TV and breakfast. Avoid the noisy rooms opening onto Maarif Caddesi.

The cheaper *Efe Hotel* (☎ 213 6166, fax 212 6080, Maarif Caddesi 13) has an air-conditioned lobby, lobby bar, and presentable rooms with shower and TV (but without air-con) for US$26/32. There's a noisy 'English Pub' in the basement.

The top hotel, right in the centre of town, is the two-star *Sultan Oteli* (☎ 225 1372, fax 225 5763, Talat Paşa Caddesi 170), half a block west of the tourist office. Rooms with shower, TV, good reading lamps and a good breakfast cost US$30/40. There's plentiful parking in the hotel's rear lot.

The two-star *Balta Hotel* (☎ 225 5210, fax 225 3529, Talat Paşa Asfaltı 97), halfway from the otogar to Hürriyet Meydanı, has the disadvantages of being 1km from the centre, facing a noisy street, and having drab rooms that catch the heat of the afternoon sun. Posted prices are a ridiculous US$60/100, including breakfast, but with a bit of banter they'll knock at least 50% off.

The *Hotel Kervansaray* (☎ 225 2195, fax 212 0462, İki Kapılıhan Caddesi 57), facing the park next to the Eski Cami, is in fact an Ottoman caravanserai built by order of Rüstem Paşa, a grand vizier of Süleyman the Magnificent, in about 1550. The camel caravans on the road between Europe, İstanbul and points further east rested here for the night, their valuable cargo safe within the building's massive stone walls and great armoured doors. Quality is variable, and often not worth the price of US$38 a double.

Places to Eat

Edirne has many small eateries, especially *köftecis* (serving *köfte*, meatballs) and *ciğercis* (serving fried liver). Among the brightest and best is *Serhad Köftecisi* on Saraçlar Caddesi just off Hürriyet Meydanı, where köfte with yogurt, salad, bread and a drink costs US$3.

Gaziantep Kebapçısı, to the right (west) of the main tourist office, near Hürriyet Meydanı, is as good a place as any for grilled kebaps and salads (it doesn't serve alcohol) for around US$3 or US$4 per meal.

There's a row of small restaurants facing a tiny park west of the Rüstem Paşa Kervansarayı by the Hotel Şaban Açıkgöz. *Serhad 1 Köftecisi* is the nicest of the four köftecis here; *Polat Lokantası* is best for stews, but serves grilled meats as well. Facing these eateries, with a name that looks like a menu, is *Edirne Lahmacun Döner Pide*, a more modern place.

More atmospheric, and only slightly more expensive, are the restaurants a five-minute walk south of the centre by the rivers. The *Yuva Restaurant* and *Gazi Baba II Meyhanesi*, between the two Ottoman stone bridges on the road to the Greek border, have white-tablecloth formality at moderate prices. But the all-time favourite is the *Emirgan Aile Çay Bahçesi*, at the southern end of the Meriç bridge, serving snacks and light meals as well as soft drinks and the ubiquitous çay (tea).

Restaurants located upriver from the bridge – the *Villa* and *Lalezar* – serve more substantial meat and fish dishes outdoors in warm weather, for US$12 to US$20 per person.

Entertainment
Edirne's nightlife revolves around the *Barcelona Disco-Bar* and *Cafe Akropol*, between the two Ottoman stone bridges on the river.

Getting There & Away
Bus & Dolmuş The new otogar is 8.5km east of the city centre on the access road to the Trans European Motorway, but at the time of writing buses to İstanbul still left from Edirne's old Otobüs Garajı, 2km southeast of the Eski Cami, every 20 minutes or so throughout the day. The 235km journey takes about 2½ hours and costs US$7. Take a city bus from the *belediye* (town hall) or along Talat Paşa Asfaltı and look for 'Terminal' on the signpost. Dolmuşes (US$0.35) run to the Otobüs Garajı quite frequently from the lot on the south-eastern side of the Rüstem Paşa Kervansarayı.

Heading south from Edirne, there are at least five buses daily to Çanakkale (3½ hours), though some require a transfer at Keşan; Truva Turizm has a direct bus (US$8, four hours).

Pazarkule, the border post for crossing into Greece, is 2km from the suburb of Karaağaç, 5km from the centre of Edirne along Saraçlar Caddesi. City buses run between Karaağaç and Edirne's belediye about every half-hour during the day; dolmuşes (US$0.25) make the same run, departing from the street between the belediye and Selimiye Camii. You'll have to walk or hitch the 2km to the border post. Alternatively, a taxi between Edirne and Pazarkule costs US$7 and takes about 15 minutes.

If you're heading for Bulgaria, to get to or from the Turkish border post at Kapıkule,

take city bus C-1 from behind the belediye, just uphill from the Eski Cami in the centre of Edirne. Alternatively, there are dolmuşes (US$0.75) every 20 minutes or so from the dolmuş station behind the Rüstem Paşa Kervansarayı to Kapıkule and, but both buses and dolmuşes are infrequent in the early morning and late at night.

For more details on the border crossings between Edirne and Bulgaria or Greece, see the Land section of the main Getting There & Away chapter earlier in this book.

Midnight Express

It's interesting to note that the original *Midnight Express* ran between İstanbul and Edirne through Greece. When the Ottoman Empire collapsed, the new border between Turkey and Greece was drawn so that the old railway line was partly in Greece. Greek border police would board when the train entered Greek territory and get off when it re-entered Turkish territory.

During the 1960s and '70s there was a slow, late-night train on this run. Foreigners convicted of drug-related offences in Turkey would be released by the Turkish government while their convictions were being appealed. They'd be given all their possessions except their passports, and told in a whisper about the *Midnight Express*.

They'd climb aboard in İstanbul and jump off the train in Greece, where Greek border police would pick them up and jail them. They'd call their consulate, arrange for a new passport, be let out of jail and sent on their way. This system allowed the Turkish government to meet the US government's demands that it be strict with drug smugglers, but it avoided the expense and bother of actually incarcerating the convicted smugglers. In the late 1970s, the Turkish State Railways built a bypass line and the Greek corridor route was abandoned.

The truth of the *Midnight Express* is quite different from that portrayed in the politically inspired anti-Turkish movie of the same name, in which a convicted drug-smuggler is magically transmuted into a suffering hero.

Train Edirne has two train stations: the city station (Edirne Garı), 3.5km south-east of the Eski Cami; and the one 18km away at Kapıkule on the Bulgarian border. Dolmuşes and city buses running south-east along Talat Paşa Asfaltı can drop you within 350m of the Edirne Garı.

The train service between Edirne and İstanbul (Sirkeci) is slow, infrequent and inconvenient. The *Edirne Ekspresi* (US$4) connects Edirne and İstanbul, departing Edirne at 8 am, and İstanbul at 3.25 pm, taking six hours (over twice as long as the bus) to make the run. The *Bosfor Ekspresi* to Bucharest comes through Edirne in the middle of the night, as does the *Balkan Ekspresi* to Budapest.

Car The highway between Europe and Edirne follows closely the Via Ignatia, the ancient road which connected Rome and Constantinople. It travels along the river valleys past Nisand Sofia, on between the mountain ranges of the Stara and Rhodope to Plovdiv, and along the Maritsa (Meriç) riverbank into Edirne.

After Edirne, the old Edirne-İstanbul highway (D100) heads east into the rolling, steppe-like terrain of Eastern Thrace towards İstanbul, still following the Via Ignatia. The E80 Avrupa Otoyol/Trans European Motorway (TEM) is a far preferable route to İstanbul in terms of condition, speed and safety. The toll of about US$4.50 to İstanbul is a small price to pay.

EAST OF EDİRNE

The ride to İstanbul is fairly uneventful, although this part of the country has had a tumultuous history. Enemy armies from the west intent on seizing Constantinople or İstanbul passed easily over this rolling countryside.

In 1877 the Russians held all of Turkish Thrace, and came within a few kilometres of İstanbul's city walls. During WWI, Allied armies marched this way; in WWII Thrace was heavily militarised by the Turks to fend off the Germans and to protect Turkey's fragile neutrality. A Turkish friend tells the story of his time on the line in Thrace:

It was late in a bitter winter. The wolves found little to eat in the countryside, and began coming dangerously close to our outpost. Ammunition was very scarce, but we asked permission to use a few rounds to defend ourselves against the wolves. Our commander said, 'You are Turkish soldiers. Use your bayonets'.

Havsa
☎ 284 • pop 10,000
The first town along the İstanbul road is Havsa, a town of some importance during Ottoman times. Its **Sokollu Kasım Paşa Külliyesi** is a mosque complex designed by Sinan and built in 1576–77 from orders of the son of Sokollu Mehmet Paşa, a grand vizier under Sultan Süleyman the Magnificent.

Lüleburgaz
☎ 282 • pop 56,000
About 75km east of Edirne is the market town of Lüleburgaz, the ancient Arcadiopolis. Unremarkable in itself, Lüleburgaz has the fine **Sokollu Mehmet Paşa Camii**, a mosque built in 1549 on the orders of Sokollu Mehmet Paşa, the *beylerbey* of Rumeli (governor of European Turkey) and later grand vizier to Süleyman the Magnificent.

Çorlu
☎ 282 • pop 75,000
Though wonderfully ancient, having been founded by the Phrygians around 1000 BC, Çorlu has little to show for its long history. A farmers' market town at best, it was a way-station on the İstanbul-Edirne road and thus received its share of mosque-building, and also a caravanserai and hamam. The **Sultan Süleyman Camii** (1521) is its most noteworthy old building. A few small hotels and restaurants provide for travellers.

Tekirdağ
☎ 282 • pop 85,000
Once known for its luxuriant vineyards and excellent wines, Tekirdağ, formerly Rodosto, today is a bustling modern place with little to hold your interest. Traces of Early Bronze Age life have been found in the vicinity.

THRACE

The tourist office (☎/fax 261 2083) is at Atatürk Bulvarı 65, on the waterfront street next to the Eski İskele (Old Dock).

The Ottomans – particularly Süleyman the Magnificent's grand vizier Rüstem Paşa – left Tekirdağ a legacy of great buildings, including the mosque, bedesten and medrese named after Rüstem.

Also here is the **Rakoczy Museum** (☎ 261 2082) on Barbaros Caddesi just in from the waterfront near the centre of the town. Prince Francis II Rakoczy (1676–1735) led rebellious Hungarians in their struggle against Hapsburg repression in the early 1700s. Forced to flee in 1711, he went into exile in Poland, then France, and finally in Turkey, where he died. Rakoczy's remains were returned to Hungary in 1906, and his Tekirdağ home became a museum in 1932.

SOUTH OF EDİRNE

The fertile Thracian landscape rolls on south from Edirne, ending in the seaside resorts of Saros and Erikli on the Gulf of Saros.

Uzunköprü
☎ 284 • pop 36,000

About 36km south of Havsa along the E87/D550 is the farming town of Uzunköprü. Named 'Long Bridge' for its Ottoman viaduct, 1270m long with 173 arches, Uzunköprü has the nearest train station to the border on the line connecting İstanbul and Athens. A daily train (US$3, 5½ hours) connects İstanbul and Uzunköprü, but buses, as usual, are faster, if a bit more expensive.

The Long Bridge itself, begun in 1427 and finished in 1443, is still in use as the town's main access road from the north, a monument to the durability of Ottoman construction. Its southern end is in the town centre, where there are simple, cheap hotels including *Hotel Ergene*, and basic *eateries*. The town's otogar is 2km south-east of the centre on the road to Keşan, 46km further south.

İpsala & Keşan
☎ 284

İpsala is the main border-crossing point between Turkey and Greece, on the E84/D110 highway; the Greek border post is Kipi. Both border posts have currency exchange facilities and are open 24 hours.

The actual Turkish border post is 5km west of the town of İpsala, reachable by taxi (US$5). A bus from İpsala to İstanbul (246km) costs US$8.50, and takes four hours. There is a tourist office (☎/fax 616 1577) at the border post. If you're coming from Greece, go straight through İpsala to Keşan (US$2 by dolmuş, US$15 by taxi), from where bus connections to Edirne (102km), İstanbul (220km), Gelibolu (77km) and Çanakkale (120km) are available.

Keşan's otogar (Belediye Terminalı) is on the E87/D550 south of the E84/D110, but most minibuses terminate at a lot just off the main square, 2.5km south-east and uphill from the intersection of these two highways, and 2.5km east of the otogar. Keşan's main square has several small köftecis, restaurants and pastanes. *Hotel Ayhan* (☎ 714 5467), just south of the main square, can put you up cheaply, though the best lodgings are at the three-star *Hotel Yener* (☎ 714 3660) on Demirciler Caddesi.

South of Keşan on the Bay of Saros is the village of **Saros** (also known as İbrikbaba or İbrice), with numerous little cheap beachfront pensions and hotels.

GALLIPOLI (GELİBOLU) PENINSULA

The slender peninsula which forms the north-western side of the Dardanelles (Çanakkale Boğazı), across the water from Çanakkale, is called Gallipoli (Gelibolu in Turkish). For a millennium it has been the key to İstanbul: the navy that could force the straits had a good chance of capturing the capital of the Eastern European world. Many fleets have tried to force the straits. Most, including the mighty Allied fleet mustered in WWI, have failed. Today the Gallipoli battlefields are peaceful places covered in scrubby brush, pine forests, and fields. But the battles fought here nearly a century ago are still alive in the memories of many people, both Turkish and foreign. Gallipoli has a special significance for Australians and New Zealanders, thousands of whom make a kind of pilgrimage here every year.

GALLIPOLI PENINSULA

1. Büyük Kemikli Picnic Area & Beach
2. Lala Baba
3. Hill 60 New Zealand Memorial
4. 7th Field Ambulance Cemetery
5. Kocaçimentepe
6. Kabatepe Information Centre & Museum
7. Gallipoli National Historic Park Visitors' Centre & Picnic Area
8. Twelve Tree Copse Cemetery
9. Redoubt Cemetery
10. Pink Farm Cemetery
11. Skew Bridge Cemetery
12. French Memorial & Museum
13. Kerevizdere Picnic Area
14. Çanakkale Şehitleri Abidesi Memorial
15. 'V' Beach Cemetery
16. İlk Şehitler & Yahya Çavuş Memorials
17. Cape Helles British Memorial
18. Lancashire Landing Cemetery

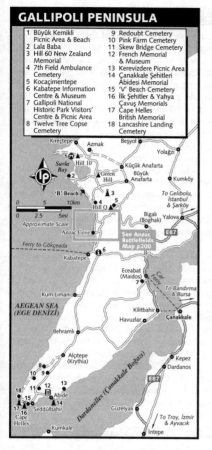

On the hillside by Kilitbahir, clearly visible from Çanakkale, are gigantic letters spelling out the first few words of a poem by Necmettin Halil Onan commemorating the momentous struggle for Gallipoli in 1915:

Dur yolcu! Bilmeden gelip bastığın
bu toprak bir devrin battığı yerdir.
Eğil de kulak ver, bu sessiz yığın
bir vatan kalbinin attığı yerdir.

Traveller, halt! The soil you heedlessly tread
once witnessed the end of an era.
Listen! In this quiet mound
there once beat the heart of a nation.

The best base for visiting the battlefields is Eceabat on the western shore of the Dardanelles, although Çanakkale on the eastern shore has a much wider range of accommodation. Gelibolu, 45km north-east of Eceabat, is another option. Most of the Gallipoli peninsula is now a national park.

History

Just 1.4km wide at its narrowest point, the Strait of Çanakkale (Çanakkale Boğazı, Hellespont, Dardanelles) has always offered the best opportunity for travellers – and armies – to cross between Europe and Asia Minor.

King Xerxes I of Persia crossed the strait here on a bridge of boats in 481 BC, as did Alexander the Great 150 years later. In Byzantine times it was the first line of defence for Constantinople.

By 1402 the strait was under the control of the Ottoman sultan, Beyazıt I, providing the means for the Ottoman armies to cross to – and conquer – the Balkans. Mehmet the Conqueror fortified the strait as part of his grand and ultimately successful plan to conquer Constantinople (1453).

The Ottomans maintained numerous fortresses: Seddülbahir and Kumkale at the southern end of the straits; Çamburun, Karaburun, Bigalı and Kilibahir within the strait; Bozcaada on the island at the southern mouth; Çimenlik in the town of Çanakkale, and Kilitbahir, the 'Lock on the Sea', on the Gallipoli side across from Çanakkale.

During the 19th century, England and France competed with Russia for influence over the 'Sick Man of Europe', as the Ottoman Empire was popularly known, and the strategic sea passages linking the Black, Marmara and Aegean Seas.

With the intention of capturing the Ottoman capital and the road to Eastern Europe during WWI, Winston Churchill, British First Lord of the Admiralty, organised a naval assault on the strait. A strong Franco-British fleet tried first to force them in March 1915 but failed. Then, on 25 April, British, Australian, New Zealand and Indian troops landed on Gallipoli, and French troops near Çanakkale. Both Turkish and

THRACE

The Hellespont

Hellespont, the ancient name of the Dardanelles, is the product of a classical myth.

Athamas, a king of Thessaly, tired of his wife, Nephele, and set her aside in favour of Princess Ino of Thebes. Ino, who had a son by Athamas, set to work to eliminate Nephele's son Phryxus, and daughter Helle, so that her own son might inherit Athamas' crown. She secretly parched all of the kingdom's seed corn before the spring sowing, resulting in a disastrous harvest.

The king sent a messenger to the nearest oracle asking what he should do to relieve the terrible distress. As the messenger returned, Ino intercepted, bribed and threatened him to forget what the oracle had said in favour of her own pronouncement. The messenger told Athamas that Phryxus must die in sacrifice to the gods before the corn would grow again.

With the boy on the altar about to go under the knife, Hermes, in answer to Nephele's prayer, sent a golden-fleeced flying ram to save him. Phryxus and Helle leapt on the ram's back and were whisked into the sky and across the strait which separates Europe from Asia. During the flight, Helle fell off and drowned in the strait, which was named Hellespont (Helle's Sea) in her memory.

Phryxus continued his flight, finally landing in Colchis at the eastern end of the Unfriendly (Black) Sea, where he sacrificed the ram in honour of Zeus, giving its priceless golden fleece to King Aeetes, who permitted Phryxus to marry one of his daughters. The golden fleece was placed in a sacred grove under the watchful eye of a sleepless dragon, obviously a set-up so that Jason would later have a quest worthy of his heroism.

The strait's other name, Dardanelles, comes from the ancient town of Dardanus, the ruins of which were discovered between Çanakkale and Güzelyalı on its Asian shore. The town was named after Dardanus, son of Zeus and the Pleiad Electra, who founded Troy and the Trojan race, or Dardani.

The Hellespont was also the setting for the legend of Hero and Leander. Leander, a youth from Abydos (Çanakkale), fell in love with Hero, a priestess in the Temple of Venus at Sestos (Kilitbahir). Each night Leander would plunge into the chill waters of the Hellespont and swim to the European shore, guided by a torch which Hero held up in the temple tower. One stormy night the torch was blown out by the wind and Leander, without guidance, was exhausted trying to find the shore, and drowned. Hero, in despair at finding his body on the shore, threw herself from her tower.

The myth was thought to be an impossible exaggeration until Lord Byron, ever the romantic, arrived in 1807 to prove it possible. Born lame, he had no trouble swimming and completed the crossing to incredulous acclaim. He later used Abydos as the setting for his verse tale 'The Bride of Abydos' (1813). Since Byron, many others have come to swim the Hellespont, including the American ambassador to Turkey, William Macomber, in 1975.

Allied troops fought desperately and fearlessly, and devastated one another. After nine months of ferocious combat but little progress, the Allied forces were withdrawn.

The Turkish success at Gallipoli was partly due to bad luck and bad leadership on the Allied side, and partly due to the timely provision of reinforcements coming to the aid of the Turkish side under the command of General Liman von Sanders. But a crucial element in the defeat was that the Allied troops happened to land in a sector where they faced Lieutenant-Colonel Mustafa Kemal (Atatürk).

He was a relatively minor officer, but he had General von Sanders' confidence. He guessed the Allied battle plan correctly when his commanders did not, and stalled the invasion by bitter fighting which wiped out his division. Though suffering from malaria, he commanded in full view of his troops and of the enemy, and miraculously escaped death several times. At one point a piece of shrapnel tore through the breast pocket of his uniform, but was stopped by his pocket watch (now in the Çanakkale Military & Naval Museum). His brilliant performance made him a folk hero and paved the way for his promotion to pasha (general).

The Gallipoli campaign lasted for nine months, until January 1916, and resulted in a total of more than half a million casualties. The British Empire suffered over 200,000 casualties, with the loss of some 36,000 lives.

French casualties of 47,000 were over half of the entire French contingent. Half of the 500,000 Ottoman troops who participated in the battle became a casualty, with more than 55,000 dead. There are now 31 war cemeteries on the peninsula as well as several important monuments.

The treaties of Sèvres (1920) and Lausanne (1923) decreed that the strait was to be demilitarised, but as WWII approached, the Montreux Convention (1936) permitted Turkey to remilitarise it.

Turkey maintained a precarious neutrality during WWII, allowing both Allied and Axis shipping to pass through, but when the course of the war seemed certain in January 1945, Allied supply ships were allowed through on their way to Russia.

Orientation

Gallipoli is a fairly large area to tour, especially without your own transport. It's over 35km as the crow flies from the northernmost battlefield to the southern tip of the peninsula.

The principal battles took place on the western shore of the peninsula near Anzac Cove and Arıburnu, and in the hills just to the east. Anzac Cove is about 12km from Eceabat, 19km from Kilitbahir, and 57km from Gelibolu. If your time is limited or if you're touring by public transport, head for Anzac Cove and Arıburnu first.

Ferries run from Çanakkale on the eastern side of the Dardanelles to Kilitbahir and Eceabat on the peninsula.

Organised Tours

With your own transport you can tour the battlefields easily in a day or less. Touring by public transport is possible, but dolmuşes serve only certain sites or nearby villages, and you must expect to do some waiting and

walking. In summer, hitching greatly facilitates getting around on your own, but in other seasons traffic may not be sufficient. The most important group of monuments and cemeteries, from Lone Pine uphill to Chunuk Bair, can be toured on foot, an excellent idea in fine weather.

Joining an organised tour is a good idea as you save time and trouble, and get the benefit of a guide who can relate the history and explain the battles. Some readers have complained that tours go too fast and allow too little time at the beach, so you'd be well advised to talk with other travellers who have just taken a tour and find out what they recommend. Most tours include a picnic and some time at a Gallipoli beach for swimming. Tours are organised by several agencies in Çanakkale and Eceabat.

The typical four- to six-hour battlefield tour includes transport by car or minibus, driver and guide, lunch and a swim from a beach on the western shore.

TJs Tours (☎ 286-814 2940, fax 814 2941, ⓔ tjs_tours@excite.com) based at TJs Hostel in Eceabat has been recommended by many travellers. İlhami Gezici, aka TJ, matches his historical knowledge with genuine enthusiasm. Tours last six hours and cost US$20. A two-person tour, costing US$110, can include the less visited sites at Cape Helles and around Suvla Bay. This agency has copies of the cemetery records if visitors want to find a particular grave.

Hassle Free Tours (☎ 286-213 5969, fax 217 2906, ⓔ hasslefree@anzachouse.com) operates from Anzac House in Çanakkale for US$21. Unless you're a military specialist or an archaeologist you should find the site tours adequate and enjoyable. Tour guide Ali Efe gets good reports. Hassle Free also runs tours out of İstanbul to Gallipoli for US$55, staying one night at Anzac House before visiting the ruins at Troy and either travelling on to Selçuk or back to İstanbul. But visiting the battlefields straight after a five-hour bus ride from İstanbul is not much fun – it might be better to take the tour from Çanakkale. Travel agencies in İstanbul tend to hustle for Hassle Free Tours even if you just inquire about travelling independently to Gallipoli.

THRACE

Troy-Anzac Tours (☎ 286-217 5849, fax 217 0196), Saat Kulesi Meydanı 6, Çanakkale, facing the clock tower, has been in business the longest but it doesn't seem to be as popular as the other two, perhaps because it is not associated with a hostel. Four-hour tours cost US$20 per person.

In Gelibolu, the Hotel Yılmaz runs tours departing at 9.30 am, returning at 1.30 pm, for US$25 per person. The drivers rarely speak English and the 'tour guide' is a tape recording! It's better, and cheaper, to take a tour from Eceabat or Çanakkale.

Diving on some of the many wrecks on the western coast of the peninsula is becoming popular. The tour agencies listed can put you in touch with local diving agencies. Mehmet Günaydın is the most experienced guide – he can be contacted through Çanakkale's Underwater and Lifesaving Club (Sualtı ve Cankurtama Külübüu) (☎ 286-212 5442). Diving costs around US$80 per day.

Shipwreck Tours (☎ 286-814 2144, ask for Timon) based at the Boomerang Bar in Eceabat offers good-value snorkelling tours of a shelled landing craft just north of Anzac Cove. It's eerie to float over the skeleton of the boat, but the water is refreshingly cool. The best time to fossick for bullets and other relics on the seabed is after a storm, when some of the sand has been cleared away. The Shipwreck Tours truck also stops at the little-visited Shell Green cemetery, and the vehicle is sturdy enough to venture to little-known trenches. The four-hour tour costs US$10 per person.

Gallipoli National Historic Park

This park, Gelibolu Tarihi Milli Parkı in Turkish, covers much of the peninsula and all of the significant battle sites. Park headquarters is 2km south-west of Eceabat (5km north-east of Kilitbahir) at the Ziyaretçi Merkezi (Visitors Centre); there's a picnic ground here as well.

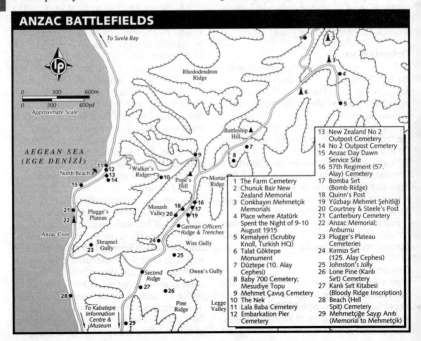

ANZAC BATTLEFIELDS

To Suvla Bay

Rhododendron Ridge

0   300   600m
0   300   600yd
Approximate Scale

Battleship Hill

AEGEAN SEA
(EGE DENİZİ)

Walker's Ridge
North Beach
Pope's Hill
Mortar Ridge

Plugge's Plateau

Monash Valley

German Officers' Ridge & Trenches

Anzac Cove
Shrapnel Gully
Wire Gully

Second Ridge
Owen's Gully

To Kabatepe Information Centre & Museum
Pine Ridge
Legge Valley

1 The Farm Cemetery
2 Chunuk Bair New Zealand Memorial
3 Conkbayırı Mehmetçik Memorials
4 Place where Atatürk Spent the Night of 9-10 August 1915
5 Kemalyeri (Scrubby Knoll, Turkish HQ)
6 Talat Göktepe Monument
7 Düztepe (10. Alay Cephesi)
8 Baby 700 Cemetery; Mesudiye Topu
9 Mehmet Çavuş Cemetery
10 The Nek
11 Lala Baba Cemetery
12 Embarkation Pier Cemetery
13 New Zealand No 2 Outpost Cemetery
14 No 2 Outpost Cemetery
15 Anzac Day Dawn Service Site
16 57th Regiment (57. Alay) Cemetery
17 Bomba Sırt (Bomb Ridge)
18 Quinn's Post
19 Yüzbaşı Mehmet Şehitliği
20 Courtney & Steele's Post
21 Canterbury Cemetery
22 Anzac Memorial; Arıburnu
23 Plugge's Plateau Cemeteries
24 Kırmızı Sırt (125. Alay Cephesi)
25 Johnston's Jolly
26 Lone Pine (Kanlı Sırt) Cemetery
27 Kanlı Sırt Kitabesi (Bloody Ridge Inscription)
28 Beach (Hell Spit) Cemetery
29 Mehmetçiğe Saygı Anıtı (Memorial to Mehmetçik)

Anzac Day

The great WWI battles of Gallipoli are commemorated each year during March and April.

Turkish Victory Day (Çanakkale Deniz Zaferi), when Ottoman cannons and mines succeeded in keeping the Allied fleet from passing through the Dardanelles, is celebrated on 18 March, with festivities from 12 to 19 March.

Most Australians and New Zealanders choose to visit on Anzac Day (Anzac Günü, 25 April), the anniversary of the Allied landings on the peninsula in 1915. A dawn service at a site on North Beach begins a day of commemorative events.

Alan Moorehead, the author of *Gallipoli*, wrote in the 1950s, 'Except for occasional organised tours not more than half a dozen visitors arrive from one year's end to the other.'.

In recent years, however, the memory of Gallipoli has most definitely come to life. The battlefields are now among the most-visited places in Turkey, particularly on Anzac Day, when upwards of 12,000 visitors crowd the cemeteries and monument sites. Long rows of buses block the narrow roads, and dignitaries as well as visitors are often unable to reach the site of an event. The traffic snarl lasts most of the day.

We've heard plenty of stories of people being ripped off trying to make it to Anzac Day on a package deal. Three-star hotels turn out to be fleapits, camp sites turn out to be a forest clearing without even the most basic facilities. 'Expert' guides turn out to be sorely lacking – our favourite story involves a guide solemnly announcing on arrival at Eceabat that the bus had arrived at Anzac Cove, until a passenger had to point out that Anzac Cove was on the other side of the peninsula. The solution is to book as early as possible with an experienced agency, and be sceptical of agencies in İstanbul, in particular, offering last-minute deals. In Çanakkale, all lodgings are booked solid at high prices months before 25 April, and other tourist services increase their prices.

Some tour operators convince visitors that it's possible to drive from İstanbul to Çanakkale in time for the Anzac Day dawn service, when in fact many people coming from Çanakkale can't even make it to the site in time.

All in all, a day which in the past was a solemn commemoration of heroic courage and sacrifice has developed more than its share of logistical problems. Anzac Day at Gallipoli has an almost sacred quality for many Australians and New Zealanders, but be aware that everyone's patience gets tested. To experience the poignant beauty of Gallipoli, you'd do well to visit at some other time.

In the national park there are several different signage systems: the normal Turkish highway signs, the national park administration signs and those posted by the Commonwealth War Graves Commission. This leads to confusion because the foreign troops had a completely different nomenclature for battlefield sites from the Turks, and the Turkish battlefield markings do not necessarily agree with the ones erected by the highway department. We've used both English and Turkish names in the text and on the Gallipoli map.

There are camping grounds at Kabatepe, Kum Limanı and Seddülbahir, and simple accommodation at Kum Limanı, Seddülbahir and Abide.

About 3km north of Eceabat a road marked for Kabatepe and Kemalyeri heads west.

Kabatepe Information Centre & Museum

This centre (Kabatepe Tanıtma Merkezi), 9km from Eceabat and 1km or so east of the village of Kabatepe, holds a small museum (US$1.30) with period uniforms, soldiers' letters, rusty weapons and other battlefield finds such as the skull of a luckless Turkish soldier with a ball lodged right in the forehead.

The road uphill to Lone Pine (Kanlı Sırt) and Chunuk Bair (Conkbayırı) begins 750m west of the information centre. Anzac Cove is about 3.5km from the information centre.

Kabatepe Village The small harbour here may have been the object of the Allied landing on 25 April 1915, and perhaps in the pitch dark of early morning the landing craft were swept northwards by uncharted currents to the steep cliffs of Arıburnu – a bit of bad luck which would have been crucial to the campaign. Today there is little here but a camping ground and the dock for ferries to the island of Gökçeada. The ferry timetable seems to be rather flexible, but in summer ferries leave Kabatepe at 9.45 and 11 am, and at 4 and 7 pm. From Gökçeada ferries leave at 7 and 8 am, and at 1.45, 4 and 7 pm. The ferry costs US$1.60 per person, US$10 per car.

Anzac Cove & Beaches Going west from the information centre, it's 3km to the **Beach Cemetery**, and another 90m to where a road goes inland to the Shrapnel Valley and Plugge's Plateau cemeteries.

Another 400m along from where the road goes inland is Anzac Cove (Anzac Koyu). The ill-fated Allied landing was made here on 25 April 1915, beneath and just south of the Arıburnu cliffs. The Allied forces were ordered to advance inland, but met with fierce resistance from the Ottoman forces under Mustafa Kemal (Atatürk), who had foreseen the landing here and, disobeyed a direct order from his commanders to send his troops south to Cape Helles. After this first failed effort, the Anzacs concentrated on consolidating and expanding the beachhead, which they did until June while awaiting reinforcements.

In August a major offensive was staged in an attempt to advance beyond the beachhead and up to the ridges of Chunuk Bair and Sarı Bair, and resulted in the bloodiest battles of the campaign, but little progress was made.

Anzac Cove is marked by a Turkish monument, another 300m along, which repeats Atatürk's famous words uttered in 1934 for the Anzac troops. As a memorial reserve, the beach here is off-limits to swimmers and picnickers.

A few hundred metres beyond Anzac Cove is the **Arıburnu Cemetery** and, 750m further along, the **Canterbury Cemetery**. Less than 1km further along the seaside road are the cemeteries at the **No 2 Outpost**, set back inland from the road, and the **New Zealand No 2 Outpost**, next to the road. The **Embarkation Pier Cemetery** is 200m beyond the New Zealand No 2 Outpost.

Lone Pine Retrace your steps to the Kabatepe information centre and follow the signs up the hill for Lone Pine (Kanlı Sırt), perhaps the most poignant and moving of all the Anzac cemeteries. It's just under 3km to Lone Pine from the junction with the beach road, and another 3km uphill to the New Zealand Memorial at Chunuk Bair (Conkbayırı).

This area, which saw the most bitter fighting of the campaign, was later cloaked in pines, but a disastrous forest fire in 1994 denuded the hills. Reforestation efforts are under way.

The first monument, **Mehmetçiğe Saygı Anıtı**, on the right-hand side of the road 1200m up from the junction, is the one to 'Mehmetçik' (Little Mehmet), the Turkish 'Johnnie' or 'GI Joe', for his contribution to national defence. Another 1200m brings you to the **Kanlı Sırt Kitabesi**, the inscription monument (in Turkish) detailing the battle of Lone Pine from the Turkish viewpoint.

At Lone Pine, 400m uphill from the Kanlı Sırt Kitabesi, Australian forces captured the Turkish positions on the evening of 6 August. In the few days of the August assault 4000 men died here. The trees which shaded the cemetery were swept away by the fire in 1994, leaving only one: a lone pine planted years ago as a memorial from the seed of the original tree which had stood here during the battle. The small tombstones carry touching epitaphs: 'Only son', 'He died for his country' and 'If I could hold your hand once more just to say well done'.

Johnston's Jolly to Quinn's Post As you progress up the hill from Lone Pine, you quickly come to understand the ferocity of the battles here. At some points the trenches were only a few metres apart. The order to attack meant certain death to all who followed it, and virtually all – on both the Ottoman and Allied sides – did as they were ordered.

At Johnston's Jolly, 200m beyond Lone Pine, at Courtney's & Steele's Post, another 300m along, and especially at Quinn's Post (Bomba Sırt, Yüzbaşı Mehmet Şehitliği), another 400m uphill, the trenches were separated only by the width of the modern road.

On the eastern side at **Johnston's Jolly** is the Turkish monument to the soldiers of the 125th Regiment who died here on 'Red Ridge' (Kırmızı Sırt/125 Alay Cephesi). At **Quinn's Post** is the memorial to Sergeant Mehmet, who fought with rocks and his fists after he ran out of ammunition, and the Captain Mehmet Cemetery.

57. Alay (57th Regiment) Just over 1km

uphill from Lone Pine is another monument to Mehmetçik on the western side of the road and, on the eastern side, the cemetery and monument for officers and soldiers of the Ottoman 57th Regiment, which was sacrificed to the first Anzac assaults. The cemetery, built only a few years ago, has a surprising amount of religious symbolism for a Turkish army site, as the republican army has historically been steadfastly secular. The statue of an old man showing his granddaughter the battle sites portrays veteran Hüseyin Kaçmaz, who fought in the Balkan Wars, the Gallipoli campaign and the War of Independence at the fateful Battle of Dumlupınar. He died in 1994 at the age of 110.

Mehmet Çavuş & The Nek About 100m

uphill past the 57th Regiment Cemetery, a road goes west to the monument for Mehmet Çavuş (another Sergeant Mehmet) and The Nek. It was at The Nek on 7 August 1915 that the eighth (Victorian) and 10th (Western Australian) regiments of the third Light Horse Brigade vaulted out of their trenches into withering fire and certain death – doomed but utterly courageous.

Baby 700/Mesudiye Topu About 300m

uphill from the road to The Nek is the Baby 700 Cemetery and the Ottoman cannon

called the Mesudiye Topu. Baby 700 was the limit of the initial attack, and the graves here are mostly dated 25 April.

Düztepe (10. Alay Cephesi) Another

1.5km uphill brings you to this monument, which marks the spot where the Ottoman 10th Regiment held the line. The views of the strait and the surrounding countryside are very fine.

Talat Göktepe Monument About 1km

further along from Düztepe is the monument to Talat Göktepe, Chief Director of the Çanakkale Forestry District, who died fighting a forest fire in these hills in 1994.

Chunuk Bair At the top of the hill, 600m

past the Talat Göktepe Monument, is a T-intersection. A right turn takes you east to the spot where, having stayed awake for four days and nights, Atatürk spent the night of 9 to 10 August, directing part of the counterattack to the August offensive, and also to **Kemalyeri** (Scrubby Knoll), his command post. A left turn leads after 100m to **Chunuk Bair** (Conkbayırı), the first objective of the Allied landing in April 1915, and now the site of the New Zealand memorial.

As the Anzac troops made their way up the scrub-covered slopes on 25 April, the divisional commander Mustafa Kemal (Atatürk) brought up the 57th Infantry Regiment and gave them his famous order: 'I order you not just to attack, but to die. In the time it takes us to die, other troops and commanders will arrive to take our places.' The 57th was wiped out, but held the line and inflicted equally heavy casualties on the Anzacs below.

Chunuk Bair was also at the heart of the struggle for the peninsula from 6 to 9 August 1915, when 28,000 men died on this ridge. The peaceful pine grove of today makes it difficult to imagine the blasted wasteland of almost a century ago, when bullets, bombs and shrapnel mowed down men as the fighting went on day and night with huge numbers of casualties. The Anzac attack on 6 to 7 August, which included the New Zealand Mounted Rifle

Brigade and a Maori contingent, was deadly, but the attack on the following day was of a ferocity which, according to Atatürk, 'could scarcely be described'.

On the western side of the road are the **New Zealand memorial** and some reconstructed **Turkish trenches** (Türk Siperleri). A sign indicates the spots at which Mustafa Kemal (Atatürk) stood on 8 August 1915, known to every Turkish schoolchild: where he gave the order for the crucial attack at 4.30 am; where he watched the progress of the battle; and the spot where shrapnel would have hit his heart, but was stopped by his pocket watch.

To the east a side road leads up to the **Turkish Conkbayırı Memorial**, five gigantic tablets with inscriptions (in Turkish) describing the progress of the battle.

Beyond Chunuk Bair the road leads to Kocaçimentepe, less than 2km along.

Southern Peninsula A road goes south from near the Kabatepe information centre past the side road to **Kum Limanı**, where there's a good swimming beach and the *Hotel Kum and Kum Camping* (☎ 286-814 1466, fax 814 1917), just over 6km southwest of the information centre. It has comfortable shower-equipped rooms for US$50 in summer, and camping places with some shade for US$3.20 per person.

From Kabatepe (Gaba Tepe) it's about 12km to the village of **Alçıtepe**, formerly known as Krythia or Kirte. Close to the village's main intersection is the privately run **Salim Mutlu War Museum**, which has a collection of relics from the northern and southern battlefields. Most of the items at the Kabatepe Museum were gifts from here. Payment is by donation. In the village, signs point out the road south-west to the **Twelve Tree Copse** and **Pink Farm** cemeteries, and north to the Turkish **Sargı Yeri Cemetery** and **Nuri Yamut monument**.

Heading south, the road passes the **Redoubt Cemetery**. About 5.5km south of Alçıtepe, south of the **Skew Bridge Cemetery**, the road divides, the right fork for the village of Seddülbahir and several Allied memorials. **Seddülbahir** (Sedd el Bahr),

1.5km from the intersection, is a sleepy farming village with a few pensions (including the *Helles Panorama*, *Evim*, *Kale* and *Fulda*), a PTT, a ruined Ottoman/Byzantine fortress; an army post and a small harbour.

Follow the signs for Yahya Çavuş Şehitliği to reach the **Helles Memorial**, 1km beyond the Seddülbahir village square. There are fine views of the straits, with ships cruising placidly up and down. Half a million men were killed, wounded or lost in the dispute over which ships should (or should not) go through.

The initial Allied attack was two-pronged, with the southern landing being here at the tip of the peninsula on 'V' Beach. Yahya Çavuş (Sergeant Yahya) was the Turkish officer who led the first resistance to the Allied landing on 25 April 1915, causing heavy casualties. The cemetery named after him, known as **Yahya Çavuş Şehitliği**, is between the Helles Memorial and 'V' Beach.

Lancashire Landing cemetery is off to the north along a road marked by a sign; another sign points south to **'V' Beach**, 550m downhill. Right next to the beach is *Mocamp Seddülbahir*, with tent and caravan sites and a few pension-like rooms.

Retrace your steps from the Helles Memorial back to the road division and then head east following signs for Abide and/or Çanakkale Şehitleri Abidesi (Çanakkale Martyrs' Memorial) at Morto Bay. Along the way you will pass the **French Memorial & Museum**. French troops, including a regiment of Africans, attacked Kumkale on the Asian shore in March 1915 with complete success, then re-embarked and landed in support of their British comrades-in-arms at Cape Helles. The French cemetery is rarely visited but quite moving, with five concrete ossuaries containing the bones of thousands of soldiers.

At the foot of the Turkish monument hill is a fine pine-shaded picnic area. The monument, known as **Çanakkale Şehitleri Abidesi**, commemorates all of the Turkish soldiers who fought and died at Gallipoli. It's a gigantic four-legged stone table almost 42m high and surrounded by landscaped grounds, which stands above a war museum (admission US$0.80). Exhibits include interesting bits of metal turned up by farmers' ploughs, such as English forks and spoons, soldiers' seals and medals, scimitars, French bayonets and machine guns. The poem on the side of the memorial translates:

Soldiers who have fallen on this land defending this land!
Would that your ancestors might descend from the skies to kiss your pure brows.
Who could dig the grave that was not too small for you?
All of history itself is too small a place for you.

The most touching exhibit at the museum is a letter from a young officer who had left law school in Constantinople to volunteer in the Gallipoli campaign. He wrote to his mother in poetic terms about the beauty of the landscape and of his love for life. Two days later he died in battle.

Gelibolu
☎ 286 • pop 25,000
If you are coming from Edirne or Keşan, or from İstanbul along the northern shore of the Sea of Marmara, the little harbour town of Gelibolu can provide transport connections, a meal or a bed. This quiet Turkish holiday spot also has an interesting collection of monuments and shrines, worthy of a day trip. However, most people stop here in the mistaken belief they have arrived at the Gallipoli battlefields, which are 60km away.

Orientation & Information The centre of Gelibolu is by the docks for the car ferry to Lapseki, and everything you may need is within 100m of here. The stone tower which looms above the ancient harbour is a remnant of the Byzantine town of Kallipolis, which gave the present town and peninsula their name. The tower is now the Piri Reis Museum, named after the famous Turkish cartographer, with changing exhibits (free admission). The otogar is 500m south-west of the stone tower on the Eceabat road.

The Gelibolu Promotion Centre is in a booth beside the fishing boat harbour, next to the bust of Piri Reis. It offers little except souvenirs and copies of the Piri Reis map. The PTT has a yellow-and-black kiosk right at the docks where you can convert currency and buy stamps. Across the road is a Yapı Kredi ATM. Other banks are along Yukarı Çarşı Sokak, the town's main shopping street, which starts opposite the Hotel Yılmaz (by the Emlak Bankası) and goes uphill.

Things to See & Do The road north past the Hotel Yılmaz veers uphill, past several military buildings. After 800m there's the shrine of **Yazıcızade Mehmet Efendi** on the right, with a mosque and the tomb of the author of a commentary on the Quran called the *Muhammadiye*. Another 200m on there is a **French Cemetery** from the Crimean War, which also contains an ossuary containing the bones of Senegalese soldiers who died in the Gallipoli campaign. The cemetery overlooks a military camp and a pleasant beach.

Continue on to the headland with the lighthouse, where a path leads down to the left to the **Bayraklı Baba Türbesi**. Karaca Bey was an Ottoman standard bearer who ate the flag in his keeping piece by piece rather than let it be captured by the enemy. When his comrades found him they asked where the flag was, but refused to believe him. He split open his stomach to prove the point, and while this cost him his life, he became a local legend and was renamed Bayraklı Baba. Today his tomb is bedecked in hundreds of Turkish flags – the attendant will sell you one to attach to the shrine's frame.

At the edge of the headland, not far from the lighthouse, is the small but elegant **Namazgah**, a mosque built in 1407, unusual for being roofless. It has some fine, if weatherbeaten, marble carvings.

Places to Stay Best in town is the two-star *Hotel Oya* (☎ 566 0392) on Miralay Şefik Aker Caddesi, 100m from the ferry docks, with TV- and shower-equipped singles/doubles for US$13/29. A block away is the older *Hotel Yılmaz* (☎ 566 1256, *Liman Meydanı 8*), with small rooms that could use a more attentive cleaner for US$12/20.

Otel Hakan (☎ *566 2424, Liman Meydanı Belediye Caddesi 8*), facing the stone tower on the main square, is simple but clean; doubles with sink go for US$6.

Camping Obidi, 1.5km from the stone tower and off the road south-west to Eceabat and Kilitbahir (follow the signs), is on the shore, has some shade, and can be pleasant for a night or two.

About 12km south of Gelibolu on the road to Eceabat, on the shore, is the two-star 48-room *Hotel Boncuk* (☎ *576 8292, fax 576 8158*), charging US$25 a double. *Cennet Camping & Motel*, 19km south of Gelibolu, is better for camping than motel accommodation, with some shady sites. *Derya Camping*, across the road, is not as good.

Places to Eat Among the hotels at the centre are many small restaurants, kebapçıs and büfes serving everything from stand-up snacks to sit-down dinners with white tablecloths and wine.

The best view and breeze are at *Café Nezih* next to the Denizyolları ferryboat ticket office by the docks, but it serves only drinks and snacks. For full meals, the *İmren*, *Boğaz*, *Liman* and *Yelken* restaurants near the Otel Yelkenci are best in the evening, with nice views, tables on the pavement, and fish menus (*sardalya* or fresh sardines are the local speciality), but no alcohol. Expect to spend from US$6 to US$15 here, the latter for fish.

Yarımada Lokantası advertises 'Ottoman cuisine' and has a nice garden dining area, and full meals for US$4 to US$8. For fine water views, try *İlhan* and also *Belediye Kafeterya Restaurant*, which serves alcohol.

As usual, the further you go from the sea, the lower the prices. Just east of the Hotel Yılmaz is *İpek Urfa Kebap Salonu* for cheap kebabs.

Entertainment Dining near the water is the prime evening entertainment here, but if you just want to sit, drink and nibble at lower prices, walk inland from the ferry docks past the cafes on the left, then turn left. This street, which heads south towards Eceabat, has two small *birahanes* (beer halls), called the *Albatros* and the *Dostlar*, as well as the coffeehouse *İkinci Adres*.

Getting There & Away Gelibolu's otogar is 500m south-west of the stone tower on the road to Eceabat. Dolmuşes or buses run hourly via Eceabat to Kilitbahir. To get to the Gallipoli battlefields, go to Eceabat, then look for a dolmuş (or hitch a ride) to Kabatepe. To get to Çanakkale (US$1, less than two hours, 49km), take the Gelibolu-Lapseki ferry then a bus or dolmuş, or take the minibus to Eceabat or Kilitbahir and then the ferry to Çanakkale from either of these towns. The table below lists other useful services from Gelibolu.

The Gelibolu-Lapseki car ferry leaves Gelibolu at 1, 2, 3, 5, 6.30, 7.30 and 8.30 am, then every hour on the hour until midnight. Departures from Lapseki are at 1, 2, 4, 5.45, 6.30, 7.30, 8.15 and 9 am, then every hour on the hour until midnight. The fare is US$0.80 per person, US$1.60 for a bicycle or scooter, US$5 for a car.

If you miss this ferry, you can go south-west to Eceabat (50 minutes, 45km) and catch the car ferry from there, or to Kilitbahir 7km beyond Eceabat and catch the

Services from Gelibolu's Otogar

destination	fare (US$)	time (hr)	distance (km)	daily services
Eceabat	0.80	1	45	hourly buses or dolmuş
Edirne	7	3	160	three direct buses daily or change at Keşan
İstanbul	10	4½	288	frequent buses
İzmir	10	6½	384	frequent buses
Keşan	4.50	2	77	frequent buses
Kilitbahir	1	1	52	hourly minibuses

small private ferry, which can take a few cars as well, and charges less than the other ferries. See Getting There & Away in the Çanakkale section for details.

Eceabat

☎ 286 • pop 5000

Eceabat (formerly Maidos) makes a more convenient base to visit the battlefields than Çanakkale. This easy-going little waterfront town has a handful of restaurants, one good hostel, some other accommodation options and two cheerfully rowdy bars. The main square, İskele Meydanı, is directly in front of the ferry dock, and around it are restaurants, a Türkiye Iş Bankası ATM and bus company offices. In the centre of the square are the dolmuş and taxi stands. The Cyberia Internet Cafe is a couple of doors from TJs Hostel, and costs US$2.50 per hour.

Places to Stay It is possible to camp for free at the *Boomerang Bar* (☎ 814 2144) and the *Vegemite Disco Bar* (☎ 814 1431) but the facilities are pretty rough – see under Entertainment for details. The Boomerang's camp site is a grubby stretch of sand, while the Vegemite's is a mostly overgrown field. Both also have seating areas outside with cushions where you can kip down, though it would get cold in winter. You can also sleep inside for free.

A rather more comfy budget option is the friendly *TJs Hostel* (☎ 814 2940, fax 814 2941, e tjs_tours@mail.excite.com, Cumhuriyet Caddesi 5), a multistorey building 100m from the main square, down the road to the right as you face inland. It's run by a friendly Turkish-Australian couple, TJ and Bernina. The rooms (US$5 per person) are clean, fairly simple, and all have bathrooms. Breakfasts, including the inevitable Vegemite toast, cost around US$1.60. Internet access costs US$1.60 per hour, and beers are just about the cheapest in town at US$0.80. TJs Tours is based here.

Boss 2 Hotel (☎/fax 814 2311) is another budget option, in a newer building which appears to have been hastily put up if the gaps in the door and window frames are anything to go by. Dorm beds cost US$5,

doubles US$14. It's a stiff 10-minute walk to the edge of town: from the ferry dock follow the road left along the seafront past the Gül Restaurant. The road eventually veers inland, at which point, take the first left and continue on.

The hotels facing İskele Meydanı are nothing special. *Hotel Ece* (☎ 814 1043) has reasonably clean but dull doubles with bath for US$14. *Hotel Eceabat* (☎ 814 2460) is much the same but doubles are US$17; some rooms have views over the busy shipping lane of the Dardanelles.

Places to Eat Next to the ferry dock is the *Murat Restaurant*, serving seafood but best known for its mezes. Next to it is the *Liman Restaurant*, with the best seafood in town for around US$7 for an appetiser, grilled fish, salad and a beer. The *Gül Restaurant* just south of the ferry dock has pide for US$1 and İskender kebap for US$5, and an unnamed, blue-tiled *köftecisi* close to TJs Hostel offers excellent köfte. The *Boomerang* and *Vegemite* bars do cheeseburgers and chips, while the Vegemite has a nightly barbecue with chicken and salad for US$3.20, which includes one beer.

Entertainment Two large, cheerful bars at opposite ends of town cater for thirsty young Aussies and Kiwis, and stay open for as long as there are customers still standing. The *Boomerang Bar* is at the northern end of town, a three-minute walk from the main square, past TJs Hostel. A tone-setting sign says 'Yes we do sell alcohol to intoxicated persons'. Beers cost from US$1.25 to $1.60.

The *Vegemite Disco Bar*, decorated with a weird mix of pictures of Gallipoli combatants juxtaposed with beer signs, also has a billiards table, nargileh (water pipes) and a disco. Beers cost US$1.60, Bundaberg rum ('Bundy') and coke a scorching US$8. The collection of Aussie and Kiwi rock CDs is impressive. It's a 10-minute walk south of the town centre, on the seafront.

Quieter types could spend an evening pondering the waterfront with the locals at the *Liman* or *Murat* restaurants over a bottle of rakı.

THRACE

Getting There & Away Long-distance buses cost the same as from Çanakkale; see the Çanakkale section for details of services.

Buses or minibuses run hourly north-east to Gelibolu (US$0.80, one hour, 45km). In summer there are several dolmuşes daily to the ferry dock at Kabatepe (US$0.80, 15 minutes, 10km) on the western shore of the peninsula, and these can drop you at the national park's Kabatepe Information Centre & Museum, or at the base of the road up to Lone Pine and Chunuk Bair.

Dolmuşes also run down the coast to Kilitbahir, from where dolmuşes travel south to Abide at the southern tip of the peninsula.

Kilitbahir

The small hamlet of Kilitbahir, at the foot of the Kilitbahir castle, is where the small private ferry from Çanakkale arrives, at a dock just north-east of the castle walls. There are a few small teahouses and restaurants, and the fortress is well worth a look, but these days Kilitbahir is a pass-through place. Dolmuşes and taxis await the ferry to shuttle you north-west to Eceabat (7km) and Gelibolu, or south-west via Alçıtepe (Krythia, 19.5km) to Çanakkale Şehitleri Abidesi (28km), the Turkish war memorial on Morto Bay in Abide.

ÇANAKKALE

☎ 286 • pop 60,000

For centuries, pilgrims, conquering armies and trade caravans stopped in Çanakkale before or after crossing the Dardanelles. Many travellers still stop here to pay a visit to the Gallipoli battlefields and to the ruins of ancient Troy. For the most part it's not a particularly handsome place, just a jumble of multistorey concrete, but the seafront is quite pleasant. Around Anzac Day (25 April) everything, from accommodation to restaurants, tours and bars, comes under intense pressure. Unless being here for Anzac Day is important to you, you'd do best to pick another date.

Orientation & Information

Çanakkale centres on its docks, and the town has spread inland. An Ottoman clock tower *(saat kulesi)* stands just west of the docks. Restored in 1995, it acts as the town's symbol and makes a convenient landmark. Hotels, restaurants, banks and bus ticket offices are mostly within a few hundred metres of the docks. The otogar is 1km inland, as is the dolmuş station for Troy. The Arkeoloji Müzesi (Archaeology Museum) is just over 2km to the south.

From the otogar, turn left, walk to the first set of traffic lights, and follow the signs for 'Feribot', which will bring you to the town centre and the docks. To reach the shops, walk behind the clock tower.

The town's useful tourist office (☎/fax 217 1187) is between the clock tower and the ferry docks.

There are lots of Internet cafes around town, especially on and around Fetvane Sokak. Bizim Ev Internet Cafe is one of the nicer ones, and cheap too for US$0.60 per hour.

Arkeoloji Müzesi

Çanakkale's Arkeoloji Müzesi (Archaeological Museum) is on the southern outskirts of town, just over 2km south-east of the clock tower, on the road to Troy. It's open 10 am to 5 pm daily except Monday. Admission costs US$1.30, half-price for students. From Atatürk Caddesi you can get any dolmuş heading towards İntepe or Güzelyalı, which run past the museum.

The museum's exhibits are arranged chronologically, starting with prehistoric fossils and continuing with Bronze Age and later artefacts. The most interesting exhibits are probably those from the ancient ruins at Troy. The exhibits from Dardanos, an ancient town near Çanakkale, are also interesting. Recent additions include a carved sarcophagus. Don't miss the glass case of painstakingly crafted bone brooches and small implements near the exit.

Museums & Fortress

In the military zone at the southern end of the quay are the **Askeri Müzesi** (Military Museum) and **Deniz Müzesi** (Naval Museum), set in a park surrounding the fortress, the Çimenlik Kalesi. The park is open 9 am to 10 pm daily; the museums are open 9 to 11 am and 2.30 to 7.30 pm daily except Monday and Thursday. Admission is free to the park and US$0.75 to the museums (half-price for students).

Beside the Naval Museum is a mock-up of the minelayer *Nusrat*, which had a heroic role in the Gallipoli campaign. The day before the Allied fleet tried to force the straits, Allied minesweepers proclaimed the water cleared. At night the *Nusrat* went out, picked up loose mines and relaid them. Three Allied ships struck the Nusrat's mines and were sunk or crippled.

Another small **museum** houses reminders of Atatürk and the battles of Gallipoli.

Mehmet the Conqueror built the impressive **Çimenlik Kalesi** in the mid-15th century. The cannons surrounding the stone walls are leftovers from assorted battles; many were made in French, English and German foundries.

Cannon Monument

In Demircioğlu Caddesi, the broad main street, stands a monument constructed of old WWI cannons. The inscription reads: 'Turkish soldiers used these cannons on 18 March 1915 to ensure the impassability of the Çanakkale strait'.

Hamams

The old Tarihi Yalı Hamamı (Turkish bath) is a few short blocks south of the clock tower. The new Ferhat Hamamı, on Atatürk Caddesi about 1.5km south of the centre of town, has much better facilities and costs around US$10.

Special Events

For one week in mid-August, the Çanakkale Trova Festivali brings dance and musical troupes to town. Art and craft exhibits, sports and chess tournaments and an underwater rubbish-pick-up contest fill the days.

Places to Stay

Çanakkale has a selection of hotels in all price ranges. You'll need to book well in advance if you're visiting on or around Anzac Day (25 April).

Places to Stay – Budget

If you want to camp, *Mocamp Trova* (☎ 232 8025), open in summer only, is 16km from Çanakkale off the Troy road at Güzelyalı, reachable by Güzelyalı dolmuş from Çanakkale.

Most of the budget hotels are near the clock tower, in the centre of town. The newly renovated *Hotel Efes* (☎ 217 3256, Aralık Sokak 5), behind the clock tower, is run by Mrs Yetimoğlu. It's bright and cheerful and charges US$5 for a bed in triple or quad rooms, and US$10/14 for a single/double with bath. The hotel doesn't look much from the outside but there's satellite TV and a nice little garden.

Anzac House (☎ 213 5969, fax 217 2906, e hasslefree@anzachouse.com, Cumhuriyet Bulvarı 61) provides clean, simple, slightly impersonal budget accommodation, with a choice of dorm beds for US$5, singles for US$9 or doubles for US$14. Most of the doubles are claustrophobic, windowless boxes, while the dorms actually have windows. Internet access costs US$1.60 per hour. Peter Weir's film *Gallipoli* and an Australian TV documentary *The Fatal Shore* are shown nightly.

Yellow Rose Pension (☎ 217 3343, e yellowrose1@mailexcite.com, Yeni Sokak 5) is 50m south-east of the clock tower in an attractive 60-year-old house along a quiet side street. Guests have access to a garden, washing machine and kitchen, as well as table tennis. Rooms, at US$6 per person, are basic, as are the bathrooms. The owner has a reputation for argumentativeness in relation to money issues. Internet access is cheap at US$0.80 an hour. *Gallipoli* and *The Fatal Shore* are shown nightly.

The other cheapies are for emergencies only. The *Hotel Kervansaray* (☎ 217 8192, Fetvane Sokak 13), the 200-year-old former home of a Turkish paşa, looks promising from the outside. The tired old rooms without running water cost US$7.50/12, and the toilets are the squat type. At least there's an attractive courtyard and garden. No alcohol is allowed on the premises. The very ordinary *Avrupa Pansiyon* (☎ 217 4084, Matbaa Sokak 8) is close to the bars.

THRACE

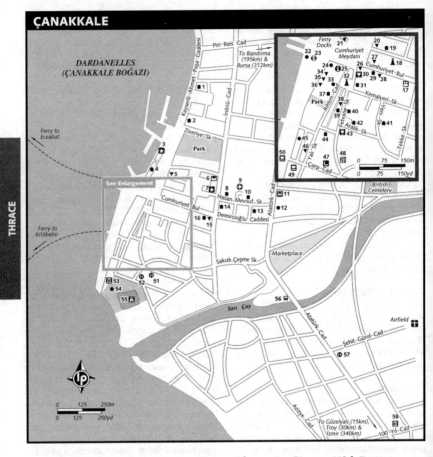

ÇANAKKALE

Konak Oteli (☎ 217 1150, Fetvane Sokak 14) boasts central heating and constant hot water. Prices for waterless rooms are US$7.50/11; US$10/14 with shower.

The *Otel Fatih 2 (☎ 217 7884, İnönü Caddesi 149)*, near the police station, charges US$12 for a double with shower.

Otel Aşkın (☎/fax 217 4956, Hasan Mevsuf Sokak 53) is a short block from the otogar but there's not much else to recommend it. A double room with shower costs US$16. Its sister establishment, the nearby *Aşkın Pansiyon* (same phone) has cheerless service and waterless rooms for US$5/8.

Places to Stay – Mid-Range

You can't miss the two-star *Otel Anafartalar (☎ 217 4454, fax 217 2622, İskele Meydanı)*, a seven-storey high-rise on the northern side of the ferry docks. Recently renovated, the front rooms with harbour views and bath are good value for US$25/ 34 a single/double, including breakfast. There's also a pleasant seaside restaurant (see Places to Eat later in this section).

Anzac Hotel (☎ 217 7777, fax 217 2018, Saat Kulesi Meydanı 8), more or less facing the clock tower, is a characterless two-star lodging with rooms, all with showers or

ÇANAKKALE

PLACES TO STAY		21	Köfteci & Pıdeci Shops	24	Bus Ticket Office
1	Büyük Truva Otelı	26	Boğaz 2000 Restaurant; Bus	25	Tourist Office
2	Hotel Akol		Ticket Offices	30	TNT Bar
4	Otel Anafartalar	27	Trakya Restaurant	32	Clock Tower
8	Hotel Kestanbol	28	Trakya Restaurant		(Saat Kulesi)
10	Otel Aşkın	34	Çekiç	33	Troy-Anzac Tours
13	Aşkın Pansiyon	35	Rıhtım	43	Depo Bar
14	Otel Fatih 2	36	Yeni Entellektüel	45	Customs Office (Gümrük)
16	Hotel Temizay	38	Gaziantep Aile Kebap ve Pide	47	Yalı Camii
19	Otel Yaldız		Salonu	48	Bizim Ev Internet Cafe
29	Anzac Hotel	46	Aussie & Kiwi Restaurant	49	Tea Garden
31	Hotel Anzac			50	Teahouses
37	Hotel Bakır	**OTHER**		51	Tarihi Yalı Hamamı (Men's
39	Hotel Konak	3	Police		Entrance)
40	Hotel Kervansaray	6	PTT	52	Tarihi Yalı Hamamı (Women's
41	Yellow Rose Pension	7	Police		Entrance)
42	Hotel Efes	9	Hospital	53	Askeri Müzesi (Military
44	Avrupa Pansiyon	11	Otogar		Museum)
		12	Belediye (Town Hall)	54	Nusrat Minelayer
PLACES TO EAT		17	Emek Sineması; Reşat Tabak	55	Çimenlik Kalesi (Fortress)
5	Sunak Restaurant	18	Cannon Monument	56	Dolmuş Station
15	Doğum Pide ve Kebap Salonu	22	Ferry Ticket Office	57	Ferhat Hamamı
20	Trakya Restaurant	23	ATMs; PTT Exchange Office	58	Arkeoloji Müzesi

THRACE

tubs, going for US$25/35; breakfast is an extra US$5.

Hotel Temizay (☎ 212 8760, fax 217 5885, Cumhuriyet Bulvarı 15) has friendly management and some futuristic design touches. Single/double/triple rooms go for US$18/27/33.

The three-star *Büyük Truva Oteli (☎ 217 1024, fax 217 0903, Mehmet Akif Ersoy Caddesi 2)*, on the waterfront 200m north of the docks, has clean, serviceable rooms, many with lovely sea views. Rates are US$48/60/73 for a room with TV, minibar and shower, including breakfast.

The ageing *Hotel Bakır (☎ 217 2908, fax 217 4090, Yalı Sokak 12)* is very near the clock tower. Rooms with shower and a view of the straits cost US$25/50/60, including breakfast.

One block east of the ferry docks is the one-star *Otel Yaldız (☎ 217 1793, fax 212 6704, Kızılay Sokak 20)*, on a side street. It's clean, simple, and offers rooms with shower for US$14/20/25.

The one-star *Hotel Kestanbol (☎ 217 0857, fax 217 9173, Hasan Mevsuf Sokak 5)*, inland a few blocks and across the street from the police station, has 26 rooms, all with bath, for US$20/30, including breakfast. It's quiet, with a pleasant rooftop bar.

Tour groups stay at the high-rise, four-star *Hotel Akol (☎ 217 9456, fax 217 2897, Kordonboyu)*, on the waterfront north of the docks. Rooms with bath cost US$60/90. Services include an outdoor pool, several restaurants and bars, a disco, and satellite TV in guest rooms.

There are a few more three-star hotels in the seaside suburb of Güzelyalı, 16km south-west of Çanakkale off the road to Troy, of which the best are the older *Tusan Hotel (☎ 232 8746, fax 232 8226)*, charging US$25 per person in an air-con room, with breakfast; and the similarly priced *İris Otel (☎ 232 8628, fax 232 8028)*.

Places to Eat

Çanakkale has cheap places to eat throughout town. Look along the main street or past the clock tower for köfteci and pideci shops. Typical places include *Gaziantep Aile Kebap ve Pide Salonu*, behind the clock tower, where a meal of soup, pide or köfte, bread and a soft drink costs US$4; or *Doğum Pide ve Kebap Salonu* along Demircioğlu Caddesi, which is popular with the locals.

There are several branches of *Trakya Restaurant*. The branch opposite Anzac House has a selection of ready-food in the steam tables and is supposedly open 24 hours a day. The branch beside Anzac House dishes up all sorts of tasty meat dishes for a US$4 to US$5 price tag.

The *Aussie & Kiwi Restaurant* in Yalı Sokak does its best to oblige Antipodeans, serving up Vegemite toast for US$2 alongside cheap kebaps and köfte.

Sunak Restaurant across from the Otel Anafartalar is a new, clean place with waiters in black ties, but good value with pide for US$2 and Adana kebap for US$3.50. The *Boğaz 2000 Restaurant*, next to the bus offices on Fetvane Sokak, is another recommended new place, with a dinner of salad, chicken kebap and a soft drink for US$7.

Look out for shops serving *peynirli helva* (a local pudding of soft, marzipan-like helva, faintly flavoured with cheese).

The best places face the quay to the north and south of the ferry docks, and include the long-standing *Rıhtım*, *Yeni Entellektüel* (Intellectuals' Restaurant) and *Çekiç*. An appetiser, fried or grilled fish, salad and a bottle of beer at any one of them might cost from US$10 to US$14.

On the northern side, the seaside restaurant at *Otel Anafartalar* is popular, with prices posted prominently.

Entertainment

Playing to its popularity with young Aussies and Kiwis, Çanakkale now has half a dozen bars, mostly clustered in Fetvane Sokak. None, however, have quite the same atmosphere as the bars over the water in Eceabat. One of the most comfortable, with live music and a snooker table, is the *TNT Bar*, round the corner from Anzac House, facing the clock tower. Watch out for happy hours with cheap grog from 7 to 9 pm.

The *Depo Bar* is the biggest disco in town, with a mostly Turkish clientele and music until the Antipodeans take over the town in late April.

A cluster of *tea gardens* at the southern end of the quay make good places to sit and observe the comings and goings across the straits. Alternatively, in Yalı Sokak, there's a pleasant *tea garden* in what was once the Yalı Han.

The town's cinema, *Emek Sinemasi*, is upstairs in the Reşat Tabak İş Merkezi shopping centre on Cumhuriyet Bulvarı. Tickets cost US$2.50.

Getting There & Away

Bus & Dolmuş Çanakkale's otogar is 1km east of the ferry docks but you probably won't need to use it as many buses pick up and drop off at the bus company offices near the clock tower. Walk straight inland from the docks to Atatürk Caddesi and turn left; the otogar is 100m along on the right. Dolmuşes to Troy (30km) leave from the dolmuş station under the bridge over the Sarı Çay.

You can buy bus tickets at the otogar or at the bus company offices on the main street, in the centre of Çanakkale near the ferry docks.

Services from Çanakkale's Otogar

destination	fare (US$)	time (hr)	distance (km)	daily services
Ankara	17	10	700	several buses
Ayvalık	7.50	3½	200	many buses
Bandırma	6.60	3	195	12 buses
Behramkale (Assos)	4	2	100	change to dolmuş at Ayvacık
Bursa	10	5	310	12 buses
Edirne	9	4	230	4 direct, or change at Keşan
İstanbul	12–15	6	340	hourly buses
İzmir	10–12	5	340	hourly buses
Truva (Troy)	1.60	½	30	frequent dolmuşes in summer

THRACE

To get to Gelibolu (US$3.20, about two hours), take a bus or minibus to Lapseki then the ferry, or take the ferry to Eceabat or Kilitbahir and then the minibus to Gelibolu. For Lapseki (US$1.60, 45 minutes, 33km), take a bus bound for Gönen, Bandırma or Bursa, but make sure you will be allowed to get off at Lapseki.

Details of some other daily bus and dolmuş services from Çanakkale are listed in the table on the previous page.

Boat Two ferries connect Çanakkale with the Gallipoli peninsula, one to Kilitbahir, the other to Eceabat; both carry cars as well as passengers. For information on the Gelibolu-Lapseki car ferry, see Getting There & Away in the Gelibolu section later in this chapter.

The car ferries between Çanakkale and Eceabat take approximately 25 minutes to cross in good weather. From 6 am to midnight boats run in each direction every hour on the hour, and every 30 minutes in summer. There are also boats at midnight and at 2 and 4 am from Eceabat and at 1, 3 and 5 am from Çanakkale. Fares are US$0.80 per person, US$1.60 per bicycle and US$5 per car.

The Çanakkale-Kilitbahir ferry is a smaller boat which takes mostly passengers and a few cars. There is only one boat which departs from near the Hotel Bakır, to the south-west of the main docks. It takes just 15 minutes to cross. It costs US$0.60 per passenger, US$4 per car.

One ferry a day leaves for Gökçeada – the tourist office might know the departure time, but even so the timetable is notoriously casual.

GÖKÇEADA
☎ 286

Once known as İmbros, this rugged, sparsely populated island guards the entrance to the Dardanelles. The largest island in Turkey, Gökçeada measures roughly 13km from north to south and 30km from east to west. During WWI it was an important base for the Gallipoli campaign. The Allied commander General Ian Hamilton was based at the village of Aydıncık (formerly Kefalos) on the island's east coast. Along with its smaller neighbour Bozcaada (see the North Aegean Turkey chapter), Gökçeada was a predominantly Greek island which Turkey held onto after 1923. It was exempted from the population exchange, at least until the 1950s when the Cyprus issue inspired the government to pressure the local Greeks to clear out. Until the 1980s Gökçeada was off-limits to foreigners. Nowadays the 7000 inhabitants mostly earn a living through fishing, or farming the narrow belt of fertile land around Gökçeada town.

The island is singularly difficult to get around without your own transport. Dolmuşes are few and far between, and sometimes don't even meet incoming ferries. Apart from some semi-deserted Greek villages, olive groves and pine forests, the island boasts some fine beaches and rugged scenery. For now Gökçeada is a rare example of an Aegean island which hasn't been completely colonised by tourism. Most visitors are well-off İstanbullus, or Greek islanders and their descendants who left for the US and Australia.

Ferries from the mainland dock at Kuzu Limanı, from where dolmuşes should be waiting (*inshallah*) to drive 6km to the island's administrative centre, also called Gökçeada. Most people head on to the beach resort of Kaleköy, 4km north, which also boasts an Ottoman-era castle.

Information
The tourist office (☎ 887 4642) is on the harbour in Kaleköy; no-one speaks English. In July and August a tourism official hands out a pamphlet when the ferries come in which has a map, as well as a list of pensions and their prices.

There are ATMs on the main square of Gökçeada town, including Türkiye İş Bankası and TC Ziraat Bankası. The Tokyay Internet Cafe is in a market complex about 500m from the centre of town on the Kuzu Limanı road, and charges US$0.80 per hour. The island's only petrol station is 2km from Gökçeada town, also on the Kuzu Limanı road.

THRACE

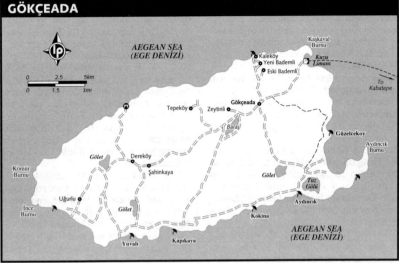

GÖKÇEADA

AEGEAN SEA (EGE DENİZİ)

Kaşkaval Burnu

Kaleköy
Yeni Bademli
Eski Bademli

Kuzu Limanı

To Kabatepe

Gökçeada

Tepeköy   Zeytinli

Baraj

Güzelcekoy

Aydıncık Burnu

Kömür Burnu

Gölet   Dereköy

Şahinkaya

Gölet

Tuz Gölü

İnce Burnu

Uğurlu

Gölet

Aydıncık

Kokina

AEGEAN SEA (EGE DENİZİ)

Yuvalı   Kapıkaya

Things to See & Do

Most visitors head straight for the **beaches** at Kaleköy and Uğurlu. Both are clean and well protected, though not exactly undiscovered. The island's first big hotel is being built at Kaleköy. It would be more adventurous to take a motorbike or scooter along the rough track hugging the south coast to the less visited coves and beaches such as Kapıkaya, Kokina and Yuvalı. Watch out for sea urchins, spiky little black creatures that live among the rocks.

The **Greek villages** of Zeytinli (3km west of Gökçeada), Tepeköy (10km west) and Dereköy (15km west) stand on hillsides overlooking the island's central valley, situated to avoid the depredations of pirate raids. Nowadays many of the houses are deserted and falling into disrepair, and the churches are usually locked. Nevertheless they hold a certain charm, and the local coffeehouses are interesting places to stop.

The coastline between Kuzu Limanı and Kaleköy has been declared a **marine national park** *(sualtı milli parkı)*.

The first week of July sees the **Yumurta Panayırı** or Egg Festival when many former Greek inhabitants return to the island, including the current Orthodox Patriarch of İstanbul.

Places to Stay & Eat

In Kaleköy, Uğurlu and Yeni Bademli a local may approach you and offer a room in their house for a negotiable price; around US$12 for a single room with breakfast is normal.

There are many informal home pensions in Kaleköy and the nearby settlement of Yeni Bademli, and some good cheap fish restaurants. In Kaleköy the *Yakamoz Pansiyon* (☎ 887 2057), perched on the hill overlooking the harbour, has a pleasant terrace restaurant and double rooms for US$17. The *Kale Motel* (☎ 887 44 04) is a comfortable place on the harbour near the tourist office with singles for US$12. The nearby *Kalimerhaba Hotel* (☎ 887 3648) has comfortable double rooms for US$25. Both the Kale and Kalimerhaba also have restaurants.

Accommodation in Uğurlu tends to be a bit pricier, reflecting the means of the wealthier clientele. *Çağiran Pansiyon* (☎ 897 6123) is cheaper than most, with doubles for US$17. *Mitat Pansiyon* (☎ 897

6108) has friendly owners and charges US$25, including breakfast, for a double room with bath.

In Tepeköy the ***Barba Yorgo Pension*** (☎ *887 3592, fax 887 3659)* is run by a Greek man who also runs a popular taverna in the village. There are only 13 rooms in this restored village house, so it's advisable to book in advance. Doubles cost US$30.

In Gökçeada town the ***Belediye Otel*** (☎ *887 3473)* on the main square is an uninspired modern concrete pile, but the rooms are quite OK. Singles/doubles cost US$12/17. Places to eat in town include the *Okya-*

nus Pide Salonu and the *Hikmetler Kebap Salonu*.

Getting There & Away

From Kabatepe ferries leave every day in summer (theoretically) at 9 and 11 am and 4 and 7 pm, returning to Kabatepe at 7 am and 1.45, 4 and 7 pm, and cost US$1.25 per person, US$7 per car. There is one ferry a day from Çanakkale as well, the *Bozcaada*, at 5 pm, returning to Çanakkale at 8 am. The four-hour journey costs US$2 per person, US$20 per car. In winter, services shrink to twice a week to and from Kabatepe.

North Aegean Turkey

The North Aegean coast, which is among the country's richest agricultural areas, has avoided the worst excesses of tourism development. There are some resorts that are an eyesore, but the coastal towns are mostly smaller and more family-oriented places than those further south.

Çanakkale is the hub for transport to Troy and across the Dardanelles to the famous Gallipoli battlefields; for this reason, we've included it in the Thrace chapter. Not far away is Assos, a beautiful old town perched on an extinct volcano, overlooking the Greek island of Lesvos. Assos also offers classical ruins and a small tidy seafront. Ayvalık, to the south, is a resort town with beaches, seafood restaurants and panoramas of Lesvos.

At Bergama (ancient Pergamum) you can see the impressive ruins of the acropolis where parchment was invented, and the Asclepion, an early medical centre. The small coastal towns of Dikili, Çandarlı and Foça are less well known and thus more pleasant seaside resorts.

İzmir, Turkey's third-largest city, is an industrial centre which is not especially interesting – a far cry from its colourful past. However, Adnan Menderes Airport, south of İzmir proper, is a useful arrival or departure point. If you come to Çeşme from the Greek island of Chios you'll probably have to transit İzmir on your way to other parts of the Aegean.

HIGHLIGHTS

- Picnicking amid the ruins of ancient Pergamum (Bergama)
- Having a fish lunch on Alibey Adası, off Ayvalık
- Enjoying the nightlife of Alsancak in İzmir
- Exploring ancient Sardis, gold-rich capital of the Lydians
- Relaxing on Bozcaada, known for its wine

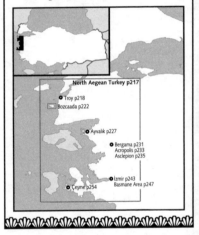

North Aegean Turkey p217

Troy p218
Bozcaada p222

Ayvalık p227

Bergama p231
Acropolis p233
Asclepion p235

İzmir p243
Basmane Area p247

Çeşme p254

TROY

The approach to Troy (Truva), 30km from Çanakkale, is across low, rolling grain fields dotted with villages. This is the ancient Troad, all but lost to legend until German-born Californian treasure-seeker and amateur archaeologist Heinrich Schliemann (1822–90) excavated it in 1871. At that time the poetry of Homer was assumed to be based on legend, not history. Schliemann got permission from the Ottoman government to dig here at his own expense and uncovered four ancient towns, more or less destroying three others in the process (for another view on the affair, see the boxed text 'Frank Calvert, Discoverer of Troy' in this section).

Schliemann had been particularly keen to uncover the treasure of King Priam and on the last day of excavations he quite literally hit gold. However, what he thought dated back to Homeric Troy is now believed to have belonged to a queen or princess living in Troy II. Schliemann's treasure disappeared during WWII and was only recently rediscovered in Russia. It's now in Moscow's Pushkin Museum and the subject of an ongoing ownership dispute.

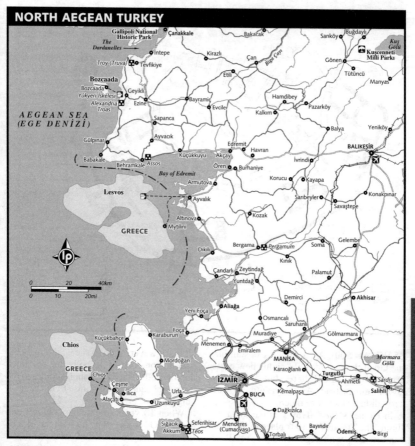

NORTH AEGEAN TURKEY

(map of North Aegean Turkey region showing towns including Çanakkale, Troy (Truva), Bozcaada, Ezine, Behramkale, Assos, Edremit, BALIKESİR, Ayvalık, Bergama, Pergamum, MANİSA, İZMİR, Çeşme, Sardis and surrounding areas; AEGEAN SEA (EGE DENİZİ); Lesvos, Chios (GREECE))

NORTH AEGEAN

History

Excavations by Schliemann and others have revealed nine ancient cities, one on top of another, dating back to 3000 BC. The first people lived here during the Early Bronze Age. The cities called Troy I to Troy V (3000–1700 BC) had a similar culture, but Troy VI (1700–1250 BC) took on a different character, with a new population of Indo-European stock related to the Mycenaeans. The town doubled in size and carried on a prosperous trade with Mycenae. As defender of the straits, it also held the key to the prosperous trade with the Greek

colonies on the Black Sea. Archaeologists argue over whether Troy VI or Troy VII was the city of King Priam which engaged in the Trojan War. Most believe it was Troy VI, arguing that the bad earthquake which brought down the walls in 1250 BC hastened the Achaean victory.

Troy VII lasted from 1250 to 1050 BC. The Achaeans may have burned the city in 1240 BC; an invading Balkan people moved in around 1190 BC and Troy sank into a torpor for four centuries. It was revived as a Greek city (Troy VIII, 700–85 BC) and then as a Roman one (Troy IX,

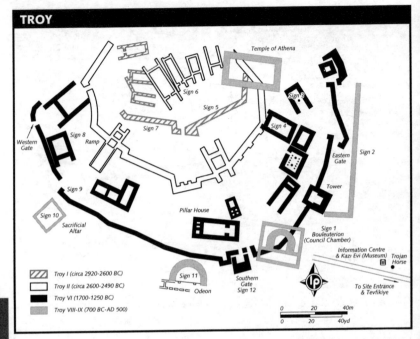

TROY

Temple of Athena

Sign 6
Sign 5
Sign 7
Western Gate
Sign 8
Ramp
Sign 3
Sign 4
Eastern Gate
Sign 2
Tower
Sign 9
Pillar House
Sign 10
Sacrificial Altar
Sign 1
Bouleuterion (Council Chamber)
Information Centre & Kazı Evi (Museum)
Trojan Horse
Sign 11
Odeon
Southern Gate
Sign 12
To Site Entrance & Tevfikiye

Troy I (circa 2920-2600 BC)
Troy II (circa 2600-2490 BC)
Troy VI (1700-1250 BC)
Troy VIII-IX (700 BC-AD 500)

0 20 40m
0 20 40yd

85 BC–AD 500). At one point Constantine the Great thought of building his new eastern Roman capital here, but he chose Byzantium instead. As a Byzantine town, Troy didn't amount to much.

In Homer's *Iliad*, Troy was the town of Ilium. The Trojan War took place in the 13th century BC, with Agamemnon, Achilles, Odysseus (Ulysses), Patroclus and Nestor on the Achaean (Greek) side, and Priam with his sons Hector and Paris on the Trojan side. Rather than suggesting commercial rivalries as a cause for the war, Homer claimed that Paris had kidnapped the beautiful Helen from her husband Menelaus, King of Sparta (his reward for giving the golden apple for most beautiful woman to Aphrodite, goddess of love), and the king asked the Achaeans to help him get her back.

During the decade-long war, Hector killed Patroclus and Achilles killed Hector. Paris knew that Achilles' mother had dipped her son in the River Styx to make him invincible. However, to do so she held him by his heel, the one part of his body that remained unprotected. Hence Paris shot Achilles in the heel and bequeathed a phrase to the English language.

When 10 years of carnage couldn't end the war, Odysseus came up with the idea of the wooden horse filled with soldiers, against which Cassandra warned the Trojans in vain. (Cassandra was a daughter of Priam who had the gift of prophecy but the curse that no-one would believe her.) The wooden horse was left outside the west gate for the Trojans to wheel inside the walls.

One theory has it that the earthquake of 1250 BC gave the Achaeans the break they needed, bringing down Troy's formidable walls and allowing them to battle their way into the city. In gratitude to Poseidon, the Earth-Shaker, they built a monumental wooden statue of his horse. So there may well have been a real Trojan horse, even though Homer's account is less than fully historical.

Frank Calvert, Discoverer of Troy

While Heinrich Schliemann is traditionally credited with rediscovering Troy, others claim that it was Frank Calvert (1828–1908), a Malta-born British expatriate and sometime American consul at the Dardanelles, who was the actual discoverer.

In 1859 Calvert, an amateur archaeologist who owned much of the land around the site, published a pioneering excavation report on his work at Hanay Tepe, a prehistoric site near Troy. He later moved on to Pınarbaşı, believing it to be the site of Troy. By 1863, however, he was convinced that the hill on his land called Hisarlık, identified in 1812 as the site of the Roman city of Ilium Novum, was the site of Troy. He began to excavate by digging a trench, in which he found numerous artefacts from several periods.

Calvert applied to the British Museum for support in his excavations but was turned down. He continued his excavations on a small scale, but was hampered by financial difficulties and family responsibilities.

In 1868 Calvert was visited by Heinrich Schliemann, who had been excavating, in vain, for Troy at Pınarbaşı. Convinced by the artefacts Calvert had uncovered that this was Troy, Schliemann began to excavate on Calvert's land at Hisarlık. The two men later had a falling out, but Calvert continued to support Schliemann's work for the sake of science, and Schliemann continued to fund Calvert's own explorations elsewhere in exchange for the benefit of Calvert's knowledge.

Schliemann, a peerless self-promoter, saw to it that his name was inscribed in the history books as the discoverer of Troy, but it was Frank Calvert who made Schliemann's success possible. In the 20th century, Calvert's priceless collection of artefacts from Troy and nearby sites was dispersed to museums in Çanakkale, London, and Boston and Worcester in the USA.

The last people to live here were Turkish soldiers and their families, subjects of the emir of Karası, in the 14th century. After them, the town disappeared.

Ruins of Troy

The *gişe* (booth) where you buy your admission ticket (US$2.50, US$1.25 for students) is 500m before the site. The ruins are open 8.30 am to 5 pm daily, until 7.30 pm from June to October.

A huge replica of the wooden Trojan horse catches your eye as you approach Troy – it should, as it was put here so you'd have something distinctive to photograph. Before that, visitors used to complain that Troy lacked anything eye-catching.

The **Kazı Evi** (Excavation House) to the right of the path was used by earlier archaeological teams. Today it holds exhibits on work in progress. The models and superimposed pictures should help you understand what Troy looked like at different points in its history. There's a small bookshop on the other side of the path.

The identifiable structures at Troy are marked by explanatory signs: the walls from various periods, including one of the five oldest still standing in the world, are especially interesting; the **bouleterion** (council chamber) built at about Homer's time (circa 800 BC); the **stone ramp** from Troy II; and the **Temple of Athena** from Troy VIII, rebuilt by the Romans.

Don't miss the beautiful views of the Troad, particularly over towards the straits. On a clear day you can see the **Çanakkale Martyrs' Memorial** on the far shore, and ships passing through the Dardanelles. You can just about imagine the Achaean fleet beached on the Troad's shores, ready to begin a battle that would be remembered over 3000 years later.

Tevfikiye

☎ 286

Facing the gates to the archaeological site are a hotel, drinks stand, restaurants, souvenir shops, and replicas of Schliemann's cabin and the Trojan treasure.

Most visitors stay in Çanakkale and visit Troy in passing, leaving their gear at the ticket office or at a restaurant. However, the atmosphere of Tevfikiye village, spreading out 500m to the north of the gates, is a pleasant change from the hassle of Çanakkale. If you decide to stay, **Deniz Pansiyon**, in a quiet street at the heart of the village (follow the signs), is tidy and relatively cheap at US$12 for two in a waterless room; you may have to ask around for the key.

Hotel Hisarlık (☎ 283 1026, fax 283 1087), opposite the site gates, has straightforward rooms (with showers) named after characters from Greek myths but is a bit overpriced at US$20/30 a single/double. The **restaurant** below is a bus tour favourite. If you come alone you might prefer to eat at the **Helen Restaurant** across the road. You are also permitted to camp in the grounds for US$3 per person.

Getting There & Away

Çanakkale is the usual base for visiting Troy and Tevfikiye. From Çanakkale, dolmuşes leave from the dolmuş station under the bridge over the Sarı Çay. Dolmuşes to Troy (US$1.50, 35 minutes, 30km) leave every 30 to 60 minutes in high summer. At other times of the year you should plan to leave Çanakkale by 9 am at the latest; any later and the chances of getting a dolmuş back are precarious.

It's worth considering taking a tour because a good guide can bring the ruins of Troy to life in a way that's difficult if you visit on your own. However tours (usually two to three hours) only eventuate if there are enough people signed up.

Hassle Free Tours (☎ 286-213 5969, fax 217 2906, @ hasslefree@anzachouse.com), at Anzac Hostel in Çanakkale, runs tours for US$14 per person.

Down Under Travel Agency (TJ Tours) (☎ 286-814 2940, fax 814 2941, @ d.under@mailex cite.com), at the Down Under Hostel in Eceabat, also has tours to Troy for US$14.

Tours by Troy-Anzac Tours (☎ 217 5847, 217 5049, fax 217 0196), Saat Kulesi Meydanı 6 in Çanakkale, cost US$15.

If you plan to visit Troy and then head south, buy a ticket on a southbound bus a day in advance. Let the ticket seller know you want to be picked up at Troy, do your sightseeing, then be out on the main highway in plenty of time to catch the bus. Without a ticket, you can hitch out to the highway from Troy and hope a bus with vacant seats comes by. This often works, though it entails some waiting and uncertainty.

If you're coming from the south, ask to be let out on the highway at the access road to Troy, which is 4.5km north of the big Geyikli/Çimento Fabrikası crossroads. From the highway it's 5km west to Troy. Hitch, walk or wait for a dolmuş (infrequent).

AROUND TROY

Heading south from Troy on the main highway (as the buses do), there's little reason to stop until you reach the town of **Ayvacık** (population 6000), from where dolmuşes run 19km west to Behramkale. If you have your own transport, consider taking a much more interesting side road through the western part of the Biga Peninsula, which takes you to little-visited minor ruins and beaches which are good for camping.

Some 4.5km south of the Troy road is a narrow, paved road heading west and marked for Alexandria Troas and Apollo Smintheion. After passing the cement factory the road proceeds south-west to the small town of **Geyikli**, 24km along, which has a few simple **restaurants** and basic **hotels**.

Alexandria Troas

About 5km south of Oduniskelesi the road passes through the widely scattered ruins of Alexandria Troas near the village of Dalyan. Some signs read 'Alexandria (Truva)', but this is not Troy.

Antigonus, one of Alexander the Great's generals, took control of this land after the collapse of the Alexandrian empire and founded the city of Antigoneia in 310 BC. He was later defeated in battle by Lysimachus, another of Alexander's generals, who took the city and renamed it in honour of his late commander. An earthquake later destroyed much of the city.

Archaeologists have identified bits of the city's theatre, palace, temple, agora, baths, necropolis, harbour and city walls amid the farmers' fields. But for most visitors Alexandria Troas is more about atmosphere, a place which, like so many in Turkey, conjures up that feeling of great antiquity slowly disappearing beneath the grinding wheels of time.

Dolmuşes run infrequently between Ezine, on the main highway, and Dalyan. Don't make a special trip, but if you pass by, it's worth pausing for the view.

Neandria
When Antigonus founded the city of Antigoneia, he forced the inhabitants of nearby Neandria, settled around 700 BC, to populate his new city. The ruins of Neandria, 1.5km north-east of the village of Kayacık and 500m inland from the sea, offer nothing to the casual visitor today, but archaeologists have discovered the oldest Aeolian temple with a clearly distinguishable plan.

Gülpınar
Just 3km south of Alexandria Troas are the hot springs of **Kestanbol Kaplıcaları** (13km south of Geyikli), with a small bathhouse. Continue south 32km to Gülpınar, a small farming town with no services beyond a petrol station. This was once the ancient city of Khrysa, famous for its Ionic temple to Apollo and its mice. An oracle had told Cretan colonists who came to this area that they should settle where 'the sons of the earth' attacked them. They awoke to find mice chewing their equipment, so they settled here and built a temple to the 'Lord of the Mice' (Smintheion). The **Apollo Smintheion**, 400m down a steep hill from the centre of the town, has some bits of marble column on top of a short flight of steps. The cult statue of the god, now disappeared, once had marble mice carved at its feet. Reliefs on the temple's walls illustrated scenes from the *Iliad*.

Gülpınar Belediyesi buses connect Gülpınar with Çanakkale and Ayvacık.

Babakale & Akliman
In Gülpınar a road heading west is signed for Babakale (Lekton), 9km away. The road

to Akliman, a coastal settlement with a nice long beach backed by olive groves, and several good, cheap camping places and motels, is 3km along. About 6km further on is Babakale, with a small village clustered at the base of a ruined fortress overlooking a long sweep of sea. A new yacht and fishing harbour has been completed, and the first tourist hotels – the **Karayel** and **Ser-Tur** – have been opened, with undoubtedly many more to follow. Some İstanbullus have already fixed up stone village houses (and one windmill) as villas.

BOZCAADA
☎ 286
Windswept little Bozcaada, formerly known as Tenedos, has always been known to Anatolian oenophiles for its wines (Ataol, Talay and Yunatçilar) and to soldiers for its defences. A huge medieval fortress towers over the north-eastern tip of the island, and vineyards blanket its sunny slopes. The island has the advantage of being small (about 5km to 6km across) and easy to explore. Bozcaada has become increasingly popular since two Turkish blockbusters were made here; some say it will become the next Bodrum. In the meantime it still has beaches where you can hide away, and a well-preserved settlement which has kept the character of a Greek village.

Information
There is no tourist office on the island, but you can pick up a map from the Ada Cafe. The Cafe at Lisa's has a collection of magazines with articles on the island.

There is only one ATM on the island and it doesn't take foreign cards. Bring sufficient cash with you. The nearest ATM that takes foreign cards is in Geyikli.

The Virus Internet Cafe is upstairs in the building next to the Ada Cafe; connections are a bit slower than on the mainland. One hour costs US$1.60.

Things to See & Do
The island's biggest attraction may be that there's not much to see or do, besides the beaches. The one official tourist site is the

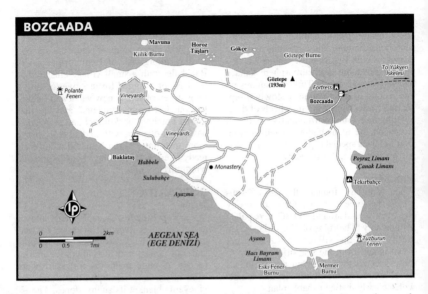

BOZCAADA

Kiilik Burnu
Mavuna
Horoz Taşları
Gökçe
Göztepe Burnu
To Yükyeri İskelesi
Polante Feneri
Vineyards
Göztepe (193m) ▲
Fortress
Bozcaada
Vineyards
Baklataş
Habbele
Monastery
Poyraz Limanı
Çanak Limanı
Sulubahçe
Tekirbahçe
Ayazma
AEGEAN SEA
(EGE DENİZİ)
Ayana
Tuzburun Feneri
Hacı Bayram Limanı
Eski Fener Burnu
Mermer Burnu

0   1   2km
0   0.5   1mi

enormous **fortress** in the town, open from 10 am to 1, 2 to 7 pm from April to November; admission costs US$1.25. There is a small ethnographical display inside. There is also the Greek **church**, in the old Greek neighbourhood directly behind the castle, but it is rarely open and the local priest is usually busy tending his goats. A dwindling number of elderly Greeks still live here.

The three **wineries** in town are not open for guided tours as such, but if you ask nicely you might be able to have a look around them. They have an intriguing mix of ancient hoists and pulleys and modern Italian equipment. The Ataol winery, in the street behind the Ada Cafe, is the biggest. Bottles of wine are half-price (US$2.50) from the wineries. Most of the wine is pretty basic stuff; the winemakers aren't paid much and none of the wine is cellared. The best wines are the reds which have been allowed to age for a couple of years.

The best **beaches** are on a 10km stretch along the south coast, including Ayana beach, Ayazma and Habbele. Ayazma is the best known, and there are several cafes here and an abandoned **Greek monastery** uphill. If a southerly wind is blowing you may have to head for the less impressive north coast, which has small coves but not much sand. Watch out for sea urchins.

Special Events

Former Greek islanders and their descendants return every year in the last week of July for the Ayazma Panayırı Festival.

Places to Stay

Camping is possible on just about any public land, provided you don't light fires or leave a mess. There is a basic camp site about 5km south of town. Many villagers offer rooms in their houses; chances are someone will approach you at the docks. The standard rate is around US$8 per person, not including breakfast. However on weekends in summer it can get crowded.

There are at least 25 pensions in town, mostly pretty similar. The **Ergin Pansiyon** (☎ 697 8429), in the neighbourhood behind the castle, costs US$8 per person, breakfast an extra US$3.20. The rooms are simple but clean. Further up the hill is the **Kale Pansiyon** (☎ 697 8617), with the same prices but with a fine breakfast terrace overlooking the town. Other options are the **Gürkol Pan-**

siyon (☎ 697 8011), **Emiroğlu Antik Pan-siyon** *(☎ 697 8037)* and the **Güler Pansiyon** *(☎ 697 8454)*. The **Tuna Pansiyon** *(☎ 697 8262)* gets good reports for hospitality.

Otel Ege *(☎ 697 8189, fax 697 8389)* was formerly the local Greek school. Follow the signs from the town's bank. There are 36 simple rooms with bath, those on the top floor with balconies. Its costs US$17 per person, with breakfast.

The **Gümüs Otel** *(☎ 697 8252, fax 697 0052)* behind the harbour has small rooms but comfy beds for US$40 for a double with breakfast.

Places to Eat

Excellent fish restaurants line Bozcaada's harbour. The **Paşa**, **Zorba** and **Şehir** restaurants are open all year; two mezes and grilled fish costs US$7.50 (depending on the type of fish, of course). The **Paşa** sells a very decent 1995 Ataol red for US$6. The **Boruzan** and **Korelli** restaurants are also good. Inland the **Ada Cafe** also sells wine – most places do – and offers snacks and light meals. The **Cafe at Lisa's**, at the end of the street behind the harbour, offers non-Turkish breakfasts, coffee and cakes.

The very cool **Salhane Bar** is an attractively converted warehouse on the bay north of the castle. Outdoor seating areas are set around large rocks and there's a platform over the sea. Drinks are on the pricey side: US$2.50 for a small Efes or a glass of wine. The best place to dance is the **Palamar Disco** inland from the town; on summer weekends minibuses shuttle partygoers from the main square.

Getting There & Away

Ferries depart from the new harbour of Yükyeri İskelesi (*not* the old harbour at Odunluk İskelesi), 5km west of Geyikli, south of Troy. Dolmuşes run every 45 minutes or so during the day between Çanakkale's otogar and Geyikli for US$1.60; some continue on to the harbour but you may have to change to an 'İskele' minibus in the main square for the last leg (US$0.25). Coming back from Bozcaada, minibuses go all the way to Çanakkale from the harbour. In

summer boats leave Yükyeri İskelesi daily at 10 am, 2, 7 and 9 pm, with a 12 pm service from Friday to Sunday. From Bozcaada the ferry leaves at 7.30 am, 12, 4.30 and 8 pm, with an 11 pm service from Friday to Sunday. The fare is US$0.80 per passenger, US$4 per car. In winter services fall to one or two ferries per day.

Getting Around

There are dolmuşes from the centre of town to Ayazma Beach in summer for US$0.80. Otherwise it is pretty easy to hitchhike on tractors. In any case it would take about 8 hours to walk around the entire island. Bicycles can be hired from the Ada Cafe for US$7 per day, though some of the bikes are a bit battered. From the town one road leads along the north shore, and another along the southern shore.

ASSOS (BEHRAMKALE)
☎ 286

Called Assos in ancient times, the ruins and village of Behramkale share a gorgeous setting, overlooking the Aegean and the nearby island of Lesvos (Mytilini or Midilli in Turkish).

Assos makes a brave sight as you approach, its craggy summit surrounded by huge remnants of a mighty wall. The main part of the village and the acropolis ruins are perched at the top, but down the far (sea) side of the hill at the *iskele* (wharf), a tiny cluster of stone buildings clings to the cliff in a romantic and unlikely setting. There's a short, narrow pebble beach. For many kilometres of wider beach head on to Kadırga, 4km to the east.

History

In its long history, Assos has flourished as a port, agricultural town and centre for Platonic learning.

The Mysian city of Assos was founded in the 8th century BC by colonists from Lesvos, who later built its great temple to Athena in 530 BC. The city enjoyed its greatest prosperity and renown under the rule of Hermeias, a one-time student of Plato who also ruled the Troad and Lesvos.

Hermeias encouraged philosophers and savants to live in Assos; Aristotle lived here from 348 to 345 BC and ended up marrying Hermeias' niece, Pythia. Assos' glory days came to an end with the advent of the Persians, who tortured Hermeias to death.

Alexander the Great drove the Persians out, but Assos' importance was challenged by the ascendancy of Alexandria Troas to the north. From 241 to 133 BC, the city was ruled by the kings of Pergamum.

St Paul visited Assos briefly during his third missionary journey through Asia Minor (AD 53–57), walking here from Alexandria Troas to meet St Luke and others before taking a boat to Lesvos.

In Byzantine times the city dwindled to a village, which it has remained ever since. Excavations of the ruins continue. Tourists, both Turkish and foreign, crowd the iskele, and the local people plough their fields and tend their olive trees, awaiting the day when a developer will buy their land at a fat price and make them rich.

Special Events

Behramkale hosts its own Camel Wrestling Festival around the second week of February – a gathering of Yörük Turks from the mountainous plateaus of the Troad that doesn't attract many tourists.

Things to See

As you approach the village there's a fine **Ottoman humpback bridge**, built in the 14th century, to the left of the road. Shortly afterwards, you'll come to a crossroads; the road left leads to the beach at Kadırga, the road right to the village of Behramkale and on to Gülpınar. Continue until you reach a fork in the road. Go left (uphill) for the old village, or right (downhill) to see the massive city walls, necropolis and iskele.

Taking the village road, you wind up to a small square with a few shops and restaurants. Continue upwards, and you'll come to a small square with a teahouse and a bust of Atatürk. At the very top of the hill there's a spectacular view, which you can enjoy after fending off villagers eager to sell you embroidery and woollen socks.

The **Murad Hüdavendigar Camii**, the 14th-century mosque beside the entrance to the ruins, is a simple pre-Ottoman work – a dome on squinches set on top of a square room – accomplished before Turks and Turkish architects had conquered Constantinople and assimilated the lessons of Sancta Sophia. The lintel above the entrance bears Greek inscriptions, a reminder that the Byzantine emperor was still on his throne when this mosque was built with parts permanently borrowed from a 6th-century church.

The principal sight on top of the hill (altitude 228m) is the **Temple of Athena**, built in Doric style, and now partly reconstructed. The short, tapered columns with plain capitals are hardly elegant, and the concrete reconstruction (and rusting scaffolding) hurts more than helps. But the site and the view out to Lesvos are, as with so many ancient cities, spectacular and well worth the admission fee of US$1.60. The Temple is open 8 am to 5 pm (until 7 pm in summer) Tuesday to Sunday.

Ringing the hill are stretches of the **city walls**, among the most impressive classical fortifications in Turkey. Scramble down the hillside to find the **necropolis**. Assos' sarcophagi ('flesh-eaters') were famous: according to Pliny the stone itself was caustic and 'ate' the flesh off the deceased in 40 days. There are also remains of a **theatre** and **basilica**. An exit gate emerges on the block-paved road which winds down the cliff side to the iskele, the most picturesque spot in Behramkale.

Places to Stay

In high summer, virtually all accommodation around the iskele is *yarım pansiyon* (half pension, ie, including breakfast and dinner). Room prices are 35% lower in the off season (April, May and October), when you may be able to wriggle out of the half-pension requirement; a double room which costs US$60 (with two meals) in August may be priced as low as US$25 in early October. The hotels in the iskele are all atmospheric old stone buildings right next to the sea.

Places to Stay – Budget

Camping The cheapest option is to camp in the olive groves just inland where a half-dozen or so charming *camping grounds* charge about US$2 per person. They change names and owners fairly regularly.

Assos Camping (☎ 721 7168) has the motto 'We like people', and offers a couple of basic but new bungalows for US$8 for two, and tent sites for US$5.

Çakır Camping (☎ 721 7048) is right by the sea and charges US$5 for a camp site.

There are many more *camping grounds* among beachfront olive groves at Kadırga, 4km to the east, and beyond it along the road which ultimately rejoins the coastal highway at Küçükkuyu.

Pensions There is only one cheap pension in the picturesque old village, the very simple *Sidar Pansiyon* (☎ 721 7047), which costs US$12 for a waterless double in summer. At other times you'll find it closed.

Old Stone House (☎ 721 7426/7, e *old bridgehouse@yahoo.com*) is a true original. Built by Cem and his Dutch wife Diana, both veteran travellers, the place is full of recycled materials put together with real imagination. There are four double rooms (US$25), each decorated in a different colour, and a six-bed dormitory costing US$6 per person, not including breakfast. Breakfast costs US$4, and dinners (which might include Thai, Indonesian, Turkish or Dutch dishes) US$12.50. There are scooters for hire (US$20 per day) and they have lots of suggestions on tours to do in the area. Internet access is available for US$1.60 per hour.

Old Stone House is next to the Ottoman humpback bridge, 1km from the village on the Ayvacık road. It's open all year, despite what the dolmuş drivers may tell you.

Timur Pansiyon (☎/fax 721 7449) has only four double rooms for US$25 each and they're fairly simple, but the views over to Lesvos are wonderful. The pension is at the top of the hill in Behramkale.

Eris Pansiyon (☎ 721 7080) is run by a semi-retired American couple. It's a fine stone house with six double rooms, for US$25 each, again with excellent views but

looking north and east rather than towards the sea. It's tricky to find on your own so you'll need to ask directions.

Dolunay Pansiyon (☎ 721 7271), run by the Arkan family, has seven spotless if plain rooms, set around a courtyard with stone tables. Singles/doubles cost US$12.50/25, and breakfast is US$4. There's also an attractive restaurant-lounge area. It's in the centre of the village, a short walk from the dolmuş stand.

Down at the iskele, the *Assos Antik Pansiyon* (☎ 721 8811) behind the Hotel Behram has four clean, quiet rooms, and is run by a couple of friendly young men. Rooms cost US$10/20.

The ivy-clad *Assos Mehtap Motel* (☎ 721 7221), at the far end of the quay behind the Hotel Assos, charges US$12.50/25 for modest but well-kept rooms.

Assos Şen Pansiyon (☎ 721 7076), behind the Ikun Ev, has a rooftop restaurant with marvellous views and interesting architectural information on the Assos ruins. The rooms are smallish but not unreasonable at US$25 for a double.

Places to Stay – Mid-Range

Assos Harbour First of the places on the quay as you turn left is *Hotel Behram* (☎ 721 7016, fax 721 7044, e *behramassos@yahoo.com*) which has comfortable rooms with satellite TV and the best bathrooms of any of the harbour hotels. It charges US$25/50 with breakfast and dinner.

Immediately behind the (not recommended) Hotel Assos is *Hotel Assos Kervansaray* (☎ 721 7093, fax 721 7200), which has a swimming pool, sauna and courtyard restaurant, but the bathrooms are old and the rooms are looking frayed. Half pension costs US$45/60.

Turn right instead of left along the harbour and you'll come to *Hotel Nazlıhan* (☎ 721 7385, fax 721 7387, e *assos.eden@garanti.net.tr*) beyond the *jandarma* (police) post, which encompasses two restored stone houses. The rooms are quite small but imaginatively decorated, with İznik-style tiles in the bathrooms. Rates are US$65/84 for rooms with sea view, slightly less without.

Kadırga There are many more hotels on the beach at Kadırga, 4km east, though reaching them is difficult without your own wheels.

Troy Otel (π *721 7154, fax 721 7241*) has four-star comforts for US$70 a double, breakfast and dinner included.

Yeni Yıldız Saray (π *721 7204*) offers air-con and an American bar for US$50.

Several kilometres further east, perched on a terrace overlooking the sea, *Assos Terrace Motel* (π *762 9885, fax 762 9884*) has comfortable rooms with excellent views for US$40 a double including two meals.

Places to Eat

If you can get out of paying for half board it's fun to pop around the hotels, trying their different restaurants. If you're not paying half board, be sure to check prices carefully, especially for fish and bottles of wine. Most of the hotels serve excellent evening meals, although breakfasts are pretty mundane, especially for the high summer prices.

The *Ev Yemekleri*, just inland from Hotel Assos, serves *gözleme* (Turkish pancakes) and *mantı* (a ravioli-like dish). The fancy *Fenerli Han Restaurant*, beside the Hotel Nazlıhan, has a beautiful harbourside setting and a set-price dinner for about US$10, plus drinks and tip. *Ikun Ev* is a cool place to wind up the evening with a drink.

If you're on a budget, you'll need to walk up to the old village where the *Cengiz Lokantası* will serve you dinner for a more reasonable US$7.

Getting There & Away

It's 73km from Çanakkale along the main highway (E87/D550) to Ayvacık (not to be confused with nearby Ayvalık), a bus ride of under two hours. Dolmuşes depart from Ayvacık for Behramkale (19km) hourly in high summer although some only run as far as the old village, leaving you to trek down to the harbour with your baggage or barter for an unofficial, and costly, 'taxi'. There are also a couple of buses each day in high summer only (US$0.80).

In the off season, dolmuşes run much less frequently and you can have trouble getting away from the village. If you visit during the off season, which is highly advisable, get to Ayvacık as early in the day as you can to catch a dolmuş (US$1.30). If you miss the last one, Ayvacık has a couple of hotels, or a taxi driver may be talked into driving you there for around US$17. Hitching is also possible.

AROUND BEHRAMKALE

From Behramkale the road west to Gülpınar (25km) passes through several small villages. From some of these, unpaved roads lead down to the coast where there's sure to be a beach shack with a primitive toilet and perhaps fresh water for the ever-increasing number of camper-van owners who have discovered this road.

The road east from Behramkale and Kadırga follows the coast to rejoin the main coastal highway at Küçükkuyu, then continues round the Bay of Edremit. Along the way at **Altınoluk** the highway passes a motley collection of hotels, motels and beachfront eateries which, though right on the water, are subject to road noise. Seaside accommodation is somewhat better at **Akçay** and **Ören**, off the highway. At Akçay there's a fine 5km-long beach featuring sulphur springs. The beach at Ören stretches for 9km.

Inland is the farming centre of **Edremit** (pop 37,000), called Adramyttium in classical times. There's nothing to draw you today except that it's an important transport hub; coming from Ayvacık to Ayvalık you may well have to change in Edremit which is also served by frequent buses to Balıkesir. Ayvalık, your most likely destination, is 130km (over two hours) south-east of Behramkale and 110km (two hours) south-east of Ayvacık, by road.

AYVALIK

π 266 • pop 30,000

Across a narrow strait from the Greek island of Lesvos, Ayvalık (Quince Orchard) is a seaside resort, fishing town, olive oil and soap-making centre, and a terminus for boats to and from Greece. The coast here is cloaked in pine forests and olive orchards, the offshore waters sprinkled with islands.

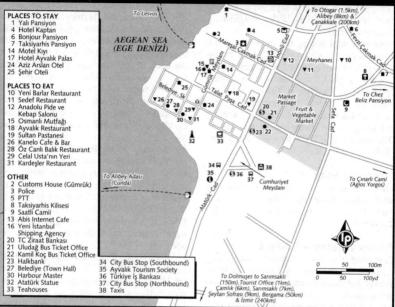

PLACES TO STAY
1 Yalı Pansiyon
4 Hotel Kaptan
6 Bonjour Pansiyon
7 Taksiyarhis Pansiyon
14 Motel Kıyı
17 Hotel Ayvalık Palas
24 Aziz Arslan Otel
25 Şehir Oteli

PLACES TO EAT
10 Yeni Barlar Restaurant
11 Sedef Restaurant
12 Anadolu Pide ve Kebap Salonu
15 Osmanlı Mutfağı
18 Ayvalık Restaurant
19 Sultan Pastanesi
26 Kanelo Cafe & Bar
28 Öz Canlı Balık Restaurant
29 Celal Usta'nın Yeri
31 Kardeşler Restaurant

OTHER
2 Customs House (Gümrük)
3 Police
5 PTT
8 Taksiyarhis Kilisesi
9 Saatli Camii
13 Abis Internet Cafe
16 Yeni İstanbul Shipping Agency
20 TC Ziraat Bankası
21 Uludağ Bus Ticket Office
22 Kamil Koç Bus Ticket Office
23 Halkbank
27 Belediye (Town Hall)
30 Harbour Master
32 Atatürk Statue
33 Teahouses
34 City Bus Stop (Southbound)
35 Ayvalık Tourism Society
36 Türkiye İş Bankası
37 City Bus Stop (Northbound)
38 Taxis

Ayvalık was inhabited by Ottoman Greeks until after WWI. During the exchange of populations between Greece and Turkey in the 1920s, Ayvalık's Turkish-speaking Greeks went to Greece, and Greek-speaking Turks came here from Lesvos, the Balkans and Crete. A few locals still speak Greek, and most of the local mosques are converted Orthodox churches. The Saatli Camii was once the church of Agios Yannis (St John); the Çınarlı Camii used to be the Agios Yorgos (St George) church.

Orientation & Information

Ayvalık is small and manageable but with a few inconveniences: the otogar is 1.5km north of the town centre and the tourist office (☎/fax 312 2122) is 1km south of the main square around the curve of the bay, across from the yacht harbour. In summer a small kiosk on the waterfront at the southern side of the main square is staffed by Ayvalık Tourism Association personnel.

A few kilometres further to the south are Çamlık and Orta Çamlık, with a scattering of pensions and camping areas popular with holidaying Turks. Sarımsaklı Plaj (Garlic Beach), also known as Küçükköy or Plajlar (The Beaches) is 7km south of the centre. Packed with hotels, motels and pensions, Sarımsaklı is very much package-holiday territory. Alibey Adası (Alibey Island) is just over 8km north-west of Ayvalık centre by road although it's more pleasant getting there by boat.

The Abis Internet Cafe, one block south of the PTT on İnönü Caddesi, has good connections and costs US$1 per hour.

The White Knight Tourist Bazaar behind the statue of Atatürk on the waterfront sells the *Turkish Daily News* and some foreign newspapers.

Things to See & Do

The quay is crowded with day-cruisers eager to take you on a daytime or evening

NORTH AEGEAN

sail around the dozens of islands in the bay. Competition is fierce in high summer, with most cruises priced at US$6 to US$8 including a meal.

As you walk along the quayside you'll also find people advertising six-hour excursions to local villages for US$12 per person.

Another goal for excursions is **Şeytan Sofrası** (Devil's Dinner Table), a hilltop south of the town offering magnificent views and a snack stand. The only regular dolmuş goes up there just before sunset. Otherwise you'll have to walk, hitch (unlikely) or take a taxi.

Places to Stay

There are some excellent pensions in the town centre. Prices are highest in July and August; at other times, look around for discounts.

Places to Stay – Budget

Camping The best camping is on Alibey Adası, with the pitches located inconveniently but quietly outside the village. The ubiquitously advertised *Ada Camp* (☎ 312 1211) is 3km to the west, as are *Ortunü Hidden Paradise* and *Cunda Motel-Camping*.

At the southern end of Çamlık, on the way to Sarımsaklı Plaj, there's a pleasant national forest camping ground, *Orman Kampı*, and several private camping grounds.

Pensions & Hotels The most interesting budget place is *Taksiyarhis Pansiyon* (☎ 312 1494, Mareşal Çakmak Caddesi 71), two renovated Ottoman houses joined together, five minutes' walk east of the PTT behind the former Taxiarkhis church. The hand-painted signs are difficult to spot – if you get stuck, phone from the PTT. Pensions don't get much better – it's a fascinating warren with handicrafts everywhere, a book exchange, a good music collection, bikes for hire and lots of information on sights in the area. There are also two terraces, wonderful views and a kitchen for guests' use. At just US$8 per person plus US$4 for breakfast, it's often full in summer. There are more rooms in an adjacent house. Don't forget to take your shoes off at the door.

Chez Beliz Pansiyon (☎ 312 4897, fax 312 2948, Mareşal Çakmak Caddesi 28) is run by exuberant former actress Beliz (İşlek) Soysal in her grandfather's old house. Singles/doubles are US$12/24 in the main house, or US$10/20 in a bungalow at the back of the charming garden. Madame İşlek's wonderful dinners cost US$8. It's open from the middle of May to November.

Bonjour Pansiyon (☎ 312 8085, Fevzi Çakmak Caddesi, Çeşme Sokak 5) is another excellent option. The house once belonged to a French priest who was ambassador to the Ottoman Sultan. Fine restoration work – the roof frescoes are especially interesting – by owner Yalçın Arga comes with great amenities including a kitchen for guests' use and a nice courtyard. There are only seven rooms; singles/doubles with breakfast cost US$12/20. Some rooms are in a modern annexe at the rear. Follow the street uphill across from the PTT.

Down on the waterfront, on the street directly behind the PTT, is *Yalı Pansiyon* (☎ 312 2423), another grand old house complete with sweeping staircase and chandeliers. The elderly owners have limited resources, so the beds and outside bathrooms are fairly basic, but the house also has a large garden lit with coloured lights, and its own jetty. Doubles/triples/quads cost US$30/35/40 with breakfast.

A few small, cheap, old-style hotels lurk in the warren of streets just north of the main square. The cheapest of them is the noisy *Şehir Oteli*, charging around US$4 per person.

The renovated *Motel Kıyı* (☎ 312 6677, Gümrük Meydanı 18) charges US$7 per person for small rooms with shower but without breakfast. Front rooms have water views. It could be a bit cleaner but it's still good value.

Places to Stay – Mid-Range

With the quality of budget accommodation, the modern hotels closer to the harbour are finding it hard to attract business.

Hotel Ayvalık Palas (☎ 312 1064, fax 312 1046, Gümrük Meydanı) charges US$15/25 per person for rooms with shower and TV, including breakfast, but is showing signs of neglect. A diving centre operates out of the hotel. The nearby 20-room *Aziz Arslan Otel* (☎ *312 5331, fax 312 6888*) is cleaner and offers spacious doubles with TV, balcony and clean bath for US$20, including breakfast. Both these hotels suffer from noise from the nearby bars.

Hotel Kaptan (☎ *312 8834, Balıkhane Sokak*) charges US$20 to US$30 for doubles whose wallpaper looks more suited to England than Turkey. Despite its harbourside position, only three rooms have sea views. Again, it's looking a bit worn.

Places to Eat

Most restaurants put out signboards listing prices, at least in the busy summer months, but it's still wise to be careful when ordering fish.

The narrow streets north of the harbour have lots of small, simple restaurants with good food and low prices. *Ayvalık Restaurant* has good soups and stews which, with bread, make a filling meal for about US$3. *Celal Usta'nın Yeri* is similar. *Osmanlı Mutfağı (Eminzade İşhanı 21),* next to the Hotel Ayvalık Palas, serves meat dishes for US$2, with vegetable stews for slightly less. *Anadolu Pide ve Kebap Salonu (İnönü Caddesi 33)* serves Turkish pizza for about US$2. *Sultan Pastanesi* is good for biscuits or pastries.

In the market to the east of İnönü Caddesi, the *Yeni Barlar* and *Sedef* restaurants are popular with locals who can be found tucking into kebaps and good cheap steamtray fare 24 hours a day. Nearby, the narrow market streets harbour various *meyhanes*, the Turkish equivalent of tavernas, patronised by local men.

Pricier fish restaurants ring the waterfront. Here you'll find the *Öz Canlı Balık* and *Kardeşler* restaurants, with spacious, airy dining rooms and nicely lit terraces with sea views. A full dinner will cost you between US$10 and US$12 per person for meat, and more for fish, drinks included. At the far end of the quay is *Kanelo Café & Bar*, a good place for a drink while you watch the sun set.

Getting There & Away

Bus Ayvalık is served by the frequent bus services running up and down the Aegean coast between Çanakkale and İzmir. If you're on a main intercity service you'll probably be dropped off and have to hitch in from the highway. For more details, see Getting Around, following.

When leaving Ayvalık, it's often easiest to buy a ticket from the otogar in Edremit and transfer there to services for Çanakkale rather than having to make your way back out to the highway to pick up one of the long-distance services. You can buy a ticket at the bus company offices in the main square. Check departure times and availability early in the day as few buses depart in the evening. Services from Ayvalık include the following:

destination	fare (US$)	time (hr)	distance (km)
Balıkesir	5	2½	104
Behramkale (Assos)	5	2	130
Bergama	3	¾	50
Bursa	10	4½	300
Çanakkale	7	3½	200
Edremit	1.60	30	56
İzmir	4	3½	240

Boat The passage by sea between Ayvalık and Lesvos is now so expensive (US$50 one way, US$65 same-day round trip) that few people use it. If you're coming from Greece (ie, not returning to Turkey after a day trip), you must also pay a 5000-drachma (US$8) Greek port tax. Turkish boats make the two-hour voyage to Lesvos at 9 am in summer (sporadic services at other times) on Tuesday, Thursday and Saturday. Usually you must buy your ticket and hand over your passport for paperwork a day in advance of the voyage, whether you're departing from Turkey or from Greece.

For information and tickets, contact one of the shipping agencies in the warren of streets north and west of the main square, including the Yeni İstanbul Shipping Agency (☎ 312 6123).

NORTH AEGEAN

Getting Around

Buses along the highway will drop you at the northern turn-off for Ayvalık, exactly 5km from the centre, unless the company specifically designates Ayvalık otogar as a stop. From the highway you must hitch into town; drivers readily understand your situation and stop to give you a lift.

If you're dropped in town, it will be at Ayvalık's otogar, which is 1.5km (15 or 20 minutes' walk) north of the main square. City buses marked 'Ayvalık Belediyesi' run all the way through the town and will carry you from the bus station to the main square, south to the tourist office, and further south to Çamlık, Orta Çamlık and Sarımsaklı, for US$0.30. A taxi from the otogar to the town centre costs US$3.

Minibuses (US$0.50) depart for the beaches from the fifth side street south of the main square.

AROUND AYVALIK
Alibey Adası
☎ 266

The island visible across the bay is Alibey Adası, called Cunda by locals, which boasts abandoned, ruined Greek churches, seaside restaurants in old stone houses, and hundreds of condominiums. The northern part of the island forms the **Patrica Nature Reserve**, with ruins of an ancient Greek temple and a Genoese watchtower.

Places to Stay Set back from the waterfront, *Günay Motel* (☎ 327 1048) is quiet, simple and reasonably priced at US$13/20 for rooms with shower but no breakfast. Tiny Lale Adası on the road to Alibey Adası is dominated by the four-star *Hotel Florium* (☎ 312 9628, fax 312 9631) where double rooms cost US$80 with breakfast.

Places to Eat Taking the boat to Alibey Adası from Ayvalık for lunch or dinner is a favoured pastime. Expect to spend around US$12 to US$18 per person for a full seafood dinner with wine.

The promenade is all restaurants, with indoor tables in old stone houses and outdoor tables lining the quay. In general, those further east are a bit cheaper, but it's easy to check as they all have signboards with prices. In the off season, it's best to patronise the busiest one because it will have the freshest food. Even though it's fun to come across on the boats, coming by bus means you avoid arriving en masse with others and might get better service.

Pizza Veranda offers an alternative to seafood and *Taşkahve* is a pleasant waterside place for a cuppa.

Getting There & Away Two causeways link the island to tiny Lale Adası and the mainland; you can get there by city bus (US$0.30) or taxi (US$10) at any time of the year, although this isn't as much fun as taking the boats which depart in summer from the centre of Ayvalık near the Ayvalık Tourism Association kiosk (US$0.50, 15 minutes).

DİKİLİ
☎ 232 • pop 20,000

Travelling 41km south from Ayvalık along the coast road, a road on the right leads to Dikili, 4km west of the coastal highway, and 30km west of Bergama. A wharf capable of serving ocean liners brings the occasional Aegean cruise ship to Dikili to see the ruins at Bergama but mostly Dikili is a summer resort for families from İstanbul and İzmir.

The town's main beach (of dark, coarse sand) starts about 600m north of the main square and goes west for about 1km. The PTT is a few steps north of the main square, towards the beach. The otogar is 400m north of the main square.

Özdemir Pansiyon (☎ 671 1295), 100m north of the main square along the main street, is good if you expect to spend only a night or two and want to do it cheaply; likewise *Güneş Pansiyon* (☎ 671 1847), a bit further north then east (inland) (follow the signs). Both charge about US$7 per person. *Dikili Pansiyon* (☎ 671 2454), further north and a bit inland (there are no street names in this new section yet) is much newer, and costs US$8 per person.

Although there are direct buses between İzmir and Dikili via Çandarlı, most long-distance bus traffic goes via Bergama. Take one of the frequent minibuses to Bergama (US$1.30, 35 minutes) for connections with more distant points.

BERGAMA (PERGAMUM)
☎ 232 • pop 50,000

Modern Bergama, in the province of İzmir, is a sleepy agricultural market town in the midst of a well-watered plain. There has been a town here since Trojan times, but Pergamum's heyday was during the period between Alexander the Great and the Roman domination of all Asia Minor. At that time, Pergamum was one of the Middle East's richest and most powerful small kingdoms.

History

Pergamum owes its prosperity to Lysimachus, one of Alexander the Great's generals, and his downfall. Lysimachus controlled much of the Aegean region when Alexander's far-flung empire fell apart after his death in 323 BC. In the battles over the spoils Lysimachus captured a great treasure, which he secured in Pergamum before going off to fight Seleucus for control of Asia Minor. But Lysimachus lost and was killed in 281 BC, whereupon Philetarus, the commander he had posted at Pergamum to protect the treasure, set himself up nicely as governor.

Philetarus was a eunuch, but he was succeeded by his nephew Eumenes I (263–241 BC), and Eumenes was followed by his adopted son Attalus I (241–197 BC). Attalus took the title of king, expanded his power and made an alliance with Rome. He was succeeded by his son Eumenes II (197–159 BC), and that's when the fun began.

Eumenes II was the man who really built Pergamum. Rich and powerful, he added the library and the Altar of Zeus to the hilltop city, and built the 'middle city' on terraces halfway down the hill. He also expanded and beautified the already famous medical centre of the Asclepion.

The Pergamum of Eumenes II is remembered most of all for its library. Said to have held more than 200,000 volumes, the library was a symbol of Pergamum's social and cultural climb. Eumenes was a passionate book

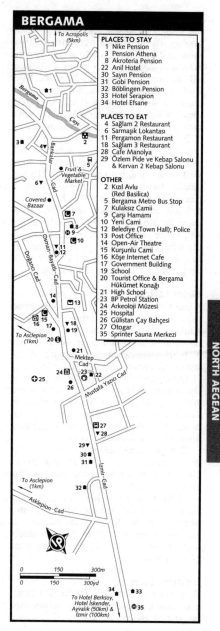

BERGAMA

To Acropolis (5km)

Bergama Çayı

Bandaki Cad

Fruit & Vegetable Market

Covered Bazaar

Osman-bayatlı Cad

Doğancı Cad

To Asclepion (1km)

Mektep Cad

Mustafa Yazıcı Cad

İzmir Cad

To Asclepion (1km)

Asclepion-Cad

0   150   300m
0   150   300yd

To Hotel Berksoy, Hotel İskender, Ayvalık (50km) & İzmir (100km)

PLACES TO STAY
1 Nike Pension
3 Pension Athena
8 Akroteria Pension
22 Anil Hotel
30 Sayın Pension
31 Gobi Pension
32 Böblingen Pension
33 Hotel Serapion
34 Hotel Efsane

PLACES TO EAT
4 Sağlam 2 Restaurant
6 Sarmaşık Lokantası
11 Pergamon Restaurant
18 Sağlam 3 Restaurant
28 Cafe Manolya
29 Özlem Pide ve Kebap Salonu & Kervan 2 Kebap Salonu

OTHER
2 Kızıl Avlu (Red Basilica)
5 Bergama Metro Bus Stop
7 Kulaksız Camii
9 Çarşı Hamamı
10 Yeni Cami
12 Belediye (Town Hall); Police
13 Post Office
14 Open-Air Theatre
15 Kurşunlu Cami
16 Köşe Internet Cafe
17 Government Building
19 School
20 Tourist Office & Bergama Hükümet Konağı
21 High School
23 BP Petrol Station
24 Arkeoloji Müzesi
25 Hospital
26 Gülistan Çay Bahçesi
27 Otogar
35 Sprinter Sauna Merkezi

NORTH AEGEAN

collector; and his library came to challenge the world's greatest in Alexandria (700,000 books). The Egyptians were afraid Pergamum and its library would attract famous scholars away from Alexandria, so they cut off the supply of papyrus from the Nile. Eumenes set his scientists to work, and they came up with *pergamen* (Latin for parchment), a writing surface made from animal hides rather than pressed papyrus reeds.

The Egyptians were to have their revenge, however. When Eumenes died, he was succeeded by his brother Attalus II. Things went well for a while, but under Attalus II's son Attalus III the kingdom began falling to pieces. With no heir he willed his kingdom to Rome and the Kingdom of Pergamum became the Roman province of Asia in 129 BC. In the early years of the Christian era the library at Alexandria was damaged by fire. Mark Antony pillaged the library at Pergamum for books to give Cleopatra.

Orientation

Almost everything you'll need in Bergama is between the otogar to the south and the market to the north, including cheap hotels, restaurants, banks and the museum. Nearly all of the more expensive hotels are west of the otogar towards the coastal highway.

The centre of town, for our purposes, is the Arkeoloji Müzesi on the main street, İzmir Caddesi, İzmir Yolu, Cumhuriyet Caddesi, Hükümet Caddesi, Bankalar Caddesi, or Uzun Çarşı Caddesi, depending upon whom and where you ask.

The handsome old part of town flanks the Bergama Çayı; the Muslim neighbourhood is on the western bank, the Ottoman Greek on the eastern bank.

Of Bergama's four main sites, only the museum is in the centre of town. The two principal archaeological sites are several kilometres out of town in different directions and require some healthy hiking or the hire of a taxi.

Information

Bergama's tourist office (☎/fax 633 1862) is at İzmir Caddesi 54, midway between the bus station and the market.

The sites at the Acropolis and Asclepion both have soft drinks for sale at a hefty premium, but no food. If you're walking, take plenty of water as you won't be able to stock up on the way.

The Köşe Internet Cafe is just up the hill from the Kurşunlu Cami, and has speedy connections for US$1 per hour.

Arkeoloji Müzesi

In the town centre next to Gülistan Çay Bahçesi is the Arkeoloji Müzesi, which has a substantial collection of artefacts for so small a town, and an excellent ethnology section. It has reopened after extensive renovation, and also has fine displays of sculpture from Pergamum, influenced by the Afrodisias school, which was known for its expressive features and lavish detailing, as well as a model of the Altar of Zeus. The museum is open 8.30 am to 5.30 pm daily; admission costs US$2.50.

Kızıl Avlu (Red Basilica)

The cathedral-sized Kızıl Avlu (Red Basilica or Red Courtyard) was originally a temple, built in the 2nd century AD, to the Egyptian gods Serapis, Isis and Harpocrates. In Revelations, St John the Divine wrote that this was one of the seven churches of the Apocalypse, singling it out as the throne of the devil.

Look out for a hole in the podium in the centre which allowed someone to hide and appear to speak through the 10m-high cult statue. The building is so big that the Christians didn't convert it into a church, but built a basilica inside it. One tower now houses the small Kurtuluş Camii, proving the theory that sacred ground tends to remain sacred even though the religion may change. The Bergama Çayı passes diagonally underneath the building through two tunnels.

The curious red flat-brick walls of the large, roofless structure are visible from midway down the road to the acropolis. You can easily walk to the Kızıl Avlu, or stop your taxi there on your way to or from the acropolis.

[Continued on page 236]

PERGAMUM: ACROPOLIS & ASCLEPION

Much of what was built by the ambitious kings of Pergamum didn't survive, but what did is impressive, dramatically sited and often beautifully restored.

Acropolis

The road up to the Acropolis winds 6km from the museum (5km from the Red Basilica), around the northern and eastern sides of the hill, to a car park at the top. Next to the car park (US$1.25 to park) are some souvenir and refreshment stands, and a ticket seller. The Acropolis is open from 8.30 am to 5.30 pm (till 7.30 pm in summer) daily; note that the road is closed outside these hours. Admission costs US$2.50.

Inset: Details of the impressive marble columns near the theatre in the Asclepion (Photo by Martin Moos)

Bottom: The re-erected columns of the Temple of Trajan

Blue dots mark a suggested route around the main structures, with multilingual signboards. The main structures include the **library** as well as the marble-columned **Temple of Trajan**, rebuilt by the German Archaeological Institute. This temple was built during the reigns of the emperors Trajan and Hadrian and was used to worship them as well as Zeus. It's the only Roman structure surviving on the Acropolis. The foundations underneath were used as cisterns during the Middle Ages.

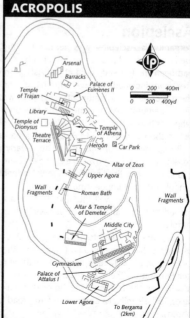

ACROPOLIS

Arsenal
Barracks
Temple of Trajan
Palace of Eumenes II
Library
Temple of Dionysus
Theatre Terrace
Temple of Athena
Heroön
Car Park
Altar of Zeus
Upper Agora
Wall Fragments
Roman Bath
Altar & Temple of Demeter
Wall Fragments
Middle City
Gymnasium
Palace of Attalus I
Lower Agora
To Bergama (2km)

0   200   400m
0   200   400yd

NEIL WILSON

The vertigo-inducing, 10,000-seat **theatre** is impressive and unusual. Pergamum borrowed from Hellenistic architecture, but in the case of the theatre made major modifications. To take advantage of the spectacular view and conserve precious building space on top of the hill, the theatre was built into the hillside. Hellenistic theatres are usually wider and rounder, but because of this one's location, rounding proved impossible and it was increased in height instead.

Below the stage is the ruined **Temple of Dionysus**. The **Altar of Zeus**, south of the theatre and shaded by evergreen trees, is in an idyllic setting. Originally it was covered with magnificent friezes depicting the battle between the Olympian gods and their subterranean foes but most of this famous building was removed to Berlin by the 19th-century German excavators of Pergamum (with the sultan's permission). Only the base remains.

Several piles of rubble on top of the Acropolis are marked as the **Palaces of Attalus I and Eumenes II**, and there's an **agora** as well as stretches of magnificent defensive **walls**.

If you want to see everything that remains of Pergamum, walk down the hill from the Altar of Zeus, through the **Middle City**, passing the **Altar & Temple of Demeter, gymnasium** or school, **Lower Agora** and **Roman Bath**. Take care as the path down is steep and not well marked.

While you're up on the Acropolis, don't forget to look for the Asclepion, across the valley to the west. You'll also see the ruins of a small and a large theatre, an aqueduct and a stadium down in the valley.

Asclepion

Pergamum's Asclepion was neither the first nor the only ancient medical centre. This one was founded by Archias, a local citizen who had been treated and cured at the Asclepion of Epidaurus in Greece. Treatment included massage, mud baths, drinking sacred waters, and the use of herbs and ointments. Diagnosis was often by dream analysis. Pergamum's centre came to the fore under Galen (AD 131–210), who was born here, studied in Alexandria, Greece and Asia Minor, and set up shop as physician to Pergamum's gladiators.

Recognised as perhaps the greatest early physician, Galen added considerably to the knowledge of the circulatory and nervous systems, and also systematised medical theory. Under his influence, the medical school at Pergamum became renowned. His work was the basis for all Western medicine well into the 16th century. Around AD 162, he moved to Rome and became personal physician to Emperor Marcus Aurelius.

There are two roads to the Asclepion. One leads up from the centre of town behind the Kurşunlu Cami. The other is at the western edge of town on the way to the highway, cutting up in front of the Böblingen Pension. By the latter road, the ruins are 3.5km from the Arkeoloji Müzesi, or about 2km from the otogar. This road passes through a large Turkish military base; be off the road by dusk and don't take photos.

ASCLEPION

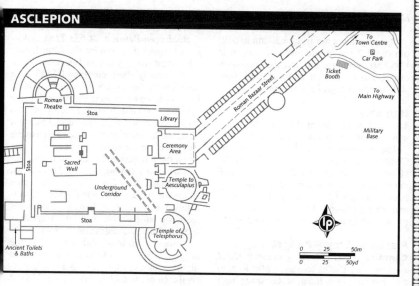

A Roman **bazaar street**, once lined with shops, leads from the car park to the centre where you'll see the base of a column carved with snakes, the symbol of Asclepios (Aesculapius), god of medicine. Just as the snake sheds its skin and gains a 'new life', so the patients at the Asclepion were supposed to 'shed' their illnesses. Signs mark a **Temple to Aesculapius**, a **library** and a **Roman theatre**.

Take a drink of cool water from the **Sacred Well**, then pass along the vaulted underground corridor to the **Temple of Telesphorus**. Patients slept in the temple hoping that Telesphorus, another god of medicine, would send a cure, or at least a diagnosis, in a dream. Telesphorus had two daughters, Hygeia and Panacea, whose names have passed into medical terminology.

Bottom: This magnificent row of columns near the theatre is just one remnant of the colonnaded walkways that patients at the Asclepion would once have walked through.

The Asclepion's opening hours and fees are the same as for the Acropolis.

MARTIN MOOS

[Continued from page 232]

Opening hours are from 8.30 am to 5.30 pm (until 7 pm in summer); admission is US$2.50. Some readers felt the admission charge wasn't worth it, and that it was possible to see enough from the outside.

Hamams

The old Çarşı Hamamı charges US$5 for a massage but it is poorly maintained.

The Sprinter Sauna Merkezi at İzmir Caddesi 85, a few doors down from the Hotel Serapion, is a modern hamam and very clean. It's open for women every day from 1 to 5 pm (there's a female masseur), and for men from 9.30 am to 12 pm and 5 pm to midnight. A massage costs US$6.

Places to Stay – Budget

Camping If you're looking to camp, *Hotel Berksoy* (see Places to Stay – Mid-Range) and, just west of it, *Karavan Camping* have sites for tents, caravans and camper vans. Sometimes cheaper places pop up for a brief life nearer to the coastal highway.

Pensions Lots of people visit Bergama on whistle-stop bus tours without spending the night, so there's only a handful of good pensions and hotels.

If you're after a place with old-fashioned character, two places near the Kızıl Avlu fit the bill. With a touching honesty, the owners of *Pension Athena* (☎ 633 3420, İmam Çikmazı 5) admits 'we are not the best but trying to get there'. Rooms are split between a 160-year-old stone house with some interesting wooden ceilings and a newer building. Rooms with/without shower cost US$7.50/5. Breakfast is another US$2. One lovely old room looks over to the Acropolis. To get there, turn down the street to the left of the Sağlam 2 Restaurant, then left again just before the stone bridge. The friendly manager can point out a shortcut to the Acropolis.

Cross the stone bridge and turn left to find *Nike Pension* (☎ 633 3901, Tabak Köprü Çikmazı 2), which has bigger rooms in a carefully restored 300-year-old Ottoman-Greek house at the back of a flower-filled yard. Rooms cost US$20 including breakfast.

Böblingen Pension (☎ 633 2153, Asklepion Caddesi 3) is run by the Altın family who spent many years in Germany. It's a quiet, friendly place, charging US$17 for a double with shower, US$14 without shower. Ideally placed for visiting the Asclepion, the pension is remote from the Acropolis. To find it, come out of the otogar and turn left along the highway until you see a sign to the Asclepion on the right. The pension is just up on the hill beside the road junction.

Akroteria Pension (☎ 633 2469) down the lane next to the Çarşı Hamamı has a nice courtyard and a good location, but unfortunately it isn't that clean. Beds and bathrooms are basic but passable, and little English is spoken. Singles/doubles cost US$8/17.

Across the highway and just south of the otogar are two run-of-the-mill pensions in high-rise blocks which would do for late arrivals. *Gobi* (☎ 633 2518) charges US$14 for a double with shower; the owner and son speak English. The *Sayın* (☎ 633 2405) costs US$17 for a substandard double and the owners don't speak English.

As a last resort, *Manolya Pension* (☎ 633 4488, 633 2583, Tanpınar Sokak 5) is managed by the people who run Café Manolya on the corner of the main street just outside the otogar. Ask at the cafe for price and availability (the pension isn't open year-round).

Places to Stay – Mid-Range

Anıl Hotel (☎ 631 1830, fax 632 6353, Hatuniye Caddesi 4) is a new dusky pink multistorey hotel in the centre of town, next to the BP petrol station. The attractive rooftop terrace has an unusual peaked roof. The facilities are excellent: air-con, modern bathrooms and comfy beds. Singles/doubles/triples cost US$37/50/65 with breakfast.

Bergama's other mid-range hotels are suffering from the downturn in tourism. The *Hotel Berksoy* (☎ 633 2595, fax 633 5346) is 2km west of the centre on the main highway. Just back from the road in flower-filled grounds, it boasts a restaurant, bar, tennis court and swimming pool for US$40/60 a modern single/double in season, breakfast included. Expect some traffic noise though. Just west of the Berksoy, *Hotel İskender* (*☎ 633 2123, fax 632 9710*) is a cuboid three-star high-rise, charging the same.

The two-star *Hotel Serapion* (*☎ 633 3434, İzmir Caddesi 75*) posts prices of US$25/40, discountable if they're not busy. Spacious rooms with shower and TV are fitted with thicker glass to deaden traffic noise from the main road outside. The pink and purple two-star *Efsane Hotel* (*☎ 632 6350, fax 632 6353, İzmir Caddesi 86*), across the road, charges US$23/35 for its bath-equipped but rather faded rooms.

Places to Eat

The recommended *Sağlam 2 Restaurant* offers more than the usual range of kebaps and pides. It specialises in spicy Urfa cuisine from south-eastern Anatolia, including *izgara köfte* (cigar-shaped meatballs). Mezes cost US$1, main dishes US$5 or so. There's a bar upstairs. The *Sağlam 3 Restaurant*, a few doors down from the post office, is a little more formal. There's a garden courtyard at the back and two old dining rooms.

Across the road from the otogar are two more reliable options. The popular *Özlem Pide ve Kebap Salonu* is reckoned to have the best pide in town (US$1 for a meat pizza, *kıymalı pide*). *Kervan 2 Kebap Salonu*, a few doors away, is one of the trendier spots for the young mobile-phone set. It plays the latest Turkish pop hits and charges a little more than the Özlem for pide and kebaps.

The *Pergamon Restaurant*, set round a tinkling fountain in an old Ottoman house, has good food though occasionally slack service. Expect to pay US$10 for a full meal here, not including drinks.

The *Sarmaşık Lokantası*, a villagers' place without streetside tables, has good hearty stews and low prices.

Café Manolya near the otogar is open late and is good for coffee and baklava for around US$1.50.

Getting There & Away

Whether you approach Bergama from the north or south, check to see if your bus ac-

tually stops *in* Bergama at the otogar. Most buses will drop you along the highway at the turn-off to Bergama, leaving you to hitch 7km into town. Hitching is pretty easy, except in the evening.

Ask the driver, *'Bergama otogarına gidiyor musunuz?'* (Do you go to Bergama's bus terminal?) Even then many drivers will nod *'Evet!'* (Yes!), and then blithely drop you on the highway. Taxis lurk here to charge outrageous sums to run you into town; wait 15 minutes and a minibus will come by to pick you up.

Bergama Metro buses stop at the otogar and then continue through town and stop not far from the Kızıl Avlu – this is very convenient if you want to stay at the Athena or Nike pensions.

Note that bus traffic dies down dramatically in the late afternoon and evening, so if you're heading onward, check schedules and reserve your seat earlier in the day. Several bus companies have ticket offices on the main street not far from the tourist office.

There are many buses to Ayvalık (US$2, 45 minutes, 50km) from the highway junction; there's also a limited but timetabled service from the otogar. Frequent minibuses go to Dikili (US$1.50, 35 minutes, 30km). Bergama Metro runs buses to İzmir (US$3, 1¾ hours, 100km) almost every 30 minutes. There are a few direct night buses to İstanbul, but it's far cheaper and, surprisingly, quicker to travel via Izmir. Buses to other destinations are not all that frequent. In winter, you may find yourself changing buses in İzmir or Balıkesir to get to Ankara, Bursa or İstanbul.

Getting Around

Bergama's sights are so spread out that you'll find the effort taxing if you're not in good shape. The Kızıl Avlu is over a kilometre from the otogar, the Asclepion is 2km, and the Acropolis is over 6km.

If you enjoy walking but have limited time, find others to share a taxi to the top of the acropolis, then walk down the hill to the Kızıl Avlu, either following the tarmac road or cutting down the slope beneath the theatre. From the Kızıl Avlu, walk through the market district into town, have lunch and take a taxi, or hitch, or walk to the Asclepion, depending upon your budget, your level of fatigue and your schedule.

The standard taxi-tour rates (per car) from town are US$6 one way to the Acropolis; US$12 return to the Acropolis, with a one-hour wait; or US$25 to go to the Acropolis (one hour wait), Kızıl Avlu (short stop), museum (15 minute wait), Asclepion (30 minute wait) and return.

Taxis for hire cluster near the Kurşunlu Cami, the Sağlam 2 Restaurant and at the otogar. A taxi from the otogar to the Athena or Nike pensions costs US$2.

ÇANDARLI
☎ 232

The little resort town of Çandarlı, dominated by a small but stately restored Genoese castle, is 11km west of the main highway, and over 18km south of Dikili. The castle and village are on a peninsula jutting into the Aegean. Although it's a pleasant place to while away a few days, the condominiums across the bay are steadily closing in on the views. Local tourism fills most of the small pensions and hotels in high summer, while the village shops cater to the owners of the villas on the outskirts. Most lodgings close between late October and April/May.

The main square, the Friday market and the shops, are to the east of the castle. The PTT is in the market square, just south of the main square.

Places to Stay

Most of the hotels and pensions are west of the castle, facing the thin strip of coarse-sand beach. To find them walk towards the castle and then skirt round the back; the Samyeli and Senger are to the right, the Martı and Philippi to the left.

One of the most prominent places is *Otel Samyeli* (☎ 673 3428), with bright, clean but somewhat spartan rooms, some with a sea view, for US$20 a double with breakfast.

A few buildings along is *Senger Pansiyon* (☎/fax 673 3117), run by a family who winter in Germany. Attractive rooms cost US$17 a double.

Inland a block from the Samyeli are several cheaper places, among them the simple *Gül Pansiyon* (☎ 673 3347) in an ordinary apartment block. Follow the signs along İncirli Çeşme Sokak to *Bağış Pansiyon* (☎ 673 2459), which has no sea views but a nice courtyard and a low price of US$12 a double, breakfast included.

Heading in the other direction along the beach towards the tip of the peninsula, *Martı Motel* (☎ 673 3441) is simple, with a rosy terrace restaurant and views of the sea. *Philippi Pansiyon* (☎ 673 3053), 200m south of the Martı, is a better choice: a modern house with a little terrace cafe and obliging owners. The rate for either place is US$20 a double, breakfast included. The *Tuna* next door is similar.

Places to Eat

Locals prefer the restaurants around the main square which, though not as pleasant as the touristy places to the west, are cheaper. *Temizocak Pide Salonu* (Tidy Hearth), between the Kaya Pansiyon and the market, serves pides for less than US$2 at a few streetside tables.

The Senger and Samyeli hotels both have fish restaurants on their ground floors, but just as good (and pretty friendly) is the independent *Kalender Restaurant* in between the two of them. A fish main course with two mezes and a cold drink costs about US$10.

Getting There & Away

Buses run frequently between Çandarlı and İzmir (US$2, 1½ hours) and Dikili. There are also four daily minibuses to and from Bergama.

FOÇA
☎ 232 • pop 12,000

Old Ottoman-Greek stone houses line a sinuous shore crowded with fishing boats. A Genoese fortress (1275) continues its slow centuries of crumbling on a hill in the town. Turkish sailors in nautical whites crowd the cheaper cafes, while the more expensive ones are a babble of European languages. This is Foça (**foh**-chah), sometimes called Eski Foça, a pleasant resort town resembling Kuşadası before it exploded into hyper-tourism.

Eski Foça, the ancient Phocaea, was founded before 600 BC and flourished during the 5th century BC. During their golden age, the Phocaeans were famous mariners, sending swift vessels powered by 50 oars into the Aegean, Mediterranean and Black seas. They were also great colonists, founding Samsun on the Black Sea as well as towns in southern Italy, Corsica, France and Spain.

Little remains of the ancient city: a ruined theatre, some bits of wall and an *anıt mezarı* (monumental tomb) 7km east of the town (west of the town of Bağarası) on the way to the İzmir highway. There are also traces of two shrines to the goddess Cybele: the first hovers between the two bays of Foça, while the second is on the hillside as you come into town from İzmir, beside the remains of two 19th-century stone windmills.

More recently this was an Ottoman-Greek fishing and trading town. It's now a prosperous, middle-class Turkish resort with yachts bobbing in the harbour and holiday villas marshalling on the outskirts. Much of the surrounding land is controlled by the military, which has saved the town from being over-developed. Rare Mediterranean monk seals lurk on the offshore islands, providing the inspiration for hundreds of souvenir mugs and T-shirts. Several fountains in the main square are renowned for the sweetness of their water, and you'll see people queuing to fill plastic bottles at them.

Orientation & Information

Foça's circular bay is partially divided by a peninsula cutting in from the south-east, dividing the eastern part of the bay into the Küçük Deniz (Small Sea) to the north and the Büyük Deniz (Big Sea) to the south. The Küçük Deniz, ringed with restaurants, is the more picturesque part, while bigger fishing vessels pull into the Büyük Deniz.

The otogar, on the eastern edge of the Büyük Deniz, is just south of the main square. Walk north through the square, passing the tourist office (☎/fax 812 1222), PTT and shady park. After 350m you'll arrive at the bay and the restaurants; continue along the left-hand (eastern) side to find the pensions, about 600m from the otogar.

Castles

West of the Küçük Deniz, Aşıklar Caddesi passes in front of some modern apartment blocks as it rounds the peninsula holding the fortress called **Beşkapılar** (Five Gates). This was built by the Genoese, repaired by the Ottomans, and partially restored in 1993.

Another fortress, the **Dışkale** (External Fortress) guards the approaches to the town from its perch at the end of the peninsula which shapes the south-western arc of the bay.

Boat Trips

In summer boats leave the Küçük Deniz every day at 10.30 am for trips around the outlying islands. Lunch and drinks are included in the US$17 price, and you'll have ample time for swimming and relaxation.

Places to Stay

Most of Foça's lodgings are pensions charging between US$8 and US$12 for double rooms with breakfast, and small hotels charging up to US$25 for double rooms with bath. Rooms can book up especially quickly at weekends when parents like to visit sons based at Foça's military bases.

Hotel Karaçam (☎ *812 1416, fax 812 2042, Sahil Caddesi 70)* is an Ottoman house (1881) with something of the air of a British seaside hotel. In addition to its location, its advantages include a roof-terrace bar, street-side cafe, fancy furniture in the lobby and plentiful plants. Rates are US$25/35 a single/ double in season, breakfast included.

Visitors speak well of *Ensar Aile Pansiyonu* (☎ *812 1777, fax 812 1401, İsmetpaşa Mahallesi, 161 Sokak 15)*, a modern building one block inland from the water, charging US$12.50 per person for rooms with showers. Internet access costs US$1.60 per hour.

The adjoining *Siren Pansiyon* (☎ *812 2660, fax 812 6620)* is equally good and costs the same. *Melaike Otel* (☎ *812 2414, fax 812 3117, 200 Sokak 20)*, at the end of the street, is run by the English-speaking

Selma Husenay. This spotless, quiet hotel has a definite feminine touch, and is good value for US$25 a double with shower and air-con.

The *Sempatik Hotel Güneş* (*☎/fax 812 1915, 163 Sokak 10*) is clean and comfortable. Rooms, some with a sofa, are US$24 a double.

Even further along, *İyigün Cafe-Pension* (*☎ 812 1182*) charges US$10 per person for very basic rooms.

A great budget option is on the street leading inland from the İyigün. *Pansiyon Iyon* (*☎ 812 1182, 198 Sokak 8*), run by two welcoming retired teachers, is a charming old house set around a leafy courtyard. Simple rooms cost US$6/8 and use of the kitchen is allowed. Mrs Tutar speaks some English.

At the northern end of the street is *Fokai Pansiyon* (*☎ 812 1765*), right on the water and a little pricey at US$25 for a simple twin room with shower. There's a kitchen for guests' use on the roof terrace, which also has some comfy couches.

The coast north of Foça is sculpted into small coves with sandy beaches, mostly backed by holiday condominiums, but a few have camping places. The closest is *Belediye Halk Plajı* (Municipal Beach), 3km north of Eski Foça.

Places to Eat

As you walk up from the main square to the Küçük Deniz you'll pass several simple Turkish restaurants where meals will cost a fraction of the bill in contrast to the restaurants by the waterside. These include *Zümrüt*, with meat stews for US$2 or so and cheap pides. *İmren Restaurant*, two short blocks to the north, is cheaper still, with good *sulu yemekler* (stews), making a two-course meal possible for US$3. For grills, try the neighbouring *Rumeli Köftecisi*, which also has a few outside tables. The popular *Sedef Restaurant* is the last of the kebap houses before you move into the harbour and the fish restaurants.

Be sure to ask prices first at any of the restaurants along the water, particularly when ordering fish. All waterfront restaurants charge from US$12 to US$20 for a full fish dinner, half that for meat (kebaps etc). The *Celep* and *Kordon* are among the better ones, though all are good for sunset dining.

Entertainment

There's a lively market on Saturdays which is when people from İzmir pop up to Foça for the day. Foça has many fashionable cafes – *Keylif Bar* seemed to be the most popular when we visited, with cool music and a groovy young clientele. A large Efes costs US$1.40. Several of the bars and restaurants have live music.

Getting There & Away

Foça is 83km south of Bergama, 70km north-west of İzmir and 25km west of the İzmir-Çanakkale highway. Virtually all bus traffic is to and from İzmir (US$2.50, 1½ hours, hourly buses in summer), with a stop midway in Menemen (US$1.60, 35 minutes, 37km). If you're bound for somewhere other than İzmir (Manisa in particular), you'll be dropped off on the highway opposite Menemen otogar where it's usually easy to pick up onward transportation.

Hanedan-Plajlar dolmuşes (US$0.60) run through town periodically in the summer, ferrying passengers between the town centre and the northern beach (Belediye Halk Plajı).

AROUND FOÇA

The road north from Eski Foça to Yeni Foça passes several camping grounds, hotels and holiday villa clusters, offering dramatic sea views, small coves and beaches, and numerous opportunities for rough or organised camping, as well as swimming and water sports.

Yeni Foça, 25km north of Foça and 12km west of the Çanakkale-İzmir highway, has a few old stone houses, many more new houses, hotels, condos and holiday villages. The sand-and-pebble beach, ranged around a picture-perfect bay, must have been created by nature expressly for water sports.

MANİSA
☎ 236 • pop 160,000

The modern town of Manisa was once the ancient town of Magnesia ad Sipylus, backed by craggy mountains. An early king was Tantalus, whose name gave us the word 'tantalise'.

As punishment for offending the gods Tantalus was left in a lake but the water receded every time he tried to take a drink. White apples hung 'tantalisingly' out of reach above his head.

The early, great Ottoman sultans favoured it as a residence, and for a while the province of Manisa was the training ground for promising Ottoman princes.

During the War of Independence, retreating Greek soldiers wreaked terrible destruction on the town, leaving only 500 of its 18,000 historic buildings still standing. The main reason to visit today is to see its historic mosques and some of the finds from Sardis in the local museum.

Orientation & Information

Doğu Caddesi is the main street in the commercial district. The historic mosques are only a few hundred metres to the south along İbrahim Gökçen Caddesi. The train station is less than 1km north-east of the centre; the otogar, 600m north-west.

The tourist office (☎ 231 2541, fax 232 7423) is in the Özel İdare İşhanı building, Yarhasanlar Mahallesi, Doğu Caddesi 14/3.

Things to See

Of Manisa's many old mosques, the **Muradiye Camii** (1585) has the most impressive tilework. The adjoining building, originally constructed as a soup kitchen, is now the **Manisa Müzesi.** It's open 9 am to noon and 1 to 5 pm, Tuesday to Sunday; admission costs US$1.25. The museum has the standard collections, including some fine mosaics from the ruins of Sardis.

More or less across the road from the Muradiye, the **Sultan Camii** (1522) has some gaudy painting, but an agreeable hamam next door with separate entrances for men and women. Perched on the steep hillside above the town centre is the **Ulu Cami** (1366), ravaged by the ages and not as impressive as the view from the teahouse next to it. Other historic mosques in town are the **Hatuniye** (1490) and the **İlyas Bey** (1363).

Special Events

For four days around the spring equinox (21 March) each year, Manisa rejoices in the **Mesir Şenlikleri,** a festival celebrating *mesir macunu* (power gum). Legend says that over 450 years ago a local pharmacist named Merkez Müslihiddin Efendi concocted a potion to cure a mysterious ailment of Hafza Sultan, mother of Sultan Süleyman the Magnificent. Delighted with her swift recovery, the queen mother ordered that the amazing elixir be distributed to the local people at her expense. In fact, the Ottomans had a long-standing custom of eating spiced sweets at Nevruz, the Persian new year.

Hafza Sultan's bank account is long closed, and these days the municipal authorities pick up the tab for the 10 tonnes of mesir, mixed from sugar and 40 spices and ingredients. Townsfolk in period costumes re-enact the mixing of the potion, then throw it from the dome of the Sultan Camii. Locals credit mesir with improving the circulation, calming the nerves, stimulating hormones, increasing appetite, immunising against poisonous stings and bites, and doubling tourist revenue.

Places to Stay

Since almost everyone stays in İzmir and drives to Manisa for the day, there are unfortunately few decent places to stay. Amid the shops of Doğu Caddesi, the two-star *Hotel Arma* (☎ 231 1980, fax 232 4501) has reasonable rooms with rather faded wallpaper for US$35/45 a single/double. Another option, as you head out of town bound for İzmir, is the four-star *Büyük Saruhan* (☎ 233 0272. fax 233 2648, Nusret Köklü Caddesi 1) with doubles for around US$65, and that's about it.

Getting There & Away

Buses leave at least every hour from İzmir's otogar for the 45 minute, 30km journey to Manisa (US$1).

İZMİR
☎ 232 • pop 2.5 million
İzmir is Turkey's third-largest city and its major port on the Aegean. It has a dramatic

setting, sprawling around a great bay and backed by mountains to the east and south. Most of the city is modern, the traffic is nightmarish, the bay polluted and for most people this is somewhere to get through as quickly as possible.

If you do take the time to explore you will find broad, modern boulevards lined with glass-fronted apartment and office blocks, and dotted with shady streetside cafes. Particularly in the bazaar area, the odd red-tile roof and bull's-eye window of a 19th-century warehouse pops up to remind you that there was an older İzmir too. But when you come upon an old mosque – so common in other Turkish cities – it hardly seems to belong here.

Most other traces of İzmir's past have been swept away by war, fire and earthquake. With just a day to spare, you can take in the few antiquities and museums, explore the labyrinthine bazaar, loiter in the cafes along the waterfront, and enjoy the wonderful, sweeping views from the 2000-year-old castle.

History

İzmir owes its special atmosphere, indeed its entire appearance, to its turbulent history. What you see today has risen from the ashes of Ottoman İzmir since 1922, when a disastrous fire razed most of the city. Before that, İzmir was Smyrna, the most Westernised and cosmopolitan of Turkish cities, where more citizens were Christian and Jewish than Muslim, and there were thousands of foreign diplomats, traders, merchants and sailors. Its connections with Greece and Europe were close. To the Turks it was *gavur* İzmir (infidel Smyrna).

İzmir's commercial connections with Europe began in 1535, but the city is far older than that. The first settlement, at Bayraklı near the eastern end of the bay, was built by Aeolians in the 10th century BC, but there were probably people here as far back as 3000 BC. The city's name comes from the goddess Myrina, the prevalent deity before the coming of the Aeolians who also worshipped Nemesis. Famous early citizens of Smyrna included the poet Homer, the founder of Western literature, who lived before 700 BC.

The city's history of war and destruction began early, for the Aeolians were overcome by the Ionians, who in turn were conquered by the Lydians from Sardis. Around 600 BC, the Lydians destroyed the city, which lay in ruins until the coming of Alexander the Great (356–323 BC).

Alexander re-founded Smyrna on Mt Pagus (now called Kadifekale, meaning 'Velvet Fortress') in the centre of the modern city, erecting the fortification which, much repaired over the ages, still crowns the hill.

Smyrna's luck changed during the struggles over the spoils of Alexander's empire. The city sided with Pergamum, the Aegean power-to-be. Later, it welcomed and benefited greatly from Roman rule. When an earthquake destroyed the city in AD 178, Emperor Marcus Aurelius sent money and men to aid in the reconstruction. During the Byzantine period, it became one of the busiest ports along the coast.

As Byzantium's power declined, the armies of the Arabs, Seljuk Turks, Genoese and crusaders marched in and, often, out again. Tamerlane arrived in 1402 and, true to form, destroyed the city. After he left, the Ottomans took over in 1415 and things began to look up.

In 1535, Süleyman the Magnificent signed the Ottomans' first-ever commercial treaty with François I of France, which permitted foreign merchants to reside in the sultan's dominions. After that humble start, Smyrna became Turkey's most sophisticated commercial city. Its streets and buildings took on a quasi-European appearance, and any worthwhile merchant was expected to be fluent in Arabic, English, French, German, Greek, Italian and Turkish. It didn't hurt to know Armenian, Ladino and Russian as well. In the 19th and early 20th centuries lowlifes flocked to the city's hashish and opium dens, birthplace of the Greek folk music style called *rembetika*.

The Ottoman Empire was defeated along with Germany in WWI, and the victorious Allies sought to carve up the sultan's vast

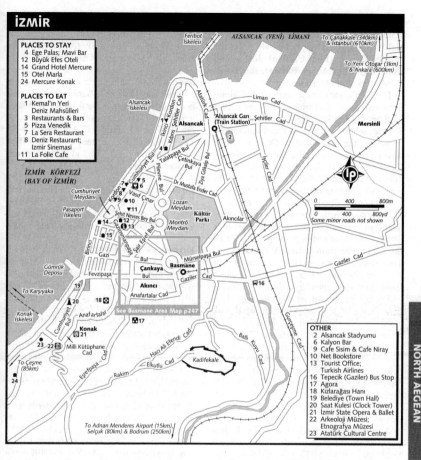

İZMİR

PLACES TO STAY
4 Ege Palas; Mavi Bar
12 Büyük Efes Oteli
14 Grand Hotel Mercure
15 Otel Marla
24 Mercure Konak

PLACES TO EAT
1 Kemal'ın Yeri
   Deniz Mahsülleri
3 Restaurants & Bars
5 Pizza Venedik
7 La Sera Restaurant
8 Deniz Restaurant;
   İzmir Sineması
11 La Folie Cafe

OTHER
2 Alsancak Stadyumu
6 Kalyon Bar
9 Cafe Sisim & Cafe Niray
10 Net Bookstore
13 Tourist Office;
   Turkish Airlines
16 Tepecik (Gaziler) Bus Stop
17 Agora
18 Kızlarağası Hanı
19 Belediye (Town Hall)
20 Saat Kulesi (Clock Tower)
21 İzmir State Opera & Ballet
22 Arkeoloji Müzesi;
   Etnografya Müzesi
23 Atatürk Cultural Centre

NORTH AEGEAN

dominions. Some Greeks had always dreamed of re-creating the long-lost Byzantine Empire. In 1920, with Allied encouragement, the Greeks took a gamble, invaded İzmir, seized Bursa and headed towards Ankara. In fierce fighting on the outskirts of Ankara, where Atatürk's provisional government had its headquarters, the foreign forces were turned around and pushed back. The Greek defeat turned into a rout and the once-powerful army, with half its men taken prisoner, scorched the earth and fled to ships waiting in İzmir. The day Atatürk took İzmir, 9 September 1922, was the moment of victory in the Turkish War of Independence. It's now the big holiday.

During the final mopping-up operations, a disastrous fire destroyed most of the city, a tragedy which paved the way for the creation of the modern city.

Orientation

İzmir has wide boulevards but is rather difficult to negotiate because the many roundabouts (traffic circles), with their streets radiating like spokes from a hub, don't give you the sense of direction a grid plan does. Nor are there many obvious landmarks.

The two main avenues run parallel to the waterfront. The waterfront street is officially Atatürk Caddesi, but locals call it the Birinci Kordon (First Cordon). Just inland from it is Cumhuriyet Bulvarı, the İkinci Kordon (Second Cordon).

The city's two main squares are along these two parallel avenues. The very centre is Konak Meydanı (Government House Square) where you'll find the municipality buildings, the *saat kulesi* or Ottoman clock tower (İzmir's symbol), the little Konak Camii mosque decorated with coloured Kütahya tiles, and a dock for ferries to Karşıyaka, the suburb across the bay.

The central district of Konak is the heart of İzmir, and opens onto the bazaar. Anafartalar Caddesi, the bazaar's main street, winds through İzmir's most picturesque quarter all the way to the train station, Basmane Garı. The Basmane area is home to dozens of small and medium-priced hotels and restaurants, and many intercity bus ticket offices.

The other main square, Cumhuriyet Meydanı, is about a kilometre north of Konak along the two main streets and holds an equestrian statue of Atatürk. The PTT, tourist office, Turkish Airlines office, car rental offices and expensive hotels are all near here. The relatively upmarket shopping, restaurant and nightclub district of Alsancak is further north.

The Çankaya district is two long blocks inland, south-east of Cumhuriyet Meydanı.

Another İzmir landmark is the Kültür Parkı (Culture Park), site of the annual İzmir International Fair. Kadifekale, the Velvet Fortress, crowns the hill directly behind the main part of town.

If you arrive in İzmir from Manisa, the road passes through the suburb of Bornova, once the summer residence of wealthy Levantine traders. Some of their mansions still stand; most are now converted for public use as municipal offices, schools and the like. Ege Üniversitesi (Aegean University) is here as well.

Information

Tourist Office The helpful tourist office (☎ 445 7390, fax 489 9278), Gaziosmanpaşa Bulvarı 1/D, is next to Turkish Airlines, close to the Büyük Efes Oteli. Opening hours are 8.30 am to 7 pm daily from June to October, till 5.30 pm in the off season.

Money Many banks have offices in Konak; Akbank and Türkiye İş Bankası have ATMs here, and there's an İş Bankası ATM in Basmane Garı. You can exchange currency at the PTT on Cumhuriyet Meydanı as well. The Bamka Döviz currency exchange office on the corner of 1369 and 1364 Sokaks, changes money quickly and efficiently.

Bookshops Net Bookstore on Cumhuriyet Bulvarı 100m north of Cumhuriyet Meydanı has a wide range of foreign newspapers and a good selection of English-language books.

Konak & the Bazaar

Konak Square was named after the Ottoman government mansion (*hükümet konağı*) which still stands here at the back of a park-like plaza. In the plaza is the late-Ottoman **saat kulesi** (clock tower) given to the city in 1901 by Sultan Abdül Hamit II. Its ornate Orientalist style may have been meant to compensate for 'infidel Smyrna's' European ambience.

İzmir's large bazaar, entered by walking along the right wall of the Konak, is fascinating. An hour or two of exploration along **Anafartalar Caddesi**, the main street, is a must, and it's worth trying to find the **Kızlarağası Hanı**, a covered market built in 1744, restored in 1995 and full of shops aimed at the tourist trade. You can also enter the bazaar from Basmane, or from Eşrefpaşa Caddesi near Çankaya after your visit to the Agora. Get well and truly lost, and when you're ready to leave, ask the way to Basmane, Çankaya or Konak. Virtually all the shops close on Sunday.

Agora

The marketplace built on the orders of Alexander was ruined in an earthquake in AD 178, but much remains of the Agora as it was rebuilt by the Roman emperor Marcus Aurelius. Colonnades of Corinthian columns, vaulted chambers and a reconstructed arch fill this conspicuously open spot in the midst of the crowded city, and give you a good idea of what a Roman 'bazaar' looked like.

To reach the Agora, walk up Eşrefpaşa Caddesi from Fevzipaşa Bulvarı, one short and one long block, to 816 Sokak on the left. This street of bakeries and radio-repair shops leads to the Agora, one short block away. You can also reach the Agora via 943 Sokak, off Anafartalar Caddesi near the Hatuniye Camii in the bazaar. Follow the signs.

The Agora is open 8.30 am to 5.30 pm daily for US$1.30. If you're only moderately interested in agoras or pinched for cash, you can see most of what there is to see from the street without paying the admission fee.

Museums

These two museums are in Bahri Baba Park, a short, unsigned walk up the hill from Konak along Anafartalar Caddesi. The entrance is positioned on the one-way road which brings traffic down the hillside, so to reach the museums, walk up that way. If you walk up the road for uphill traffic, you'll walk all the way around the museums but you won't be able to enter.

The **Arkeoloji Müzesi** (Archaeological Museum) is in a modern building. You enter on a floor with fine exhibits of Greek and Roman statuary, then move to an upper level dedicated to terracotta objects, tools and vessels, glassware, metalwork and jewellery of silver and gold. The lower level has tomb statuary and sarcophagi, and also the head of a gigantic statue of Domitian which once stood at Ephesus. Be sure to see the beautiful frieze depicting the funeral games from the mausoleum at Belevi (250 BC), south of İzmir, and also the high relief of Poseidon and Demeter dating from AD 200.

Even more interesting is the **Etnografya Müzesi** (Ethnography Museum) next door. Once İzmir's Department of Public Health, this fine old stone building now houses colourful displays demonstrating local folk arts, crafts and customs. You'll learn about camel wrestling, the potter's craft, the important task of tin-plating which renders toxic copper vessels safe for kitchen use, felt making, embroidery, and wood-block printing for scarves and cloth. You can even see how those curious little blue-and-white 'evil eye' beads are made, a craft going back hundreds, perhaps even thousands, of years.

Other exhibits include an Ottoman chemist's shop, a fully decorated salon from a 19th-century Ottoman residence, an Ottoman bridal chamber, a circumcision celebration room from the same period and a kitchen. There are also displays of armour, weapons, carpets and local costumes.

The Arkeoloji Müzesi is open 8.30 am to 5 pm (US$2.50), the Etnografya Müzesi 9 am to noon, 1 to 5 pm (US$1.30). Both are open Tuesday to Sunday.

Kadifekale

The time to ride up the mountain is an hour before sunset. Catch a city bus south of Konak (it may say only 'K Kale' on the sign), allowing 20 minutes for the ride. The view on all sides is spectacular. At sunset, as the muezzins give the call to prayer from İzmir's minarets the wave of sound rolls across the city as the lights twinkle on. The surrounding neighbourhood is pretty rough, so don't walk back from here after dark.

Near the gate are a few terrace teahouses for tea, soft drinks or beer.

Other Things to See & Do

As you make your way around town, you'll certainly see the **equestrian statue of Atatürk** in Cumhuriyet Meydanı. It symbolises Atatürk's leadership as he began the counteroffensive from Ankara during the War of Independence. His battle order to the troops on the first day (26 August 1922) read 'Soldiers, your goal is the Aegean'.

The Catholic **Church of St Polycarp**, on Gaziosmanpaşa Bulvarı (the entrance is down a side street), is a lavishly decorated 19th-century French church. Ancient Smyrna was the site of one of the seven original churches named in Revelations, and St Polycarp was Smyrna's first bishop, dying in AD 153. The Roman proconsul Quadratus ordered St Polycarp, who had served for more than 50 years, to renounce his faith publicly, and when he refused the bishop was burned at the stake. Mass is held here every Sunday morning.

Had it with the crowded, noisy city? Head down to the dock on the Konak waterfront and board a ferry for **Karşıyaka**, on the far side of the bay. The view is beautiful, the air fresh and cool. The return trip takes up to 75 minutes, and costs less than US$1.

Special Events

From mid-June to mid-July, the International İzmir Festival offers performances of music and dance in Çeşme and Ephesus as well as İzmir. Check with the İzmir Kültür Vakfı (İzmir Culture Foundation; ☎ 463 0300, fax 463 0077), Şair Eşref Bulvarı 50/4, Alsancak, or the tourist office for what's on where.

The annual İzmir International Fair is an amusement and industry show which takes place from late August to mid-September in the Kültür Parkı, at which time hotel space may be tight.

Places to Stay

Although İzmir has dozens of hotels, the choice isn't wonderful. Because so few tourists stay here, there are few of the cheap, pleasant pensions you find in İstanbul or even Kuşadası. Instead, İzmir's cheapies tend to be grungy places with little to recommend them except low prices.

The better hotels are certainly more comfortable but remain pretty mundane and overpriced in comparison to elsewhere. Some hotels post prices so high it hardly seems worth trying to argue them down.

There are lots of small, cheap hotels, and a good selection of mid-priced places just a few steps from Basmane Garı. The top-end hotels are mostly grouped around Cumhuriyet Meydanı, with the odd straggler in Alsancak.

Places to Stay – Budget

The Akıncı quarter, also called Yenigün, is bounded by Fevzipaşa Bulvarı, Basmane Meydanı, Anafartalar Caddesi and Eşrefpaşa Caddesi. Several streets are lined with cheap places to stay and equally cheap places to eat. The Basmane Hamamı, adjoining the Basmane Camii facing the station, is a convenient Turkish bath (men only). Bus ticket offices for your onward journey are only 50m away in Dokuz Eylül Meydanı. The better bus companies have shuttle buses to take you between Dokuz Eylül Meydanı and the otogar.

Note that there are also a lot of bars and nightclubs and, with them, a lot of prostitute activity in this area.

In the bazaar area, the best is the quaint *Otel Hikmet* (☎ 484 2672, 945 Sokak 26, Tilkilik/Dönertaş), up the side street opposite the Hatuniye Camii. It's clean and reasonably comfortable, and the manager is helpful. Rooms without shower cost US$6.60/12 a single/double, rooms with shower are US$8/14.

Just past the Hatuniye Camii is the slightly grubby but cheap *Otel Saray* (☎ 483 6946, Anafartalar Caddesi 635, Tilkilik), charging US$8 for a double with sink, opening onto a small enclosed central courtyard. Get a room on the upper floor if you can.

Cheap hotels line 1369 Sokak and the neighbouring lanes, but most are dives. The best of the lot is *Hotel Oba* (☎ 441 9605, fax 483 8198, 1369 Sokak 27), a respectable place with good bathrooms and air-con. It has luggage storage and a bar, with cushions to relax on. Rooms with shower cost US$12.50/20.

Güzel İzmir Oteli (☎ 483 5069, 1368 Sokak 8) is another decent option – reasonably clean and respectable. Rooms with shower cost US$8/15.

Places to Stay – Mid-Range

Basmane Try the two-star *Hotel Baylan* (☎ 483 1426, fax 483 3844, 1299 Sokak 8), with accommodating staff, clean modern (if small) air-con rooms with shower and TV, and private car park. Hefty posted prices of US$55/70 are subject to negotiation. Walk up 1296 Sokak and enter through the car park, or turn left onto 1299 Sokak by the (not recommended) Otel Gümüş Palas.

Another good choice is the new *Otel Antik Han* (☎ 489 2750, fax 483 5925, Ana-

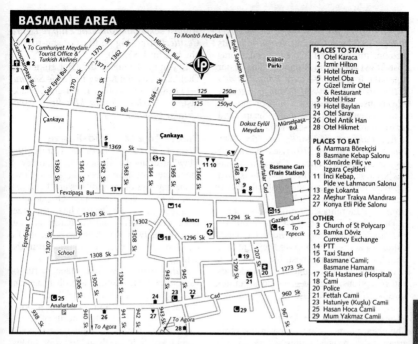

BASMANE AREA

To Montrö Meydanı

To Cumhuriyet Meydanı,
Tourist Office &
Turkish Airlines

Kültür
Parkı

Gazi Bul

Çankaya

Çankaya

Dokuz Eylül
Meydanı

Mürselpaşa
Bul

Basmane Garı
(Train Station)

Fevzipaşa Bul

Akıncı

To
Tepecik

Gaziler Cad

School

To Agora

To Agora

PLACES TO STAY
1 Otel Karaca
2 İzmir Hilton
4 Hotel İsmira
5 Hotel Oba
7 Güzel İzmir Otel
  & Restaurant
9 Hotel Hisar
19 Hotel Baylan
24 Otel Saray
26 Otel Antik Han
28 Otel Hikmet

PLACES TO EAT
6 Marmara Börekçisi
8 Basmane Kebap Salonu
10 Kömürde Piliç ve
  İzgara Çeşitleri
11 İnci Kebap,
  Pide ve Lahmacun Salonu
13 Ege Lokanta
22 Meşhur Trakya Mandırası
27 Konya Etli Pide Salonu

OTHER
3 Church of St Polycarp
12 Bamka Döviz
  Currency Exchange
14 PTT
15 Taxi Stand
16 Basmane Camii;
  Basmane Hamamı
17 Şifa Hastanesi (Hospital)
18 Cami
20 Police
21 Fettah Camii
23 Hatuniye (Kuşlu) Camii
25 Hasan Hoca Camii
29 Mum Yakmaz Camii

fartalar Caddesi 600), in a restored house right in the bazaar. Rooms with baths, TVs, ceiling fans and plenty of character cost US$20/30.

Down Fevzipaşa Bulvarı, a block from the station, is the three-star *Hotel Hisar* (☎ *484 5400, fax 425 8830, Fevzipaşa Bulvarı 153, or 1368 Sokak 2),* older but serviceable, with 63 rooms with bath, TV, minibar and air-con for US$42/64, including breakfast.

Cumhuriyet Meydanı Although this area is undeniably central and convenient, prices are extremely high. It would be wise to book through a travel agent or be prepared for some hard bargaining.

The three-star *Otel Karaca* (☎ *489 1940, fax 483 1498, Necati Bey Bulvarı, 1379 Sokak 55, 35210 Alsancak,)* is between the Hilton and the Büyük Efes. The quiet location, comfortable modern rooms and English-speaking staff make this a long-time

favourite of NATO military and diplomatic families. Rooms cost US$75/100, breakfast included. There's a restaurant and cinema attached.

The three-star *Hotel İsmira* (☎ *445 6060, fax 445 6071, Gaziosmanpaşa Bulvarı 28),* across from the Hilton, charges US$75/100 for similar comforts.

Otel Marla (☎ *441 4000, fax 441 1150, Kazım Dirik Caddesi 7, 35210 Pasaport)* has 68 rooms with marble bath, trendy decor, satellite TV, minibar and air-con. The location is quiet, yet only a block from Cumhuriyet Meydanı. Rooms cost US$60/80.

Places to Stay – Top End
As you enter İzmir, you can't help noticing the *İzmir Hilton* (☎ *441 6060, fax 441 2277, Gaziosmanpaşa Bulvarı 7),* which soars 40 storeys above the city centre. The complex includes a shopping centre. Posted room rates are as high as the building: US$230/265/300 for single/double/triple rooms.

The five-star *Grand Hotel Mercure* (☎ 489 4090, fax 489 4089, *Cumhuriyet Bulvarı 138*) faces Cumhuriyet Meydanı. Its air-con, minibar and TV-equipped rooms cost US$140/180 in summer. The sister hotel, the four-star *Mercure Konak (☎ 489 1500, fax 489 1709, Mithatpaşa Caddesi 128)* is just south-west of Konak on the way to the museums. It's marginally cheaper and many rooms have fine sea views.

Ege Palas (☎ 463 9090, fax 463 8100, Cumhuriyet Bulvarı 210) rises 20 storeys above northern Alsancak. Close to Alsancak's cafes and nightlife, its rooms cost US$130/190 for a sea view, about US$10 less for a land view. There are great views from the Panorama Cafe on the top floor.

The *Büyük Efes Oteli (☎ 484 4300, fax 441 5695, Gaziosmanpaşa Bulvarı 1)* faces out to sea across Cumhuriyet Meydanı. For decades it was İzmir's best, but now seems to concentrate on revenues from weddings and receptions. Double rooms cost an absurd US$170 to US$200.

Places to Eat – Budget

The cheapest meals are found in the same areas as the cheapest hotels.

The Basmane Garı area isn't exactly a glamorous place to eat out. The clientele in the many eating places in this area is almost entirely male. *Basmane Kebap Salonu (Fevzipaşa Bulvarı)* is a step above; it's clean and has good service, and is reasonably priced at US$4 for a large pide, salad and drink.

Ege Lokanta (1363 Sokak) is another good choice, with meat dishes for around US$2; dinner might cost US$4.

Güzel İzmir Restaurant in front of the hotel of the same name, has kebaps and ready meals, streetside tables and low-ish prices. A three-course meal costs about US$5 or US$6.

A few steps away at the junction of 1368 and 1369 Sokaks, *Marmara Börekçisi* serves large portions of flaky *börek* (filled pastry) and freshly baked pide with a soft drink for US$3.

On 1369 Sokak, look for the similarly cheap *İnci Kebap, Pide ve Lahmacun Salonu* – the restaurant's name is its menu. Almost next door, *Kömürde Piliç ve Izgara Çeşitleri* offers big portions of spit-roasted chicken for US$2.50.

If you're staying at the Otel Hikmet or Otel Saray, try the *Konya Etli Pide Salonu*, between the two hotels. For a good breakfast, try *Meşhur Trakya Mandırası (Anafartalar Caddesi 451)*.

Places to Eat – Mid-Range

Birinci Kordon North of Cumhuriyet Meydanı along the Birinci Kordon, many of the restaurants have streetside tables, views of the bay, lots of meze dishes and fresh fish prepared in various ways. On summer evenings, this is the place to be as the street is closed to traffic and the cafes spill out into the roadway. At other times, the traffic and the sea defence wall detract from the setting.

Cafe Sisim, the first place north of Cumhuriyet Meydanı, is a posh restaurant offering full meals for under US$10, occasional live music and the best people-watching in the city. Just north of it, the *Cafe Niray* serves draught beer (US$2), snacks and light meals at streetside tables.

The *Deniz Restaurant* is on the corner of Vasıf Çınar Bulvarı, on the ground floor of the Otel İzmir Palas. Prices are reasonable (about US$10 to US$18 for a full meal), with outdoor tables more or less regardless of the weather.

Across Vasıf Çınar from Deniz is *La Sera*, which also serves full meals at the tables closest to the building; the ones further out in the street are usually filled with drinkers.

Inland from the Kordon on Şehit Nevres Bey Bulvarı is *La Folie Cafe*, a modern bistro with great coffee, and a range of pastas and salads so big they alone suffice for lunch (US$5).

Alsancak North of Cumhuriyet Meydanı, inland from the water, is the wealthy district of Alsancak, with many good restaurants. A taxi from Basmane to Alsancak costs less than US$1.50.

For Italian fare in attractive surroundings, try the very popular *Pizza Venedik (☎ 422*

NORTH AEGEAN

2735, 1382 or Gül Sokak 10-B), half a block inland from the Birinci Kordon. Dining rooms and outdoor tables are open from 11 am to 11 pm daily. The menu lists 20 types of pizzas (US$4 to US$6 for fairly small portions) and several reasonably priced Italian main courses. Alcohol is served.

Even further north, several streets and squares have been closed to traffic (which in Turkey means fewer cars rather than no cars) and *streetside cafes* and *restaurants* are flourishing. Start at Gündoğdu Meydanı at the intersection of İkinci Kordon (Cumhuriyet Bulvarı), Plevne and Ali Çetinkaya Caddesi, walk east on Ali Çetinkaya and bear left on Kıbrıs Şehitleri Caddesi. You'll pass everything from McDonald's and İskender kebap places to cafes and bars accommodating İzmir's elite. The side streets hold some of the city's better restaurants, some in restored 19th-century stone houses.

A small street running west off Kıbrıs Şehitler Caddesi called 1444 Sokak is filled with restaurants, like the large *Altınkapı*, specialising in grilled lamb & köfte, and so popular it has taken over both sides of the street. Placemats bear pictures of the dishes. If you're tired of lamb, have the *piliç şiş* (chicken kebap) for US$4. The adjoining *Sofra* is also good.

A bit further north along Kıbrıs Şehitleri brings you to 1453 Sokak, a street of prettily restored houses. Several restaurants put tables out in the evening, including *Kemal'ın Yeri Deniz Mahsülleri* (☎ 422 3190 No 20/A), noted for its reasonably priced seafood. As fish are subject to market fluctuations, ask prices before you order.

Entertainment

Dining at the waterfront cafes along the Birinci Kordon, and taking a stroll along Kıbrıs Şehitleri Caddesi, are the prime evening activities.

Alsancak is the centre of the club scene. Some of the waterfront places along the Birinci Kordon have evening entertainment of high amplification and low quality, but the small indoor clubs off Kıbrıs Şehitleri Caddesi tend to be better. A good place to start looking is 1482 Sokak, full of attractive old

houses, but *Mavi*, beside the Ege Palas Hotel, is also inviting. *Kalyon*, opposite McDonald's on Cumhuriyet Bulvarı, has the air of an English pub – and you'll be hard-pressed to get a seat on a Saturday night.

For highbrow entertainment, the *İzmir Devlet Opera ve Balesi* (☎ 484 1562, venue ☎ 489 3692), the İzmir State Opera and Ballet, performs in a 1920s converted neoclassical cinema on Milli Kütüphane Caddesi, just north of the museums. The *İzmir Devlet Senfoni Orkestrası* (☎ 484 5172), or İzmir State Symphony Orchestra, performs every Friday and Saturday night at the cultural centre, the *Atatürk Kültür Merkezi* (☎ 483 8520, Mithatpaşa Caddesi 92, Konak). Tickets to the symphony cost US$10 to US$17, and US$5 for students. The *Turkish Daily News* usually carries schedules.

For less enlightening entertainment, the İzmir Sinemasi on Cumhuriyet Bulvarı next to the Deniz Restaurant shows recent Hollywood shlockbusters; tickets cost US$2.50.

Getting There & Away

Air Turkish airlines offers flights to İstanbul and Ankara, with connections to other destinations. There are also numerous flights between İzmir and Europe with various European airlines. The Adnan Menderes Airport information number is ☎ 274 2626.

Turkish Airlines (☎ 445 5363) is in the row of shops in the Büyük Efes Oteli at Gaziosmanpaşa Bulvarı 1, open seven days. Offices of some of the major airlines include the following:

British Airways (☎ 441 3829, fax 441 6284)
    Şair Eşref Bulvarı 3/304, Alsancak
Delta (☎ 421 4262) Cumhuriyet Bulvarı 143
Lufthansa (☎ 422 3622) 1379 Sokak 23,
    Alsancak

Bus İzmir's mammoth yet efficient new otogar is 6km north-east of the city centre; there are buses to almost every corner of the country. Long-distance buses and their ticket offices are on the lower level, regional buses (Selçuk, Bergama, Manisa, Sardis etc) and their ticket offices are on the upper level. City buses and dolmuşes leave from a separate courtyard on the lower level – this

Services from İzmir's Otogar

destination	fare (US$)	time (hr)	distance (km)	daily services
Ankara	14	8	600	every 30 minutes
Antalya	14	9	550	at least every hour
Bergama	3	1	100	at least every 30 minutes
Bodrum	10	4	250	every 30 minutes in summer
Bursa	8	6	375	every 30 minutes
Çanakkale	10	6	340	at least every hour
Denizli	7.50	4	250	every 30 minutes
İstanbul	17–25	8	610	at least every 30 minutes
Konya	13	8	575	every hour
Kuşadası	4	1½	95	at least every 30 minutes in summer
Marmaris	9	6	320	at least every hour
Sardis	2	1¼	90	buses for Salihli at least every 30 minutes
Selçuk	2	1¼	80	every 15 minutes in summer

includes bus No 605 to Üçkuyular otogar, from where buses run to Çeşme.

The larger bus companies provide *servis arabası* (shuttle services) between the otogar and Dokuz Eylül Meydanı next to Basmane Garı. For other transport to and from the otogar, see the following Getting Around section.

In the city centre, bus companies with ticket offices around Dokuz Eylül Meydanı include Hakiki Koç, İzmir Seyahat, Kamil Koç, Karadeveci, Kent, Kontur, Metro, Pamukkale, Uludağ and Vantur. Premium companies Pamukkale, Ulusoy and Varan have offices on Gaziosmanpaşa Bulvarı opposite the entrance to the Büyük Efes Oteli.

Details of daily bus services to selected destinations are listed in the table above.

Buses for Çeşme (US$2.50, 1½ hours, 85km) depart at least hourly from a separate bus station in Üçkuyular, 6.5km south-west of Konak; take a Balçova minibus from Konak to Üçkuyular.

Train Most intercity trains come into Basmane Garı (☎ 484 8638, for reservations 484 5353). İzmir's other terminus, Alsancak Garı (☎ 433 5897), at the northern end of the city near the port, is mostly for commuter and suburban lines but has frequent trains to Adnan Menderes Airport.

For information on trains, don't ask at the prominent Anahat (Main Lines) ticket kiosk in Basmane. Instead, consult the agent at Danışma (Information), who has all the schedules in his head.

The fastest and most comfortable train to Ankara is the *Ankara Mavi Tren*, departing at 6.20 pm, arriving in Ankara at 8.25 am. The one-way fare is US$11; sleeping compartments cost US$12/10 per person for one/two people. Dinner on board costs from US$6 to US$10. The next best train is the *İzmir Ekspresi*, departing at 7 pm, arriving in Ankara at 10.17 am. The one-way fare is US$10/7 in 1st/2nd class.

All Ankara-bound trains stop at Kütahya and Eskişehir, a major railway junction. In addition, the *Ege Ekspresi* (Aegean Express) departs İzmir each morning at 6.55 am for Eskişehir (US$6), and rail-buses depart for Manisa (US$1) at 2.40 and 6.30 pm daily. Some Ankara-bound trains stop at Afyon – check at Danışma. There's also a rail-bus from Basmane for Afyon daily at 12.15 pm.

Express trains depart for Denizli (near Pamukkale; US$4 one way) at 9 am (arriving at 2.25 pm), 3.10 pm (arriving at 10 pm) and 6.50 pm (arriving at 11.50 pm), stopping at Adnan Menderes Airport, Selçuk (US$1.30 one way), Aydın and Nazilli (for Afrodisias).

One train a day leaves for Isparta (US$5) at 9.30 pm, arriving at 6.30 am. The same service also calls at Burdur.

There are also daily services to Aliağa (6.30 am, 11.30 am, 4.25 pm), Ödemiş (5.15 pm) and Söke (7.20 pm), and *banliyö* (suburban) trains to Karşıyaka, across the bay.

Boat The İstanbul-İzmir car ferry service operates each weekend throughout the year, leaving İzmir on Sunday at 2 pm and arriving in İstanbul on Monday at 9 am. One-way fares (per person) range from US$23 for Pullman seats to US$155 for deluxe cabin berths. Meals are extra. The fare for a car is US$60 one way; it's less than half that for a motorcycle.

There are also ferry services between İzmir and Italy – see the Sea section of the Getting There & Away chapter for more information.

If arrive by sea, you'll see İzmir at its best as you glide into Alsancak Limanı (Alsancak Harbour), also called Yeni Liman (New Harbour), at the northern tip of Alsancak. The harbour is about the same distance (2km) from the otogar and from Konak. For transport, turn left as you leave the dock area and walk the block to Alsancak Gari, from where buses (US$0.40) and taxis (US$4) take you to the centre.

Getting Around

To/From the Airport You can travel between the centre of İzmir and Adnan Menderes Airport (18km south of the city near Cumaovası on the road to Ephesus and Kuşadası) by airport bus, city bus, intercity bus, commuter train or express train.

Havaş airport buses (US$2.50) leave for the 30-minute trip from the Turkish Airlines (THY) office in İzmir about 90 minutes before each Turkish Airlines departure. If you're not flying THY, ask for the schedule and catch a bus that leaves at least 90 minutes before your domestic departure, or two hours before an international departure.

Cheaper city buses trundle fairly slowly between Menderes airport and Montrö Meydanı, at the Kültür Parkı end of Şehit Nevres Bey Bulvarı, every 30 minutes throughout the day, but the trip takes twice as long.

A taxi between İzmir and the airport can cost between US$20 and US$40, depending upon your haggling abilities and whether or not the driver actually runs the meter.

More or less hourly suburban trains (US$0.50) connect Menderes airport with Alsancak Garı. Most travellers prefer to take a dolmuş as this is likely to be faster and more dependable.

To/From the Otogar If you've come on one of the bigger bus lines, there should be a *servis arabası* to take you to Dokuz Eylül Meydanı; as you descend from your bus, ask '*Servis arabası var mı?*'

Most convenient is the dolmuş marked 'Çankaya-Mersinli', which will take you to the bus ticket offices at Dokuz Eylül Meydanı, just a few steps from Basmane Garı, then to Çankaya. City bus Nos 601, 603 and 605 run from the city centre to the otogar.

If you're arriving in İzmir by bus from the south, ask to be let out at Tepecik, which is 700m east of Basmane Garı, and closer to the centre than the otogar. Minibuses and dolmuşes run from Tepecik along Gaziler Caddesi to Basmane. Conductors sometimes call this stop 'Gaziler'.

To get to Çeşme, catch any bus or dolmuş bound westward from Konak to Güzelyalı, Altay Meydanı or Balçova, and get out at Güzelyalı/Altay Meydanı to board a Çeşme-bound bus. Bus No 605 runs between Yeni Garaj (the main otogar) and Üçkuyular otogar, the bus station for Çeşme.

Bus & Dolmuş City buses lumber along the major thoroughfares. Two major terminal/transfer points are at Montrö Meydanı by the Kültür Parkı, and at Konak in front of the Atatürk Kültür Merkezi. You must buy a ticket (US$0.40) from a white kiosk in advance and place it in the box by the driver.

Metro Work on the İzmir metro has been going on for some years. The first 9.2km-long stretch of the metro will connect Basmane with Konak, then run west along the shore via Üçyol to Altay Meydanı in Güzelyalı, the beginning of the Çeşme highway.

Car Rental The large international franchises and many small local companies all have offices in İzmir. There's a cluster of offices on Şehit Fethi Bey Caddesi, the street between the Büyük Efes Oteli and the İkinci Kordon; and on the İkinci Kordon north of Cumhuriyet Meydanı.

Some addresses are:

Avis (☎ 441 4417, fax 441 4420) Şair Eşref Bulvarı 18-D, Alsancak; (☎ 274 2172, fax 274 2174) Adnan Menderes Airport
Budget (☎ 482 0505, fax 441 9375) Şair Eşref Bulvarı 22/1, Alsancak; (☎ 274 2203, fax 274 2260) Adnan Menderes Airport
Europcar (☎ 441 5141, fax 483 0031) Esin Turizm, Şehit Fethi Bey Caddesi 122-F, Alsancak; (☎/fax 274 2163) Adnan Menderes Airport
Hertz (☎ 464 3440, fax 464 5215) 1377 Sokak 8/F, Alsancak; (☎ 274 2193, fax 274 2099) Adnan Menderes Airport

Taxi To ensure a reliable driver it's best to take a taxi from a *durak* (taxi stand), or to have your hotel call one.

SARDIS (SART) & SALİHLİ
☎ 236

The important ruins of Sardis lie 90km east of İzmir. The great capital of the wealthy Lydian kingdom lies next to the Pactolus River, whose waters carry specks of gold which were collected with fleeces by the Lydians. It is here that coinage appears to have been invented, and the phrase 'rich as Croesus' originated. Croesus (560–546 BC) was the King of Lydia. No doubt the Greeks thought Croesus rich because he could store so much wealth in such a small form. Rather than having vast estates and far-ranging herds of livestock, Croesus kept his wealth in his seemingly bottomless pockets.

For all his wealth, Croesus was defeated and captured by Cyrus and his Persians, after which he leapt onto a funeral pyre, proving that not even he could take it with him.

The Lydian Kingdom dominated much of the Aegean before the Persians came. Besides being the kingdom's wealthy capital, Sardis was a great trading centre because its coinage facilitated trade.

After the Persians, Alexander the Great took the city in 334 BC and embellished it even more. Unfortunately, the inevitable

earthquake brought its fine buildings down in AD 17, but it was rebuilt by Tiberius and developed into a thriving provincial Roman town. It became part of the Ottoman Empire at the end of the 14th century.

Orientation & Information
About 90km east of İzmir, there are actually two small villages at Sardis, nestled in a valley rich in vineyards (producing sultanas, not wine grapes), olive groves, melon fields and tobacco fields. Sartmustafa (usually just called Sart) is the village on the highway, with a few teahouses and grocery shops. Sartmahmut is 1km north of the highway, clustered around the train station.

During the day the farmers come into town, park their tractors in front of the teahouses, sit down for a few glasses and discuss the crops. In early August when the harvest is in progress, children sell huge bunches of luscious, crisp, sweet sultanas to passers-by from streetside stalls. This is one of those areas where whole families careen around on motorcycles with sidecars attached.

A short hop further east, Salihli (population 71,000) is a local farming town with a sizeable otogar, an open-air marketplace, and three hotels to suit all budgets clustered around the otogar.

Archaeological Sites
The ruins of Sardis are scattered throughout the valley that lies beneath the striking ragged mountain range to the south, but two areas are particularly interesting.

At the eastern end of Sart, immediately north of the highway, lies the most extensive area of ruins, open virtually all the time during daylight hours, for US$1.75.

Buy your ticket at the little booth, then enter the ruins along the **Roman road**, past a well-preserved **Byzantine latrine** and rows of **Byzantine shops**. Many of these once belonged to Jewish merchants and artisans, as they backed onto the wall of the great synagogue. Note the elaborate drainage system, with pipes buried in the stone walls. Some of the shops have been identified from inscriptions. There's a restaurant, Jacob's Paint Shop, an office, a hardware shop, and shops belonging to Sabbatios and Jacob, an elder of the synagogue. At the end of the Roman Road is an inscription on the marble paving stones done in either AD 17 or 43, honouring Prince Germanicus.

Turn left from the Roman Road and enter the **synagogue** (*havra*), impressive because of its size and beautiful decoration. It was built over the site of the old baths and gymnasium and has lots of fine geometric mosaic paving, and coloured stone on its walls. A plaque lists donors to the Sardis American Excavation Fund who supported excavation work between 1965 and 1973.

From the synagogue, cross a grassy area to reach the striking, two-storey facade of a building described as the **Marble Court of the Hall of the Imperial Cult**. Whether you like the restoration or not, it's certainly imposing – and provides plentiful nesting sites for local birds. Note the finely chiselled inscriptions in Greek, and the serpentine fluting on the columns. Behind it you'll find an ancient swimming pool and rest area.

A yellow sign points south down the road beside the teahouses to the **Temple of Artemis**, just over 1km away. Today only a few columns of a once-magnificent building, which was never completed, still stand, but the temple's plan is clearly visible and very impressive. Next to it is an **altar** used since ancient times, refurbished by Alexander the Great and later by the Romans. Clinging to the south-eastern corner of the temple is a small brick **Byzantine church**. From archaic times until the Hellenistic, Roman and Byzantine periods, this was a sacred spot, no matter what the religion. You may have to pay another admission fee if there's anyone in the booth to collect it.

As you're going back to İzmir, look to the north of the highway and you'll see a series of softly rounded **tumuli**, the burial mounds of the Lydian kings.

Places to Stay & Eat

Snacks are available at the crossroads in Sart although the noise and dust of the main road discourages lingering. For full meals and hotel rooms, catch any bus going east from Sart along the E96/D300 to Salihli (9km).

In Salihli, *Hotel Yener* (☎ *712 5003, fax 714 3207, Zafer Mahallesi, Dede Çelik Sokak 7*) is a block south of the otogar across the open-air marketplace. Clean singles/doubles with shower cost US$8/12. *Toros Et Lokantası* shares the ground floor and terrace with the hotel.

Across the road is the smart two-star *Otel Berrak* (☎ *713 1452, fax 713 1457, Belediye Caddesi 59*), much more comfortable but charging US$45/60 for rooms with shower.

Finally, behind the *belediye* (town hall) and in sight of the otogar is the impersonal *Otel Akgül* (☎*/fax 713 3787*) which offers pretty ordinary rooms but with panoramic views of Salihli for US$17/29 with breakfast, shower and TV.

Getting There & Away

Buses depart for the 1½-hour, 90km journey to Sart at least every 30 minutes from İzmir's otogar. There's no need to buy a ticket in advance – just go to the otogar and buy a ticket for the next bus to Salihli (US$2). Tell them you want to get out at Sart.

Dolmuş minibuses run between Salihli, Sart, and Manisa, the provincial capital (US$1.75, 1½ hours).

Several daily trains from İzmir (Basmane) stop here but they're slower than the buses. Take the bus out to Sardis, but ask in town about return trains to İzmir, as you may find one at a convenient time.

ÇEŞME

☎ 232 • pop 100,000

Çeşme, 85km due west of İzmir, means 'fountain' or 'spring'. From the town, it's only about 10km across the water to the Greek island of Chios. The resort area encircling the town is popular with weekendtrippers from İzmir. Çeşme's tourism industry has struggled in recent years – bad for local business, but good for the travellers who make the effort to come here.

Çeşme itself is a pleasant seaside town, and the land to the east of it is rolling steppe, a foretaste of Anatolia. This barrenness subsides as you approach İzmir, giving way to wheat fields, lush orchards, olive groves and tobacco fields. About 23km east

NORTH AEGEAN

of Çeşme is the pretty Uzunkuyu Piknik Yeri, a roadside picnic area in a pine forest. About 50km east of Çeşme you pass the official city limits of İzmir, a full 30km west of Konak Meydanı.

Ilıca, a seaside resort town 6km to the east, has numerous hotels in all price ranges. There are frequent dolmuşes running between Ilıca and Çeşme (US$1) – and buses from İzmir call in there first – but unless you want to spend all your time at the beach you're better off staying in Çeşme proper.

Orientation

Çeşme is right on the coast and its otogar is less than 1km south of the main square, Cumhuriyet Meydanı, although you can pick up a bus to İzmir from immediately west of the monument at the western end of İnkilap Caddesi. Everything you need is near the main square on the waterfront, with its inevitable statue of Atatürk. The tourist office, customs house (gümrük), ferry ticket offices, bus ticket offices, restaurants and hotels are all within two blocks.

Information

The tourist office (☎/fax 712 6653) is down by the dock at İskele Meydanı 6. It doesn't have much to offer besides a free map. You can change money at Bamka Döviz (☎ 712 0853), İnkilap Caddesi 80, and there are ATMs on Cumhuriyet Meydanı, the main square. The Çeşme International Pop Song Contest is held during the third week of July, and the Çeşme Film Festival is held during the third week of August.

Kalesi ve Müzesi

The Genoese fortress dominating the centre of town was repaired by Sultan Beyazıt, son of Sultan Mehmet the Conqueror (Mehmet Fatih), to defend the coast from attack by pirates and by the Knights of St John of Jerusalem based on Rhodes. It is now the Çeşme Kalesi ve Müzesi (Çeşme Fortress &

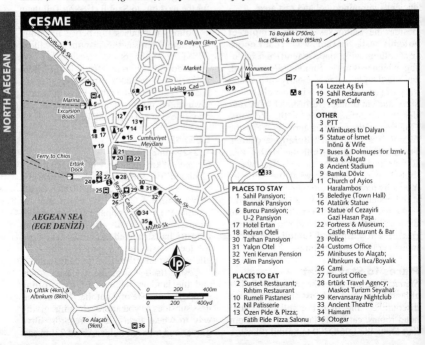

ÇEŞME

To Boyalık (750m),
Ilıca (5km) & İzmir (85km)

To Dalyan (3km)

Market

Monument

Inkilap Cad

Cumhuriyet Meydanı

Marina

Excursion Boats

Ferry to Chios

Ertürk Dock

AEGEAN SEA
(EGE DENİZİ)

Kale Sk

Beyazit Cad

Müftü Sk

To Çiftlik (4km) & Altınkum (8km)

To Alaçatı (9km)

0   200   400m
0   200   400yd

PLACES TO STAY
1 Sahil Pansiyon;
   Barınak Pansiyon
6 Burcu Pansiyon;
   U-2 Pansiyon
17 Hotel Ertan
18 Rıdvan Oteli
30 Tarhan Pansiyon
31 Yalçın Otel
32 Yeni Kervan Pension
35 Alim Pansiyon

PLACES TO EAT
2 Sunset Restaurant;
   Rıhtım Restaurant
10 Rumeli Pastanesi
12 Nil Patisserie
13 Özen Pide & Pizza;
   Fatih Pide Pizza Salonu

14 Lezzet Aş Evi
19 Sahil Restaurants
20 Çeştur Cafe

OTHER
3 PTT
4 Minibuses to Dalyan
5 Statue of İsmet
   İnönü & Wife
7 Buses & Dolmuşes for İzmir,
   Ilıca & Alaçatı
8 Ancient Stadium
9 Bamka Döviz
11 Church of Ayios
   Haralambos
15 Belediye (Town Hall)
16 Atatürk Statue
21 Statue of Cezayirli
   Gazi Hasan Paşa
22 Fortress & Museum;
   Castle Restaurant & Bar
23 Police
24 Customs Office
25 Minibuses to Alaçatı;
   Altınkum & Ilıca/Boyalık
26 Cami
27 Tourist Office
28 Ertürk Travel Agency;
   Maskot Turizm Seyahat
29 Kervansaray Nightclub
33 Ancient Theatre
34 Hamam
36 Otogar

NORTH AEGEAN

Museum), open 8.30 am to noon, 1 to 5 pm daily; admission costs US$1.30. The entrance is up the hill by the steps more or less opposite the tourist office.

Most of the castle's interior is empty, with the exception of the north tower, which displays some rather paltry local archaeological finds, many relating to Çeşme's maritime history, others from nearby Erythrae. You can climb up on the battlements for a good look around. One of the towers houses the Castle Restaurant & Bar, open in summer only (see Places to Eat in this section).

Facing the main square, with its back to the fortress, is a statue of Cezayirli Gazi Hasan Paşa (1714–90), together with a lion which symbolises his temperament. As a boy he was captured in a battle on the Iranian border, sold into slavery by the Ottoman army and bought by a Turkish tradesman who raised him with his own sons. Having joined the Janissaries at the age of 25, he began a brilliant military, naval and political career which included fierce battles with the Russian fleet off Çeşme. He retired an extremely wealthy man, having served as the sultan's grand vizier and having built public monuments, fountains and mosques on Lesvos, Lemnos, Chios, Kos and Rhodes (all Ottoman possessions at the time).

Other Things to See & Do

Çeşme's caravanserai was built in 1528, during the reign of Süleyman the Magnificent. It was restored and converted into a hotel with limited success – it now functions as a nightclub, the Kervansaray Nightclub. It's worth taking a look around.

On İnkilap Caddesi is the ruined orthodox Church of Ayios Haralambos, sometimes used for shows and exhibitions.

In the evening the people of Çeşme still observe the old Mediterranean custom of piyasa vakti (promenading): dressing up and coming down to the main square for a stroll, a glass of tea, a bit of conversation and some people-watching. The men, some with their wives, then linger in the seaside restaurants and teahouses.

Vessels moored along Çeşme's waterfront make day excursions up and down the coast, stopping at good swimming spots. Trips cost around US$15 per person, lunch included.

Çeşme has a hamam, just past the Kervansaray Nightclub. However, it charges US$20 for a wash and massage.

Dalyan, 4km north of Çeşme, is a fishing village on a fine natural harbour (but with no beach), with some reasonable seafood restaurants.

Beaches

The best beaches are at Boyalık, 1.5km east of Çeşme's main square, and Ilıca, 6km east. Both beaches are heavily developed with hotels, but are still good for a swim in the sun.

Places to Stay

The lack of tourists means accommodation in Çeşme is a buyers' market. There are inexpensive pensions and hotels, and several moderately priced hotels.

Places to Stay – Budget

Two of the best pensions are 600m north of Cumhuriyet Meydanı, uphill from the marina, but they are only open from May to November. *Barınak Pansiyon* (☎ 712 6670, *Kutludağ Sokak 62*) is a family-run pension with a glorious panorama of the harbour and Chios from the roof terrace. The rooms are basic, but clean. Singles/doubles/triples cost US$11/17/24. The owner, Suat Cı, speaks a little English.

Sahil Pansiyon (☎ 712 6934, fax 712 6237, *Kutludağ Sokak 64*) is next door. There's no roof terrace but the rooms have small balconies where you can soak in the views. Rooms (all with bath) cost US$12/17.

South of the Kervansaray is the cheap *Alim Pansiyon* (☎ 712 8319, *Mütfü Sokak 3*). Rooms cost from US$5 to US$7 per person, breakfast US$2.50. The building is no great beauty but all the rooms have baths and there's a kitchen at the back that guests can use.

Tarhan Pansiyon (☎ 712 6599), behind the Kervansaray, charges US$8/15 for single/double rooms in a pretty house draped with bougainvillea and centred on a courtyard. The same family runs the more modern *Yeni Kervan Pension* (☎ 712 8496, *Kale Sokak*). All rooms (US$8/15) have baths and balconies, and there's a large downstairs lounge and a kitchen that guests can use.

There are a couple of simple pensions in the midst of the action just off İnkilap Caddesi. In a narrow lane of crumbling old houses, *Burcu Pansiyon* (☎ 712 0387) has a fine terrace and shower-equipped rooms, as does the nearby *U-2 Pansiyon* (☎ 712 6381). Both charge US$8/12 for singles/doubles.

Places to Stay – Mid-Range

Yalçın Otel (☎ 712 6981, fax 712 0623, *Musalla Mahallesi, Kale Sokak 38*) is perched on the hillside overlooking the town. Its 16 pleasant rooms, all with showers, some with excellent views, cost US$14/18/23 a single/double/triple. Guests return here year after year.

On the shore, facing the main square, the two-star *Hotel Ertan* (☎ 712 6795, fax 712 7852, *Cumhuriyet Meydanı 12*) has a lift, open-air terrace bar, air-con, restaurant and rather ordinary guest rooms with baths, some of them facing the sea. Rooms are US$20/25, including breakfast.

Next door to the Ertan, the newer *Rıdvan Oteli* (☎ 712 6336, fax 712 7627) charges the same for rooms with similar facilities, but usually with balconies. The lobby is decorated with works by local photographer Çavit Kürnek.

Places to Eat

Çeşme's restaurants are all reasonably cheap, but of varying standards. Virtually all restaurants post their prices prominently. For a local taste treat, try the *sakızlı dondurma*, ice cream flavoured with locally grown mastic, the same stuff they put in Greek retsina. If you like retsina, you should like this weird reincarnation of the flavour.

The belediye runs the *Çeştur Cafe* on the square in front of the castle. It's a popular local tea garden, and an old lady makes gözleme for US$0.50 each.

Behind the old church are numerous small eateries, including *Özen Pide &*

Pizza, which serves grills and Turkish pizza, also the speciality of *Fatih Pide Pizza Salonu* next door. Both places have outdoor tables by the church.

Lezzet Aş Evi (İnkilap Caddesi) is still hanging on as one of the cheapest eateries in town, with vegetable dishes for US$1, and *salçalı köfte* (meatballs in tomato sauce) for US$1.25.

Nearby, *Nil Patisserie* serves excellent baklava (pastry with nuts and honey) and *lokum* (Turkish delight) for US$1 to US$2, and has a few streetside cafe tables. *Rumeli Pastanesi (İnkilap Caddesi)* specialises in the local *reçel* (jams), which include *patlıcan* (aubergine), *turunç* (orange), *incir* (fig), *limon çiçeği* (lemon-flower), *sakız* (pine gum, an unusual white jam), *ayva* (quince), *gül* (rose) and *karpuz* (watermelon).

The *Castle Restaurant & Bar* (☎ 712 8339), in a tower in the fortress, is a romantic place to watch the sunset, especially on your last night in Turkey before catching the ferry bound for Greece. A full dinner will cost you between US$10 to US$15 but it's only open from late May to September.

Down on the waterfront across from the castle, the *Sahil* restaurants have the best location but higher prices: pizza is US$3.50, şiş kebap and similar simple grills are US$4 and fish is substantially more. Both restaurants have outdoor tables, some facing the sea. There are other harbour restaurants further north towards the marina, including the *Rıhtım* and *Sunset*. The latter offers salads for US$3, seafood mezes for US$4 and steaks for US$8. As for the others, the following rule applies: the more they thrust menus in your face as you walk by, the more they overcharge.

Getting There & Away

Bus The opening of the Çeşme-İzmir otoyol has made it harder to get to Çeşme without transiting İzmir. If you're coming from Selçuk or Kuşadası, don't think you can avoid İzmir by taking a bus to Urla – there's no longer any onward public transport from Urla to Çeşme.

This is a drag because the bus to Çeşme doesn't leave from the main İzmir otogar.

FERGUS BLAKISTON

The memorial at Anzac Cove, erected by Atatürk, honouring the Allied troops who fell

TROY FLOWER

The magnificent acropolis at Pergamum

Although concrete has definitely made its mark on Turkey's urban landscape, many architectural treasures remain, such as Edirne's superb mosques (top left and right) and traditional wooden houses (bottom right), and this beautiful old windmill in Alaçatı (bottom left).

Ferry Schedule from Çeşme to Chios

time of year	departure days
16 to 30 April; throughout October	Tuesday, Thursday
1 to 15 May	Tuesday, Thursday, Sunday
16 May to 30 June	Tuesday, Thursday, Friday, Saturday, Sunday
1 July to 10 September	daily
11 to 30 September	Tuesday, Thursday, Friday, Sunday
1 November to 15 April	Thursday

You'll have to come into the otogar, and then catch city bus No 605 across town to the separate terminal for Çeşme in Üçkuyular, a neighbourhood 6.5km south-west of Konak. This can add a good hour to the journey time (see Bus under Getting There & Away in the İzmir section earlier).

Once you've got to the Çeşme terminal it's simple. Çeşme buses and minibuses (US$2.50, 1¼ hours, 85km) run every 15 minutes or so from 6 am to 6 pm, stopping at Ilıca and Alaçatı on the way.

From Çeşme, there are services to İstanbul (US$18 to US$25, nine hours, 700km, four daily) and Ankara (US$15, nine hours, 690km, two daily).

Ferry Many people visit Çeşme on their way to or from Chios. The boat schedule (see the table on this page) depends on the time of the year. Departure is at 9 am on Tuesday, Thursday and Saturday, 4 pm on other days. Return journeys are at 6 pm daily.

A one-way fare between Çeşme and Chios is US$30 but a same-day return is also US$30, making for a nice day trip. An open-date round trip costs US$40; a US$8 Greek port tax is levied if you stay overnight. Children aged from four to 12 years get a 50% reduction in fare (but not tax). Motorcycles, cars, even caravans, minibuses and buses can be carried on the ferries. Car fares cost US$70 or US$90, depending upon length.

You should buy tickets at least a day in advance. For details, reservations and tickets, contact Ertürk Travel Agency (☎ 712 6768, fax 712 6223), Beyazıt Caddesi 6/7; or Maskot Turizm Seyahat (☎ 712 7654, fax 712 8435) next door.

These agencies can also provide information about onward connections by sea and air from Chios to other Aegean islands, Athens, Bari, Brindisi and Venice. From Chios there are usually close connections with ships for Athens (Piraeus), Lesvos, Samos and Thessaloniki, as well as flights to Athens, Samos, Mykonos and Venice.

Çeşme is also served by direct car/passenger ferries to and from Italy. See the Getting There & Away chapter for details.

Getting Around

Ertürk Rent a Car (☎ 712 6768, fax 712 6223), Beyazıt Caddesi 6/7, has perhaps been in business the longest; look for it beside the fortress.

AROUND ÇEŞME

Altınkum consists of a series of coves 9km to the south-west beyond the town of Çiftlik, reached by dolmuşes which depart from behind Çeşme's tourist office. There are simple restaurants and camping grounds here, as well as some rental equipment for water sports, especially windsurfing.

Alaçatı is a well-preserved village of old stone houses populated by Ottoman Greeks a century ago, 9km to the south-east of Çeşme. It is backed by three windmills and equipped with a few small restaurants, pensions and hotels. The nearest beach is 4km away, but, like many other spots along this coast, it's famed for its windsurfing. Alaçatı Sörf Cenneti (Surf Paradise) in the Çark Mevkii district rents sailboards, bicycles, mopeds and camp sites. Dolmuşes run from Ilıca to Alaçatı, a distance less than 4km.

The unimpressive ruins of ancient **Erythrae**, famed for its cult temples of Cybele and Hercules, are within and around the modern village of Ildır, 27km north of Çeşme. A few small fish restaurants provide sustenance.

SIĞACIK
☎ 232

Sığacık, a pretty port village backed by a crumbling castle, is on its way to becoming just another town surrounded by ranks of villas, apartments and package-tour resorts. For now most people pass through quickly on their way to the white sands of Akkum, just over the hills to the west.

The centre of Sığacık is Atatürk Meydanı, the park bordered by the PTT, tea-houses and restaurants.

The best place to stay is the inviting *Teos Pension-Bar-Restaurant* (☎ 745 7463) behind the castle. Attractive rooms painted in autumnal colours cost US$10 per person, including breakfast. There's cool Turkish music in the bar, and Internet access for US1.60 per hour. Alternatively, in the main square, *Burg Pansiyon* (☎ 745 7464, Atatürk Meydanı 14) is in a modern building, charging US$12 for a double with shower. Some rooms have harbour views.

Lined up by the yacht harbour are the *Burç* and the fancier *Liman* restaurants, where businessmen babble into mobile phones while tucking into fish for around US$6 a portion. For a good view of the village, go around the harbour to *Deniz Restaurant*, on the road to Akkum. Cut in from the square to find *Şadırvan Pide Salonu* and more down-to-earth prices.

From Seferihisar, regular dolmuşes and city buses run west to Sığacık (4.5km). Since the construction of the expressway, the only way to get from Çeşme to Seferihisar is via İzmir; no dolmuşes run along the coast road from Çeşme to Urla any more. Coming from Selçuk, catch a minibus to Seferihisar (72km).

AKKUM
☎ 232

Just 2km around the bay and over the hills is the turn-off west to Akkum, another 700m along. The protected cove draws sailboarders in summer. Two small but smooth sand beaches, Büyük Akkum and Küçük Akkum, backed by olive groves, accommodate non-sailing companions.

For accommodation, there's the gorgeous but rather exclusive *Neptun Holiday Village Windsurf Center* (☎ 745 7455, fax 745 3038), the sailboarders' hotel behind Büyük Akkum. When available, rooms cost from US$35 to US$55 per person with full board. Also backing on to the beach is *Belediye Tesisleri*, a holiday village run by the Seferihisar town government. Slightly up the hillside, *Yakamoz Restaurant* provides meals with a view of the cove.

Regular dolmuşes and city buses run from Seferihisar to Akkum (7.2km).

TEOS

Scattered amid the farmers' fields and olive groves, 3km from Akkum, are the ruins of ancient Teos. The few fluted column fragments and chunks of marble rubble suggest that this was once a major Ionian city. It was home to the poet Anacreon and noted for its devotion to Dionysus, the Greek god of wine and fruitfulness, and the pleasures of the cup and the table.

From Akkum, go up to the road and turn right to reach the **Teos Orman İçi Dinlenme Yeri**, 1km east of the turn-off, a pine-shaded picnic grove run by the forestry department. Entry costs less than US$1 per person, and about US$1 per car.

Another 600m along, the road splits: the left fork goes to the ruins of Teos (800m); the right, to the Teos-Emeksiz Plajı and *Çadırlı Kamp-Günnübirlik Plaj* (beach, day-use and tent camping ground), 1km over the hill.

South Aegean Turkey

South of İzmir the Aegean coast is thickly studded with beaches and ancient ruins, most of them easily accessible by the fast coastal road. The area immediately south of İzmir was ancient Ionia where colonists from Greece arrived around 1000 BC, fleeing an invasion by the Dorians. Not surprisingly the main attractions are the many ruined Ionian cities, most obviously Ephesus, the best-preserved classical city in the Mediterranean, but also Priene, Miletus, Didyma, and several others which are all the more pleasant for being less well known.

If you're coming to visit Ephesus, the most obvious bases are Selçuk or Kuşadası. The pleasant small town of Selçuk is only 3km from Ephesus and is packed with cheap pensions and eateries aimed at backpackers. Just 7km west is Pamucak, with a 4km-long wide swathe of sandy beach.

Alternatively, Kuşadası is a sprawling resort town and port for Aegean cruise ships doing the Greek Islands route. Although this is solid package-holiday territory, Kuşadası makes a decent base for exploring Ionia.

The far south-western corner of the coast is mountainous and somewhat isolated. In ancient times this was the Kingdom of Caria, with its own customs and people. Nowadays most people come here to stay in Bodrum, which is, like Kuşadası, geared primarily to the needs of package holiday-makers. Even so, the wonderful crusader castle and pretty sugar-cube houses make Bodrum an enjoyable place to visit if you travel outside peak season (July to mid-September).

If you prefer something smaller and quieter you'd do better to head for resorts like Ören, Güllük or Iasos where development is still relatively low-key. One or two of the smaller resorts of the Bodrum Peninsula, especially Gümüşlük, are enjoyable.

SELÇUK
☎ 232

Once a modest farming town with a sideline in tourism, Selçuk has been transformed by

HIGHLIGHTS

- Touring the marble ruins of Ephesus
- Exploring the less well-known ruins at Priene, Miletus and Didyma
- Visiting the crusader Castle of St Peter at Bodrum, now the Museum of Underwater Archaeology
- Eating a sunset supper at Gümüşlük, near Bodrum

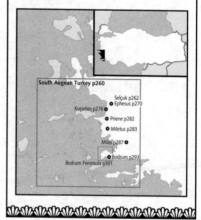

the tourism boom of the 1990s. Tourism is now the driving force in the local economy, though the lush fields of cotton and tobacco and the orchards of apples and figs surrounding the ever-growing town attest to the continuing efforts of the farmers.

Orientation

Ayasoluk Hill, with its castle, is north-west of the centre. Cengiz Topel Caddesi, the pedestrian way which is the heart of the commercial district, runs from an elaborate round fountain at the intersection with the main road (Atatürk Caddesi) to the train station. A few hundred metres south of the fountain on the main road is the otogar. On the western side of the main road is a shady

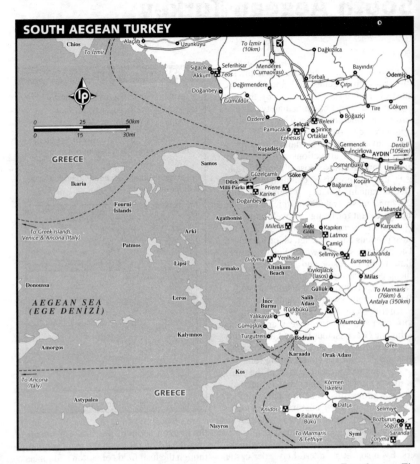

SOUTH AEGEAN TURKEY

park, and west of the park is the famous Ephesus Müzesi (Ephesus Museum). On the southern side of the park is the tourist office.

Information
Tourist Office Selçuk's tourist office (☎ 892 6328, fax 892 6945) is at Efes Müzesi Karşısı 23, across Atatürk Caddesi from the otogar. It is open 8.30 am to 12 pm and 1 to 5 pm daily between April and October; otherwise it is closed on weekends.

Money The PTT on Cengiz Topel Caddesi is open 24 hours every day, and will change cash, travellers cheques or Eurocheques. Ziraat Bankası has an office with an ATM on Cengiz Topel Caddesi; İş Bankası and Akbank have ATMs on Namık Kemal Caddesi, a block north. There are foreign exchange offices along Cengiz Topel Caddesi as well.

Email & Internet Access There are a few Internet cafes on Cengiz Topel Caddesi but they charge more than the pensions or hostels, and the connections are slower.

Medical Services We've had complaints of outrageous overcharging at Selçuk's hospital, so if you require nonurgent medical attention you're probably better off going to Kuşadası's private hospital (see under Information in the Kuşadası section for details) instead.

Parking If you park a car near the tourist office, Ephesus Müzesi or St John Basilica, you may be approached by a man wanting to collect a parking fee of up to US$1.50. Although the charge is official, ask for a *bilet* (ticket) or *makbuz* (receipt) to make sure the cash is going into the right pockets. Alternatively, move your car and park a few blocks away for free.

Ayasoluk Hill

It is said that St John came to Ephesus at the end of his life and wrote his Gospel here. A tomb built in the 4th century was thought to be his, so Justinian erected a magnificent church, **St John Basilica**, on the top of the hill above it in the 6th century. Earthquakes and scavengers for building materials had left the church a heap of rubble until a century ago when restoration began; virtually all of what you see now is restored. The church site is open 8 am to 5.30 pm (later in summer) daily; admission costs US$2.50. Look for signs pointing the way to 'St Jean'.

This hill, including the higher peak with the fortress, is called Ayasoluk and it offers an attractive view. Look west: at the foot of the hill is the **İsa Bey Camii**, built in 1375 by the Emir of Aydın in a transitional style which was post-Seljuk and pre-Ottoman. Keep a picture of it in your mind if you plan to venture deep into Anatolia for a look at more Seljuk buildings. There's a bust of İsa Bey more or less opposite. The mosque is usually only open to visitors just after prayer services, the most convenient of which are at midday and early evening. Leave your shoes at the door. Local Muslims seem used to visitors dressing inconsiderately, but it is polite to cover up anyway.

Beyond the mosque you can see how the Aegean Sea once invaded this plain, allowing Ephesus to prosper from maritime commerce. When the harbour silted up, Ephesus began to lose its famous wealth.

The hilltop **citadel** to the north of St John Basilica was originally constructed by the Byzantines in the 6th century, rebuilt by the Seljuks and 'restored' in modern times. A Seljuk mosque and a ruined church are inside. The citadel has been closed for several years after a chunk of wall fell down. Given that the restoration hasn't been a total success it will probably remain closed for the foreseeable future.

As at Ephesus, you may be approached in this area to buy grimy 'ancient' coins. In fact the coins are modern. Some local genius discovered that when coins pass through the digestive tract of a sheep or cow, they emerge with a convincingly aged appearance.

Early in the town's existence it earned money from pilgrims paying homage to Cybele/Artemis. The Anatolian fertility goddess had a fabulous temple, the **Artemision**, to the south-west of the St John Basilica. A sign on the road to Ephesus marks the spot today, and you can see a re-erected column and the outline of the foundation. If you visit the huge temple at Didyma you will get an idea of what this great temple must once have looked like, as Didyma's is thought to have been similar. If you walk to Ephesus you can take in the Artemision on the way.

Ephesus Müzesi

Don't miss Selçuk's beautiful museum, across from the tourist office. The collection is significant, and its statuary, mosaics and artefacts are attractively displayed. Highlights include the small, bronze figure of the Boy on a Dolphin in the first room; the marble statues of Cybele/Artemis adorned with rows of testicles (the Cybele cult included a castration rite); several effigies of Priapus, the phallic god; and pieces from a gigantic statue of the emperor Domitian. Beyond the courtyard is the ethnographic section set up in an *arasta* (row of shops) concentrating on traditional Turkish and Ottoman life with tools, costumes and a *topuk ev* (tent-like dwelling) used by Turkic nomads.

It's open from 8.30 am to noon and 1 to 5 pm; admission costs US$5. You'll probably appreciate it most if you visit the site at Ephesus first.

SOUTH AEGEAN

SELÇUK

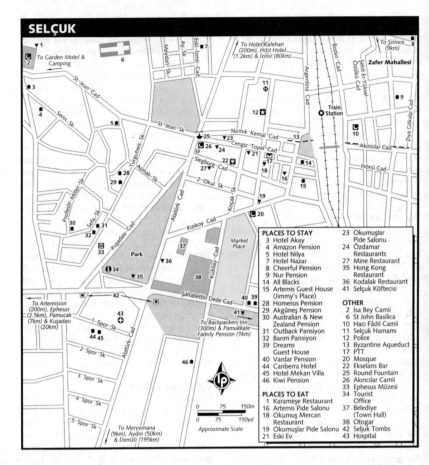

PLACES TO STAY
3   Hotel Akay
4   Amazon Pension
5   Hotel Nilya
7   Hotel Nazar
8   Cheerful Pension
9   Nur Pension
14 All Blacks
15 Artemis Guest House
    (Jimmy's Place)
28 Homeros Pension
29 Akgüneş Pension
30 Australian & New
    Zealand Pension
31 Outback Pansiyon
32 Barım Pansiyon
39 Dreams
    Guest House
40 Vardar Pension
44 Canberra Hotel
45 Hotel Mekan Villa
46 Kiwi Pension

PLACES TO EAT
1   Karameşe Restaurant
16 Artemis Pide Salonu
18 Okumuş Mercan
    Restaurant
19 Okumuşlar Pide Salonu
21 Eski Ev

23 Okumuşlar
    Pide Salonu
24 Özdamar
    Restaurants
27 Mine Restaurant
35 Hong Kong
    Restaurant
36 Kodalak Restaurant
41 Selçuk Köftecisi

OTHER
2   İsa Bey Camii
6   St John Basilica
10 Hacı Fâdıl Camii
11 Selçuk Hamamı
12 Police
13 Byzantine Aqueduct
17 PTT
20 Mosque
22 Ekselans Bar
25 Round Fountain
26 Akıncılar Camii
33 Ephesus Müzesi
34 Tourist
    Office
37 Belediye
    (Town Hall)
38 Otogar
42 Seljuk Tombs
43 Hospital

Other Sites

Selçuk has some **tombs** and a little **mosque**, dating from the Seljuk period, just south of the otogar. On Namık Kemal Caddesi are the remains of a **Byzantine aqueduct**, now a favourite nesting place for *leylekler* (storks). Eggs are laid in late April or May, and the storks are there right into September.

Hamams

The Selçuk Hamamı is north of the police station. Traditionally, women bathe on Friday; there's a female masseuse on Fridays from 12 to 5 pm (be there by 3.30 pm). The

fee is US$2 for a simple wash, US$6 for the works; everything is thoroughly clean and respectable. It stays open until midnight.

Places to Stay – Budget

Camping On the western side of Ayasoluk Hill 200m beyond the İsa Bey Camii, *Garden Motel & Camping* (☎ 892 6165, fax 892 2997) offers grassy pitches in the shade of aspen trees. At US$7 for a two-person tent, it's only a bit cheaper than the cheapest pensions, but the setting is delightful. There are also some pension rooms with a few dorm beds for US$3 per person. Carpets are made here for export to Italy, so you get the chance to see the dyeing and weaving in progress without pressure to buy.

Hotels & Pensions The competition between Selçuk's many pensions is intense, and the services on offer are much better than other towns.

Some of the pensions have their own carpet shops, either on the premises or elsewhere in town. They'll do their best to get you to shop at their particular outlet, which is fine if you want a carpet. If you don't, remember that there's rarely such a thing as a free lunch and one way to soften people up so they'll be ready to shop is to run them to Ephesus or help in similar ways.

The town authorities set most pension and hotel prices, so in high season (July to mid-September) they compete not on price but on extras like cheap home-made meals, views, and free transport to Ephesus and Meryemana. When business is slow, they compete on price as well. Dorm beds are around US$2.50 to US$4. Waterless singles/doubles cost from US$6/8 to US$8/10; or from US$8/12 to US$10/15 with shower.

Behind the Museum There are many pensions up the hill behind the museum. *Homeros Pension* (☎ 892 3995, fax 892 8392, e *homeros_turkey@hotmail.com, Asmalı Sokak 17*), has lots of character and a nice terrace and rooftop bar with a panoramic view. The owner, Derviş, is a carpenter and built most of the furnishings himself. Internet access costs US$1.60 per hour, and they let guests borrow bicycles too.

Outback Pansiyon (☎/fax 891 4039, *Turgutreis Sokak 5)* has 10 rooms, including some singles and some with showers. The hospitable owner Mark Mercan lived for many years in Australia. He has a carpet shop, hence the carpets and kilims decorating the rooms.

Akgüneş Pension (☎ 892 3869, *Turgutreis Sokak 14)* has nine simple rooms, all with bath, and a reasonable roof terrace.

Barım Pansiyon (☎ 892 6923, *Turgutreis Sokak 34)* is thoroughly kitschy on the outside (iron camels slouching along the fa-

cade) but inside it's an old stone house with a mixture of rooms with and without bath. The rear courtyard makes an inviting place to sit and read at the end of a long day. The owners have a hands-off approach to guests.

Sefa Sokak winds uphill to the large *Australian & New Zealand Pension* (☎ 892 1050, fax 892 1594, e *oznzpension@su peronline.com, Profesör Mitler Sokak 17)*, run by the Toparlak family. It's popular with younger travellers, and offers a rooftop terrace, kitchen, washing machine and Internet access (US$1 per hour). There's a range of rooms from doubles with bath to dorm beds.

Provided it's open, the quiet *Amazon Pension* (☎ 892 3215, *Serin Sokak 8)*, near the İsa Bey Camii and Hotel Akay, has seven bathless rooms and a pretty garden courtyard where breakfast is served. It's an old farmer's house with real character, run by a charming lady.

East of Ayasoluk Hill East of Ayasoluk Hill and the castle are several other possibilities, including the *Hotel Nazar* (☎ 892 2222, fax 892 4016, *Eski İzmir Caddesi 14)*, a midrange hotel that is willing to offer discounts in slow times. The rooms are tidy and there's a roof terrace with views of the castle.

Town Centre The best choice here is *Artemis Guest House (Jimmy's Place)* (☎ 892 6191, fax 892 9537, e *enquiries@ artemisguesthouse.com, 1012 Sokak 2)*. Clean, simple rooms are supplemented by a large lounge with DVD player and satellite TV, Internet access (US$1 per hour), a courtyard and unusually helpful management. The location is central but quiet. There are two deluxe rooms with air-con and flash bathrooms for US$30. They offer free pickup from Kuşadası harbour.

Close to the market, Seval Demirel runs the *Vardar Pension* (☎ 891 4967, fax 891 4099, *Şahabettin Dede Caddesi 7)*, with 16 small, clean rooms, most with bath, and a nice dining terrace where breakfast and dinner are served. Mrs Seval speaks some Dutch, English, French, German and Japanese. There is some street noise though. Close by is *Dreams Guest House* (☎/fax 892 2278,

Şahabettin Dede Caddesi 3), with very similar facilities.

The five-storey *All Blacks* (☎/fax 892 3657, 1011 Sokak 1), named after the New Zealand rugby team, suits people who want to drink a few beers and stay up late. They offer an all-you-can-eat barbecue.

South of the Town Centre South of the centre are quiet neighbourhoods of modern apartment blocks. *Kiwi Pension* (☎ 891 4892, fax 892 9516, Kubilay Caddesi 8) is a friendly little backpacker pension run by an English woman. There's a pool table in the basement, and a swimming pool nearby. Most rooms share bathrooms but are quite spacious. There's a washing machine and kitchen facilities.

East of the Town Centre Rooms are good if a bit characterless at the *Backpackers Inn* (☎ 892 3736, fax 892 6589, ⓔ backpackers inn.ephesus@turkey.com, 14 Mayıs Mahellesi, Kobuleti Caddesi 8), which used to be a mid-range hotel. Internet use is free. Budget package tours sometimes stay here. From the otogar walk along Şahabettin Dede Caddesi, turn right as soon as you cross the railway lines, and it's about 100m along.

For Turkish hospitality *Pamukkale Family Pension* (☎ 892 2388, ⓔ pamukkale pension@yahoo.com, 14 Mayıs Mahellesi, Sedir Sokak 1), run by Mehmet İrdem, has been described as 'awe-inspiring'. Mehmet is an all-singing, all-dancing one-man show. His wife's cooking also comes in for high praise. The rooms are simple but adequate. Perched on the hill east of town, the views from here are great.

Nur Pension (☎ 892 6595, Zafer Mahallesi, 3004 Sokak 16) gets glowing reports for its hospitality. Mrs Sukran Kiraci's cooking is recommended in particular. The clean rooms all have baths. Again, this pension will pay for a taxi from the otogar.

The *Cheerful Pension* (☎ 892 2732, Zafer Mahallesi, Çimenlik Sokak 3) is another quiet, friendly family-run place. It has eight bathless rooms and gives excellent service.

Places to Stay – Mid-Range
Selçuk has several one- and two-star hotels in quiet locations with private facilities.

The atmospheric *Hotel Kalehan* (☎ 892 6154, fax 892 2169, ⓔ ergirh@superonline .com, İzmir Caddesi), is north of the town centre on the main road near the Shell station. Built to resemble a group of old Turkish houses, it's decorated with antiques, local crafts and textiles. Rooms with double-glazing are set back from the road around a small swimming pool and verdant terrace. The best rooms have showers, mini-fridges and air-con, and cost US$35/50/65 a single/double/triple, but there are also a few bungalows costing US$20. The air-conditioned restaurant is excellent (see Places to Eat).

The welcoming *Hotel Akay* (☎ 892 3172, fax 892 3009, İsa Bey Camii Karşısı, Serin Sokak 3) is close to the İsa Bey Camii. Simple guest rooms are built around an interior courtyard and reached by walkways. All have tiled baths with showers, and cost US$17/25, including breakfast. The rooftop has a restaurant, bar and cushioned divan, and lovely views of the mosque. It's a fine place for an evening drink.

Readers recommend *Hotel Nilya* (☎ 892 9081, fax 892 9080, 1051 Sokak 7), close to the St John Basilica. It has a peaceful courtyard, small but comfortable rooms, fine breakfast and a good collection of jazz CDs. Doubles cost US$40.

One block south of Atatürk Caddesi, the *Canberra Hotel* (☎/fax 892 7668, 1 Spor Sokak 13) is a high-rise hotel with practically budget prices – US$8 for a single, US$14 for a double. The rooms are rather sterile but the views are good. Next door the *Hotel Mekan Villa* (☎ 892 6299, fax 892 6331, 1 Spor Sokak 11) is basically the same, with a flashier lobby. Doubles cost US$12.

Places to Stay – Top End
The four-star *Hitit Hotel* (☎ 892 6075, fax 892 2490, ⓔ hitithotel@anet.net.tr) is 1.5km north of town on the İzmir road. A new hotel with all mod cons (swimming pool, satellite TV, air-con, acres of marble), rooms cost US$40/60, dinner an extra US$5. You can spend a day at the pool with

a free meal for US$6.60. The pool closes for nonguests at 6.30pm.

Places to Eat

In high season Selçuk's restaurant prices can soar towards İzmir or İstanbul levels. Out of season, they drop considerably. On average, soups cost US$1.25, meze from US$1.50 to US$2 and meat dishes from US$2.50 to US$4. The simple *pide* (Turkish-style pizza) and *köfte* (meatball) places may not serve alcohol. A speciality of this region is *çöp şiş*, small bits of lamb or beef skewered on a sliver of bamboo and grilled on charcoal.

All the restaurants along Cengiz Topel Caddesi between the highway and the train station have tables outdoors in good weather, and most display prices prominently.

Many pensions will prepare meals for you – great food at low prices, especially when served on a roof terrace.

For cheap pide, try *Artemis Pide Salonu*, half a block south of the teahouse at the eastern end of Cengiz Topel Caddesi, where pide costs US$1.50 to US$2.50. Similar is *Okumuşlar Pide Salonu* on Namık Kemal Caddesi, across from the Akbank; Okumuşlar has another excellent branch opposite the mosque on the road to the bus station. *Kodalak Restaurant* at the otogar serves cheap stews, but ask for prices before you order.

The *Karameşe Restaurant* behind the İsa Bey Camii is more interesting than most, with pavilions decorated with carpets and a menu of *gözleme* (Turkish-style pancakes) and çöp şiş, washed down with *ayran* (yogurt drink).

At the popular *Okumuş Mercan Restaurant*, in the small square south of the post office, the food is freshly prepared and it's cheap: US$3 for kebap, rice and salad; US$1 for a serving of a meze dip and bread. Milk puddings, cake, baklava and biscuits from a neighbouring *pastane* (pastry shop) can be brought to your table and included in the bill.

Selçuk Köftecisi, opposite Dreams Guesthouse, is a reliable, modestly priced eatery, noted locally for its exceptionally clean kitchen. It serves kebabs, salads, rice and steam-tray fare; dinner costs around US$3.

Several tourist-oriented places lie on Cengiz Topel Caddesi, including the perennial *Özdamar Restaurant*. The nearby *Hanımeli Restaurant* advertises vegetarian food. On the next block, *Eski Ev* is another option.

Mine Restaurant at Siegburg Caddesi 4 has lots of inside tables and a few outside for tucking into good cooking. *Peynirli börek* (pastry filled with cheese) followed by a kebap washed down with wine will come to around US$8.

The *Hong Kong Restaurant* on Atatürk Caddesi across from the otogar is a branch of a well-known Chinese restaurant in İstanbul. It isn't cheap (US$3 for wonton soup, US$9 for ginger prawns), but it has air-con.

Even if you aren't staying at *Hotel Kalehan*, you can drop in for the excellent table d'hote dinner, a carefully prepared three-course meal for less than US$8 with a simple main course, US$10 with a fancier one, plus drinks. *Hotel Akay*, on a quiet street near the İsa Bey Camii, also has a pleasant rooftop restaurant.

By the train station there are several shaded *tea gardens* where you can sip tea and watch the storks on top of the aqueduct.

Entertainment

Sipping drinks and talking are the main evening entertainments in Selçuk. Besides the restaurants on Cengiz Topel Caddesi, you'll find *Ekselans Bar* on Siegburg Caddesi with outdoor tables.

Getting There & Away

Bus & Dolmuş Selçuk's otogar is across from the tourist office. While it's easy enough to get to Selçuk direct from İzmir, coming from the south or east you may have to change at Aydın. Most services from the otogar are local. Long-distance services usually start somewhere else (İzmir, Kuşadası, Bodrum) and pick up passengers on the way through.

There are frequent bus services from the otogar to Ephesus (US$0.50, 30 minutes, 3km), İzmir (US$3.20, 1¼ hours, 80km), Kuşadası (US$1.25, 30 minutes, 20km), Pamucak (US$0.80, 10 minutes, 7km) and Söke (US$1.60, 40 minutes, 35km).

There are dolmuş minibus services to Kuşadası, Pamucak, Şirince, Söke and other nearby points. Many pensions offer free lifts to Ephesus.

Taxi Taxi drivers charge about US$4 per car to take you the 3km to the Ephesus ruins, and about US$17 to Meryemana and back. For US$25 per car, they'll take you to the main ruins, wait, take you to Meryemana, and return you to Selçuk. Perhaps the best plan is to take a taxi to Meryemana for a short visit, then have it drop you at Ephesus' southern entrance so you can walk downhill through the ruins rather than up. You'll get as long a visit as you want, after which you can walk the 3km back to Selçuk.

Minibus Tours Minibus tours to Priene, Miletus and Didyma cost around US$17 per person from Selçuk's otogar. The tours may cost a bit more than normal dolmuş and bus fares, but save the time you'd spend waiting for a lift or an onward minibus. When booking the tour, try and persuade the driver to allow an hour at each site, as often they'll try to rush you through.

In spring and autumn, tours to Priene, Miletus and Didyma may run on Wednesday, Saturday and/or Sunday, or only when a group can be gathered.

MERYEMANA (MARY'S HOUSE)

Since at least the Renaissance, some people have believed that the Virgin Mary came to Ephesus with St John towards the end of her life (AD 37–45). In the 19th century Catherine Emmerich of Germany had visions of Mary at Ephesus. Using her descriptions, clergy from İzmir discovered the foundations of an old house in the hills near Ephesus, later verified by Pope Paul VI on a visit to the site in 1967. A small traditional service is held in the chapel on the site every 15 August to honour Mary's Assumption into heaven. Mass is held in the tiny chapel here at 7.15 am Monday to Saturday, and at 10.30 am on Sunday. To Muslims, Mary is Meryemana, Mother Mary, who bore İsa Peygamber, the Prophet Jesus. Below the chapel an entire wall is covered in rags tied to a frame

– Turkish villagers tie on the bits of cloth and make a wish.

It costs US$3.50 to get into the site, which is usually mobbed by coach parties in the mornings; however, by late afternoon the feeling of serenity returns.

A small restaurant and snack stand provide meals at relatively moderate prices. Alternatively, bring along some picnic supplies and enjoy lunch in the shady park.

The site is 9km from Selçuk, perched on the high wooded slope of Bulbul Dağı (Nightingale Mountain, Mt Coressos). It's 7km from Ephesus' Lower (northern) Gate and 5.5km from the Upper (southern) Gate. There's no dolmuş service so you'll have to hitch, rent a taxi (around US$17 for the round trip from the otogar) or take a tour.

EPHESUS (EFES)

Ephesus is the best-preserved classical city in the eastern Mediterranean, and among the best places in the world to get a feel for what life was like in Roman times. Needless to say, it's a major tourist destination.

Ancient Ephesus was a great trading and religious city, a centre for the cult of Cybele, the Anatolian fertility goddess. Under the influence of the Ionians, Cybele became Artemis, the virgin goddess of the hunt and the moon, and a fabulous temple was built in her honour. When the Romans took over and made this the province of Asia, Artemis became Diana and Ephesus became the Roman provincial capital. Its Temple of Diana was counted among the Seven Wonders of the World.

As a large and busy Roman town with ships and caravans coming from all over, it quickly acquired a sizeable Christian congregation. St Paul visited Ephesus and later wrote the most profound of his epistles to the Ephesians.

Ephesus was renowned for its wealth and beauty before it was pillaged by Gothic invaders in AD 262, and it was still an important enough place in AD 431 for a church council to be held there. Much of the city remains for you to see.

In high summer it gets very hot here. It's best to start your tramping early in the morning, then retire to a shady restaurant for lunch during the heat of the day. Unfortunately this is what the coach parties also do; lunch time is when you're most likely to avoid the bedlam of tour groups. Late afternoon can still be hot but it's usually less crowded.

If your interest in ancient ruins is slight, half a day may suffice, but real ruins buffs will want to continue their explorations in the afternoon. Take a water bottle as drinks at the site are expensive.

The site is open from 8.30 am to 5.30 pm (7 pm in summer) daily. Admission to the archaeological site costs US$6.60; parking costs US$1.60.

History

Earliest Times According to a legend related by Athenaeus, Androclus, son of King Codrus of Athens, consulted an oracle about where he should found a settlement in Ionia. The oracle answered, in typically cryptic style, 'choose the site indicated by the fish and the boar'.

Androclus sat down with some fishermen near the mouth of the Cayster River and Panayır Dağı (Mt Pion), the hill into which Ephesus' Great Theatre was later built. As they grilled some fish for lunch, one of the fish leapt out of the brazier, taking with it a hot coal which ignited some shavings, which in turn ignited the nearby brush. A wild boar hiding in the brush ran in alarm from the fire; and the spot at which the fishermen killed it became the site of Ephesus' Temple of Artemis.

For many years thereafter the wild boar was a symbol of the city. Until the 1970s it was still common to see wild pigs in scrub thickets near Ephesus.

In ancient times the sea came much further inland, almost as far as present-day Selçuk, even lapping at the feet of Panayır Dağı. The first settlement, of which virtually nothing remains, was built on the hill's northern slope, and was a prosperous city by about 600 BC. The nearby sanctuary of Cybele/Artemis had been a place of pilgrimage since at least 800 BC, which probably had more to do with the selection of the site than the fish and the pig.

Croesus & the Persians Ephesus prospered so much that it aroused the envy of King Croesus of Lydia, who attacked it around 600 BC. The Ephesians, who neglected to build defensive walls, stretched a rope from the Temple of Artemis to the town, a distance of 1200m, hoping thus to place themselves under the protection of the goddess. Croesus responded to this quaint defensive measure by giving some of his famous wealth for the completion of the temple, which was still under construction. But he destroyed the city of Ephesus and relocated its citizens inland to the southern side of the temple, where they rebuilt the city and lived through classical times.

Neglecting again (or perhaps forbidden) to build walls, the Ephesians were tributaries of Croesus' Lydia and, later, of the Persians. They then joined the Athenian confederacy, but later fell back under Persian control.

Rebuilding the Temple In 356 BC the Temple of Cybele/Artemis was destroyed in a fire set by one Herostratus, who claimed to have done it to get a mention in history, proving that modern society has no monopoly on a perverted sense of celebrity.

The Ephesians planned a new grander temple, the construction of which was well under way when Alexander the Great arrived in 334 BC. Much impressed by the plans, Alexander offered to pay the cost of construction if only it would be dedicated to him. The Ephesians declined his generous offer, saying with monumental tact that it was not fitting for one god to make a dedication to another. When the temple was finished, it was recognised as one of the Seven Wonders of the World.

Under Lysimachus After Alexander the Great's death, Ionia came under the control of Lysimachus, one of his generals. As the Cayster brought more silt into the harbour, it became clear that the city would have to move westward or die a commercial death. Lysimachus, unable to convince the Ephesians to budge, blocked the sewers of the old city during a downpour causing major flooding of their homes. The Ephesians then reluctantly moved to a site on the western side of Mt Pion, where the Roman city now stands.

Little survives of Lysimachus' city, though it finally got a defensive wall almost 10km long which served it well as it allied itself first with the Seleucid kings of Syria, then with the Ptolemies of Egypt, later with King Antiochus, then Eumenes of Pergamum, and finally with the Romans. Long stretches of the wall survive on top of Bülbül Dağı (Mt Coressos), the high ridge of hills on the southern side of Ephesus. A prominent square tower, nicknamed 'St Paul's Prison', also survives, on a low hill to the west.

Roman Ephesus Roman Ephesus boasted that it was the 'first and greatest metropolis of Asia', with a population nearing 250,000. It became the Roman capital of Asia Minor, honoured and beautified by succeeding emperors. With its brisk sea traffic, rich commerce and right of sanctuary in the Temple of Artemis, it drew many immigrants of various nations and creeds. It's said that St John came here with the Virgin Mary, followed by St Paul, whose Letter to the Ephesians was written to people he had known during his three-year stay.

Its prosperity from commerce and temple pilgrimage was unrivalled, but the Cayster continued to bring silt down into the harbour. Despite great works by Attalus II of Pergamum, who rebuilt the harbour, and Nero's proconsul, who dredged it, the silting continued. Emperor Hadrian had the Cayster diverted, but the harbour continued to silt up, ultimately pushing the sea back to Pamucak, 4km to the west. Cut off from its commerce, Ephesus lost its wealth. By the 6th century AD, when the Emperor Justinian was looking for a site for the St John Basilica, he chose Ayasoluk Hill in Selçuk, which became the new city centre.

Special Events

The Ephesus Festival, held at varying times in the year, brings top performers to the Great Theatre at Ephesus and other venues.

St Paul in Ephesus

St Paul lived at Ephesus for three years, perhaps in the 60s AD. According to the Bible (Acts 19:24–41), his mission was so successful that the trade in religious artefacts for the Artemis cult dropped off precipitously. Hurt by the slump, a silversmith named Demetrius, who made Artemis shrines, gathered a group of other artisans who had lost business. At first they grumbled about the effects of Paul's preaching on their incomes, but they soon sought a higher rationale and blamed him for a loss of respect for the goddess herself.

Rumours spread throughout the city that someone was being disrespectful of Artemis. People flooded into the Great Theatre, sweeping along several of Paul's Christian travelling companions. Paul, set on entering the theatre (perhaps to give the sermon of his life to a packed house), was dissuaded from doing so by his disciples.

Unclear on the cause of the uproar, the mob in the theatre shouted 'Great is Artemis of the Ephesians!' for an hour before the secretary of the city council calmed them down enough to speak. The Christians, having broken no law, were released and the uproar subsided, but Paul left Ephesus shortly thereafter for Macedonia.

From mid-June to mid-July, performances of music and dance are organised under the rubric of the International İzmir Festival and there are some performances at Ephesus.

Getting There & Away

It's 3km from the tourist office in Selçuk to the admission gate at Ephesus, a pleasant 30- to 45-minute walk along a shady lane at the side of the highway. The lane, actually the old road, is named after Dr Sabri Yayla, who had the foresight to plant the trees earlier in the century.

Alternatively, there are frequent buses (US$0.50) and taxis (US$4 per car) from Selçuk, and many pensions in Selçuk offer free lifts to the site.

[Continued on page 274]

EPHESUS – A WALKING TOUR

As you walk into the site from Dr Sabri Yayla Bulvarı, a road to the left is marked for the Grotto of the Seven Sleepers, on the north-eastern side of Panayır Dağı about 1km away.

Grotto of the Seven Sleepers

According to legend, seven persecuted Christian youths fled from Ephesus in the 3rd century AD and took refuge in this cave. Agents of the Emperor Decius, a terror to Christians, found the cave and sealed it. Two centuries later an earthquake broke down the wall, awakening the sleepers, and they ambled back to town for a meal. Finding that all their old friends were long dead, they concluded that they had undergone a sort of resurrection – Ephesus was by this time a Christian city. When they died they were buried in the cave, and a cult following developed.

The grotto is actually a fairly elaborate Byzantine-era **necropolis** with scores of tombs cut into the rock. Many people feel it's hardly worth paying the extra admission charge (at least in season).

Gymnasium of Vedius & Stadium

Back on the entry road you pass the Gymnasium of Vedius (2nd century AD), with its exercise fields, baths, toilets, covered exercise rooms, a swimming pool and a ceremonial hall, on your left. Just south of it is the Stadium, dating from about the same period. Most of its finely cut stones were taken by the Byzantines to build the citadel and walls of the castle on Ayasoluk Hill. This 'quarrying' of pre-cut building stone from older, often earthquake-ruined structures continued throughout the history of Ephesus.

Double Church

The road comes over a low rise and descends to the car park, where there are teahouses, restaurants, souvenir shops, a PTT and banks. To the right of the road are the ruins of the Church of the Virgin Mary, also called the Double Church. The original building was a museum, a Hall of the Muses – a place for lectures, teaching and educated discussions and debates. Destroyed by fire, it was rebuilt in the 4th century AD as a church, later to become the site of the third Ecumenical Council (AD 431) which condemned the Nestorian heresy. Over the centuries several other churches were built here, somewhat obscuring the original layout.

Harbour St

As you walk down a lane bordered by evergreen trees, a few colossal remains of the **harbour gymnasium** are off to the right (west) before you reach the marble-paved Harbour St. This, the grandest street in Ephesus, had water and sewer lines beneath the marble flags, 50 streetlights along its colonnades, shops along its sides, and near its western (harbour) end a **nymphaeum** (fountain and pool) and triumphal columns. It was and is a grand sight – a legacy of the Byzantine emperor Arcadius (AD 395–408).

Inset: Detail from the facade of the Temple of Hadrian (photo by Peter Ptschelinzew)

EPHESUS

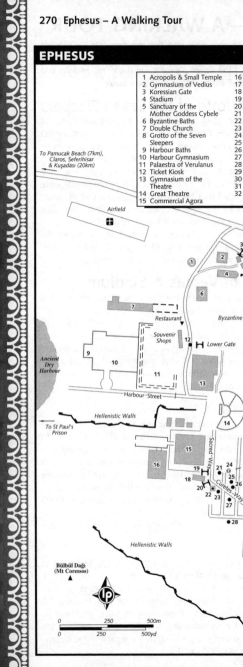

1	Acropolis & Small Temple
2	Gymnasium of Vedius
3	Koressian Gate
4	Stadium
5	Sanctuary of the Mother Goddess Cybele
6	Byzantine Baths
7	Double Church
8	Grotto of the Seven Sleepers
9	Harbour Baths
10	Harbour Gymnasium
11	Palaestra of Verulanus
12	Ticket Kiosk
13	Gymnasium of the Theatre
14	Great Theatre
15	Commercial Agora
16	Temple of Serapis
17	Round Monument
18	Library of Celsus
19	Gate of Augustus
20	Gate of Hadrian
21	Brothel
22	Tomb of Androclus
23	Octagon
24	Public Toilets
25	Temple of Hadrian
26	Baths of Skolastika
27	Shops & Mosaic
28	Terrace Houses
29	Fountain of Trajan
30	Gate of Hercules
31	Tomb of Memmius
32	Temple of Domitian & Museum of Inscriptions
33	Museum of Memmius
34	Prytaneum (Town Hall)
35	Odeum
36	Fountain of Pollio
37	Water Palace
38	Basilica & Bouleuterion
39	State Agora
40	6th Century BC Necropolis
41	Baths
42	Fountain
43	Magnesia Gate
44	Ticket Kiosk
45	Tomb of St Luke
46	Souvenir Shops
47	East Gymnasium
48	Tomb of Androcius

Airfield

To Pamucak Beach (7km),
Claros, Seferihisar
& Kuşadası (20km)

Dr-Sabri-Yayla Bul

To Selçuk

To Temple of Artemision
& Selçuk (3km)

Byzantine Walls

Restaurant

Souvenir
Shops

Lower Gate

Panayır Dağı
(Mt Pion)

Ancient
Dry
Harbour

Harbour Street

Hellenistic Walls

To St Paul's
Prison

Highway

Byzantine Walls

Hellenistic
Walls

Sacred Way

Curetes Way

Hellenistic Walls

Bülbül Dağı
(Mt Coressos)

To Meryemana (Virgin
Mary's House) (5km)

0   250   500m
0   250   500yd

Great Theatre

At the eastern end of Harbour St is the Great Theatre, skilfully reconstructed by the Romans between AD 41 and 117, which means that the riot of Demetrius the Silversmith (see the boxed text 'St Paul in Ephesus' earlier) took place in a theatre under reconstruction.

The first theatre here dates from the Hellenistic city of Lysimachus, and many features of the original building were incorporated into the Roman structure. Among these is the ingenious design of the *cavea* (seating area), capable of holding 25,000 people: each successive range of seating up from the stage is pitched more steeply than the one below it, thereby improving the view and acoustics for spectators in the upper seats. Among other modifications, the Romans enlarged the stage, pitched it towards the audience, and built a three-storey decorative stage wall behind it, further improving the acoustics.

The Great Theatre is still used for performances, although it was partly closed for restoration at the time of writing.

Behind the Great Theatre is Panayır Dağı, which bears a few traces of the **ruined city walls** of Lysimachus.

Sacred Way

From the theatre, walk south along the marble-paved Sacred Way, also called the Marble Way. Note the remains of the city's elaborate water and sewer systems beneath the paving stones, and the ruts made by wheeled vehicles (which were not permitted along Harbour St). The large, open space to the right (west) of the street, once surrounded by a colonnade and shops, was the **commercial agora** (3 BC) or marketplace, heart of Ephesus' business life.

On the left as you approach the end of the street is an elaborate building which some archaeologists call a **brothel** and others describe as a private house. Either way, its main hall contains a rich mosaic of the Four Seasons.

The Sacred Way ends at the **embolos**, with the Library of Celsus and the monumental Gate of Augustus to the right (west), and Curetes Way heading east up the slope.

Library of Celsus

Tiberius Julius Celsus Polemaeanus was the Roman governor of Asia Minor early in the 2nd century AD. In 114, after the governor's death, his son, Consul Tiberius Julius Aquila, erected this library in his father's honour, according to an inscription in Latin and Greek on the side of the front staircase. Celsus was buried under the western side of the library.

The library held 12,000 scrolls in niches around its walls. A 1m gap between the inner and outer walls protected the valuable books from extremes of temperature and humidity. Though it now stands alone, the library was originally built between other buildings, and architectural trickery was used to make it look bigger than it is: the base of the facade is convex, adding height to the central elements; and the central columns and capitals are larger than those at the ends.

Niches on the facade hold statues (the originals are in Vienna's Ephesus Museum) representing the Virtues: Arete (Goodness), Ennoia (Thought), Episteme (Knowledge) and Sophia (Wisdom). The library was restored with the aid of the Austrian Archaeological Institute.

As you leave the library, on the left is the **Gate of Augustus**, also called the Gate of Mazaeus & Mithridates, which leads into the 110m-square commercial agora where food and craft items were sold. The monumental gate, dedicated to the Emperor Augustus and members of his family, was apparently a favourite place for Roman ne'er-do-wells to relieve themselves, as a bit of ancient graffiti curses 'those who piss here'.

Curetes Way

As you head up Curetes Way, a passage on the left (north) leads to the **public toilets**. These posh premises were for men only; the women's

Top: The impressive facade of the Library of Celsus, which once held 12,000 valuable scrolls, is evidence of the prosperity of Ephesus during Roman times, before the harbour silted up.

Bottom: One of the beautiful friezes on the facade of the Temple of Hadrian

were elsewhere. The famous figure of Priapus (now in the Ephesus Müzesi in Selçuk) with the penis of most men's dreams was found in the nearby **well**, right next to the presumed brothel.

You can't miss the impressive Corinthian-style **Temple of Hadrian**, on the left, with beautiful friezes in the porch and a head of Medusa to keep out evil spirits. It was dedicated to Hadrian, Artemis and the people of Ephesus in AD 118, but greatly reconstructed in the 5th century. Across the street is a row of 10 shops from the same period, fronted by an elaborate 5th-century mosaic.

On the right side of Curetes Way across from the Temple of Hadrian, excavation and restoration work is still in progress on the **Yamaç Evleri** (Terrace Houses). These are usually closed to visitors although some of the finds can be seen in Ephesus Müzesi. Should you get the opportunity, be sure to see the rare **glass mosaic** in a niche off the atrium of one of the houses.

Further along Curetes Way, on the left, is the **Fountain of Trajan**. A huge statue of the emperor (AD 98–117) used to tower above the pool; only one foot now remains.

Curetes Way ends at the two-storey **Gate of Hercules**, constructed in the 4th century AD, with reliefs of Hercules on both main pillars.

To the right is a side street leading to a colossal temple dedicated to the Emperor Domitian (AD 81–96), part of which serves as a rarely accessible **Museum of Inscriptions**.

Up the hill on the left (east) are the very ruined remains of the **Prytaneum**, a municipal hall; and the **Temple of Hestia Boulaea**, in which the perpetual flame was guarded. Finally you come to the **odeum**, a small 1400-seat theatre dating from AD 150 and used for lectures, musical performances and meetings of the town council. Its lower seats of marble show something of the magnificence of the original.

To the east of the Odeum are more **baths** and, further east, the **East Gymnasium** and **Magnesia Gate**, of which virtually nothing remains.

Bottom: The well-preserved marble carving of Winged Victory on the Gate of Hercules at the end of Curetes Way

MARTIN MOOS

[Continued from page 268]

PAMUCAK
☎ 232

About 7km west of Selçuk (3km west of the highway junction with the Kuşadası and Seferihisar roads) lies Pamucak beach, a long, wide crescent of soft sand. As you approach the beach from Selçuk or Kuşadası, the signs are not very encouraging, with a dirt track cutting down to the sea opposite some half-built villas. However, persevere and you may be pleasantly surprised. The beach is crowded with free campers and Turkish families on summer weekends, but mostly deserted at other times, except for the weekend litter.

Places to Stay

The shady *Dereli Motel* (☎ *893 1204, fax 893 1203*) offers rooms with bath and shady camping facilities. It may be stretching it to compare the Dereli to a Thai beach resort, but when you're sitting on your verandah sipping a drink, this is the comparison that most readily comes to mind. Smaller cabins cost US$22 for two people, larger ones will set you back US$32. Some face onto a rose garden instead of the sea. The complex incorporates a restaurant, food shop and camping area – US$9 for a tent, free for caravans or camper vans.

Right beside the Dereli, the *Selçuk Belediyesi Halk Plajları* (☎ *852 3836*) is the municipal beach and camping ground but looks thoroughly miserable. You'll pay about US$6 for up to four people in a tent but it's only open in the summer months (from June to September).

If you must stay in a hotel, the four-star *Otel Tamsa* (☎ *892 1190, fax 892 2771, Çorak Mevkii*) has all the exterior charm of a military barracks, although the interior is comfortable enough at US$45/60 a single/double during the high season.

Getting There & Away

There are regular minibuses from Selçuk and Kuşadası in summer; at other times, if you are coming from Kuşadası, you may have to change to a Pamucak dolmuş in Selçuk, or get out at the Pamucak road and walk 3km. Be sure to find out when the last minibus departs from the beach as it may leave well before sunset.

ŞİRİNCE
☎ 232 • pop 800

Up in the hills 9km east of Selçuk, amid grapevines, peach and apple orchards, sits Şirince. The old-fashioned stone-and-stucco houses have red-tile roofs, and the villagers, who were moved here from Salonica and its vicinity during the exchange of populations in 1924, are ardent fruit farmers who also make interesting grape and apple wines. Locals regale you with the story that in Ottoman times, when it was populated mostly by Greeks, the village was called Çirkince (Ugliness), but that it was changed to Şirince (Pleasantness) shortly after they arrived. A century ago it was also much larger and more prosperous – the economic focus for seven monasteries in the hills around.

In recent years the village has become an 'authentic Turkish village' on the tour-bus circuit, with the result that the bazaar is filled with the usual souvenir shops. If a local woman invites you to inspect her 'antique house', you can be sure she'll have lace for sale. The less-visited corners of the village are still good for a stroll though, or you could take a walk among the nearby hillside vineyards and orchards. The best reason to come is to dine at the Artemis Şirince Şarapevi Restaurant.

Places to Stay & Eat

Şirince's pensions are quite pricey, usually with only three or four rooms. Expect to pay at least US$13 per person at the *Huzur Pansiyon* (☎ *898 3060*) or the *Şirin Pansiyon* (☎ *898 3167*).

The picturesque *Hotel Şirince Evleri* (☎/*fax 898 3099*) has two houses with lovely traditional sitting rooms and nicely decorated rooms for US$80 a double, including breakfast.

The minibus from Selçuk drops you at the centre of the village near the restaurants. *Köy Restaurant* and *Sultan Han Café* have the best shade and views, and specialise in village dishes like *mantı* (Turkish ravioli), *gözleme*, *yayık ayran* (churned yogurt and spring water) and *ev şarapı* (home-made wine).

The **Artemis Şirince Şarapevi Restaurant** is in the old Greek school perched overlooking the valley as you come into the village. It looks expensive but it isn't; mezes cost US$1.50 and main courses around US$4, and it sells bottles of apple, strawberry and cherry wine for US$6.

Getting There & Away
From 8 am to 7 pm hourly minibuses connect Selçuk and Şirince (US$0.70) in summer.

BELEVİ
About 9km out of Selçuk on the İzmir highway is the village of Belevi, and about 2km east of the village, just to the side of the İzmir-Aydın road, stands the **Belevi Mezar Anıtı** (Belevi Mausoleum), an ancient funerary monument resting on a base of about 30 square metres cut from the limestone bedrock. The roof was decorated with lion griffins (now in Selçuk's Ephesus Müzesi and in İzmir's Arkeoloji Müzesi), and the interior held a large sarcophagus with a carved effigy of its occupant; this, too, is now in the Selçuk museum. Archaeologists are not certain who built this great tomb; possible candidates include the Seleucid ruler Antiochus II Theos (261–46 BC), or Persian invaders a century or more earlier.

Just west of the mausoleum are scant remains of a tumulus, or burial mound, thought to date from the 4th century BC.

KUŞADASI
☎ 256 • pop 50,000

About 20km from Selçuk is Kuşadası, a seaside resort town so tacky it's almost good. Like Marmaris it becomes swollen out of all recognition throughout the summer with package holiday-makers from Europe.

Many cruise ships on the Aegean Islands circuit stop at Kuşadası so passengers can tour Ephesus and haggle for trinkets in the bazaar. The town centre is all shops and 'hello, one question, yes please!' sales pitches. The easy-going atmosphere which made it popular in the 1970s is long gone, even though a few businesses still hang on to serve the farmers, beekeepers and fishermen who make up an ever-dwindling portion of the population. On the other hand the nightlife has a lot to offer, and the city's taxi fleet includes a number of very cool bright yellow 1960s Chevrolet Impalas.

Kuşadası, which means 'Bird Island', gets its name from a small island now connected to the mainland by a causeway, called Güvercinada, or Güvercin Adası (Pigeon Island). It's recognisable by the small stone fort which is its most prominent feature.

Like Selçuk, Kuşadası makes a good base for excursions to the ancient cities of Ephesus, Priene, Miletus, and Didyma, to Altınkum Beach and Dilek Milli Parkı, and even inland to Afrodisias and Pamukkale.

History
The natural port here may have been in use for several centuries BC, and was probably known to the Byzantines, but modern Kuşadası's history begins in medieval times when Venetian and Genoese traders came here, calling it Scala Nuova. Two centuries after the Ottoman conquest in 1413, Öküz Mehmet Paşa, vizier and sometime grand vizier to sultans Ahmet I and Osman II, ordered the building of the Kaleiçi Mosque and Hamam, the city walls, and the caravanserai in order to improve the city's prospects as a trading port with Europe and Africa.

Useful for exporting agricultural goods, Kuşadası was also an important defensive port along the Ottoman Aegean coast. In 1834 the Güvercinada fortress was restored and improved. Kuşadası maintained its modest trade, farming and fishing economy and its quiet character until the tourism boom of the late 1980s turned it into the brash resort you see today.

Orientation
Kuşadası's central landmark is the Öküz Mehmet Paşa Kervansarayı, an Ottoman caravanserai which is now a hotel. It's 100m inland from the cruise-ship docks, at the intersection of the waterfront boulevard,

Atatürk Bulvarı, and the town's main street, the pedestrianised Barbaros Hayrettin Cadesi which cuts inland from the caravanserai.

Just beyond the PTT on the northern side of Barbaros Hayrettin Bulvarı, a passage leads to the Öküz Mehmet Paşa Camii and the Kaleiçi Hamamı. Further along at the stone tower, Barbaros Hayrettin Caddesi crosses Sağlık Caddesi and becomes Kahramanlar Caddesi, lined with shops and restaurants. Turn left onto Sağlık Caddesi to explore Kuşadası's market and the old Kaleiçi neighbourhood of narrow streets packed with restaurants and bars. Turn right

off Barbaros Hayrettin Caddesi to find raucous Barlar Sokak (Bars Street), and the hillside pensions overlooking the harbour.

The Hacı Hatice Hanım Camii (Hanım Camii for short) about 100m along Kahramanlar Caddesi is a convenient landmark.

The otogar and dolmuş station are over 1km east of the caravanserai on the bypass road.

Information

The tourist office (☎ 614 1103, fax 614 6295), on İskele Meydanı, is right near the wharf where the cruise ships dock, about

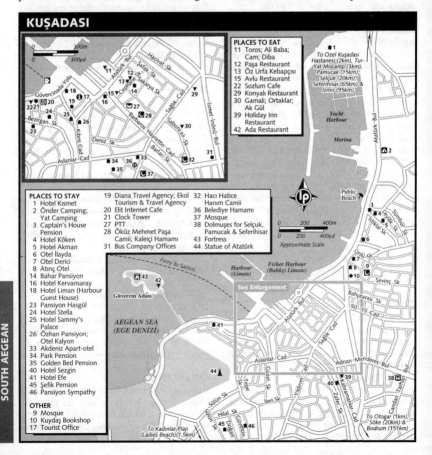

KUŞADASI

PLACES TO EAT
11 Toros; Ali Baba; Cam; Diba
12 Paşa Restaurant
13 Öz Urfa Kebapçısı
15 Avlu Restaurant
22 Sozlum Cafe
29 Konyalı Restaurant
30 Gamali; Ortaklar; Ak Gül
39 Holiday Inn Restaurant
42 Ada Restaurant

PLACES TO STAY
1 Hotel Kısmet
2 Önder Camping; Yat Camping
3 Captain's House Pension
4 Hotel Köken
5 Hotel Akman
6 Otel İlayda
7 Otel Derici
8 Atınç Otel
14 Bahar Pansiyon
16 Hotel Kervansaray
18 Hotel Liman (Harbour Guest House)
23 Pansiyon Hasgül
24 Hotel Stella
25 Hotel Sammy's Palace
26 Özhan Pansiyon; Otel Kalyon
33 Akdeniz Apart-otel
34 Park Pension
35 Golden Bed Pension
40 Hotel Sezgin
41 Hotel Efe
45 Şefik Pension
46 Pansiyon Sympathy

OTHER
9 Mosque
10 Kuydaş Bookshop
17 Tourist Office
19 Diana Travel Agency; Ekol Tourism & Travel Agency
20 Elit Internet Cafe
21 Clock Tower
27 PTT
28 Öküz Mehmet Paşa Camii; Kaleiçi Hamamı
31 Bus Company Offices
32 Hacı Hatice Hanım Camii
36 Belediye Hamamı
37 Mosque
38 Dolmuşes for Selçuk, Pamucak & Seferihisar
43 Fortress
44 Statue of Atatürk

100m west of the caravanserai. This office is usually open from 8 am to noon and 1.30 to 5.30 pm but sometimes keeps longer hours in summer.

There are several banks (Akbank, Garanti, Yapı Kredi and Ziraat) with ATMs on Barbaros Hayrettin Caddesi. The PTT on Barbaros Hayrettin Caddesi near the caravanserai changes money as well.

Kuydaş (☎ 614 1828), İsmet İnönü Bulvarı 8/B, has a good selection of English-language books on Turkey, as well as novels, newspapers and periodicals.

There are quite a few Internet cafes around but most are expensive. The Elit Internet Cafe next to the clock tower on Güvercinada Yolu charges a more reasonable US$1.60 per hour.

Kuşadası has an excellent private hospital, the Ozel Kuşadası Hastanesi ☎ 613 1616, at Turkmen Mahallesi, Anıt Sokak, with English-speaking doctors. The hospital is 3km north of the centre on the Selçuk road.

Beaches

You can swim from the rocky shores of Güvercin Adası and its causeway, but **Yılancı Burnu**, the peninsula less than 1km to the south, is more enticing. Alternatively, catch the *şehiriçi* (intracity) dolmuş to the northern beach near the yacht marina or further north, past the Kuştur holiday village, to the beach opposite the Tur-Yat Mocamp.

Kuşadası's most famous beach is **Kadınlar Plajı** (Ladies Beach), 2.5km south of town and served by dolmuş minibuses running along the shore road. Kadınlar Plajı is a small beach crowded by big hotels and woefully inadequate for the crowds in high summer, when the hotel pool is often more inviting. The coast south of Kadınlar Plajı has several more small beaches, each backed by ranks of big hotels.

Hamams

Kuşadası's hamams are the un-Turkish type, where men and women bathe at the same time, and charge an outrageous US$20 for the full works.

The Belediye Hamamı (☎ 614 1219) is up the hill behind the Akdeniz Apart-otel; take the street which goes along the left side of the hotel. It's open from 9 am to 9 pm. The Kaleiçi Hamamı (☎ 614 1292), just west of the Öküz Mehmet Paşa Camii, is open from 7 am to 10 pm.

Places to Stay

At last count Kuşadası had no less than 673 hotels, with still more being built. Rooms inevitably cost most in July and August, but drop by about 20% in June and September, and up to 50% in other months. Only a few places remain open from November to March.

The centre is well stocked with small, moderately priced hotels and cheap pensions which tend to get cheaper the further you head inland.

Most of the big package-holiday places are on the outskirts; for a longer stay check the prices in the package holiday brochures before booking.

Places to Stay – Budget

Camping North of the centre, about 1km inland from the yacht marina, are three decent camping areas. Best is *Önder Camping* (☎ *618 1590, fax 618 1517, Atatürk Bulvarı 84)*, open year-round, with lots of facilities: tennis, swimming pool, laundry and a good restaurant (open from March to October only).

A tent site is US$2, a two-person bungalow US$15. If the Önder is full, the adjoining *Yat Camping (☎ 618 1516)* takes the overflow.

The larger *Tur-Yat Mocamp (☎ 256-614 1087)*, several kilometres north of these, is open from mid-April or late May until mid- to late October. Across the road from a small beach, it charges US$8 for two people in a tent. Motel rooms cost US$36/42/50 a single/double/triple, including breakfast and dinner. There are a few restaurants and a petrol station close by.

Pensions Most cheaper pensions have pleasant rooms, sometimes with sinks, sometimes with a bathroom. Expect to pay between US$16 and US$24 a double in the high season.

Pension touts and owners wait at the otogar and ferry dock. Many of them are perfectly helpful, but there is a small number of sleazy characters, so it's good to size up a pension carefully before choosing to stay there.

Harbour & Kıbrıs Caddesi The first place as you get off the boat is also one of the best: **Hotel Liman** (☎ 614 7770, fax 614 6913, ⓔ hasandegirmenci@usa.net, Kıbrıs Caddesi, Buyral Sokak 4), also called the Harbour Guest House, is tucked just off the corner of Kıbrıs Caddesi and Güvercinada Yolu. Dorm beds cost US$5, doubles without air-con US$15, and singles/doubles with air-con US$17/30, including breakfast. It's an attractive building with a lift, tiled bathrooms and even suites for US$40. Manager Hasan Degirmenci, alias Mr Happy, is more fun than a barrel of monkeys. There's no-one better to show you Kuşadası's nightlife.

Hotel Sammy's Palace (☎ 612 2588, fax 612 9991, Kıbrıs Caddesi 14) is busy but gets very mixed reports – some people have a ball, others say they were overcharged. They push Fez Bus (a hop-on, hop-off bus service round the most popular parts of Turkey) tickets heavily, so take their travel advice with a pinch of salt. When the Fez Bus horde hits town, it gets noisy and a bit sleazy. Dorm beds are US$5, singles/doubles US$12/18, and laundry an exorbitant US$2.50/kg.

Across the street from Sammy's is **Özhan Pansiyon** (☎ 614 2932, Kıbrıs Caddesi 15). It's very central and normally quiet, with a nice roof terrace with bar. Doubles cost US$17. Next door is **Otel Kalyon** (☎ 614 3346), which charges the same and has a friendly English-speaking manager.

Above Kıbrıs Caddesi is Bezirgan Sokak. Past the Hotel Stella you'll find **Pansiyon Hasgül** (☎/fax 614 3641, Bezirgan Sokak 53), up steep steps in a quiet area but with tremendous sea views. The rooms are simple but clean and cost US$8/17. The family is friendly and you can use the Hotel Stella's swimming pool for free.

Central Kuşadası Tucked away in a quiet cul-de-sac, **Golden Bed Pension** (☎ 614 8707, fax 612 6667, ⓔ goldenbed_anzac@hotmail.com, Aslanlar Caddesi, Uğurlu 1 Çıkmazı 4) is at the top of a steep hill; they'll pay for a taxi to the pension. Run by a Turkish-Australian couple, this newly renovated pension is spotlessly clean and has a terrific rooftop terrace with a bar overlooking the town. It's a friendly, peaceful retreat which would suit solo women travellers. Dorm beds cost US$3, singles around US$8 and doubles around US$16 with breakfast. Internet access costs US$1.60 per hour.

On Aslanlar Caddesi itself is the **Park Pension** (☎ 614 3917, Aslanlar Caddesi 17), run by Welsh woman Helen Topcu, with simple rooms in a restored house set around a shady courtyard with orange trees, and a little bathing pool at the back. This Ottoman Greek house, over a century old, is a bit rickety but exudes character, especially compared with the concrete sprawl surrounding it. Doubles cost from US$8 to US$12 with breakfast. Mrs Topcu also runs a lively cafe.

Instead of walking towards the harbour from Hanım Camii you can cut up a block, past the end of Barlar Sokak, to **Hotel Sezgin** (☎ 614 4225, fax 614 6489, ⓔ sezgin@ispro.net.tr, Zafer Sokak 15). Dorm beds costs US$5, and rooms with shower US$8 per person. The Sezgin has lots of services for backpackers, including a laundry, movies in several languages and an Internet link-up for US$2 an hour.

Upper Kuşadası At the top of Aslanlar Caddesi, turn left into Güzel Sokak. At the end of the road, turn right into İleri Sokak. Continue along İleri Sokak, which rises steeply, until you come to a modern residential district on the left. Turn left down Güvercin Sokak for the **Pansiyon Sympathy** (☎ 614 4388, Güvercin Sokak 14), run by Güngür Gencer, a smiling dynamo of a woman who provides tasty cheap meals in a rooftop dining room as well as clean, cheap accommodation. Rates are from US$8/17 in summer, including breakfast.

One block further up the hill, **Şefik Pension** (☎ 614 4222, Doğan Sokak 11) has comparable rates, with good food and friendly family proprietors.

Places to Stay – Mid-Range

Mid-range hotels are scattered throughout town, with some inland from the yacht marina, some on Aslanlar Caddesi and Bezirgan Sokak, and many more along Atatürk Bulvarı and İstiklal Sokak.

Cephane (**jehp**-hah-neh) Sokak leads off Barbaros Hayrettin Caddesi opposite the caravanserai. *Bahar Pansiyon* (☎ *614 1191, fax 614 9359, Cephane Sokak 12*) is a reasonable choice. Rooms with air-con and bright bedcovers cost US$18/26 per person. The Bahar is closed from November to February.

The airy, two-star *Hotel Stella* (☎ *614 1632, fax 612 2406, Bezirgan Sokak 44*) has fabulous views of the town and the harbour. Rooms cost US$40/50, and there's a swimming pool.

Facing the sea, on Atatürk Bulvarı just less than 1km north of the caravanserai, are several convenient modern hotels. The three-star *Otel İlayda* (☎ *614 3807, fax 614 6766, Atatürk Bulvarı 46*) has rooms with bath (and many with sea-view balconies) for US$25/40 with breakfast. The nearby *Otel Derici* (☎ *614 8222, fax 614 8226, Atatürk Bulvarı 40*) also has three stars, and comfortable rooms (some with sea views) at rates of US$50 a double with breakfast. Right next door *Atınç Otel* (☎ *614 7608, fax 614 4967, Atatürk Bulvarı 38*) charges US$34/42 for its rooms.

Continue along the seafront and, about 1km north of the centre, you'll come to another group of moderately priced lodgings on İstiklal Sokak. *Captain's House Pension* (☎/*fax 614 4754, İstiklal Sokak 1*) is a bright little place decked out with pictures of yachts and nautical charts. There's also a small bathing pool, jokingly called the aquarium by staff. Rooms, some with balconies overlooking the sea, cost US$17/29. There's a bar and cafe on the ground floor.

Next along, the *Hotel Köken* (☎ *614 1460, fax 614 5723, İstiklal Sokak 5*) is the standard Turkish two-star: rooms with bath cost US$25.

The nearby two-star *Hotel Akman* (☎ *614 1501, İstiklal Sokak 13*) is tidy if soulless. It's open from mid-March to the end of October and is used by tour groups. Rooms, some with bathtubs, cost US$22/32, including breakfast.

Facing Güvercin Adası is the *Hotel Efe* (☎ *614 3660, fax 614 3662*), a waterfront place with balconies lined up to scoop the sunsets. Readers have enjoyed staying in rooms which are very reasonably priced at US$42 a double, including breakfast, but basically it's a tour group place and independent travellers will be lucky to get a bed.

Places to Stay – Top End

The *Hotel Kısmet* (☎ *614 2005, fax 614 4914, Akyar Mevkii*), just north of the yacht marina perched on a little peninsula, is the best place for a splurge. It's well run and has the feel of a private club. Indeed, there are no signs displaying its name – it gets enough custom by word of mouth. Rates are US$100/135/155 a single/double/triple, including breakfast.

It would be good to be able to recommend *Hotel Kervansaray* (☎ *614 4115, fax 614 2423*), also called Club Caravansérail, near the harbour, but the interior is spoiled by tourist shops, and the 'Turkish Nights' in the courtyard means music until midnight on most summer evenings (see Entertainment). The rate for pleasant small stone rooms is US$50/80, including breakfast.

The coast to the north and south of Kuşadası is crowded with huge, gleaming five-star hotels for the package-holiday trade. Rooms cost from US$90 to US$120 a double in summer.

South of the centre on Kadınlar Plajı are comfortable hotels priced from US$50 to US$100 a double. These include the four-star *İmbat Oteli* (☎ *614 2000, fax 614 4960*), and the much cheaper three-star *Martı Oteli* (☎ *614 3650, fax 614 4700*), an older place that offers a superb location and good value for money.

About 5km south of the centre beyond Kadınlar Plajı at Yavansu Mevkii, the five-star *Onura Hotel* (☎ *614 8505, fax 614 3727*) is perched on a cliff right above the sea, offering luxury rooms and full facilities. Next door is the similar *Fantasia Otel* (☎ *614 8600, fax 614 2765*).

SOUTH AEGEAN

Places to Eat

Kuşadası is fish and chips and 'full English breakfast' country. In summer, its restaurant prices are even higher than Selçuk's, which are already higher than İstanbul's but at least most places post prices prominently so you can make comparisons.

The cheapest food is in the low-budget pensions mentioned in Places to Stay – Budget earlier; ask about meals when you book a room. For other cheap eats, you usually have to search well inland and find places patronised mostly by locals.

On Güvercinada Yolu there are a couple of inexpensive cafes around the clock tower. The *Sozlum Cafe* has big gözleme for US$2 and seafood salads for US$4.

The restaurants on Sağlık Caddesi between Kahramanlar Caddesi and İsmet İnönü Bulvarı tend to be popular with Turks and so are cheaper than many others. Check prices at the *Konyalı*, beside the big Kalyon Restaurant, and nearby shopfront places.

Walk along Sabuncalı Sokak off Sağlık Caddesi to the Hotel Karasu and Gündoğdu Restaurant and turn left. The row of grills *Gamali*, *Ortaklar*, *Ak Gül* etc specialise in the regional favourite, çöp şiş, for around US$2.50 per portion.

For atmospheric cheap eats you could do worse than pop inside the castle on Güvercin Adası, where several small *eateries* sell döner kebap (roasted lamb slices), pide and köfte for prices only US$0.50 or so more than in town.

One pleasant surprise is the *Ada Restaurant*, on Güvercin Adası, which offers good food at low prices right on the water. Set meals cost around US$6. The *Holiday Inn Restaurant* on Karamanlar Caddesi is recommended by readers for its service; a Turkish main course costs around US$5.

On Kadınlar Plajı, *Chris & Nil's Roof Restaurant* is a popular American-run steakhouse with American-sized steaks for US$10, and great fish and chips as well. There's a complimentary bottle of wine on your first visit. It's on top of the Umut Bufe mini market, close to the Erkin Hotel.

There are many atmospheric places to eat in Kaleiçi, the old section behind the PTT.

On Cephane Sokak, the *Avlu Restaurant* has outdoor tables and low-ish prices for soups and stews. The *Paşa Restaurant* is a family-run establishment in the courtyard of an old house, with mezes around US$1 and a wide range of grills for US$5. Some evenings the cook comes out and plays an accordion. Another favourite is the nearby *Öz Urfa Kebapçısı*, on Cephane Sokak, which is strong on roast meats, with dishes from US$4 to US$5.

The town's prime dining location is on the waterfront by the harbour, but competition ensures that prices are about the same as those further inland. Just be careful to get the price on any seafood you order. A full fish dinner with wine at the *Toros*, *Ali Baba*, *Cam* or *Diba* is likely to cost from US$15 to US$25 per person.

Entertainment

Barlar Sokak (not to be confused with Barhar Sokak) went Irish in 2000, with *Molly Malone's*, *Kitty O'Shea's* and *O'Neills*. Unfortunately some of the bars didn't have the time or money to fully renovate after the line-dancing craze finished, leading to weird hybrids like the *Log Cabin Irish Bar* (which is actually one of the better places to go). Barlar Sokak sure ain't classy but with the right group of people it can be fun, if you can handle karaoke and cheesy pick-up lines.

There's a more interesting mix of clubs and bars on Sakarya Sokak in Kaleiçi, including the *Woodstock Rock Bar*, several Turkish music venues like the *Roman Bar* and the *Samata Bar*, and the city's best dance club *Ecstacy*.

Out on Güvercin Adası, the fort is often let to disco organisers. Even if the latest incarnation is not to your liking, the walk out to the island and back is pleasant. This is certainly the place to come for a sunset rakı (the local aniseed-flavoured spirit) or two.

If you're into organised entertainment, *Hotel Kervansaray* plays host to a Turkish night most evenings during summer. To watch the music and dancing without eating costs US$25; with a meal you're looking at US$45. Either way there's free booze.

Shopping

Kuşadası's bazaar offers the full range of Turkish souvenirs: leather clothing and accessories, onyx, meerschaum, copper, brass, carpets and jewellery. If you're heading on, save your shopping for later as almost anywhere else will be cheaper. If you must shop here, do it before or after the cruise ships are in port, as prices are even higher when the cruise-ship crowd is in town, and dealers are ruder.

Getting There & Away

Bus & Dolmuş In summer frequent şehir-içi (intracity) minibuses run from the otogar to the centre, and up and down the coast. Kadınlar Plajı minibuses head along the shore road to the beach. For either, the fare is US$0.40.

Kuşadası's otogar is situated at the southern end of Kahramanlar Caddesi on the bypass highway. Direct buses depart for several far-flung parts of the country, or you can change at İzmir. For Adnan Menderes airport (US$2.75, 1¼ hours, 80km), take an İzmir bus and ask to be dropped off at the airport.

For Selçuk, Pamucak and Seferihisar you needn't bother going to the otogar; instead you can pick up a minibus on Adnan Menderes Bulvarı. For Didyma, Priene and Miletus, change at Söke.

Several companies have ticket offices on İsmet İnönü Bulvarı. When you purchase a ticket, try to ascertain if it's really a direct service: your 'bus to Priene' may turn out to be a minibus to Söke, where you must change to another for Priene. Bus and minibus services to some major destinations are listed in the table below.

In summer, minibus drivers organise tours to Priene, Miletus and Didyma for about US$20 per person. The drivers at the otogar also run tours to Ephesus and Meryemana for about US$15 per person.

Boat You can walk into any travel agency in Kuşadası and purchase a ticket for a boat to Samos. You can go over for the day and return in the evening, or you can stay. Boats depart from Samos and Kuşadası at 8.30 am and 5 pm daily from April to October, with less frequent services in winter. The trip costs US$30 one way, US$35 same-day return, or US$55 for a return ticket valid for a year (not including US$8 tax when you leave Greece). Some agencies discount these tickets, so ask, and flash your student card if you have one. You must be at the harbour 45 minutes before sailing time for immigration formalities.

You can book through Ekol Tourism & Travel Agency (☎ 614 5591, fax 614 2644) at Buyral Sokak 9 and Diana Travel Agency (☎ 614 3859, fax 614 7295), at the harbour end of Kıbrıs Caddesi. These agencies also handle tickets for car ferries to Greece and Italy.

DİLEK PENINSULA

About 30km south of Kuşadası, the Dilek Peninsula juts westwards into the Aegean, almost touching the Greek island of Samos. West of the village of Güzelçamlı the land has been set aside as **Dilek Milli Parkı** (National Park), a nature reserve with some areas for day visitors; no camping is allowed. The mountain slopes here are clad in pines, the wildlife is abundant, the air is clean and the sun is bright.

Sevices from Kuşadası's Otogar

destination	fare (US$)	time (hr)	distance (km)	daily services
Bodrum	6	2	151	frequent buses in summer
İzmir	3.20	1½	95	buses every 20 minutes in summer
Pamukkale	6.60	3	220	some direct buses, or change at Denizli
Seferihisar	2	1½	65	a few minibuses
Selçuk	1.30	½	20	frequent minibuses in summer
Söke	1	½	20	frequent minibuses

The park is open from 8 am to 6 pm daily for US$0.50 per person, US$2.50 per car.

Approaching Dilek from Kuşadası or Söke, the road passes through the villages of Davutlar and **Güzelçamlı**. The latter, once a sleepy village, is now backed by thousands of holiday villas. Among the ranks of flats are several small two- and three-star hotels. There's a good pension here, the *Ecer* (☎ 256-646 1017, fax 646 2737), in a big garden near the main road. Doubles cost US$20, not including dinner on the roof terrace. The English-speaking owner organises horse riding through the park.

It's 2km from Güzelçamlı to the national park entrance, then another 1km to **İçmeler Köyü**, a protected cove with a small but cigarette-butt-strewn beach, lounge chairs and umbrellas, a restaurant and picnic area.

About 3km beyond İçmeler Köyü an unpaved road heads 1km downhill on the right to **Aydınlık Beach**, a quieter pebble-and-sand strand about 800m long with surf, backed by pines, and served by a small cafe.

Less than 1km further along is a jandarma post. Another 1km brings you to **Kavaklı Burun**, another sand-and-pebble surf beach 500m to the right of the road. As at Aydınlık, there's a second entrance to the beach at the far end, another 1km along. West of that is a military zone where entry is forbidden. It's 8.5km back to the park entrance.

Getting There & Away

You can walk the 3km from Güzelçamlı to İçmeler Köyü in about 30 minutes. Otherwise, without your own transport you must rely on dolmuşes from Kuşadası and Söke (45 minutes, US$1.25). They run from 8 am to dusk in summer and usually go all the way to the far end of Kavaklı Burun. Don't leave the park too long after mid-afternoon, as the later dolmuşes fill up quickly.

PRIENE, MILETUS & DIDYMA

Ephesus may be the *creme-de-la-creme* of the Aegean archaeological sites but south of Kuşadası are the ruins of three other very ancient and important settlements well worth a day trip. Priene occupies a dramatic position overlooking the plain of the Büyük Men-

deres (Meander) River; Miletus preserves a great theatre; and Didyma's Temple of Apollo is among the world's most impressive religious structures. These sites are also much less visited than Ephesus. You might consider seeing them in the reverse order (Didyma, Miletus, Priene) to catch the sunset at Priene.

Beyond Didyma is Altınkum Beach, one of Turkey's busiest beaches, good for an after-ruins swim off season but usually festooned with cigarette butts.

Priene
☎ 256

Priene was important around 300 BC when the League of Ionian Cities held congresses and festivals here. Otherwise, it was smaller and less important than nearby Miletus, which means that its Hellenistic buildings were not buried by Roman buildings.

Priene was a planned town, with its streets laid out in a grid, a system which originated

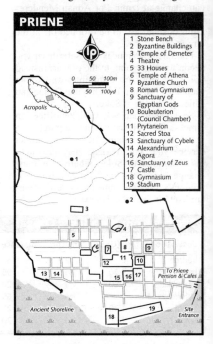

PRIENE

1	Stone Bench
2	Byzantine Buildings
3	Temple of Demeter
4	Theatre
5	33 Houses
6	Temple of Athena
7	Byzantine Church
8	Roman Gymnasium
9	Sanctuary of Egyptian Gods
10	Bouleuterion (Council Chamber)
11	Prytaneion
12	Sacred Stoa
13	Sanctuary of Cybele
14	Alexandrium
15	Agora
16	Sanctuary of Zeus
17	Castle
18	Gymnasium
19	Stadium

0   50   100m
0   50   100yd

Acropolis

Ancient Shoreline

To Priene Pension & Cafes

Site Entrance

in Miletus. Of the buildings that remain, the **bouleuterion** (city council meeting place) is in very good condition. The five standing columns of the **Temple of Athena**, designed by Pythius of Halicarnassus and looked upon as the epitome of an Ionian temple, form Priene's most familiar landmark; the view from here is superb. Take a look at the **theatre** with its finely carved front seats for VIPs, the ruins of a **Byzantine church**, the **gymnasium** and **stadium**.

Although the ruins are good there's a strong chance you'll remember Priene's magnificent setting the most, with steep Mt Mykale rising behind it, and the broad flood plain of the Büyük Menderes River spread out at its feet.

Priene is open from 8 am to 7.30 pm daily in summer (from 8.30 am to 5.30 pm in winter); admission costs US$2.

The well-signed *Priene Pension (☎ 547 1725)*, run by Nevin Çataltuğ and her son, offers 11 pleasant pine-ceilinged rooms set around a rose and orange-tree garden. A twin room with breakfast costs US$16, or you can camp for US$4.

Near the site entrance is a shady rest spot with water cascading from an old aqueduct next to the *Şelale Restaurant*, where you can get a cool drink or hot tea, make a telephone call or have a meal. A *teahouse* opposite competes fiercely with the Şelale for the drinks traffic. There are several smaller, cheaper restaurants as well.

Miletus

Miletus is 22km south of Priene. Its **Great Theatre** rises to greet you as you approach the flood plain's southern boundary and turn left (east), riding through swampy cotton fields to reach the site. It's the most significant reminder of a once-grand city, which was an important commercial and governmental centre from about 700 BC to AD 700. After that time the harbour filled with silt, and Miletus' commerce dwindled. The 15,000-seat theatre was originally a Hellenistic building, but the Romans reconstructed it extensively during the 1st century. It's still in good condition and exciting to explore.

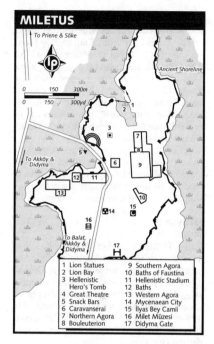

MILETUS

1	Lion Statues	9	Southern Agora
2	Lion Bay	10	Baths of Faustina
3	Hellenistic	11	Hellenistic Stadium
	Hero's Tomb	12	Baths
4	Great Theatre	13	Western Agora
5	Snack Bars	14	Mycenaean City
6	Caravanserai	15	İlyas Bey Camii
7	Northern Agora	16	Milet Müzesi
8	Bouleuterion	17	Didyma Gate

Climb to the top of the theatre where the ramparts of a later Byzantine castle provide a viewing platform for several groups of ruins scattered around. Look left and you'll see what remains of the **harbour**, called Lion Bay after the stone statues of lions which guarded it. Look right and you'll see the **stadium**; the northern, western and southern **agoras**; the vast **Baths of Faustina**, constructed on the order of Emperor Marcus Aurelius' wife; and a **bouleuterion** between the northern and southern agoras.

Some of the site is underwater for much of the year and although that makes it hard to walk around, it also makes it more picturesque. Note that the northern gateway to the southern agora is now one of the prized exhibits in Berlin's Pergamum Museum.

To the south of the main ruins is the **İlyas Bey Camii** (1404), dating from a period after the Seljuks but before the Ottomans when this region was ruled by the Turkish emirs of Menteşe. The doorway and mihrab are well worth noticing, and you'll probably have this neglected corner of Miletus to yourself.

The site is open from 8 am to 7.30 pm in summer (to 5.30 pm in winter) for US$2. The **Milet Müzesi** (Miletus Museum), about 1km south of the theatre, is open from 8.30 am to 12.30 pm, and 1.30 to 5.30 pm and costs US$1, but it's hardly worth it. Across the road from the Great Theatre are a couple of small *snack bars* where you can get sandwiches and drinks.

A Seljuk caravanserai, 100m south of the ticket booth, has been restored and converted to shops, although it's been unoccupied for so long one wonders whether any shopkeepers will ever move in now.

Didyma
☎ 256

Called Didim in Turkish, this was the site of a stupendous temple to Apollo, occupied by an oracle as important as the one at Delphi. The ruins you see today belong to a temple started in the late 4th century. This replaced the original temple, which was destroyed in 494 BC by the Persians, and a later construction that was completed under Alexander the Great.

The Temple of Apollo was never finished, though its oracle and priests were hard at work until, after 1400 years of soothsaying, Christianity became the state religion of the Byzantines and brought an end to pagan practices.

Ancient Didyma was never a real town. Only the priests who specialised in oracular temple management lived here. Originally from Delphi, they had a pretty cushy life, sitting on the considerable temple treasure.

When you approach Didyma today, you come into the town of Yenihisar, which has grown phenomenally in the last few years to engulf both Altınkum, the beach to the south, and Didim, formerly the Ottoman-Greek town of Yeronda. It's a popular place with tour groups, and carpet shops gush forth touts at the approach of each new bus.

Temple of Apollo The temple porch held 120 huge columns with richly carved bases vaguely reminiscent of Luxor in Egypt. Be-

hind the porch is a great doorway where oracular poems were written and presented to petitioners. Beyond the doorway is the cella (court), where the oracle sat and prophesied after drinking from the sacred spring. We can only speculate on what that water contained to make the prophesies possible. The cella is reached today by covered ramps on both sides of the porch.

The temple grounds contain fragments of rich decoration, including a photogenic head of Medusa (she of the snakes for hair). There used to be a road lined with statues which led to a small harbour but after standing unmoved for 23 centuries the statues were taken to the British Museum in 1858.

Admission is from 9 am to 7 pm in summer (8 am to 5.30 pm in winter) and costs US$2.

Places to Stay & Eat There are two good pensions beside the temple. The 10-room *Oracle Pension* (☎ 811 0270) is perched above the temple precinct to the south, with close-up views of the marble pile. If you don't stay here (US$15/30/40 for single/double/triple for rooms with bath), at least come for a drink on the terrace for the view.

Just around the corner from the temple, on the Altınkum road, *Medusa House* (☎ 811 0063) is a pretty restored stone village house with lovely gardens. Inviting rooms cost US$22 a double, including breakfast. Although it's only steps from the temple, it has no temple view.

The vast *restaurants* across the road from the temple entrance are geared up for the tourist trade, with prices to match.

Getting There & Away
If you start early in the morning from Kuşadası or Selçuk, you can get to Priene, Miletus and Didyma by dolmuş and return to your base at night. If you have a car, you can see all three sites, have a swim at Altınkum Beach and be back by mid-afternoon.

It is possible but difficult to do the trip yourself, as dolmuş services can be infrequent. Catch a dolmuş to Söke from Kuşadası (20km, US$1) or Selçuk (40km, US$2), then another onward to Priene (US$0.75).

When you've finished at Priene, wait for a passing dolmuş (US$1) or hitch across the flat flood plain to Miletus (22km). Take any dolmuş saying 'Balat' (the village next to Miletus), 'Akköy' (a larger village beyond Balat) or 'Yenihisar'.

From Miletus, fairly frequent dolmuşes head south to Akköy (4.5km, US$1.25) where you can pick up a minibus to Söke or Didyma, 14km beyond Akköy. There's not much traffic about, so it may take some time to hitch to Akköy. South of Akköy there's more traffic, most of it heading on past Didyma to Altınkum Beach.

Alternatively, minibus drivers at the Selçuk otogar organise tours to Priene, Miletus, Didyma and Altınkum Beach during summer. The tour should take a whole day, with the minibus departing from the bus station between 8.30 and 9.30 am, spending an hour at Priene, 1½ hours at Miletus, 2½ hours at Didyma and its museum, and about 1½ hours at Altınkum Beach before returning to Selçuk between 5.30 and 6.30 pm. Often the drivers hope to squeeze in two trips by halving these times, which is not really enough. Some travellers recommend doing the trip in reverse order, to enjoy the sunset at Priene.

The cost is between US$18 and US$25, depending on how many people there are. Lunch isn't usually included in this price. It's a good idea to reserve your seat in advance.

SÖKE
☎ 256

Söke is a mostly cheerless modern town, livened by its market every Wednesday. You may be forced to come here to change buses as you travel around the coast.

If you arrive in Söke too late to move on, the modern *Hotel Akalın* (☎ 512 7793), opposite the otogar, has singles/doubles for US$12/20, including breakfast.

The big otogar is divided into separate bus and dolmuş sections. From the bus side of the station, Söke municipal buses depart for İzmir (US$3) every hour on the half-hour until 7.30 pm. Others head east to Denizli and Pamukkale, south to Bodrum and to Muğla (for Marmaris).

Services from the dolmuş side of the station include the following:

destination	fare (US$)	distance (km)	services
Aydın	1.60	55	every 15 mins
Balat	1	35	every 30 mins
Davutlar	1	13	every 30 mins
Didyma	1.60	56	every 30 mins
Güllübahçe	0.60	14	every 15 mins
Güzelçamlı	1	22	every 30 mins
Kuşadası	1	20	every 15 mins
Milas	2.50	82	every 30 mins

HERAKLEIA (LATMOS)
☎ 252

About 30km south of Söke the highway skirts the southern shore of the huge Bafa Gölü (Bafa Lake). This was once a gulf of the Aegean Sea, but became a lake as the sea retreated. At the south-eastern end of Bafa Gölü is a village called Çamiçi, from which a paved road on the left is marked for Kapıkırı, 10km to the north, though it's actually less than 9km; watch carefully for the sign, which is easily missed.

At the end of the wonderful, twisting, rock-dominated road, you'll come to the ruins of Herakleia ad Latmos in and around the village of Kapıkırı. Behind the village looms the dramatic, five-peaked Beşparmak Dağı, the Five-Fingered Mountain (1500m). This was the ancient Mt Latmos.

History

Latmos is famous because of Endymion, the legendary shepherd boy. The story relates how the handsome Endymion was asleep on Mt Latmos when Selene, the moon goddess, fell in love with him. Myths differ as to what happened next. It seems that Endymion slept forever, and Selene (also called Diana) got to come down and sleep with him every night. She also saw to the care of his flocks, while he slept on. And that's about it.

Ringed by mountains, this area was one of refuge for Christian hermits during the Arab invasions of the 8th century AD, hence the ruined churches and monasteries. The monks reputedly thought Endymion a Christian saint because they admired his powers of self-denial, though catatonia seems a more appropriate word.

Things to See

As you enter the village in summer, you may be asked to pay an admission fee of US$1.25. Bear right at the ticket booth, pass the Pelikan Restaurant, and you'll come to the Agora Restaurant.

A path behind the Agora car park leads westwards up to the **Temple of Athena**, on a promontory overlooking the lake. Also from the car park, paths lead eastwards to the **agora**, the **bouleuterion** and then several hundred metres through stone-walled pastures and across a valley to the unrestored **theatre**. The badly ruined theatre is oddly sited, with no spectacular view. Its most interesting feature is the several rows of seats and flights of steps cut into the rock. You will also see many remnants of the **city walls** dating from 300 BC.

Much of the fun of a visit to Latmos is to observe Turkish village life. Beehives dot the fields, and camomile flowers (*papatya*) grow wild by the roadsides in spring and summer. During the day women sit by the road, making lace which they then attempt to sell to passers-by. In the evenings villagers herd their animals along the main street.

When you're finished in the village, walk down the road to the lake, past the **Endymion Temple** built partly into the rock, the ruins of a **Byzantine castle** and the city's **necropolis**.

Down at the lakeside, near the ruins of a Byzantine church, are several small fish restaurants (if they've caught any that day), including the **Zeybek**, **Kaya** and **Selene**. All offer camping and boat tours of the lake. There's a small beach of white coarse sand. Just offshore is an island which can sometimes be reached from the shore on foot as the level of the lake falls. Around its base are foundations of ancient buildings.

Places to Stay & Eat

Of the several pensions in the village the best is certainly the 14-room **Agora Pansiyon** (*☎/fax 543 5445*), which charges US$15 for a waterless double and has clean shared bathrooms. Included in the price is a village breakfast of fresh eggs, local butter and honey (no packets). Three wooden bungalows are also available for the same price. The pension and its restaurant are surrounded by flowers, and the owners have lots of information on the ruins and birds of the area.

The 10-room **Pelikan Pansiyon** (*☎ 543 5158*) has more basic rooms but with lake views and showers for US$12. Its **restaurant** also offers panoramic lake views.

When it comes to **camping**, the less well-kept lakeside sites are preferable because of their position.

Getting There & Away

Minibuses from Söke or Milas will drop you at the road junction but you'll have to hike or hitch along the side road unless you manage to catch one of the very infrequent dolmuşes.

MİLAS

☎ 252 • pop 35,000

Milas is a very old town. As Mylasa, it was capital of the Kingdom of Caria, except during the period when Mausolus ruled the kingdom from Halicarnassus (present-day Bodrum). Today it's a fairly sleepy agricultural town, with many homes where carpets are handwoven. Don't be put off by what you see from the otogar – the town is actually quite attractive, and makes a good break from the bright lights of the coastal resorts. On Tuesdays there is an excellent local market held here.

Since Milas is actually closer to the new Bodrum international airport than Bodrum itself, you could stay the night in Milas if you arrive late in high season when Bodrum is likely to be full.

Orientation

Approaching Milas from Söke, you pass the new otogar on 19 Mayıs Bulvarı 1km before coming to Labranda Bulvarı to the left. To the right İnönü Caddesi is marked for 'Şehir Merkezi' (City Centre). It's another 1km to the centre of town at the Milas Belediye Parkı.

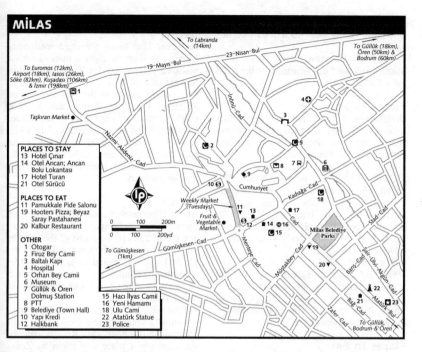

MİLAS

To Labranda (14km)
To Güllük (18km), Ören (50km) & Bodrum (60km)
23-Nisan-Bul
19-Mayıs-Bul
To Euromos (12km), Airport (18km), Iasos (26km), Söke (82km), Kuşadası (106km) & İzmir (198km)
Taşkıran Market
İnönü-Cad
Nazmi-Akdeniz-Cad
Cumhuriyet
Kadıağa-Cad
Stad-Cad
Milas Belediye Parkı
Weekly Market (Tuesdays)
Fruit & Vegetable Market
Menteşe-Cad
Muğlabey-Cad
Gümüşkesen-Cad
To Gümüşkesen (1km)
Zafer-Cad
Bağ-Cad
Barış-Cad
Şair-Ulvi-Akgün-Cad
Atatürk-Bul
To Güllük, Bodrum & Ören

PLACES TO STAY
13 Hotel Çınar
14 Otel Arıcan; Arıcan Bolu Lokantası
17 Hotel Turan
21 Otel Sürücü

PLACES TO EAT
11 Pamukkale Pide Salonu
19 Hooters Pizza; Beyaz Saray Pastahanesi
20 Kalbur Restaurant

OTHER
1 Otogar
2 Firuz Bey Camii
3 Baltalı Kapı
4 Hospital
5 Orhan Bey Camii
6 Museum
7 Güllük & Ören Dolmuş Station
8 PTT
9 Belediye (Town Hall)
10 Yapı Kredi
12 Halkbank
15 Hacı İlyas Camii
16 Yeni Hamamı
18 Ulu Cami
22 Atatürk Statue
23 Police

0   100   200m
0   100   200yd

Things to See & Do

Coming into town from the otogar along İnönü Caddesi, watch for signs pointing to the right for the *belediye* (town hall) and, opposite, turn left for the **Baltalı Kapı** (Gate with an Axe). Cross a small bridge and look left to see the well-preserved Roman gate, which has marble posts and lintel and Corinthian capitals. The eponymous double-headed axe is carved into the keystone on the northern side.

Return to the road and continue south past the forgettable **museum**, bearing right at the traffic roundabout next to the shady Milas Belediye Parkı, in the centre of which is a marble scale model of the Gümüşkesen monumental tomb.

Continue straight on for three blocks, turn right, then turn again at Gümüşkesen Caddesi to reach the tomb, 1.4km from the roundabout on a hill west of the centre.

The **Gümüşkesen** (meaning either 'That Which cuts Silver' or, construed as Gümüş-kese, 'Silver Purse') is a Roman monumental tomb dating from the 1st century, thought to have been modelled on the great Tomb of Mausolus at Halicarnassus. As in the Mausoleum, Corinthian columns here support a pyramidal roof, beneath which is a tomb chamber, which you can enter. A hole in the platform floor allowed devotees to pour libations into the tomb to quench the dead soul's thirst.

The tomb enclosure, in a little park, is usually open. If he's around, the guardian will charge you the US$1.25 admission fee.

You might also want to see some of Milas' fine mosques, especially the **Ulu Cami** (1378) and **Orhan Bey Camii** (1330), built when Milas was the capital of the Turkish principality of Menteşe. The larger, more impressive **Firuz Bey Camii** (1394) was built shortly after Menteşe became part of the new and growing Ottoman Empire.

Like Muğla, Milas has kept some of its older houses, and especially along Atatürk

SOUTH AEGEAN

Bulvarı there is some very impressive **architecture** dating back to the start of this century.

The **Yeni Hamamı**, across Hacı İlyas Sokak from the Otel Arıcan, fills the need for a Turkish bath.

Places to Stay

Otel Arıcan (☎ 512 1215), next to the Hacı İlyas Camii (and, alas, its minaret), has cheap rooms for US$8 a double without bath, or US$12 with shower.

A better option is *Hotel Çınar (☎ 512 5525, fax 512 2102, Kadıağa Caddesi 52)*, which offers much more congenial accommodation, with a lobby one flight up. Singles/doubles with bath are US$12/18, including breakfast. *Hotel Turan (☎ 512 1342, Cumhuriyet Caddesi 26)* has comparable rooms for US$6.50/12.

The *Otel Sürücü (☎ 512 4001, fax 512 4000)*, on Atatürk Bulvarı opposite the statue of Atatürk, is slightly more comfortable, with bigger rooms than the Çınar or Turan, for US$12/18. The lobby is imposing and some rooms have TV.

Places to Eat

The *Kalbur Restaurant* on Atatürk Bulvarı is quite a stylish little bistro. A dinner of lamb şiş kebap, salad and a drink costs about US$6 per person. Otherwise the town's culinary offerings don't run much beyond pide. The market area has several pidecis, including the locally esteemed *Pamukkale Pide Salonu*, where a pide and soft drink sell for US$1.75. Otel Arıcan has its own *Arıcan Bolu Lokantası* with soups, stews and kebaps. *Hooters Pizza* on the main intersection is the most happening place in town for the youth of Milas, with fairly ordinary pizzas for US$2, but it at least it stays open late and plays music. *Beyaz Saray Pastahanesi* next door is a more traditional option. The *Milas Belediye Parkı* across the road has a pleasant tea garden.

Getting There & Away

The new otogar is on 19 Mayıs Bulvarı, 1km before Labranda Bulvarı. There are frequent dolmuş services from Söke (US2.50, 82km).

AROUND MİLAS

Beçina

Just over 1km along the Ören road from Milas, a road on the right is marked with a black-on-yellow sign for **Beçina Byzantine fortress** on a rocky outcrop, which was later pressed into service by the Turkish emirs of Menteşe. It's open from 8 am to dusk (US$1), but there's not a lot to see inside. Less than 500m on are remnants of the 14th-century Menteşe settlement, including the Kızıl Han caravanserai, Orhan Bey Camii, and the Ahmet Gazi tomb and medrese (religious seminary).

Euromos

About 12km north-west of Milas, 1km from the village of Selimiye, is the picturesque **Temple of Zeus** in the midst of the ancient city of Euromos. Of the town, only the temple and a few scattered ruins remain. The Corinthian columns set in an olive grove seem too good to be true, like a Hollywood set of a classical scene.

First settled in the 6th century BC, Euromos held a sanctuary to a local deity. With the coming of Greek, then Roman, culture, the local god's place was taken by Zeus. Euromos reached the height of its prosperity between 200 BC and AD 200. Emperor Hadrian, who built so many monuments in Anatolia, is thought to have also built this one. The several unfluted columns suggest that the work was never finished.

If you're interested in ruins, you can clamber up the slopes to find other bits of the town. Look up behind the ticket booth at the big stone fortification wall on the hillside. Climb up through the olive groves, go over the wall, and continue at the same altitude (the path dips a bit, which is OK, but don't climb higher). After 100m you'll cross another stone wall and find yourself on flat ground which was the stage of the ancient **theatre**. It's badly ruined now, with olive trees growing among the few remaining rows of seats. Besides the theatre, the town's **agora** is down by the highway, with only a few toppled column drums to mark it.

The site is open from 8.30 am to 5.30 pm (7 pm in summer); admission costs US$1.25.

Aegean Turkey offers charming seaside resorts (top; Bodrum), memorable coastal panoramas (bottom left; Bodrum Peninsula) and picturesque old houses (bottom right; Şirince), as well as some less obvious attractions, such as these storks on a Selçuk rooftop (middle right).

STUART WASSERMAN

DIANA MAYFIELD

Ephesus is the largest and best-preserved classical city in Turkey. Highlights of the site include the Library of Celsus (top), with its elegant two-storey facade, and the suitably impressive Great Theatre (bottom), capable of holding 25,000 people.

There are no services except soft drinks sales in summer only.

To get here, take the Milas to Söke bus or dolmuş and ask to get out at the ruins. Alternatively, take a dolmuş from Milas to Kıyıkışlacık, get out at the road junction for Iasos and walk the short distance north along the highway until you see the Euromos ruins on the right.

Kıyıkışlacık (Iasos)
☎ 252

About 4km south-west of Euromos (8km north-west of Milas) is a road on the right (west) marked for Kıyıkışlacık (Iasos), about 18km further on. The Turkish name means 'Little Barracks on the Coast', but Iasos was in fact a fine city set on its dramatic perch several centuries before Christ. Earliest settlement may date from the Old Bronze Age, and may have included a civilisation much like the Minoan one on Crete.

Today Iasos is a sleepy Aegean fishing village set amid the tumbled ruins of an ancient city. As you approach it, past a cluster of visually unfortunate half-built concrete villas, the road forks. The right fork leads to the **Balıkpazarı Iasos Müzesi** holding the village's most interesting ruin, a monumental Roman tomb; the left fork leads to the port, up over the hill and along the coast.

Iasos was built on a hill at the tip of a peninsula framed by two picture-perfect bays. Excavations have revealed the city's bouleuterion and agora, a gymnasium, a basilica, a Roman temple of Artemis Astias (AD 190) and numerous other buildings besides the prominent Byzantine fortress.

Today the hill above the port is covered with ruins, including a walled acropolis-fortress (admission is US$1.25 if there's anyone to collect it). Olive groves surround the town and reach nearly to its centre. South-west of the hill on the bay is a small yacht harbour. Fishing boats crowd the quay, and a handful of small pensions and restaurants cater to travellers who want to get away from it all for a few days. Have çipura (gilt-head bream), if it's in season, at *Iasos Deniz Restaurant*, right down on the water, or at the less interesting *Yıldız*, behind it.

Climb the hill behind the restaurants to find the delightful *Cengiz* (☎ 537 7181) and *Zeytin* (☎ 537 7008) pensions, both clean and modern with simple rooms for US$20 a double, including breakfast. Their biggest pluses are the views down over Iasos to the sea.

In summer boats come to Iasos from Güllük to the south. Otherwise you can get there by infrequent dolmuş from Milas (US$1.60).

Labranda
Labranda was a sanctuary to Zeus Stratius, controlled for a long time by Milas. There may have been an oracle here; it's certainly known that festivals and Olympic games were held at the site. Set into a steep hillside at 600m elevation in an area from which the ancient city of Mylasa and the modern town of Milas took their water supplies, Labranda today is surrounded by fragrant pine forests peopled by beekeepers. Late in the season (October) you can see their tents pitched in cool groves as they go about their business of extracting the honey and rendering the wax from the honeycombs. It's a beautiful site, worth seeing partly because so few people come here.

Labranda was a holy place, where worship of a god was going on by the 7th century BC, and perhaps long before. The site seems to have been abandoned around AD 1000. Today a caretaker will welcome you, have you sign the guest book and show you around the site; he speaks only Turkish, with a few words of other languages, but the site is well marked. Admission costs US$1.25.

The great **Temple of Zeus** honours the god's warlike aspect (Stratius, or Labrayndus, meaning 'Axe-Bearing'). Two men's religious gathering places, the **First Andron** and the **Second Andron**, are in surprisingly good condition, as is a large 4th-century **tomb** of fine construction, and other buildings. The ruins, excavated by a Swedish team in the early part of this century, are interesting, but it's the site itself, with its spectacular view over the valley, which is most impressive.

The junction for the road to Labranda is just north-west of Milas on the road to Söke.

It's 14km to the site: the first 6km are tarmac and easy to travel on, the remaining 8km are along a rough but scenic road deep in dust which winds tortuously up into the mountains. In rainy weather (October to April) the road turns to a slurry of mud that may require a 4WD. The village of Kargıcak is 8km along the way, and though you may be able to get a dolmuş from Milas to Kargıcak, that still leaves 6km to walk. Hitching is possible but not at all reliable, particularly later in the day. A taxi from Milas costs about US$40 for the round trip but drivers are reluctant to subject their cars to the punishment even for such a sizeable sum.

ÖREN
☎ 252

Ören has hung on to the tranquil atmosphere which was once common to villages along the Turkish coasts. The village is in two parts. About 1.5km inland from the beach is the centre, with its PTT, shops, and old Ottoman houses with geranium-filled gardens set amid the ruins of the ancient city of **Keramos** (or Ceramus), which flourished from the 6th century BC until at least the 3rd century AD. There is a Yapı Kredi ATM at the power station's front gate, about 4km from town on the road to Milas.

The 1km-long sand-and-pebble **beach** is the centre of visitor interest and draws Turkish holiday-makers from the big cities who come for stays of a week, two weeks or more. If you take the time to travel the 50km from Milas to the village, you too will want to linger more than a night.

Hamile Dağ (meaning, literally, 'Pregnant Woman Mountain') stretches behind the town. With a bit of imagination the jagged western hump is the face, the swollen middle hump is the belly, and the long ridge closest to town makes up the legs. Paragliders launch from the 'knees', topped with radio towers.

Places to Stay & Eat
Although the number of pensions is steadily increasing, so far it's all fairly low-key, with not a high-rise on the horizon. If you plan to stay in high summer, come early in the morning to find a room, or call ahead and reserve one.

Among cheap lodgings, try **Karya Oteli** (☎ 532 2115), **Otel Göksu** (☎ 532 2112) or **Hotel Marçalı** (☎ 532 2063), with double rooms for US$15. **Hayat Pansiyon** (☎ 532 2992), inland from the eastern end of the beach is run by the cheerful Celal Baş. All charge around US$8 per person. Many other houses have rooms for rent, so if all these are full a bit of asking around will turn up something.

For more comfort there's **Hotel Nur** (☎ 532 2839) across from the dolmuş stop, with smallish but clean rooms (US$12.50/25 for a single/double with shower) and a friendly English-speaking manager. **Keramos Motel** (same telephone as the Hotel Nur) next door costs the same and has a rooftop terrace with sea views. **Hotel Salihağa** (☎ 532 2138) has similar rates.

Best of the lot in terms of comfort is the new three-star **Hotel Alnata** (☎ 532 2813, fax 532 2381), at the western end of the beach, where modern rooms come with air-con, marble floors, marble bathtubs and sea views. Some rooms have wheelchair access. There's a pool and the hotel can arrange all sorts of water sports for you, but none of this comes cheap; expect to pay US$36/48 for rooms with half-board.

Ören also has a few restaurants, including the waterfront **Café Palmiye** which dishes up burgers for US$1 and **Kerme Restaurant** with şiş kebap for US$2. The **Hotel Nur** has a cheap cafe serving pide for US$1.60.

There's also a small shop for putting together a picnic.

Getting There & Away
A timetabled minibus service runs from Milas to Ören and back roughly every 45 minutes from 8 am to 6 pm. If you ask, the driver may drop you right at the beach instead of in the village. The journey takes an hour and costs US$1.60.

GÜLLÜK
☎ 252

About 18km south-west of Milas is Güllük, a mining port and minor seaside resort town which retains a semblance of authentic daily life. Güllük is spread along three bays. The road brings you and a steady stream of bauxite ore trucks to the central bay and the centre of town, where the ore is loaded onto waiting ships. Fishing boats are moored south of the ore dock, and beyond them more fishing craft are built in the traditional way at simple open-air boat yards. Though there's a yacht mooring area, the harbour is mostly for working vessels.

Güllük is a working town with a sideline in tourism, which is its main attraction. There's sufficient accommodation and other services but none of the hassle encountered in hyper-resorts like Kuşadası, Marmaris or Bodrum. If you'd like a few days in a traditional Turkish seaside town with swimming and ruins nearby, Güllük should do nicely.

Orientation & Information
The bay to the south of the central one is monopolised by a Türk Petrol company resort; to the right, the northern bay is lined with posh summer villas. The northern bay is best for swimming, and there's a small beach here. On the main square just inland from the central bay there's a small tourist office (☎ 522 2776) in the belediye building, the PTT and a Yapı Kredi ATM.

Day trips by boat to Iasos and nearby beaches can be arranged from the restaurants along the waterfront. To hire a whole boat to Iasos is likely to cost about US$25.

Places to Stay & Eat
Nicest of the pensions is **Passala Motel** (☎ 522 2822, fax 522 2026), on the northern bay, far from the rumbling ore-laden lorries. Owner Selçuk Orkun runs a relaxed little pension set around a garden, with plenty of old books and magazines to read. Singles/doubles cost US$10/13 with breakfast. Another good option is **Kemer** (☎ 522 2143) on the hillside above the harbour. Clean, simple rooms cost US$12 to US$16. There's a pleasant front garden and good views from the terrace. **Kordon Motel** (☎ 522 2356), attached to the harbourside restaurant of the same name, has basic sea-view rooms with balconies for US$4 per person.

Of the mid-range hotels, the three-star **Ikont Hotel** (☎ 522 2427, fax 522 2426) is way out on the hillside amid the holiday homes on the southern side of the bay.

Two four-star hotels dominate the northern side of the bay. Rooms at the **Corinthia Labranda Hotel** (☎ 522 2911, fax 522 2009) cost US$60/80, including breakfast. Just down the hill the newer **Corinthia Güllük Hotel** (☎ 522 3746, fax 522 3756) has rooms costing the same as the Labranda, and a fine rooftop bar with views over the bay. Both have swimming pools.

A few Ottoman-era buildings survive in the centre, including the fine house now inhabited by Tekel, the national alcohol and tobacco company, and, north of it, a stone *han* (caravanserai) and warehouse, the latter fronted with restaurants, including **Çiçek**, **Kücük Ev**, **Kordon** and **Eski Depo**, all of which post prices, serve alcohol, have good sunset water views and can arrange boat excursions. **Nazar** is popular with yachters and has good meals for around US$7 (one meze, kebap and salad).

Just inland on the market square (the market begins at dawn on Friday) is the cheaper **Barış Pide Pizza Kebap Salonu**.

Getting There & Away
Dolmuşes run to Güllük from Milas (US$2), and also from the village of Koru, on the highway a few kilometres north of the Güllük turn-off.

BODRUM
☎ 252 • pop 30,000
Bodrum owes its fame to a man long dead and a building long disappeared. It is, however, the South Aegean's most picturesque resort, with a yacht harbour and a port for ferries to the Greek island of Kos.

The man long dead is King Mausolus, and the building is his tomb, the Mausoleum, but Bodrum has many other attractions. Most striking is the Castle of St Peter in the middle of town, guarding twin bays now busy with yachts. Palm-lined streets ring the bays, and white sugar-cube houses, now joined by ranks of villas, crowd the hillside. Yachting, boating, swimming, snorkelling and scuba diving are prime Bodrum activities. Daytime diversions include boat or minibus trips to nearby beaches and villages, or over to the Greek island of Kos.

At night, Bodrum's famous discos throb, boom and blare. As a former provincial governor was quoted in the newspaper as asking, 'If (visitors) want peace and quiet, why do they come to Bodrum?'. Come in spring or autumn and Bodrum reverts to a pleasant, relatively low-key resort.

The local economy is now dedicated to tourism, though winter brings a bounteous citrus crop (especially tangerines). A few sponge-fishing boats survive as well.

History

Following the Persian invasion, Caria was ruled by a satrap named Mausolus (circa 376–353 BC), who moved the capital here from Mylasa and called this town Halicarnassus. After the satrap's death, his wife undertook construction of the monumental tomb which Mausolus had planned for himself. The Mausoleum, an enormous white-marble tomb topped by a stepped pyramid, came to be considered one of the Seven Wonders of the World. It stood relatively intact for almost 19 centuries, until it was broken up by the crusaders and the pieces used as building material in 1522.

Bodrum's other claim to fame comes from Herodotus (circa 485–425 BC), the 'Father of History', who was born here. Herodotus was the first person to write a comprehensive world history; all later historians of Western civilisation are indebted to him.

Orientation

The road to Bodrum winds through pine forests, finally cresting a hill to reveal a panorama of the town with its striking crusader castle.

The otogar is several hundred metres inland from the sea, on Cevat Şakir Caddesi, the main street into the centre of town. Walk down from the otogar towards the castle, passing the fruit and vegetable market, and you'll come to a small white mosque called the Adliye Camii (Courthouse Mosque) or Yeni Cami. Turn right, and you'll be head-

ing west on Neyzen Tevfik Caddesi towards the Yat Limanı (Yacht Marina), passing various restaurants and the quieter pensions. If you turn left at the Adliye Camii and go through the bazaar, then walk along Doktor Alim Bey Caddesi, which later becomes Cumhuriyet Caddesi, you reach the noisier hotels and pensions. Lodging places continue all the way around the bay, then along the shore of another bay further on.

Go straight on from the Adliye Camii towards the castle and you'll be walking along Kale Caddesi, the tourist axis of Bodrum, lined with boutiques selling clothing, carpets, souvenirs and trinkets. At the end of Kale Caddesi, beneath the castle walls, is the main plaza, Oniki Eylül Meydanı (12 September Square), also called İskele Meydanı (Dock Square). Here you'll find the tourist office, customs office, teahouses and, along the wharf, day-excursion boats. The ferry company ticket offices are further along on the pier.

Information

The informationless tourist office (☎ 316 1091, fax 316 7694) is on Oniki Eylül (İskele) Meydanı. Opening hours are flexible, to say the least.

The Neşe-i Muhabbet (Happy Chat) Internet Cafe on Türkkuyusu Sokak charges US$1.60, as does the Palmiye Internet Cafe on Neyzen Tevfik Caddesi.

There are several laundries near the marina, catering for yachters, including the Neyzen Laundry on Neyzen Tevfik Caddesi. To wash and dry a full load costs US$4.

Castle of St Peter

When Tamerlane invaded Anatolia in 1402, throwing the nascent Ottoman Empire temporarily off balance, the Knights Hospitaller or Knights of St John of Jerusalem based on Rhodes took the opportunity to capture Bodrum. They built the Castle of St Peter, which defended Bodrum (not always successfully) until the end of WWI.

The castle now holds Bodrum's excellent **Museum of Underwater Archaeology**. Opening hours are from 8.30 am to 5 pm with an hour off for lunch between noon and 1 pm daily except Monday. Admission is an exorbitant US$5.50; students pay half price. The Glass-Shipwreck exhibit is open between 10 to 11 am and from 2 to 4 pm Monday to Friday only, for an additional US$2.50. The Carian Princess Exhibit is open the same hours and also costs US$2.50.

Signs are in Turkish and English. The occasional maps of the castle and the directional signs are not always clear or helpful.

Head up the stone ramp into the castle past crusader **coats of arms** carved in marble and mounted on the stone walls. Keep an eye out for bits of marble taken from the

ancient Mausoleum. The ramp leads to the castle's main court, centred on an aged, ivy-covered mulberry tree. To the left are **exhibits of amphorae** and other artefacts dating from the 14th century BC recovered from the waters of south-western Turkey. At a small stall, **artisans** demonstrate techniques used centuries ago. The courtyard cafe, amid displays of Greek and Roman statuary, provides a shady resting place for those who have climbed the stone towers.

The chapel contains a full-sized reconstruction of the stern half of a 7th-century eastern **Roman ship** discovered off Yassıada

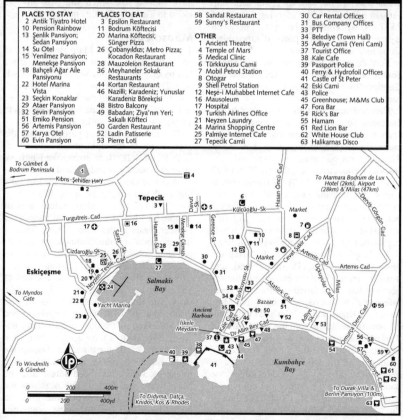

BODRUM

PLACES TO STAY	PLACES TO EAT		OTHER	
2 Antik Tiyatro Hotel	3 Epsilon Restaurant	58 Sandal Restaurant	1 Ancient Theatre	30 Car Rental Offices
10 Pension Rainbow	11 Bodrum Köftecisi	59 Sunny's Restaurant	4 Temple of Mars	31 Bus Company Offices
13 Şenlik Pansiyon;	20 Marina Köftecisi;		5 Medical Clinic	33 PTT
Sedan Pansiyon	Sünger Pizza		6 Türkkuyusu Camii	34 Belediye (Town Hall)
14 Su Otel	26 Çobanyıldızı; Metro Pizza;		7 Mobil Petrol Station	35 Adliye Camii (Yeni Cami)
15 Yenilmez Pansiyon;	Kocadon Restaurant		8 Otogar	37 Tourist Office
Menekşe Pansiyon	28 Mauzoleion Restaurant		9 Shell Petrol Station	38 Kale Cafe
18 Bahçeli Ağar Aile	36 Meyhaneler Sokak		12 Neşe-i Muhabbet Internet Cafe	39 Passport Police
Pansiyonu	Restaurants		16 Mausoleum	40 Ferry & Hydrofoil Offices
22 Hotel Marina	44 Kortan Restaurant		17 Hospital	41 Castle of St Peter
Vista	46 Nazilli; Karadeniz; Yunuslar		19 Turkish Airlines Office	42 Eski Cami
23 Seçkin Konaklar	Karadeniz Börekçisi		21 Neyzen Laundry	43 Police
29 Ataer Pansiyon	48 Bistro Balcony		24 Marina Shopping Centre	45 Greenhouse; M&Ms Club
32 Sevin Pansiyon	49 Babadan; Ziya'nın Yeri;		25 Palmiye Internet Cafe	51 Fora Bar
51 Emiko Pension	Sakallı Köfteci		27 Tepecik Camii	54 Rick's Bar
56 Artemis Pansiyon	50 Garden Restaurant			55 Hamam
57 Karya Otel	52 Ladin Patisserie			61 Red Lion Bar
60 Evin Pansiyon	53 Pierre Loti			62 White House Club
				63 Halikarnas Disco

To Gümbet & Bodrum Peninsula

Kıbrıs-Şehitler Hwy

To Marmara Bodrum de Lux Hotel (2km), Airport (28km) & Milas (47km)

Tepecik

Turgutreis Cad

Külcüoğlu-Sk

Market

Cizdaroğlu-Sk

Market

Eskiçeşme

Salmakis Bay

To Myndos Gate

Yacht Marina

Ancient Harbour

İskele Meydanı

Bazaar

To Windmills & Gümbet

Kumbahçe Bay

To Durak Villa & Berlin Pansiyon (100m)

To Didyma, Datça, Knidos, Kos & Rhodes

0   200   400m
0   200   400yd

SOUTH AEGEAN

and excavated by a University of Pennsylvania team between 1961 and 1964. Visitors can walk the decks, stand at the helm, look below decks at the cargo of wine, and peek into the galley where the cook prepared meals for the crew.

Follow the path on the left side of the chapel to ascend to the towers past flocks of pigeons, roosters and peacocks. Up the ramp is the **Glass-Shipwreck exhibit**. As you enter, look for the castle-like dovecote on the castle wall beyond.

Discovered by a sponge diver in 1973 and excavated from 1977 to 1979 by Professor George Bass of Texas A&M University and his international team of marine archaeologists, the 16m-long, 5m-wide ship sank in AD 1025 while carrying a cargo of 25 tons of commercial glass between Byzantine and Fatimid ports. It's the oldest shipwreck ever discovered.

Further up in the castle are the **Snake Tower**, with an amphora exhibit, and the **German Tower**, decked out in medieval European style.

Descend past the Ottoman toilets to the **Gatineau Tower** and the dungeons beneath. Over the inner gate is the inscription 'Inde Deus abest' (Where God does not exist). The dungeon was used as a place of confinement and torture by the Knights of St John from 1513 to 1523. A PT Barnumesque sign warns that the exhibits of torture implements might not be suitable for children, but most video-hardened visitors will find the display of dummies and a tape of groaning sounds amusing rather than disturbing.

The **English Tower** was built during the reign of King Henry IV of England, and bears his arms above the entrance to the uppermost hall, now fitted out as a medieval refectory. The standards of the Grand Masters of the Knights of St John and their Turkish adversaries hang from the walls. Suits of Turkish chain mail and authentic crusader graffiti carved into the stones (especially prominent in the window niches) serve as decoration. The long wooden tables are handy for taking a breather and enjoying a glass of wine (at US$1 it's cheaper than in the town below) while listening to recordings of *Carmina Burana*, lute music, or other pseudo-medieval strains.

Within the **French Tower**, the highest point in the castle, are the remains and sarcophagus of Queen Ada, a Carian princess whose intact tomb was discovered by Turkish archaeologists in 1989. The princess, who died sometime between 360 and 325 BC aged about 40, was of the Hecatomnid dynasty, probably the sister of Satrap Mausolus and the wife of Idreus. She was buried with a gold crown, necklace, bracelets, rings, and an exquisite wreath of gold myrtle leaves. Using modern reconstruction techniques, experts at Manchester University modelled what the princess' face might have looked like when she was alive; a video in Turkish explains their work.

Mausoleum

Though most of the Mausoleum is long gone, the site is still worth visiting. It's a few blocks inland from Neyzen Tevfik Caddesi. Turn right near the little white Tepecik Camii on the shore of the western bay, then left onto Hamam Sokak, which leads up to Turgutreis Caddesi, following the signs.

The site has pleasant gardens, with the excavations to the right and a covered arcade to the left. Here archaeologists have arranged models, drawings and translations of documents to give you an idea of why this tomb was among the Seven Wonders of the World. Exhibits also include bits of sculpted marble found at the site, a model of Halicarnassus at the time of King Mausolus, a model of the Mausoleum and its precincts, plus various diagrams and plans.

A description written in 1581 and supposedly taken from an eyewitness account of 1522 tells the alarming, if barely credible, story. The Knights Hospitaller from Rhodes discovered the Mausoleum, largely buried and preserved by the dust of ages. They uncovered it, admired it for a while, then went back to the castle for the night. During the night, pirates broke in and stole the tomb treasures, which had been safe while the Mausoleum was buried. The next day the knights returned and broke the tomb to pieces for use as building stone. Some bits were pulverised to make lime for mortar which was used to repair their castle in anticipation of an attack by Süleyman the Magnificent. They knew they would lose the battle and have to abandon the castle, but saw the effort as a holding action. So the Mausoleum was supposedly sacrificed to the honour of a crusader military order. In reality, earlier earthquakes had probably shattered it long before the Knights set foot in Turkey.

The arcade contains a copy of the famous frieze mainly recovered from the castle walls; the original is now in the British Museum in London, UK. The four original fragments on display were discovered more recently.

Of the actual remains, there's little to impress: a few pre-Mausolean stairways and tomb chambers, the Mausolean drainage system, the entry to Mausolus' tomb chamber, a few bits of precinct wall and some large, fluted marble column drums.

The site is open from 8 am to noon and 1 to 5 pm daily except Monday. Admission costs US$2.50. Most information is written in English and Turkish, with some in French.

Ancient Theatre

The theatre is cut into the rock of the hillside behind town on the Gümbet road, but lies next to the busy main road and is fenced off.

Boat Trips

Dozens of yachts are moored along Neyzen Tevfik Caddesi on the western bay, and most have sales agents who will try and cajole you into taking a day trip. Most boat excursions depart at 10 or 11 am, return at 4.30 or 5 pm and cost US$12.

Typically, you sail to **Karaada** (Black Island) south of Bodrum, where hot springs issue in a strong current from a cave. Swimmers rub the orange mud from the springs on their bodies, hoping for some aesthetic improvement. After a 30-minute stop at Karaada, the boat makes for the coarse sand-and-pebble beach at **Ortakent Yalısı**, west of Bodrum. The lovely cove is backed with beachfront restaurants, small pensions and camping areas, but there are big hotels nearby as well.

After Ortakent, the boat sails to the Aquarium, a small cove deserted except for other excursion boats, for its last stop. The water is beautifully clear, and the idea is that you'll see lots of fish, although the boating and swimming activity usually scares them away.

Special Events

The Bodrum Festival is held annually during the first week in September. Accommodation may be especially scarce then.

Places to Stay

In high summer, especially at weekends, Bodrum can fill up with holiday-makers. Try to arrive early in the day to find a room. The tourist office may be able to help you find a room if space is tight. If you're planning to stay a week or so, especially if you're thinking of a hotel rather than a pension, check the package holiday brochures before leaving home since they may offer a cheaper deal than you'll get in the resort itself.

Places to Stay – Budget

The narrow streets north of the western bay harbour have pleasant family run pensions which tend to be quieter than those on the eastern bay because they're further from the Halikarnas Disco. Pensions charge from US$18 to US$25 for a double in high summer (July to mid-September). Off season, prices drop, and the breakfast which costs extra in season may be included in the price.

Some of the smaller villages on the peninsula, such as Bitez Yalısı and Ortakent Yalısı, have camp sites. There are more on the peninsula's north shore.

Western Bay Türkkuyusu Sokak, with its tongue-twister name, starts just north of the Adliye Camii and goes north past several good, cheap, convenient pensions, mostly with shady courtyards.

Şenlik Pansiyon (☎ 316 6382, Türkkuyusu Sokak 115), is just off the street, with cosy doubles for US$12 including breakfast. There's a kitchen on the roof which offers fine views of Bodrum. Behind it (down the same narrow alley – watch for potholes when coming back in the dark) is the friendly, family-run *Sedan Pansiyon* (☎ *316 0355, Türkkuyusu 121*). The Sedan's courtyard, shaded by grapevines heavy with fruit in August, connects two buildings. In the newer one, double rooms with shower cost US$24; in the older building, waterless doubles are US$16.

Signs on Türkkuyusu Sokak point to the right to Gencel Çıkmazı, a narrow alley harbouring the passable *Pension Rainbow* (☎ *316 5170*), which has a nice shady terrace but annoying little signs everywhere telling you what you can and can't do. Singles/doubles cost US$8/17.

Close to the seafront, *Sevin Pansiyon* (☎ *316 7682, Türkkuyusu Caddesi, Gencel Çıkmazı 12*) is the least inviting, its basic rooms overpriced at US$30 a double.

Menekşe Çıkmazı is a narrow alley which begins between Neyzen Tevfik Caddesi 84 and 86. At its very end are two nearly identical plain, quiet, modern pensions, *Yenilmez* (☎ *316 2520*) at No 30, and *Menekşe* (☎ *316 5890*) at No 34. Both have doubles with showers for US$17. During the low season, breakfast is included. They're set around picturesque gardens, and the Menekşe in particular has lots of cats.

Ataer Pansiyon (☎ *316 5357, Neyzen Tevfik 102*) is just east of the Tepecik Camii, back from the street, with clean, simple rooms for US$8/17.

Set back from Neyzen Tevfik Caddesi at the end of a passage beside the Turkish Airlines Office is the friendly, family-run *Bahçeli Ağar Aile Pansiyonu* (☎ *316 1648*). There is a kitchen that guests can use. Doubles/triples/quads cost US$17/25/30 with breakfast. There are bathrooms on every floor.

Eastern Bay *Emiko Pension* (☎/*fax 316 5560, Uslu Sokak 11*) is just off Atatürk Caddesi. Run by a Japanese woman, the eight rooms in this peaceful haven are almost frighteningly clean. Rooms cost US$20.

If you want to be in the midst of the nightlife, look on Rasathane Sokak, a narrow alley beginning between Cumhuriyet Caddesi 147 and 149, uphill from the Ha-

likarnas Disco. *Durak Villa* (☎ *316 1564*) has doubles for only US$10; the neighbouring *Berlin Pansiyon* (☎ *316 2524*) is similarly priced. The nearby *Evin* (☎ *316 1312*) is swathed from top to bottom in bougainvillea, but isn't open year-round.

Places to Stay – Mid-Range

Western Bay Best is the charming *Su Otel* (☎ *316 6906, fax 316 7391,* e *suotel@ superonline.com, 1201 Sokak*), at the end of a cul-de-sac and an oasis of quiet and charm. Decorated with local crafts and an abundance of bougainvillea, rooms overlook a courtyard with a small central swimming pool. Rooms cost US$35/60, buffet breakfast included. With only 30 beds, it's often full, so it's best to make a reservation if you can. Follow the street opposite the Tepecik Camii, turn right at the 'T' intersection, and walk several hundred metres following the signs.

The cheerful *Seçkin Konaklar* (☎ *316 1351, fax 316 3336, Neyzen Tevfik Caddesi 246*), facing the marina, has multi-bed apartments sleeping up to six people, as well as some normal bedrooms set around a central pool. It's often busy with tour groups, so ring ahead to be on the safe side. Rooms cost from US$50/70.

Eastern Bay East along Cumhuriyet Caddesi are a couple of similar places facing the narrow beach. *Artemis Pansiyon* (☎ *316 2530, fax 316 2907, Cumhuriyet Caddesi 117*) has rooms with air-con for US$25/32. There's a cafe right in front.

A few steps east, *Karya Otel* (☎ *316 1535, fax 316 4814, Cumhuriyet Caddesi 127*) charges US$40 a double. Its front rooms are double-glazed against noise, and have ceiling fans and TVs with satellite channels; there's also a popular cafe-bar at the front.

Places to Stay – Top End

The four-star *Hotel Marina Vista* (☎ *313 0356, fax 316 2347, Neyzen Tevfik Caddesi 226*) faces the marina and boasts lots of marble, two pools and many other services. Singles/doubles are US$83/110, including breakfast.

Antik Tiyatro Hotel (☎ 316 6053, fax 316 0825, Kıbrıs Şehitler Highway, **e** theatre hot@superonline.com) is, as the name suggests, close to the amphitheatre. Set around a swimming pool perched overlooking the town, it's run by two escapees from İstanbul. Elegant doubles cost US$120, and the food is highly recommended.

If you want the five-star treatment, *Marmara Bodrum de Lux* (☎ 313 8130, fax 316 1642, Milas Yolu) is on a hillside outside town on the way to Milas. The hotel has won acclaim for its architecture. Doubles cost US$260.

Places to Eat
You'll have no trouble finding places to eat, but because many of the restaurants are seasonal, with inexperienced part-time staff, food and service are often mediocre. In July and August, prices are double those of İstanbul, but at least they're usually available for inspection before you sit down. As ever, check the price before ordering fish.

Restaurants open and close all the time in Bodrum. Those described in the following sections are mostly dependable long-established ones.

Places to Eat – Budget
During the low season you should have no problem finding cheap eats. You can buy a *dönerli sandviç* (sandwich with roast lamb) for less than US$2 at a streetside *büfe* (snack bar).

In July and August, the cheapest food is at simple local eateries well inland, without menus in English and German. Most places don't serve alcohol.

On Türkkuyusu Sokak the *Bodrum Köftecisi* has a nice little upstairs terrace and a friendly owner who produces a tiny handheld fan on hot days. Köfte and salad costs US$2.50, beers US$1.30.

In the grid of small market streets just east of the Adliye Camii are several restaurants which serve reasonable döner kebap and pizza. *Babadan* and *Ziya'nın Yeri* are patronised by locals as well as foreigners, and serve plates of döner for about US$3, beer for US$1.50. Around the corner from

Üsküdarlı by the Garanti Bankası is the *Sakallı Köfteci*, serving full meals of grilled lamb meatballs, salad, bread and a drink for US$4, but no booze.

Just east of the bazaar is Hilmi Uran Meydanı, called Kilise Meydanı (Church Square) by locals because it once had an Orthodox church on its eastern side. Here the *Nazilli* and *Karadeniz* both serve pide (US$3 to US$4), pizzas and kebaps.

For cheap breakfast or lunch, try *Yunuslar Karadeniz Börekçisi*, just east of Karadeniz Restaurant at the eastern edge of Kilise Meydanı on Taşlık Sokak. Peynirli börek costs US$1.50 a serving in the morning. There's a grander branch of this börekçi on Dr Alim Bey Caddesi.

For a sweet, try *lokma*, the traditional Aegean fritters, light balls of deep-fried dough dipped in syrup and sold in a paper cone for less than US$1. *Ladin Patisserie* at Cumhuriyet 75–77 serves them as well as böreks, pastries, puddings, fruit cups and other light fare.

Inland along Cevat Şakir Caddesi are several little *grill shops* where locals eat; some open for lunch only. Food for picnics is available at the *fruit market* just south of Çarşı Sokak and the Shell station, and in the shops behind the market.

Places to Eat – Mid-Range
Meyhaneler Sokak Walk from the Adliye Camii along Kale Caddesi towards İskele Meydanı and turn left just after the Tütünbank into Meyhaneler Sokak (Taverna Street), a narrow alley shaded by foliage, crowded with long rows of wooden tables, and cooled by ceiling fans. On summer evenings the mixed crowd of locals and foreigners is jolly without being raucous. The half-dozen restaurants, *Hades*, *Erkal*, *No 7 Orhan*, *Ibo*, *Ayaz*, *Farketmez*, all serve alcohol and a varied menu of Turkish and continental dishes. Look at a few menus, find a seat, meet your neighbours, and get into the scene. The bill for a long dinner with drinks might be from US$12 to US$18, perhaps more if you have fish. There may well be live music to keep you company.

SOUTH AEGEAN

Western Bay Neyzen Tevfik Caddesi has several good places, all serving alcohol. *Mauzoleion* is a modest but long-established place with a simple indoor dining room (used in winter), and a seaside open-air dining area across the street. Meat dishes are priced from US$4 to US$6, and the fish, though more expensive, is usually good.

Çobanyıldızı (☎ 316 7060, Neyzen Tevfik Caddesi 164), across from the marina, has streetside tables and an interior dining room in an old stone commercial building. Turkish carpets add colour, and bits of seafaring equipment provide visual interest. Start with a plate of mixed mezes for US$4 and go on to grilled meat or fish (US$4 to US$10).

Metro Pizza offers good Italian-style pizzas for around US$4 and cheerful, willing service.

Across from the Marina shopping centre are two justly popular places side by side. *Marina Köftecisi* offers authentic Turkish food for reasonable prices; salads for US$1, İnegol köfte US$2. *Sünger Pizza* offers good pastas for US$3, large pizzas for US$5 and large beers for US$1.25.

Eastern Bay Adliye Sokak runs inland off Cumhuriyet Caddesi opposite a break in the buildings which allows access to the sea. *Pierre Loti (Adliye Sokak 5)* in an old stone house, has a pretty courtyard and set-price French-style table d'hote three-course meals from US$8 to US$35. A la carte, main course steak and chicken dishes cost US$18 to US$22.

Inland on Rasathane Sokak and set around a nice courtyard, *Sunny's Restaurant (☎ 316 0716)* has a Turkish and Continental menu on which most main courses (chicken Kiev, Mexican beef) cost US$8; vegetarian plates are US$1 less.

The *Sandal Restaurant* on Atatürk Caddesi is a long-running Thai restaurant, with reasonably authentic decor and highly authentic chefs (they're Thai). It has set menus from US$10 to US$20 featuring a wide range of spicy salads and fiery curries – you can set the chilli level when you order. There are also Chinese dishes on offer.

Places to Eat – Top End
The restaurants along Dr Alim Bey Caddesi have pleasant seaside dining areas but can be very pricey. In high summer, a full meal with drinks would cost US$25 to US$30 per person. In May, June, September and October when the restaurants are competing for custom, you can do better on price.

Worth looking at are *Bistro Balcony*, with its wonderful display of fish, *Kortan Restaurant* in an old stone house, and the cheaper *Garden* which serves Turkish staples like İskender kebap for perhaps US$2 more than you'd normally pay.

Kocadon Restaurant (☎ 316 3705, Neyzen Tevfik Caddesi 160), is the place for a romantic dinner. Sheltered from the street by atmospheric old stone houses, a quiet courtyard is filled with soft music and lighting. Try the revived Ottoman dishes, such as *hünkar beğendi* (grilled şiş kebap over buttery aubergine puree). Dinner for two with a bottle of wine should cost around US$25 or US$30 per person. It's open daily in summer from 8 pm to midnight.

Epsilon Restaurant (☎ 313 2964, Keleş Çıkmazı 5) is on a laneway off Turgutreis Caddesi. This elegant courtyard restaurant offers Turco-European cuisine, from *tekke kebap* (shin of lamb on a bed of aubergine puree) for US$8 to chicken fillet with pistachios for US$7.50. It has an excellent wine list, including Turkey's finest, Sevilen, for US$30 per bottle.

Entertainment
In summer, bars are everywhere, opening and closing with revolving-door frequency. Most are on the eastern bay along Dr Alim Bey Caddesi/Cumhuriyet Caddesi, or in narrow alleys off it, or in Gümbet. Most are empty until around 10 pm, after which the currently favoured places fill up. Local drinks (beer, rakı, Turkish gin and vodka) are always significantly cheaper than foreign liquor.

İskele Meydanı is a good place to sit, sip a beer and watch the passing parade. *Kale Cafe*, just past the western entrance to the castle, has boat and water views, and drinks and food at prices a bit below most.

The roads east of Adliye Camii are dotted with clubs, pubs and bars which come thicker and faster the further east you go. At the time of writing happening places included *Fora Bar*, with Top 40 tunes on the dance floor and tables by the sea; the more alternative *Greenhouse*; perennial favourites like the *Red Lion* and *Rick's Bar*; and the *White House Club* for its sound system and lights show. *M&Ms Club* owns the bizarre floating nightclub yacht anchored in the eastern bay. It costs US$30 to take to the water, or US$15 to enter the landlubbers club.

The *Halikarnas Disco*, on the eastern bay at the end of Cumhuriyet Caddesi, is the biggest and loudest. Staff look you up and down for proper trendy dress and take a cover charge of US$17 before admitting you. Inside it's like a Hollywood set, with a laser light show on most evenings.

These days the most garish karaoke bars, ABBA theme nights, even drag shows with British transvestites, are in Gümbet, over the hill to the west.

Getting There & Away

Air Bodrum international airport lies between Milas and Bodrum. Turkish Airlines has daily flights from İstanbul for US$94. Many charter airlines fly here; check the brochures for bargains, especially at the start and end of the season.

Havaş buses leave Bodrum otogar two hours before each Turkish Airlines flight and the journey takes 45 minutes (US$4.50).

However if you are coming or going on another airline, a taxi is virtually the only option. There is no information at the airport about when or from where Havaş shuttle buses leave. Arriving, you could get a taxi from the airport to the highway for US$4, and wave down a passing minibus into Bodrum. A taxi to/from the airport costs US$32.

Bus As usual, Bodrum's bus service is frequent and far flung. The table on this page lists some useful summer daily services. For Gökova, change at Marmaris. For Kaş, take a bus to Fethiye and change there.

Boat Ferries leave Bodrum's western bay for Datça, Didyma and Knidos, and for the Greek islands of Kos and Rhodes. For information and tickets contact Bodrum Express Lines (☎ 316 1087, fax 313 0077) or the Bodrum Ferryboat Association (☎ 316 0882, fax 313 0205), on the docks past the western entrance to the castle.

Ferries depart Bodrum daily except Wednesday at 8.30 am in summer on the two-hour voyage to Didyma (US$12 return); the return leg departs Didyma at 4.30 pm.

Car-and-passenger ferries (two hours) operate daily from May to September between Bodrum and Datça; the fare is US$21 return. The ferry actually docks at Körmen on the peninsula's northern coast, from which Datça is only a 10- to 15-minute drive south; bus transport to Datça is included in your fare.

Services from Bodrum's Otogar

destination	fare (US$)	time (hr)	distance (km)	daily services
Ankara	15	13	785	a dozen buses
Antalya	13	11	640	1 bus
Fethiye	7	4½	265	6 buses
İstanbul	22–28	13	830	hourly buses
İzmir	11	4	250	buses at least every hour
Konya	16	12	750	1 bus daily
Kuşadası	6	2½	151	buses every half-hour
Marmaris	5	3	165	hourly buses
Milas	1.30	1	66	frequent minibuses
Pamukkale	7	5	310	2 direct buses
Söke	6	2	171	frequent buses

Hydrofoils (20 minutes) and ferries (50 minutes) carry passengers and cars across to Kos daily from May to September. Buy tickets (US$20 one way, US$25 same-day return, US$30 open return by hydrofoil; US$15 one way, US$18 same-day return, US$25 open return by ferry) at least a day in advance. Limited ferry services (usually two or three days per week, weather permitting) continue throughout winter. Both hydrofoil and ferry leave Bodrum at 9 am, and Kos at 4.30 pm.

Hydrofoils (two hours) depart Bodrum for Rhodes at 8.30 am on Monday from May to September. The return trip departs Rhodes at 4 pm. Buy tickets (US$45 one way, US$48 same-day return, open return US$56) a day in advance.

BODRUM PENINSULA

The volcanic landscape of the Bodrum Peninsula is one of high hills, dramatic rock outcrops, surprising marine panoramas and ugly concrete tourist developments. It comes as a surprise to see traditional life in the midst of all the villas, all-inclusive resorts and leather emporia, but in a few peninsula villages you may still see local women wearing the traditional *şalvar* (pantaloons) and white headscarves. Donkeys laden with sticks for fuel plod stubbornly to the domed, beehive-shaped earthen ovens still used to bake bread and roast mutton. But many of the distinctive *gümbet* (igloo-shaped stone cisterns) are falling to ruin, having been superseded by the ubiquitous tank trucks supplying *kullanma su* (non-drinking water). On the hilltops the ruins of old windmills tell a similar story of changing lifestyles.

Several of the beach villages, notably Gümüşlük, are good for day trips. If you've come to stay for a while, you might even move your base from Bodrum.

Frequent dolmuşes depart from Bodrum's otogar to most places on the peninsula in high summer. Fares are rarely more than US$1. Off season, be aware of departure times for the last minibus back to Bodrum. You could hire a scooter in Bodrum and ride around, but the main road from Bodrum to Turgutreis has a lot of traffic.

Note that there's no road from Gümüslük to Yalıkavak and no dolmuş service from Yalıkavak to Gölköy, so you'll have to keep returning to Bodrum to proceed along the northern coast.

Gümbet
☎ 252

Just 5km west of Bodrum, Gümbet is the quintessential package tour resort; mass-produced package tour habitation cuboids, souvenir shops, bars decked out with European flags and a rash of Chinese-Mexican-Indian restaurants. If you do want to stay you'd do well to consult the brochures at home before setting out.

Gümbet is a 10-minute dolmuş ride from Bodrum otogar (US$0.60) or you can walk there in about 45 minutes over the hills west of the yacht marina. The water is not all that clean, but it's always crowded in summer nevertheless.

Bitez, Ortakent & Yahşi Yalısı
☎ 252

West of Gümbet, past the next peninsula, are the bays of **Bitez Yalısı**, **Ortakent Yalısı** and **Yahşi Yalısı**, backed by white hotels, pensions, camping grounds and resort villas ,and offering small but good beaches and services. At Bitez Yalısı there's a windsurfing school. Dolmuşes run direct from Bodrum to Bitez Yalısı and to Yahşi Yalısı.

From Ortakent and Yahşi beaches you must travel inland via Gürece to continue your circuit of the peninsula, as there's no coastal road west of Yahşi.

Akyarlar
☎ 252

Akyarlar, 30km from Bodrum, is a pretty harbour village, formerly inhabited by Ottoman Greeks. There's a narrow beach, and a small yacht and fishing port. Holiday villas crowd the hillsides above – you may get the feeling the developers won't stop until the whole coast is covered in Legoland architecture.

If you want to stay, *Babadan Hotel-Restaurant* (☎ 393 6002), just off the main road, has clean, simple rooms with shower,

BODRUM PENINSULA

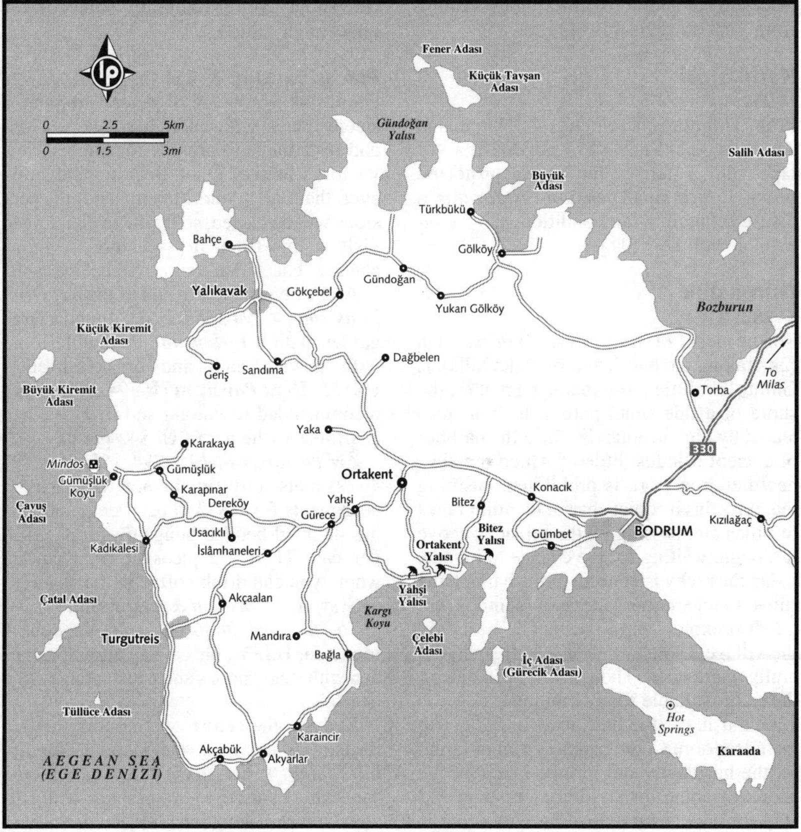
0 2.5 5km
0 1.5 3mi
Fener Adası
Küçük Tavşan Adası
Gündoğan Yalısı
Salih Adası
Büyük Adası
Türkbükü
Bahçe
Gölköy
Gündoğan
Yalıkavak
Gökçebel
Yukarı Gölköy
Bozburun
Küçük Kiremit Adası
Dağbelen
Geriş
Sandıma
To Milas
Büyük Kiremit Adası
Torba
Yaka
Karakaya
330
Mindos
Gümüşlük
Gümüşlük Koyu
Ortakent
Karapınar
Konacık
Çavuş Adası
Dereköy
Yahşi
Bitez
Gürece
Kızılağaç
Usacıklı
Bitez Yalısı
Gümbet
BODRUM
Kadıkalesi
İslâmhaneleri
Ortakent Yalısı
Yahşi Yalısı
Akçaalan
Çatal Adası
Kargı Koyu
Mandıra
Çelebi Adası
Turgutreis
Bağla
İç Adası (Gürecik Adası)
Tüllüce Adası
Hot Springs
Karaincir
Karaada
Akçabük
Akyarlar
AEGEAN SEA (EGE DENİZİ)

some with sea view, for US$12/25 a single/double. There's a big rear car park. You could eat here too, or at ***Küçük Ev*** which does fish and kebap meals. Be sure to check prices before ordering.

The next bay to the east is **Karaincir**, a similar cove with a grey gravel beach, hotels, a few pensions and a holiday village but far less inviting than Akyarlar.

Following the coastal road west from Akyarlar brings you to **Akçabük**, with another cove and beach. North of Akçabük all the way to Turgutreis the coast is lined with holiday villages.

Turgutreis

☎ 252

Old Turgutreis is about 3km inland from the newly developed modern town 20km west of Bodrum. The great Turkish admiral Turgut Reis (who died in 1560) was born here and a monument to him stands south of the town on the shore. The modern town is a tawdry strip of Ye Olde Englande bars, restaurants and shops selling downmarket sportswear. A new marina is being built to try to raise the tone of the place.

Dolmuşes (US$0.75) from Bodrum leave you at the main square right on the thin strip of beach. The square is surrounded with places to eat and drink, offering everything from Turkish standards to pizza.

Kadıkalesi
☎ 252

From Turgutreis, a road travels 1km inland and then 3.5km north to Kadıkalesi, a village with a narrow but partly protected beach, several small *pension-restaurants*, a disused church in fair condition, and the inevitable holiday villages.

Gümüşlük
☎ 252

To the north of Kadıkalesi, 3km by road (2km along the beach and over the hills), is Gümüşlük, little more than a hamlet on the shore of a fine small natural harbour protected by high headlands. Once the harbour of ancient Mindos, little of which remains, new building work is prohibited, ensuring that it retains its quiet charm. Identikit ranks of villas are massing on the hillsides above it though, waiting for the chance to invade.

On the rocky islet north of the hamlet, the ruins (some underwater) of Mindos are good to explore on a swim. The beach on the village's southern side is long and generally uncrowded. Though weedy in places, the sea is suitable for swimming.

Gümüşlük is the best goal for a day trip from Bodrum. Come here to swim or climb on the headlands and to take lunch on the shore; or come for an afternoon swim and stay for a sunset dinner. The waterfront is lined with restaurants, all with excellent sea, island and sunset views; there are tables ranged along the water under shady vines. Most post their prices and start to fill up an hour before sunset.

Diving Based at the Gümüşlük Motel, Feridun Boruk (☎ 0542 575 3520) is a former diving instructor in the Turkish navy who offers diving courses for novices for US$42 per day, and four-day courses for US$280. Nondivers can tag along and go snorkelling for US$15. Although diving over the ruins of Mindos is banned, it is possible to go snorkelling. Feridun rents out snorkelling gear for US$1.60 per day, and can supply rough maps of some of the underwater relics.

Places to Stay & Eat In the off season, Gümüşlük is a haven of peace and quiet, a sleepy place with enough small pensions and restaurants to provide for the very few visitors who seek it out. Bear in mind, however, that before mid-May many of the pensions will be closed, so if you're planning to visit at this time, it's sensible to phone ahead to check that rooms will be available.

At the quiet southern end of the bay *Özak Pansiyon* (☎ 394 3388) is set around a large garden with a *restaurant*. A double room with private bath and breakfast costs US$25. *Hera Pansiyon* (☎ 394 3065) has a recommended restaurant and four five-bed apartments which cost US$42 per day.

Arriba Apart-otel (☎ 394 3654, fax 394 4039) rents fully fitted, somewhat spartan apartments for US$250 per week, and also has doubled-bedded bungalows for US$30 per day. There's a pleasant front garden where you can drink coffee in the shade.

Sysyphos Pansiyon & Restaurant (☎ 394 3016, fax 394 3656) has simple double rooms for US$21, plus a very attractive garden with shady nooks and a restaurant on the beach.

Right in the centre overlooking the fish restaurants and open year-round is *Gümüşlük Motel* (☎ 394 3045) where two people can share a simple room, perhaps with balcony and sea view, for US$28.

At the northern end of the beach are a group of pretty stone villas *Villa Magnolia*, *Jasmine Cottage* and *Mindos Cottage* right on the beach but contracted to the British tour company Simply Turkey.

As you walk to the beach from the dolmuş stand the first thing you see is a row of fish restaurants, *Akvaryum*, *Yakamoz*, *Siesta* and *Gümüşlük*, all much the same. Be sure to ask the price of fish before ordering; you should be able to find a main course for around US$6 but a full fish meal is likely to cost between US$12 and US$15 per person.

Head north along the beach and you'll come to smaller places like *Mimoza* and

Gümüs Café where prices may be marginally lower and the throngs less pressing. Set back from the shore, right in the centre, is *Dalgiç Restaurant* which serves kebaps and stuffed vine leaves for those days when fish isn't what you fancy.

Getting There & Away Gümüşlük is accessible by dolmuş from Bodrum (US$1) or from Turgutreis (US$0.50). Vehicles are banned from entering the village. The last dolmuş to Bodrum departs at midnight (10 pm out of season). You may want to leave before then in case it's full.

Yalıkavak
☎ 252

The northern shore of the peninsula is the least overdeveloped and the trickiest to get around by public transport.

In the north-western corner, 18km from Bodrum, is Yalıkavak. As you approach you'll see the ruins of three old windmills on the hill; another has been reconstructed on the waterfront. As Datça is to Marmaris, so Yalıkavak is to Bodrum: a smaller, quieter version with the constant threat of similar development looming over it. In the meantime it's surprisingly pleasant, with no high-rise buildings to spoil the harbour and several attractive hotels and restaurants.

Cruise boats will take you out to hidden bays along the peninsula and as far as Gümüşlük to see the ruins of Mindos. A day trip costs about US$16.

Places to Stay & Eat There are a handful of pensions in and around the village where you can expect to get a bed for about US$6 per person. One of the most central is *Yalıkavak Pansiyon* but it's likely to be noisy because of the restaurants and bars. Walk east along the promenade and you'll come to *Yüksel Pension*, with chickens in the backyard. Most of these places only open during the height of the season (July to mid-September).

Otherwise, Yalıkavak has several very comfortable, attractive hotels and apartment blocks, all with swimming pools and all east of the restaurants along the promenade

(Plaj Yolu Caddesi). These are contracted to European tour operators for most of the season but in April/early May and again at the end of September/early October individual travellers may be able to find a bed.

Most attractive is *Otel Taşkule (☎/fax 385 4935)* as you head out along the eastern promenade. Pretty rooms with tiled showers cost US$22, including breakfast. There's also a swimming pool. Also inviting, though one block in from the sea, is *Yeldeğirmen Konuk Evi (☎ 385 4805)*, Windmill Hotel, with a stream flowing through the grounds. Doubles cost US$30.

Lavanta Hotel (☎ 385 2167, fax 385 2290, [e] satelco@netone.com.tr), perched above the village on the Bodrum road, comes highly recommended by guests for its hospitality, food and gardens. Rooms cost US$66/130 with breakfast.

Altınköy Apart Hotel (☎ 385 2685, fax 385 4909) is a gorgeous, glistening white pile set around a central pool, with bright, beautifully equipped apartments to sleep four for US$100 a night.

There's a cluster of seafood restaurants beside the harbour. The *Liman* and *Windmill* are good but *Çakıroğlu Çardak* wins first prize both for its presentation and for delicious food such as seafood croquettes for US$2 and shrimp casseroles for US$6.

As usual, to find food at lower prices cut inland a block and look for places like *Devecıoğlu Lokantası* offering *ev yemekleri* (home cooking). The *Margül Restaurant* does gözleme and pide from US$2.25, while *Meltem* does İskender kebap for US$3.

Getting There & Away Frequent dolmuşes ply back and forth between Bodrum and Yalıkavak, taking just over 30 minutes and charging US$1. Surprisingly, although the road is good, there's no onward dolmuş to Gölköy; you'll have to take a taxi for around US$12, or return to Bodrum and catch another dolmuş from there.

Gölköy
☎ 252

About 17km north of Bodrum, the village of Gölköy is arrayed around a narrow grey beach, backed by a sprawl of concrete motels and pensions, plus the inevitable villas. In July and August family pensions open to accommodate most arrivals. Otherwise *Sahil Motel* (☎ 357 7183) and *Sultan Motel* (☎ 357 7260) guard the bay. Both have pretty gardens, and simple, furnished rooms with shower for US$16 per person, including breakfast.

Wooden docks serve the fishing boats; the boat owners will also take you out for short excursions if you wish.

About 1.5km around the point from Gölköy, and served by the same dolmuş from Bodrum, is **Türkbükü**, another village with a few modest pensions and motels, a PTT, the *Ship Ahoy* restaurant and shops for the yachters who anchor in its harbour.

TURKISH TILES

Tiles are one of the most striking features of Turkish architecture. Tile-making played a major role in Ottoman art and architecture between the 14th and 17th centuries and was most prominent in İznik and Kütahya.

Most of the designs were inspired by flowers with turquoise, green, yellow, dark blue and red as the dominant colours; geometric shapes and calligraphy were also popular. Tiles were mainly used in mosques, hamams, palaces, mansions, fountains and churches. They were intended to enhance the architectural effect of buildings, not just to cover up surfaces. The unique styles and designs inspired enormous pride among the Turkish people, particularly the master artisans.

Some of the oldest Ottoman tiles can be seen today in the minaret of Bursa's Yeşil Cami. The architecture of this impressive construction heralded the emergence of a distinctly Turkish style, and features yellow and green encaustic tiles made by architect Hacı İvaz. But perhaps the best-known tiles can be found on İznik's Yeşil Cami, about 150km from İstanbul.

Good quality tilework is painted carefully by apprentices under the direction of a master. The master's own work is the highest quality available, and is often signed. Painting a single tile or plate is a painstaking job, taking several days for each one. (Inset photo by Greg Elms)

By the mid-16th century Turkey's tiles were becoming more multi-coloured. Instead of mosaic and gilded tiles of one distinct colour, a new glazing technique was adopted for the rectangular-shaped tiles which introduced a burst of different colours to the designs. It was around this time that 'İznik red' – brilliant red tiles made from an Anatolian clay rich in iron oxide – became popular. One of the finest examples of İznik tilework is in İstanbul's Süleymaniye Camii.

During the second half of the 16th century, tiles were made using another new glazing technique. İstanbul's Süleymaniye Camii houses some exquisite examples as does the Topkapı Palace, the Piyale Paşa Camii in Kasımpasa, Yeni Valide Camii in Üsküdar and the Selimiye Camii in Edirne.

Tile-making became less popular at the start of the 17th century only to be rejuvenated when factories producing hard-glaze delftware and porcelain were opened in İstanbul's Beykoz and Yıldız districts. Today Kütahya has become the centre of tile producing with walls, floors and facades decorated in this uniquely Turkish way.

OLIVIER CIRENDINI

GEOFF STRINGER

Flower motifs were popular in tile designs, shown by these exquis examples from Topkap Palace in İstanbul. Calligraphy was also often incorporated into the designs.

Western Anatolia

Western Anatolia inland from the coast holds a wealth of historical and agricultural riches. It's a good place to escape the urban and seaside crowds and explore the 'real' Turkey.

İznik (Nicaea) and Bursa, just south of the Sea of Marmara, offer history, architecture, cuisine and shopping. Eskişehir is the world centre of meerschaum mining and artistry. Kütahya is Turkey's centre for the production of coloured tiles, and Afyon for opium (carefully controlled). In the southern reaches of the region, Afrodisias and Pamukkale have excellent archaeological sites and Pamukkale also has the famous calcium-laden hot springs. The great lakes in the south-eastern part of the region, especially Eğirdir, are great for a peaceful break from a hectic trip.

YALOVA
☎ 226 • pop 60,000
Yalova is a farming and transportation centre. The highway between the industrial cities of Bursa and Kocaeli (İzmit) passes near here, as does the car ferry/bus link between Bursa and İstanbul. Yalova was badly damaged in the earthquake of 1999, but has been rebuilt.

There's nothing to detain you in Yalova. Head for the spa at Termal, or to Bursa or İznik without delay.

Getting There & Away
Bus The centre, just in from the dock, is marked by a traffic circle centred on an enormous statue of Atatürk. Just off the dock to the left are rows of buses and minibuses. Buses to İznik (US$2.75) and Bursa (US$4) leave about every 30 minutes or less.

Yalova city bus No 4 (Taşköprü-Termal) takes you to Termal for US$0.60, a dolmuş charges US$0.75.

Boat The dock for catamarans to İstanbul's Yenikapı docks (US$7, one hour) is just off Yalova's main square, with the fast *hızlı feribot* (car ferry) dock just to the east of it.

HIGHLIGHTS

- Touring Bursa's great mosques, the Ulu Cami and Yeşil Cami
- Walking the city walls and gates in İznik
- Shopping for painted tiles in Kütahya
- Admiring the brilliant-white travertine pools at Pamukkale
- Joining a fisherman for an early morning voyage on the lake at Eğirdir

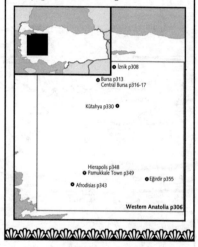

İznik p308
Bursa p313
Central Bursa p316-17
Kütahya p330
Hierapolis p348
Pamukkale Town p349
Eğirdir p355
Afrodisias p343
Western Anatolia p306

By catching a ferry to İstanbul, you'll save yourself a 100km drive round the eastern side of the Sea of Marmara along chaotic roads through an industrial wasteland.

The Yalova-Yenikapı fast car-ferry gets you to İstanbul in under an hour for US$28 per car and driver, US$7 per pedestrian/passenger. Ferries leave about every two hours from 7.30 am to 9 pm. A cheaper, slower alternative is the traditional car ferry between Eskihisar (near Darıca, south-west of Gebze on the northern side of the Sea of Marmara) across the Bay of İzmit to Topçular, on the southern shore, east of Yalova. Ferries run every 30 minutes around the

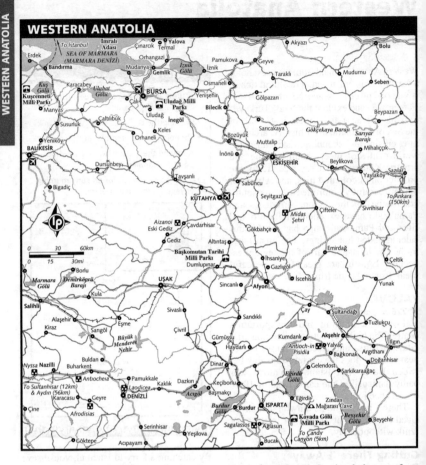

WESTERN ANATOLIA

clock on the 25-minute voyage; the fare for car and driver is US$12.

TERMAL

About 12km south-west of Yalova, off the road to Çınarcık, is the spa town of Termal. The baths here take advantage of the hot, mineral-rich waters that gush from the earth, and were first exploited in Roman times. The Ottomans used the baths from the 16th century. Abdül Hamit II repaired and refurbished them in 1900 in a gaudy Ottoman baroque style to celebrate the 25th anniversary of his accession to the throne.

Later, Atatürk added a simple but comfortable spa hotel.

Atatürk had a small house here, which is now a **museum**. At the **Valide Banyo** you get a locker for your clothes, before taking a shower and entering a pool. An admission charge of less than US$2 gets you 1½ hours of bathing. Soap and shampoo cost extra, so bring your own. The **Sultan Banyo** is even grander and much pricier, but you can rent a swimsuit here. The **Kurşunlu Banyo** features an open-air pool for US$2.50, an enclosed pool and sauna for US$3, and small private cubicles for about the same.

The *Yalova Termal Tesisleri* (☎ 675 7400, fax 675 7413) operates the Çamlık and Cınar hotels right at the spa, which charges from US$30/40 to US$40/60 for singles/doubles, including breakfast. Lunch or dinner costs US$10. The front rooms are the more expensive. Other hotels are at nearby Gökçedere.

There are frequent buses (US$0.60) and dolmuşes (US$0.75) from Yalova.

İZNİK
☎ 224 • pop 18,000

The 60km, one-hour trip from Yalova to İznik takes you along fertile green hills punctuated by tall, spiky cypress trees, passing peach orchards, cornfields and vineyards.

As you approach İznik you may notice fruit-packing plants among the orchards. You will certainly have admired the vast İznik Gölü (İznik Lake). Watch for the great Byzantine city walls: one entrance to the city is through the old İstanbul Kapısı (İstanbul Gate) on Atatürk Caddesi, which leads directly to the centre and the ruined church Aya Sofya (Hagia Sophia), now a museum.

History

This ancient city may have been founded around 1000 BC. We know that it was revitalised by one of Alexander the Great's generals in 316 BC. Another of the generals, Lysimachus, soon got hold of it and named it after his wife Nikaea. It became the capital city of the province of Bithynia.

Nicaea lost some of its prominence with the founding of Nicomedia (today's Kocaeli/İzmit) in 264 BC, and by 74 BC the entire area had been incorporated into the Roman Empire.

Nicaea flourished under Rome, but invasions by the Goths and the Persians brought ruin by AD 300.

Ecumenical Councils With the rise of Constantinople, Nicaea took on a new importance. In AD 325, the first Ecumenical Council was held here to condemn the heresy of Arianism. During the reign of Justinian I (527–65), Nicaea was grandly refurbished with new buildings and defences, which served the city well a few centuries later

when the Arabs invaded. Like Constantinople, Nicaea never fell to its Arab besiegers.

In 787 another Ecumenical Council, the seventh, was held in Nicaea's Hagia Sofia church. The deliberations solved the problem of iconoclasm: henceforth it would be church policy not to destroy icons. Theologians who saw icons as 'images' prohibited by the Bible, were dismayed, but Byzantine artists were delighted, and went to work on their art with even more vigour.

Nicaea and Constantinople did, however, fall to the crusaders. From 1204 to 1261, when a Latin king sat on the throne of Byzantium, the true Byzantine emperor Theodore I (Lascaris) reigned over the Empire of Nicaea. When the crusaders left, the imperial capital returned to Constantinople.

The Turks The Seljuk Turks had a flourishing empire in Central Anatolia before 1250, and various tribes of nomadic warriors had circulated near the walls of Nicaea during those times. In fact, Turkish soldiers had served as mercenaries in the interminable battles that raged among rival claimants to the Byzantine throne. At one point, a Byzantine battle over Nicaea ended with a Turkish emir as its ruler.

On 2 March 1331, Orhan, son of Osman and second sultan (1326–61) of the Ottoman Empire conquered İznik. The city soon had the honour of harbouring the first Ottoman theological school. Prusa (Bursa) had fallen to the Ottomans on 6 April 1326, and became their first capital city. In 1337 they took Nicomedia and effectively blocked the Byzantines from entering Anatolia.

Sultan Selim I (1512–20), a mighty conqueror nicknamed Selim the Grim, rolled his armies over Azerbaijan in 1514 and took the Persian city of Tabriz. Packing up all of the region's artisans, he sent them west to İznik. They brought with them a high level of expertise in the making of coloured tiles. Soon İznik's kilns were turning out faience, unequalled even today. The great period of İznik faience continued almost to 1700. At one point, artisans were sent to Tunisia, then an Ottoman possession, to begin a high-quality faience industry.

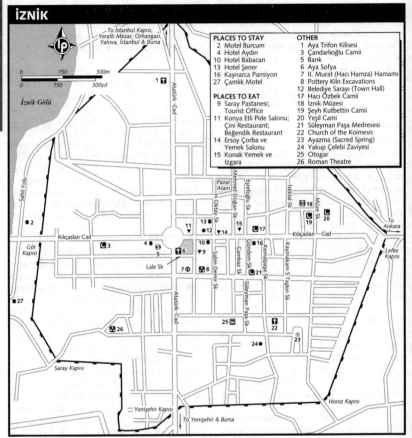

İZNİK

PLACES TO STAY
2 Motel Burcum
4 Hotel Aydın
10 Hotel Babacan
13 Hotel Şener
16 Kaynarca Pansiyon
27 Çamlık Motel

PLACES TO EAT
9 Saray Pastanesi;
  Tourist Office
11 Konya Etli Pide Salonu;
  Çini Restaurant;
  Beğendik Restaurant
14 Ersoy Çorba ve
  Yemek Salonu
15 Konak Yemek ve
  Izgara

OTHER
1 Aya Trifon Kilisesi
3 Çandarlıoğlu Camii
5 Bank
6 Aya Sofya
7 II. Murat (Hacı Hamza) Hamamı
8 Pottery Kiln Excavations
12 Belediye Sarayı (Town Hall)
17 Hacı Özbek Camii
18 Iznik Müzesi
19 Şeyh Kutbettin Camii
20 Yeşil Cami
21 Süleyman Paşa Medresesi
22 Church of the Koimesis
23 Ayazma (Sacred Spring)
24 Yakup Çelebi Zaviyesi
25 Otogar
26 Roman Theatre

The art of coloured tile-making is being revived in İznik today, but it's at nowhere near the scale of the trade in Kütahya. Though new tiles make good purchases, 17th- and 18th-century İznik tiles are considered antiquities, and cannot legally be exported from Turkey.

Orientation

Aya Sofya (known for centuries as Hagia Sophia) is a good vantage point from which to consider the town's Roman layout: two straight boulevards, north-south (Atatürk Caddesi) and east-west (Kılıçaslan Cad-

desi), leading to the four principal gates (kapısı) in the city walls. To the north is the İstanbul Kapısı, to the south Yenişehir Kapısı, to the east Lefke Kapısı and to the west, Göl Kapısı.

The *otogar* (bus station) is a few blocks south-east of the church.

Information

The tourist office (☎/fax 757 1933), just east of Aya Sofya, is open from 9 am to noon and from 1 to 5.30 pm daily in the warm months, with shorter hours (closed weekends) off season.

Aya Sofya

Aya Sofya, the Church of the Divine Wisdom, is hardly striking in its grandeur, but it has a fascinating past.

What you see is the ruin of three different buildings. Inside is a mosaic floor and a mural of Jesus with Mary and John the Baptist which dates from the time of Justinian. That original church was destroyed by an earthquake in 1065 and was later rebuilt. Mosaics were set into the walls at that time. With the Ottoman conquest, the church became a mosque. A fire in the 16th century ruined everything, but reconstruction was carried out under the expert eye of Mimar Sinan, who added İznik tiles to the decoration.

Aya Sofya is open from 9 am to noon and from 2 to 5 pm daily except Monday. If there's no-one about when you visit, ask at the İznik Museum to be let into the church, as the key is often there.

To the south-east of Aya Sofya is the II. Murat Hamamı, also called the 'Hacı Hamza Hamamı', a Turkish bath constructed during the reign of Sultan Murat II, in the first half of the 15th century, and still in operation.

Kılıçaslan Caddesi

İznik's main street, Kılıçaslan Caddesi, leads eventually to the Lefke Kapısı. Walking from Aya Sofya, on the left is the *belediye sarayı* or town hall, with a sign out the front that reads (in Turkish) 'Our motto is, Clean City, Green City'. The motto is carried out in the small but agreeable park with its big poplars shading the commercial district from the hot summer sun.

A bit further along on the left is the Hacı Özbek Camii, one of the town's oldest mosques, dating from 1332.

Walk one block south along Gündem Sokak, opposite the Hacı Özbek Camii, to reach the Süleyman Paşa Medresesi. Founded by Sultan Orhan shortly after he captured Nicaea, it has the distinction of being the very first college (actually a theological seminary) founded by a member of the Ottoman dynasty.

Back on the main street, continue eastwards and soon, to the left, you can see the tile-covered minaret of the Yeşil Cami.

Yeşil Cami

Built in 1492, the year of Columbus' first voyage to America, the Yeşil Cami, or Green Mosque, has Seljuk Turkish proportions influenced more by Persia (the Seljuk homeland) than by İstanbul. The green-glazed bricks of the minaret foreshadowed the tile industry that arose a few decades after the mosque was built.

İznik Museum & Underground Tomb

Opposite the Yeşil Cami is the Nilüfer Hatun İmareti (Soup Kitchen of Lady Nilüfer), now the İznik Museum (İznik Müzesi). It's open from 8.30 am to noon and 1 to 5 pm daily except Monday (usually). Admission costs US$1.50.

Begun in 1388, it was built by Sultan Murat I for his mother, Nilüfer Hatun, who was born a Byzantine princess but was married off to Orhan, second sultan of the Ottoman state, to form a diplomatic alliance.

Though intended as a place where the poor could come for free food, it now dispenses culture to the masses. The front court is filled with marble statuary, bits of cornice and column, and similar archaeological flotsam and jetsam. In the lofty, cool halls are exhibits of İznik faience, Ottoman weaponry, embroidery and calligraphy, and several items from the city's Roman past. Many of the little signs are in French and English, but you'll need to know the word *yüzyıl* (century), as in XVI. Yüzyıl (16th century).

While at the museum, ask about a visit to the Underground Tomb (Yeraltı Mezar), a Byzantine tomb on the outskirts of town. You must have a museum official accompany you with the key; there is a small charge for admission, and the official should receive a small tip. Also, you will have to haggle with a taxi driver for a price for the return trip.

The little tomb, discovered by accident in the 1960s, has delightful Byzantine murals covering its walls and ceiling.

Across the road to the south of the museum is the Şeyh Kutbettin Camii (1492), in ruins.

City Walls

Return to Kılıçaslan Caddesi and continue east towards the **Lefke Kapısı**. Lefke, now a small town called Osmaneli, was a city of considerable size in Byzantine times. This charming old monument is actually three gates in a row, dating from Byzantine times. The middle one has an inscription which tells us it was built by Proconsul Plancius Varus in AD 123. It's possible to climb to the top of the gate and the walls here, a good vantage point for inspecting the ancient walls.

Outside the gate is an **aqueduct**, and the **tomb of Çandarlı Halil Hayrettin Paşa** (late 14th century), with the graves of many lesser mortals nearby.

Re-enter the city through the Lefke Kapısı, and turn left. Follow the walls south and west to the **Yenişehir Kapısı**. On the way you will pass near the ruined **Church of the Koimesis**, on the western side of Kaymakam S Taşkın Sokak, which dates from about AD 800. Only some of the foundations remain, but it is famous as the burial place of the Byzantine emperor Theodore I (Lascaris). When the crusaders took Constantinople in 1204, Lascaris fled to Nicaea and established his court here.

Lascaris built Nicaea's outer ring of walls, supported by over 100 towers and protected by a wide moat. No doubt he didn't trust the crusaders, having lost one city to them. The emperor died and was buried here, and when the court finally returned to Constantinople in 1261, it was under the leadership of Michael VIII Palaeologus. Lascaris never made it back to his beloved capital.

Half a block east of the church is an *ayazma* or **sacred fountain**, also called *yeraltı çeşme* (underground spring).

After admiring the Yenişehir Kapısı, start towards the centre along Atatürk Caddesi. Halfway to Aya Sofya, a road on the left leads to the ruins of a Roman theatre. To the south-west is the **Saray Kapısı**, or Palace Gate. Sultan Orhan had a palace near here in the 14th century.

Places to Stay

The few hotels in İznik may fill up with Turks from nearby cities on summer weekends, and you may need to reserve a room in advance. Bursa has a much better selection of hotels and restaurants than İznik, so unless you're unusually interested in İznik, you're better off going there.

İznik has a few modest hotels good for an overnight stay. *Kaynarca Pansiyon* (☎ 757 1753, fax 757 1723, Gündem Sokak 1), run by the irrepressible Ali Bulmuş, is clean and central, charging US$10/14/19 a single/double/triple with bath and TV; breakfast costs an additional US$2. There's an adjoining Internet cafe.

In the centre, just across the street from the belediye, is the plain, drab *Hotel Babacan* (☎ 757 1211, Kılıçaslan Caddesi 104). There are 30 rooms with sinks for US$8/10 a single/double. With shower, the prices are US$12.50/16.

Hotel Şener (☎ 757 1480, fax 757 2280, Belediye Arkası, H Oktay Sokak 7) has a lift, lounge, restaurant, and comfortable rooms going for US$11/22/33 with shower. You can sometimes haggle for a lower rate.

The *Hotel Aydın* (☎ 757 7650, fax 757 7652, Kılıçaslan Caddesi 64) charges US$20/30, including breakfast, for the newest rooms in town.

Motel Burcum (☎ 757 1011, Sahil Yolu) has verdant grounds and tidy rooms, some with views of the lake, for US$22 a double, including breakfast. Get a room on the 2nd or 3rd floor if you want the view. You can also camp in the garden for a few dollars per night.

Çamlık Motel (☎ 757 1631, Sahil Yolu), at the southern end of the street, has good rooms and a restaurant that serves alcohol, and a room price of US$26 a double. There's camping here as well.

Places to Eat

On Kılıçaslan Caddesi, opposite Aya Sofya, there are three small eateries, including the *Konya Etli Pide Salonu*, which serves good, cheap, freshly made Turkish-style pizzas for US$2 to US$3, and the *Çini* and *Beğendik* restaurants serving full meals. The *Ersoy Çorba ve Yemek Salonu* is also presentable.

Konak Yemek ve Izgara, further east along Kılıçaslan Caddesi, is the fancy version of a Turkish grill, with a greater variety of lamb and chicken grills but only slightly higher prices.

There are also several *pastanes* (patisseries), including **Saray Pastanesi** east of Aya Sofya, good for breakfast, dinner or a snack.

Getting There & Away

There are hourly buses from the city's otogar to Bursa. Don't wait until too late in the day, however, as the last bus heads out at 6 or 7 pm on the 1½ hour trip. A ticket costs US$2.75. There are also frequent buses to Yalova (US$2.75).

BURSA

☎ 224 • pop 1 million

Bursa has a special place in the hearts of the Turks. It was the first capital city of the Ottoman Empire and, in a real sense, the birthplace of modern Turkish culture. The city has its pretty parts despite its industrial base.

History

Called Prusa by the Byzantines, Bursa is a very old and important city, dating from at least 200 BC. According to legend, it was founded by Prusias, the King of Bithynia. It soon came under the sway of Eumenes II of Pergamum, and thereafter under direct Roman control.

Bursa grew to importance in the early centuries of Christianity, when the thermal baths at Çekirge were first developed on a large scale and when a silk trade was founded here. The importation of silkworms and the establishment of looms began an industry which survives to this day. However, it was Justinian I (AD 527–65) who really put Bursa on the map. Besides favouring the silk trade, he built a palace for himself and bathhouses in Çekirge.

With the decline of the Byzantine Empire, Bursa's location near Constantinople drew the interest of would-be conquerors, including the Arab armies (circa AD 700) and the Seljuk Turks. The Seljuks, having conquered much of Anatolia by 1075, took Bursa with ease that same year, and planted the seeds of the great Ottoman Empire to come.

With the arrival of the First Crusade in 1097, Bursa reverted to Christian hands, though it was to be conquered and reconquered by both sides for the next 100 years. When the rapacious armies of the Fourth Crusade sacked Constantinople in 1204, the Byzantine emperor fled to İznik and set up his capital there. He succeeded in controlling the hinterland of İznik, including Bursa, until the capital was moved back to Constantinople in 1261.

After the Turkish migration into Anatolia during the 11th and 12th centuries, small principalities had risen here and there around Turkish military leaders. A *gazi* (chieftain or 'hero of the faith') would rally a group of followers, gain control of a territory, govern it and seek to expand its borders. One such prince was Ertuğrul Gazi, who formed a small state near Bursa. Under the rule of his son Osman Gazi (1281–1326) the small state grew to a nascent empire and took Osman's name, Osmanlı (Ottoman). Bursa was besieged by Osman's forces in 1317 and was finally starved into submission on 6 April 1326 when it became the Ottoman capital.

After Osman had expanded and enriched his principality, he was succeeded by Orhan Gazi (1326–61) who, from his base at Bursa, expanded the empire to include everything from what is now Ankara in Central Anatolia to Thrace in Europe. The Byzantine capital at Constantinople was thus surrounded, and the Byzantine Empire had only about a century to survive. Orhan took the title of sultan, struck the first Ottoman coinage and near the end of his reign was able to dictate to the Byzantine emperors. One of them, John VI Cantacuzene, was Orhan's close ally and later even his father-in-law (Orhan married the Princess Theodora).

Although the Ottoman capital moved to Adrianople (Edirne) in 1402, Bursa remained an important, even revered, Ottoman city throughout the long history of the empire. Both Osman and Orhan were buried there; their tombs are still important monuments in Turkish history.

With the founding of the Turkish Republic (1923), Bursa's industrial development began in earnest. What really brought the

Karagöz

Bursa is traditionally regarded as the 'birthplace' of the Turkish Karagöz shadow puppet theatre. The puppets – cut from camel hide treated with oil to promote translucency, and brought to life with coloured paint – are manipulated behind a white cloth onto which their images are cast by a light behind them.

Legend has it that one of the construction foremen working on Bursa's Ulu Cami was a hunchback called Karagöz. He and his straight man Hacivat indulged in such humorous antics that the other workers abandoned their tasks to watch. This infuriated the sultan, who had the two miscreants put to death. Their comic routines (many of them bawdy) live on in the Karagöz shadow puppet theatre, a Central Asian tradition brought to Bursa from where it spread throughout the Ottoman lands.

Once commonly performed in tea and coffeehouses, salons and parks throughout the empire, the traditional Karagöz show has long since succumbed to the ravages of cinema, video and television.

In the Eski Aynalı Çarşı in the centre of Bursa's Kapalı Çarşı (Covered Market) is a shop called Karagöz (☎ 221 8727), open daily except Sunday, and run by a man named Şinasi Çelikkol. He sells Turkish antiques and handicrafts, including the Karagöz shadow puppets. Şinasi Bey has led efforts to revive and perpetuate the Karagöz show, including the establishment of the Karagöz Sanat Evi (Karagöz Art House) and organisation of the annual Karagöz Festival.

The Karagöz Sanat Evi, on the south side of Altıparmak Caddesi, opposite the Karagöz monument, hosts exhibits of local and regional arts and crafts and organises Karagöz shows.

The Karagöz Festival, held in mid-November, brings Karagöz *hayali* (shadow puppeteers), Western puppeteers and marionette performers from Turkey and neighbouring countries to Bursa for five days of festivities and performances.

MICK WELDON

boom was the automobile assembly plants, set up in the 1960s and '70s. Large factories still assemble Renaults, Fiats and other motor vehicles. Also, as Bursa has always been noted for its fruit, it is logical that a large fruit juice and soft drink industry should be centred here. Tourism is also important.

Orientation

Bursa clings to the slopes of Uludağ and spills down into the fertile valley. The major boulevards are Kıbrıs Şehitler Caddesi and Atatürk Caddesi, which is the main axis in the commercial district. Both run across the slope, not up and down it.

Bursa's main square is Cumhuriyet Alanı (Republic Square), with its statue of Atatürk. Most people refer to the square as Heykel (Statue). Bursa's main street, Atatürk Caddesi, runs west from Heykel through the commercial centre to the Ulu Cami (Great Mosque), a distance of about 700m. Heavy traffic makes it almost impossible to cross the street, so use the *altgeçidi* (pedestrian subways), each of which bears a name. To the north-west, Atatürk Caddesi becomes Cemal Nadir Caddesi, then Altıparmak Caddesi, then Çekirge Caddesi. It leads to the spa suburb of Çekirge, about a 10-minute bus ride away.

South-east of Heykel at Setbaşı, Namazgah Caddesi crosses the Gök Deresi trickling along the bottom of a dramatic gorge. Just after the stream, Yeşil Caddesi branches off to the left to the Yeşil Cami and Yeşil Türbe, after which it changes names to become Emir Sultan Caddesi.

From Heykel, Setbaşı and Atatürk Caddesi you can get dolmuşes and buses to all other parts of the city.

Information

The tourist office (☎ 220 1848) is beneath Atatürk Caddesi at the northern entrance to the Orhan Gazi Altgeçidi, facing the Koza Han and Orhan Gazi Camii across the park.

Internet House Cafe (☎ 532-406 4868) on Sanatçılar Sokak can make the connection for you.

TAŞ Kitapçılık Bookshop (☎ 222 9453), Adliye Karşısı, Kültür Sokak 8/A, just a few steps uphill from Heykel, has Penguin books and a number of other English titles.

Just downhill at Elt Kitabevi are English-language newspapers and periodicals.

Emir Sultan Camii

You can see most of Bursa's sights in one full day, though a leisurely tour will take a little more time. Start with the city's most famous architectural monuments, east of the city centre.

The Emir Sultan Camii is a favourite of Bursa's pious Muslims. Rebuilt by Selim III in 1805 and restored in the early 1990s, it echoes the romantic decadence of Ottoman rococo style. The setting, next to a large hillside cemetery surrounded by huge trees and overlooking the city and valley, is as pleasant as the mosque itself.

To reach the mosque, take a dolmuş heading for Emirsultan or any bus with 'Emirsultan' in its name, such as No 1, 1A, 2A, 6 or 18, and head east. You'll pass by the Yeşil Cami and Yeşil Türbe before coming to the Emir Sultan Camii, but this

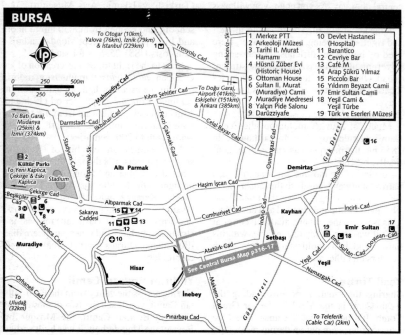

BURSA

To Otogar (10km),
Yalova (76km), İznik (79km)
& İstanbul (229km)

1 Merkez PTT
2 Arkeoloji Müzesi
3 Tarihi II. Murat Hamamı
4 Hüsnü Züber Evi (Historic House)
5 Ottoman House
6 Sultan II. Murat (Muradiye) Camii
7 Muradiye Medresesi
8 Yalçın Pide Salonu
9 Darüzziyafe
10 Devlet Hastanesi (Hospital)
11 Barantico
12 Cevriye Bar
13 Café M
14 Arap Şükrü Yılmaz
15 Piccolo Bar
16 Yıldırım Beyazit Camii
17 Emir Sultan Camii
18 Yeşil Cami & Yeşil Türbe
19 Türk ve Eserleri Müzesi

To Doğu Garaj, Airport (41km), Eskişehir (151km) & Ankara (385km)

To Batı Garaj, Mudanya (25km) & İzmir (374km)

Kültür Parkı
To Yeni Kaplıca, Çekirge & Eski Kaplıca

Altı Parmak

Demirtaş

Sakarya Caddesi

Kayhan

Muradiye

Emir Sultan

Setbaşı

Hisar

İnebey

Yeşil

To Uludağ (32km)

See Central Bursa Map p316-17

To Teleferik (Cable Car) (2km)

0   250   500m
0   250   500yd

way you get to walk downhill back to the Yeşil Cami, not up.

Yeşil Cami

After the disastrous victories of Tamerlane, Beyazıt's sons argued over the succession to the weakened Ottoman throne. The civil war between them lasted for 10 years until 1413, when one son, Mehmet Çelebi, was able to gain supreme power. Six years after becoming sultan, Mehmet I (1413–21) ordered his architect Hacı İvaz to begin construction on Bursa's greatest monument, the Yeşil Cami or Green Mosque. It was finished in 1424.

The mosque, a few minutes' walk from Setbaşı, is a supremely beautiful building in a fine setting and represents a turning point in Turkish architectural style. Before this, Turkish mosques echoed the style of the great Seljuks which was basically Persian, but in the Yeşil Cami a purely Turkish style emerges. Notice the harmonious facade and the beautiful carved marblework around the central doorway. As you enter, you will pass beneath the sultan's private apartments into a domed central hall. The rooms to the left and right, if not being used for prayer, were used by high court officials for transacting government business. The room straight ahead, with the 15m-high mihrab (niche indicating the direction of Mecca), is the main prayer room. Greenish-blue tiles on the interior walls gave the mosque its name.

Much of Bursa, including the Yeşil Cami, was destroyed in an earthquake in 1855 but the mosque was restored, authentically, by 1864.

Just inside the mosque's main entrance, a narrow stairway leads up to the *hünkar mahfili*, or sultan's loge, above the main door. The loge is sumptuously tiled and decorated. This is where the sultan actually lived (or at least it was one of his residences), with his harem and household staff in less plush quarters on either side.

Yeşil Türbe

Sharing the small park surrounding the Yeşil Cami is the Yeşil Türbe, or Green Tomb. It's not green, of course. The blue exterior tiles were put on during restoration

work in the 19th century; the lavish use of tiles inside is original work, however. The tomb is open from 8.30 am to noon and 1 to 5.30 pm. There is no admission charge and no need to remove your shoes.

The most prominent tomb is that of the Yeşil Cami's founder, Mehmet I (Çelebi). Other tombs include those of his children. Take a walk around the outside of the tomb to look at the tiled calligraphy above several windows. The huge tiled mihrab here is very impressive.

After seeing the mosque and the tomb, you might want to take a rest and have something to drink at one of the cafes on the eastern side of the mosque, which have wonderful views of the valley, although you pay a premium for them.

Türk ve İslam Eserleri Müzesi

Down the road a few steps from the Yeşil Cami is its medrese, or school, which is now the Türk ve İslam Eserleri Müzesi (Turkish & Islamic Arts Museum). The building is in the Seljuk style of religious schools, and is open from 8.30 am to noon and 1 to 5 pm daily except Monday; admission costs US$1.25, less for students.

Start to the right to see a re-creation of an Ottoman *sünnet odası* (circumcision room), then, in the *eyvan* or hall, an exhibition of ceramics from the Seljuk period (12th and 13th centuries), İznik ware from the 14th to 18th centuries, and more modern Kütahya ware (18th to 20th centuries).

Next comes an exhibit of Karagöz shadow puppets. It's thought that these originated in China and Mongolia, and were brought to the Middle East by the Turks.

After Karagöz, museum displays include costumes, carpets, jewellery, metalwork and arms; *dergah* (dervish hall) musical instruments, turbans and other paraphernalia; illuminated Qurans, carpet weaving and embroidery.

Yıldırım Beyazıt Camii

Gazing across the valley from the Emir Sultan Camii, you'll see the two domes of the Yıldırım Beyazıt Camii, the Mosque of Beyazıt the Thunderbolt. It was built earlier (in 1391) than the Yeşil Cami, and forms part of the same architectural evolution.

Next to the Yıldırım Beyazıt Camii is its *medrese*, once a Muslim theological seminary, now a public health centre. Here also are the tombs of the mosque's founder, Sultan Beyazıt I, and his son İsa. This peaceful spot gives one no sense of the turbulent times which brought Beyazıt to his death.

Yıldırım Beyazıt (Sultan Beyazıt I, who reigned from 1389–1402) led his Ottoman armies into Yugoslavia and Hungary, and captured even more of Anatolia for the Ottomans. But he was brought down by Tamerlane, who defeated him and took him prisoner at the Battle of Ankara in 1402. Beyazıt died a year later in captivity, and Tamerlane marched all the way to İzmir and Bursa. With this blow, the Ottoman Empire all but collapsed.

Markets

From the plaza at Heykel, walk down the hill on the eastern (right) side of İnönü Caddesi one very long block. Cross Kirişkızı Sokak and turn right onto the next street, Kayhan Caddesi, to enter a warren of little streets called the **Bat Pazarı** (Goose Market), or, more appropriately, the **Demirciler Çarşısı** (Ironmongers' Market).

After a half-hour stroll, head back to İnönü Caddesi and ask someone to point the way to the **Kapalı Çarşı** or Covered Market. Cross İnönü Caddesi and head into the side streets, following the directions given. The actual covered market is surrounded by a network of small shopping streets.

The *bedesten* (vaulted market enclosure), at the centre of the Kapalı Çarşı, was originally built in the late 14th century by Yıldırım Beyazıt, but the earthquake of 1855 brought it down. The reconstructed bedesten retains the look and feel of the original, though it is obviously much tidier. This is not a tourist trap; most of the shoppers are local people. As you wander around, look for the **Eski Aynalı Çarşı** which, though now a market, was originally built as the Orhangazi Hamamı (1335), the Turkish bath of the Orhan Camii Külliyesi. The domed ceiling with many small skylights shows this.

Koza & Emir Hans

The raising of silkworms is a cottage industry in Bursa. Each April, villagers buy the worms from their cooperatives, take them home and raise them on mulberry leaves. After a month the worms spin their cocoons and are soon ready for the trip to the Koza Han or Silk Cocoon Caravanserai just outside the bedesten's eastern entrance. Built in 1451, this han is lively with cocoon dealers in June and also in September when there is a second harvest.

When you visit, you may well see huge sacks of the precious little white cocoons being haggled over by some of the 14,000 villagers who engage in the trade. In the centre of the Koza Han's courtyard is a small mosque constructed by Yıldırım Beyazıt in 1393, restored by the guild of silk traders in 1948, and again in 1985 by the Aga Khan. The product of all this industry, *ipek* (silk cloth), is for sale in the bedesten.

Adjoining the north-eastern corner of the Ulu Cami is the Emir Han, used by many of Bursa's silk brokers today, as it has been for centuries. There's a lovely fountain in the centre of the courtyard, and a tea garden for refreshments. Camels from the silk caravans used to be corralled in the courtyard, while goods were stored in the ground-floor rooms and drovers and merchants slept and did business in the rooms above.

Ulu Cami

Next to the bedesten and Emir Han is Bursa's Ulu Cami. This one is completely Seljuk in style, a big rectangular building with immense portals and a forest of supporting columns inside, similar to the much older Ulu Cami in Erzurum. The roof is a mass of 20 small domes. A fountain plays peacefully at the centre of the interior. Yıldırım Beyazıt put up the money for the building in 1396. Notice the fine work of the *mimber* (pulpit) and the preacher's chair, also the calligraphy on the walls.

Hisar

This section of town, the oldest in Bursa, was once enclosed by stone ramparts and walls, bits of which still survive.

WESTERN ANATOLIA

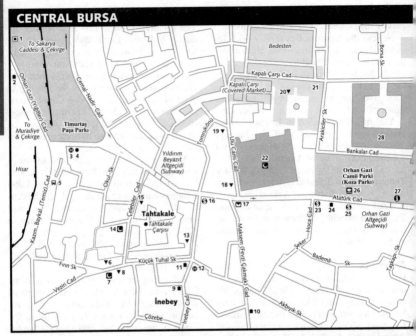

CENTRAL BURSA

PLACES TO STAY
2 Safran Oteli & Restaurant
9 Otel Çamlıbel
10 Hotel Dikmen
11 Otel Güneş
24 Kent Hotel
36 Hotel Çeşmeli

PLACES TO EAT
6 Yeşil İnci Lokantası
8 Şölen Ocakbaşı
13 Şehir Lokantası
15 Aliş Izgara
18 Ömür Köftecisi
19 Marmara Lokantası
20 Emirhan Çay Evi
30 Çiçek Izgara
33 Kebapçı İskenderoğlu Nurettin

34 İnegöl Köftecisi; Kamil Koç Co
Bus Tickets
37 Okyanus Fırın Salonu
43 Adanur Hacıbey
44 Kebapçı İskender

OTHER
1 Osman Gazi & Orhan Gazi
Tombs
3 Çakır Ağa Hamamı
4 Uludağ Co Bus Tickets
5 Muradiye Dolmuş
7 Hacı Sevinç Camii
12 Tarihi İnebey Hamamı
14 Mecnundede Camii
16 Türkiye Emlak Bankası
17 PTT
21 Emir Han

22 Ulu Cami
23 Türkiye İş Bankası
25 Osmanlı Bankası
26 Cafe Koza
27 Tourist Office
28 Koza Han
29 Mahmutpaşa (Fidan) Han
31 Belediye Sarayı (Town Hall)
32 Internet House Cafe
35 Karaşeyh Camii
38 Elt Kitabevi
39 TAŞ Kitapçılık & Yayıncılık
40 Dolmuşes to Devlet Hastanesi,
Emir Sultan, Muradiye &
Teleferik
41 Ahmet Vefik Paşa Tiyatrosu
42 TC Ziraat Bankası
45 Karakedi Camii

From the Ulu Cami, walk west and up Orhan Gazi (Yiğitler) Caddesi, a ramp-like street that leads up to the section known as Hisar (Fortress) or Tophane. To ride there, take any bus marked for Devlet Hastanesi (Dev. Hst.), Muradiye or Hamzabey and get out at the 'Tophane' stop. (The Devlet Hastanesi is a large government hospital just

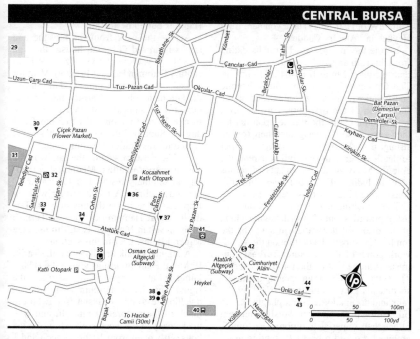

CENTRAL BURSA

west of the tombs of sultans Osman and Orhan.)

Near a sign which reads 'İstiklal Savaşı Şehitler', in a little park near the edge of the cliff overlooking Cemal Nadir Caddesi and the valley, are the **Osman Gazi ve Orhan Gazi Türbeleri** (Tombs of Sultans Osman and Orhan), founders of the Ottoman Empire. The original structures were destroyed in the earthquake of 1855 and rebuilt in Ottoman baroque style by Sultan Abdül Aziz in 1868.

Osman Gazi's tomb is the more richly decorated of the two. A small donation is requested, and you should remove your shoes before entering.

The tomb of Orhan Gazi was built on the foundations of a small Byzantine church, and you can see some remnants of the church's floor.

The park here is attractive, as is the view of the city. Snack bars and patisseries across Osmangazi Caddesi provide sustenance.

Hop in a bus or dolmuş marked 'Muradiye' to continue along Hasta Yurdu Caddesi to Muradiye, about 2.5km to the west. You'll dip down into the valley of the Cılımboz Deresi before arriving in the verdant residential quarter of Muradiye.

Sakarya Caddesi, north of the Hisar district, was once the main street of Bursa's Jewish quarter, which thrived from 1492 until recent times. There are still several operating synagogues on the street, most notably the 500-year-old Geruş Havrası at No 59 (visits by special arrangement only).

Muradiye Complex

With a shady park in front and a quiet cemetery behind, the **Sultan II. Murat (Muradiye) Camii**, also called the Hüdavendigar Camii, is pretty and peaceful. The mosque proper dates from 1426 and follows the style of the Yeşil Cami. A vegetable and fruit market fills the neighbouring street on Tuesday.

Dolmuşes (to Muradiye) and buses (to Muradiye or Hamzabey) take you here from Heykel and Atatürk Caddesi.

Beside the mosque are 12 tombs dating from the 15th and 16th centuries, including that of Sultan Murat II (1404–51) himself. The Ottoman dynasty, like other Islamic and Asiatic dynasties, was not based on the succession of the first-born. Any son of a sultan could claim the throne upon his father's death, so the designated heir (or the strongest son) would have his brothers put to death rather than see civil war rend the empire. Many of the occupants of tombs here, including all the şehzades (imperial sons), were killed by close relatives.

Tomb-visiting may not be high on your list of priorities, but it's worth having a look at the beautiful decoration in some of the tombs. The superb decoration on the woodwork porch of the **II. Murat Türbesi** contrasts with the rest of the tomb's austerity. The sultan's tomb has an opening to the sky so that his grave could be washed by the rain, and his unadorned sarcophagus has no lid, following common Muslim custom rather than imperial tradition. The tomb's architect did add a bit of Byzantine grandeur by borrowing some old Corinthian columns, but he used capitals as both capitals and plinths.

The beautiful İznik tilework in the gaudy **Cem Türbesi** celebrates Cem Sultan (1459–95), the youngest son of Sultan Mehmet the Conqueror. Cem reigned for 18 days, but was chased from the throne by Beyazıt II and fled to Europe, where he became a hostage of the pope and a pawn in Ottoman-European diplomacy.

The İznik tiles in the **Şehzade Mustafa Türbesi** are as fine as those in the Rüstem Paşa Camii in İstanbul. Mustafa (1515–53), son of Süleyman the Magnificent, was governor of Amasya when Süleyman's wife Roxelana plotted against him, causing the sultan to order his execution – which he soon regretted bitterly.

The **Şehzade Ahmet Türbesi** is elegant in its simplicity of light- and dark-blue tiles framed by a vine-patterned blue-and-white border. The stained glass window is restrained as well. Ahmet's mother Bülbül Hatun is buried beside him.

Across the park from the mosque and tombs is an old **Ottoman house** (the sign says '17. y. y. Osmanlı Evi Müzesi' or 17th-century Ottoman House Museum). Visit for a fascinating glimpse into the daily life of the Ottoman nobility. Carpets and furnishings are all authentic. It used to be open from 8.30 am to noon and 1 to 5 pm Tuesday to Sunday but the house has been closed for restoration for some time.

On the western side of the tombs is the 15th-century **Muradiye Medresesi**, a theological seminary restored in 1951 as a tuberculosis clinic. A block further west on Kaplıca Caddesi near the bus stop, the **Tarihi II. Murat Hamamı**, or Historic Turkish Bath of Sultan Murat II, is still in use (see Mineral Baths, later in this section).

A minute's walk uphill behind the Tarihi II. Murat Hamamı brings you to the **Hüsnü Züber Evi** at Uzunyol Sokak 3 (follow the signs). This 'living museum' is an Ottoman dwelling restored by Hüsnü Bey, who did much of the restoration himself, and who made many of the woodwork exhibits in the house. It's open from 10 am to noon and 1 to 5 pm daily except Monday, but you may find no-one at home. Admission costs US$1.25, less for students.

Kültür Parkı

Bursa's Kültür Parkı or 'Cultural Park', is laid out to the north of the Muradiye Complex, down the hill some distance. You can reach it from Heykel by any bus or dolmuş going to Altıparmak, Sigorta or Çekirge. Besides offering a pleasant stroll, the Kültür Parkı has a fun park with children's rides, a small zoo, an open-air theatre, a rose garden, many tea gardens, and shady outdoor restaurants.

The park also houses the **Arkeoloji Müzesi**. Bursa's history goes back to the time of Hannibal (200 BC), and Roman artefacts are preserved here. The collection is nice, but not at all exceptional. If you've seen another good Turkish collection, this is more of the same. The museum (US$0.50) is open from 8.30 am to noon and 1 to 5 pm daily except

Monday. Find the 'Arkeoloji Müzesi' bus stop, and enter the park by the gate nearby.

I. Murat (Hüdavendigâr) Camii

In this city of early Ottoman mosques, the I. Murat (Hüdavendigâr) Camii behind the Ada Palas Oteli in Çekirge is among the more unusual. Its basic design is the early Ottoman inverted 'T' plan which first appeared in the *imaret* (soup kitchen for the poor), built in 1388 by Murat's mother Nilüfer Hatun in İznik. Here, however, the 'T' wings are barrel-vaulted rather than dome-topped. On the ground floor at the front are the rooms of a *zaviye*, or 'dervish hostel'. The 2nd-floor gallery on the facade, built as a medrese, is not evident from within except for the sultan's loge in the middle at the back of the mosque.

Sultan Murat I (1359–89), who died after a victorious battle against his rebellious Albanian, Bosnian, Bulgarian, Hungarian and Serbian subjects at Kosovo, is buried in the tomb across the street. On the eastern side of the Tuğra Termal Oteli, the rather grand mosque toilet is all that is left of the mosque's imaret.

Mineral Baths

The warm, mineral-rich waters that spring from the slopes of Uludağ have been famous for their curative powers since ancient times. Today the ailing and the infirm come here for several weeks at a time, take a daily soak or two in the tub, and spend the rest of the time chatting, reading and dining. Most people stay in hotels which have their own mineral bath facilities. There are independent *kaplıca* (thermal baths) as well, some of historical importance.

Baths will be crowded on Friday, the Muslim holy day, as local people clean up for it.

The Yeni Kaplıca (☎ 236 6955), Mudanya Caddesi 10, on the north-western side of the Kültür Parkı, is a bath renovated in 1522 by Sultan Süleyman the Magnificent's grand vizier, Rüstem Paşa, on the site of a much older one built by Justinian. Besides the Yeni (New) baths, you'll find the Kaynarca (Boiling), limited to women; and the Karamustafa, which has facilities for

family bathing. All baths in the complex are open from 6 am to 11 pm (last admission at 10 pm).

Perhaps the most attractive place is the Eski Kaplıca (☎ 233 9300) next door to the Kervansaray Termal Hotel on Çekirge's eastern outskirts. Beautifully restored, the baths now cater to an upmarket clientele of business travellers, tourists and local notables who stay at or socialise in the hotel.

The bathing rooms are covered in creamy marble. In the hot room are plunging pools; use of the nice swimming pool downstairs is subject to a hefty additional charge. The cool room has lounge chairs for relaxing, and a bar with waiter service.

Prices are higher here than at unrestored local baths, but the building is beautiful, though service is fairly inattentive. Hours are daily from 7 am to 11 pm for men, from 7.30 am to 11 pm for women. There's an entry fee of US$6, and US$4 for a massage or to have an attendant wash you; the cost of soap is additional, so figure on spending US$20 for the works, including massage and tips. You can bring your own soap and wash yourself for little more than the basic entry fee. To get to the Eski Kaplıca baths, take a bus or dolmuş marked for 'SSK Hast(anesi)' or 'Sigorta'.

For a simpler, less expensive bath near the hotels in the centre of Bursa, try Çakır Ağa Hamamı, on the corner of Atatürk Caddesi and Kazım Baykal (Temiz) Caddesi, just west of the Tahtakale/İnebey district. Posted prices are US$3 for a wash, another US$1.75 for soap and scrub, US$2 for a massage, US$4 for use of a resting cubicle, or the works for US$12 or so. The hamam is open daily from 7 am to 11 pm.

The Tarihi İnebey Hamamı on İnebey Caddesi is even closer to several recommended hotels.

Next to the Muradiye mosque is the Tarihi II. Murat Hamamı ('II. Murat' is said 'İkinci Murat'), open to men on Friday and Sunday, to women *(kadınlara)* all other days, from 10 am to 6 pm. The Tarihi Keçeli Hamamı opposite the Yıldız Oteli and the Askeri Hastanesi (Military Hospital) is for women only.

The Hamam Experience

The history of steam baths goes back thousands of years when many of Turkey's natural spas were enjoyed by the ancient Greeks and Romans. Turks built beautiful, elaborate *hamams* (baths) to serve their communities, partly because Islam demands high standards of personal hygiene, and partly because bathing is such a pleasure.

Public baths used to be required because private homes didn't have bathing facilities. Everybody, rich and poor alike, went to the baths. For a workman, it was simply to get clean. For a high-born woman, it was a ritual of attendants and polite courtesies, and many museums display the gorgeous gold-embroidered towels, mother-of-pearl pattens and lovely accessories she would have taken with her.

Most Turkish towns still have hamams of varying degrees of fanciness, although they are becoming scarcer in the west as homes acquire plumbed-in bathrooms. The custom of going to the hamam continues because the public facilities are so much grander than those available at home, and because, for Turks, it is still a social occasion. To steam clean, have a massage, relax, watch television, sip tea and chat with friends is looked upon as wonderful, affordable luxury.

What happens in a hamam? Well, you will be shown to a *camekan* (cubicle) where you can undress, store your clothes, lock up your valuables and wrap the cloth that's provided (the *pestemal*) around you. A *tellak* (attendant) will lead you through to the hot room where you sit and sweat for a while.

Then you have to make a choice. It's cheapest to wash yourself with the *sabun* (soap), *sampuan* (shampoo) and *havlu* (towel) you brought with you. The hot room will be ringed with individual basins which you fill from the taps above before sluicing the water over yourself with a plastic scoop. You should try not to get soap into the water in the basin, and avoid splashing your neighbours, especially on a Friday when someone who has completed their ritual wash would have to start all over again if soaked by a non-Muslim.

But it's far more enjoyable to let an attendant wash you. In the hot room you'll be doused with warm water and then scrubbed with a coarse cloth *kese* (mitten), loosening dirt you never suspected you had. Afterwards you'll be lathered with a sudsy swab, rinsed off and shampooed.

When all this is done you'll be offered the chance of a massage, an experience worth having at least once during your trip. Some massages are carried out on the floor or a table, but often you'll be spread out on the great marble bench (or *göbektasi*) beneath the dome. In touristy areas (other than İstanbul) the massage is likely to be pretty cursory and unless you're prepared to pay the extra

Places to Stay

Because of its industrial and touristic prosperity, hotels in Bursa can be somewhat expensive.

Places to Stay – Budget

Central Bursa The Tahtakale/İnebey district just south of the Ulu Cami is an interesting area with many narrow streets and historic houses. Some of the houses are being restored, and will no doubt soon be turned into expensive shops and moderately priced 'boutique' hotels. There's a good produce market here as well.

The cheapest rooms in Tahtakale are at *Otel Güneş (☎ 222 1404, İnebey Caddesi 75)*, where waterless singles/doubles are US$7/14, with a shower down the hall.

Though somewhat overpriced, the nearby *Otel Çamlıbel (☎ 221 2565, fax 223 4405, İnebey Caddesi 71)* is a renovated hotel in a quiet location, with rooms with constant hot water and good cross-ventilation, a lift and even a few parking places in front of the hotel. Single/double/triple rooms with shower are US$25/30/40.

Çekirge Most Çekirge hotels have their own facilities for 'taking the waters'. You may find that the bathtub or shower at your hotel runs only mineral water, or there may be private or public bathing rooms in the

The Hamam Experience

for an 'oil massage' you may be disappointed. Elsewhere, however, a Turkish massage can be an unforgettable, if occasionally rough, experience.

The massage over, you'll be led back to the cold room, there to be swathed in towels and taken to your cubicle for a rest. Tea, coffee, soft drinks and beer are usually available.

Traditional hamams have separate sections for men and women or admit men and women at separate times. As the number of baths declines, it's usually the ones for women that go first as there is some ambivalence about how desirable it is for women to be out of the home. Opening hours for women are almost invariably more restricted than for men.

Bath etiquette dictates that men should keep the pestemal on at all times, washing their own private parts without ever removing this modesty wrap. In the women's section, the amount of modesty expected varies considerably: in some baths total nudity is fine, in others it would be a blunder to remove your knickers. Play it safe by keeping your underwear on under your pestemal until inside the hot room where you can decide what is appropriate. Women also wash their own private parts. If you want to shave your legs or armpits, you should do this in the outer warm room rather than in the bath.

In the touristy areas, most hamams are more than happy for foreign men and women to bathe together, usually for a premium price. In traditional hamams, women are washed and massaged by other women. No Turkish woman would let a male masseur anywhere near her, however, while Turkish men continue to frequent baths used by tourists, the Turkish women vanish, and with them go the female masseuses.

Sexual activity has no place in the traditional bath ritual. Women who accept a masseur should have their massage within view of their male companions or friends. At the first sign of impropriety, they should protest loudly.

MICK WELDON

basement of the hotel. A day's dip in the mineral waters is no great thrill; the therapeutic benefits are supposedly acquired over weeks. All the same, a soak in the bath may be included in the price of the room so take advantage of it.

Çekirge's main street is I. Murat Caddesi (Birinci Murat Caddesi). To get to the Çekirge hotels, take a bus or dolmuş from Heykel or along Atatürk Caddesi to Çekirge or SSK Hastanesi.

Most Çekirge hotels suffer from street noise; in this section we've listed the ones that don't.

Öz Yeşil Yayla Oteli (☎/fax 239 6496, *Çekirge Caddesi, Selvi Sokak 6*), between

the Boyugüzel and Yıldız II hotels at the upper end of the village, is old-fashioned and simple – a living piece of 1950s Çekirge – charging US$24 for a double with sink, including free use of the mineral baths.

Next door, the *Boyugüzel Termal Otel* (☎ 239 9999, fax 239 6767, Selvi Sokak) charges US$32 for a double room with sink and toilet, with a half-hour mineral bath downstairs included each day.

Hotel Gold 2 (☎/fax 236 8099, I. Murat Caddesi, Cami Aralığı 2) is behind the more visible Ada Palas. It has quiet rooms with showers, and a terrace in front, and charges US$25/35 a single/double.

Places to Stay – Mid-Range

In central Bursa noise is a big problem, but the best hotels are off the main streets. If you need to, ask for *sakin bir oda* (a quiet room).

Hotel Çeşmeli (☎ 224 1511, *Gümüşçeken Caddesi 6*), a few steps north of Atatürk Caddesi near Heykel, is friendly, simple, fairly quiet, very clean, run by God-fearing Muslims and conveniently located. Singles/doubles/triples with shower cost US$27/36/45, including breakfast. Though expensive, this is a good choice for women travellers.

Hotel Dikmen (☎ 224 1840, *fax 220 4085, Maksem, or Fevzi Çakmak, Caddesi 78*) is further west, then south. This three-star hotel's lobby is pleasant, with a small enclosed garden terrace, complete with fountain, at the back; a lift takes you up to your room. Singles/doubles with little luxuries such as bathtubs, TVs and minibars are US$40/55, which is a bit expensive. The hotel is about 50m uphill on the street which starts beside the PTT.

Places to Stay – Top End

Central Bursa At the nominally three-star *Kent Hotel* (☎ 223 5420, *fax 224 4015, Atatürk Caddesi 69*) all rooms have air-con, showers, minibars and satellite TVs. Although posted prices may be as high as US$75/100 a single/double, ask for a reduction as rates are negotiable.

Opposite the Osman and Orhan tombs, *Safran Oteli & Restaurant* (☎ 224 7216, *fax 224 7219, Kale Sokak*) is a restored Ottoman house in a historic neighbourhood. Rooms with bath and TV cost US$45/60, including breakfast. The adjoining restaurant and Mavi Bar are good, too.

Çekirge The three-star *Termal Hotel Gönlü Ferah* (☎ 233 9210, *fax 233 9218, I. Murat Caddesi 24*) is in the centre of the village. Some of the rooms have fine views over the valley. The ambience here is 'European spa', and the service is experienced. Singles/doubles are US$86/104, including breakfast, with reductions if they're not busy.

Next door, the four-star *Hotel Dilmen* (☎ 233 9500, *fax 235 2568, I. Murat Caddesi*) boasts a garden terrace, restaurant/bar, an exercise room with sauna and mineral-water baths, and 100 posh rooms with TVs and minibars for about the same as the Gönlü Ferah.

Places to Eat

Bursa's culinary specialities include fresh fruit (especially *şeftali* – peaches – in season), *kestane şekeri* (candied chestnuts) and two types of roast meat. *Bursa kebap*, or *İskender kebap*, is döner kebap laid on a bed of fresh pide bread and topped with savoury tomato sauce and browned butter (see the boxed text 'İskender Kebap' in the Food section of the Facts for the Visitor chapter). İnegöl *köftesi* is a rich grilled meatball in the style of the nearby town of İnegöl.

Kebapçıs & Other Grills Cost differences among restaurants of the same class are small due to fixed municipal prices. A *bir porsyon* (one-serving) plate of kebap with yogurt costs US$5 or US$6, soft drink included (alcohol is not normally served at kebapçıs). Add US$2 if you order *bir buçuk porsyon* (1½ portions). All these places are open seven days a week from 11 am until 9 or 10 pm.

The owners of *Kebapçı İskender* (☎ 221 4615, *Ünlü Caddesi 7*), half a block southeast of Heykel on a pedestrian-only street, claim to be descendants of the eponymous İskender Usta himself. The elaborate Ottomanesque facade and semi-formal waiters belie moderate prices (US$6 to US$8 for Bursa kebap with yoghurt, plus a soft drink). İskender kebap and a few salads and sweets are all that is served.

Directly across the road is *Adanur Hacıbey* (☎ 221 6440, *Ünlü Caddesi*), a simpler place where the Bursa kebap comes with a dab of smoky aubergine puree on the side. Don't begin eating your kebap until the waiter brings the tomato sauce and browned butter.

Bursa kebap was invented in a small restaurant now called *Kebapçı İskenderoğlu Nurettin* (*Atatürk Caddesi 60*), meaning 'İskender's Son', between Heykel and the Ulu Cami. The surroundings are basic and simple, the kebap good but unremarkable.

For İnegöl köftesi, try *İnegöl Köftecisi (Atatürk Caddesi 48)*. Variations of the basic grilled lamb meatball include those stuffed with onions or cheese. A full lunch costs US$5.

Çiçek Izgara (☎ 221 6526, Belediye Caddesi 15), one block from the Koza Parkı behind the half-timbered belediye, doesn't specialise in Bursa kebap, but serves excellent grills in a white-tablecloth setting. Prices range from US$3 for *köfte* (meatballs) to US$8 for the big mixed grill; a *bonfile* (small beef filet steak) costs US$6.

Okyanus Fırın Salonu (Pars Çıkmazı), on the side street between the Vakıfbank and Atatürk Caddesi 44, is shiny and modern, specialising in *Konya fırın kebap* – rich joints of roasted mutton. A filling meal costs US$6.

Ömür Köftecisi, on the western side of the Ulu Cami, is in the historical *arasta* (complex of shops attached to a mosque). The grills range from *kaşarlı köfte* (lamb meatballs with yellow cheese) for US$2.25 to a *karışık ızgara* (mixed grill) for US$3.50. The nearby *Marmara Lokantası* has a wider selection of dishes.

Hazır Yemek Ready-food *(hazır yemek)* restaurants have steam tables and precooked soups, stews, *pilavs* (rice dishes) and stuffed vegetables. Many close by 7 pm. The Tahtakale/İnebey district is a particularly good place to look for a good, cheap meal. *Şehir Lokantası (İnebey Caddesi 85)*, half a block up the hill from Atatürk Caddesi, serves hazır yemek meals for around US$3 or US$4, as does the neighbouring *Ümit*.

Further up the street from the Şehir, turn right (west) and walk to the market area known as the Tahtakale Çarşısı. To the north-west is the *Ali Izgara (Çelebiler Caddesi 18)* and the adjoining *Ali Baba Baklavacısı*. Walk uphill two blocks on Çelebiler Caddesi to a T-intersection, turn right and walk half a block to the *Yeşil İnci Lokantası* (Green Pearl), which has a separate 10-table *aile salonu* (family dining room). This restaurant, facing the Hacı Sevinç Camii, stays open later than many other local eateries and serves delicious ready food accompanied by its own freshly baked pide bread. You need spend no more than US$4 to fill up. *Şölen Ocakbaşı* across the street is also good.

Fish Restaurants Sakarya Caddesi's fame was made by one Arap Şükrü who opened a restaurant here decades ago. It was so popular and successful that, as with İskender and his kebap, Arap Şükrü's descendants have gone into the business. The street, now generally known as Arap Şükrü Sokak, has no less than five restaurants with that name, all run by relatives or descendants. Among them, perhaps the favourite is *Arap Şükrü Yılmaz (☎ 221 9239, Sakarya Caddesi 4)*. Fish is the speciality, but grills are always served, and a full meal with rakı, beer or wine need cost no more than US$12 to US$20 per person.

The street is on the northern side of the Hisar district, just south of Altıparmak Caddesi. To find it, take a bus or dolmuş from Heykel bound for Çekirge and get out at the Çatal Fırın bus stop across from the Sabahettin Paşa Camii. Cross to the southern side of Altıparmak Caddesi and walk west into Sakarya Caddesi. If you're walking, go downhill from the Ulu Cami along Atatürk/Altıparmak on the Hisar side of the road; it's less than 10 minutes.

Restaurants Facing the park before the Muradiye mosque is *Darüzziyafe (☎ 224 6439, II. Murat Caddesi 36)*, a restaurant serving classic Turkish cuisine. Order the plate of assorted Turkish specialities and your lunch bill might be US$7 or US$8. Even cheaper meals are available up the street at the *Yalçın Pide Salonu*, at No 24.

Strolling around the Kültür Parkı is pleasant, and having a meal here is more so. The *Seljuk Restaurant (☎ 220 9695)* near the mosque is good, quiet, shady, serves alcoholic beverages, and is not overly expensive, with three-course meals for US$8 to US$15.

Cafes Above Koza Parkı on Atatürk Caddesi near the Ulu Cami, *Cafe Koza* is Bursa's central people-watching place, but it's not cheap. A simple tea costs US$0.60, coffee twice as much.

Self-Catering The Tahtakale Çarşısı is the nicest and most convenient market area in central Bursa. Walk west from the Ulu Cami along Atatürk Caddesi to the pedestrian underpass named Yıldırım Beyazıt Altgeçidi. From the southern end of the subway, go left or right a few steps, then south along a narrow street to the market area.

Another market lies downhill (north) of the Çiçek Pazarı (Flower Market) behind Koza Parkı and the belediye. Come here for fruits (fresh and dried), nuts, vegetables, meats, bread and biscuits.

Entertainment

Sakarya Caddesi is a small street lined with *meyhanes* (taverns), some of them serving fish. At many restaurants and bars the clientele is heavily male, but most nightspots post signs reading 'Damsız Girilmez', which means that a man unaccompanied by a woman will not be admitted, to keep things more in proportion. The *Piccolo Bar* at No 16 puts tables outdoors in fine weather, as indeed do most of the places on the street.

Cafe M which is among the nicer places, and a good choice for women travellers. *Barantico* (☎ 222 4049, Sakarya Caddesi 55) has a long menu of drinks, grills, light meals and sweets, and offers a popular dance floor. The *Cevriye Bar*, at No 47, is chic like the Barantico.

Another place for drinks is in the *Mavi Bar* at the Safran Oteli & Restaurant (see Places to Stay – Top End).

Shopping

Bursa's specialities are silk cloth (especially scarves), hand-knitted woollen mittens, gloves and socks, Karagöz shadow puppets and candied chestnuts. Other good items are thick Bursa Turkish towels (some say they were invented here), for those taking the Çekirge waters. If you have lots of room in your luggage, buy a *bornoz*, a huge, thick, heavy terry-towelling bathrobe. You can find all these things in the Kapalı Çarşı (Covered Market).

Getting There & Away

The best way to reach Bursa from İstanbul is by fast catamaran and bus. A new airport is being readied at Yenişehir, 40km east of Bursa, but it may not be finished for years.

Bursa's otogar, the Bursa Şehirlerarası Otobüs Terminalı, is 10km north of the centre on the Yalova road. Special 'Terminal' buses (grey with a blue stripe) shuttle between the bus station and the city centre.

The Doğu Garaj (Eastern Garage) and Batı Garaj (Western Garage) – separate, small minibus terminals to the east and west of the city centre – serve regional routes.

The fastest way to İstanbul (US$10, 2½ to three hours) is a bus to Yalova, then a catamaran or fast car-ferry to İstanbul's Yenikapı docks. Get a bus that departs from Bursa's bus terminal at least 90 minutes before the scheduled boat departure. There are frequent buses from Yalova to Bursa (US$4). Otherwise, it takes four to five hours by road (230km) to İstanbul.

For other destinations, buy your ticket in advance to ensure a good seat and departure

Services from Bursa's Otogar

destination	fare (US$)	time (hr)	distance (km)	daily services
Afyon	10	5	290	8 buses
Ankara	11	5½	400	hourly buses
Bandırma	5	2	115	12 buses
Çanakkale	10	5	310	12 buses
İzmir	8	5½	375	hourly buses
İznik	2.75–3.50	1½	82	hourly buses
Kütahya	6.50	3	190	several buses
Yalova	4	1¼	60	buses every 30 mins

time. The table lists some daily services on some selected routes from Bursa.

Getting Around

To/From the Otogar Take the silver-and-blue 'Terminal' bus (US$0.75) from special stops to travel the 10km between the otogar and the city centre. A taxi costs US$8.

City Bus Bursa's city buses (BOİ; US$0.40) have destinations and stops marked on the front and kerb side. A major set of stops is by Koza Parkı on Atatürk Caddesi. Catch a bus from *peron* (gate) 1 for Emir Sultan and Teleferuç (Uludağ cable car); from peron 2 for Muradiye; from peron 4 for Altıparmak and the Kültür Parkı; from the BOİ Ekspres Peron for the Osman Gazi and Orhan Gazi tombs and Muradiye.

Dolmuş In Bursa, cars operate as dolmuşes along with the minibuses. The destination is indicated by the illuminated sign on the roof. The minimum fare is US$0.50.

A major dolmuş starting-point is just south of Heykel. Among other destinations, cars go to Çekirge via the Kültür Parkı, Eski Kaplıca and I. Murat Camii.

Taxi A ride from Heykel to Muradiye costs about US$2; about US$4 to Çekirge.

ULUDAĞ
☎ 224

In the ancient world, a number of mountains bore the name Olympus. Uludağ (Great Mountain, 2543m) was on the outskirts of the ancient city of Bithynia (now Bursa), so this was the Bithynian Olympus.

The gods no longer live on top of Uludağ, but there is a *teleferik* (cable car), a selection of hotels, a national park, cool forests and often snow. Even if you don't plan to hike to the summit (three hours each way from the hotel area) or to go skiing (in winter only), you might want to take the cable car or a dolmuş up for the view and a draught of cool air. If you take a picnic, beware of groups of boy thieves, aged seven to 13, who circulate in the summer. Report any such groups to the police.

Though a fairly sleepy place in summer, the hotel and ski area on Uludağ comes to life during the skiing season from December to early April.

At the cable-car terminus at Sarıalan there are a few snack and refreshment stands, a national-park camping ground (usually full), some walking trails and the occasional dolmuş to the *oteller mevkii* (hotel zone), 6km further up the mountain slope.

Getting There & Away

Cable Car For a summer visit to Uludağ, getting there is most of the fun. Take a Bursa city bus from Koza Parkı (peron 1), or a dolmuş, marked for 'Teleferik' (☎ 221 3635), to the lower terminus of the cable car – a 15-minute ride from Heykel at Bursa's eastern edge. In summer, the cable cars depart when full or at least every 30 to 45 minutes, weather and winds permitting. The trip to the top takes about 30 minutes and costs US$5 each way, half price on Wednesday.

The cable car stops at an intermediate point named Kadıyayla, from where you continue upwards to the terminus at Sarıalan at an altitude of 1635m.

Dolmuş Dolmuşes run from central Bursa to the hotel zone on Uludağ (32km) several times daily in summer (more frequently in winter) for US$7 per person each way.

At the 11km marker you must stop and pay an entry fee for the national park of US$0.50 per person, US$1.50 for a car and driver. The hotel zone is 11km further up from the national park entrance. Almost half of the entire drive from Bursa is on rough granite-block pavement.

The return ride can be difficult in summer as there are few dolmuşes or taxis in evidence. In winter there are usually plenty, and they are eager to get at least some fare before they head back down, so you may be able to get back to Bursa for less.

Car If you're driving, you'll need to have tyre chains in winter (December to early April) when the road is icy or snowy; look out for signs saying 'Zincir Takmak Mecburidir' (Chains are Required).

BANDIRMA
☎ 266 • pop 80,000

The port town of Bandırma has an ancient history, but nothing to show for it. What you see is a 20th-century creation which might well be nicknamed Betonbol (Concreteville). It has little to offer the tourist except the junction between the İzmir to Bandırma train line and the Bandırma to İstanbul ferry line. You'd do well to pass straight through, but if you must stop, there are hotels and restaurants in the town.

Orientation & Information

Bandırma's otogar is 1.8km south-east of the centre, out by the main highway by *servis arabası* (shuttle bus).

If you arrive by train or ferry, walk east for 250m to reach the main square.

From the main square, the main road going east is İnönü Caddesi, which has cheap hotels, restaurants and bus ticket offices.

Places to Stay & Eat

The *Çetin Otel* (*☎ 718 8750, Haydarçavuş Sokak 5-B*), opposite the Kamil Koç bus office, is relatively quiet, charges US$8/11 for singles/doubles with sink, US$14/16 with shower, and has rooms with TV. Its sister hotel, the *Sahil* (*☎ 718 4485, İnönü Caddesi 10*), faces the noisy town square.

The older *Hotel Eken* (*☎ 714 7800, fax 712 5355, Uğur Mumcu Caddesi 9*), half a block west of the main square up the hill, charges US$40 to US$46 for a double with shower and TV, including breakfast. It's overshadowed by the fancier four-star *Hotel Eken Prestige* (*☎ 714 7600, Mehmet Akif Ersoy Caddesi 7*), which thinks it's the Hilton: rooms are US$100/180.

İnönü Caddesi, the main shopping street, has many little restaurants. Try the *Moby Dick Restaurant* off the main traffic circle, or *Kapıdağ* off İnönü, towards the water.

Getting There & Away

Hızlı feribot (fast car-ferries) connect Bandırma with İstanbul's Yenikapı docks thrice daily, making the run in under two hours. The fare for a car and driver is US$45, for a pedestrian or passenger US$13.

Bandırma is midway on the bus run between Bursa (US$5, two hours, 115km, 12 buses daily) and Çanakkale (US$7, three hours, 195km, 12 buses daily). There are also buses south to Balıkesir and points beyond. For route, schedule and fare information, ask at the otogar, or at the bus-company ticket offices on İnönü Caddesi.

The daily train to İzmir's Basmane station (US$4.50, six hours) departs in the late afternoon.

KUŞCENNETİ MİLLİ PARKI

Though Bandırma will not hold your interest for very long, bird enthusiasts will want to make a detour (18.5km) to Kuşcenneti Milli Parkı (Bird Paradise National Park). This 64-hectare reserve on the shores of Kuş Gölü (Bird Lake, the ancient Manias), due south of Bandırma, boasts from two to three million feathered visitors, of 255 different varieties, each year.

The annual migrations take place in April to June and September to November. In high summer and mid-winter there is little to see. Avoid weekends, when it's very crowded and noisy – the birds do. Bring binoculars if you have them. Admission costs US$1 (half price for students).

The visitor centre has exhibits – reminiscent of 19th-century natural history museums – of stuffed birds in simulated habitats. From the centre, walk to the observation tower for the view over the lake. No camping or picnicking is permitted, so your visit may be cut short by hunger.

From the Bandırma-Bursa highway, turn south 13km east of Bandırma centre. After 3km, turn west following signs for the park, which is 2.5km further along.

BALIKESİR
☎ 266

At least 5000 years old, the city of Balıkesir was known as Palaeokastron to the Romans and Byzantines. Though there are a few old buildings, including the **Zağanos Paşa Camii** (1461), the **Yıldırım Camii** (1388), the **Umur Bey Camii** (1412) and the **Karesi Bey Türbesi** (1336), this is not really a tourist town. You'll probably whip through it on the bus or train. There are several cheap hotels near the otogar. The one-star *İnanöz Hotel (☎ 241 4265, fax 245 2124)*, just opposite the Garaj Karşısı, offers singles/doubles with bath for US$8/14. The two-star *İmanoğlu Hotel (☎ 241 1302, fax 243 7137, Örücüler Caddesi 18)* has rooms with bath for US$15/22.

ESKİŞEHİR
☎ 222 • pop 430,000

Despite its name, Eskişehir (Old City) is a thoroughly modern centre. The scant ruins of the earlier Graeco-Roman city of Dorylaeum mostly lie beneath recent buildings.

This has always been an important transit point on the natural routes from north to south and east to west. Railway locomotives manufactured here haul trains throughout Turkey, sometimes laden with the products of Eskişehir's other industries: cement, sugar, textiles and more. The crack and whoosh of fighter jets announce a major air force base on the outskirts. The Anadolu Üniversitesi (Anatolia University) is also here, and the large student population gives the city more of a kick than many other provincial centres. Several hotels feature thermal bathing pools, advertised as curing all manners of ills and popular with Turkish tourists.

A riverside promenade with streetside cafes and a bustling market brighten the unremarkable city centre. Make sure you sample the local *nuga helvası* (nougat), on sale at the many confectioners' shops in the otogar.

Orientation & Information

Really there are two Eskişehirs: the modern city you whip through on the bus and the older Ottoman city hidden away to the south of Atatürk and İki Eylül Caddesis. The modern city centre is easily negotiated on foot. Hotels, restaurants, banks and other services are not far from the train station, which is north-west of the centre, but the new otogar is 3km from the centre by the sugar factory; take bus No 13 (US$0.25). Buses into town run along Sivrihisar Caddesi. Ask to be dropped at the old (eski) otogar and you'll be put off at the junction with Yunus Emre Caddesi.

The most historically interesting part of town can be found by walking south along Şeyh Sahabettin Caddesi towards the Kurşunlu Camii complex.

The tourist office (☎ 220 4227) is in the *vilayet* (provincial government headquarters) at İki Eylül Caddesi 175. There's no sign, so you may have trouble locating it but when you do, it can supply a basic map and directions to local sights.

Things to See & Do

At the southern end of İki Eylül Caddesi next to the post office is the Yunus Emre Kültür Sarayı with, on the fourth floor, the **Lületaşı Müzesi**, a fine collection of old and new meerschaum pipes, and photos of the mine at Sepetçi Köyü. You may have to wait for someone to find the key; and having them hover while you look around hardly makes for a relaxing visit. If you don't manage to get in, the modern pipes on sale in Eskişehir are mostly copies of these originals.

All along Şeyh Sahabettin Caddesi a wonderful **fruit and vegetable market** features stalls selling tomatoes the size of a man's fist and stripy aubergines and runner beans. Look out for a baker's cart offering *haşhaşlı*, a flat bread seasoned and stuffed with potato – utterly delicious when hot (US$0.60).

Narrow streets are lined with crumbling, colourful old Ottoman houses. The gracious **Osmanlı Evi Müzesi** in Yeşilefendi Sokak is open to the public (free of charge) from 9 am to noon and 1 to 4 pm – knock if the door is closed. In theory the nearby **Etnografya Müzesi** is open the same hours.

At the heart of this old district the large **Kurşunlu Camii** (1525) is surrounded by pretty, flower-filled gardens and old tombs.

Still south of Atatürk Caddesi but west along H. Polatkan Bulvarı, the **Arkeoloji Müzesi** is open from 8.30 am to noon and from 1.30 to 5 pm (admission US$1.30). Here you'll see the finds from Dorylaeum including several crude mosaic floors, together with Roman statuettes of Cybele, Hecate and Mithras.

Dream Pipes

Most travellers who stop in Eskişehir are looking for meerschaum (German for 'sea foam', *lületaşı* in Turkish). This soft, light, porous white stone, a hydrous magnesium silicate called sepiolite by mineralogists, is mined at numerous villages east of Eskişehir, including Başören, Karahöyük (Karatepe), Kemikli, Kozlubel Köyü, Nemli, Sarısıva, Sepetçi Köyü, Söğütçük and Yarmalar. Eskişehir has the world's largest and most easily accessible deposits of the mineral.

Miners are lowered into vertical shafts which penetrate the meerschaum beds to depths of between 10 and 150m. The miners fill buckets with heavy mud, which is hauled to the surface, dumped and sluiced, revealing rough chunks of meerschaum. There are no veins where large blocks can be cut. The larger the chunk, the higher its value.

Though once pulverised and made into tooth powder, meerschaum is now used for carving. While the stone is still wet and as soft as soap, carvers in the villages and in Eskişehir work it into fanciful shapes and decorative objects, most of which are exported. Block meerschaum was also exported until 1979, when someone figured out that to export the material was to export the carving jobs as well, and so it became illegal to export it. Prayer beads, necklaces, cigarette-holders, belts, earrings and baubles are commonly made items, but the most popular is the meerschaum pipe.

A good carver can make about four pipes a day, while highly elaborate pieces can take a week. Meerschaum pipes are valued because the strong, light, porous material smokes cool and sweet, drawing off the burning tobacco's heat and some of the tar. Devoted meerschaum pipe smokers wear special gloves while smoking to protect their prized pipes from being tarnished by skin oils. With time, a coddled pipe will take on an even nut-brown patina that is highly valued by devotees.

You can view carvers at work and buy their art in Eskişehir, from 9 am to about 7 pm Monday to Saturday, at Işık Pipo (☎ 323 8702), Sakarya Caddesi, Konya İşhanı 12/17, and Pipo Burhan Yücel, both in Eskişehir city centre near the Büyük Otel. Burhan Yücel also has a shop beneath the otogar.

Places to Stay

There's no problem finding somewhere central to stay although the real cheapies are very basic and not very used to non-Turkish travellers. Some of the other hotels are relatively pricey, considering their universally drab decor, but may be open to haggling.

Across Yunus Emre Caddesi from the old otogar are two two-star hotels. The *Soyiç Hotel* (☎ 230 7190, fax 230 5120) at No 101 charges US$17/30/36 for a single/double/triple with bath. *Hotel Arslan* (☎ 231 0909, fax 231 5018), at No 107 charges US$15/22 a single/double. At No 93 is *Atışhan Otel* (☎ 220 1666, fax 232 4547), undoubtedly the smartest place in town but they charge US$60/75.

Turn left at the northern end of Yunus Emre Caddesi and you'll soon arrive at the confluence of İnönü, Cengiz Topel, Sakarya, Muttalip and Sivrihisar Caddesis (in the district called Köprübaşı). Here you'll find *Eskişehir Büyük Otel* (☎ 230 6800, fax 234 6508, Sivrihisar Caddesi 40), an older three-star place charging US$35 for doubles with all mod cons (TV, minibar, radio, shower, hairdryer) but the same drab, brown decor. Get a room at the back to avoid street noise.

The one-star *Otel Şale* (☎ 231 4144, İsmet İnönü Caddesi 17/1), across the street from the prominent Ordu Evi (Army Building; ask for that to find the hotel), is central but quite noisy. It charges US$15/25 for a room with shower.

There are a couple of cheapies near here too. *Otel Divan* (☎ 231 1728, İsmet İnönü Caddesi 13) costs US$7.50/15 but its clientele is solidly male. If you're down to your last few million liras, *Otel Çiçek* (☎ 234 4056, Sivrihisar Caddesi 29) charges just US$3.20 per person but a female guest would be an oddity.

In the heart of the shopping district you'll find a pair of hotels with natural spring water that is said to help rheumatism, lumbago and other health problems. *Termal Otel Sultan* (☎ 231 8371, Hamamyolu Caddesi 1) offers shabby rooms for US$15/24. Better is *Has Hotel Termal* (☎ 231 9191, fax 234 6488, Hamamyolu Caddesi 7) which charges exactly the same for cleaner, quieter rooms. It's another US$5 to use the attached hamam (women admitted Tuesday only).

Places to Eat

The stretch of road between the Büyük Otel and the Otel Şale is full of cheap kebap shops. Turn down Köprübaşı Caddesi for the bright, cheerful and busy *Şahin İşkembe Salonu* where a bowl of beans and rice with bread and a soft drink will come to about US$2.50. Across the road, *Nasir* is truly a family-friendly place whose upstairs *aile salonu* (family room) boasts a swing, slide and other child-diverting playthings; İskender kebap with a soft drink will cost US$4.

A few doors away from the Nasir is the *Altı Kardeşler* pastry shop which stocks, among other gooey desserts, the two puddings made with chicken: *tavukgögsü* and *kazandibi* (US$1 a bowl).

There's a delightful *çay bahçesi* (tea garden) beside the market off Şeyh Sahabettin Caddesi where men sip their tea around a fountain surrounded by pine and plane trees, closely observed by white ducks.

Getting There & Away

The vast otogar in the outskirts is served by innumerable city buses along Sivrihisar Caddesi (look for signs saying 'Terminal' or 'Yeni Otogar') or by dolmuş from Yunus Emre Caddesi. Details of some long-distance services to selected destinations are listed in the table below.

As Eskişehir is an important stop on the İstanbul-Ankara line, there are frequent train services throughout the day and night.

AROUND ESKİŞEHİR

Meerschaum is collected in lumps from opencast mines up to 100m deep, which are scattered for 5km in every direction around the villages of **Sepetçi Köyü** and **Kozlubel**. While there are poultry and grain farmers here, 85% of Sepetçi's wealth comes from meerschaum and the village now prefers to be called Beyaz Altın (White Gold) in honour of its most valuable commodity.

There are no services in either village, but if you ask for Mr Bülent Girgin in Sepetçi, he will take you to his prominent carving workshop at the eastern edge of the village. If you're lucky he may also show you a *lületaşı ocağı* (mining pit) further east.

Getting there can be tricky without your own vehicle. There are a few daily buses to the village of Yakaboyu which continue to Sepetçi and then Kozlubel (US$1.30), but you either have to go straight back when the driver's had his tea or hang around for several hours. Hitching is likely to be time-consuming as there's hardly any traffic out here. With your own wheels, drive northeast from Eskişehir on the road to Alpu as far as Çavlum (18km), then turn left (north) and go via Kızılcaören, Yakakayı and Gündüzler to Sepetçi/Beyaz Altın (40km) and, 6km beyond it, to Kozlubel.

KÜTAHYA

☎ 274 • pop 150,000

Spread beneath the walls of an imposing hilltop fortress in the midst of hill country, Kütahya is a small city famous for the manufacture of coloured tiles and pottery. Faience (*çini* means coloured tile) is used everywhere – on building facades, in floors and walls, and in unexpected places. Every

Services from Eskişehir's Otogar

destination	fare (US$)	time (hr)	distance (km)	daily services
Ankara	7	3¼	230	hourly buses
Bursa	5	2½	155	hourly buses
İstanbul	8	6	310	hourly buses
Konya	10	6	420	several direct buses, or change at Afyon
Kütahya	4	1¼	91	hourly buses

year scholars flock from around the world to attend the International Faience & Ceramics Congress. The Dumlupınar Fuarı, held each year in the fairgrounds of the same name near the otogar, is Turkey's largest handicrafts fair. Kütahya's factories also turn out more mundane clay products such as water pipes, conduits and other industrial ceramics.

The Temple of Zeus at Aizanoi, one of Anatolia's best-preserved Roman temples, is one hour away.

History

No-one is sure when Kütahya was founded; its earliest known inhabitants were Phrygians. In 546 BC it was captured by the Persians, and then saw the usual succession of rulers, from Alexander the Great to the kings of Bithynia and the emperors of Rome and Byzantium, who called the town Cotiaeum.

The first Turks to arrive were the Seljuks in 1182. Later they were pushed out by the crusaders but returned to found the Emirate of Germiyan (1302–1428), with Kütahya as its capital. The emirs cooperated with the Ottomans in nearby Bursa, and, upon the death of the last emir, his lands were incorporated in the growing Ottoman Empire. When Tamerlane swept in at the beginning of the 15th century, he upset everyone's applecart, made Kütahya his headquarters for a while and then went back to where he came from.

As an Ottoman province, Kütahya settled down to tile-making. After Selim I took Tabriz in 1514, he brought all of its ceramic artisans to Kütahya and İznik, and set them to work. The two towns rivalled one another in the excellence of their faience.

After the collapse of the 1848 Hungarian revolution, the great leader Lajos Kossuth fled to the Ottoman Empire, where he was given refuge and settled in Kütahya for a short time. His house is now a museum, Kossuth Evi.

Orientation & Information

The roundabout centred on a huge tiled fountain in the shape of a vase is Belediye Meydanı, the city's main square. Overlooking it are the vilayet and the belediye. The otogar, Kütahya Çinigar (Tile Station – you'll see why), is less than 1km north-east of Belediye Meydanı; leave the otogar's front gateway, turn right and walk straight on. Hotels, restaurants and tile shops cluster within 100m of the square.

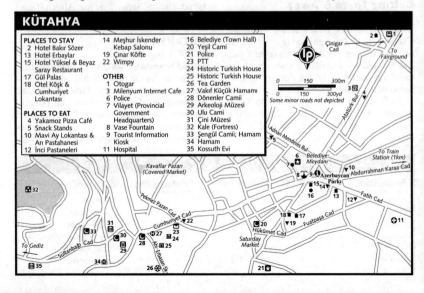

KÜTAHYA

PLACES TO STAY
2 Hotel Bakır Sözer
13 Hotel Erbaylar
15 Hotel Yüksel & Beyaz Saray Restaurant
17 Gül Palas
18 Otel Köşk & Cumhuriyet Lokantası

PLACES TO EAT
4 Yakamoz Pizza Café
5 Snack Stands
10 Mavi Ay Lokantası & Arı Pastahanesi
12 İnci Pastaneleri
14 Meşhur İskender Kebap Salonu
19 Çınar Köfte
22 Wimpy

OTHER
1 Otogar
3 Milenyum Internet Cafe
6 Police
7 Vilayet (Provincial Government Headquarters)
8 Vase Fountain
9 Tourist Information Kiosk
11 Hospital
16 Belediye (Town Hall)
20 Yeşil Cami
21 Police
23 PTT
24 Historic Turkish House
25 Historic Turkish House
26 Tea Garden
27 Vakıf Küçük Hamamı
28 Dönenler Camii
29 Arkeoloji Müzesi
30 Ulu Cami
31 Çini Müzesi
32 Kale (Fortress)
33 Şengül Camii; Hamam
34 Hamam
35 Kossuth Evi

Çinigar Cad
To Fairground

0   150   300m
0   150   300yd
Some minor roads not depicted

Kavaflar Pazarı (Covered Market)

Adnan Menderes Bul

Belediye Meydanı

To Train Station (1km)

Azerbaycan Parkı
Abdurrahman Karaa Cad

Fatih Cad

Pekmez Pazarı Cad

Cumhuriyet Cad

Fuatpaşa Cad

Hükümet Cad

Saturday Market

Sultanbağı Cad

Arı Erbakan Sok

To Gediz

Kütahya Tilework

The Kütahya çini (faience, coloured tile) industry was founded in the late 14th century, and given a boost in the early 16th century when Sultan Selim I brought expert tile-makers here from his newly conquered city of Tabriz in Persia.

Tilemaking thrived until the cataclysm of WWI, which resulted in the closure of all but two of the city's pottery ateliers. One of these was run by David Ohannessian, an Ottoman Armenian. When he was called to Jerusalem to repair the tiles in the famous Dome of the Rock, he took a team of Kütahya's best artisans. Instead of returning, they established a traditional Turkish faience industry in Jerusalem, where it thrives today.

That left one working atelier in Kütahya whose master, Hafız Mehmet Emin, died in 1922. Luckily, he had a skilled and inspired apprentice, Ahmet Şahin (born 1907), who, with another young and enthusiastic tile-maker named Hakkı Çinicioğlu, worked to maintain the traditions of Kütahya tile-making. Though still a tenuous industry in 1950, Kütahya faience has since grown to include some 50 ateliers producing plates, vases and other decorative tableware, flat tiles for wall mounting, and many other objects.

Kütahya tiles are made of kaolin, quartz, chalk, clay and sand. Refined in a time-consuming, laborious process, the base material is covered with an even more refined slip, then painted, glazed and fired again. The designs are mostly floral, geometric or based on Quranic inscriptions.

From the beginning, Ahmet Şahin insisted on creating coloured tiles of the highest standards of artisanship and aesthetics. Though he is master of every part of the complicated and laborious process, Şahin is renowned mostly as a designer. His patterns for the designs and calligraphy used on Kütahya faience fill nine trunks. About 70% of all Kütahya designs are his, or have been derived from his designs.

The sons of Ahmet Şahin, Faruk Şahin and Zafer Şahin, are çinicis (master tile-makers) as is Zafer Bey's son Ahmet Hürriyet Şahin. Nurten Şahin, Ahmet Hürriyet Şahin's wife, is an acknowledged çinici of the first rank, even though she had never painted a tile before her marriage. Look for their work from the former Işıl Çini atelier, their present work from Metin Çini, and that of other masters such as Ali Özker and İhsan and İbrahim Erdeyer of Süsler Çini, and Hakkı Ermumcu and Mehmet Gürsoy of İznik Çini.

Kütahya ware comes in three general grades. Turist işi (tourist work) is the lowest, painted quickly to basic designs and sold to souvenir shops. Normal or fabrika işi is good quality work, painted carefully by apprentices under the direction of a master. Özel işi (special work) is the master's own, often signed. Painting a single özel plate can take four or five days.

The town's main commercial street is Cumhuriyet Caddesi which runs south-west from the vilayet, past the PTT, and on to the Ulu Cami.

In summer there's a tourist information kiosk in the Azerbaycan Parkı, just east of Belediye Meydanı.

The Milenyum Internet Cafe on Atatürk Bulvarı, across from the Yakamoz Pizza Cafe, costs US$0.80 per hour.

Ulu Cami & Bazaar

The Ulu Cami, at the far end of Cumhuriyet Caddesi from Belediye Meydanı, has been restored several times since it was built in 1410. From a distance it still manages to look a bit like Aya Sofya in İstanbul. It's surrounded by a colourful bazaar, in which you might stumble upon the **Kavaflar Pazarı**, a 16th-century market building, the **İshak Fakih Camii** (1434) and the **İmaret Mescidi** (1440), a former medrese.

Arkeoloji Müzesi

The Arkeoloji Müzesi (Archaeology Museum) is housed in the Vacidiye Medresesi right next door to the Ulu Cami. The medrese was built by Umur bin Savcı of the princely family of Germiyan in 1314 and has a fine central dome above a marble pool. Apart from a small medley of artefacts from the Chalcolithic to Ottoman periods, the museum also contains finds from the great Temple of Zeus (see the Aizanoi section later in this chapter), including a magnificent Roman sarcophagus carved with scenes of battling Amazons. Otherwise the collection is nothing special.

The museum is open from 8 am to noon and 1.30 to 5.30 pm daily except Monday. Admission costs US$1.25.

Çini Müzesi

This new museum, devoted to Kütahya's tilework and pottery, is housed in the İmaret Camii on the opposite side of the Ulu Cami to the Arkeoloji Müzesi. Some of the collection dates back to the 14th century. The museum is open from 8 am to noon and 1.30 to 5.30 pm daily except Monday. Admission costs US$1.25.

Kossuth Evi

Follow the signs behind the Ulu Cami to the Kossuth Evi (Kossuth House), also called the Macar Evi (Hungarian House). It's more or less 250m straight on up the hill; look for the house on the left, marked by plaques in Turkish and Hungarian. On the way you'll pass the 16th-century Şengül Camii and its thriving hamam.

Lajos Kossuth (1802–94) was a prominent member of the Hungarian parliament. In 1848, chafing at Hapsburg rule from Vienna, he and others rose in revolt, declaring Hungary an independent republic in 1849. When Russian troops intervened on the side of the Austrians, he was forced to flee. The Ottomans offered him a refuge and he lived in Kütahya from 1850–51.

His house, with its perfectly preserved kitchen, dining room, bedroom and office, is open from 8 am to noon and 1.30 to 5.30 pm daily except Monday. Admission costs US$1.25. The first floor verandah offers lovely views over a rose garden complete with statue of Kossuth and of the encircling hills. This is how upper-class Kütahyans lived in the mid-19th century.

Kütahya Fortress

The ruins of the fortress are accessed by a steep path from the neighbourhood of the Ulu Cami, or by a road which winds around the hill and approaches the top from the far side (follow black-on-yellow signs reading 'Döner Gazino').

Built in two stages by the Byzantines, the castle was restored and used by their successors, the Seljuks, the emirs of Germiyan, and the Ottomans. The latest building work seems to have taken place in the 15th century. One look at the remains of the dozens of cylindrical towers makes it easy to imagine what a formidable obstacle this would have been to any army.

Tea gardens with splendid views, and the Döner Gazino, a cylindrical restaurant/nightclub, reward your climb.

Places to Stay

Most of Kütahya's hotels are clustered around the central square, Belediye Meydanı. The cheaper ones are quite basic.

Hotel Yüksel (☎ 212 0111, Belediye Meydanı 1) is a well-worn hostel charging US$7/11 for a single/double without shower. *Otel Köşk* (☎ 216 2024, Lise Caddesi 1) offers simple double rooms with sinks for US$10 or US$14 with shower; the carpets are grubby but the sheets are clean and you'll get a TV, towels, soap and a fair amount of space for your money.

Kütahya's best hotel, *Gül Palas* (☎ 216 1759, fax 216 2135, Belediye Meydanı), is tiled in light blue and navy. Pleasant singles/doubles with showers and reasonably up-to-date decor cost US$20/30. There's a sauna in the basement.

The three-star *Hotel Erbaylar* (☎ 223 6960, fax 216 1046, Fatih Caddesi 14) has decent rooms with shower for an outrageous US$42/66; these prices should drop by half when you threaten to go elsewhere. Some rooms have TV and minibar.

For peace and quiet you might be better off at the *Hotel Bakır Sözer* (☎ 224 8146, fax 224 8149, Çinigar Caddesi), on the southern side of the otogar, but away from the main roads. Clean rooms with bath cost US$12/17.

Places to Eat

Çınar Köfte (Lise Caddesi 7), near the Otel Köşk, serves köfte, soup, salad, bread and beverages for US$4 or less.

Cumhuriyet Lokantası, on the ground floor of the Otel Köşk, is a quiet eatery open from breakfast time and serving three-course meals for under US$8.

The *Meşhur İskender Kebap Salonu (Fatih Caddesi 6)* is also popular, though portions are quite small. A few doors further along is the cheerful *İnci Pastaneleri*, selling coffee and thick chocolate mousse for around US$1.50.

On the north-eastern side of Belediye Meydanı, across Abdurrahman Karaa and Fatih Caddesis, are several other cheap restaurants (try the popular *Mavi Ay Lokantası*) and a pastry shop, *Arı Pastahanesi*, where coffee and a dessert cost US$1.50.

Kütahya's bright young things flock to *Yakamoz Pizza Cafe* on Atatürk Bulvarı, which also serves coffee and pastries on its umbrella-shaded terrace. Pizzas cost from US$5.

At night a few booths selling köfte, *gözleme* (Turkish pancakes) and other snacks open at the fountain end of Adnan Menderes Bulvarı. For conventional Western snacks, Kütahya has its own *Wimpy*, serving up standard burgers and fries. It's on Cumhuriyet Caddesi, close to the PTT.

For fresh fruit, vegetables and picnic supplies, browse the open-air market up the hill on Lise Caddesi; it's at its liveliest on Saturday and has a pleasant *çay bahçesi* attached.

Shopping

You can find Kütahya pottery in any Turkish souvenir shop, but the shops around Belediye Meydanı in Kütahya have the widest selection of the best work. Each pottery has its authorised shop.

As well as the expected tourist stuff, shops have fine mid-range pieces in a variety of designs, plus some masterworks for connoisseurs. Heading out of town towards Eskişehir or Afyon you'll also find vast porcelain warehouses all geared up for the coach party trade.

If you're really into pots, it should be easy to arrange a factory visit if you ask at a shop and give a bit of notice.

Getting There & Away

Kütahya is a provincial capital, so its otogar supports fairly busy traffic. Details of daily bus services to selected destinations from Kütahya are listed in the table below.

AİZANOİ (ÇAVDARHİSAR)
• pop 4100

The village of Çavdarhisar, 60km south-west of Kütahya, is home to Aizanoi (or Aezani), the site of one of Anatolia's best-preserved Roman temples. The great **Temple of Zeus** (or Jupiter) dates from the reign of Hadrian (AD 117–38), and was dedicated to the worship of Zeus and to the Anatolian fertility goddess Cybele (Artemis).

Hours are officially from 9 am to noon and 1 to 5 pm daily, but there's no fence so the friendly custodian, Mr Nazim Ertaş, will come to find you and sell you a ticket for

Services from Kütahya's Otogar

destination	fare (US$)	time (hr)	distance (km)	daily services
Afyon	4	1½	100	frequent buses and minibuses
Ankara	8	5	315	a dozen buses
Antalya	12	8	375	a few buses
Bursa	6.50	3	190	5 buses
Çavdarhisar	2	1	60	10 buses and minibuses
Eskişehir	4	1¼	91	very frequent
İstanbul	10	6	355	a dozen buses
İzmir	9	6	385	a dozen buses
Konya (via Afyon)	10	5	335	several direct, or change at Afyon

US$1.25. He'll also unlock the gate and take you down to the crypt-like sanctuary of Cybele beneath the temple.

The temple stands on a broad terrace built to serve as the temple precinct. Like some ancient Hollywood set, the north and west faces of the temple have their double rows of Ionic and Corinthian columns intact, but the south and east rows have fallen in a picturesque jumble. The three columns at the north-eastern corner were toppled by the disastrous Gediz earthquake of 1970, but have since been re-erected. The cella (inner room) walls are intact enough to give a good impression of the whole. A wire enclosure on the north-western edge of the temple precinct holds some of the best bits of sculpture found here.

The road out of Çavdarhisar towards Aizanoi is lined with chunks of fallen Roman masonry, but turn right along the path into the fields opposite the temple and you'll come first to remains of a 2nd-century **palaestra** or gymnasium, and then to more substantial remains of a linked **theatre** and **stadium**. The stones have crumbled badly and now provide a home for innumerable wheatears and the odd woodpecker. Look out on the right for a stretch of wall with the names of Olympic winners inscribed in medallions.

Return to the road and turn left back into the village, crossing a bridge over a small stream; divert down beside it and you'll realise much of the stonework that you'll see dates back to Hadrian's reign. Turn left after the bridge and you'll come to the remains of a **bath complex**. The locked shed contains a fine mosaic pavement, mostly covered with geometric patterns but with a representation of a satyr and maenad too; ask Mr Ertaş to let you in.

Go back to the road by the bridge and take the path right along the stream. Eventually you'll emerge by the remains of the Roman **forum**, or marketplace, with fine standing columns and a marble pavement.

Around the corner from the Eski Pazar Camii are the remains of an unusual **circular market building** with a little turret reconstructed beside it. Look closely at the walls and you'll see the fixed prices for market goods inscribed in Roman numerals.

At the Çavdarhisar crossroads there are a few *eateries* and shops although the village itself boasts only a basic teahouse. You may be able to get permission to camp somewhere at the edge of the village, but there are no facilities except at the petrol stations and the toilets opposite the temple.

Getting There & Away

Çavdarhisar is on the Kütahya to Gediz road. A few direct buses from Kütahya's otogar take one hour to get to the village (US$2). Alternatively, take a Gediz or Emet minibus and ask to be dropped at Çavdarhisar.

Driving, take the Afyon road for 10km, then turn right (west) on the road marked for Aizanoi and Çavdarhisar another 50km. At the Çavdarhisar crossroads turn right towards Emet. The Temple of Zeus is 800m along this road on the left.

To make a day of it, start early and bring a picnic. As soon as you arrive in Çavdarhisar, check the times of return buses or minibuses to Kütahya (they run pretty infrequently). Alternatively, there are onward minibuses to Gediz (37km) and Uşak (65km more); from Uşak you can easily catch a bus to Afyon, Ankara, Denizli, İzmir, Konya or Manisa.

MİDAS ŞEHRİ

The rock-hewn monuments at Midas Şehri, midway between Afyon and Eskişehir, are the most impressive we've inherited from the civilisation of the Phrygians.

If you have your own transport, it's worth a half-day detour to see the site. It's best done in the early morning, the only time when sunlight bathes the Midas Tomb at Midas Şehri. Without your own wheels, you must have an intense interest in things Phrygian as public transport is slow and uncertain.

What archaeologists call Midas Şehri is in the village of **Yazılıkaya** (meaning 'Inscribed Rock'), 72km north of Afyon or 107km south of Eskişehir, not to be confused with the Yazılıkaya at the Hittite capital of Boğazkale, east of Ankara.

The Phrygians

The Phrygians emigrated from Thrace to central Anatolia around 1200 BC. They spoke an Indo-European language, used an alphabet similar to Greek, and established a kingdom with its capital at Gordion, 106km west of Ankara (see the Central Anatolia chapter). Phrygian culture was based on that of their neighbours the Greeks, but with strong Neo-Hittite and Urartian influences.

The Phrygians are credited with having invented the frieze, embroidery and numerous musical instruments including cymbals (for which Turkey is still famous), *aulos* (double clarinet), flute, lyre, syrinx (panpipes) and triangle.

The Phrygian Empire flourished under its most famous king, Midas (circa 725–675 BC), one of many Phrygian monarchs to have that name, until the empire was overrun by the Cimmerians (676–585 BC).

Phrygian art and culture flourished from around 585 to 550 BC, when the rock-cut monuments at Midas Şehri – the most impressive Phrygian monuments still in existence – were carved. The area was later ruled by the Lydian kings from Sardis, and still later by the kings of Pergamum.

Phrygian art, executed in ceramics, wood, mosaics, metal and rock, is vigorous, spirited and original, and seems to have influenced later Greek vase painters in the Aegean Cyclades islands.

The Phrygians' most notable exports seem to have been metal objects, textiles, slaves and the names of their kings: Midas and Gordios. Several kings bore these names, and archaeologists have found it difficult to solve the mystery of which Midas was which.

Most prominent of the works in Midas Şehri is the so-called **Midas Tomb**, a 17m-high relief carved into the soft tufa representing the facade of a temple covered in geometric patterns. At the centre near the base of the facade is a niche where an effigy of the Anatolian fertility goddess Cybele would be displayed during festivals. Inscriptions in the Phrygian alphabet, one bearing the name of Midas, decorate the facade. A small **museum**, which you pass on the walk up to the Midas Tomb, holds a few finds from the site, and diagrams. A portion of the ancient road, visible from the wagon-wheel ruts worn into the rock, connects the museum with the Midas Tomb.

Beside the Midas Tomb is a later rock-cut **monastery**, with tombs beneath.

A few hundred metres to the west is **Küçük Yazılıkaya**, another 6th-century BC rock-hewn cult monument which was never completed.

About 150m south of the Midas Tomb on the plateau's eastern side, a rock-hewn stairway decorated with reliefs of figures leads to the acropolis atop the 30m-high plateau. Here there are signs of a rock-hewn throne-altar, defensive walls, and other stairways leading down into the rock to a well. The site guardian will show you around for a tip.

Getting There & Away

Bus & Dolmuş You can get to Midas Şehri from Eskişehir or Afyon. From Eskişehir, take a bus or dolmuş south to Seyitgazi, then ask for directions. There may be a dolmuş south from Seyitgazi via Şükranlı and Çukurca to Yazılıkaya along the paved road. If not, take something bound for Gazlıgöl or Afyon along road 03-78, get out at the Kümbet turn, and hope to hitch a ride, or expect a long walk along the unpaved road eastward.

From Afyon, dolmuşes go as far as Gazlıgöl and perhaps İhsaniye, where you'll probably have to change for onward rides. A few trains can take you to İhsaniye and Döğer; after visiting Arslankaya and Kapı-kayalar, you'll probably find it easiest to return to Afyon by dolmuş.

Car From Eskişehir, it's faster to take the Ankara highway (E90) east for 37km to the turn-off south for Mahmudiye and Çifteler. At Çifteler, 60km south-east of Eskişehir, turn right (west) on the one-lane macadam road for Gökçeköyü and Yazılıkaya, another 36km along.

From Afyon, if you're driving, head due north following signs for 'Organize Sanayi

Bölgesi', 'Gazlıgöl' and 'Seyitgazi' and turn right off the road towards Kümbet. Head east from Kümbet to reach Midas Şehri.

AROUND MİDAS ŞEHRİ

There are several more Phrygian sites nearby, but public transport is very limited. You'll almost certainly have to hitch rides at some point, and these roads have little traffic. Plan to spend the whole day on this excursion. With your own vehicle, transport is easy enough, and you can visit most of these sites in less than a day.

At **Arezastis**, about 1km away on the Seyitgazi road, there's another Phrygian cult temple.

Even more Phrygian rock carvings are to be found east and south of Midas Şehri along the roads to Afyon. Heading west from Midas Şehri along unpaved roads, the village of **Kümbet** (17km) has a *kümbet* (Seljuk tomb) and a Phrygian shrine with a relief of a lion (Aslanlı Mabet).

Just 2km west of Kümbet is the narrow but paved Seyitgazi-Afyon road (03-78). Go south towards Afyon (21km) to an unpaved road on the right (west) marked for the **Göynüş Vadisi**, a valley of tuff outcrops bearing several Phrygian reliefs, including Aslantaş (a lion), Yılantaş (a snake) and Maltaş (a sheep).

Continue along the poor unpaved road to İhsaniye (or go back to the Afyon road), and head south to the hot-springs town of **Gazlıgöl** (14km), then north-west to İhsaniye (16km) via road 03-77. From İhsaniye take the unpaved road north towards Döğer (13km) to reach other Phrygian carvings at **Kapıkayalar** and **Arslankaya** (Cybele with a lion at each side).

About 5km south of the Göynüş Vadisi turn on the way to Gazlıgöl and Afyon, is a turn on the left (east) at Kayahan for **Ayazinköyü**, the site of an ancient rock-hewn settlement called Metropolis. The village, 5km east of Kayahan, is set amid Cappadocia-like rock formations of soft tuff which have been hollowed out to make dwellings, storerooms and churches. These troglodyte dwellings and the decoration in the churches are not nearly as well preserved

as those in the Göreme valley but are worth a look if you won't reach Cappadocia. There are also a few minor Phrygian lion reliefs.

AFYON

☎ 272 • pop 100,000

Formerly called Afyonkarahisar (meaning 'Black Fortress of Opium'), this tidy agricultural and carpet-weaving town, capital of the province of the same name, hardly lives up to its sinister moniker.

Although still an important region for producing opium for pharmaceutical use, these days the opium poppies are grown by the 'poppy straw' method, which is easier to police and control. The young plants are cut down before the narcotic sap begins to flow, and the 'straw' is processed in special government-operated factories. Afyon produces more than a third of the world's legally grown opium.

Cream from Contented Cows

Afyon's claim to fame among Turks is not its opium, but its *kaymak* (clotted cream).

The story is this: Afyon's opium farmers rarely use the drug themselves, but they use every other part of the plant. The poppy seeds are sprinkled on bread and pastries, the tender leaves are good in salads and the left-over opium plants are fed to the cattle. The cattle become very contented and produce rich cream in abundance.

Early each morning, near the Ot Pazarı Camii just a few blocks from Hükümet Meydanı, you can see the dairy farmers carrying their cylindrical kaymak containers. Brokers and restaurant owners meet them in front of the mosque and haggle over prices for the precious cream, carefully protected in flat circular dishes of glass or plastic. Later in the day, the kaymak will end up atop a serving of *kadayıf* (crumpet in syrup), in *kaymaklı baklava*, or even stuffed in lokum.

The popularity of eating kaymak on, in and with sweets may have inspired many locals to open confectioners' shops, *şekerleme*. Afyon has dozens of them, on Millet Caddesi off Hükümet Meydanı, and at the otogar.

Nature and art: the incredible travertine terraces at Pamukkale (top); the dramatic Temple of Athena at Priene (middle left); exquisite carvings from Afrodisias (middle right); and one of the striking tombs in the atmospheric necropolis at Hierapolis (bottom)

The warm waters of the peaceful Ölüdeniz lagoon are perfect for all sorts of water sports.

A view to die for: the striking Lycian rock tombs above the town of Fethiye

The eponymous fortress stands atop the massive rock in the historic centre of town with crumbling wooden houses at its base. It's a pleasant enough place to pause, and you're unlikely to bump into many other tourists.

History

As with so many Anatolian towns, Afyon's history starts some 3000 years ago. After occupation by the Hittites, Phrygians, Lydians and Persians, it was settled by the Romans and then the Byzantines, who called the town Akroenos, and later Nikopolis. Following the Seljuk victory at Manzikert (Malazgirt) in 1071, Afyon was governed by the Seljuk Turks. The important Seljuk vizier, Sahip Ata, took direct control of the town, and it was called Karahisar-i Sahip even through Ottoman times (1428–1923).

During the War of Independence, Greek forces occupied the town on their push towards Ankara. During the Battle of the Sakarya, in late August 1921, the republican armies under Mustafa Kemal (Atatürk) stopped the invading force within earshot of Ankara in one of history's longest pitched battles. The Greek forces retreated and dug in for the winter near Eskişehir and Afyon.

On 26 August 1922 the Turks began their counteroffensive, advancing rapidly on the Greek army. Within days Atatürk had set up his headquarters in Afyon's belediye building and had half the Greek army surrounded at Dumlupınar, 40km to the west. The Battle of the Commander-in-Chief, as it came to be known, destroyed the Greek expeditionary army as a fighting force, and sent its survivors fleeing towards İzmir and the ships waiting in the harbour.

In 2000 Afyon celebrated when native son Ahmet Necdet Sezer became the 10th president of Turkey, replacing Isparta's Suleyman Demirel.

Orientation & Information

The main square, called Hükümet Meydanı, lies east of the citadel, at the intersection of Ordu Bulvarı and Milli Egemenlik (usually called Bankalar) Caddesi; you'll recognise it by a fountain in the shape of a revolving ball of marble. About 250m south is another traffic roundabout, the starting point for Ambar Yolu (which goes north-east 2km to the otogar) and other streets.

Almost everything important is on or just off Bankalar Caddesi between the two traffic roundabouts, including the PTT, several hotels, restaurants and the local hamam.

The train station is 2km from the centre, at the north-eastern end of Ordu Bulvarı. Minibuses (US$0.25) connect both the train station and the otogar to the centre.

The tourist office (☎ 215 5447) in Hükümet Meydanı is quite helpful and some staff speak English. It's open from 8 am to 12 pm, 1.30 to 5.30 pm Monday to Friday.

Walking Tour

Start at the İmaret Camii, Afyon's major mosque, just south of the traffic roundabout at the southern end of Bankalar Caddesi. Built on the orders of Gedik Ahmet Paşa in 1472, its design shows the transition from the Selçuk to the Ottoman style. The strangely futuristic spiral-fluted minaret is decorated, Seljuk style, with blue tiles. The entrance on the eastern side is like an *eyvan* (vaulted recess) and leads to a main sanctuary topped by two domes, front and back, a design also seen in the early Ottoman capitals of Bursa and Edirne. A shady park with fountain provides a peaceful refuge from bustling Bankalar Caddesi. The mosque's medrese is on the western side; its hamam, still popular with both men and women, is nearer to the busy traffic roundabout.

Walk north along Bankalar Caddesi to Hükümet Meydanı, named after the neighbouring *hükümet konağı*, or provincial government headquarters. The hükümet konağı used to be the building facing the dramatic black Zafer Anıtı (Victory Monument; 1936). Today the government resides in a modern building beside the old one, and the former headquarters is the **Zafer Müzesi** (Victory Museum), with exhibits relating to the battles of the War of Independence which were fought nearby. It's rarely open though.

From Hükümet Meydanı opposite the Hotel Oruçoğlu, walk south-west up Millet (or Uzunçarşı) Caddesi, lined with a range

The Battle of Dumlupınar

The decisive battle of the Turkish War of Independence was fought along a front 80km long, running due west from Afyon.

During the War of Independence, Greek armies intent on claiming Ottoman lands for Greece pushed inland from İzmir, threatening the fledgling Turkish republican government at Ankara. Twice the Greek advance was checked by the Turks at the village of İnönü, north-east of Kütahya, but the invading forces finally broke through, took Eskişehir and Afyon, and made them strong points in a defensive line that stretched 500km from the Sea of Marmara to the valley of the Büyük Menderes (Meander) River.

Since the beginning of WWI, Turkish soldiers had been fighting defensive battles. In the Battle of the Sakarya, the longest pitched battle in history, the Greek armies were brought to a standstill, with many casualties on both sides. The republican capital at Ankara had been successfully defended. The time had come for a Turkish offensive.

Plans were carried out with the utmost secrecy. Mustafa Kemal (Atatürk) got all his generals together at a football game, so spies would never suspect that high-level consultations were under way. Troops were moved at night, under cover of darkness, resting by day beneath trees and in houses, away from the prying eyes of Greek reconnaissance flights. Small troops of soldiers were sent out to raise great clouds of dust to simulate larger troop movements. The Greek occupiers were so lulled into complacency that many of the commanders attended a dance in Afyon on the evening of 25 August 1922.

At first light the next morning, the Turkish forces began a bold and risky counterattack, with a thunderous barrage of artillery. The Turkish generals directed their troops from the front lines, not from observation points in the rear. By 9.30 am, the Turkish forces had taken all but two of their hilltop objectives, breaking through the Greek defences along the valley of Dumlupınar, near the highway from Afyon to İzmir. They followed up quickly and relentlessly on this advantage, driving the enemy soldiers just as quickly from their second and third lines of defence.

In the battle for the valley, half of the Greek expeditionary force was annihilated or captured, while the other half beat a hasty retreat towards İzmir. The Dumlupınar victory (30 August 1922) was the turning point in the war.

of confectionery shops, several short blocks to the small park in front of the Ot Pazarı Camii, where the makers of *kaymak* (clotted cream) sell their wares to confectioners in the early morning hours. Turn right and follow the main road (Köprübaşı and Camii Kebir Caddesi) uphill until you come to a fork. Take the left route and look for the **Mevlevihane Camii** on your left.

This was the site of the Afyonkarahisar Mevlevihanesi, or dervish meeting place, dating from Seljuk times (13th century). Sultan Veled, son of Celaleddin Rumi, the founder of the Mevlevi whirling dervish order, established Afyon as the second most important Mevlevi centre in the empire. The present mosque, with twin domes, twin pyramidal roofs above its courtyard and a rather church-like aspect, dates only from 1908, when it was built on the orders of Sul-

tan Abdül Hamit II. It's usually locked except at prayer times.

Continue walking up the main road to the square Ulu Cami (1273), about 1km from Hükümet Meydanı. On your way to the Ulu Cami notice the many old **Ottoman houses**. Those in some other cities, including Kütahya, may be in better repair, but Afyon boasts an interesting variety of styles of domestic architecture.

The **Ulu Cami** is one of the most important surviving examples of the Seljuk architectural style which called for brick walls and a roof supported by carved wooden columns and beams – here you'll find 40 columns with stalactite capitals and a flat beamed roof. Note the green tiles on the minaret. Unless you come just after prayer time, you may have to ask around for the *bekçi* (custodian) to let you in.

Across the street from the Ulu Cami, a lane marked by a sign to the *kale* (fortress) leads up towards the rock and its fortress. At the end of the lane is the first of some 700 steps to the summit, 226m high.

Despite its eventful history, there's little left to see inside the **citadel**. The Hittite king Mursilis II is thought to have built the first fortress by around 1350 BC, and every other conqueror elaborated on it afterwards. The views are spectacular and it's well worth coming up here at prayer time to listen to the wraparound calls of the muezzins from Afyon's many mosques.

Arkeoloji Müzesi

Take a dolmuş along Kurtuluş Caddesi, the continuation of Bankalar Caddesi, for almost 2km and you'll see Afyon's museum, the Arkeoloji Müzesi, on the right-hand side, near the intersection with İnönü Caddesi. It has a fine collection of Roman artefacts, including a cache of small marble statues of gods, unearthed when a road was being built. There are some good explanations of exhibits in English, including one on the castration cult of the Anatolian fertility goddess Cybele. A highlight of the museum is the massive head and torso of Hercules in a shelter at the back of the building. Carved sarcophagi and Ottoman headstones are scattered around the grounds. It's open from 8 am to noon and 1.30 to 5.30 pm daily; admission is US$1.25.

Places to Stay

In this pious town it'll be difficult to miss the muezzins' wake-up call wherever you stay. If you're planning a brief visit you might as well stay in one of the hotels overlooking the otogar.

Otel Mesut (☎ 212 0429, Dumlupınar Caddesi 5), on the northern side of the PTT half a block east of Bankalar Caddesi, offers presentable accommodation at the heart of things, although the lift doesn't inspire confidence. Singles/doubles/triples with shower are US$9/15/23. The rooms are beat-up and a bit depressing, but will do for a night.

Royal Turan Hotel (☎ 213 1227, Dumlupınar Caddesi 2) is a step above, with brightly painted rooms and comfy beds for US$15 20/27. There are several cheaper hotels further along this street.

Otel Hocaoğlu (☎ 213 8182, fax 213 0188, Ambaryolu 12) is closer to the İmaret Camii. Its reasonably comfortable singles/doubles with shower cost US$10/18.

The two-star *Otel Oruçoğlu (☎ 212 0120, fax 213 1313, Bankalar Caddesi)*, facing Hükümet Meydanı on the corner of Ordu Bulvarı, is well-used but serviceable. Rooms with shower cost US$22/33/50. The top-floor restaurant offers decent food.

Hotel Soydan (☎ 215 6070, fax 212 2111, Turan Emeksiz Caddesi 2) is a clean two-star place charging US$15/18/30. Its rooms boast such luxuries (for Afyon) as frilly bedcovers, TVs and minibars.

Afyon's best hotel is the new *Grand Ozer Termal Otel (☎ 214 3300, fax 214 3309, Suleyman Gonçer Caddesi 2)*, one block east of Hükümet Meydanı. Rooms with satellite TV and air-con cost a reasonable US$32/44. There's a luxurious hamam in the basement and a swimming pool.

For four-star comforts you must head out of Afyon on the Kütahya road 14km to *Termal Resort Oruçoğlu (☎ 251 5050, fax 213 9895)*, where comfy rooms can be had for US$40/60.

Places to Eat

The little street called Ziraat Bankası Geçidi, across Bankalar from the Hotel Oruçoğlu, just south of Hükümet Meydanı, has a good assortment of eateries, including the *Narin*, *Arzu* and *Doyum* restaurants and *Zümrüt Etli Pide Salonu*. The first three are good for cheap, simple, filling meals (US$3 to US$4), including, of course, kaymak on your sweet. The pide salonu is cheaper still. Another popular pide place is the *Lale Pide Salonu* on Bankalar Caddesi, half a block from the İmaret Camii.

İkbal Lokantası (Millet or Uzunçarşı Caddesi 21), half a block south-west of Hükümet Meydanı, was founded in 1956, and is an interesting period piece, well worth trying for its old-time atmosphere. They're particularly proud of their sweet cherry-flavoured bread pudding.

Services from Afyon's Otogar

destination	fare (US$)	time (hr)	distance (km)	daily services
Ankara	6	4	260	at least hourly buses
Antalya	6.50	5	300	frequent buses
Eskişehir	3.20	3	191	hourly buses
Isparta	6	3	175	several buses
İstanbul	12	8	455	hourly buses
İzmir	7.50	5½	340	hourly buses
Konya	7	3¾	235	several buses
Kütahya	4	1½	100	hourly buses
Denizli (for Pamukkale)	6.60	4	240	several buses

A set dinner in the top-floor dining room of *Hotel Oruçoğlu* on Bankalar Caddesi costs US$12.

Don't forget to pop into one of the local şekerleme for a taste of Afyon's famous *lokum*. Free samples are usually on offer – point to something and say *'Deneyelim!'* (Let's try it!). A 500g portion costs around US$2, depending upon the type.

Getting There & Away

Afyon is on the inland routes connecting İstanbul with Antalya and Konya, and İzmir with Ankara and the east, so bus traffic is heavy. Details of daily bus services to selected destinations are listed in the table above.

Trains will take you to Denizli, Eskişehir, İstanbul, İzmir, Konya and Kütahya.

Pamukkale Region

At Pamukkale (meaning 'Cotton Castle'), hot calcium-laden mineral waters flowed through a ruined Hellenistic city before cascading over a cliff. As the water cooled, the calcium precipitated and clung to the cliffs, forming snowy white travertine, the waterfalls of white stone which gave the spa its name. Despite what a million tourist promotion posters show, it is no longer possible to bathe in the travertine pools, and most of the area is off-limits. But the ruins of Hierapolis, scattered along the top of the ridge at Pamukkale are still a remarkable sight, well worth visiting in their own right.

From Pamukkale you can visit several other important archaeological sites, including the hilltop city of Nyssa about 100km east of Kuşadası. About 150km east of Kuşadası is Afrodisias, one of Turkey's most complete and absorbing archaeological sites. Near Pamukkale itself are the ruins of Laodicea, one of the Seven Churches of Asia.

AYDIN

☎ 256 • pop 120,000

Framed by the mountains of Aydın Dağı to the north and Menteşe Dağı to the south, Aydın is at the centre of the agriculturally rich Büyük Menderes River valley. The valley has always been an important natural travel route, which today includes an east-west highway and the railway to Denizli, Burdur and Isparta.

During the War of Independence Aydın was occupied by the invading Greek forces and then burned to the ground when they left. Being at the centre of an earthquake zone hasn't helped Aydın's appearance either. What you see today is mostly modern and charmless, and nearly everyone passes it by. You could spend an hour or two looking at the **Süleyman Bey Camii** (1683), designed by one of Sinan's apprentices. It's between the train station and the park on the main square. The **Archaeology Museum**, 750m uphill from the main square, houses finds from Afrodisias, Didyma, Miletus, Priene and Tralles, including good statues of Athena and Nike, and a fine bust of Marcus Aurelius.

NYSSA

East of Aydın, you're deep in the fertile farming country of the Büyük Menderes River valley. Cotton fields sweep away from the road, and during the late October harvest the highways are jammed with tractors hauling wagons overloaded with the white puffy stuff. Other important crops include pomegranates, pears, citrus fruits, apples, melons, olives and tobacco.

About 31km east of Aydın is the town of Sultanhisar where a 3km uphill walk to the north brings you to ancient Nyssa, set on a hilltop amid olive groves. When you get there you'll find public toilets, a soft-drink stand and a guard who will charge you US$1.50 admission during daylight hours and show you around the site in return for a tip.

The ruins consist of the **theatre**, and a 115m-long **tunnel** beneath the road and the parking area which was once the ancient city's main square. Walk another five minutes up the hill along the road and through a field and you'll come to the **bouleuterion** (place of assembly), which has some nice fragments of sculpture.

But what you're most likely to remember about Nyssa is the site's peaceful beauty, so different from the hubbub at honeypot metropolises like Ephesus. The walk back down to Sultanhisar and the highway is very enjoyable in the late afternoon.

Though Sultanhisar has a few simple eateries, there are no real hotels. The İzmir-Denizli trains stop in town, and the highway carries many east-west buses. Dolmuşes run to Sultanhisar from Nazilli every 15 minutes (US$0.70).

NAZİLLİ

☎ 256 • pop 100,000

The market town of Nazilli, 14km east of Nyssa and Sultanhisar, is a possible transfer point for a trip to Afrodisias, though most people visit Afrodisias from Pamukkale. The otogar is just north of the main highway, one block west of the main traffic roundabout. The train station is south of the highway.

Places to Stay & Eat

Unfortunately, Nazilli has no cheap hotels around its otogar, though there are a few small places near the train station. The two-star *Hotel Metya* (☎ 312 8888, fax 312 8891, 92 Sokak 10) in Karaçay Mahallesi, just across from the otogar, facing the Shell petrol station, has singles/doubles with bath for US$15/25, including breakfast.

Go north 200m from the main traffic roundabout on the highway east of the otogar to reach the comfortable two-star *Nazilli Ticaret Odası Oteli* (☎ 313 9678, fax 313 9681, Hürriyet Caddesi). Decent rooms with bath and balcony cost US$18/30, including breakfast. There's a *restaurant* and *bar*, and a decent *pastry shop* adjoins the hotel.

The little *eateries* around the otogar are good for snacks if you're passing through.

Getting There & Away

Bus Nazilli is the local transportation hub, with buses to and from İzmir and Selçuk

Services from Nazilli's Otogar

destination	fare (US$)	time (hr)	distance (km)	daily services
Ankara	12	8	545	several buses
Antalya	10	6	360	several buses
Bodrum	6	4	225	several buses
Denizli	2	1	65	very frequent buses and dolmuşes
İstanbul	15	12	600	several buses
İzmir	4	2½–3	170	very frequent buses
Konya	12	8	505	several buses
Kuşadası	4	2½	150	several buses
Pamukkale	2	1½	85	several buses
Selçuk	3.50	1½	130	buses at least every hour

WESTERN ANATOLIA

about every 45 minutes or so until early evening. The table on the previous page lists some useful daily services.

You're most likely to be transiting in Nazilli on the way to or from Afrodisias, although you can also visit Nyssa from here.

Train The three daily trains between Denizli and İzmir stop at Nazilli.

AROUND NAZİLLİ

On the road between the main Nazilli to Denizli highway and Karacasu you may notice signs pointing the way to **Antiocheia**; to get there you turn north at the centre of the village of Başaran, which is 18km northwest of Karacasu. From Başaran it's 1km to the impressively sited and extensive ruins of an ancient hilltop city. Unlike Afrodisias, it is totally unexcavated and unrestored so you get an idea of what the archaeologists see on the day they begin their fieldwork.

With your own vehicle, you can return to the Nazilli-Denizli highway, 6km to the north, by continuing past Antiocheia across the intensely fertile flood plain of the Büyük Menderes River and through the farming village of **Azizabat**, with some fine fieldstone walls and houses. You regain the highway at a point 5.6km east of the Karacasu turn-off, 21km east of Nazilli. Turn right (east) for Denizli.

Alternatively, you could continue on to the town of **Karacasu**, which is surrounded by tobacco fields, fig trees and orchards. Besides farming, Karacasu is famous for its potters, who work with the local reddish-brown clay, firing it in wood-fired kilns. To see the potters at work, ask to be directed to the 'çanakçı ocakları'.

AFRODİSİAS
☎ 256

The city's name quickly brings to mind 'aphrodisiac'. Both words come from the Greek name for the goddess of love, Aphrodite, called Venus by the Romans. Aphrodite was many things to many people. As Aphrodite Urania she was the goddess of pure, spiritual love; as Aphrodite Pandemos she was the goddess of sensual love, married to Hephaestus but lover also of Ares, Hermes, Dionysus and Adonis. Her children included Harmonia, Eros, Hermaphroditus, Aeneas and Priapus, the phallic god. All in all, she was the complete goddess of fertility, fornication and fun.

History

Excavations have proved that the Afrodisias acropolis isn't a natural hill but a prehistoric mound built up by successive settlements beginning in the Early Bronze Age (2800–2200 BC). From the 8th century BC, its famous temple was a favourite goal of pilgrims, and the city prospered. But under the Byzantines the city changed substantially: the steamy Temple of Aphrodite was transformed into a chaste Christian church, and ancient buildings were pulled down to provide building stones for defensive walls (circa AD 350).

Diminished from its former glory, the town was attacked by Tamerlane on his Anatolian rampage in 1402 and never recovered. The village of Geyre sprang up on the site sometime later. In 1956 an earthquake devastated the village, which was rebuilt to the west at its present location, allowing easier excavation of the site. The pleasant plaza in front of the museum was the main square of pre-1956 Geyre.

Preliminary explorations of Afrodisias were carried out by French and Italian archaeologists early in the 20th century. After the earthquake of 1956, US and Turkish archaeologists began to resurrect the city. They found a surprisingly well-preserved stadium, odeum and theatre. From 1961 to 1990 Professor Kenan T Erim of New York University directed work at the site. His book, *Afrodisias: City of Venus Aphrodite* (1986), tells the story of his work. After his death, Professor Erim was buried at the site which he had done so much to reveal and explain.

Information

The site at Afrodisias is open from 9 am to 8 pm (5 pm in winter) daily. Admission costs US$3, with another US$2.50 required for visiting the museum. The museum closes at 6.30 pm in summer. No photography is permitted in the museum, nor are you allowed to photograph excavations in progress. Signs in the car park prohibit camping; they're afraid of antiquity thieves.

Museum

During Roman times Afrodisias was home to a famous school for sculptors who were attracted by the beds of high-grade white and blue-grey marble 2km away at the foot of Babadağ mountain. The statuary in the museum reflects the excellence of their work. Note the 'cult statue of Aphrodite, second century' and the 'cuirassed statue of an emperor or high official, second century, signed by Appolonius Aster'. The 'portrait statue of Flavius Palmatus, governor of the province of Asia', looks like a man with big problems. Did they make his head that small on purpose, or as an insult? One of the finest pieces is the tomb of C Julius Zovios, a freedman from Afrodisias who died in the 1st century AD.

The Ruins

Follow the path to the right as you come from the museum. Most of what you see dates back to the 2nd century AD or later.

Unfortunately quite a lot of the site is fenced off behind barbed wire and is inaccessible.

The first site you pass, on your left, is an unmarked collection of serpentine **columns** in a murky pool. Further along on the left is the magnificently elaborate **tetrapylon**, or monumental gateway, which greeted pilgrims as they approached the Temple of Aphrodite. The tomb of Professor Erim is just south-west of it.

Follow the footpath until you come to a right turn which leads across the fields to the well-preserved **stadium**. Most of its 30,000 seats are overgrown but still in usable condition and you can almost imagine the football-crowd atmosphere when games were in progress. The stadium has a slightly ovoid shape so that spectators would have a better view of events, which were usually sports in Greek times, blood sports in the Roman era. As the city dwindled in the 5th century, one end of the stadium was converted into a theatre.

Return to the main path and continue to the **Temple of Aphrodite**, completely rebuilt when it was converted into a basilica (circa AD 500). Its cella (inner room) was removed, its columns shifted to form a nave,

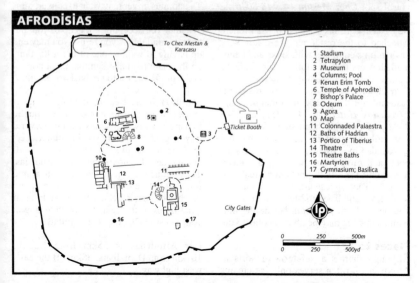

AFRODİSİAS

To Chez Mestan & Karacasu

Ticket Booth

City Gates

1 Stadium
2 Tetrapylon
3 Museum
4 Columns; Pool
5 Kenan Erim Tomb
6 Temple of Aphrodite
7 Bishop's Palace
8 Odeum
9 Agora
10 Map
11 Colonnaded Palaestra
12 Baths of Hadrian
13 Portico of Tiberius
14 Theatre
15 Theatre Baths
16 Martyrion
17 Gymnasium; Basilica

0   250   500m
0   250   500yd

and an apse added at the eastern end, making it difficult to picture the place in which orgies to Aphrodite were held. Near the temple-church is the **Bishop's Palace**, dating from Byzantine times.

Just south of the Bishop's Palace a path leads east to the beautiful marble **odeum**, preserved almost undamaged for a thousand years in a bath of mud.

South of the odeum was the **agora**, once enclosed by Ionic porticoes but now little more than a grassy field. Next the path leads you to the **Baths of Hadrian**, five large **galleries** and a **colonnaded palaestra** or playing field, and the grand **Portico of Tiberius**.

Climb up the earthen mound to find the white marble **theatre**, complete with stage and individually labelled seats, and at least as impressive as the one at Aspendos. South of it stood a large **baths** complex.

Because Afrodisias is so isolated and so much of it still survives, here more than in most places you get a very real sense of the grandeur and extent of the lost classical cities.

Places to Stay

About 500m before you reach the ruins, on the main road from Karacasu to Tavas, you'll spot *Chez Mestan* (☎ 448 8046), a restaurant with a shady front porch. Mestan Bey is Turkish; his wife Nicole is French. Attached to the restaurant are a few very basic rooms equipped with sinks and hand-held showers (but not toilets) for US$8/17 a single/double, including breakfast.

Walk another 500m back towards Karacasu and you'll see Mestan's other offering, *Afrodisias Hotel* (☎ 448 8132, fax 448 8422), on the right-hand side of the road. The building itself is uninspiring but it's surrounded by gardens, with a wisteria arbour, and olive trees. Inside smart, clean rooms cost US$20/25, including breakfast. There's a rooftop restaurant, a good place to wind down and listen to Mestan's stories. If you phone from the booth beside the museum, someone may be able to collect you.

Places to Eat

Although there's a cafeteria of sorts at Afrodisias, it often serves only ice creams and cold drinks. Your best bet for a meal is to walk back along the highway to *Chez Mestan* where lunch in the shady garden will cost about US$4. The rooftop restaurant at *Afrodisias Hotel* is also very inviting; a buffet lunch or dinner costs US$6.

If you're hanging about in Karacasu, there's no problem picking up a simple kebap meal, although the surroundings won't be anything special.

Getting There & Away

Bus A few direct buses link Karacasu with İzmir (US$10, 3½ hours, 210km) and Selçuk (US$8.50, two hours, 130km).

Otherwise, take a bus from İzmir, Selçuk, Ortaklar, Aydın or Denizli to Nazilli, and from there pick up a dolmuş to Afrodisias or to Geyre, the village next to the ruins. If you can't find a dolmuş to Geyre or Afrodisias, there are services to Karacasu from Nazilli every 20 minutes (US$1.40) during the main part of the day. Then take a dolmuş (US$0.60), hitch a ride or hire a taxi (US$12 return) for the final 13km to the ruins. Hitching should be easy in summer.

If you arrive at the ruins by dolmuş, be sure to check the time of the service back. The dolmuş driver may want to convert himself into a private taxi service at this point. Whether you accept or not is up to you, but bear in mind that if you refuse you may end up having to walk to one of the restaurants on the main road and summoning a normal taxi from Karacasu to get back to Nazilli.

Minibus Tours Bearing in mind the difficulties of getting to Afrodisias by public transport it's worth knowing that several travel agencies operate special minibus services from Pamukkale. These leave at 10 am and take 1½ hours to get to Afrodisias. They return at 3 pm, leaving you ample time to explore the ruins and have a picnic lunch. The cost is US$8 per person. Even at quiet times of the year it's worth asking at your pension about special minibuses.

Car Afrodisias is 55km from Nazilli, 101km from Denizli and 38km off the east-west highway.

DENİZLİ
☎ 258 • pop 250,000

Denizli is a prosperous, busy agricultural city with some light industry. There's not much need to hang about here. In the unlikely event that every hotel and pension in Pamukkale is full, there are some accommodation options.

Orientation & Information

The train station is on the main highway near the roundabout with the statue of a rooster, one block west of the otogar and a short distance west of the three-point traffic roundabout called Üçgen.

There's a tourist office (☎ 264 3971) in the otogar, theoretically open 8 am to 5 pm daily, from May to October, closed on weekends at other times. In reality working hours are somewhat shorter.

Places to Stay

Denizli's best pension is in Deliktaş Mahallesi, about 1km from the otogar on the eastern side of the highway to the south of the Üçgen Çarşısı. The *Denizli Pansiyon* (☎ 261 8738, 1993 Sokak 14) is clearly signposted. All rooms have showers and toilets and cost US$17 a double, including breakfast. The pension has a nice courtyard with a fountain and lots of fruit trees. The owner, Süleyman Can (pronounced 'john'), also sells carpets. Call from the otogar and he'll pick you up to save you the 25-minute walk. The one drawback might be the minaret right beside the back wall.

The three-star *Otel Laodikya* (☎ 265 1506, fax 258 2005) overlooks the otogar. If you don't mind paying US$12.50/22 for a single/double, you'll get comfortable air-con and TV-equipped rooms. Expect to pay more at busy times of the year.

The nearby two-star *Otel Yıldırım* (☎/fax 263 3590, 632 Sokak 3) has rooms with baths for similar prices, less when it's quiet. Rooms vary in smartness and quietness, and beware the restaurant's air-conditioning unit roaring away at the back.

Grand Hotel Keskin (☎ 263 6361, fax 242 0967, İstasyon Caddesi 11), just a block from the otogar, boasts three stars, a garage and air-con rooms, all with bath and satellite TV. Rates are US$32/50.

Cumhuriyet Caddesi, the street cutting across İstasyon Caddesi 100m uphill from the otogar, has a rash of other top-end hotels catering primarily to the tour group market. Best is probably *Bellona* (☎ 241 9828, fax 242 0655) which charges US$32/44, but other possibilities include *Otel Den-Tur* (☎ 241 7189, fax 241 1969) and *Aygören Otel* (☎ 264 7896, fax 263 9153).

Places to Eat

Denizli's big otogar is ringed with inexpensive restaurants, including *Doyuran Kafeterya*, serving freshly made *kıymalı pide* (Turkish pizza with meat topping) for US$1.75. *Çiçek Hamburg Lokantası* is open long hours, and is good for ready-made meals such as soups, stews and salads. Two plates with bread and drink costs around US$3. At the front of the otogar is *Özlem Lokantası*, another cheap dining possibility, with köfte for under US$1.

On İstasyon Caddesi a popular place is *Özen Lokantası*, serving roasted chicken to an appreciative local clientele.

Getting There & Away

Bus There are frequent buses between İzmir and Denizli via Selçuk, Ortaklar, Aydın and Nazilli. The otogar has an *emanetçi* (left-luggage room) next to the PTT and the toilets.

You can catch a bus in Denizli for virtually any major city in Turkey. Some daily services to selected destinations are listed in the table over the page.

Warning

Most people come to Denizli en route to Pamukkale. Some bus companies, particularly in Selçuk, sell tickets for Pamukkale which actually drop you in Denizli where you must change to a city bus or dolmuş for the onward journey. Sometimes the price is included in your ticket, sometimes it isn't. Often you'll be hanging around Denizli waiting for the dolmuş to fill up.

Services from Denizli's Otogar

destination	fare (US$)	time (hr)	distance (km)	daily services
Ankara	12	7	480	frequent buses
Antalya	6.50	5	300	several buses
Bodrum	6.50	5	290	several buses
Bursa	13	9	532	several buses
Fethiye	8	5	280	several buses
Isparta	5	3	172	frequent buses
İstanbul	15	12	665	frequent buses
İzmir	5	4	250	frequent buses
Konya	11	7	440	several buses
Kuşadası	4	3½	215	frequent buses
Marmaris	6.50	3	185	several buses
Nevşehir	14	11	674	at least one night bus
Selçuk	3.50	3	195	hourly buses

There are two separate services from Denizli to Pamukkale. The local bus service leaves from inside the otogar and runs roughly every 30 minutes with no waiting about for it to fill up. It also passes many of the pensions and hotels. Denizli's otogar is one of the few places where touts who take commissions from hotels still operate. These hustlers will try and get you to take the dolmuş minibuses which wait just beside the otogar. In summer these fill up quickly, but at other times you'll have to wait around. The hustlers use this waiting time to try and divert you to their favoured pensions, spinning lies about why you shouldn't or can't stay at your chosen accommodation. Stick to your guns and insist on going where you originally planned. If in doubt, head for a *kontürlü telefon* (metered phone) in the otogar and phone to get someone from the pension to collect you. The buses and dolmuşes cost exactly the same (US$1) to Pamukkale. Be warned that some of the touts can be aggressive, so don't lose your temper.

Train Three trains a day ply between Denizli and İzmir. Tickets (US$3) go on sale at Denizli station an hour before departure.

The nightly *Pamukkale Ekspresi* between Denizli and İstanbul via Afyon hauls sleeping, couchette and Pullman cars. It leaves from İstanbul (Haydarpaşa) at 5.35 pm and from Denizli at 5.05 pm. The journey takes 14 hours. A 1st/2nd-class seat costs US$9/6.50; fares for sleeping compartments range from an additional US$10 in a one-person compartment to US$8 in a three-person compartment.

There's also a daily *mototren* (motor train) between Denizli and Afyon, departing from Denizli at 7.30 am and from Afyon at 11.10 pm for a five-hour journey.

When you arrive at the train station, walk out the front door, cross the busy highway, turn left and walk one block to the otogar, where you can catch a dolmuş or bus to Pamukkale.

PAMUKKALE
☎ 258

One of the most familiar images of Turkey is of the gleaming white calcium formations (travertine pools) of Pamukkale, 19km north of Denizli. From a distance these form a white scar on the side of a ridge. As you come closer, they take on a more distinct shape, giving credence to the name, which means 'Cotton Castle'.

Pamukkale was formed when warm calcium-rich mineral water cascaded over the cliff edge, cooling and depositing its calcium in the process. The calcium built natural shelves, pools and stalactites in which tourists delighted to splash and soak. The Romans built a large spa city, Hierapolis, above the travertine pools to take advantage of the water's curative powers, and from the 1960s to the 1980s modern hotels were built on the ridge to serve visitors. So special was Pamukkale that Unesco declared it a World Heritage Site. The tourist boom of the 1990s brought so many tourists to Pamukkale that the travertine pools and water supply were threatened.

A conservation plan has been partly carried out; most of the hotels have been demolished or (almost) closed, and the travertine pools have been closed in order to preserve them. However the foundations of the demolished hotels are still there. Care to explore the ruins of modern tourism? Features include empty swimming pools and tiled bathroom floors. Still, it's an improvement on the situation in the mid-1990s when the travertine pools were drying up and becoming discoloured.

Without being able to bathe in the pools, why go to Pamukkale? Well, the travertine pools are just as beautiful and interesting as ever, and the ruins of Hierapolis still as impressive. Pamukkale also makes a good base for day trips to Afrodisias and Laodikya. Pension owners organise picnic excursions to Ağlayan Kayalar, a waterfall at Sakızcılar between Denizli and Çal for about US$10 per person. Haydar Baba Mağarası, a bizarre travertine-filled cave, is another possible day trip. The village itself is on the edge of a fertile agricultural area and is well-stocked with small family-run pensions and hotels, most with their own pools and perfect for a few days of relaxation.

Orientation

Pamukkale and Hierapolis constitute a national park with entrances and visitor centres on the northern and southern sides. To the west, at the base of the travertine ridge, is Pamukkale town, once a farming village but now a small town with many pensions.

About 5km west of the northern entrance (*kuzey girişi*) is the village of Karahayıt where you'll find most of the luxury hotel development.

Cars can reach the southern entrance (*güney girişi*) of the national park via Pamukkale town (2km), or the northern entrance via Karahayıt. It's a short walk from the hideous carbuncle of a building at the southern entrance to the centre of the site, but 2.5km from the northern entrance.

Information

Although Pamukkale has a tourist office (☎ 272 2077) on the plateau, it doesn't offer much. There's also a PTT, souvenir shops, a museum and a first aid post. The nearest banks are in Denizli.

Travertine Pools

It costs US$6.40 to enter the national park; tickets are valid for two days. A sign at the ticket kiosk warns against entering the travertine pools to protect their natural beauty. From the kiosk you have to walk 250m barefoot up to the plateau along a calcium-covered path lined with artificial concrete pools. Tiny sharp ridges of calcium make this a delicate task on tender feet. The route to the southern entrance is much longer, about 3km, but it is on bitumen. The site is (supposedly) open 24 hours, which means you can visit for sunrise and sunset.

You can still swim in the beautiful pool at the Pamukkale Termal (formerly the Pamukkale Motel), with its submerged fragments of fluted marble columns. A two-hour dip costs US$5 (children half price), but they rarely check your pass so you may be able to stretch it out a bit. A safe box for your belongings costs another US$0.80.

The Motel Koru also has a swimming pool, but the manager said it was not open. Mysteriously, though, the rooms were still furnished and rumour has it this place takes guests when they can get away with it.

Hierapolis

Hierapolis was a cure centre founded around 190 BC by Eumenes II, King of Pergamum, which prospered under the Romans and even more under the Byzantines. It had a large Jewish community and therefore an early Christian church. Earthquakes brought disaster a few times; after the one in 1334 the locals finally called it a day and moved away.

These days the main reason for coming to Pamukkale should be to explore the ruins of

HIERAPOLIS

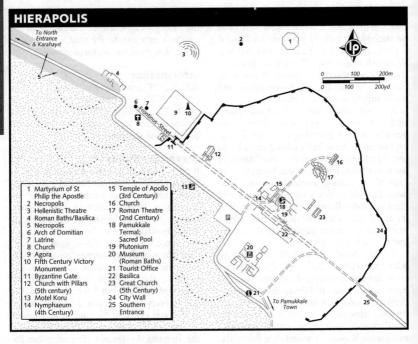

Legend:

1. Martyrium of St Philip the Apostle
2. Necropolis
3. Hellenistic Theatre
4. Roman Baths/Basilica
5. Necropolis
6. Arch of Domitian
7. Latrine
8. Church
9. Agora
10. Fifth Century Victory Monument
11. Byzantine Gate
12. Church with Pillars (5th century)
13. Motel Koru
14. Nymphaeum (4th Century)
15. Temple of Apollo (3rd Century)
16. Church
17. Roman Theatre (2nd Century)
18. Pamukkale Termal; Sacred Pool
19. Plutonium
20. Museum (Roman Baths)
21. Tourist Office
22. Basilica
23. Great Church (5th Century)
24. City Wall
25. Southern Entrance

Hierapolis where Fiat is sponsoring on-going excavations and restoration work. The ruins sprawl over a wide area within the national park. To inspect everything carefully could take the best part of a day, although most visitors settle for an hour or two.

The centre of Hierapolis may have been the **sacred pool**, now the swimming pool in the courtyard of the Pamukkale Termal. If the motel had been torn down as planned, the pool would have become visible as it was to the ancients, instead of being ringed with overpriced ice cream stands.

The city's **Roman baths**, parts of which are now the **Pamukkale Museum**, are in front of the Pamukkale Termal. The museum has a fine collection of Roman-era statuary, identified as having come from the Afrodisias school, and a few sarcophagi and architectural fragments unearthed by Italian archaeologists. The museum is open from 8.30 am to noon and 1.30 to 5 pm daily except Monday. Admission is US$1.25.

Near the museum stands a ruined **Byzantine church** and the foundations of a **Temple of Apollo**. As at Didyma and Delphi, the temple had an oracle attended by eunuch priests. The source of inspiration was an adjoining spring called the Plutonium, dedicated appropriately to Pluto, god of the underworld. The spring gives off toxic vapours, lethal to all but the priests, who would demonstrate its powers to visitors by throwing small animals and birds in and watching them die.

To find the spring, walk up towards the Roman theatre but enter the first gate in the fence on the right, then follow the path down to the right about 30m. To the left and in front of the big, block-like temple is a small subterranean entry closed by a rusted grate and marked by a sign reading 'Tehlikelidir Zehirli Gaz' (Dangerous Poisonous Gas). If you listen, you can hear the gas bubbling up from the waters below. Note that the gas is still deadly poisonous. Before the grate was installed there were several fatalities among those with more curiosity than sense.

The spectacular **Roman theatre**, capable of seating more than 12,000 spectators, was built in two stages by the emperors Hadrian and Septimius Severus. Much of the stage survives, along with some of the decorative panels and the front-row 'box' seats for VIPs. It was carefully restored by Italian stonecutters in the 1970s.

From the theatre take one of the rough tracks heading uphill and eventually you'll come to the extraordinary octagonal **Martyrium of St Philip the Apostle**, built on the site where it's believed that St Philip was martyred. The arches of the eight individual chapels are all marked with crosses. Views from here are wonderful and you'll probably share them only with the goldfinches and skylarks.

If you hack across the hillside in a westerly direction, eventually you'll come to a completely ruined **Hellenistic theatre** along unmarked goat tracks.

Standing beside the theatre and looking down you'll see the 2nd-century **agora**, one of the largest ever discovered. On three sides, marble porticoes with Ionic columns surrounded it, while a basilica closed off the fourth side.

Walk down the hill and through the agora, and you'll re-emerge on the main road along the top of the ridge. Turn right towards the northern exit and you'll come to the remains of the marvellous colonnaded **Frontinus Street**, still with some of its paving and columns intact. Once the city's main north-south commercial axis, this street was bounded at both ends by monumental archways. The ruins of the **Arch of Domitian**, with its twin towers, are at the northern end, but just before them don't miss the surprisingly large **latrine** building, with two channels cut into its floor, one to carry away sewage, the other for fresh water.

Beyond the Arch of Domitian you come first to the ruins of the **Roman baths** and then to the Appian Way of Hierapolis, an extraordinary **necropolis** (cemetery), extending several kilometres to the north, with

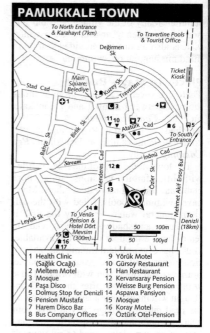

PAMUKKALE TOWN

1 Health Clinic (Sağlık Ocağı)	9 Yörük Motel
2 Meltem Motel	10 Gürsoy Restaurant
3 Mosque	11 Han Restaurant
4 Paşa Disco	12 Kervansaray Pension
5 Dolmuş Stop for Denizli	13 Weisse Burg Pension
6 Pension Mustafa	14 Aspawa Pansiyon
7 Harem Disco Bar	15 Mosque
8 Bus Company Offices	16 Koray Motel
	17 Öztürk Otel-Pension

many striking, even stupendous, tombs in all shapes and sizes. Look out in particular for a cluster of circular tombs, supposedly topped with phallic symbols in antiquity. Hierapolis was a health spa, but obviously the cure didn't work for everyone.

Special Events

In late May or early June, the Pamukkale Festival brings spectators to Hierapolis' restored Roman theatre for musical and folkloric performances.

Places to Stay

With the razing or (supposed) closure of the motels on top of the ridge, accommodation is now in Pamukkale town or in Karahayıt, the building site of choice for large hotels catering to the tour-group trade.

Prices vary according to the season, being highest in mid-summer. To avoid the crush, and find a bargain, come during the week, or very early on Friday or Saturday, and preferably in spring or autumn, not high summer. Many of the village pensions and hotels stay open year-round, so a winter visit is also an option, provided you don't mind missing out on swimming.

Places to Stay – Budget

There are several camping grounds along the road between Denizli and Pamukkale, including *Çankur Kamping* (☎ 272 2784), attached to the Şafak Restaurant, as you come into Pamukkale from Denizli and *Ege Camping* nearby.

The town at the base of the ridge is filled with little family pensions, some more elaborate and expensive than others. Many have swimming pools, filled with the calcium mineral water – cool by the time it gets there – and shady places to sit, read, sip tea or have a meal. If rooms are available, you'll have no problem finding one, as pension owners will crowd around your bus as it arrives and flood you with offers. Those with rooms available after the initial onslaught will intercept you as you walk along the road into the village. If you have your heart set on somewhere specific you may have to be very determined to rid yourself of the touts and hotel owners.

A cluster of welcoming, family-run pensions can be found at the junction of İnönü and Menderes Caddesis. The honeysuckle-scented *Kervansaray Pension* (☎ 272 2209, fax 272 2143, e kervansaray2@superonline.com) offers cheerful double rooms with shower for US$18, including breakfast, a swimming pool, and a friendly family atmosphere. It's been a favourite for years and the central heating system makes it a year-round possibility.

Very close to the Kervansaray is the friendly *Aspawa Pansiyon* (☎ 272 2094, fax 272 2631, e aspawa@mail.koc.net.tr), with singles/doubles/triples for US$8/12/18, a front pool and an upstairs restaurant. It, too, has central heating and is open year-round. Gurel's cooking is another bonus – dinner costs US$5 or so. There's satellite TV and free Internet for guests.

The *Weisse Burg Pension* (☎ 272 2064) has eight ground-floor rooms, a small pool

and a rooftop restaurant where Haçer's cooking is particularly warmly endorsed. She can cater for vegetarians if you ask. Singles/doubles cost US$6/12, breakfast is US$2 and dinner will set you back US$5.

As you come into town from Denizli there are several other pensions in a quiet location. *Hotel Dört Mevsim* (☎ 272 2009, Namık Cemal Caddesi) is on the very edge of town, overlooking the fields of the Büyük Menderes valley. It offers simple rooms with bath, costing from US$10 per person in high season down to as low as US$3.50 in low season. There's a swimming pool, bar and a relaxed atmosphere courtesy of the friendly, unflappable owner Hassan.

Across the road is the *Venüs Pension* (☎ 272 2152), with very clean, modern bedrooms (with balconies on three floors) for US$6/10. The pool here is very inviting and you can eat out around it on sunny evenings (the food is good too).

Almost at the southern entrance to town is *Pension Mustafa* (☎ 272 2240, fax 272 2830), with an interesting front terrace and clean simple rooms, all with their own shower, for US$5 per person. Breakfast is another US$2 and a sizeable dinner costs US$4. There's satellite TV and Internet access for US$2.

The *Meltem Motel* (☎ 272 2413/4, e meltemmotel@superonline.com, Kuzey Sokak) is a 22-room backpacker-oriented place. Dorm beds cost US$3.20, singles US$5 and doubles US$8. It has a rooftop bar with satellite TV and video and there's a swimming pool. We've had some complaints of overcharging for local tours though.

Places to Stay – Mid-Range

Pamukkale also has a few extremely inviting motels. One of the nicest is Rifat Durmuş's *Koray Motel* (☎ 272 2300, fax 272 2095), with a pool romantically set in a central courtyard surrounded by trees. Well-kept and friendly, it offers double rooms with shower and bath for US$20; for US$10 more you get breakfast, lunch and dinner as well.

Next door the *Öztürk Otel-Pension* (☎ 272 2116, fax 272 2838), run by a large traditional family, also has plenty of greenery set around a swimming pool, pleasant if dull rooms, and it charges a little less than the Koray.

The *Yörük Motel* (☎/fax 272 2073), a short walk down the hill in the village centre, is more inviting than its lobby initially suggests. Rooms are on two levels, surrounding a courtyard with swimming pool. The restaurant is often busy with tour groups. Rooms with shower, balcony and breakfast cost US$20/32 a single/double in summer. A couple of four-bedded rooms can be snapped up for US$40.

Places to Eat

Most of Pamukkale's restaurants have closed in recent years, not that they had a reputation for fine dining anyway. The few that survive are worth a look, but it's not a bad idea to take a room with breakfast and dinner included. Chances are that your pension will serve you better food, with larger portions at lower prices.

Gürsoy Restaurant faces the Yörük Motel on the main street. With its small, shady front terrace, it's good for people-watching. A meal with a drink costs about US$8. Similarly priced is the *Han Restaurant*, facing the main square. The menu has many popular dishes, such as grills for around US$4. There are a couple of pide places around the main square.

Entertainment

Local bars and discos seem to change hands rather often; at the time of research there was the subterranean *Paşa Disco*, not unlike a small-town disco anywhere in the world, with local spirits for US$2. It's on the main road to Karahayıt a short distance from the corner with Atatürk Caddesi.

Otherwise there's the *Harem Disco Bar*, with nargileh pipes and a basement disco. Beers are cheaper in the bar on the ground floor. It's across the main street from the bus company offices.

Getting There & Away

Bus In summer, Pamukkale has a number of direct buses to and from other cities, many of them continuing to Pamukkale from Denizli. Companies serving the town with direct buses include Kamil Koç and Pamukkale. At other times of year it's best to assume you'll have to change in Denizli.

Pamukkale has no proper otogar. Buses stop at the dolmuş stop for Denizli. Ticket offices are on the town's main street.

Municipal buses make the half-hour trip between Denizli and Pamukkale every 30 minutes or so, more frequently on Saturday and Sunday, for US$1; the last bus runs at 10 pm in summer, around sunset in other seasons. A few of these buses actually go to the top of the ridge for no extra charge. In summer dolmuşes go more frequently but see the warning on delays and pension touts in the Denizli section earlier in this chapter.

Taxi A taxi between Denizli and Pamukkale costs about US$8, but don't take one until you're *sure* the bus and dolmuş services have stopped for the day, which is what you're liable to hear from every taxi driver. The drivers will most likely then try to take you to a hotel where they take a commission.

AROUND PAMUKKALE
Laodicea (Laodikya)

Laodicea was a prosperous commercial city at the junction of two major trade routes running north to south and east to west. Famed for its black wool, banking and medicines, it had a large Jewish community and a prominent Christian congregation. It's one of the Seven Churches of Asia mentioned in the New Testament Book of Revelation. Cicero lived here a few years before he was put to death at the request of Mark Antony.

Though the city was a big one, as proved by the ruins spread over a large area, there's not much of interest left for the casual tourist. The **stadium** is visible, but most of the cut stones were purloined to construct the railway. One of the two **theatres** is in better shape, with many of its upper tiers of seats remaining, though the bottom ones have collapsed.

The site is open from 8.30 am until 7 pm (5.30 pm in winter) daily. Admission costs US$1.60.

To reach the ruins of Laodicea on your own, you'll need a car, a taxi, a hired minibus, or good strong legs. Head north towards Pamukkale from the Üçgen, the large traffic roundabout near Denizli's otogar. Take the left turn marked for Pamukkale, and then almost immediately (just before the village of Korucuk) another left marked for Laodicea.

From this point it's a bit more than 3km to the edge of the archaeological site, or just more than 4km from Laodicea's most prominent theatre. There are several possible routes to the ruins, but this one takes you through a little farming village; the road is unmarked, so ask, or when in doubt, bear right. You should soon come to a railway level crossing; on the other side of the tracks, the ruins are visible. (Another route leaves the main road closer to Pamukkale, and brings you to the theatre first.)

Without your own transport you might want to sign up for a tour from Pamukkale. The Koray Motel, in Pamukkale, organises trips to Laodicea for around US$10 per person, depending on the number of people. These tours also take in the Ak Han.

Ak Han
En route to Laodicea, you can also visit the Ak Han (White Caravanserai), a marble Seljuk Turkish caravanserai just 1km past the Pamukkale turn-off from the main road. Heading north from the Üçgen in Denizli, don't take the Pamukkale road, but continue in the direction marked for Dinar for another 1km. The caravanserai is set just off the highway on the left as you come down the slope of a hill. It is in quite marvellous shape considering that it dates from the early 1250s.

Baba Haydar Mağarası
Sunk inconspicuously in a field, the Father Haydar cave is a bizarre, sulphur-smelling cavity with its own calcium creation. Calcium-rich water flows from near the surface into a large sinkhole, creating a bright, white pyramid, with warm travertine pools at the bottom where you can bathe. You enter down a rickety set of stairs and steps cut into the calcium.

Getting here is a bit tricky. Catch a bus or dolmuş (about US$1.60) west from Denizli on the Isparta highway until you approach the village of Kaklık, where a yellow and black sign reading 'Baba Haydar Mağarası' points down a road to the left (north). It's a 4km walk along this road to the cave, unless you can hitch a ride on a farmer's tractor. The cave is close to two white concrete structures, one marked 'DSI', on the left-hand side of the road, which continues on to a cement factory. Turn left down the dirt track and look for the top of the stairwell, or follow the sound of the falling water. There is no admission charge, and no souvenir stalls or cafes (yet), so it's a good idea to bring supplies with you.

Lake District

East of Denizli and north of Antalya, Turkey has its own Lake District, with three main lakes (*gölü*) – Burdur Gölü, Eğirdir Gölü and Beyşehir Gölü – and several smaller ones. The main town in the lakes area is Isparta, but neither it, nor Burdur, is especially interesting. Eğirdir, on the other hand, lives for tourism. Its beautiful freshwater lake is ringed with mountains, and two islands linked to the mainland by a causeway jut into the lake. Beyşehir is also well worth a visit for its wonderful 13th-century lakeside mosque.

The ruined cities of Sagalassos and Antioch-in-Pisidia are reasons to linger a while longer, and many people enjoy treks into the nearby mountains or a visit to Çandır Canyon in Kovada Gölü Milli Parkı (Kovada Lake National Park).

Spring is a good time to visit the lakes. The apple trees are in blossom in April, while the annual rose harvest begins on 20 May.

ISPARTA
☎ 246 • pop 125,000
Famous for its kilims, carpets and attar of roses, Isparta is at an important highway junction on the way east to Eğirdir (36km). Isparta is the home town of former president Süleyman Demirel.

Orientation & Information
The main road, Süleyman Demirel Bulvarı, sweeps from the Kaymakkapı Meydanı traffic roundabout, near the Otel Bolat, all the way up to the statue of the rotund Demirel (waving his hat in front of the Büyük Isparta Oteli), changing its name to Mimar Sinan Caddesi somewhere along the way. Here you'll find the banks and exchange offices and most of the bus company offices.

The otogar is 1.5km away and the train station is a little further.

Things to See & Do
Should you need to spend time here, stop in at the **Ulu Cami** (1417) and the **Firdevs Bey Camii** (1561) with its neighbouring **bedesten** (covered market), the latter two buildings attributed to Mimar Sinan. Also, wander into the huge **Halı Saray** (Carpet Palace) on Mimar Sinan Caddesi. On four days each week, fine Isparta carpets are auctioned to dealers and anyone else with the money to buy them.

The **Archaeology Museum** on Kenan Evren Caddesi, is open from 8.30 am to 6 pm Monday to Friday for US$1.25, but is way out from the centre.

Places to Stay & Eat
Süleyman Demirel Bulvarı/Mimar Sinan Caddesi has several hotels from which to choose.

Hotel Yeni Gülistan (☎ 218 4085, *Mimar Sinan Caddesi 31)* is new only in name. Basic but serviceable singles/doubles with shower cost US$10/20.

The two-star *Otel Akkoç* (☎ 232 5811, *fax 232 5810)*, across the road, has clean, spacious rooms for US$12/18.

The six-storey *Büyük Isparta Oteli* (☎ 232 0176, fax 232 4422) is a tired-looking mid-range hotel, facing the Belediye İşhanı. Singles/doubles cost US$25/35.

The *Otel Bolat* (☎ 223 9001, fax 218 5506, Süleyman Demirel Bulvarı 71) is the best in town. Singles/doubles with modern decor and satellite TV cost US$34/48, including breakfast. The rooftop *Teras Restaurant* has good views over the city. Mezes cost US$1.30, köfte US$3.

Near the Bolat is the popular *Başkent Döner Kebap ve Pide Salonu*, a moderately priced eatery. *37 Pide ve Borek Salonu* is another cheap joint between the Başkent and the Otel Bolat.

Getting There & Away
Isparta's otogar is the main transit point for the lakes, although the most frequent services to Eğirdir leave from a minibus terminal in town. Coming north from Antalya you may find yourself dropped on the outskirts of Isparta and ferried to the otogar in a *servis* minibus.

Dolmuşes to Ağlasun (for Sagalassos, US$1) and Bucak leave from the Çarşı terminal. Catch a Çarşı city bus from in front of the otogar. Note that the hourly minibus service to Burdur leaves from the otogar.

To get to Eğirdir (US$1.10, 30 minutes, 36km), take a Konya-bound bus from the otogar; alternatively, there are minibuses every 30 minutes from the Çarşı terminal.

Some daily services to selected destinations are listed in the table below.

SAGALASSOS
Dramatically sited, Sagalassos is an ancient city perched on a plateau backed by the

Services from Isparta's Otogar

destination	fare (US$)	time (hr)	distance (km)	daily services
Afyon	6	3	175	frequent buses
Antalya	4	2	175	hourly buses
Burdur	1.50	0.75	50	hourly minibuses
Denizli	5	3	175	several buses
İzmir	10	7	425	several buses
Konya	7.50	4	270	every hour

sheer rock of ragged mountains. Since 1990 a Belgian team of archaeologists and volunteers have been excavating and restoring parts of the city, which some believe will one day rival Ephesus.

Founded by a warlike tribe of the 'People from the Sea', Sagalassos became an important Pisidian city, which was second only to Antioch-in-Pisidia near Yalvaç. Archaeologists are still excavating the site but the late Hellenistic Fountain House and the Roman library with a fine mosaic floor have been rebuilt and opened to the public. The fountain house is functioning again with the original water supply.

There's also a 9,000-seat Roman theatre, and a temple with two walls standing. The massive Roman baths, dating from AD 180, are also being reconstructed. Much of the rest of the site looks to the untrained eye like a pile of rubble but the archaeologists say Sagalassos is in fact unusually well preserved, as the city wasn't pillaged for building material. There is no admission charge to the site, and parking is also free.

To get to the site, take the road south from Isparta which passes through the town of **Ağlasun** after 35km. Here a turn-off on the right leads 7km uphill. If you have your own wheels, it's worth following the narrow but paved road to visit the site. Otherwise you can take a dolmuş to Ağlasun from Isparta, and take a taxi to and from the site for about US$15. Dolmuşes run between Ağlasun and Isparta's Çarşı terminal every 30 minutes during the day, and cost US$1.60.

EĞİRDİR
☎ 246 • pop 18,000

Eğirdir (eh-**yeer**-deer) enjoys a beautiful situation on the road from Konya to the Aegean, near the southern tip of Eğirdir Gölü (Lake Eğirdir). The lake is Turkey's fourth largest, covering 517 sq km, with an average depth of 12m and a maximum depth of 16.5m. On the hillside by the road into town from Isparta is a large Turkish army commando training base, the commando slogan emblazoned in gigantic letters on the slope above: 'Komandoyuz, Güçlüyüz, Cesuruz, Hazırız' (We're Commandos: Strong, Brave

and Ready). On their day off, the commandos' blue berets are a common sight about town.

In Lydian times this highway was the Royal Road, the main route between Ephesus and Babylon, and Eğirdir was a beautiful and convenient place to stop, so the town prospered.

Today's town, clinging to the base of the steep slopes of Davras Dağı (2635m), serves something of the same purpose. Travellers on their way to or from Konya stop for a day or two to enjoy views of the lake, dine on fish, and generally relax in one of the pensions in the town or on Yeşilada, the small island connected to the shore by a causeway. More active types can hike around Davras Dağı – or take a little rowing boat onto the silvery blue waters of the lake.

The town is proud of its carpet and kilim weaving, mostly carried out by descendants of the Yörük nomads, and of its apple orchards and rose gardens, but really what it excels at is helping people to relax.

History
Founded by the Hittites, Eğirdir was taken by the Phrygians (circa 1200 BC), and was later ruled by the Lydians, captured by the Persians, and conquered by Alexander the Great, followed by the Romans who called it Prostanna. Documents from the period hint that it was large and prosperous, but no excavations have been done at the site, which lies within a large military enclave.

In Byzantine times, as Akrotiri (meaning 'Steep Mountain'), it was the seat of a bishopric. With the coming of the Turks, it became first a Seljuk city (circa 1080–1280), then the capital of a small principality covering the Lakes region and ruled by the Hamidoğulları (1280–1381). Most of the historic buildings in town date from the Seljuk and Hamidoğulları periods. The Ottomans took control in 1417, but the population of Yeşilada remained mostly Greek Christian.

Under the Turks, Akrotiri was transformed into Eğridir, a word meaning 'crooked' and 'wrong'. In the 1980s, public relations caught up with Eğridir and the town officially changed its name to Eğirdir,

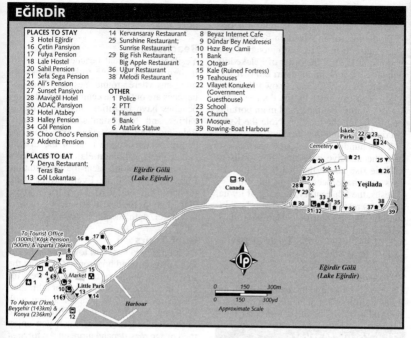

EĞİRDİR

PLACES TO STAY
3 Hotel Eğirdir
16 Çetin Pansiyon
17 Fulya Pension
18 Lale Hostel
20 Sahil Pension
21 Sefa Sega Pension
26 Ali's Pension
27 Sunset Pansiyon
28 Mavigöl Hotel
30 ADAC Pansiyon
32 Hotel Atabey
33 Halley Pension
34 Göl Pension
35 Choo Choo's Pension
37 Akdeniz Pension

PLACES TO EAT
7 Derya Restaurant;
    Teras Bar
13 Göl Lokantası

14 Kervansaray Restaurant
25 Sunshine Restaurant;
    Sunrise Restaurant
29 Big Fish Restaurant;
    Big Apple Restaurant
36 Uğur Restaurant
38 Melodi Restaurant

OTHER
1 Police
2 PTT
4 Hamam
5 Bank
6 Atatürk Statue

8 Beyaz Internet Cafe
9 Dündar Bey Medresesi
10 Hızır Bey Camii
11 Bank
12 Otogar
15 Kale (Ruined Fortress)
19 Teahouses
22 Vilayet Konukevi
    (Government
    Guesthouse)
23 School
24 Church
31 Mosque
39 Rowing-Boat Harbour

Eğirdir Gölü
(Lake Eğirdir)

Eğirdir Gölü
(Lake Eğirdir)

*To Tourist Office
(300m), Köşk Pension
(500m) & Isparta (36km)*

*To Akpınar (7km),
Beyşehir (143km) &
Konya (236km)*

Market
Little Park
Harbour

İskele
Parkı
Cemetery
Yeşilada
Canada

0   150   300m
0   150   300yd
Approximate Scale

which evokes much nicer images, of spinning, sweet flag (a flower) and propolis (a sticky sap produced by bees).

Orientation & Information

Eğirdir stretches along by the lake for several kilometres. Its centre is on a point of land jutting into the lake, marked by the statue of Atatürk, the historic Hızır Bey Camii, Dündar Bey Medresesi and the otogar. The Hotel Eğirdir is at the northern side of the town centre. The police station and PTT are in between the Hotel Eğirdir and the tourist office.

A few hundred metres north-west of the centre, the *kale* (fortress) rises at the beginning of the isthmus and the causeway which leads to tiny Canada (**jahn**-ah-da) and Yeşilada, 1.5km north-west of the otogar. Many of the town's best pensions are on Yeşilada, or around the kale's crumbling walls. The train station is 3km from the centre of town on the Isparta road.

The tourist office (☎ 311 4388, fax 312 2098) is at 2 Sahilyolu 13, 600m north-west of the otogar on the shore road towards Isparta. It's open 8.30 am to 12 pm and 1.30 to 6 pm Monday to Friday; the manager speaks English.

The Beyaz Internet Cafe is about 75m from the Derya Restaurant on the northern shore of the peninsula. It charges US$1 per hour.

Historic Architecture

You can walk round Eğirdir's sights in an hour or so, starting from the Hızır Bey Camii, a Seljuk construction built as a warehouse in 1237, but restored as a mosque in 1308 by Hızır Bey, a Hamidoğulları emir. Note especially the finely carved wooden doors, and the bits of blue tile still to be seen on the minaret. Otherwise, the mosque is quite simple, with a clerestory (row of windows) above the central hall. The tiles around the mihrab are new.

Facing the mosque is the **Dündar Bey Medresesi**, a theological school built first by the Seljuk sultan Alaeddin Keykubat as a caravanserai in 1218, but converted to a medrese in 1285 at the order of Felekeddin Dündar Bey, a Hamidoğulları emir. It was last restored in 1979, and is now filled with shops. You can enter by the door near the **Atatürk statue**, but the grand main portal is the one facing the mosque. Note the Kufic inscription around the doorway.

A few hundred metres out towards Yeşilada, the massive but crumbling walls of the **kale** rise above the beach. Its foundations may have been laid on the order of Croesus, the 5th-century BC king of Lydia, but it was restored by successive rulers, including the Byzantines, Hamidoğulları, Seljuks and Ottomans. On the causeway side of the walls is the **Tomb of Devran Dede**, a local Muslim mystic.

Hamams

The town's venerable hamam is behind the Hotel Eğirdir, with separate entrances for men and women. The full works costs about US$15, though you should agree on the price first.

Beaches

Yeşilada has no real beaches to speak of, though there's nothing to stop you swimming anywhere around Yeşilada. The best beaches are out of the centre. The following beaches have facilities such as changing cabins and food stands or restaurants. **Belediye Plajı** is less than 1km from the centre on the Isparta road in the district called Yazla. **Altınkum Plajı** is several kilometres further north, near the train station. Entry costs US$0.30. Even further north (about 11km) on the road to Barla is **Bedre Plajı**, perhaps the best of all – 1.5km of sand and water, with adequate facilities.

Boat Tours

As soon as you arrive in town you'll be offered pensions and boat tours. Choosing the first is often choosing the second as well, for each pension owner has a boat or a brother, cousin or son with a boat, or a deal with someone who has a boat. Offerings are fairly standard, and how much you enjoy the voyage may depend more on the force of the wind that day than on the boat or owner.

Places to Stay

Yeşilada essentially consists of lots of small, family-run pensions and restaurants, interspersed with second homes for the İstanbul elite who come here for a fortnight every year. There are more inviting pensions clustered near the kale (castle) on the mainland, though this part of town isn't as scenic. Prices are fixed by the municipality; expect to pay around US$8/9 for a single/double without bath or US$12/13 with private facilities. The island is small enough to walk around in 15 minutes, so you might want to make a quick circuit and weigh up the relative positions and views before deciding.

If you arrive at the start or end of the season, bear in mind that nights can be cold; the pensions with central heating come into their own then. Most places have hot water, although you may need to tell your host so they can turn it on for your shower.

The Yörük Markets

The weekly market in Eğirdir is every Thursday, but from the end of July to the middle of October, there are markets every Sunday for the Yörük people of the mountain villages. The Yörüks come to Eğirdir to sell their apples, goats and yogurt, and to buy supplies for the winter. It's an important opportunity for people from different villages to meet and mix. These markets are held for 10 Sundays in a row. On the Saturday before the last Sunday market, when the trading is nearly done, there is a market attended only by women. During this day, mothers with sons of marriageable age approach the mothers of acceptable potential daughters-in-law and offer them a handkerchief. If the handkerchief is accepted, then the process of introductions between the families and the prospective bride and groom can begin. If all goes well, the marriage can go ahead in the spring of the following year.

In high season you may find Eğirdir pension owners, especially on Yeşilada, biased against single travellers. Even if you offer to pay the double rate for just one person, they may turn you down because they won't be able to sell two meals.

In the unlikely event that everywhere in town is full, many of the restaurants on Yeşilada rent out rooms.

Yeşilada This island, the 'Green Island', is the best place to stay because of its scenery and ambience. At the time of writing there were no noisy discos or importunate carpet sellers to disturb its tranquillity. Let's hope it stays that way.

There are three excellent pensions on the south side of the island. *Halley Pension* (☎ 312 3625) offers airy rooms with showers and some rooms have double beds. Several readers have written to recommend the welcome here and to praise Mehmet and Esna's home-cooked meals. You can hire bicycles for US$5 per day, or borrow their little rowing boat for free.

Göl Pension (☎ 312 2370), run by the Davras family, has nine spotlessly clean and comfortable rooms, a cut above many on the island and therefore slightly more expensive. The best rooms are on the top floor. Doubles cost US$20, including breakfast on the downstairs terrace.

Choo Choo's Pension (☎ 311 4926, fax 311 6764) was designed by an eccentric American. There are only five rooms, each named after Choo Choo's favourite artists, including Rembrandt and Utrillo. The rooms are nicely decorated and there's a fine terrace on the top floor. It's often booked out. Doubles cost US$25.

Just where the causeway joins the island is *ADAC Pansiyon* (☎ 312 3074), another cheerful little pension with strategic balconies looking west and south over the lake and mainland. Some of the rooms are a bit small, but at least they offer free boat trips. There's a restaurant on the ground floor.

Taking the road to the left as you reach the island there are a couple more choices. *Sunset Pansiyon* (☎ 311 4315) has nine rooms all with balconies. The bathrooms are a bit small but the rooms have lots of light and have wood-panelled ceilings. *Sahil Pension* (☎ 312 2167) has some nice rooms on the top floor, but it seems their restaurant is now the focus of their business.

Perhaps the most charming pension, if you don't mind foregoing the lake views, is Mustafa and Ayşe Gökdal's *Sefa Sega Pension* (☎ 311 1877), a traditional village house. Though retired, Ayşe Hanım works hard to keep it tidy, and Mustafa provides a warm welcome. Remove your shoes as you enter, in the old-fashioned way.

Akdeniz Pension (☎ 311 2432), which is also run by a nice old couple who don't speak much English, has three simple but tidy rooms and a vine-shaded terrace.

Ali's Pension (☎ 312 2547) is another family-run place, but we've had complaints that they can be unfriendly if you don't eat there every night. It's on the eastern side of the island.

Yeşilada has two conventional hotels. The hulking modern *Mavigöl* (☎ 311 6417, fax 311 6303) is no architectural masterpiece but the rooms have all mod cons. Doubles cost from US$22 to US$35 in high season. On the south side of the island, the *Hotel Atabey* (☎ 312 4628, fax 312 8977) is a little older but it's quiet and comfortable. Doubles cost US$28.

Mainland As you pass the kale on the way to Yeşilada, look up to the left to see the *Lale Hostel* (☎ 312 2406, fax 311 4984, ⓔ lale hostel@hotmail.com). It's a popular backpacker's haunt, run by the sincere and helpful Ibrahim. Dorm beds cost from US$4, doubles are US$10; all rooms have bathrooms. There's a great view of the lake from the rooftop terrace and bar. Internet access costs US$1.50 per hour, and there's a useful book with tips on local excursions. Bicycle hire is US$4 per day, boat trips cost US$5.

Close by there's the very friendly *Çetin Pansiyon* (☎ 312 2154), which has six rooms with bathrooms. It's right by the lake's edge and they offer free boat trips. *Fulya Pension* (☎ 312 2175) is one of the best in town with its roof terrace, restaurant and panoramic views. Big double rooms with shower cost US$7 per person, including breakfast.

About 800m west of town past the tourist office is the **Köşk Pension** (☎ 311 4382), which gets good reports. Rooms cost between US$5 and US$10 per person. It offers free trips to and from the centre of town.

The **Hotel Eğirdir** (☎ 311 4992, fax 311 4219), facing the water beside the PTT, is looking a bit battered but it's clean, with smallish singles/doubles for US$25/40, including breakfast.

Places to Eat

Many pension owners have their own restaurants, usually specialising in fish, but if you don't want to dine 'at home' there are plenty of good restaurants on Yeşilada.

The excellent **Melodi Restaurant**, next to the Akdeniz Pension at the tip of the island, has a good range of fresh mezes for US$2 and delicious grilled fish for around US$7. There are also good lake views.

If you turn left at the end of the causeway you'll come to the **Big Fish Restaurant** and the **Big Apple Restaurant**. Both these places have biggish restaurants and the Big Fish in particular seems very popular with the locals, always a good sign.

On the other side of the island there's the **Sunrise Restaurant** and the adjoining **Sunshine Restaurant**, both catering mostly to visitors from Isparta and İstanbul. They're perfectly good if there are enough visitors in town, otherwise the mezes aren't always as fresh as you'd like.

On the mainland, **Kervansaray Restaurant** has a lakeside terrace, grills for around US$5, fish for up to US$10 and a good selection of booze.

The **Derya Restaurant**, across the street from the Hotel Eğirdir, has outdoor tables set by the water and a sprawling indoor dining room as well. The **Teras Bar** upstairs turns into the local nightclub on summer evenings.

For cheaper eats, try the **Göl Lokantası** near the otogar, on the main road leading to Yeşilada. Standard steam-tray fare costs about US$3.20 for lunch or dinner. The **Uğur Restaurant** sometimes has live Turkish folk music, with much clapping, dancing and balancing of glasses of rakı on heads.

Getting There & Away

Bus If there's no bus leaving straight away for your destination, hop on a minibus to Isparta and catch one there (see Isparta Getting There & Away earlier). The table below lists some useful daily services.

Train One train a day leaves for İstanbul at 5.30 pm; it costs US$7 for the 13-hour journey. The train station is 2km west of town.

AROUND EĞİRDİR
Davras Dağı

High on the steep slopes of Davras Dağı is the tiny Yörük village of Akpınar, with apple orchards and photogenic views over the lake. To get there head 3km south of Eğirdir along the lake-shore road to the suburb of Yeni Mahalle, where a road begins to wind 4km up the mountain to the village. It's a steep walk, but you might be able to hitch a lift. It takes about two hours if you're in reasonable shape. The village has about

Services from Eğirdir's Otogar

destination	fare (US$)	time (hr)	distance (km)	daily services
Ankara	8	7	457	3 buses
Antalya	3	2½	186	hourly buses
Denizli	5	3	203	change at Isparta
Isparta	1.25	½	36	every 15 minutes
İstanbul	12	11	638	1 bus
İzmir	8	7	418	several buses
Konya	6	4	236	several buses
Nevşehir	10	8	443	4 buses

50 houses, and sometimes there's a yurt (tent) selling *ayran* (yogurt drink) and gözleme. The local kids have become accustomed to visitors giving them gifts.

Serious hikers can continue up to the top of Davras Dağı, but some of the rocks are unstable so you should take care.

Kovada Gölü Milli Parkı

When the citizens of Eğirdir take an outing, they usually head 25km south to Kovada Gölü Milli Parkı, the small (40 sq km) lake filled by the runoff from Eğirdir Gölü. Noted for its flora and fauna, it's a pleasant place for a hike and a picnic. Further along the Çandır road from the lake is the Çandır Canyon, 73km from Eğirdir, a spectacular mountain gorge carved out of marble. It's a great place to swim.

The easiest way to get to Kovada Gölü and Çandır is to sign up with a tour from one of the pensions. Out of season taxi tours to Kovada Gölü and the canyon, including a three-hour wait will cost around US$40 per carload. You could also try hitching on a Sunday in summer, when locals make excursions.

Zından Mağarası

Another excursion is to Zından Mağarası (Zından Caverns), 30km to the south-west, 1km north of the village of Aksu across a fine Roman bridge. The 1km-long cave has Byzantine ruins at its mouth, lots of stalactites and stalagmites, and a curious room dubbed the Hamam. It's rather muddy though. Bring a powerful torch if you plan to explore more than superficially. There's a pleasant walk along the river if you don't fancy getting dirty. Once again the pensions organise tours in summer, or taxis will take you there for about US$25 per carload.

BURDUR

☎ 248 • pop 60,000

Despite its proximity to the saltwater Burdur Gölü, Burdur is a dreary small town you're only likely to want to visit if you'd like to see the finds from Sagalassos in the museum. Buses from Isparta drop you on the eastern outskirts. Come out of the otogar,

turn right and walk along Gazi Caddesi for 15 minutes to the town centre, or catch a Burdur Belediyesi bus from just outside.

To find the **Burdur Müzesi** turn right opposite the Haci Mahmut Bey Camii in Gazi Caddesi. The most impressive exhibits are Hellenistic and Roman statues from Kremna and Sagalassos, although there are also Neolithic bits and pieces from the nearby Hacılar and Kuruçay mounds. One of the finest exhibits is a 2nd-century bronze torso of an athlete, but there are also some fine bronze jugs. The museum is open from 8.30 am to noon and 1.30 to 5.30 pm daily except Monday. Admission costs US$1.30.

If you need to stay there are several hotels along Gazi Caddesi. One fairly basic place is *Otel Altın* (☎ 234 4942, Gazi Caddesi 61), where beds cost US$7 per person. Much better value for money is *Hotel Özeren* (☎ 233 9607, Gazi Caddesi 51). Although not geared for foreign visitors, this is a smart, clean place, which is a good deal at US$10/16 for singles/doubles with showers.

Gazi Caddesi also has plenty of places to eat simple meals. Try *Özgü Restaurant* with its frilly chair covers, or the popular *Ege Lokantası* which has pictures of beach resorts on its walls. In neither will a meal cost more than US$4.

There are hourly minibuses from Isparta (US$1.50, 45 minutes, 50km).

BEYŞEHİR

☎ 332 • pop 32,000

If Burdur disappoints, Beyşehir is a charming lakeside town with a mixture of traditional and modern houses and one of the best medieval mosques in central Anatolia. From 1071 Beyşehir was a local administrative centre, but its glory days came at the end of the 13th century. Şeyheddin Süleyman Bey was responsible for creating the **Eşrefoğlu Camii**, with its 39 soaring wooden pillars and beautiful blue-tiled mihrab, second only in architectural importance to the Ulu Cami in Afyon. Süleyman is buried beside the mosque. Nearby are a contemporary **medrese**, with an impressive portal, and the many-domed **Dokumacılar Hanı** (Cloth Hall).

Since the mosque and Beyşehir Gölü are right beside the otogar you could easily visit en route from Eğirdir to Konya or vice versa. If you want to make a longer trip of it, come out of the otogar and bear right onto the main highway. When you reach the bridge, drop down on the left for the town centre with its hotels and restaurants.

At the time of writing the most promising place to stay was *Beyaz Park Motel* (☎ *512 3865)*, an old house with a riverside restaurant in Atatürk Caddesi. Singles/doubles with shower cost US$10/16. The smaller *Park Oteli* (☎ *512 4745)*, which overlooks the main square, has simple rooms with bath for US$5/8.

Atatürk Caddesi is also the place to look for food. Popular places include the big *Kanarya Restaurant*, serving *etli ekmek* (flat bread with minced lamb), and *Anıt Restaurant*, with spit-roasted chicken.

Beyşehir is two hours by bus from Eğirdir (US$4) and one hour from Konya (US$2).

YALVAÇ & ANTIOCH-IN-PISIDIA
☎ 532

The little-known, but extensive ruins of Antioch-in-Pisidia are perched on a stark mountainside, 72km north-east of Eğirdir, about 2km north-east Yalvaç, on the road to Hisarardi village. Archaeological work is ongoing. The small museum in Yalvaç has a useful plan of the ruins.

The main feature of the site is the acropolis, with the scant remains of a triumphal archway. In Roman times this featured an Imperial cult temple dedicated to Augustus. There are some details carved into the foundations of this temple.

The stonework of the theatre below the acropolis now makes up some of the houses in Yalvaç, but you can still see where the hillside was carved away.

St Paul preached at the synagogue here, and provoked such a strong reaction that he and St Barnabus were expelled from the city. The city was abandoned in the 8th century after Arab attacks.

Set on a windswept plain at an altitude of 1100m, the market town of Yalvaç doesn't have a lot to offer visitors, but it's certainly not a tourist trap and the authorities are trying their best to encourage visitors. There are two hotels, should you want to stay overnight: the *Otel Pisidia Antiochia* (☎ *441 4375)* with singles/doubles for US$10/23, and the more comfortable *Otel Oba* (☎ *235 53 06)* with doubles for US$28.

There are about 10 buses a day between Yalvaç and Eğirdir (US$2, one hour, 72km).

Western Mediterranean Turkey

The south-western coast of Turkey is a succession of scenic roads and dramatically sited ancient ruins interspersed with resort towns which range from charming to overwhelming. Until the 1970s, parts of this coast could only be explored with a pack animal, boat or sturdy 4WD. Highway construction during the 1980s changed all that. The advent of convenient transportation has brought on the ruin of some otherwise delightful places, as crowds out of all proportion to a town's carrying capacity pour in during the warm months. Other, more remote places are just now coming into their own as enjoyable resorts. A handful of places remain sleepy fishing villages with a few pensions – at least for now.

MUĞLA

☎ 252 • pop 50,000

If only all of Turkey's provincial capitals were like Muğla, a compact, attractive city with lots of trees set in a rich agricultural valley. An obviously prosperous town, Muğla prides itself on having had Turkey's first female *vali* (governor). Though tourism and farming are important sources of wealth, most people seem to be employed as bureaucrats.

It's well worth dropping your bags at a bus company office in the *otogar* (bus station) and walking around the historic quarter for a couple of hours – Muğla's old Ottoman neighbourhoods, tea gardens and markets are a breath of fresh air after too many concrete seaside resorts.

First settled around 1200 BC, Muğla was known as Alinda until Seljuk times. Captured by the Turkish emirs of Menteşe in 1261, it was seized by the Ottomans in 1390, but was returned to Menteşe control by the victorious Tamerlane in 1402. Mehmet the Conqueror regained control for the Ottomans in 1451. The town seems to have been called Mabolla, Mobella or Mobolia in later Ottoman times, yielding the Muğla of today.

HIGHLIGHTS

- Sailing along the coast
- Walking through the Saklıkent Gorge
- Exploring the ruins at Xanthos or Pınara
- Lazing on Patara beach
- Enjoying a boat ride through the reed beds of Dalyan to İztuzu
- Lingering at the mysterious flames of the Chimaera on a moonless night
- Strolling the labyrinthine streets of Kaleiçi (Old Antalya)
- Climbing through the mountainside ruins of Termessos

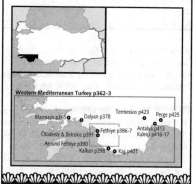

Western Mediterranean Turkey p362-3

Marmaris p365 • Dalyan p378 • Termessos p423 • Perge p425 •
Ölüdeniz & Belcekız p391 • Fethiye p386-7 • Antalya p413 • Kaleiçi p416-17 •
Around Fethiye p390
Kalkan p398 • Kaş p401 •

Orientation & Information

Muğla's centre is Cumhuriyet Meydanı, the traffic roundabout with the statue of Atatürk. Everything you're likely to need is within walking distance: the otogar a few blocks south-west, the PTT 500m northwest along Recai Güreli Bulvarı, and the bazaar and historic quarter 500m due north along İsmet İnönü Caddesi.

The tourist office (☎ 214 1244, fax 214 1261) is in the İl Turizm Mudurluğu (Provincial Tourism Directorate) on Marmaris Bulvarı, the road running south-east from Cumhuriyet Meydanı. From the otogar walk up to the meydanı and go down the

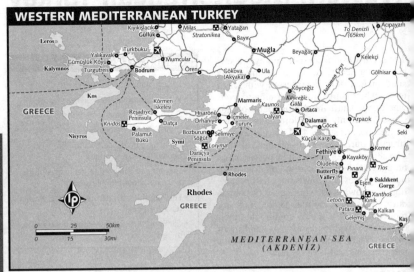

WESTERN MEDITERRANEAN TURKEY

main road leading off to the right. The office is on the right-hand side about 100m past the Hotel Petek. The staff speak English and can provide a useful town map.

Things to See & Do

Go north along İsmet İnönü Caddesi from Cumhuriyet Meydanı to the **Kurşunlu Cami**, built in 1494, repaired in 1853 and with a minaret and courtyard added in 1900. Nearby is the **Ulu Cami** (1344), dating from the time of the Menteşe emirs, although 19th century repairs have rendered its pre-Ottoman design almost unrecognisable.

Continue walking north into the **bazaar**, its narrow lanes jammed with artisans shops and some very basic restaurants. Proceed up the hill to see Muğla's **Ottoman houses**, some still in good condition. Centuries ago there was a small fortress at the top of the hill, but not a stone remains.

The **Vakıflar Hamamı**, on the corner of Tabakhane and General Mustafa Muğlalı Caddesis and built in 1258, is still operating. It has a separate women's entrance. Near it stands a curiously church-like clock tower.

Muğla's **Müzesi** displays finds excavated from fossil beds at Özlüce in 1993. It's in-

teresting to discover that animals looking much like the rhinoceros once roamed these parts. There are also rooms devoted to ethnographical displays and a few archaeological bits and pieces. The museum is open from 9 am to noon and from 1 to 5 pm daily except Monday. Admission costs US$0.80. It's close to the *belediye* (town hall) and faces the impressive **Konakaltı İskender Alper Kültür Merkezi** which houses small craft shops.

Places to Stay – Budget

Follow Tabakhane Caddesi into the bazaar to find the very simple *Doğan Pansiyon* (☎ 214 3960), above a *kiraathane* (coffeehouse) half a block from the Ulu Cami. It has waterless doubles for US$8.

Otel Tuncer (☎ 214 8251, Saatli Kule Altı, Kütüphane Sokak 1) is a long block north-east of the Kurşunlu Cami (follow the signs). It's relatively clean, fairly quiet and well priced, with singles/doubles with shower for US$6/10.

Otel Zeybek (☎ 214 1774, fax 214 3156, Turgutreis Caddesi 5), one short block west of the Kurşunlu Cami, is older and a bit noisier, charging US$7 for a bed in a waterless room and US$8 for one with a shower.

Head along Cumhuriyet Caddesi to the large Orgeneral Mustafa Muğlalı İşhanı building and then turn left and cut through the market to find *Hotel Saray* (☎ 214 1594, fax 214 1950, Açik Pazar Yeri 11). Good, clean rooms with shower and views of the market go for US$10/18.

Places to Stay – Mid-Range

On a quiet street opposite the otogar, the *Hotel Yalçın* (☎ 214 1599, fax 214 1050, Garaj Caddesi 7) is Muğla's best value-for-money lodging. Although some 30 or so years old, It's well maintained, and charges US$15/25 for comfortable rooms with shower, including breakfast.

The three-star *Hotel Petek* (☎/fax 214 1897, Marmaris Bulvarı 27), 400m east of Cumhuriyet Meydanı, is a good choice for solo travellers. Its smaller single rooms, aimed at business travellers, cost US$14 (you can get a whole suite for that price when it's quiet), while doubles are US$25.

Muğla's fanciest – and the only place with swimming pool, hamam and sauna – is the three-star *Hotel Grand Brothers* (☎ 212 2700, fax 212 2610), 1km west of Cumhuriyet Meydanı along the Yatağan-İzmir high-

WESTERN MEDITERRANEAN

way. The posted rates are US$45/65, but it's seldom busy so ask for a discount.

Places to Eat

The bazaar holds numerous *köfte* (meatball) grills, *pide* (Turkish-style pizza) makers and ready-food eateries. *Hotel Yalçın* has a terrace restaurant noted for its good food, service and alcoholic beverages. You're likely to spend between US$5 and US$10 here.

Walking along Cumhuriyet Bulvarı you'll come to a big office building called the Orgeneral Mustafa Muğlalı İşhanı which is virtually ringed with mid-range eating places. Worth trying are *Bulvar Ocakbaşı Restaurant* and *Köşem Restaurant*, both with indoor and outdoor seating. A good meal should cost no more than US$5 to US$8.

Walk up İsmet İnönü Caddesi to the Kurşunlu Cami and turn right. Hidden away on the right is the pleasant *Saklı Bahçe Restaurant* where you can tuck into kebaps beneath wisteria and bougainvillea for US$4.

Local students tend to hang out in shady open-air cafes along the İzmir highway, between Cumhuriyet Meydanı and the Grand Brothers Hotel. *Serpil Park Cafe* is about 150m from the square, with cheap meals (eg, hamburgers for US$2), soft drinks and cool house music beats over the PA.

Getting There & Away

Muğla's busy otogar offers fairly frequent services to all major destinations in the region. For points along the Mediterranean coast east of Marmaris, you may have to take a bus to Marmaris and change there. Details of some services follow:

destination	fare (US$)	time (hr)	distance (km)
Aydın	3.20	1¾	100
Bodrum	3.20	2	110
Dalaman	3	1½	86
Denizli	4	2	130
Gökova	0.80	¾	35
İstanbul	20	14	875
İzmir	7	4½	265
Köyceğiz	1.60	1	57
Marmaris	1.25	1	55
Milas	2	1	57

AROUND MUĞLA

Just west of Yatağan at Eskihisar are the ruins of **Stratonikea**. The city was founded under the Seleucids, important under the Romans, and is now threatened by a huge open-cut mine producing lignite. Bits of ruin are visible from the road as you pass through, but you must follow the signposted road 1km down to the abandoned former village of Eskihisar to reach the centre of Stratonikea.

It's worth a visit if you have your own transport, as there are two ruined settlements: the Roman city, and the ghost village of **Eskihisar**, abandoned as the mine tailings crept nearer.

Of Stratonikea, bits of the walls and gates, gymnasium and tomb survive, hidden in the grass and scrub and extending up the slope to the other side of the highway.

The abandoned Turkish village has houses of beautiful stonework and a remarkable absence of modernity: no wires, commercial signs or cars. There is one building, on the shady former village square, maintained and used as a teahouse, which may not be open. At the end of the village road another stone house is the museum/storehouse for archaeological finds from the site. (Admission costs US$1 and is hardly worth it.) Otherwise, Eskihisar is a museum village of Turkish rural life a century ago.

GÖKOVA (AKYAKA)

☎ 252

About 30km north of Marmaris the road from Muğla to Marmaris comes over the Sakar Geçidi (Sakar Pass, 670m) to reveal breathtaking views of Gökova Bay from a parachute platform. It then descends by switchbacks into a fertile valley.

At the base of the hill, signs point the way west to the village of Akyaka, often called Gökova after the beautiful bay nearby. Backed by mountains, this fast-growing resort village is built on a hillside which descends to a little grey-sand beach with good bathing beside a river mouth. Instead of the usual high-rises, development here has centred on attractive two-storey houses with wooden balconies. However, as so often,

creation of an infrastructure hasn't kept pace with the building work and many roads are still dirt tracks.

Places to Stay & Eat

The western side of the waterfront is dominated by **Otel Yücelen** (☎ 243 5108, fax 243 5435), a beautiful complex mainly aimed at tour groups but with attractive rooms set around a pool. It costs US$40/55 a single/double for half board, or there are some bungalows available for US$40.

Inland a bit but with its own pool is the well-signed **Hotel Engin** (☎ 243 5727, fax 243 5609) at the end of Sefa Sokak, offering clean doubles with shower for US$26.

Otherwise, there are several small apartment complexes which let rooms as pensions when they're not needed by tour groups. Typical of these are **Murat** (☎ 243 5279), which costs US$12.50 per person in bungalows with small kitchens, and **Deniz** (☎ 243 5553) in the centre of the village.

For a meal with a view, a couple of restaurants overlook the beach. **Umut** has mezes for around US$1, and chicken kebaps for US$4. **Sahil Kafeterya** is similar. **Kösem Restaurant**, slightly inland, advertises a few choices for vegetarians.

About 700m beyond the village of Akyaka is an *orman piknik yeri* (forest picnic ground), and another 500m beyond that is the port hamlet of İskele, with a few basic *restaurants* serving the tiny beach at the end of the small cove.

Getting There & Away

Regular minibuses ply back and forth between Muğla and Akyaka (note that they say 'Gökova' on the front even though the road is signposted to Akyaka). The fare is US$0.80 and the journey takes 45 minutes.

MARMARİS

☎ 252 • pop 18,000

The once-sleepy fishing village of Marmaris is situated on the marvellous natural harbour where Lord Nelson organised his fleet for the attack on the French at Abukir in 1798. The setting may still be glorious but the picturesque old part of town around the harbour

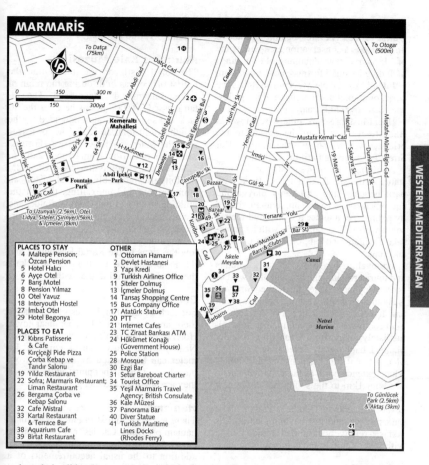

MARMARIS

To Datça (75km)

To Otogar (500m)

Datça Cad

Canal

0 150 300 m
0 150 300yd

Kemeraltı Mahallesi

Hacı Abdi Cad

Konfil Ilgaz Sk

Ulusal Egemenlik Bul

Nuri Nur Sk

Yeniyol Cad

Mustafa Münir Elgin Cad

Mustafa Kemal Cad

Hacılar

19 Mayıs Sk

Sakarya Sk

Dumlupınar Cad

H Mehmet

Seha Neray

69 Sk

İrmiçi Sk

Hasan Işık Cad

Abdi İpekçi Park

Dereüstü

Çavuşoğlu Sk

Bazaar

Güzpınar Sk

Gül Sk

Fountain Park

Atatürk Cad

To Uzunyalı (2.5km), Otel Lidya, Siteler (Sirinyer)(5km), & İçmeler (8km)

Bazaar

Tersane Yolu

Kordon Cad

Hacı Mustafa Sk Bars & Clubs

Bars St

İskele Meydanı

Canal

Barbaros

Netsel Marina

To Günlücek Park (2.5km) & Aktaş (3km)

PLACES TO STAY	OTHER
4 Maltepe Pension; Özcan Pension	1 Ottoman Hamamı
5 Hotel Halıcı	2 Devlet Hastanesi
6 Ayçe Otel	3 Yapı Kredi
7 Barış Motel	9 Turkish Airlines Office
8 Pension Yılmaz	11 Siteler Dolmuş
10 Otel Yavuz	13 İçmeler Dolmuş
18 Interyouth Hostel	14 Tansaş Shopping Centre
27 İmbat Otel	15 Bus Company Office
29 Hotel Begonya	17 Atatürk Statue
	20 PTT
PLACES TO EAT	21 Internet Cafes
12 Kıbrıs Patisserie & Cafe	23 TC Ziraat Bankası ATM
16 Kırçiçeği Pide Pizza Çorba Kebap ve Tandır Salonu	24 Hükümet Konağı (Government House)
19 Yıldız Restaurant	25 Police Station
22 Sofra; Marmaris Restaurant; Liman Restaurant	28 Mosque
26 Bergama Çorba ve Kebap Salonu	31 Setur Bareboat Charter
32 Cafe Mistral	34 Tourist Office
33 Kartal Restaurant & Terrace Bar	35 Yeşil Marmaris Travel Agency; British Consulate
38 Aquarium Cafe	36 Kale Müzesi
39 Birtat Restaurant	37 Panorama Bar
	40 Diver Statue
	41 Turkish Maritime Lines Docks (Rhodes Ferry)

WESTERN MEDITERRANEAN

and castle is all but lost now in the concrete sprawl trailing off to the west. In summer the town's population swells to between 150,000 and 200,000, mostly budget package-holiday-makers. The bazaar is full of expensive souvenirs and cheap tourists, the streets are full of traffic, and the restaurant scene is based on fish and chips with beer by the gallon.

If it's a last night out, a boat cruise or a ferry to Greece you're after, this is the place. Marmaris still has Turkey's largest and most modern yacht marina and is consequently the country's busiest yacht-charter port, and the bar district and harbour have a great range of places to drink. When you need to escape, hire a car or motorcycle and cruise around the rugged Reşadiye and Daraçya Peninsulas.

Orientation

From the otogar dolmuşes run down the wide Ulusal Egemenlik Bulvarı and deposit arrivals at the Tansaş Shopping Centre, a useful landmark. At the end of Ulusal Egemenlik Bulvarı, marked by the obligatory Atatürk statue, Kordon Caddesi veers left along the seafront for 300m to the İskele

Meydanı, the harbourside plaza with the tourist office. The area behind and above this office is a conservation area with some of Marmaris' few remaining old buildings including its small fortress, now a museum.

Inland from İskele Meydanı stretches the çarşı, or market district, much of it a pedestrianised covered bazaar.

Hacı Mustafa Sokak, otherwise known as Bar Street, runs from the bazaar to the bridge, over which lies the marina. Bar Street keeps going until the early hours.

A few hundred metres west of the Atatürk statue is the small Abdi İpekçi Park, with park benches and children's playground equipment around a dolphin fountain shaded by palms. Yet another few hundred metres south-west is Fountain Park, with its namesake fountain and bits of ancient columns and statues.

Uzunyalı, a beach district full of hotels and tourist restaurants, is about 3km west of İskele Meydanı; Siteler, also called Şirinyer, is about 5km south-west of İskele Meydanı; and İçmeler, another beach resort area, is 8km south-west of the centre. The area immediately inland from Uzunyalı is a badly planned, haphazardly developing wasteland of apartment blocks, pensions and hotels which extends north as far as Armutalan.

About 1km to the south-east is the new harbour for ferries to Rhodes; 3.5km south-east of the centre is Günlücek Park, a forest park reserve, and just beyond Günlücek is Aktaş, a relatively unspoiled seaside village with several hotels and camping grounds.

Information

The tourist office (☎ 412 1035) is at İskele Meydanı 2. It's open from 8 am to 7.30 pm daily in summer and 8 am to noon and 1 to 5 pm from Monday to Friday in winter.

Banks with ATMs are situated along the shore north and west of the tourist office; others are inland, in the bazaar. There's a Yapı Kredi branch 1½ blocks inland along Ulusal Egemenlik Bulvarı, on the right-hand side.

The PTT, on 49 Sokak, is open until 6 pm but the phones are accessible 24 hours a day. There is a cluster of Internet cafes in the laneway beside the PTT, with costs around US$1.60 per hour.

Marmaris Kale Müzesi

The small castle on the hill behind the tourist office was built during the reign of Sultan Süleyman the Magnificent. The sultan massed 200,000 troops here for the attack and siege of Rhodes, defended by the Knights of St John, in 1522. The fortress is now the Marmaris Kale Müzesi (Fortress Museum), open from 8 am to noon and 1 to 5.30 pm daily; admission costs US$1.25. Exhibits are predictably nautical, historical, ethnographic and unexciting, though the building itself and the views are nice, and the resident free-ranging peacocks and tortoises delight children.

From the harbour end of the bazaar, follow the signs to the Kartal Restaurant and the Panorama Bar up Eski Cami Sokak, then continue uphill to the castle.

Beaches

For such a major holiday resort it's strange there aren't any good beaches near town. Hotel swimming pools provide the solution. Nearby beaches at Günlücek Park and İçmeler can be reached by dolmuşes from outside the Tansaş Shopping Centre, though they are smallish and can get crowded.

Hamams

There's a very tourist-oriented 'Ottoman' hamam off Datça Caddesi not far from the devlet hastanesi (government hospital). In addition to the usual accoutrements of a Turkish bath, this one boasts a sauna and alarmingly cold 'shock' pool. It's open from 8 am to 11 pm daily and charges a hefty US$20 for a bath, including assisted wash, massage and drink afterwards. If you find the massage too cursory, you can have a 20-minute massage with baby oil for another US$8. The bath is mixed and all the masseurs are male.

Boat Trips

Besides the daily boats and hydrofoils to Rhodes, numerous yachts along the waterfront offer day tours of the harbour, its

A Blue Voyage

Between the world wars, writer Cevat Şakir Kabaağaç lived in Bodrum and wrote an account of his idyllic sailing excursions along Turkey's Carian (southern Aegean) and Lycian (western Mediterranean) coasts, an area completely untouched by tourism at the time. Kabaağaç called his book *Mavi Yolculuk* (Blue Voyage), a name now co-opted for any cruise along these shores.

Marmaris is a good place to charter a *gulet* (a Turkish wooden yacht) to explore the coastline. There are several ways to do this. If you don't want to do the crewing yourself and can get a party of up to 16 people together, you can charter a gulet complete with skipper and cook. In May, the cheapest month, chartering the whole boat is likely to cost between US$400 and US$1000 per day, with prices rising to US$800 to US$1750 in August, the most expensive month. Meals might cost an extra US$25 per person per day. Obviously the more people to share the costs, the less each individual will have to pay.

If you're not able to put together a large enough group of people to charter the entire boat, you can still opt for a cabin charter where you just pay for the berths you use, about US$500 to US$600 per person per week, all meals included.

Finally, experienced sailors can opt for a bareboat charter where you do the crewing (and cooking) yourself. To hire a bareboat sleeping six to 11 passengers for one week in spring costs US$1400 to US$3400. In high summer expect to pay US$1900 to US$4900. Extra charges for one-way journeys, employing a skipper, cleaning up at the end of the voyage etc can bump up the price even more.

The Interyouth Hostel in Marmaris organises cruises to Fethiye (US$200, five days, four nights, not including alcohol). Lots of drinking and partying goes on, if that's your scene. Numbers are limited to 12 people (six double cabins).

For more information on yachting and lists of yachts and brokers, contact the Marmaris International Yacht Club (☎ 412 3835), PO Box 132, 48700 Marmaris. You can usually book through a yacht broker or travel agency near your home. If not, contact Yeşil Marmaris (☎ 252-412 6486, fax 412 5077, e yesilmarmarisiris.com.tr), Barbaros Caddesi 249 (PO Box 8), 48700 Marmaris. For bareboat charters, contact Setur Bareboat Charter (☎ 412 6530, fax 412 4608), Barbaros Caddesi 223, 48700 Marmaris.

beaches and islands. Summer departures are usually at 9 am. Before deciding on your boat talk to the captain about where the excursion goes, what it costs, whether lunch is included and, if so, what's on the menu. A day's outing usually costs around US$16 or US$20 per person, much less in the off-season when boats leave later in the day.

The most popular daily excursions are to Dalyan and Kaunos or to the bays around Marmaris. In the latter case beware an extended lunch stop at Amos Bay where the only eating options available are extremely expensive. Pack a picnic or hang on until you get to Turunç Bay where there's more of a choice.

You can also take longer, more serious boat trips to Datça and Knidos, out along the hilly peninsula west of Marmaris.

Scuba Diving

There are several places in Marmaris where you can learn to dive on short courses for between US$35 and US$65, depending on the time of year. Look for the Marmaris Diving Centre on a boat moored near the tourist office. There are several others nearby.

Special Events

The Marmaris Yacht Festival is usually held in the second week of May. Though this is a private convention for yacht owners and brokers, anyone interested in yachts will enjoy seeing all the boats in the harbour and marina. Race Week, at the end of October, provides another chance to see the harbour full of yachts in full sail. For information contact the Marmaris International

Yacht Club (☎ 412 3835), PO Box 132, 48700 Marmaris.

Places to Stay

Although Marmaris has several hundred hotels and pensions, the cheaper places are being squeezed out by the relentless rise in the number of hotels serving package holiday-makers. There are several moderately priced hotels a short walk from İskele Meydanı. Most of the really expensive hotels are well around the bay from the town, some as far out as İçmeler.

Places to Stay – Budget

The **Interyouth Hostel** (☎ 412 3687, fax 412 7823, e interyouth@turk.net, Tepe Mahallesi, 42 Sokak 45) is deep in the bazaar in the town centre. Shopkeepers will usually point the way, though touts may try to mislead you. It's a clean, well-managed place with dorm beds for US$4.50 and doubles for US$12, all with shared bathrooms. Internet access costs US$2.50 per hour. They sell cheap ferry tickets to Rhodes, and the friendly staff gladly lead expeditions into local nightlife. Once the bazaar shuts down around 11 pm it's very quiet.

There are a couple of cheap pensions in Kemeraltı Mahallesi. Walk along the waterfront to Abdi İpekçi Park. Turn inland just past the park and left at the first street, then right and past the Ayçe Otel. Cross a footbridge and you'll find the **Maltepe Pension** (☎ 412 1629, 64 Sokak 7), with doubles for US$10 with shared bathrooms, US$14 with shower. There's a small garden and free use of a kitchen. The **Özcan Pension** (☎ 412 7761, Çam Sokak 3) next door charges the same prices but the bathrooms are a bit grubby. Some rooms have balconies.

Barış Motel (☎ 413 0652, 66 Sokak 10) is a new family-run place with tiled bathrooms for US$8 per person. Readers report that the family are very friendly.

If you don't mind roughing it a bit there's the **İmbat Otel** (☎ 412 1413, Eski Çarşı, 39 Sokak 5), a worn-out backpacker hotel with showers in each room but squat toilets outside. Singles cost US$5, doubles US$10 to US$14.

Pension Yılmaz (☎ 412 3754, 107 Sokak) is just inland from the little park (Fountain Park) that's east of the Turkish Airlines office (124 Sokak goes alongside the park). For US$15 a double and being this close to the centre, it's a real find.

Places to Stay – Mid-Range

If you're in Europe and planning to stay more than a few days in a mid-range Marmaris hotel in summer, check the price of package holidays on sale through travel agencies before booking. The market is so competitive that these may work out cheaper than buying a flight and then booking the room yourself. In July and August most of these hotels are block-booked for groups and it is often difficult to find a room for just one or two nights.

The aptly named **Hotel Halıcı** (☎ 412 1683, fax 412 9200, Cem Sokak 1), Carpet-dealer Hotel, is run by a firm that owns three carpet shops in Marmaris' bazaar. Rooms set amid fine gardens in a relatively quiet location cost US$60 a double, including breakfast. It has a swimming pool and some fine antique furniture and maps.

Around the corner from Abdi İpekçi Park is **Ayçe Otel** (☎ 412 3136, fax 412 3705, 64 Sokak 11). It's a small, quiet and comfortable family-run hotel with a small swimming pool. Rooms cost US$30/44 a single/double.

Otel Yavuz (☎ 412 2937, fax 412 4112), further west along Atatürk Caddesi, has three-star comforts, 55 rooms and a small swimming pool on top of the building. Your room (with bath) may well have a balcony with a view of the bay. In high season the price is US$48 a double, including breakfast.

Hotel Begonya (☎ 412 4095, fax 412 1518, Hacı Mustafa Sokak 101) is a delightful place, with a walled courtyard filled with plants and birdsong. Attractively decorated air-con doubles cost US$30 to US$35. There are heaps of bars nearby, but the management has installed double-glazing and can offer earplugs. There's a restaurant as well.

Places to Stay – Top End

The first luxury hotel to be built in Marmaris decades ago was **Otel Lidya** (☎ 412 2940, *fax 412 1478)* in Siteler just past Uzunyalı. Its ageing comforts are now superseded by the many luxury palaces nearby. It has the advantage of mature gardens with shady palms in front of the hotel, many luxury hotel services, and sea-view guest rooms priced at only US$65/80 a single/double in summer.

Places to Eat

Marmaris has an astonishing number of eating places so you certainly won't starve. There are concentrations of restaurants all along the harbour, along Kordon Caddesi and out along the shore to Uzunyalı, with more places to eat in the bazaar and along Hacı Mustafa Sokak. Small restaurants open, operate and go out of business at an alarming rate. The following suggestions merely scratch the surface.

For the very cheapest fare, head for the bazaar and the streets beyond it looking for 'untouristy', local Turkish places selling pide, kebaps and ready food. Find where the farmers eat and you'll save 40% on the price of your meal.

For a cheap breakfast, try the bakery in the Tansaş Shopping Centre, where fresh rolls and mini-pizzas cost a pittance.

Head for the PTT on 51 Sokak in the bazaar. Just inland from it are several good, cheap restaurants including *Sofra*, *Marmaris Restaurant* and *Liman Restaurant* just off 51 Sokak at 40 Sokak 32. Any of these places will serve you a good lunch or dinner for US$4 to US$7 or so. Even further inland, *Yıldız Restaurant* is, if anything, less crowded and a bit cheaper.

Bergama Çorba ve Kebap Salonu, in the bazaar on 44 Sokak at the corner with 49 Sokak, on the north-east (inland) side of the police station, is another good choice.

Aquarium Cafe on Barbaros Caddesi is always full because it's at the centre of the action. Ask prices before ordering, and you'll do alright with a drink here.

Walk inland from the Atatürk statue along Ulusal Egemenlik Bulvarı and turn right opposite the Tansaş Shopping Centre to find *Kırçiçeği Pide Pizza Çorba Kebap ve Tandır Salonu*. Its name reflects the menu and it's always crowded with locals who like the food and the prices. A bowl of soup and a baked pide need cost no more than US$3.

For pastries and drinks near Abdi İpekçi Park, try *Kıbrıs Patisserie & Cafe*, which serves ice cream, cappuccino and pastries.

Waterfront restaurants to the south and east of the tourist office have pleasant outdoor dining areas, but prices are inevitably higher than those inland and the extra money pays for the setting rather than the quality of the food. Assume you'll spend between US$10 and US$20 per person for a full meal with wine.

Birtat Restaurant (Barbaros Caddesi 19) has indoor and outdoor seating and full meals based on meat main courses for US$12 to US$16, or fish for US$18 to US$24. Portions of seafood are small and, as at most of the places facing the harbour, drinks are expensive.

Further around the harbour toward the marina, the trendy *Cafe Mistral* has live jazz most nights and a varied, interesting menu which includes six vegetarian dishes. It's a bit quieter here and a good dinner might cost US$14 to US$20. The courtyard restaurant at the *Hotel Begonya* is another quiet refuge, with a good wine list and Turkish-European main courses for around US$10.

If the crowds and stench of the water along the harbour prove unpleasant, follow the signs up to Kartal Restaurant & Terrace Bar. You'll pass a number of small restaurants with fine views of the town, quiet dining rooms and terraces and moderate prices. The owner of *Kartal Restaurant & Terrace Bar (Eski Cami Sokak)* has been in the restaurant business for more than three decades. Come early to get a table with a good view. A three-course meal with drinks might cost US$12 to US$18.

Entertainment

The nightlife in Marmaris rivals anything on the Turkish coast. Hacı Mustafa Sokak (aka Bar Street) boasts a good supply of bars and discos which keep the music pumping until the early hours. If you can't find music to your taste, there's bound to be somewhere close by. Places on the eastern side of the street usually have terrace seating areas overlooking the harbour. 'Damsız girilmez' means 'No admittance to men not accompanied by women' but this applies mostly to local Romeos and the seriously drunk.

The fashions, inspirations, owners and names change from each year to the next. *Greenhouse* is the biggest club, a popular techno den which wins on sheer volume.

The Backstreet has live music in a garden setting most nights and attracts a hyperactive young crowd. *Davy Jones's Locker* opposite is a more solid drinking club with a nautical theme.

Amid all the bars churning out Western music you might think there was no room for anything traditionally Turkish, but head down to the yacht harbour and hunt out *Ezgi Bar* which has live Turkish music nightly and draws rapturous local audiences.

On Barbaros Caddesi further along from the Ezgi Bar, the *Escape Bar* is a longstanding favourite, with friendly staff, a pool table and tables overlooking the rows of charter yachts.

Finding somewhere for a quiet drink is a tall order, but the *Panorama Bar* has views that more than justify its name. Drinks cost a stiff US$4 for domestic and US$5 for imported stuff. To find it, follow the signs from the kale (castle) end of the bazaar uphill on Eski Cami Sokak.

Shopping

Marmaris has several shops selling excellent local honey in jars priced from US$2 to US$5, or in larger tins for US$6 to US$12. Well worth visiting is Nur-Bal, 51 Sokak 9-C, one block inland from the PTT on the same side of the street. Because the boats from Rhodes bring hordes of shoppers on day trips, Marmaris merchants stock everything: onyx, leather clothing and accessories, carpets, jewellery, crafts, Turkish delight, meerschaum pipes and baubles, sandals, apple-tea powder, copper and beach wear.

Getting There & Away

Air The region's principal airport is at Dalaman, 120km east of Marmaris. A Havaş bus (US$7) runs from the Turkish Airlines office in Marmaris to Dalaman airport, de-

parting about 3½ hours before each Turkish Airlines flight. Alternatively, catch one of the hourly buses to Dalaman from Marmaris' otogar, then take a short but relatively expensive taxi ride to the airport.

See the Dalaman section for flight details. Turkish Airlines (☎ 412 3751, fax 412 3753), Atatürk Caddesi 26-B, is a short stroll west of the Atatürk statue along the waterfront.

Bus Marmaris' otogar is 2km from the centre of town on Mustafa Münir Elgin Caddesi. Dolmuşes run to and from the otogar along Ulusal Egemenlik Bulvarı every few minutes in summer. There are convenient bus company ticket offices for Pamukkale, Kamil Koç, Uludağ and Metro on and off Ulusal Egemenlik Bulvarı just inland from the Tansaş Shopping Centre.

In summer, buses roll in and out of town all day, but in winter services drop to that required by a small farming town. The table on the facing page lists some useful services.

Boat Hydrofoils to Rhodes operate daily in summer, departing at 9.15 am and taking 45 minutes to reach Rhodes Town. From Rhodes Town hydrofoils leave at 3 pm. Tickets cost US$32 one way or same-day return and US$45 open-date return. Buy your ticket at any travel agency in Marmaris (you'll see them along Kordon Caddesi) at least a day in advance. Leaving Turkey you have to pay a US$10 port tax. Leaving Greece you have to pay a US$8 tax, and another US$10 port tax for Turkey (for same-day and open return this means a total of US$28 in taxes!). When returning from Rhodes to Turkey, you may have to buy a new visa (depending on your nationality and type of visa – see Visas & Documents in the Facts for the Visitor chapter for more information) if you've stayed overnight but not if you went on a day trip.

In high summer, motorboats also run to and from Rhodes three times a week, taking 2½ hours for the voyage. Turkish boats depart from Marmaris in the morning, returning from Rhodes in the late afternoon; Greek boats depart from Rhodes in the morning,

Services from Marmaris' Otogar

destination	fare (US$)	time (hr)	distance (km)	daily services
Adana	22	16	1025	change buses at Antalya
Ankara	17	10	780	12 buses in summer
Antalya	12	7	590	a few buses
Bodrum	5	3	165	hourly buses/minibuses in summer
Dalaman	3.20	2	120	hourly buses in summer
Datça	3.20	1½	75	hourly buses/minibuses in summer
İstanbul	20–24	13	900	12 buses in summer
İzmir	8	4½	320	hourly buses in summer
Fethiye	5	3	170	hourly buses/minibuses in summer
Kaş	8	4	305	several buses
Köyceğiz	2	1	75	at least 9 buses/minibuses in summer
Muğla	1.25	1	55	frequent buses and dolmuşes
Pamukkale	8	4	185	via Muğla and Tavas; several buses

returning from Marmaris in the late afternoon. Some of these ferries are capable of carrying cars as well as passengers. Most places selling hydrofoil tickets also sell boat tickets for the same price and these too must be booked at least a day in advance.

Getting Around
Dolmuşes run frequently around the bay, picking up and dropping passengers near the Tansaş Shopping Centre on Ulusal Egemenlik Bulvarı. They go to Uzunyalı (US$0.30, 3km), Turban-Siteler (US$0.40, 4km) and İçmeler (US$0.50, 8km), as well as to more distant towns on the Reşadiye and Daraçya Peninsulas such as Turunç, Hisarönü, Bozburun and Orhaniye. The dolmuş for Datça leaves from in front of the Pamukkale bus office just inland from the Atatürk statue.

Taxi boats run from a dock just west of the tourist office to İçmeler for US$3 per person.

AROUND MARMARİS
Once a separate fishing village, İçmeler, 8km west and south around the bay, is now little more than a beach suburb of Marmaris. However, it feels a much classier place, not least because it has been better planned, with roads laid out to a plan, and a relatively clean beach and sea.

These days İçmeler is nearly as popular with package holiday-makers as Marmaris

itself so there's not a lot of cheap accommodation available for independent travellers.

REŞADİYE & DARAÇYA PENINSULAS
A narrow, mountainous finger of land stretches west from Marmaris for about 100km into the Aegean between the Greek islands of Kos and Rhodes. Known in ancient times as the Peraea, it is now called the Reşadiye Peninsula, Datça Peninsula or Hisarönü; its southern branch is known as the Daraçya or Loryma Peninsula, with the ruins of the ancient city of Loryma at its tip. A road twists its way from Marmaris west to the tip of the Reşadiye Peninsula, but a voyage by boat is preferable. Besides the joy of sailing near the peninsula's pine-clad coasts and anchoring in some of its hundreds of secluded coves, visitors come to explore Bozburun, a fishing town 56km from Marmaris; Datça, a resort town about 75km west of Marmaris; and the hamlet and ruins of Knidos, the ancient city of the great sculptor Praxiteles, 35km west of Datça.

Orhaniye & Selimiye
Set on a beautiful bay, Orhaniye is about 10km south from the main Marmaris to Datça road. You could stop for a meal here at *İskele Motel, Cafe-Bar & Swimming Pool* (☎ 252-487 1013) or *Palmiye Motel & Restaurant* (☎ 252-487 1134, fax 487 1167).

Daraçya Peninsula by Scooter

The mountainous, deeply indented Daraçya or Loryma Peninsula is the perfect place to escape the bedlam of Marmaris and get some fresh air.

It's a rugged, wild place with remarkably varied landscapes; lush pine forests on a high plateau inland from Turunç give way to steep bare rocky hillsides as you approach Bozburun. You can go via the main road to Bozburun but it's more fun to do a loop, heading down on village roads and coming back on the main road.

Setting off from Marmaris head for İçmeler along Atatürk Caddesi. In İçmeler the main road branches; take the left-hand road which leads around the back of the town and begins a steep, winding ascent towards Turunç. Take the road to the right through the pine forest before you get to Turunç. The road narrows and gets steeper, slowly winding down to the inland village of Bayır (meaning 'Hill' or 'Slope'). There couldn't be a sharper contrast between the concrete playhouses of Marmaris and İçmeler and rustic Bayır. Signposts are a rarity in Bayır so you may have to ask directions for the correct road to Söğüt (Willow), where there are a handful of pensions and seafood restaurants. After Bayır the landscape becomes much drier, and the land falls steeply away into inaccessible coves. From tiny Söğüt the road is relatively level on the way to Bozburun, which has several good cafes for lunch.

From Bozburun a good road leads back along the western side of the peninsula, past the idyllic bays of Selimiye and Hisarönü, before rejoining the main Datça-Marmaris road.

The whole circuit of the peninsula is about 120km, and takes about eight hours with rests and photo stops. Many places in Marmaris rent scooters by the day, most for around US$30. A bigger motorcycle is unnecessary; the roads are steep and winding so speed is hardly an asset. The Interyouth Hostel rents scooters for US$20 per day. Just bear in mind that Turkey has one of the highest road traffic accident rates in the world; it's advisable to wear a helmet and appropriate clothing to protect against road rash if you come off.

There are no petrol stations on the peninsula except at the eminently missable tourist town of Turunç. Fill up in Marmaris at the Shell service station on Seyfettin Elgin Bulvarı, the extension of Atatürk Caddesi. A full tank is sufficient for doing the circuit and costs around US$6.

About 9km south of Orhaniye is an intersection with roads to Bayır and Bozburun. Follow the Bozburun road to reach the village of Selimiye, a traditional boatbuilders' village on its own lovely bay facing an islet topped by bits of ancient ruin. The piles of rough-hewn boards which you see here and there will be turned into shapely sea craft through the artisans' magic.

Though backed by craggy mountains and with no good beach to speak of, Selimiye has a few pleasant cheap restaurants supplying the yachters, including *Balıkçı Kardeşler*, *Falcon* and *Sardunya* restaurants and *Can Pide Salonu*. The inexpensive *Selim Han Apart Hotel* (☎ 252-446 4069) has a swimming pool and restaurant; *Güvercin Pansiyon* (☎ 252-446 4274) at the western end of the village is another option.

There are minibuses to Orhaniye from Marmaris and to Selimiye from Bozburun.

Bozburun
☎ 252

From Selimiye the road twists onward until, after 12km, you reach Bozburun. At the time of writing, the seaside village of Bozburun was a perfect antidote to the tourist madness of Marmaris. Fishing and farming still employ most villagers, though some work in bars and shops set up to serve the yachters who drop anchor in Sömbeki Körfezi (Sömbeki Bay). There are a few small pensions and restaurants, and a PTT. Some of the shops do currency exchange.

Bozburun is not known for its beaches, but you can swim from the rocks by the primary school south-east of the bust of

Atatürk. At the moment there are not enough tourists to justify regular excursion boats but you can charter private vessels to explore the surrounding bays. There are also many interesting walks in the surrounding countryside.

Places to Stay Bozburun's simple pensions charge from US$5 to US$10 per person, depending upon season and demand.

The pensions along the shore from the Atatürk statue are quieter, and have better sea views. First along the shore is the well-kept *Yılmaz Pension* (☎ 456 2167), and 50m beyond it the *Esengül Pansiyon* (☎ 456 2153) with fine views from its terrace.

There are several similar pensions further along this beach such as *Yılmaz Kaptan* (☎ 456 2112), the upmarket *Naturland*, *Yalçın* (☎ 456 2151) and finally *Pembe Yunus* (☎ 456 2154), 250m beyond the primary school. Pembe Yunus (Pink Dolphin) has a roof terrace for sunning and dining, and the inimitable Fatma Doğanyılmaz as a manager. She will rent you one of her clean but basic, shower-equipped singles/double rooms for US$8/17.

For complete seclusion you can't do better than *Sabrinas Haus* (☎ 456 2045, fax 456 2470, ✉ sabrinashaus@superonline.com), only reachable by boat or a long 30-minute walk. There are 20 rooms in three buildings and a beautiful garden; doubles cost US$80, including breakfast.

Places to Eat Of the restaurants, *Sahil Pide ve Pastane*, just across the street to the north-east of the Atatürk statue, is among the cheapest, though *Paradise* on the main promenade is better. *Kandil* on the main square is popular with trendy folks from İstanbul but is good value with grilled fish for US$7, mezes US$1.50 each. *Roguish Osman's Place* gets the prize for best name. Full meals are not as cheap as you might imagine because of the need to import most of the raw materials by truck or boat. The restaurant at *Sabrina Haus* is recommended. It is open to nonguests for dinner only. If you call from town they'll send a boat to fetch you. Fish and meat dishes cost

around US$10, and there are vegetarian options as well.

Getting There & Away Minibuses leave Bozburun for Marmaris (US$2) at 6.30 and 11 am, 12.30 and 4.30 pm. Return trips from Marmaris are in the afternoon, the last being at 7 pm. Services are most frequent in summer. At other times of the year day trips from Marmaris can be tricky.

Datça
☎ 252

Once a small port village, the quiet resort town of Datça has its share of villa development but it hasn't completely lost its soul. Though it has a rather exposed setting, it has some good beaches and bars and an easy-going mix of yachters, backpackers, trendy escapees from İstanbul and families with flocks of kids.

The road from Marmaris has some spectacular turns along the Reşadiye Peninsula.

Orientation The main street, İskele Caddesi, runs downhill from the highway, passing several teahouses, restaurants, the tourist office and the PTT before arriving at a small roundabout with a big tree. Immediately before the roundabout, Buxerolles Sokak on the right has several small pensions.

After the roundabout İskele Caddesi forks left and runs to Cumhuriyet Meydanı, the main square with a market and otogar. From there it continues to the harbour, with a cluster of small pensions on the left, finally running out at the end of a short peninsula, once an island called Esenada, which features an open-air cinema (summer only). Just after the main square, Kargı Yolu turns right, skirts Taşlık Plajı and climbs up the hill.

Some buses drop you at the otogar on the highway next to the *jandarma* (police) post. If that happens, turn right and follow the highway around until you see the signs for Şehir Merkezi. It's about 1km from the otogar to the main square.

Datça has two small beaches: Kumluk Plajı, tucked away behind the shops on İskele Caddesi; and Taşlık Plajı, running west from the end of the harbour.

Information Datça's tourist office (☎ 712 3546) is just off the main street into town, in the same building as the police station. It's open daily from May to October but closes on weekends in winter. When we say it's open daily, the staff did warn it is 'generally' open daily. When in attendance the staff are helpful and can supply a map and they keep lists of accommodation.

Things to Do Datça has no specific sights but it's a pretty place to hang around and relax. With its fine yacht-filled harbour, it's a bit like a smaller, quieter, laid-back version of Marmaris.

In the summer there are daily excursion boats to Knidos, with less frequent boats to the Greek islands of Simi, Kos and Rhodes, depending on demand.

Places to Stay – Budget If you walk along Taşlık Plajı on the eastern bay you'll come to *Ilıca Camping*, right on the beach, where a camp site costs US$3 per person in high season. There are also some wooden bungalows with beds for US$6, a laid-back bar facing the sea, and a restaurant. You can hire a canoe for US$1.60 per hour or just chat to the friendly owners at the bar. It's arguably the best budget option in town.

Off the main road to Marmaris, *Surf Camping* (☎ 712 2355) is on a stretch of beach good for windsurfing.

Many of Datça's small pensions have closed in recent years, but those that remain are good value. Among the surviving pensions is the *Huzur* (☎ 712 3052) on a bluff above Kumluk Plajı, with a pleasantly shady breakfast terrace. Single/double rooms cost US$13/20 in season. The nearby *Kader* (☎ 712 3553) is also good.

Quiet places on Buxerolles Sokak include *Aşkın Pansiyon* (☎ 712 3406, *Buxerolles Sokak 8*) with rooms for US$7, including breakfast. Across the street is *Tunç Pansiyon* (☎ 712 3036), attractively decorated and with satellite TV. Rooms cost US$13 per person. Other options on this street include the *Sahil Pansiyon* and *Gülhan Pansiyon*.

On İskele Caddesi itself *Tuna Pansiyon* (☎ 712 3931) has comfortable twin rooms

with bath and balcony for US$8. Rooms at the back with sea views are particularly good value and quieter than the front rooms. Across the road is *Antalyalı Pansiyon* (☎ 712 3810), which has clean modern rooms for US$5/12.

Places to Stay – Mid-Range Datça's best is the *Villa Tokur* (712 8728, fax 712 8729), a few minutes' walk up the hill from Taşlık Plajı. Owned by a German-Turkish couple, it has 13 double rooms for US$35, a swimming pool, and tremendous views.

Hotel Club Dorya (☎ 712 3593, fax 712 3303) is out on the peninsula at the end of the main street amid lovely gardens. There's a pool at the front and swimming off the rocks at the back. The setting may be great but the rooms are looking dowdy and could use refurbishment. Singles/doubles cost US$25/42.

At the eastern end of Kumluk Plajı, *Datça Öğretmen Evi* (☎ 712 2341), or Teachers' House, is a teachers' social club and hotel and a big tan eyesore. If it's not full of teachers, they'll usually rent you a pleasant modern room with views for US$25 a double, including breakfast.

The three-star *Hotel Mare* (☎ 712 3211, fax 712 3396), Yanık Harman Mevkii, is further east from the Öğretmen Evi, near Club Datça. It has a pretty, circular swimming pool and comfortable rooms with tiled showers and balconies with sea views for US$50/67. The beach is only metres away.

Places to Eat As is usual in a harbour town, food prices rise the closer you get to the water.

The harbour is ringed with fish restaurants where you should expect a meal to cost at least US$15. Near the harbour on İskele Caddesi, *Taraça* and *Küçük Ev* don't look much from the street, but have nice terraces offering lovely harbour views and menus listing meze plates for US$1.50, chicken curry for US$5 and steaks for just a bit more.

On the quayside the aptly named *Sunrise Cafe Bar* is already serving all sorts of breakfasts for US$2 to US$4 when nearby restaurants are just opening up.

Looking down on the quayside is the popular and rather cool *Kristina Bistro* which serves pizza, lasagne and chicken curry for US$6 to US$12 each. Their nonalcoholic fruit cocktails go down a treat too.

Set apart from the other restaurants is *Yasu Restaurant & Bar* in an old Greek-style stone house on Kargı Yolu where you can eat chicken in ginger or beef fillet at taverna-style tables overlooking the harbour. A meal here will cost at least US$12, probably more.

Speaking of views, *Karaoğlu Garden Restaurant* on the hillside behind (east of) the Huzur Pansiyon has good sunset views of Kumluk Plajı.

On Kumluk Plajı, *Dutdibi Pide Salonu* is run by friendly people and does good, cheap food (pides for US$1) with beach views.

İskele Caddesi also has several restaurants where you can eat without worrying about the bill. *Kemal Restaurant* boasts home-cooked dishes including vegetarian options but is closed on Sundays. *Mandalina Pide Salonu* in the modern Mandalina Pansiyon on İskele Caddesi is another possibility for a cheap pide supper.

Entertainment Datça's nightlife certainly can't match Marmaris' but that's not to say you can't dance, drink and carouse until the early hours. Bars around the harbour include *Bolero*, *Gallus*, *Sunrise Cafe Bar*, the popular *Eclipse*, which plays a more interesting selection of music than the usual top 40 hits you hear everywhere, with the funkier *Gitanes* up the hill.

Getting There & Away In summer there are hourly buses and dolmuşes to Marmaris during the day (US$3.20, 1¾ hours, 75km), and you can change there for a bus to other destinations. There are also daily buses to İzmir and Muğla and overnight services to Ankara and İstanbul. Kamil Koç, Uludağ and Ulusoy have ticket offices along İskele Caddesi between Buxerolles Sokak and Kargı Yolu.

There are often boat excursions to Datça from Marmaris and sometimes you can buy a one-way ticket.

During the summer months, the Bodrum Ferryboat Association (☎ 252-316 0882) operates scheduled ferry services between Bodrum and Datça. Ferries leave Bodrum on Saturday at 9 am, returning from Datça at 5 pm. Tickets are sold in the office in Turgut Özul Meydanı (☎ 712 2143) opposite the Deniz Motel. The ferry actually leaves from Körmen, a 15-minute ride north of Datça on the peninsula's northern coast but there are bus connections with the town.

Knidos

At Knidos, 35km west of Datça at the very tip of the peninsula, are ruins of a prosperous port city dating from about 400 BC. The Dorians who founded it were smart: the winds change as one rounds the peninsula and ships in ancient times often had to wait at Knidos for good winds, giving Knidos a prosperous trade in ship repairs, hospitality and trading. The ship taking St Paul to Rome for trial was one of the many which had to stop for a while in Knidos.

Being rich, Knidos commissioned the great Praxiteles to make a large cult statue of Aphrodite to go in a circular temple within sight of the sea. The statue, said to have been the sculptor's masterpiece, has been lost, though copies or derivative versions exist in museums in Munich, New York and Rome.

The ruins aside, Knidos consists of a tiny jandarma post with a telephone for emergencies, a single restaurant unimaginatively called *Restaurant* and a repository for artefacts found on the site (no entry). Overnight stays in the village are not allowed, so, unlike in Praxiteles' time, today there are no facilities. You can swim in the bays from wooden piers, but the beaches are several kilometres out of town. The nearest PTT is in Çeşme Köyü, the last village you pass through before coming to Knidos.

Excursion boats to Knidos often stop for lunch in the village of Palamutbükü; of the scattering of restaurants here *Merhaba*, along the beach, is cheaper than *Liman* (close to where the boats dock).

Things to See The ruins of Knidos are scattered along the 3km at the end of a peninsula, occupied only by goatherds, their flocks, and the occasional wild boar. The setting is dramatic: steep hillsides terraced and planted with groves of olive, almond and fruit trees rise above two picture-perfect bays in which a handful of yachts rest at anchor.

Few of the ancient buildings are easily recognisable, but you can certainly appreciate the importance of the town by exploring the site. The guardian will show you around for a small tip. Don't miss the ruins of the temple of Aphrodite and the theatre, the 4th century BC sundial and the fine carvings in what was once a Byzantine church.

Getting There & Away Knidos Taxi, near Cumhuriyet Meydanı in Datça, will take up to three people from Datça to Knidos and return, with up to two hours' waiting time, for US$45.

Ask in Datça's harbour about excursions to Knidos. Boats tend to leave around 9 to 9.30 am and return early evening, and cost about US$14 per person.

KÖYCEĞİZ
☎ 252 • pop 6500

Less than 50km east of the turn-off from the Muğla-Marmaris road lies quiet, pretty Köyceğiz, a small town at the northern end of a large lake, Köyceğiz Gölü, which is joined to the Mediterranean Sea via the Dalyan Çayı. The main attraction here is the lake itself – broad, beautiful and serene. Except for its small (but growing) tourist trade, Köyceğiz is a farming town producing citrus fruit, olives, honey and cotton. This region is famous for its liquidambar trees, source of the precious petrified amber gum.

Orientation & Information
The otogar and local hospital are near the highway turn-off. To reach the waterfront, head south past a roundabout and then along tree-lined Atatürk Bulvarı for 2km, passing the new precinct with the belediye, *adliye* (court house) and *hükümet konağı* (government house) on the right. You'll come to the main square with the inevitable bust of Atatürk and then to a small mosque

right by the waterfront. Kordon Boyu, the road skirting the lake, has several hotels, pensions and restaurants.

The tourist office (☎ 262 4703), opposite the mosque on the main square's eastern edge, stocks a simple map.

Things to See & Do
Stroll along the lakeshore promenade past the pleasant town park, an imaginative children's playground, shady tea gardens and several restaurants. If there's not much activity on the lake, you may see the fish jump.

When you get restless you can take a boat excursion from the promenade to the thermal baths, the **Sultaniye Kaplıcaları**, 30km by road or eight nautical miles across the lake on the southern shore (see the following Dalyan section for more details).

Other than the hot baths, you can take boat trips to Dalyan and the Kaunos ruins for about US$10 per person.

Places to Stay
In general, the better accommodation and camping options are off to the west (right) as you approach the mosque when coming into town.

About 1km west of the mosque, just beyond the Panorama Plaza, is *Anatolia Camping* (☎ 262 4750), a forest camping ground among liquidambar trees, with a small beach nearby.

Tango Pansiyon (☎ 262 2501, fax 262 4345, ⓔ tangopension@superonline.com) on Ali İhsan Kalmaz Caddesi is an upbeat pension in a clean modern building; if someone doesn't meet you at the bus stand, walk down the lake, turn right, walk 200m and follow the signs inland. The dynamic management offer daily boat trips for US$10, maps of hikes in the surrounding hills and sometimes a male belly-dancer in the evenings. Dorm beds cost US$5, single/double rooms are US$7/14.

A little further along from Tango is *Fulya Pension* (☎ 262 2301). It's also clean and new but not much English is spoken. We were quoted rates of US$6/8 for a room.

Back on the waterfront on Emeksiz Caddesi is the charming *Alila Hotel* (☎/fax 262

1150), an attractive place overlooking the lake with fine bath-equipped rooms for US$28 a double, including breakfast.

Further along in the same direction (west) is the two-star *Hotel Kaunos* (☎ *262 4288, fax 262 4836, Cengiz Topel Caddesi 37)*, even older but well kept, where the double rooms with showers and balconies overlooking the placid lake are priced at US$30, including breakfast.

Finally, *Panorama Plaza* (☎ *262 3773, fax 262 3633, Cengiz Topel Caddesi 69)*, almost 1km west of the mosque, is perhaps the best in town, with comfy double rooms a bargain for US$36 in summer.

If you turn left (east) when approaching the mosque, you'll find a mixed bag of places to stay.

Cutting inland and following the signs you'll come to the welcoming *Oba Pansiyon* (☎ *262 4181, Gülpınar Mahallesi, Gümüşlük Caddesi 10)*, a relatively quiet spot (only rooster noise) somewhat overpriced at US$20 for a double with shower.

Places to Eat

As always, the market area has the cheapest eats. Try *Meşhur Ali Baba Pide, Kebap ve Yemek Salonu*, on the southern side of the Atatürk statue in the central park, for good cheap Turkish pizza (US$1), kebaps and ready food (US$1.50 to US$2.50). To the north up the same street through the market are *Güven Restaurant* for ready meals, and *Penguen Pide Salonu* for Turkish pizza.

The lake shore is lined with pricier outdoor fish restaurants and cafes. To the east, try *Çınaraltı* while to the west *Paşa Cafe Bar Restaurant* and *Şamdan* do good fish and grills. *Çiçek Restaurant* on the main square is a bit overpriced but the outdoor tables are good for a drink and a spot of people-watching.

Getting There & Away

Most buses will drop you at the Köyceğiz otogar on the outskirts of town. Unless you fancy a 2km walk to the lake, you'll need to take a dolmuş from there to the smaller central bus station west of the main street behind the Kamil Koç bus company office.

Kamil Koç runs 14 buses daily to Marmaris (US$2, one hour, 75km), and 17 to Fethiye (US$3.20, 1¾ hours, 95km). Pamukkale has several buses to Marmaris and Fethiye. It also has one night bus to İstanbul and one to Ankara. Köyceğiz Minibüs Kooperatifi has frequent minibuses to Marmaris, Muğla (US$2, one hour, 57km), Ortaca (for Dalyan, US$1, 25 minutes, 20km) and Dalaman (US$1.75, 40 minutes, 34km).

DALYAN
☎ 252

Rapidly being colonised by the package-tour market, Dalyan is struggling to keep its once peaceful atmosphere. On top of those who choose to stay here, summer afternoons bring an armada of excursion boats from Marmaris and Fethiye carving a path through the reedbeds of the Dalyan Çayı (Dalyan Creek) on their way to the ruins of ancient Kaunos and the beach at İztuzu. Above the river the weathered facades of Lycian rock tombs gaze silently down on all this activity. Dalyan may be filling up with identical restaurants boasting obsequious staff and mediocre food, but away from the centre the quiet, lazy riverside character of the place still lingers.

Orientation & Information

It's 13km from the highway at Ortaca to Dalyan's centre by the mosque and the PTT building. Minibuses stop behind the main square where the statue of Atatürk is overshadowed by a statue of a pair of turtles.

To the north along the riverbank are the requisite bars and, inland from them, pensions, hotels and restaurants. To the south, most of the town's better hotels and pensions are along Maraş Caddesi, which runs for 1km south and ends at the riverbank.

The Dalyan tourist office (☎ 284 4235) is on Maraş Caddesi in the centre. It's open from 9.30 am to noon and from 2.30 to 6 pm Monday to Saturday in summer

The Yapı Kredi ATM is on the south-east side of the big ugly PTT building in the centre, and the Sağlık Ocağı (Medical Clinic) is near the Hotel Dalyan, south of the centre off Maraş Caddesi.

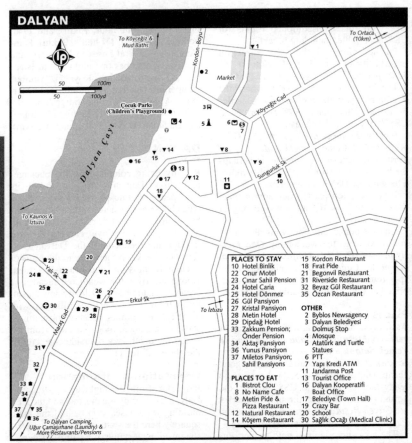

DALYAN

To Köyceğiz &
Mud Baths

To Ortaca
(10km)

Kordon Boyu

0   50   100m
0   50   100yd

Çocuk Parkı
(Children's Playground)

Market

Dalyan Çayı

Köyceğiz Cad.

Sungurluk Sk

To Kaunos &
İztuzu

To Dalyan Camping,
Uğur Çamaşırhane (Laundry) &
More Restaurants/Pensions

Yalı Sk.

Maraş Cad.

Erkul Sk.

To İztuzu

PLACES TO STAY
10 Hotel Binlik
22 Onur Motel
23 Çınar Sahil Pension
24 Hotel Caria
25 Hotel Dönmez
26 Gül Pansiyon
27 Kristal Pansiyon
28 Metin Hotel
29 Dipdağ Hotel
33 Zakkum Pension;
     Önder Pension
34 Aktaş Pansiyon
36 Yunus Pansiyon
37 Miletos Pansiyon;
     Sahil Pansiyons

PLACES TO EAT
1 Bistrot Clou
8 No Name Cafe
9 Metin Pide &
    Pizza Restaurant
12 Natural Restaurant
14 Köşem Restaurant

15 Kordon Restaurant
18 Fırat Pide
21 Begonvil Restaurant
31 Riverside Restaurant
32 Beyaz Gül Restaurant
35 Özcan Restaurant

OTHER
2 Byblos Newsagency
3 Dalyan Belediyesi
    Dolmuş Stop
4 Mosque
5 Atatürk and Turtle
    Statues
6 PTT
7 Yapı Kredi ATM
11 Jandarma Post
13 Tourist Office
16 Dalyan Kooperatifi
     Boat Office
17 Belediye (Town Hall)
19 Crazy Bar
20 School
30 Sağlık Ocağı (Medical Clinic)

The Byblos newsagency on Kordon Boyu sells foreign newspapers and magazines.

Boat Trips

Every day in summer, excursion boats leave the quayside at 10 am to cruise to Köyceğiz Gölü and the Sultaniye Kaplıcaları and mud baths, the ruins of Kaunos and the beach at İztuzu on the Mediterranean coast. Inclusive tickets cost US$5 per person.

If you can organise a small group, it may be more economical to hire an entire passenger boat which holds from eight to 12 people. Haggle to get the best price, particularly if it's early or late in the season and many boats are standing idle. A two-hour tour just to Kaunos costs from US$30 to US$40 for the entire boat; if you want to visit the Sultaniye hot springs as well, figure on three hours and US$50 for the boat.

Boats belonging to the various boat cooperatives operate a 'river dolmuş' service between the town and İztuzu Beach, charging US$2.50 for the return trip. In high summer there may be five or more boats per day, heading out from 9 am to 2 pm and returning between 1 and 6 pm. (In high summer minibuses make the 13km run to İztuzu

Turtle Alert

Some years ago Dalyan's İztuzu Beach shot to world fame when a serious threat to one of the last Mediterranean nesting sites of *Caretta caretta*, the loggerhead turtle, was identified.

The loggerhead turtle (*deniz kaplumbağa* in Turkish) is a large flat-headed reptile, reddish brown on top and yellow-orange below. An adult can weigh up to 130kg.

Between May and September the female turtles come ashore at night to lay their eggs in the sand. Using their back flippers they scoop out a nest about 40cm deep, lay between 70 and 120 soft-shelled white eggs approximately the size of ping-pong balls, and then cover them over again. If disturbed, the females may abandon the nests and return to the sea.

The eggs incubate in the sand for 50 to 65 days and the temperature at which they do so determines the gender of the ensuing young: below 30°C all the young will be male; above 30°C they will be female. At a steady 30°C an even mix of the genders will hatch out.

As soon as they're born (at night when it's cool and fewer predators are about), the young turtles make their way towards the sea, drawn by the light (the sea reflects more light than land). If hotels and restaurants are built too close to the beach, their lights can confuse the youngsters, leading them to move up the beach towards danger instead of down to the sea and safety. So when it was discovered that developers wanted to build a hotel right on the beach there was an outcry which eventually lead to the plans being abandoned.

At the same time, rules were introduced to protect the turtles. Although the beach is still open to the public during the day, night-time visits are prohibited from May to September. A line of wooden stakes on the beach indicates the nest sites and visitors are asked to sunbathe behind the stakes to avoid disturbing the nests. It's particularly important not to leave any litter on the beach which could hamper the turtles' struggle for survival.

The loggerhead turtle also nests on the beaches at Dalaman, Fethiye, Patara, Kale, Kumluca, Tekirova, Belek, Kızılot, Demirtaş, Gazipaşa and Anamur and in the Göksu Delta.

A second larger species of sea turtle, *Chelonia mydas*, the hard-shelled green turtle, also nests in Turkey, at Kazanlı, Akyatan and Samandağ, along the eastern Mediterranean coast. Hunting of these turtles for their flesh (for turtle soup) and eggs has reduced their numbers to danger point.

For more information, contact The Society for the Protection of Sea Turtles (☎ 242-825 7260) in Çıralı.

KATE NOLAN

by land as well.) Take some food as you might not like the kebap stands on the beach.

Boat cooperatives also provide dolmuş boats to Kaunos, three times a day, for US$6 return, and to the mud baths in the early evening for US$2.

Kaunos

Founded around the 9th century BC, Kaunos became an important Carian city by 400 BC. Right on the border with the Kingdom of Lycia, its culture reflected aspects of both kingdoms. The **tombs**, for instance, are in Lycian style (you'll see many more of them at Fethiye, Kaş and other points east). If you don't take a river cruise, walk south from town along Maraş Caddesi to get a good view of the tombs.

When Mausolus of Halicarnassus was ruler of Caria, his Hellenising influence reached the Kaunians, who eagerly adopted that culture. Though of good size, Kaunos suffered from endemic malaria; according to Herodotus, its people were famous for their yellowish skin and eyes. The Kaunians' prosperity was also threatened by the silting of their harbour. The Mediterranean, which once surrounded the hill on which the archaeological site stands, has now retreated 5km to the south, pushed back by silt from the Dalyan Çayı.

Apart from the tombs, the **theatre** is very well preserved; parts of an **acropolis** and other structures (baths, a basilica and defensive walls) are nearby.

Your boat pulls up to the western bank, then it's a five-minute walk to the site which is open from 8.30 am to 5.30 pm and costs US$1.60. The curious wooden structures in the river are *dalyanlar* (fishing weirs). No doubt the ancient Kaunians also benefited from such an industry.

Sultaniye Kaplıcaları & Mud Baths

The Sultaniye Kaplıcaları lie south-west of Köyceğiz Gölü. The hot, mildly radioactive mineral waters are rich in calcium, sulphur, iron, nitrates, potassium and other mineral salts and are said to be good for skin complaints and rheumatism; temperatures sometimes reach 40°C. Admission costs US$1.25. At the smaller mud baths, just before Dalyan Çayı joins the lake, you can give yourself a body pack of mud and then wash it all off again in a sulphur pool with temperatures as hot as in the Sultaniye baths.

İztuzu Beach

About 13km south of the town, this 5km sand bar separating the sea from the mouth of the Dalyan Çayı is an excellent swimming beach with some camping possibilities. A parking fee of US$1 is charged. The beach is important as one of the last nesting sites in the Mediterranean of the loggerhead turtle – for more details, see the boxed text on the previous page. Special rules to protect the turtles are strictly enforced.

Places to Stay

Once known for its many cheap *ev pansiyonu* (private home pensions), Dalyan is fast repositioning itself upmarket. Rooms are being fitted with plumbing, pensions are being razed to make way for hotels and hotels are acquiring swimming pools. At present, however, there are still some good places to stay in all price ranges. Most of the town's accommodation is south of the centre along Maraş Caddesi. The road continues for just more than 2km before ending at the riverbank.

Dalyan's swampy surroundings can produce zillions of mosquitoes at certain times of the year, so check whether the windows in your room have insect screens, and buy some industrial-strength repellent anyway.

Places to Stay – Budget

South along Maraş Caddesi is *Dalyan Camping* (✿/fax 284 4157), which charges US$5 for a single-person tent site in summer and US$8 for a small wooden two-person bungalow without running water. There's some shade, the showers and toilets are clean and it fills up early in high summer. Uğur Çamaşırhane across the road will do your laundry for you.

There are several pensions in the centre, but the ones along Maraş Caddesi to the south are quieter and some have views of the river and the rock-cut tombs. Prices are generally US$7 per person in waterless rooms, US$9 to US$10 with shower. Small hotels are usually priced from US$18 to US$22 for a double with shower.

Turning left after the school down Erkul Sokak are two excellent pensions, close to the centre but quiet. The only drawback is that they aren't on the river. *Kristal Pansiyon* (✿ 284 2263, fax 284 2743) has a small swimming pool and a lovingly tended garden. Simple singles/doubles with balconies cost US$7/10. Breakfast is on the roof terrace.

Gül Pansiyon (284 2467, fax 284 4803) across the lane has 20 rooms and a vine-shaded roof terrace. Rooms cost US$7/13 and air-con doubles are US$18.

Dipdağ Hotel (✿ 284 4572, fax 284 2526) is near the corner of Maraş Caddesi and Erkul Sokak. The spacious rooms have showers, and cost US$24 to US$28 a double. The rooms in the rear wing are quieter.

Turn right towards the water at the Dipdağ. Here on Yalı Sokak you'll find the **Hotel Dönmez** (☎ 284 2107, fax 284 2201). Hotel rooms with bath and ceiling fans cost US$20 a double, and there's a roof terrace with a bar and pool. The neighbouring **Hotel Caria** (☎ 284 2075, fax 284 3046, Yalı Sokak 82) has big, cool rooms for US$16/28. Buffet meals can be eaten on a roof terrace with terrific views.

Onur Motel (☎ 284 3074, fax 284 2787) is a welcoming family-run place with clean rooms for US$15/19 and an attractive roof bar. Also on Yalı Sokak, on the shore, is the pleasant, similarly priced **Çınar Sahil Pension** (☎ 284 2117), with a shady terrace from where you can gaze at the river.

Keep heading south along Maraş Caddesi and you'll pass yet more cheap pensions, including **Zakkum** (☎ 284 2111), a simple, friendly family-run place with shower-equipped rooms for US$19; and the similar **Önder** next door.

Aktaş Pansiyon (☎ 284 2042, fax 284 4380) is on the water, with views of the river and tombs; all rooms have showers. **Miletos Pansiyon** (☎ 284 2532) and **Sahil Pansiyon** (☎ 284 2187) are also on the riverbank. **Yunus Pansiyon** (☎ 284 2102) inland from the Sahil is quieter.

Even further south, follow the signs to **Kilim Pansiyon** (☎ 284 2253, 284 3464), decorated, as you'd expect, with kilims. This is among the nicest pensions in town, with a clean swimming pool and some of the biggest rooms in Dalyan for U$30 a double, including breakfast. There's a ramp for wheelchair access too. Similar to the Kilim is **Bur-Al Motel** (☎ 284 4885) on Balıkhane Sokak, charging a bit less.

Further down this road are several other pensions right on the river, including **Likya Pension** and **Midas Pension**. **Happy Caretta** (☎/fax 284 2109) is one of the best, with a large garden and friendly hosts. Doubles cost US$25. It's about a 10-minute walk into town.

Places to Stay – Mid-Range
In Sungurluk Sokak, down from the belediye, is the three-star **Hotel Binlik** (☎ 284 2148, fax 284 2149) with comfortable air-con rooms set around two pools for US$40 to US$50. It's usually booked by groups.

The **Metin Hotel** (☎ 284 2040, fax 284 2066, Erkul Sokak 14) is a modern, well-kept hotel centred on a swimming pool; doubles cost US$43.

Places to Stay – Top End
Dalyan now has one four-star hotel, **Asur Oteli** (☎ 284 3232, fax 284 3244). Although it's 1km south of the centre at the end of Maraş Caddesi, this is a superb place, designed as a collection of 32 single-storey octagonal units around a big pool by the award-winning architect Nail Çakırhan. The rooms are quite small, but they all have air-con and minibars, TVs and all mod cons. Prices are high at US$75 to US$105 depending on the season, so look to see if any tour operators are offering competitively priced packages before booking.

Places to Eat
Virtually all the restaurants in Dalyan seem to serve alcohol.

Bistrot Clou is an intimate little place north of the centre of town on the edge of the market area. Candlelight and cool jazz goes down well with a menu of well-prepared Turkish standards, which include mezes for US$1.50, grills for US$5 and salads for US$2.

Natural Restaurant is tucked down an alleyway near the tourist office. Despite its name there's nothing especially 'natural' about its food, the best of which is döner kebap and toasted sandwiches. Prices are good: US$5 for İskender kebap and a fresh orange juice. **No Name Cafe** nearby looks as if it should be expensive but isn't. Pizzas here cost about US$5. Inland, **Metin Pide & Pizza Restaurant** has even cheaper food.

Fırat Pide, in the warren of shops near the tourist office, is among the cheapest eateries in town.

Facing a terrace leading down to the river at the centre of town are two nice semi-open-air restaurants, **Köşem** and **Kordon**. The prices are nearly identical, with breakfast costing less than US$3, meat-based meals for US$7 to US$10 and fish meals for a bit more.

On Maraş Caddesi *Beyaz Gül Restaurant* serves outdoor grills on the riverbank in the shade of olive and orange trees. Just north of it, *Riverside Restaurant* is almost as pleasant. *Begonvil Restaurant* a bit further north is more expensive, but atmospheric. The *Özcan Restaurant* across from the Miletos Pansiyon has the usual unimaginative tourist menu (fillet steak US$6, aubergine kebap US$4) but the lush garden setting is very enticing.

Entertainment

Sitting at a riverside cafe and drinking seems to be the main pursuit for Dalyan's tourists, but there are a couple of smallish clubs in the town centre. At the time of writing, the busiest was *Crazy Bar* on Maraş Caddesi, designed as a grotto and so tacky it's really quite fun. The music is all the standard summer hits but it's worth a look.

Getting There & Away

Every day in summer minibuses leave the dolmuş stop in Dalyan at 10 and 11 am for Marmaris, Muğla and Fethiye and at 10 am for Göcek. Otherwise you usually need to take a minibus to Ortaca (US$0.40) and change to another bus there. The minibuses leave Dalyan and Ortaca every 15 minutes during the day in summer, but the last one to Dalyan is at 7 pm. Services stop even earlier in winter.

At Ortaca otogar you can connect with buses to Köyceğiz (US$1, 25 minutes, 20km) and Dalaman (US$0.50, 15 minutes, 5km). You can sometimes catch buses to more distant points at the highway in Ortaca. If not, take a bus or minibus to Dalaman and change there.

DALAMAN

☎ 252 • pop 16,500

This agricultural town was quite dozy until the regional airport was built on the neighbouring river delta. Now it stirs whenever a jet arrives, before slumping back to sleep again. Most visitors pass straight through

and bus connections are good. The only conceivable reason to linger would be to take the turn-off from the airport road to the beach at Sarıgerme.

There are hotels in Dalaman but they have the double bogey of being both expensive and poorly run. If at all possible it's better to head on straight away.

Orientation & Information

It's 5.5km from the airport to the town, and another 5.5km from the town to the east-west highway. The road connecting the highway with the town centre is called Kenan Evren Bulvarı, and beyond the town it's called Havaalanı Yolu (Airport Road). A large mosque marks its junction with the town's main street, Atatürk Caddesi; a Yapı Kredi ATM is here as well. Atatürk Caddesi is about 500m long, running east from Kenan Evren Bulvarı, with banks, shops and simple restaurants. The otogar, served by the Pamukkale, Aydın and Köseoğlu companies, is near the junction of Evren Bulvarı and Atatürk Caddesi. The PTT is a block north on Atatürk Caddesi.

Places to Stay

The well-kept *Otel Hafızoğlu* (☎ 692 5078, *Meltem Sokak*), one block south of the otogar across from Atatürk Caddesi, charges US$20/30/36 a single/double/triple for its standard one-star rooms with bath.

The cheapest choice is *Dalaman Pansiyon* (☎ 692 5543), 200m south of the traffic roundabout near the otogar, where a double room costs US$12/18 without/with bath. The town has several other cheap pensions as well.

Getting There & Away

Air Besides flights to many European cities during the tourist season, there are two daily flights from Dalaman to İstanbul year-round, costing US$83 one way.

Bus At Dalaman's small otogar you can buy tickets to many destinations. All routes north and east pass through either Muğla or Fethiye. Details of some services are as follows.

destination	fare (US$)	time (hr)	distance (km)
Antalya (inland)	8	5½	272
Bodrum	8	3½	201
Denizli	5	4	221
Fethiye	2	1	50
Göcek	1	½	23
Gökova	2	1½	80
İstanbul	20	15	966
İzmir	11	5	356
Kalkan	5	2½	131
Kaş	6	3	160
Köyceğiz	1.50	¾	34
Marmaris	5	2	120
Muğla	4	1½	91
Selçuk	9	4½	285

For Pamukkale (US$8, four hours, 240km), take the bus to Denizli, then a city bus or dolmuş from there.

Getting Around
In summer, several bus companies pick up passengers outside the airport. At other times you may need to get a taxi into Dalaman for an expensive US$7 to US$9.

GÖCEK
☎ 252
This delightful small yachting and fishing port lies on a bay at the foot of the mountains. With a reputation as a rather exclusive port of call for the yachting set, it is scrupulously well manicured and a little pricey. It's about 23km east of Dalaman.

Orientation & Information
Buses drop you at a petrol station on the main road, from there it's a 1km walk to the centre. Minibuses drive right down to the main square with the bust of Atatürk and a collection of small restaurants, laundries and a PTT with money-changing facilities. The square aside, Göcek mainly consists of the road running alongside the harbour which is lined with pensions, hotels and restaurants.

Things to Do
Göcek is really a place for relaxing. There's only a fairly scrubby beach at the western end of the quayside, although you can take a '12-Island Cruise' to beaches on nearby islands. The Göcek Club Marina boasts a Turkish bath of the modern variety which you can use for US$18.

Places to Stay
There isn't much for the budget traveller besides *Taştepe* (☎ 645 1372) on Atatürk Caddesi – luckily it's very nice, and some rooms have views of the harbour. Doubles cost US$14.

At the western end of the harbour *Başak Pansiyon* (☎ 645 1024, fax 645 1862) has a good restaurant and connecting rooms with four beds for US$25, ideal for families. A double with shower costs US$25 in high summer but only half that during low season.

Also good is *Sultan Pansiyon* (☎ 645 1557), above the food store of the same name. It's clean and proper; some rooms facing the sea have one double and one single bed, and one room on the street side has four beds. Two people pay US$24 in season, half that in low season.

Demir Pansiyon (☎ 645 1060) is a modest, homey place on the inland side of the street, charging a few dollars less and including breakfast in the price.

Dim Pansiyon (☎ 645 1294) is fairly new and clean, with a swimming pool and aircon in some rooms.

Deniz Hotel (☎ 645 1902, fax 645 1903) facing the marina is posh, pleasant and priced accordingly at US$50/60 a single/double, including breakfast. *A&B Home Hotel* (☎ 645 1820, fax 645 1843) and *Yonca Resort* (☎ 645 2255, fax 645 2275) charge similar rates.

Yağmur Apart Otel (☎/fax 645 1080), located inland a block on the north-western side of town, is new and nice, with small apartments for US$40 a double.

In the hills above Göcek, accommodation with a difference is provided at *Huzur Vadisi* (☎ 645 2429), a settlement of felt *yurts* (tents).

Places to Eat
Göcek has plenty of places to eat along the waterfront but most cater to yachters and

tend to be on the pricey side. *Blue Bar & Restaurant* does fish kebaps for about US$10 (the price changes with the fish and the season). *Nanai Restaurant-Bar* offers meat dishes for an expensive US$8 each. You eat them in cool, trendy surroundings. For something cheaper but less atmospheric, head inland to the main square.

Getting There & Away
Dolmuşes from Fethiye run to Göcek several times daily and frequently on summer weekends. In summer there is also one minibus a day from Dalyan at 10 am. There are also excursion boats from Marmaris, Dalyan and Fethiye.

AROUND GÖCEK
At **Küçük Kargı**, 33km east of Dalaman, a forest picnic area has a *camping ground* and beach. About 2km further east at **Katrancı** is another picnic and *camping ground* with a small restaurant, on a beautiful little cove with a beach. Another 18km brings you to Fethiye.

FETHİYE
☎ 252 • pop 25,000
Fethiye is a very old town with few old buildings. An earthquake in 1958 levelled the town, leaving very little standing. Most of what was left were tombs from the time when Fethiye was called Telmessos (400 BC). It's a fairly relaxed place despite its size, often visited at the beginning or end of a gulet cruise.

Fethiye's inner bay is an excellent natural harbour, protected from storms by the island called Şövalye Adası. The much larger outer bay has 11 more islands. North of town is the soulless beachside package tour resort of Çalış. The beaches are good here, but even better at nearby Ölüdeniz, one of Turkey's seaside hot spots. The Fethiye region has many interesting sites to explore, including the ghost town of Karmylassos, just over the hill (see Kayaköy, later in this chapter).

Orientation
Fethiye's otogar is 2km east of the centre of town, with a separate station for minibuses

1km east of the centre. Mid-range and top-end hotels are near the centre, but most inexpensive pensions are west of the centre overlooking the yacht harbour, with a couple of stragglers east of the centre near the stadium. Dolmuşes run to the centre along the main street, Atatürk Caddesi.

The all-important beach at Ölüdeniz is 15km south of Fethiye (see the Ölüdeniz section later in this chapter for more details).

Information
Fethiye's tourist office (☎ 614 1527), open from 8 am to 7 pm (5 pm in winter) daily, is on İskele Meydanı next to Otel Dedeoğlu, near the marina. The staff can sometimes help with accommodation and inexpensive yacht charters, but they may well just fob you off with a map and a few brochures.

The Imagine Bookshop on Atatürk Caddesi sells foreign newspapers and magazines, and there's a small Internet cafe next door (US$1.60 per hour).

Atatürk Caddesi has banks with ATMs, foreign exchange offices and shops that change money. Double-check that the rate advertised is actually the rate used to calculate your transaction; shops that advertise surprisingly good rates of exchange are the most suspect.

Where there's a yacht marina, there's a laundry. Look for the Güneş Laundry between the Prenses Hotel and the marina.

Ancient Telmessos
Throughout the town you will notice curious Lycian stone **sarcophagi** dating from around 450 BC. There's one sarcophagus near the PTT and others in the middle of streets or in private gardens; the town was built around them. All were broken into by tomb robbers, centuries ago of course.

Carved into the rock face behind the town is the **Tomb of Amyntas** (350 BC), a Doric temple facade carved in the sheer rock face. It's open from 8 am to 7 pm for US$1.30, and gets crowded at sunset in summer, the most pleasant time to visit. It's a steep climb up steps to get there; on a hot day it's worth first considering how much Lycian funerary monuments really mean to you. Other smaller tombs are nearby to the left. Follow the signs from the otogar or take a taxi for a look at the tomb and the fine view of the town and bay.

Behind the harbour as you turn up Liman Caddesi you'll see the excavated remains of a **theatre** dating from Roman times.

On the hillside behind the town, just north of the road to Kayaköy, notice the ruined tower of a **crusader fortress** built by the Knights of St John on earlier foundations dating back to perhaps 400 BC.

Fethiye Müzesi

Fethiye's museum is open from 8.30 am to 5 pm daily except Monday and charges US$1.30 for admission. The most interesting exhibits are some small statues and votive stones (the Stelae of Graves and Stelae of Promise) and the trilingual stele (Lycian-Greek-Aramaic) from Letoön, which was used to decipher the Lycian language. King Kaunos gave money to do some good work in honour of the gods and the trilingual stele described his benefaction.

Beaches

About 5km north-east of the centre is **Çalış**, a wide swathe of beach several kilometres long solidly lined with mass-produced hotels and pensions catering mostly to Germans. Once very popular, it's now overshadowed by nearby Ölüdeniz. If you want to stay for more than a day or so, it's probably cheaper to book through a European tour operator. Dolmuşes depart for Çalış from the minibus station throughout the day.

12-Island Tour

Be sure to sign up for the 12-Island Tour, a boat trip around Fethiye Körfezi which takes most of a day (9 am to 6 or 7 pm) and costs around US$13 per person. Any hotel or travel agency can sign you up, or ask around at the harbour. The boats usually stop at six islands and cruise by the rest. The most popular backpacker hostels sell tickets on booze-cruise style tours, which can be fun if your liver is prepared for it.

A normal tour visits **Şövalye Adası**, an island at the mouth of the inner bay, with a

The Lycians

Ancient Lycia extended along the Mediterranean coast roughly from Köyceğiz in the west to Antalya in the east. The Lycians first crop up in history when Homer records their presence during an attack on Troy in the *Iliad*. It is thought they may have been descendants of an Anatolian tribe called the Luvians. A matrilineal people with their own language, the Lycians lived in city-states, 23 of which formed the Lycian Federation to make communal decisions about 'foreign affairs'.

By the 6th century BC the Lycians had come under the loose control of Persia. In the 5th century BC the Athenians briefly drove the Persians out of Lycia, which became part of the Delian Confederacy. All too soon, however, the Persians were back in charge, followed in turn by Alexander the Great, the Ptolemies, the Romans and the Rhodians. After Alexander's conquest, the Lycians abandoned their own language in favour of Greek.

In the 2nd century BC Lycia was governed by the Pergamene kings. When the last of the kings died without an heir, he bequeathed Lycia to the Romans who incorporated it in their province of Asia. In spite of this nominal loss of independence, the Lycians seem to have continued their own way until, in AD 42, the resurgent Lycian League made the unwise decision not to support Brutus, leading to the destruction of Xanthos.

In AD 43 the Romans joined Lycia to adjacent Pamphylia as a single province, a union that survived until the 4th century. Lycia never again regained its independence, succumbing in turn to invading Arab and Turkish armies.

The most obvious reminders of ancient Lycia are the monumental sarcophagi littering the Mediterranean coast and the rock-cut tombs, sometimes resembling temples, high up on the hillsides at Dalyan, Xanthos, Fethiye, Kaş and Myra. At Letoön there are ruins of a huge temple built by the Lycian Federation to commemorate Leto, their supreme deity. Fethiye Müzesi also contains a trilingual stele which was used to decipher the Lycian language.

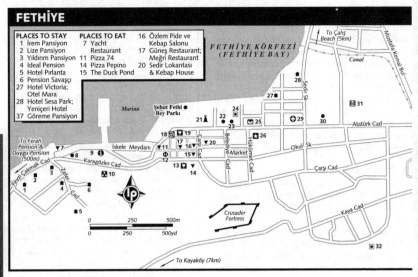

FETHİYE

PLACES TO STAY	PLACES TO EAT	16 Özlem Pide ve
1 İrem Pansiyon	7 Yacht	Kebap Salonu
2 Lize Pansiyon	Restaurant	17 Güneş Restaurant;
3 Yıldırım Pansiyon	11 Pizza 74	Meğri Restaurant
4 Ideal Pension	14 Pizza Pepino	20 Sedir Lokantası
5 Hotel Pırlanta	15 The Duck Pond	& Kebap House
6 Pension Savaşçı		
27 Hotel Victoria;		
Otel Mara		
28 Hotel Sesa Park;		
Yeniçeri Hotel		
37 Göreme Pansiyon		

FETHİYE KÖRFEZİ
(FETHİYE BAY)

To Çalış Beach (5km)

Canal

Mustafa Kemal Bul

Sedir Sk

Atatürk Cad

Okul Sk.

Çarşı Cad

Kaya Cad

Crusader Fortress

To Kayaköy (7km)

To Ferah Pension & Duygu Pension (500m)

İskele Meydanı

Karagözler Cad

Şehut Fethi Bey Parkı

Marina

Fevzi Çakmak Cad

Zafer Cad

Belediye Cad

Hükümet Cad

Market Cad

0 250 500m
0 250 500yd

---

beach and restaurant; **Gemile Adası**, with the unrestored ruins of an ancient city; **Katrancık Adası**, offshore from the beach of the same name to the west of Fethiye; **Göcek Adası**, opposite the town 27km west of Göcek, and the **islands** of Kızılada, Tersane, Domuz, Yassıcalar, Delikli, Şeytanlı and Karacaören.

Scuba Diving

The European Diving Centre (☎ 614 9771), a scuba-diving company located on a boat and founded by two Welshmen, offers day trips for US$60, including two dives and lunch. The diving is well organised and visibility is excellent, though the seabed is somewhat littered, and overfishing and dynamite fishing have robbed the area of much of its marine life. If you don't have a diver's certificate, you can take a certification course for US$300. There are other diving companies as well.

Organised Tours

You can arrange to take a boat or minibus tour to some of the archaeological sites and beaches along the nearby coasts. Standard tours go west to Günlük (Küçük Kargı),

Pınarbaşı, Dalyan and Kaunos, and east to Letoön, Kalkan, Kaş, Patara and Xanthos. Bear in mind that it will often be cheaper just to take a minibus direct to the site.

Places to Stay

Fethiye has a good selection of budget and mid-range accommodation, but little in the way of luxury. Most of the better places are block-booked by European tour operators in summer.

Places to Stay – Budget

Fethiye has lots of small hotels and pensions so you're sure to find something. Pension owners with vacant rooms await buses at the otogar.

East of the Centre *Göreme Pansiyon* (☎/fax 614 6944, Dolgu Sahası, Stadyum Yanı 25) is run by the friendly, helpful Mrs Duvarcı who once lived in England and speaks English fluently. Spotless rooms cost US$10/16 a single/double, including breakfast. From the minibus station, cross Atatürk Caddesi to the northern side and walk 450m north to the northern side of the stadium.

FETHİYE

To Dalaman
(50km) &
Marmaris (170km)

■ 37

To Kaş (110km),
Muğla (150km)
& Antalya (220km)

● 36

Ölüdeniz
Cad

🚌 38

To Hisarönü (5.5km),
Ölüdeniz (8.5km) &
Kayaköy (14km)

35 ⛽
34 🚌

■ 33

OTHER
8   Güneş Laundry
9   Tourist Office;
    Harbour Master
10 Roman Theatre
    Ruins
12 Hamam
13 Ottoman Bar
18 Internet Cafe;
    Imagine Bookshop
19 Yes Bar
21 Atatürk Statue
22 Belediye
    (Town Hall)
23 Hükümet Konağı
    (Government House)
24 Lycian Rock Tombs
25 PTT
26 Police
29 Government
    Hospital
30 School
31 Fethiye Müzesi
32 Tomb of Amyntas
33 Lycian Rock Tombs
34 Minibus Station
35 Petrol Station
36 Stadium
38 Otogar

WESTERN MEDITERRANEAN

West of the Centre The main concentration of pensions near the centre is west of the tourist office, up the hill inland from the yacht marina in the districts called 1 Karagözler Mahallesi and 2 Karagözler Mahallesi: look for the 'pansiyon' signs. Dolmuşes run along Fevzi Çakmak Caddesi every few minutes.

Up the steep hill from Fevzi Çakmak Caddesi (follow signs for Hotel Pırlanta) is the popular *İdeal Pension* (*☎/fax 614 1981, Zafer Caddesi 1*), with a fine terrace overlooking the bay. All rooms have showers and cost US$6.60/14, including breakfast. Dinner costs US$4. Some of the rooms are a bit battered but the manager works hard to ensure everyone enjoys their stay. They offer a range of incentives to stay longer: a free boat tour after two nights with half board; boat tour and free hamam after four nights; and boat tour, hamam and free laundry after five nights. They'll pick you up from just outside the otogar if you call (they'd prefer to collect you from the otogar itself but the taxi rank there doesn't like it). They should have Internet access by the time you read this.

Ferah Pension (*☎ 614 2816, fax 612 7398, 2 Karagözler Mahallesi, Ordu Cad-*

desi 2), the main rival of İdeal Pension, is in the next neighbourhood west of 1 Karagözler Mahallesi, on the street up the hill running parallel to Fevzi Çakmak Caddesi. It's a smaller, more homely pension with hammocks and a colourful bar, but the management isn't always as relaxed as at İdeal. Rooms cost US$10/15, and there's a dormitory on the glass-enclosed terrace with views over the harbour; dorm beds cost US$6.60. Again there's a free pick-up service from the otogar. Internet access costs US$1.60 per hour.

The other pensions in this area aren't chasing the backpacker dollar so hard, so while they don't offer everything from cheap beer to laundry service, you can escape the conversations about how much everybody drank on the boat cruise. Close to the Ferah Pension is the small *Duygu Pension* (*☎ 614 3563, 2 Karagözler Mahallesi, Ordu Caddesi 54)*, the family don't speak much English but it's a quiet retreat. Simple, clean rooms cost US$8/10.

Back on Fevzi Çakmak Caddesi, you'll come to a row of pensions in 1 Karagözler Mahallesi. *Yıldırım Pansiyon* (*☎ 614 3913, Fevzi Çakmak Caddesi 37)* charges US$10 for a double with shower, slightly more for rooms with views at the front. *Lize Pansiyon* (*☎ 614 6411)*, next along in the row, is similar, with rooms for US$6.60/14. *İrem Pansiyon* (*☎ 614 3985, fax 614 5875)* at No 45 is the nicest of the lot, charging US$24 a double with shower, including breakfast served on the comfy terrace with a sea view.

On the hill to the left of the İdeal Pension is the *Pension Savaşçı* (*☎ 614 6681)* which charges only US$5/10 for fairly basic rooms, some with spectacular harbour views.

Places to Stay – Mid-Range
Fethiye's mid-range places are struggling to compete with hotels at Belcekız near Ölüdeniz. If you want to be near the beach you're better off staying there.

The area behind the PTT and between the hükümet konağı and the museum has several reasonably good three-star hotels including *Hotel Sesa Park* (*☎ 614 4656, fax 614 4326, Akdeniz Caddesi 17)*. It overlooks a small park and the sea, with comfortable rooms for US$45 a double, including breakfast. Nearby, the **Yeniçeri Hotel** (☎ 614 8583, fax 614 1324, Akdeniz Caddesi 15) has modern rooms for US$17/27.

The three-star **Hotel Victoria** (☎ 614 4501, fax 614 4596, Hastane Caddesi 7/A) has a swimming pool and rooms for US$22/33. The adjoining **Otel Mara** (☎ 614 9307, fax 614 8039, Kral Caddesi, Yalı Sokak 2) is the best of the lot, charging US$28/42/56 a single/double/triple.

The three-star **Hotel Pırlanta** (☎ 614 4959, fax 614 1686, 1 Karagözler Mevkii) is up the hill from the yacht marina. The rooms have baths and balconies, many with wonderful water views. We were quoted rates of US$12/23, including breakfast, but if business picks up these are likely to double.

Places to Eat

There is no shortage of places to eat in Fethiye but you should always ask prices, at least for the main course, and especially for fish, before you order. As usual the places around the harbour change every year and can be prone to overcharging. If you haven't ordered something don't let waiters put it on your table. If they do, ask *'Bedava mı?'* (Is it free?) It rarely is. Check your bill carefully for 'errors'.

Pizza 74 on Atatürk Caddesi has mezes for US$1, pides for US$1.60, delicious freshly baked bread and cheap beer (a large Efes for US$1).

On Çarşı Caddesi a block off Atatürk Caddesi, **Özlem Pide ve Kebap Salonu** will serve you köfte, salad, and soda for less than US$5. A bit further south on Çarşı Caddesi is *Pizza Pepino* if you prefer your pide Italian-style. Pepino serves tasty pizzas under a shady vine for reasonable prices; a good vegetarian pizza costs US$6.

Across Çarşı Caddesi from the Özlem, on Tütün Sokak, is **Sedir Lokantası & Kebap House**, a local favourite serving pizzas for around US$3 and meat plates for US$5.

Around the corner from the Özlem, the gimmick at **The Duck Pond** is just that: as you dine you can watch the ducks who live in the pond.

For serious dining, however, go to the heart of the bazaar and **Güneş Restaurant**, with indoor dining rooms as well as open-air cafe dining, in good weather. There's a good range of meat and fish dishes and cold starters here and prices aren't bad either (chicken kebap for US$5), but service can be slow. The adjoining **Meğri** is similar, and popular with locals.

For atmosphere at a price, try **Yacht Restaurant**, facing the yacht marina. The outdoor tables are pleasant, service polite and the food quite good. A fish dinner might cost about US$20, drinks included. Turkish music and dancing are sometimes laid on at no extra charge.

Entertainment

The **Ottoman Bar**, behind the bazaar up a short flight of steps, is lavishly decorated with traditional furniture and household items, most of which is for sale. A nargileh pipe which can last a group of eight for up to an hour costs US$3.20, a large Efes US$1.60.

The **Yes Bar** on Cumhuriyet Caddesi in the bazaar is a popular dance venue, with less conventional music than most Turkish discos. It's open until late.

Getting There & Away

Air The nearest airport is 50km to the west at Dalaman. Antalya airport, a four-hour bus ride to the east, has far more flights. The Turkish Airlines agent in Fethiye is Fetur (☎ 614 2443, fax 614 3845), Fevzi Çakmak Caddesi, Körfez Apt No 9/1, near the Otel Dedeoğlu and the yacht harbour.

Bus The mountains behind Fethiye force transport to go east or west and for many destinations you must change buses at Antalya or Muğla. However, buses head east along the coast at least every two hours in summer. Bus fares along this stretch of coast tend to be higher than usual as the passengers are mostly tourists. The highways in this region are being improved, with new routes, wider curves and more gentle grades. These improvements shorten highway distances and decrease travel times.

For intermediate distance destinations, go to the minibus garage off Atatürk Caddesi 1km east of the centre. Destinations served by minibuses include Çiftlik, Esenköy, Eşen, Göcek, Günlüklü Plajlar, Hacıosmanlar, Hisarönü, Kadıköy, Karadere, Karamersin, Kargı, Katrancı, Kaya, Kayadibi, Kemer, Kumluova, Otel Tuana, Ovacık, Ölüdeniz (stops at main otogar as well), Saklıkent, Tlos, Yanıklar and Yonca Camping.

The otogar, which is 2km east of the centre, handles services to main destinations like İstanbul, Ankara, Antalya and Alanya. There are hourly services in summer to Marmaris (US$5, three hours, 170km). Some approximate times and distances for other routes from the main otogar include:

destination	fare (US$)	duration (hr)	distance (km)
Antalya (coastal)	8	7½	295
(inland)	6	4	222
Dalaman	2.50	1	50
Demre	5	3	155
Denizli	5	4½	290
Kalkan	3.25	2	81
Kaş	3.50	2½	110
Letoön	2	1¼	60
Ölüdeniz	1.20	¼	7
Pamukkale	6	5	309
Patara	3.25	1½	75
Pınara	2	1	52
Tlos	2	1	40
Xanthos (Kınık)	2.25	1½	65

For Pamukkale, it's better to take a bus to Denizli and a dolmuş from there.

Boat In high summer a hydrofoil service operates between Rhodes (Greece) and Fethiye on Tuesday and Thursday. A one-way ticket will cost you US$50; a same-day return US$57 and an open return US$83. The travel agencies in town can book tickets but will need your passport 24 hours in advance. For information on entry/exit taxes see Getting There & Away in the Marmaris section earlier in this chapter.

Getting Around

Minibuses ply the one-way system along Atatürk Caddesi and up Çarşı Caddesi to the otogar all day. There's a fixed charge of US$0.30 however far you go. A taxi from the otogar to the pensions east of the centre will cost about US$5.

ÖLÜDENİZ
☎ 252

Ölüdeniz (Dead or Calm Sea), 8.5km southeast of Fethiye, is not devoid of life like its biblical namesake. Rather, it's a sheltered lagoon hidden from the open sea. The scene as you come down from the pine-forested hills is absolutely beautiful: in the distance open sea; in the foreground a peaceful lagoon bordered by forest; in the middle a long spit of perfect sandy beach.

Don't mistake Ölüdeniz, the lagoon, with Belcekız, the nearby beach resort. Both have a party atmosphere in high summer but Belcekız is mostly package-tour territory.

As most accommodation at the beach fills early in the day in high summer, you may want to plan your first night's stay in Fethiye. Then come out to Ölüdeniz and find something for the next few nights.

Orientation

As you approach Ölüdeniz, the road passes through the almost surreal package tour colonies of Ovacık and Hisarönü, packed with bars with names like 'The Rover's Return' and 'Hamish McTurks'. The main road descends steeply from Hisarönü another 3km to the beautiful swathe of beach. The road terminates at the free, public, Belcekız Plajı.

The beach is very much the centre of things. To your right, on the road from Fethiye, you pass a jandarma post, a PTT and the entrance to the Ölüdeniz Tabiat Parkı, with a pay beach (US$1) winding around the lagoon. This stretch has been laid out with paths, showers, toilets and makeshift cafes. The road continues behind the park to several camping grounds and the expensive Hotel Meri high above the lagoon.

To your left as you arrive the beach promenade is closed to traffic and backed with restaurants and a tightly packed cluster of hotels.

At the eastern end of the beach, the road climbs up and clings to the mountainside

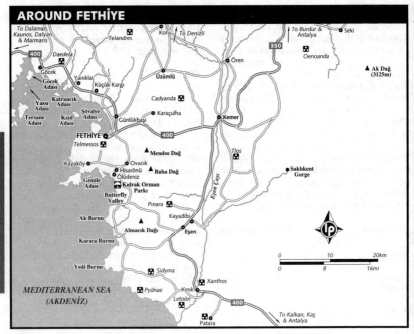

AROUND FETHİYE

To Dalaman, Kaunos, Dalyan & Marmaris
Telandres
Koru
To Denizli
To Burdur & Antalya
Seki
Daedela
400
Ören
350
Oenoanda
Ak Dağ (3125m)
Göcek
Göcek Adası
Yanıklar
Küçük Kargı
Üzümlü
Yassı Adası
Katrancık Adası
Cadyanda
Tersane Adası
Kızıl Adası
Şövalye Adası
Günlükbaşı
Karaçulha
Kemer
FETHİYE
Telmessos
400
Kayaköy
Ovacık
Mendos Dağ
Tlos
Hisarönü
Ölüdeniz
Baba Dağ
Sakhkent Gorge
Gemile Adası
Kıdrak Orman Parkı
Butterfly Valley
Pınara
Kayadibi
Ak Burnu
Almacık Dağı
Eşen
Karaca Burnu
Yedi Burnu
Sidyma
MEDITERRANEAN SEA (AKDENİZ)
Pydnae
Kınık
Xanthos
Letoôn
400
To Kalkan, Kaş & Antalya
Patara

0   10   20km
0   8   16mi

for 2km before descending to Kıdrak Orman Parkı (Kıdrak Forest Park).

Information
The Ölüdeniz Turizm Geliştirme Kooperatifi (☎ 617 0438, fax 617 0135) or 'Ölüdeniz Tourism Development Co-operative' maintains an information booth on the access road just inland from the beach. Far more useful than any government-run tourist office, they can quickly rustle up a cheap room in a resort hotel in Belcekız, Ovacık and Hisarönü. But don't pay them – pay at the hotel. They can also give advice on paragliding and boat trips.

Boat Trips
Throughout summer, boats set out to explore the coast, charging about US$10 for a day trip. A typical trip might take in Gemile Beach, the Blue Cave, Butterfly Valley (for more details, see the section later in this chapter) and St Nicholas Island, with time for swimming as well. Some readers have not thought this trip good value for money. If you want to snorkel, ask how much equipment will be available before you make a bookiing.

Sports
You can rent water-sports equipment on the main beach. Several agencies offer tandem paragliding flights for US$100, if you like the idea of plummeting off a cliff with a Turk strapped to your back. The descent from Baba Dağ can take as long as an hour. Parasailing comes much cheaper at a mere US$30.

Places to Stay – Budget
The camp sites are the only budget option, and fortunately there are plenty of them, most offering fixed tents and cabins with or without running water for those who don't want the trouble of carting the equipment around with them.

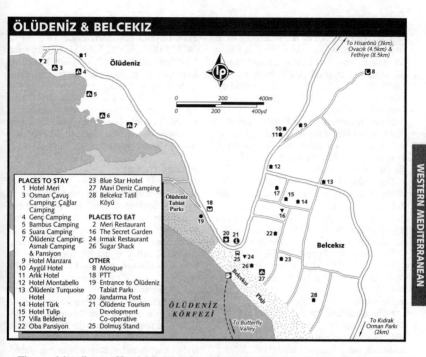

ÖLÜDENİZ & BELCEKIZ

To Hisarönü (3km),
Ovacık (4.5km) &
Fethiye (8.5km)

Ölüdeniz

0   200   400m
0   200   400yd

Ölüdeniz
Tabiat
Parkı

ÖLÜDENİZ
KÖRFEZİ

Belcekız
Plajı

Belcekız

To Butterfly
Valley

To Kıdrak
Orman Parkı
(2km)

PLACES TO STAY	23 Blue Star Hotel
1 Hotel Meri	27 Mavi Deniz Camping
3 Osman Çavuş	28 Belcekız Tatil
Camping; Çağlar	Köyü
Camping	
4 Genç Camping	PLACES TO EAT
5 Bambus Camping	2 Meri Restaurant
6 Suara Camping	16 The Secret Garden
7 Ölüdeniz Camping;	24 Irmak Restaurant
Asmalı Camping	26 Sugar Shack
& Pansiyon	
9 Hotel Manzara	OTHER
10 Aygül Hotel	8 Mosque
11 Arlık Hotel	18 PTT
12 Hotel Montabello	19 Entrance to Ölüdeniz
13 Ölüdeniz Turquoise	Tabiat Parkı
Hotel	20 Jandarma Post
14 Hotel Türk	21 Ölüdeniz Tourism
15 Hotel Tulip	Development
17 Villa Beldeniz	Co-operative
22 Oba Pansiyon	25 Dolmuş Stand

WESTERN MEDITERRANEAN

The road heading to Hotel Meri winds past six camping grounds. *Ölüdeniz Camping* (☎ 617 0048, fax 617 0181, ✉ oludeniz camping@superonline.com) is the most popular, managed by the unforgettable Merv from Adelaide. In summer there are dorm beds in an open-sided pavilion for US$1.60. Otherwise they supply tents for US$3, bungalows with common bathroom US$6, and bungalows with bath US$8. Dinners cost around US$3. Naturally, there's a bar.

Adjoining it, *Asmalı Camping & Pansiyon* (☎ 617 0137) has tents and a few bungalows for rent, but mostly sites for tents and caravans. *Genç Camping* is similar. About 100m further on, *Suara Camping* (☎ 617 0123) is about the best place to stay if you have your own tent. *Bambus Camping* (☎ 617 0655) has showerless bungalows for US$8. Facilities are basic and the beach is nice.

Osman Çavuş Camping (☎ 616 6002) and *Çağlar Camping* (☎ 617 0017), across from Hotel Meri, have waterless bungalows for US$17 as well as tent sites. The Osman also has a waterfront restaurant.

Mavi Deniz Camping (☎ 617 0045, fax 617 0054), just inland from Belcekız Plajı, has a big restaurant, book exchange, a bar and a range of lodgings, including waterless wooden cabins for US$15 a double.

Inland from Belcekız Plajı *Oba Pansiyon* (☎ 617 0470, fax 617 0522) has a grassy lawn and cabins with showers for US$6 per person. It costs less during low season and for waterless cabins. There's also a good bar and restaurant.

Finally, *Kıdrak Orman Parkı*, 2km to the south-east, has cheap tent sites in a pine grove, simple facilities and a good beach, but the huge Club Likya World resort just south of it encroaches on its serenity.

Places to Stay – Mid-Range

Most of Belcekız's hotels have their sights firmly fixed on package holiday-makers but if they're not full they'll gladly take individual travellers. All of the following have swimming pools, air-con rooms and bars (of course), and in season some host 'Turkish nights' – cultural pastiches in sparkly costumes. The Ölüdeniz Tourism Development Co-operative will happily arrange somewhere to stay.

Hotel Manzara (☎ 617 0207, fax 617 0049) at the top of the hill leading down to Belcekız is hard to miss; there's a model of Tyrannosaurus Rex by the front gate. Singles/doubles cost US$25/33.

The *Arlık Hotel* (☎ 617 0119, fax 617 0669) is close by, perched on the side of the hill. Doubles were US$15 when we were there; there's a great view from the pool. *Aygül Hotel* (☎ 617 0086, fax 614 9091) next door is similar, with doubles for US$17.

The *Ölüdeniz Turquoise Hotel* (☎ 617 0178, fax 617 0307) has a larger swimming pool than most and rooms in shades of, well, turquoise. Rooms cost US$27, including breakfast.

Villa Beldeniz (☎ 617 0103, fax 617 0109) is older than most Ölüdeniz hotels and therefore not quite up to the group-tour standards, so it charges less (US$25 for a double with bath) and may have rooms when you want them. There's a small swimming pool. *Hotel Montabello* (☎ 617 0022, fax 617 0109) is under the same management and costs the same.

The two-star *Blue Star Hotel* (☎ 617 0069, fax 617 0128) is new, with a good swimming pool, a kids pool and a price of US$40 a double, including breakfast. *Hotel Tulip* (☎ 617 0074, fax 617 0221) is similar, as is *Hotel Türk* (☎ 617 0444).

Places to Stay – Top End

At the end of the road winding around the lagoon stands the snooty *Hotel Meri* (☎ 617 0001, fax 617 0010) with 75 rooms tumbling down the hillside amid picturesque gardens. The views from many of the rooms, especially those at the top, are magnificent. The oldest hotel at Ölüdeniz, single/double rooms cost US$63/105. The hotel has its own beach and a seaside eatery called *Meri Restaurant*.

At the far end of Belcekız Plajı there's an even flashier place, *Belcekız Tatil Köyü* (☎ 617 0077, fax 617 0372), formerly the Club Belcekız Beach. Rooms here have tiled floors, modern decor and fabrics, pleasant bathrooms and small terraces. There's a huge pool, a Turkish bath and several dining areas. The rooms don't come cheap – US$80 a double (about the same for single occupancy) – but you might get a better deal through a tour operator.

Places to Eat

As staff and ownership change frequently at beachside restaurants, the best approach is to do the beachfront stroll, looking at menus and prices, seeing which restaurants are full or empty and even asking the opinion of other diners (particularly those who, having paid their bill, are just leaving). For lower prices, as always, go inland away from the beach.

The *Sugar Shack* and *Irmak* restaurants, facing Belcekız beach, seem to be the most popular places. *The Secret Garden*, inland, is a pleasant restaurant hidden away in dense foliage. Meals may not be particularly cheap here but they will be enjoyable.

Getting There & Away

In summer minibuses leave Fethiye for Ölüdeniz roughly every 15 minutes (US$1.20, 20 minutes, 8.5km), passing through Hisarönü.

BUTTERFLY VALLEY

Although you can get to Butterfly Valley, home of the unique Jersey Tiger butterfly, on a tour, if you want to spend the night there, boats leave Ölüdeniz daily at 11 am and 2 and 6 pm, charging US$5 return. Once there, you can spend the night in a *treehouse*, where beds cost US$3 per person, and eat at the *beach cafe*. Alternatively a relatively dangerous path winds up a cliff to *George's Pension*, where beds cost US$1.60 and better food is available. It is possible to get to the valley by a dolmuş from Fethiye's minibus station. A few dolmuşes run every day to the mountain village of Faralya and pass the top of the gorge, but it's a long hard walk down.

KAYAKÖY (KARMYLASSOS)
☎ 252

Called Levissi for much of its history, this town of 2000 stone houses, just over 5km west of Hisarönü, was deserted by its mostly Ottoman-Greek inhabitants after WWI and the Turkish War of Independence. The League of Nations supervised an exchange of populations between Turkey and Greece, with most Greek Muslims coming from Greece to Turkey and most Ottoman Christians moving to Greece. The people of Levissi, most of whom were Orthodox Christians, moved to the outskirts of Athens and founded Nea Levissi there.

As there were far more Ottoman Greeks than Greek Muslims, many of the towns vacated by the Ottoman Greeks were left unoccupied after the exchange of populations. Kayaköy, as it is called now, has only a handful of Turkish inhabitants.

With the tourism boom of the 1980s, a development company wanted to restore Kayaköy's stone houses and turn the town into a holiday village. Scenting money, the local inhabitants were delighted, but Turkish artists and architects were alarmed, and saw to it that the Ministry of Culture declared Kayaköy, or Kaya as it's called locally, a historic monument, safe from unregulated development.

There are plans for careful restoration of the town, and its use as a venue for cultural presentations.

Two churches are still prominent: the Kataponagia in the lower part of the town and the Taxiarkis further up the slope. Both retain some of their painted decoration and black and white pebble mosaic floors.

In summer there are hourly minibuses from Fethiye to Kaya (US$1, 30 minutes). Alternatively it's about a one-hour walk downhill through pine forest from Hisarönü. There's also a marked trail to Ölüdeniz which should take two to 2½ hours (8km) – although some readers have taken much longer!

If you want to stay at Kaya (a pleasant and certainly quieter alternative to staying in Hisarönü or Belcekız) *Çavuşoğlu Motel* (☎ 616 6749), with a big swimming pool

about 100m west of the Kayaköy entrance, has simple rooms for US$15 a double with bath and breakfast. The *Selçuk Pension* (☎ 616 6757) is a bit further along, with doubles for US$12.

TLOS
☎ 252

Tlos was one of the oldest and most important cities in ancient Lycia. Its prominence is matched by its promontory, as the city has a dramatic setting high on a rocky outcrop. As you climb the winding road to Tlos, look for the fortress-topped **acropolis** on the right. What you see is Ottoman-era work, but the Lycians had a fort in the same place. Beneath it, reached by narrow paths, are the familiar **rock-cut tombs**, including that of Bellerophon, a pseudo-temple facade carved into the rock face which has a fine bas-relief of the hero riding Pegasus, the winged horse. You can reach the tomb by walking along a stream bed, then turning left and climbing a crude ladder.

The **theatre** is 100m further up the road from the ticket kiosk, and is in excellent condition, with most of its marble seating intact, though the stage wall is gone. There's a fine view of the **acropolis** from here. Off to the right of the theatre (as you sit in the centre rows) is an ancient **Lycian sarcophagus** in a farmer's field. The **necropolis** on the path up to the fortress has many stone sarcophagi.

The site is open from 8 am to 5 pm daily for US$1.30. One of the men at the ticket kiosk will offer to be your guide (for a tip), which is a good idea if you want to see all the rock-cut tombs.

Places to Stay & Eat

A meal of trout in garlic sauce, salad, bread and a cold drink will cost you US$10 at *Cafe Tlawa Restaurant* opposite the site. Simple rooms are available here in an emergency, or you could try *Mountain Lodge* or *Çağrı Pension* back down the road to the highway.

With your own transport you could press on for another 2km to the lovely *Yaka Park Restaurant* (☎ 638 2011), where tables cascade down the hillside, shaded with plane trees and cooled with running water. The bar counter here has a channel cut into it along which trout swim so visitors can tickle them. How much the trout enjoy this experience is open to question of course.

Getting There & Away

The easiest way to get to Tlos is to take a dolmuş from Fethiye to Saklıkent. This passes within 4km of the site. This 4km would be a tough walk because the road climbs steadily uphill but you might be able to get a lift or negotiate with the driver to drop you off.

If you are driving, follow the signs to Saklıkent from Kayadibi and watch for the yellow ancient monument sign on the left.

SAKLIKENT GORGE

Another 12km after the turn-off to Tlos you will come to the spectacular Saklıkent Gorge cut into the Akdağlar mountains. The gorge is 18km long and so steep and narrow that the sun doesn't penetrate, so the water is icy-cold, even in summer.

You approach the gorge along a wooden boardwalk above the river which opens out into a series of wooden platforms suspended above the water where you can buy and eat trout. From there you wade across the river, hanging onto a rope and then continue into the gorge proper, sometimes walking in mud, sometimes in the water. Plastic shoes can be hired for US$0.50, but you're better off bringing your own shoes with good grip.

The gorge is open daily from 8 am to 5 pm for US$2. Get there in summer by taking a dolmuş from Fethiye. It takes about 45 minutes, past lovely fields of cotton, and costs US$2.

If there's no direct minibus, take one to Kayadibi and change. Alternatively you can sign up for an excursion from Fethiye, Kaş or Kalkan.

Back on the highway heading south towards Kaş, the road takes you up into fragrant evergreen forests and down into fertile valleys. You'll see herds of sheep and goats (and a few cattle) along the road near the villages. The road is curvy and the journey somewhat slow.

PINARA

Some 46km south-east of Fethiye, near the village of Eşen, is a turn-off (to the right) for Pınara, which lies another 6km up in the mountains. Infrequent minibuses from Fethiye (US$1.75, one hour) drop you at the start of the Pınara road and you can walk to the site, or bargain with the driver to take you all the way.

The road winds through tobacco and cornfields and across irrigation channels for more than 3km to the village of Minare, then takes a sharp left turn to climb the slope. The last 2km or so are extremely steep. If you decide to walk make sure you stock up on water first. There's a cafe at the foot of the slope and nothing after that.

At the top of the slope is an open parking area and near it a cool, shady spring with refreshing water. The guardian will probably appear and offer to show you around the ruins and it would pay to take up the offer as the path around the site (which is always open) is not easy to follow. You should probably tip the guardian if you have a tour.

Pınara was among the most important cities in ancient Lycia but, although the site is vast, the actual ruins are not Turkey's most impressive. Instead it's the sheer splendour of the isolated setting which makes the journey so worthwhile, the new toilet block providing the one jarring note.

The sheer column of rock behind the site, and the rock walls to its left, are honeycombed with **rock-cut tombs**. To reach any of them would take several hours. Other **tombs** are within the ruined city itself. The one called the Royal (or King's) Tomb has particularly fine reliefs, including several showing walled cities. Pınara's **theatre** is in good condition, but its **odeum** and **temples** of Apollo, Aphrodite and Athena (with heart-shaped columns) are badly ruined.

The village at Eşen, 3km south-east of the Pınara turn-off, has a few basic *restaurants*.

SIDYMA

About 4km from Eşen, a rough dirt road to the left goes 12km to Sidyma. The ruins are not spectacular. If you've seen all the other Lycian cities and are simply aching for more, then take the time to visit Sidyma. Otherwise, press onward.

LETOÖN

About 17km south of the Pınara turn-off is the road to Letoön. The turn-off is on the right-hand (south-west) side near the village of Kumluova. (Dolmuşes run from Fethiye via Eşen to Kumluova. Get out at the Letoön turn-off.) Turn right off the highway, go 3.2km to a T-junction, turn left, then right after 100m (this turn-off is easy to miss) and proceed 1km to the site through fertile fields and orchards and past greenhouses full of tomato plants. If you miss the second turn you'll end up in the main square of the village. There are no services as this is still a farming village largely unaffected by tourism.

When you get to the ruins (open from 8.30 am to 5 pm daily) a person selling soft drinks and admission tickets (US$1.30) will greet you.

Letoön takes its name and importance from a large shrine to Leto, who according to legend was loved by Zeus. Unimpressed, Zeus' wife Hera commanded that Leto spend an eternity wandering from country to country. According to local folklore she spent much of this enforced holiday time in Lycia, becoming the Lycian national deity. The federation of Lycian cities then built this very impressive religious sanctuary to worship her.

The site consists of three **temples** side by side: Apollo (on the left), Artemis (in the middle) and Leto (on the right). The Temple of Apollo has a nice mosaic showing a lyre and a bow and arrow. The **nymphaeum** is permanently flooded (and inhabited by frogs), which is appropriate as worship of Leto was somehow associated with water. Nearby is a large Hellenistic **theatre** in excellent condition.

XANTHOS

At Kınık, 63km from Fethiye, the road crosses a river. Up to the left on a rock outcrop is the ruined city of Xanthos, once the capital and grandest city of Lycia, with a fine **Roman theatre** and Lycian pillar **tombs**

with Lycian inscriptions. Dolmuşes run here from Fethiye and Kaş and some long-distance buses will stop if you ask.

It's a short walk up the hill to the site, which is open from 8.30 am to 5.30 pm; admission is US$1.30. For all its grandeur, Xanthos had a chequered history of wars and destruction. Several times, when besieged by clearly superior enemy forces, the city was destroyed by its own inhabitants. You'll see the **theatre**, with the **agora** opposite. Despite Xanthos's importance, the **acropolis** is now badly ruined. As many of the finest sculptures and inscriptions were carted off to the British Museum in 1842, many of the inscriptions and decorations you see today are copies of the originals. However, French excavations in the 1950s have made Xanthos well worth seeing.

PATARA
☎ 242

Patara is a slightly scruffy, rambling village that attracts an interesting mix of Turkish and foreign eccentrics. Its ruins come with a bonus in the form of a wonderful white sand beach some 50m wide and 20km long. While there are plenty of pensions and a few mid-range hotels, traditional village life still continues. Transport here can be irregular, so hopefully this means it will stay the way it is.

Patara was the birthplace of St Nicholas, the 4th-century Byzantine bishop who later passed into legend as Santa Claus. Before that, Patara was famous for its temple and oracle of Apollo, of which little remains.

Orientation

Look for the Patara turn-off just east of the village of Ovaköy; from here it's 3.5km to Gelemiş, commonly called Patara, and another 1.5km to the Patara ruins. The beach is another 1km past the ruins and some dolmuşes will take you there.

As you come into Gelemiş, on your left is a hillside holding various hotels and pensions. A turn to the right at Golden Pension takes you to the village centre, across the valley and up the other side to more pensions and the three-star Hotel Beyhan Patara.

The Ruins

Admission to the ruins and beach costs US$3, valid for a week, possibly longer if you remember to wave to the man at the ticket gate every day. Patara's ruins include a triple-arched **triumphal gate** at the entrance to the site with a **necropolis** with several **Lycian tombs** nearby. Next are the **baths** and much later, a **basilica**.

The good-sized **theatre** is striking because it is half-covered by wind-driven sand, which seems intent on making a dune out of it. Climb to the top for a good view of the whole site.

There are also several other **baths**, two **temples** and a **Corinthian temple** by the lake, although the swampy ground may make them difficult to approach. Across the lake is a **granary**. What is now a swamp was once the city's harbour. When it silted up in the Middle Ages, the city declined.

Patara Beach

The beach is simply splendid. You can get there by following the road past the ruins, or by turning right at Golden Pension and following the track which heads for the sand dunes on the other (western) side of the archaeological zone. It's about a 30-minute walk. Sometimes you can hitch a ride with tractors passing along the main road.

Be sure to bring footwear for crossing the 50m of scorching sand to the water's edge, and also something for shelter as there are few places to escape the sun. If you don't have your own shelter, rent an umbrella on the beach for US$2.

Behind the beach Patara Restaurant provides shade and sustenance, and there's a wooden shack on the sand selling kebaps. The beach closes at dusk as it is a nesting ground for sea turtles. Note that camping is prohibited.

Çayağzı Beach

On the western side of the stream by the access road from the highway to Gelemiş (Patara), a sign points the way to Çayağzı Beach 5km away, the alternative to Patara, where there are basic beach services and camping facilities.

Places to Stay – Budget

Patara has accommodation in all price ranges. The places at higher elevation have fewer mosquitoes, which are a pest here in summer. Bilal's Shop in the village advertises 'We have everything you need to be bite-free'.

Medusa Camping (☎ *843 5193)* has tent sites with basic facilities for US$1.60 per person. Fortunately there's a large and attractively decked out bar with cushions – large Efes cost US$1.60.

Flower Pension (☎ *843 5164)*, on the road into town from Gelemiş, is a cheerful little place owned by the ebullient Mustafa Kirca. Simple single/double rooms cost US$6.60/14, and there's a nice garden.

The *St Nicholas Pension* (☎ *843 5024)* in the centre of town has 15 rooms, all with fan and balcony, for US$7/14. The boys who run it are friendly and arrange canoe trips for US$17 for a full day.

Hotel Sisyphos (☎ *843 5043)* close by has pleasantly decorated rooms and a small swimming pool, with doubles for US$20.

Golden Pension & Restaurant (☎ *843 5162, fax 843 5008)*, in the village centre, is OK but seems to be resting on its laurels. Rooms, some with fan, cost US$8/14.

On the hill to the left as you face the beach are a string of good places to stay. *Likya 1* and *Likya 2* (☎ *843 5068)* both have rooms for US$8/17 (less for longer stays), and lovely gardens.

Turn right into the village and continue up the hill to *Eucalyptus Pension* (☎ *843 5076)*; the building won't be winning any prizes for aesthetic charm but the family who run it are friendly, and there's a shady terrace. The clean rooms cost US$7/12.

Places to Stay – Mid-Range

On the left-hand side of the valley on the road to Hotel Beyhan Patara is the *Apollon Otel* (☎ *843 5048, fax 843 5079)*, with a large swimming pool and a cosy bar. Rooms cost US$14/25, more with air-con.

On the hill above the Eucalyptus Pension is the *Hotel Lighthouse* (☎ *843 5107, fax 843 5175)*, good value with a bar, swimming pool and rooms with fan for US$12/20.

Patara's biggest hotel is the three-star *Hotel Beyhan Patara* (☎ *843 5098, fax 843 5097)*, high up on the hill to the west of town. The building is a standard-issue ugly cuboid and it's looking a bit run-down. However it's set in pretty gardens and facilities include a tennis court and swimming pool. Doubles cost US$50, if it's not full with tour groups.

Places to Eat

Florya Restaurant, near the Golden Pension, has good food and reasonable prices – about US$8 for a full meal. About 50m north of the Golden Pension on the road into the village, *Tlos Terrace Bolu'lu Osman'ın Yeri* has a chef-owner from Bolu, where many of Turkey's great chefs come from. New places come and go every year.

Patara also has a fun collection of bars. The *Sarpedon Bar* near the Florya plays jazz and has an open fireplace. Large Efes cost US$1.60. If you're hungry they can order gözleme from the little cafes across the road.

The bar at *Medusa Camping* has a good collection of music, as does the nearby *Voodoo Bar*.

Getting There & Away

If you come to Patara by bus, be warned that it may drop you on the highway 3.5km from the village.

The dolmuş station may post schedules but that doesn't mean they're adhered to. Theoretically minibuses run four times a day to Fethiye in summer (at least three per day at other times) for US$3.20. Around eight per day run to Kalkan (US$1.60, 25 minutes, 15km) and maybe five per day to Kaş (US$2.50, one hour, 42km).

KALKAN
☎ 242

Kalkan was once a fishing village, called Kalamaki, occupied by Ottoman Greeks but it's now completely devoted to tourism. Discovered by travellers in the 1980s in search of the simple, cheap, quiet life, this perfect Mediterranean village soon boasted a yacht marina, then some modern hotels and finally a vast holiday village complex (Hotel Patara Prince and Club Patara) covering an entire hillside to the south. It attracts a rather upmarket crowd, though it's still possible to stay here on a budget.

Orientation & Information

Kalkan is built on a hillside sloping down to the bay and you'll find yourself trekking up and down it all day. Coming in from the highway the road zigzags down to a central parking lot with a taxi rank, bus offices, the PTT and banks. It then enters the main commercial area and descends the hill as Hasan Altan Caddesi (also called 6 Sokak).

The town's health clinic is out to the west past the Diva and Dionysia Hotels. More hotels and pensions can be found around the east of the bay.

Kalkan doesn't have a tourist office but it has a Web site (www.kalkan.org.tr).

The local Internet cafe, the Cımbırık Pub, is really just a bar with two computer terminals perched on the terrace. It's up the hill from the bus and dolmuş stops, next to the Tespa Shopping Centre. Internet access costs US$1.30 per hour.

Places to Stay – Budget

Although cheap pensions are vanishing in favour of hotels suitable for the package-holiday market, there are still quite a few relatively cheap places to stay right in the centre of Kalkan and in prime positions on the waterfront.

Up a path next to the PTT is the *Öz Pansiyon* (☎ *844 3444, fax 844 3306)*, an attractive modern building with airy rooms. Singles/doubles cost US$13/17, and in season they open another building next door with cheaper rooms for US$10/13.

The nearby *Çelik Pansiyon* (☎ *844 2126, Yalıboyu 9)* is a standard simple pension charging US$8/12 a room; it's looking a bit worn but it's passable. Up the hill across the street is the slightly rustic *Gül Pansiyon* (☎ *844 3099)*, with clean simple rooms for US$10/14, including breakfast.

Continue along Süleyman Yılmaz Sokak to the end for the delightful *Holiday Pension* (☎ *844 3154)*, run by Ahmet Bozburt and his family. They have eight rooms in

KALKAN

PLACES TO STAY
3 Öz Pansiyon
6 Türk Evi
7 Gül Pansiyon
8 Çelik Pansiyon
12 Kervan Han Pansiyon
13 Daphne Pansiyon
14 Zinbad Hotel
15 Hotel Pirat
18 Holiday Pension
19 Kalamaki Pension
21 Balıkçı Han
24 Çetin Pansiyon
25 Patara Pansiyon
26 Çetinkaya Pension

PLACES TO EAT
2 Ali Baba Lokantası;
   Doyum
9 Merkez Café
10 Belgin's Kitchen
11 Kervan Han Pideci
17 Alternatif Restaurant
20 Steps Terrace
   Cafe-Bar
22 Patara Restaurant
28 Korsan Restaurant
29 Yakamoz Restaurant

OTHER
1 Bus and Dolmuş
   Stops
4 PTT
5 Moonlight Bar
16 Mosque
23 Atatürk Bust
27 Mosque
30 Lighthouse;
   Cafe Fener

To Belediye, TC
Ziraat Bankası ATM,
Cımbırık Internet Cafe
& Bar, Health Clinic, Diva,
Diana, Dionysia Apartments
& Highway

MEDITERRANEAN SEA
(AKDENİZ)

0   50   100m
0   50   100yd
Approximate Scale

adjoining houses, one a 150-year-old Greek house with handsome wooden balconies. It's a peaceful location with great views, and cheap at US$8/12 for rooms.

In the centre of town *Kervan Han Pansiyon* (☎ 844 3033) is a pleasant old family home with handsome white rooms for US$12/17, including breakfast.

Çetin Pansiyon (☎ 844 3094), in the southern part of town, is out of the central bustle, quieter, cheaper and done in traditional style. Rooms cost US$17 a double.

Kalamaki Pension (☎ 844 3649, fax 844 3654), run by Christine and Durmuş Uşaklı,

is an excellent choice, charging US$22 for a double with bath and breakfast. They have a rooftop restaurant as well.

Places to Stay – Mid-Range

Zinbad Hotel (☎ 844 3404, fax 844 3943, Yalıboyu Mahallesi 18) is newish, family run, pleasant and well priced at US$38 for a double room, including breakfast; the higher price buys you a sea view. Good dinners are served in the rooftop restaurant.

At the upper end of town *Türk Evi* (☎ 844 3129, 844 3492) has nine charmingly decorated rooms and a huge centre living area.

Single rooms cost US$18, doubles between US$25 and US$35, including breakfast.

Balıkçı Han (☎ 844 3075, fax 844 3640) is another house designed to look like an older building, with stone fireplaces, red-tiled floors, and panels of coloured faience in the walls. Some rooms have brass beds. Rooms with shower cost US$34 a double, including breakfast.

On the road winding down past the mosque to the harbour is **Daphne Pansiyon** (☎ 844 3547, Kocakaya Caddesi), nicely decorated with kilims and carpets, and with good reading lights in the bedrooms. You pay US$12/25 a single/double, including breakfast on a pleasant roof terrace.

Almost hidden beneath its veil of bougainvillea is **Patara Pansiyon** (☎ 844 3076), a lovely old stone house with views from the roof terrace. Rooms cost US$13/25 with shower and breakfast.

Close by is **Çetinkaya Pension** (☎ 844 3307) with pleasant rooms for US$22/34, including breakfast.

Out towards the west, Aldi Hotels runs three nice small modern hotels on Cumhuriyet Caddesi: **Diva, Dionysia** and **Diana Apartments** (☎ 844 3175, fax 844 3139). They're all fine, and prices are reasonable, averaging US$30 to US$40 a double, breakfast included. All are usually filled with groups, but they'll take your reservation within 10 days or a week of the date you intend to stay if they have a vacancy.

The three-star **Hotel Pirat** (☎ 844 3178, fax 844 3183), Kalkan Marina, has an older 1980s building and a newer complex built to look like a row of village houses. Altogether there are 136 comfortable, modern air-con rooms for US$38/50, breakfast included.

Places to Eat

Kalkan's eateries can be pricey because of their yachting clientele but choose carefully and you can still have a pleasant and not overly expensive meal.

One way to avoid the high prices is to eat where the locals do, which would be at **Ali Baba Lokantası** and **Doyum** just north-west of the PTT. This is not the tourist district, so a full meal can be enjoyed for US$4 or US$5.

Steps Terrace Cafe-Bar, opposite the bust of Atatürk at the foot of Hasan Altan Caddesi, has a varied cafe menu and takeaway sandwiches. Find **Kervan Han Pideci** for a decent pide for US$1.50 to US$3.50.

The rooftop restaurant at **Zinbad Hotel** has good views and reasonable prices.

The **Alternatif Restaurant** near the mosque has a slightly more interesting menu than most, with appetisers including samosas and felafel for US$3, and mains such as sea bass for around US$10.

For food in a 'Turkish' setting with tables at floor level and lots of kilims, head for **Belgin's Kitchen** where you can sample traditional dishes like mantı (Turkish ravioli) and çiğ börek (raw ground lamb in a pastry roll). Expect to spend US$10 to US$16 for a meal.

Down on the waterfront by the marina are numerous restaurants which are fun to patronise in the evening, but tend to be more expensive. **Cafe Fener** is beneath the lighthouse and along the quay are **Korsan, Yakamoz** and **Patara**. In season, you may have to grab a seat where you can find one. Expect to spend from US$15 to US$22 per person for a meal with wine or beer.

The **Moonlight Bar** near the PTT is about as exciting as local nightlife gets, with a small dance floor and a good choice of music.

Getting There & Away

In summer, minibuses connect Kalkan with Fethiye (US$3.20, two hours, 81km) and Kaş (US$1.30, 35 minutes, 29km) throughout the day. There are also irregular minibuses to Patara (US$1.60, 20 minutes, 15km) – around eight per day.

AROUND KALKAN

Kaputaş, about 7km east of Kalkan and just over 20km west of Kaş is a striking mountain gorge crossed by a small highway bridge. The plaques each side of the bridge commemorate four road workers who were killed during the construction of this part of the highway. Below the bridge is a perfect little sandy cove and beach, accessible by a long flight of stairs. A dolmuş from Kalkan will take you there in summer for US$0.50.

A short distance east of Kaputaş, **Mavi Mağara** (Blue Cave) lurks beneath the highway, marked by a sign. Look out for boats bringing tourists for a glimpse of this Turkish Capri.

KAŞ
☎ 242 • pop 5000

Fishing boats and a few yachts in the harbour, a town square with teahouses and restaurants in which one can hear half a dozen languages spoken, inexpensive pensions and hotels, classical ruins scattered about: this is Kaş, the quintessential Turkish seaside town.

Kaş is not popular because of its beaches – they are small, pebbly and some are a good way out of town – but because it is pleasant in itself and makes an ideal base for boat excursions to several fascinating spots along the coast.

Life centres on the town square by the harbour, with its teahouses, restaurants, mosque and shops.

A well-preserved ancient theatre is about all that's left of ancient Antiphellus, which was the Lycian town here. Also, on the sheer rock mountain wall above the town are a number of Lycian rock tombs, which are illuminated at night.

Orientation
The otogar is a few hundred metres uphill from the town centre. Descend the hill along Atatürk Bulvarı to get into the town centre. Cheap pensions are mostly to your right (west), the more expensive hotels to the left (east). At the Merkez Süleyman Çavuş Camii, turn left to reach the main square, Cumhuriyet Meydanı, and the tourist office. İbrahim Serin Caddesi strikes north to the PTT and a bank with an ATM dispensing foreign currency, while Uzun Çarşı Caddesi cuts north-east past lovely shops in restored wooden houses to a Lycian sarcophagus. Beyond the main square over the hill are more hotels and a small pebble beach.

Turning right at the mosque onto Necip Bey Caddesi and Hastane Caddesi takes you to the hospital, theatre and camping ground.

Information
The tourist office (☎/fax 836 1238) is on the main square. The unusually helpful staff speak English and have numerous handouts on local lodgings and sights.

The Net House and MagicCom Internet cafes on Çukurbağlı Caddesi both charge US$1.60 per hour, with good connections. The Galileo Bookshop in the warren of lanes off İbrahim Serin Caddesi has second-hand books in English, French and German for around US$4.

Antiphellus Ruins
Walk up the hill on the street to the left of the tourist office to reach the **Monument Tomb**, a Lycian sarcophagus mounted on a high base. It is said that Kaş was once littered with such sarcophagi but that over the years most were broken apart to provide building materials.

The **theatre**, 500m west of the main square, is in very good condition and was restored some time ago. Over the hill behind the theatre is the **Doric Tomb**, cut into the hillside rock in the 3rd century BC. You can also walk to the rock tombs in the cliffs above the town, but as the walk is strenuous go at a cool time of day.

Excursions
Several standard excursions will take you along the coast for cruising and swimming. No matter which you take, check to see whether lunch is included in the price. If you're watching your budget you may prefer to pack a picnic or to pick your own place to eat when you reach the lunch stop at around noon.

One popular excursion is to Kekova and Üçağız, about two hours away by boat, where there are several interesting ruins (see Üçağız and Kaleköy, following). The cost is from US$10 to US$14 per person.

You can also visit Kastellorizo (Meis Adası in Turkish), the Greek island just off the coast and visible from Kaş, either returning to Kaş in the evening, or perhaps using it as a base to enter Greece and go on to other islands. If you want to do this, the travel agency making the arrangements will

WESTERN MEDITERRANEAN

KAŞ

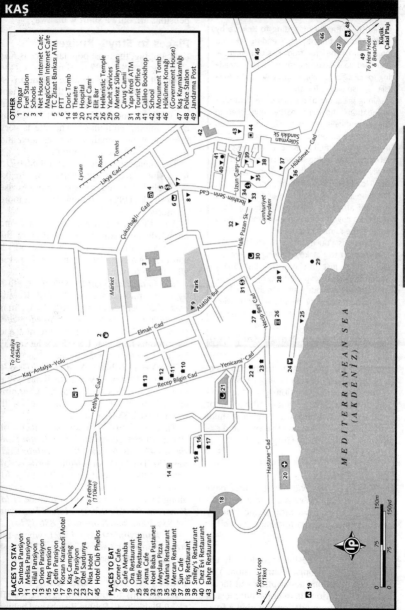

PLACES TO STAY
10 Santosa Pansiyon
11 Melisa Pansiyon
12 Hilal Pansiyon
13 Orion Pansiyon
15 Ateş Pension
16 Çetin Pansiyon
17 Korsan Karakedi Motel
19 Kaş Camping
22 Ay Pansiyon
23 Otel Sardunya
27 Nisa Hotel
45 Hotel Club Phellos

PLACES TO EAT
7 Corner Cafe
8 Cafe Merhaba
9 Ora Restaurant
25 Little Restaurants
28 Asma Cafe
32 Noel Baba Pastanesi
33 Meydan Pizza
35 Marina Restaurant
36 Mercan Restaurant
37 Sun Cafe
38 Eriş Restaurant
39 Smiley's Restaurant
40 Chez Evi Restaurant
43 Bahçe Restaurant

OTHER
1 Otogar
2 Fuel Station
3 Schools
4 Net House Internet Cafe;
  MagicCom Internet Cafe
5 TC Ziraat Bankası ATM
6 PTT
14 Doric Tomb
18 Theatre
20 Hospital
21 Yeni Cami
24 Elit Bar
26 Hellenistic Temple
29 Yacht Services
30 Merkez Süleyman
31 Çavuş Camii
34 Yapı Kredi ATM
34 Tourist Office
41 Galileo Bookshop
42 School
44 Monument Tomb
46 Hükümet Konağı
  (Government House)
47 Kaş Kaymakamlığı
48 Police Station
49 Jandarma Post

MEDITERRANEAN SEA
(AKDENİZ)

Kekova Boat Trips

Given the difficulty of getting to Kekova by public transport most people end up taking a boat tour of the area from Kaş or Kalkan. A standard boat excursion might start by heading for Üçağız, passing Kekova Adası (Kekova Island, also called Tersane).

Along the shore of the island are Byzantine foundations and ruins, partly submerged in the sea and called the Batık Şehir, the Sunken City. Some tour operators have become slack in recent years and cruise over the most interesting parts of the sunken city without actually telling anyone they're doing so. Signs say 'No Skin-Diving Allowed', indicating that this is an archaeological zone and the authorities are afraid of antiquity theft. The boat stops in a cove so you can swim and perhaps explore the ruins on land.

Afterwards you head for lunch in Üçağız and then on to Kaleköy, passing sunken Lycian tombs just offshore. There's usually about an hour to explore Kaleköy and climb up to the eponymous castle. On the way back to Kaş there should be time for another swim. Tours generally leave at 10 am and charge around US$8 or US$10 per person.

need your passport 24 hours in advance. The fare to Kastellorizo is about US$26.

Other standard excursions go to the Mavi Mağara (Blue Cave), Patara and Kalkan or to Liman Ağzı, Longos and several small nearby islands. There are also overland excursions to Saklıkent Gorge and villages further inland.

Special Events

The Kaş Lycia Festival runs for three days at the end of June every year, featuring folk-dancing troupes from around the country and sometimes international acts as well.

Places to Stay

As you step off the bus people will approach you to patronise their pension. You could ask questions about price and facilities and then follow them home but most of the town's accommodation is within a five-

or 10-minute walk and some of the best pensions are only a short walk away.

Places to Stay – Budget

For camping, the most popular place is *Kaş Camping* (☎ 836 1050), 1km west of the centre of town along Hastane Caddesi past the theatre. Two people in their own tent pay US$5 but you can rent a waterless cabin for US$12 a double if you don't have your own camping equipment. The site is very pleasant, with a small swimming area and bar and a good pizza restaurant.

The cheapest pensions charge US$10/16 for a single/double with bathroom (breakfast included) in high season but prices rise to more like US$12/20 in places with more comforts.

Ateş Pension, run by the friendly and knowledgeable Ahmet, is uphill from the Yeni Cami. Simple rooms cost US$6.60/12, and there's a comfy rooftop lounging area with DVD player.

The *Çetin Pansiyon* (☎ 836 5673) close by is an option if the Ateş is full. Rooms cost US$7 per person. Opposite the Çetin is the slightly pricier *Korsan Karakedi Motel* (☎ 836 1887) with a lovely roof terrace and bar. Rooms here cost US$15/23 but it may be full with tour groups in peak season.

The YHA-affiliated *Nisa Hostel* (☎ 836 3581) on Necip Bey Caddesi has great views from its rooftop terrace. The rooms are spartan and the bathrooms are small; rooms cost US$8/16.

There's a string of similar places on Recep Bilgin Caddesi, including *Orion Pansiyon* (☎/fax 836 1286, Recep Bilgin Caddesi 18). The top floor is a quiet terrace with a view of the town and the sea. Rooms go for US$13/22, breakfast included. Other places along this street or just off it include *Hilal Pansiyon* (☎ 836 1207), *Melisa Pansiyon* (☎ 836 1068) and *Santosa* (☎ 836 1714).

Ay Pansiyon (☎ 836 1562), where the front rooms have sea views, is a bit rough around the edges but cheap at US$7/10.

Places to Stay – Mid-Range

Over the hill to the south-east is Küçük Çakıl Plajı (Small Pebble Beach) and behind it, along with the big hotels, are about 40 small one- and two-star hotels offering good simple rooms, vine-shaded terraces with sea views and congenial atmosphere. Prices depend upon season and demand, but average US$20 a single, US$40 to US$50 a double with bath and breakfast, with reductions off season. Immediately above the beach try *Lale* (☎ 836 1074), *Patara* (☎ 836 1328) or *Nur* (☎ 836 1203). One level higher up are *Cemil* (☎ 836 1554), *Antiphellos* (☎ 836 1136), *Talay* (☎ 836 1101) and *Defne* (☎ 836 1932).

Hotel Kayahan (☎ 836 1313, fax 836 2001, Koza Sokak 9), located up the hill from Küçük Çakıl Plajı, is two-star, attractive and family run, with front rooms that have fine sea views. All have baths and cost US$28/34 a single/double, including breakfast. There's a roof terrace as well.

Otel Sardunya (☎ 836 3080, fax 836 3082), Hastane Caddesi, on the western 'pension' side of town, charges US$25 a double, including breakfast, and is very popular.

The three-star *Hotel Club Phellos* (☎ 836 1953, fax 836 1890), on Doğruyol Sokak, up from Küçük Çakıl Plajı, was designed to recall the historic houses of Kaş, now mostly swept away. It has a nice airy restaurant and swimming pool, and air-con rooms with bath, going for US$70/100/135 a single/double/triple, including breakfast.

The new *Hera Hotel* (☎ 836 3062, fax 836 3063) facing Küçük Çakıl Plajı is a hilarious confection of a building with the facade of a Greek temple. Comfortable rooms cost US$70/90, including breakfast. It has a small private beach, a swimming pool and a hamam.

Places to Eat

For breakfast, snacks, pastries and puddings, *Noel Baba Pastanesi* on the main square is a favourite and best for people-watching when its outdoor tables are in the shade. Also very popular is *Corner Cafe*, at the PTT end of Ibrahim Serin Caddesi (a pedestrian way at this point), where you can get juices, yogurt with fruit and honey and vegetable omelettes. Immediately opposite is *Cafe Merhaba*, run by two women, and

offering a choice of home-made cakes to eat with coffee or juice. You can buy your foreign-language newspapers here to read while you're tucking in.

For cheap, good quality Turkish food try the *Ora Restaurant* on Elmalı Caddesi, with kebaps for US$2 to US$3 and pides for US$1.50.

Just down from the tourist office at the water's edge, *Mercan Restaurant* is generally regarded as the town's best place to dine because of its longstanding service, waterfront location and seafood. Choose a fish, have it weighed, get the price, then say '*evet*' if you want it, or '*hayır*' if you don't. A fish dinner with mezes and wine can cost from US$12 to US$18 per person. The *Sun Cafe* across the road gets good reports from long-term residents; main courses cost around US$6.

Just back from the main square is *Eriş Restaurant*, with shady pseudo-rustic tables in front. Prices are not bad, the food is good and the atmosphere makes it very popular in the evenings. Full meals run from US$7 to US$12. Above the Eriş, *Marina Restaurant* has the best views because of its height. The *Dolphin Cafe* is also good and very popular, with terrific views from the terrace and seafood meals for around US$15.

Beside Eriş in the main square is *Smiley's Restaurant*, a brasher but popular place serving pizza for around US$3 to US$6. *Meydan Pizza* by the tourist office is even cheaper.

Up behind the Lycian sarcophagus it's also worth looking out for *Bahçe* (Garden) *Restaurant*, set, as its name suggests, in a garden with an excellent selection of cold mezes to choose from and prices similar to those at Eriş.

The *Chez Evi Restaurant* on narrow Terzi Sokak offers French cuisine such as *calamar Provençale* (squid) for US$6, wild boar for US$9 and Yakut wine for US$11. It's open evenings only.

South of the mosque, the tiny *Asma Cafe* also receives the local seal of approval for its salad lunches and pleasant ambience. Beyond it, out towards the quay and on the right, is a row of little restaurants that are

Services from Kaş's Otogar

destination	fare (US$)	time (hr)	distance (km)	services
Antalya	4	4	185	frequent
Demre/Kale	2	1	45	frequent
Fethiye	3.50	2½	110	frequent
İstanbul	20–25	12	1090	
Kalkan	1.30	½	29	frequent
Patara	2.50	1	42	frequent

great for breakfast or a sunset drink. *Elit Bar*, at the western end of the row along from the marina has a concrete sun deck and unobstructed view of Kastellorizo.

Getting There & Away
Most tourists arrive and leave Kaş by bus. Most buses in and out of Kaş are handled by the Pamukkale, Kaş Turizm and Kamil Koç companies. Some daily bus and dolmuş services are listed in the table above.

For other destinations, connect at Fethiye or Antalya.

ÜÇAĞIZ
About 14km east of Kaş is a road on the right (south) to Üçağız. A 19km ride along a paved road brings you to the village of Kale/Üçağız, the Lycian Teimiussa, in an area of ancient ruined cities, some of them partly submerged in the Mediterranean Sea. This area is regularly visited by day-trippers on boats and yachts from Kaş and Kalkan but you can also stay overnight.

Declared off-limits to development, Üçağız was until recently an unspoilt Turkish fishing and farming village in an absolutely idyllic setting, on a bay amid islands and peninsulas. Nowadays it's becoming an up-market 'undiscovered hideaway', with prices to match.

Here and there are remnants of ancient Lycian tombs. Near the Koç Restaurant in particular, look for two Lycian sarcophagi (one of them in the shape of a house) and a rock-cut tomb.

Orientation
The village you enter is Üçağız (meaning 'Three Mouths'), the ancient Teimiussa.

Across the water to the east is Kale (Kaleköy), a village on the site of the ancient city of Simena, accessible by boat. South of the villages is a harbour called Ölüdeniz (not to be confused with the famous beach spot near Fethiye), and south of that is the channel entrance, shielded from the Mediterranean's occasional fury by a long island named Kekova Adası.

Streets in the village are barely wide enough for one vehicle. If you're driving, park your vehicle well outside the village.

Boat Trips
Boats from Üçağız will take you on a tour of the area lasting from one to 1½ hours. Chartering an entire boat costs around US$10 to US$16, but haggle as prices are negotiable. Although the water is very clear some readers have thought it worth paying a bit extra to sail past the 'sunken city' ruins in a glass-bottomed boat.

Places to Stay & Eat
You can camp on the western outskirts at *Kekova Camping*.

Üçağız's small pensions charge around US$10 per person. The tidy *Ekin Pansiyon* (☎ 874 2064) at the western end of the village is right next to the water, with a pretty garden and insect screens on the windows. *Flower Pension* (☎ 874 2043) above the restaurant of the same name is ramshackle but cheap. *Onur Pension* (☎ 874 2071) on the harbour has decent double rooms. *Koç Pansiyon* (☎ 874 2080) at the eastern end of the village is the fanciest.

There's a small store selling groceries in the village centre, opposite an information booth which is open in high summer.

Though they cater mostly to yachters and boat groups, Üçağız's restaurants are not outrageously priced and a meal for US$4 or US$5 is possible. A short stroll through the village shows you the restaurant situation, which changes from year to year. *Koç* on the main square is usually reliable and *Flower Pansiyon Restaurant* is worth a try. The restaurant at *Onur Pension* is another option.

Getting There & Away

Very occasional minibuses link Kaş to Üçağız in winter, but services in summer are sometimes nonexistent, as most traffic goes by boat. If there's no bus and you don't want to take an excursion you could get a taxi as far as Üçağız and then take a taxi boat to Kaleköy for US$5 each way. In summer there's also a water taxi direct from Kaş; the Kaş tourist office has details.

Coming from Demre, motorboats can be chartered at the western beach, called Çayağzı, for US$30; sometimes it's possible to buy one place in the boat for a one-way journey for about US$3. You may be able to do this from Kaş as well.

KALEKÖY
☎ 242

Tours from Kaş normally arrive in Üçağız and then head for Kaleköy to see the ruins of ancient **Simena** and the Byzantine **fortress** perched above the picture-perfect hamlet. Within the fortress a little theatre is cut into the rock and nearby are ruins of several temples and public baths, several sarcophagi and Lycian tombs; the **city walls** are visible on the outskirts. It's a delightfully pretty spot, accessible by motorboat from Üçağız (10 minutes) or on foot (one hour).

Kaleköy has a couple of pensions, including the delightfully sited *Mehtap Pansiyon* (☎ 874 2146, fax 874 2261), high on the hill with spectacular views over the harbour and a sunken Lycian tomb. Beds cost US$8 in waterless rooms. Closer to the harbour there's also *Kale Pansiyon* (☎ 874 2111) with beds for US$7. The harbourside restaurants tend to be pricey because of their yachting clientele.

KYANEAİ

From the main highway at the Üçağız turn-off, it's 8km east and south to the turn-off for Kyaneai. About 2km off the highway, Roman and Lycian ruins stand amid the houses and paddocks of the farming hamlet called Yavı. A track starts in the town and leads 3km uphill to the main part of this ancient city, founded in Lycian times, which flourished under the Romans and was the seat of a bishop during the Byzantine era. It was abandoned in the 10th century.

The site has some interesting tombs, a theatre and traces of other buildings, but the rough terrain and undergrowth make exploration difficult. This is one for dedicated antiquities buffs who enjoy having little-visited sites to themselves.

DEMRE
☎ 242

Demre (Kale) is 24km east of the Kyaneai turn-off. Winding past rocky, scrubby terrain from Kaş, the road descends from the mountains to a fertile river delta, much of it covered in greenhouses. Demre, 46km east of Kaş, was the Roman city of Myra (the name comes from 'myrrh') and by the 4th century was important enough to have its own bishop (one of them St Nicholas, later immortalised as Santa Claus). Several centuries before that, St Paul stopped here on his voyage to Rome.

Though Myra had a long history as a religious, commercial and administrative town, Arab raids in the 7th century and the silting of the harbour led to its decline. Today that same silting is the foundation of the town's wealth. The rich alluvial soil supports the intensive greenhouse production of flowers and vegetables.

Though lots of tourists pass through Demre, few stay for long. Those who do find that the prices of services such as hotels, taxi rides and boat tours are usually negotiable.

Orientation & Information

Demre sprawls over the alluvial plain. At the centre is the main square, near which are several cheap hotels and restaurants. The street going west from the square to the

Santa Claus

The legend of Father Christmas (Santa Claus or Noel Baba in Turkish) is believed to have begun in Demre when a 4th-century Christian bishop, later St Nicholas, gave anonymous gifts to dowryless village girls. He would drop bags of coins down the chimneys of their houses, and this 'gift from heaven' would allow them to marry, which is perhaps why he's the patron saint of virgins. He went on to become the patron saint of sailors, children, pawnbrokers, Holy Russia and others.

St Nicholas' fame grew and in 1087 a raiding party from the Italian city of Bari stole his remains from the church. They missed a few bones which are now in Antalya Museum.

To judge from the carvings on its top, what is touted as St Nicholas' tomb in Demre church is more likely to be that of a Byzantine couple.

Church of St Nicholas is Müze Caddesi (also called St Nicholas Caddesi). Going north is Alakent Caddesi, which leads 2km to the Lycian rock tombs of Myra. PTT Caddesi (also called Ortaokul Caddesi) heads east to the PTT and the town's best hotel, Grand Hotel Kekova. The street going south from the square passes the otogar (100m) and continues to a cluster of hotels (800m) across from the primary school, at the junction with the road to Antalya.

Looming above the town on a hilltop to the north is the huge kale, which looks especially impressive in the late afternoon sun.

Church of St Nicholas

The Church of St Nicholas (Noel Baba in Turkish), a block west of the main square, was first built in the 3rd century, held St Nicholas' remains after he died in 343 and became a Byzantine basilica when it was restored in 1043.

Later restorations sponsored by Tsar Nicholas I of Russia in 1862 changed the St Nicholas church even more. More recent work by Turkish archaeologists was designed to protect it from deterioration.

Not vast like Aya Sofya, nor brilliant with mosaics like İstanbul's Chora Church, the Church of St Nicholas at Demre is, at first, a disappointment. What redeems it is the venerable dignity lent it by its age and the stories which surround it.

Admission to the church (open 8 am to 5.30 pm, to 7 pm in summer, daily) is overpriced at US$3.

Myra

About 2km inland from Demre's main square lie the ruins of Myra, with a striking honeycomb of rock-hewn **Lycian tombs** and a well-preserved **Roman theatre**. Climb the ladders for a closer look at the tombs, which were thought to have been carved to resemble Lycian houses, wood beams and all. Around to the left as you climb is a tomb topped by a deathbed scene; there are other reliefs to discover as well.

Opening hours are from 7.30 am to 7 pm in summer and 8 am to 5.30 pm the rest of the year. Admission costs US$1.30.

Taxi drivers in town will offer to take you on a tour, but the walk from the main square only takes about 20 minutes and the site is fairly self-explanatory.

Andriake (Çayağzı)

About 5km west of Demre centre is Çayağzı (Stream Mouth), called Andriake by the Romans. In Roman times this port was an important entrepot for grain on the sea route between the eastern Mediterranean and Rome.

The ruins of the ancient town cover a wide area around the present settlement, which is little more than a dozen boat yards and a beachfront restaurant with decent food and fine sea views. Some of the land is swampy, so the great granary built by Hadrian (finished in AD 139), to the south of the beach access road, can be difficult to access in wet weather.

Besides the ruins and the 1km-long beach, it's interesting to watch the boatbuilders at work. You can usually find an excursion boat or a taxi boat to Üçağız departing from Çayağzı as well.

Dolmuşes run out here occasionally from the centre of Demre, but it's more likely that you'll have to take a taxi (US$5).

Beaches

On the eastern outskirts of Demre, about 5km from the centre are more fine beaches, named Kömürlü and Sülüklü, in the district called Beymelek.

Places to Stay & Eat

Despite its several points of interest, Demre doesn't have much accommodation. Most people are passing through.

Hotel Şahin (*☎ 871 5686, fax 871 5781, Müze Caddesi)*, just west off the main square on the way to the St Nicholas Church, is convenient and usable, though hardly beautiful. Rooms with bath and breakfast cost US$14/20 a single/double.

About 300m south of the Myra ruins (and 1.7km north of the main square), *Kent Pansiyon* (*☎ 871 2042)* has pleasant gardens and costs US$10/12 for a room.

Two more hotels are 800m south of the main square near the junction with the highway to Antalya: *Otel Kıyak* (*☎ 871 2092, fax 871 2093)*, charging US$9/12 a room with bath; and the cheaper *Kekova Pansiyon* (*☎ 871 2804)* with rooms for US$5 per person.

Across the highway from this duo, the three-star *Hotel Andriake* (*☎ 871 2249, fax 871 5440, Finike Caddesi)* is the town's best at US$32 a double.

The food from the little restaurants near the main square (*Çınar* and *Şehir*) and along Müze Caddesi between the square and the church (*İpek* in particular and *İnci Pastanesi* for sweets) can fill you up. *Simena* on Müze Caddesi serves wine and beer with meals; *Güney Han* is fancied up, but the food is no better.

Getting There & Away

There are frequent buses and dolmuşes between Demre and Kaş (US$2, one hour, 45km).

ÇAĞILLI & GÖKLİMAN

East from Demre towards Antalya is Çağıllı, a small cove with a nice pebble beach overlooked by the highway. At Gökliman, another 4km east (and 4km before Finike), a longer, wider beach is good for a swim.

FİNİKE
☎ 242 pop 7000

About 30km further along the twisting mountain road is Finike, the ancient Phoenicus, now a sleepy fishing port and way-station on the tourist route. Finike itself is uninteresting and not really worth making a special stop for. Most of the tourists are Turks who have built ramshackle dwellings on the long pebble beach to the east of the town. The beach looks inviting but parts of it are polluted and bugs can be a problem at certain times of year.

The ruins of ancient **Limyra** are 11km inland along the Elmalı road in the village of Hasyurt. They're not really worth the effort unless you're out to see every ancient town along the coast. The theatre is fairly well preserved, as are some tombs 200m further north, but beware the bees! Other ruined buildings are scattered among the modern farms and houses.

Arycanda, 35km north along the Elmalı road, is well worth seeing with its dramatic setting and many well-preserved buildings, but requires a special excursion.

If you decide to stay here, there are several options. *Paris Pansiyon* (*☎ 855 1488)*, 200m inland from the highway off the Elmalı road, is up a flight of steps. Beds here cost just US$7, including breakfast.

In the market district behind the belediye stand several inexpensive hotels, including the *Hotel Bahar* (*☎ 855 2020)*, the friendly *Hotel Bilal* (*☎ 855 2199)* and the older *Hotel Sedir* (*☎ 855 1183, Cumhuriyet Caddesi 37)*. All three places charge around US$12/20 a single/double with shower, including breakfast.

KUMLUCA TO OLİMPOS

As you leave Finike the highway skirts a sand-and-pebble beach which runs for about 15km. Once past the long beach, at 19km from Finike, the road transits Kumluca (population 17,000), a farming town surrounded by citrus orchards and plastic-roofed greenhouses, particularly worth visiting on Fridays for its lively market. A few small pensions can provide a room in an emergency.

After Kumluca the highway winds back up into the mountains with an especially good panorama about 28km from Finike. About 3km later you enter **Beydağları Sahil Milli Parkı** (Bey Mountains Coastal National Park).

Just east of Kumluca, a road on the right goes 2km to the small farming towns of Beykonak, and then another 8km to Mavikent. A narrow but scenic road continues from Mavikent through a broad alluvial valley paved in plastic-sheeted greenhouses to Adrasan, another 15km along, and then continues to Olimpos/Çıralı.

OLİMPOS & THE CHIMAERA
☎ 242

Midway between Kumluca and Tekirova three roads lead from the main highway towards Çavuşköy, Olimpos and Çıralı, to Adrasan beach, and to the ruins of ancient Olimpos and the site of the Chimaera, all set within the glorious Beydağları Sahil Milli Parkı. The turn-off to the treehouse camps at Olimpos is the second road. Confusingly, the road to Çıralı is signposted 'Olimpos-Çıralı-Yanartaş/Chimaera 7km' – useful if you want to go to Çıralı, not useful if you want to go to Olimpos. Every bus or dolmuş between Kaş and Antalya passes this turn-off. Tell the driver you want to stop at Olimpos and you'll arrive at the right turn-off. If you take the Çavuşköy turn-off it will be 11km to the village.

Olimpos

Though a very ancient city, the early history of Olimpos is shrouded in mystery. We know that it was an important Lycian city by the 2nd century BC, and that the Olympians worshipped Hephaestos (Vulcan), the god of fire. No doubt this veneration sprang from reverence for the mysterious Chimaera, an eternal flame which still springs from the earth not far from the city. Along with the other Lycian coastal cities, Olimpos went into a decline in the 1st century BC. With the coming of the Romans in the 1st century AD, things improved, but in the 3rd century pirate attacks brought impoverishment. In the Middle Ages the Venetians, Genoese

and Rhodians built fortresses along the coast (bits of which still remain), but by the 15th century Olimpos had been abandoned.

Today the site is fascinating, not just for its ruins (which are fragmentary and widely scattered among the thick verdure of wild grapevines, flowering oleander, bay trees, wild figs and pines), but for its site, just inland from a beautiful beach along the course of a stream which runs through a rocky gorge. The stream dries to a rivulet in high summer and a ramble along its course, listening to the wind in the trees and the songs of innumerable birds, is a rare treat, with never a tour bus in sight.

The site is effectively open all the time but during daylight hours a custodian awaits to collect US$3.20 from those wishing to climb to the acropolis. There's a car park at the nonbeach end of the site.

The Chimaera

The Chimaera, a cluster of spontaneous flames which blaze from crevices on the rocky slopes of Mt Olimpos, is the stuff of legends. It's not difficult to see why ancient peoples attributed these extraordinary flames to the breath of a monster – part lion, part goat and part dragon. Even today, they have not been explained.

In mythology, the Chimaera was the son of Typhon. Typhon was the fierce and monstrous son of Gaia, the earth goddess; he was so frightening that Zeus set him on fire and buried him alive under Mt Etna, thereby creating the volcano. Typhon's offspring, the Chimaera, was killed by the hero Bellerophon on the orders of King Iobates of Lycia. Bellerophon killed the monster by aerial bombardment – mounting Pegasus, the winged horse, and pouring molten lead into the Chimaera's mouth.

Today gas still seeps from the earth and bursts into flame upon contact with the air. The exact composition of the gas is unknown, though it is thought to contain some methane. Though the flames can be extinguished by being covered, they will reignite when uncovered. In ancient times they were much more vigorous, being easily recognised at night by mariners sailing along the coast.

These days there are about 20 or 30 flames in the main area, and a less impressive collection at the top of the hill. The best time to visit is after dark. Various pensions in Olimpos run tours here for a modest fee in the evening, but it's worth making the journey here in a smaller group to appreciate it. It's about a 7km walk from Olimpos. From Çıralı, follow the track marked for the Chimaera (Yanartaş, Burning Rock) along a valley to a car park, then climb up a dirt track through the forest (bring a torch) for another 20 to 30 minutes to the site.

Places to Stay & Eat
Olimpos The rustic treehouse camps of Olimpos have become one of the most popular backpacker stops in Turkey, because they're cheap, because there are no carpet shops (or any other shops or banks for that matter), and because of the rumoured availability of a certain herb. Add to this a fine beach, interesting ruins and fabulous setting in a steep forested valley, and you can understand why lots of people stay here for longer than they had planned. Its popularity may well be its eventual downfall, though. It's going to take careful management to see that the meagre infrastructure doesn't become overburdened.

All the treehouse camps include meals in the price, though drinks are extra, and while some have rooms with bathrooms, the authentic experience is staying in a wooden shack with common bathrooms. Few treehouses have locks, so store valuables at reception. Unless otherwise noted, treehouses cost US$7 per person and rooms or bungalows with bathrooms US$10 per person. Incidentally, the chickens and turkeys picking around the place serve the useful purpose of eating the local scorpions.

A dozen or so camps line the track along the valley down to the ruins. The original that all the others imitated is **Kadir's Yörük Treehouses** (☎ 892 1250, fax 892 1110, ℯ treehouse@superonline.com). It's also the biggest (room for 200!) and has the most interesting design, not unlike a set from *Xena: Warrior Princess*. Dorms ranging from four to 12 beds cost US$6, cabins

US$8, bungalows with attached bathroom and shower US$12. The Bull Bar in one corner of the compound is the valley's busiest and loudest – lots of people stay in other camps and party here.

Next along from Kadir's treehouses towards the beach is **Olympos Çamlık Pansiyon** (☎ 892 1257), a small family-run place. **Sheriff's** (☎ 892 1301) is similar.

Further along is **Türkmen Pansiyon** (☎ 892 1249), which actually has a few real treehouses in trees rather than a row of huts like a Japanese prisoner-of-war camp. It's a large place with a good reputation for food, and many comfy lounging areas.

Tucked in next to Turkmen is **Caretta Caretta** (☎ 892 1295), with a capacity for 25 people or so, aiming a tiny bit upmarket by offering cappuccino and espresso coffee.

Across the stream is **Şaban Pansiyon** (☎ 892 1265), with a nice female manager, a garden, and treehouses set on spacious grounds backing onto the pine-covered hillside. The food gets good reports.

Next along is **Orange Pansiyon** (☎ 892 1242), run by friendly young Turkish guys with disturbingly accurate Australian accents. It isn't the cleanest place, but it seems popular. **Bayram's Treehouses & Pension** (☎ 892 1243, fax 892 1399, ℯ bayrams1@ turk.net) is another large camp with treehouses in an orange orchard and comfortable lounging areas.

Next to Bayram's is the **Gypsy Restaurant**. Does it actually sell food? We were never certain. Pink Floyd gets a flogging on the stereo though.

The last (at least for now) is **Zeus Treehouses** (☎ 892 1347), more rustic than most with staff who are effortlessly friendly but slightly incompetent in the nicest possible way.

Çıralı Arriving in Çıralı, you cross a small bridge where a few taxis wait to run people back up to the main road. Continue across the bridge and you'll come to a junction in the road disfigured with innumerable signboards – there are about 60 pensions here. Go straight on for the pensions nearest to the path up to the Chimaera. Turn right for the pensions closest to the beach and the Olimpos ruins.

The standard price for a pension double room here – actually more like a one-star hotel room with bath and breakfast – is US$24.

In Çıralı village, **Orange Pansiyon** (☎ 825 7128) is quite nice, as is **Aygün Pansiyon** (☎ 825 7146) beyond it (not to be confused with the neighbouring Grand Aygün). There are six other decent places here as well.

An even better location is down by the beach. Follow the signs to **Fehim Pansiyon** (☎ 825 7250), an older place with more spacious, shady grounds and a full *restaurant*. Adjoining it is **Sima Peace Pansiyon** (☎ 825 7245), a tidy collection of little honey-coloured pine cabins.

Barış Pansiyon (☎ 825 7080) has eight double rooms, a large garden and a pleasant terrace. **Yıldız Pansiyon** (☎ 825 7160) at the southern end of the beach is cheaper than most at US$14 for a comfortable double room, and has a large garden.

The small and friendly **Rüya Pansiyon** (☎ 825 7055), tucked away behind a school and run by a friendly family, is another good choice.

Walking along the beach towards the Olimpos ruins you'll come to the delightful **Olympos Lodge** (☎ 825 7171, fax 825 7173, e olimposlodge@superonline.com), a beautiful lodge and villas set among citrus orchards and well-tended gardens near the beach. Sculpture and a flock of peacocks augment the scene. Rooms cost US$87/134 a single/double, all meals included.

In summer there are plenty of small beach restaurants serving up simple kebap meals but most close by the end of October.

Adrasan/Çavuşköy South along the coast from Olimpos about 10km is Çavuşköy, more commonly called by its historical name of Adrasan, a tiny little-known coastal resort with a growing collection of beachfront hotels and pensions. Like Çıralı, Adrasan is a farming village, but turn in the main square and follow the sign pointing east 5km to the Adrasan Turistik Tesisleri (Tourism Facilities).

The relatively clean, unpolluted beach is lined with little pensions and hotels, including **İkizler Pansiyon Restaurant** (☎ 883 5227), **Atıcı Motel & Pension**, **Çizmeci Hotel** and **Gelidonya Pension**. The fancier **Sözen Motel** (☎ 883 5153), **Koreli Motel** (☎ 883 5413) and the adjoining **Hotel Ford** (☎ 883 5121, fax 883 5097) all charge about US$35 for a double room with bath and breakfast and perhaps air-con. These three places have swimming pools, and all are only a few steps from the beach.

Getting There & Away

Buses plying up and down the main road linking Antalya and Fethiye will drop you at either of the road junctions leading to Çıralı, Olimpos or Adrasan/Çavuşköy.

Dolmuşes wait at the Olimpos turn-off until enough passengers arrive, which can sometimes take a couple of hours, unless you want to charter and pay for the whole vehicle. Assuming enough people show up, the dolmuş passes all the camps until it reaches the one the driver gets paid to stop at. It costs US$1.30.

Taxis usually wait at the Çıralı junction, charging US$8 for the short run. There are a couple of dolmuşes as well. In summer boats run from Adrasan beach to Demre and Kaş. On Friday there are dolmuşes from Çıralı to Kumluca market.

TEKİROVA
☎ 242

About 13km north-east of Olimpos is the turn-off for Tekirova, a resort area with several large luxury hotels (**Phaselis Princess, Corinthia Club Hotel Tekirova**, etc) and more under construction. Of the many pensions here, **Phaselis Pension** (☎/fax 821 4507) is off the highway on the old road next to a stream. The benefits are a quiet location, swimming pool and being 750m from the beach. The decent double rooms with bath for US$25, breakfast included, are good value. Follow the signs to get there.

A reader recommends **Aloha Otel** (☎/fax 821 4450), with a garden, terrace and swimming pool and a friendly young owner. Doubles cost US$20.

Lycian Way

Turkey's first walking trail, the Lycian Way, is a 30-day, 500km walk around the coast and mountains of Lycia, starting at Fethiye and finishing near Antalya. It gets progressively more difficult as it winds around the coast, into the mountain ranges and finishes at a height of 1500m with a spectacular view over the tourist beaches.

However, it's easy to walk a bit at a time – every time the route crosses a road, be it ever so tiny, it's marked by a yellow-and-green signpost. And the whole length of the path is marked every 100m with red-and-white paint flashes. Good places for starting from are Ölüdeniz, Kaş, Adrasan or Olimpos.

The route starts at Ölüdeniz with a stiff climb up the shoulder of Baba Dağı mountain until you are looking down on the hang-gliders. Around Kaş you can choose level but rocky walking past overgrown ruined Roman watchtowers as far as Üçağız. The walk from Çıralı to Ulupınar, via the flames of the Chimaera is a well-known day-walk. From Olimpos to Adrasan, the path leads you past hilltop ruins where orchids flourish and down a green gorge. From Adrasan south, a tough day's hiking takes you to the lighthouse at Gelidonia – the southernmost part of the route. If you are staying in Antalya, day walks up the Göynük Valley are a cool choice – you can splash in the clear waters of the canyon.

The peak attraction, however, is the summit of Tahtalı – Mt Olimpos – rearing 2388m above the Mediterranean. The path is waymarked from the main road near Ulupınar, or from Beycik village, right up and over the main pass at 1800m. If you want to reach the summit, you have to branch up and north-east, following a cairned path up the scree. But Tahtalı can be dangerous – don't climb in bad weather or alone, take waterproofs, food and water, mark your route or take compass bearings so you can return safely if cloud descends, and report in to the locals and take their advice.

There are pensions available at only a few points on the route; to tackle some of the major sections (for example, Myra to Finike or Olimpos to Adrasan), camping is essential, and you'll need to take all your own supplies, as there are very few places to buy food. The Antalya end is more difficult than the Fethiye end; from Myra onwards, experience in hard trekking with a full rucksack is essential. Walkers should also be careful not to tackle difficult sections when the weather is too hot (June to August) – walk early or late in the day or just do day walks.

Up to now, trekking has been restricted by the army because their excellent maps are stamped 'secret' and not allowed out to play. However, there is now a walking guide, *Turkey's First Long Distance Walk – the Lycian Way* by Kate Clow, pioneer of the Lycian Way, available in the UK or check out their Web site (www.lycianway.da.ru). The route also has to be maintained; if you are interested in maintaining a section or helping to find alternative sections or day walks, contact Kate Clow via the Web site.

Kate Clow

WESTERN MEDITERRANEAN

PHASELIS

About 3km north of the Tekirova turn-off, 12km before the turn-off to Kemer and about 56km from Antalya, is a road marked for Phaselis, a ruined Lycian city 2km off the highway on the shore.

Phaselis was apparently founded by Greek colonists on the border between Lycia and Pamphylia around 334 BC. Its wealth came from being a port for the shipment of timber, rose oil and perfume.

Shaded by soughing pines, the ruins of Phaselis are arranged around three small perfect bays, each with its own diminutive beach. The ruins are not particularly exciting, and are all from Roman and Byzantine times, but the setting is incomparably romantic.

The site is open from 7.30 am to 7 pm in summer for US$1.60. About 1km from the highway is the entrance to the site, with a small modern building where you can buy soft drinks, snacks, souvenirs, use the toilet and visit a one-room museum. The ruins and the shore are another 1km further on. The nearest accommodation is in Tekirova.

KEMER
☎ 242 • pop 10,000

Kemer is a burgeoning beach holiday resort with its face turned to the rough, rocky beaches of the Mediterranean and its back to the steep, pine-clad Beydağları (Bey Mountains). It was designed as a holding tank for planeloads of sun-seeking charter and group tours, and built to a government master plan. For the rest of us it has little to offer. Passing through, you can stop for a meal and a look at the Yörük Parkı, an outdoor ethnological exhibit.

Yörük Parkı

On a promontory north of the cove beach is Kemer's Yörük Parkı, an ethnographic exhibit meant to introduce you to some of the mysteries of the region. Local *yörüks* (nomads) lived in these black camel-hair tents now furnished with carpets and grass mats. Typical nomad paraphernalia includes distaffs for spinning woollen yarn, looms on which Turkish carpets are being woven, musical instruments and churns for butter and *ayran* (yogurt drink). Among the tents, in the shade of the pines, are little rustic tables with three-legged stools at which a 'nomad girl' will serve you refreshments and snacks.

Keep walking through the park and you'll emerge above the cove to enjoy the view. At night, Antalya, to the north, is a long string of shore lights in the distance.

Adjoining the Yörük Parkı, the Moonlight Park, between the sea and the Özkaymak Hotel, has a beach and yacht marina.

Getting There & Away

Frequent dolmuşes run from Antalya to Tekirova and Phaselis along the highway (marked 'Üst yoldan ekspres', which means they stop only on the highway, not at otogars). There are also dolmuşes to Kemer's otogar from Antalya otogar, some of which follow parts of the old highway via Göynük and Beldibi (see the following section).

Approaching Kemer from Fethiye, Kaş and Kalkan, you're likely to find yourself dropped off on the main highway, 2km from the otogar. The taxi fare, if you don't want to walk or wait for a dolmuş, is about US$3.

BELDİBİ/GÖYNÜK

North of Kemer, the old Antalya highway follows the shoreline more closely than the new highway, further inland. About 12km north of Kemer is the centre of Beldibi, another planned resort area. The beach here consists of stones, not even pebbles, but the water is clear, the pines cool and the mountain backdrop dramatic. Unfortunately there's also a lot of construction and piles of rubbish here and there.

Among the resorts is *Göynük Çadırlı Kamp Alanı* (Tent Camping Ground), about 400m north of Sultansaray Antalya Hotel & Resort on the old road and 23km south-west of Antalya. Take the Göynük exit from the highway, then turn left (north, back towards Antalya) to find it.

ANTALYA
☎ 242 • pop 600,000

The biggest urban centre on the coast between Izmir and Adana, Antalya has all the activity of a big city but has managed to preserve its peaceful old quarter. The first impressions of a concrete sprawl displacing the orange trees that once grew here are not so enticing, but Antalya is worth a few days of anyone's time. The city has a relaxed, liberal air about it, with good restaurants and pensions and an active nightlife.

Though always a busy port (trading to Crete, Cyprus and Egypt), Antalya has grown explosively since the 1960s because of the tourism boom. Its airport, the busiest on the Turkish Mediterranean, funnels travellers to the whole coast and beyond.

Rough pebble beaches (several kilometres from the centre to east and west) cater for the seaside crowd and the commercial centre provides necessities. Though Antalya has a historic Roman-Ottoman core, the ancient cities on its outskirts – Perge, Aspendos, Side, Termessos, Phaselis, Olimpos – offer more to see in the way of historic buildings. Antalya is a good base from which to visit them.

History

This area has been inhabited since the earliest times. The oldest artefacts, found in the

Karain caves 25km inland from Antalya, date back to the Palaeolithic period. As a city, Antalya is not as old as many other cities that once lined this coast, but it is still prospering while the older cities are dead.

Founded by Attalus II of Pergamum in the 1st century BC, the city was named Attaleia after its founder. When the Pergamene kingdom was willed to Rome, Attaleia became a Roman city. Emperor Hadrian visited here in AD 130 and a triumphal arch (no known as Hadriyanüs Kapısı) was built in his honour. The Byzantines took over from the Romans.

In 1207 the Seljuk Turks based in Konya took the city from the Byzantines and gave Antalya a new version of its name, and also its symbol, the Yivli Minare (Grooved Minaret). After the Mongols broke Seljuk power, Antalya was held for a while by the Turkish Hamidoğulları emirs. It was later taken by the Ottomans in 1391.

During WWI the Allies made plans to divide up the Ottoman Empire and at the end of the war they parcelled it out. Italy got Antalya in 1918, but by 1921 Atatürk's armies had put an end to all such foreign holdings in Anatolia.

WESTERN MEDITERRANEAN

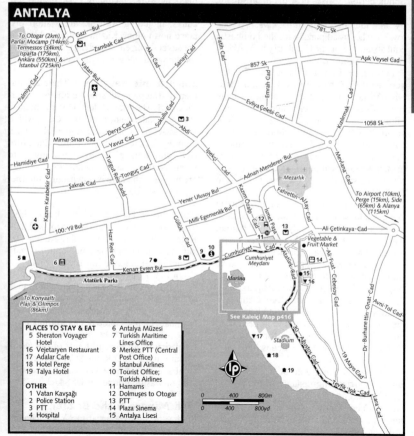

ANTALYA

PLACES TO STAY & EAT
5 Sheraton Voyager Hotel
16 Vejetaryen Restaurant
17 Adalar Cafe
18 Hotel Perge
19 Talya Hotel

OTHER
1 Vatan Kavşağı
2 Police Station
3 PTT
4 Hospital
6 Antalya Müzesi
7 Turkish Maritime Lines Office
8 Merkez PTT (Central Post Office)
9 İstanbul Airlines
10 Tourist Office; Turkish Airlines
11 Hamams
12 Dolmuşes to Otogar
13 PTT
14 Plaza Sinema
15 Antalya Lisesi

Orientation

At the centre of the historic city is the Roman harbour, now the yacht marina. Around it is the historic district called Kaleiçi, which features Ottoman houses sprinkled with Roman ruins. Many of the graceful old houses have been restored or reconstructed, and converted to restaurants, pensions and small hotels – some simple, some quite luxurious.

Around Kaleiçi, outside the Roman walls, is the commercial centre of the city. Antalya's central landmark and symbol is the Yivli Minare, a grooved minaret from the Seljuk period. It rises near the main square, called Kale Kapısı (Fortress Gate), marked by an ancient stone *saat kulesi* (clock tower). The broad plaza with the bombastic equestrian statue is Cumhuriyet Meydanı (Republic Square).

From Kale Kapısı, Cumhuriyet Caddesi goes west past the tourist office and Turkish Airlines office, then becomes Kenan Evren Bulvarı, which continues for several kilometres to the Antalya Müzesi, and Konyaaltı Plajı, a 10km-long pebble beach now partly sullied by industrial development. Antalya's new *tramvay* (tram) runs from the museum along Cumhuriyet Caddesi, Atatürk Caddesi and Fevzi Çakmak Caddesi to the stadium.

North-west from Kale Kapısı, Kazım Özalp Caddesi, formerly Şarampol Caddesi, is a pedestrian way. Antalya's small bazaar, which seems to be mostly jewellery shops, is east of Kazım Özalp Caddesi.

East from Kale Kapısı, Ali Çetinkaya Caddesi goes to the airport (10km), Perge, Aspendos, Side and beyond. Atatürk Caddesi goes south-east from Ali Çetinkaya Caddesi, skirting Kaleiçi through more of the commercial district to the large Karaalioğlu Parkı before heading for Lara Plajı (12km from the centre) which is lined with hotels.

A *çevreyolu* (ring road or bypass), Gazi Bulvarı, carries long-distance traffic around the city centre. The big, modern Antalya otogar (Yeni Garaj) is 4km north of the centre on the D650 Hwy to Burdur, Ankara and İstanbul.

Information

Tourist Office The tourist office (☎/fax 241 1747) is at Cumhuriyet Caddesi 91. It's 600m west of Kale Kapısı on the right-hand side in the Özel İdare Çarşısı building (which also houses Turkish Airlines and Varan bus company). This building is after the jandarma headquarters but before the pedestrian bridge over the roadway. Look for 'Antalya Devlet Tiyatrosu' emblazoned on it.

Money The Yapı Kredi office at the southern end of Kazım Özalp Caddesi, just off Kale Kapısı, has an ATM connected to the major networks, including Visa, MasterCard, Eurocard, Cirrus and Plus Systems. Other banks, including Akbank, are a short distance north along Kazım Özalp Caddesi, as are several currency exchange houses (look for the word 'Döviz' in the name).

Email & Internet Access There are numerous Internet cafes in the alleys and arcades off Atatürk Caddesi. One of the best is Hayat Kahvehanesi Internet Cafe, which has air-con, cool music and real coffee. Leaving Kaleiçi from Hadrian's Gate, turn right and walk along by the tramway to where Atatürk Caddesi bends. Look for the green sign – the cafe is downstairs. Internet access costs US$1.60 per hour.

Bookshops Try the Owl Bookshop, Barbaros Mahallesi, Akarçeşme Sokak 21, in Kaleiçi. The engaging owner, Kemal Özkurt, stocks old and new books in English, French, German and Turkish.

On Fevzi Çakmak Caddesi, near the corner with Atatürk Caddesi, there's a branch of the D&R music and bookshop chain, with a wide selection of foreign magazines and newspapers, plus some books in English.

Laundry In Kaleiçi, just east of the Kesik Minare in the Ünal Rent-a-Car office is the Ünal Laundry where you can have a 5kg load of washing done for US$4.

Yivli Minare & the Bazaar

Start your sightseeing at the Yivli Minare, just downhill from the saat kulesi. The hand-

WESTERN MEDITERRANEAN

some and unique minaret was erected by the Seljuk sultan Alaeddin Keykubat I in the early 13th century, next to a church which the sultan had converted to a mosque. It is now the **Güzel Sanatlar Galerisi** (Fine Arts Gallery) with changing exhibits. To its north-west is a Mevlevi tekke, or whirling dervish monastery, which probably dates from the 13th century, and nearby are two **tombs**, that of Zincirkıran Mehmet Bey (1377) and the lady Nigar Hatun.

The view from the plaza, taking in Kaleiçi, the bay and the distant ragged summits of the Beydağları (Bey Mountains), is spectacular. Teahouses behind Cumhuriyet Meydanı and the Atatürk statue offer the opportunity to enjoy the view.

Kaleiçi (Old Antalya)

Go down Uzun Çarşı Sokak, the street by the saat kulesi. On the left is the **Tekeli Mehmet Paşa Camii**, built by the Beylerbey (Governor of Governors) Tekeli Mehmet Paşa. The building was repaired extensively in 1886 and 1926. Note the beautiful Arabic inscriptions in the coloured tiles above the doors and windows.

Wander further into Kaleiçi, now a historic zone protected from modern development. Many of the gracious old Ottoman houses have been restored, then immediately converted to pensions, hotels or, inevitably, carpet shops.

Roman Harbour The Roman Harbour at the base of the slope was restored during the 1980s and is now used for yachts and excursion boats. It was Antalya's lifeline from the 2nd century BC up until late in the 20th century when a new port was constructed about 12km west of the city, at the far end of Konyaaltı Plajı. Today it's lined with restaurants, tavernas and shops. Day-excursion boats tie up here and tout for passengers.

Kesik Minare & Korkut Camii In the eastern reaches of Kaleiçi is the Kesik Minare (Cut Minaret), a stump of a minaret which marks the ruins of a substantial building. Built originally as a 2nd-century Roman temple, it was converted in the 6th century to the Byzantine Church of the Virgin Mary. Destroyed during the Arab raids of the 7th century, it was repaired and converted to a mosque by the Seljuks in the 9th century. When Antalya fell to the Christian king of Cyprus, Peter I in 1361, it became a church again, but reverted to a mosque under Sultan Beyazid II's son Prince Dede Korkut (1470–1509). The mosque served the neighbourhood's Muslim population until 1896, when it was mostly destroyed by fire, including the wooden superstructure of its minaret.

Gates and walls prevent entry, but it's possible to see bits of marble decoration in Roman and Byzantine styles from a walk around.

Hıdırlık Kulesi At the south-western edge of Kaleiçi, on the corner with Karaalioğlu Parkı, rises the Hıdırlık Kulesi, a 14m-high tower in the ancient walls which dates from the 1st century AD, and may have been used as a lighthouse.

Hadriyanüs Kapısı & Karaalioğlu Parkı

Down Atatürk Caddesi is Hadriyanüs Kapısı (Hadrian's Gate, also called Üçkapılar, the Three Gates) erected during the Roman emperor Hadrian's reign (AD 117–38). The monumental marble arch, which now leads to Kaleiçi, is set in a shady park.

Further along Atatürk Caddesi towards the sea is Karaalioğlu Parkı, a large, attractive, flower-filled park good for a stroll and its sea views. Sunset, the prettiest time, is when Turks come here to stroll. Steps lead down the cliffs to the Adalar Cafe, where there are bathing platforms.

Antalya Müzesi

Antalya's large and rich museum is west of the centre, just over 2km from the Yivli Minare, and can be reached by tram. The collections include fascinating glimpses into the popular life of the region, with crafts and costume displays as well as a wealth of ancient artefacts. Opening hours are from 9 am to 6 pm daily except Monday. Admission costs US$3.50.

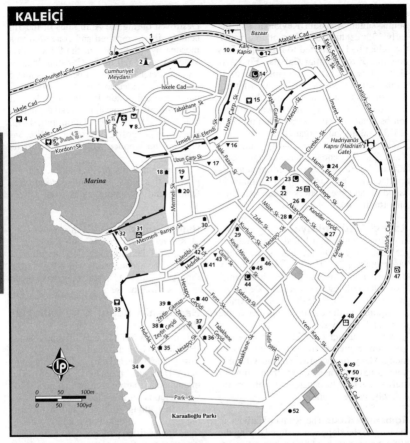

KALEİÇİ

Many exhibits, most of them labelled in English as well as Turkish, are arranged according to where they were found. They start with fossils, proceed chronologically through the Stone and Bronze ages (in which Turkey is especially rich in artefacts) and continue through the Mycenaean, classical and Hellenistic periods. The Gallery of the Gods has statues of 15 classical gods from Aphrodite to Zeus, some of them very fine. Among the exceptionally good smaller objects are jewellery, vases, glass items and statuettes. Note the surprising sophistication and beauty of the Phrygian (Frig) ornaments, figurines and utensils from the 8th to 7th centuries BC.

The museum has a small collection of Christian art, including a room for icons which also contains pieces of the skull and jaw of St Nicholas, the original Santa Claus. There are also several sections of mosaic pavement.

The collection continues through Seljuk and Ottoman times with costumes, armour, calligraphy, implements, faience, musical instruments, carpets and saddlebags. The ethnographic exhibits are fascinating and include a fully furnished nomad's tent, a

PLACES TO STAY	6 Yat Restaurant	7 Tourism Police
18 Türk Evi Otelleri	8 Kral Sofrası	9 PTT
20 Marina Residence	11 Parlak Restaurant; Plaza Fast	10 Yivli Minare
21 Pansiyon Mini Orient	Food Self Service	(Grooved Minaret)
22 Atelya Pension	13 Azim Döner ve İskender	12 Saat Kulesi (Clock Tower)
24 Ninova Pension	Salonu	14 Tekeli Mehmet Paşa Camii
26 Villa Perla	16 Favorit Restaurant; Sunset	15 Rock Bar
28 Hotel Alp Paşa	Restaurant; Cafe Alba	23 Mosque
29 Erken Pansiyon	17 Sırrı Restaurant	25 Research Institute for
30 Doğan Hotel	19 Kırk Merdiven	Mediterranean Civilisations
35 Senem Family Pension	32 Mermerli Restaurant	27 Owl Bookshop
36 Lazer Pansiyon	42 Sim Restaurant	31 Kültür Taxi
37 Sabah Pansiyon	43 Restaurant 36	33 Garden Cafe-Bar
38 Özmen Pansiyon	50 Stella's Bistro	34 Hıdırlık Kulesi (Tower)
39 Hadriyanus Pansiyon	51 Burger King	44 Kesik Minare
40 White Garden Pansiyon		& Korkut Camii
41 Pansiyon Dedekonak	**OTHER**	45 Ünal Laundry
46 Hodja Pansiyon	2 Atatürk Statue	47 Hayat Kahvanesi
	3 Hükümet Konağı	Internet Cafe
PLACES TO EAT	(Government House)	48 Kültür Sinema
1 Şehir Ocakbaşı Restaurant;	4 Club Ally	49 D&R Bookshop
Can İnegöl Köftecisi	5 Club 29	52 Belediye (Town Hall)

room with a carpet loom from a village home and several rooms from a typical Ottoman household.

A shady patio has tables where you can sit and have a cool drink or hot tea.

Research Institute for Mediterranean Civilisations

The Koç Foundation's Akdeniz Medeniyetleri Araştırma Enstitüsü (☎ 243 4274, fax 243 8013), Kaleiçi, Kocatepe Sokak 25, is dedicated to the study of the archaeology, art, ethnography, history and philology of Turkey's Mediterranean coast. Permanent and changing exhibits highlight the institute's projects.

Beaches

Antalya's reputation as a tourist centre is built not on its own beaches, but on those nearby, like Side's. Antalya's Konyaaltı Plajı to the west is pebbly, shadeless and relatively cheerless. Lara Plajı to the east is somewhat better; dolmuşes run from Fevzi Çakmak Caddesi to Lara Plajı for US$0.30.

Boat Trips

Excursion yachts tie up in the Roman Harbour in Kaleiçi, waiting for customers. They offer a variety of itineraries ranging in length from three to nine hours. Some trips go as far as Kemer, Phaselis, Olimpos, Demre and Kaş. A normal tour of the nearby coast takes 4½ or five hours, visits the Lower Düden Falls, Gulf of Antalya islands and some beaches for a swim. It includes lunch and costs US$14 to US$20 person. It's a good idea to ask in detail about lunch when comparing prices; there's a big difference between a sandwich and a three-course seafood feast.

Special Events

Antalya is famous in Turkey for its Altın Portakal Filim Festivali (Golden Orange Film Festival), held in late September or early October, and the Akdeniz Şarkı Festivali (Mediterranean Song Festival), a performance contest that is held immediately afterwards. Hotels are heavily booked during the festivities.

The Aspendos Opera and Ballet Festival, held in the Roman theatre at nearby Aspendos, runs from mid-June to early July. In 2000 there were 12 performances held, including the operas *Carmen* and *Fidelio*. The tourist office should be able to provide you with details of upcoming festivals.

Places to Stay

Antalya has a huge number of places to stay in all price ranges. Kaleiçi is the most atmospheric district, with pensions and small hotels in three categories. Cheapest are the run-down old houses and modern concrete buildings with minimal charm and similar plumbing, costing US$12 to US$16 for a double room (about 25% less for a single), probably with a common bathroom, perhaps including breakfast. Next come the houses renovated or rebuilt in Ottoman style, more or less atmospheric, with private bathrooms, occasionally air-conditioning, and rates of US$16 to US$40 double (25% less for a single). Finally come the 'boutique' hotels, usually one or more adjoining lavishly furnished Ottoman-style houses, perhaps with a swimming pool, for US$60 to US$150. Surprisingly, you don't get much more of a guest room for US$100 than you do for US$30.

All prices listed are for a room with shower and toilet and include breakfast, unless otherwise stated.

Some taxi drivers will swear that the pension of your choice is full, or has closed, or they don't know where it is, and try to take you to another place where – surprise! – they take a 50% commission.

Places to Stay – Budget

Camping is expensive (US$8 per tent) and inconvenient. *Parlar Mocamp*, 14km north on the Burdur highway (D650), is designed for caravans and cars, but there are tent sites as well. Stopping a bus for transport to and from the city can be a problem.

Bambus Motel, Restaurant & Camping (☎ 321 5263, fax 321 3550), 300m west of Hotel Dedeman Antalya on the coast road, is small and crowded but shady, with room for only eight or 10 caravans at most, but with some tent spaces at similar prices. It's on the road closest to the coast, which at this point is one way heading east.

To reach the pension section in Kaleiçi, walk downhill from Kale Kapısı past the Tekeli Mehmet Paşa Camii along Uzun Çarşı Sokak and turn left onto Balık Pazarı Sokak. Another route is through Hadriyanüs Kapısı and along Hesapçı Sokak. Once in Kaleiçi, signs at street corners point the way to most pensions.

Senem Family Pension (☎ 247 1752, fax 247 0615, Kılınçaslan Mahallesi, Zeytin Geçidi Sokak 9) is near the Hıdırlık Kulesi. Mrs Seval Ünsal is everyone's mama, offering clean, simple rooms for US$13/25 for a single/double. Breakfast is served on the roof terrace, with one of the best westward views in the neighbourhood.

Özmen Pansiyon (☎ 241 6505, fax 248 1534, Zeytin Çıkmazı 5), run by Aziz Barış, gets good reports from guests. The rooms are carpeted and some have air-con, and at night the convivial roof terrace glows with coloured neon. Ordinary rooms cost US$10/15, rooms with air-con cost US$15/20. In summer you can sleep on the terrace for US$5.

Not far away, *Sabah Pansiyon* (☎ 247 5345, Hesapçı Sokak 60/A) is a popular backpacker's place with 16 rooms with shower from US$16 to US$18 a double, or US$10 a double for rooms with shared bath. Tours, car and motorcycle rental and other useful services are available as well. The mother cooks good cheap meals for US$6.

Across from Sabah is *Lazer Pansiyon* (☎ 242 7194, fax 243 9353, Hesapçı Sokak 60), cheap for around US$8 per person. Some rooms are better than others, but it has a small, candlelit garden.

Erken Pansiyon (☎ 247 6092, fax 248 9801, Hıdırlık Sokak 5) is a well-preserved (not restored) Ottoman house of dark wood and white plaster charging US$16 a double.

Pansiyon Dedekonak (☎ 247 5170, fax 244 0427, Hıdırlık Sokak 13) is full of well-preserved character and a good choice at US$15/20 a room.

Hadriyanus Pansiyon (☎ 244 0030, Kılınçarslan Mahallesi, Zeytin Çıkmazı 4/A-B) is a series of old, mostly unrestored buildings around a refreshingly large and green walled garden. The friendly owners charge US$12/18 for a room or *sivit* (suite).

White Garden Pansiyon (☎ 241 9115, fax 241 2062, Hesapçı Geçidi 9) has a nice garden and a good price of US$20 a double for more modern, pleasant rooms.

Places to Stay – Mid-Range

The 12-room *Villa Perla* (☎ 248 9793, fax 241 2917, e villaperla@hotmail.com, Hesapçı Sokak 26), has lots of style in a well-preserved old house of great character. The swimming pool is in the garden. Hostess İnci Akduman also runs one of the best restaurants in town. Rooms cost US$40/50 with shower and breakfast.

Ninova Pension (☎ 248 6114, Hamit Efendi Sokak 9) is an artistically restored house with a peaceful garden renting double rooms for US$32, breakfast included.

Atelya Pension (☎ 241 6416, fax 241 2848, Civelek Sokak 21) is a beautifully restored stone house with a vine-shaded garden on a quiet street. Room rates are US$22/30, breakfast included – excellent value.

For nice but slightly cheaper rooms, walk a few steps further to *Pansiyon Mini Orient* (☎/fax 244 0015, Civelek Sokak 30), an old house nicely restored but still simple. The four double and six triple rooms grouped around the small courtyard all have tiny private facilities, and there's a cosy dining room for meals. Prices in summer are US$20/28/36 for a single/double/triple, with reductions in the low season.

Hodja Pansiyon (☎ 248 9486, fax 248 9485, Hesapçı Sokak 37) is newish and clean, renting double rooms with shower for US$30, breakfast included.

Hotel Alp Paşa (☎ 247 5676, fax 248 5074, Hesapçı Sokak 30–32) has been restored into a posh Ottoman dream of comforts, from its hamam and courtyard swimming pool to its suites with whirlpool baths. Rooms with bath and breakfast cost US$45 or US$90 a single, depending upon the room.

The more luxurious places are along Mermerli Sokak, to the east of the yacht harbour. They are reasonably close to Club Ally and Club 29 though.

Doğan Hotel (☎ 247 4654, fax 242 4006, e doganhotel@superonline.com, Mermerli Banyo Sokak 5) is exceptionally good value with rooms for US$25/50, including breakfast. There are 28 rooms with satellite TV and air-con in three houses, a swimming pool and an attractive garden.

Türk Evi Otelleri (☎ 248 6591, fax 241 9419, Mermerli Sokak 2) was closed at the time of research. It features three restored Ottoman houses with 20 guest rooms, all done in late Ottoman Baroque decor with lots of gold leaf and Turkish carpets. Rooms should cost around US$60/100.

South of Karaalioğlu Parkı the *Hotel Perge* (☎ 244 0025, fax 241 7587, Fevzi Çakmak Caddesi, 1311 Sokak 5) is a handsome 1950s-era hotel perched on the cliff's edge in a quiet part of town. The rooms are large but not particularly fancy, but the views across Antalya Körfezi (Antalya Gulf) are superb. Rooms with air-con cost US$45/ 60. Steps lead down to the hotel's private bathing area at the water's edge.

Places to Stay – Top End

Without doubt, Antalya's most prestigious and luxurious address is the five-star *Sheraton Voyager Hotel* (☎ 243 2432, fax 243 2462, 100 Yıl Bulvarı), at the western end of Kenan Evren Bulvarı about 2.5km west of Kale Kapısı. This strikingly modern, appealing building with terraced gardens has all the five-star services. Rooms cost from US$120 to US$210 a single, US$180 to US$260 a double, including breakfast. Occasionally promotional rates are lower.

In Kaleiçi the smartest hotel is the *Marina Residence* (☎ 247 5490, fax 241 1765, Mermerli Sokak 15). The posted prices were US$150/200 for a room with all mod cons, though there's a 30% discount with reservations. There's a sauna and fitness centre, a swimming pool with a glass wall, a pricey cafe and a bar.

The five-star *Talya Hotel* (☎ 248 6800, fax 241 5400, Fevzi Çakmak Caddesi 30) is a large modern place overlooking the sea. For US$120 a single or from US$140 to US$200 a double, you get a modern air-con room, swimming pool, tennis court, restaurant, bar and other services.

Places to Eat

Town Centre The closer you get to the harbour, the more expensive the food gets. Quite a few places around the harbour charge exorbitant prices, so check the menu first.

Go to the intersection of Cumhuriyet and Atatürk Caddesis and find the little street (parallel to Atatürk Caddesi) called Eski Sebzeciler İçi Sokak. The name means 'the Old Inner Street of the Greengrocers Market'. The narrow street is now shaded by a huge and unsightly but effective canopy and lined with little restaurants and pastry shops, many of which have outdoor tables. It's very touristy, but still enjoyable if you're careful not to let yourself be cheated.

The food is kebaps, mostly the ever-popular döner kebap, but you'll also find Antalya's speciality, *tandır kebap* – mutton baked in an earthenware pot buried in a fire pit; it's rich, tasty and greasy, served on a bed of fresh pide with vegetable garnish. It's sold by weight so you can have as many grams as you like. A normal portion is *yüz elli gram* (150g), a small portion is *yüz gram* (100g). Some or much of the portion may be fat. A full meal costs anywhere from US$5 to US$10; ask prices before you sit down.

A 150g portion of döner kebap, *soslu* (with sauce), and a glass of ayran costs US$5 at *Azim Döner ve İskender Salonu* (☎ 241 6610, *Eski Sebzeciler İçi Sokak 6*).

The clientele at *Şehir Ocakbaşı Restaurant* (☎ 241 5127), not far from Kale Kapısı, is mostly local high rollers who come to talk business and politics. In fine weather street-side tables are set up and many diners make a meal of mezes and drinks (about US$10 or so). From Kale Kapısı cross Cumhuriyet Caddesi to its northern side, climb to the pedestrian walkway, turn left, then right at the second street.

Just around the corner (inland) from the Şehir is the cheaper *Can İnegöl Köftecisi*, a small grill where you can eat for US$4.

On Fevzi Çakmak Caddesi there's the popular *Stella's Bistro*, with air-con and a good wine list. Pizzas cost US$5, satay chicken US$7 and baked sea bass US$8.

The only vegetarian restaurant on Turkey's Mediterranean coast, cunningly titled the *Vejetaryen* (☎ 247 4952, *1295 Sokak 5*), is on an alley off Atatürk Caddesi. Look for the Antalya Lisesi (Antalya High School) on Atatürk Caddesi, turn down the lane on the south side of the school and then take the first right. Salads and soups cost US$1.60, main courses US$3.20. It's open every day except Monday for lunch and dinner.

Kaleiçi Kaleiçi has many small restaurants, mostly catering to foreign tourists with Continental-style menus. There are even two Chinese restaurants in Kaleiçi, both of which set high prices and give small servings.

Villa Perla (☎ 248 9793, fax 241 2917, Hesapçı Sokak 26), in the pension of the same name, is well regarded, with tables out in a verdant courtyard. Have the Caucasian *şaşlık* (skewered meat and vegetables) for US$7, or the chicken *şiş kebap* (roast skewered meat) for less. Full meals may be had for US$10 to US$16.

Hotel Alp Paşa has a popular buffet dinner every night for US$8, set around the hotel swimming pool.

Restaurant 36 on Hıdırlık Sokak is one of the best and most reliable, with large servings of Turkish standards like *tavuk şiş* (roast skewered chicken) and excellent salads. A full dinner with non-alcoholic drinks costs around US$8.

Sim Restaurant on Kaledibi Sokak is small and simple, and when tables are set out in the street it's pleasant. They serve şiş kebap for US$3.50, 'garlicky beefsteak' for US$4.25, or a four-course set menu for US$8.

Walk along Balık Pazarı Sokak to Uzun Çarşı Sokak to find more restaurants, including *Favorit*, *Sunset* and *Cafe Alba*, all on shaded terraces above the street. Prices are posted prominently. *Sırrı Restaurant* (☎ 241 7239, Uzun Çarşı Sokak 25) has cheap meals like spaghetti for US$2 or steaks for up to US$8. The decor is Ottoman, the atmosphere welcoming.

Deeper into Kaleiçi, *Kırk Merdiven* (Forty Steps) across from the Türk Evi Otelleri, has a Euro-Turk menu featuring mushroom soup and various Continental-style grills served on a vine-shaded terrace. Your bill might come to US$18 per person for dinner here.

Yacht Harbour For splendid unobstructed sunset views of the bay and Beydağları mountains, the tidy *Mermerli Restaurant*, perched above the eastern end of the harbour, can't be beaten. The bonus is lower prices than at most harbour restaurants: full meals for US$8 to US$12.

If you really want to dine down in the harbour area, try *Yat Restaurant*, which has been here for years, serving meals for US$12 to US$20. Even cheaper is *Kral Sofrası* (☎ 241 2198), just up from the waterside by the little PTT. It's not quite so fancy, but the food is good and meals cost US$9 to US$15.

Kazım Özalp Caddesi Just a few steps up Kazım Özalp Caddesi from Kale Kapısı on the left-hand side is the entrance to a courtyard which holds *Parlak Restaurant* (☎ 241 6553), an old Antalya stand-by for grills. The impressively long grill pit belches smoke generated by its load of skewered chickens and lamb kebaps. Talk and rakı flow freely and the evening passes quickly. If the decor is too basic (there is none), escape to the *aile salonu* (family room) on the left. A full meal of meze, grills and rakı costs from US$8 to US$16 a person. The neighbouring *Plaza Fast Food Self Servis* is the sanitised version of the Parlak.

Entertainment

Long dinners are the rule. Kaleiçi and the yacht harbour have numerous bars and lounges good for drinks and conversation. However, some places around the harbour in particular overcharge massively, so it's probably best to avoid the bars in this area. Some places have a high 'Natasha' (as call girls from the former Soviet Union are dubbed) presence as well.

A great place for a quiet drink at sunset is the *Garden Cafe-Bar*, right on the cliff's edge behind the Hıdırlık Kulesi, with reasonable prices, laid-back music and trees strung with lights. Walk to the end of Hesapçı Sokak and turn right to find it.

It won't take long to notice Antalya's clubs, which boom all night. *Club Ally* above the harbour is the main culprit, a large outdoor venue with eight different bars, a bright green laser and a massive

sound system. The choice of music is a bit disappointing though; just the usual top 40 stuff you hear everywhere. Dress to impress; entrance costs US$14.

Down at the harbour is *Club 29*, the second biggest in town, with a better range of dance music and a crowd of beautiful young people. Entry costs US$12 on weekends, slightly less during the week.

Antalya's disaffected youth head to the *Rock Bar*, where local bands thrash out covers of Nirvana, The Doors and every band espousing disaffected lyrics between. It's loud, the ceiling is alarmingly bowed and the toilets don't bear thinking about – a real rock club in other words. It's just off Uzun Çarşı Sokak, in a little lane leading off to the right as you walk downhill. Look for the rusty old ship's gangplank you must climb to enter.

The annual film festival means the city has some good cinemas. The modern three-screen *Plaza Sinema* is in the new city; from Hadrian's Gate cross the street and walk straight ahead; the building is one block down on the left. The two-screen *Kültür Sinema* is on Atatürk Caddesi; turn right from Hadriyanüs Kapısı (Hadrian's Gate). Both show recent Hollywood movies.

Getting There & Away

Air Antalya's airport is 10km east of the city centre on the Alanya Highway. Turkish Airlines (☎ 243 4383, fax 248 4761), Cumhuriyet Caddesi 91, in the same building as the tourist office, has at least eight nonstop flights daily in summer to/from İstanbul (US$92) and at least two from Ankara. There are also nonstop flights to Tel Aviv (Israel) and Zürich (Switzerland) at least weekly.

Bus Antalya's otogar (Yeni Garaj), 4km north of the city centre on the highway to Burdur, consists of two large terminals fronted by a park. Approaching the otogar along the access road, the Şehirlerarası Terminalı (Intercity Terminal) is to the right; go here for all long distance buses. The İlçeler Terminalı (Provincial Terminal) to the left handles minibuses to nearby points such as Kemer, Side and Alanya.

The otogar has a left luggage room (Emanet/Trustee) which is open 24 hours, a PTT which changes foreign currency, a Yapı Kredi ATM and a currency exchange office. There are also shops, snack stands and a restaurant. The table below lists some useful daily services from Antalya.

Minibuses rocket eastwards from Antalya to Perge, Aspendos, Side, Manavgat, Alanya and Gazipaşa every 20 minutes throughout the day in summer.

Many bus and dolmuş routes go through the Vatan Kavşağı (the intersection of Vatan and Gazi Boulevards), so it serves as an informal bus and minibus station for regional traffic. Take an 'Aksu' dolmuş for Perge (US$0.75), or a 'Manavgat' for Side (US$1.75).

Boat Fener Tours has introduced a ferry service from Antalya to Girne (Kyrenia) in Northern Cyprus, leaving on Wednesday, Friday, Saturday and Sunday. The crossing takes 4½ hours and costs US$70 return. Fener Tours also offers ferry services from Antalya to Rhodes (US$70 return), leaving on Tuesday and Thursday.

Getting Around

To/From the Airport The airport is 10km east of the city centre. There's plenty of bus and minibus traffic along the highway, but the terminal is almost 2km south of the highway. If you don't favour walking you can take a taxi (US$7 or US$8 to the city centre). Havaş runs seven to nine airport buses (US$2) a day from the Turkish Airlines office on Cumhuriyet Caddesi.

To/From the Otogar To get to the city centre from the otogar, walk along the otogar access road to the boulevard and catch a dolmuş to Kale Kapısı. The dolmuş will probably go along Güllük Caddesi to Cumhuriyet Caddesi. To return to the otogar, catch a dolmuş marked 'Yeni Garaj', 'Otogar' or 'Terminal' (US$0.40) heading north on Güllük Caddesi just north of the corner of Cumhuriyet Caddesi. You can also get a red-and-beige Özel Halk Otobüsü (private bus) for the same fare.

AROUND ANTALYA

You can use Antalya as a base for excursions to Olimpos and Phaselis, Termessos, Perge,

Services from Antalya's Otogar

destination	fare (US$)	time (hr)	distance (km)	services
Adana	14	11	555	several buses
Alanya	4	2	115	every 20 mins in summer
Ankara	14	8	550	frequent
Bodrum	12	11	640	1 bus
Denizli (Pamukkale)	6.50	4	300	several buses
Eğirdir	3	2½	186	buses every hour
Fethiye (coastal)	8	7½	295	several buses
(inland)	6	4	222	several buses
Göreme/Ürgüp	15	10	485	1 or 2 buses
İstanbul	18–20	12	725	frequent buses
İzmir	10	9	550	several buses
Kaş	4	4	185	frequent in summer
Kemer	1	¾	35	every 10 mins
Konya (via Isparta)	10	6	365	several buses
(via Akseki)	11	5	349	several buses
Marmaris	12	7	590	a few buses
Olimpos/Çıralı	2.50	1½	79	several minibuses and buses
Side/Manavgat	3	1½	65	every 20 mins in summer

Aspendos and Side, but you might find it easier to visit Olimpos and Phaselis on your way to or from Kaş, and Perge and Aspendos on your way to Side or Alanya. With your own car you can stop at Termessos on your way north or west to Ankara, Denizli/Pamukkale, Eğirdir, İstanbul or İzmir.

Travel agencies in Antalya operate tours to all of these sites. For instance, a half-day tour to the Düden Şelalesi (Düden Falls) and Termessos costs US$25 per person and is perhaps a bit rushed – there's a lot to see at Termessos. A full-day tour to Perge, Aspendos and Side costs almost US$50. The Sabah Pansiyon in Kaleiçi has competitive rates for car tours, or you could try any of the numerous taxi ranks around town.

Düden Falls

The Yukarı Düden Şelalesi (Upper Düden Falls), less than 10km north of the city centre, can be reached by dolmuş. Within view of the falls is a nice park and teahouse. This can be a relaxing spot on a hot summer afternoon, but avoid Düden on summer weekends when the park is crowded.

The Aşağı Düden Şelalesi (Lower Düden Falls) are down where the Düden Çayı meets the Mediterranean at Lara Plajı. Excursion boats include a visit to Lower Düden Falls on their rounds of the Gulf of Antalya. See Boat Excursions in the Antalya section for details.

Termessos

High in a rugged mountain valley 34km inland from Antalya lies the ruined city of Termessos. The warlike Termessians, a Pisidian people, lived in their impregnable fortress city and guarded their independence fiercely. Alexander the Great was fought off in 333 BC and the Romans accepted Termessos as an independent ally, not as a subject city, in 70 BC. Termessos is arguably the most spectacularly sited ruined city in Turkey; the mountain backdrop to the theatre is unforgettable.

Start early in the day as you have to walk and climb a good deal to see the ruins. Though it's cooler up in the mountains than on the shore, the sun is still quite hot. Take

good shoes, a supply of drinking water and perhaps some food.

The Termessos archaeological site, within the Güllük Dağı Milli Parkı (Güllük Mountains National Park), is open from 8 am to 6 pm daily from May to September, until 5 pm in winter; admission costs US$3.20 per person, or US$5 for a car and driver. It's possible to see the site quickly in two hours, but a leisurely, thorough visit takes more like four or five hours.

At the car park are the remains of a small **Artemis-Hadrian Temple** and **Hadrian Propyleum**, now little more than a doorway. From the car park, it's a steep 20-minute hike up via the lower city walls and the city gate to the **lower gymnasium** and **colonnaded street** which leads to the **quarry** and some **sarcophagi**. It's a full hour's walk all the way to the **southern necropolis** with a detour to the **upper agora** and its five large **partitions**, and stops at the **theatre** – the most dramatically sited ever – and the

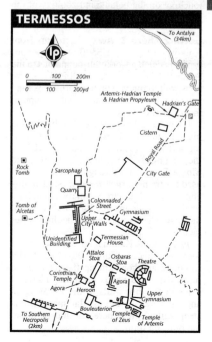

TERMESSOS

To Antalya (34km)

Artemis-Hadrian Temple & Hadrian Propyleum

Hadrian's Gate

Cistern

Royal Road

Rock Tomb

Sarcophagi

City Gate

Quarry

Tomb of Alcetas

Colonnaded Street

Gymnasium

Upper City Walls

Termessian House

Unidentified Building

Attalos Stoa

Osbaras Stoa

Theatre

Corinthian Temple

Agora

Agora

Heroon

Upper Gymnasium

To Southern Necropolis (2km)

Bouleuterion

Temple of Zeus

Temple of Artemis

bouleuterion of finely cut limestone. South of it, the **Temple of Artemis** is badly ruined, but clamber over it to the ruined **Temple of Zeus**, on the south-eastern side of the bouleuterion, to enjoy the spectacular view of the mountains and steep valley. Note the narrow ancient road up the ramp just below the small circular foundation.

The **southern necropolis** or *mezarlık* is at the very top of the valley, 3km up from the car park. It's a vast field of huge stone sarcophagi tumbled about by earthquakes and grave-robbers. The scene is reminiscent of medieval paintings portraying the Judgement Day, when all tombs are to be cast open.

Most famous is the **tomb of Alcetas** (follow the signs), a successor general of Alexander's, with fine reliefs on its facade.

Güllük Dağı Milli Parkı is also worth a visit. Pay the park admission fee at teh entrance and check out the small museum, the Flora ve Fauna Müzesi, with photographs and artefacts from the ruins, plus displays touching on the botany and zoology of the park. Near the museum are picnic sites.

Getting There & Away Taxi tours from Antalya cost around US$30. A cheaper option is to catch a Korkuteli-bound bus to the entrance of Güllük Dağı Milli Parkı, where taxis wait to run you up the Termessos road and back for US$10. This is only an option in summer, however.

If you're driving, leave Antalya by the highway towards Burdur and Isparta, turning left after about 11km onto E87/D350, the road marked for Korkuteli, Denizli and Muğla. Follow this through a stretch of road used for training *sürücü adayı* (student drivers). About 25km from Antalya, look for a road on the right marked for Karain (12km), the cave where important Palaeolithic artefacts were found.

Just after the Karain road, look on the left for the entrance to Güllük Dağı Milli Parkı. Continue another 9km up the road to the ruins. The road winds up through several gates in the city walls to the lower agora and car park, the largest flat space in this steep valley. From here you must explore the ruins on foot.

Karain Cave

The antiquity of the Karain Cave borders on the incredible. Archaeological evidence has convinced scientists that this cave was continuously occupied for 25,000 years.

Set in a steep rock face 150m above the floor of a fertile, temperate valley and 650m above sea level, the cave offered tolerable year-round living conditions for primitive humans. The valley below was well-watered and fertile, abundant with wild fruit trees, grains and vegetation, and good hunting.

The little museum at the site (open from 8 am to 6 pm daily for US$1.30) has an exhibit of ancient animal bones and teeth, wild wheat, small game, rhinoceros, hippopotamus and elephant bones found in the cave. The cave was first excavated in 1946.

The cave proper is a 15- or 20-minute hike up the steep hillside from the museum. It's an eerie place, three large interconnected chambers with a common entrance and many signs of long human habitation, not the least of which is a startling relief mask of a human face carved high up on the main 'pillar' of the main inner room.

Getting There & Away Karain is difficult to access by public transport. With your own car you can visit Termessos and Karain in the same day trip; a taxi tour combining the two costs around US$30. Descending from Termessos, take the Karain road just outside the national park. After 1.4km the road forks; take either road, they rejoin at 4km. At 8km, turn left (there's a sign) and continue 3km to Karain.

Coming from Antalya on the highway to Burdur and Isparta, pass the road on the left to Korkuteli, Denizli and Muğla, and take the next road on the left marked for Yeşilbayır, Yeniköy and Karain.

Salda Gölü

If your itinerary takes you north from Termessos towards Denizli, you pass through Korkuteli and Tefenni, two undistinguished farming towns on the Anatolian plateau. But onward, near Yeşilova, is Salda Gölü, a beautiful lake with a few simple camp sites and restaurants with signs in German.

Kurşunlu Şelalesi

About 14km north-east of Antalya and 1km north of Aksu is Kurşunlu Şelalesi (meaning 'Leaded Waterfall'), a shady park set in a pine forest with a waterfall and pool. It's a good place to get away from the noise and activity of Turkish cities, except on weekends, when the city folk move here. Opening hours are from 8 am to 5.30 pm; admission costs US$0.60.

Bring a picnic (there are lots of tables), then follow the *geziyolu* (scenic trail) down the steps to the pool and the falls, actually a number of rivulets cascading down a rock wall festooned with ferns, vines and moss.

Perge

Perge, 15km east of Antalya and 2km north of the town of Aksu, is one of those very ancient towns. Greek colonists came here after the Trojan War and probably displaced even earlier inhabitants. The city prospered under Alexander the Great and the Romans but dwindled under the Byzantines before it was abandoned. The ruins are open from 7.30 am to 7 pm from May to October and from 8 am to 5.30 pm in winter; admission is US$2.50.

As you walk around, recall the grand Tomb of Plancia Magna, the city's great benefactress, which you should have seen in the Antalya Museum. Also, note the fine detailed carving in the marble throughout the city.

The great **theatre** and **stadium** are quite impressive, but Perge is famous for its huge **Roman and Hellenistic gates** and an impressive **colonnaded street**. The Roman gate is oddly off axis, so walk through it to the Hellenistic Triumphal Gate to get the full effect of the city's original plan: looking through the Hellenistic Triumphal Gate down the colonnaded street.

The **southern baths** are quite impressive, as is the **agora** with the odd circular structure at its centre. At the **acropolis**, on a rise behind the other ruins, there is nothing much to see. For a fine view of the site climb to the top of the theatre.

Getting There & Away A visit to Perge can be included in the trip eastward to As-

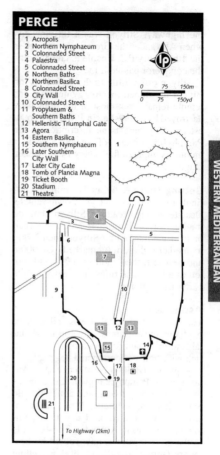

PERGE

1 Acropolis
2 Northern Nymphaeum
3 Colonnaded Street
4 Palaestra
5 Colonnaded Street
6 Northern Baths
7 Northern Basilica
8 Colonnaded Street
9 City Wall
10 Colonnaded Street
11 Propylaeum & Southern Baths
12 Hellenistic Triumphal Gate
13 Agora
14 Eastern Basilica
15 Southern Nymphaeum
16 Later Southern City Wall
17 Later City Gate
18 Tomb of Plancia Magna
19 Ticket Booth
20 Stadium
21 Theatre

To Highway (2km)

pendos and Side, doing it all in a day if you're pressed for time. Leave early in the morning.

Dolmuşes leave for Aksu from the Antalya otogar and Vatan Kavşağı. Ride the 13km east from Antalya to Aksu and the turn-off for Perge, then walk (20 to 25 minutes) or hitch the remaining 2km north to the ruins. You can include Perge in a taxi tour to Aspendos for US$40.

Sillyon

About 7km east of Perge and Aksu, a road on the left (north) is marked for Gebiz and

Sillyon. Set on a mesa usually visible from the highway, Sillyon was a thriving city when Alexander the Great came through in the 4th century BC. Unable to take the city, the conqueror passed it by.

Sillyon offers little to the casual visitor. Bits of the ruined theatre, gymnasium and temple remain, but most of the ruins were destroyed by a landslide in 1969. The greatest curiosity here is an inscription in the Pamphylian dialect of ancient Greek, a unique example of this otherwise little-seen language.

Getting There & Away The ruins are difficult to reach without your own vehicle. Despite the sign reading 'Sillyon 8km' on the highway, it is further: 7.2km to a road on the right marked for Sillyon, then 2.2km to another right turn (unmarked). Go 900m and bear left, then another 100m, and turn left at a farm. The ruins are clearly visible 1km further along.

Aspendos

The land east of Antalya was called Pamphylia in ancient times. The Taurus Mountains form a beautiful backdrop to the coast, rich with fields of cotton and vegetables.

Aspendos (Belkis) lies 47km east of Antalya in the Pamphylian plain. Go as far as the Köprü Çayı stream, and notice the old Seljuk humpback bridge. Turn left (north) along the western bank of the stream, following the signs to Aspendos. The 4km ride to the great theatre is now sullied by bus-tour restaurants and all sorts of shops selling leather apparel, jewellery, carpets and the like. Better, simpler, cheaper restaurants serve you in the village just south of the site.

Aspendos is open from 8 am to 7 pm daily in summer and to 5.30 pm in winter; admission is US$3.50.

What you see here remains from Roman times, though the history of the settlement goes back to the Hittite Empire (800 BC). In 468 BC the Greeks and Persians fought a great battle here (the Greeks won, but not for long). Under the Romans, during the reign of Marcus Aurelius (AD 161–80), Aspendos got its theatre.

There are many fine Hellenistic and Roman theatres in Anatolia but the one at Aspendos is the finest of all. Built by the Romans, maintained by the Byzantines and Seljuks, it was restored after a visit by Atatürk. A plaque by the entrance states that when Atatürk saw the theatre he declared that it should be restored and used again for performances and sports.

Purists may question the authenticity of the restorations, but more than any other, the theatre at Aspendos allows the present-day visitor to see and feel a true classical theatre: its acoustics, its lighting by day and night, and how the audiences moved in and out. Don't miss it.

Facing the theatre from the car park, a path to the right of the theatre is marked for Theatre Hill, which takes you up above the theatre for the stunning view. Follow the 'Aqueduct' fork in the trail for a good look at the remains of the city's aqueduct and of the modern village to the left of it. You can also follow the unpaved road north for 1km for fine views of the aqueduct.

The ruins of the ancient city are extensive and include a stadium, agora and basilica, but they offer little to look at. Follow the aqueduct trail along the ridge to reach them.

Getting There & Away Minibuses going to Serik pick up passengers at the Vatan Kavşağı in Antalya (see Getting There & Away in the Antalya section). They'll drop you at the Aspendos turn-off, from which you can walk (45 minutes) or hitch the remaining 4km to the site. Taxis waiting at the highway junction will take you to the theatre for an outrageous US$5, or you can take a taxi tour from Antalya for US$40, perhaps stopping in Perge along the way.

Selge & Köprülü Kanyon

High in the mountains north of the lush Mediterranean littoral, 96km north-east of Antalya, a Roman bridge spans the picturesque canyon of the Köprü Irmağı (Bridge River). Above it, less than 12km away, are the ruins of the Roman city of Selge, scattered amid the stone houses of the Turkish village of Altınkaya in a forest of Mediterranean cypresses. The setting, high in the mountains, is spectacular, with rock formations reminiscent of south-western USA. The local people make their living cultivating wheat, corn, barley, apples, plums, chestnuts, walnuts and vetch for fodder.

Roman Selge was thought to have a population of about 20,000 at its peak, though how such a thriving city was sufficiently supplied with water in these arid mountains is something of a mystery. Selge was famous for storax, the balsam of the Asiatic liquidambar tree, which was highly prized for medicinal purposes and for use in perfumes. The city survived into Byzantine times.

Selge Ruins The vine-covered theatre rises dramatically behind the town. Though it is fairly well preserved, with only some rows of seats collapsed, the rest of the city is badly ruined. According to locals, the stage wall of the theatre stood intact until 1948, when it was felled by lightning. As you approach the theatre's left side, traces of the stadium are visible to the left. Climb up past the hamam to the agora. Not much remains, but the situation and views are satisfying. On a hill near the agora is a ruined church and, on a higher hill behind it, a temple of Zeus now completely ruined. Traces of the 2.5km of city walls are still visible.

Hiking Villagers can guide you on hikes up from Köprülü Kanyon along the original Roman road, about two hours up, or 1½ hours down, for about US$10 each way. They can also arrange mountain treks for groups to Bozburun Dağı (2504m) and other points in the Kuyucuk Dağları (Kuyucuk Range), with a guide, *katırcı* (muleteer) and *yemekçi* (cook) for about US$50 per day.

Canoe & Raft Trips Medraft (☎ 248 0083, fax 242 7118), Cumhuriyet Caddesi 76/6, Işık Apt, Antalya, operates daily multi-person raft and two-person inflatable 'canoe' trips in summer along the Köprü River in Köprülü Kanyon for US$55.

There's also Antalya Rafting (☎ 321 8631, fax 321 8233), Ali Çetinkaya Caddesi 107/4, Antalya.

The company's buses pick you up at your hotel in the morning and drive you to the river. You paddle about 15km downstream, stopping on the way for a picnic. Buses return you to your hotel late in the afternoon. The price per person is US$50 (half price for children under 13 years), which includes lunch, insurance, guides and equipment.

Places to Stay You can sleep on the concrete-slab porch of *Davut Çevik's house*, which acts as a drinks stand, for US$1 or US$1.50, if you have your own bedding. By the time you visit there may be a few spartan rooms for rent, but Altınkaya will not develop in a hurry because there is a shortage of water; the village's meagre supply is now brought from many kilometres away.

Otherwise, stay at one of the pensions about 15km below on the western bank of the river, *Selge Pension* or *Kanyon Pension*.

Getting There & Away Köprülü Kanyon and Selge are included in some tours run from Antalya, Side and Alanya for about US$25 per person. If you'd rather do it independently, the one daily minibus departs from Altınkaya in the morning for Serik (1½ hours, US$4) on the Antalya-Alanya highway, returning to Altınkaya in the evening. Thus you must plan to spend the night in the mountains, or haggle for a return fare, if you take the minibus.

With your own vehicle, you can make the visit in half a day, though it deserves a lot more time. About 5km east of the Aspendos road (48km east of Antalya) along the main highway, a paved road on the left (north) is marked for Beşkonak, Selge and Köprülü Kanyon Milli Parkı (Bridge Canyon National Park).

The road is paved and travelling is fast for the first 33km. Then, about 4km before the town of Beşkonak, the road divides, with the left fork marked for Altınkaya, the right for Beşkonak. If you take the Altınkaya road along the river's western bank, you'll pass Medraft Outdoor camp, Öncü Turizm Air Raft camp, Selge Restaurant & Pension, and Kanyon Restaurant & Pension, at the river's edge. About 11km from the turn-off is the graceful old arched Oluk bridge, an Ottoman work.

If instead you follow the road through Beşkonak, it's 6.5km from that village to the canyon and the Oluk bridge. The un-paved road on the western bank of the river marked for Altınkaya or Zerk, the modern Turkish names for Selge, climbs 11.7km from the bridge to the village through ever more dramatic scenery.

Eastern Mediterranean Turkey

Around Side and Alanya are some of Turkey's most built-up stretches of coast. Further development eastwards has been restricted by the soaring Taurus Mountains which plough right down to the cliff edges, squeezing out everything but the road. But wherever the land lies low and flat, you'll find developments of modern holiday homes. The resorts at Anamur and Kızkalesi have grown up rapidly around stretches of beach with interesting ruins.

The far eastern end of the coast is heavily industrialised and the cities of Mersin (İçel), Adana and İskenderun offer little; agriculture, commerce and shipping rather than tourism are their *raison d'être*. Cut inland, however, and you can explore relatively little visited Hittite and Roman sites at Karatepe, Anavarza and Hierapolis-Castabala.

Things brighten up south of İskenderun, with the Arab influence getting stronger with each kilometre. Antakya, the ancient Antioch, is not a beautiful city but does have a couple of gems (the museum and the cave-church of St Peter) that are well worth pausing for.

A good road runs all the way along the coast from Antalya to Antakya and then down to the Syrian border, and there are airports at Antalya, to the west, and Adana, to the east. If you want to combine a trip to Turkey with one to Northern Cyprus, there are daily boats and hydrofoils from Taşucu, near Silifke, and Mersin, as well as more sporadic services from Alanya and Anamur in high summer.

SİDE

☎ 242 • pop 18,000

Once upon a time Side (**see**-deh) was a small Turkish village with a fine sand beach on either side of it and some wonderful Hellenistic ruins. Legend even had it that Cleopatra and Mark Antony had chosen it as the spot for a romantic tryst. Unfortunately the world soon wised up to Side's potential and these days first impressions are not nearly so

HIGHLIGHTS

- Admiring the magnificent mosaics in the Antakya Arkeoloji Müzesi
- Visiting the off-the-beaten-track archaeological sites at Seleukeia, Uzuncaburç and Anavarza
- Enjoying the views from the Kale in Alanya
- Wading through wild flowers at Anamurium in spring
- Taking the boat to Northern Cyprus from Taşucu
- Having lunch beside a waterfall at Harbiye (Daphne)

Adana to Antakya p459

Eastern Mediterranean Turkey p430-1

Side p432
Alanya p435
Mersin (İçel) p452
Adana p456
Silifke p446
Antakya (Hatay) p465
Anamur p441

MEDITERRANEAN SEA

CYPRUS

SYRIA

EASTERN MEDITERRANEAN

alluring as you step into a tractor-drawn, advertisement-bedecked *tramvay* (tram) to be hauled down to a main street lined with shops selling jewellery, carpets and lurid pink leopard-print leather jackets.

But first impressions can be deceptive. Dive down the side streets to escape the touts and you'll find the sort of small family-run pensions that Alanya has so completely lost, along with enough ruins to keep you happy for a few days. Traditional village life continues in the midst of all the hotels and shops, the beaches are as good as ever, and you're never far from a meal or a drink.

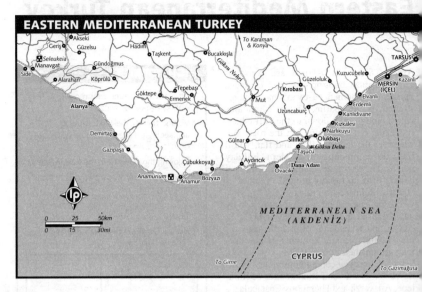

EASTERN MEDITERRANEAN TURKEY

History

No one knows where Side got its name, though it probably means 'pomegranate' in some ancient Anatolian language. The site was colonised by Aeolians (a Hellenic people) around 600 BC but by the time Alexander the Great swept through, the inhabitants had abandoned much of their Greek culture and language.

Many of Side's great buildings were raised with the profits of piracy and slavery, which flourished under the Greeks, only to be stopped when the city came under Roman control. After that, Side managed to prosper from legitimate commerce; under the Byzantines it was still large enough to rate a bishop. The 7th-century Arab raids diminished the town, which was dead within two centuries. During the late 19th century it had another brief flowering under Ottoman rule.

Orientation & Information

Side is set on a promontory, 3km south of the east-west highway. The road to the town is littered with trashy signs and dotted with hotels; it then passes the museum, continues under an arch and winds around the theatre. Vehicle access is tightly controlled and if you're driving, you'll almost certainly have to park (for a fee) in the car park outside the village, before the ruins.

The main street, Liman Caddesi, cuts straight through the village to the harbour, which is fronted by a bust of Atatürk with a lion and lioness in front of it. On either side of the promontory are small beaches, although the main beach extends to the west.

The otogar is past the archaeological zone and the way to the village is not clearly indicated. Follow signs for the tramvay and you'll find the main road. Turn left if you want to walk, or board the tramvay for US$0.25.

The tourist office (☎ 753 1265, fax 753 2657) is inconveniently positioned about 800m from the village centre, on the road in from Manavgat.

The Side Internet Cafe on Nergis Caddesi costs US$1.60 per hour.

The Ruins

One reason why it makes sense to stay in the village proper is that Side's impressive ruins are just a short walk away. Look first at the **theatre**, one of the largest in Anatolia, with 15,000 seats. Originally constructed during

Hellenistic times, it was enlarged under the Romans. At the time of writing it was closed for restoration. Locals will try and persuade you to clamber up the walls, which is probably not a good idea.

Next to the theatre and across the road from the museum is the **agora**, with many columns still standing. The **museum**, established in the old Roman baths, has an excellent small collection of statuary and reliefs. Opening hours are from 8 am to noon and 1 to 5 pm daily except Monday; admission costs US$2.50.

To the east, between these buildings and the Hellenistic city walls, is a Byzantine **basilica** and the so-called **colonnaded street**, with some evocative foundations of Byzantine houses with mosaic floors. At the edge of the eastern beach, overlooked by snooty tourist camels, is another **agora**.

At the southern tip of the point of land upon which Side stands are two ruined buildings, the **Temples of Apollo and Athena**, which date from the 2nd century AD. Some of the columns were re-erected by an American woman who had come here many times with her husband and wanted to commemorate him. Restoration work continues. They have something of the atmosphere of Cape Sounion, near Athens in Greece, and are especially magical at dusk.

Later, the Byzantines constructed an immense basilica over and around the temple sites and parts of the walls remain. Wandering among these marble remains at dusk is one of the most atmospheric things to do here.

Boat Trips
As well as the usual sailing and swimming excursions from the waterfront, you can take a cruise from Side to Manavgat to see the Manavgat waterfalls on Monday, Wednesday and Friday, leaving at 10 am and returning at about 5 pm. The cost is US$14 per person, including lunch. The Monday trip allows time to explore Manavgat's market too.

Places to Stay
Side is one of those places where many hotels and pensions (and restaurants) change hands every year. The town is slow to get going at the start of the tourist season, but although you may find many pensions closed or only half-heartedly open, April is a good time to visit since prices will be roughly half what they are in summer and the crowds won't be so oppressive. October is much the same as April. From June to September you may have trouble finding a room so try and arrive early in the day. Only a few places stay open year-round.

Places to Stay – Budget
There are small, simple *camping grounds* on the roads going to motels on the western beach; names and management seem to change from year to year.

In the side streets of the village proper, there are dozens of small pensions to choose from. In general, you'll pay US$5 to US$10 for a bed out of peak season, and up to twice that in high season (July to mid-September). Look for signs reading 'Boş Oda Var' (Empty Room Available).

On Menekşe Caddesi (commonly known as Cami Caddesi) *Pettino's Pension* (☎ 753 3608) is an Australian-Turkish owned enterprise which offers rooms in a cheerfully

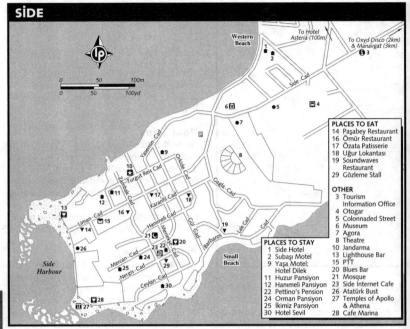

SİDE

PLACES TO EAT
14 Paşabey Restaurant
16 Ömür Restaurant
17 Özata Patisserie
18 Uğur Lokantası
19 Soundwaves Restaurant
29 Gözleme Stall

OTHER
3 Tourism Information Office
4 Otogar
5 Colonnaded Street
6 Museum
7 Agora
8 Theatre
10 Jandarma
13 Lighthouse Bar
15 PTT
20 Blues Bar
21 Mosque
23 Side Internet Cafe
26 Atatürk Bust
27 Temples of Apollo & Athena
28 Cafe Marina

PLACES TO STAY
1 Side Hotel
2 Subaşı Motel
9 Yaşa Motel; Hotel Dilek
11 Huzur Pansiyon
12 Hanımeli Pansiyon
22 Pettino's Pension
24 Orman Pansiyon
25 İkimiz Pansiyon
30 Hotel Sevil

decorated house for just US$5 per person with breakfast. All rooms have showers, there's a kitchen for guests to use, Internet access costs US$0.80 per hour, and they rent scooters for US$15 per day.

Hotel Sevil *(☎ 753 2041, fax 753 3186)* on Zambak Caddesi has 15 very clean wood-panelled rooms with air-con for US$20.

İkimiz Pansiyon *(☎ 753 23 22)* on Mercan Caddesi is a quiet, green retreat with eight bungalows for US$12.50 for two people. There's an amenities block in one corner of the lush garden.

Orman Pansiyon *(☎ 753 5024)* close by on Mercan Caddesi is basic but cheap, with a very laid-back manager and simple rooms in a two-storey concrete building for US$8/12 for singles/doubles without breakfast.

More pensions can be found just off Liman Caddesi on the right-hand side as you walk towards the waterfront. One promising one, designed in wood and overlooking a pleasant garden is ***Yaşa Motel*** *(☎ 753 4024,*

fax 753 2299) in Turgut Reis Caddesi. Beds here can cost as little as US$6 each. Next door the ***Hotel Dilek*** *(☎ 753 1084)* has rooms for between US$7.50 and US$10 per person.

Continue down Turgut Reis Caddesi to ***Hanımeli Pansiyon*** *(☎/fax 753 1789)*, a beautifully restored stone house, surrounded by gardens scented by jasmine. It's quiet, full of character, and reasonably priced at US$24 a double with shower and breakfast. ***Huzur Pansiyon*** opposite is considerably cheaper at US$16 per double.

Places to Stay – Mid-Range

There are several comfortable hotels on the western beach. One of the best is ***Side Hotel*** *(☎ 753 3824, fax 753 4671)*. Close to the village, with a nice patio restaurant and pool, it charges US$24/36 for singles/doubles, including breakfast and dinner.

Inland from the Side Hotel is the comfortable, modern ***Subaşı Motel*** *(☎ 753 1047, fax 753 1855)*, a 15-minute walk from the village. The rooms have balconies facing east and west to take full advantage of sunrises and sunsets. Doubles with bath cost from US$27, including breakfast.

The western beach is lined with three- and four-star hotels catering for the package-holiday market.

Places to Stay – Top End

There are also scores of four- and five-star hotels along the western beach. One of the best is the five-star *Hotel Asteria* (☎ 753 1830, fax 753 1830), set on a rise overlooking the beach about 3km north-east of the village proper. Its extensive grounds have swimming pools, sunning areas, bars and cafes, and lots of equipment for water sports. Each comfortable room has a small terrace; ask for one with an eastern sea view. Singles/doubles start at US$80/100, including breakfast.

Places to Eat

Many pensions have cooking facilities. At the larger hotels you may be required to buy at least two meals a day, so the food problem is solved whether you like it or not. As for cheap restaurants, you need to duck down the backstreets of the village proper and look for the smaller, simple places like *Uğur Lokantası*, where you can still get a kebap for US$4. There's a *gözleme stall* on Nergis Caddesi near the corner with Menekşe Caddesi.

The waterfront restaurants are more atmospheric but also more expensive; again most of them change hands every year. It makes sense to inquire carefully what you're getting for your money. A portion of grilled fish should cost between US$6 and US$8.

On Barbaros Caddesi, *Soundwaves Restaurant* is a long-established restaurant with Turkish-Australian management, which keeps its menu lively with dishes like garlic prawns and onion steak to top up the Turkish standards. The woody pine interior offers soft lighting and classical music. Full meals cost from US$10 to US$20 per person, including drinks.

If you have a sudden yearning for pork, *Ömür Restaurant* on Zambak Caddesi rather bravely touts a menu with all sorts of non-Islamic dishes for around US$5 per person.

Liman Caddesi has several mouth-watering patisseries. Look in particular for *Özata* which serves cakes downstairs and fast food on a terrace upstairs.

Entertainment

Side has more than its share of bars, including the large *Lighthouse* at the far end of the promontory which also has a dance floor. Side's biggest disco is *Oxyd*, 3km from town, a bizarre place with an exterior like a West African mosque and a science fiction interior. On a good night it's on a par with any club in Turkey. Entry is US$7, a beer costs US$3, and a taxi out there about US$8.

Atmospheric places in town to go for a drink include the *Blues Bar*, built around the shell of an old village house on Menekşe Caddesi, and *Cafe Marina* with lots of pieces of statuary and a platform overlooking the Temple of Apollo.

In Liman Caddesi, look in at *Paşabey Restaurant*, a masterwork of kitsch with mock travertine pools, where it could be fun to have a drink on a sunny evening.

Getting There & Away

In summer, Side has direct bus services to Ankara, İzmir and İstanbul. Otherwise, the numerous buses and dolmuşes which run between Antalya (US$3, 1¼ hours, 65km) and Alanya (US$3, 1¼ hours, 63km) will drop you right in Side or at least in Manavgat, the town on the highway. From Manavgat dolmuşes travel the 4km down to the shore every 20 minutes (US$0.50). There are no direct buses from Side to Konya, but you can catch one in Manavgat (US$10, 5½ hours, 296km) or at the junction with D695 (the road up to Konya), 12km east of Manavgat.

AROUND SİDE

The coast east and west of Side is package-holiday territory, filled by charter flights landing at Antalya's airport. About 12km east of Manavgat (50km west of Alanya) the D695 highway heads north-west up to the Anatolian plateau and Konya (280km) via Akseki, curving through some beautiful

EASTERN MEDITERRANEAN

mountain scenery. The once-narrow, curvy road has been greatly improved and is now the preferred route to Konya from this part of the coast. The route via Antalya and Isparta takes seven hours from Side.

About 6km to the north and east of Side, **Manavgat** is a commercial town with a thriving Monday market, worth visiting in the unlikely event that you couldn't find exactly the right pink leather jacket in Side. The otogar is immediately to the west of the bridge in the main street and, except at the height of summer, you'll have to come here from Side to connect with bus services to Antalya, Alanya, Konya and the lakes.

Walk through the otogar to get to the Manavgat River and you'll find boats waiting to run you upriver to Manavgat's two waterfalls. An 80-minute round trip costs US$6 per person, providing there are at least four people.

About 4km north of Manavgat is **Manavgat Şelalesi**, a horseshoe-shaped waterfall on the Manavgat River, with teahouses, snack shops and restaurants. Although it's a terrible tourist trap, with camels in straw hats, monkeys and donkeys lined up for photographs, it's also a pleasant place to have lunch on a hot summer day. Admission costs US$0.40, and a meal of şiş kebap, salad and a cold drink will cost you US$6. A dolmuş from Manavgat costs US$0.50.

About 2km north of the waterfall the road crosses a bridge over a stream. To the left is a fine old five-arched **Ottoman bridge** built next to a bastion which appears to be much older. Another 1km along on the left are the remains of the **Roman aqueduct** which brought water from Dumanlı to Side.

About 2km past the Ottoman bridge a road on the left is signposted 7km for **Seleukeia**. Follow it through the village of Şıhlar, with many old fieldstone houses, some with bits of columns incorporated into the walls. Take the road to the right opposite the minaret. It's over 3km uphill to the ruins along an increasingly rough track, which may be impassable for low-slung cars at some times of the year. The walk is pleasant provided you bring plenty of water. The last place to buy a drink is in Şıhlar.

The ruins, scattered amid soughing pines in a beautiful and easily defensible hilltop location, include baths, a necropolis, a bouleuterion (place of assembly), a temple and many unidentified buildings, all badly ruined. Most impressive is the large market hall with a ruined hamam to one side, but really you could come here as much for the natural beauty of the site, where you pick your way over pine cones with only birdsong as an accompaniment.

For years this was believed to be the Seleukeia in Pamphylia which was founded during Hellenistic times, but the recent discovery of an inscription in both Greek and the language of ancient Side (which predated Alexander the Great) makes it more likely that the ruins are of the city of Lyrbe. For the time being the signs are sticking with Seleukeia.

If you don't have your own transport, taxi drivers wait both at the otogar and across the bridge in Manavgat to run you up, with a stop at the waterfall thrown in. Expect to pay US$15 for the return trip.

ALANYA
☎ 242 • pop 200,000

There's evidence of people living in the Alanya area as far back as the Palaeolithic period. The Romans and Byzantines also settled it, but present-day Alanya is really the handiwork of the Seljuk Turks who stamped their mark so firmly on the hilltop promontory. The Seljuks built a powerful empire, the Sultanate of Rum (Rome), which thrived from 1071 to 1243. Its capital was in Konya, but its primary port was Alanya.

Like Side, Alanya occupies a point of land flanked by two great sweeping beaches. Once a sleepy agricultural, fishing and tourist town, it has grown beyond all recognition since the late 1980s. A town with a winter population of 200,00 has to cope with three times that number in summer. With a wide swathe of sandy beach stretching 22km east from the town, Alanya is a Marmaris clone with a similar clutter of high-rise towers and resort hotels, lots of carpet-shop touts and high prices. It's big with Scandinavian and German package holiday groups.

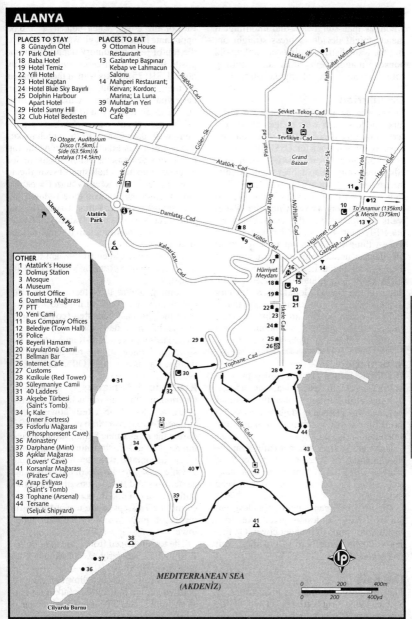

ALANYA

PLACES TO STAY
8 Günaydın Otel
17 Park Otel
18 Baba Hotel
19 Hotel Temiz
22 Yili Hotel
23 Hotel Kaptan
24 Hotel Blue Sky Bayırlı
25 Dolphin Harbour
     Apart Hotel
29 Hotel Sunny Hill
32 Club Hotel Bedesten

PLACES TO EAT
9 Ottoman House
     Restaurant
13 Gaziantep Başpınar
     Kebap ve Lahmacun
     Salonu
14 Mahperi Restaurant;
     Kervan; Kordon;
     Marina; La Luna
39 Muhtar'ın Yeri
40 Aydoğan
     Café

OTHER
1 Atatürk's House
2 Dolmuş Station
3 Mosque
4 Museum
5 Tourist Office
6 Damlataş Mağarası
7 PTT
10 Yeni Cami
11 Bus Company Offices
12 Belediye (Town Hall)
15 Police
16 Beyerli Hamamı
20 Kuyularönü Camii
21 Bellman Bar
26 Internet Cafe
27 Customs
28 Kızılkule (Red Tower)
30 Süleymaniye Camii
31 40 Ladders
33 Akşebe Türbesi
     (Saint's Tomb)
34 İç Kale
     (Inner Fortress)
35 Fosforlu Mağarası
     (Phosphoresent Cave)
36 Monastery
37 Darphane (Mint)
38 Aşıklar Mağarası
     (Lovers' Cave)
41 Korsanlar Mağarası
     (Pirates' Cave)
42 Arap Evliyası
     (Saint's Tomb)
43 Tophane (Arsenal)
44 Tersane
     (Seljuk Shipyard)

To Otogar, Auditorium
Disco (1.5km),
Side (63.5km) &
Antalya (114.5km)

Kleopatra Plaji

Atatürk
Park

Azaklar Sk.

Sugözü Cad.

Güler Sk.

Şevket Tekoş Cad.

Tevfikiye Cad.

Grand
Bazaar

Atatürk Cad.

Pınarı Cad.

Eczacılar Sk.

Yayla Yolu

Hacet Cad.

Fatih Sultan Mehmet Cad.

Bebek Sk.

Damlataş Cad.

Bostancı Cad.

Müftüler Cad.

Hükümet Cad.

To Anamur (135km)
& Mersin (375km)

Gazipaşa Cad.

Kültür Cad.

Kalearkası Cad.

Hürriyet
Meydanı

İskele Cad.

Tophane Cad.

Kale Cad.

MEDITERRANEAN SEA
(AKDENİZ)

Cilyarda Burnu

0   200   400m
0   200   400yd

EASTERN MEDITERRANEAN

At first sight those who want more from a holiday than sun, beach and multilingual menus might decide to press straight on. But the Kale district, with its crumbling old houses, magnificent ruins and inviting cafes, is worth a day of anyone's time.

Orientation

The otogar is on the coastal highway (Atatürk Caddesi) 3km west of the centre. It is served by city buses, which take you into town every half-hour for US$0.60.

Having gone from a small town to a 20km-long city almost overnight, Alanya has no real main square or civic centre. The centre – such as it is – lies inland (north) from the promontory on which the citadel walls sit. Scattered in this central area are the PTT, tourist office and museum. The closest thing to a main square is Hürriyet Meydanı, a nondescript traffic junction at the northern end of İskele Caddesi.

Development inland is limited by the slopes of the Taurus Mountains, so the city sprawls east and west along the coast. The ranks of beach hotels barely thin out until you reach the districts of Mahmutlar and Kargıcak, 15km east of Alanya's centre.

Information

The tourist office (☎ 513 1240, fax 513 5436), Çarşı Mahallesi, Kalearkası Caddesi, is at the north-western foot of the promontory, near the Damlataş Mağarası (Cave). It has little to offer other than maps and brochures.

There are several Internet cafes near the Hotel Kaptan, on İskele Caddesi. You'll be charged US$1 for an hour on the terminals, with coffee and fast food on offer to keep you going.

The area between Atatürk Caddesi and Şevket Tekoş Caddesi is given over to a vast bazaar, some of it under cover. On Friday villagers come here to sell their fruit and vegetables.

The Kale

Alanya's most exciting historical site is, of course, the Kale (Fortress) on top of the promontory. It's 3km to the top, so it's best to take transport up and save the walking for coming down, when you'll be able to appreciate the splendid views. City buses to the top of the promontory depart from opposite the tourist office every hour on the hour (US$0.25). Taxis wait at the bottom of all the approach roads (and halfway up in case you think you can't make it); they charge US$6 to run you to the top.

The ancient city was enclosed by a rambling wall (dating from 1226) which makes its way all around the peninsula. At the top is the **Ehmedek Kapısı**, which was the major gateway into the enclosure. From the **İç Kale** (inner fort or keep) you get a panoramic view of the peninsula, walls, town and great expanses of coastline backed by the blue Taurus Mountains. Inside you'll find ruins of a Byzantine church, cisterns and storerooms.

The İç Kale is open from 8 am to 7 pm daily. Admission costs US$3, or US$2 for students.

Coming down, look for a sign on the right which cuts slightly inland to what was once the Ottoman **bedesten** (covered market) and is now the Club Hotel Bedesten (see Places to Stay – Mid-Range later in this section). Beside it, the red-brick **Süleymaniye Camii** is another Ottoman work.

Kızılkule & Tersane

Overlooking the harbour is the five-storey, octagonal Kızılkule (Red Tower), constructed by a Syrian Arab architect in 1226 during the reign of the Seljuk sultan, Alaeddin Keykubad I. Now restored to its former glory, it contains a somewhat dull ethnographic museum with lots of old carpets and camel bags and translations of verse by the 13th-century Turkish poet Yunus Emre. Climb the 78 steps to the top of the battlements for fine views of the harbour and the town.

The tower is open from 8 am to noon and 1.30 to 5.30 pm daily except Monday; admission is US$1.70.

Afterwards, you can follow the sea walls until you come to the old Seljuk *tersane* or shipyard (1228). The views are some of Alanya's best.

Atatürk's House

While Atatürk was president of the republic, he spent the night of 18 February 1935 in a house on Azaklar Sokak, off Fatih Sultan Mehmet Caddesi. His stay was of little historical importance, but the owner of the house, Mr Rifat Azakoğlu, left it to be preserved as a museum. The downstairs rooms are filled with so-so photographs illustrating the great man's life. Upstairs, however, the rooms are furnished to show how a well-to-do Alanya family lived during the 1930s.

Opening hours are from 8.30 am to noon and 1.30 to 5.30 pm Monday to Friday; admission costs US$1.25. It'll be surprising if you don't have the house to yourself.

Museum

Alanya has a tidy little museum on the western side of the peninsula, near the tourist office. Exhibits span the ages from Old Bronze through Greek and Roman to Ottoman. Don't miss the Ethnology Room at the back, with a fine assortment of kilims (woven mats), *cicims* (embroidered mats), Turkish carpets, wood- and copper-inlay work, gold and silver and beautifully illuminated religious books.

The museum is open from 8 am to noon and 1.30 to 5.30 pm daily except Monday; admission costs US$1.25.

Damlataş Mağarası

About 100m towards the sea from the tourist office is the entrance to Damlataş Mağarası (Dripping-Stone Cave) noted for its 95% humidity and constant high temperatures. The stalactites do indeed drip, encouraged by the heavy-breathing exhalations of troops of curious tourists. The humid atmosphere is supposed to be good for asthma sufferers, but it's hardly a world-class thrill.

The cave is open from 10 am to 7 or 8 pm daily; admission costs US$1.25.

Hamams

The Beyerli Hamamı beside the mosque in Hürriyet Meydanı is open daily until midnight. It's for women only on Tuesday from 9am to 5 pm. A wash with massage costs US$18, or you can wash yourself for US$6.

Beaches

Alanya's sandy beaches are perfectly good, although if you're staying east or west of the centre they're fronted by a busy main road. Kleopatra Plajı (Cleopatra's Beach) is accessible on foot from the western side of the promontory, behind the tourist office. It's sandy and more secluded – at least outside high summer – and has fine views of the citadel up above.

Boat Trips

Every day at 11 am boats leave from in front of Gazipaşa Caddesi for excursions around the promontory. Tours approach several caves, including Aşıklar Mağarası (Lovers' Cave), Korsanlar Mağarası (Pirates' Cave) and Fosforlu Mağarası (Phosphorescent Cave), as well as Kleopatra Plajı (Cleopatra's Beach) on the western side of the promontory. The cost per person for a five-hour voyage is US$18, including lunch.

Places to Stay

Alanya has hundreds of hotels and pensions, almost all of them designed for and catering to group visitors and those in search of *apart-otels* (self-catering flats). If you want to stay for more than a day or so it's worth checking the package holiday brochures at home first since tours inclusive of flights and transfers may well be cheaper than booking privately. In any case most of these places will be block-booked by tour operators throughout the summer.

On your own, you really need to arrive by early afternoon at the latest to be sure of a bed in one of the few places still catering for individual travellers.

Places to Stay – Budget

In high season your best bet may be to go with a pension owner who approaches you at the otogar. However, make sure you know how far from the centre you'll be staying before going with them. There are still a handful of small hotels and pensions around Hürriyet Meydanı which rent rooms for less than US$20 a double. On the whole these are shabby places, too old-fashioned to be snapped up by the tour companies.

EASTERN MEDITERRANEAN

As you head down İskele Caddesi the first you'll come to is **Baba Hotel** (☎ *513 1032, İskele Caddesi 6*), where mundane rooms cost US$6.60/10.

More expensive but infinitely preferable is the **Hotel Temiz** (☎ *513 1016, İskele Caddesi 12*), a few steps further along towards the Kızılkule. Comfortable singles/doubles with showers cost US$10/20. Rooms at the front have balconies; for a better night's sleep ask for one at the back. This place is used by groups in high season.

A little further along and upstairs on the right is **Yili Hotel** (☎ *513 1017*), which advertises itself as a hostel and does indeed offer the most basic of waterless rooms for US$6 per person. There's a pleasant breakfast terrace.

Günaydın Otel (☎ *513 1943, Kültür Caddesi 26/B*), one long block inland towards the Damlataş Mağarası, provides reasonably comfortable accommodation for US$10/20.

Places to Stay – Mid-Range

Snazziest of the centrally placed hotels along İskele Caddesi is the three-star **Hotel Kaptan** (☎ *513 4900, fax 513 2000*), which charges US$46/60 for modern rooms with TVs, minibars, air-con and spotless bathrooms. Rooms at the back are cheaper at US$32/43.

A block closer to the Kızılkule is **Hotel Blue Sky Bayırlı** (☎ *513 6487, fax 513 4320*), with shower-equipped rooms for US$25/39, many with nice balconies overlooking the town and the bay. If you'd like to rent an apartment, the **Dolphin Harbour Apart Hotel** (☎ *513 2996, fax 512 2835, İskele Caddesi 88*) charges US$32 to US$40 per day.

On Hürriyet Meydanı at the northern end of İskele Caddesi, **Park Otel** (☎ *513 1675, fax 513 2589, Eski PTT Caddesi 6*) charges US$25 a double for rooms with the luxury of a swimming pool.

The three-star **Hotel Sunny Hill** (☎ *511 1211, fax 512 3893, Çarşı Mahallesi, Damlataş Mevkii, Sultan Alaaddin Caddesi 3*) clings to the hillside above the tourist office, on the Kale bus route. It boasts a beautiful swimming pool, terrace restaurant and

bar and comfortable single/double rooms (some with views) for US$32/48, breakfast included.

Better still is **Club Hotel Bedesten** (☎ *512 1234, fax 513 7934*), higher up on the hill and created out of the old Ottoman covered market. Rooms are small and low-lit but this is a thoroughly atmospheric place to stay, with marvellous views from its rooftop restaurant and pool. There's even an echoing 12m-deep cistern underneath. Of course all this clocks up a rate of US$54 a double, including breakfast – worth it to stay in a completely different Alanya from the tacky one below. Any snags? Perhaps the call to prayer from the mosque next door.

Places to Eat

There's no danger of starving since every other building seems to serve food or drink of some description. The problem is trying to stay within a tight budget. Although they're vanishing fast, there are still a few small places to eat in the narrow streets of Alanya's bazaar, in the centre of town on the eastern inland side of the promontory. Look for signs saying *'İnegöl Köftecisi'*, and snap up *köfte* (grilled meatballs) and salad for around US$5. In fine weather, streetside tables are set up.

Many of these places are patronised by tourists, but if you search you may find one that has a mostly Turkish clientele. One such place is **Gaziantep Başpınar Kebap ve Lahmacun Salonu**, inland from the eastern end of the row of water-view restaurants. Head straight inland to the bazaar and you'll find the **Ravza** and **Şölen** restaurants where something like an İskender kebap and a cold drink will cost US$4. Another area worth exploring for cheap restaurants is behind the Kuyularönü mosque, off Hürriyet Meydanı.

The waterfront promenade has a string of restaurants with attractive terraces looking out towards the sea. **Mahperi Restaurant** has been serving meals here for more than 30 years. Seafood is the speciality, of course, but it also does a good chicken *şiş kebap* (skewered roast chicken) for US$5. **Kervan**, **Kordon**, **Marina** and **La Luna** are similar, with prices posted prominently.

For an escape from fish kebaps and schnitzel, walk along Kültür Caddesi to the **Ottoman House Restaurant**, which has specialities such as *beğendili kebap* (chunks of lamb on pureed aubergine), and *kağit kebap*, lamb cooked in special paper with green pepper, carrot and tomato, for around US$7 for each dish. You can eat these while you sit in the gardens of the attractive old wooden house.

The road up to the Kale is lined with small places to eat and drink, often serving *ayran* (a yogurt drink) and *gözleme* (Turkish pancakes). The higher you go, the nicer the places, partly because of the views and partly because of the surrounding gardens. Two especially good choices are **Aydoğan Café**, where you can sip a cold drink beneath wisteria, and **Muhtar'ın Yeri**, which has spectacular views.

At the entrance to the Damlataş Mağarası a **stall** serves piping hot gözleme for US$1.75 a portion.

Entertainment

Each district – indeed, each hotel – in this sprawling city has its own collection of bars, tavernas, discos and jazz clubs. The ones in the centre change ownership (and theme) frequently.

South of Gazipaşa Caddesi there's a cluster of disco bars, including **Bellman**, with an uninspired light show and relentlessly predictable tunes – Ricky Martin, Tom Jones and the mysteriously popular *Take My Breath Away* by 1980s hair disasters,

Berlin. Sunburned Nordic girls flirt with overheated Turkish boys while the bar rakes it in with beers for US$6. Out in the western outskirts, Alanya's most impressive disco is currently the **Auditorium** which has a stream running through the middle. A taxi back afterwards will cost about US$8.

Getting There & Away

Much of Alanya's bus traffic travels via Antalya and you may find yourself switching buses there. Compared with the rest of Turkey, traffic is sparse around the eastward 'bulge' of Anamur. Few buses originate in Alanya so you have to rely on passing buses having empty seats; make your departure arrangements as far in advance as possible. Also keep in mind that the road east is mountainous and curvy and takes a good deal longer to traverse than you might think from looking at the map. Nor is it good for anyone suffering from motion sickness.

Many local operators organise tours to the ruins along the coast west of Alanya and to Anamur. A typical tour to Aspendos, Side and Manavgat will cost around US$24 per person, while a village-visiting jeep safari into the Taurus Mountains will cost about US$20 per person.

Details of some of the main services are listed in the table; note that most services are less frequent outside summer.

Getting Around

Frequent dolmuşes shuttle along the coast, transporting passengers from the outlying

Services from Alanya's Otogar

destination	fare (US$)	time (hr)	distance (km)	daily services
Adana	12	10	440	8 buses
Anamur	5	3	135	several buses
Antalya	4	2	115	hourly buses
İstanbul	23	16	840	several buses
İzmir	15	12	660	via Antalya
Konya	9	6½	320	Akseki-Beyşehir route
Mersin (İçel)	10	8½	375	8 buses
Side	3	1¼	63	frequent buses and dolmuşes
Silifke	6.60	7	275	8 buses
Ürgüp	15	10	590	Akseki-Beyşehir-Konya route

hotel areas to the centre. Dolmuşes to the otogar (US$0.25) can be picked up in the bazaar, north of Atatürk Caddesi.

AROUND ALANYA

About 23km west of Alanya is İncekum (Fine Sand) and Avsallar, these days virtual extensions of Alanya with little to recommend them. At İncekum the *İncekum Orman İçi Dinlenme Yeri* (Fine Sand Forest Rest Area) has a camping ground in a pine grove near the beach.

About 13km west of Alanya notice the **Şarapsa Hanı**, a Seljuk caravanserai. Further west towards Side, there's another one, the **Alarahan**, accessible by a side road heading north for 9km.

Heading east towards Silifke (275km), the twisting, turning road is cut into the cliffs. Every now and then it passes through the fertile delta of a stream, planted with bananas (as at Demirtaş) or crowded with glass greenhouses. It's a long drive with few places to stop until you get to Anamur but the sea views and the cool pine forests are extremely beautiful.

This region was the ancient Cilicia, a somewhat forbidding part of the world because of the mountains. Anyone wanting to conquer Cilicia had to have a navy, as the only practicable transport was by sea. Pirates preyed on ships from the hidden coves along this stretch of coast. In the late 1960s the government completed the good road running east from Alanya, and since then tourism has grown rapidly.

ANAMUR

☎ 324 • pop 60,000

At the southernmost point along the Turkish Mediterranean coast, Anamur is a sprawling and architecturally uninspiring town but it does make a possible base for exploring the ruined Byzantine city of Anamurium and the wonderfully imposing Mamure Kalesi (Mamure Castle), which is impossible to miss as you sweep along the coast road. Due south of Anamur the İskele district has its own beach and all of the decent hotels, and there are a few places to stay near Mamure Kalesi too.

Orientation & Information

Anamur town centre lies to the north of the highway, 1km from the main square. The otogar is at the junction of the highway and the main street. The tourist office (☎ 814 3529) is on the first floor of the otogar; open 8 am to 12 pm and 1 to 5 pm Monday to Friday. Not much English is spoken but the staff try hard to help. If you need to get money you'll have to visit the PTT or the Türkiye İş Bankası ATM in the town centre.

To reach the beach at İskele, head east from the otogar and turn right (south) at the signs; the beach is 2km south of the highway and 4km from the main square.

Mamure Kalesi is 7km east of the town centre; the ruins of Anamurium are 8.5km west of the centre.

Anamurium

Approaching Anamur from the west or down from the Cilician mountains, the highway finally reaches some level ground and a straight section. At this point, before you reach Anamur itself, a road on the right points south towards the ruins. The road bumps 3km past fields and through the ruins to a dead end at the beach.

Founded by the Phoenicians, Anamurium flourished throughout the Roman period. Its Golden Age may have been around AD 250, after which it lost some importance. When the Arab armies stormed out of Arabia in the 7th century they raided and pillaged this coast, including Anamurium. Despite its mighty walls and remote location, the city fell. It never recovered from the devastation and no-one was interested in settling here afterwards.

Had new settlers come, they no doubt would have torn down these old buildings and used the cut stones to build their settlement. Anamurium escaped this destruction and survives as a sprawling Byzantine ghost town, with dozens of buildings perched on the rocky hillside above an unsullied pebble beach. Churches, aqueducts, houses and defensive walls stand silent and empty, their roofs caved in but their walls largely intact.

The **public baths** are well preserved, even retaining some wall decorations and mosaic

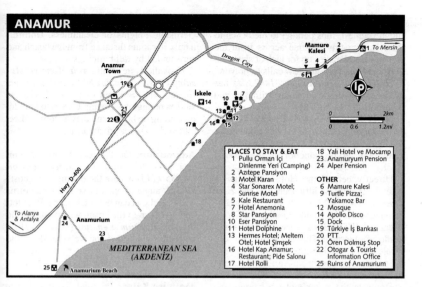

ANAMUR

MEDITERRANEAN SEA (AKDENİZ)

Anamurium Beach

PLACES TO STAY & EAT	
1 Pullu Orman İçi Dinlenme Yeri (Camping)	18 Yalı Hotel ve Mocamp
2 Azitepe Pansiyon	23 Anamuryum Pension
3 Motel Karan	24 Alper Pension
4 Star Sonarex Motel; Sunrise Motel	**OTHER**
5 Kale Restaurant	6 Mamure Kalesi
7 Hotel Anemonia	9 Turtle Pizza; Yakamoz Bar
8 Star Pansiyon	12 Mosque
10 Eser Pansiyon	14 Apollo Disco
11 Hotel Dolphine	15 Dock
13 Hermes Hotel; Meltem Otel; Hotel Şimşek	19 Türkiye İş Bankası
16 Hotel Kap Anamur; Restaurant; Pide Salonu	20 PTT
17 Hotel Rolli	21 Ören Dolmuş Stop
	22 Otogar & Tourist Information Office
	25 Ruins of Anamurium

floors. Many of the tombs in the vast **necropolis** have traces of decoration as well, but treasure-hunters have been hard at work, wreaking havoc as they go. You can also visit the ruins of a **theatre** and **stadium**, and make out the remains of shops too.

The site is particularly wonderful in spring when the air is sweet-scented and you can walk ankle-deep in wild flowers. Although there are signs forbidding picnicking, they're primarily aimed at stopping people lighting stoves and causing fires. It's unlikely anyone will object if you bring out your sandwich box. The beach here is coarse white sand and the water pristine, so you may want to make a day trip. The site is open 8 am to 8 pm daily; admission is US$2.50.

Mamure Kalesi

About 7km east of Anamur, the moat-girdled Mamure Kalesi, a maze of crenellated walls and towers with one foot in the Mediterranean, stands right beside the highway. The castle is made up of three courtyards, with a mosque in the western one.

There has been a fortress here since the Romans built one in the 3rd century AD, but the present structure dates from the time

of the crusades when the crusader rulers of Cyprus used it. Later it became a stronghold of the 13th-century Karamanoğlu emirs.

The Ottomans took over in the middle of the 14th century and kept the castle in good repair until their empire finally collapsed. Inside there's little to see except the mosque, built by the Karamanoğlu emirs in 1300 but restored many times, and flocks of grazing sheep, but the fortifications, with crenellated walls and towers, are as impressive as any in Turkey and you can walk right around them providing you don't mind steep drops.

The castle is open 8 am to 5 or 6 pm daily; admission is US$2.50.

Places to Stay

There are cheap pensions and camping grounds at İskele and near Anamurium and Mamure Kalesi.

İskele In the İskele (Harbour) district, there are numerous pensions and hotels along İnönü Caddesi, the main waterfront street, and even more lurking in various stages of completion on the road running down from the highway. The dolmuş drops you at the main intersection across from the Hotel Kap

Anamur. The main hotel and restaurant strip, İnönü Caddesi, runs parallel to the beach to the left. The tiny mosque across from the Hermes Hotel makes up for lack of size with very loud and very tuneless calls to prayer.

Hotel Kap Anamur (☎ 814 2374) has rather small singles/doubles with fan and bathroom for US$13/25.

Hotel Dolphine (☎ 814 3435, fax 814 1575, İnönü Caddesi 17) is quite cheap for the facilities it provides. There is a pleasant restaurant serving alcohol on the ground floor.

Directly behind the Hotel Dolphine is İskele's friendliest little pension, the *Eser Pansiyon* (☎ 814 2322), run by retired teachers. There are 10 rooms, costing US$7/10. Breakfast (US$1.30) is served on the vine-shaded roof terrace. They sometimes prepare meals with vegetables plucked straight from the garden. It is open from April until the end of October.

Opposite the waterfront tea garden, the prominent *Meltem Otel* (☎ 814 2316, fax 814 4814) and *Hotel Şimşek* (☎ 814 3978) look more expensive than they actually are. Rooms with bath cost US$10/16.

About 200m further on from the Hotel Dolphine the *Star Pansiyon* (☎ 816 4605), on İnönü Caddesi, is covered in morning glory, has a shady front terrace restaurant and a rooftop terrace with water views and shower-equipped rooms for US$12 a double.

At the end of İnönü Caddesi is the *Hotel Anemonia* (☎ 814 4000, fax 814 1443), an attractive mid-range hotel which has rooms for US$20/27.

The three-star *Hermes Hotel* (☎ 814 3950, fax 814 3995) on İnönü Caddesi was closed at the time of writing, but when it re-opens, prices are likely to be around the US$25/50 mark, including breakfast. The hotel has a swimming pool but is painfully close to the mosque.

Hotel Rolli (☎ 814 4978, fax 814 7821), in the Yalıevleri Mahallesi district, has 22 rooms, six with wheelchair access. It is popular with disabled tourists from Germany. The simple but attractive rooms cost US$25 per person for disabled people, US$17 per person in the other rooms. There's a bar and a swimming pool, and everything is kept to Germanic heights of cleanliness. Unfortunately it's some distance from the beach and surrounded by tall buildings.

Near the Hotel Rolli, *Yalı Hotel ve Mocamp* (☎ 814 3474, fax 814 1435) has space for tents (US$4) and caravans (US$6) as well as bungalows costing US$20 to US$24, depending on how many they accommodate, all overlooking a private beach.

Anamurium On the road to Anamurium you pass the family-run *Alper Pension* (☎ 835 1113), where the double room costs US$12, a bed in one of two four-bed dorms US$6, and you can use the kitchen. Bear left and go 650m to the beach where you'll find the *Anamuryum Pension* (☎ 835 1191), perfectly positioned for walking along the beach to the ruins. Camping costs US$4 per person, and simple double rooms US$10.

Mamure Kalesi The road east to Mamure Kalesi is dotted with pensions. The one major drawback, however, is the busy road in front. Noise is one inevitable snag. The other, for children especially, is the danger from traffic.

Two of the first places you'll come to are *Sunrise Motel* (☎ 827 1352) and the more basic *Star Sonarex Motel* (☎ 827 1219), both with scenic gardens and charging around US$12 a double with shower.

Even if the site, immediately beside a BP station, is not inspiring, *Motel Karan* (☎ 827 1027, fax 827 1349) has the great advantage of being on the beach side of the main road. Cheerful air-con rooms with balconies and bathrooms cost US$17 a double, or US$25 for a suite with a large living room, and look straight onto the beach. So, too, does the adjacent restaurant.

Next up is the very basic *Azıtepe Pansiyon* (☎ 827 1100) where bed and breakfast is available for just US$4 per person.

Finally 1.5km east of the castle, you'll find *Pullu Orman İçi Dinlenme Yeri*, a delightful, shady forest camping ground with an amenities block and a restaurant. The cost is US$5 for a tent, US$7 for a caravan. There's a fine sandy beach just below.

EASTERN MEDITERRANEAN

Places to Eat

Many pensions provide meals, as do the hotels and motels. Otherwise the best dining is along the waterfront in İskele, where the restaurant on the ground floor of the *Hotel Kap Anamur* serves fish dinners for US$8. There's also a small *pide salonu* in the same building, with *kıymalı pides* (meat pizzas) for US$1.

Turtle Pizza in front of the Hotel Dolphine is a popular local eatery, with pizza for US$6 and beers for US$1.30. In summer there are numerous simple cafes between İnönü Caddesi and the beach, serving tea, *pides* (Turkish pizzas), kebaps and gözleme.

Across the road from Mamure Kalesi there are several small restaurants which can do you simple meals of kebap and salad. One such spot is *Kale Restaurant*, almost opposite the gates, where a quick lunch shouldn't cost more than US$5.

Entertainment

In İskele there's the *Yakamoz Bar* next to Turtle Pizza, with all your favourite Turkish pop hits and beers for US$1.60. But the biggest joint in town is the *Apollo Disco*, the red castle on the road from Anamur town to İskele, open June to October. The DJs play a mix of Turkish and European dance music to get the open-air dance floor shaking. Entry costs US$8, beers US$3.

Getting There & Away

There are several buses daily in summer to Alanya (US$5, three hours, 135km) and Silifke (US$5, 3½ hours, 160km).

Getting Around

Anamur is spread out and tricky to get around without your own transport.

Dolmuşes to Ören leave from the road next to the otogar and can drop you off at the Anamurium turn-off on the main highway. Alternatively, you'll need to take a taxi from Anamur otogar or from İskele. Expect to pay about US$15 to go there and back, with an hour's waiting time – barely enough time to see the site highlights.

There are dolmuşes between İskele and Anamur centre every 30 minutes or so for US$0.25. Taxis want about US$8 to run you there.

East of Anamur the transport situation brightens. Frequent dolmuşes to Bozyazı leave the otogar and travel past the town centre hotels and out to Mamure Kalesi and the eastern beach.

AROUND ANAMUR
☎ 324

About 20km east of Anamur, you'll come to the town of **Bozyazı**, spread across a fertile alluvial plain backed by rugged mountains. Bozyazı manages several small pensions and some condominiums, as well as the two-star *Alinko Motel (☎/fax 851 3998)*, the four-star *Vivanco Hotel (☎ 851 4200, fax 851 2291)* and the shiny new three-star *Hotel Mamure (☎ 851 5400, fax 851 4604)* on the western outskirts.

East across the plain and clearly visible from miles around, is **Softa Kalesi**, impossibly perched on the rocks above the little hamlet of Çubukkoyağı. This castle, built by the Armenian kings who ruled Cilicia for a short while during the crusades, is now fairly ruined inside but the walls and location are mightily impressive. As you leave Bozyazı, a sign on the left points inland to the castle, but the road doesn't go all the way to the top.

About 75km from Anamur you come to **Aydıncık**. Although not perhaps the most exciting town, Aydıncık, with its greenhouses and forestry, does at least have the feel of a real town with a life beyond tourism. There's a small harbour with a *camp site* and small *pensions* and then the highway toils up into the mountains again.

If you'd like to climb into the mountains and see yet another medieval castle, turn left at Sipahili 3km south-west of Aydıncık and head up towards Gülnar (25km) for a look at the **Meydancık Kalesi**, which has stood here in one form or another since Hittite times.

TAŞUCU
☎ 324

Taşucu, the port of Silifke, lives for the ferries. Hotels put up travellers, while car ferries and hydrofoils take them to and fro across the sea. It's a working town rather

EASTERN MEDITERRANEAN

than a tourist resort – no carpet shops or leather emporia – yet the beach is quite nice and it definitely has a laid-back atmosphere. We liked the middle-aged man in tweed cap and woollen cardigan who, while riding along on his bicycle, suddenly decided to pull over and take a nap on the beach. He was still asleep five hours later, his bicycle lying where it fell.

Orientation & Information

The main square by the ferry dock accommodates a bust of Atatürk, the PTT, various banks, a customs house, assorted shipping offices, restaurants and a small museum of amphoras. It's one block south of the highway. The beach, backed by a waterfront street (Sahil Yolu) and several good pensions, stretches out east of the docks.

Places to Stay

There are some cheap places to stay on Atatürk Caddesi, the main highway. *Yuven Pansiyon* (☎ 741 4101) has clean, simple rooms for US$7 per person, US$8 with aircon. Triples cost US$15. Right next door, the *Hotel Konak* (☎ 741 2999, fax 741 6180) is a little smarter and a little more expensive (US$13/17 a single/double, including breakfast), with cool tiled floors.

Further along, *Hotel Fatih* (☎ 741 4125) has rooms with shower and balcony for US$13/20/25 a single/double/triple, though you can haggle them down out of season.

If you don't mind paying a bit more, *Lades Motel* (☎ 741 4008, fax 741 4258) also on Atatürk Caddesi, boasts a swimming pool and restaurant with fine harbour views. At US$25/32, rooms are a little pricey but they do share the views. Halls are decorated with kilims and there's a lot of information about the birdlife of the Göksu Delta.

A few hundred metres west of the Lades and designed to look like a giant ocean-going ship, the five-star *Taşucu Best Resort Hotel* (☎ 741 6300, fax 741 3005) is Taşucu's best by far, with stylish modern rooms overlooking a huge pool and the harbour. Expect to pay for the comfort, but not as much as the posted prices; you'll be quoted US$45/60 for half board if you ask.

A couple of other places are east of the otogar overlooking the harbour. The best is *Holmi Pansiyon* (☎ 741 2321, Sahil Caddesi 25), a spotlessly clean place with a large, pleasant restaurant on the ground floor, run by a German couple. The attractive rooms cost US$12.50/25. *Barış Pansiyon* (☎/fax 741 5378) next door is simpler and cheaper for US$10/17.

If you fancy a spot of sunbathing before you catch your ferry, a couple of other places face the pebble beach about 500m east of the docks. The family-run *Meltem Pansiyon* (☎ 741 4391, Sahil Caddesi 75) charges US$8 per person in rooms with sea-facing balcony, fridge and sink for washing clothes. The pleasant *Olba Cafe-Bar* is next door. Unfortunately the view along the coast is marred by a paper factory jutting out into the sea to the east.

Places to Eat

Denizkızı Restaurant, opposite the bust of Atatürk in the main square, is the locals' favourite for lunch and dinner, and is fairly cheap. Next to the otogar, *İstanbul Restaurant*, with its sea-view terrace, is popular with travellers waiting for the boat. The *100. Yıl Restaurant* on the main square is a bit more expensive, with full meals costing US$8 to US$12, but it's a pleasant place to come just for a drink. For the cheapest meals, pick up a pide at *Gaziantep Lahmacun ve Pide Salonu* for less than US$2.

Getting There & Away

There are frequent dolmuşes between Silifke and Taşucu, and good long-distance services from Silifke to major destinations.

Three companies run *feribotlar* (car ferries) and/or *ekspresler* (hydrofoils) between Taşucu and Girne (Kyrenia) in Northern Cyprus, selling tickets from offices in the main square. Hydrofoils are faster but the ride can be stomach-churning. Passenger tickets cost less on the car ferry, but the trip is longer (four hours rather than two). Provided your visa allows for multiple entries within its period of validity you shouldn't have to pay for a new one when you come back into Turkey. If you do need a new visa, expect long queues, so try and be off the boat early.

The best ferry company is Fergün Express (☎ 741 2323, fax 741 2802; in Girne ☎ 815 2344, fax 815 1989) which has a hydrofoil at 11 am and a car ferry leaving at midnight daily. The express service return from Girne runs daily at 9.30 am, while the car ferry's return is at 11 am. A one-way ticket on the express service costs US$23 and a return ticket will set you back US$42. On the car ferry, the passenger fare is US$19/33 (single/return); a car costs US$38.

Başak Denizcilik (☎ 741 2976, fax 741 6296; in Girne ☎ 815 6632, fax 815 8858) has a hydrofoil at 11.30 am and a car ferry at midnight, returning from Girne at 9 am and 12 pm, respectively. Hydrofoil tickets cost $24/34, while a passenger ticket on the car ferry costs US$19/32, plus US$38 for a car.

Hoca Bey Deniz Jeti (☎ 741 4874, fax 741 4876, Girne ☎ 815 9865) has a ferry which leaves Taşucu at 12 pm, returning from Girne at 9.30 am daily. Tickets cost US$23/41.

Getting Around

Frequent dolmuşes (US$0.30) run between Taşucu and Silifke's otogar. You can pick them up at the fuel station across the road from the otogar in Silifke or from the southern side of the bridge near the PTT.

SİLİFKE

☎ 324 • pop 50,000

Silifke was the ancient Seleucia, founded by Seleucus I Nicator in the 3rd century BC. Seleucus was one of Alexander the Great's most able generals and founder of the Seleucid dynasty which ruled Syria after Alexander's death.

The town's other claim to fame is that Emperor Frederick Barbarossa (1125–90) drowned in the river near here while leading his troops on the Third Crusade – an ignominious end for a soldier.

Silifke is a down-to-earth country town, an honest example of the 'real' Turkey. A striking castle dominates the town from a Taurus hillside, and there are some fascinating archaeological relics in the vicinity.

Orientation & Information

The otogar is near the junction of the highways to Alanya, Mersin and Konya, exactly 1km along İnönü Caddesi from the town centre. Halfway between the otogar and the town centre you pass the Temple of Jupiter.

The town is divided by the Göksu River, called the Calycadnus in ancient times. Most of the services, including the otogar, are on the southern bank of the river. Exceptions are the tourist office, Internet cafe and the bus stop for Uzuncaburç, which are on the northern bank. The stone bridge over the Göksu dates back to AD 78, and has been restored many times.

The useful tourist office (☎ 714 1151, fax 714 5328) is at Veli Gürten Bozbey Caddesi 6, a few steps north of Atatürk Caddesi and the Hotel Çadır. The staff speak some English, French and German. An excellent guidebook, *Silifke (Seleucia on Calycadnus) and Environs*, written by a retired director of

Sacrifice at the Bridge

Once a year the citizens of Silifke throw the lungs of slaughtered animals from the top of the stone bridge over the Göksu River. This gory custom is designed to prevent a repeat of the tragedy of the bride sealed in the bridge's foundations.

A legend tells that when the bridge was being built, the chief engineer was unable to fix the central pillar in the riverbed. He had sacrificed many goats and camels to appease the spirits, but to no avail. One day while pondering the problem he saw a black-eyed bride with henna on her hands coming to the river to collect water. A solution occurred to him. He grabbed the young woman and buried her alive in the masonry of the main pillar. Another version tells that the unfortunate woman was burned alive and her ashes buried in the pillar. Either way, the central pillar was secured and the bridge completed.

Once a year the terrified scream of a woman is said to be heard in Silifke, which is taken to be a demand for another human sacrifice. To appease the bloodthirsty spirits, the people of Silifke offer goats and camels instead.

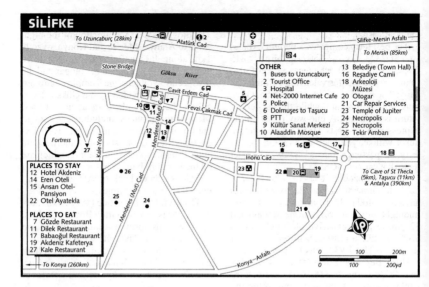

SİLİFKE

To Uzuncaburç (28km)
Atatürk Cad
Silifke-Mersin Asfaltı
To Mersin (85km)
Stone Bridge
Göksu River
Cavit Erdem Cad
Fevzi Çakmak Cad
Menderes (Mut) Cad
İnönü Cad
Fortress
Kale Yolu
Menderes (Mut) Cad
Konya Asfaltı
To Konya (260km)

OTHER
1 Buses to Uzuncaburç
2 Tourist Office
3 Hospital
4 Net-2000 Internet Cafe
5 Police
6 Dolmuşes to Taşucu
8 PTT
9 Kültür Sanat Merkezi
10 Alaaddin Mosque
13 Belediye (Town Hall)
16 Reşadiye Camii
18 Arkeoloji
   Müzesi
20 Otogar
21 Car Repair Services
23 Temple of Jupiter
24 Necropolis
25 Necropolis
26 Tekir Ambarı

PLACES TO STAY
12 Hotel Akdeniz
14 Eren Oteli
15 Ansan Otel-
   Pansiyon
22 Otel Ayatekla

PLACES TO EAT
7 Gözde Restaurant
11 Dilek Restaurant
17 Babaoğul Restaurant
19 Akdeniz Kafeterya
27 Kale Restaurant

To Cave of St Thecla
(5km), Taşucu (11km)
& Antalya (390km)

0   100   200m
0   100   200yd

the tourist office, Celal Taşkıran, is on sale here for US$10.

The Net-2000 Internet Cafe (US$1.60 per hour) is on the north side of the river, one block past the hospital down the street on the right.

Things to See

The **fortress** on the hill dates from medieval times. Officially it isn't open, but no-one seems to mind if you clamber inside. Curiously it seems to lack a gate – entry is through a breach in the northern wall. From it you can gaze down at the **Tekir Ambarı**, an ancient cistern some 46m long, 23m wide and 12m deep, carved from the rock. A circular stone staircase provides access to what was an important feature of the ancient city's water supply. To get to the Tekir Ambarı from the junction of İnönü and Menderes Caddesis, walk up the hill on the street to the left of the Emlak Bankası. A female reader reported being hassled in the fort, so it's probably best only to visit in the middle of the day and preferably with other people.

Perhaps the most striking ruin in Silifke is that of the **Temple of Jupiter**, which dates from the 2nd or 3rd century AD. A pair of

storks are almost guaranteed to be in residence on the most prominent column throughout the summer months.

The **Arkeoloji Müzesi**, near the otogar, has the usual mix of archaeological and ethnographical exhibits, including some gold jewellery and a good collection of coins, including some of Alexander the Great. The museum is open from 8 am to 5 pm daily except Monday for US$1.30.

The town's mosques include the **Ulu Cami**, originally constructed by the Seljuks but much modified, and the **Reşadiye Camii**, an Ottoman work which re-uses Roman columns in its porches.

A site of interest for those up on their biblical lore is the **Cave of St Thecla**. The saint (Ayatekla in Turkish) is known as St Paul's first Christian convert. She was also the first woman to be threatened with death for the young faith. An outcast from her family and society, she supposedly retreated to a cave outside present-day Silifke, where she pursued good works, particularly healing the sick. The Byzantines built a church over the cave in her honour in AD 480.

The site is 5km from the Silifke otogar, south past the museum, then to the right up a narrow road. Rubble from the Byzantine settlement is scattered over a large area. Ruins of the basilica and a nearby cistern are evident, but the entrance to the cave is not. With luck when you arrive, a guardian will appear, sell you a ticket (US$1.30) and unlock the iron gate to the cave. It contains several vaulted chambers, arches and columns – exciting if you're a fan of the saint.

To get there from Silifke take a Taşucu dolmuş and ask to be dropped off at the Ayatekla junction, 1km from the site (the yellow sign is easier to see on the way back to Silifke).

Special Events

Silifke hosts a Turkoman folkloric song and dance festival every year from 20 to 26 May.

Places to Stay

Most accommodation options are at Taşucu, 11km west of Silifke. Silifke's own hotels tend to be quite modest.

At the cheaper end of the price scale the *Hotel Akdeniz* (☎ *714 1285, Menderes Caddesi 76)*, at the western end of İnönü Caddesi, is simple but presentable. It charges US$4/6/7.50 for a waterless single/double/triple, a dollar more per room with shower.

The nearby *Eren Oteli* (☎ *714 1289)*, in a quiet location north of İnönü Caddesi, charges US$6/10 for singles/doubles with shower.

Newer and more cheerful is the *Arısan Otel-Pansiyon* (☎/fax *714 3331, İnönü Caddesi 89)*, which charges just US$4.50/10 for large clean rooms with shower (hot water most of the time).

Opposite the otogar Silifke now has a two-star hotel, *Otel Ayatekla* (☎ *715 1081, fax 715 1085, Otogar Yanı)*, where smart but rather cluttered rooms with TV, air-con, minibar and showers cost US$15/30. There's a ground-floor restaurant and a first-floor lobby bar.

Places to Eat

Silifkelis aren't the types to waste money on eating out much. Nevertheless there are a few decent little eateries, which offer value for money. *Babaoğul Restaurant*, on the traffic circle at the eastern end of İnönü Caddesi, is regarded as the best in town, though it isn't open late. Generous servings of Adana kebap and salad cost just US$4.

Near the PTT there's the simple but clean *Gözde Restaurant*, a straightforward kebap joint which wouldn't dare to stint on big servings to local clients. A *tavuk şiş* (chicken kebap), salad and drink costs US$4.

Dilek Restaurant one block from the PTT stays open when nearly everything else is closed, serving a standard array of kebaps, stews and pides. Watch for overcharging. The last place open at night seems to be the *Akdeniz Kafeterya* at the otogar, with servings of *börek* (filled pastry) for US$1.30.

Near the hilltop fort above the town is the aptly named *Kale Restaurant* (☎ *714 1521)*, right at the upper end of the road. It's a great place for lunch or dinner in summer, with meals costing around US$8 per person.

Otherwise there's a restaurant at *Otel Ayatekla* where a full dinner of starter, fish and dessert will cost upwards of US$10; wine and beer are available here.

Entertainment

Clubs? Hip bars? Not around here. The Kültür Sanat Merkezi next to the PTT, also the local cinema, recalls a high-school assembly hall. The dodgy sound and wonky projection just add to the fun. Tickets cost US$2.50.

Getting There & Away

At the junction of the coastal highway and the road into the mountains and up to the plateau, Silifke is an important transportation point with good bus services.

The highway east from Silifke to Adana is well travelled by buses. Silifke Koop company buses depart for Adana about every 20 minutes throughout the morning and afternoon and will stop to pick up those who've been visiting one of the many archaeological sites east of town. Heading west can be more problematic since you're dependent on long-distance buses coming from Adana and Mersin which can be full. Reserve ahead if possible.

Services from Silifke's Otogar

destination	fare (US$)	time (hr)	distance (km)	daily services
Adana	4	2	155	14 buses
Alanya	7	6	275	a dozen buses (in summer)
Anamur	5	3½	160	a dozen buses (in summer)
Ankara (via Konya)	12	8	520	5 buses
Antalya	10	9	390	a dozen buses (in summer)
Kızkalesi	0.60	½	20	3 buses per hour
Konya	8	4½	260	frequent buses
Mersin	2	2	85	3 buses per hour
Narlıkuyu	0.60	½	23	3 buses per hour
Ürgüp (via Mersin)	10	6½	400	several buses

Dolmuşes to Taşucu for the Cyprus ferries depart about every half-hour from the Mobil station across the highway from the otogar or from a stand on the south bank of the Göksu.

Other services from Silifke are listed in the table above.

AROUND SİLİFKE

Immediately south of Silifke is the Göksu Delta, a world-renowned wetland area, rich in birdlife. East of Silifke the Cilician plain opens to an ever-widening swathe of arable land which allowed civilisation to flourish.

Atakent (Susanoğlu)

☎ 324

Atakent is a holiday village 16km east of Silifke with a nice beach backed by a million holiday flats. What with all the condos for well-to-do holiday-makers from Mersin and Adana, there's little room for the passing traveller. The four-star *Altınorfoz Banana Hotel* (☎ 722 4211, fax 722 4215), set around its own private bay, has not-too-outrageous rates of US$65/86 a single/double, including breakfast and dinner.

Narlıkuyu

About 3km east of Atakent, Narlıkuyu is a pretty village set around a rocky harbour and ringed with fish restaurants. A small museum contains the remains of a 4th-century Roman bath with a fine mosaic of the Three Graces – Aglaia, Thalia and Euphrosyne. Admission costs US$1.60, only worth it if you're a real mosaic freak. Several houses in the village offer *ev pansiyon* (home pension) arrangements for around US$8 per person. There's a small shop for snacks and necessities and that's about it. The restaurants are excellent but your bill is likely to come to at least US$10 if you have fish.

Cennet ve Cehennem

Above Narlıkuyu, the road winds 2km up the mountainside to the Cennet ve Cehennem (Caves of Heaven and Hell).

This limestone coast is riddled with caverns but the Cennet is one of the most impressive. According to legend, this may be the Korykos cave in which the gigantic half-human, half-animal monster Typhon held Zeus captive, though the king of the gods later emerged victorious in this battle between good and evil.

To enter the 250m-long cave, walk through the drinks and souvenir complex and descend the 452 hefty steps to the cavern mouth. Along the way notice the strips of cloth and paper tied to twigs and branches by those who have come to this 'mystical' place in search of cures; they're supposed to remind a saint or spirit that a supplicant has asked for help.

At the mouth of the cave are the ruins of a 5th-century Byzantine church dedicated to the Virgin. Recently installed lighting allows you to go about 100m into the cavern.

Follow the path above the gorge for about 75m and you'll come to Cehennem, or Hell, a 128m-deep sinkhole where Zeus

The Göksu Delta

Accessible from Silifke or Taşucu, the 14,500-hectare Göksu Delta contains several lagoons, most importantly the freshwater Akgöl and the smaller Karadeniz lake. A large area of salt marsh is used for growing rice, while in other parts of the delta strawberries are a popular crop. At the far south of the delta at İncekum a sandspit which changes shape over the years provides the most easterly breeding ground in the Mediterranean for the rare monk seal. Loggerhead and green turtles also nest here.

The Göksu Delta is a paradise for bird-watchers. Of Turkey's 450 species, 332 have been recorded here, while of the 24 globally endangered species found in Turkey, 17 have been seen here. The symbol of the delta is the purple gallinule, but other rare birds found here include marbled teals, black francolins and Audoin's gulls. Whether you visit in summer or winter, something interesting is bound to be on the move.

Unfortunately, despite all sorts of legislation to protect the delta (even the European Union has become involved), its survival is still threatened by dam projects and the never-ending spread of summer housing blocks. To find out more, contact the Society for the Protection of Nature (☎ 212-281 0321, fax 279 5544), Doğal Hayatı Koruma Derneği, PK 18 Bebek, 80810 İstanbul.

is supposed to have imprisoned Titan temporarily until he could bury him permanently beneath Mt Etna in Italy. Local legend also holds that this is one of the entrances to the underworld.

As you arrive at the entrance to the complex a custodian will give you a ticket for US$1.60. He'll be standing beside the remains of a temple to Zeus which was later turned into a church. Turn left here and walk 500m to yet another cave, this one credited with the power to cure asthma.

UZUNCABURÇ

With time, and preferably with your own transport, it's well worth making a detour 28km north of Silifke to the remote village of Uzuncaburç, with its woodpeckers, wild flowers and sense of solitude a world away from the hubbub of the coast.

What is now Uzuncaburç was once the ancient temple-city of Olbia, renamed Diocaesarea in Roman times. It probably began its history as a centre of worship to Zeus Olbius and was ruled by a dynasty of priest-kings, who managed the ceremonies in the large temple.

Because it was a holy place, many people wanted to be buried near it and the priest-kings organised this too. Only 8km up the road from Silifke you encounter the first group of tombs, and then, shortly afterwards, in the village of Demircili, the elegant two-storeyed **Çifte Anıt Mezarları** (Twin Monument Tombs) are plainly visible from the road. Turn right at 23km and proceed through a lovely pine forest to the archaeological site, almost 6km on. Entry costs US$1 but opening hours seem pretty flexible.

Just before the car park there are remains of a peaceful Roman **theatre** to the left of the road. From the car park you enter the main site along a colonnaded way, passing the famous **Temple of Zeus Olbius** on your left. The temple offers one of the earliest examples of Corinthian architecture (circa 300 BC), but was converted to a church by the Byzantines, who removed its central portion, the cella. Just past the temple, on the right, is a **city gate**, after which you come to the **Temple of Tyche** (circa 100 BC).

Come out of the site and turn left through the village. On your right a road leads to the imposing Hellenistic *burç* (city tower), while, further on, a path to the left winds down 500m to the **necropolis**.

Places to Stay & Eat

The village has a small restaurant, the *Burç Kafeterya*, a couple of shops and a *teahouse*. If you get stuck, the ticket office-cum-summer-cafe will put you up but only in the simplest style – it's not a real pension.

Getting There & Away

Only one bus a day (at 2 pm, US$1, one hour) connects Silifke with Uzuncaburç, so to get there and back in the same day you're

EASTERN MEDITERRANEAN

dependent on finding someone ready to run you back when you've finished sightseeing. It's safer to round up a few other explorers and hire a taxi (for about US$25 return, waiting time included). This also lets you stop and inspect the tombs along the way.

UZUNCABURÇ TO KONYA

From Uzuncaburç the road continues via Kırobası to Mut and then to Karaman and Konya. Winding up into the forests you may pass huge stacks of logs cut by the Tahtacılar, the mountain woodcutters who live a secluded life in the forest.

About 40km before Mut the road skirts a fantastic limestone **canyon** which extends for several kilometres. High above in the limestone cliffs are **caves** which were probably once inhabited. The land in the valleys is rich and well-watered, exploited by diligent farmers. The air is cool, clean and sweet.

About 20km north of Mut a turn-off on the right leads 5km to the ruins of another **medieval castle** at Alahan.

KIZKALESİ

☎ 324

Boasting one of the finest beaches along this stretch of coast, Kızkalesi, 26km east of Silifke, takes its name from the striking offshore Maiden's Castle (Kızkalesi). Other ruins are scattered around the foreshore and the inland fields. A site as inviting as this couldn't stay secret for long and a concrete resort village of restaurants, hotels, pensions, souvenir shops and camping areas has grown up all the way around the bay.

Things to See

Though massive, **Maiden's Castle** seems to float on the blue waves, especially when viewed from the mountain road leading to the Cennet ve Cehennem caves. Strong swimmers can make it out to Maiden's Castle (about 150m) alone. The rest of us need to pay a boatman US$2.50 to get there.

Facing it on the shore is the ruined **Korkyos Castle** which was linked to the sea castle by a causeway in ancient times. Admission costs US$2.50 although there's no labelling and you'll need to do a bit of

scrambling over rocks. The builders pillaged nearby ruins for material, and some of the walls are studded with bits of columns.

These twin castles crop up in many legends, but historically they were built by the Byzantines and extensively rebuilt in the 1200s by the Armenian kings of Cilicia with the support of the crusaders. The throne of Cilicia passed through two Armenian dynasties in the 1300s before being taken by Peter I of Cyprus while the Mamluks of Egypt took the rest of Armenian Cilicia to the east.

Immediately across the road from Korkyos Castle is an ancient **necropolis**, with giant sarcophagi scattered among the rocks. Look out for the carving of a soldier with a sword.

Places to Stay

Virtually every building in Kızkalesi is a pension or hotel. Inevitably, the best places are right by the beach and most of them reflect their location in their price. An exception is the small *Hotel Hantur* (☎ 523 2367), halfway around the bay, where singles/doubles with frilly decor and bathrooms cost US$17/25; most have side sea views at least and the owner is extremely welcoming. In the streets running down to the beach you'll find many similarly priced pensions (including the *Holiday*, *Mavideniz*, *Star* and *Nisam*), often calling themselves motels, and with signs up reading 'Boş Oda Var' indicating they have rooms available.

Hotel İnka (☎ 523 2182) near the bars on the middle section of the beach, charges US$13 for a double room, US$17 with aircon. It's close to the beach and every room has a balcony.

West of the bay the *Kilikya* (☎ 523 2116, fax 523 2084) and the *Admiral* (☎ 523 2518, fax 523 2158) are similar three-star hotels with pools, geared mainly to tour groups but with rooms for around US$50/75.

Snazziest of all the places on the bay is *Club Hotel Barbarossa* (☎ 523 2364, fax 523 2090), with pieces of Roman stonework decorating a lawn which sweeps down to the beach. At US$19 per person, it's remarkable value for money.

EASTERN MEDITERRANEAN

Places to Eat

Many of the pensions have their own restaurants and there are one or two private *lokantas* down on the beach, including *Çağdaş Restaurant* which is good for people-watching over an Adana kebap. On the highway the *Honey Restaurant & Bar* is run by a friendly German woman who serves hamburgers for US$1.50 and large Efes for US$1.50. But really you're better off paying the US$0.20 bus fare to hop 10 minutes back to Narlıkuyu (see the Around Silifke section earlier in this chapter) and eat at one of the fish restaurants there.

On the central stretch of Kızkalesi's beach the *Botanik Restaurant*, also known as the *İncirlik F-16 Cafe*, caters to personnel from the American airforce base near Adana with beers for US$1.60 and CDs from Nashville country to East Coast rap. The *Oxyd Disco* next door is tiny compared with its Side namesake, but it's cheap and easy-going.

Getting There & Away

There are frequent buses to Silifke (US$0.60, 30 minutes, 20km).

AROUND KIZKALESİ

East of Kızkalesi the Cilician Plain is littered with ruins, some fairly grand, others little more than fields of cut limestone. About 3km east of Kızkalesi at Ayaş are the extensive but badly ruined remains of ancient **Elaiussa-Sebaste**, a city with its foundations dating from at least the early Roman period, and perhaps even the Hittite era.

About 8.5km east of Kızkalesi at Kumkuyu is the road to Kanlıdivane and a fairly grubby beach with a handful of hotels and plenty of apartment blocks. About 4km north of the highway are the ruins of ancient **Kanytelis**. This ancient city, founded in Hellenistic times, occupies a vast site around limestone caverns. As you ride into the hills the ruins, mostly dating from Roman and Byzantine times, become more extensive.

Kanytelis thrived through Byzantine times, as indicated by several Greek churches and inscriptions. Its extensive necropolis (cemetery) has many Roman tombs built in the form of miniature temples.

MERSİN (İÇEL)

☎ 324 • pop 1.5 million

This city has been officially renamed İçel although the buses, dolmuşes and tourist office brochures are sticking with Mersin. It is the capital of the province of İçel and is a sprawling modern city built half a century ago to give Anatolia a port close to Adana and its rich agricultural hinterland. Until the 1991 Gulf War, the city was a major port for goods going to and from Iraq. Since then, the port and the city have been in something of a slump. It has several good hotels in each price range and, since traffic here is less alarming than in Adana, it makes a more manageable stopping point on your way through to Kızkalesi, Anamur or Antakya.

The suburbs of Mersin now sprawl out as far as Mezitli where a road on the right (south) leads to Viranşehir, the ancient Soles or Pompeiopolis. About 2km down the road a row of Corinthian columns stand in a field, while in the distance is part of an aqueduct, all dating from the 3rd century AD.

Orientation

The town centre is Gümrük Meydanı, the plaza occupied by the ugly modern Ulu Cami (Great Mosque) and with the four-star Mersin Oteli on its eastern side. On the western side is Atatürk Caddesi, a pedestrianised shopping street, while two blocks north is İstiklal Caddesi, the main thoroughfare.

To get to the centre from the otogar, leave by the main exit, turn right and walk up to the main road. Cross to the far side and catch a bus travelling west (US$0.25) which will drop you at the train station.

Information

The tourist office (☎ 238 3271, fax 238 3272) is open 8 am to 12 noon and 1 to 5pm daily and is by the entrance to the docks, east of Atatürk Parkı, at Yenimahalle, İsmet İnönü Bulvarı, Liman Giriş Sahası. Next to it is the stop for buses to Mezitli and Viranşehir.

If you're planning a visit to Northern Cyprus, the Turkish Republic of Northern Cyprus consulate (☎ 237 2482), on the corner of Silifke and Atatürk Caddesis, is open

EASTERN MEDITERRANEAN

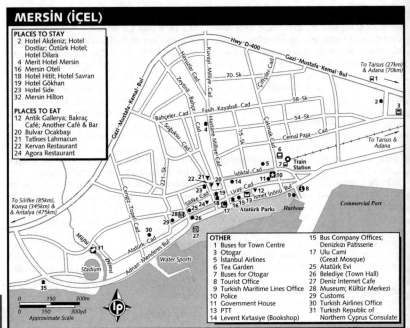

MERSİN (İÇEL)

PLACES TO STAY
2 Hotel Akdeniz; Hotel
   Dostlar; Öztürk Hotel;
   Hotel Dilara
4 Merit Hotel Mersin
16 Mersin Oteli
18 Hotel Hitit; Hotel Savran
19 Hotel Gökhan
23 Hotel Side
32 Mersin Hilton

PLACES TO EAT
12 Antik Gallerya; Bakraç
   Café; Another Café & Bar
20 Bulvar Ocakbaşı
21 Tatlıses Lahmacun
22 Kervan Restaurant
24 Agora Restaurant

OTHER
1 Buses for Town Centre
3 Otogar
5 İstanbul Airlines
6 Tea Garden
7 Buses for Otogar
8 Tourist Office
9 Turkish Maritime Lines Office
10 Police
11 Government House
13 PTT
14 Levent Kırtasiye (Bookshop)
15 Bus Company Offices;
   Denizkızı Patisserie
17 Ulu Cami
   (Great Mosque)
25 Atatürk Evi
26 Belediye (Town Hall)
27 Deniz Internet Cafe
28 Museum; Kültür Merkezi
29 Customs
30 Turkish Airlines Office
31 Turkish Republic of
   Northern Cyprus Consulate

8 am to 1 pm, and 2 to 4 pm weekdays, and has a useful collection of tourist information.

Exchange offices and bank ATMs are clustered around Gümrük Meydanı and the Ulu Cami. Look for signs for Kanarya Döviz, Kiraz Döviz and many others keen to change dollars and deutschmarks.

Levent Kırtasiye in İstiklal Caddesi, near the junction with Hastane Milliye Caddesi, sells the *Turkish Daily News* as well as foreign newspapers and magazines.

The Deniz Internet Cafe is a building in Atatürk Parkı, across from the *belediye* (town hall). Connections are quite fast, and it costs US$1 for one hour.

Things to See

At the eastern end of Atatürk Caddesi a fine stone house, the **Atatürk Evi**, is open 9 am to noon and 1 to 4.30 pm daily except Sunday for US$1.60.

A little further west, beside the Kültür Merkezi, is Mersin's small **museum**, open the same hours as the Atatürk Evi but closed on Monday rather than Sunday (US$2.50). This has a reasonably good archaeological collection with many Roman artefacts on the ground floor and the usual ethnographical bits and bobs on the first floor. There's some English labelling.

The **waterfront** makes for a pleasant promenade.

Places to Stay – Budget

Unfortunately, hotels near the otogar tend to be in the middle range. For a good cheapie, you'll have to trek into the centre. Many cheap and medium-priced hotels are in Soğuksu Caddesi, just north of the Ulu Cami. The cheaper hotels tend to rent rooms by the hour and most of the restaurants double as meeting places for prostitutes and their clients.

On Soğuksu Caddesi the clean but simple *Hotel Hitit* (☎ 231 6431, *Soğuksu Caddesi 12*), across from the old municipal market, charges US$12/17 for single/double rooms. Nearby, the *Hotel Savran* (☎ 232 4473, Soğuksu Caddesi 46) offers similar standards and the same prices. Further north *Hotel Side* (☎ 231 1773, Soğuksu Caddesi 27) is a little more expensive at US$15/20.

Soğuksu Caddesi also has a couple of mid-range choices, including the two-star *Hotel Gökhan* (☎ 231 6256, fax 237 4462, Soğuksu Caddesi 20) with pleasant Art Deco interiors. Rates of US$40/75 are posted, but discounts aren't hard to come by. Rooms boast TV, minibar and air-con and some have balconies.

Lined up outside the otogar gates are 15 hotels, most of them two-star places charging US$17/25/35 for a single/double/triple room with bath, including breakfast. It's worth shopping around since the same money will buy you something bright and new at *Hotel Akdeniz* (☎ 238 0188) or perhaps something more in need of renovation at *Hotel Dostlar*. The Akdeniz boasts a decent restaurant and hamam (men only).

Other reasonable choices include *Öztürk Hotel* (☎ 233 9318) and *Hotel Dilara* (☎ 238 6190).

The four-star *Mersin Oteli* (☎ 238 1040, fax 231 2625, Gümrük Meydanı 112) is on the waterfront a few steps east of the Ulu Cami. Its air-con rooms have comfortable beds, bath, minibar, telephone and balcony. Rates are posted at US$140/160, but 50% reductions are not uncommon.

For luxury, there's the five-star *Merit Hotel Mersin* (☎ 336 1010, fax 336 0722, Kuvayi Milliye Caddesi 165), with rooms in Mersin's tallest building. If you don't mind braving the airport-style security gates, there's nothing to stop you dropping in for a drink in the 46th floor Panorama Bar. Rooms nominally cost US$100/130, but again discounts of up to 50% are possible, we were told.

The *Mersin Hilton* (☎ 326 5000, fax 326 5050, Adnan Menderes Bulvarı), right on the waterfront, is the best in town, with swimming pool, health centre and restaurants. The manager said it had opened just a year before the Gulf War and hadn't exactly been busy since. Rooms cost US$163/183.

Places to Eat

Soğuksu Caddesi boasts several small fish restaurants, such as *Agora*, in the old municipal market building across from the Hotel Hitit. With outdoor tables in fair weather and full meals for US$5 to US$10, these are very popular places although the portions won't go far if you're really hungry.

North of the Hotel Gökhan, *Kervan Restaurant*, opposite the Hotel Side, serves a wide variety of dishes, and alcoholic beverages to wash them down.

The western reaches of İstiklal Caddesi have a number of *lahmacun* (Arabic-style pizza) places, including a branch of *Tatlıses Lahmacun* where people queue for instant *ayran* (yogurt drink) and lahmacun. Along here *Bulvar Ocakbaşı*, beside the Etibank at No 85, serves delicious pides and *döner kebap* (spit-roasted lamb slices) for US$3.

The *Antik Gallerya*, on a small lane between Uray Caddesi and İsmet İnönü Bulvarı next to the PTT, is a collection of bars and outdoor cafes set around a courtyard, popular with trendy young locals. The *Bakraç Cafe* has *mantı* (Turkish ravioli) for US$1.20 and köfte lunches for US$1.70. For somewhere to have a drink and hear a few tunes we liked *Another Cafe & Bar* on the first floor of the building.

For cakes and coffee try *Denizkızı Patisserie* on İsmet İnönü Bulvarı near the Mersin Oteli and the bus company offices.

If you're just passing through, there are lots of *restaurants* mixed in with the hotels outside the otogar. There's something to suit most budgets, plus *stalls* selling fruit and nuts, and several *beer halls*.

Getting There & Away

Bus From Mersin's otogar, on the eastern outskirts of the city, buses depart for all points, including up to the Anatolian plateau through the Cilician Gates. Distances, travel times and prices are similar to those from Adana, 70km to the east on a fast four-lane highway – see Getting There & Away in the Adana section later in this chapter. Several of the main companies serving İstanbul, Ankara and İzmir have offices on İsmet İnönü Bulvarı.

EASTERN MEDITERRANEAN

Train There are frequent services to Tarsus (US$0.50), Adana (US$1) and İskenderun (US$3). The daily *Çukurova Ekspresi* between Ankara and Adana stops at Mersin (US$9/12 in a coach/couchette, 12 hours).

Boat Turkish Maritime Lines (☎ 233 9858) has ferries every Monday, Wednesday and Friday at 10 pm from Mersin to Mağusa in Northern Cyprus. Chair class costs US$25, a cabin US$34 per person, a car US$50. The trip takes 10 hours. The ferry leaves Mağusa on Tuesday, Thursday and Saturday at 10 pm. The Turkish Maritime Lines office is near the tourist office, and the ferry departs from the adjacent dock. Tickets must be bought a day in advance.

TARSUS
☎ 324 • pop 160,000

Tarsus is one of those towns with a name inextricably linked with the memory of one man: St Paul, born here almost 2000 years ago. Unusually, Tarsus has managed to hang on to the same name from antiquity to the present day, despite just as tumultuous a history as anywhere else along the coast.

One reader wrote that Tarsus 'might have done for Saul/Paul but it's come down in the world since then', and at first sight, few people would disagree with his assessment. However, this is one of those towns that repays perseverance and you could certainly while away three or four hours here quite happily.

Things to See & Do

Buses drop you off beside **Cleopatra's Gate**, a Roman city gate which has nothing to do with the famous Cleopatra, although the Egyptian queen is thought to have met Mark Antony in Tarsus. In any case, restoration carried out in 1994 has robbed it of any sense of antiquity.

Walk straight ahead and just before the *hükümet konağı* (government house) you'll see a sign pointing left to the **Senpol Kuyusu** (St Paul's Well). There's little to see except a water-filled hole in the ground, although you can pay US$0.20 to down a cup of water.

At the same road junction a second sign to the left points to the **Antik Şehir** (Old City). Follow it and you'll come to Cumhuriyet Alanı where ongoing excavations have uncovered a wonderful stretch of Roman road, with heavy basalt paving slabs covering a lengthy drain.

Return to the *hükümet konağı* and continue heading north until you come to the 19th-century **Makam Camii** on the right. Turn right beside it and you'll come to the small **Tarsus Müzesi**, housed in the 16th-century Mehmet Efendi Medresesi, extensively restored in 1972; admission costs US$1. Continue along the side street and you'll find the 16th-century **Ulu Cami**, with a curious 19th-century clock tower.

Cross the car park beside it and eventually you'll come to the ruins of **St Paul's Church**. The existing church is 19th century and has nothing whatsoever to do with the saint.

Retrace your steps to the Makam Camii and across the road you'll see the more interesting **Eski Cami** (Old Mosque), a medieval structure which may originally have been a church dedicated to St Paul. Right beside it looms the barely recognisable brickwork of a huge old **Roman bath**.

Beside the Eski Cami you can catch a dolmuş (US$0.20) to Tarsus' other main sight, the **Şelale** (Waterfall) on the Tarsus Çayı (Cydnus River) which cascades over rocks right in the town, providing the perfect setting for tea gardens and restaurants.

Places to Stay & Eat

Tarsus is not brimming over with lovely places to stay. At the time of writing your best hope was *Hotel Zorbaz* (☎ 622 2166) Eski Belediye Karşısı, right beside the hükümet konağı. It has acceptable, basic rooms with shower for US$6/9 a single/double. Ask for a room at the back to escape traffic noise. The nearby *Cihan Palas Hotel* (☎ 624 1623) is a step up in quality, with rooms for US$10/20.

If you're prepared to pay more, the ugly *Tarsus Mersin Oteli* (☎ 614 0600, fax 614 0033, Şelale Mevkii), is right beside the waterfall, with all its smart, modern rooms overlooking it. Single/double/triple rooms cost US$75/105/130. Among other facilities there's a disco and open-air pool. What St Paul would have made of the St Paul Bar is a question probably better not asked

There are plenty of basic *lokantas* (restaurants) on the road up from Cleopatra's Gate, but it makes more sense to come and eat by the waterfall, taking care to check prices before ordering.

Getting There & Away

There are plenty of buses and dolmuşes connecting Tarsus with Adana and Mersin, so you could take a break here while travelling between the two.

ADANA

☎ 322 • pop 1.7 million

Turkey's fourth largest city, Adana, is a big, brash commercial city with a distinct social and physical divide. North of the D400 highway (also called Turan Cemal Berıker Bulvarı) new cars cruise the leafy streets, lined with apartment blocks with air-conditioners hanging from every second window. The further south of the highway you go the poorer the city becomes, until the modern city dissolves into a sprawl of unplanned houses crammed together, with itinerant lottery ticket salesmen on every corner. Unfortunately nearly all the hotels are on the south side of town.

Adana's wealth comes from local industry (especially the Sabancı conglomerate), from the traffic passing through the Cilician Gates, and from the intensely fertile Çukurova, the ancient Cilician plain deposited as silt by the Seyhan and Ceyhan Rivers.

Adana's growth has been rapid and chaotic, and nearly all of the old neighbourhoods have been demolished. The constant high temperature and humidity from May to October does little to boost its limited appeal and the barely controlled traffic is positively terrifying.

Most likely you'll only wind up in Adana because it has an airport, a train station, a large otogar and hotels. Its few sights are just enough to fill the few hours between transport in and transport out.

Orientation

The Seyhan River skirts the city centre to the east. Adana's airport (Şakirpaşa Havaalanı) is 4km west of the centre on the D400 highway. The otogar is 2km further west on the northern side of the D400. The train station is at the northern end of Ziyapaşa Bulvarı, 1.5km north of İnönü Caddesi, the main commercial and hotel street.

The E90 expressway skirts the city to the north. If you approach from the north or west, take the Adana Küzey (Adana North) exit to reach the city centre. This brings you south to the D400 highway which ploughs right through the city centre.

At the western end of İnönü Caddesi is Kuruköprü Meydanı, marked by the highrise Çetinkaya shopping centre. There are several hotels on Özler Caddesi between Kuruköprü Meydanı and Küçüksaat Meydanı to the south-east, a plaza marked by a statue of Atatürk.

Information

The tourist office (☎ 359 1994, fax 352 6790), open Monday to Friday, is at Atatürk Caddesi 13, a block north of İnönü Caddesi, in the centre of town. Don't expect much help. There's a smaller office at the airport (☎/fax 436 92314).

Mosques

The attractive 16th-century **Ulu Cami**, off Abidin Paşa Caddesi, is in a style reminiscent of Syria or the Mamluk mosques of Cairo, with black and white banded marble and elaborate surrounds to its windows. The tiles in the mihrab came from Kütahya and İznik.

The **Yeni Cami** (New Mosque, 1724), follows the general square plan of the Ulu Cami, with 10 domes, while the **Yağ Camii** (1501), with its imposing portal, started life as the church of St James.

More conspicuous than either of these is the brand-new **Sabancı Merkez Cami**, a six-minaret monster right beside the Girne Köprüsü (Girne Bridge), built by industrial magnate Sakip Sabancı. It's worth a look around to marvel at the sheer quantity of gold leaf and marble.

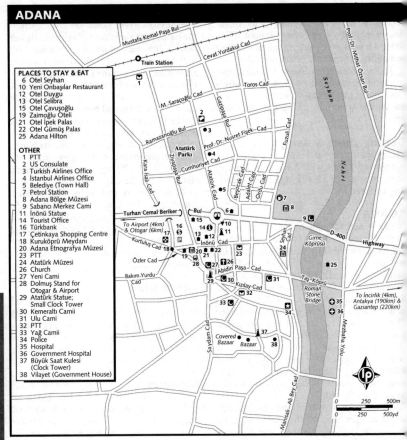

ADANA

PLACES TO STAY & EAT
6 Otel Seyhan
10 Yeni Onbaşılar Restaurant
12 Otel Duygu
13 Otel Selibra
15 Otel Çavuşoğlu
19 Zaimoğlu Oteli
21 Otel İpek Palas
22 Otel Gümüş Palas
25 Adana Hilton

OTHER
1 PTT
2 US Consulate
3 Turkish Airlines Office
4 İstanbul Airlines Office
5 Belediye (Town Hall)
7 Petrol Station
8 Adana Bölge Müzesi
9 Sabancı Merkez Cami
11 İnönü Statue
14 Tourist Office
16 Türkbank
17 Çetinkaya Shopping Centre
18 Kuruköprü Meydanı
20 Adana Etnografya Müzesi
23 PTT
24 Atatürk Müzesi
26 Church
27 Yeni Cami
28 Dolmuş Stand for
   Otogar & Airport
29 Atatürk Statue;
   Small Clock Tower
30 Kemeraltı Camii
31 Ulu Cami
32 PTT
33 Yağ Camii
34 Police
35 Hospital
36 Government Hospital
37 Büyük Saat Kulesi
   (Clock Tower)
38 Vilayet (Government House)

Museums

Adana's two main museums are a cut above most of Turkey's provincial museums. The **Adana Etnografya Müzesi** (Adana Ethnography Museum), on a little side street off İnönü Caddesi, is housed in a small, nicely restored crusader church. It now holds displays of carpets and kilims, weapons, manuscripts, inscriptions and funeral monuments.

The **Adana Bölge Müzesi** (Adana Regional Museum) on Fuzuli Caddesi is rich in Roman statuary as the Cilician Gates were an important transit point even in Roman times. Note especially the 2nd-century Achilles sar-

cophagus, decorated with scenes from the *Iliad*; the Roman and Byzantine mosaics and the bronze statuary. Hittite and Urartian artefacts are also on display.

Both museums are open from 8.30 am to noon and 1 to 4.30 pm daily except Monday; admission to each costs US$1.

The small **Atatürk Müzesi** on the riverside Seyhan Caddesi is one of the city's few remaining traditional houses, this one a mansion that once belonged to the Ramazanoğulları family. Atatürk stayed here a few nights in 1923. Some of the furniture is quite attractive, but otherwise it's hardly

Kaş (top and bottom right), on the Mediterranean coast, makes an excellent base for cruises in a *gulet*, a traditional Turkish yacht (middle). Further east and inland in the Taurus Mountains, a girl makes goat's milk cheese (bottom left), a world away from the hustle and bustle of the coastal resorts.

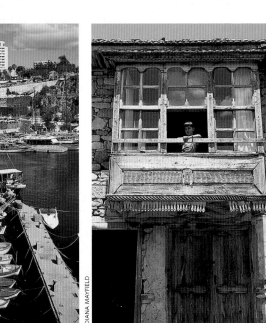

Mediterranean Turkey has it all – picture-perfect yacht harbours (top left; Antalya), charming old wooden houses (top right; Aspendos) and dramatic ancient sites (bottom; Termessos).

must-see. The museum is open 8 am to 12 pm, 1.30 to 5 pm daily except Monday. Admission is US$1.

Other Things to See

Have a look at the 16-arched **Roman stone bridge** (taş köprü) over the Seyhan, at the eastern end of Abidin Paşa Caddesi. Built by Hadrian (AD 117–38), repaired by Justinian, and now sullied by modern traffic, it's still an impressive sight.

The **Büyük Saat Kulesi** (Great Clock Tower) dates back to 1881. Around it you'll find Adana's **covered bazaar**.

Places to Stay

Though Adana has lodgings in all price ranges, there are no hotels near the airport, otogar or train station. The budget hotel scene is pretty dire. Most hotels are on İnönü Caddesi, with a few others on nearby Özler Caddesi. All but the cheapest post high prices, then slash them if they're not busy. All suffer from traffic noise, especially when the muggy heat forces you to keep your window open. The top places have half-hearted air-con.

If you fly into Adana and arrive reasonably early, you could take a bus to more manageable Mersin and stay there instead.

Places to Stay – Budget

Adjoining Otel İpek Palas in İnönü Caddesi is the *Otel Gümüş Palas* (☎ 363 0126) with small but clean singles/doubles for US$6.50/12. The single rooms are very small.

The one-star *Otel İpek Palas* (☎ 363 3512, fax 363 3516, İnönü Caddesi 103) charges US$14/20 for rooms with bath and ceiling fan. It's characterless but clean enough.

Opposite the İpek, *Otel Duygu* (☎ 363 1510, fax 363 0905, İnönü Caddesi 14/1) has been recently refurbished. All rooms have baths and fans for US$21/32.

The *Otel Selibra* (☎ 363 3676, fax 363 4283, İnönü Caddesi 40) is clean, modern and recently renovated. Rooms are US$40/55, with a 50% discount if you can prove you are in Adana on business.

Hotel Princess Maya (☎ 453 7213, fax 453 7299, Turhan Cemal Beriker Bulvarı) is a small new hotel on the main road through town. The rooms are brightly painted and the bathrooms are spotless. Rooms with air-con cost US$40/60. There's also car parking.

The two-star *Otel Çavuşoğlu* (☎ 363 2687, fax 363 3281, Ziyapaşa Bulvarı 115) is at the southern end of the overpass which spans the D400 Highway. It has a restaurant and bar and rooms with bath for US$30/40.

The most comfortable hotel in town is the *Zaimoğlu Oteli* (☎ 363 5353, fax 363 5363, Özler Caddesi 22), a smart, richly decorated modern hotel charging US$140/180 for rooms with air-con, TV, minibar and bath. Hesitate and they'll work with you to discover face-saving reasons for a discount to US$70/90.

The unmissable five-star *Otel Seyhan* (☎ 457 5810, fax 454 2834, Turhan Cemal Beriker Bulvarı 18) is not far from the new Sabancı Merkez Cami. The interior is looking tired, but it still has all mod cons including an outdoor swimming pool. Rooms cost US$88/105, including breakfast.

The massive *Adana Hilton* should be open by the time this book is printed. It's on the east bank of the Seyhan River.

Places to Eat

The local speciality is Adana kebap, minced lamb mixed with hot pepper, squeezed on a flat skewer then charcoal-grilled. It's served with sliced purple onions dusted with fiery paprika, handfuls of parsley, a lemon wedge and flat bread.

For decades the favoured city-centre restaurant has been *Yeni Onbaşılar Restaurant* (☎ 351 4178), on Atatürk Caddesi just south of D400 Highway, opposite the tourist office (enter on the southern side). Adana kebap, a salad and a big Efes beer comes to US$8.

Otherwise, İnönü Caddesi and its side streets have numerous small kebapçıs and even a few *birahanes* (bars). Crossing the highway and walking north along Atatürk Caddesi you can find a better class of döner kebap shops and ice cream vendors.

If the noise and bustle of Adana are too much for you, hop on a dolmuş to nearby İncirlik where there's an American air-force base. Ask to be dropped off at the *Mutlu Evi* (Happy House), a carpet- and kilim-covered restaurant which serves excellent bread with cheese baked onto it to go with the house speciality, a variation on *saç kavurma* (wok-fried lamb) with prawns and börek thrown in. Expect to pay around US$10.

Around town you'll see stands selling beetroot-coloured liquid. This is *şalgam*, a bitter local drink made from turnips, carrots, garlic and lettuce.

Getting There & Away
Adana is an important transfer point, and as such is served by all means of transport.

Air Turkish Airlines (☎ 457 0222, fax 454 3088), Stadyum Caddesi 32, operates daily nonstop flights between Adana and Ankara (one hour), İzmir (1½ hours) and İstanbul (US$75, 1½ hours). There are also at least weekly flights to and from Amsterdam, Athens, Frankfurt, Hanover and Munich, Jeddah and Lefkoşa (Nicosia).

Bus Adana's large otogar offers direct buses or dolmuşes to pretty well anywhere. Some useful daily services are listed in the table below.

Train The facade of the Adana train station (☎ 453 3172), north of İnönü Caddesi at the northern end of Ziyapaşa Bulvarı, is decor-

ated with pretty faience panels. Trains depart frequently throughout the day for Mersin (US$1, 1¼ hours) via Tarsus between 5.15 am and 10.30pm.

Adana is served by three express trains which make their way up onto the Anatolian plateau. The *Erciyes Ekspresi* departs for Kayseri each evening at 5.30 pm, arriving at midnight. Departure from Kayseri is at 4.40 am, arriving in Adana at 10.46 am. One-way tickets cost US$4.

The *Çukurova Ekspresi* runs between Ankara and Adana (12 hours) daily. One-way tickets between Ankara and Adana cost US$9/12 in a coach/couchette, or US$20/34/45 for one/two/three people in a sleeping compartment. The *Toros Ekspresi* from İstanbul's Haydarpaşa station stops at Adana (US$10) on its way to Gaziantep three times weekly. The fare is US$10 to İstanbul and US$13 to Gaziantep.

Getting Around
A taxi from the airport into town costs about US$4 and about US$2 to the otogar. Make sure the meter is on.

AROUND ADANA
The far eastern end of the Turkish Mediterranean coast swoops around the Bay of İskenderun (İskenderun Körfezi) to the cities of İskenderun and Antakya, in the province of Hatay. Inland from the bay are ruins of

Services from Adana's Otogar

destination	fare (US$)	time (hr)	distance (km)	daily services
Adıyaman (for Nemrut Dağı)	11	6	370	7 buses
Alanya	12	10	440	8 buses (n summer)
Ankara	12	10	490	hourly buses
Antakya	5	3½	190	hourly buses
Antalya	14	12	555	a few buses
Diyarbakır	15	10	550	several buses
Gaziantep	5.50	4	220	several buses
Halab (Aleppo, Syria)	25	12	300	at least one bus
Kadirli	1.60	1	75	frequent dolmuşes
Kayseri	10	6½	335	several buses
Konya	10	6½	350	frequent buses
Şanlıurfa	10	6	365	several buses
Van	18	18	950	at least one bus

an ancient Hittite city at Karatepe, and of a later Roman one (Anazarbus). Along the road stand assorted medieval fortresses.

Yılankale

If you're driving look out for the hilltop Yılankale (Snake Castle), about 45 minutes (35km) east of Adana and 2.5km south of the highway. Built by Armenians and crusaders in the 12th or 13th century, it's said to have taken its name from a serpent which was once entwined in the coat of arms above the main entrance (today you'll see a king and lion, but no snake); other tales claim that this area was once full of snakes. If you have the time, it's about a 20-minute climb over the rocks and up to the fort's highest point. There are no services, no guardian and no admission charge.

To continue on to Anazarbus (Anavarza) and Karatepe, head north and east just after the Yılankale turn-off. About 37km east of Adana an intersection is signed on the left

(north) for Kozan and Kadirli, on the right (south) for Ceyhan. Take the Kozan/Kadirli road.

Anazarbus (Anavarza)

When the Romans moved into this area around 19 BC they built this fortress city on top of a hill dominating the fertile plain and called it Caesarea ad Anazarbus. Later, when Cilicia was divided in two, Tarsus remained the capital of the west, and Anazarbus became capital of the east. In the 3rd century AD Persian invaders destroyed the city along with lots of others in Anatolia. The Byzantine emperors rebuilt it as they did over and again when later earthquakes destroyed it several times.

The Arab raids of the 8th century gave Anazarbus new rulers and a new Arabicised name, Ain Zarba. The Byzantines reconquered and held it for a brief period, but Anazarbus was an important city at a strategic nexus, and other armies came through

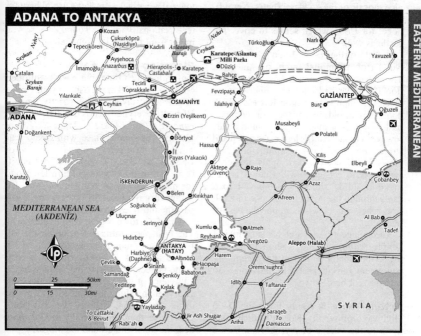
ADANA TO ANTAKYA

and snatched it, including those of the Hamdanid princes of Aleppo, the crusaders, a local Armenian king, the Byzantines again, the Turks and the Mamluks. The last owners didn't care about it much and it fell into decline in the 15th century. Today it's called Anavarza.

After 5km you reach a road junction and a large **gateway** set in the city walls. Through this gate was the ancient city, now given over to crops and pasture but strewn with ancient stones. Turn left through a village where every other gatepost re-uses a Roman column, and after walking 650m you'll reach the remains of an **aqueduct** with several arches still standing. Sometimes there's a gypsy camp set up around them.

Go back to the junction and turn right and after 200m you'll come to a little private **open-air museum** on the right-hand side of the road. Bits of column and sarcophagi are set in the garden, and an ancient pool has a nice **mosaic** of the goddess Thetis (Nereid), a sea nymph. Here you'll be asked to buy a ticket for US$1 which seems to cover the castle as well.

A little further on and you'll come to a wonderful **triumphal arch** on the left. Through here you can walk back to the junction if you've had enough. Otherwise, to reach the impressive hilltop **fortress** which dominates the old city and the plain, continue past the open-air museum for 2km to a narrow pass cut in the hill. Here a steep path and stone steps lead to the summit and fine views. You'll need a good supply of energy and water to get up on a hot day – not to mention sturdy shoes. An unpaved road leads through the cut to the far side of a hill from where a track winds around the base of the rock.

The village of Anavarza has a couple of simple *teahouses* and a shop with cold drinks but that's it. If you have *camping* equipment you can probably find a place to set up a tent here.

Getting There & Away From the D400 Highway follow the Kozan/Kadirli road north to the village of Ayşehoca, where a road on the right is marked for Anavarza/Anazarbus, 5km to the east. If you're in a dolmuş or bus you can get out here and usually hitch a ride pretty easily in the morning.

Heading on towards Kadirli, hitch back the 5km to Ayşehoca and take the 817 road north to Naşidiye/Çukurköprü where the road divides. The left fork is marked for Kozan and Feke, the right for Kadirli.

Kadirli
☎ 322 • pop 55,000

Kadirli, 20km east of Çukurköprü, is a farming town with a useful bazaar, and a few small restaurants and hotels. *Aktürk Lokantası*, facing the shady park with the teahouses in the centre, is simple and cheap but there are plenty of other options near the otogar.

OSMANİYE
☎ 322

Osmaniye lies on the E90 linking Adana with Gaziantep. An uninspiring modern town, it nevertheless makes a useful base for getting to Hierapolis-Castabala, the Karatepe National Park and Toprakkale, so you might want to spend a night here.

Places to Stay & Eat

Unfortunately Osmaniye hasn't cottoned onto the potential of tourism so your choice of places to stay and eat is strictly limited. Virtually everybody ends up at *Hotel Kervansaray (☎ 814 1310, Palalı Süleyman Caddesi)*, a simple place with clean, reasonably comfortable rooms with shower for US$5/8, or US$4/7 without. To find it, come out of the otogar and turn left along the main highway. When you reach the BP garage turn right and the hotel is on the left past the mosque and the MHP office.

This is a town where people eat early. The best place turns out to be on the 7th floor of a building across from the PTT where the *R & A Restaurant* is a vast, white-tablecloth place, with friendly service and views of the rooftops as you tuck into your kebap. Hummus, kebap and a soft drink cost US$4. Beer is also available. Otherwise, there are several basic *lokantas* near the hotel and around the otogar.

Getting There & Away

Without your own transport your best bet for seeing Hierapolis-Castabala and Karatepe in one day is to organise a taxi. There's a handy taxi rank outside the otogar. To go to Hierapolis for an hour, then to Karatepe for two hours and either on to Kadirli or back to Osmaniye should cost about US$28.

From the centre of Osmaniye, road 01-08 is signposted north-west for Hierapolis-Castabala and the Karatepe-Aslantaş Müzesi. Follow the road until you come to a sign on the right for Hierapolis-Castabala which is 6km along a bumpy road. About 10km beyond Hierapolis-Castabala, a road on the left is marked for Karatepe (9km).

Heading south, to get to İskenderun from Osmaniye by dolmuş takes one hour (US$4). There are also frequent connections west to Adana and east to Gaziantep.

AROUND OSMANİYE
Karatepe-Aslantaş Milli Parkı

The Karatepe-Aslantaş Milli Parkı (Karatepe-Aslantaş National Park) incorporates the **Karatepe-Aslantaş Müzesi** (Black-Hill Lion-Stone Museum), a site which has been inhabited for al most 4000 years. The ruins date from the 13th century BC when this was a summer retreat for the neo-Hittite kings of Kizzuwatna (Cilicia), the greatest of whom was named Azitawatas.

From its beautiful, forested hilltop, the park overlooks the **Ceyhan Gölü** (Lake Ceyhan), an artificial lake used for hydroelectric power and recreation.

The 2km park access road leads to a car park and, nearby, picnic tables, charcoal grills and camping sites. Entry to the park costs US$1.60 per person and US$3 for a car.

From here it's a five-minute, 400m walk uphill through the forest to the hilltop archaeological zone. A building above the car park has toilets, and there are soft drinks for sale. Entrance to the Hittite ruins, open from 8 am to noon and from 2 to 5.30 pm (1 to 3.30 pm in winter), costs an extra US$1.60 per person. Be warned that on top of the difficulty of getting to Karatepe without your own transport, the opening hours are rigorously adhered to, and the custodi-

ans will only take you around in a group, which can involve hanging about waiting for other people to arrive. Nor are you allowed to take photographs at the site.

The Hittite remains here are certainly significant, although you shouldn't come expecting something on the scale of Hattuşa. The city was defended by **walls** 1km long, traces of which are still evident. Before arriving at the southern gate there's a **lookout** giving a fine view of the lake which was dammed and filled during the 1980s.

The city's **southern entrance** is protected by four lions and two sphinxes and lined with fine reliefs showing a coronation or feast complete with sacrificial bull, musicians and chariots. Across the hill at the **northern gate** the lions look scarier and the reliefs sharper as the stones were buried for centuries and thus protected from weathering. The eyes in the volcanic lion statue are of white stone, held in place by lead.

There are several **inscriptions** in Hittite script. A particularly long one with Phoenician translation was deciphered, which is how we know the city's history.

Hierapolis-Castabala

About 19km south of Karatepe and 15km north of Osmaniye are the ruins of Hierapolis-Castabala, set in the midst of cotton fields. A castle (kale) tops a rocky outcrop above the plain about 1km east of the road. Admission to the site, which is open during daylight hours, costs US$1.30 and the ticket seller will lend you a leaflet in English to take around in about an hour. You can see everything in about an hour.

Hierapolis-Castabala flourished during the Hellenistic period and was later the capital of a semi-independent principality paying tribute to Rome. Unfortunately one of its kings, Tarcondimotus I, unwisely sided with Antony in his struggle with Octavian and was defeated at the great sea battle of Actium in 31 BC. Though he was followed by Tarcondimotus II, the dynasty died out in the 1st century AD, as did the city in early Byzantine times.

From the ticket-seller's shed, walk along a **colonnaded street** which once boasted 78

EASTERN MEDITERRANEAN

paired columns; some still bear their fine Corinthian capitals. You'll pass a badly ruined **temple** and **baths** on the right. Keeping the kale on your left, walk past the rock outcrop to the theatre, also badly ruined. Beyond it to the south in the fields is a ruined Byzantine **basilica**. Further along the same path is a spring *(çeşme)* and, in the ridge of rocks further on, some **rock-cut tombs**. The site is especially beautiful in spring when it's covered in wild flowers and skylarks twitter above the stones.

The kale has a road cut straight through the rock and good views from the summit.

Toprakkale

About 9km west of Osmaniye the highway divides, skirting the Toprakkale (Earth Castle), built of dark volcanic stone about the same time as the Snake Castle near Adana. Take a bus to İskenderun or a dolmuş to Dörtyol and ask to be dropped off at the kale; it's 400m to the fortress walls, then an easy few minutes walk into the ruins.

Issos

From Toprakkale the E98 expressway runs south to Erzin, bypassing the ruins of the ancient city of Issos. If you follow the older road (817), 8km south of Toprakkale just east of Erzin, you'll notice a long **aqueduct** in the fields to the right, all that remains of the city.

Payas

At Payas, also called Yakacık, 35km south of Toprakkale, look for the inconspicuous signs in the centre of town (north of Payas' big steel factory) pointing right towards the Cinkale Kervansaray, 1km towards the sea.

The huge Ottoman **Sokullu Mehmet Paşa Kervansaray** was built for the grand vizier of Süleyman the Magnificent and Selim II in the 1570s. Opening hours are from 8 am to 4 or 5 pm daily. It's an elaborate complex of courtyards, Turkish baths, mosque, *medrese* (theological seminary) and covered bazaar – a fortified city in what was then recently conquered and still hostile territory. Parts of it look positively Burgundian, and it was possible that Sokullu Mehmet Paşa's

architects, who worked under the guidance of Sinan's school, may have restored and expanded the ruins of a crusader church.

Next to the caravanserai is the **Cin Kalesi** (Fortress of the Genies), a restored bastion protected by a moat. The main gate is a double-bend defensive one which leads to a grassy interior now used as cattle pasture. The ruins of a small mosque are the only other item of interest. If you walk around the outside you can descend and pick figs in the moat by means of a stone subterranean stairway at its westernmost point.

Further along the tarmac road is another little **fortress** with a bent-gate entrance, a keep and gun ports. The ruins of a third fortress are down by the water's edge. You can visit all three forts at any time.

After Payas the road is lined with smoke-belching factories turning out steel, cement and fertiliser, all taking advantage of the port of İskenderun, 22km to the south.

İSKENDERUN
☎ 326 • pop 160,000

İskenderun, 130km east of Adana, was founded by Alexander the Great in 333 BC; İskenderun is a translation of its original name, Alexandretta. Until Mersin was developed in the 1960s, this was the most important port on this part of the coast. Its continued importance was emphasised during the 1980s with the opening of the oil pipeline from Iraq, and then the shutting of that pipeline during the Gulf War of 1991.

İskenderun was occupied by the English in 1918, turned over to the French in 1919, and incorporated into the French Protectorate of Syria as the Sanjak of Alexandretta. In 1938 Atatürk reclaimed it for the Turkish Republic, knowing it would be of great strategic importance in WWII.

There's nothing to detain you in modern İskenderun, an unexciting sailors, brokers and shippers town. If you have to stop, there are several places to stay near the waterfront, the one attractive part of town.

Orientation & Information

Assuming you arrive by bus, come out of the otogar and head due south, passing the minibus station before you reach the main highway. To find the sea you'll need to cross the highway and take a turn on the right, towards Şehit Pamir Caddesi which is lined with hotels, banks and restaurants. Once on this road, head north until you come to Atatürk Bulvarı, the waterfront boulevard, and the sea. The main square at the top of Şehit Pamir Caddesi is marked by a huge monument on the waterfront, pretentious or imposing depending on your viewpoint. Most hotels are within a few blocks of this monument.

The tourist office (☎ 614 1620, fax 613 2879) is at Atatürk Bulvarı 49/B, 100m west of the monument.

Places to Stay
The clean, central *Hotel Açıkalın (☎ 617 3732, Şehit Pamir Caddesi 13)* has single/double rooms with showers and fans for US$14/19.

Nearby, *Hotel Altındişler (☎/fax 617 1011, Şehit Pamir Caddesi 11)* is similar, if marginally more pricey at US$13/26 with shower and TV. A step up in comfort is the nearby *Hotel İmrenay (☎ 613 2117, fax 613 5984, Şehit Pamir Caddesi 5)*, charging US$24/33 with shower and TV.

The best in town – although that's not saying too much – is the *Hotel Cabir (☎ 612 3391, fax 612 3393, Ulucami Caddesi 16)*, a block east of Şehit Pamir Caddesi, with comfortable rooms with shower for US$21/28.

From İskenderun the coastal road continues south-west to Assos; the few *hotels* and the *camp site* overlooking a pleasant beach might make alternatives to staying in the city.

Places to Eat
The town's best is the big *Saray Restaurant*, a few blocks west of the tourist office on Atatürk Bulvarı. For cheaper meals, stroll along the narrow lane which runs between Şehit Pamir Caddesi at Hotel Açıkalın, and Ulucami Caddesi at the Hotel Cabir. The street has half a dozen cheap restaurants serving kebaps, stews etc. *Yeni Lokanta* is long-established and serves a renowned

döner kebap for US$2; also popular is *Yeşil Dörtyol* which serves pides as well.

Getting There & Away
There are frequent minibus and dolmuş connections to both Adana and Antakya (US$1.30, one hour, 58km). A dolmuş to Osmaniye costs US$4 and takes one hour.

AROUND İSKENDERUN
Some 15km south of İskenderun, on the road south to Antakya, is the town of **Belen**, at the head of a gorge. Archaeological excavations nearby have unearthed evidence of settlements dating back to the time of Hammurabi, King of Babylon (1728–1686 BC).

ANTAKYA (HATAY)
☎ 326 • pop 130,000
Until 1938, Antakya (Hatay) was Arabic in culture and language. Many people still speak Arabic as a first language and Turkish as the second. The city also has a heterogenous religious mix – Muslims, Alevis and a small Syrian Orthodox Christian community. Modern Antakya is hardly a beautiful place but its museum is one of Turkey's finest, justifying a lengthy detour. In the cave-church of St Peter, Antakya can also lay claim to possessing 'the world's first cathedral', where the apostle is said to have preached and the term 'Christian' was first used (Acts 11, verse 26). The city is still the titular seat of five Christian Patriarchs; three Catholic (Syrian Catholic, Maronite and Greco-Melchite), as well as Greek Orthodox and Syrian-Jacobite, although none are based here any longer.

Throughout Antakya's long history violent earthquakes have shattered the town, most notably in AD 526 when around 250,000 people were killed. It explains why so little remains of the old city.

The town's relatively small size means that more of the Roman city has been excavated than has been possible in other major Roman towns; hence the splendid collection of floor mosaics in the museum.

Antakya is backed by the Altınözü Mountains, with the snowcapped peak of Mt Silpius dominating the surrounding area.

EASTERN MEDITERRANEAN

History

Antakya is the ancient Antioch ad Orontes, which was founded by Seleucus I Nicator in 300 BC and soon became a city of half a million people. Under the Romans an important Christian community developed out of the already large Jewish one. At one time this was headed by St Paul.

Persians, Byzantines, Arabs, Armenians and Seljuks all fought over Antioch, as did the crusaders and Saracens. In 1268 the Mamluks of Egypt took the city and wiped it out. It never regained its former glory.

The Ottomans held the city until Mohammed Ali of Egypt captured it in 1831, but with European help the Ottomans eventually managed to drive their rebellious vassal back. Antakya was part of the French protectorate of Syria until 1939 and then had a brief flowering as the independent State of Hatay. But when Atatürk saw WWII approaching he wanted the city rejoined to the republic as a defensive measure. His campaign to reclaim it reached fruition when parliament voted for union with Turkey and on 23 July 1939 Hatay became part of Turkey.

Orientation

The Asi (Orontes) River divides the town. The modern district is on the west bank, with the PTT, government buildings and museum circling the Cumhuriyet Alanı traffic roundabout; the Büyük Antakya Oteli, best in town, is just up the street.

The older Ottoman town on the eastern bank is the commercial centre, with most of the hotels, restaurants and services, especially along Hürriyet Caddesi. The otogar is a few blocks north-east of the centre. Continue north-east along İstiklal Caddesi for dolmuşes to Bakras, Samandağ and Harbiye.

Information

The tourist office has been relocated to the former French Assembly Rooms, on the west bank of the Asi River, near the museum.

There's a Yapı Kredi ATM on the east bank of the Asi River, one block from the Jasmin Hotel. The Ferah Kırtasiye ve Kitabevi at Hürriyet Caddesi 17/D stocks the *Turkish Daily News* and other newspapers.

The Data-Net Internet Cafe is in an arcade off Hürriyet Caddesi, between the Saray Hotel and the Ferah Kırtasiye ve Kitabevi. Connections were a bit slow when we visited (US$1.60 per hour).

Antakya Arkeoloji Müzesi

The Antakya Arkeoloji Müzesi (Antakya Archaeology Museum) is the prime reason for journeying all the way to Antakya. Here you'll see as fine a collection of Roman/Byzantine mosaics as graces any museum in the world, covering a period from the 1st century to the 5th century AD. While some are inevitably fragmentary, others were recovered almost intact.

Salons I to IV are tall, naturally lit rooms, perfect for displaying mosaics so fine that at first glance you could mistake some of them for paintings; check out particularly the Oceanus and Thetis mosaic (2nd century) and the Buffet Mosaic (3rd century). As well as the standard scenes of hunting and fishing there are also stories from mythology (Narcissus admiring his reflection in a pool; Orpheus playing his harp to the animals). Other mosaics have quirkier subjects; don't miss the priapic happy hunchback, the black fisherman or the mysterious portrayal of a raven, a scorpion and a pitchfork attacking the 'evil eye'. Many of the mosaics came from Roman seaside villas or from the suburban resort of Daphne (Harbiye), although some are from Tarsus.

After the mosaics you might expect everything else to pale into insignificance but Salon V has some interesting artefacts recovered from the tells (mounds) at Açana and Cüdeyde. The lovely pair of lions serving as column pediments, dating from the 8th century BC, are especially noteworthy.

Salon VI contains Roman and Byzantine coins, statues, pots, glassware and tools, some dating from the Eski Tunç Devri II (Second Old Bronze Age, 2600–2500 BC), together with cuneiform inscriptions from the Açana excavations.

Opening hours are 8.30 am to noon and 1.30 to 5 pm daily except Monday; admission costs US$2.50. Most labels are in English and Turkish.

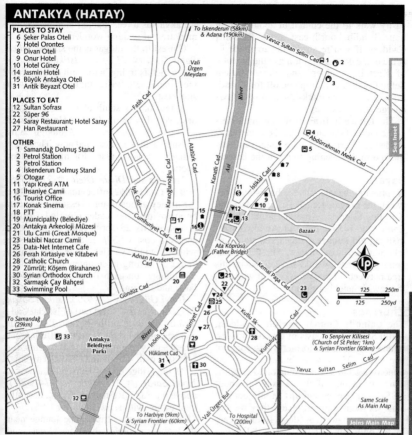

ANTAKYA (HATAY)

PLACES TO STAY
6 Şeker Palas Oteli
7 Hotel Orontes
8 Divan Oteli
9 Onur Hotel
10 Hotel Güney
14 Jasmin Hotel
15 Büyük Antakya Oteli
31 Antik Beyazıt Otel

PLACES TO EAT
12 Sultan Sofrası
22 Süper 96
24 Saray Restaurant; Hotel Saray
27 Han Restaurant

OTHER
1 Samandağ Dolmuş Stand
2 Petrol Station
3 Petrol Station
4 İskenderun Dolmuş Stand
5 Otogar
11 Yapı Kredi ATM
13 İhsaniye Camii
16 Tourist Office
17 Konak Sinema
18 PTT
19 Municipality (Belediye)
20 Antakya Arkeoloji Müzesi
21 Ulu Cami (Great Mosque)
23 Habibi Naccar Camii
25 Data-Net Internet Cafe
26 Ferah Kırtasiye ve Kitabevi
28 Catholic Church
29 Zümrüt; Köşem (Birahanes)
30 Syrian Orthodox Church
32 Sarmaşık Çay Bahçesi
33 Swimming Pool

EASTERN MEDITERRANEAN

Senpiyer Kilisesi

About 3km from the centre on the north-eastern outskirts of town, you'll find the Senpiyer Kilisesi, also known as the Cave-Church of St Peter. Tradition has it that this cave was the property of St Luke the Evangelist, who was from Antioch, and that he donated it to the burgeoning Christian congregation as a place of worship. Saints Peter and Paul lived in Antioch for a few years and are thought to have preached here. When the Crusaders marched through in 1098, they constructed the wall at the front, and a narthex.

To the right of the altar faint traces of fresco can still be seen, and some of the simple mosaic floor survives. Mass can be celebrated here if a tour group of pilgrims requests it. Contact the Capuchin fathers at the Catholic Church (fax 214 1851), Kurtuluş Caddesi, Kutlu Sokak 6.

The Orthodox liturgy is on Sunday at 8 am in summer and 8.30 am in winter. Avoid visiting on public holidays when you may be shocked to see local people climbing on the altar to have their picture taken.

The church is open from 8 am to noon and from 1.30 to 6 pm daily except Monday.

Admission is free. If it's not too hot you can easily walk to the church in about half an hour, heading north-east along Kurtuluş Caddesi. If you're struggling to make it, some of the dolmuşes waiting at the junction of Kurtuluş Caddesi and Yavuz Sultan Selim Caddesi will drop you off for a handful of lira – a sign marks the turn-off. Taxis charge US$2 one way.

The terrace in front of the church offers a fine view of the city. Note the many vine-shaded roof terraces, where Antakyalı families go in the evening to catch the breeze.

Bazaar

A sprawling **bazaar** fills the backstreets between the otogar, Kemal Paşa Caddesi and Kurtuluş Caddesi. Around **Habibi Naccar Camii** you'll find most of Antakya's remaining **old houses**, with carved stone lintels or wooden overhangs. The Capuchins believe St Peter would have lived in this area between 42 and 48 AD, as it was then the Jewish neighbourhood.

Churches

The **Catholic Church**, Kurtuluş Caddesi, Kutlu Sokak 6, consists of two old houses, with a chapel in the former living room of one house. Mass is celebrated here every Sunday at 5 pm. A maximum of 20 pilgrims can stay in one of the houses for about US$10 per person. Groups should book at least six months in advance if they want to visit during major feast days. Bookings are by fax only (fax 214 1851). The Italian Capuchin fathers can also arrange visits for pilgrims to the **Syrian Orthodox Church**, which is not normally open to visitors.

Park & City Walls

If it's hot, a good place to hang out is the riverside **Antakya Belediyesi Parkı** a few blocks south-west of the museum. Here you'll find tea gardens such as the **Sarmaşık Çay Bahçesi** and ice cream booths, as well as shady promenades.

On the high mountain to the south-east are remnants of the long **city walls** and a badly ruined **acropolis**. It's worth the climb for the view.

Places to Stay – Budget

Antakya has a reasonable range of accommodation, if nothing wonderful.

Closest to the otogar is the simple **Şeker Palas Oteli** (*☎ 215 1603, İstiklal Caddesi 79)*, which is trying hard, with display cabinets in the hall. Basic singles/doubles with sink cost US$4/6.

A few blocks south along İstiklal Caddesi, you'll come to **Jasmin Hotel** (*☎ 212 7171, İstiklal Caddesi 14)*. Although baths are shared, they're clean and new. The lobby lounge is a good place for meeting other people.

The one-star **Divan Oteli** (*☎ 215 1518, İstiklal Caddesi 62)* offers reasonable value for money although unnecessary noise can be annoying. One reader reported a frosty reception. Its 23 serviceable rooms with showers cost US$9/18. Some rooms are without windows (let alone fan) which could be stifling in summer, but the large TV lounges on each floor are well ventilated and inviting.

Hotel Güney (*☎ 214 9713, İstiklal Sokak 28)* is on a narrow street east of İstiklal Caddesi on the edge of the bazaar. Big, bright and bare rooms show signs of suffering but it's friendly enough and has rooms for US$8/12 with shower and US$6/10 without.

At the bridge end of Hürriyet Caddesi is **Hotel Saray** (*☎ 214 9001, fax 214 9002)*, above the Saray Restaurant. Clean, decently kept rooms with showers go for US$12/15/18 a single/double/triple. The lounge near the lobby is a comfortable place to read, and the managers are friendly.

Places to Stay – Mid-Range

The **Hotel Orontes** (*☎ 214 5931, fax 214 5933, İstiklal Caddesi 58)* is comfortably modern, with satellite TVs and sizeable showers. Front rooms get the traffic noise and the restaurant sometimes has live music but it's a reasonable mid-range choice at US$31/44/55 a single/double/triple. It can get booked out with tour groups though.

The two-star **Onur Hotel** (*☎ 216 2210, fax 216 2214, İstiklal Caddesi, İstiklal Sokak 14)* is on the edge of the bazaar but despite this, it's quiet at night. Comfortable rooms have modern bathrooms, TV and air-con, and cost US$31/44/55.

Places to Stay – Top End

Officially Antakya's best is the four-star *Büyük Antakya Oteli* (☎ *213 5860, fax 213 5869, Atatürk Caddesi 8*), with 72 air-con rooms, some with river views. As you'd expect, all rooms have TV and bath, but the US$70/100 is a bit much for a place which seems to have skimped on the updating. The only credit card they'll accept is Visa.

For somewhere with more character try the *Antik Beyazıt Otel* (☎ *216 2900, fax 214 3089, Hükümet Caddesi 4*), a French colonial building dating from the 1920s. The decorations clash a bit – Scandinavian pine here, 1920s French there – but it's a comfortable and interesting place to stay. The posted prices are US$70/90/110, but discounts of 30% can be negotiated. There's a nice bar downstairs.

Places to Eat

The Syrian influence permeates Antakya's cuisine. Handfuls of mint and wedges of lemon accompany many kebaps. Hummus, rare elsewhere in Turkey, is readily available here. Many main courses and salads are dusted with fiery pepper; if this isn't to your taste, ask for yours *acısız* (without hot pepper). For dessert, try the local speciality, *künefe*, a cake of fine shredded wheat laid over a dollop of fresh, mild cheese, on a layer of sugar syrup, topped with chopped walnuts and baked. Shops at the northern end of Hürriyet Caddesi sell it. Try and get it hot, straight from the oven.

Many small, cheap *eateries* line İstiklal Caddesi, near the otogar. Otherwise, try Hürriyet Caddesi, İnönü Caddesi or, across the river, Cumhuriyet Caddesi, which has lots of small kebapçıs.

The tiny *Süper 96* on Kutlu Sokak is a popular place to tuck into lahmacun and other local delicacies for a couple of dollars.

In Hürriyet Caddesi most places have tiny street-level rooms, with larger dining rooms one flight up. First up is the big, two-part *Saray Restaurant*, friendly, and with a good selection of dishes and a modern salon

to eat them in. Full meals can be enjoyed for US$2 to US$3.50. Have your döner served rolled up in flat village bread.

Perhaps the best all-round choice is *Han Restaurant* (☎ *215 8538, Hürriyet Caddesi 19/1*). Go upstairs to either of the two open-air terraces (the rear one with shady trees is the nicest) and order döner kebap, served with flat peasant bread, chopped parsley and pepper-dusted sliced red onions. This is also a good place to try künefe; tell them early in the meal that you'll want it for dessert. A full meal of döner, salad, künefe and a beer comes to US$5.

Entertainment

For a drink, try the *Zümrüt* or the *Köşem*, two birahanes at the southern end of Hürriyet Caddesi, where local men come to sip and talk sports and politics. There are other birahanes on Hürriyet Caddesi as well.

The *Konak Sinema*, beside the PTT, shows English-language films subtitled in Turkish. It's the second cinema on the right as you walk up from the traffic circle; the first shows soft porn movies.

Getting There & Away

Bus There are frequent dolmuşes and city buses along Kurtuluş Caddesi to Harbiye (US$0.40, 15 minutes, 9km), where they stop (briefly) to pick up passengers. Dolmuşes to Samandağ (US$0.60, 35 minutes, 29km) leave from an unmarked stand on Yavuz Sultan Selim Caddesi, near the corner with İstiklal Caddesi. In Samandağ you can catch another dolmuş to Çevlik for US$0.30.

The otogar has direct buses to most western and northern points (Ankara, Antalya, İstanbul, İzmir, Kayseri and Konya), usually travelling via Adana (US$5, 2½ hours, 190km) and up through the Cilician Gates. There are also frequent services to Gaziantep (US$8, four hours, 200km) and Şanlıurfa (US$12, seven hours, 345km), either direct or via Gaziantep. Minibuses and dolmuşes for İskenderun (US$1.30, one hour, 58km) leave from a stand just north of the otogar.

There are also direct buses across the border to Syria, though you may find it faster to buy a ticket only as far as the border, cross on your own, and catch something on the other side, thus avoiding the tedium of waiting until everyone on your bus has undergone border formalities. Everyone needs a visa to enter Syria, which you will need to get in advance. There are three buses a day to Damascus (US$15, eight hours, 465km) and five buses a day to Halab (Aleppo; US$8, four hours, 105km). These journey times don't include border formalities, which may add several hours to the trip.

AROUND ANTAKYA
Harbiye (Daphne)

The hill suburb of Harbiye, 9km to the south of Antakya, is the ancient Daphne where, according to classical mythology, the virgin Daphne prayed to be rescued from the attentions of the god Apollo and was turned into a laurel tree. There are no laurels to be seen nowadays, although pine trees ring a large pool of water, very popular as a picnic place.

Most visitors will find the litter strewn around the pool very off-putting. Instead, get off the dolmuş opposite the Hotel Çağlayan and walk down into the wooded valley on the left, which is usually full of Antakyalı vacationers enjoying the cool shade, the tea gardens, and the pools and rivulets of cooling water. Some people find the souvenir stalls tacky, but most will enjoy sipping tea or having a fish lunch with curtains of water falling behind them and bottles of beer cooling in the streams around them. Check prices before ordering, though, since it's easy to pay more than what you bargained for. Harbiye used to be a pleasant alternative to staying in Antakya, but it is rapidly developing into a noisy concrete town and the hotels aren't very good.

Dolmuşes (US$0.30, 30 minutes) and less frequent city buses run from the Samandağ dolmuş stand north of Yavuz Sultan Selim Caddesi along Kurtuluş to Harbiye.

Yayladağı Yazılıtaş Orman Piknik Yeri

About another 42km past Harbiye is the Yayladağı Yazılıtaş Orman Piknik Yeri, a forest picnic spot near some ancient inscriptions. Along the way the road passes near the village of **Sofular**, next to which is a crusader castle.

Samandağ & Çevlik

Samandağ is a seaside suburb 29km south of Antakya. It's a conspicuously ugly concrete town, but if you continue for 6km north along the beach you'll come to Çevlik and the scant ruins of **Seleucia ad Piera**, the port of Antioch in ancient times. Çevlik itself is pretty dejected, its litter-strewn beach unlikely to seduce you. There are several sea-facing restaurants and a few simple pensions but none of them is anything to write home about. Nor is the water the cleanest if you're hoping to swim.

What you really come here for is the **Titüs ve Vespasiyanüs Tüneli**, an astonishing feat of Roman engineering. During its heyday, Seleucia lived with the constant threat of inundation from a stream which descended the mountains and flowed through the town. To counter this threat, the Roman emperors Titus and Vespasian ordered their engineers to dig a diversion channel around the town.

From the car park in Çevlik, ascend the steps to the gate. If there's anybody in the booth you'll have to pay a US$1 admission fee, after which a guide will accompany you up the hillside, along the channel and through a great gorge. The walk is over rocks and is definitely sturdy shoe rather than sandal terrain. If you're not up to it, follow the channel until you come to a metal arch on the right; take the path behind the arch (right fork) which follows an irrigation canal past some rock-cut shelters, finally arriving at a humpback Roman bridge across the gorge. Here steps lead down to the tunnel. Bring a torch since the path is still pretty treacherous. At the far end of the channel an inscription provides a date for the work.

The slopes above the Roman bridge provide a perfect picnic spot.

To get to Samandağ (US$0.60, 35 minutes), head north-east along İstiklal Caddesi to the dolmuş stand at the junction with Yavuz Sultan Selim Caddesi. Dolmuşes run from Samandağ to Çevlik (US$0.30).

Central Anatolia

Central Anatolia is the Turkish heartland, a great antidote to the coast where it can sometimes seem that the 'real' Turkey has vanished altogether. Here, amid the vast, rolling, seemingly deserted plains, you will find some of modern Turkey's most important towns, places like Kayseri and Konya, which, for all their social conservatism, are growing so fast that they have been dubbed 'the Anatolian tigers'.

The armies of a dozen empires swept across this 'land bridge' between Europe and Asia; a dozen civilisations have risen and fallen here, including the very earliest established human communities, which date from 7500 BC. Crumbling caravanserais scattered along the modern highways testify to the rich trade routes of yesteryear. The legacy of all this turbulence is a region rich in historic monuments.

These days, not surprisingly, most visitors to Turkey make a beeline for Cappadocia (Kapadokya), four hours' drive south of Ankara. Here you can find spectacular scenery, wonderful walking country and historic monuments galore: rock-cut churches, restored caravanserais and even whole cities cut out of the earth.

But Central Anatolia is much more than Cappadocia. Not many people choose to linger in Ankara, the modern Turkish capital, although if you do it will give you an understanding of the frequently opposing currents of thought and lifestyle tugging at Turkey. Ankara also makes a good base for visiting the Phrygian sites around Gordion and the Hittite sites around Boğazkale.

North of Ankara is a crescent of small towns – Safranbolu, Kastamonu, Amasya, Tokat and Sivas – all well worth visiting for their historic attractions and to get a feel for life in small-town Turkey. If you have time for only one town, then Safranbolu, with its wonderful Ottoman houses, is a great place to break a journey between İstanbul and Ankara. The other towns are just as interesting, albeit in a more low-key way.

HIGHLIGHTS

- Staying in a restored Ottoman house in Safranbolu
- Visiting the Mevlâna Museum in Konya
- Walking through the Ihlara Gorge
- Exploring the Cappadocian valleys, especially Göreme
- Visiting Ankara's Museum of Anatolian Civilisations
- Hittite-spotting at Hattuşa
- Staying in a rock-cut cave room in Cappadocia
- Trying not to get lost in the underground cities of Kaymaklı or Derinkuyu

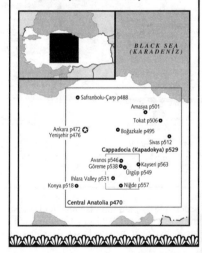

Central Anatolia can be freezing cold in winter and baking hot in summer, so the most pleasant times to visit are spring, when the wild flowers are out, and autumn. Rain is common in April and if you come early or late in the season, you should pack warmer clothes to see you through the chilly nights.

Getting around the region by bus could hardly be easier, and Ankara is easily

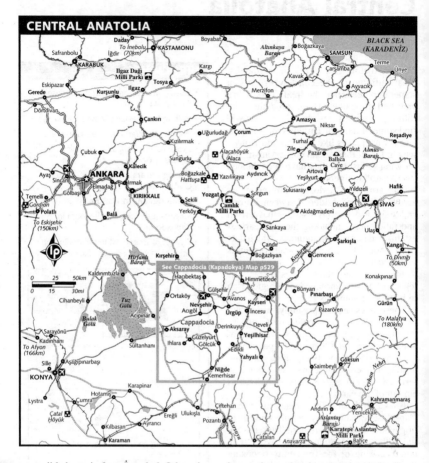

CENTRAL ANATOLIA

accessible by train from İstanbul. Otherwise train services are liable to be slower and less convenient than the buses. The airports at Kayseri and Tüzköy (Nevşehir) are handy if you want to get to Cappadocia without enduring an overnight bus journey.

Ankara

☎ 312 • pop 4 million

A disaffected resident was once heard to say that the best view of the modern Turkish capital was the one from AŞTİ, the huge

bus station and main exit point. Ankara was once called Angora, and had a thriving trade in the fine, soft hair of Angora goats. Today, its prime concern is government. It's a city of ministries, embassies, universities, medical centres and some light industry. Sprawling suburbs march across the surrounding hillsides, most of them filled with country people who have moved here in search of work and a better life.

Whether they want to or not, many travellers need to stop in Ankara to pick up visas. And anyone who will be visiting the Hittite sites, or Gordion in particular, will want to see the superb Museum of Anatolian Civilisations. Those interested in modern Turkey may also want to visit the Anıt Kabir, the striking monument to Atatürk, the father of modern Turkey. A day or so should be sufficient, although you may find Ankara grows on you with a longer acquaintance.

History

Although Hittite remains dating back to before 1200 BC have been found in Ankara, the town was really a Phrygian foundation prospering because it was at the intersection of the north-south and east-west trade routes. Later it was taken by Alexander the Great, claimed by the Seleucids and finally occupied by the Galatians who invaded Anatolia around 250 BC. Augustus Caesar annexed it to Rome in 25 BC as Ankyra.

The Byzantines held the town for centuries, with intermittent raids by the Persians and Arabs. When the Seljuk Turks came to Anatolia after 1071, they took over the city but held it with difficulty.

Ottoman possession of Angora did not go well, for it was near here that Sultan Yıldırım Beyazıt was captured by Tamerlane – the sultan later died in captivity. After the Timurid state collapsed and the Ottoman civil war ended, Angora became a quiet backwater town, famous only for its goats.

Modern Ankara is a planned city. When Atatürk set up his provisional government here in 1920, it was a small, dusty settlement of some 30,000 people, strategically sited at the heart of the country. After his victory in the War of Independence, Atatürk declared it the new Turkish capital (October 1923), and set about developing it. European urban planners were consulted, and the result was a city of long, wide boulevards, a forested park with an artificial lake, and numerous residential and diplomatic neighbourhoods. From 1919 to 1927, Atatürk never set foot in İstanbul, preferring to work at making Ankara the country's capital in fact as well as in name.

Orientation

The main boulevard through the city is, of course, Atatürk Bulvarı, which runs from Ulus in the north to the Presidential Mansion in Çankaya, 6km to the south.

The old city of Ankara is near Ulus Meydanı, called simply Ulus and marked by a large equestrian statue of Atatürk. The most important museums and sights are near Ulus, as are numerous budget and mid-range hotels and restaurants. The first goal of most visitors is Ankara Kalesi, the citadel atop the hill 100m east of Ulus, and the nearby Museum of Anatolian Civilisations. The train station *(gar)*, also the terminus for Havaş airport buses, is 1400m south-west of Ulus along Cumhuriyet Bulvarı.

Kızılay, the intersection of Atatürk Bulvarı and Gazi Mustafa Kemal Bulvarı/Ziya Gökalp Caddesi, is the centre of new Ankara (Yenişehir, New City), with mid-range and top-end hotels, restaurants, airline and bus ticket offices, travel agencies and department stores. The Kocatepe Camii is one of the largest in the world.

Kavaklıdere, halfway up the slope south from Kızılay to Çankaya, is a fashionable district with embassies, trendy bars, smart shops, and the Hilton and Sheraton hotels.

Up in the hills at the southern end of Atatürk Bulvarı is Çankaya, the residential neighbourhood which hosts the Presidential Mansion and many of the most important ambassadorial residences. Its most prominent landmark is the Atakule, a tall tower with a revolving restaurant in its bulbous top that is visible throughout the city.

AŞTİ, Ankara's *otogar* (bus station), is 6.5km south-west of Ulus and 6km west of Kızılay.

Information

For addresses of diplomatic missions in Ankara, see Embassies & Consulates in the Facts for the Visitor chapter.

Tourist Office The tourist office (☎ 231 5572) at Gazi Mustafa Kemal Bulvarı 121, opposite the Maltepe Ankaray station, is mainly a glorified souvenir shop.

Money There are lots of banks with ATMs in Ulus, Kızılay and Kavaklıdere. With cash, you may prefer to use a *döviz bürosu*

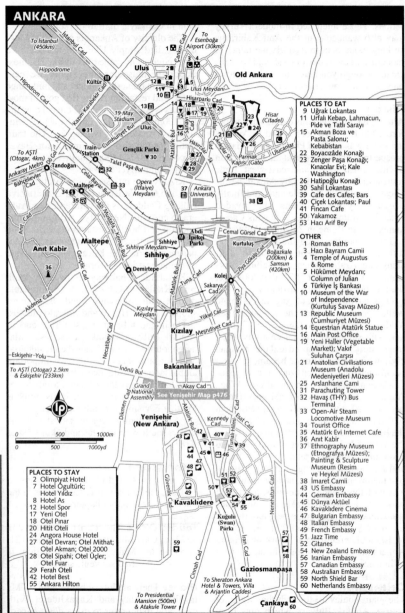

ANKARA

PLACES TO EAT
9 Uğrak Lokantası
11 Urfalı Kebap, Lahmacun, Pide ve Tatlı Sarayı
15 Akman Boza ve Pasta Salonu; Kebabistan
22 Boyacızâde Konağı
23 Zenger Paşa Konağı; Kınacılar Evi; Kale Washington
26 Hatipoğlu Konağı
30 Sahil Lokantası
39 Cafe des Cafes; Bars
40 Çiçek Lokantası; Paul
41 Fincan Cafe
50 Yakamoz
53 Hacı Arif Bey

OTHER
1 Roman Baths
3 Hacı Bayram Camii
4 Temple of Augustus & Rome
5 Hükümet Meydanı; Column of Julian
7 Türkiye İş Bankası
10 Museum of the War of Independence (Kurtuluş Savaşı Müzesi)
13 Republic Museum (Cumhuriyet Müzesi)
14 Equestrian Atatürk Statue
16 Main Post Office
19 Yeni Haller (Vegetable Market); Vakıf Suluhan Çarşısı
21 Anatolian Civilisations Museum (Anadolu Medeniyetleri Müzesi)
25 Arslanhane Cami
31 Parachuting Tower
32 Havaş (THY) Bus Terminal
33 Open-Air Steam Locomotive Museum
34 Tourist Office
35 Atatürk Evi Internet Cafe
36 Anıt Kabir
37 Ethnography Museum (Etnografya Müzesi); Painting & Sculpture Museum (Resim ve Heykel Müzesi)
38 İmaret Camii
43 US Embassy
44 German Embassy
45 Dünya Aktüel
46 Kavaklıdere Cinema
47 Bulgarian Embassy
48 Italian Embassy
49 French Embassy
51 Jazz Time
52 Gitanes
54 New Zealand Embassy
56 Iranian Embassy
57 Canadian Embassy
58 Australian Embassy
59 North Shield Bar
60 Netherlands Embassy

PLACES TO STAY
2 Olimpiyat Hotel
7 Hotel Oğultürk; Hotel Yıldız
8 Hotel As
12 Hotel Spor
17 Yeni Otel
18 Otel Pınar
20 Hitit Oteli
24 Angora House Hotel
27 Otel Devran; Otel Mithat; Otel Akman; Otel 2000
28 Otel Sipahi; Otel Üçler; Otel Fuar
29 Ferah Oteli
42 Hotel Best
55 Ankara Hilton

See Yenişehir Map p476

(exchange office); look near the corner of Sakarya Caddesi and Atatürk Bulvarı for Sakarya Döviz, Sakarya Caddesi 6-A, which has good rates but is often crowded. Near Ulus, Erol Döviz, Alsancak Sokak 2, opposite the Yeni Haller, also has good rates.

Post & Communications For most travellers the most useful post offices will be those at the train station, the AŞTİ otogar (bus station) or the main post office in Ulus on Atatürk Bulvarı. All have foreign exchange facilities and public phone booths nearby.

Email & Internet Access The densest concentration of Internet cafes can be found in Yenişehir, around Karafil and Olgunlar Sokaks, but the one in the Atatürk Evi bookshop at Gazi Mustafa Kemal Bulvarı 133, near the tourist office, could be useful if you're staying in Ulus. The Esra Internet cafe is upstairs in the D&R Konur bookshop (see below). Use of the cafe is cheap – you shouldn't need to spend more than US$1.50 an hour.

Bookshops The branch of Dünya Aktüel (☎ 467 1633) at Tunalı Hilmi Caddesi 82/A2, Kavaklıdere, sells foreign newspapers and a few foreign language novels. For a wider choice of foreign language books try D&R Konur (☎ 419 7946), Konur Sokak 8/A-B, Kızılay, which also has a pleasant cafe. At least one of the Olgunlar Sokak second-hand bookstalls sells foreign language novels.

Medical Services Ankara is Turkey's major medical centre. The city's most up-to-date facility is the private Bayındır Hospital (☎ 428 0808), Atatürk Bulvarı 201, Kavaklıdere. The City Hospital (☎ 466 3346), Büklüm Sokak 53, near Tunalı Hilmi Caddesi, is also good and has a beautiful modern Kadın Sağlığı Merkezi (Women's Health Centre). Call your embassy for other suggestions.

Museum of Anatolian Civilisations

Ankara's premier museum, the Museum of Anatolian Civilisations (☎ 324 3160), or Anadolu Medeniyetleri Müzesi, is a must-see for anyone interested in Turkey's ancient past. It is housed in a beautifully restored 15th-century covered market and warehouse. Exhibits concentrate on the earlier Anatolian civilisations: Urartian, Hattian, Hittite, Phrygian and Assyrian. Among the most interesting items are those brought from Çatal Höyük, the earliest known human community. You'll also enjoy the striking Hittite figures of bulls and stags, one of which has become the emblem of Ankara. Note that MÖ is the Turkish abbreviation for BC.

The museum is open from 8.30 am to 5 pm daily, 'closed' on Monday in winter unless you pay twice the $3 entry fee. Photography is only permitted (free) in the central room; in the others it must be approved by the director and a substantial fee paid. You will probably be approached by several would-be guides. Agree a price in advance, and be sure it's understood that it's for your entire group, not per person.

You can buy drinks but not food in the museum.

If it's not too hot, you can climb the hill from Ulus to the museum (12 to 15 minutes, 1km); head east from Ulus on Hisarparkı Caddesi and turn right into Anafartalar Caddesi, then bear left along Çıkrıkçılar Sokak to reach the museum. A taxi from Ulus should cost about US$2.50.

Hisar (Castle)

The imposing Hisar (also called Ankara Kalesi), just up the hill from the museum, took its present form in the 9th century when the Byzantine emperor Michael II constructed the outer walls. The inner walls date from the 7th century.

Walk up Gözcü Sokak from the Museum of Anatolian Civilisations past the octagonal tower, then turn left to enter the Hisar through the **Parmak Kapısı** (Finger Gate), also called the Saatli Kapı (Clock Gate). Inside is a traditional Turkish village, parts of it under restoration.

As you wander about the Hisar, you'll notice broken column drums, bits of marble statuary and inscribed lintels all incorporated into the mighty walls. The Hisar's small mosque, the **Alaettin Camii**, dates from the 12th century but has been extensively rebuilt. Wander into the village, following any upward path and you'll soon arrive at a flight of concrete stairs on the right leading to the **Şark Kulesi** (Eastern Tower), with panoramic city views. The tower at the north, **Ak Kale** (White Fort), also offers fine views.

There are some excellent restaurants inside the Hisar – see Places to Eat later in this section for more details.

Railway Museums

Rail enthusiasts arriving at Ankara's train station will want to have a look at the **Railway Museum** (Demiryolları Müzesi), a small station building on platform one which served as Atatürk's residence during the War of Independence. It's open from 9 am to noon and from 1 to 5 pm daily (closed on holidays). If it's locked, find an official and ask '*Müzeyi açar mısınız?*' (Would you open the museum?). Right beside it is Atatürk's private railway coach, a gift to the Turkish leader from Adolf Hitler.

A second railway museum is the **Open-Air Steam Locomotive Museum** (Açık Hava Buharlı Lokomotif Müzesi), a collection of slowly rusting vintage locomotives on the south-western side of the station. To find them, descend the underpass as though you were going to the train platforms, but keep walking straight on. Just before entering the Tandoğan Kapalı Çarşı shopping area, turn left up the steps and then right along Celal Bayar Bulvarı for less than 1km.

Roman Ankara

Roman Ankyra (Ankara) was an important city and several significant Roman structures remain. Start your tour in Hükümet Meydanı (Government Square), just off Ulus; to find it head north along Çankırı Caddesi and take the right turning beside the beautiful old Türkiye İş Bankası building. In the square, ringed by government offices, stands the **Column of Julian** (Jülyanüs Sütunu). The Roman Emperor Julian the Apostate (AD 361–63) visited Ankara in the middle of his short reign and the column was erected in his honour. Turkish inhabitants with vivid imaginations later dubbed it Belkız Minaresi, the Queen of Sheba's Minaret.

From the square, walk uphill behind the clock tower and upstairs through the shopping complex surrounding the Hacı Bayram Camii. The mosque was built next to the ruins of the **Temple of Augustus & Rome**, of which only the remains of the cella (inner sanctum) still stand. The Roman temple was built over an earlier shrine to Cybele, the Anatolian fertility goddess, and Men, the Phrygian phallic god. Later the Byzantines converted the temple into a church.

Hacı Bayram Camii is Ankara's most revered mosque. Hacı Bayram Veli was a Muslim saint who founded the Bayramiye order of dervishes around AD 1400. Ankara was the centre of the order and Hacı Bayram Veli is still revered by pious Muslims. The mosque precincts are ringed with shops selling religious paraphernalia (including wooden toothbrushes as, supposedly, used by Mohammed). For US$0.20 you can buy food to feed the pigeons in a designated feeding area (Güverçin Yemleme Alanı).

From Hacı Bayram Camii, walk north on Çiçek Sokak until it meets Çankırı Caddesi. Across this main road, up the hill on the opposite side, are the sprawling ruins of the 3rd-century **Roman Baths** (Roma Hamamları), about 400m north of Ulus Meydanı. Opening hours are from 8.30 am to noon and from 1 to 5 pm daily except Monday; admission costs US$1.

The layout of the baths and the system for heating them is clearly visible; look for the standard Roman facilities – an apoditerium (dressing room), frigidarium (cold room), tepidarium (warm room) and caldarium (hot room). Remains dating back to Phrygian times (8th to 6th centuries BC) have been found beneath the baths.

Republican Ankara

In the 1920s, at the time of the War of Independence, Ankara consisted of the citadel and a few buildings in Ulus. Atatürk's new city grew with Ulus as its centre, and many of the buildings here witnessed the birth and growing pains of the Turkish Republic.

Museum of the War of Independence

The War of Salvation Museum (Kurtuluş Savaşı Müzesi) is on Cumhuriyet Bulvarı on the north-western corner of Ulus, where the republican Grand National Assembly held its early sessions. Before it was Turkey's first parliament, this building was the Ankara headquarters of the Committee of Union & Progress, the political party which in 1909 overthrew Sultan Abdülhamid and attempted to bring democracy to the Ottoman Empire. At the time of writing the museum was closed for restoration.

Republic Museum

The Republic Museum or Cumhuriyet Müzesi, on Cumhuriyet Bulvarı just down the hill from Ulus, was the second headquarters of the Grand National Assembly and its early history appears in photographs and documents; the captions are in Turkish but you can visit the assembly's meeting room and get a sense of its modest beginnings. The Grand National Assembly is now housed in an imposing building in Yenişehir. It's open from 8.30 am to noon and from 1 to 5 pm daily except Monday; admission costs US$1.

Facing the museum is the former **Ankara Palas** hotel, built as the city's first luxury lodging for dignitaries in the early days of the republic. It now serves as guest accommodation for important official visitors.

Ethnography Museum

The Ethnography Museum (Etnografya Müzesi) is perched above Atatürk Bulvarı, to the east of the boulevard and south of Ulus. Walk up Talat Paşa Bulvarı to reach it. At the time of writing it was closed for restoration, but when it reopens, hopefully it will still display the same fine collection of *hattat* (Islamic calligraphy), woodwork, weapons, metalwork, costumes, embroidery and musical instruments.

The building, which once housed Atatürk's offices, is a white marble post-Ottoman structure (1925) with an equestrian statue of the great man in front. Upon entering, you confront a marble slab with an inscription which translates as: 'This is the place where Atatürk, who entered into eter-

nity on 10-xi-1938, lay from 21-xi-1938 until 10-xi-1953'. After this period his body was transferred to the just completed Anıt Kabir.

Next door to the Ethnography Museum is the **Painting & Sculpture Museum** (Resim ve Heykel Müzesi). This, too, was closed for restoration at the time of writing.

Anıt Kabir

Atatürk's mausoleum, the Anıt Kabir or Monumental Tomb, stands on top of a small hill in a park about 2km west of Kızılay along Gazi Mustafa Kemal Bulvarı. A visit to the tomb is one of the 'must-sees' of Ankara. Opening hours are 9 am to 5 pm (4 pm in winter) daily although the museum closes from noon to 1.30 pm; admission is free. The nearest Ankaray station is Tandoğan, which is 1500m north of Anıt Kabir. You can walk uphill to the mausoleum (about 20 minutes), or take a taxi (US$2).

Up the steps from the car park you pass between statues and two square kiosks; the right-hand kiosk holds a model of the tomb and photos of its construction. Then you pass along a monumental avenue flanked by neo-Hittite stone lions to the courtyard.

To the right as you enter the courtyard, beneath the western colonnade, is the **sarcophagus of İsmet İnönü** (1884–1973), Atatürk's close friend and chief of staff, a republican general (hero of the Battle of İnönü, from which he took his surname), diplomat, prime minister and second president of the republic.

Across the courtyard, on the eastern side, is a **museum** of memorabilia and personal effects of Atatürk. You can also see his official automobiles. A video about Atatürk's life and times is shown from 10 am to noon and 2 to 4.30 pm.

As you approach the tomb proper, the high-stepping guards will jump to action. Past the colonnade, look left and right at the gilded inscriptions, which are quotations from Atatürk's speech celebrating the republic's 10th anniversary in 1932. As you enter the tomb through its huge bronze doors, you must remove your hat (if you don't, a guard will remind you of the correct

CENTRAL ANATOLIA

protocol). The lofty hall is lined in red marble and sparingly decorated with mosaics. At the northern end stands an immense marble **cenotaph**, cut from a single piece of stone. The actual tomb is beneath it.

Incorporating echoes of several great empires, from the Hittite to the Roman and Seljuk, the design of the Anıt Kabir seeks to capture the spirit of Anatolia. The final effect is one of true Turkish timelessness.

Presidential Mansion

At the far southern end of Atatürk Bulvarı in Çankaya is the Presidential Mansion. Within its beautiful gardens is the **Çankaya Köşkü**, or Çankaya Atatürk Müzesi, a quaint chalet that was Atatürk's country residence, set amid vineyards and evergreens. In the early days of the republic it was a retreat from the town, but now the town spreads beyond it. Visits to the mansion's grounds and to the museum are permitted on Sunday from 1.30 to 5.30 pm, and on holidays from 12.30 to 5.30 pm, free of charge. Bring your passport.

Take any Çankaya-bound bus or taxi to the southern end of Atatürk Bulvarı, where you will find an entrance to the grounds. Tell the bus or taxi driver you want to go to the Çankaya Köşkü (**chahn**-kah-yah kursh-kur). At the guardhouse, exchange your passport for an identity badge, leave your camera, and a guide will accompany you through the museum.

Atakule

Within walking distance of the Presidential Mansion is Atakule, the thin tower with a revolving restaurant on top which dominates views of Ankara. From 10 am to 2 am daily a lift whisks you to the top and great views of the city; admission is US$1.50.

What's Free

Walk south from Ulus along Atatürk Bulvarı and you'll soon reach the entrance to **Gençlik Parkı** (Youth Park), where Atatürk had a swamp converted into an artificial lake. There's a funfair with amusements for children and several pleasant outdoor cafes; single women should look for one with the word *aile* (family) in its name.

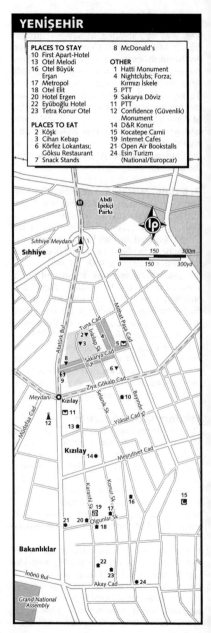

Other oases in an often wearing city are **Kuğulu Parkı** (Swan Park) at the southern end of Tunalı Himli Caddesi and the **Botanical Garden** beneath the Atakule in Çankaya.

Places to Stay

Despite being the Turkish capital, Ankara is not well-geared for western tourists; anyone opening a half-decent budget travellers' place would soon scoop the market. Most of the hotels cater for business travellers on expense accounts. Those that don't are often shabby and old-fashioned. On a tight budget you will have to stick with Ulus, which has numerous budget and mid-range hotels. Yenişehir has several good mid-range hotels. The top-end hotels are in Kavaklıdere.

Places to Stay – Budget

Facing İtfaiye Meydanı (also called Opera Meydanı), on the eastern side of Atatürk Bulvarı across from the opera house, is a line of relatively cheap hotels. To find them, ask anyone to point the way to Gazi Lisesi, the high school on the eastern side of the square. During the day Opera Meydanı is full of second-hand stalls; at night it's creepily quiet, dimly lit and not a very suitable area for lone women to walk around.

The **Hotel Devran** (☎ 311 0485, Tavus Sokak 8), **Otel Mithat** (☎ 311 5410, Tavus Sokak 2) and **Otel 2000** (☎ 324 6995, Kosova Sokak 3) all post rates of US$12/19 for singles/doubles with bath. The Otel 2000 has the distinct advantage of newness but the Mithat is also trying hard with its decor.

The two-star **Otel Akman** (☎ 324 4140, Tavus Sokak 6) charges a bit more (US$16/ 25 with shower) for slightly more comfort and has a pide/kebap restaurant attached.

A step down in price and quality is the dingy **Otel Sipahi** (☎ 324 0235, Kosova Sokak 1) which has rooms with shower for US$10/15.

For rock-bottom budgets the **Otel Üçler** (☎ 310 6664, Kosova Sokak 7) and **Otel Fuar** (☎ 312 3288, Kosova Sokak 11) both charge US$6/10 for very basic rooms with shared baths and smelly toilets.

One street east of Kosova Sokak, there are a few more cheapies including the de-

cent **Ferah Oteli** (☎ 309 1174, Denizciler Caddesi 58), where some rooms have balconies overlooking Ankara. Rooms with showers cost US$10/15.

If you can afford to pay a bit more, there are better choices on the northern side of Ulus. To find them walk along the western side of Çankırı Caddesi and take the first turn on the left (Rüzgarlı Sokak). The one-star **Hotel As** (☎ 310 3998, fax 312 7584, Rüzgarlı Sokak 4) has pleasantly decorated rooms for US$13/20 with shower, but suffers from some street noise.

Turn right for the **Olimpiyat Hotel** (☎ 324 3331, Rüzgarlı Eşdost Sokak 18), where serviceable rooms with bath cost US$30 a head, less if you barter at quiet times.

Another quietish possibility right behind Ulus Meydanı is the **Yeni Otel** (☎ 310 4720, Sanayı Caddesi 5) where comfortable, if dimly lit, rooms with bath cost US$13/25. This place is popular with tour groups.

If you want to be near the museum and the Hisar, try **Otel Pınar** (☎ 311 8951, Hisarparkı Caddesi 14), on the steep road leading up from Ulus to the Hisar, which charges just US$7/12 for basic singles/doubles.

Places to Stay – Mid-Range

Near Ulus Compared with the mid-range hotels in Yenişehir, those near Ulus offer similar comfort for less money, with the advantage of being within walking distance of the Hisar and museum. All offer private bathrooms and include breakfast in their (negotiable) rates.

With the **Angora House Hotel** (☎ 309 8380, fax 309 8381, Kalekapısı Sokak 16–18) Ankara has at last what it has long lacked – a truly interesting place to stay. Tucked inside the Hisar, this place offers beautiful, individually decorated rooms in a restored house, convenient for Ankara's more interesting places to eat and with an atmosphere more like that of a home than a hotel. With only five rooms priced from US$40 to US$60 a single and US$55 to US$75 a double, advance reservation is certainly recommended.

There are lots of two- and three-star hotels north of Ulus on the western side of

Çankırı Caddesi, but most are hopelessly noisy. For the quieter places, go one street west of Çankırı Caddesi to Rüzgarlı Eşdost Sokak and try the **Hotel Yıldız** (☎ 312 7581, fax 312 7584, Rüzgarlı Eşdost Sokak 4), which has singles/doubles for US$35/50. Mattresses are rather lumpy though.

Better is the three-star **Hotel Oğultürk** (☎ 309 2900, fax 311 8321, Rüzgarlı Eşdost Sokak 6), whose boldly modern architecture – including a suspended lobby bar – contrasts sharply with the general workaday look of the street. Spotless modern rooms cost US$40/60.

Better still is the **Hotel Spor** (☎ 324 2165, fax 312 2153, Rüzgarlı Plevne Sokak 6), one street further west, where similarly priced rooms come with decent breakfast. This place is popular with French tour groups.

Up Hisarparkı Caddesi towards the Hisar is the **Hitit Otel** (☎ 310 8617, fax 311 4102, Hisarparkı Caddesi 12), a slightly faded but still serviceable hotel in a quieter setting with rooms for US$45/58, some with pleasant views over the hills.

Near Kızılay If you can afford the prices it would be better to stay in the quiet tree-shaded streets south-east of Kızılay, in the district called Bakanlıklar, close to lots of restaurants, cinemas and Internet cafes. All the hotels here offer private bath and TV, and many have air-con and minibars as well. Most will negotiate discounts if they're not busy, especially for stays of more than one night.

Karanfil Sokak is a pedestrian-only street one block east of Kızılay. **Otel Melodi** (☎ 417 6414, fax 418 7858, Karanfil Sokak 10) is relatively quiet, very convenient and charges US$55/80. The three-star **Eyüboğlu Hotel** (☎ 417 6400, fax 417 8125, Karanfil Sokak 73) is used by Turkish groups, and offers comfortable modern rooms for US$67/87. The simple one-star **Hotel Ergen** (☎ 417 5906, fax 425 7819, Karanfil Sokak 48) has a terrace cafe and charges only US$35/47 for rooms with rather feminine decor, some of them a bit smallish.

Cutting across Karanfil Sokak is tree-lined Olgunlar Sokak, with a row of second-hand book stalls. The two-star **Otel Elit** (☎ 417 4695, fax 417 4697, Olgunlar Sokak 10) is pleasingly decorated with rooms of moderate comfort for US$73/98. The lift is twice the usual width, which might make access easier for some guests. Facing it, the attractive **Metropol** (☎ 417 3060, fax 417 6990, Olgunlar Sokak 5) is marginally cheaper and boasts a pleasing restaurant and lobby.

The **Otel Büyük Erşan** (☎ 417 6045, fax 417 4943, Selanik Caddesi 74) has standard rooms on a quiet street with several cafes for a reasonable US$30/45.

Places to Stay – Top End

The excellent **First Apart-Hotel** (☎ 425 7575, fax 419 2714, İnkilap Sokak 29), a small modern building on a quiet backstreet three blocks east of Kızılay, has five types of accommodation: standard rooms with bath and TV for US$65, deluxe rooms for US$75, corner rooms for US$85, suites for US$110, and fully equipped apartments for US$145. Discounts of at least 20% are often available, especially if you stay several days.

Otherwise, try **Hotel Best** (☎ 467 0880, 468 1122, fax 467 0885, Atatürk Bulvarı 195), across the street from the US embassy. Rates are US$75/104, including breakfast. Advance reservations are usually necessary.

On a quiet street, the **Tetra Konur Otel** (☎ 419 2946, fax 417 4915, Konur Sokak 58) has four-star comforts and understated elegance. The posted prices of US$140/180 are usually subject to 30% discounts if it's quiet.

The **Ankara Hilton** (☎ 468 2888, fax 468 0909, Tahran Caddesi 12) has 327 plush rooms and suites on 16 floors near Çankaya and the embassies. The hotel's bold, modern architecture uses traditional Anatolian coloured stone, brass, glass and lots of greenery. Rates are US$230/250.

The **Sheraton Ankara Hotel & Towers** (☎ 468 5454, fax 467 1136, Noktalı Sokak) in Gaziosmanpaşa is a landmark cylindrical high-rise building which towers above a pleasant residential neighbourhood. Views from the upper-floor rooms in the Sheraton Towers section are superb. Rates are from US$217 to US$270 a single, and US$235 to US$287 a double.

Places to Eat

Arcund Ulus North of Ulus, along Çankırı Caddesi, the left-hand (western) side of the street has several big, bright restaurants featuring rotisserie chicken and other dishes; many serve beer and have a strictly male clientele. The *Uğrak Lokantası* will do you a big helping of chicken for just US$2.50.

Round the corner on Rüzgarlı Sokak is a big branch of the popular *Urfalı Kebap, Lahmacun, Pide ve Tatlı Sarayı* where a decent İskender kebap and cold drink costs US$2.50.

Walk south on the eastern side of Atatürk Bulvarı and turn into the second courtyard to find the smoky *Akman Boza ve Pasta Salonu*. Breakfasts, light lunches (sandwiches, omelettes etc) and pastries are a bit pricey, but this is a very popular place and always busy. *Boza*, the fermented millet drink, though traditionally a winter favourite, is served all year here. Expect to spend from US$4 or US$5 for a light lunch, less for tea and a pastry.

Right above the Akman Boza is the long-established *Kebabistan* (Kebap-Land), a family-oriented kebap and pide parlour serving fresh, cheap pide (US$1.25 to US$2) and kebaps (US$2 to US$3). The food is good any time but make sure you come before 3 pm for a full choice of dishes.

Escape the noise and fumes of the city by heading for Gençlik Parkı and the wistfully named *Sahil Lokantası* (Shore Restaurant), on the north side of the lake, near the open-air theatre. There are pleasantly shaded tables and inexpensive mezes cost around US$1.25, kebaps around US$2.50.

Citadel (Hisar) Within the citadel, several old houses have been converted into atmospheric restaurants serving alcohol. Come here for lunch after a visit to the Museum of Anatolian Civilisations, or for a special dinner. All are open daily in summer from 11 am to midnight.

The historic restaurant boom started off with the *Zenger Paşa Konağı* (☎ 311 7070, *Doyran Sokak 13*), which is still the best of the lot. A virtual museum of old-time Ankara, with a dining room on top, the Zenger's cuisine is Ottoman and fiercely authentic – right down to having local women knead, roll and bake the wafer-thin village bread before your eyes. Try *gözleme* (filled pancake), *mantı* (Turkish ravioli), or *şiş* kebap served on a hot tile. Full meals cost US$8 to US$12. The views from the dining room are spectacular, the museum rooms drenched with atmosphere. It's downhill beyond the Kale Washington restaurant.

If you go through Parmak Kapısı and walk straight on for several hundred metres you will come to the *Kınacılar Evi* (☎ 324 2500, *Kalekapısı Sokak 28*), on the right. Popular with tour groups, this lofty Ottoman *konak* (mansion) seems to place greater emphasis on a party atmosphere than on its food. Full meals cost from US$8 to US$15 per person, drinks included.

Although the interior decoration is nothing to write home about and the prices can be quite steep, the *Kale Washington* (☎ 311 4344, *Doyran Sokak 5–7*) currently offers the best-quality meals of the various Hisar restaurants. The menu is Turkish-style Continental, which means things like *şatobrian* (chateaubriand), *böf straganoff* (beef stroganoff), and *chicken kievski* (chicken kiev). Expect to pay around US$15 a head.

Come out of Parmak Kapısı and turn left for the promising new *Hatipoğlu Konağı* (☎ 311 3696, *Sevinç Sokak 3*), which has nightly live music from 9 pm and set menus from US$11 to US$15 a head.

Signposted up a side street close to the Museum of Anatolian Civilisations is the wonderfully atmospheric *Boyacızâde Konağı* (☎ 310 1515, *Berrak Sokak 7*), another converted mansion-restaurant set round a courtyard and specialising in fish dishes from about US$7.

Around Kızılay The streets north of Ziya Gökalp Caddesi and east of Atatürk Bulvarı are closed to motor vehicles and lined with places to eat and drink. Cheap, filling snacks such as *balık-ekmek* (a fried-fish sandwich) and *dönerli sandviç* (döner kebap in bread) sell for about US$1.25. *Kumpir*, a huge baked potato with a sauce or topping, is another favourite. Selanik Sokak north of Ziya

Gökalp Caddesi is best for cheap kebaps with dozens of places to choose from – you can hardly go wrong!

South of Yüksel Caddesi, Selanik Sokak boasts a row of pavement cafes that draw the capital's moneyed youth.

Sakarya Caddesi is parallel to and one block north of Ziya Gökalp Caddesi. Walk along it to the big Sakarya Süper Marketi, the ground floor of which is devoted to *snack stands*. Just to the right of the market are more snack stands (try the *Otlangaç*) selling İstanbul Çiçek Pasaj-style fried mussels on a stick, *bodrum lokması* (sweet fritters), *kuzu kokoreç* (grilled sheep's intestines) and similar treats.

For good kebaps and a place to sit down, find *Cihan Kebap (Selanik Caddesi 3/B)*, between Sakarya and Tuna Caddesis. A full meal with soup, bread and kebap costs from US$4 to US$6.

Even better is the spotless *Köşk (İnkilap Sokak 2)*, just round the corner, a veritable kebap palace with unbeatable prices. This huge two-storey eatery blazes with light, shining crystal and burnished brass, and canaries even manage to out-sing the mobile phones. İskender kebap costs US$3.50, İnegol *köfte* (a type of grilled meatballs) US$3 and chicken şiş US$4.

You can't go wrong at the *Körfez Lokantası (Bayındır Sokak 24)*, a half-block north of Ziya Gökalp Caddesi. Fish specialities cost around US$5 to US$9 per plate, but many kebaps cost less than US$4. Your meal comes with plentiful *lavaş*, freshly made unleavened village bread.

Next door to the Körfez is the *Göksu Restaurant (Bayındır Sokak 22/A)*, a long-standing favourite, with fancier surroundings and diligent service for much the same prices as the Körfez.

For those who just can't live without a Big Mac fix, there's a *McDonald's (Atatürk Bulvarı 89)* just north of Kızılay, on the eastern side of the boulevard.

Kavaklıdere This posh residential district up the hill towards Çankaya has several good restaurants and a flourishing cafe scene on Arjantin Caddesi behind the Sheraton Hotel. Take a bus south (uphill) along Atatürk Bulvarı and get out at Kuğulu Parkı next to the Polish embassy. Cross the park to reach Tunalı Hilmi Caddesi, the district's main commercial street.

In general this is not the cheapest area to eat out. However, at *Hacı Arif Bey (Güniz Sokak 48)*, right in the shadow of the Hilton Hotel, a meal of hummus, kebap and soft drink, overlooking a terrapin pool, costs a bargain US$6 or so. Not surprisingly this is a very popular place.

Yakamoz (Tunalı Hilmi Caddesi 114/J 2–3), right at the edge of Kuğulu Parkı, is a big, busy place specialising in seafood. The best deal is the set menu with drinks for US$15 per couple. Ordering a la carte, seafood plates cost around US$8 to US$10.

The popular *Cafe des Cafes (Tunalı Hilmi Caddesi)* is a Parisian-style, wood-floored cafe where you can eat dishes such as chicken and spinach crepe and drink a cappuccino for around US$7.

Cross the road and turn left down Bülten Sokak to find several pleasing cafes and restaurants. Long-time Ulus resident, *Çiçek Lokantası (Bülten Sokak 9)* has just moved here. Soup, kebap, salad and a drink at the familiar white-clothed tables costs around US$6 to US$10.

Right beside it is a branch of the popular *Paul* patisseries, while across the road, hidden inside an apartment block (you'll need to ring the bell) is *Fincan Cafe*; either place is perfect for coffee and cakes after a movie.

For a romantic dinner with low lights and soft music, seek out *Villa (☎ 427 0838, Boğaz Sokak 13)*, a pizza and steak house on a quiet residential street up the hill behind the Sheraton. Dinner with drinks won't be much more than US$15 to US$20 per person. There's live music on Wednesday, Friday and Saturday night.

On Sunday morning few things could be more pleasant than heading up Arjantin Caddesi beside the Sheraton Hotel for brunch alongside Ankara's elite. There's a string of places to choose from; the following are simply favourites. Try the *Cafe Turkish Daily News (☎ 468 4513, Arjantin Caddesi)* which is everything the newspaper is not – stylish, colourful and modern. Expect to pay around US$10 for a giant Mexican chicken sandwich with fries – newspaper thrown in free, of course!

Nearby is *Paul (☎ 427 6811, Arjantin Caddesi 18)*, a French-style patisserie selling chocolate eclairs, strawberry tarts, croque monsieur and full breakfasts for US$6.

Up the hill is *Cafe Kristiansen (☎ 466 1346, Arjantin Caddesi 24)* where you can eat Danish-style open sandwiches.

Çankaya For dinner with a view, head straight for the *Dönen (Revolving) Restaurant (☎ 440 7412, Atakule)* at the top of the Atakule Tower. Expect to pay at least US$20 a head for a meal, less for coffee and a cake – making a restaurant reservation exempts you from paying the tower admission fee.

Entertainment

Most visitors don't hang around Ankara long enough to get to grips with the nightlife. However, in a big city with several universities it's easy enough to find a good night's entertainment.

Gazinos, Bars & Discos To mingle with Turkish students, head for Kızılay and Bayındır Sokak, between Sakarya Caddesi and Tuna Caddesi. The street is lined with Turkish *gazinos* (nightclubs), among them *Forza* and *Kırmızı İskele*, which usually have live Turkish pop music and beers for little more than US$1.50.

South of the pool in Gençlik Parkı are several more traditional *gazinos* with live entertainment, drinks and food at low to moderate prices; to the north are mostly *teahouses* which vie with one another to advertise the lowest-priced beer.

The upmarket nightlife scene is concentrated in Kavaklıdere, Ayrancı, Gaziosmanpaşa and Çankaya. From Kuğulu Parkı in Kavaklıdere, go north on Tunalı Hilmi Caddesi one block to Bilir Sokak and turn right to find *Jazz Time (Bilir Sokak 4/1)*, which usually has live Turkish pop or folk artists and, behind it, the quieter *Gitanes* bar. Local drinks are the standard US$2.50 for rakı or gin and tonic, and about US$1.50 for

beer. The heaving *North Shield* on Güvenlik Caddesi does its best to emulate the atmosphere of a British pub.

Cult (☎ 447 6390, Küpe Sokak 8) in Gaziosmanpaşa is one of those trendy clubs where you need to arrive before 10 pm to be able to see the bar. When it closes at midnight, locals in the know often head on to the *Dip Club (☎ 468 5783, Güvenlik Caddesi 97)* underneath the Süleyman Nazıf restaurant in Ayrancı. The US$8.50 entry fee is hardly needed to pay the wages of the robot bar-tender!

Also popular is the *Home Club (☎ 424 0400, Esat Caddesi 37)* in Küçük Esat where admission costs a hefty US$10 (free entry for women on Fridays).

Dancers may also want to seek out relative newcomer *Kashmere (☎ 466 4400, Farabi Sokak 34)*, a dress-to-kill venue in Çankaya.

Cinema Several cinemas show recently released Western films, usually in the original language with Turkish subtitles. Try *Akün Sineması (☎ 427 7656, Atatürk Bulvarı 227, Kavaklıdere)*; the *Kavaklıdere (☎ 468 7193, Tunalı Hilmi Caddesi 105)*, and the *Metropol (☎ 425 7478, Selanik Caddesi 76, Kızılay)*. See the *Turkish Daily News* for program details.

Opera, Ballet & Classical Music Beginning in the autumn and running through until spring, Ankara has regular seasons of opera, ballet, symphony and chamber music, often with visiting foreign artists. The performances, though not necessarily world-class, are enthusiastically done, and tickets are ridiculously cheap – usually around US$4 to US$6.

The small *opera house* is on Atatürk Bulvarı, just past the entrance to Gençlik Parkı. Atatürk fell in love with opera while serving as military attache in Sofia, and was determined to introduce it to Ankara. Try the Web site www.devtiyatro.gov.tr for program details

Bilkent University is a keen sponsor of classical music concerts; call ☎ 266 4539 for program details.

CENTRAL ANATOLIA

Shopping

Ulus is the cheaper part of town to shop in, but to see what fashionable Turkey likes to spend its money on, you'll need to head south to Kızılay and Kavaklıdere.

To shop for a picnic, walk up Hisarparkı Caddesi, out of Ulus, and turn right at the first traffic signal onto Susam Sokak; a Ziraat Bankası will be on your right. Bear left, then turn left and on your right will be Ankara's lively, colourful Yeni Haller vegetable market.

Behind the vegetable market, on Konya Caddesi, is the Vakıf Suluhan Çarşısı, a restored *han* (caravanserai) with lots of clothes shops, a cafe, toilets and a small free-standing mosque in its courtyard.

The area around the Parmak Kapısı entrance to the Hisar was traditionally a centre for trading in Angora wool. Right by the gate is a row of dried-fruit stalls. Turn left to find the carpet and antique shops, though you'll need to be wary of the prices.

Tunalı Hilmi Caddesi in Kavaklıdere is a great place to watch wealthier Ankaralıs shopping. It even has a branch of the British department store Marks & Spencer. Nearby on İran Caddesi, just before you reach the Sheraton Hotel, is Kanum, a flashy shopping mall which wouldn't look out of place in London.

The tourist offices in Maltepe and Gesav, at Kireçli Sokak 6, inside the Hisar are good places to pick up traditional Turkish arts and crafts.

Getting There & Away

Air Ankara's Esenboğa airport (☎ 398 0100), 33km north of the city centre, is the hub for Turkey's domestic flight network.

Turkish Airlines (☎ 428 1700, fax 428 1681) has an office at Atatürk Bulvarı 154, Kavaklıdere.

Most one-way fares (on Turkish Airlines) from Ankara to various destinations within Turkey cost between US$70 and US$100. The following table lists nonstop summer flights on Turkish Airlines (THY); many more cities can be reached via connections in İstanbul. All schedules are subject to change.

destination	timetable
Adana	3 daily
Antalya	3 daily
Bodrum	daily
Diyarbakır	2 daily
Erzurum	2 daily
İstanbul	over 14 flights daily
İzmir	more than 12 daily
Samsun	daily except Saturday
Trabzon	3 daily
Van	2 daily

Other international airlines sometimes have flights to Ankara, or connections with Turkish Airlines' flights from İstanbul. Contact details of the offices of some of the major airlines are as follows:

Air France (☎ 467 4404) Atatürk Bulvarı 231/7, Kavaklıdere
British Airways (☎ 467 5557) Atatürk Bulvarı 237/29, Kavaklıdere
KLM (☎ 417 5616, fax 440 6108) Atatürk Bulvarı 199, 2nd floor, Kavaklıdere

Bus Every city or town of any size has direct buses to Ankara. From İstanbul there's a bus to Ankara every 15 minutes throughout the day and late into the night.

AŞTİ (Ankara Şehirlerarası Terminalı İşletmesi), Ankara's gigantic bus station, is also known as the Yeni Terminal, Yeni Otogar and Yeni Garaj. It's at the western end of the Ankaray underground train line, 5km due west of Bakanlıklar and the Grand National Assembly building, on Bahçelerarası Caddesi (Konya Devlet Yolu) just north of İsmet İnönü Bulvarı (Eskişehir Yolu).

The terminal follows the traditional airport plan with departure gates on the upper level and arrivals on the lower but it's already starting to fray at the edges; escalators rarely work, nor does the huge airport-style arrivals and departures board.

Nevertheless, AŞTİ has most services a traveller might want, including several restaurants, a mosque, a first-aid post, a nursery, ATMs, telephones and a newsstand selling the *Turkish Daily News*. The *emanet* (left-luggage room) on the lower level charges according to the value of the item stored! Also on the lower level are empty benches where you can spread out and have a rest if you've got a longish wait.

As Ankara has many buses to all parts of the country, it's often fine to arrive at the otogar, buy a ticket, and be on your way within the hour. Don't try this over public holidays though.

AŞTİ has 80 *gişe* (ticket counters). The major companies are:

bus company	gişe no
Kamil Koç	17, 18
Köseoğlu	48
Metro	41
Pamukkale	58, 59
Uludağ	45
Ulusoy	13
Varan	12

If these companies don't go to your destination, one of the bus company runners will direct you to another one that does.

Many bus companies also maintain city-centre ticket offices near Kızılay on Ziya Gökalp Caddesi, Gazi Mustafa Kemal Bulvarı, İzmir Caddesi and Menekşe Sokak. Several premium bus companies, including Varan and Ulusoy, have their own terminal facilities near the otogar. The Varan ticket office (☎ 312-426 9753) is south of Kızılay on the eastern side of Atatürk Bulvarı. The table below lists details of some useful daily routes from Ankara.

Train The top trains between İstanbul and Ankara are quite good, and there are useful services to Adana, Kayseri, Sivas and a few other cities. Ankara Garı (☎ 311 0620) has a PTT with exchange facilities, a restaurant, snack shops, ATMs, telephones and a left-luggage room. The newsstand sells the *Turkish Daily News* but you'll need to ask. Havaş buses to Esenboğa airport depart from the station forecourt.

The nightly *Anadolu Ekspresi* to İstanbul (Haydarpaşa) via Eskişehir has couchette (US$8), Pullman (US$6.50) and sleeping (US$26 to US$30) cars. It leaves Ankara at 10 pm and arrives at 7.15 am. A similar sleeping-car train leaves at 10.30 pm.

Services from Ankara's Otogar

destination	fare (US$)	time (hr)	distance (km)	daily services
Adana	10	10	490	frequent buses
Amasya	7	5	335	frequent buses
Antalya	from 12	8	550	frequent buses
Bodrum	from 12	13	785	a dozen buses (summer)
Bursa	10	5½	400	hourly buses
Denizli (for Pamukkale)	9	7	480	frequent buses
Diyarbakır	20	13	945	several buses
Erzurum	18	12	925	several buses
Gaziantep	12	10	705	frequent buses
İstanbul	10–23	5–5½	450	shuttle bus service
İzmir	10	8	600	at least hourly buses
Kayseri	9	4½	330	very frequent buses
Konya	8	3	260	very frequent buses
Marmaris	15	10	780	a dozen buses (summer)
Nevşehir (for Göreme, Uçhisar, Ürgüp)	8	5	285	frequent buses
Samsun	12	7	420	frequent buses
Sivas	10	6	450	frequen buses
Sungurlu (for Boğazkale)	5	2½	175	hourly buses
Trabzon	from 18	12	780	several buses

CENTRAL ANATOLIA

The nightly *Ankara Ekspresi* to İstanbul's Haydarpaşa station is an all-sleeping-car express. Private compartments cost US$30/40 a single/double. It departs Ankara at 10.30 pm and arrives in İstanbul at 7.35 am.

The *Başarı Ekspresi* departs Ankara at 1.15 pm and gets to İstanbul (Haydarpaşa) about 7½ hours later, arriving at 8.55 pm. It's an air-conditioned, all-1st-class day train. The fare is US$14, or US$10 for students.

The *Başkent Ekspresi* (Capital Express), pride of the Turkish State Railways, departs Ankara at 10 am and makes the run to İstanbul (Hydarpaşa) in 6½ hours, the fastest train of all. This air-conditioned, super-1st-class day train has Pullman seats, video, and meals served at your seat. The fare is US$14; US$10 for students. The *Fatih Ekspresi* is a night train to İstanbul (Haydarpaşa), departing Ankara at 11.30 pm, arriving in İstanbul at 7.20 am, otherwise similar to the *Başkent* in comfort, speed and price.

The *Boğaziçi Ekspresi* (Bosphorus Express) is a comfortable, if faded, 1st-class Pullman-car train costing US$10 between Ankara and İstanbul (Haydarpaşa), departing at 1.30 pm, and arriving in İstanbul at 10.27 pm.

The *Çukurova Ekspresi* departs Ankara daily in the evening hauling one-class coaches, couchette cars and sleeping cars to Mersin and Adana, arriving about 12 hours later. One-way tickets between Ankara and Adana or Mersin cost US$9/12 in a coach/couchette. Fares in a sleeping compartment cost US$20/34/45 for one/two/three people.

The *Doğu Ekspresi* stops at Ankara on its long trip from İstanbul to Kars, via Sivas, Erzincan and Erzurum.

You can also pick up the *Güney-Vangölü Ekspresi* as it makes its way east to Elazığ Junction via Kayseri, Sivas and Malatya. At the junction, the train continues as the *Vangölü* (Lake Van) *Ekspresi* to Tatvan, or the *Güney* (Southern) *Ekspresi* to Diyarbakır and Kurtalan (east of Diyarbakır), depending upon the day. For the *Vangölü Ekspresi* eastbound, board in Ankara on Tuesday, Thursday or Sunday. For the *Güney*, board in Ankara on Monday, Wednesday, Friday or Saturday. A ticket from Ankara costs US$8 to Tatvan and US$6 to Diyarbakır. The fare in a sleeping car is from US$20/34/45 for one/two/three people.

Getting Around

To/From the Airport Esenboğa airport is 33km north of the city. Havaş buses (US$3.50) depart about every 30 minutes from AŞTİ otogar, stopping at the train station, Ankara Garı, but as they may leave sooner if they fill up, claim your seat at least two hours before flight time. Minimum check-in time for domestic flights is 45 minutes before departure.

When your flight arrives in Ankara, grab your luggage and board the Havaş bus quickly as it will depart within half an hour. Taxis between the airport and the city cost about US$25.

To/From AŞTİ Otogar Most good bus companies provide a free *servis* bus into the city centre; ask '*servis var mı?*'.

Otherwise the easiest way to get into town is on the Ankaray underground train, which has a station right next to AŞTİ otogar. Take it to Maltepe station for the tourist office or the train station (a 10-minute walk), or to Kızılay for the three- and four-star hotels in Kızılay and Bakanlıklar. Change at Kızılay for Ulus and the cheap hotels.

City bus No 198 leaves from the arrivals level of the bus terminal for the Gar and Ulus; bus No 623 goes via Kızılay to Gaziler.

For a dolmuş to Ulus, go to the avenue in front of AŞTİ otogar, cross to the other side, and catch an 'Ulus-Balgat' dolmuş to Ulus. 'Gölbaşı-Opera Meydanı' dolmuşes take you to Opera Meydanı and its cheap hotels.

A taxi between the otogar and the train station costs about US$4; about US$4.50 to Ulus or Kızılay.

To/From Ankara Garı The train station is about 1.25km south-west of Ulus and 3km north-west of Kızılay. Any bus or dolmuş heading north-east along Cumhuriyet Bulvarı (straight out the station door), such as No 411 or 281, will take you to Ulus. Many buses (such as No 411) heading east along Talat Paşa Bulvarı which runs past the station, go to Kızılay and/or Kavaklıdere; look on their signboards for your destination.

It's about 1km from the station to Opera Meydanı's hotels; any bus headed east along Talat Paşa Bulvarı will drop you within a few hundred metres if you ask for Gazi Lisesi, the high school nearby.

To go from the train station to the AŞTİ otogar, follow the underpass in the train station through several shopping areas and you'll eventually end up at the Maltepe Ankaray station. Take the Ankaray line to the AŞTİ otogar.

Bus Ankara has a good and frequent bus and minibus network. Signs on the front and side of the bus are better guides than route numbers. Buses marked 'Ulus' and 'Çankaya' ply the entire length of Atatürk Bulvarı. Those marked 'Gar' go to the train station; those marked 'AŞTİ', or one of the otogar's other names, will drop you off there.

City bus tickets costing US$0.50 can be bought from ticket kiosks at major bus stops or from shops and vendors displaying a sign reading 'EGO Bilet Bayii' or 'EGO Bileti Satılır', or some other phrase with 'EGO Bilet' in it. These can be used on buses with 'EGO' written on the front; on non-EGO buses you pay the conductor. Cards for five or 10 journeys cost a flat US$2.50/5, and can be used on the underground trains as well.

Underground Ankara's underground train network has two lines: the Ankaray line running between AŞTİ otogar in the west through Kızılay to Dikimevi in the east; and the Metro line running from Kızılay northwest via Sıhhiye, Maltepe and Ulus to Batıkent. The two lines interconnect at Kızılay.

Single journey tickets cost US$0.50 or you can buy a card for five or 10 journeys also valid on 'EGO' buses (see Bus earlier).

Car Don't rent a car to drive around Ankara, and if you've got one, do yourself a favour and use public transport instead. Driving is chaotic and signs are woefully insufficient.

If you plan to hire a car to drive out of Ankara, there are many small local com-

panies, and the major international firms have offices at Esenboğa airport and in the city centre. Details of some of these follow:

Avis (☎ 467 2315, fax 467 5703) Tunus Caddesi 68/2, Kavaklıdere

Budget (☎ 417 5952, fax 425 9608) Tunus Caddesi 39/A, Kavaklıdere

Europcar (☎ 418 3430, 418 3877, fax 417 8445) (National, Interrent, Kemwel) Akçay Yokuşu 25/C, Bakanlıklar

Hertz (☎ 418 8440) Akay Caddesi, Kızılırmak Sokak 1/A, Bakanlıklar

Thrifty (☎ 436 0505, 436 0606) Köroğlu Caddesi 65/B, Gaziosmanpaşa

Taxi Every other vehicle on the road seems to be a taxi and they all have meters. The drop rate is US$0.60; an average trip costs around US$3 during daylight hours, 50% more at night.

AROUND ANKARA

If you need to stay in Ankara for a few days it's worth considering a side trip to the Phrygian remains at Gordion or the Hittite sites near Boğazkale.

Gordion & Polatlı

The capital of ancient Phrygia, Gordion lies 106km west of Ankara in the village of Yassıhöyük.

Gordion was occupied by the Phrygians as early as the 9th century BC, and soon afterwards became their royal capital. Although destroyed during the Cimmerian invasion, Gordion was later rebuilt, only to be conquered first by the Lydians and then by the Persians. Alexander the Great came through and cut the Gordian Knot in 333 BC, but the Galatian occupation of 278 BC put an end to what was left of the city. (For more on the Phrygians, see Midas Şehri in the Western Anatolia chapter.)

The landscape around Yassıhöyük is dotted with tumuli (burial mounds) that cover the graves of the Phrygian kings. Of 80 identified tumuli roughly half have been excavated, as has the site of the Gordion acropolis, which revealed 18 different levels of civilisation from the Bronze Age to Roman times.

Golden Touch & Gordian Knot

The Phrygians left us two enduring legends. The first is of King Midas, who showed hospitality toward Silenus, chief of the satyrs, and was rewarded by the god with a wish – anything he desired. Midas asked that everything he touch turn to gold.

Granted his wish, at first Midas was delighted to be able to turn common objects into precious ones but he soon discovered to his shock that the food he picked up to eat also turned to gold, and that he was in danger of starvation. When he embraced his beloved daughter, she became a lifeless golden statue. He pleaded to be relieved of the golden touch, and was told to bathe in the Pactolus stream, which he did. The sands of the Pactolus supposedly turned to gold, and gold dust continued to be found there for centuries afterwards.

The second story concerns the Gordian Knot. Legend says that during a period of civil unrest, a man named Gordius, his wife and his son Midas arrived at the site of Gordion in a wooden peasant's cart. An oracle had declared that the ruler who would save Phrygia from its turmoil would arrive in such a cart, and so Gordius was immediately proclaimed king of Phrygia, with Midas as his successor. Subsequent rulers took the names Gordius and Midas in succession.

The cart that had brought Gordius and his family to glory was enshrined in a temple, and an oracle foretold that whoever could untie the knot that bound the pole to the yoke of the cart would be the ruler of all Asia. Arriving in Gordion in 333 BC, intent on the conquest of Asia, Alexander the Great attempted to untie the knot but quickly became frustrated, and severed it with his sword. He went on to conquer all of Asia anyway but his early death was often attributed to this piece of impetuousness.

The sites can easily be visited on a day trip from Ankara. Otherwise the small town of Polatlı, 18km away, has hotels and restaurants.

Acropolis Although excavations here have yielded a wealth of data on Gordion's many civilisations, the 8th century BC acropolis itself (across the road from a petrol station on the far side of the village as you approach from Polatlı) is not particularly exciting for the casual visitor.

The lofty main, or Phrygian, Gate on the city's western side was approached by a 6m-wide ramp. Within the fortified enclosure were four large square halls (megara) from which the king and his priests and ministers ruled the empire. Coloured mosaics found in one of these halls are now on display outside the museum.

Midas Tümülüsü & Gordion Müzesi

In 1957 archaeologists discovered the intact tomb of a Phrygian king probably buried sometime between 750 and 725 BC. The tomb is actually a gabled 'cottage' of pine surrounded by juniper logs, buried beneath a tumulus 60m high and 300m in diameter. It's the oldest wooden structure ever found in Anatolia, and perhaps in the world. The tunnel and tomb entrance are modern additions to ease access for visitors.

Having first drilled into the tumulus from above to determine the placement and composition of the tomb, the archaeologists then tunnelled in from the side. Inside the tomb they found the body of a 61- to 65-year-old man, 1.59m tall, surrounded with burial objects but without weapons or jewellery of silver or gold. The occupant's name remains unknown although both 'Gordius' and 'Midas' are good bets; most Phrygian kings seem to have been called one or the other.

Across the road the museum houses finds from the Bronze Age (3000–2000 BC), Hittite period (2000–1000 BC), and Phrygian and Hellenistic times (1000–330 BC), especially fibulae (brooches), whistles, decorations and arrowheads. (The best objects were removed to Ankara's Museum of Anatolian Civilisations.)

In the grounds are several simple mosaics together with a reconstructed Galatian tomb.

Both tomb and museum are open from 8.30 am to 5.30 pm, daily. Joint admission costs US$3.75. Cafe Gordion, by the gate, sells cold drinks and gözleme.

Getting There & Away Buses run from Ankara otogar to Polatlı at least every half an hour (US$1.75, one hour) but, once there, you'll be lucky to find a dolmuş. Taxi drivers charge about US$25 to run you to Gordion and back, including waiting time.

To get to Gordion from Polatlı, drive out on the Ayaş road until you come to a sign on the left, 7km before Yassıhöyük village.

North Central Anatolia

The region north-east of Ankara and north-west of Sivas has a little of everything: ancient Hittite ruins, gritty industrial cities, graceful old Ottoman towns, mountain scenery and plains. Most travellers only stop here on their way to somewhere else, but it's worth visiting the well-preserved Ottoman town of Safranbolu; the Hittite ruins at Boğazkale, near Sungurlu; and the historic towns of Amasya, situated in a dramatic river gorge, and Tokat.

SAFRANBOLU
☎ 370 • pop 32,500

Hidden in the hill country 225km north of Ankara, Safranbolu boasts a glorious collection of old Ottoman houses, so beautifully preserved that it qualifies as a Unesco World Heritage Site, on a par with Florence in Italy. It's a world away from the grim steel-manufacturing city of Karabük just 10km to the south. These days Safranbolu is well and truly on the Turkish tourist map although still not much visited by foreigners. It's a place to enjoy walking along narrow cobbled lanes and observing traditional trades and crafts practised just as they were in Ottoman times.

History
During the 17th century, the main Ottoman trade route between Gerede and the Black Sea coast passed through Safranbolu, bringing commerce, prominence and wealth to the town. During the 18th and 19th centuries Safranbolu's wealthy inhabitants built spacious mansions of sun-dried mud bricks, wood and stucco. The families of the large population of prosperous artisans built less impressive but similarly sturdy, harmonious homes, and an unusually large number of these buildings survive today. During the 19th century about 20 to 25% of Safranbolu's population were Ottoman Greeks, most of whom moved to Greece during the exchange of populations following WWI. Their principal church, dedicated to St Stephen, has been restored as Kıranköy's Ulu Cami (Great Mosque).

Orientation & Information
Coming from Karabük, you arrive in Kıranköy (Yenişehir), the modern part of Safranbolu, arrayed along the ridge of a hill. If you continue uphill from the traffic roundabout you will reach the section called Bağlar, with its centre at Köyiçi, which has many interesting old houses.

Turn right (south-east) at the roundabout and go 1.7km, down the hill, up the other side and down again to reach the centre of Old Safranbolu (Eski Safranbolu), which is called Çarşı (Market). On Saturday a busy market takes place in the main square, marked by the Kazdağlı Camii (1779). Although there are a few modern hotels in Kıranköy, most of what you've come to see lies in Eski Safranbolu and in Bağlar which has more wonderful old houses.

Çarşı's tourist office (☎ 712 3863) is 300m from the main square in the *arasta* or market place. A second information office sponsored by the Kültür ve Turizm Vakfı or Safranbolu Culture & Tourism Association (☎ 712 1047) is on the corner of the road leading up to Kıranköy.

To use the Natural Internet Cafe you'll need to take a bus up to Kıranköy and look for it near the Metro bus office.

Historic Architecture
In Ottoman times, prosperous residents of Safranbolu maintained two households. In winter they occupied their town houses in Çarşı, situated at the meeting point of three valleys and protected from the winter winds. During the warm months they moved to

summer houses amid the vineyards of Bağlar (Vines). After the iron and steel works at Karabük were established in 1938, modern houses built by factory staff encroached on the old neighbourhoods of Bağlar, although Çarşı remained virtually untouched.

Some of the largest houses had indoor pools, which, though big enough to be swimming pools, were not used as such. The running water cooled the room and gave a pleasant background sound. The best and most accessible example of this is the **Havuzlu Asmazlar Konağı** (Mansion with Pool), now run as a hotel by the Turkish Touring & Automobile Association. See Places to Stay later in this section for details.

Several historic houses have been restored and as time goes on, more and more are being saved from deterioration. At the time of writing the following old houses were open to the public: the **Kaymakamlar Müze Evi, Mümtazlar Konağı, Kileciler Evi** and **Karaüzümler Evi**. Most are open during daylight hours, charge US$0.75 for admission and serve tea in their gardens. In winter some of them may be closed but as there's little to see inside the houses, apart from their architecture, that isn't such a disaster.

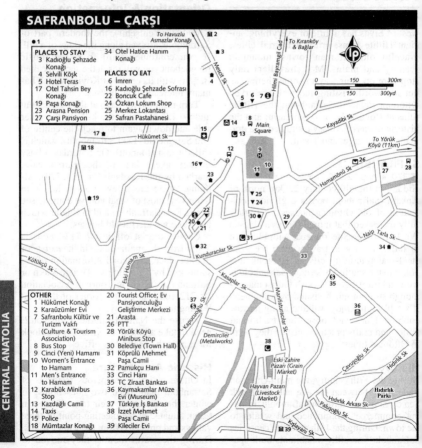

SAFRANBOLU – ÇARŞI

PLACES TO STAY
3 Kadıoğlu Şehzade Konağı
4 Selvili Köşk
5 Hotel Teras
17 Otel Tahsin Bey Konağı
19 Paşa Konağı
23 Arasna Pension
27 Çarşı Pansiyon
34 Otel Hatice Hanım Konağı

PLACES TO EAT
6 İmren
16 Kadıoğlu Şehzade Sofrası
22 Boncuk Cafe
24 Özkan Lokum Shop
25 Merkez Lokantası
29 Safran Pastahanesi

OTHER
1 Hükümet Konağı
2 Karaüzümler Evi
7 Safranbolu Kültür ve Turizm Vakfı (Culture & Tourism Association)
8 Bus Stop
9 Cinci (Yeni) Hamamı
10 Women's Entrance to Hamam
11 Men's Entrance to Hamam
12 Karabük Minibus Stop
13 Kazdağlı Camii
14 Taxis
15 Police
18 Mümtazlar Konağı
20 Tourist Office; Ev Pansiyonculuğu Geliştirme Merkezi
21 Arasta
26 PTT
28 Yörük Köyü Minibus Stop
30 Belediye (Town Hall)
31 Köprülü Mehmet Paşa Camii
32 Pamukçu Hanı
33 Cinci Hanı
35 TC Ziraat Bankası
36 Kaymakamlar Müze Evi (Museum)
37 Türkiye İş Bankası
38 İzzet Mehmet Paşa Camii
39 Kileciler Evi

To Havuzlu Asmazlar Konağı
To Kıranköy & Bağlar
Mecit Sk
Hilmi Bayramgil Cad
Hükümet Sk
Main Square
Kayadibi Sk
To Yörük Köyü (11km)
Hamamönü Sk
Naip Tarla Sk
Kunduracılar Sk
Kütükçü Sk
Eski Hamam Sk
Kasaplar Sk
Manifaturacılar Sk
Kapucuoğlu Sk
Demirciler (Metalworks)
Eski Zahire Pazarı (Grain Market)
Çavuşoğlu Sk
Hayvan Pazarı (Livestock Market)
Hıdırlık Sk
Hıdırlık Arkası Sk
Paluoğlu Sk
Kışlayanı Sk
Hıdırlık Parkı

0   150   300m
0   150   300yd

CENTRAL ANATOLIA

TURKEY'S WOODEN HOUSES

These days most Turkish towns are vanishing beneath a blanket of brick and concrete. It wasn't always like this, of course, and in the 19th century most towns and villages boasted fine wooden houses. Enthusiasts for such houses will find many in Afyon, Amasya or Tokat, but the best are in Safranbolu, declared a Unesco World Heritage Site due to its domestic architecture.

Ottoman wooden houses generally had two or three storeys, the upper storeys jutting out over the lower ones on carved corbels (brackets). Their timber frames were filled with adobe and then plastered with a mixture of mud and straw. Sometimes the houses were left unsealed but in towns they were usually given a finish of plaster or whitewash,

Inset: Antlers hanging, to ward off bad luck, above the wooden shutters of an old house in Yörük Köyü.

Bottom: The large Ottoman houses of Yörük Köyü, east of Safranbolu, reflect the historic wealth of this small town.

BOTH PHOTOS BY PAT YALE

with decorative flourishes in plaster or wood. The wealthier the owner, the fancier the decoration.

Lower storey windows often had ornamental grilles on them, while the upper ones were decorated with fretwork. The houses of the wealthy sometimes had a stained-glass skylight above the door. Many houses had double doors allowing carts through into a courtyard.

Inside, the larger houses had 10 to 12 rooms, divided into *selamlık* (men's quarters) and *haremlik* (women's quarters). Rooms were often decorated with built-in niches and cupboards, and had fine plaster fireplaces with *yaşmaks* (conical hoods). Sometimes the ceilings were very elaborate; that of the Paşa Odası of Tokat's Latifoğlu Konağı, for example, is thought to emulate a chandelier in wood.

The houses rarely had much furniture beyond a low bench or *sedir* around the walls. Families dined at a table board which was brought out and placed on a stand at mealtimes and covered with a cloth which also covered the diners' laps and doubled as a napkin. Bedding was spread out at night and stored in cupboards during the day. Washing facilities were usually concealed inside closets.

Many Turks now see these old houses as draughty fire hazards, lacking in modern conveniences and expensive to maintain. Cheaper, sturdier, more convenient apartment blocks are preferred. But a conservation movement has taken hold, and government aid is often available to help people maintain these charming historic houses.

OLIVIER CIRENDINI

Many Ottoman wooden houses are dilapidated and left to fall into disrepair. Even so, they retain much of their original charm.

There are more fine houses in **Bağlar**, but they're much more spread out and difficult to visit. Ask at the tourist office for more information.

Other Historic Buildings

Çarşı's most famous and imposing structure is the large stone **Cinci Hanı**, a caravanserai dating from 1645. Work on converting it into a luxury hotel had come to a halt at the time of writing.

Right by Çarşı's main square is the **Cinci Hamamı**, built along with the Cinci Hanı and still in service, with lots of creamy marble and glass dome lights which let in dramatic rays of sunshine. There are separate baths for men (Erkekler Kısmı) and women (Kadınlar Kısmı); the women's section may look closed but if you ask, someone will come and open it for you. This is a great place to get cleaned up for between US$2 and US$4 depending on what extras you choose.

The large **Köprülü Mehmet Paşa Camii** beside the arasta was built in 1662; the **İzzet Mehmet Paşa Camii** in 1796.

Walk uphill past the Kaymakamlar Evi to reach **Hıdırlık Parkı**, which offers excellent views of the town. Peek through the windows of the locked Tomb of Ahmet Lütfi and you'll see a heap of coins left by the faithful. Safranbolu's kale was demolished early in the last century to make way for the ornamented **hükümet konağı** (government building) on the hilltop across the valley.

Places to Stay

Safranbolu is very popular with Turkish tourists at weekends and holidays, and prices are on average US$10 a head higher at those times; the prices given in this section are for midweek. If you can't visit midweek, be sure to book ahead to guarantee a bed.

Even if you're on a tight budget, consider splashing out a bit in Safranbolu since staying in one of the converted Ottoman houses is a rare and reasonably priced treat. With the exception of the Havuzlu Asmazlar Konağı, most of the hotels are run like Turkish homes, which means you must remove your shoes before going upstairs, sometimes even before reaching the check-in desk.

If you need to catch an early bus there are a few basic pensions in Kıranköy, but for some odd reason the better new hotels there actually charge more than the lovely restored Ottoman hotels of the old town.

Places to Stay – Budget

Çarşı Pansiyon (☎ 725 1079, Babasultan Mahallesi, Bozkurt Sokak 1) is a small place not far from the Cinci Hanı. Rooms with baths come with low-level beds, carpets and pretty curtains for US$14/27 a single/double (breakfast included). Similar and charging the same prices is the *Hotel Teras* (☎ 725 1748, Mescit Sokak 4).

Arasna Pension (☎ 712 4170, Arasta Arkası Sokak 7) has a restaurant and live music on Wednesday, Friday, Saturday and Sunday nights in summer, when an early night might be out of the question. Rooms go for US$14/27 with shower and breakfast.

Places to Stay – Mid-Range

The *Ev Pansiyonculuğu Geliştirme Merkezi* (☎ 712 7236, Yemeniciler Arastası 2), or Home Pension Development Centre, next to the tourist office, makes reservations for overnight stays in restored houses. Rates are US$19 to US$26 a single, US$29 to US$38 a double, breakfast included. Some rooms have private baths; in others you share with the family. Use their scrapbook of photos to help you choose.

The most atmospheric of the old house-hotels is the *Havuzlu Asmazlar Konağı* (☎ 725 2883, fax 712 3824, Mescit Sokak), restored and operated by the Turkish Touring and Automobile Association. It's enclosed behind high walls 400m uphill from Çarşı's main square, opposite the turn off for the Bartın-Zonguldak road. As soon as you enter you glimpse the fine pool that gives the house its name (*havuzlu* means 'with pool'), right in the centre of the main room, surrounded by low sofas and small brass-tray tables at which guests take breakfast and afternoon tea.

The 11 guest rooms are beautifully furnished with brass beds, sedirs, brass tables and kilims; rooms 14, 15, 20 and 21 upstairs are the nicest. Rooms cost US$30/50 midweek. Bathrooms are minuscule and sound-proofing minimal but these are minor inconveniences. Overflow rooms in a house across the road and in the Cevizli Konaği in the grounds are cheaper but much less atmospheric.

A block from the Cinci Hanı, *Otel Hatice Hanım Konağı* (☎ 712 7545, Naip Tarla Sokak 6), charges US$29/39 for rooms decorated in Ottoman style with bath and breakfast; rooms without bath cost a bit less. The public rooms are nicely decorated and atmospheric as well.

Otel Tahsin Bey Konağı (☎ 712 2065, Hükümet Sokak 50) and *Paşa Konağı* (same phone) just 50m further up the road and to the left, offer light, airy rooms with built-in cupboards, plastered fireplaces and period decoration. The Tahsin Bey has good views from some rooms, the Paşa Konağı a secluded garden and rather spooky bar. In both cases some of the bathrooms are inside cupboards with high doorsteps, which might trouble some guests; check before agreeing to take your room. When it's quiet you can expect to pay US$17 per person for bed and breakfast.

Six more converted properties scattered about Safranbolu are all called *Kadıoğlu Şehzade Konağı* (☎ 725 2762, fax 712 5657). They're managed from Mescit Sokak 24 where you can see pictures of all the houses before deciding where to stay. Rooms cost US$35/50 for half board.

Across the road the *Selvili Köşk* (☎ 712 8646, fax 725 2294, Mescit Sokak 23) is similar.

Places to Eat

In the arasta, *Boncuk Cafe* is one of the town's most congenial places for lunch, a modern Safranbolulu's conception of what an 'antique' cafe should be. Here you can watch gözleme being made; to sample it will cost you about US$1.50. Opposite the Cinci Hanı the friendly *Safran Pastahanesi* makes another congenial place to stop for breakfast or a cake.

Near the arasta, the *Kadıoğlu Şehzade Sofrası* has two entrances, a courtyard around a fountain and lots of attractive indoor dining rooms. You can get pide here but the house speciality is *kuyu kebap*, lamb cooked in an underground oven. Kebap, salad and a soft drink will set you back about US$5 or US$6. Unfortunately the food is not always served very hot.

The vast basement restaurant of *Havuzlu Asmazlar Konağı* has marble floors and an arched fireplace. The menu lists such Ottoman delights as *mıklama* (fried eggs, tomatoes, spinach and ground lamb) and *pastırma,* Turkish pastrami, but they may only be available when the hotel is busy. Otherwise it's şiş kebab. Portions are large and prices moderate: less than US$8 for soup, salad, main course and beer.

Among the older places favoured by locals is *Merkez Lokantası*, which is plain, clean and typical, with three-course meals for US$3.50. For a wider choice of simple dishes take the bus up to Kıranköy.

These days those shops that are not selling handicrafts are selling sweets – big trays of Turkish delight laid out enticingly in their windows. A Safranbolu speciality is *yaprak helvası*, layers of helva interspersed with walnuts. Buy it at *Özkan* or at *İmren* which has a sprawling Ottoman-style cafe upstairs.

Shopping

Safranbolu is a great place to pick up handicrafts (especially textiles, metalwork, shoes and wooden artefacts) either made locally or shipped in from around the country to supply holidaying İstanbullus. The restored **Yemeniciler Arastası**, meaning 'Peasant-Shoe-Makers' Bazaar', is a good place to start looking. The makers of light flat-heeled shoes who used to work here have now moved into the surrounding streets, leaving the little wooden shops to handicraft sellers, particularly textile sellers. Otherwise most of the shops and workshops line the streets south of the Cinci Hamamı and the Köprülü Camii. Be a little careful about prices, but you should find something you like.

Getting There & Away

There are a few direct buses to Safranbolu but most drop you at Karabük's flashy new otogar. Minibuses (US$0.50) ply up and down the road outside to run you the last 10km to Kıranköy. Regular daily services to Ankara (US$7, four hours, 225km) and İstanbul (US$12, five hours, 390km) leave from Kıranköy; sadly there are no longer *servis* buses from Çarşı so you will need to take a bus up the hill to catch them. There are also services from Karabük to Kastamonu (US$3.50, two hours, 100km) and Bartın (for Amasra, US$4, 1½ hours, 92km).

If you're driving, exit the Ankara-İstanbul highway at Gerede and head north, following the signs for Karabük.

Safranbolu is also reachable by taking the *Karaelmas* (Ankara-Zonguldak) train and disembarking at Karabük.

Getting Around

Every 30 minutes or so until 10 pm local buses (US$0.30) roll along the route from Çarşı's main square over the hills to Kıranköy and up to the Köyiçi stop in Bağlar. Buy a ticket in advance from the booth in the square.

AROUND SAFRANBOLU
Yörük Köyü

Along the Kastamonu road, 11km east of Safranbolu, is a village of old houses called Yörük Köyü (which translates oddly enough as 'Nomad Village'). The villagers grew rich, somewhat surprisingly, on making bread and some of the houses are truly enormous. Ask around and someone may point out the old village *çamaşırlık*, or laundry, with arched hearths where the water was heated in cauldrons and a huge stone table, rather like the *göbektaşı* in a hamam which was used for the actual scrubbing.

Yörük Köyü has a traditional **teahouse** and a weekends-only cafe selling *ayran* (yogurt drink), baklava and gözleme. Otherwise tourism has hardly touched it.

If you have your own car, there's an excellent restaurant, *Çevrik Köprü* (☎ 372-737 2119), on the right side of the road just before the turn off for Yörük Köyü. Here you can tuck into juicy kuyu kebap in shady gardens with fountains and pools.

Dolmuşes depart from Safranbolu from a stop on Hamamönü Sokak near the Çarşı

Pansiyon. Start out early to get a return dolmuş before nightfall. Failing that, you'll need to haggle with a Safranbolu taxi driver to take you there, wait for an hour or so while you explore the village, then return. This will cost around US$15 depending on your bargaining skills.

KASTAMONU
☎ 366 • pop 58,000

Heading from Safranbolu to Ankara or the Black Sea, you may need to stop in Kastamonu, an important transport connection point with enough of interest – a small museum, castle and some ancient market buildings – to while away a few hours. There's also a reasonable range of places to stay so you could linger and make a side trip to see one of Turkey's finest surviving wooden mosques in the nearby village of Kasaba.

History

Kastamonu's history has been as chequered as that of most central Turkish towns. Archaeological evidence suggests there was a settlement here as far back as 2000 BC, but the Hittites, Persians, Macedonians and Pontic (Black Sea) kings all left their mark. In the 11th century the Seljuks descended, followed by the Danışmends. In the late 13th century the Byzantine emperor John Comnenus tried to hold out here but the Mongols and the Ottomans soon swept in and by 1459 Kastamonu was secured as an Ottoman town. More recently, Kastamonu played an unexpected role as the town where Atatürk chose to launch his hat reforms. As of 25 November 1925 old-fashioned fezzes were out, their place taken by European-style hats as part of Atatürk's drive to modernise Turkey.

Orientation & Information

Kastamonu's small otogar is on the western side of the city centre, as you come in from Samsun or Sinop. It's about 1km from the centre, reachable by dolmuş or taxi (US$2).

A stream runs through the centre of the town. The road along its northern bank is Yalçın Caddesi, which becomes Plevne Caddesi as it reaches the centre and then

CENTRAL ANATOLIA

Atatürk Caddesi. The road along the southern bank is Kışla Caddesi, which becomes Cumhuriyet Caddesi towards the centre.

The centre of town is Cumhuriyet Meydanı, with an imposing *valilik* (provincial government headquarters) building and statue of Atatürk. This is where you'll find the PTT and local bus stops.

Just to the west of Cumhuriyet Meydanı the stream passes under the restored Nasrullah Köprüsü (Nasrullah Bridge). To the southern side a road leads to Nasrullah Meydanı and the bazaar.

The unhelpful tourist office (☎ 212 0162, fax 214 6159) in Nasrullah Meydanı can sell you a map for US$0.45.

There's an Internet cafe round the corner from the Ilgaz Oteli in Özbeli Sokak.

Kastamonu Müzesi

About 100m east of Cumhuriyet Meydanı along Cumhuriyet Caddesi is the Kastamonu Museum, which was closed for restoration at the time of writing, but which is housed in the attractive building where Atatürk announced his planned headgear reforms.

There's the usual mildly depressing collection of dusty Roman and Byzantine relics, including a gruesome sarcophagus opened to reveal the skeleton inside, still with a full head of hair. Upstairs, look out for some of the wood blocks used to make the printed cloths on sale around here and for some fine carved wood and horn spoons. Among the costumes on display, a couple of fezzes are more interesting when you know the history of the building.

If the custodian doesn't immediately offer, ask him to unlock the Atatürk Salonu on the ground floor so you can see the photos of the 1925 visit. Some were taken in İnebolu and show his entourage looking silly in hats with turned-up brims. Two days later they are marching into Kastamonu looking much more confident in their Panamas. There are also assorted quotations from Atatürk's speech, but in Turkish only.

Historic Buildings

Kastamonu is dominated by its **kale**, built on a rock above the town. Parts of it date from Byzantine times, but most of what you see belongs to the later Seljuk and Ottoman reconstructions. A family still lives inside the castle so you should be able to visit it at reasonable times. It's a steep 1km climb up through the streets of the old town and you'll be rewarded with fine views. Otherwise, you can appreciate the outline of the walls better from down below.

Nasrullah Meydanı centres on the Ottoman **Nasrullah Camii** and the fine double fountain in front of it. The area immediately south of Nasrullah Meydanı is filled with old market buildings, several of them still in use. The present-day bazaar takes place in and around the **Karanlık Bedesten**, the **Balkapanı Hanı** and the **İsmail Bey Hanı** (1466) which was restored in 1972 to provide workshops. Wander down any of the side streets in this area and you'll come across old hamams, fountains and other buildings.

Places to Stay

Kastamonu's hotels are clustered around Belediye and Cumhuriyet Caddesis, right in the centre of town.

One of the cheapest is **Ilgaz Oteli** (☎ 214 1170, Belediye Caddesi 4), which has very basic waterless rooms for US$4.50 a head.

Nearby, **Otel İdrisoğlu** (☎ 214 1757, Cumhuriyet Caddesi 25) has shabby singles/doubles with bathtubs for US$13/20 per person. Street-facing rooms are noisy. A few doors away is the cheerier **Rugancı Otel** (☎ 214 9500, fax 212 4343), which has rooms for US$17/27 including breakfast. Ask for one of the newer rooms, but watch for noise here too.

Just off Nasrullah Meydanı is **Otel Selvi** (☎ 214 1763, fax 212 1164, Banka Sokak 10) with a range of rooms with and without bath. Some top-floor rooms have good views of the castle. Bigger rooms with TV cost US$10/17.50; without TV and bath, rooms are US$7.50/13.50.

Kastamonu's best hotel is undoubtedly the two-star **Otel Mütevelli** (☎ 212 2018, fax 212 2017, Cumhuriyet Caddesi 10), across the road from Cumhuriyet Meydanı. The rooms are good and clean, and although the price might seem a bit high

(US$24/35) there are lots of extras like bathtubs and a decent restaurant.

Places to Eat

Across the road from the Ilgaz Oteli is an alleyway with several small restaurants. The *Ender* does *saç kavurma* (lamb fried in a flat pan), while *Uludağ Pide ve Kebap Salonu* on the corner serves more standard fare on a pleasant upstairs balcony; a meal at either can be had for US$3 or so.

Worth a look if you like gözleme is *Frenkşah Sultan Sofrası*, in an old han in Nasrullah Meydanı, where you tuck into your meal in an alcove surrounded by handicrafts for sale. Depending on filling, you'll pay from US$1.50 for gözleme.

In Cumhuriyet Caddesi, near Otel Mütevelli, is the cheerful *Ömür Pastanesi* where you can sample *tavuk göğsü*, a dessert made from milk, rice and pounded chicken breast (which you won't be able to find or taste).

Across the other side of the stream, Plevne Caddesi has several *beer houses*.

Getting There & Away

Kastamonu's small otogar offers regular departures for Ankara (US$7, four hours, 245km), İstanbul (US$15, 10 hours, 507km) and Samsun (US$11, six hours, 312km). To get to Sinop you usually have to travel via Boyabat. There are hourly departures for Karabük (US$3, two hours, 100km), with some buses continuing to Safranbolu. Minibuses for İnebolu (US$1.75, two hours) and Cide also leave from the otogar.

AROUND KASTAMONU

The tiny village of **Kasaba**, 17km from Kastamonu, is an unlikely place to find one of Turkey's finest surviving wooden mosques. Mahmudbey Camii was built in 1366. Externally there is nothing other than the lovely wooden doors to suggest there is anything special about this mosque. Get the *hoca* to unlock it, however, and you'll find a stunning, recently restored interior with four painted wooden columns, a wooden gallery and fine painted ceiling rafters.

To get to Kasaba, take a minibus to Daday from Kastamonu otogar and ask to be let off at Subaşı (US$1). From there it's 3km to Kasaba. If there's no sign of a lift, walk through Subaşı and out the other side, bearing right when the road forks and walking through the village of Göçen. After Göçen the road is signposted 'Mahmudbey Camii' on the right. In the village you'll see a bridge on the right. The mosque is the second alongside the stream.

BOYABAT
☎ 368

Heading for the Black Sea from Kastamonu you may need to transit Boyabat (US$2, 1½ hours), a small town with a large brick-making industry. Boyabat's otogar is just off Adnan Menderes Bulvarı, the main road through town. Chances are you'll be passing through, but with an hour or so to spare, go out of the otogar and turn right along the highway towards a road bridge. Just to the left of the bridge you'll find a pleasant pine-tree shaded tea garden to while away the time. From the bridge itself there's a fine view of Boyabat's **castle**, built to guard a prominent gorge. Beneath the bridge are some unexpectedly clean toilets.

Alternatively, leave the otogar, cross the highway and cut through any of the breaks in the shops to find the **bazaar** behind. Interspersed amid the shops are some fine old timber buildings. You'll also see women wearing a white, black and red headscarf that looks like an Indian bedspread, called a *pita*.

If you need to spend the night here, come out of the otogar, turn right towards the bridge, cross the highway and turn left following the sign marked 'Şehir'. Just past the PTT on the right you'll find *Merkez Oteli* (☎ 315 1119), with very basic rooms at US$5 a head. There are several simple places to eat opposite the otogar.

The road north from Boyabat passes through some stunning forested scenery, zigzagging up to 1370m, so that it takes 2½ hours to reach Sinop.

BOĞAZKALE, HATTUŞA & YAZILIKAYA

Anyone interested in the Hittites, who played such an important role in early Anatolian history (see the boxed text 'The Hittites'), will want to visit Hattuşa (or Hattuşas), once the Hittite capital and a designated Unesco World Heritage Site, as well as nearby Yazılıkaya, a Hittite religious sanctuary with fine rock carvings.

The best base for visiting Hattuşa and Yazılıkaya is Boğazkale (formerly Boğazköy), a farming village 200km east of Ankara, 86km south of Çorum and 30km east of Sungurlu. Boğazkale has adequate, though hardly fancy, travellers' services. Çorum, a provincial capital, is the nearest city with a full range of hotels and a big otogar.

The Hittites

Before this century little was known about the Hittites, a people who commanded a vast Middle Eastern empire, conquered Babylon, and challenged the Egyptian pharaohs over 3000 years ago. Apart from a few written references to them in the Bible and Egyptian chronicles, there were few clues to their existence until 1834 when a French traveller, Charles Texier, stumbled on the ruins of the Hittite capital of Hattuşa, next to the Turkish village of Boğazköy (today called Boğazkale).

In 1905 excavations began and turned up notable works of art, most of them now preserved in Ankara's Museum of Anatolian Civilisations. Also brought to light were the Hittite state archives, written in cuneiform on thousands of clay tablets. From these tablets, historians and archaeologists were able to construct a history of the Hittite Empire.

Speaking an Indo-European language, the Hittites swept into Anatolia around 2000 BC, conquering the Hatti from whom they borrowed both their culture and name. They established themselves at Hattuşa, the Hatti capital, and in the course of a millennium enlarged and beautified the city. From about 1375 to 1200 BC, Hattuşa was the capital of a Hittite Empire which, at its height, incorporated parts of Syria as well.

The Hittites worshipped over a thousand different deities but among the most important were Teshub, the storm god, and Hepatu, the sun goddess. The cuneiform tablets revealed a well-ordered society with more than 200 laws. The death sentence was prescribed for bestiality, while thieves got off more lightly provided they paid their victims compensation.

From about 1250 BC the Hittite Empire seems to have gone into a decline, its demise hastened by the arrival of the Phrygians. Only the city-states of Syria survived until they, too, were swallowed by the Assyrians.

Boğazkale
☎ 364 • pop 2100

Sleepy little Boğazkale has one pension, a handful of restaurant-hotel-camping complexes, the odd small shop and a post office. In summer it's a dry, dusty place but in spring the surrounding hills are covered in lush greenery, making it a fine time to visit.

It's an easy village to get around and the extensive ruins of ancient Hattuşa cover a hilltop to the south. If you're a hiker and the day is not too hot, you'll happily trek around the extensive ruins, but most visitors will want to ride at least some of the way.

Boğazkale's small **museum** is on the left as you come into the village. It has a large topographical map of Hattuşa, and some Hittite artefacts worth seeing: fascinating cuneiform tablets, signature seals, arrows and axeheads, a saw and whimsically shaped pots and vessels. High on the walls are large photographs of the site and Hittite objects found during excavation. The few Byzantine crosses come from a later church on the site. There's some German labelling. It's open from 8 am to 5.30 pm, entry is US$1.75.

Hattuşa

Hattuşa was once a great and impressive city, defended by stone walls over 6km in length. Today the ruins consist mostly of reconstructed foundations, walls and a few rock carvings, but there are several more interesting features, including a tunnel and some fine hieroglyphic inscriptions preserved in situ. The site itself is strange, almost eerie, exciting for its ruggedness and high antiquity rather than for its buildings or reliefs. Chances are that you'll share it with the birds for much of the day.

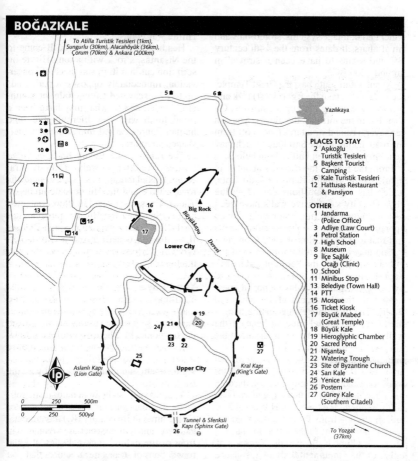

BOĞAZKALE

To Atilla Turistik Tesisleri (1km),
Sungurlu (30km), Alacahöyük (36km),
Çorum (70km) & Ankara (200km)

Yazılıkaya

Big Rock

Büyükkaya Deresi

Lower City

Aslanlı Kapı
(Lion Gate)

Upper City

Kral Kapı
(King's Gate)

Tunnel & Sfenksli
Kapı (Sphinx Gate)

To Yozgat
(37km)

0   250   500m
0   250   500yd

PLACES TO STAY
2 Aşıkoğlu
   Turistik Tesisleri
5 Başkent Tourist
   Camping
6 Kale Turistik Tesisleri
12 Hattusas Restaurant
   & Pansiyon

OTHER
1 Jandarma
   (Police Office)
3 Adliye (Law Court)
4 Petrol Station
7 High School
8 Museum
9 İlçe Sağlık
   Ocağı (Clinic)
10 School
11 Minibus Stop
13 Belediye (Town Hall)
14 PTT
15 Mosque
16 Ticket Kiosk
17 Büyük Mabed
   (Great Temple)
18 Büyük Kale
19 Hieroglyphic Chamber
20 Sacred Pond
21 Nişantaş
22 Watering Trough
23 Site of Byzantine Church
24 Sarı Kale
25 Yenice Kale
26 Postern
27 Güney Kale
   (Southern Citadel)

It's exactly 1km from the Aşikoğlu Turistik Tesisleri to the Hattuşa ticket kiosk. From there the road looping around the entire site from the ticket kiosk (not including Yazılıkaya) is another 5km. The walk itself takes at least an hour, plus time spent exploring the ruins, so figure on spending a good three hours here. Take drinking water and start early in the day before the sun is too hot as there's little shade. Local taxis will take you all the way around for about US$10. You may want to haggle for an all-day tour including Hattuşa, Yazılıkaya and Alacahöyük.

Hattuşa is open from 8 am to 5 pm daily, with a theoretical break for lunch from noon to 1.30 pm; in practice you enter when you like and let the ticket-seller catch up with you. Admission costs US$2 and the ticket is valid for Yazılıkaya, 3km uphill from the Hattuşa ticket kiosk, as well.

The following description assumes you do the loop in an anticlockwise direction.

Exploring Hattuşa The first site you come to, 300m up (south-west) from the ticket kiosk, is the **Büyük Mabed**, or the Great Temple of the storm god, a vast complex that's almost a town in itself, with its own water and drainage systems, storerooms and ritual altars. It dates from the 14th century BC and seems to have been destroyed in around 1200 BC.

About 350m south past the Great Temple, the road forks; take the right (west) fork and follow the winding road up the hillside. On your left in the midst of the old city you can see several ruined structures fenced off from the road, including the **Sarı Kale**, which may be a Phrygian fort on Hittite foundations.

From the fork in the road it's about 1km uphill to the **Aslanlı Kapı**, or Lion Gate, which has two stone lions defending the city. The city's defensive walls have been restored along the ridge, allowing you to appreciate the scope of the construction effort that took place almost 4000 years ago.

Continue another 700m to the top of the hill and you'll find the **Yer Kapı** or **Sfenksli Kapı** (Earth or Sphinx Gate), once defended by two great sphinxes, who are now domesticated in the museums of İstanbul and Berlin. The most interesting feature here is the 70m-long **tunnel** running beneath the walls to a **postern** on the southern side of the hill. As the true arch was not discovered until much later, the Hittites used a corbelled arch, two flat faces of stones leaning towards one another. Primitive or not, the arch has done its job for millennia, and you can still pass down the tunnel as Hittite soldiers did, emerging from the postern. Your reward is a toilet, off to the left at the base of the slope. Climb back up to the Yer Kapı by either of the **monumental stairways** placed on either side of the wide stone glacis beneath the walls. Once back on the top, enjoy the wonderful view from this highest point, sweeping down over Hattuşa, Boğazkale and beyond. Below you'll see the **Yenice Kale**, where Hittite engineers transformed the very uneven site into a plain on which to build their structures.

Another 600m eastward down the slope brings you to the **Kral Kapı**, or King's Gate, named after the regal-looking figure in the relief carving. The one you see is an obvious copy; the original was removed for safekeeping to the Ankara museum. Actually, the figure is not a king at all, but the Hittite war god.

Heading downhill again you'll come to the **Nişantaş**, a rock with a long Hittite inscription cut into it, in sore need of conservation. Immediately opposite a path leads up to the excavated **Güney Kale**, or Southern Citadel, and to what may have been a royal tomb with fine hieroglyphics and human figures carved into another tunnel-shaped structure.

The ruins of the **Büyük Kale**, or Great Fortress, are 800m downhill from the Kral Kapı. This elaborate fortress also held the royal palace and the Hittite state archives. The archives, discovered in 1906, contained a treaty between the Hittite monarch Hattusili III and the Egyptian pharaoh Ramses II, written in cuneiform on a clay tablet. From the fortress it's just over 1km back to the ticket kiosk.

Yazılıkaya

Yazılıkaya means 'Inscribed Rock', and that's what you'll find at this site just under 3km from Boğazkale (follow the signs from the ticket kiosk). The road circles a hillock called Ambarlı Kaya, on top of which once stood more Hittite buildings, before crossing a stream and climbing the hill past the Başkent Motel.

Yazılıkaya was always a naturalistic religious sanctuary open to the sky, but in later Hittite times (13th century BC) monumental gateways and temple structures were built in front of the **natural rock galleries**. It's the foundations of these late structures that you see as you approach from the car park.

There are two natural rock galleries, the larger one to the left, which was the empire's sacred place, and a narrower one to the right, which was the burial place of the royal family. In the large gallery, the fast-fading low reliefs of numerous cone-headed gods and goddesses marching in procession indicate that this was the Hittites' holiest religious sanctuary. Rock ledges were probably for sacrifices.

The best preserved carvings are in the narrower rear gallery so make sure not to miss them. Supposedly you should ask permission of the lion carved onto the rock by the entrance before penetrating his lair.

Places to Stay & Eat

Boğazkale is a pleasant place to spend the odd night, with such noise as there is coming from honking geese, crowing cockerels and braying donkeys.

If you want to be at the heart of Boğazkale's limited action, a good first choice is the *Hattuşas Restaurant & Pansiyon (☎ 452 2013, fax 452 2957)*, on the main square in the village. Simple but spacious rooms above a carpet shop and restaurant are US$7/13 a single/double (some rooms have showers). You can easily walk to the museum and to Hattuşa from here, and Ahmed, the friendly proprietor, speaks good English. The restaurant is pleasingly decorated with old kilims and boasts BBC TV. The pension is open year-round. If you're having trouble getting from Sungurlu, give Ahmed a call and he may be able to help.

The *Aşıkoğlu Turistik Tesisleri (☎ 452 2004, fax 452 2171)*, on the right as you enter Boğazkale and also within easy walking distance of the museum and shops, is partially open year-round. Cheerful rooms with baths cost US$25/40, breakfast included. The hotel also has a capacious restaurant with acceptable food for around US$5 a head. At the back a pretty basic *camping ground* charges US$5 for a tent or US$8.50 for a caravan. In summer the hotel may be full with groups.

Up the hill, 1km from the museum on the road to Yazılıkaya and Yozgat, is *Başkent Tourist Camping (☎ 452 2037, 452 2567, Yazılıkaya Yolu Üzeri)*, with pleasant motel-style rooms with twin beds and showers for US$20, including breakfast. To camp here costs US$5. The restaurant has good views of the ruins and is popular with groups.

Just 400m further up the hill along the Yazılıkaya road is *Kale Turistik Tesisleri (☎/fax 452 2189)* with big but very simple rooms for US$10/15 a single/double. The *camping ground* is primitive, but there's a *restaurant* here as well.

Atilla Turistik Tesisleri (☎ 452 2101), just over 1km north of the Aşıkoğlu Turistik

Tesisleri on the Sungurlu road, may or may not be open when you arrive, but it charges less for its simple motel, restaurant and primitive camping ground with little shade.

Getting There & Away

Unfortunately getting round the Hittite sites without your own transport is likely to prove time-consuming. Until 6 pm on weekdays regular minibuses run to Hattuşa from Sungurlu (US$0.30); at weekends you may well have to hitch or take a taxi for around US$12.

Travellers coming from Cappadocia may want to travel via Yozgat. Once again, direct minibuses to Boğazkale are thin on the ground; a taxi will cost about US$17.

SUNGURLU

Sungurlu is a forgettable small town 30km west of Boğazkale, on the thundering highway linking Ankara with Samsun. If you arrive too late to catch the dolmuş onward to Boğazkale, you could stay at the simple but clean *Hotel Fatih (☎ 364-311 3488)*, across the road from the PTT and right beside the dolmuş stand. Singles/doubles cost US$11/17, not including breakfast. The *Hitit Motel (☎ 364-311 8042, fax 311 3873)*, 1km east of the centre on the Ankara-Samsun road between an Ofisi petrol station and a Renault garage, was once fine enough to attract Prince Charles as a guest. Although it looks pretty faded these days, tour groups still sometimes stop here. Rooms cost US$19/29 with bath but no breakfast.

Be warned that many buses from Ankara to Sungurlu drop their passengers on the highway rather than at Sungurlu otogar. Taxi drivers waiting there will then deny the existence of any dolmuşes to Boğazkale. To be sure of making a connection, travel from Ankara with Sungurlu Birlik (gişe 1 at the otogar); they run a *servis* bus into Sungurlu that drops you at a small park across from the Boğazkale dolmuş stand.

ALACAHÖYÜK

There's less to see at Alacahöyük, 36km north of Boğazkale and 52km south of Çorum, than at Boğazkale, but it is a very old site settled from about 4000 BC. As at the other Hittite sites, movable monuments have been taken to the museum in Ankara, though there is a small site museum, and a few worn sphinxes and good bas-reliefs have been left in place.

Modern Alacahöyük is a farming hamlet with a PTT, a souvenir shop, a bakery, a modest grocery shop and the *Hitit Cafe* opposite the site entrance, handy for tea or a cool drink. The museum is right by the ruins and both are open, officially, from 8 am to noon, and from 1.30 to 5.30 pm daily, though the lunch break is not always observed. The admission fee for everything is US$1.75.

In the small **museum** you can inspect tools used in the excavations, and finds from the Chalcolithic and Old Bronze ages. A handy ant-farm-style glass case shows the stratigraphy of Alacahöyük's 15 layers of history. The ethnography section upstairs may or may not be open.

At the ruins, the **monumental gate**, with its sphinxes guarding the door and very fine reliefs along the walls, is what you've come to see. The reliefs show storm-god worshipping ceremonies and festivals with musicians, acrobats, priests and the Hittite king and queen. Off to the left across the fields is a **secret escape tunnel** supposedly leading to a postern as at Hattuşa, but nowadays just a culvert.

Getting There & Away

Alacahöyük is 36km north-west of Boğazkale and there's no public transport between the two sites. To get to Alacahöyük you can take a bus or dolmuş from Çorum to Alaca and then another from Alaca to Alacahöyük (no service at weekends). To take a taxi from Boğazkale to Alacahöyük, have it wait for an hour and then run you on to Alaca, will cost about US$18. There are frequent buses and dolmuşes along the Sungurlu-Çorum highway.

To get to Alacahöyük by car from Boğazkale, head out on the Sungurlu road and after 13.5km turn right at the road marked for Alaca and Alacahöyük. (Coming from Sungurlu, turn left about 11km after turning onto the Boğazkale road.) Go another

11.5km and turn left for Alacahöyük, another 9km along. Heading back, signs for Sungurlu lead you 7km out to the Sungurlu-Çorum highway. Turn left (south-west) for Sungurlu (27km), right for Çorum (42km) and Samsun (210km).

YOZGAT
● **pop 50,000**

About 35km south-east of Boğazkale and on the Ankara-Sivas highway is Yozgat, with a few very basic, rundown hotels, restaurants and an otogar.

If you're heading to the Hittite sites from Cappadocia you may need to transit Yozgat. Otherwise it's an unprepossessing provincial capital, the main highway lined with modern Turkish waffle-front apartment buildings. The one building of passing interest is the **Nizamoğlu Konağı**, a 19th-century Ottoman house converted to hold ethnographic exhibits.

ÇORUM
☎ 364 ● **pop 150,000**

Set on an alluvial plain on a branch of the Çorum River, Çorum is an agricultural town and provincial capital, its origins lost in the mists of history. People have been living here for at least 4000 years.

You probably thought a chickpea was just a chickpea but that was before you came to Çorum, the chickpea capital of Turkey. The town's main street is lined with *leblebiciler* (chickpea roasters) and sacks upon sacks of the chalky little pulses, all sorted according to fine distinctions obvious to a chickpea dealer but not, perhaps, to anyone else. Turks love to munch *leblebi* (dry roasted chickpeas) while sipping rakı. They're served plain, sugared, salted, peppered, or flavoured with clove. Shops in the otogar sell them freshly roasted.

If you're travelling north or east by bus you may have to stop in Çorum. Given the shortage of transport to Boğazkale from Yozgat and the paucity of accommodation in Sungurlu, it also makes a handy base for getting to the Hittite sites. Çorum has a small Byzantine kale on a hilltop, and a Seljuk mosque, the 13th-century Ulu Cami.

Most of its other old buildings are Ottoman, and there are some fine, if crumbling, old houses near the clock tower.

Orientation & Information
The clock tower marks the centre of Çorum, with the PTT, *belediye* (town hall) and tourist office all within 100m. Nearby is Eğridere Sokak, a small street lined with shops selling gold jewellery and changing money.

The otogar is 1km south-west of the clock tower along İnönü Caddesi, where there are a few banks with ATMs. Most hotels are within a 10-minute walk of the otogar.

To pick up your email, the Small House Internet Cafe is near the clock tower, just past the PTT on the right.

Çorum Müzesi
Close to the otogar is Çorum Müzesi (Çorum Museum),open from 8 am to 5.30 pm daily for US$1.75, with a small, mildly interesting collection of Hittite, Byzantine-Roman and Ottoman exhibits. Ethnographic exhibits cover Turkish life during the last century. If you're stuck for an hour or two between buses, go out of the main entrance of the otogar, turn left, then left again at the traffic roundabout. The museum is in the copse of pines on the right-hand side at the next roundabout, across the street from the Çorum Büyük Otel.

Places to Stay
Most hotels are along the İnönü Caddesi (the main street), either near the otogar or the clock tower. Middle-range accommodation seems to be getting squeezed out in favour of three-star places catering to the business brigade.

Otel Aygün (☎ 213 3364, *İnönü Caddesi 115*), opposite the Otel Anitta, is not very welcoming but the rooms – when not full with sports groups – are reasonably clean and cheap at US$9/15 a single/double with private shower.

The friendlier *Hotel Merih* (☎ 213 8379), near the clock tower on İnönü Caddesi, is oldish but serviceable, with waterless rooms for US$9/15, or US$11/17 with private facilities.

The two-star *Hotel Kolağası* (☎ 213 1971, fax 224 1556, *İnönü Caddesi 97*) charges US$20/30, including breakfast, for rooms with shower. It's clean and has a lift.

The three-star *Otel Anitta* (☎ 213 8515, fax 212 0613, *İnönü Caddesi 80*), looming above the otogar from its perch on İnönü Caddesi, is cheerful and modern, with a good restaurant, a shop, a barber and a bar with wide-screen TV. Decent rooms with bath cost US$60/100, including breakfast.

Across from the otogar is the three-star *Çorum Büyük Otel* (☎ 224 6092, fax 224 6094, *İnönü Caddesi 90*), where spacious, reasonably modern rooms with pleasant baths cost US$45/70/85 a single/double/triple. There are plenty of extras, including two restaurants, an American bar, a billiards room, a TV lounge and a sauna.

Another good three-star, *Hotel Sarıgül* (☎ 224 2012, fax 224 0396, *Azap Ahmet Sokak 18*), is hidden away off Gazi Caddesi behind the PTT. Comfortable rooms cost US$49/67, breakfast included. There's a restaurant, bar and Turkish bath.

The new *Otel Pithana* (☎ 224 3661, fax 213 1648, *Nurettinbey Caddesi 1/A*) is hidden away at the far end of the pedestrian street running down from the clock tower. It has big, modern rooms with baths for US$17 a head, including breakfast. There's a lift and the hotel is used to guests in wheelchairs.

Places to Eat
There are restaurants all along İnönü Caddesi; good choices include *Bursa Hacıbey Kebap ve Yemek Salonu* and the *Sultan Sofrasi* right next door; *Özler Lokantası*, further up towards the clock tower, with good roast chicken; and *Kılıçlar Kebap ve Pide Salonu* across the street. Men wanting a slice of the slightly sleazy side of Çorum should try the *Sevdalım Restaurant* which has live music nightly.

Catering to the business brigade in the gorgeous setting of an old restored Çorum house is the *Konak ZD Restaurant* (☎ 213 6993), opposite the Hotel Sarıgül. Despite the beautiful surroundings and attentive service, a three-course meal won't necessarily break the bank (perhaps US$7). If you want

Services from Çorum's Otogar

destination	fare (US$)	time (hr)	distance (km)	daily services
Alaca	1.75	1	60	several minibuses
Amasya	3.50	1½	95	several buses
Ankara	from 3.50	4	242	buses every 1½ hours
Kayseri	7.50	4	274	several buses
Samsun	5.50	3	176	frequent buses
Sungurlu	1.75	¼	70	very frequent buses

to try the künefe, a type of sweet, you need to order it when you sit down.

The *Kültür Restaurant*, on the top floor of the imaginatively designed Kültür Sitesi in Gazi Caddesi, is only open for party bookings. There's a more normal restaurant on the floor below, but it lacks the views.

Getting There & Away

Being on the main Ankara-Samsun highway, Çorum has good bus connections. The table above lists some useful daily services.

AMASYA

☎ 358 • pop 63,000

Set in a rocky ravine with the Yeşilırmak (Green River) running through it, Amasya is a great place to spend a day or so. Set apart from the rest of Anatolia in its tight mountain valley, it has a feeling of independence, self-sufficiency and civic pride, and surely deserves a prize as one of the nicest small towns in all Turkey.

Capital of the modern province of the same name, Amasya was once the capital of a great Pontic Kingdom and its dramatic setting adds interest to its numerous historic buildings, especially the rock-hewn tombs of the kings of Pontus and some fine old mosques and *medreses* (theological seminaries). But what makes Amasya so special is the survival of so many picturesque Ottoman half-timbered houses, especially along the north bank of the river. What's more, sensitive restoration and reconstruction is actually improving the landscape.

History

Once a Hittite town, Amasya was conquered by Alexander the Great, and then be-

came the capital of a successor-kingdom ruled by a family of Persian satraps. By the time of King Mithridates II (281 BC), the Kingdom of Pontus was entering its golden age and dominated a large part of Anatolia.

During the latter part of Pontus' flowering, Amasya was the birthplace of Strabo (circa 63 BC to AD 25), the world's first historian. Perhaps feeling restricted by the surrounding mountains, Strabo left home to travel in Europe, west Asia and north Africa, writing 47 history and 17 geography books as a result of his journeys. Though most of his history books have been lost, we know something of their content because many other classical writers chose to quote him.

Amasya's golden age ended when the Romans decided it was time to take over all of Anatolia (47 BC). After them came the Byzantines, who left little mark on the town, the Seljuks (1075) and the Mongols (early 14th century), who built numerous fine buildings which still stand. In Ottoman times, Amasya was an important base when the sultans led military campaigns into Persia. By tradition the Ottoman crown prince had to be taught statecraft in Amasya, and test his knowledge and skill as governor of the province. The town was also noted as a centre of Islamic theological study, with as many as 18 medreses and 2000 theological students in the 19th century.

After WWI, Mustafa Kemal (Atatürk) escaped from the confines of occupied İstanbul and came to Amasya where he secretly met with friends on 12 June 1919 and hammered out basic principles for the Turkish struggle for independence. The monument in the main square commemorates the meeting; other scenes depict the unhappy state of

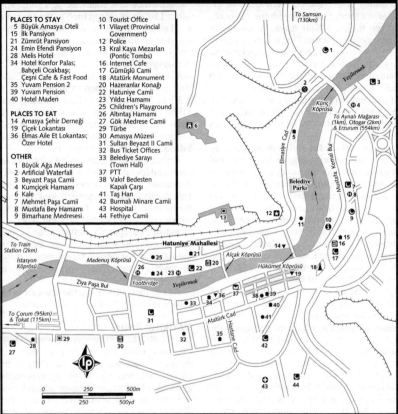

AMASYA

PLACES TO STAY
5 Büyük Amasya Oteli
15 İlk Pansiyon
21 Zümrüt Pansiyon
24 Emin Efendi Pansiyon
28 Melis Hotel
34 Hotel Konfor Palas;
  Bahçeli Ocakbaşı;
  Çeşni Cafe & Fast Food
35 Yuvam Pension 2
39 Yuvam Pension
40 Hotel Maden

PLACES TO EAT
14 Amasya Şehir Derneği
19 Çiçek Lokantası
36 Elmas Aile Et Lokantası;
  Özer Hotel

OTHER
1 Büyük Ağa Medresesi
2 Artificial Waterfall
3 Beyazıt Paşa Camii
4 Kumçiçek Hamamı
6 Kale
7 Mehmet Paşa Camii
8 Mustafa Bey Hamamı
9 Bimarhane Medresesi
10 Tourist Office
11 Vilayet (Provincial
  Government)
12 Police
13 Kral Kaya Mezarları
  (Pontic Tombs)
16 Internet Cafe
17 Gümüşlü Cami
18 Atatürk Monument
20 Hazeranlar Konağı
22 Hatuniye Camii
23 Yıldız Hamamı
25 Children's Playground
26 Altıntaş Hamamı
27 Gök Medrese Camii
29 Türbe
30 Amasya Müzesi
31 Sultan Beyazıt II Camii
32 Bus Ticket Offices
33 Belediye Sarayı
  (Town Hall)
37 PTT
38 Vakıf Bedesten
  Kapalı Çarşı
41 Taş Han
42 Burmalı Minare Camii
43 Hospital
44 Fethiye Camii

Turks in Anatolia before the War of Independence. Each year, Amasyalıs commemorate the meeting with a week-long art and culture festival beginning on 12 June.

Orientation & Information

The otogar is at the north-eastern edge of town and the train station at the western edge. It's 2km from either to the main square, marked by the statue of Atatürk and a bridge across the river. Most of the town (including the main square, the bazaar and the museum) is on the southern bank of the river. On the northern bank are various government and military offices, the tombs of the Pontic kings and the kale. You may want to take a bus, minibus, or taxi to and from the otogar and train station; otherwise everything is within walking distance, even the Gök Medrese, 1200m from the main square.

The summer-only tourist office (☎ 218 7428) is in a kiosk on the river bank, more or less opposite the İlk Pansiyon and just north of the main square.

There's an Internet cafe just east of the main square as you walk towards the İlk Pansiyon and another over the river in Hatuniye Mahallesi, near the Emin Efendi Pansiyon.

Pontic Tombs

Looming above the northern bank of the river is a sheer rock face with the easily observed rock-cut Kral Kaya Mezarları, or Tombs of the Pontic Kings, carved into it. Cross the river, climb the well-marked path towards them and you'll come to the Kızlar Sarayı, or Palace of the Maidens, now a cafe. Though there were indeed harems full of maidens here, the palace which stood on this rock terrace was not theirs, but that of the kings of Pontus and later of the Ottoman governors.

As you follow the path upward you may find your footsteps dogged by a youthful unappointed guide repeating a few words of German and hoping for a tip. In a few minutes you will reach the Pontic tombs, cut deep into the rock as early as the 4th century BC, and used for cult worship of the deified rulers. There are 14 tombs in this area but there's nothing inside any of them. Opening hours are from 8.30 am to 8.30 pm daily in summer. Admission costs US$1.

One of the best of the Pontic tombs, the Aynalı Mağara (Mirror Cave) is apart from the others, signposted to the left on the road in from Samsun, a pleasant 1km walk away. Although you can't hope to get inside the lofty entrance, you can walk right around it to see how the tomb was cut clean away from the rock face. There's also a Greek inscription high above the commonplace graffiti below. If you're feeling lazy, a taxi will run you there and back from the centre for about US$6, waiting time (not much needed) included.

Citadel

Above the tombs is the kale, perched precariously on the cliffs and offering magnificent views. The remnants of the walls date from Pontic times, perhaps around the time of King Mithridates. The fortress was repaired by the Ottomans, and again in the late 1980s. On a ledge just below the citadel is an old Russian cannon which is fired during the Ramazan month to mark the ending of the fast.

To reach the kale, cross the northern bridge near the Büyük Ağa Medresesi and follow the Samsun road for 850m to a street on the left marked 'Kale'. It's 1.7km up the mountainside to a small car park, then another 15-minute steep climb to the summit, marked by a flagpole. Women are not advised to go up there unaccompanied.

Amasya Müzesi

Amasya's small museum on Atatürk Caddesi is open from 8 am to noon and from 1.30 to 5.30 pm (closed on Monday) for US$1.75. The collection includes artefacts from Pontic, Roman, Byzantine, Seljuk and Ottoman times, and the usual collection of kilims, costumes and weaponry.

Perhaps the most interesting exhibits are the wooden doors of the ancient Gök Medrese Camii, the carpets and the strange baked-clay coffins. Upstairs, look out for the bronze figure of Teshub, the Hittite storm god, with pointed cap and huge almond-shaped eyes. A Seljuk tomb in the garden contains some gruesome mummies dating from the Seljuk period which were discovered beneath the Burmalı Cami – an exhibit not for the squeamish.

At the time of writing the museum was closed for restoration.

Walking Tour

It's possible to spend a very pleasant couple of hours exploring the minor sights of Amasya which are spread out along both banks of the river. The following walk starts at the Gök Medrese, to the west, and follows the southern bank of the river as far as the Beyazıt Paşa Camii. It then crosses the river at the Künç Köprüsü and returns along the north bank as far as the Altıntaş Hamamı.

About 1200m west of the main square is the Gök Medrese Camii, or Mosque of the Blue Seminary, built in 1266–67 for Seyfettin Torumtay, the Seljuk governor of Amasya. The eyvan (vaulted recess) serving as its main portal is unique in Anatolia. The adjoining kümbet (dome) was once covered in blue (gök) tiles, hence its name. The unfinished Torumtay Türbesi (1278) in front of the mosque is the final resting-place of Seyfettin Bey.

Head east along Atatürk Caddesi, passing a türbe (tomb) on the right, and on the left you'll see the graceful **Sultan Beyazıt II Camii** (1486), Amasya's principal mosque, with a medrese, *kütüphane* (library) and sweet-scented garden.

Keep heading east along Atatürk Caddesi and on the right you'll come to the partly ruined **Taş Han** (1758), an Ottoman caravanserai still used by local artisans. Behind it to the south is the **Burmalı Minare Camii**, or Spiral Minaret Mosque, a Seljuk construction (1237–47) with elegant spiral carving on the minaret, true to its name. Across the road, towards the river, is the **Vakıf Bedesten Kapalı Çarşı** (Covered Market), built in 1483 and still in use today.

Eventually you'll emerge in Amasya's main square with its imposing memorial to the War of Independence. Perched on a rise to the north-eastern side of the main square is the **Gümüşlü Cami** (Silvery Mosque) which was built in 1326. It was rebuilt in 1491 after an earthquake, in 1612 after a fire, and again in 1688, then added to in 1903, and restored yet again in 1988.

Cross the square and head east along Mustafa Kemal Bulvarı, which follows the river bank. On the right you'll come to the **Bimarhane Medresesi** which was built for Ilduş Hatun, the wife of the Ilkhanid Sultan Oljaytu in 1309. The İlkhans were the successors to the great Mongol Empire of Ghengis Khan, which had defeated the Seljuks of Anatolia, and their architecture reflects styles and motifs borrowed from many conquered peoples. Today only the outer walls of the building are original, the rest having been restored to serve as a sporadically functioning **Fine Arts Gallery** (Güzel Sanatlar Galerisi). On the northern side of the Bimarhane is the **Mustafa Bey Hamamı** (1436).

Next along the river is the pretty **Mehmet Paşa Camii**, an early Ottoman mosque built in 1486 by Lala Mehmet Paşa, tutor to Şehzade Ahmet, the son of Sultan Beyazıt II. The complex originally included the builder's tomb, and a soup kitchen *(imarethane)*, hospital *(tabhane)*, hamam and inn *(handan)*.

The **Beyazıt Paşa Camii**, a few hundred metres north and just past the bridge, was finished in 1419 and bears many similarities to the famous early Ottoman Yeşil Cami in Bursa. Note especially the porch with coloured marble arches, the entrance with gold and blue and the carved doors.

Cross the Künç Köprüsü to the north bank of the river and just to the right you'll see the octagonal **Büyük Ağa Medresesi**, built in 1488 by Sultan Beyazıt II's chief white eunuch Hüseyin Ağa. Nicely restored, it still serves as a seminary for boys who are training to be *hafız* (theologians who have memorised the entire Quran). It's not open to the public, but if the door is open you may be able to peep in to see local boys at their Quranic studies.

Turn back and start walking west along Elmasiye Caddesi, passing a **waterfall** on the right. You'll soon pass a police station and the *vilayet* (provincial government building) on the left with the shady **Belediye Parkı** beside it, a good place to stop for a drink. Many of the old wooden houses nearby are still occupied. Walk beneath the railway line behind the huge military building (near the Büyük Amasya Oteli) to explore a neighbourhood of such houses.

East of the Hükümet Köprüsü (Government Bridge) you enter the **Hatuniye Mahallesi**, a wonderful neighbourhood of old Ottoman houses and good modern repros. Just past the steps up to the Pontic Tombs you'll see (on the left) the **Hazeranlar Konağı**, constructed in 1865 and restored in 1979. It's usually open from 9 to 11.45 am and 1.15 to 4.45 pm; admission costs US$1. It often hosts good travelling exhibitions.

Continue walking west until you come to the **Altıntaş Hamamı**. Cross at the footbridge and stop for a refreshing drink in the little square in front of the Hotel Konfor Palas.

Places to Stay – Budget

It's almost worth coming to Amasya just to stay in the gorgeous *İlk Pansiyon* (☎ 218 1689, fax 218 6277, Hitit Sokak 1). Its architect-proprietor, Ali Kamil Yalçın, discovered the once grand but then dilapidated mansion of a one-time Armenian priest, rented it and restored it beautifully. The five light, airy, spacious salons are now fitted with beds and bathrooms. At just US$13 to

US$26 a single, US$17 to US$36 a double, depending upon the room, they're a positive snip. There's one smaller, cheaper room with bath off a courtyard that provides a convivial setting for breakfast and dinner. The İlk is by the river east of the Atatürk statue (follow the signs).

If the İlk Pansiyon is full, try *Yuvam Pension* (☎ *218 1324, fax 218 3409, Atatürk Caddesi 24/5*) on the main thoroughfare, 2½ blocks south-west of the Atatürk statue. Ask about the rooms at the *eczane* (pharmacy) at street level, which is where the owners are during the day. Clean rooms with shower, in a family atmosphere, cost US$15/20.

If the Yuvam is full, the friendly owners may take you to *Yuvam Pension 2*, their 1930s Amasya-style house, about 300m further to the south-west (follow the signs uphill marked 'Hastane' and then turn right at the top). The house, with its quiet garden, is preferable to the apartment rooms on Atatürk Caddesi, though baths are shared.

The cheap, quiet *Zümrüt Pansiyon* (☎ *218 2675, Hazeranlar Sokak 28*), just across the road from the Yıldız Hamamı (men only), has rooms with showers but no toilet or sink for US$10 per person. The real bonus is the roof terrace with uninterrupted views of the Pontic Tombs, especially impressive when floodlit at night.

Nearby, *Emin Efendi Pansiyon* (☎ *212 0852, Hazeranlar Sokak 73*) is a small wooden house furnished with nice old carpets and handicrafts. The rooms, all without bath and thus overpriced at US$22/33, have river views. Potentially this could be a good place to stay, although at the time of writing it didn't seem to be anticipating visitors.

On a tighter budget the choice is not so great. The inaptly named *Konfor Palas* (☎ *218 1260, Ziya Paşa Bulvarı 2/C*), meaning 'Comfort Palace', is close to the river and has rooms for US$8/12. The bedrooms are clean, the communal toilets less so. The *Özer Hotel* across the way has bunk beds for just US$4.50.

Places to Stay – Mid-Range

About 60m east of the Gök Medrese Camii, the *Melis Hotel* (☎ *212 3650, fax 218 2082,* *Torumtay Sokak 135)* is a veritable Aladdin's Cave of Ottoman artefacts, utensils and knick-knacks. Bright, clean rooms with bath cost US$35/49 with breakfast.

The two-star *Büyük Amasya Oteli* (☎ *218 4054, fax 218 4056, Elmasiye Caddesi 20*), north of the centre near the Büyük Ağa Medresesi, is right on the river bank, with a restaurant, a bar and fine views of the river. Rooms with shower cost US$39/57, breakfast included, but it's often filled by tour groups.

The run-of-the-mill two-star *Hotel Maden* (☎ *218 6050, fax 212 6343, Atatürk Caddesi 5*), above the Ford-Tofaş car showroom, is surprisingly reasonable at US$17/26 with breakfast.

Places to Eat

Amasya is famed for its apples; don't miss them if you visit during the autumn harvest.

Look for small restaurants in the narrow market streets off the main square (the one with the statue of Atatürk). The *Çiçek Lokantası* is cheap and serviceable, with decent roast chicken and ready meals for little more than US$3. *Elmas Aile Et Lokantası*, on the same street, does kebaps and pides, and stays open late.

There are many small kebapçıs north of the Yuvam Pension in the bazaar streets around the covered market. *Beslen Kebap ve Pide Salonu* (*Kocacık Çarşısı 18*) has good food and friendly staff.

The *Bahçeli Ocakbaşı*, in front of the Konfor Palas, is friendly enough and has outdoor tables to enjoy freshly baked pide (US$2) while gazing across the river. Even better is the adjacent *Çeşni Cafe & Fast Food* which does excellent Italian-style pizza for just US$1.75.

For nicer dining at a higher price (around US$8 for a full meal, depending on how much you drink), go to the restaurant in *Büyük Amasya Oteli* which specialises in kebaps from south-eastern Turkey.

Foreign tourists are also welcome at *Amasya Şehir Derneği*, overlooking the river at the northern end of the Hükümet Köprüsü, opposite the main square. A stark, quasi-private club, it offers good service and moderately priced food and drink. Amasya's prominent citizens (all male, of course) come here to eat, drink, talk business and while away the evening. A biggish portion of baked trout costs around US$4.

Getting There & Away

Amasya is not far off the busy route between Ankara and Samsun, so buses are frequent. It's also on the railway line between Samsun and Sivas, but the daily trains are quite slow. Some bus companies maintain ticket offices on Atatürk Caddesi across from the belediye building, just east of the Sultan Beyazıt II Camii. The table lists some useful daily services.

To get to Safranbolu (US$16, nine hours, 450km), take a minibus to Gerede, then a minibus to Karabük and, from there, another minibus to Safranbolu – a long day!

AROUND AMASYA
Yassıçal, Saraycık Koyü & Kaleköy

Occasional buses run to villages in the surrounding hills, where residents still make lovely striped kilims from sheep and goat's hair. At **Yassıçal** there's a pleasant *restaurant* (☎ 358-241 6003) set around an artificial pool full of fish near the new hotel; you dine in wooden kiosks amid flowers. You can get here easily at any time with your own transport but the last bus back to Amasya goes at 5 pm.

Further along the road, but without reliable bus links, are **Saraycık Köyü** and **Kaleköy**. Of the two, Kaleköy has the most interesting buildings (the eponymous castle,

an old wooden mosque, and a crumbling hamam and stone laundry), but the villagers are moving away, so Saraycık is livelier.

Ali Kamil Yalçın, proprietor of the İlk Pansiyon (see Places to Stay in the Amasya section), may be able to advise on arranging a taxi excursion to some of these villages.

Yedi Kuğular Gölü

About 15km west of town is the artificial Yedi Kuğular Gölü (Seven Swans Lake), a favourite stopping-place for birds on their spring and autumn migrations. Trees have been planted and as they mature, this *kuş cenneti* (bird paradise) may become as welcoming to humans as to birds.

TOKAT
☎ 356 • pop 100,000

The quintessential Turkish town, Tokat is half-Ottoman, half-modern, and liberally sprinkled with crumbling ruins, many of them now below ground level. Between the 13th and 20th centuries Tokat's ground is thought to have risen by up to 5m as silt from the hills was carried down into the valley by rain and floods, and debris from earthquakes added to the accumulation.

The town doesn't get many tourists, and those who do come usually have a quick look at the Gök Medrese and then leave, which is a shame since they miss the wonderful Latifoğlu Konağı, as excellent an example of a restored Ottoman house as you'll find in Turkey.

Provided you're not desperate for major monuments, Tokat makes a fine place to

Services from Amasya's Otogar

destination	fare (US$)	time (hr)	distance (km)	daily services
Adıyaman (for Nemrut Dağı)	12	10	650	1 bus
Ankara	10	5	335	very frequent buses
Çorum	4.50	1½	95	at least 8 buses
İstanbul	20	10	685	12 buses
Kayseri	13	8	405	3 buses
Malatya	13	8	460	5 buses
Samsun	3.50	2	130	10 buses
Sivas	9	3½	225	5 buses
Tokat	3.50	2	115	9 buses

CENTRAL ANATOLIA

while away at least a day, more if you use it as a base for exploring some of the lesser-known sites nearby.

History

Tokat's history kicks off in about 3000 BC and proceeds through the sovereignty of 14 states, including the Hittites and Phrygians, the Medes and the Persians, the empire of Alexander the Great, the Kingdom of Pontus, the Romans, the Byzantines, the Turkish principality of Danışmend, the Seljuks and the Mongol İlkhanids.

By the time of the Seljuk Sultanate of Rum, Tokat was Anatolia's sixth-largest city and on important trade routes. The approach roads are littered with great Seljuk bridges and caravanserais testifying to its earlier importance.

After the Mongols rushed in and upset everyone in the mid-13th century, their İlkhanid successors took over, followed by a succession of petty warlords who did little for Tokat.

Under the Ottomans, who took the town in 1402, Tokat resumed its role as an important trading entrepot, agricultural town and copper-mining centre. Significant non-Muslim populations (Greek, Armenian, Jewish) were in charge of the town's commerce until the cataclysm of WWI. There's still a small but active Jewish congregation.

Orientation & Information

The town centre is Cumhuriyet Alanı, a big open square where you will find the old vilayet, the belediye and the PTT. An underground shopping centre has added lots of retail space without ruining the spaciousness of the square. Across the main street from the shopping centre is the Tarihi Ali Paşa Hamamı.

Looming above the town is a rocky promontory crowned by the obligatory ancient fortress. Beneath it cluster the bazaar and the town's old Ottoman-style houses.

The main street, Gazi Osman Paşa Bulvarı (universally abbreviated to G.O.P. Bulvarı), runs downhill from the main square past the Gök Medrese to a traffic roundabout. The otogar is nearby, 2km from the main square.

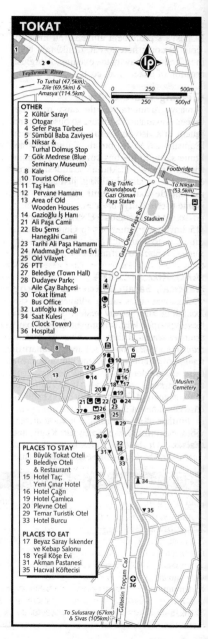

TOKAT

To Turhal (47.5km),
Zile (69.5km) &
Amasya (114.5km)

Yeşilırmak River

Footbridge

To Niksar
(53.5km)

Big Traffic
Roundabout;
Gazi Osman
Paşa Statue

Stadium

Muslim
Cemetery

OTHER
2 Kültür Sarayı
3 Otogar
4 Sefer Paşa Türbesi
5 Sümbül Baba Zaviyesi
6 Niksar &
   Turhal Dolmuş Stop
7 Gök Medrese (Blue
   Seminary Museum)
8 Kale
10 Tourist Office
11 Taş Han
12 Pervane Hamamı
13 Area of Old
    Wooden Houses
14 Gazioğlu İş Hanı
21 Ali Paşa Camii
22 Ebu Şems
    Hanegâhi Camii
23 Tarihi Ali Paşa Hamamı
24 Madımağın Celal'ın Evi
25 Old Vilayet
26 PTT
27 Belediye (Town Hall)
28 Dudayev Parkı;
    Aile Çay Bahçesi
30 Tokat İtimat
    Bus Office
32 Latifoğlu Konağı
34 Saat Kulesi
    (Clock Tower)
36 Hospital

PLACES TO STAY
1 Büyük Tokat Oteli
9 Belediye Oteli
   & Restaurant
15 Hotel Taç;
    Yeni Çınar Hotel
16 Hotel Çağrı
19 Hotel Çamlıca
20 Plevne Otel
29 Temar Turistik Otel
33 Hotel Burcu

PLACES TO EAT
17 Beyaz Saray İskender
    ve Kebap Salonu
18 Yeşil Köşe Evi
31 Akman Pastanesi
35 Hacıvalı Köftecisi

Gazi Osman Paşa Bulvarı

Gültekin Topçam Cad

To Sulusaray (67km)
& Sivas (105km)

Many bus companies have offices on G.O.P. Bulvarı south of the main square.

The tourist office (☎ 211 8252) is a booth in front of the Taş Han with erratic opening hours.

Gök Medrese

The Gök Medrese (Blue Seminary), next to the Taş Han and the Belediye Oteli several hundred metres down the hill from Cumhuriyet Alanı, was constructed in 1277 by Pervane Muhineddin Süleyman, a local potentate, after the fall of the Seljuks and the coming of the Mongols. Used as a hospital until 1811, it's now the town museum and is open from 8.30 am to 12 pm and 1 to 5 pm daily except Monday; admission costs US$1.75.

Gök (sky) is an old word for blue, and it is the building's blue tiles which occasioned the name. Very few of these are left on the facade, which is now well below street level, but there are enough tiles on the interior walls to give an idea of what it must have looked like in its glory days. Museum exhibits include Stone Age and Bronze Age artefacts from excavations at Maşat Höyük, relics from Tokat's churches (most curious is a wax effigy of the Christian Christina, martyred during the reign of Diocletian), tools and weapons, Qurans and Islamic calligraphy and an excellent costume display. An ethnographic section also displays local kilims and explains Tokat's famous art of wood-block printing on *yazmalar*, or gauze scarves.

The seminary contains the Kırkkızlar Türbesi (Tomb of 40 Maidens), actually an assembly of 20 tombs, probably of the seminary's founders, though popular belief would have it that they are the tombs of 40 girls.

Taş Han & Around

Near the Gök Medrese, on the other side of the Belediye Oteli, is the Taş Han (1631), an Ottoman caravanserai and workshop. At the time of writing it had been sold and was being converted into a hotel. If work proceeds as slowly as on a similar project in Safranbolu, it's unlikely to be accessible again this side of 2005.

Behind the Taş Han are bazaar streets lined with old half-timbered Ottoman houses. The shops have lots of copperware, yazmalar and local kilims and carpets, some with Afghani designs because of the many Afghani refugees who settled here during the Soviet invasion of their country during the 1980s.

It used to be possible to see yazmalar being made in the crumbling Gazioğlu İş Hanı, behind the Taş Han, but in an astonishingly short-sighted move the han has been closed down and the yazma-makers relocated to the outskirts of town.

In the fruit and vegetable market, across Gazi Osman Paşa Bulvarı from the Taş Han, stands the **Hatuniye Camii** and **medrese**, dating from 1485 and the reign of Sultan Beyazıt II.

Several hundred metres north, down the hill from the Gök Medrese, on the same side of the street, look out for the portal of the **Sümbül Baba Zaviyesi** dervish lodge, probably built in 1292 and now incorporated into a house. Another block further north is the octagonal **Sefer Paşa Türbesi**, a Seljuk-style tomb dating from 1251. Beside it a road leads up to the kale, of which little remains but the fine view.

Tarihi Ali Paşa Hamamı

Go into any Turkish hamam and ask the masseur where he came from and chances are he'll answer Tokat. So while in Tokat you should certainly not miss the chance to bathe in the wonderful Tarihi Ali Paşa Hamamı. These baths, with breast-like glass bulbs set into the domes to admit light, were built in 1572 for Ali Paşa, and have separate bathing areas for men and women. A simple bath costs US$2.50. Near the bath is the Ali Paşa Camii, built between 1566 and 1572.

Historic Houses

On the main street south of Cumhuriyet Alanı stands the **Latifoğlu Konağı**, one of the most splendid 19th-century houses on view in Turkey. Its large, gracious rooms are surrounded with low sedir sofas. In the bedrooms, bedding was taken up and stored in cabinets during the day, Asian-style. The most spectacular rooms are upstairs: the Paşa Odası (Pasha's Room) for the men of the house, and the Havuzbaşı room for the women. The light, airy upstairs hall would have been used in summer only.

It's open from 8 am to noon and 1.30 to 5 pm daily except Monday for US$1.75.

Sulu Sokak

The houses to the east of Gazi Osman Paşa were mainly owned by Tokat's wealthier citizens, but to the west you can find many streets of simpler but elegant houses. Take the street running west beside the Ali Paşa Camii in Cumhuriyet Alanı (it's signposted to the Bedesten) and you'll arrive in Sulu Sokak, which used to be Tokat's main thoroughfare before the Samsun-Sivas road was improved in the 1960s. The further along you go, the more interesting it gets, with the crumbling remains of a bedesten and several medreses, *türbes* (tombs) and mosques. At the western end of the road, smaller cobblestone streets fan out in all directions. Here you can lose yourself amid wonderful old wooden houses, their upper storeys jutting out at all angles to suit the geography of the street.

Places to Stay – Budget

The old, bleak *Belediye Oteli* (☎ 212 8983, G.O.P. Bulvarı) is only worth staying in if you can beat them down from the official US$9/14 for a noisy, waterless single/double.

The situation improves as you move towards the centre. *Hotel Taç* (☎ 214 1331, G.O.P. Bulvarı), in the İnci Vakıf İş Hanı building opposite the Taş Han, charges US$10/13 for waterless rooms with peeling wallpaper, or US$17/26 for rooms with shower. Choose between noisy front rooms with fine kale views or quieter back rooms with hillside views.

If you can afford a bit more the new *Yeni Çınar Hotel* (☎ 214 0066, fax 213 1927, G.O.P. Bulvarı İş Bankası Yanı 2) is a good choice, with cheerful rooms that have fairly modern decor and nice bathrooms for US$22/30, including breakfast.

Hotel Çağrı (☎ 212 1028, G.O.P. Bulvarı 92) is more promising inside than out; all rooms have showers and go for US$10/15 – a good value option.

At *Plevne Otel* (☎ 214 2207, G.O.P. Bulvarı 83), named after the great general's most famous battle, the best rooms are the big, quiet ones at the back, with spacious bathrooms. Posted prices are US$10/14 with sink, US$14/17 with shower, though lower rates are usually offered. Across the street, the *Hotel Çamlıca* (☎ 214 1269, G.O.P. Bulvarı 86) is in need of modernisation and is overpriced at US$20/38. If you want to stay, haggle like mad.

Next to the Ziraat Bankası, facing the old vilayet building, is the *Temar Turistik Otel* (☎ 212 7755, Cumhuriyet Meydanı 10). The rooms with showers are old but clean, relatively quiet and cost US$10/14. For convenience the position is unbeatable.

Places to Stay – Mid-Range

A block south of the Latifoğlu Konağı and just north of the clock tower is the two-star *Hotel Burcu* (☎ 212 8494, fax 212 2327, G.O.P. Bulvarı 48). The posted rates for a comfortable single/double with bath and breakfast are US$35/60, but drop considerably if it's quiet.

Were it not for its inconvenient position, 3km from the city centre on the north-western outskirts, the four-star *Büyük Tokat Oteli* (☎ 228 1661, fax 228 1660, Demirköprü Mevkii) would no doubt charge more than US$38/51 for its comfortable rooms. As it is this is mainly an option for the car-owning/renting fraternity who will be able to enjoy oodles of space, a big swimming pool, a Turkish bath, a barber's shop and a pastry shop on site.

Places to Eat

Tokat is surprisingly short of good places for eating out. For alcoholic drinks with your meal, you may have to trek out to the Büyük Tokat Oteli.

Beyaz Saray İskender ve Kebap Salonu, across the street from the Taş Han and the Belediye Oteli, is a simple split-level place where a helping of chicken and rice and a soft drink will set you back about US$2.50. Behind it, in the *sebze halı* (fruit and veg-table market) near the Hatuniye Camii, are several little *köfte and kebap shops* with even lower prices.

Tokat has its very own kebap: skewers of lamb, sliced potato and aubergine (eggplant) hung vertically and baked in a wood-fired oven. Tomatoes and pimentos, which take less time to cook, are baked on separate skewers. As the lamb cooks, it releases juices that baste the potato and aubergine. The first-floor restaurant at the *Yeni Çınar Hotel* serves an excellent Tokat kebap for US$3.50, but its yawning empty spaces can be daunting when there are no big parties gathered. You might try the nearby *Yeşil Köşe Et Lokantası* for a less intimidating environment.

Keep walking down G.O.P.. Bulvarı, past the clock tower, and eventually you'll reach *Macıval Köftecisi*, a modern-looking place which can do you a nice bowl of *menemen* (scrambled eggs with vegetables) for just US$0.75.

Of the various *pastanes* (pastry shops), *Akman*, across the road from the Hotel Burcu, is especially congenial.

Getting There & Away

Tokat's small otogar is not as busy as some, especially in the morning (there are, for example, fewer buses to Sivas than you might anticipate), but buses still manage to get you where you want to go pretty easily, especially if you don't mind going via Ankara. The better bus companies provide *servises* to ferry you into town. Otherwise, if you don't want to wait for the infrequent ordinary buses, a taxi will cost about US$2 to the main square. To walk, go 400m west to the traffic roundabout, turn left (south)

and it's just over 1km to the cluster of hotels, 1.5km to the main square. Several bus companies have ticket offices on the southern side of the main square, saving you a trip to the otogar to buy onward tickets. Some useful daily bus services from Tokat are listed in the table.

AROUND TOKAT
Niksar

Formerly Neocaesarea, Niksar, 54km north-east of Tokat, was a city of the Pontic kings, then of the Romans. For 40 years after its conquest in 1077 by the Seljuk general, Melik Ahmet Danışmend Gazi, it was the capital of the Danışmend Turkish Emirate and today preserves several rare examples of Danışmendid architecture, as well as many Ottoman works.

Turhal

About 48 kilometres west of Tokat and an easy break of journey between Amasya and Tokat, Turhal has an impressive citadel with a network of subterranean tunnels. It, too, was a Danışmendid town, and has several mosques, baths and other buildings to show for it, as well as a neighbourhood of fine old Ottoman houses.

Zile

About 70km west of Tokat, Zile is near where Caesar battled Pharnaces and afterwards sent his famous one-liner – *Veni, Vidi, Vici* – back to Rome (see the boxed text over the page). The actual battle site was along the Amasya-Zile road. The town of Zile has a very old citadel, and mosques and hamams dating from the Danışmend, Seljuk and Ottoman periods.

Services from Tokat's Otogar

destination	fare (US$)	time (hr)	distance (km)	daily services
Amasya	3	2	115	frequent buses
Ankara	8	6½	440	frequent buses
Erzurum	12	8½	493	a few direct or change at Sivas
İstanbul	15	12	800	several buses
Samsun	6	4	245	frequent buses
Sivas	3	1½	105	frequent buses

He Came, He Saw, He Conquered

It may come as quite a surprise to learn that Julius Caesar was at Zile, near Tokat, when he delivered his immortal message back to the Roman Senate, *Veni, Vidi, Vici* (I came, I saw, I conquered).

During the 1st century BC, Tokat lay within the kingdom of Pontus, which had held out against the Romans, indeed declared war against them, even after the rest of Anatolia had submitted. In 47 BC, while Julius Caesar was distracted in Egypt, King Pharnaces II launched an attack on the Roman provinces of Galatia, Armenia and Cappadocia with the intention of recreating the earlier Pontic kingdom of his ancestors. Caesar was forced to retaliate and marched on Pharnaces with his army. At a site between the modern villages of Yünlü and Bacul on the Zile to Amasya road, the two armies clashed. During a fierce five-hour battle, Pharnaces's army drove chariots with scythes fitted to their wheels against the Romans, but despite heavy losses Caesar's troops have eventually triumphed. The tourist office has been playing fast and loose with his words ever since.

Ballıca Cave

About 26km west of Tokat, near Pazar, is Ballıca Cave (Ballıca Mağarası), one of the finest Turkish caves open to the public, with fine stalactite and stalagmite formations.

Sulusaray

The Roman city of Sebastopolis (present-day Sulusaray) lay 67km south-west of Tokat, on the banks of the Çekerek river. Excavations here have produced extensive remains and the museum contains some fine mosaics. Getting to it without your own transport is difficult because it's 49km off the Tokat to Sivas road.

SİVAS

☎ 346 • pop 225,000

The highway comes through Sivas, the railway comes through Sivas, and over the centuries dozens of invading armies have come through Sivas, often leaving the town i ruins in their wake. The Seljuks left perhap the most obvious mark and the centre o town is liberally sprinkled with some of th finest Seljuk Turkish buildings ever erected

Nowadays Sivas is fairly modern, wit bicycle lanes along its main thoroughfar and even some kerbstone ramps for wheel chairs. That said, few tourists come her and it's where you'll feel modern wester Turkey starting its seamless merger with th more exotic eastern Turkey.

History

The tumulus at nearby Maltepe shows evi dence of settlement as early as 2600 BC Sivas itself was probably founded by th Hittite king Hattushilish I in around 150 BC, and was ruled in turn by the Assyrians Medes and Persians, before coming withi the realms of the kings of Cappadocia an Pontus. Eventually it fell to the Romans wh called it Megalopolis, later changed to Se bastea and shortened to Sivas by the Turks

Byzantine rule lasted from 395 to 1075 when the city was taken by the Danışmen emirs. Danışmend rule was disputed by th Seljuks, and Sivas changed allegiance fron one side to the other several times betwee 1152 and 1175, when the Seljuks finall took it – until the Mongol invasion of 1243

Even after the Mongols were succeede by the İlkhanids, Sivas' travails weren' over. Taken by the Bey of Eretna in 134 it succumbed to Tamerlane in 1400, an soon after (in 1408) to the Ottomans.

In more recent times Sivas gained fame a the location for the Sivas Congress, whic opened on 4 September 1919. Atatürk cam here from Samsun and Amasya, seeking t consolidate the Turkish resistance to Allie occupation and partition of his country. H gathered delegates from as many parts of th country as possible, and confirmed decision that had been made at the earlier Erzuru Congress. These two congresses heralded th War of Independence.

Orientation & Information

The centre of town is Konak Meydanı, ju in front of the attractive *vilayet konağ*

The Alevis

A significant minority of Sivas' population are Alevis, Muslims whose traditions are very different to those of the majority Sunni Muslims.

On 17 June 656, mutinous Muslim soldiers from Egypt burst into the private chambers of Caliph Uthman in Medina and wounded him mortally. The Prophet's cousin and son-in-law Ali was immediately hailed by his supporters as the new caliph, but political factions loyal to Uthman's appointed successor, Muawiya of the Umayyad clan, disputed Ali's claim and accused him of complicity or at least a passive role in Uthman's murder. The dispute continued a clan rivalry which had existed before Mohammed, and the commonwealth of Islam erupted into clan warfare. After Ali's murder, his son Hasan ceded the caliphate to Muawiya, who founded the Umayyad dynasty of caliphs.

Ali's clan, however, nurtured the dream that at some stage one of Ali's descendants would recover the caliphate and re-establish the 'legitimate' line of succession from the Prophet. Ali's son Hussein was the hope of those disaffected with Umayyad rule, but in 680 at the Battle of Kerbela (in present-day Iraq) the victorious Umayyad forces killed Hussein.

The bitter disappointments of Ali's followers resulted in the first great schism of Islam, with those who followed the Umayyad succession known as Sunnis, and those who believed in the legitimacy of Ali's succession as Shiis (Shiites) and Alevis (Alawites).

The debate and antipathy between the two factions continue to this day – the Sunnis gathering for prayer in a *cami* with men and women separated; the Alevis in a *cemevi* with men and women together in equality. A Sunni village holds its *imam* (preacher) in high regard; an Alevi village reveres its *dede* (sheikh, leader).

Many Alevi beliefs are congruent with those espoused by Hacı Bektaş Veli, the 13th-century Muslim mystic whose tomb is in northern Cappadocia. The Alevi *sema* ceremony involves the chanting of Alevi poetry; and men and women dressed in colours of green and red dancing together. 'If their hearts are pure', says one Alevi dede, 'the gathering of men and women together is pure'.

(provincial government headquarters). Near it are most of Sivas' important sights, hotels and restaurants.

The train station, Sivas Garı, is about 1.5km south-west of Konak Meydanı along İstasyon Caddesi (formerly İnönü Bulvarı). Walk out of the station to the bus stop on the station side of İstasyon Caddesi and any bus running along this major road will take you to the centre. If in doubt, ask the driver, '*Konak?*'. Sivas' otogar is over 2km south-east of the centre, reachable by dolmuş.

Most of the sights are conveniently grouped in a pleasant park at Konak Meydanı. The Gök Medrese (Blue Seminary) is a short walk away.

Bus company ticket offices and banks with ATMs are located along Atatürk Caddesi between Konak Meydanı and the PTT.

The tourist office (☎ 221 3135, fax 222 2252) is on the ground floor of the vilayet konağı building, facing the main square. It's only open weekdays.

Of Sivas' several Internet cafes the Blue Moon, around the corner from Otel Ergin, is likely to be the most convenient.

Kale Camii

Heading down İstasyon Caddesi from Konak Meydanı, the first building you'll probably come to is the Kale Camii (1580), an Ottoman work constructed by Sultan Murad III's grand vizier Mahmut Paşa.

Seljuk Architecture

Bürüciye Medresesi A few steps east of the Kale Camii, near a gazebo with an ablutions fountain on top and a toilet beneath, is the Bürüciye Medresesi, built in 1271 by Muzaffer Bürücerdi, who is entombed inside it (to the left, with the fine tilework).

Şifaiye Medresesi Across the park from the Bürüciye Medresesi is the Şifaiye Medresesi (İzzettin Keykavus Şifahanesi, Darüş-şifa), a medieval medical school that ranks as one of the city's oldest buildings. It dates from 1217, when it was built for the Seljuk sultan İzzettin Keykavus I, whose architect used stylised sun/lion and moon/bull motifs in the decoration.

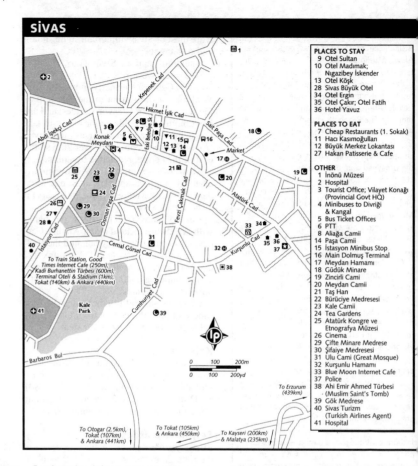

SİVAS

PLACES TO STAY
9 Otel Sultan
10 Otel Madımak;
 Nıgazibey İskender
13 Otel Köşk
28 Sivas Büyük Otel
34 Otel Ergin
35 Otel Çakır; Otel Fatih
36 Hotel Yavuz

PLACES TO EAT
7 Cheap Restaurants (1. Sokak)
11 Hacı Kasımoğulları
12 Büyük Merkez Lokantası
27 Hakan Patisserie & Cafe

OTHER
1 İnönü Müzesi
2 Hospital
3 Tourist Office; Vilayet Konağı
 (Provincial Govt HQ)
4 Minibuses to Divriği
 & Kangal
5 Bus Ticket Offices
6 PTT
8 Aliağa Camii
14 Paşa Camii
15 İstasyon Minibus Stop
16 Main Dolmuş Terminal
17 Meydan Hamamı
18 Güdük Minare
19 Zincirli Cami
20 Meydan Camii
21 Taş Han
22 Bürüciye Medresesi
23 Kale Camii
24 Tea Gardens
25 Atatürk Kongre ve
 Etnografya Müzesi
26 Cinema
29 Çifte Minare Medrese
30 Şifaiye Medresesi
31 Ulu Cami (Great Mosque)
32 Kurşunlu Hamamı
33 Blue Moon Internet Cafe
37 Police
38 Ahi Emir Ahmed Türbesi
 (Muslim Saint's Tomb)
39 Gök Medrese
40 Sivas Turizm
 (Turkish Airlines Agent)
41 Hospital

Konak Meydanı

Kale Park

To Train Station, Good
Times Internet Cafe (250m),
Kadi Burhanettin Türbesi (600m),
Terminal Oteli & Stadium (1km),
Tokat (140km) & Ankara (440km)

To Otogar (2.5km),
Tokat (107km)
& Ankara (441km)

To Tokat (105km)
& Ankara (450km)

To Kayseri (200km)
& Malatya (235km)

To Erzurum
(439km)

0   100   200m
0   100   200yd

CENTRAL ANATOLIA

Look to the right as you enter the courtyard to see the porch which was closed up and made into a tomb for Sultan İzzettin when he died in 1219. Note the beautiful blue tilework and Arabic inscriptions.

The main courtyard has four eyvans, with sun and moon symbols on either side of the eastern one. It's now grassed over and surrounded by tea tables and leather, carpet and souvenir shops. If you're looking for Turkish souvenirs, this is a good place to start.

Çifte Minare Medrese Directly opposite the Şifaiye Medresesi, the Çifte Minare

Medrese (Seminary of the Twin Minarets) has, as its name states, a *çift* (pair) of minarets. Along with its grand Seljuk-style gateway, that's about all it has, as the medrese behind the portal has long been ruined. Finished in 1271, it was commissioned by the Mongol-İlkhanid vizier Şemsettin Güveyn who ruled here. If you stand between the two opposing medreses, you will be able to see clearly what a difference half a century made to the exuberance of Seljuk architecture.

Ulu Cami (Great Mosque) The town's other sights are south-east of Konak Mey danı along Cemal Gürsel and Cumhuriyet Caddesis. To find them, walk to the southern end of the park and turn left (east) onto Cemal Gürsel Caddesi.

The Ulu Cami (1197) is Sivas' oldest significant building. Built during the reign of Kutbettin Melikşah, it's a large, low room with a forest of 50 columns. The brick minaret was added in 1213. Though it's not as grand as the more imposing Seljuk buildings, it has a certain old-Anatolian charm.

Gök Medrese Just east of the Ulu Cami, turn right (south) on Cumhuriyet Caddesi to reach the Gök Medrese, or Blue Seminary. It was built in 1271 at the behest of Sahip Ata, the grand vizier of Sultan Gıyasettin II Keyhüsrev, who funded the grand Sahip Ata mosque complex in Konya. The facade was decorated with wild exuberance, with tiles, brickwork designs and carving covering not just the doorway, but the windows and walls as well. The blue tilework gave the school its name, *gök* (sky) being an old Turkish word for 'blue'.

Atatürk Congress & Ethnography Museum

Across İstasyon Caddesi from the Kale Camii is the Ottoman school building which hosted the Sivas Congress on 4 September 1919. Today it's the Atatürk Kongre ve Etnografya Müzesi, open from 8.30 am to noon and 1.30 to 5.30 pm daily except Monday. Admission is US$1.75. The entrance is round the back of the building.

The ethnographical collection is pleasantly displayed on the ground floor and includes a fine selection of kilims and carpets; some magnificent embroideries; the old wooden doors from the Ulu Cami/Darüşşifa complex in Divriği; a 12th-century wooden *mimber* (pulpit) from the Kale Camii in Divriği; and relics collected from dervish *tekkes* (monasteries) closed in 1925.

Upstairs, the Congress Hall is preserved as it was when the Sivas Congress met, with photos of the delegates touchingly displayed on old school desks. You can also see Atatürk's bedroom and the cable room which played a more important role in de-

velopments than you might imagine. The other displays (mainly photographs and documents) are captioned in Turkish only.

Ahi Emir Ahmed Türbesi & Kurşunlu Hamamı

On Kurşunlu Caddesi just south-west of the budget hotels is the Ahi Emir Ahmed Türbesi, the tomb of a Muslim saint who died in 1333.

Across the street, the women's section of the Kurşunlu Hamamı (Turkish bath) is open from 8.30 am to 5 pm; the men's opens earlier and closes later.

Places to Stay – Budget

Sivas has one or two decent cheap hotels and any number of less decent ones. There's one basic high-rise hotel, the aptly named *Terminal Oteli* (☎ 226 2909), near the otogar if you have to make an incredibly early start.

The budget hotels in the first 500m southeast of Konak Meydanı, along Atatürk Caddesi, are drab, dingy and expensive. The better cheap hotels are 700m south-east of Konak Meydanı, at the junction of Atatürk and Kurşunlu Caddesis.

Perhaps the best of the newer places in this area is *Hotel Yavuz* (☎ 225 0204, *Atatürk Caddesi 86*), south-east of the intersection with Kurşunlu Caddesi. You'll pay US$12.50/17 for a single/double with shower in averagely comfortable rooms. The restaurant downstairs is a plus.

Around the corner, *Otel Çakır* (☎/fax 222 4526, *Kurşunlu Caddesi 20*) charges the same for clean but basic rooms with bath. The lobby was under reconstruction at the time of writing. The nearby *Otel Fatih* (☎ 233 4313, *Kurşunlu Caddesi 22*) also charges the same for slightly cheerier rooms in an atmosphere of Islamic propriety.

Across Kurşunlu Caddesi is the rock-bottom budget hotel, *Otel Ergin* (☎ 221 2301, *Atatürk Caddesi 80*), formerly the Hotel Evin, offering rooms for US$6/10, subject to bartering. The lobby is grubby but the waterless rooms are not too bad. Single women would probably be better off at the Çakır or Fatih.

Places to Stay – Mid-Range

The two-star *Otel Madımak (☎ 221 8027, Eski Belediye Sokak 2)* is a phoenix literally arisen from the ashes of a fire deliberately set in 1995 amid the furore over Salman Rushdie's *Satanic Verses*. It resulted in the deaths of 37 people. Many people might think it would have been more sensitive to close it completely, but if you want to stay it charges US$30/50 for quite comfortable rooms with bath, TV and breakfast. Some of the doubles are very spacious.

A few steps further down the same street, *Otel Sultan (☎ 221 2986, fax 221 9346, Eski Belediye Sokak 18)*, across from the German consulate, is beginning to look its age but still offers comfortable rooms with shower (copious hot water) for US$25 a head, subject to discussion when it's quiet.

Around the corner on the main avenue, the two-star *Otel Köşk (☎ 221 1150, fax 223 9350, Atatürk Caddesi 7)* has a restaurant, a lift and reasonably modern rooms for US$25/33, breakfast included. Ask for a room at the back if you're a light sleeper.

The city's newest and most luxurious hotel is the four-star *Sivas Büyük Otel (☎ 225 4762, fax 225 2323, İstasyon Caddesi)*, which charges US$22/30/37 a single/double/triple with all mod cons and breakfast. There's a nice pastry shop off the lobby.

Places to Eat

Sivas has plenty of good inexpensive places to eat. For a range of foods at the lowest prices, find 1. Sokak (Birinci Sokak), behind the PTT just off the eastern side of Konak Meydanı. The Aliağa Camii is halfway up the slope, and below it are several small, cheap restaurants good for a quick feed for US$2 to US$4. *Nimet* and *Anadolu* are the nicest, the Nimet having a particularly inviting upstairs *aile salonu* (room for families and single women). *Güleryüz Kebap* is good for a variety of kebaps, including grills, İskender kebap and spicy-hot Adana kebap, as is the newer *Gonca* right on the street corner.

Right beside the Madımak hotel, the *Nıyazıbey İskender* serves, as its name would suggest, excellent İskender kebab on silvery platters, with the butter and yogurt poured on afterwards. Expect to pay around US$4 for a kebap and soft drink.

Around the corner on Atatürk Caddesi, near the Otel Köşk, is the spacious *Büyük Merkez Lokantası* serving a wide range of ready meals. Order their speciality, the *sebzeli Sivas kebabı*, lamb cooked with aubergines, tomatoes, peppers and garlic and served with flaps of soft flat bread, for US$4.

Another bright, popular option is *Hacı Kasımoğulları* in nearby Afyon Sokak where you can get the usual range of kebaps plus an İskender if you get there early.

In the evenings İstasyon Caddesi is the place for promenading and on summer evenings you'll find stalls set up serving everything from gözleme to popcorn. Also on İstasyon you'll find the newest branch of *Hakan Patisserie & Cafe* where Sivas' students meet to chat in congenial surroundings – not a headscarf in sight!

For fancy meals with drinks, try the dining rooms of the Otel Köşk and the Sivas Büyük Otel.

Getting There & Away

Air Twice-weekly Turkish Airlines flights on Wednesday and Friday connect Sivas with Ankara and, by a connection there, to İstanbul. The ticket agency is Sivas Turizm (☎ 221 1147, fax 223 1659), İstasyon Caddesi 50, near the Sivas Büyük Otel. A bus to the airport departs from this office 90 minutes before flight time.

Bus Sivas' otogar is 2.5km south of Konak Meydanı. 'Yenişehir' dolmuşes pass by the otogar and end their run at a stop just uphill from the Paşa Camii near the Sivas Pide Fırını, a five-minute walk from either Konak Meydanı or the budget hotels on Kurşunlu Caddesi.

The otogar has its own PTT branch, a restaurant and pastry shop, a shoe repair shop and an *emanetçi* (left-luggage room).

The main dolmuş terminal in the centre is behind (north of) the Paşa Camii, just off Atatürk Caddesi.

Sivas' otogar can be an eerily empty place. Many buses are passing through from other towns, which makes it hard to be sure seats will be available until they actually arrive. Although most companies run *servis* buses into town, few run them back to the otogar.

Since many travellers will be heading east to Erzurum, it's a shame to have to report a poor choice of services. Metro is probably the best company operating the route but they offer only a night service. It's hard to recommend Esatas/Dadaş, which runs during the day but takes six hours to complete the journey, stopping only once for 20 minutes and that a mere 1¼ hours into the trip.

Some useful daily services are listed in the table below.

Train Sivas is a main rail junction for both east-west and north-south lines. The main east-west express, the *Doğu Ekspresi*, goes through Sivas daily, the *Güney Ekspresi* (from İstanbul to Diyarbakır) and the *Vangölü Ekspresi* (from İstanbul to Tatvan) on alternate days. You could travel by train to Kangal (US$0.75) and Divriği (US$1.50) or to Zile (US$2), Turhal (US$2) and Amasya (US$2.75) but buses are generally quicker and more convenient; Kangal station, for example, is 8km out of town, although Divriği station is relatively handy.

Getting Around
'İstasyon' dolmuşes run from Sivas Garı to Konak Meydanı and the city centre dolmuş terminal by the Paşa Camii.

To get to the otogar catch a 'Universite' bus from Konak Meydanı (buy your ticket in advance from the white booth; US$0.30); or a less-crowded dolmuş from Fevzi Çakmak Caddesi.

AROUND SİVAS
East of Sivas you move straight into the less developed atmosphere of eastern Turkey. However, Balıklı Kaplıca and Divriği are described here since both are most easily visited from Sivas.

Balıklı Kaplıca
There's absolutely no reason to stop in Kangal, a dreary, dusty farming town east of the Sivas-Malatya road which gave its name to the famous white Kangal sheepdogs. But 15km east of Kangal at Balıklı Kaplıca (the name means 'Hot Spring with Fish'), off the Divriği road, is a curious – even bizarre – health spa for those with psoriasis, an itchy, flaky skin condition. A shepherd boy is said to have discovered the magical healing qualities of the local warm mineral water, especially when combined with the action of the 'doctor fish' that nibble at sufferers' scaly skin. The fish are supposed to be able to distinguish skin with psoriasis from all other types of skin defect, but one of the authors of this book found they were just as happy to feast on her sweaty feet!

The complex at Balıklı Kaplıca has several pools (segregated by sex) set amid trees, together with a *hotel* with restaurant, and a small shop. Single rooms cost US$38 per night, doubles US$43, on top of which

Services from Sivas' Otogar

destination	fare (US$)	time (hr)	distance (km)	daily services
Amasya	7	3½	225	5 buses
Ankara	10	6	450	frequent buses
Divriği	4	3	175	several minibuses
Diyarbakır	10	8	500	several buses
Erzurum	12	6	485	several buses
İstanbul	20	11	900	several buses
Kayseri	5	3½	200	hourly buses
Malatya	7	4½	235	several buses
Samsun	10	5½	341	several buses
Tokat	5	1½	105	hourly buses
Yozgat	5	3	224	frequent buses

you should budget US$8 for full board, essential if you're to do what the brochure tells you and spend eight hours a day in the pool for three weeks. At the time of writing new, more modern rooms were being added to the complex and the road to the resort was being upgraded. Contact their Web site (www.balikli.com) for more information.

Getting There & Away Minibuses from the Konak Meydanı in Sivas run to Kangal (US$2, one hour) from where you can take a taxi to the resort (US$8). In summer the minibuses continue direct to the resort.

Divriği
☎ 346

If Pamukkale is Turkey's most over-visited World Heritage Site, the mosque-medrese complex at Divriği is certainly its least visited. A typically old-fashioned mountain town, Divriği is hidden beyond a mountain pass (1970m high) in a fertile valley and still has an agricultural economy. The narrow streets are laced with grapevines and paved in stone blocks, and as yet no concrete high-rises have eaten into the skyline.

Divriği has a few very basic hotels, some simple restaurants and banks with ATMs.

Ulu Cami & Darüşşifa Uphill from the town centre stands the beautifully restored complex of the Ulu Cami and Darüşşifa (hospital), both founded in 1228 by the local emir Ahmet Şah and his wife, the lady Fatma Turan Melik.

The northern entrance to the Ulu Cami is stupendous, a sort of exuberant rococo Seljuk style, with geometric patterns, medallions, luxuriant stone foliage and intricate Arabic inscriptions bursting free of the facade's flatness in a richness that is astonishing. It's the sort of doorway which only a provincial emir with more money than sense would ever have dreamt of building. In a large Seljuk city, this sort of extravagance would have been ridiculed as lacking in taste. In Divriği, it's a petty potentate's wonderful, fanciful whim shaped in stone.

The northern entrance is really what you've come to see, although the north-

western one has some fine work as well. The mosque's interior is very simple, with 16 columns and a plain mihrab (niche indicating the direction of Mecca), but you're unlikely to see it as it's kept locked outside prayer times.

Adjoining the Ulu Cami is the hospital, equally plain and simple outside except for the requisite elaborate entrance. Inside, eclecticism and odd ingenuity reigns: the floor plan is asymmetrical, the four columns all dissimilar. The octagonal pool in the court has a spiral runoff, similar to the one in Konya's Karatay Medresesi, which allowed the soothing tinkle of running water to break the silence of the room and soothe the patients' nerves. A platform raised above the main floor may have been for musicians who likewise soothed the patients with pleasant sounds.

In theory the Darüşşifa is open from 8 am to 5 pm Monday to Friday but in the absence of tourists you may find it locked. If so ask around and someone is bound to come up with the key.

Other Things to See & Do As this was once an important provincial capital, you will notice several drum-like **kümbets** (Seljuk tombs) scattered about town. Ahmet Şah's tomb is near the Ulu Cami, as are several earlier ones dating from 1196 and another from 1240.

Trailing down the sides of the hill dominating Divriği are the ruined walls of a vast medieval **castle**, with the Kale Camii a solid but equally ruinous structure on the summit.

The no-frills **Tarihi Çifte Kapı Hamamı** is open for women from noon until 5pm, much longer for men, daily except Sunday. A basic bath costs just US$0.75.

Places to Stay Neither of Divriği's two hotels is truly recommendable, but of the two, the better is probably *Belediye Oteli* (☎ 418 1825), which does at least have setting in its favour. Beds in big but shabby rooms with showers cost about US$5 each. Rooms at the back have balconies overlooking the kale ruins. The hotel is along a side turn-off, on the left, off the main road into town. Ask to be dropped off, otherwise a taxi back from the otogar will cost about US$1.50.

The other possibility is just off the main commercial street in the centre of town. You could be forgiven for thinking the *Otel Ninni* (☎ *418 1239*) had ceased trading but in fact it's still open and charges US$3 for a dorm bed in a waterless room; the common shower and toilet, though reasonably clean, are down one floor from some of the rooms.

Getting There & Away Minibuses to Divriği (US$4, three hours) depart from the Konak Meydanı in Sivas several times a day and are easier to get onto than the bigger buses from Ankara and İstanbul, which are often full before they get to Sivas. If you catch the first minibus at 9.30 am you'll arrive in plenty of time to look round and catch the last bus back at 5 pm.

You might prefer to take a train, even though it will take longer than the bus. The rail line from Sivas to Erzurum passes through Divriği. In theory you could look round and then continue eastwards to Erzurum (roughly 6½ hours); in practise you'll probably have to stay overnight in Divriği and catch an onward connection the next day. Divriği train station is about 2km south of the Ulu Cami.

Drivers should note that there's no road onward towards Erzincan from Divriği, forcing you to backtrack.

South Central Anatolia

KONYA
☎ 332 • pop 680,000
Standing alone in the middle of the vast Anatolian steppe, Konya is like a traditional caravan stopping-place. The wind-swept landscape gives way to patches of greenery in the city, and once in town you forget the loneliness of the plateau. In recent years Konya has been booming. The barren-looking steppe is in fact good for growing grain and Konya is the heart of Turkey's very

rich 'bread-basket'. Light industry provides jobs for those who are not farmers.

Much of the city was built within the last two decades but the centre is very old. Were it not for Konya's reputation for religious conservatism it would no doubt attract many more visitors. If you really couldn't bear to go without alcohol for a day or so, Konya may not be the best place for you. On the other hand if you're interested in the Seljuks or in seeing another side of life in modern Turkey, then there's enough to see and do here to fill at least a day – avoid Monday as the museums will be closed.

Konya is devoutly Muslim, self-satisfied and proud of it. A motto emblazoned on the city's buses proclaims locals' desire for 'All of Turkey to be just like Konya'. At first, locals in Konya will treat you with chilly formality. In most cases this quickly fades into the warm glow of the familiar Turkish hospitality, but occasionally you may get the feeling that you're being regarded as a *gavur* (infidel).

Take special care not to upset the pious especially when you enter mosques and the Mevlâna Museum. If you visit during Ramazan, don't eat or drink in public during the day as a courtesy to those who are fasting. (For the dates of Ramazan and other religious holidays, see Public Holidays & Special Events in the Facts for the Visitor chapter.) Ironically, women may encounter more hassles in this bastion of propriety than in many other Turkish cities. Most travellers quickly tire of the aggro from touts hanging about Mevlâna Caddesi.

Note that the dervishes only whirl during the Mevlâna Festival in December (see Special Events later in this section).

History
The city has been here a very long time and Çatal Höyük, 50km to the south, has claims to being the oldest known human community, dating back to 7500 BC.

The Hittites called this city 'Kuwanna' almost 4000 years ago. It was Kowania to the Phrygians, Iconium to the Romans and then Konya to the Turks. Under the Romans, Iconium was an important provincial

KONYA

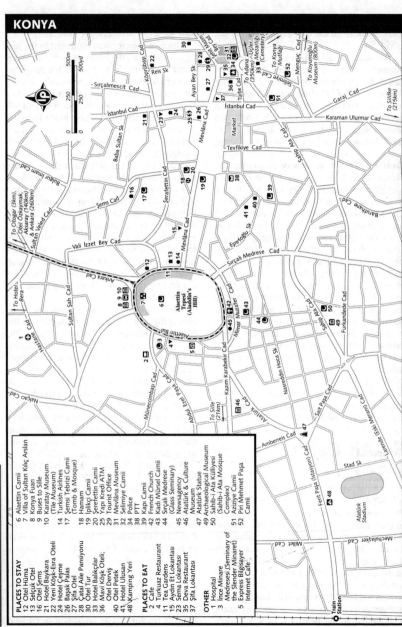

PLACES TO STAY
12 Otel Hüma
13 Selçuk Otel
16 Otel Şems
21 Hotel Baykara
22 Yeni Köşk-Esra Oteli
24 Hotel Çeşme
26 Başak Palas
27 Şifa Otel
28 Çatal Aile Pansiyonu
30 Otel Tur
33 Hotel Balıkçılar
36 Mavi Köşk Oteli;
40 Otel Petek
41 Hotel Ulusan
48 Kamping Yeri

PLACES TO EAT
2 Cafe
4 Turkuaz Restaurant
9 Tea Gardens
15 Aydın Et Lokantası
23 Sema Lokantası
35 Deva Restaurant
37 Şifa Lokantası

OTHER
1 Hospital
3 İnce Minare
  Medressesi (Seminary of
  the Slender Minaret)
5 Express Bilgisayer
  Internet Cafe

6 Alaettin Camii
7 Villa of Sultan Kılıç Arslan
8 Konya Fuarı
9 Buses to Sille
10 Karatay Museum
  (Tile Museum)
14 Turkish Airlines
17 Şemsi Tebrizi Camii
  (Tomb & Mosque)
18 Hamam
19 İplikçi Camii
20 Şerefettin Camii
25 Yapı Kredi ATM
29 Tourist Office
31 Mevlâna Museum
32 Selimiye Camii
34 Police
38 PTT
39 Kapı Camii
42 French Church
43 Kadı Mürsel Camii
44 Sırçalı Medrese
  (Glass Seminary)
45 Newsagency
46 Atatürk & Culture
  Museum
47 Atatürk Statue
49 Archaeological Museum
50 Sahib-i Ata Küllivesi
  (Sahib-i Ata Mosque
  Complex)
51 Aziziye Camii
52 Piri Mehmet Paşa
  Camii

town visited several times by saints Paul and Barnabas, although its early Christian community doesn't seem to have been very influential.

Konya's heyday was during the 13th century, when it was capital of the Seljuk Sultanate of Rum, one of the successor states to the Great Seljuk Turkish Empire of the 11th century. The Sultanate of Rum encompassed most of Anatolia and had Konya as its capital from about 1150 to 1300. During that period, the Seljuk sultans built dozens of fine buildings in an architectural style decidedly Turkish, but with its roots in Persia and Byzantium.

Orientation

The city centre is the hill Alaettin Tepesi, crowned with a great Seljuk mosque and surrounded by the city's best Seljuk buildings. From the hill, Mevlâna Caddesi goes south-east 500m to Hükümet Alanı (Government Plaza, also called Konak), with the provincial and city government buildings, the main PTT and a vast underground gold jewellery market.

East of Hükümet Alanı, the boulevard continues another 500m to the tourist office and the Mevlâna Museum, Konya's prime attraction.

Hotels are located along Mevlâna Caddesi and near the Mevlâna Museum. The otogar, 3.5km due north of the centre, is connected to it by regular minibuses. The train station is about 3km due west.

Information

Konya's tourist office (☎ 351 1074) is at Mevlâna Caddesi 21, across the square from the Mevlâna Museum. Opening hours are from 8.30 am to 5 pm Monday to Saturday in summer. The staff speak English, French and German. Across the street, the Konya Kültür ve Turizm Derneği or Konya Culture & Tourism Association (☎ 351 8288) can help Turkish speakers with information about the dervishes.

Banks with ATMs can be found in or around Hükümet Alanı. The Express Bilgisayer Internet Cafe (☎ 350 7866) is on Alaettin Bulvarı at Baybal Apt 21/4.

Mevlâna Museum

The first place to visit in Konya is the Mevlâna Museum (Mevlâna Müzesi), the former lodge of the whirling dervishes, open from 9 am to 5.30 pm daily (10 am to 5 pm on Monday); admission is US$2.50. On religious holidays the museum (really a shrine) may be open longer. For Turkish Muslims, this is a very holy place and more than 1.5 million people visit it a year, most of them Turkish. You will see many people praying and pleading for Mevlâna's intercession. When entering, women should cover their heads and shoulders, and both sexes should avoid wearing shorts.

The gorgeous lodge is visible from some distance, its fluted dome of turquoise tiles one of Turkey's most splendid sights. After walking through a pretty courtyard with an ablutions fountain and several tombs, you remove your shoes and pass into the **Mevlâna Türbesi**. Look out for the big Nisan tası, or 'April bowl', on the left as you enter. April rainwater, so important to the farmers of this region, was considered sacred, and was collected in this bowl. The tip of Mevlâna's turban was dipped in the water and offered to those in need of healing.

Mevlâna's sarcophagus (the largest) is flanked by those of his son, Sultan Veled, and his father. All are covered in velvet shrouds heavy with gold embroidery, and those of Mevlâna and Sultan Veled bear huge turbans, symbols of spiritual authority.

The Mevlâna Türbesi dates from Seljuk times. The mosque and room for ceremonies were added later by Ottoman sultans (Mehmet the Conqueror was a Mevlevi adherent and Süleyman the Magnificent made large charitable donations to the order). Selim I, conqueror of Egypt, donated the Mamluk crystal lamps.

In the small chapel and semahane (hall), attached to the sepulchral chamber, are articles of clothing used by Mevlâna, Sultan Veled and Şemsi Tebrizi, as well as dervish paraphernalia like musical instruments, vestments, prayer mats, illuminated manuscripts and ethnographic artefacts. In the museum's last room, look on the left near the mihrab for a seccade (prayer carpet)

Mevlâna & the Whirling Dervishes

In Celaleddin Rumi (Mevlâna, 'Our Guide' to his followers), the Seljuk Sultanate of Rum produced one of the world's great mystic philosophers. His poetry and religious writings, mostly in Persian, the literary language of the day, are among the most beloved and respected in the Islamic world.

Celaleddin was born in 1207 in Balkh (Afghanistan). His family fled the impending Mongol invasion by moving to Mecca and then to the Sultanate of Rum, reaching Konya by 1228. His father, Baha' uddin, was a noted preacher and Celaleddin became a brilliant student of Islamic theology. After his father's death in 1231, he studied in Aleppo and Damascus, returning to live in Konya by 1240.

In 1244 he met Mehmet Şemseddin Tebrizi, called Şemsi Tebrizi, one of his father's Sufi (Muslim mystic) disciples. Tebrizi had a profound influence on Rumi, who became devoted to him. Jealous of his overwhelming influence on their master, an angry crowd of Rumi's own disciples put Tebrizi to death in 1247. Stunned by the loss, Rumi withdrew from the world to meditate and, in this period, wrote his great poetic work, the *Mathnawi* (called *Mesnevi* in Turkish). He also wrote many *ruba'i* and *ghazal* poems, collected into his 'Great Opus', the *Divan-i Kebir*.

His ecumenical teachings were summed up in this beautiful verse:

> Whoever you may be, come
> Even though you may be
> An infidel, a pagan, or a fire-worshipper, come
> Our brotherhood is not one of despair
> Even though you have broken
> Your vows of repentance a hundred times, come.

Rumi died late in the day on 17 December 1273, the date now known as his 'wedding night' as he was finally united with Allah. His son, Sultan Veled, organised his followers into the brotherhood called the Mevlevi, or whirling dervishes.

Though the Mongol invasion put an end to Seljuk sovereignty in Anatolia, the Mevlevi order prospered. In the centuries following Mevlâna's death, over 100 dervish lodges were founded throughout the Ottoman domains, and numerous Ottoman sultans were Mevlevi Sufis.

Under the Ottoman Empire, dervish orders exerted considerable influence on the country's political, social and economic life. In most cases their world-view was monarchist, conservative and xenophobic. Committed to democracy and the separation of religion and state, Atatürk saw the dervishes as an obstacle to advancement for the Turkish people, and in 1925 he banned all the dervish orders.

Though outlawed, several of the dervish orders survived as fraternal religious brotherhoods. The dervishes were revived in Konya in 1957 as a 'cultural association' intended to preserve a historical tradition. The annual Festival of Mevlâna is officially encouraged as a popular rather than a religious event. Groups of dervishes are also sent on cultural exchange tours to other countries, performing the ceremony from Hawaii to Helsinki.

bearing a picture of the Kaaba at Mecca. Made in Iran of silk and wool, it's extremely fine, with an estimated three million knots.

The rooms surrounding the courtyard, once offices and quarters for the dervishes, are furnished as they would have been at the time of Mevlâna, with mannequins dressed in dervish costumes.

Across from the museum entrance is the **Selimiye Camii**, endowed by Sultan Selim II in 1567 when he was still just the governor of Konya.

Seljuk Turkish Architecture

Central Konya forms Turkey's best 'outdoor museum' of Seljuk architecture. On a tight budget you can walk round and study the imposing exteriors for free but most of the buildings now house museums that are well worth a look.

Alaettin Camii The ancient Alaettin Camii is right on Alaettin Tepesi, or Aladdin's Hill, at the western end of Alaettin Bulvarı. The mosque of Alaeddin Keykubat I, Seljuk Sultan of Rum from 1219 to 1231, is a great rambling building designed by a Damascene architect in Arab style and finished in 1221. Over the centuries it was embellished, refurbished, ruined and restored. It reopened again recently after decades of restoration.

The main entrance on the northern side incorporates bits of decoration from earlier Byzantine and Roman buildings. To the right of it a tomb chamber holds the remains of a dozen Seljuk sultans. The entrance led to a door into the mosque, which was between two huge Seljuk türbes; today a less imposing entrance on the east is used.

While the exterior of the mosque is fairly plain, the interior is a forest of old marble columns surmounted with recycled Roman and Byzantine capitals, with a fine, carved wooden mimber (1156) and an old marble mihrab, framed by beautiful modern Seljuk-style blue and black calligraphy.

You can visit the mosque from 8.30 am to 6 pm, but remember that it's still a place of worship: leave your shoes at the door and avoid entering at prayer times.

On the northern side of the Alaettin Tepesi, the scant ruins of the **Villa of Sultan Kılıç Arslan** are protected by a concrete shelter. The hill's eastern slopes are dotted with tea gardens, pleasant places to relax in summer.

Karatay Müzesi The Büyük Karatay Medresesi (Great Karatay Seminary), now called the Karatay Müzesi, is a Seljuk theological school just north of Alaettin Tepesi. Housing an outstanding collection of ceramics and tiles, it's open from 9 am to noon and from 1.30 to 5.30 pm daily. Admission costs US$1.25.

The school was constructed in 1251–52 by Emir Celaleddin Karatay, a Seljuk general, vizier and statesman who is buried in the south-western corner room.

Beyond the magnificent marble entrance the central dome and the eyvan contain masterpieces of Seljuk light and dark blue

tilework, interspersed with snatches of white and black. The Kufic-style Arabic inscription ringing the dome is the first chapter of the Quran while the triangles below are decorated with the stylised names of the prophets (Mohammed, Jesus, Moses and David) and of the four caliphs who succeeded Mohammed.

Notice the curlicue drain for the central pool: its curved shape made the sound of running water a pleasant background noise in the quiet room where students studied.

The tile collection includes interesting coloured examples from the Seljuk palace on Alaettin Tepesi and from the Palace of Kubadabad near Beyşehir Lake. Compare these with the later Ottoman tiles from İznik.

İnce Minare Müzesi On the western side of Alaettin Tepesi is the İnce Minare Medresesi (Seminary of the Slender Minaret), now the Museum of Wood & Stone Carving. This religious school was built in 1264 for Sahip Ata, a powerful Seljuk vizier, who may have been trying to outdo the patron of the Karatay Medresesi, built only seven years earlier. Hours and fee are the same as at the Karatay; labels are in Turkish only.

Don't enter the building immediately, for half of what you've come to see is the elaborate doorway, with bands of Arabic inscription running up the sides and looping overhead, which is far more impressive than the small building behind it. The minaret beside the door is over 600 years old and gave the seminary its popular name, Slender Minaret. Since most of it was knocked down by lightning in 1901, the latest restorative efforts included installation of a lightning conductor.

Inside, many of the carvings in wood and stone feature motifs similar to those used in the tile and ceramic work. You'll quickly see that the Seljuks didn't let Islam's famous condemnation of images of creatures with souls (humans and animals) stand in the way of their art; there are plenty of images of birds (the Seljuk double-headed eagle, for example), men and women, lions and leopards here. The eyvan in particular contains two delightful carvings of Seljuk angels with distinctly Mongol features. Be sure to visit the Ahşap Eserler Bölümü (Carved Wood Section) to see the intricately worked doors.

South of Alaettin Tepesi

Several other Seljuk monuments lurk in the warren of streets to the south of the city. Ask for the Kadı Mürsel Camii, then walk south along Ressam Sami Sokak, the street which begins just east of a small French church and opposite a large white mansion housing offices of the Milli Eğitim Bakanlığı.

A few minutes' walk south along Ressam Sami Sokak is another Seljuk seminary, the Sırçalı Medrese (Glass Seminary), named after its tiled exterior. Sponsored by Bedreddin Muslih, a Seljuk vizier, construction was completed in 1242. It's now the small Mezar Anıtlar Müzesi (Museum of Tombstones). The main entrance is grand but formal and restrained compared to the exuberance of those in Konya's other great medreses. In the courtyard, the great eyvan on the western side was used for classes; its arch is decorated with a band of particularly fine calligraphic tilework. The students' cells are on two floors.

The inscriptions on the tombstones are often very fine. Symbols of rank served to indicate the deceased's role in life.

A few blocks further south along Ressam Sami Sokak is the Sahib-i Ata Külliyesi (Sahib-i Ata Mosque Complex), founded in 1285. Behind its requisite grand entrance – with its own minaret – is the Sahib-i Ata Camii, originally constructed during the reign of Alaettin Keykavus by the Seljuk soldier and statesman Hacı Ebubekirzade Hüseyinoğlu Sahib-i Ata Fahreddin Ali. Destroyed by fire in 1871, it was razed and rebuilt to the same style. The mihrab is original and a fine example of Seljuk light-and-dark blue tilework.

On the south-eastern side of the mosque is another grand gateway which once led to a dervish lodge, now in ruins.

Other Mosques & Tombs

Dotted about town are other interesting buildings. The Şemsi Tebrizi Camii, containing the elegant 14th-century tomb of Rumi's spiritual mentor, is just north of Hükümet Alanı, not far from Alaettin Bulvarı. The Aziziye Camii (1875) in the bazaar was rebuilt in baroque late-Ottoman-style after a fire; it's the one with twin minarets bearing little sheltered balconies. The İplikçi Camii (1202) on Mevlâna Caddesi, perhaps Konya's oldest mosque, was built for the Seljuk vizier Şemseddin Altun-Aba in plain, unadorned style: a forest of columns, arches and vaulting. The Şerefettin Camii, off Mevlâna Caddesi near Hükümet Alanı, was built in the 1200s and rebuilt in 1636. The Piri Mehmet Paşa Camii (1523) and adjoining Siyavüş Sultan Türbesi face the Piri Mehmet Paşa Zaviyesi, a dervish hostel, restored in 1996.

Other Museums

Archaeological Museum

The small but interesting Archaeological Museum is to the west of the Sahib-i Ata Külliyesi and is open from 9 am to noon and 1.30 to 5.30 pm daily except Monday for US$1.75. The forecourt is filled with statuary and sarcophagi from Konya's long history. Some of the small, simple funeral monuments have an appealing primitive directness.

The museum has several fine sarcophagi decorated with bold, lively high-relief carvings. The Pamphylian one resembles a small temple; the Roman Sidamara sarcophagus dating from AD 250–60 bears striking reliefs of the labours of Hercules.

Koyunoğlu Müzesi

This museum, at Kerimler Caddesi 25, 500m from the Mevlâna Müzesi, was donated to the city by a private collector who seemed to collect everything. Opening hours are from 9 am to 5 pm; admission costs US$1. The few labels are in Turkish only.

The modern museum building has three levels. Downstairs has collections of minerals, weapons, fossils and stuffed birds, and an atrium filled with plants and live birds. The main floor displays ancient coins, sculptures, glass, jewellery, Bronze Age implements and photos of old Konya. Upstairs, the ethnographic section displays kilims and carpets (one bears a map of Turkey); illuminated manuscripts and Qurans; miniature paintings and clocks; and 19th-century clothing, bath clogs, weapons, household items, coffee sets, musical instruments, embroidery and needlework.

Next door to the museum is the **Koyunoğlu Konya Evi**, a delightful old house which shows how a Konyalı family lived a century ago. Leave your shoes at the carved wooden door, put on sandals and inspect the small ground-floor room with its silk carpet. The upstairs rooms are traditionally furnished with lots of carpets, kilims, low

benches, pillows, a fine tray-table and lots of turned wood.

The quickest way to the museum lies through the **Üçler Mezarlığı**, the cemetery between the Selimiye Camii and the Mevlâna Müzesi. If you want to walk through, do so only in daylight when other people are about. Women are not advised to walk through alone.

Special Events

The Mevlâna Festival, when visitors can see the famous whirling dervishes in action,

Whirling to Ecstasy

The Mevlevi worship ceremony, which traditionally takes place on a Monday evening (Tuesday morning in Islamic thinking), is a ritual dance, or sema, representing union with God. The dervishes enter the semahane, or whirling hall, dressed in long white robes with full skirts that represent their shrouds. Over them they wear voluminous black cloaks symbolising their worldly tombs; their conical felt hats represent their tombstones.

The ceremony begins when the *hafız*, a celebrant who has committed the entire Quran to memory, intones a prayer for Mevlâna and a verse from the Quran. A kettledrum booms out, followed by the plaintive song of the *ney*, or reed flute. The breathy, haunting music of the ney is perhaps the most striking sound during the ceremony. Each musician 'opens' (makes) his own instrument from a carefully chosen length of bamboo-like reed, burning the finger holes to a mathematical formula. The ney is thought to have its own soul, and 'opening' it allows the soul to come out in its music.

MICK WELDON

The *şeyh* (sheikh or master) bows, then leads the dervishes in a circle around the hall. As they pass the sheikh's ceremonial position at the head of the hall, they bow to one another. After three circuits, the dervishes drop their black cloaks to symbolise their deliverance from the attachments of this world. One by one, arms folded on their breasts, they approach the sheikh, bow, kiss his hand, receive whispered instructions, then spin out onto the floor as they relinquish the earthly life to be reborn in mystical union with God. The male choir and the orchestra of small *bendir* (drums), *rebap* (gourd viol) and *kemençe* (bow), and ney begin the music, and the dervishes unfurl their arms and begin to whirl.

By holding their right arms up, palms upwards, they receive the blessings of heaven, which are communicated to earth by holding their left arms down, palms downwards. Pivoting on their left heels, the dervishes whirl ever faster, reaching ecstasy with a blissful expression. As they whirl, they form a 'constellation' of revolving bodies which itself slowly rotates. The sheikh walks among them to make sure each dervish is performing the ritual properly. After about 10 minutes, they all stop and kneel down. Then, rising, they begin again.

The dance is repeated four times, with the sheikh joining the last circuit. The whirling over, the hafız again chants poetical passages from the holy book, sealing the experience of mystical union with God.

runs for a week from about 10 December. The last night commemorates Mevlâna's 'wedding night' with God.

Tickets should be bought well in advance; contact the tourist office or the Konya Culture & Tourism Association for assistance. Reserve your hotel room in advance as well. These days the *semas* (ceremonies) take place in a basketball stadium which robs them of atmosphere for many people; you may well enjoy the twice-monthly semas at the Galata Mevlevihanesi in İstanbul much more. (See the Tünel section in the İstanbul chapter for details). Don't worry too much if you can't get a ticket for the main event because during the Festival other groups of dancers usually perform in the Cultural Centre behind the Mevlâna Müzesi – look for advertisements near the museum.

Places to Stay

Given Konya's character as a conservative Muslim city with a healthy pilgrimage trade, it's not surprising that alcoholic drinks are banned from most lodgings. Konya's hotels boast their own mosques, not bars; it's best to assume your minibar will be filled with soft drinks rather than beer and wine.

Places to Stay – Budget

In summer you can camp at the *Kamp Yeri* in the grounds of the Atatürk Stadium, 600m east of the train station.

Look for signs off Mevlâna Caddesi to the *Yeni Köşk-Esra Oteli* (☎ 352 0671, fax 352 0901, Yeni Aziziye Caddesi, Kadılar Sokak 28), run by Mustafa Sarıoğlan. Clean, tidy and fairly quiet, it features rooms with showers and TV for US$14/20 a single/double. The newer rooms in the Esra Otel are most comfortable.

On a tight budget one of the best choices is Ali Ulusan's *Hotel Ulusan* (☎ 351 5004, Kurşuncular Sokak 2), signposted behind the PTT. Rooms here are simple but spotless and cost US$6/12. The shower is Indian-style, stoked with wood from the bottom.

Nearby is the *Otel Petek* (☎ 351 2599, Çırıkçılar İçi 40), squeezed between a shop selling helva and another selling nuts and dried fruit. Clean, simple rooms with shower

cost US$11/14 with breakfast, a little less without the showers.

Nearer to the Mevlâna Museum, the welcoming *Otel Derviş* (☎/fax 351 1688, Mevlâna Caddesi, Bostançelebi Sokak 11/D) is simple but serviceable with shower-equipped rooms for US$13/16, subject to negotiation. The neighbouring *Mavi Köşk Oteli* (☎ 350 1904, Bostançelebi Sokak 13) is dingier, but charges about the same.

In the narrow street beside the tourist office look out for the *Çatal Aile Pansiyonu* (☎ 351 4981, Mevlâna Caddesi, Naci Fikret Sokak 14/A), where a kilim-decorated lobby leads to rooms for US$14/16, less without shower. The plant-filled *Hotel Çeşme* (☎ 351 2426, İstanbul Caddesi, Akifpaşa Sokak 35) nearby is relatively quiet, clean and charges the same.

The *Otel Tur* (☎ 351 9825, fax 352 4299, Mevlâna Caddesi, Eş'arizade Sokak 13) charges US$17/20 for clean, reasonably quiet rooms. There's a car park at the rear.

The one-star *Başak Palas* (☎ 351 1338, Hükümet Alanı 8), facing the provincial government building midway along Mevlâna Caddesi, has been here for decades if not centuries. Its well-used rooms cost US$26/30.

Places to Stay – Mid-Range

The *Otel Şems* (☎ 350 5738, fax 351 1771, Şems Caddesi 10), across the street from the Şemsi Tebrizi Camii and Türbesi, is comfortable and well located, if not especially exciting. The posted prices of US$30/34 a single/double with bath are probably negotiable. The same people run the adjoining *Hotel Ani*.

Proving that even holy Konya is not immune to irony, the three-star *Hotel Balık-çılar* (☎ 350 9470, fax 352 3259, Mevlâna Karşısı 1), the closest hotel to the Mevlâna Museum, is one of the few places in town with a proper bar! All its rooms have air-con, minibars and TV sets, and cost US$79/107. The quieter rooms are at the back, but some of the front rooms have views of the Mevlâna Museum.

Near the Büyük Karatay Medresesi, the three-star *Otel Hüma* (☎ 350 6618, fax 351

0244, Alaettin Bulvarı 8) is another good choice, its architecture designed to echo that of Konya's Seljuk buildings. Rooms here are bright and modern, with minibars and TVs, and cost US$35/50 with breakfast.

The *Selçuk Otel* (☎ *353 2525, fax 353 2529, Alaettin Bulvarı 4)*, near Alaettin Tepesi, rents air-con rooms with pleasant bathrooms, boozeless minibars and TV for US$75/100. Front rooms have views of Alaettin Tepesi.

Just east of Hükümet Alanı, the two-star *Şifa Otel* (☎ *350 4290, fax 351 9251, Mevlâna Caddesi 55)* has surprisingly old-fashioned decor but charges US$35/50, including breakfast. There's a strong undercurrent of infidel xenophobia, and street noise is a problem.

Sharing the same management, the three-star *Hotel Baykara* (☎ *353 6030, fax 353 6035, İstanbul Caddesi 181)*, three short blocks north of Mevlâna Caddesi, is reasonably comfortable, if in need of modernising, and charges US$60/80.

Places To Stay – Top End

The new *Hotel Bera* (☎ *238 1090, fax 238 1099, Kemerli Caddesi 13)* is in the commercial district behind the fairground – not necessarily the best position although the comforts offered here are Konya's best. Comfortable, modern rooms cost US$70/100. The top-floor restaurant has panoramic views of Konya. There's an Ottoman-style coffeehouse but no alcohol on the premises.

The four-star *Otel Özkaymak* (☎ *233 8720, fax 237 8729)*, across the park from the otogar, charges US$70/100 for superior rooms.

Places to Eat

Konya's speciality is *fırın kebap*, a deliciously tender, fairly greasy oven-roasted joint of mutton. The city bakers also make excellent fresh pide topped with minced lamb, cheese or eggs, but in Konya pide is called *etli ekmek* (bread with meat). A *dürüm* (roll) is thin flat bread topped with a filling, then rolled up.

This being a conservative, religious town, few places serve alcohol, and those few

places which do serve alcohol are so debased that they make one think the teetotallers may have a point. To buy booze, look for shops marked 'Tekel Bayii'. There's one near the French church on Mimar Muzaffer Caddesi.

The bright, popular *Şifa Lokantası (Mevlâna Caddesi 30)* is only a short stroll west of the Mevlâna Museum. They'll serve you a fırın kebap and cold drink for US$4.50.

The cheerful, airy *Deva Restaurant (Mevlâna Caddesi 3)*, across from the Otel Derviş, serves an assortment of Turkish dishes including *tandır kebap* (pit-roasted lamb). With salad, bread and soft drink a meal might cost US$4 or so.

In the backstreets near the Hotel Çeşme, the welcoming *Sema Lokantası (İstanbul Caddesi 107)* serves the usual kebaps and stews but also more exotic dishes like *aşure* (Noah's Ark Pudding).

For Italian-style pizzas try *Aydın Et Lokantası (Tolunay Sokak 5)*, just off Mevlâna Caddesi near the İmar Bankası.

Konya Mutfağı or Konya Kitchen (☎ *352 8547, Akçeşme Mahallesi, Topraklık Caddesi 66)*, across from the Akçeşme İlkokulu school, is in a restored house just a few minutes' walk from the Hotel Balıkçılar, down towards the Koyunoğlu Museum. It's very popular with the locals and service is polite, though the absence of a written menu makes it a bit daunting for non-Turkish-speakers. A good traditional meal is unlikely to cost more than US$10 per person.

A great night out is promised at the low-lit, first-floor *Turkuaz Restaurant* (☎ *0532-357 9474, Adliye Bulvarı)*, beside the İnce Minare. By 10.30 pm the place is packed with locals downing beers and joining in the live music. A meal of mezes and a main course like lamb chops need only cost around US$7.

Immediately behind the İnce Minare, in the basement of a reconstructed 'old' house, there's a nameless *cafe* serving tea and coffee and renting out nargilehs (water pipes). It's extremely popular with young Turks and students.

In summer few things could be more pleasurable than drinking tea in one of the innumerable *tea gardens* dotting the slopes of Alaettin Tepesi.

Shopping

Konya's market area, behind the modern PTT building, is divided up in very medieval fashion: here a section for plastic flowers, there one for teapots, here one for coils of rope. Shops at the eastern end of Mevlâna Caddesi sell carpets and other souvenirs. A kiosk in the Mevlâna Museum sells books and cassettes related to the dervishes.

Getting There & Away

Air Turkish Airlines (☎ 351 2000, fax 350 2171), at Alaettin Bulvarı 9, on the northern side of the street not far from Alaettin Tepesi, has daily flights to and from İstanbul. An airport bus (US$1.75) leaves from Alaettin Bulvarı to connect with flights, but you should check the time carefully.

Bus Konya's Otobüs Terminali (otogar) is 3.5km north of Hükümet Alanı (Konak). To get to the centre take a minibus (US$0.30) from the rank outside the otogar. For Selçuk Otel and Otel Hüma, get out at İş Bankası/THY; for most of the others, the stop is Valilik/Konak/PTT. Some of the minibuses continue to Mevlâna Meydanı, next to the tourist office and the Mevlâna Museum. A taxi to the centre costs about US$4. The table below lists some daily services.

Train There's no direct rail link across the plateau between Konya and Ankara. The best way to make this journey is by bus. Between İstanbul (Haydarpaşa) and Konya you can ride either the *Meram Ekspresi* or the *Toros Ekspresi* or the *İç Anadolu Mavi Tren*.

City buses, running at least every half hour, connect the train station with the centre of town. If you take a taxi from the train station to Hükümet Alanı, it will cost about US$4.

Getting Around

As most of the city centre sights are easily reached on foot, you only need public transport to get to the otogar and train station. Konya's efficient system of minibuses does this well; a run from the otogar to the centre costs just US$0.30. The tram runs from the otogar to Alaettin Tepesi but doesn't continue down Mevlâna Caddesi.

To return to the otogar, catch a minibus on Mevlâna Caddesi opposite the post office.

AROUND KONYA
Çatal Höyük

Between 1961 and 1965, British archaeologist James Mellaart excavated two Neolithic mounds at Çatal Höyük, 50km south-east of Konya. He discovered a community from the dawn of civilisation 9000 years ago, and proclaimed it to be the world's oldest known human community.

The 13 layers of remains, dating from 6800 to 5500 BC and thought to be what's left of 150 mud-brick houses, yielded shrines with bulls' horns, painted murals and plaster reliefs, mother-goddess figurines, polished

Services from Konya's Otogar

destination	fare (US$)	time (hr)	distance (km)	daily services
Adana	10	6½	350	frequent buses
Aksaray	5	2½	140	frequent buses
Alanya	10	6½	320	change at Silifke or Antalya
Ankara	7	3	260	very frequent buses
Antalya (via Isparta)	10	6	365	several buses
Denizli (Pamukkale)	10	8	440	several buses
Eğirdir	7	4	236	several buses
İstanbul	18	10	660	frequent buses
İzmir	12	8	575	buses at least every 2 hours
Nevşehir	8.50	2½	226	several buses

obsidian mirrors, tools and the earliest known pottery. Most of the finds are now in Ankara's Museum of Anatolian Civilisations, but recently efforts have been made to make the site more visitor-friendly with on-site exhibits, explanations and basic visitors' facilities.

To get there without your own car, take a dolmuş to Çumra and then hire a taxi for the last 10km.

Lystra (Kilistra/Gökyurt)

Konya may be well south of central Cappadocia but the landscape at Lystra (50km to the south-west) is reminiscent of what you'll see in Güzelyurt or Ihlara: gorges with medieval churches cut into the rock face. There's even one particularly fine church cut completely out of the rock.

Without a car it's not easy to reach Lystra, but you could try asking Ahmet Bilge in the Karavan carpet shop, Mevlâna Caddesi 63, in Konya for advice.

Driving, you should take the road towards Hatunsaray and look for a tiny yellow sign on the left to Gökyurt-Kilistra (called Lystra on most maps). Drive to Kayalı and turn left behind the fountain. Continue through Kumralı. It's a dirt track for most of the way. Cyclists need to be aware of the large number of sheepdogs roaming about.

Sille

The pretty village of Sille, 9km north-west of Konya, has an old stone bridge, several huge old churches and medieval frescoes rotting away in the barns.

You can get there from Konya on bus No 64 from in front of the fairground on Alaettin Bulvarı.

SULTANHANI
☎ 382

The highway between Konya and Aksaray crosses quintessential Anatolian steppe: undulating grassland, sometimes with mountains in the distance. Along the way, 110km from Konya and 42km from Aksaray, is the village of Sultanhanı, which has one of several Seljuk caravanserais bearing that name.

This Sultanhanı is 100m from the highway and can be visited on any day in summer from 7 am to 7 pm for US$1.50. You can explore it thoroughly in about half an hour.

It was constructed in 1229, during the reign of the Seljuk sultan Alaettin Keykubat I, restored in 1278 after a fire (when it became Turkey's largest caravanserai) and restored again and re-roofed 20 years ago. Note the wonderful carved entrance, the raised central *mescit* and the huge *ahır*, or stable, at the back. Other rooms once served as baths, bedrooms and an accounting house.

Immediately opposite the Sultanhanı, *Sultan Restaurant & Kafeterya* offers a complete touristic service: restaurant, toilets, exchange facilities, shops, stamps, phone cards and somewhere to leave your bag while you look around...all this and a smile too!

About 150m east of the Sultanhanı is *Kervansaray Pansiyon & Camping* (☎ 242 2008) with beds for US$8 and an adequate camping ground.

Walk south-east 850m through the village centre to find *Kervan Pansiyon, Restaurant & Camping* (☎ 242 2325), which has perhaps the nicest camping ground, separate from the pension, enclosed by a wall with its own toilets and showers. Though a bit out of the way, this makes it quieter. Beds in the pension cost US$7 per person including breakfast. Camping costs US$6 per site.

Sultanhanı Belediyesi buses run from Aksaray otogar (US$1.25, 45 minutes). Alternatively catch a Konya bus and ask to be dropped off; to be sure of a seat on to Konya afterwards, make a reservation in Aksaray and ask to be picked up on the main road.

Sultanhanı pension owners sometimes organise excursions to the nearby Acı Gölü crater lake and to see the flamingoes on Tuz Gölü.

Cappadocia

Cappadocia, the region between Ankara and Sivas, and between Konya and Malatya, was once the heart of the Hittite Empire, later an independent kingdom, then a vast Roman province mentioned in the Bible.

Today the name survives as a convenient label to describe one of Turkey's most visited tourist areas, particularly the moonscape around the town of Ürgüp and the Göreme Valley. Since it doesn't appear on official road maps, you'll need to know that today's 'Kapadokya' is the area bordered by Kayseri in the east, Aksaray in the west, Hacıbektaş to the north and Niğde to the south.

In spite of its seeming barrenness, the mineral-laden volcanic soil is very fertile and Cappadocia is a prime agricultural region with many fruit orchards and vineyards. Little wineries experiment with the excellent grapes, with sometimes pleasing results.

These days, however, tourism is Cappadocia's industry par excellence. People come from all over the world to visit the churches and chapels of the Göreme, Zelve and Soğanlı Open-Air Museums; to explore the rock-hewn dwellings in surrounding valleys; to gaze on the fairy chimneys; to walk the Ihlara Valley; and to plumb the depths of the underground cities at Derinkuyu and Kaymaklı.

The sights fall into three main groups. Aksaray is the main entry point for exploring Western Cappadocia and the Ihlara Valley; for the fairy chimneys and the Göreme Open-Air Museum you're best based in Uçhisar, Göreme, Ürgüp or Avanos; while Niğde or Kayseri are possible bases for getting to the Soğanlı Valley.

Getting Around

Although you could see something of central Cappadocia on a lightning day trip, it's much better to stay a few days. Indeed you could easily spend a week here and still not see everything.

Most people come to Cappadocia by bus, although there are train services to Kayseri and Niğde. There's also an airport at Tüzköy near Gülşehir; or you can fly into more distant Kayseri.

The most convenient bases for exploring central Cappadocia are Göreme (favourite of backpackers and budget travellers), Ürgüp (with a good mix of lodgings, including many group hotels) and Avanos, a

---

Cappadocia from the Air

There's nothing quite like it: you get up before dawn, grab a quick cup of coffee, climb into an all-terrain vehicle and set out for the launch site. As the sky lightens, you watch a pile of fabric the size of a small car swell into a huge, graceful balloon. Standing in the basket below, your pilot turns a valve, flames roar upward into the void, and you lift off into the chill morning air to float across the Cappadocian landscape just as the warming sun makes its way above the horizon.

If you've never taken a flight in a hot-air balloon, Cappadocia is one of the best places in the world to try it. Flight conditions are especially favourable here, with gentle winds most mornings between April and November, and the views are simply unforgettable.

Though the balloon depends on air currents for lateral movement, a good pilot can control the height with surprising precision. Kaili Kidner and Lars-Eric Möre of Kapadokya Balloons (☎ 384-271 2755, e fly@kapadokyaballoons .com) boast that they can even descend into a Cappadocian valley and 'pick apricots off the trees'. Because of the winds and the vertical control, every flight is an adventure. No two flights are ever exactly the same.

Flights take place at dawn (weather permitting), last for approximately 1¼ hours, and are followed by the traditional champagne toast. Sturdy all-terrain vehicles follow your flight and assure that wherever the balloon lands it can be recovered. To avoid disappointment it's wise to reserve a place in the basket well in advance. The office is in Göreme, uphill on the Uçhisar road to the left of Cafedoci@.

Transport to and from your hotel to the balloon launch site is included in the price of US$210 per person. The cost may seem high but life offers few more exhilarating adventures so easily achieved and so thoroughly enjoyable.

---

pottery-making centre. Uçhisar, popular with French travellers, is sleepier despite its dramatic volcanic rock kale. Ortahisar has a handful of hotels and pensions but

CAPPADOCIA

The history of Cappadocia began with the eruptions of three volcanoes (Erciyes Dağı near Kayseri, Hasan Dağı near Aksaray amd Melendiz Dağı near Niğde), as much as 10 million years ago. The eruptions spread a thick layer of hot volcanic ash over the region, which hardened into a soft, porous stone called tuff.

Over aeons of geological time, wind, water and sand erosion wore away portions of the tuff, carving it into elaborate, unearthly shapes. Boulders of hard stone, caught in the tuff and then exposed by erosion, protected it from further erosion from below. The result was a column or cone of tuff with a boulder perched on top, whimsically called a peribaca, or 'fairy chimney'. Entire valleys are filled with these formations, many of them amusingly phallic in appearance.

Inset: One of the wonderful frescoes that decorates the rock-cut churches in Göreme Valley, and which form an important record of Byzantine art. (Anders Blomqvist).

Bottom: This cave dwelling, carved out of a single cone of tuff, is typical of Cappadocia; its maze of rooms and connecting tunnels would have provided shelter for a whole community.

DIANA MAYFIELD

The tuff was easily worked with primitive tools and the inhabitants quickly learned how simple it was to carve out sturdy dwellings; a cave could be excavated very quickly and, if the family expanded, more carving could produce a nursery or storeroom in next to no time.

When Christianity arrived in Cappadocia, its adherents found that cave churches, complete with elaborate decoration, could be carved from the rock as easily as dwellings. Large Christian communities thrived here and the sheer quantity of rock-hewn churches they left behind is unparalleled. When the Arab armies swept across Anatolia in the 7th century, the Christians retreated into vast underground settlements that the Hittites may originally have excavated.

Many of the caves and villages were inhabited by the descendants of these early settlers right up until 1923, when the crumbling of the Ottoman Empire finally culminated in an exchange of populations between Greece and Turkey.

Cappadocia is one of Turkey's most extraordinary treasures. The utter improbability of the landscape really has to be seen to be believed, with its fairytale cave dwellings (top left), amusingly phallic tuff cones (top right) and the warm colour and texture of the rock (bottom).

CAPPADOCIA (KAPADOKYA)

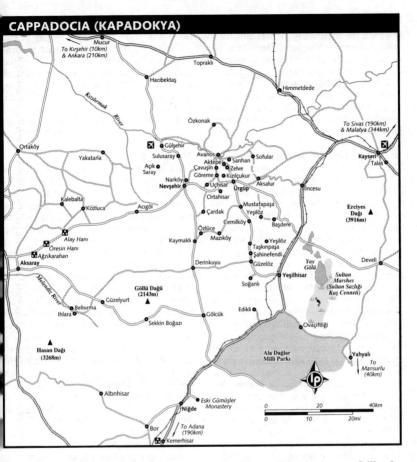

few tourists. Nevşehir, the provincial capital, is little more than a transfer point.

In summer, travelling between these places by public transport is relatively straightforward. In winter, transport is less frequent, and you may want to consider a tour or a hire car or taxi if time is tight.

Tours organised by travel agencies allow you to see all the sights cheaply and conveniently, but may dump you in a carpet or souvenir shop in the middle of nowhere for two hours. The tour company gets as much as 30% commission on everything you buy but the tea is free and the 'shopping' can be a rest from walking in the sun. Still, why pay to be fleeced? Find a tour with no shopping stop, shop on your own, and pocket the tour company's 30%.

To hire a taxi or minibus, with driver, for a full-day tour of central Cappadocia starting from Ürgüp or Göreme costs from US$50 to US$80. Alternatively, you can rent a bicycle, moped or motorbike to help you get about; see Getting Around in the Göreme section, later. With more time than money, plan to walk and hitch through the region, a wonderful way to do it, although it can be tiring in the hot sun.

However you go, wear flat shoes for climbing the metal-rung ladders and stairways to the cave churches, and carry a torch (flashlight). Snacks and light meals are available at all major sites.

The Ihlara Valley in western Cappadocia can be visited on a day trip from Göreme or by bus from Aksaray. Alternatively you can make the attractive village of Güzelyurt your base.

Getting There & Away

The new Nevşehir international airport (☎ 384-214 2800) at Tuzköy has made it much easier to reach Cappadocia from İstanbul, although at the time of writing flights were still only twice weekly. The alternative is to fly to Kayseri airport, which has twice-daily flights. In both cases Turkish Airlines operates transfer buses to meet the flights, although particularly in the case of Kayseri these need to be pre-booked through Argeus Tours in Ürgüp (☎ 384-341 4688, fax 341 4888, e inform@argeus.com.tr); if you don't pre-book you may be forced to take an expensive taxi to your final destination.

Although it's very easy to get from İstanbul or Ankara by bus, many people arrive in İstanbul and are persuaded to book a package tour. Although if you're pushed for time this may not be a bad idea, be warned that some of the tours are hugely overpriced, especially if they still involve travelling by public bus and staying in local pensions.

Buses from İstanbul to Cappadocia travel overnight and bring you to Nevşehir where there should be a *servis* bus to run you onto Uçhisar, Göreme, Avanos or Ürgüp. From Ankara you can travel more comfortably during the day.

The nearest you can get to Cappadocia by train is Konya or Kayseri.

AKSARAY

☎ 382 • pop 101,000 • elevation 980m

Aksaray is a fast-growing modern town with few reminders of the Roman town of Archelais, but with sites enough to while away the odd hour or so. It also makes a possible base for visits to nearby Selime, Ihlara and Güzelyurt in western Cappadocia.

Orientation & Information

It's 500m from Aksaray's otogar to the main square, with nicely restored government buildings behind an equestrian statue of Atatürk; to get there, leave the otogar and take a sharp left. Continue straight along Bankalar Caddesi for places to eat and the Ulu Cami.

The Altamira Kültür Evi sells some English novels.

Things to See & Do

The **Ulu Cami** in the town centre has decoration characteristic of the post-Seljuk Beylik period. It dates from 1408–09, but was repaired extensively in 1483 and later again when the original minaret was replaced with the present Ottoman model. Little of the original yellow stone remains in the grand doorway. Inside the mosque is a finely worked wooden mimber brought here from the older, ruined Kılıçarslan II mosque.

Aksaray Müzesi is housed in the Zinciriye Medresesi, which was built in Seljuk style by the local Karamanoğulları emir Yahşi Bey in 1336. The courtyard contains a selection of Hittite, Greek, Roman, Seljuk and Ottoman stonework, including the gravestone of St Mamas, patron saint of Kayseri, rescued from the village of Mamasos when it was drowned by the Mamasos Baraj. The museum is open from 8 am to noon and from 1.30 to 5.30 pm daily; admission is free. To find it, walk from the Ulu Cami across the main street and down Vehbibey Caddesi towards the river.

The adjoining **Tarihi Paşa Hamamı** is a restored Ottoman bath with separate sections for men and women (US$4.50 for the full works).

The older part of town along Nevşehir Caddesi has a few **old stone houses** and the curious **Eğri Minare** (Crooked Minaret), next to the Kızıl Minare Camii, built in 1236 and leaning at an angle of 27 degrees. Inevitably it's known locally as the 'Turkish Tower of Pisa'.

Places to Stay

Cross the road outside the otogar and take the first left to find the simple *Aksaray*

Pansion (☎ 212 4133, Kılıçaslant Sokak), with clean beds in rooms with showers for US$9.25 per person with breakfast. The nearby *Hitit Pansion (☎ 213 1312)* is more basic but charges only US$5 per person.

Otel Yoğuran (☎ 212 0280, Nolu Hükümet Caddesi 3) is in the bazaar on a street crowded with jewellery shops (turn off the main street opposite the Merkez Lokantası/ Beko and follow the signs). Rooms with shower cost US$9/14, breakfast included. It's quiet at night. The *Otel Tezcanlar (☎ 213 8482, fax 215 1234, Kızılay Sokak 5)* charges the same for pleasant rooms with spacious bathrooms. Immediately opposite, the one-star *Çakır İpek Oteli (☎ 213 7053)* is drab but slightly cheaper.

Right on the main square, next to the modern Hacıbektaş Kurşunlu Camii, is the *Otel Yuvam (☎ 212 0024, fax 213 2875, Eski Sanayı Caddesi)*. Minaret and traffic noise might make the US$10/20 prices seem a bit steep but they're negotiable out of season.

The big glass-fronted *Otel Üçyıldız (☎ 214 0404, fax 212 5003, Bankalar Caddesi 6)* is Aksarary's best, with nice modern decor and cheerful rooms with smart bathrooms for US$35/50/60 a single/double/triple.

Places to Eat
The *Yeni Merkez Lokantası* on Bankalar Caddesi is deservedly popular for its stews and kebaps for around US$4 a serve.

Excellent Italian-style pizzas cost just US$2 at the enterprising *Pizza & Net* Internet cafe beside Aksaray's wedding salon; for a takeaway phone ☎ 212 9895.

Of Aksaray's many pastry shops, most popular in summer is the *Park Pastanesi*, right beside the Ulu Cami with a long terrace overlooking the small park. The *Golden Apple* on Bankalar Caddesi is also popular and does delicious sweets for around US$2 each.

Getting There & Away
There are direct buses from Aksaray to Ankara (US$7, 4½ hours, 230km), Nevşehir (US$3, 1½ hours, 65km), Niğde (US$4, two hours, 115km), Sultanhanı (US$1.25, 40 minutes, 42km) and Konya (US$5, 2½ hours, 140km).

There are also dolmuşes and some buses in summer to Ihlara (US$0.75, one hour, 45km), to Güzelyurt (US$1) and to Selime (US$0.75).

IHLARA (PERISTREMA)
☎ 382
About 45km south-east of Aksaray is Ihlara, at the head of the Peristrema Gorge, a remote valley which was once a favourite retreat of Byzantine monks. Dozens of painted churches carved from the rock have

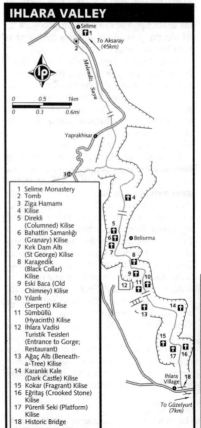

IHLARA VALLEY

1 Selime Monastery
2 Tomb
3 Ziga Hamamı
4 Kilise
5 Direkli (Columned) Kilise
6 Bahattin Samanlığı (Granary) Kilise
7 Kirk Dam Altı (St George) Kilise
8 Karagedik (Black Collar) Kilise
9 Eski Baca (Old Chimney) Kilise
10 Yılanlı (Serpent) Kilise
11 Sümbüllü (Hyacinth) Kilise
12 Ihlara Vadisi Turistik Tesisleri (Entrance to Gorge; Restaurant)
13 Ağaç Altı (Beneath-a-Tree) Kilise
14 Karanlık Kale (Dark Castle) Kilise
15 Kokar (Fragrant) Kilise
16 Eğritaş (Crooked Stone) Kilise
17 Pürenli Seki (Platform) Kilise
18 Historic Bridge

CENTRAL ANATOLIA

survived, but this wildly beautiful place is still less touristy than Göreme, if only because access is more time-consuming. Allow a full day to walk the gorge from end to end. If you're coming from Aksaray, the drive will also take some time.

Ihlara Gorge (Ihlara Vadisi)

You come here to follow the course of the Melendiz Suyu stream as it flows for 16km through the Ihlara Gorge from Selime to Ihlara village; an unforgettable experience, with a sea of greenery hugging the banks of the stream at the base of a dramatic canyon. Many people visit on day tours from Göreme, which allow only a few hours to walk the central part of the gorge, but to walk the whole thing is likely to be a highlight of your trip to Turkey.

If you're planning to walk all the way it's best to start early in the day, particularly in summer. Especially good times to visit are midweek in May or September when fewer people are about. Roughly midway along the valley, near Belisirma village, a couple of restaurants mean that you needn't come weighed down with provisions.

If you plan to walk the length of the gorge you can enter from behind the Pansion Anatolia in Ihlara village or from Selime. If, like most people, you only want to walk the short stretch with most of the churches, then you enter via a very long flight of steps leading down from the Ihlara Vadisi Turistik Tesisleri, perched on the rim of the gorge 2km from Ihlara village. To park here costs US$0.75. A ticket to enter the gorge costs US$1.75. It's open from 8 am to 7 pm daily.

Along the valley floor, signs mark the different **churches**, the most interesting, with the best paintings, being the Yılanlı Kilise, Sümbüllü Kilise, Kokar Kilise and Eğritaş Kilise. Further down the valley are the Kırk Dam Altı Kilise, Bahattin Samanlığı Kilise, Direkli Kilise and Ala Kilise. Some of the churches may be closed because of the risk of structural damage.

Monastery

The monastery at Selime is an astonishing rock-cut structure incorporating a vast kitchen with soaring chimney, a church with a gallery all around it and all sorts of evidence of the troglodyte lifestyle. Claims that it was used in the making of the *Star Wars* film should be taken with a big pinch of salt.

Hot Springs

There are two local hot springs with baths attached to them. The first, at Ilısu near Ihlara, is tiny, with tepid water; the other, at Ziga near Selime, is trying to turn itself into a centre for thermal treatments and has water that pours out at an unbelievable (and unbearable) 50°C (just 40°C in winter!). Cabins at the site should have opened as pension rooms by the time you read this but they're not at all visually inviting.

Places to Stay & Eat

If you want to walk all the way along the gorge there are pensions handily placed at both ends, in Ihlara and Selime. You can also break your journey into two parts with an overnight stay either camping in the gorge itself or staying in a pension in Belisirma village.

Ihlara In Ihlara village itself the *Star Otel & Restaurant* (☎ 453 7676) was undergoing a refit at the time of writing. What was a simple village pension may well reopen as something a bit smarter, in which case it might make a good base, with the river running right under its windows and a restaurant serving fresh trout in the garden.

Otherwise, there are a few pensions above the actual village, along the roads to the gorge entrance and to Aksaray. The welcoming *Pansion Anatolia* (☎ 453 7440, fax 453 7439) is on the road running between the village and the entry to the gorge. Pleasant rooms with bathroom cost US$16 a double, or you can camp in the grounds for US$3 per person. There's a washing machine for guests' use and plenty of parking space.

The *Akar Pansiyon* (☎ 453 7018, fax 453 7511), on the road to Aksaray, offers clean, comfortable rooms. The shop downstairs sells picnic ingredients and there's a restaurant behind. Right beside it the *Bişginler Ihlara Pansiyon* (☎/fax 453 7077) is another good choice with clean, simple rooms with bath. Both charge US$16 a double with breakfast, subject to some negotiation if it's quiet. *Pansiyon Famille* (☎ 453 7098) across the road is more basic, but charges the same.

Belisırma Midway along the gorge, near Belisırma village, you can camp in the grounds of three restaurants with just the birds to keep you company. *Aslan Camping & Pansiyon* (☎ 213 3033) offers six beds in pre-erected tents for US$8 a double. Otherwise, you may be asked to pay US$1.50 to put up your own tent. *Anatolya Valley* and *Peristrema Restaurant* are similar. All three serve cheap, if hardly imaginative, meals.

In Belisırma itself there's also a small *ev pansiyon* (☎ 457 3037), or private pension, with tiny, waterless rooms for US$8 including breakfast. The house itself is not particularly pretty but staying here allows you a glimpse of rural life.

Selime At the northern end of the gorge you can pitch a tent in the grounds of the *Çatlak* and *Konak* restaurants. The *Çatlak* has a pleasant setting, right by the river, and the food is good, though the service slow. The camp sites are by the bridge but just a few metres away, right by the entrance to Selime monastery, is *Piri Pansiyon* (☎ 454 5114) where US$9 buys you bed and breakfast. The carpet shop in front will not delight everyone and it's a crying shame that the owners were allowed to build a modern concrete structure here, when lovely old stone houses right behind it are crumbling into dust. *Çatlak Pansiyon* (☎ 454 5065) is way away from the restaurant of the same name. It's clean and new, with bed and breakfast for US$10, and the owner emphasises that Selime-Aksaray buses pass right by the door, but not everyone would want to be so isolated.

Getting There & Away
Bus There are several buses a day from Aksaray otogar to Selime and Ihlara village, but you should aim to get to Aksaray

as early as possible to avoid an enforced overnight stay there.

Car From the Aksaray-Nevşehir highway, turn south (right, if you're coming from Aksaray) at a point 11km east of the intersection of the Ankara-Adana and Aksaray-Nevşehir highways. After turning, go about 23km to another right turn marked for Ihlara Vadisi. The road passes through Selime and Yaprakhisar villages, both of them dramatically surrounded by rock and marked by fairy chimneys. After another 13km you come to Ihlara village, where you turn left to reach the main entrance to the gorge.

Alternatively you can drive to Ihlara from Derinkuyu (53km), or from the village of Gölcük (60km) between Derinkuyu and Niğde.

Organised Tours Most of the travel agencies in Göreme and Ürgüp offer tours to Ihlara. Göreme's Zemi Tours (☎ 384-271 2576, fax 271 2577) runs a two-day camping tour that takes in the Derinkuyu underground city, Nargölü crater lake, Güzelyurt, a hike through Ihlara gorge, camping overnight at Belisırma, the Ağzıkarahan caravanserai and Uçhisar for US$50. This includes some meals, camping equipment and admission fees.

If it's not too busy, tour companies may be happy to agree a one-way fare to leave you in the valley, usually after a visit to Derinkuyu underground city.

GÜZELYURT
☎ 382
About 14km from Ihlara village, on the road east to Derinkuyu, is Güzelyurt, a quiet, interesting old Cappadocian farming village with stone houses, orthodox churches converted to mosques, lush fields, valleys, streams and gardens. In Ottoman times this was the town of Karballa (Gelveri), inhabited by 1000 Ottoman-Greek families, many of them wealthy from goldsmithing, and 50 Turkish-Muslim families. In the exchange of populations between Turkey and Greece in 1924, the Greeks of Gelveri went to Nea Karvali near Kavala in Greece, while

Turkish families from Kozan and Kastoria in Greece moved to Güzelyurt. Once there were some 50 churches here, but most are now badly ruined.

Today Güzelyurt is a conservation area where all new building must be of natural stone and no more than two storeys high. You may see other tourists in July or August, but most of the time Güzelyurt is refreshingly under-visited.

Things to See & Do
Walk or drive downhill from the main square following the signs to **Manastır Vadisi** (Monastery Valley). About 300m from the square a sign points up on the left to a small **underground city** *(yeraltı şehri)*, actually more of an underground village. Other such dwellings are marked as you go along the road, as are churches: the Koç (Ram), Cafarlar (Rivulets) and, most interesting of all, the Aşağı or Büyük Kilise Camii, built as the **Church of St Gregory of Nazianzus** in 385, and restored and modernised in 1896. St Gregory (330–90) grew up in Güzelyurt and went on to become a theologian, patriarch, and one of the Four Fathers of the Greek Church. Plans call for the church to become a museum, and the whitewash to be removed from its frescoes. In the garden, a subterranean stairway leads to an *ayasma*, or sacred spring. The bell is gone from the bell tower (though the imam proudly guards the clapper), which is now the mosque's minaret. Inside the ancient building, the iconostasis has been moved from the front wall to the side to serve as a frame for the mihrab. A guardian may charge you US$1 to see the church and nearby buildings.

Across the valley and up the hill from the Kilise Camii is the **Sıvışlı Kilise** (Anargyros Church), a much later rock-hewn church with clean lines, square pillars, and some badly ruined frescoes.

To enter the Monastery Valley (a sort of Ihlara in miniature) you must pay a US$1.50 entrance fee. Just walking through this quiet unspoilt valley is pleasant, but there are also more rock-cut churches to explore.

Perched on a rock overlooking the Güzelyurt Göleti lake is the **Kızıl Kilise** (Red Church), named for the colour of its stone. Its three naves and deteriorating frescoes are accessible off the access road to Güzelyurt.

Places to Stay & Eat
Tovi and Ahmet Diler of Kirkit Voyage in Avanos have converted a 19th-century Greek monastery into the quiet, rather special *Otel Karballa* (☎ *451 2103, fax 451 2107)*, with its own swimming pool. Bed and breakfast costs US$17 per person and half board US$24; you eat your meals in what was once the monks' refectory. Horse riding, mountain biking and hiking (with snowshoes in winter) tours can all be arranged.

Getting There & Away
Several dolmuşes a day link Güzelyurt with Aksaray (US$0.75).

UZUN YOL
The drive from Aksaray to Nevşehir takes you along one of the oldest trade routes in the world, the Uzun Yol (Long Road) which linked Konya, the capital of the Seljuk Sultanate of Rum, with its other great cities (Kayseri, Sivas and Erzurum) and ultimately with the birthplace of Seljuk power in Persia.

Following the Long Road today takes you past the remains of several hans, including the impressive and well-preserved **Ağzıkarahan** (1243; open daily from 7.30 am to 8 pm for US$0.75) on the southern side of the road 10km east of Aksaray; the 13th-century **Tepesidelik Hanı** also on the southern side about 13km east of Aksaray; and the 12th-century **Alay Hanı**, badly ruined, on the northern side of the highway about 33km east of Aksaray.

NEVŞEHİR
☎ 384 • pop 55,000 • elevation 1260m
Nevşehir, the provincial capital, is an ugly modern town where you're unlikely to want to linger. The otogar is 1.5km north of the town's main intersection, on the road towards Gülşehir, but buses and dolmuşes to most local towns and villages leave from near the tourist office (☎ 213 3659) on Atatürk Bulvarı, the main drag. Nevşehir

hotels cater mainly for the business fraternity. Almost everyone else heads straight on to the more atmospheric hotels and pensions of the Cappadocian villages.

Things to See & Do

With half an hour to spare you might visit the **Damat İbrahim Paşa Külliyesi**. Sultan Ahmet III's grand vizier İbrahim Paşa (1662–1730) was a great builder who supplied his sovereign with many romantic palaces and lodges in İstanbul. Born in humble conditions in the village of Muşkara, he later returned there to found a new city (*nev*, new; *şehir*, city) and the mosque complex (1726). The mosque and hamam are still in business. Bath hours are from 7.30 am to 9 pm (Wednesday for women).

Nevşehir Müzesi is 1km out along Yeni Kayseri Caddesi, on the road to Göreme and Ürgüp. Opening hours are from 8 am to noon and from 1 to 5 pm daily except Monday; admission is US$1.75. There's an archaeological section with Phrygian, Hittite and Bronze Age pots and implements, then Roman, Byzantine and Ottoman articles; and an ethnographic section with costumes, tools, manuscripts and jewellery.

Places to Stay & Eat

Nevşehir's hotels mostly cater for local business travellers and bus tour groups. Even if you arrive late you're unlikely to want to stay here when the accommodation options in Göreme, Uçhisar, Ürgüp and Avanos are so much more inviting even at the top end of the market.

About 3km east of the centre on the Ürgüp road stands the five-star **Kapadokya Dedeman Hotel** (☎ 213 9900, fax 213 2158). It's hardly a pretty building but the rooms have every comfort, including air-con, TV and minibar, for US$90/120 a single/double. Nicer to look at is the similarly pricey **Kapadokya Lodge** (☎ 213 9945, fax 213 5092), near where the road turns off towards Göreme. In either case, those without their own transport could feel pretty cut-off.

Nevşehir's eating out options are also pretty limited, though if you have the odd hour or so between buses it's worth walking up the high street to find the big tea garden with fountain in front of the **Park Bostan Restaurant**. Whether you're after a quick drink or a full meal indoors or outdoors, this is a good place to come, and popular with local families at weekends.

Getting There & Away

Nevşehir's Adnan Menderes Terminali, its otogar, handles both bus and dolmuş services, but you can usually flag down the dolmuşes outside the tourist office as well. Local buses connect Nevşehir with all the surrounding villages and with Kaymaklı, Derinkuyu and Niğde.

Many passengers who buy intercity bus tickets to Göreme, Ürgüp or other local destinations are bewildered when their bus stops at Nevşehir. Decent bus companies provide *servis* minibuses to run you the rest of the way but see the boxed text 'Warning' in the Göreme section later in this chapter.

UÇHİSAR

☎ 384

East of Nevşehir, the panorama of Cappadocia begins to unfold: across the sandy landscape, distant rock formations become visible as the so-called fairy chimneys and valleys with undulating walls of soft, volcanic ash fall away from the road. In the distance, the gigantic snowcapped summit of volcanic **Erciyes Dağı** (Mt Argeus) floats above a layer of cloud.

After 8km you come to pretty little Uçhisar which is dominated by its **kale**, a tall volcanic rock outcrop riddled with tunnels and windows, and visible for miles around. Now a tourist attraction (open from 8 am to sunset for US$1.25), it provides panoramic views of the Cappadocian valleys and countryside.

Especially popular with French tourists, old Uçhisar is in some ways less spoilt than the more popular Göreme. It makes a good alternative base for exploring Cappadocia, although many pensions don't open until May. There's less to see and do here than in Göreme or Ürgüp, but that also means there are fewer tourists, except around the kale which is on every tour itinerary.

You can pick up your email at the Altın Internet Cafe, which is behind Belediye Meydanı in town.

The fine walk along the signposted **Pigeon Valley** (Güvercinlik Vadisi) is easier heading towards Göreme than in the other direction. Along the way look out for rock-cut holes high in the valley wall that served as pigeon-houses in the days when villagers kept the birds for their valuable droppings (used as fertiliser).

Places to Stay

Although Uçhisar has a few simple pensions east of the main square (Belediye Meydanı), it would be a shame to come here and not stay in one of the more picturesque places in the older part of the village.

Heading west from the main square, Göreme Caddesi turns downhill through the old village. One of the first places you'll come to is the clean, simple **Kilim Pansiyon** (☎ 219 2774, fax 219 2660) where beds in arched rooms with great views cost US$20 a double, including breakfast. Beyond that and with a fine restaurant attached is **Les Terrasses d'Uçhisar** (☎ 219 2792, fax 219 2762). Attractive rooms with modern decor cost US$25 a double, including breakfast, and there's a great terrace and bar for soaking up the views in the evening.

Further down the hill the pretty **Le Jardin des 1001 Nuits** (☎ 219 2293, fax 219 2505) was created out of a cluster of cones so that each room is different. Beds vary in price, with the cheapest costing US$9 and the most expensive US$22. Tucked away between Le Jardin and the road is **Tekelli Evi** (☎ 219 2929), a tiny place with three inviting rock-cut rooms run by Sinan Önengüt, himself a Turkish backpacker. Depending on the room the price is US$20/30/40 including breakfast.

Near the entrance to Le Jardin is **Kaya Pension** (☎ 219 2441, fax 219 2079), with a lovely plant and kilim-filled restaurant, a big terrace, fine views, and double rooms with shower and breakfast for US$20.

Yet further down the hill, **Buket Pansiyon** (☎ 219 2490, fax 219 3047) has several very nice cave rooms with interesting features and a big cave dining room. The simplest doubles cost US$17 with breakfast, but more luxurious Jacuzzi-equipped rooms cost US$33.

Right by the main square on the edge of Güvercinlik Vadisi, is **Pension Méditerranée** (☎ 219 2210, fax 219 2669), a hotel-like modern place with fabulous views, a nice rooftop restaurant and shower-equipped rooms – some of them surprisingly spartan – for US$14/18/29, including breakfast.

Also east of the main square is the swish **Kaya Oteli** (☎ 219 2007, fax 219 2363), a Club Med hotel carved into the volcanic tuff with fabulous views. Comfortable rooms cost US$40 per person half board. The Kaya closes from October to April.

The **Villa Pansion** (☎ 219 2089, fax 219 2680) and the **Erciyes Pension** (☎ 219 2090), both near the PTT, are friendly enough and cheaper because they lack the views. The same is true of the **Anatolia Pension** (☎ 219 2339) on the road leading into Uçhisar.

Uçhisar's finest places to stay are the villas called **Les Maisons de Cappadoce** (☎ 219 2813, fax 219 2782, Belediye Meydanı 24), rented from an office in the main square. Exquisitely renovated, fully furnished and decorated by French architect Jacques Avizou, the villas sleep between two and eight people and can be rented for four days or longer. Prices range from US$90 (two persons) to US$300 (six persons) per night, with reduced rates for longer stays. Check out their Web site www.cappadoce.com for more details.

Places to Eat

Most of the pensions have their own restaurants, usually sited to scoop spectacular views. In the main square the **Uçhisar 96** restaurant has a large garden in which to tuck into a range of mezes and kebaps.

Uçhisar's finest restaurant is the one in the **Kaya Oteli** where buffet-style meals offer a vast choice of European-style cuisine. Right next door the **Yeni Bindallı Restaurant** (☎ 219 2690) serves a magnificent buffet lunch for US$10. It's very popular with tour groups.

CENTRAL ANATOLIA

For a quick tea in an atmospheric *cafe* look out for the converted six-storey fairy chimney in front of Le Jardin des 1001 Nuits; you sip your drink while sitting on floor cushions. Near the kale, *La Meze* and *Oase Cafe-Bar* will also sell you a reviving beverage while you drink in the view.

Getting There & Away

Regular Uçhisar Belediyesi buses link Uçhisar with Nevşehir, or you can take the half-hourly Nevşehir bus from Göreme and get out at the road junction for Uçhisar (US$0.45).

GÖREME

☎ 384 • pop 2000

Just 12km east of Nevşehir is Göreme village, a magical place set amid towering tuff cones and honeycomb cliffs and surrounded by vineyards. It's deservedly popular with backpackers.

Once a sleepy farming village named Avcılar, Göreme grew explosively during the 1980s as Turkey's tourism boom swept over it. These days village life is an odd mixture of the modern and the ultra-conservative, with veiled women in the traditional baggy *şalvar* trousers rubbing shoulders with scantily clad tourists throughout the summer. Göreme is chock-a-block with pensions, camping grounds, restaurants and tour agencies. It's the prime place for budget travellers because the beds and meals are cheap and good, and the sights are within walking distance; Göreme Open-Air Museum is just 1.5km to the south-east.

Orientation & Information

Buses and minibuses drop you off at the otogar-cum-shopping mall. Across from the bus ticket offices is a booth with information on all the local accommodation options. There are also several travel agencies where you can change money.

Immediately in front of the otogar is the main Nevşehir to Avanos road, with a cluster of eating places mainly aimed at the group trade. Beside and behind the otogar, floodwater channels cut through the village, with pensions leading off on either side.

The Türkiye İş Bankası ATM in front of the belediye is always busy. The post office beyond the SOS Restaurant tends to have the best exchange rates for a range of currencies, as well as providing phone and fax services. The Nese Internet Cafe, midway along the main road, is popular and busy; you can have a drink and read the papers while you wait.

Göreme Open-Air Museum

One of Turkey's World Heritage Sites, the Göreme Open-Air Museum (Göreme Açık Hava Müzesi) is a cluster of rock-cut Byzantine churches, chapels and monasteries 1.5km uphill from the centre of the village.

The site is open from 8.30 am to 5.30 pm (4.30 pm in winter) and it's good to try and get there early in the morning in summer and space yourself between tour groups – when lots of people crowd into one of these little churches they block the doorway, which is often the only source of light. Admission costs US$5 (students US$3) plus another US$6 for the Karanlık Kilisesi, the best of the churches inside the main site. Car parking costs US$1.50; for motorcycles and mopeds it's US$0.60.

It's easy to spend most of the day walking the paths here, climbing stairways or passing through tunnels to reach the various monastery churches with their wonderful, primitive 11th- and 12th-century **frescoes**. Between the churches, the utter improbability of the landscape floods over you: the lovely, soft textures in the rock, the fairytale cave dwellings, the spare vegetation growing vigorously from the stark but mineral-rich soil.

First off, you come to the **Rahibeler Manastırı**, or Nun's Convent, a large plain room with steps up to a smaller domed chapel with frescoes. To the right past the cafe is the similar Monk's Monastery. From this point you can follow a loop path around the valley in either direction. The following are the main sights you come to if you walk clockwise, although the path also winds past various vistas and unmarked churches.

The **Çarıklı Kilise**, or Sandal Church, is named for the footprints marked in the floor

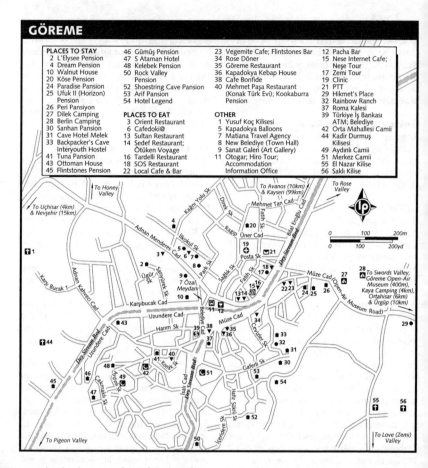

GÖREME

PLACES TO STAY
2 L'Elysee Pension
4 Dream Pension
10 Walnut House
20 Köse Pension
24 Paradise Pension
25 Ufuk II (Horizon) Pension
26 Peri Pansiyon
27 Dilek Camping
28 Berlin Camping
30 Sarıhan Pansion
31 Cave Hotel Melek
33 Backpacker's Cave Interyouth Hostel
41 Tuna Pansion
43 Ottoman House
45 Flintstones Pension

46 Gümüş Pension
47 S Ataman Hotel
48 Kelebek Pension
50 Rock Valley Pension
52 Shoestring Cave Pansion
53 Arif Pansion
54 Hotel Legend

PLACES TO EAT
3 Orient Restaurant
6 Cafedoki@
13 Sultan Restaurant
14 Sedef Restaurant; Ötüken Voyage
16 Tardelli Restaurant
18 SOS Restaurant
22 Local Cafe & Bar

23 Vegemite Cafe; Flintstones Bar
34 Rose Döner
35 Göreme Restaurant
36 Kapadokya Kebap House
38 Cafe Bonfide
40 Mehmet Paşa Restaurant (Konak Türk Evi); Kookaburra Pension

OTHER
1 Yusuf Koç Kilisesi
5 Kapadokya Balloons
7 Matiana Travel Agency
8 New Belediye (Town Hall)
9 Sanat Galeri (Art Gallery)
11 Otogar; Hiro Tour; Accommodation Information Office

12 Pacha Bar
15 Neşe Internet Cafe; Neşe Tour
17 Zemi Tour
19 Clinic
21 PTT
29 Hikmet's Place
32 Rainbow Ranch
37 Roma Kalesi
39 Türkiye İş Bankası ATM; Belediye
42 Orta Mahallesi Camii
44 Kadir Durmuş Kilisesi
49 Aydınlı Camii
51 Merkez Camii
55 El Nazar Kilise
56 Saklı Kilise

---

opposite the doorway. One of the best frescoes shows Judas' betrayal (in the arch over the door to the left). Near the Sandal Church a small unmarked chapel has a fresco of a man on horseback – probably St George.

The **Karanlık Kilise**, or Dark Church, among the most famous and fresco-filled, was restored at great expense, hence the charge of US$6. Although some people get very upset about the extra charge, the church is very small and it makes sense to preserve it for those most interested in the art. The church took its name from its former condition when it had very few windows. The

lack of light preserved the vivid colour of the frescoes, which include, among others, scenes of Christ as Pantocrator, Christ on the cross and his betrayal by Judas.

Beneath the Dark Church are a larder, kitchen and refectory with tables and benches cut from the rock. Another smaller nameless church here retains a rock-cut iconostasis.

The **Yılanlı Kilise** (Snake Church, or Church of St Onuphrius) has 11th-century frescoes on part of the vault. On the left wall, St George and St Theodore attack the dragon yet again. Look out, too, for paintings of Constantine the Great and his mother Helena holding the True Cross.

The **Azize Barbara Şapeli**, or Chapel of St Barbara, has such plain decoration that it has sometimes been attributed to the iconoclastic period (725–842) when images were outlawed. There are a few fairly worn frescoes of the Virgin Mary and St Barbara. On the right three more chapels have carved crosses in the apse and primitive line drawings.

The **Elmalı Kilise**, or Apple Church, has a stunning display of frescoes. There are eight small domes and one large one, and lots of well-preserved paintings. Where's the apple? Some say the Angel Gabriel, above the central nave, is holding it. There's also some iconoclastic decoration – red ochre painted on the stone without any images of people or animals.

The **Aziz Basil Şapeli**, or Chapel of St Basil, the last church on the loop, is rather dark inside because the main room is off to the left away from the door. The grate-covered grooves in the floor were burial places.

Don't miss the **Tokalı Kilise**, or Buckle Church, outside the enclosure and back down the hill towards Göreme. This is among the biggest and finest of the Göreme churches, with frescoes telling the stories of Christ's miracles and a fine chapel downstairs. If a guardian is not on duty and the gate is locked, ask someone to open it and turn on the *ışıklar* (lights).

Other Churches

If you can't afford to visit the Open-Air Museum, that doesn't mean you need leave Göreme without seeing any rock-cut churches. To the right of the Open-Air Museum road a sign points to the **Saklı Kilise** (Hidden Church), tucked away behind Hikmet's Place (if he's not busy Hikmet may be prepared to help you find it). Also off to the right in the Zemi Valley is the **El Nazar Kilise** (Church of the Evil Eye), expensively restored and now kept locked; you need to apply to the museum in Nevşehir for permission to visit.

Continue uphill past the museum and towards Ortahisar and on the right you'll see

signs to the secluded **Aynılı** and **Fırkatan** churches.

There's another group of churches to the west of Göreme village. Look for signs to the **Yusuf Koç Kilisesi** and the **Kadir Durmuş Kilisesi** in particular.

Göreme Village

Göreme village, set amid cones and pinnacles of volcanic tuff, is its own biggest attraction. At its centre is the so-called **Roma Kalesi**, a tall volcanic column with the remains of a rock-cut Roman temple facade high up. The tops of the columns are intact, but the *bottoms* are missing!

You might also look at the **Konak Türk Evi** or Turkish Mansion House (1826), now a fine restaurant hidden in the maze of cobbled streets to the east of the village. Once the home of Mehmet Paşa, the local Ottoman grandee, it has two beautifully decorated rooms, the *selamlık* (men's room) and *haremlik* (women's room). The frescoes on the walls were apparently created by the artist responsible for the paintings in the dining room of İstanbul's Topkapı Palace. Unfortunately the Konak Türk Evi is not always open to visitors.

Walks Around Göreme

Göreme village is surrounded by the magnificent Göreme National Park. Valleys with gorgeous scenery and a mixture of ancient pigeon houses and even more ancient rock-cut churches fan out from all around the village.

Particularly popular valleys are **Güllüdere** (Rose Valley) connecting Göreme and Çavuşin; **Güvercinlik Vadısı** (Pigeon Valley), connecting Göreme and Uçhisar; **Ballıdere** (Honey Valley), running behind Göreme village; **Swords Valley**, running off the Open-Air Museum road; and **Zemi Valley**, behind the Turist Hotel (and with some particularly spectacular rock formations).

Most of the valleys have signposts directing you to them, but nothing to keep you on the straight and narrow once you get inside. Nor are they all particularly easy to walk. Mehmet Güngör (☎ 0532-382 2069) is one local guide with an encyclopaedic knowledge of Göreme's highways and by-ways. For US$10 he will lead you through any of the local valleys, perhaps in company with Hashmet, the famous local guide dog.

Organised Tours

Göreme is overrun with travel agents but prices are agreed at the start of each season and vary little from shop to shop. The agencies tend to offer a standard daily tour which takes in one of the underground cities and a stretch of the Ihlara Valley, as well as various photogenic viewing points and one of the caravanserais, with perhaps a final stop in Avanos to shop for pottery. At the start and end of the season when customers are thin on the ground, the tour companies tend to join forces, rather than have a fleet of half-empty minibuses plying back and forth. Most of the pensions either operate their own tours or work with one of the travel agencies.

If you want to go to Mustafapaşa and Soğanlı you will probably have to shop around. But Göreme agents are good at spotting a market opening; at certain times of year you may find them organising ski trips to Erciyes Dağı or visits to the Hacıbektaş Festival (see Hacıbektaş later in this chapter). They also organise evening trips to the hamam in Ürgüp and to the hot springs at Bayramhacılar (women may want to forgo the massage here though).

Expect to pay US$20 to US$25 for a day tour by minibus. To save arguments, check whether any visits to carpet shops or onyx factories are scheduled. Reliable agencies which have been in business for years include Ötüken Voyage (☎ 271 2588), Neşe Tour (☎ 271 2525), Zemi Tour (☎ 271 2576), Turtle Tours (☎ 271 2388) and Hiro Tour (☎ 271 2542), but others may well be equally good. Matiana (☎ 271 2900), beside Cafedoci@, offers an interesting range of tours, some of them to eastern Turkey.

Rainbow Ranch (☎ 271 2413), uphill on the road to Cave Hotel Melek, rents horses (no hard hats) for US$15 for two hours.

Places to Stay

These days Göreme has 60-plus pensions whose owners have formed a cooperative with an office in Göreme bus station. Head straight there and you'll be guided to the pension of your choice without hassle or deception. The cooperative agrees prices at the start of the season, so wherever you go you should get quoted about the same maximum rates for basic accommodation: US$4 to US$5 for a dorm bed, US$6 for a bed in a waterless room and US$7 or US$8 per person in a room with private facilities. Some pensions have areas where you can camp for even less money; others are upgrading some rooms to small-hotel comforts, and raising prices accordingly. Out of season, the discounts may vary.

These days even the tuff cones are increasingly being fitted out with private bathrooms and central heating, which means you can have the romance of cave living without having to forgo modern comforts. Some people find the rooms cut into the rock a bit claustrophobic, although they're far cooler than those in modern buildings. Some of the pensions are cut into the rock face, so you can get a feel for cave living in more spacious surroundings.

If you're coming to Göreme from October to May, make sure you pack warm clothes since it gets very cold at night and pension owners may delay putting the heating on.

Dollar for dollar, what you get in Göreme is much better value than what's on offer in many other parts of Turkey. Many of the hostels run book exchanges, offer videos and/or satellite TV, and serve a choice of breakfast second to none. No wonder people come for the day and end up staying for weeks.

Places to Stay – Budget

Camping Best is *Kaya Camping* (☎ 343 3100, fax 343 3984), uphill from the Göreme Open-Air Museum, on the Ortahisar road. Although it's 2km from the centre of Göreme, it's the closest to the Göreme Valley and has spectacular views, as well as a swimming pool, solar-heated showers, restaurant, caravan hook-ups, and other services. Camp sites cost US$3.50 per person plus US$1.75 per tent, US$2.25 per caravan.

Dilek Camping (☎ 271 2395) and *Berlin Camping (☎ 271 2249)*, side by side across from Peri Pansiyon on the Open-Air Museum road, are less fancy but more conveniently positioned for those without cars. Two people can pitch a tent for US$6. Even if you're not staying you can use the Berlin pool for US$3.50.

Pensions Backpackers have long made a beeline for *Köse Pension (☎ 271 2294, fax 271 2577)*, close to the PTT. It's run by Dawn and Mehmet Köse and has a big roof dorm with mattresses on the floor, as well as comfortable bedrooms with balconies and showers. Evening meals cost US$4.50 and there's always one vegetarian and one meat option. The gorgeous swimming pool is a distinct plus in summer. Dawn runs a book-swap scheme and keeps a visitor's book filled with travel tips rather than adulatory comments.

Also very popular and well worth visiting if you want to experience the real troglodyte lifestyle is Ali Yavuz's flower-bedecked *Kelebek Pension (☎ 271 2531, fax 271 2763, ℮ ali@kelebekhotel.com)*, up a steep flight of steps in the old part of the village but with views to die for. A wide choice of accommodation includes a few dorm beds for US$5 and a beautiful honeymoon suite with Jacuzzi for US$60. Fairy-chimney rooms without bath cost US$12; others with stone arches and bath US$18 to US$25. There's a nice rooftop bar, and excellent evening meals are usually available.

Just off the road leading to the Göreme Open-Air Museum there's a cluster of pensions set amid the fairy chimneys. At *Peri Pansiyon (☎ 271 2136, fax 271 2589)*, Fairy Pension, rooms in fairy chimneys stand on one side of a pretty flower-filled courtyard and there's also an inviting cave bar. Meals here are thoroughly enjoyable too. Also deservedly popular are *Paradise Pension (☎ 271 2248)* and *Ufuk II (Horizon) Pension (☎ 271 2157)*, tucked up behind Peri.

A road cuts inland from behind the Sultan Carpet Shop. Follow it to find, on the left, the inviting *Backpacker's Cave Interyouth Hostel (☎ 271 2705)*, with a pretty, flower-filled courtyard and lots of cave rooms. Although it calls itself a hostel it's really little different from the other pensions, although a six-bed dorm has beds for US$4.50 a head.

Keep going past the Rainbow Ranch to find *Sarıhan Pansion (☎ 271 2216)*, with good views of the town and rock-cut rooms. At the time of writing it was being used by Fez Bus groups. High up above it is *Arif Pansion (☎ 271 2361)*, with several rock-cut rooms and panoramic views.

Also up here at the back of the village is the popular new *Shoestring Cave Pansion (☎ 271 2450)* which has rock-cut rooms set around a flowery courtyard.

Very close to the otogar on the road leading to the Pigeon Valley, *Walnut House (☎ 271 2564, fax 271 2235)* has six comfortable rooms designed with traditional vaulted stone ceilings and lots of character. There's a cosy, kilim-filled lobby, too.

Continue up the road and turn right up a lane opposite the Ottoman House Hotel for the *L'Elysee Pension (☎ 271 2244)*, set back from a pretty rose garden. The owners speak French, English and Turkish, and the meals get good write-ups.

Even further along on the left the *Gümüş Pension (☎ 271 2438)* has a pretty garden and a small rock-cut bar. Alone on the right-hand side of the road is the popular *Flintstones (☎ 271 2555)* with a swimming pool and cave rooms.

Another long-lived favourite is the *Rock Valley Pension (☎ 271 2153)*, well up the valley from the village centre – follow the bed of the dry canal to find it. As well as the standard double rooms, it has a four-bed dorm in a stone-vaulted room, a laundry service, a restaurant and a swimming pool.

Heading up towards the Kelebek Pension you pass *Tuna Pansion (☎ 271 2681)* with cave rooms, and *Kookaburra Pension (☎ 271 2549)*, with comfortable rooms set round yet another courtyard awash with flowers.

On the left as you come into Göreme from Uçhisar is *Dream Pension (☎ 271 2282)*, with more cave rooms and pleasant views.

Places to Stay – Mid-Range

For a bit more comfort at marginal extra cost, try the *Cave Hotel Melek (☎/fax 271 2463)*, 150m uphill from the main street. A small multi-level courtyard leads to a lounge with low seats and a fireplace adjoining the dining room. Single/doubles with shower, in the buildings or carved into the tuff, cost US$15/25 with breakfast.

Ottoman House (☎ 271 2616, fax 271 2351, e ottoman@indigoturizm.com.tr) boasts luxury at affordable prices: US$15/30 a room. A scrumptious buffet breakfast costs another US$5; a set menu dinner US$10. Marble steps lead off a comfortable lobby to pleasant modern rooms, with photographs of Cappadocia on the walls. In the basement both the restaurant and the Harem Bar are decked out with carpets, kilims, old costumes and other handicrafts.

Hotel Legend (☎ 271 2059, fax 271 2192), above the Arif Pansion in a quiet position with fine views, has comfortably furnished rooms (Jacuzzis in the bathrooms) on both sides of the road. Bed and breakfast costs US$30 per person. Several rooms have four beds suitable for families.

Göreme House Hotel (☎ 271 2668, fax 271 2669) has comfortable modern rooms in a building carefully designed to mimic the style of the older village houses. A suite with Jacuzzi costs US$60, normal singles/doubles cost US$20/30.

Places to Stay – Top End

At the end of the road running past the Ottoman House is the *S Ataman Hotel (☎ 271 2310, fax 271 2313, e info@atamanhotel.com)* created out of a 200-year-old stone building. The rooms are individually decorated with carpets and handicrafts but boast all mod cons (including TV, fridge and hairdryer) as well; however at US$120/150 a single/double for half board, they are way overpriced. There's a basement disco, a decent restaurant and a library crammed full of books about Cappadocia.

Places to Eat

Most Göreme pensions provide good, cheap meals and often serve wine and beer too.

If you want to eat out you'll find a line-up of restaurants along the main Avanos road. They're mainly geared to the bus-tour trade but offer pleasant terraces where you can sit and eat while gazing on the fairy chimneys. The *Sultan Restaurant* is popular with locals for its excellent *domates çorbası* (tomato soup) for US$1. The *Sedef Restaurant* does good pizzas and a long list of mezes; the *Tardelli Restaurant* and *Mercan* are similar. A full dinner with drinks (which are relatively expensive) can cost around US$10 in any of them. The *SOS Restaurant*, just before you reach the post office, is less flashy and a bit cheaper.

One of Göreme's best places to eat is *Orient Restaurant*, on the left-hand side of the road heading out towards Uçhisar. An excellent, filling four-course meal with soft drink costs US$4.75, but you can also pick and choose from the main menu and eat inside or out depending on the weather. The ambience is relaxing, even occasionally romantic.

The drolly named *Cafedoci@*, across the road from the Orient, offers big portions of burgers and salads alongside Internet terminals, movies on a big-screen TV and a range of beers and spirits.

Close to the Vegemite Cafe is the big new *Local Cafe & Bar*, with indoor and outdoor tables and excellent food to soak up the atmosphere. For US$4 the Osman Special (chicken or beef rolls stuffed with mushrooms, cheese and garlic) is to die for, as is the melt-in-your-mouth chocolate cake.

On a tighter budget head across to the other side of the channel and look for *Kapadokya Kebap House* or *Rose Döner*, both offering a range of cheaper, snack-type meals. The pleasant outdoor *Cafe Bonefide*, overlooking the amphitheatre, serves burgers as well as the usual kebaps.

Also on this side of the channel is *Göreme Restaurant* which tries its best with floor cushions, carpets and live music but isn't always as good at getting the food to the tables piping hot.

When you stagger back from the Open-Air Museum you can collapse in the friendly *Vegemite Cafe* which serves – as its name suggests – Vegemite with anything as well as gözleme, fruit juices and a range of sandwiches.

If it's open, Göreme's most historic eatery is **Mehmet Paşa Restaurant** (*☎/fax 271 2207*) in the Konak Türk Evi, where two beautiful frescoed rooms have been turned into private dining rooms. There's also an open-air terrace with fine views and a bar. The menu offers a fairly standard range of Turkish mezes and kebaps for which you should expect to pay around US$8 a head.

The restaurant at the **S Ataman Hotel** (*☎ 271 2310*) is good but clearly aimed at tour groups. The rock-hewn dining rooms are decorated with Turkish crafts. Expect to pay around US$10 a head.

Some of the best food in Cappadocia is to be had in the beautiful basement dining room of the **Ottoman House** (*☎ 271 2616*). The US$10 per person set menu offers four courses and an interesting array of Turkish dishes – well worth splashing out.

Entertainment
For a small village Göreme has a great range of places to while away your evenings. First off there's the homely **Pacha Bar**, right beside the otogar, with big-screen TV, decent music and a good range of drinks. Then there's **Flintstones Bar** at the start of the Open-Air Museum road, which is cut right into the rock face. Then there's **Cafedoci@**, which screens recent Hollywood movies to go with its drinks. Finally, in high summer there's the **Escape** disco in a converted donkey stable behind the otogar. Watch out for the male belly-dancer – he's said to be hot stuff!

Warning

A warning is needed about so-called direct bus services to Göreme. Several readers have complained that they bought tickets on buses which, they were told, were going 'directly to Göreme', only to find themselves deposited at Nevşehir otogar in the early hours. Worse still, people are sometimes dumped on the roadside near Avanos or outside Nevşehir long before daybreak.

Unless you travel with the Göreme, Nevtur or Kapadokya bus companies, which run free *servis* buses from Nevşehir to the surrounding villages, it's probably best to assume you are going to have to find your own way from Nevşehir or Avanos to Göreme. Buses from Pamukkale are particularly notorious for leaving Göreme-bound customers in the lurch.

Getting There & Away
There are daily buses to all sorts of places from Göreme otogar, although normally you're ferried to Nevşehir otogar to pick up the main service (which can add a good half-hour to your travelling time). Half-hourly dolmuşes connect Göreme with Nevşehir year-round (US$0.45, 15 minutes). There are also hourly buses to Çavuşin and Avanos and two-hourly buses to Ortahisar and Ürgüp (US$0.45). Details of some useful daily services are listed in the table.

Services from Göreme's Otogar

destination	cost (US$)	time (hr)	distance (km)	daily services
Adana	9	5	285	several buses
Aksaray	2.50	1½	65	frequent minibuses and buses
Aleppo (Syria)	30	10	580	1 night bus
Ankara	9	4	285	several buses
Denizli (Pamukkale)	14	11	674	1 bus
İstanbul	17	11	715	a few night buses
Kayseri	3.50	1½	105	frequent buses
Konya	9	3	226	several buses
Yozgat (via Kayseri, for Boğazkale)	6	4	300	a few buses

Getting Around

There are several places to hire mountain bikes, mopeds and motor scooters. Bikes cost around US$8; mopeds and scooters go for US$15 for four hours, US$25 for 12 hours, or US$30 for 24 hours. For a couple, two scooters will thus cost about the same as a rental car. You must leave your passport as a security deposit.

To avoid argument later take only a machine that's in good repair, even if it's more expensive. Beware rental places that rent bikes with dents in them, then charge you for causing the dents when you return the machine. (They'll charge the next renter as well; in effect, one dent can pay for a whole bike.) Ötüken and Zemi Tour are reputable places to hire bikes.

Since there are no petrol stations in Göreme and the bike rental companies will hike petrol prices, fill up the tank in Nevşehir, Avanos or Ürgüp before returning the bike.

ÇAVUŞİN
☎ 384

Midway between Göreme and Avanos is sleepy little Çavuşin. Walk through the new housing and out the back to find the old village, with houses cut into a steep rock face. The cathedral-sized **Church of John the Baptist**, near the top of the cliff, is one of the oldest in Cappadocia. Right beside the main road is the other **Church of St John** (also known as the Great Pigeon House), up a steep iron stairway and with fine frescoes. It's open from 8 am to 5.30 pm daily; admission costs US$1.75.

Çavuşin is the starting point for **scenic hikes** through the volcanic Güllüdere Vadisi (Rose Valley) and Kızılçukur (Red Gulch Valley), to the east of the village. You can even go as far as the Zindanönü viewpoint (6.5km), then walk out to the Ürgüp-Ortahisar road and hitch or catch a dolmuş back to your base.

Places to Stay & Eat

Right in the main square is the **In Pension** (☎ 532 7070) in a converted village house, with an old loom set up in a kilim-covered salon. Beds in clean, simple rooms cost US$9.50 each, including breakfast.

Set back behind gardens is the much bigger **Green Motel** (☎ 532 7228, fax 532 7032) with inviting rooms for US$20/30, some with great views of the cliff.

Panorama Pansion (☎ 532 7002) has simple rooms for US$9/17. The nearby **Turbel Pension** (☎ 432 7084, fax 532 7083) has attractive, spacious rooms decorated with handicrafts, some of them with lovely, peaceful, rural views. Any of these places would make a good choice if you were looking for somewhere quieter to base yourself than Göreme.

Right in the main square the **Konak Restaurant** does its best with a limited menu and live music most nights. Up in the old village the **Walnut Kafeterya** offers cold drinks beneath shady ancient walnut trees.

ZELVE

A side road from Çavuşin runs 5km to Zelve, where three valleys of abandoned homes converge. At Paşabağ, halfway along the road, a cluster of fairy chimneys, one of them 'three-headed', stands in a vineyard near a row of souvenir stalls. This is a popular place to come to watch the sun set.

Zelve was another monastic retreat. The **Balıklı Kilise**, or Fish Church, has fish figuring in one of the primitive paintings, and the more impressive **Üzümlü Kilise** (Grape Church) has obvious bunches of grapes, but in general the valleys here don't have as many impressive painted churches as Göreme. Still, you can while away many happy hours exploring tunnels and houses and gazing on gorgeous vistas. There's also an old **değirmen** (mill). Unfortunately, erosion continues to eat into the structures in the valley, and some parts may be closed because of the danger of collapse. There are also some sections included in tours that involve walking in the pitch dark and scrambling down a frightening ladder. Take a torch (flashlight) and be prepared.

Zelve's opening hours are from 8 am to 6 pm (last admission at 5.30 pm) and admission costs US$2.50. There are cafes and tea gardens in the car park outside.

VALLEY OF THE FAIRY CHIMNEYS

From Zelve, go 400m back down the access road and turn right on a paved road marked for Ürgüp. After 2km you'll come to the village of **Aktepe** (Yeni Zelve). Bear right, follow the Ürgüp road uphill and, after less than 2km, you'll find yourself in the Valley of the Fairy Chimneys (Peribacalar Vadisi).

Though many Cappadocian valleys boast collections of strange volcanic cones, these are the best-formed and most thickly clustered. Most of the rosy rock cones are topped by flattish, darker stones of harder rock that sheltered the cones from the rains until all the surrounding rock was eaten away, a process known as differential erosion.

If you continue to the top of the ridge, you'll reach the Avanos-Ürgüp road, with Avanos to the left, Ürgüp to the right.

AVANOS

☎ 384 • pop 12,000 • elevation 910m

North of Göreme, on the banks of the Kızılırmak River (Red River), lies Avanos, once called Venessa, another potential base for exploring the Cappadocian valleys. Avanos is more coy about revealing its charms than Göreme, but head up into the signposted old village behind the central square and you'll find lovely old stone houses, some of them decorated with ancient motifs – a rural setting inside a small town.

Modern Avanos is famous for its pottery, and for once the most prominent statue is not of Atatürk but of an anonymous potter and his observers. The town's workshops still turn out pots, ashtrays, lamps, chess sets and other utensils and souvenirs moulded from the red clay of the river, as they have been doing for centuries. Most of these workshops welcome visitors.

Some people find Göreme too touristy and prefer the more low-key charms of Avanos where a life beyond tourism is still much in evidence. Even if you're not staying overnight, it still makes a good place for lunch or a çay (tea) break.

Orientation & Information

Most of the town is on the northern bank of the river, with Atatürk Caddesi providing the main thoroughfare. The otogar is south of the river, although many of the dolmuşes also stop outside the PTT, across from the main square which is marked by the large monument to the potter. The tourist office (☎ 511 4360) is on Atatürk Caddesi.

Things to See

Tour groups tend to find themselves shopping for pots in vast warehouses on the outskirts of town. It's much more enjoyable to patronise one of the smaller **pottery workshops** right in town, most of which will happily show you how to throw a pot or two. To find them, go behind the pottery monument and turn right just after the Şanso-Panso restaurant. Along this street are several potteries, including **Chez Galip** with its infamous, shades-of-Bluebeard Hair Museum. Other potteries are scattered throughout the town; look for **Chez Efe** on Atatürk Caddesi near the Kirkit Pension.

Activities

The Alaaddin Turkish Bath (☎ 511 5036), west of the Sofa Hotel on the river bank, was built at the end of the 1980s with tourists in mind and is a Disneyfied version of the real thing. A bath with full works costs US$10. In summer this place is very popular with tour groups. It's open daily from 8 am to 2 am.

Kirkit Voyage (☎ 511 3259, fax 511 2135), Atatürk Caddesi 50, run by the owners of the Kirkit Pension, can arrange walking, biking, rafting, canoeing, horse riding and even snowshoe trips, as well as the more usual guided tours. To hire a horse for a day costs US$26; a mountain bike is US$17.

You can also rent horses from Akhal-Teke (☎ 511 5171, 532 7135 in Çavuşin, fax 511 3000), Camikebir Mahallesi, Kadı Sokak 1. Horse-riding trips to the Sarıhan (Yellow Caravanserai), Rose Valley (Güllüdere Vadisi) and other local sights cost about US$50 a day.

Places to Stay – Budget

You can camp in the riverside grounds of *Mesut Restaurant* (☎ 511 3545) for US$5 a tent.

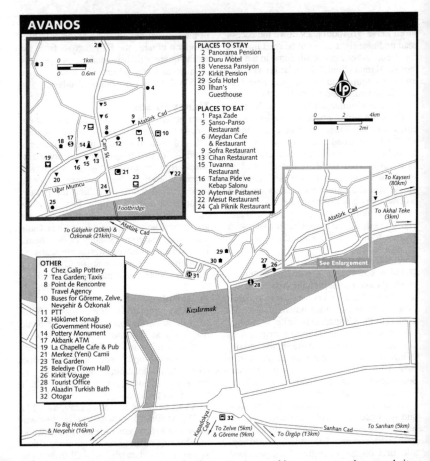

AVANOS

PLACES TO STAY
2 Panorama Pension
3 Duru Motel
18 Venessa Pansiyon
27 Kirkit Pension
29 Sofa Hotel
30 İlhan's Guesthouse

PLACES TO EAT
1 Paşa Zade
5 Şanso-Panso Restaurant
6 Meydan Cafe & Restaurant
9 Sofra Restaurant
13 Cihan Restaurant
15 Tuvanna Restaurant
16 Tafana Pide ve Kebap Salonu
20 Aytemur Pastanesi
22 Mesut Restaurant
24 Çalı Piknik Restaurant

OTHER
4 Chez Galip Pottery
7 Tea Garden; Taxis
8 Point de Rencontre Travel Agency
10 Buses for Göreme, Zelve, Nevşehir & Özkonak
11 PTT
12 Hükümet Konağı (Government House)
14 Pottery Monument
17 Akbank ATM
19 La Chapelle Cafe & Pub
21 Merkez (Yeni) Camii
23 Tea Garden
25 Belediye (Town Hall)
26 Kirkit Voyage
28 Tourist Office
31 Alaadin Turkish Bath
32 Otogar

Perhaps the best place to stay is the charming **Kirkit Pension** (☎ 511 3148, fax 511 2135) where four old, stone houses have been turned into a pension full of nooks and crannies where backpackers can meet and chat. Beds cost US$8.50 in waterless rooms, US$10 in rooms with shower, breakfast included. There's a rock-cut restaurant at the back where good food and wine (as you'd expect in a place popular with the French) is served with ad hoc music sessions.

A promising newcomer is **Venessa Pansiyon** (☎ 511 3840, Hafızağa Sokak 20) in a beautifully restored old house with several terraces and its very own underground city, complete with rolling door stones. The owner, Mükremin Tokmak, is very knowledgeable about local history and keeps all sorts of interesting knick-knacks and photographs. Beds in rooms with showers cost US$10 including breakfast.

Immediately in front of the Sofa Hotel is **İlhan's Guesthouse** (☎ 511 4828, Zafer Sokak 1), with similar prices to the Kirkit. Ask for the slightly more expensive special room at the back, with a fireplace and antique furniture. The breakfast terrace boasts great river views. İlhan speaks English.

Another low-price favourite is **Panorama Pension** (☎ 511 4654), a five-minute walk 250m uphill through the backstreets of the old town, with impressive views from the terrace. Bed and breakfast costs from US$6 to US$11, depending upon the room and whether it has a shower.

Places to Stay – Mid-Range
The inviting **Sofa Hotel** (☎ 511 5186, fax 511 4489, Orta Mahalle 13) consists of three old stone houses joined into one, renovated and fitted with mod cons. Several of its shower-equipped rooms are partially built into the rock, and there's a small TV lounge. You can live the troglodytic life here for US$30/50/70 a single/double/triple, including breakfast, but book ahead because tour groups like this place.

High above the town stands **Duru Motel** (☎ 511 4005, fax 511 2402, Cumhuriyet Meydanı 15), a two-storey white block with grassy terrace and wonderful views over the town and the river. Rooms have insect screens, showers and stoves for cold spring days. Prices are US$17/25, breakfast included; a good home-made four-course dinner goes for US$5. To find the Duru, follow the signs up the winding, narrow street to the top, or ask at the Duru Carpet Shop at the back of the main square.

Across the bridge, on the road to Göreme, are several three- and four-star hotels aimed at tour groups but available to individual travellers as well. These include the four-star **Hotel Altınyazı** (☎ 511 2010), **Yıltok Oteli** (☎ 511 5210) and **Avrasya Oteli** (☎ 511 5181) and the three-star **Hotel Palansaray** (☎ 511 4044).

Places to Eat
The **Sofra Restaurant**, facing the hükümet konaği building, serves mantı, pizza and pide, as well as a range of kebaps and stews. The **Cihan Restaurant** on the main square is smaller but just as popular. Lunch or dinner at either place will cost your about US$3 or US$4.

The **Tuvanna Restaurant** is more popular for nights out and prices are higher, with şiş kebap costing US$2.50 and a small steak

US$3; a full meal is likely to cost about US$10, although a pizza need only set you back US$2.50.

The **Paşa Zade** (☎ 511 4560, Kayseri Caddesi Kız Meslek Lisesi Karşısı) looks set to scoop the summer trade in wedding and circumcision parties, although an İskender kebap and a cold drink still only costs US$3.

The friendly **Şanso-Panso Restaurant**, on the right up the slope of the main square behind the pottery monument, serves Efes Pilsen beer (US$1.25). Given Avanos' pottery trade it's hardly surprising that the speciality is *güveç*, beef stew with potatoes, tomatoes, garlic, paprika and cumin, baked in a clay pot (US$2.75). The **Meydan Cafe & Restaurant**, to the left of the Point de Rencontre travel agency, serves cheap pide at outdoor tables. Another popular pide joint is **Tafana Pide ve Kebap Salonu** on Atatürk Caddesi.

Facing the river is **Mesut Restaurant** where you can eat gözleme and other popular home-cooked dishes while looking out on the sweep of the Kızılırmak.

Aytemur Pastanesi, near the Tuvanna, serves a tasty banana roll with a large glass of tea for less than US$1.50.

Entertainment
An excellent place to stop for a tea, coffee or something stronger, is the tiny **La Chapelle Cafe & Pub** on Atatürk Caddesi. The decor, provided by a local artist, mimics that of the ancient rock-cut chapels. If you're lucky you'll hit an evening with live music.

Getting There & Away
Avanos Belediyesi buses travel to Nevşehir via Çavuşin, Göreme and Uçhisar every hour in summer from 7 am to 6 pm (US$0.50). Between times there are also direct buses to Nevşehir. Services are less frequent in winter.

AROUND AVANOS
Sarıhan
The Seljuk-era Sarıhan (Yellow Caravanserai) is signposted 6km east of Avanos. The elaborate gateway, with a small mosque above it, is impressive and inside there's a

large courtyard where animals were loaded and unloaded, and a great hall where people and animals could escape the weather.

The caravanserai was restored in the late 1980s, and is open as a museum from 9 am to 1 pm and 2 to 6 pm daily; admission costs US$1.75. These days it also serves as a cultural centre, offering well-thought of nightly performances of dervish dancing in summer (☎ 511 3785 for more details) for US$25 a head.

Getting to the Sarıhan without your own transport is difficult, as there are no dolmuşes and few vehicles with which to hitch a ride. You may have to haggle with an Avanos taxi driver.

Özkonak Underground City

North of Avanos the village of Özkonak hosts a smaller version of the underground cities to be seen at Kaymaklı and Derinkuyu, with the same wine reservoirs, air shafts, rolling stone doors, grindstones etc. It's not nearly as dramatic or impressive as the larger ones, but is much less crowded.

The site is open from 8 am to 5.30 pm; admission costs US$1.75. Take a jacket and a torch (flashlight) if you have them. Some of the passages from room to room require you to bend almost double.

The easiest way to get to Özkonak is by dolmuş from Avanos (US$0.60, 30 minutes). Özkonak is a straggly village with no clear centre so you'll need to watch for the village sign and ask the way to the '*yeraltı şehri*' (underground city). It's on the left immediately opposite the Petrol Ofisi as you come in from the Kayseri road. From there it's about 500m to the car park.

ORTAHİSAR
☎ 384

The village of Ortahisar, 3km south-east of the Göreme Valley, is near the intersection of the Nevşehir to Ürgüp and Göreme roads. Somehow mainstream tourism has bypassed Ortahisar and it remains a Cappadocian farming village, with a thriving trade in storing citrus fruits in its caves. Its main claim to fame is its **kale**, an 18m-high rock used as a fortress in Byzantine times and a great place

to come for sunset panoramas provided you have a good head for heights (US$1.75). From Ortahisar you can also hike to various lesser churches in the surrounding countryside, especially in the Pancarlık Valley.

Places to Stay & Eat

There are limited accommodation choices in the village centre, 1.5km from the main road intersection. Try the simple *Hotel Gümüş* (☎ 343 3127), to the right of the PTT, which charges US$6 per person in a room with shower.

Continue up the hill past the PTT and turn left for the *Hotel Yavuz* (☎ 343 3995, fax 343 3346), an atmospheric hotel with rooms set around a courtyard. Comfortable singles/doubles with immaculate bathrooms cost US$35/50.

Tour groups are often taken to the unmissable *Kapadokya Inn* (☎ 343 3470, fax 343 3480) out on the main road at the junction with the road to Göreme. Rooms clock in at US$85/105 for which you get the necessary comfort even if it's in the middle of nowhere. The *restaurant* here has a particularly good reputation locally.

Getting There & Away

There are regular Ortahisar Belediyesi buses from Nevşehir (US$0.75), and plenty of dolmuşes along the Ürgüp-Nevşehir road.

ÜRGÜP
☎ 384 • pop 13,500

About 23km east of Nevşehir and 7km east of Göreme Valley is the small town of Ürgüp, with some magnificent old houses left over from the (pre-1923) days when it still had a large Greek population.

Ürgüp has many large tour-group hotels on its eastern outskirts, but the centre of town retains many honey-coloured stone buildings, which are slowly being converted into fine hotels and pensions.

Orientation & Information

Ürgüp is set within a steep valley. The otogar is right in the centre off the main street, Kayseri Caddesi, which is sprinkled with antique shops, carpet shops and restaurants.

ÜRGÜP

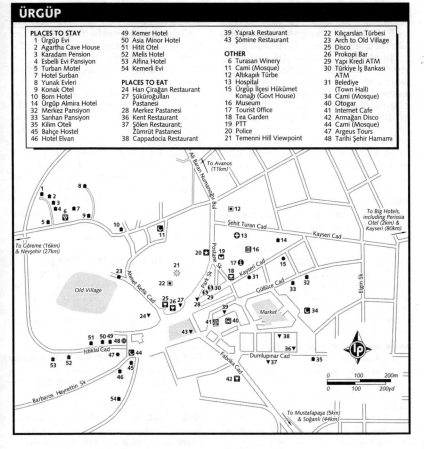

PLACES TO STAY
1 Ürgüp Evi
2 Agartha Cave House
3 Karadam Pension
4 Esbelli Evi Pansiyon
5 Turban Motel
7 Hotel Surban
8 Yunak Evleri
9 Konak Otel
10 Born Hotel
14 Ürgüp Almira Hotel
32 Merkez Pansiyon
33 Sarıhan Pansiyon
35 Kilim Oteli
45 Bahçe Hostel
46 Hotel Elvan

49 Kemer Hotel
50 Asia Minor Hotel
51 Hitit Otel
52 Melis Hotel
53 Alfina Hotel
54 Kemerli Evi

PLACES TO EAT
24 Han Çirağan Restaurant
27 Şüküroğulları
   Pastanesi
28 Merkez Pastanesi
36 Kent Restaurant
37 Şölen Restaurant;
   Zümrüt Pastanesi
38 Cappadocia Restaurant

39 Yaprak Restaurant
43 Şömine Restaurant

OTHER
6 Turasan Winery
11 Cami (Mosque)
12 Altıkapılı Türbe
13 Hospital
15 Ürgüp İlçesi Hükümet
   Konağı (Govt House)
16 Museum
17 Tourist Office
18 Tea Garden
19 PTT
20 Police
21 Temenni Hill Viewpoint

22 Kılıçarslan Türbesi
23 Arch to Old Village
25 Disco
26 Prokopi Bar
29 Yapı Kredi ATM
30 Türkiye İş Bankası
   ATM
31 Belediye
   (Town Hall)
34 Cami (Mosque)
40 Otogar
41 Internet Cafe
42 Armağan Disco
44 Cami (Mosque)
47 Argeus Tours
48 Tarihi Şehir Hamamı

CENTRAL ANATOLIA

The helpful and well-informed tourist office (☎ 341 4059) is at Kayseri Caddesi 37, down the hill from the main square behind a tea garden and open from 8 am to 6 pm (8 pm in summer), every day. The uninspiring museum, open daily from 8 am to 5 pm, is right next door. Admission costs US$1.75.

Across the road from the hamam, the excellent Argeus Tours (☎ 341 4688, fax 341 4888, ⓔ inform@argeus.com.tr), İstiklal Caddesi 13, can help with cycling, walking and riding holidays as well as with day tours, airport transfers and flights. Check their Web site at www.argeus.com.tr for details.

Things to See & Do

West of the main square is the oldest part of the town, reached through a stone arch, with many fine **old houses**. It's worth a stroll, after which you can hack up Ahmet Refik Caddesi and turn right to reach the **Temenni hilltop**, with a saint's tomb, a terrace cafe, an Ottoman library with photos of pre-1923 Ürgüp (note the huge old Greek church) and fine views of the town. North of the centre is the historic **Altıkapılı Türbe** (Six-Gated Tomb).

Overlooking the main square is the **Tarihi Şehir Hamamı**, the local hamam, partly housed in what was once a small church. Foreign men and women can bathe together for US$5 a scrub. It's a good place to come for your first experience of a Turkish bath.

The abundant sunshine and fertile volcanic soil of Cappadocia produce delicious sweet grapes, and several small local **wineries** carry on the Ottoman-Greek tradition of wine-making. Try Turasan's Peribaca light red, Duyurgan's dry white Algan, the hearty red Cappadocia from Mustafapaşa, or Tekel's Ürgüp white and Çubuk red. You can sample the produce at the big **Turasan Winery**, uphill on the Nevşehir road out of town or in the shops just off the main square.

Places to Stay – Budget

If you stay in Ürgüp it's worth splashing out a bit to take advantage of some of the excellent accommodation available.

The streets south and east of the otogar harbour several small family-run pensions which are perfectly pleasant, although it seems almost wilfully perverse to opt for suburbia when you could stay in a pension in an old stone house north or west of the otogar, for very little more money.

If you don't mind a modern building **Kilim Oteli** (☎ 341 3131, fax 341 5758, Dumlupınar Caddesi 47), south of the market, offers clean simple singles/doubles for US$12/20 without breakfast. There are more similarly priced cheapies in Güllüce Caddesi, the street south of Kayseri Caddesi. Look, in particular, for the **Sarıhan Pansiyon** (☎ 341 8813, fax 341 5820) and **Merkez Pansiyon** (☎ 341 2746).

Assuming you'd rather stay in an old stone house, one of the cheapest options is the **Bahçe Hostel** (☎ 341 3314, fax 341 4878, e bahce@altavista.net), across the road from the hamam, which has basic waterless rooms for US$4.50 a head and pension rooms with baths for US$7/13 a single/double, set round a pleasant courtyard.

Up the hill a bit is the homely **Hotel Elvan** (☎ 341 4191, fax 341 3455, İstiklal Caddesi, Barbaros Hayrettin Sokak 11), run by Ahmet and Fatma Bilir, with nicer rooms arranged around a small courtyard and good views from the roof terrace.

There's a lounge with carpets and sedirs. Rooms cost US$15/25, breakfast included.

Continuing up İstiklal Caddesi, on the right you'll see the fairly simple but friendly **Kemer Hotel** (☎ 341 2168, Hamam Sokak 19), with small arched rooms for US$9 a head.

Heading up the hill towards Nevşehir you soon come to the **Born Hotel** (☎ 341 4756), an old pasha's house fallen on hard times. It's in need of renovation but the big rooms are pleasant enough for US$4.50 a head.

Further up is the **Konak Otel** (☎ 341 3222, fax 341 3223, Yunak Mahallesi) with basic singles/doubles for US$9 a head set round a courtyard. Even further up is the modern **Hotel Surban** (☎ 341 4603, fax 341 3223, Yunak Mahallesi), which is popular with groups and charges US$17 per person for comfortable rooms with baths.

Places to Stay – Mid-Range

Heading up İstiklal Caddesi on the right you'll come to an excellent choice: the **Asia Minor Hotel** (☎ 341 4645, fax 341 2721, e cappadocia50@hotmail.com), with a pleasant garden, fine frescoes in the hall and stylishly decorated double rooms (no singles) for US$40. The neighbouring **Hitit Otel** (☎ 341 4481, fax 341 3620, İstiklal Caddesi 46) has a lovely garden and is marginally cheaper but nowhere near as nicely decorated.

Further up the hill on the left is the new **Melis Hotel** (☎ 341 2495, Karahan Dere Sokak 75), which offers pleasantly decorated rooms in an old house with wooden floors for US$20 a head, including breakfast.

The **Alfina Hotel** (☎ 341 4822, fax 341 2424, İstiklal Caddesi 25), further up the hill, has 32 comfortable rooms hewn from the rock for US$36/53.

Places to Stay – Top End

First, and still foremost, of all the boutique hotels in old village houses is Süha Ersöz's **Esbelli Evi Pansiyon** (☎ 341 3395, fax 341 8848, e suha@esbelli.com.tr). Six old village houses cut into the rock have been combined and lovingly restored, and now constitute one of Turkey's finest places to stay. The pristine rooms, many fashioned from caves, have modern bathrooms with showers and direct-dial phones. Two sundeck terraces, two lounges, a modern kitchen and laundry facilities are at your disposal. Several of the rooms, including the one for honeymooners, have fine iron bedsteads. One room is in what was once a rock-cut kitchen complete with soaring chimney. Another would be ideal for families, with a big double bed, a single and a cot. Singles/doubles/triples are US$70/85/100 (no discounts), including an excellent breakfast. Advance reservations are essential. Check out their Web site at www .esbelli.com.tr for more details.

To find the Esbelli head up the long hill from the main square and take the turning beside the huge, ugly old Turban Motel (which may have reopened under new ownership by the time you read this).

The success of the Esbelli has spawned imitators, several of them close by. The lovely *Ürgüp Evi* (☎ *341 3173, fax 341 6080,* e *Faruk@urgupevi.com.tr)* is a group of stone houses spilling down terraces with fine views. Standard rooms with lovely fittings cost US$65/85. There's also a self-catering suite with its own sauna for US$180. The *Agartha Cave House* (☎ *341 6000, 341 8089,* e *agartha@turkeytours .com)* is similar, as is the *Kayadam Pansiyon* (☎ *341 6673, fax 5982).*

Heading back down towards the centre, and taking a small turning on the left beside the Konak Otel, you'll come to the wonderful new *Yunak Evleri* (☎ *341 6920, fax 341 6924,* e *yunak@yunak.com).* It's a group of old village houses cut into a rock face pierced with ancient pigeon houses. One central house serves as a restaurant with twin sitting rooms, while the rock-cut houses provide the rooms, one of them a suite with a Jacuzzi. This is a surprisingly quiet, private corner of Ürgüp and the US$90 a double price tag can only go up. Take advantage of it while you can. Check their Web site at www.yunak.com for details.

Across the other side of town in the backstreets, south-west of the main square, is the *Kemerli Evi* (☎ *341 5445, fax 341 5446,* *Dutlu Camii Çıkmaz Sokak 12),* another splendid conversion set round a courtyard, this time with a subtly Italianate feel reflecting its owner's origins. Rooms are decorated with antique carpets and textiles, some of them from Bali. Rooms cost US$50/70.

There are numerous upmarket hotels on the eastern outskirts catering almost exclusively to groups. Most upmarket of all, but way out of the centre, is the *Perissia Otel* (☎ *341 2930, fax 341 4524, Kayseri Caddesi)* where visiting celebrities tend to stay. Right in town on Kayseri Caddesi, just past the museum, is the four-star *Ürgüp Almira Hotel* (☎ *341 8990, fax 341 8999, Kayseri Caddesi 43),* with its own swimming pool. You get air-con, but for the US$70/100 price tag you'd do better staying in one of the lovely old places described above.

Places to Eat

The long-serving *Cappadocia Restaurant* offers fairly attentive service and decent three-course meals for around US$4 or US$5. It's in the street running down from the market to Dumlupınar Caddesi.

For cheaper meals continue to Dumlupınar Caddesi where the *Şölen Restaurant* specialises in kebaps and good cheap pide and pizza – including vegetarian – for under US$2. The drearier *Kent Restaurant*, more or less across the street from the Kilim Oteli, serves staples like *kuru fasulye* (beans) for US$1.50 a shot.

Facing the entrance to the otogar are several restaurants catering to marooned travellers. Probably best is *Yaprak Restaurant* where you can get a pleasant chicken döner with rice, salad and a soft drink for US$3.

Ürgüp also has many pastry shops near its main square. The longstanding *Merkez Pastanesi* is the best in town. A large glass of tea and a portion of cake cost less than US$2. Flashier is *Şüküroğulları Pastanesi*, facing the main square.

The town's most prominent eatery is the *Şömine Restaurant*, on the main square with indoor and outdoor tables. Ürgüp-style kebaps baked on tiles are a speciality and the trout casserole is a rare treat. Full meals with drinks cost from US$8 to US$12.

CENTRAL ANATOLIA

Han Çirağan Restaurant is at the far end of the main square in an old stone house behind a vine-covered garden. In summer you can dine outside in a pleasant small courtyard. One reader particularly rated their chicken güveç (stew).

Entertainment
Ürgüp has one delightful – if hardly cheap – place to drink: the *Prokopi Bar* is set round a courtyard behind the shops facing the main square. Of the two discos, the *Armağan* was most in favour at the time of writing.

The *Karakuş Entertainment Centre* (☎ 341 5353, fax 341 5356), on the outskirts of Ürgüp signposted off the Mustafapaşa road, offers dinner with unlimited drinks and a Turkish folklore show for US$15 if you make your reservation, twice as much if you reserve through your hotel or a travel agency.

Getting There & Away
Argeus Tours (☎ 341 4688, fax 341 4888), Ürgüp's Turkish Airlines representative, runs minibus transfers to and from THY flights. Contact them to reserve your place in advance, especially if you're arriving at Kayseri airport rather than Tuzköy (Nevşehir).

Bus and minibus services are frequent in high summer, much less so in winter. Some daily services are listed in the table below.

Getting Around
Minibuses link Ürgüp with the Göreme Valley, Göreme village, Zelve, Avanos etc hourly every day from May to September.

You can hop on and off anywhere around the loop, but each hop costs US$0.45.

The major international car companies – Avis, Europcar (National), Hertz and Interrent – all have offices near Ürgüp's main square, within one block of the otogar.

Agencies in town rent bicycles, mopeds and motorcycles at prices similar to those listed in the Göreme section.

AYVALI & DAMSA GÖLÜ
Heading south from Ürgüp to Mustafapaşa look out for a turn-off to Ayvalı, a tiny unspoilt Cappadocian village where İbrahim and Sabina have set up their delightful Gamırasu Hotel (☎ 384-354 5815, fax 354 5815, e gamirasu@hotmail.com). It's a series of simple rooms with futon-style mattresses. There's a church with frescoes and an ancient winery on the premises and a path immediately behind runs 7km to Golgoli Hill. You can hire horses, donkeys or bikes to explore the surrounding countryside. Breakfasts use fresh local produce, and dinners are designed to suit individual preferences. It's a perfect place for a real get-away-from-it-all holiday. They charge US$40/50 for singles/doubles including breakfast. İbrahim can fetch you from Kayseri or Nevşehir airport free of charge.

If you have your own car it might be worth stopping for a picnic at the nearby Damsa Gölü, formed by a newly built dam.

MUSTAFAPAŞA
☎ 384
Called Sinasos when it was an Ottoman Greek settlement before WWI, Mustafapaşa

Services from Ürgüp's Otogar

destination	fare	time	distance	daily services
Adana	9	5	308	1 bus
Ankara	9	4½	300	at least 7 buses (in summer)
Antalya	15	10	485	1 or 2 buses
İstanbul	17	11	725	at least 2 buses
Kayseri	2.50	1½	80	hourly minibuses between 7 am and 6 pm
Konya	7.50	3	250	two-hourly buses between 8 am and 8 pm
Nevşehir	1	¼	18	minibuses every half-hour
Pamukkale	15	11	690	at least 1 bus (in summer)

is the sleeping beauty of Cappadocia, a quiet village with lovely old stone-carved houses, a few minor rock-cut churches and several good places to stay.

Driving from Ürgüp (5km), you may want to stop to inspect the **Pancarlık Kilisesi**, reached by an unpaved road on the right 2km out of Ürgüp. The church is built into a volcanic cone and has wonderful frescoes of saints whose visages are relatively undamaged by the stones of shepherds. Admission costs US$1.75, and you'll often have it to yourself.

Back on the road, you pass turnings for the **Sarıca and Kepez Churches** before entering the village and reaching a large plaza with a dry central fountain. A shop here doubles as a tourist office of sorts and there's a signboard indicating the whereabouts of the local **rock-cut churches**. Follow the road downhill and you'll come to Cumhuriyet Meydanı, the centre of the village with the habitual bust of Atatürk and several teahouses.

Things to See & Do

There's a 19th-century **medrese** with a fine carved portal (including stone columns that swivel) to the south-west.

Right in the town centre is the imposing 19th-century **Church of Sts Constantine and Helena** with a stone grapevine running round its entrance. Sadly, it's rarely unlocked.

To find Mustafapaşa's older churches walk past the Monastery and Atasoy pensions and into the Monastery Valley. First up on the right is **Ayios Stefanos Church** (St Stephen's), with fine carving and painted decoration. An easy path continues to a fork on the right where you'll find the **Ayios Nikolaos Manastırı** (Monastery of St Nicholas). The partially collapsed **Sinasos Church** is another 150m uphill from Ayios Nikolaos. Despite the large direction signs, you'll probably arrive to find all the gates locked. It's a lovely walk nonetheless.

Places to Stay & Eat

Mustafapaşa has a couple of cheap pensions on the road leading to Monastery Valley.

The **Atasoy** (☎ 353 5378) has simple shower-equipped rooms with beds for US$5/8 a single/double, including breakfast. The more cheery **Monastery** (☎ 353 5005) next door charges US$9 per head for comfy if simple rooms and use of a big cave bar and restaurant.

The best place to stay must be the **Old Greek House** (☎ 353 5306, fax 353 5141), a wonderful old Ottoman-Greek house which still bears some of the original 19th-century painting and decoration. A small hamam was created out of a private chapel. The public areas are much more atmospheric than the rather prosaic bedrooms which cost US$25/35. If you don't stay, it's still worth coming here to sample tasty Turkish home cooking in attractive surroundings.

A close runner-up in the local charm contest is **Hotel Pacha** (☎/fax 353 5331), another restored Ottoman-Greek house with flower-filled courtyard and top-floor terrace with lovely views. Rooms with showers accommodate two to four people and cost US$7 a head, including breakfast. Home-cooked evening meals are US$5.

Also pleasant is the refurbished **Hotel Cavit** (☎ 353 5186), with a nice garden terrace shaded by grapevines. For US$13/22 you get a bed and a decent breakfast with no packet of jam in sight. It's on the southern side of town as you head out to Soğanlı.

Mustafapaşa's fanciest hotel is theoretically the **Otel Sinasos** (☎ 353 5009, fax 353 5435), where the bedrooms are in a modern extension to an old Greek house. Service seems pretty half-hearted, although at US$13 a head it's hardly overpriced. The real gem is the restaurant in the old house itself, with its wonderful painted wooden ceilings painstakingly restored and a balcony overlooking a lovely garden.

Follow the signs to find **Lamia** (☎ 353 5413), a home-from-home run by Lamia, a retired İstanbullu who brought all her bits and bobs with her when she came. Rooms cost US$30/50, including breakfast, and there's a pretty, secluded garden.

Getting There & Away

Mustafapaşa Belediyesi buses leave Ürgüp for Mustafapaşa roughly every two hours (US$0.30). A brief stop in Mustafapaşa is

CENTRAL ANATOLIA

Going Underground

For sheer fascination and mystery, you could hardly beat the underground cities of Cappadocia. While in the area it should be one of your top priorities to take in a visit to one of the estimated 36 underground cities that have been identified (if not always excavated).

Some archaeologists date the earliest portions of these underground cities to Hittite times 4000 years ago. The German archaeologist Martin Urban believes they were occupied by at least the 7th century BC and the ancient Greek historian Xenophon mentioned the underground dwellings of Cappadocia in his *Anabasis*.

In times of peace the people of this region lived and farmed above ground, but when invaders threatened they took to their troglodyte dwellings where they could live safely (if not always happily) for up to six months at a time.

When you arrive at one of the underground cities, little arrows guide you into the cool depths. As you go down, it's like entering a huge and very complex Swiss cheese: holes here, holes there, 'windows' from room to room, paths going this way and that and more levels of rooms above and below. Without the arrows and the electric wires, it would be frighteningly difficult to find the way out again. If you wander off along another passage, you may be separated from your group by only a few metres, and able to hear what they say and converse with them, but unable to find your way back to them! Suddenly a foot comes into view and you realise that they're on the next level, almost above your head!

Signs of the troglodyte lifestyle are everywhere: storage jars for oil, wine and water, communal kitchens blackened by smoke, stables with mangers, and incredibly deep wells. Soon it's easy to believe that tens of thousands of people could have lived here for months on end, deep within the earth. Some people even think that underground passages connected Kaymaklı with its sister city of Derinkuyu, 10km away, though the tunnels have yet to be excavated.

Even if you don't normally like having a guide, it's well worth having one take you around the underground cities, since they can conjure up the details of life below ground in a way which is virtually impossible to achieve on your own.

Kaymaklı and Derinkuyu are by far the most visited of the underground cities. When visiting them you may need to try and space yourself into a gap between larger groups. Alternatively, head for one of the less-visited sites, such as Özlüce or Mazıköy.

Kaymaklı

Kaymaklı itself is an unprepossessing farming town, notable only for its underground city and a handful of old stone houses. You can use Kaymaklı as a base to get to the less well-known underground cities at Özlüce and Mazıköy.

An unimpressive little cave in a low mound leads down into a maze of tunnels and rooms carved four levels deep into the earth. From the highway, follow the signs which indicate a left (east) turn, or ask for the '*yeraltı şehri*' (underground city). The entrance is one block east of the highway and it's open daily from 8 am to 5 pm (6.30 pm in summer); admission costs US$2.50. As this is the most convenient and popular of the underground cities, you should be here early (7.30 am is not too early) in July and August to enjoy it properly.

Özlüce

Turn right as you enter Kaymaklı from the north and you'll be headed for Özlüce, 7km further away. Özlüce also has an underground city. More modest than those of Kaymaklı or Derinkuyu, it is also less developed and less crowded, and still a good example of troglodytic living. In July and August, this is the place to come if there are long lines at the more famous sites. Don't forget to tip the guardian for showing you around.

Going Underground

Mazıköy

Just north of the turn-off for Kaymaklı's yeraltı şehri is another turn-off east marked for Mazıköy yeraltı şehri, 10km away. Nestled in a valley enclosed by the now-familiar sheer rock cliffs is the village of Mazıköy, with its central town square. Buy your ticket here (US$1.75) whenever there's anyone around, then head for the entrance just off the town square. On top of the valley wall is a necropolis with slot-like graves. A guide will probably show you the stone shelter supposedly used for the *güvercin postası* (carrier-pigeon mail service). The village has few services beyond food and drinks shops.

Derinkuyu

The name Derinkuyu means 'deep well', and this underground city, 10km south of Kaymaklı, has larger rooms arrayed on eight levels. When you get all the way down, look up the ventilation shaft to see just how deep you are – not for claustrophobics!

Like Kaymaklı, Derinkuyu is popular with tour groups and can be horribly crowded in peak season. Prices and opening times are the same as at Kaymaklı.

Derinkuyu has several restaurants and a couple of basic hotels near the main square. With time on your hands it's worth taking a look at the huge monastery church, 100m south of the entrance to the underground city, which was built in the 19th century when the local Greek culture was undergoing a revival. At the time of writing the entire area between the church and the underground city was being re-landscaped. It should look much nicer by the time you read this.

Finally, if you can get the caretaker to unlock the town mosque you'll get a pleasant surprise. Like so many local mosques it started life as a church and the marvellous 19th-century wooden screen separating nave and apse is still in situ.

Getting There & Away

Although you can visit one of the 'cities' on a day tour from Göreme, Avanos or Ürgüp, it's also easy to visit them on your own by taking a Niğde-bound bus out of Nevşehir. Niğde buses transit Kaymaklı and Derinkuyu, homes to the most popular underground cities; or there are local Kaymaklı and Derinkuyu buses from Nevşehir. All these buses leave from outside the tourist office in Nevşehir. On your own, you could easily visit Kaymaklı and Derinkuyu and then continue onto Niğde in the same day using the local buses.

KELLI HAMBLET

CENTRAL ANATOLIA

also included in many day trips to Soğanlı. Strangely enough no buses continue down the road to Soğanlı.

SOĞANLI

The twin valleys of Soğanlı, about 30km south of Mustafapaşa, are much less visited than Göreme or Zelve. Indeed, in recent years the number of visitors to Soğanlı has actually diminished, probably because it's on the road to nowhere. It's a beautiful and interesting place to explore, and unless your visit coincides with one of the day trips from Göreme, you may well have the valleys to yourself.

To reach Soğanlı turn off the main road from Mustafapaşa to Yeşilhisar and proceed 5km to the village, paying an admission fee of US$1.75 near the *Soğanlı Restaurant*, which boasts tables set under shady trees and sometimes reasonable food at reasonable prices. The village square is backed by the *Kapadokya Restaurant,* toilets, a teahouse and a line of women selling knitted gloves and socks, and the dolls for which Soğanlı is supposedly famous. Facing the square is the solitary pension, the tiny *Emek*.

The Churches

The valleys of **Aşağı Soğanlı** (Lower Onion Valley) and **Yukarı Soğanlı** (Upper Onion Valley) were largely monastic, like Göreme and Zelve. Their ancient rock-cut churches are open from 8.30 am to 5.30 pm.

At the point where the valleys divide a billboard indicates all the churches. Signs point to the **Tokalı Kilise** (Buckle Church), on the right, reached by a steep flight of worn steps, and the **Gök Kilise** (Sky Church), to the left across the valley floor. The Gök has twin naves separated by columns and ending in apses. The double frieze of saints is badly worn.

Of the other churches, one of the most interesting is No 4, the **Karabaş** (Black Head), in the right-hand valley and covered in paintings showing the life of Christ, with Gabriel and various saints. A pigeon in the fresco reflects the importance of pigeons to the monks, who wooed them with dovecotes cut in the rock. Many of the dovecotes have

white paint around their small windows to attract the birds; the sides of the entrance are smoothed so the birds cannot alight, but must enter. Inside, a grid of poles provides roosting space for hundreds of birds, which used to dump manure by the kilo onto the floor below. The monks gathered the manure, put it on the grapevines and got the sweetest grapes and the best wine for miles around. In the yard between the Karabaş church and the dovecote is a refectory, with clay ovens in the ground (note the air-holes for the fires). The monks lived alone but dined communally.

Also in the right-hand valley, across the valley floor and high on the far hillside, are the **Kubbeli and Saklı** (Cupola and Hidden Churches). The Kubbeli is interesting because of its unusual eastern-style cupola cut clean out of the rock. The Hidden Church is just that: hidden from view until you get close to it.

Farthest up the right-hand valley is the **Yılanlı** (Snake Church), its frescoes deliberately painted over with black paint, probably to protect them. You can still make out the serpent to the left as you enter.

Getting There & Away

It's not easy to get to Soğanlı by public transport. Buses run from Ürgüp to Mustafapaşa and no further, so you could try to hitch from there, or take a taxi. Otherwise you must take a bus from Kayseri to Yeşilhisar and thence to Soğanlı. The easiest way to get there, of course, is to sign up for a day tour costing roughly US$25.

SULTAN MARSHES BIRD PARADISE
☎ 352

At the Sultan Marshes Bird Paradise (Sultan Sazlığı Kuş Cenneti), 35km south-east of Soğanlı, well over 250 species of birds, including cranes, eagles, herons, spoonbills and storks have been recorded. Unfortunately a visit is likely to be both time-consuming and pricey.

Unless you have your own car or can find enough people to arrange a private excursion through a Cappadocian travel agency, you will first need to take a Yeşilhisar bus from Kayseri and then an onward bus to Ovaçiftliği, the very simple village on the edge of the marshes. Here an observation tower offers good views across the marshy lake, Eğri Göl, and a fairly risible 'museum' about the local bird life.

Sultan Pansion & Camping (*☎/fax 658 5549*) offers bed and breakfast for about US$10 per person. If you want to take a boat on the lake they can arrange it for US$30 for two people (US$40 for four), but you'll need to make an early start. Readers have also recommended **Atilla's Pension** (*☎ 658 5576*).

North of Eğri Göl is Yay Gölü, a lake noted for the big flocks of flamingos that arrive every summer. Sultan Pansion can also arrange a boat trip on this lake for US$60 for two people (US$100 for four).

Note that there are snakes and leeches around the lakes so if you plan to walk here bring sturdy footwear.

NİĞDE
☎ 388 • pop 68,700 • elevation 1216m

Niğde, 85km south of Nevşehir, was built by the Seljuks. Backed by snowcapped mountains, Niğde is a farming centre with a small but impressive selection of historic buildings.

İstasyon Caddesi is the main axis of the commercial district, bounded by Cumhuriyet Meydanı, the main traffic roundabout at its western end, and a hill bearing the lofty *saat kulesi* (clock tower), kale and the Alaeddin Camii near its eastern end.

The otogar is 1km north-east of İstasyon Caddesi, the train station 1km south-east. Look around Atatürk Meydanı for hotels, restaurants and shops, and on the aptly named Bankalar Caddesi for banks. The tourist office (☎ 232 3393, fax 232 2326) is on İstiklal Caddesi, just off the main square.

The Dünya Internet Cafe at Çetintürk Sitesi on Bor Caddesi has a remarkable 52 terminals and charges US$1 an hour.

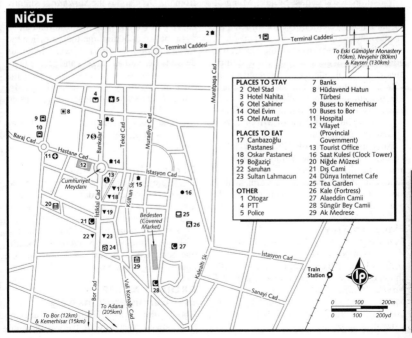

Things to See

The Seljuk **Alaeddin Camii** (1223), on the hill crowned with the fortress, is the town's grandest mosque but the **Süngür Bey Camii**, on a terrace at the end of the marketplace, is more interesting.

Built by the Seljuks but restored by the Mongols in 1335, the Süngür Bey Camii is a curious and affecting blend of architectural styles. The rose window above the northern entrance has a six-pointed 'Star of David', a motif used elsewhere in the building, and all the ground-floor windows are slightly different. The wooden doors are finely carved.

Recent restorations have done wonders for the exterior stonework but have filled the interior with ugly reinforced concrete, which breaks the spell cast by this ancient work. Look particularly at the mihrab, which is wonderfully carved and almost Chinese in appearance.

The attractive **Ak Medrese** (1409) is in a transitional style: post-Seljuk, Mongol, Beylik, with an ogee arch above the main portal. It houses a cultural centre which may or may not be open when you arrive.

In **Niğde Müzesi**, west of the Dış Cami, pride of place goes to the 10th-century mummy of a blonde nun discovered in the 1960s in Yılanlı church in the Ihlara Valley. The museum also houses finds from the excavations at Acem Höyük and Köşk (Bahçeli) Höyük but at the time of writing it was closed for restoration.

Also take a look at the **Hüdavend Hatun Türbesi** (1312), a fine Seljuk tomb with human-headed monsters carved on the facade; and at the Ottoman **Dış Cami**, which has a carved mimber inlaid with mother-of-pearl.

Places to Stay

Otel Stad (☎ 213 7866, Yeni Terminal Yanı), one block west of the otogar, charges US$8/13 for a basic single/ double with shower. Also west of the otogar, the *Hotel Nahita* (☎ 232 5366, Terminal Caddesi) boasts a bar, and rooms priced at US$12/17, breakfast included, but it's sadly in need of a facelift.

Of the hotels in the centre, the real cheapies are not at all appealing. The new *Otel Sahiner* (☎ 232 2121, Ziraat Bankası Karşısı) is probably the best choice with comfortable rooms for US$15/29 with shower. *Otel Murat* (☎ 213 3978, Eski Belediye Yanı 5), with its facade on the main street but its entrance at the back, has perfectly serviceable rooms for US$10/15 (less without shower).

The three-star *Otel Evim* (☎ 232 3536, fax 232 1526, Cumhuriyet Meydanı) has a lift, and simple but comfortable rooms with baths for US$30/40, breakfast included – open to negotiation.

Places to Eat

For a decent meal head south along İstiklal Caddesi. Very popular with families is the *Boğazici* which serves kebabs and excellent pides for just US$2. Further along the road is the cheerful *Sultan Lahmacun*, serving just what its name suggests. Across the road from the Dış Cami is the *Saruhan*, a slightly overbright place which is trying hard to serve cheap pides and kebaps in a restored han.

In the street behind the tourist office the *Canbazoğlu Pastanesi* serves delicious desserts (as well as burgers and pizza) in an inviting upstairs aile salonu – ignore the off-putting grungy stair carpet. The nearby *Oskar Pastanesi* is where the local cops go for breakfast.

Niğde has a surprising number of *beer houses* – look for them behind the Otel Evim.

Getting There & Away

There are frequent bus services from the otogar at Niğde to Adana (US$6, three hours, 205km), Aksaray (US$2, 1½ hours, 115km), Kayseri (US$4.25, 1½ hours, 130km) and Konya (US$8.50, 3½ hours, 250km). Minibuses to Nevşehir (US$2.50, one hour, 85km) depart every hour on the hour from 5 am to 6 pm.

AROUND NİĞDE
Eski Gümüşler Monastery

About 10km east of Niğde is the ancient rock-hewn monastery of Eski Gümüşler, with some of the best-preserved paintings in Cappadocia. The village of Gümüşler itself is in rich apple country, which yield mountains of fruit in October.

The Eski Gümüşler monastery was only rediscovered in 1963. You reach it along a rock-cut passage that opens onto a large courtyard surrounded by rock-hewn dwellings, crypts, a kitchen and a refectory with deep reservoirs for wine and oil. A small hole in the ground acts as a vent for a mysterious 9m-deep shaft beneath.

The lofty main church has wonderful Byzantine frescoes painted between the 7th and 11th centuries. The Virgin and Child to the right of the apse is particularly affecting, with the elongated Mary given a Mona Lisa smile. The church's great columns are completely unnecessary, but were left when the rock was cut away to mimic the appearance of a traditional church. The cross-hatch motif was favoured during the Iconoclastic period (725–842) when sacred images were prohibited and artists resorted to geometrical designs, a preference soon picked up by Islam.

The monastery is open in summer from 9 am to noon and from 1.30 to 6.30 pm daily; from October to May it's open from 8 am to noon and 1.30 to 5.30 pm. Admission costs US$1.75.

Hourly Gümüşler Belediyesi minibuses (US$0.30, 15 minutes) depart from the minibus depot beside Niğde's otogar.

Kemerhisar

Kemerhisar, site of the Roman town of Tyana, is 15km south-west of Niğde. Of ancient Tyana few traces now remain with the exception of the dramatic *su kemer* or **aqueduct** that stretches along the road for almost a kilometre to neighbouring Bahçeli, providing a garden wall and gates for innumerable houses.

Hourly buses to Kemerhisar via Bor (US$0.50, 30 minutes) depart from immediately behind the Hüdavend Hatun Türbesi in Niğde. Get out when you see the 'welcome to Kemerhisar' sign, cross the road and bear left behind the cemetery and petrol station to find the aqueduct.

KARAMAN
☎ 338

After the fall of the Great Seljuk Empire central Anatolia was split into several different provinces with different governments, and for some time Karaman served as a regional capital. Although little visited these days, it boasts a selection of fine 13th- and 14th-century buildings and makes a base for excursions to Binbirkilise (see the Around Karaman section, following).

Things to See

The **Hacıbeyler Camii**, dating from 1358, has a magnificent squared-off entrance with decoration that looks like a baroque variant on Seljuk art. The **Mader-i Mevlâna (Aktepe) Cami** dating from 1370 is the burial place of the great Mevlâna's mother and has a dervish-style felt hat carved above its entrance. The adjacent **hamam** is still in use (open to women on Wednesday).

The **İbrahim II Bey Imareti**, built in 1423, has a partially tiled minaret. Behind it is a conical tomb with a stork's nest on top.

The tomb of the great Turkish poet Yunus Emre (1320) is beside the **Yunus Emre Camii**. Extracts from his verses are carved into the walls of a poetry garden to the rear.

Karaman Müzesi houses finds from nearby Taşkale and Canhasan and has a fine ethnography section. It's housed behind the magnificent frontage of the **Hatuniye Medresesi**, built in 1382 and one of the finest examples of Karaman art. The museum is open from 8 am to noon and 1.30 to 5.30 pm, daily except Monday; admission costs US$1.75.

Places to Stay & Eat

Karaman is not geared for tourists, which means it has several really rough budget hotels along the main street and one two-star hotel, the *Nas Otel* (☎ 213 8200, İsmetpaşa Caddesi 30), which is inclined to ask a hefty US$27 a head for comfortable rooms, subject to bargaining.

There's a selection of simple eateries along İsmetpaşa Caddesi, none of them especially memorable. Coffee, snacks and Internet access are available at the *Pusula Cafe* on Yunus Emre Caddesi.

Getting There & Away

Frequent buses link Karaman with Konya (US$3.50, two hours, 113km) and Ereğli (US$2.50, two hours, 118km). Onward buses from Ereğli to Niğde are few and far between.

AROUND KARAMAN

Just before WWI the great British traveller Gertrude Bell travelled to **Binbirkilise**, 42km north-west of Karaman, and recorded the existence of a cluster of Byzantine churches set high up on a lonely hillside and rather generously known as Binbirkilise or One Thousand and One Churches. You can still visit today and find goats and tortoises peacefully grazing amid the ruins.

It's easiest to reach the churches with your own transport. Drive out of Karaman on the Karapınar road and turn off at the yellow sign on the left saying 'Binbirkilise 5km' (in fact it's more like 15km). The first sizeable ruin pops up in the village of Madenşehir after which the road becomes increasingly rough.

Without a car you'll probably have to take a taxi from Karaman otogar for around US$35 for the return trip; the taxi drivers know where the churches are.

From Nevşehir to Ankara

Most buses from Nevşehir to Ankara take the fast road skirting the Tuz Gölü (Salt Lake). With more time on your hands you could make a day of it and travel north-west via the small towns of Gülşehir, Hacıbektaş and Kırşehir.

GÜLŞEHİR

☎ 384 • pop 9000

Gülşehir, 19km north of Nevşehir, is a sleepy small town with several rocky attractions nearby.

Right in the centre of town stands the Ottoman **Karavezir Mehmet Paşa Camii & Medrese** (1778). On the southern outskirts is the impressive **Karşı Kilise**, or church of St John, with some of the best local frescoes. A good 4km south-west of Gülşehir is the **Açık Saray** (Open Palace), with a fine rock-cut monastery and a strange mushroom-shaped rock formation.

Gülşehir ought to be well-placed to cash in on the new Nevşehir airport at nearby Tuzköy. On our most recent research visit, however, the manager of the comfortable **Kepez Hotel** (☎ 411 3163, fax 411 3639) – the crenellated building on the flat hilltop in the centre of town – declined to show us around his empty hotel which, with its barbed-wire gate and beware-of-the-dog notice, had a Colditz air about it.

If you must stay, the **Hotel Gülşehir** (☎ 411 3028, fax 411 3906) 1km out on the road north to Hacıbektaş might prove more welcoming.

Getting There & Away

At the time of writing there were twice-weekly flights from İstanbul to and from Cappadocia's new airport at Tuzköy, 12km north-west of Gülşehir. Tour groups will be met and transferred from the airport to their hotels, almost certainly south in Göreme, Avanos, Uçhisar or Ürgüp. Otherwise you can arrange a private transfer through Argeus Tours in Ürgüp (☎ 348-341 4688, fax 341 4888, @ inform@argeus.com.tr).

You can pick up a bus or dolmuş to Gülşehir from outside the Alibey Camii in Nevşehir (US$0.75, 20 minutes). If you just want to scramble round the Açık Saray, ask to be dropped off on the road before Gülşehir to save the walk back. Onward buses to Hacıbektaş leave from Gülşehir's small otogar opposite the Karavazir Mehmet Paşa Camii (US$0.85, 30 minutes).

HACIBEKTAŞ

☎ 384

Hacıbektaş is right on the edge of Cappadocia, 27.5km north-west of Gülşehir. For most of the year it slumbers undisturbed, then from 16–18 August it bursts into life to host the annual festival in memory of Hacı Bektaş Veli, founder and spiritual leader of the Bektaşi order of dervishes (see the boxed text for more information), an extremely

CARAVANSERAIS & HANS

Literally 'caravan palace', the grand Seljuk Turkish *kervansaray* was a luxury 'motel' on the 13th-century Silk Road through Anatolia.

The Seljuk sultans of Rum, with their capital at Konya, realised the importance of commerce to the prosperity of their empire, so they built camel caravan staging posts a day's travel (about 15km to 30km) apart to facilitate trade. Expenses for construction and maintenance of the caravanserais were borne by the crown, and paid for by the taxes levied on the rich trade in goods.

The finest examples of Seljuk caravanserais are the Sultanhanı (the largest in Anatolia) 45km west of Aksaray on the Konya-Aksaray highway, the Sarıhan 6km east of Avanos, and the Karatay Han 48km east of Kayseri on the Pınarbaşı-Malatya highway. Dozens of other caravanserais dot the Anatolian landscape, including the Ağzıkarahan 13km east of Aksaray on the Nevşehir highway, and the Sultan Han 45km north-east of Kayseri off the Sivas highway.

The typical Seljuk caravanserai is a monumental stone building with a huge, highly decorated main portal which provided access through the two-storey-high buttressed walls to a large open court and a slightly smaller, but still grand and lofty, vaulted hall.

The open court, where the caravans loaded and unloaded, was surrounded by rooms which served as refectory, treasury, repair shop, accounting and exchange office, store rooms, hamams for men and women, and toilets. In the centre of the open court, raised to second storey level on stone piers, there might be a *mescit* (small mosque) to

Inset: Detail of stairway in the Sarıhan

Bottom: The impressive Seljuk-era Sarıhan or Yellow Caravanserai has been restored and is now open as a museum. In summer, it's the venue for nightly performances of dervish dancing.

BOTH PHOTOS BY OLIVIER CIRENDINI

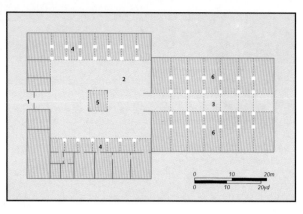

Sultanhanı
1 Main portal
2 Large open court
3 Vaulted hall
4 Refectory, treasury, repair shop, accounting and exchange office, store rooms, hamams for men and women and toilets
5 Mescit (small mosque)
6 Shelter for people and goods in bad weather

serve the travellers. In some caravanserais the mescit is above the grand main portal; in others it is in a room off the court. The vaulted hall was used to shelter people and goods in bad weather.

When the valuable cargoes reached cities and towns, the caravan unloaded in the urban equivalent of the caravanserai, called a han. Here the plan was more simple: a two-storey building, usually square, surrounding an open court with a fountain or raised mescit at its centre. On the upper storey, behind an open arcaded gallery, were offices and rooms for lodging and dining.

The most beautiful hans are the early Ottoman ones in Bursa – the Koza Han and Emir Han – but in fact every Anatolian town has at least a few hans in its market district. İstanbul's vast Kapalı Çarşı is surrounded by dozens of hans still used by traders and artisans.

Though the Ottomans built hundreds of hans in cities, their vast empire, with its command of the sea lanes, had less need for caravanserais, so they did not extend the Seljuk network.

The grand portal of the Karatay Han (1219-40), near Kayseri: Inside is a fine unmarked tomb.

Hacı Bektaş Veli & the Bektaşi Sect

Born in Nishapur in Iran sometime in the 13th century, Hacı Bektaş Veli inspired a religious and political following that blended aspects of Islam (both Sunni and Shiite) with Orthodox Christianity. During his life he is known to have travelled around Anatolia and to have lived in Kayseri, Sivas and Kırşehir, but eventually he settled in the hamlet which is now the small town of Hacıbektaş.

Although not much is known about Hacı Bektaş himself, the book he wrote, the *Makalât*, describes a mystical philosophy less austere than mainstream Islam. In it he laid out a four-stage path to enlightenment (the Four Doors). During the first stage dervishes came to know the difference between right and wrong. In the second they prayed constantly. In the third they came to understand God's love. During the fourth and final stage they arrived at an understanding of reality through constant awareness of God and through self-effacement. Though often scorned by mainstream Islamic clerics, Bektaşi dervishes attained considerable political and religious influence in Ottoman times. Along with all the other dervishes, they were outlawed in 1925.

The Bektaşi spiritual philosophy developed in the borderlands between the Turkish and Byzantine empires, where guerrilla fighters from both sides had more in common with one another than they had with their sovereigns in Konya or Constantinople. Their liberal beliefs caught on with the common people, and Bektaşi ideas are still important to the Alevis today. Every August, in what has been described as a 'mini haj', up to 100,000 believers descend on the saint's tomb in Hacıbektaş. His rehabilitation has been so complete that these days politicians try to muscle in alongside the singing and dancing with speeches claiming the great man for themselves.

important event to the modern Alevi community. Politicians tend to hijack the first day's proceedings, but days two and three are given over to music and dance. During the festival Göreme travel agencies sometimes organise special day trips. Watch out around town; the Pathfinder travel agency (☎ 271 2910) is one possibility.

Hacıbektaş Müzesi

Normally you come to Hacıbektaş to see the **Hacıbektaş Müzesi**, set up around the tomb of the great man and open from 8 am to noon and from 1.30 to 5 pm daily except Monday. Admission costs US$1.75.

Several rooms are arranged as they might have been when the dervishes lived here, including the **Aş Evi**, or kitchen, with its outsize implements, and the **Meydan Evi**, where novice dervishes were inducted into the order. Other rooms display musical instruments, costumes, embroidery, turbans and other artefacts of the order, as well as relevant old photographs.

Remove your shoes before stepping inside the **saint's tomb** in the garden at the far end of the building, as this is a place of prayer. Needless to say, the area around the shrine is awash with stalls selling Lourdes-style religious paraphernalia. Clock showing the Twelve Imams, anyone?

Immediately across the road the new cultural centre, the **Hacıbektaş Veli Kültür Merkezi**, about which visiting politicians love to brag, is still being built a good five years after work first began.

Places to Stay & Eat

If you're planning a visit in August around the time of the annual pilgrimage, you'll need to plan well ahead as Hacıbektaş is down to its last hotel.

Across the street from the shrine, down the steps leading behind the row of small shops is the simple *Hotel Hünkar* (☎ *411 3344*), with clean rooms (with bath) for US$9 a head without breakfast, a price surely negotiable except in August.

Getting There & Away

At least one bus a day from Nevşehir to Ankara passes through Hacıbektaş. Alternatively, you can pick up a Kırşehir Belediyesi minibus from Gülşehir (US$0.85, 30 minutes) which also passes through. The last bus back to Nevşehir leaves at 5 pm.

KIRŞEHİR
☎ 386 • pop 75,000

Midway along the road from Ankara to Cappadocia lies Kırşehir, an ancient city, now a provincial capital with a few old buildings and several cheap, basic hotels. Kırşehir was famous in Ottoman times as the centre of the mystical Ahi (Akhi) brotherhoods, the Muslim equivalent of the Masonic lodges. The Ahi brotherhoods were founded in the 14th century as secret religious societies among members of the crafts guilds, particularly the tanners' guild. Their political power grew to a point where sultans had to reckon with them. The founding father and inspiration for the Ahi brotherhoods was Ahi Evran (1236–1329), a tanner whose family came from Horasan. He lived and died in Kırşehir and his tomb is a Muslim place of pilgrimage.

Orientation & Information

The city centre is Cumhuriyet Meydanı, the main traffic roundabout with a modern clock tower. Almost everything you'll need is within a five-minute walk of the roundabout. The main commercial street running out of the square is Ankara Caddesi, with the PTT a few steps along it. Hotels, restaurants and the Ahi Evran Türbesi are a short walk further along Ankara Caddesi. The Cacabey Camii is on the opposite side of Cumhuriyet Meydanı from Ankara Caddesi.

The otogar is 1.5km south of the centre. Local buses stop rather more conveniently within 100m of Cumhuriyet Meydanı.

The tourist office (☎ 213 1416, fax 213 6808), Cumhuriyet Meydanı, Aşık Paşa Bulvarı, is right in the city centre but the chances of finding it open are minimal.

Things to See

The Ahi Evran Camii ve Türbesi (Ahi Evran Mosque & Tomb), also called the Ahi Evran Zaviyesi (Dervish Lodge), are simple stone structures, obviously very old. Pilgrims in their 'Friday best' are usually crowded into the small rooms in prayer.

Just off the traffic roundabout is the brown and white Cacabey Camii, built by the Seljuk Turks in 1272 as a meteorolo-gical observatory and theological college and now used as a mosque with a wonderful gateway. The Alaettin Camii also dates from Seljuk times, and there are several 14th-century tombs dotted about town.

Places to Stay & Eat

The Otel Anadolu (☎ 213 1826, Ankara Caddesi 20), across the main street from the Ahi Evran Camii, has well-worn rooms with bath for US$8/12 a single/double. The neighbouring Otel Banana (☎ 213 1879) is virtually identical.

Going upmarket, the three-star Büyük Otel Terme (☎ 212 2404, Terme Caddesi), on the outskirts of town near the Terme Kaplıcaları hot springs, offers bath-equipped rooms for US$30/42. Follow the signs to find it.

Meşhur Kebap 49, with döner kebaps for US$2.50, is more or less opposite the Otel Banana, while the Sofra Lokantası is down an alley beside it.

Getting There & Away

In summer four buses a day travel to and from Kırşehir from Nevşehir, making a day trip possible.

KAYSERİ
☎ 352 • pop 425,000

Standing in the shadow of Erciyes Dağı (Mt Argeus, 3916m) and the Kara Dağı (Black Mountain), Kayseri, 105km due east of Nevşehir, used to be a sleepy, conservative town, but is rapidly metamorphosing into a bustling city of modern, apartment-lined boulevards. These two aspects of Kayseri aren't completely comfortable together, and something of the city's old conservative soul lingers. After 9 pm, for example, many restaurants shut up shop, and lone female visitors seem to be viewed with wholly unnecessary suspicion – it's not wise for them to walk the streets alone after 10 pm.

Most people whip through Kayseri en route to Cappadocia and certainly the off-putting approach roads hardly encourage anyone to linger here. However, not only does the city have enough sights of its own to fill a day, it also makes a good base for

KAYSERİ

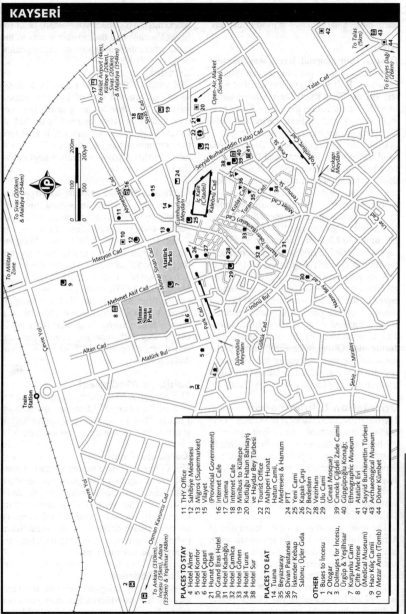

PLACES TO STAY
4 Hotel Almer
5 Hotel Konfor
6 Hotel Çapari
21 Hunat Oteli
30 Grand Eras Hotel
31 Hotel Kadıoğlu
32 Hotel Camlıca
33 Hotel Gönen
34 Hotel Turan
38 Hotel Sur

PLACES TO EAT
14 Tuana
35 Beyazsaray
36 Divan Pastanesi
37 İskender Kebap
   Salonu; Üçler Gıda

OTHER
1 Buses to İncesu
2 Otogar
3 Dolmuşes for İncesu,
   Ürgüp & Yeşilhisar
7 Kurşunlu Cami
8 Çifte Medrese
   (Medical Museum)
9 Hacı Kılıç Camii
10 Mezar Anıtı (Tomb)
11 THY Office
12 Sahibiye Medresesi
13 Migros (Supermarket)
15 Vilayet
   (Provincial Government)
16 Internet Cafe
17 Cinema
18 Internet Cafe
19 Minibus to Kültepe
20 Kurtuluğu Hatun Bahsayiş
   ve Haydar Bey Türbesi
22 Tourist Office
23 Mahperi Hunat
   Hatun Camii
   Medresesi & Hamam
24 PTT
25 Yeni Cami
26 Kapalı Çarşı
27 Bedesten
28 Vezirhanı
29 Ulu Cami
   (Great Mosque)
39 Cıncıklı Çiğdeli Zade Camii
40 Güpgüpoğlu Konağı;
   Ethnographic Museum
41 Atatürk Evi
42 Sayyid Burhanettin Türbesi
43 Archaeological Museum
44 Döner Kümbet

exploring the surrounding area, with frequent buses and dolmuşes in most directions.

History

The first Hittite capital, Kaniş, was the chief city of the Hatti people and you can visit the remains at Kültepe, 20km north-east of Kayseri, off the Sivas road. There was probably an early settlement on the site of Kayseri as well, though the earliest traces that have come to light are from Hellenistic times.

Under the Roman emperor Tiberius (AD 14–37), the town was renamed Caesarea. It later became famous as the birthplace of St Basil the Great, who was responsible for organising the monastic life of Cappadocia. Its early Christian history was interrupted by Arab invasions from the 7th century. The Seljuks took over in 1084 and held the city until the Mongols' arrival in 1243, except for a brief period when the crusaders captured it on their way to the Holy Land.

After Kayseri had been part of the Mongol Empire for almost 100 years, its Mongol governor set up his own emirate (1335) that lasted a mere 45 years. It was succeeded by another emirate (that of Seyyid Burhaneddin), then captured by the Ottomans (seized during the Ottoman interregnum by the Karamanid emirs), taken by the Mamluks, and finally conquered by the Ottomans again in 1515, all in just over 100 years.

Orientation & Information

The basalt-walled citadel at the centre of the old town just south of Cumhuriyet Meydanı, the huge main square, is a good landmark. Another convenient point of reference is Düvenönü Meydanı, 350m west of the citadel along Park Caddesi. Mimar Sinan Parkı, a vast expanse north of Park Caddesi, has some of the city's most outstanding Seljuk buildings.

The train station is at the northern end of Atatürk Bulvarı, over half a kilometre north of Düvenönü Meydanı. Kayseri's otogar is just under 2km north-west of the citadel along Osman Kavuncu Caddesi.

The helpful tourist office (☎ 222 3903, fax 222 0879) is beside the Hatun Hunat Mahperi Camii, and is open from 8.30 am to 5.30 pm daily in summer (closed winter weekends). To collect your email, head for Sivas Caddesi and the smaller streets to the north where there are heaps of Internet cafes.

Citadel

The walls of the citadel (*hisar* or *iç kale*) were constructed out of black volcanic stone by Emperor Justinian in the 6th century, and extensively repaired by the Seljuk sultan Keykavus I around 1224. In 1486, the Ottoman sultan Mehmet the Conqueror made further repairs, a practice kept up by the modern city fathers.

Mahperi Hunat Hatun Complex

Kayseri has several important building complexes which were founded by Seljuk queens and princesses. East of the Hisar is a complex which includes the Mahperi Hunat Hatun Camii (1228), built by the wife of the Seljuk sultan Alaettin Keykubat.

Next to the mosque is the Hunat Hatun Medresesi (1237), currently closed to the public. Within the medrese is Lady Mahperi Hunat's tomb, an octagonal room with a high-domed ceiling. The Turkish bath is still in use, with separate sections for men and women (open from 8.30 am to 5 pm daily, longer for men).

Sahibiye Medresesi

The Sahibiye Medresesi, on the northern side of Cumhuriyet Meydanı, dates from 1267 and has an especially beautiful Seljuk gateway. It's now used as a book bazaar.

Kurşunlu Cami

The Ottoman-style Kurşunlu Cami (Lead-Domed Mosque) stands just north of Park Caddesi and west of Cumhuriyet Meydanı. Also called the Ahmet Paşa Camii after its founder, it was completed in 1585 possibly following plans drawn up by the great Sinan (who was born in a nearby village), but certainly influenced by him.

Çifte Medrese

Two adjoining religious schools, the Gıyasiye ve Şifaiye Medreseleri, are sometimes called the Twin Seminaries. Set in Mimar

Sinan Parkı north of Park Caddesi, they were founded at the bequest of the Seljuk sultan Giyasettin I Keyhüsrev and his sister Gevher Nesibe Sultan (1165–1204), daughter of the great sultan Kılıçaslan. Today they house a **museum of medical history**.

Princess Gevher Nesibe Sultan is entombed in a chamber on the right side of the courtyard with a *mescit* (prayer-room) above it. Topping the mescit outside is a Seljuk-style dome surrounded by an inscription in Arabic which instructs the medrese's administration to accept medical students and patients into the seminary without regard to religion: Muslim, Jew and Christian were to study and be healed side by side.

A doorway on the left side of the courtyard leads to the medical section, which gives fascinating insights into the medical practices of the 13th-century Seljuks. Look out for a replica of an original stone carving of snakes (symbols of medicine and healing since ancient times) and the Seljuk *çark-ı felek* (wheel of fortune), which determined someone's fate in life and presumably their chances of recovering from disease.

The **Ameliyathane** (Operating Room) has a hole in the ceiling which acted as a 'spotlight' on the patient during operations (presumably Seljuk doctors only operated on sunny days). In the **Akıl Hastanesi** (Mental Hospital) is a suite of tiny cells for mental patients, who were kept one to a cell if violent, an unbelievable four to a cell otherwise.

The central heating system for the hamam, combined with an insulating layer of earth on top of the roof, kept the entire medical side of the building warm during Kayseri's sometimes freezing winters. The rooftop earth was used to grow vegetables and fruits to feed the patients. After it was removed during restoration, water penetrated the ceilings below and caused the plaster to flake. The Seljuks knew more about preservation than we do.

The museum is open from 8 am to noon and 1 to 5 pm Wednesday to Sunday; admission costs US$1.75. Most of the signs explaining Seljuk medical practices are in Turkish only, which is disappointing, as is the state of many of the exhibits.

Hacı Kılıç Camii

North of the Çifte Medrese on İstasyon Caddesi is the Hacı Kılıç Camii (1249) built for the Seljuk vizier Abdülgazi and with some fine Seljuk architectural detail, especially in the doorways.

Ulu Cami

Kayseri's Great Mosque is near Düvenönü Meydanı. It was begun in 1142 by the Danışmend Turkish emirs and finished by the Seljuks in 1205. Despite all the 'restoration' over the centuries, it's still a good example of early Seljuk style.

Seljuk Tombs

Scattered about Kayseri are several conical tombs dating from Seljuk times. Most famous is the so-called **Döner Kümbet** (Revolving Tomb), about 1km south-east of the Hisar along Talas Caddesi, but you'll spot many others as you walk around.

Archaeological Museum

The city's small, neglected Archaeological Museum, not far from the Döner Kümbet, houses the finds from Kültepe (ancient Kaniş-Karum), including baked cuneiform tablets which told historians much about the Hittite Empire. Opening hours are from 8 am to noon and from 1 to 5 pm daily except Monday; admission costs US$1.75.

Historic Houses

Just south-east of the citadel is the wonderful **Güpgüpoğlu Konağı**, a fine stone mansion dating from the 18th century, now housing the city's **Ethnographic Museum**. The sofa (main hall), bride's room, kitchen and guest room have been decorated in period style, and the fine woodwork on the ceilings and walls has been beautifully restored.

The house was home to Ahmet Mithat Güpgüpoğlu, a poet, composer and officer in the Ottoman government. His son Arif Güpgüpoğlu founded Anatolia's first maternity and paediatric hospital in 1921.

Nearby is the smaller **Atatürk Evi**, where Atatürk stayed when he visited Kayseri. The first floor rooms are attractively decorated in early 20th-century style.

Both houses are open from 8 am to 5 pm daily except Monday. Admission to each costs US$1.75.

Places to Stay – Budget

You won't get much cheaper than *Hunat Oteli* (☎ 232 4319, Zengin Sokak 5), behind the Hunat Mosque and near the tourist office. It's quiet, clean and convenient, with waterless rooms for US$7 per person. The proprietor, Ömer Bey, is a kindly soul well used to travellers, but some single women might find this place a bit too basic.

Hotel Gönen (☎ 222 2778, fax 231 6584, Nazmi Toker Caddesi 15), on a busy shopping street, posts prices of US$20/30 for a single/double, but may be ready to negotiate.

Hotel Sur (☎ 222 4367, fax 231 3992, Talas Caddesi 12) is conveniently positioned just inside the city walls. Rooms on the street side have windows but are liable to be noisy; those on the inside have no windows but will be quieter. Rooms are pretty expensive at US$26/32 with private shower but try bartering. To find it, look up above the walls for the illuminated sign.

The smart *Hotel Turan* (☎ 222 5537, fax 231 1153, Turan Caddesi 8) is an old faithful which has served travellers for many decades. Some of the spacious rooms have bathtubs instead of showers. They usually cost US$18/28 but the staff may be ready to haggle if business is slack. The top-floor breakfast room has pleasant views of Erciyes Dağı.

Hotel Çamlıca (☎ 231 4344, Bankalar Caddesi, Gürcü Sokak 14) is tidy and fairly quiet, with serviceable rooms for US$12 a head with sink, US$16 with shower.

Hotel Kadıoğlu (☎ 231 6320, fax 222 8296, Kiçikapı Serdar Caddesi 45), more or less across the street from the Kayseri Lisesi, offers views of Erciyes Dağı. from its noisy front rooms – there are quieter rooms at the back – all for US$18/30.

Places to Stay – Mid-Range

Kayseri has several serviceable if potentially noisy hotels around Düvenönü Meydanı, all with private baths and TVs, and including breakfast in their prices.

The *Hotel Çapari* (☎ 222 5278, fax 222 5282, Donanma Caddesi 12) is a good choice, hidden on a quiet backstreet one block north-east of Düvenönü Meydanı. Cheerful rooms cost US$33/50 a single/double.

The *Hotel Konfor* (☎ 320 0184, fax 336 5100, Atatürk Bulvarı 5) has car parking at the rear of the building and comfortable rooms for US$26/40.

Facing Düvenönü Meydanı on its western side is the three-star *Hotel Almer* (☎ 320 7970, fax 320 7974, Osman Kavuncu Caddesi 15). Modern rooms with TV, minibar and air-con cost US$50/75. Unfortunately, the staff are tip-hungry and you must check your bills carefully.

Places to Stay – Top End

The four-star *Grand Eras Hotel* (☎ 330 5111, fax 330 4949, Şehit Miralay Nazım Bey Caddesi 6) offers rooms with air-con and all the trimmings in a reasonably quiet but central location. Singles/doubles/triples cost US$75/90/120.

Places to Eat

Kayseri boasts a few special dishes, among them *pastırma* – salted, sun-dried veal coated with *çemen,* a spicy concoction of garlic, red peppers, parsley and water. It takes about a month to prepare, has a very strong flavour, tends to stick in your teeth and rules your breath despotically for hours afterwards. The darker the pastırma, the longer it has been allowed to age. Many shops in the centre sell it, among them *Üçler Gıda*, at street level in the same building as the İskender Kebap Salonu.

İskender Kebap Salonu (Millet Caddesi 5), just inside the city walls and one floor above street level, has been serving good Bursa-style döner kebap for several decades. It has a pleasing view of the busy street, and low prices of about US$3 to US$4 for a meal of kebap, ayran and salad. The general dining room is one flight up, the aile salonu up a second.

Across the road is the *Beyazsaray (Millet Caddesi 8)* where the İskender kebap is just as good and costs about the same.

There's a very popular takeaway place downstairs.

Facing the Beyazsaray is the **Divan Pastanesi** *(Millet Caddesi)*, a popular pastry shop. Try their *şam fıstıklı baklava* (pastry layers stuffed with pistachio nuts and soaked in syrup) and a large glass of tea for about US$2. There's a second branch on Sivas Caddesi.

Behind the post office facing Cumhuriyet Meydanı is a block of fast food and takeaway kebap places. Upstairs is the attractive **Tuana** *(Sivas Caddesi)*, whose big, bright dining room offers a great view towards Erciyes. Tuana is popular with the business fraternity but prices are still reasonable – US$4 for *kiremit tavuk* (chicken baked on a tile) with a soft drink. The entrance is via a lift on the south side of the block.

Shopping

Set at the intersection of age-old trade routes, Kayseri has been an important commercial centre for millennia and its Ottoman covered-markets beside the citadel have been beautifully restored. Even today they're great places to shop for cheap T-shirts, shoes etc.

The Bedesten, built in 1497, was first dedicated to the sale of textiles, but now sells all sorts of things. The Vezirhanı was constructed in 1727 on the orders of Damat İbrahim Paşa, and now sells wool and cotton on the ground floor and carpets on the upper. The Kapalı Çarşı (Covered Bazaar) was built in 1859, restored in 1988, and now sells mainly gold jewellery. Look out also for the Pamuk Han or Cotton Bazaar.

If you don't find what you want in the Kapalı Çarşı, head inside the walls of the citadel for yet more streets of stalls.

Getting There & Away

Air Turkish Airlines connects Kayseri's Erkilet airport with İstanbul by two daily nonstop flights. Buy your tickets at the THY office (☎ 222 3858, fax 222 4748) at Sahibiye Mahallesi, Yıldırım Caddesi 1. An airport bus (US$1.50) connects the ticket office with the airport; catch it 1½ hours before flight departure time, or be at the airport at least 30 minutes before the scheduled departure time. Local bus No 2 also runs to the airport from Atatürk Caddesi.

Bus On an important north-south and east-west crossroads, Kayseri has lots of bus services. If there's no *servis* bus, walk out of the front of the otogar, cross the avenue and board any bus marked 'Merkez' (Centre), or take a dolmuş marked 'Şehir'. A taxi to the citadel should cost less than US$3.

The otogar has a PTT, shops and a 24-hour restaurant. Details of some useful daily services are listed in the table.

Train The *Vangölü/Güney Ekspresi* (between İstanbul and Tatvan or Diyarbakır, depending on the day) and the *Doğu Ekspresi* (between İstanbul and Kars) and *Yeni Doğu Ekspresi* stop at Kayseri, as does the *Çukurova Ekspresi* between Ankara and Adana.

To reach the centre from the train station, walk out of the station, cross the big avenue and board any bus heading down Atatürk Bulvarı to Düvenönü Meydanı.

Services from Kayseri's Otogar

destination	fare (US$)	time (hr)	distance (km)	daily services
Adana	7	5	335	several buses
Ankara	9.50	4½	330	frequent buses
Gaziantep	7	6	371	several buses
Kahramanmaraş	7	5½	291	several buses
Malatya	9	6	354	several buses
Nevşehir	3.50	1½	105	frequent buses
Sivas	5	3½	200	frequent buses
Ürgüp	2	1½	80	frequent buses

CENTRAL ANATOLIA

AROUND KAYSERİ

Kayseri makes a good base for exploring the eastern fringes of Cappadocia. Most of the places described below can be visited on easy day and half-day excursions.

Kültepe (Kaniş-Karum)

Appropriately named 'Hill of Ashes' in Turkish, this archaeological site 20km north-east of Kayseri was originally settled around 4000 BC. The town of Kaniş came to prominence during Old Bronze Age times (around 2500–2000 BC). By around 1850 BC, it was the centre of Anatolia's most powerful kingdom. The neighbouring Assyrian trading colony of Karum was among the oldest and richest bazaars in the world, specialising in metals. Eventually a great fire destroyed Kaniş-Karum. It was rebuilt and by around 1720 BC was the Hittite city of Nisa, capital of King Anitta who conquered the pre-Hittite rulers of Hattuşa (Boğazkale) and made it a Hittite city.

Kaniş-Karum is actually two sites across the road from each other. The size and height of the palace mound at Kaniş is impressive but signs warn you not to enter the excavation trenches. Across the road at Karum it's easier for the nonspecialist to pick out the houses, shops and roads of the old Assyrian colony. Since the best finds are in the Archaeological Museum in Kayseri and the Museum of Anatolian Civilisations in Ankara, it's only worth coming out here if you're very interested in the Hittites.

To get to Kültepe take a half-hourly Bünyan bus or minibus from Sivas Caddesi in Kayseri (US$0.50, 30 minutes). About 18km along, just before a BP petrol station (with a cafe and toilets), a road to the left is marked for 'Kültepe Kaniş Karum'. It's a 2km walk to the site where the custodian will find you to collect the US$1.75 admission.

Sultan Han

The Sultan Han, built in the 1230s, is a striking old Seljuk caravanserai on the old Kayseri-Sivas highway, 45km north-east of Kayseri and 1km off the new highway. Besides being a fine example of a Seljuk royal caravan lodging and the second-largest in Anatolia (after the Sultanhanı near Aksaray), it has been beautifully restored.

As you walk round, look out for the elegant snake motif on the little mosque's arches. Climb onto the roof, but don't neglect a walk around the exterior as well. Note the lion-faced water spouts on the walls, and the plain towers of varying design.

Official opening hours are from 9 am to 1 pm and from 2 to 6 pm daily except Monday, but shortly after you arrive a boy will come running with the key and a ticket; admission costs US$1.75.

To get here, take any bus or dolmuş heading along the Sivas road and ask to be put off at the Sultan Han turn-off.

Karatay Han

Yet another fine example of high Seljuk art, the Karatay Han was built from 1219 to 1236 for the Seljuk vizier Emir Celaleddin Karatay. The open court dates from 1240, during the reign of Gıyaseddin Keyhüsrev.

Inside the grand portal to the left is a fine unmarked tomb with exquisite animal figures along the top of its decoration. Inside the tomb, above the cenotaph, is a ceiling star pattern painted blue to mimic the heavens.

The new Kayseri-Pınarbaşı-Malatya highway passes right through the village of Karadayı, with the Karatay Han easily visible. Take any bus or dolmuş following the Malatya road and get out at Karadayı. The han is open whenever visitors arrive; admission costs US$0.50.

Erciyes Dağı

Erciyes Dağı, or Mt Argeus (3916m) as it was known in Roman times, is the extinct volcano 26km south of Kayseri which gave rise to the fairy chimneys of Göreme. It's one of Turkey's few **ski centres**, with a chairlift, nursery slope and ski rental facilities. Though reasonable for skiing (for Turkey), Erciyes is rather inhospitable to hikers. Treks require planning, good equipment and a guide.

From November to May the **Dedeman Erciyes Ski Centre** (☎ 352-324 2116, fax 342 2117) caters for ski enthusiasts, with singles/doubles/triples for US$90/120/150.

CENTRAL ANATOLIA

Some of Central Anatolia's diverse highlights: the extraordinary underground city of Derinkuyu (top left); the impressive Mevlâna Müzesi in Konya (top right), shrine to a great mystic philosopher; and the regal Anıt Kabir (bottom), Atatürk's mausoleum, in Turkey's capital, Ankara (middle)

Snapshots of traditional Turkey: 'rush hour' in Sivas (top left and right), home to a fine collection of Seljuk buildings; socialising around the samovar in Amasya (middle left); traditional village life on the Black Sea Coast (bottom left); and well-preserved Ottoman houses in Safranbolu (bottom right)

To get to the ski centre take a Develi dolmuş (US$1, 30 minutes) from Talas Caddesi in Kayseri. A good time to come would be the last weekend in March/first week in April when the Kayseri tourist office organises a winter tourism festival on the slopes.

İncesu

İncesu, 35km south-west of Kayseri, was a new town built in 1667 for Emir Kara Mustafa Pasa who led the Ottoman forces in the failed assault on Vienna. The ruins of much of the old town still survive along with a magnificent complex consisting of a vast caravanserai, a mosque and a hamam. They don't get many visitors here so be prepared for an entourage of children as you explore the backstreets. To get here take a bus or dolmuş from opposite the Kayseri otogar (US$0.75, 30 minutes).

Yahyalı

Yahyalı is a fast-growing settlement 70km due south of Kayseri on the fringes of the Sultan Marshes Bird Paradise. Early every Friday morning from spring through to autumn it hosts one of Turkey's last remaining carpet markets, although prices are higher than in many proper carpet shops.

There are several impressive waterfalls on the Zamantı River near Yahyalı, which is also the access point for exploring the nearby **Ala Dağlar Milli Parkı**, the middle range of the Taurus Mountains, and the beautiful **Yedigöller** (Seven Lakes). Zemi Tours in Göreme (☎ 384-271 2576) sometimes organises tours to the waterfalls.

To get here take a bus or dolmuş from Kayseri otogar (US$2, 45 minutes). There's one extremely basic, emergencies-only hotel (the *Turaç*).

Black Sea Coast

Turkey's Black Sea coast is a unique part of the country, lush and green throughout the year with plenty of rain even in summer. Dairy farming, fishing and tea production are big industries, and there are bumper crops of *tütün* (tobacco), *kiraz* (cherries) and *fındık* (hazelnuts); during the summer, roadsides are lined with hazelnuts laid out to dry in the sun.

You'll catch the occasional glimpse of crumbling old Ottoman houses of wood and plaster, but for the most part the towns of the Black Sea coast, especially those to the east, are conspicuous for their ugly brick and concrete construction.

At the eastern end of the Black Sea the culture differs markedly from elsewhere in Turkey. The area around Rize is home to the Laz people whose women wear colourful shawls and aprons, while Ayder is home to the Hemşins whose assertively upfront women wear lovely silky headscarves (for more information about both groups of people see the boxed text 'The Laz & Hemşin Peoples' later in this chapter). The museum in Rize has a display of the traditional dress of both peoples.

Restaurants in Rize and Ayder offer Black Sea delicacies such as *muhlama* (a thick cheese soup), *sarma* (stuffed cabbage rolls), *lahana lobia* (cabbage and beans), corn bread and *Laz böreği*, flaky pastry sandwiched with confectioner's custard and sprinkled with icing sugar.

Even the spoken word is different here; you'll hear Ayderlis call out 'jel' and 'jit' instead of 'gel' and 'git' for 'come' and 'go'.

The Black Sea coast waters are chillier than those of the Aegean or the Mediterranean and this part of Turkey is most popular with local holiday-makers and those from the former Soviet republics.

Assuming you start out from İstanbul, the coast west of Amasra is difficult to get to and not especially interesting. Its chief city, Zonguldak, is a gritty industrial centre and port town. East of Amasra the road is slow

HIGHLIGHTS

- Eating Black Sea hazelnuts
- Dining in one of Amasra's fine fish restaurants
- Climbing up to Sumela Monastery near Trabzon
- Sipping tea where it's grown in Rize
- Hiking in the Kaçkar Mountains from Ayder

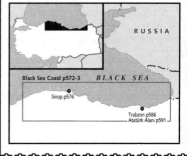

and twisting, but the countryside and sea views range from beautiful to spectacular. It takes all day to get from Amasra to Sinop.

The coastal road between Sinop and Bafra also passes beautiful, unspoilt scenery, with fields of sunflowers and racks of drying tobacco to catch the eye in summer.

East of Sinop, and especially east of Samsun as far as Trabzon, road-widening operations are doing nothing to improve the landscape and trucks bearing stone from the Kaçkar Mountains thunder up and down all day. Once the work is completed, traffic will move more quickly albeit at considerable cost to the coastal environment.

The 360km ride from Samsun to Trabzon can be done in a day and you'll find camp sites, tea gardens and fish restaurants at regular intervals all along the way. The most attractive stretch of coast is between Ünye and Ordu where development has been kept to a minimum and there are several attractive small ports; it's worth pausing at Bolaman, Yalıköy, Mersin or Perşembe.

Trabzon itself is a fascinating town, facing emphatically towards the Caucasus. Beyond Trabzon is Rize, the heart of Turkey's tea-growing area, but after that the scenery deteriorates into a sequence of ugly modern towns running all the way to the Georgian border.

From Rize it's fairly easy to get to Çamlıhemşin and from there to the northern side of the spectacular Kaçkar mountain range, perhaps using the village of Ayder as a base. From Hopa you can climb inland to Artvin in Anatolia's north-eastern corner, a region of exceptionally beautiful mountain scenery.

From June to September Turkish Maritime Lines runs a weekly car ferry service

The Laz & Hemşin Peoples

The mountainous north-eastern corner of Turkey is home to two minority peoples: the Laz and the Hemşin. The Laz people mainly inhabit the valleys between Trabzon and Rize, the Hemşin those further to the east.

The Laz

East of Trabzon you can hardly miss the Laz women in their vivid red and maroon striped shawls. Laz men are less conspicuous, although they were once among the most feared of Turkish warriors; for years black-clad Laz warriors were Atatürk's personal bodyguards.

The Laz are a Caucasian people who speak a language related to Georgian. There are perhaps 250,000 of them in Turkey today. It is believed that they originally lived along the coast of Georgia and were, perhaps, the people of Colchis who guarded the Golden Fleece of Greek myth. (The Turks claim that they were nomads who arrived with other Turkic groups from Central Asia.) In the Middle Ages they were probably driven west by Arab invaders and settled in north-eastern Turkey where they became so assimilated that they eventually forgot not only where they had come from but also that they had been Christians until the 16th century.

Just as speaking Kurdish was prohibited until 1991, so was speaking Lazuri, a language which, until recently, had not been written down. Since the 1960s, however, Wolfgang Feuerstein, a German, has been working to preserve Laz culture. As part of that effort he has created an alphabet with Latin and Georgian characters. With the Kaçkar Working Group he is also compiling a Lazuri dictionary and a history of the Laz people. If his hope was to create a sense of Laz nationalism, there are small signs that his work may be bearing fruit: Lazuri words have appeared on placards at student demonstrations in İstanbul and a Laz pop band has had modest commercial success.

Today the Laz have a reputation for their business ability and many of them are involved either in the shipping or construction industries.

The Hemşin

Hemşin women are even more eye-catching than Laz women although you're less likely to see them unless you make the ascent to Ayder in August. Even then many of the women, with their lovely leopard-print scarves tied over coin-draped black headdresses, are simply returning to visit their old homes. Most villages in this area are fast losing their young people to the cities. There may be as few as 15,000 Hemşin people still living in the area.

Caucasians like the Laz, the Hemşin may have arrived in Turkey from parts of what is now the Republic of Armenia. Like the Laz, they too were originally Christian and their relatively recent conversion could explain why they seem to wear their Islam so lightly. You won't see women wearing veils or chadors in Ayder.

The Hemşin have a great reputation as bread and pastry makers. These days many of the patisseries in İstanbul, Ankara and İzmir are owned by Hemşin people.

BLACK SEA COAST

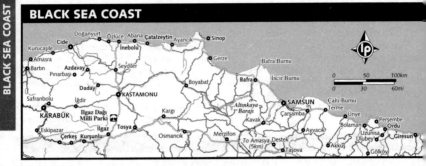

linking İstanbul, Samsun, Trabzon and Rize. Provided the weather holds, this is a very pleasant way of travelling along the Black Sea coast. Otherwise you're best off taking the buses. East of Samsun buses are fast, frequent and cheap. West of Samsun it's another story. The narrow, winding roads, coupled with a paucity of transport, can result in relatively short journeys taking the best part of a day to complete.

The only passenger train serving the Black Sea coast, the *Karaelmas* express between Ankara and Zonguldak, is of little interest to travellers.

History

The coast was colonised in the 8th century BC by Milesians and Arcadians, who founded towns at Sinop, Samsun and Trabzon. Later it became the Kingdom of Pontus. Most of Pontus' kings were named Mithridates. The most famous Mithridates (VI Eupator) gave the Romans a run for their money in 88–84 BC by conquering Cappadocia and other Anatolian kingdoms, and getting as far as Nicomedia (İzmit), which was allied with Rome. When the latter came to its defence, Mithridates pushed onward to the Aegean. The Roman response was hampered by civil war at home but they finally drove into Cappadocia and Pontus (83–81 BC) and forced Mithridates to agree to a peace based on pre-war borders.

From 74–64 BC he was at it again, this time encouraging his son-in-law Tigranes I of Armenia to grab Cappadocia from the Romans. The Roman response was to conquer Pontus whereupon Mithridates was forced to flee and later committed suicide. The Romans left a small kingdom of Pontus at the far eastern end of the coast, based in Trebizond (Trabzon).

The coast was ruled by Byzantium, and Alexius Comnenus, son of Emperor Manuel I, proclaimed himself emperor of Pontus when the crusaders sacked Constantinople and drove him out in 1204. His descendants ruled this small empire until 1461, when it was captured by Mehmet the Conqueror.

While Alexius was in Trabzon, Samsun was under Seljuk rule and the Genoese had trading privileges. But when the Ottomans came, the Genoese burned Samsun to the ground and sailed away.

After WWI the Ottoman Greek citizens of this region attempted to form a new Pontic state with Allied support. Disarmed by the Allied occupation authorities, Turkish inhabitants were persecuted by ethnic Greek guerrilla bands who had been allowed to keep their arms. In these circumstances, the Turks proved very responsive to calls for revolution. Using a bureaucratic ruse, Mustafa Kemal (Atatürk) escaped the sultan's control in İstanbul and landed at Samsun on 19 May 1919. He soon moved inland to Amasya and began to organise what would become the battle for independence.

AMASRA
☎ 378 • pop 7000

Amasra is surely the prettiest small town on the Black Sea coast, its relative isolation pre-

BLACK SEA
(KARADENİZ)

Batumı
Hopa
Arhavi
Pazar
Çamlıhemşin
Beşikdüzü
TRABZON
Rize
Kaçkar Dağı
(3937 m)
Tirebolu
Yomra
Şenyuva
Espiye
Of
Ayder
Yusufeli
Maçka
Kürtün
Sümela
Çaykara
Uzungöl
Çamlıkaya

serving it from the sort of overdevelopment it might have suffered were it on the Aegean. With two harbours and a sandy beach, it sits in the shadow of a fortified promontory, which juts out assertively towards the sea.

Amasra is 90km north of Safranbolu (see the Central Anatolia chapter) and 100km east of Zonguldak, and should not be confused with the similarly named inland city of Amasya 130km south of Samsun.

If you're planning to visit out of season, be warned that many of the restaurants and hotels close at the end of October and don't open again until May at the earliest.

Orientation & Information

As you come into Amasra, you pass the museum on the left in an old stone building. Most of the buses stop in Atatürk Meydanı, the main square, with a park stretching down to the Küçük Liman (Small Harbour) with a few hotels and pensions. Head away from the park and through the shops to find the Büyük Liman (Large Harbour) and a strip of sandy beach. Turn right and walk to the end of the beach for a few more places to stay, left for places to eat.

The entrance to the citadel lurks amid the souvenir shops, just past the Belvü Palas pension.

Kale (Citadel)

Two massive but crumbling gateways lead to the kale, the promontory fortified by the Byzantines when this small commercial port was known as Sesamos Amastris. The greater fortress seems to have replaced a

smaller one erected against Russian adventurers around 861. Rented by the Genoese as a trading station in 1270, Amasra was taken by Mehmet the Conqueror in 1460 without a fight. During Napoleon's invasion of Ottoman Egypt in 1798, French traders doing business in Anatolia were gathered together and interned here for five years as potential enemy agents. Under Ottoman rule, Amasra lost its commercial importance to other Black Sea ports.

Most of the area inside the citadel is now residential. Make your way to the north-western outcrop to sip tea and soak up views of a seagull colony on an offshore islet. All around will be the scent of figs, irises, bay trees, thistles, wild mint and sage. Since Amasra is crawling with cats you'll no doubt have one to keep you company.

Amasra Müzesi

The museum, north of the park, contains a fairly standard collection of Roman, Byzantine and Hellenistic odds and ends, as well as gold-embroidered bed linen and some fine costumes. It's open from 9 am to 5.30 pm daily except Monday and admission costs US$1.75.

Places to Stay

The *Belvü Palas* (☎ 315 1237, *Küçük Liman Caddesi 20*), just before the entrance to the citadel, has two floors of clean, simple rooms with bath for US$9 per person. Sunset views are best from room Nos 6, 7 and 8.

Until recently there were two reliable choices overlooking the Küçük Liman but at the time of writing neither the *Paşakaptan Oteli* (☎ 315 1011) nor the *Nur Turistik Pansiyon* (☎ 315 1015) was open. The Paşakaptan seems likely to reopen but the Nur may be a permanent casualty of the appalling tourist season of 1999. If neither is open, the *Huzur Otel* (☎ 315 2618) in the road behind is new and cheerful and offers beds for US$10 a head though without the benefit of the sea views.

Amasra Oteli (☎ 315 1722, fax 315 3025, *Çekiciler Caddesi 49*) is disappointingly inland from the Büyük Liman and charges US$9 a head for so-so rooms. The nearby

Otel Timur (☎ *315 2589, fax 315 3290, Çekiciler Caddesi 57)* offers very simple rooms with bath for US$13 a head, including breakfast. More cheerful, though lacking baths (or hot water), are the rooms in the nearby *Balkaya Pansiyon* (☎ *315 1434)*, costing US$9 a head.

Amasra's best is the *Amastrist Otel* (☎ *315 2465, fax 315 2629, Büyük Liman Caddesi 94)*, in a quiet location at the southern end of Büyük Liman near the naval base, about 250m from the centre. Singles/doubles are comfortable, although hardly luxurious, and all have balconies. Bed and breakfast costs US$13 a head; half board is US$20.

There are a couple of *ev pansiyons* (pensions in private homes) right beside the Amastrist and an extremely basic eyesore of an ev pansiyon right out on the promontory. Great setting, shame about the brickwork!

Places to Eat

Good, cheap food is served at *Köşem Pide Kebap Salonu* (*Amiral Celal Eyüceoğlu Caddesi 23)* between the park and the Büyük Liman. A cheese *pide* (Turkish pizza) and soft drink costs less than US$2; *döner kebap* (slices of spit-roasted lamb) and stews cost up to US$5 for a full meal.

Amasra has several pleasant seafront fish restaurants at which you should reckon on paying US$6 to US$8 for a meal. Overlooking the main harbour at Büyük Liman Caddesi 26 is the upstairs *Çesm-i Cihan* fish restaurant with great views. Walk right to the end of the promenade for the big, brightly lit *Liman Restaurant*.

Çınar Restaurant, across Küçük Liman Caddesi from the Belediye, used to be a great place to eat but nowadays contents itself with dumping a piece of fish on the plate without even such pretence at presentation as a slice of tomato. Not surprisingly the inviting seaside dining room at nearby *Mustafa Amca'nın Yeri* was stealing the trade at the time of writing.

The cheerful *Sormagir Cafe* near the entrance to the citadel is the place to go for piping hot *gözleme* (Turkish pancake) made in front of your eyes for around US$1.50.

The nearby *Kupa Birahanesi* is a favourite local drinking place that serves food as well. Otherwise the shady park is the place to enjoy a cool drink or bracing glass of *çay* (tea) dispensed by the *Cafe Kumsal*.

Shopping

Amasra has always been known for turning out wooden trinkets. Originally the woodworkers carved everyday items like spoons, forks and spatulas, and indeed you can still find these no-nonsense items for sale. But nowadays most carvers have switched to producing statuettes, lampshades and key rings for the tourist market.

Recently several embroidery shops have opened to supplement the wood shops. They sell a mixture of old and new handiwork, much of it very beautiful and not at all badly priced.

Getting There & Away

If you plan to travel east along the coast from Amasra, start early in the morning. Minibuses become increasingly difficult to find as the day wears on.

Big intercity bus companies don't operate to Amasra. Instead regular minibuses to Bartın (16km south) leave from the eastern side of the park daily from 8 am onwards. From Bartın you can catch a bus to Safranbolu (US$3.50, two hours, 92km), Ankara (US$10, five hours, 280km) and İstanbul (US$14, seven hours, 340km). The town of Bartın is interesting only for its expertise in making carved wooden walking sticks, so you're unlikely to want to stay.

AMASRA TO SİNOP
☎ 366

Travelling the narrow and twisty but scenic coastal road from Amasra east to Sinop (312km) is slow going (average 40km/h to 50km/h), with the road surface often broken and the occasional *heyelan* (landslide) to hinder progress. To get about by public transport means picking up local services from small town to small town – start early in the morning!

If you have your own transport it's fun to explore this relatively untouristy part of the coast, stopping for a swim at **Bozköy beach** west of Çakraz, or to see the boat-builders at work in the town of **Kurucaşile**, 45km east of Amasra which has several modest hotels and pensions. The picturesque village of **Kapısuyu** is another good spot to break your journey and the tiny harbour of **Gideros** is idyllic.

About 63km east of Amasra the road descends to a broad sand-and-pebble beach which stretches for several kilometres to the aptly named village of **Kumluca** (meaning 'Sandy'). The beach continues 8km eastward to **Cide**, a dreary small town where the dolmuş service could just leave you stranded. The *Yeni Alkan Otel* (☎ 366-866 1192) is there for just such an emergency.

Likewise, if you arrive in equally uninspiring **İnebolu** in late afternoon you may not be able to find onward transportation. Unfortunately both *Otel Altınöz* (☎ 811 4502, Cumhuriyet Caddesi 47), inland from the PTT opposite the Ziraat Bankası, and the nearby *Otel Özlü* (☎ 811 4198) are grungy, uninviting places, a fact reflected in prices of US$4.50 a head. It's better to walk east along the seafront to the *Oğretmen Evi*, which has a few clean, spacious hotel rooms with bath for US$7 a head. At the time of writing the *İnebolu Belediyesi Moteli* (☎ 811 4305, fax 811 3232), right on the pebble beach 500m west of the centre, was closed for refurbishment. Singles/doubles used to cost US$15/24 but will no doubt jump in price accordingly.

West of İnebolu the road improves, and after 22km is **Abana**, a fast-growing resort with a decent beach. About 41km east of İnebolu near Çatalzeytin a long pebble beach is surrounded by beautiful scenery. At Ayancık the road divides, with the left (northern) fork offering the more scenic route to Sinop, about 2½ hours from İnebolu.

SİNOP
☎ 368 • pop 29,000

Sinop, on a promontory jutting into the Black Sea, is a natural site for a port and has been one for a thousand years.

The town takes its name from the legend of Sinope, daughter of the river god Asopus. Zeus fell in love with her and, in order to win her heart, promised to grant her any wish. Sinope, who didn't fancy marrying him, asked for eternal virginity. Outwitted, Zeus allowed Sinope to live out her days in happy solitude at the tip of the peninsula.

History
Colonised from Miletus in the 8th century BC, Sinop's trade slowly grew and successive rulers – Cimmerians, Phrygians, Persians, the Pontic kings (who made it their capital), Romans and Byzantines – turned it into a busy trading centre. The Cynic philosopher Diogenes (circa 412–323 BC) was born here, then lived in Athens.

The Seljuks used Sinop as a port after taking it in 1214 but the Ottomans preferred to develop Samsun, which had better land communications.

On 30 November 1853, Sinop was attacked without any warning by a Russian armada and the local garrison was overwhelmed with great loss of life. The battle of Sinop hastened the beginning of the Crimean War in which the Ottomans allied with the British and French to fight Russian ambitions in the Near East.

Orientation & Information
Sinop is at the narrow point of the peninsula, with the road continuing east beyond the town to beaches and land's end. The otogar is at the western entrance to the town by the fortified walls. From here the unattractive main street, Sakarya Caddesi, cuts east through the centre 800m directly to the Sinop *valilik* (provincial government headquarters), just north of which are the museum and Temple of Serapis.

To reach Kurtuluş Caddesi and the cheap hotels (800m from the otogar), come out of the otogar and walk north along Sakarya Caddesi (the main road), bearing right just past the minaret and going straight on downhill.

From the valilik, Atatürk Caddesi turns right (south) and heads downhill past the clock tower and *belediye* (town hall) to the PTT, the Hotel Melia-Kasım and the harbour. East of here the road leads along the shore 3km to Karakum Plajı, a municipal beach.

BLACK SEA COAST

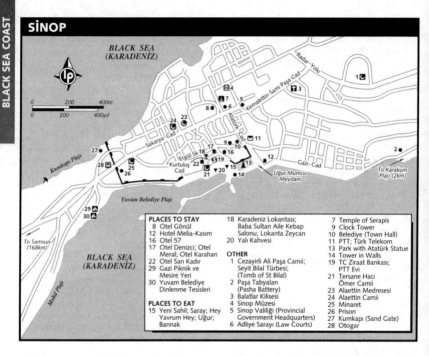

SİNOP

BLACK SEA (KARADENİZ)

PLACES TO STAY
8 Otel Gönül
12 Hotel Melia-Kasım
16 Otel 57
17 Otel Denizci; Otel Meral; Otel Karahan
22 Otel San Kadır
29 Gazi Piknik ve Mesire Yeri
30 Yuvam Belediye Dinlenme Tesisleri

PLACES TO EAT
15 Yeni Sahil; Saray; Hey Yavrum Hey; Uğur; Barınak

18 Karadeniz Lokantası; Baba Sultan Aile Kebap Salonu; Lokanta Zeycan
20 Yalı Kahvesi

OTHER
1 Cezayirli Ali Paşa Camii; Seyit Bilal Türbesi; (Tomb of St Bilal)
2 Paşa Tabyaları (Pasha Battery)
3 Balatlar Kilisesi
4 Sinop Müzesi
5 Sinop Valiliği (Provincial Government Headquarters)
6 Adliye Sarayı (Law Courts)

7 Temple of Serapis
9 Clock Tower
10 Belediye (Town Hall)
11 PTT; Türk Telekom
13 Park with Atatürk Statue
14 Tower in Walls
19 TC Ziraat Bankası; PTT Evi
21 Tersane Hacı Ömer Camii
23 Alaettin Medresesi
24 Alaettin Camii
25 Minaret
26 Prison
27 Kumkapı (Sand Gate)
28 Otogar

You can try asking for tourist information at an office on the fourth floor of the valilik (☎ 261 5207, fax 260 0310), but you'll be lucky to find anyone who speaks English.

You can pick up your email at the Dreamshop Internet Cafe on Gazi Caddesi, behind the Hotel Melia-Kasım.

Fortifications

Open to easy attack from the sea, Sinop seems to have been fortified since earliest times but the existing walls are developments of those originally erected in 72 BC by Mithridates IV, king of Pontus. At one time the walls, some 3m thick, were more than 2km long. If you keep walking west along Kurtuluş Caddesi you'll come to a stretch which, in its length and state of preservation, is vaguely reminiscent of the great walls of İstanbul.

Across Sakarya Caddesi, south of the otogar, a Seljuk building turned into a

prison by the Ottomans in 1877 is still in use as such. Near the shore on the northern side of the otogar is an ancient bastion called the Kumkapı (Sand Gate). Another square tower looms above the harbour on the southern side of town.

East of the centre almost at Karakum Plajı is the Paşa Tabyaları (Pasha Battery), a gun emplacement built to defend the town during the Crimean War.

Religious Buildings

In the town centre on Sakarya Caddesi stands the **Alaettin Camii** (1267), also called the Ulu Cami. It was constructed for Muinettin Süleyman Pervane, a powerful Seljuk grand vizier. The mosque has been repaired many times; its marble mihrab and *mimber* (pulpit) were added in 1429 by the local Candaroğlu emir.

Next to the Alaettin Camii is the **Alaettin Medresesi**, also called the Süleyman Pervane or Alaiye Medresesi, built in the late

13th century by Süleyman Pervane to commemorate the Seljuk conquest of Sinop.

Go uphill (east) from the valilik along Kemalettin Sami Paşa Caddesi to reach the **Balatlar Kilisesi**, a Roman temple converted to a Byzantine church in the 7th century. A few traces of frescoes are visible.

Further uphill, 1km from the valilik, is the **Cezayirli Ali Paşa Camii** (Mosque of Ali Pasha the Algerian). Inside is the **Seyit Bilal Türbesi**, or tomb of St Bilal, built for Emir Tayboğa in 1297. Seyit Bilal, grandson of Hüseyin (who was a grandson of the Prophet Mohamed), was blown ashore here in the 7th century and put to death by the Byzantines.

Near the harbour is the **Tersane Hacı Ömer Camii** (1903) with, next to it, a touching monument, the Şehitler Çeşmesi (Heroes' Fountain), built in memory of the many Turkish soldiers who died in the surprise Russian attack of 1853. The fountain was built using the money recovered from the soldiers' pockets.

Temple & Sinop Müzesi

Just north of the valilik is the museum, Sinop Müzesi, open noon to 5.30 pm Monday, 8 am to 5.30 pm Tuesday to Friday and 9 am to 5 pm Saturday and Sunday. Admission costs US$1.75. The collection spans Sinop's history from the Bronze Age to the Turkish War of Independence. A collection of 19th-century Greek Orthodox icons are reminders that the Black Sea coast was heavily populated by Ottoman Greeks until the War of Independence and the subsequent exchange of populations with Greece.

In the museum's garden are mosaics, tombstones and a few remains of an ancient **Temple of Serapis** (the Egyptian embodiment of Apollo) excavated in 1951.

Beaches

As you approach Sinop, turn right (south) a few hundred metres west of the otogar and prison and descend to the shore to find the Yuvam Belediye Plajı (Yuvam Municipal Beach), a forest camping area, and the Yuvam Motel. On the northern side of the peninsula near the Kumkapı is another small beach where the water is cooler.

About 3km east of the harbour on the southern shore is Karakum Plajı, officially styled the Özel İdare Karakum Yüzgeç Tatil Köyü, with a pay beach of black sand, a restaurant, a nightclub and a nice camping ground with shady tent sites and electrical hook-ups.

Across the peninsula on the northern shore is Akliman, a long beach backed by forest and adjoined by the Hamsaroz fjord.

Places to Stay

Camping South-west of the otogar near the Yuvam Belediye Plajı are two camping grounds. At *Gazi Piknik ve Mesire Yeri*, 300m south-west of the main road (750m from the otogar), you camp in full shade with fine views of the sea and there are tables and benches and even a playground. There's easy transport to the town centre along the main road. The charge of US$3 per site is rarely levied at slow times of the year.

Further along the same road, 700m off the main road (2km west of the valiliği), *Yuvam Belediye Dinlenme Tesisleri* camping ground is fairly dismal, with shadeless sites with hook-ups, but has a reasonable restaurant with a shady terrace.

The *camp sites* (☎ 261 5117) at Karakum, 3.5km east of the valilik along the southern shore, are pleasantly shady, with hook-ups, and cost US$3 per site.

Hotels Start looking by the harbour in Kurtuluş Caddesi, with the PTT Evi (Postal Workers' Club), TC Ziraat Bankası and Tersane Hacı Ömer Camii as landmarks.

A good choice, provided you can handle stairs, is *Otel Sarı Kadır* (☎ 260 1544, Derinboğazağzı Sokak 22), the continuation of Kurtuluş Caddesi, across from the Tersane Hacı Ömer Camii. Clean, simple singles/doubles cost US$12/17, including breakfast; those at the front have fabulous harbour views, as does the breakfast terrace.

Otel Denizci (☎ 261 0904) and *Otel Meral* (☎ 261 3100) are right across the street from the TC Ziraat Bankası. Both are clean and presentable, though the Denizci has the larger rooms. Both charged US$4.50 a head at the time of writing but this was likely to rise, especially at the Meral where smaller rooms have baths.

Around the corner from the Denizci, the rock-bottom *Otel Karahan* (☎ 261 0688) is in a courtyard, which should cut down some of the street noise.

The *Otel 57* (☎ 261 5462, *Kurtuluş Caddesi 29*) charges US$12/17 for rooms with bath, TV and phone. In Turkish, the name is pronounced 'ho-**tehl** ehl-**lee** yeh-**dee**'.

The big, harbour-facing *Hotel Melia-Kasım* (☎ 261 4210, fax 261 1625, *Gazi Caddesi 49*) tries hard with lurid pink paint which can hardly disguise the fact that it's past its prime. Still, the location is good, with sea views from many rooms. Lighter sleepers should ask for a top-floor room to avoid the live Turkish music in the downstairs nightclub, which tends to go on late. Posted prices are US$50/70 but you're more likely to be charged around US$17 a head.

If all these places are full the *Otel Gönül* (☎ 261 1829, fax 261 4497, *Meydankapı Mahallesi 11*) announces its existence with flashing lights from a side road beside the Adliye Sarayı (Law Courts).

Places to Eat

Sinop has a lively restaurant scene. To take advantage of the best, head straight on down to the harbour. If you're on a tightish budget try the *Karadeniz Lokantası*, one street back from the waterfront on Kurtuluş Caddesi and serving breakfast, lunch and dinner. Nearby, *Baba Sultan Aile Kebap Salonu* opposite Otel 57, and *Lokanta Zeycan* right beside it are also promising, as is the *ocakbaşı* near the Otel Denizci.

The waterfront is lined with Mediterranean-style open-air restaurants. *Yeni Sahil, Saray, Hey Yavrum Hey* and *Uğur* all serve beer, wine and food on shady terraces. *Barınak* can also rustle up hamburgers, pizza, or steak and eggs. Breakfast goes for less than US$2. Lunch or dinner costs from US$4 to US$8, slightly more for fish.

The *Yalı Kahvesi* is an excellent waterside tea-and-beer garden right behind the Tersane Hacı Ömer Camii. The *Sinema Cafe* across the road and up from the taxi rank was closed at the time of writing but looked to be worth a try should it reopen.

Getting There & Away

Most services leaving Sinop's small otogar are heading for Ankara or Samsun, with some buses continuing to Trabzon. For other destinations, you'll probably have to change buses en route. There are no direct services to Amasra (US$5, eight hours, 312km), you'll need to take point-to-point minibuses. The table below lists some useful daily services.

Getting Around

Dolmuşes (US$0.35) run through the town from the otogar in the west to Karakum Plajı on the south-eastern shore. A taxi to the otogar from Kurtuluş Caddesi costs about US$2.

SAMSUN

☎ 362 • pop 333,000

Burnt to the ground by the Genoese in the 15th century, Samsun has little to show for its long history. A major port and commer-

Services from Sinop's Otogar

destination	fare (US$)	time (hr)	distance (km)	daily services
Ankara	17	9	443	frequent buses
Boyabat	4.50	2½	80	frequent dolmuşes
İnebolu	5	3	156	1 bus at 8 am
İstanbul	from 17	10½	700	several buses
Kastamonu	7	3½	235	few minibuses or change at Boyabat
Safranbolu	12.50	6	340	change at Karabük
Samsun	7.50	3	168	frequent minibuses
Trabzon	9	6	365	frequent buses via Samsun

cial centre, it's the largest city on the coast, a grim and often dusty place. There's little reason to stop here except to change buses, have a meal or find a bed.

Orientation & Information

The city centre is Cumhuriyet Meydanı (Republic Square), just north-west of a large park with an equestrian statue of Atatürk. Just south-east of the statue stands the old *vilayet* (government headquarters). A handy landmark is the Hotel Yafeya on the north-western side of Cumhuriyet Meydanı. The new vilayet complex is across the coastal highway to the north.

The main business street with banks, a PTT and restaurants is Kazımpaşa Caddesi (sometimes called Bankalar Caddesi), one block inland from Atatürk Bulvarı, cutting north-west from Cumhuriyet Meydanı.

The large building like a celestial ski jump on the waterfront is the Kültür Sarayı (Cultural Centre), the venue for ballet, concerts and theatre.

The train station is 1km south-east of the Kültür Sarayı and the otogar is just over 2km south-east of Cumhuriyet Meydanı along the shore road, Atatürk Bulvarı. Any city bus or dolmuş heading north-west through Samsun will drop you at Cumhuriyet Meydanı (US$0.35).

The tourist office (☎ 431 1228) is at Talimhane Caddesi 6.

Museums

There's not much to detain you in Samsun, but with an hour or so to spare it's worth visiting the **Arkeoloji ve Etnografya Müzesi** (Archaeological and Ethnography Museum), just off Atatürk Bulvarı, west of the big new vilayet buildings. The most striking exhibit is a huge Romano-Byzantine mosaic depicting Thetis and Achilles and the Four Seasons, found nearby at Karasamsun.

Other exhibits include Bronze Age, Chalcolithic and Hittite finds from the twin mounds at İkiztepe, a bronze statue of an athlete dating from the 2nd century BC and some wonderful embroidery.

Right next door is the **Atatürk Müzesi**. On 19 May 1919 Atatürk arrived in Samsun from İstanbul, preparing the way for the War of Independence. A statue near the Büyük Samsun Oteli commemorates this event, as does this museum, mainly full of photographs and items of Atatürk's apparel. One look at his portable shaving kit and you'll realise this was not a man who believed in travelling light!

Both museums are open from 8 am to noon and from 1.30 to 5.30 pm. You should get into both for US$1.75.

Places to Stay

Samsun is not great for cheap places to stay. Although there are lots of cheap hotels in the central district called Kale Mahallesi, most of them seem to be anticipating guests other than tourists. Make your way to the Atatürk statue and old vilayet building just one block south-east of Cumhuriyet Meydanı. Across the road is a line of good cheap restaurants. The narrow streets behind them contain most of the budget hotels.

The *Otel Sönmez* (☎ 431 2669, Hürriyet Sokak 20) is one passable possibility that tries to charge US$8.50 a head, too much for what you get. Nearby, the *Stad Otel* (☎ 0542-892 0432, Hürriyet Sokak 14) is another possibility, charging slightly more and promising a bowl of soup for breakfast. Otherwise there's the borderline *Otel Menekşe* (☎ 431 9835) or the emergencies-only *Otel Bahar*.

Much better than any of these is the presentable *Otel Gold* (☎ 431 1959, Orhaniye Geçidi 4), a good, quiet, clean place renting rooms with shower and TV for US$13.50/23 a single/double, including breakfast.

If nothing takes your fancy, there are more cheap hotels around Gaziler Meydanı in the bazaar. Walk north-west along Kazımpaşa Caddesi, turn left through the shops and walk a few blocks to find them.

The three-star *Hotel Yafeya* (☎ 435 1131, fax 435 1135, Cumhuriyet Meydanı) has comfortable, if old-fashioned, rooms which suffer from constant traffic noise. Rooms with bath, TV and minibar cost US$35/55 a single/double, including breakfast.

Just around the corner is the three-star *Vidinli Oteli* (☎ 431 6050, fax 431 2136,

Kazımpaşa Caddesi) that promises more than it actually delivers. Rooms for US$47/74 are comfortable enough but in sore need of an update. The rooftop restaurant has fine views and works of art on the walls.

The completely refitted *Büyük Samsun Oteli* (☎ 432 4999, fax 431 0740, Atatürk Bulvarı 629), just north-west of Cumhuriyet Meydanı, is decidedly swish and comfortable. Rooms with air-con, TV, flash bathrooms and all mod cons cost US$100/130. There's a disco on Friday and Saturday nights.

Places to Eat

For a bite to eat head straight for Irmak Caddesi which runs along the south side of the park and is lined with restaurants and *pastanes* (pastry shops).

Look for the *Sila Restaurant* on the corner of Hürriyet Sokak, directly opposite the old vilayet, which offers meals for about US$4. A few steps back along Irmak Caddesi (towards the Hotel Yafeya) are the *Ravza Restaurant*, which serves good meals and cheap *lahmacun* (Arabic-style pizza) for US$1, and the *Zirve Pide ve Kebap Salonu*, another kebap, pide and lahmacun place. On the corner of Osmaniye Caddesi is the popular *Oba Restaurant*. Turn down Osmaniye Caddesi for *Ovalı Restaurant*, where you can have wine or beer with your meal. Another good place with attentive service is *Özlem Restorant* where a good helping of chicken and rice will cost around US$3.

After dinner *Kent Pastanesi* is there for the coffee and cakes, although on a sunny day the outside tables at the *Divan Pastanesi*, closer to Cumhuriyet Meydanı, might be more inviting.

The *Terminal Cafe* at the otogar offers good food, friendly service and clean toilets.

Getting There & Away

Air Turkish Airlines has nonstop daily flights between Samsun and İstanbul for about US$80. Their office is at Kazımpaşa Caddesi 18/A (☎ 432 2330, fax 431 8260).

Bus Samsun seems to offer at least one daily bus service to every important destination in Turkey and very frequent buses to logical next destinations. Most bus ticket offices are around Cumhuriyet Meydanı. If there's no *servis* (shuttle minibus) to the otogar, dolmuşes ply up and down Atatürk Bulvarı (look for signs saying 'Garaj'). Bus services to major destinations are listed in the table below.

Train Though there are daily trains between Samsun and Sivas, the journey takes more than 12 hours, hardly worth it when the bus does the same trip in half the time.

Boat Weekly car ferries operate between İstanbul and Samsun from mid-June to the end of August, leaving İstanbul at 2 pm on Monday, arriving in Samsun at 5 pm on Tuesday, and leaving for Trabzon and Rize at 7 pm.

Services from Samsun's Otogar

destination	fare (US$)	time (hr)	distance (km)	daily services
Amasya	4	2½	130	10 buses
Ankara	12	7	420	frequent
Artvin	10	10	615	several buses
Giresun	7	3½	220	frequent buses
İstanbul	17	11	750	several buses
Kayseri	14	9	530	a few buses
Sinop	7.50	3	168	frequent buses
Sivas	9	6½	345	a few buses
Trabzon	9	6	365	frequent buses
Ünye	1.50	1½	95	frequent buses

EAST TO TRABZON

Two of Anatolia's great rivers, the Kızılırmak and the Yeşilırmak, empty into the sea on either side of Samsun, but urban sprawl is slowly eating into what used to be inviting scenery. The road east of Samsun is being widened to four lanes, with construction virtually completed to **Çarşamba**, 37km to the east, where you might want to stop and examine an unusual wooden-framed and tile-roofed mosque.

If you plan to break your journey and spend a night before reaching Trabzon, Giresun is certainly the most pleasant place to do it although Ordu has one gem of a hotel worth considering.

Ünye

☎ 452 • pop 55,000

Ünye, a small port town amid hazelnut groves, is 95km east of Samsun. Its biggest claim to fame is that the great Turkish mystical poet Yunus Emre, who wrote during the early 14th century, is thought to have been born here.

About 7km inland from the town, along the Niksar road, stands **Ünye Kalesi**, a fortress built by the Byzantines to protect this pass to the interior, with an ancient tomb cut into the rock face below.

The tourist office (☎/fax 323 4952) is in a booth on the seafront beside the Ünyespor football pitch. In the centre of Ünye, the Eski Hamam was once a church. It's open to men in the morning and women in the early afternoon (US$2). Cut up the hill behind the hamam and you'll find the last old wooden Ottoman houses of Ünye slowly crumbling to nothing.

Places to Stay As you approach Ünye from Samsun, the road skirts the beaches and passes several camping grounds, pensions and seaside motels.

Black Sea Camping and **Güler Kamping** are side by side on the coast 3km west of the centre.

The comfortable two-star **Kumsal Hotel** (☎ 323 1602, fax 323 4490), 5km west of Ünye town centre, charges US$50 a double with bath, including breakfast.

Çamlık Motel (☎ 312 1333), in a pine forest on the shore 2km west of Ünye, is well used but pleasantly situated. A double room with bath and sea view costs US$16 and a two-room suite with small kitchen US$20.

There are other small hotels in the town itself. Facing the belediye is **Otel Burak** (☎ 324 5216) which has clean singles/doubles with shower and TV for US$9/14. A few doors along is the cheerfully decorated **Güney Otel** (☎ 323 8406) where even some of the singles are a fair size and the roof terrace has good views. Rooms with shower cost US$10/14.

Otel Kılıç (☎ 323 1224, Cumhuriyet Meydanı, Hükümet Yanı 4) is just off the main square. A rather run-down lobby belies good, clean rooms with showers which cost US$10/14. Some front rooms have balconies but beware minaret noise from the neighbouring Saray Camii.

Places to Eat Unusually, Ünye seems to have more jewellers and pharmacies than good eating places. **Adana Mutfağı Kebap House**, near Otel Burak and directly opposite the belediye's front door, offers meals for US$4 to US$6. **Günaydın Restaurant**, near the Güney Otel, is an alternative.

Better than either is the seafront **Park Restaurant** across Yunus Emre Parkı and facing a thin strip of beach. There's an outdoor terrace for sunny days and live music on Friday and Saturday nights.

Getting There & Away Minibuses and dolmuşes ply up and down the coastal road to Samsun (US$1.50, 1½ hours) and Ordu (US$3, two hours) via Fatsa and Perşembe.

Around Ünye

About 4km east of Ünye, the road passes a huge cement factory and, 14km further along, the town of **Fatsa**, with the four-star **Otel Yalçın**. **Bolaman**, a bit further east, has many fine though dilapidated Ottoman wooden houses. **Perşembe** faces a pretty harbour with a lighthouse on a sea wall. The wood-fronted **Dede Evi Hotel** might make a good place to break your journey.

Ordu

☎ 452 • pop 103,000

About 78km east of Ünye is Ordu, a seaside town whose centre is being tastefully tarted up and which has a pleasant tree-lined seafront boulevard.

The centre of town, at the Atatürk bust by the Aziziye (Yalı) Camii, has a town plan on a signboard. The bazaar is just inland.

The tourist office (☎ 223 1607) is conveniently situated on the sea-facing side of the belediye, just east of the mosque on the main road. Nearby, Tarakçıoğlu sells hazelnuts with chocolate, and hazelnuts with honey as well as just plain hazelnuts.

The otogar is 1.5km east of the main square but the dolmuş station for local routes is just east of the main square. You can buy bus tickets at offices a few steps inland from the mosque by the main square. The Saklı Bahçe Internet Cafe is out towards the otogar.

There's a small forest picnic spot (*orman piknik yeri*) west of the town.

Museum The Paşaoğlu Konağı ve Etnografya Müzesi (Pasha's Palace & Ethnographic Museum) is 500m uphill from Ordu's main square past the Aziziye Camii. Follow signs reading 'Müze – Museum'.

This late 19th-century house, a pale yellow box decorated with wedding-cake trim, has a fairly tame ethnographic exhibit downstairs. The 1st-floor bedrooms, guest rooms and salon, however, are fully furnished with period pieces, costumes and embroidery, and bring to life the Ottoman lifestyle of the 19th century. In the garden at the back, don't miss the old stone grill for Ottoman banquets.

This is a gem of a place and it's a shame that it doesn't get more visitors. It's open from 8 am to 5 pm daily; admission costs US$1.75.

After visiting, follow the signs saying 'Boztepe' for fine views over the town.

Places to Stay With one exception, Giresun is a much nicer place to spend the night than Ordu, so if you can make it that far, go on.

Ordu's *Otel Kervansaray (☎ 214 1330, Kazım Karabekir Caddesi 1)*, just east of the Aziziye Camii and inland from the dolmuş station, is old-fashioned, with lackadaisical staff. Singles/doubles with shower cost US$7/13. The Kervansaray Lokantasi downstairs is much cheerier.

Across the street from the Kervansaray, and a big step down in standard, is *Otel Başar Palas (☎ 214 4165)*, charging from US$4 per person, if it's actually open. Others are in the bazaar nearby.

The two-star *Turist Otel (☎ 214 9115, fax 214 1950, Atatürk Bulvarı 134)*, 350m east of the Aziziye Camii on the highway, is a bit noisy but moderately priced at US$15/28, including breakfast.

Fancier and newer is the three-star *Belde Hotel (☎ 214 3987, fax 214 9398)*, several kilometres west of Ordu on a promontory at Kirazlılimanı, charging US$30/45 for rooms with bath, TV and minibar. There's a swimming pool as well.

But Ordu's best by far is the *Karlıbel İkizevler Hotel (☎ 225 0081, fax 225 0575, Sıtkıcan Caddesi 45)* newly created out of a pair of old Ottoman houses and overlooking the sea and a stone church restored to serve as a theatre. Rooms are small but pretty and cost US$26/40, including breakfast.

Places to Eat The best place to eat if you can afford it is the restaurant attached to the Karlıbel Hotel which is just up the road in a wonderful 19th-century mansion, finely restored and with great sea views.

For more casual dining strike out west along the coastal road and you'll find the *Cafe Bulvar*, serving pizza and spaghetti for about US$2 a plate. Across the road the sea-facing *Kumsal Cafe-Bar* has live music on Wednesday, Friday and Saturday night, while the *Pikola Cinema Cafe* shows films as well as serving food.

Giresun

☎ 454 • pop 75,000

The town of Giresun, 46km east of Ordu, was founded some 3000 years ago. Legend has it that Jason and the Argonauts passed by on their voyage to the fabled Kingdom of Colchis (Georgia), on the eastern shores of the Black Sea, in search of the Golden Fleece. The Argonauts supposedly stopped at a nearby island (Büyük Ada) where Amazon queens had erected a shrine to Ares, god of war.

After the Romans conquered the Kingdom of Pontus, they discovered that the locals had orchards full of trees bearing delicious little red fruits. One theory holds that the ancient name for the town, Cerasus, is the root for many of the names for the fruit – *cherry* in English, *cerise* in French, *kiraz* in Turkish – as well as for the town's modern name. Cherries are still important here 2000 years later.

Orientation & Information The centre of Giresun is the Atapark on the main road. The belediye is just inland from the park. The main commercial street is Gazi Caddesi, climbing steeply uphill from the belediye. The bus station is 4km west of the centre; if you're coming from the east and heading west, have the bus drop you at the Atapark. Bus companies have ticket offices near the belediye.

Dolmuşes heading east to the towns of Görele, Espiye and Tirebolu use a more convenient lot, one long block east of the Atapark on the main road. Those to Ordu stop on the main highway opposite the Atapark.

Seed of a Myth?

In ancient times what is now Georgia was known as Colchis. Greek myth relates how Jason and the Argonauts sailed there in search of a Golden Fleece, supposedly owned by the Colchian king Aeetes. After many adventures along the coast of the Pontus Euxinus (the Black Sea), Jason was helped to acquire the Fleece by the king's sorceress daughter, Medea, whom he married.

Complete fantasy, you might think. However, it's likely that the myth grew out of folk memory of a 13th-century BC trading voyage during which sailors saw the Colchians laying fleeces in the river beds to gather alluvial gold.

The tourist office (☎ 212 3190, fax 216 0095) is at Gazi Caddesi 72, but there's a more convenient kiosk in the Atapark.

The PTT is 500m uphill from the belediye with several Internet cafes nearby.

Things to See & Do With time to kill in Giresun, the things to do are to eat hazelnuts and chocolate bars containing hazelnuts, and walk 1.5km uphill to the **Kalepark** (Castle Park) perched on the steep hillside above the town. The beautiful shady park offers panoramic views of the town and the sea, tables for picnickers and tea-sippers, groves for lovers, and barbecues for grillers. It's busy on weekends.

No public transport serves the park, so you'll need to walk inland uphill from the Atapark on Gazi Caddesi and turn left one block past the Otel Kit-Tur (a short cut, not passable for cars). If in doubt, ask directions for the vilayet or the kale. The prominent mansion on the hillside above the minibus lot is the vilayet, near a mosque which was obviously once a church.

The **City Museum** (Şehir Müzesi), with its run-of-the-mill collection, is housed in the disused 18th-century Gogora church, 1.5km around the promontory east of the Atapark on the main road. The most interesting exhibits are old French photographs of turn-of-the-century Giresun.

The museum administration is housed in a lovely restored Ottoman building next door. Cold drinks are sometimes available on the terrace in between.

Special Events Locals will tell you that the grandly named International Black Sea Giresun Aksu Festival, held annually on 20 May, dates from the days of the Hittite fertility gods, including Priapus, the phallic god, and Cybele, the Anatolian earth-mother goddess. The festival hails rebirth, fecundity and the start of the new growing season.

Festivities begin at the mouth of the Aksu creek where participants pass through a trivet, then through seven double pieces and one single piece of stone to boats waiting at the shore. The boats sail around Büyük Ada while the voyagers cast pebbles representing the last year's troubles into the water. Returning to the town, everyone eats and drinks, and drinks some more.

Places to Stay Giresun has a much better choice of middle range places to stay than budget places. *Hotel Bozbağ (☎ 216 1249, Eski Yağcılar Sokak 8)* is in a quiet location one block up the street from the belediye. The rooms are pretty grungy and overpriced at US$9/14 a single/double with shower. There's only hot water in the evenings.

For a few real bargain-basement prices, walk up Gazi Caddesi and turn left after the post office for places like the *Hotel Kristal* with nothing but cheapness to recommend them.

The two-star *Otel Çarıkçı (☎ 216 1026, fax 216 4578, Osmanağa Caddesi 6)*, half a block east of the Belediye, is a good choice. The century-old building has been carefully restored and provides small but comfortable if slightly dowdy rooms with bath for US$25/33, including breakfast. Attentive service is a plus and strong windows keep out most of the street noise.

Around the corner is the quietish, one-star *Er-Tur Otel (☎ 216 1757, fax 216 7762, Çapulacılar Arastası 8)*, an excellent choice with clean, more modern rooms for US$10/18, including breakfast.

The three-star *Otel Kit-Tur (☎ 212 0255, fax 212 3034, Arifbey Caddesi 27)* is two short blocks uphill from the belediye along Gazi Caddesi. Rooms have TV, smart baths and modern decor for a very reasonable price of US$25/35.

Just round the corner is the *Otel Serenti (☎ 212 9434, fax 212 9555, Arifbey Caddesi 12)* which, although new, has decor vaguely reminiscent of an old people's home. Bathrooms are good though. Rooms cost US$20/33, including breakfast.

Half a block uphill from the Kit-Tur is *Otel Ormancılar (☎ 212 4391, fax 212 7105, Gazi Caddesi 37)*, charging marginally less for equally modern rooms. Beware of the noisy front rooms.

The faded *Giresun Oteli (☎ 216 3017, fax 216 6038)*, on the Black Sea side of the highway to the east of the Atapark, has had its nose put right out of joint by the arrival of the flash Hotel Başar right on its doorstep. Rooms cost US$14/20, including breakfast. Breakfast is served in the 6th-floor restaurant which has wonderful sea views.

The swanky new *Hotel Başar (☎ 212 9920, fax 212 9929, Atatürk Bulvarı, Liman Mevkii)*, right on the seafront beside the Gireseun Oteli, is Giresun's best with big brick atrium, open-sided lift and all mod cons. Rooms with pleasant decor and inviting baths cost US$75/100.

Places to Eat *Deniz Lokantası*, next to the belediye and the Ulusoy bus ticket office, serves good helpings of Turkish staples in a clean, bright dining room.

In warm weather, a narrow street directly behind Hotel Bozbağ (on the other side of the block) is crowded with dining tables served by several small restaurants including the good, cheap *Halil Usta Pide ve Kebap*, *Kahramanmaraş Pide ve Kebap* and *Garipoğlu 2 Restaurant*. The restaurants remain open year-round, though the tables come inside during winter.

Heading up Gazi Caddesi you'll find several bright, cheerful shops serving cakes, coffee and ice cream. Even better is the *Adı Yok Café*, upstairs at Gazi Caddesi 32. Young Giresunlus gather here to drink mugs of coffee for US$1 and listen to nightly live music.

Several *beer halls* on Osmanağa Caddesi near Otel Çarıkçı serve light meals and snacks.

The best non-hotel dining in town is at *Tibor Sosyal Tesisleri (☎ 212 2878)*, a private club which accepts tourists. Walk up the street to the right of the belediye for 30m to No 4 (on the right); take the lift to the 4th floor in cool weather, the 5th floor (roof) in summer. Local worthies (mostly men) chatting about business and football fill the other tables. Service is attentive, alcohol is served, and a full meal of meat, salad and a drink only costs about US$5.

Getting There & Away Frequent buses and minibuses shuttle between Trabzon and Giresun (US$4.50, 2½ hours). Buses and minibuses between Girseun and Ordu are similarly frequent (US$1, one hour).

Giresun to Trabzon

From Giresun it's another 150km to Trabzon. Along the way, the road passes through several small towns, including **Espiye**, with the Andoz Kalesi castle, and the attractive town of **Tirebolu**, with a chirpy small harbour, a Friday market and two castles (the St Jean Kalesi and Bedrama Kalesi). The Çaykur tea-processing plant signals your arrival in Turkey's tea country.

Just east of Tirebolu is a stretch of pebble beach. Take a Görele dolmuş to reach it.

Görele is the next town eastward, and after it is **Akçakale**, where you'll see the ruins of a 13th-century Byzantine castle on a little peninsula, marked by a prominent sign.

TRABZON

☎ 462 • pop 200,000

Immortalised in Rose Macaulay's classic novel *The Towers of Trebizond*, the modern town of Trabzon is the largest port along Eastern Turkey's Black Sea coast. Goods arrive here by sea and continue overland by road to Georgia, Armenia, Azerbaijan and Iran, a 20th-century commerce that has given Trabzon new life and a rapidly swelling population.

Modern Trabzon is thoroughly cosmopolitan. Since the collapse of the Soviet Union and the opening of formerly closed borders, traders from the Soviet Union's successor republics, particularly Georgia and Armenia, have flooded into Turkey in search of a quick buck. In their wake came an influx of prostitutes, dubbed 'Natashas' by the Turks. The traders and prostitutes are still very much in evidence, but fortunately for Trabzon they have been followed by a new wave of Russian tourists, and several agencies catering to their needs have now opened up. You'll hear Russian spoken about town and see shop signs advertising in Cyrillic script. One or two restaurants have even added a Russian twist to their menus.

Most people come to Trabzon to visit the medieval church of Aya Sofya, poke around in the old town, visit Atatürk's lovely villa

on the outskirts, and to make an excursion through the alpine scenery to Sumela, a dramatic Byzantine monastery carved out of a sheer rock cliff.

The modern town is bright, bustling and very pleased with itself, its pavements so thronged with people that you can hardly move along them. The nightmarish traffic problem could be solved by replacing the fleet of old-fashioned car-dolmuşes with the minibuses favoured by most cities, but presumably the toll in terms of unemployed drivers is too high to contemplate.

History

Trabzon's recorded history begins around 746 BC, when colonists originally from Miletus (south of Kuşadası) came from Sinop and founded a settlement (Trapezus) with its acropolis on the *trápeza*, or 'table' of land above the harbour.

The town did reasonably well for 2000 years, occupying itself with port activities, until 1204 when the soldiers of the Fourth Crusade seized and sacked Constantinople, driving its noble families to seek refuge in Anatolia. The imperial family of the Comneni established an empire along the Black Sea coast in 1204, with Alexius Comnenus I reigning as the emperor of Trebizond.

The Trapezuntine rulers became skilful at balancing their alliances with the Seljuks, the Mongols, the Genoese and others; it didn't hurt to be cut off from the rest of the country by a protective wall of mountains either. Prospering through trade with Eastern Anatolia and Persia, the empire reached the height of its wealth and culture during the reign of Alexius II (1297–1330), after which it then fell to pieces in factional disputes. Even so, the Empire of Trebizond survived until the coming of the Ottomans in 1461.

When the Ottoman Empire was defeated after WWI, Trabzon's many Greek residents sought to establish a Republic of Trebizond echoing the old Comneni Empire, but Atatürk's armies were ultimately victorious.

Orientation

Modern Trabzon is built on a mountainside. Its throbbing heart is Atatürk Alanı (or

Meydan Park) which is ringed with airline offices, hotels, restaurants, banks and Internet cafes. The port is directly east of Atatürk Alanı, down a steep hill. The Meydan Oto Parkı, just east of the İskender Paşa Camii, charges US$3.50 to park for 24 hours.

There are more cafes, bookshops and restaurants west of Atatürk Alanı along Uzun Sokak (Long Lane), and more banks along Maraş Caddesi. The lively bazaar is also to the west, in the Çarşı (Market) quarter. Even further west is Ortahisar, a picturesque old neighbourhood straddling a ravine.

Trabzon's otogar is 3km east of the port on the landward side of the shore road, Devlet Karayolu. The airport is 8km east of the town. Buses bearing the legend 'Park' or 'Meydan' go to Atatürk Alanı.

Information

The tourist office (☎/fax 321 4659) is between the Hotel Nur and Hotel Benli, behind the İskender Paşa Camii. The Tourism Police office (☎ 326 3077) is beside Atatürk Alanı, attached to the belediye.

Most banks, ATMs and exchange offices are along Maraş Caddesi. Esas Döviz accepts sterling, francs and several other currencies. Other exchange offices are on the northern side of Atatürk Alanı and in the bazaar.

The post office (PTT) is on Maraş Caddesi. For letters and cards there's also a handy booth in Atatürk Alanı.

You can buy the *Turkish Daily News* and foreign newspapers in the D&R newsagent in Uzun Sokak behind the Grand Zorlu Hotel.

Walking Tour

A pleasant way to get to grips with Trabzon's sometimes confusing topography is to start at Atatürk Alanı and walk across the city to the Gülbahar Hatun Camii.

Set off from the north-western corner of Atatürk Alanı. Walk north along Gazipaşa

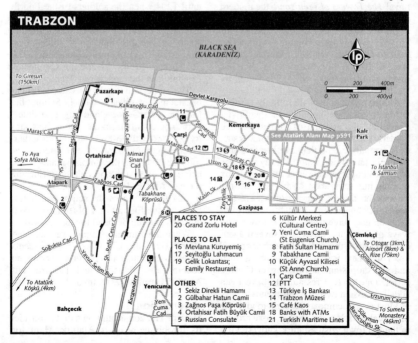

TRABZON

BLACK SEA (KARADENİZ)

To Giresun (150km)

See Atatürk Alanı Map p591

Kale Park

To İstanbul & Samsun

Çömlekçi

To Otogar (3km), Airport (8km) & Rize (75km)

To Aya Sofya Müzesi

To Atatürk Köşkü (4km)

To Sumela Monastery (46km)

PLACES TO STAY
20 Grand Zorlu Hotel

PLACES TO EAT
16 Mevlana Kuruyemiş
17 Seyitoğlu Lahmacun
19 Gelik Lokantası; Family Restaurant

OTHER
1 Sekiz Direkli Hamamı
2 Gülbahar Hatun Camii
3 Zağnos Paşa Köprüsü
4 Ortahisar Fatih Büyük Camii
5 Russian Consulate
6 Kültür Merkezi (Cultural Centre)
7 Yeni Cuma Camii (St Eugenius Church)
8 Fatih Sultan Hamamı
9 Tabakhane Camii
10 Küçük Ayvasıl Kilisesi (St Anne Church)
11 Çarşı Camii
12 PTT
13 Türkiye İş Bankası
14 Trabzon Müzesi
15 Café Kaos
18 Banks with ATMs
21 Turkish Maritime Lines

Caddesi and turn left at the first street, Kunduracılar Sokak which cuts through the **bazaar**. Keep going until you reach the recently restored **Çarşı Camii**. Enter the mosque by the northern door. On either side above the inner door, note the little 'dove temples', a fairly common feature of Ottoman architecture. The mosque's interior, adorned with crystal chandeliers, is rich in arabesques painted on domes and pillars, and trompe l'oeil 'stonework' painted on pillars and walls.

Just south-east of the Çarşı Camii is the **Taş Han** (or Vakıf Han), a collection of traders and artisans' shops set around a courtyard entered by a portal from the street and reminiscent of the hans around İstanbul's Kapalı Çarşı.

A block south-west of the Çarşı Camii on Paşahamam Sokak is the **İskender Paşa Hamamı**, an ancient Turkish bath still in use by local men.

Walk west past the İskender Paşa Hamamı and turn left at the second street, Kazazoğlu Sokak, to reach busy Maraş Caddesi and the 19th-century Müftü İsmail Efendi Camii. Follow Maraş Caddesi uphill for one block and then turn right. The crumbling **Küçük Ayvasıl Kilisesi** (Church of St Anne) is among the city's oldest buildings, having been built during the reign of Byzantine emperor Basil I in 884–5, with later renovations. It's closed to visitors.

To reach the 13th-century **Church of St Eugenius** (now the Yeni Cuma Camii), walk south to Uzun Sokak, then right (west) to the Tabakhane Köprüsü, the bridge across the steep-sided Tabakhane ravine with the big Tabakhane Camii beside it. At the eastern end of the bridge, take Sarafoğlu Sokak uphill following the signs to the Fatih Sultan Hamamı. Cami Sokak is the first right, before the hamam, and halfway up you'll see the old stones of the church-mosque on the right.

Tradition holds that Eugenius, an early Christian living here, raged against the priests of Mithra and was martyred. His skull was miraculously discovered here soon after the arrival of the Comneni imperial family, driven from Constantinople by the Fourth Crusade. St Eugenius thus became the patron saint of Trabzon.

The church was built in the 13th century, but was badly damaged in a fire in 1340, and modified during repairs. After Mehmet the Conqueror took the city in 1461, he performed his Friday ablutions in the nearby baths, proclaimed the church a mosque, prayed there, and ordered the construction of the minaret.

The mosque's north door is often locked, but the east door, reached by the courtyard to the left, may be open if the *bekçi* (guardian) is about. The building is elegantly simple, lofty and light, with three parallel naves and a transversal topped by a cupola.

Retrace your steps to the Tabakhane bridge and cross over it to reach the Ortahisar (Middle Castle), so called from its position within the old city walls and halfway up the slope. Just up the slope is the **Ortahisar Fatih Büyük Camii**, formerly the Panaghia Chrysokephalos (Gold-Topped Church of the Virgin). The building you see dates mostly from the 13th century, the time of the Comneni Empire of Trebizond, though there was probably an earlier church here. It took its name, meaning 'Gold-Topped', from gold-plated copper cladding on the cupola, an affordable Comneni extravagance as this was the principal church for imperial ceremonies. The Byzantine splendour of its decoration, however, has long since been replaced by Islamic austerity, which aids appreciation of the church's architecture.

As you enter, turn right and walk to the western end, which was the original entrance. Then walk slowly east, watching as the succession of seven arches and pseudo-arches opens above you, culminating in the dome, which, in Byzantine times, would have been ablaze in gold mosaics.

Continue west along Uzun Sokak for several hundred metres, cross the Zağnos Paşa Köprüsü (Zağnos Paşa Bridge) and go up the slope on the southern side of the Atapark to find the **Gülbahar Hatun Camii**, built by Selim the Grim, the great Ottoman conqueror of Syria and Egypt, in honour of his mother Gülbahar Hatun in 1514. Gülbahar Hatun, a princess of the Comneni imperial family, was much loved for her charitable works, which she performed for the benefit of Christians and Muslims alike. Her tomb is the little building to the east of the mosque.

The **Atapark** has a tea garden for refreshments after your walk. It also shelters a reconstructed wooden *serander* (granary) from Çağlayan, a village near Fındıklı. Afterwards, dolmuşes (US$0.30) run from beside the Gülbahar Hatun Camii along Uzun Sokak to Atatürk Alanı.

Trabzon Müzesi

Just south of Uzun Sokak at Zeytinlik Caddesi 10 is a marvellous Italian-designed mansion built for a Russian merchant in 1912 and lived in briefly by Atatürk. Inside you can examine a series of impressive living rooms, provided the curator can be found to turn on the lights.

The museum is open from 8 am to 4 pm Sunday to Thursday and admission is free.

Aya Sofya Müzesi

The Aya Sofya Müzesi, originally Hagia Sophia or Church of the Divine Wisdom, is 4km west of the centre on a terrace that once held a pagan temple. The site is above the coastal highway, reachable by city bus or dolmuş from Atatürk Alanı (look for a dolmuş saying 'Aya Sofya' on the northern side of the square).

Built between 1238 and 1263, the church was clearly influenced by eastern Anatolian and Seljuk design, although the excellent wall paintings and mosaic floors follow the style of Constantinople. Tombs were built into the northern and southern walls. Next to the church, the gloomy bell tower was finished much later, in 1427. Nothing remains of the monastery that once stood here.

The church is now a museum, open from 8 am to 5 pm daily (closed on Monday in winter); admission costs US$1.75.

Beside the museum is a tea garden set up around a reconstructed Black Sea coast farmhouse and a serander from Of county, set on tall posts to prevent mice from entering. Local women favour this place for doing their knitting.

Atatürk Köşkü

The Atatürk Köşkü or Atatürk Villa (Atatürk Pavilion on some signs), accessible by city bus or dolmuş, is 5km south-west of Atatürk Alanı. Set above the town, it has a fine view and lovely gardens. The white villa, designed in a Black Sea style popular in the Crimea, was built between 1890 and 1903 for the Karayannidis, a wealthy Trabzon banking family.

The family gave it to Atatürk when he visited the city in 1924, although he only actually visited Trabzon and stayed here on three brief occasions, the last being in 1937. When he died in 1938 the villa, and the rest of his estate, became national property. It's now a museum with Atatürk memorabilia, primarily photos of the great man in his plus-fours. There's a pleasant tea garden surrounded by hydrangeas at the back.

The villa and its well-kept gardens are open from 9 am to 7 pm (5 pm in winter) daily; admission costs US$0.50. Take a city bus (US$0.30) or dolmuş from the lower (northern) side of Atatürk Alanı. Buses depart at 20 minutes past the hour, passing the Gülbahar Hatun Camii along the way, and arriving at the villa 25 minutes later.

Sekiz Direkli Hamamı

The Sekiz Direkli (Eight-Pillared) Hamamı, near the Çarşı Camii off Kalkanoğlu Caddesi, is among the city's most pleasant Turkish baths. The rough-hewn pillars are said to date from Seljuk times, although the rest of the building has been modernised. The bath is open from 8 am to 5 pm daily for men except on Thursdays when women get their turn. It costs US$6 to use the bath and US$4 more for a wash and massage.

Boztepe

On the hillside 2km south-east of Atatürk Alanı is the Boztepe Piknik Alanı with fine views of the city and the sea. In ancient times Boztepe harboured temples to the Persian sun god Mithra and to Apollo. Later the Byzantines built several churches and monasteries here, of which the ruins of the Convent of Panaya Theoskepastos, or Kızlar Manastırı, are the most prominent.

To get there from Atatürk Alanı, take a bus labelled 'Park-Boztepe Bld Dinlenme Tesisleri' or a Boztepe dolmuş (from beside the Halkbank on the northern side of Atatürk Alanı). The route goes uphill 1.5km to the local orthopaedic hospital, then another 700m to Boztepe park.

Kaymaklı Manastırı

The former Armenian monastery at Kaymaklı makes an interesting excursion to the semi-rural outskirts of Trabzon. Catch any bus or dolmuş going uphill on Taksim Caddesi just above Atatürk Alanı and headed for Çukurayır; tell the driver you want to get out at the Mısırlı Camii. Keep walking along the same road for 100m, then turn left downhill on a rutted, unpaved, unmarked road. Follow the road for 800m, bearing right at a fork and later turning sharp right at a concreted intersection. Soon you'll see on the left the farm buildings of Mr İdris and Mrs Sevgi Kantekin, overlooking the steep valley up which the Erzurum highway passes.

With your own vehicle, in dry weather you can drive right to the farm, but you could get trapped if the road is muddy.

İdris Bey and Sevgi Hanım are used to visitors, but during the busy farming season it may be one of their children who shows you the fine frescoes (in better condition than most of those at Sumela) in the former *katholikon* (monastery church), now used as a barn. Government archaeologists have apparently studied the building, but have allotted no money for its preservation.

To return to Trabzon, it's best to retrace your steps uphill, although you can continue following the very rough, stony track downhill for almost 1km to the highway, and hope to catch a bus or dolmuş for the 4.5km ride back to Atatürk Alanı.

Places to Stay – Budget

Unfortunately, many of Trabzon's cheap hotels are filled with traders and prostitutes from the former Soviet republics, and with so much willing custom, there's little incentive to maintain standards.

Most of the cheapies are off the north-eastern corner of Atatürk Alanı on Güzel-hisar Caddesi. Whether you'll want to stay here is probably a matter of personal taste but some women have reported being frighteningly hassled. At the time of writing the following hotels seemed to be 'Natasha'-free zones but the situation can easily change.

Hotel Anıl (☎ 326 7282, Güzelhisar Caddesi 10) is a good choice, with clean singles/doubles with shower and TV for US\$12/20, including breakfast. Some rooms have harbour views.

Hotel Gözde (☎ 321 9579, Salih Yazıcı Sokak 7), just off Güzelhisar Caddesi, could certainly do with a makeover but the rooms, for US\$4.50 a head, are tolerable and the owner is doing his best to resist temptation to sell up.

The aged *Hotel Benli (☎ 321 1022, Cami Çıkmazı 5)* is just off the eastern end of Atatürk Alanı, uphill behind the belediye. It looks as if nothing much has changed since the day it opened but beds could hardly be cheaper, at US\$3.50 a head, plus another US\$1 for a hot shower.

Better than this is the nearby *Hotel Nur (☎ 321 2798, fax 321 9576, Cami Sokak 4)*, where clean singles cost US\$12/20 with shower; the rooms in the eaves have fine views.

Travellers can also stay in the hostel of the *Sankta Maria Katolik Kilisesi (☎ 321 2192, Sümer Sokak 26)*, a few blocks downhill (north) from Atatürk Alanı. Built by French Capuchins in 1869 when Trabzon was a cosmopolitan trading port, the hostel offers clean simple rooms and the use of hot showers in exchange for a (realistic) donation. You needn't be Catholic to stay here.

Places to Stay – Mid-Range

The comfortable four-star *Hotel Usta (☎ 326 5700, fax 322 3793, Telgrafhane Sokak 1)* is close to the İskender Paşa Camii, near the north-eastern corner of Atatürk Alanı in a fairly quiet yet convenient location. It has singles/doubles with bath, TV and minibar for US\$45/60, including breakfast. If they're not busy, prices might drop by up to 25%.

Just as good is the fairly quiet, three-star *Otel Horon (☎ 326 6455, fax 321 6628,*

The Natasha Syndrome

The collapse of the Soviet Union in 1990 and the liberation of the ethnic nation-states of Georgia, Armenia and Azerbaijan brought a sudden influx of 'Russians' into north-eastern Turkey. The early traders were soon followed by a flood of women who saw the potential for enriching themselves in Turkey's sexually conservative society.

Of course there's nothing new about prostitution in Turkey. Almost every town of any size has a *genelev* (brothel) on the outskirts where many a Turkish male has received his sexual initiation. It's a testimony to the popularity of these places that throughout the 1980s and early 1990s Turkey's single highest tax-payer was Matild Manukyan, a Turkish-Armenian entrepreneur who, along with her fashion apparel enterprises, was madam of a string of brothels.

But whereas traditional brothels have always kept a low profile, the Russians operate quite openly in the centre of towns, and to such an extent that it's very hard to find a legitimate hotel in Trabzon, Rize, Pazar, Ardeşen, Hopa or Artvin.

With their bleach-blonde hair, halter-neck tops and mini skirts, the 'Natashas' – as they have been dubbed for obvious reasons – are virtual parodies of themselves. Venture into a *gazino* (nightclub) in any of the aforementioned towns and you'll see them in action, but don't expect to get away with your curiosity free of charge, especially if you're male.

Old-style Turkish brothels are controlled by the government and women working in them are required to undergo regular health checks. With the new-style arrangements, however, anything goes. Reliable *prezervatif* (condoms) are readily available in pharmacies but the Turkish male is no better known for his readiness to wear one than his counterparts elsewhere. The 'Natashas' therefore represent one very obvious way for AIDS to get its teeth into Turkey.

Some 'Natashas' look upon their youthful years as a time to make good money and save it for later. One such immigrant told a Turkish reporter that she had a husband and children back home, and would return and open a shop when she'd saved up enough capital.

The influx of 'Natashas' has caused consternation among Turkish call girls who work (illegally) outside the brothels. One Turkish newspaper ran a story on two such girls who had been arrested in İstanbul. They had bleached their hair and learned a few words of Russian. When asked why, they answered, 'Are you kidding? We can charge three or four times as much! Turkish men think Natashas are exotic and think they know how to do different things than we do.'.

Sıramağazalar Caddesi 125), with comfortable modern rooms for US$50/65.

Places to Stay – Top End

The five-star **Grand Hotel Zorlu** (☎ 326 8400, fax 326 8458, Maraş Caddesi 9) is centrally positioned and charges US$142/193 for nice, comfortable, modern rooms with all mod cons. There's a grand glass-ceilinged atrium sitting area, a health club, an indoor swimming pool and a restaurant that's not quite as expensive as you might fear.

Places to Eat

Atatürk Alanı is surrounded by places to get a quick, cheap bite. On the southern side is **Çınar Lokantası**, reliably good and cheap, with prices posted prominently and a good selection of ready meals, best eaten at lunch time, when they're fresh.

Across the other side of the square is the hectic, crowded, cheap and noisy **Meydan Kebap Salonu**, with full meals for less than US$4. In season (ie, in winter) this is a good place to sample a *hamsi* (anchovy) omelette; one portion should be enough for two people. At other times of year try the nearby **Murat Balık Salonu** for a choice of reasonably priced fish dishes.

Also on this side of the square are **Derya Restaurant**, across from the belediye, with a good selection of ready food and tasty İskender kebap (US$2.50), **Volkan 2 Lokan-**

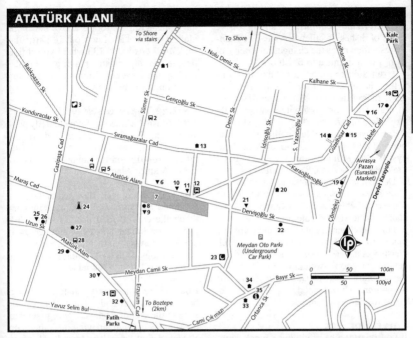

ATATÜRK ALANI

PLACES TO STAY		16	Hisar Kafeterya (Russian		17	Karden Line Office

ATATÜRK ALANI

PLACES TO STAY
1   Sankta Maria Hostel
13   Otel Horon
14   Hotel Gözde
15   Hotel Anıl
20   Hotel Usta
33   Hotel Nur
34   Hotel Benli

PLACES TO EAT
6   Meydan Kebap Salonu
9   Kıbrıs Restaurant
10   Murat Balık Salonu
11   Volkan 2 Lokantası; Güloğlu

16   Hisar Kafeterya (Russian
     Restaurant)
21   Derya Restaurant
25   Çardak Pide Salonu
30   Çınar Lokantası

OTHER
2   Havaalanı (Airport) Dolmuş
3   Georgian Consulate
4   Boztepe Dolmuş
5   Aya Sofya Dolmuş
7   Belediye (Town Hall)
8   Tourism Police
12   Garajlar Dolmuş to Otogar

17   Karden Line Office
18   Maritime Passenger Terminal
19   Afacan Tur
22   Entrance to Car Park
23   İskender Paşa Camii
24   Atatürk Statue; Tea Gardens
26   Turkish Airlines Office
27   Gümüşsu Kuşburnu
     Showroom
28   Dolmuş to Sumela
29   Trabzonspor Supporters Shop
31   Sumela (Ulusoy) Otogar
32   Metro Bus Ticket Office
35   Tourist Office

tası, and the big, bright **Güloğlu** which sells pastries as well as the usual kebaps.

On the eastern side of the square **Kıbrıs Restaurant** has a small dining room at street level and a bigger one upstairs which tends to fill up with male drinkers at night. Dishes include the Turkish classics, and a meal with a beer might cost from US$6 or US$8.

More imaginative fare is available along Uzun Sokak. **Seyitoğlu Lahmacun**, just over a block west of Atatürk Alanı, serves good, cheap lahmacun, and is friendly to both men and women. Likewise **Çardak Pide Salonu**, directly behind the Turkish Airlines building in a vine-shaded courtyard away from the traffic noise. Freshly baked pide costs US$1.50 to US$2. Further down the road *Gelik Lokantası* has an impressive range of dishes, if sullen service. The *Family* restaurant rings the changes on a range of dishes with tiramisu to finish off.

Uzun Sokak also has a number of shops selling hazelnuts, *lokum* (Turkish delight), helva (a traditional sweet) and *pestil* (sheets of dried fruit) for those with a sweet tooth. Try *Mevlana Kuruyemiş* at No 31, four shops west of Seyitoğlu Lahmacun. Splash out and buy some of the pricey local honeys; *kestane balı* (chestnut honey) is one of the cheaper ones at US$11 a kilo.

Down a few steps on the northern side of Güzelhisar Caddesi you'll find *Hisar Kafeterya* which serves a range of 'Russian' cuisine at moderate prices.

For a quick tea or cold drink there are few places to beat Atatürk Alanı itself, which consists of a series of shady *tea gardens*, excellent for people-watching. Look out, on the southern side, for *Gümüşsu Kuşburnu Showroom*, a health-food shop selling packets of rosehip syrup and blackberry juice.

Entertainment

If you're after a beer without a meal, Trabzon boasts several basement *gazinos* (nightclubs) of varying degrees of seediness. If you're after a glimpse of a side of Turkey the tourist offices keep very quiet about, these could prove illuminating, and sometimes action-packed. Lone women would be unwise to go near them.

Recently, several more presentable cafes have opened in the rooms above the shops along Uzun Sokak. Look out in particular for *Cafe Kaos* at No 133 where you'll find people making music, playing Scrabble, reading the papers and just plain lounging about on floor cushions.

Getting There & Away

Air Turkish Airlines has frequent daily nonstop flights between Trabzon and Ankara and İstanbul. The Turkish Airlines office (☎ 321 1680) is on the south-western corner of Atatürk Alanı.

Bus Trabzon's otogar, 3km east of the port, is served by buses and dolmuşes running along the coastal road and up to Atatürk Alanı. The otogar has a left-luggage area, post office, restaurant, cafeteria, barber and simple shops. Details of some useful daily services are listed in the table.

Boat There's a weekly car-ferry service between Trabzon and İstanbul from mid-June to the end of August, leaving İstanbul on Monday at 2 pm, arriving in Trabzon on Wednesday at 8 am. The ferry heads on to Rize, arriving at noon on Wednesday, then stops at Trabzon at about 7pm on the way back. It leaves Trabzon for İstanbul on Wednesday at 8 pm, arriving in İstanbul on Friday at 1 pm.

Per-person fares between İstanbul and Trabzon are US$21 for a Pullman seat,

Services from Trabzon's Otogar

destination	fare (US$)	duration (hr)	distance (km)	daily services
Ankara	18–20	12	780	frequent buses
Artvin	7	4½	255	occasional buses
Baku (Azerbaijan)	45	28	–	1 bus nightly
Erzurum	10	6	325	several buses
Hopa	4.50	3	165	half-hourly buses
İstanbul	24–32	18	1110	several buses
Kars	12	12	525	change at Erzurum or Artvin
Kayseri	22	12	686	several buses
Rize	2.50	1	75	shuttle dolmuşes
Samsun	9	6	365	frequent buses
Tflis (Georgia)	25	20	–	1 bus nightly

US$44 to US$104 for cabin berths; breakfast is US$5, US$12 for lunch or dinner. Cars cost US$102; motorcycles are US$42.

In high summer ferries go between Trabzon and Sochi in Russia at 6 pm daily except Saturday. They're operated by three different companies but Karden Line (☎ 326 9072, fax 326 1401), İskele Caddesi 55, down by the harbour, can sell tickets for all of them. The Turkish Maritime Lines office is at the harbour (☎ 321 1156).

A berth in a four-berth cabin costs US$60, a berth in a three-berth cabin with toilet US$70. A few Pullman seats at US$50 each may also be available. You will probably need to have sorted out your Russian visa before leaving home to use this service, however. Check with the Russian consulate.

Organised Tours Usta Tour (☎ 326 1870, fax 326 1871), İskele Caddesi 4, offers reasonably priced trips to Sumela and Karaca Cave (US$6; departs daily at 9 am), Uzungöl (US$8.50; Saturdays, 9 am), and Rize and Ayder (US$10; Sundays, 9 am). Afacan Tur (☎ 321 5804, fax 321 7001), İskele Caddesi 40/C, has a similar program. If you're on your own or pushed for time these could be worth trying.

Getting Around

To/From the Airport The airport (*havaalanı*) is 5.5km east of Atatürk Alanı. Dolmuşes to the airport leave from a side street on the northern side of Atatürk Alanı, near the Toros Hotel.

Bus To reach Atatürk Alanı from the otogar, cross the shore road in front of the terminal, turn left, walk to the bus stop and catch any bus with 'Park' or 'Meydan' in its name; the dolmuş for Atatürk Alanı is marked 'Garajlar-Meydan'. A taxi between the otogar and Atatürk Alanı costs US$4.

Getting to the otogar, the easiest way is to catch a dolmuş marked 'Garajlar' or 'KTU' from the north-eastern side of Atatürk Alanı.

Dolmuş Dolmuşes mainly leave from Atatürk Alanı, although you can flag them down along their routes. Whatever your destination, the fare should be about US$0.30.

Away from Atatürk Alanı beware of dolmuş drivers who suddenly claim they're driving private taxis. If the vehicle has 'taksi' written on the roof, it's a taxi; if it has a named destination, it's a dolmuş and that should be the end of it.

AROUND TRABZON
Sumela Monastery

The Greek Orthodox Monastery of the Virgin Mary at Sumela, 46km south of Trabzon, was founded in Byzantine times and abandoned in 1923 after the creation of the Turkish Republic put paid to hopes of creating a new Greek state in this region. The monastery clings to a sheer rock wall high above evergreen forests and a rushing mountain stream. It can be a mysterious, eerie place, especially when mists swirl among the tops of the trees in the valley below.

If you want good photographs, come as early in the morning as possible. Note that on Wednesdays in summer, when the ferry from İstanbul arrives in Trabzon, Sumela is crowded with cruise passengers. It's very busy over summer weekends too.

To get to Sumela take the Erzurum road and turn left for Sumela (16km) at Maçka, 29km south of Trabzon. It's also signposted as Meryemana, because the monastery was dedicated to the Virgin Mary.

The road then winds into dense evergreen forests, following the course of a rushing mountain stream interrupted by commercial trout pools. Village houses reminiscent of those in alpine areas of central Europe are interspersed with more modern brick blocks. The road is subject to landslides, and may be impassable after heavy rains.

At the entrance to Altındere National Park you pay an admission fee of US$1.75 (half price for students) to visit the monastery. Opening hours depend on the time of year, but are 9 am to 6 pm from June to August.

At the end of the road you'll find a shady park with picnic tables and fireplaces by a roaring brook, a post office, the Sumela Restaurant and several A-frame shelters for rent (no camping is allowed).

The head of the trail up to the monastery begins in the picnic area and is steep but easy to follow. A second trail begins further up the valley. To get to it, follow the unpaved road 1km uphill and across two bridges (after the second one turn and look up for a good view of the monastery) until you come to a wooden footbridge over the stream on the right, marked by a sign reading 'Manastıra gider' (To the monastery). This trail cuts straight up through the trees, past another small, abandoned church. On busy days it's likely to be much quieter than the one pointed out by the guides.

If you drive even further up the road, you reach a small muddy parking lot from which it's only a five- or 10-minute walk to the monastery.

As you climb through forests and alpine meadows, catching occasional glimpses of the monastery above you, the air gets noticeably cooler. In all you'll ascend 250m in about 30 to 45 minutes (if you're in moderately good shape). In autumn just before the snow arrives, a beautiful variety of crocus, called *kar çiçeği* (snowflower) blooms in the meadows.

Over the last five years the monastery has been restored (some would say rebuilt). Purists probably won't like it but the effect has been to make more sense of the various chapels and rooms (look out for the old lavatories). The main chapel, cut into the rock, is covered both inside and outside with frescoes. The earliest examples date from the 9th century but most of them are actually 19th-century work. Sadly, bored shepherd boys used the paintings as targets for their catapults and later, visitors who should have known better scratched their names into them. On top of all that antiquity thieves have also been a problem so it's perhaps surprising there's anything left to admire.

Beside the ticket office there's a small teahouse (twice the usual price per glass) offering limited light refreshments and toilets.

Places to Stay & Eat Ask at the National Park (Milli Parkı) office (☎ 531 1061) beside the parking lot at Sumela and you might be able to rent one of the five A-frame *bungalows* that sleep four people for US$12.50 per night.

With your own transport another possibility is to stay in Coşandere, a tiny village 5km out of Maçka. You can camp in the grounds of the **Coşandere Restaurant** (☎ 531 1190) where *canlı alabalık* (fresh trout) is a popular menu item; or stay in one of several small pensions, the most interesting housed in three seranders with picnic tables on terraces in front of them.

About 3km from Maçka (12km from Sumela) is **Sumela Camping** (☎ 512 1581), a camping ground beside a stream.

In Maçka itself there's the four-star hotel **Büyük Sumela** (☎ 512 3542) with an Internet cafe right next door.

Getting There & Away In summer Ulusoy runs buses from Trabzon to Sumela, departing at 10 am (returning at 3 pm) from the town-centre Sumela otogar just uphill from Atatürk Alanı (US$7, 45 minutes).

Dolmuşes for Coşandere village (US$3) depart all day from the Çömlekçi dolmuş ranks down on the coastal highway next to the Avrasya Pazarı. They often go as far as Sumela, or you can pay them to do so.

Trabzon travel agencies (for more details, see Organised Tours in the Trabzon Getting There & Away section earlier in this chapter) run 'tours' to Sumela. They tend to hustle visitors back down from the monastery and leave them at the restaurant for two hours. Perhaps the best thing to do is to check the time of the return journey and then let the guide know you can manage without them. In summer Usta Tour combines the trip to Sumela with one to the recently opened Karaca Cave near Gümüşhane.

Taxis leaving from opposite McDonald's in Atatürk Alanı charge US$30 to US$35 for a carload of people there and back, with two hours of waiting time.

TRABZON TO ERZURUM

Heading south into the mountains, you're in for a long (325km) but scenic ride. The atmospheric pressure at sea level is much greater than it is in the mountains. If you have a full water bottle in your pack at Trabzon, it will have burst or leaked by the time you reach Gümüşhane. If you're descending from Erzurum to Trabzon, the water bottle will collapse and leak due to the increase in pressure as you descend. Try and remember to adjust the pressure as you travel.

Along the highway south, you zoom straight to Maçka, 35km inland from Trabzon. About 1.5km north of Maçka look out along the roadside for basaltic rock columns resembling California's Devil's Postpile or Northern Ireland's Giant's Causeway. From Maçka, you begin the long, slow climb along a serpentine mountain road through active landslide zones to the breathtaking **Zigana Geçidi** (Zigana Pass) at an altitude of 2030m. The landscape is one of sinuous valleys and cool pine forests with dramatic light. Just before the pass there's a small *restaurant*, shop and holiday village.

The dense, humid air of the coast disappears as you rise and becomes light and dry as you reach the southern side of the Eastern Black Sea Mountains. Along with the landscape, the towns and villages change: Black Sea towns look vaguely Balkan, while places higher up appear much more Central Asian. Snow can be seen in all months except perhaps July, August and September.

Gümüşhane, about 125km south of Trabzon, is a small town in a mountain valley with a few simple travellers services, but not much to stop for except the scenery.

By the time you reach the provincial capital of **Bayburt**, 195km from Trabzon, you're well into the rolling steppe and low mountains of the high Anatolian plateau. A dry, desolate place, Bayburt has a big medieval fortress and simple travellers services. The road from Bayburt passes through green, rolling farm country with stands of poplar trees and flocks of brown-fleeced sheep. Wayside stalls sell locally made pestil, sundried fruit pressed into sheets. In early summer wild flowers are everywhere.

Exactly 80km west of Erzurum is the **Kop Geçidi** (Kop Pass) at an altitude of 2370m. A monument here commemorates the countless Turkish soldiers who lost their lives fighting for this pass under the most dire conditions during the War of Independence.

From Kop Pass, the open road to Erzurum offers fast, easy travelling.

EAST FROM TRABZON
Uzungöl
☎ 462 • elevation 1100m
About 56km east of Trabzon is a town called Of. Go south 25km up the Solaklı creek valley past the town of Çaykara, then another 16km along a rough road to Uzungöl (Long Lake) to enjoy the mountain air and perhaps hike in the countryside.

Uzungöl is a popular destination for local people on weekend outings, so try and come midweek if you want to stay. In Uzungöl village right beside the lake is *Özkan Otel ve Restoran (☎ 656 6197)*, a simple place with singles/doubles for US$10/18. The more basic *Uzungöl Pansiyon (☎ 656 6129)* is even closer to the water. Beyond the actual lake, *Sezgin Motel (☎ 656 6175)* charges US$10 per person for room, breakfast and dinner in pine cabins, with trout from the adjacent fish farm served up in the restaurant. *İnan Kardeşler Tesisleri (☎ 656 6021)* charges much the same and serves delicious meals of local trout for around US$10.

At weekends you may be able to get a dolmuş direct from Trabzon to Uzungöl. Failing that, take a Rize-bound dolmuş to Of and then wait for another heading inland. Afacan Tur and Usta Tour in Trabzon (see Organised Tours in the Trabzon Getting There & Away section earlier in this chapter) run tours to Uzungöl every weekend. They're popular with locals but tend to focus more on lunch than on seeing the best of the scenery. Tours cost US$10, give or take the cost of lunch.

Rize
☎ 464 • pop 74,000
About 75km east of Trabzon, Rize lies at the heart of Turkey's tea plantation area. Rize has been growing rapidly and is not, at first sight, an appealing place but if you have a few hours to spare there are a couple of interesting places to visit, especially around the Merkez Seyh Camii.

The summer-only tourist office (☎ 213 0407) is next to the beautifully reconstructed central post office, with two grand Ottoman houses soaring above it. The one on the right houses the museum, the one on the left an excellent cafe (see Places to Eat later in this section).

Ritur (☎ 217 1484, fax 217 1486, [e] i.h.yil diz@ihlas.net.tr) at Cumhuriyet Caddesi 93 is a local trekking company offering trips over the top of the Kaçkar Mountains between Erzurum and Trabzon, and into neighbouring Georgia.

Rize Müzesi Up the hill behind the tourist office is Rize Müzesi in a fine reconstructed Ottoman house. The rooms upstairs have been decorated in Ottoman style, with all sorts of textiles on display. Mannequins also model Laz costume from central Rize and Hemşin costume from around Ayder, but without conceding the separate ethnicity of the wearers.

The museum is open from 9 am to 4 pm daily for US$1.75.

Tea Research Institute The steep hillsides above the town are thickly planted with tea, which is cured, dried and blended here, then shipped throughout the country. Not surprisingly, one of Rize's main attractions is the Tea Research Institute (Atatürk Çay Araştırma Enstitüsü), 800m above town via the steep, sticky road behind the Merkez Seyh Camii. Keep walking up until you come to a crossroads, then take the turn to the right that doubles back above you and keep climbing. A taxi from outside the mosque will run you there for US$1.

The institute's grounds are a *tea garden* set amid hollyhocks, roses and hydrangeas. The views are great, the tea even better. In summer you can sit out here until 10.30 pm.

Places to Stay There are plenty of reasonably priced hotels although many double as brothels.

One of the cheapest is *Otel Akarsu*, in an excellent position right beside the main square with most of the sights nearby. The staff don't seem to be anticipating any guests but rooms cost only about US$5 per person.

Otel Efes (☎ 214 1111, Atatürk Caddesi) has a pretty kilim-filled lobby and clean, presentable singles/doubles with bath for US$15/30, including breakfast.

For two-star comfort, try the *Otel Keleş* (☎ 217 4612, fax 217 1895, Palandöken Caddesi 2) which has spacious rooms with a weird array of furnishings for around US$12 a head, good value for money.

The three-star *Hotel Asnur* (☎ 214 1751, fax 214 0397, Cumhuriyet Caddesi 165) is a bit pricey at US$45/74/90 a single/double/triple but rooms have fairly modern decor and all the trimmings: TV, minibar, hair dryer etc. The surroundings are not great but it's a good deal more convenient than the four-star *Hotel Dedeman Rize* (☎ 223 4444, fax 223 5348, Alipaşa Köyü), right out on the western outskirts with all the usual mod cons and prices to match.

Places to Eat There are plenty of simple kebap and pide places along Cumhuriyet Caddesi, including the vast *Bekiroğlu* and two branches of *Mis Lahmacun* where you can expect to get away with a quick bite for around US$2. For something classier try *Müze Kafeterya* in a restored Ottoman building up the hill behind the main post office and popular with young Rizelis. Here you can sample Black Sea delicacies such as muhlama (thick melted cheese soup) and sarma (stuffed cabbage leaves) for about US$2 per serving. The upstairs *Konak Restaurant* serves the same food in more formal surroundings.

Getting There & Away Although Rize does have an otogar, many of the buses and dolmuşes plying the coastal highway drop passengers off along the seafront. Minibuses to Hopa (US$2.50, two hours, frequent) leave from out on the main highway to the east, those to Trabzon (US$2, one hour, every 20 minutes) further to the west.

The harbour for ferries to İstanbul (in the summer months only) is even further west; arriving by ferry, turn right at the harbour gate to walk into town (about 1km), or flag down a dolmuş. Ferries arrive in Rize from Trabzon at noon on Wednesday and leave later the same day, arriving in İstanbul at 1 pm on Friday.

KAÇKAR DAĞLARI

The Kaçkar Dağları (Kaçkar Mountains) is a range in the north-east of Turkey with its highest point at **Kaçkar Dağı**, Mt Kaçkar (3937m). The Kaçkars are increasingly popular for trekking trips of anything from one to 10 days. Provided you bring a tent, sleeping bag and good shoes you could even spend a month exploring the mountains and alpine summer villages.

The Kaçkar trekking season is short and it's unwise to arrive at any time outside mid-May to mid-September without phoning first to ensure the place you want to stay in is open. It's possible to arrive in Ayder even in early May, and find only one or two pensions and no restaurants open, and no organised transport to get you back down to Çamlıhemşin either. Someone is bound to come to your assistance but it's best to plan ahead accordingly.

Trekking Guides

Although some people are happy striking off into the mountains alone, others will want a guide. Adnan Pirikoğlu at the Pirikoğlu Aile Lokantası in Ayder (☎ 657 2021, 655 5084) is a mountain guide who knows the area like the back of his hand and can be found in the village year-round. Another guide well worth talking to is Mehmet Demirci who runs the Fora Pansiyon in Ayder (☎ 657 2153) and the Türkü Tourism Travel Agency (☎ 464-651 7230) in Çamlıhemşin.

The Mountains of Turkey by Karl Smith (Cicerone Press) has detailed information on hiking in the Kaçkar Dağları but is not very up-to-date. Check Cicerone's Web site (www.cicerone.co.uk) for more details.

Çamlıhemşin

About 40km east of Rize (124km east of Trabzon), just within the western limits of Ardeşen, a road on the right is signposted for Çamlıhemşin (20km), a village deep in the Kaçkars. As you head along the valley, you'll pass several ancient humpback bridges across the Fırtına Çayı, restored in

honour of the 75th anniversary of the Turkish Republic in 1999 so that they look like garden ornaments.

Unfortunately the stones needed to widen the coastal road are being quarried in this area and heavy trucks laden with rocks trundle up and down, detracting from enjoyment of the scenery. The Çamlıhemşin area also has the cloud of yet another giant engineering project hanging over it. If the brains behind this scheme get their way, two-thirds of the water of the Fırtına Cayı will be diverted through a tunnel in the mountains to create a giant power-generating waterfall. At the time of writing the project was on hold but no-one seemed very convinced that it wouldn't be revived.

There's nothing much to linger for in Çamlıhemşin itself, unless perhaps you need to use an ATM or get something to eat in which case the *Park Lokanta* serves the usual array of grills and soups. The *Hoşdere Restaurant*, with a wooden terrace over the river at the back, used to be a good choice but seems to have fallen on hard times. For a trout lunch you'd be better off walking through the village and following the signs for Şenyuva about 100m for the *Yeşilvadi* and a much nicer setting.

Just beyond Çamlıhemşin the road forks and you'll have to decide whether to go straight ahead (signposted 'Zil Kalesi') for Şenyuva or left (signposted 'Ayder Kaplıcaları') for Ayder.

Şenyuva
☎ 464

Şenyuva is beautiful but has limited public transport. You may have to walk to and from Camlıhemşin or take a taxi for about US$5 each way.

About 5km from Camlıhemşin you'll find *Otel Doğa* (☎ 651 7455) run by İdris Duman who speaks French and English. Some of the simple rooms here have balconies overlooking the river, and there are two suites for up to six people, one with a double balcony. Beds cost US$7 each without meals, US$12.50 for half board. There's a big, inviting lounge and a restaurant overlooking the river.

Another 2km along the road, reached by a chairlift across the river, is *Sisi Pansiyon* (☎ 653 3043), operated by Doris Güney, who organises treks into the nearby mountains. Beds in A-frame bungalows will set you back US$16, or use your own tent for much less. This place is only open in July and August though.

Immediately across from the Sisi Pansiyon the old primary school buildings were being converted into the *Fırtına Pansiyon* (☎/fax 653 3111) at the time of writing. Beds in cheerfully painted rooms in the former school or in new pine cabins will cost around US$20 per person for half board.

From Şenyuva the road continues past the ruins of Zilkale castle to **Çat** (1250m), a mountain hamlet used as a trekking base. There's one simple hotel there, the *Cancık* (☎ 651 4120), open only in high summer.

AYDER
☎ 464 ● elevation 1300m

Ayder is a high-pasture village with two *kaplıcalar* (hot springs). However, if you're anticipating an alpine village of picturesque wooden chalets, forget it. Sadly, the build-it-quick-cheap-and-high merchants had already set to work with their concrete and brick before a halt to their activities was called, and now the Rize town planners have stepped in to bring pink pavements and city street lights to a once-pastoral settlement. The setting is still glorious, with the snow-capped mountains soaring over the village, and water cascading down from a dozen small waterfalls, and in theory new buildings must now be in 'traditional style' (ie, sheathed in wood), but at the time of writing a big new restaurant and chalet complex of wholly inappropriate materials was being built beside the baths. The irony of it is that beneath the Sis Hotel a new more environmentally sensitive building had just been erected – but for government officials only.

In August the village can hardly cope with the flood of local tourists, especially at weekends when, despite the growing number of hotels, most places will be full by mid-afternoon. At other times of year there may be only three or four local families living here.

Orientation & Information

About 4.5km below Ayder is a gate where you must pay an admission fee of US$1.50 in season.

The village is scattered for 2km on both sides of the road but nowadays some of the better accommodation choices are actually past Ayder itself, along the new road, which is being driven ever further up into the mountains.

There is nowhere to change money in Ayder.

Things to See & Do

Most people come to Ayder as a base for trekking in the mountains, but even if you don't have time to do that it's still worth popping up here for a day or so to take in the wonderful scenery.

When you return from your trek it will feel like heaven to be able to soak in the **kaplıca** (hot spring) where the water reaches temperatures of 56°C (133°F); it's said to be good for ulcers, skin complaints, cuts and allergies. The separate sections for men and women are open from 7 am to 8 pm daily. A session in a general bath costs US$2.50; private family pools cost US$7 per hour; children under seven get to bathe free.

Once inside the baths you'll encounter a plethora of official-looking signs in Turkish only. For those still struggling, the gist of these signs is that you must wash before bathing, you mustn't wear your ordinary day clothes in the pool, you mustn't swim in the pool, and if you want to stay in for more than an hour you should buy a second ticket. One final sign advises against staying in the water for more than 10 minutes at a time.

If you visit Ayder over a summer weekend you may also get the chance to see reminders of the **Hemşin culture** (see the boxed text 'The Laz & Hemşin Peoples' at the start of this chapter). Wander into the meadow south of Ayder to see groups of Hemşin holiday-makers dancing a conga-like dance to the whining rhythm of the *tulum*, a type of bagpipes made out of a goatskin. Everywhere you will see women in their splendid headdresses, incongruously topping off cardigans, long skirts and trainers.

Places to Stay

All of Ayder's hotels are pretty basic. Beds in waterless rooms usually cost between US$5 and US$7 in summer but at other times you can virtually name your price.

Coming in from the north, the first place you come to on the right is the ugly new *Sis Hotel* with its own restaurant. A bit further up on the left is the similar *Otel Ayder* (☎ 657 2039), with clean, simple rooms, some with nice views, also with its own restaurant.

Beside the Ayder a chairlift carries bags up to the far more inviting *Fora Pansiyon* (☎ 657 2153, fax 651 7570). Rooms here may be simple but they're quieter, with good views, besides which the pension is a much more attractive wooden chalet. You'll pay US$12 for half board, less if you want to cook for yourself.

Next up on the left is *Otel Pirikoğlu* (☎ 657 2021) with pine beds in clean rooms. There's a kitchen for guests to use, and more pleasant mountain views. This is usually one of the cheaper places to stay, charging perhaps US$3.50 a head.

A sign on the right points to one of the better choices, *Otel Yeşil Vadi* (☎ 657 5051), where clean, simple rooms are more spacious than usual. The newer pine ones on the top are best if you can get one.

One of Ayder's more visually distinguished hotels is *Hotel Saray* (☎/fax 657 2002), on the left on a bluff. Inside, however, it's not much different from the others and the fact that the rooms open off a central area with TV could mean noisy nights.

Don't let the name of the *Ayder Hilton Hotel* (☎ 657 2024) fool you. There's nothing remotely luxurious about this place, a large, prominent, ugly but serviceable building.

A path running up beside the run-down Hotel Saray leads to *Hotel Kaçkar* (☎ 657 2041). Washing facilities here are pretty rudimentary but there are a couple of single rooms if you arrive late and the other places want to sting you for two beds.

Continue past the baths and you'll come to *Otel Çağlayan* (☎ 657 2073), a family-run place in a wooden building on the right.

At this point you might think Ayder finishes but press on up the hill and on the right you'll see the *Kuşpuni* pension (☎ 657 2052, fax 657 2151) where rooms are still very simple but mainly designed for small groups; a room for three people costs US$40, one for four US$55 and one for six US$75. Six people can also rent the stilted wooden serander, or granary, beside the main building. In the past every house would have had one of these buildings to store food throughout the winter.

Further up and on the left is the *Ahşap Pansiyon* (☎ 657 2162), a family-run place with cabin-like rooms boasting stout bedding at US$12.50 a head for bed and breakfast; it's a good choice.

Still further up on the right is the *Üçhanlar Yıldırım Aile Pansiyonu* (☎ 657 2121) with a few double rooms (US$17) and a kitchen for guest use.

Places to Eat

These days many people eat in their pensions but if you want to be different, right beside the ford is the *Nazlı Çiçek* restaurant which specialises in trout; two fish, some rice and a non-alcoholic drink will cost about US$4. At the time of writing the adjacent *Otel Saray Et ve Balık Restoran* was being rebuilt but it should have reopened by the time you read this. Food is also available at the *Yeşil Vadi Café*.

Shopping

Ayder is a good place to buy pretty patterned woollen socks made by the local women; ask and there's a fair chance your pension owner will have a cache awaiting your perusal. Socks are reasonably priced but the scarves the Hemşin women wear are pricier than you might expect, as is Ayder *balı* (honey) which can cost around US$25 a kilo (a snip compared with honey from Anzer in the Rize Valley which costs a cool US$160 a kilo).

Getting There & Away

In summer there are hourly dolmuşes between Pazar on the coast and Çamlıhemşin, some of which continue on to Ayder. On summer Sundays the trickle of minibuses up to Ayder turns into a flood. Otherwise, passengers are mostly shoppers from the villages, so dolmuşes descend from the villages in the morning and return from Pazar in early afternoon. Space in the minibuses can be reserved, so if you want to leave on a weekend or Monday morning you'd do well to buy your ticket in advance from the Ayder Turizm booth in the village centre.

Even out of season there are still four bus services daily to and from Çamlıhemşin. From there you may have to take a taxi to Ayder for around US$17.

In summer one bus a day travels direct to Trabzon from Ayder, leaving at 4 pm.

To get from Camlıhemşin to Ayder (17km), turn left and cross a modern bridge, following the sign for Ayder Kaplıcaları. The road, imperilled by rockslides, winds steadily uphill, crossing and re-crossing the stream, passing small trout farms and restaurants, until finally it reaches Ayder.

HOPA
☎ 466 • pop 14,300
The easternmost of Turkey's Black Sea ports is Hopa, 165km east of Trabzon, a pit stop of a place which lays few claims on your time. Since the opening of the Georgian border at Sarp, 30km to the east, Hopa has existed to serve the army of traders and truckers who parade through night and day. You're only likely to want to stay if you're heading to/from Georgia and arrive too late to move on.

Hopa supplies the standard needs of any army: places to change money, to sleep, to get fuel, to get food and to get laid. In the budget range, the places to sleep and to get laid are usually the same. Unfortunately sleep tends to suffer.

There's a PTT right in the centre of town.

Places to Stay & Eat
Although the bus terminal is on the western side of the Sundura Çayı, most of the hotels are on the eastern side, along the waterfront street called Orta Hopa Caddesi. Walk through the market and cross the seafront bridge to reach them.

The best cheapie that's not a brothel is the *Otel Huzur* (☎ 351 4095, Cumhuriyet Caddesi 25) with singles/doubles with shower for US$12/17, including breakfast. The rooms are cheerier than the lobby might suggest.

Otel Cihan (☎ 351 2333, fax 351 4898, Orta Hopa Caddesi 5) has clean, comfortable rooms with shower and TV, for US$30/40 (negotiable). The decor is nothing to get excited about.

One of the first places you'll come to as you cross the bridge and head east is *Otel Ustabaş* (☎ 351 5220, fax 351 4507), a good choice with presentable rooms with baths for US$18/24, including breakfast. The upstairs restaurant has good views and there's a lobby shop selling shampoo etc.

Hopa's best hotel is 700m out of town to the west: the three-star *Hotel Terzioğlu* (☎ 351 5111, fax 351 5115), which charges US$30/40 for comfortable rooms with shower, TV and breakfast. Handy safe deposit boxes right at the reception desk hold your firearms while you're in the building.

As you walk along Orta Caddesi you'll pass plenty of small kebap and pide places. But for a better meal cut inland one block and try the vast *Cennet*, beside the small park, which serves everything from soups and stews to burgers and pizza. Across the road and also popular with the locals is the smaller *Ulaş Restaurant* which settles for a standard range of kebaps.

Getting There & Away
Direct buses from Hopa to Erzurum leave early in the morning. If you miss the direct bus, you can catch a later one to Artvin (US$5, 1½ hours), then an onward bus from Artvin. There are also regular minibuses to Rize (US$2.50) and Trabzon (US$4). Frequent minibuses to Sarp (US$2) and the Georgian border leave from the big petrol station on the waterfront beside the Otel Cihan. Minibuses also run from Hopa up to the Posof border crossing, which is an alternative way of getting to Georgia. For more details on crossing to Georgia, see under Georgia in the Land section of the Getting There & Away chapter.

MARTI N MOOS

IZZET KERIBAR

Two of the not-to-be-missed sights in eastern Turkey: the superbly situated İshak Paşa Sarayı in Doğubayazıt (top) and snowcapped Mt Ararat (bottom)

Eastern Turkey is a land of adventure: see vast Lake Van (top left) and the magical Akdamar Kilisesi (top right); meet the people (middle left); marvel at the colossal statues atop Nemrut Dağı; and savour the occasional splash of colour (bottom left) in an otherwise sparse landscape.

DAVOR PAVICHICH

IZZET KERIBAR

IZZET KERIBAR

IZZET KERIBAR

IZZET KERIBAR

Eastern Anatolia

These days serious travellers are often inclined to write off Turkey as 'too touristy'. In reality, it's only western Turkey that can be seen in that way – eastern Turkey is a whole different ball game. Whatever the rights and wrongs of the struggles that have torn the east apart over the last 16 years, their lasting legacy is a vast area of the country where investors have been reluctant to tread. Consequently, eastern Turkey is far less developed than the west, something you appreciate more or less as soon as you strike out from Sivas. For travellers the plus is a landscape that's far less degraded than it is in the west – no fields of plastic bags or canyons of half-built apartment blocks to spoil the views. The downside is that for the locals life in the east is often extremely hard.

Eastern Turkey is a land of adventure where every day brings some new surprise. You might go to bed at night disappointed because Mt Ararat was covered in cloud, then early next morning the sun will be up and the mountain will take your breath away. Or you might be riding along a rough road and suddenly come upon the ruins of a medieval castle, not marked on any map or described in any guidebook.

The people are no less friendly than elsewhere in Turkey, but they're often more reticent and not as used to dealing with foreigners, except in the hotels and tourist offices. It may take longer for the friendliness of the adults to emerge, although every single child will have to find out where you come from and what language you speak.

In the past it was undoubtedly cheaper to travel in eastern than western Turkey. Food prices are still low, but transport costs have been rising quite sharply and, with few tourists to cater for, hoteliers have been upgrading their properties to suit Turkish business travellers and holiday-makers. The rock-bottom places just about survive, getting grimier and less inviting by the year, but the good one-star places are becoming two-star, the good two-star places are becoming

HIGHLIGHTS

- Getting lost in the bazaars of Şanlıurfa
- Driving through the Georgian valleys
- White-water rafting out of Yusufeli
- Visiting the İshak Paşa Sarayı in Doğubayazıt
- Hiking around the ruins of Ani
- Watching the sun set over the colossal statues atop Nemrut Dağı
- Getting an early morning view of snow-capped Mt Ararat
- Driving up the 'other' Mt Nemrut near Lake Van
- Lunching in Hasankeyf
- Hiking in the Kaçkar Mountains

three-star, and so on, so it's getting harder to find decent, bargain-priced accommodation.

The line separating west from east is also moving inexorably eastwards. These days towns like Malatya, Gaziantep, Kahramanmaraş and Adıyaman are no more exotic than Afyon and Eskişehir, although Erzurum and Urfa still echo the Middle East.

The eastern mountains and high plateau are subject to long, severe winters. Although south-eastern Turkey can be mild and pleasant in the winter, we don't recommend travelling in the north-east or central-east except from May to mid-October as the weather is usually too bad. If you go in May or September/October, be prepared for some chilly nights. A trip to the summit of Nemrut Dağı should not be planned for early morning except in July and August. In other months the summit can be cold at any time and bitterly cold in early morning. The snow may be metres deep.

In general eastern bus companies are less sophisticated than those in the west and you may be expected to sit for many hours without a break and without refreshment. Gone, too, are the mini shopping-mall service stations of the west. Hereabouts you'll often be grateful if they can rustle up a bowl of soup.

If you are thinking of driving in eastern Turkey, you need to be aware that petrol stations are fewer, roads can be significantly worse and you will have to run the gauntlet of innumerable police and army roadblocks. As you approach a roadblock, slow right down and be sure you interpret the signals correctly: a red sign reading 'DUR' means stop, a green one reading 'GEÇ' means pass. If you're in the slightest doubt, it's always best to stop. To misread a signal and run a roadblock could have serious consequences.

Fill your petrol tank before setting out, carry bottled water and snacks and expect the ride to be longer than you think. Do most of your travelling in the earlier part of the day, reaching your destination by mid-afternoon. Avoid driving in the evening or at night. Roads in the extreme east and particularly in the north-east, are often riddled with potholes which break tyres and dent rims if hit at speed. When they're filled with rainwater it's impossible to judge their damage capacity. Potholes occur at random

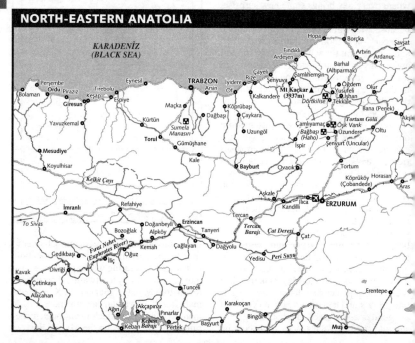

NORTH-EASTERN ANATOLIA

in otherwise smooth roads and necessitate slow driving even on good stretches.

When travelling, never underestimate the distances. You may ride for hours to get from one town to the next, only to arrive and find few hotels to choose from and the one you want – particularly if it's the best in town – fully booked. Travelling in eastern Turkey is certainly not as easy as it is in the west but if you're adaptable and out for adventure, this is the place to find it.

North-Eastern Anatolia

Mountainous and remote from the cosmopolitan atmosphere of Ankara and İstanbul, north-eastern Anatolia is a large slice of the 'real' Turkey, relatively unchanged by the tourist flood that has swept over the western and central sections of Anatolia during the past two decades.

As with much of Anatolia, cities and towns here date their existence in millennia rather than centuries. The Hittites, Romans, Persians, Armenians, Georgians, Arabs and Russians have all battled for control of these lands but this is Seljuk country *par excellence*. Sultans of the first Turkic empire in Anatolia (during the mid-1200s) built impressive mosques, *medreses* (theological seminaries) and caravanserais in Erzurum which shouldn't be missed by anyone interested in architecture. The beautiful mountain scenery and historic Armenian and Georgian churches of extreme north-eastern Anatolia (around Yusufeli, Artvin and Kars) are among the most striking attractions. The mountain trekking in the Kaçkar Dağları (Kaçkar Mountains) between Erzurum and Artvin is excellent and you can ride the white waters of the Çoruh River near Yusufeli.

The following description of north-eastern Anatolia moves from west to east, from Erzurum to Kars and then north to Artvin and south to Doğubayazıt.

FROM SİVAS TO ERZURUM
Heading east from Sivas you'll be struck immediately at how relatively under-developed north-eastern Turkey is, the roads far less impressive, the service stations generally primitive but the landscape wild and beautiful.

The first big town you'll pass through is **Erzincan** but there's nothing here to detain you. In 1939 Erzincan was devastated by an earthquake as severe as the one that struck north-western Turkey in 1999. Almost 33,000 people died and the town was levelled. Other quakes, most recently in 1993, have destroyed almost everything of historical or architectural interest. What you see today is a modern farming town whose people await the next catastrophe with San Francisco-style nonchalance.

Given that your stay in Erzincan is likely to be brief, it's good to be able to report a pleasant, shady *çay bahçesi* (tea garden) and the *Sila Restoran* right beside the otogar.

East of Erzincan the road ploughs through **Tercan**, yet another ancient settlement with a momentous history but little to show for it today. Tercan is set in a fertile river valley punctuated by huge rocky outcrops to the south. With your own transport you might want to stop and inspect the impressively restored 13th-century **Mama Hatun Kervansarayı**, topped by a forest of chimneys, and the adjacent **Mama Hatun Türbesi** (Tomb of Mama Hatun), uphill through the town 250m off the highway.

The caravanserai boasts a long entrance hall lined with *eyvans* (large recesses) leading to a particularly large eyvan across the courtyard from the entrance. The tomb is surrounded by a high wall that you enter via a gateway decorated with bands of Kufic script. Inside, the wall is pierced by 12 more eyvans in which lesser notables could be entombed. If the tomb is unlocked, climb the stairs to the right of the entrance to get a view of the surrounding cemetery. The eight-lobed tomb proper stands in the centre of the circle, oriented to the points of the compass, with the door to the south. Its roof resembles an umbrella. The space above the actual burial chamber is still used for prayers.

East and south of Tercan, you pass through more dramatic mountain scenery before arriving in Erzurum.

ERZURUM

☎ 442 • pop 300,000 • elevation 1853m

Erzurum is the largest city on the eastern Anatolian high plateau. It has always been a transportation centre and military headquarters, and was the command post for the defence of Anatolia from Russian and Persian invasion. Now it's assuming a new role as an eastern cultural and commercial city.

With its severe climate and sparse landscape, Erzurum is a city that seems to face in two directions at once: a town of God-fearing, meat-eating, mosque-going, patriotic, conservative men whose women wear voluminous black drapes or at least headscarves; but also a university town and an important base for the outspokenly secular military. Although the old city of Erzurum used to huddle beneath the walls of the *kale* (fortress), the new Erzurum, which has grown up around the old, has broad boulevards, traffic roundabouts and an open, airy

feeling. Its orderly, tree-lined boulevards provide a welcome contrast to the aridity of the surrounding steppe.

For most tourists, Erzurum is a transit point with air, rail and bus connections, but if you stay one or two nights, you'll be able to visit some fine Turkish buildings and a lively market. You can also take an excursion to the Tortum Valley and the mountain village of Yusufeli on the way to Artvin, visit the hot springs at Pasinler and, in winter, ski at nearby Palandöken.

History

During the Byzantine era Erzurum was called Theodosiopolis after the emperor who founded it in the late 5th century on the ruins of an earlier settlement. The Byzantine emperors had their hands full defending this town from Arab attack on several occasions. The Seljuk Turks took it after the Battle of Manzikert in 1071, effectively opening Anatolia to Turkish settlement.

Being in a strategic position at the confluence of roads to Constantinople, Russia and Persia, Erzurum was conquered and lost by armies of Arabs, Armenians, Byzantines, Mongols, Persians, Romans, Russians, Saltuk Turks and Seljuk Turks. As for the Ottomans, it was Selim the Grim who conquered the city in 1515. It was captured by Russian troops in 1882 and again in 1916.

In July 1919 Atatürk came to Erzurum to hold the famous congress which, along with the one at Sivas, provided the rallying cry for the independence struggle. The Erzurum Congress is most famous for determining the boundaries of what became known as the territories of the National Pact, the lands that became part of the Turkish Republic. Atatürk and the Congress claimed the lands which, in essence, form the present Turkish state and rejected claims to other formerly held Ottoman lands. The phrase at the time was, 'We want no more, we shall accept no less'.

Orientation

Two separate areas of Erzurum are of interest to visitors. Modern Erzurum's main thoroughfare is Cumhuriyet Caddesi, renamed Ömer Nasuhi Bilman Caddesi along

ERZURUM

PLACES TO STAY	PLACES TO EAT	OTHER	20 Turkish Airlines;	29 Üç Kümbetler
2 Hotel Fatih	5 Meram Lokantası	1 BP Station	Erzurum Döviz;	(Three Tombs)
3 Örnek Otel	19 Salon Asya	8 Türkiye İş Bankası	Türkiye İş Bankası	30 Çifte Minareli Medrese
4 Hitit Otel	24 Sultan Sekisi Şark Sofrası	9 Petrol Ofisi Station	& ATM	31 Ulu Cami (Great Mosque)
6 Otel Polat	32 Üçler Kebap Salonu	10 Gölbaşı Semt	21 Yakutiye Medresesi	33 İbrahim Paşa Camii
7 Hotel Sefer;	34 Mulenruj Kebap Salonu	Garajı	& Müzesi	40 PTT
Vatan Lokantası	35 Güzelyurt Restorant;	13 Mosque	22 Lala Mustafa Paşa Camii	41 Tourist Office
11 Yeni Otel Çınar	Dönerci Hacıbey	14 Rüstem Paşa	23 Caferiye Camii	42 Belediye (Town Hall)
12 Otel Arı	37 Salon Çağın;	Çarşısı	25 Hamam	43 Erzurum Müzesi
15 Hotel Dilaver	Kılıçoğlu Baklavaları	16 Akbank & ATM	26 Erzurum Kale (Citadel)	44 Hospital
36 Kral Otel	38 Dönerci Canbaba;	17 Hospital	27 Mosque	45 Buses to Pasinler
39 Otel Dede	Patisserie Zirve	18 Çağ Internet Cafe	28 Gümüşlü Kümbet	46 Hospital

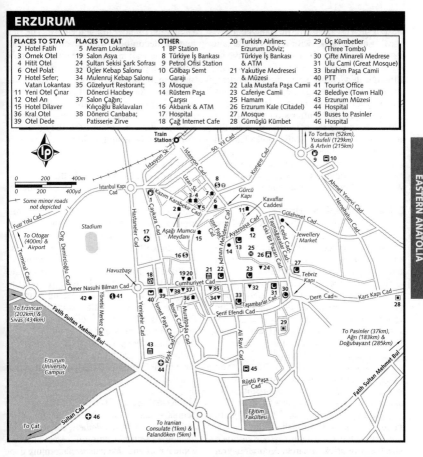

EASTERN ANATOLIA

its western reaches. The streets are divided by the Havuzbaşı traffic roundabout with a large statue of Atatürk and a pool of water. It's almost 2km from the otogar to the Havuzbaşı roundabout. Cumhuriyet and Ömer Nasuhi Bilman Caddesis are lined with restaurants, cafes, banks with ATMs and other useful amenities. Most of the older mosques and medreses are here too.

Most of the cheap hotels are a little way to the north, downhill along Adnan Menderes Caddesi around Gürcü Kapı in Old Erzurum, once the 'Georgian Gate' in the city walls and marked by a chunky stone fountain at a

traffic intersection 600m uphill from the train station.

You can walk to everything in Old Erzurum, including the train station, but you will need transport to get to the otogar (3km west of the centre) and the airport. The train station is 2.5km north-east of the otogar.

The minibus garage, the Gölbaşı Semt Garajı on the north-eastern outskirts, offers local services to points north and east.

Information

The tourist office (☎ 218 5697) is inconveniently positioned on the southern side of

Ömer Nasuhi Bilman Caddesi at 9/A, a block west of the Havuzbaşı traffic roundabout.

Most of the banks with ATMs are in and around Cumhuriyet Caddesi. If you have no ATM card some of them will change cash, although they're not so keen on travellers cheques. With nothing else, your best bet is probably a branch of Türkiye İş Bankası.

After 3 pm in the afternoon you can get copies of the *Turkish Daily News* in the newsagent next door to the Otel Dede on Cumhuriyet Caddesi.

Erzurum has lots of Internet Cafes, several of them, including the Çağ and the Blue White, on Cumhuriyet Caddesi.

Çifte Minareli Medrese

At the eastern end of Cumhuriyet Caddesi is the Çifte Minareli Medrese, or Twin Minaret Seminary, now housing the museum administration and with its courtyard half-heartedly open as a tea garden.

The Çifte Minareli dates from the 1200s when Erzurum was a wealthy Seljuk city which suffered attack and devastation by the Mongols (1242). It's believed to have been finished in 1253 on orders of Huand Hatun, daughter of Sultan Alaeddin Keykubat.

The facade is a good example of the way the Seljuks liked to try out variation even while aiming for symmetry: the panels on either side of the entrance are identical in size and position, but different in motif. The panel to the right bears the Seljuk eagle, to the left the motif is unfinished.

Enter via the towering limestone entrance with the twin brick minarets decorated with small blue tiles soaring above it. The tops of the minarets are gone, having succumbed to the vagaries of Erzurum's violent history even before the Ottomans claimed the town.

The main courtyard has four large niches and a double colonnade on the eastern and western sides, though some of the columns were never fully carved. Stairways in each of the corners lead to the students' cells on the upper level. The doorway to each cell is decorated differently, adding a liveliness and interest to the otherwise monumental design.

At the far end of the courtyard is the grand 12-sided domed hall that served as the Hatuniye Türbesi, or Tomb of Huant Hatun, the founder of the medrese. The rich marble decoration was never completed; look at the wall inside on the left to see how it was supposed to have looked, polished and creamy-white.

Beneath the domed hall is a small room with ingenious vents to allow light and air in. This may have been a *mescit* (prayer room) with a cenotaph, the lady's actual tomb being beneath the floor.

Ulu Cami

Next to the Çifte Minareli is the Ulu Cami (1179). The contrast between the two buildings is striking: unlike the elaborately decorated Çifte Minareli, the Ulu Cami, built almost a century earlier by the Saltuklu Turkish emir of Erzurum, is restrained but elegant, with seven aisles running north-south and six running east-west, resulting in a forest of columns. You enter from the north along the central aisle. Above the fourth east-west aisle a stalactite dome is open to the heavens. At the southern end of the central aisle are a curious wooden dome and a pair of bull's-eye windows.

Walking along Cumhuriyet Caddesi towards the Ulu Cami you'll pass (on the left) the small Ottoman **Caferiye Camii**, constructed in 1645.

Üç Kümbetler (Three Tombs)

Scholars believe that the design of Saltuk and Seljuk tombs, or *kümbets*, echoes that of the nomad tents of Central Asia, with a near-conical roof and side panels elaborately decorated as though hung with tapestries. Erzurum has numerous fine kümbets. Walk south between the Çifte Minareli and the Ulu Cami until you come to a T-junction. Turn left then immediately right and walk a short block up the hill to the Üç Kümbetler in a fenced enclosure to the right. The best decoration, dating from the 12th century, is on the octagonal Emir Sultan Saltuk Türbesi.

Erzurum Kale (Citadel)

The citadel, or kale, erected by the Emperor Theodosius around the 5th century, is on the hilltop to the north of the Çifte Minareli and the Ulu Cami. It's open from 8.30 am to 5.30 pm daily and admission costs US$0.30.

Near the entrance to the kale is a curious old clock tower topped by a Turkish flag that was built as a minaret in the time of the Saltuks but was later converted to its current time-keeping function.

If you climb the clock tower (preferably taking a torch/flashlight with you) be sure to open the cupboard doors at the top of the stairs and you'll find the clock, which was made in Croydon in England, and given to the Ottomans by Queen Victoria in 1877.

The walls harbour a few old cannons with Russian or Ottoman inscriptions, a disused prayer room and a lit-up picture of Atatürk. Steep steps lead up to the rough top of the walls where there's a fine view, especially of the Çifte Minareli huddled beneath the surrounding mountains, provided you don't suffer from vertigo. This is an especially fine place to be at prayer time, with the call to prayer seemingly coming at you from all sides.

Every July wrestling bouts take place in front of appreciative audiences in the grounds of the kale.

Yakutiye Medresesi & Müzesi

Just west of the Lala Mustafa Paşa Camii is the Yakutiye Medresesi (Yakutiye Seminary), a Mongol theological seminary dating from 1310, built in the reign of the Mongol Khan Oljaytu for Gazan Khan and his wife Bolugan Hatun by Cemaleddin Hoca Yakut Gazani. The medrese now serves as Erzurum's **Türk-İslâm Eserleri ve Etnografya Müzesi** (Turkish-Islamic Arts & Ethnography Museum). It's open from 8.30 am to 5 pm daily except Monday for US$1.75.

The Mongol governors borrowed the basics of Seljuk architecture and developed their own variations, as is evident in the entrance to the medrese. Of the two original minarets, only the base of one and the lower part of the second have survived. The *türbe* (tomb) at the back was to be the emir's.

Inside, the central dome is supported by faceted stalactite work, which catches the light from the central opening to make a delightful pattern. The northern eyvan has two levels, which is unusual. The southern eyvan was the mosque, with its mihrab. The room at the south-eastern corner was probably the refectory, the rear (north-eastern) entrance was for traders and artisans. Exhibits include Ottoman jewellery and ornaments, calligraphy, religious objects, Seljuk ceramics, local embroidery and lace, and samples of *oltutaşı*, the locally mined black amber.

Right next to the Yakutiye Medresesi is the **Lala Mustafa Paşa Camii** (1562). Lala Mustafa Paşa was a grand vizier during the golden age of the Ottoman Empire, and his mosque follows classical lines, perhaps having been designed by the great Sinan or one of his followers.

Erzurum Müzesi

Erzurum's museum is several long blocks south-west of the Yakutiye Medresesi. Walk west along Cumhuriyet Caddesi to the Havuzbaşı roundabout, then turn left (south) and walk up the hill. The museum is just before the next intersection, on the left (eastern) side of Paşalar Caddesi. It's a 15-minute walk, or you can take any bus climbing the hill from Havuzbaşı. The museum is open from 8 am to noon and 1.30 to 5.30 pm daily except Monday; admission costs US$1.75.

The museum has never really recovered from losing much of its collection to the Yakutiye Medresesi in 1994. It's now mostly an archaeological collection, with finds from digs at nearby Büyüktepe Höyük and Sos Höyük, Urartian and Trans-Caucasian pottery, jewellery from Hellenistic and Roman tombs, and fragments of Seljuk tiles.

Labelling is sporadically in English until you get to a room at the back that is devoted to exhibits concerning the massacre and mass burial of the Muslim inhabitants of local villagers by Armenian insurgents at the beginning of the century. In order to get across the message about 'this disgusting and shameful crime', a large English notice is provided. There is, of course, another side to this story that goes unmentioned.

Hamams

Once the sightseeing is done you may feel in need of a good scrub. The men-only **Erzurum**

Hamamı at the bazaar end of İstasyon Caddesi has been praised by many male readers. Continue along the road winding past the kale and you'll come to two small baths for women: the **Hanım** and the **Kırkçeşme**. Neither is brilliant, although the Hanım may be slightly cleaner.

Places to Stay – Budget
Despite a relative dearth of tourists, Erzurum still manages to offer lots of cheap places to stay not too far from the town centre. If you're on a really tight budget, start your room search in Kazım Karabekir Caddesi, where the **Hitit Otel** (☎ *218 1204, Kazım Karabekir Caddesi 27)* and **Örnek Otel** (☎ *218 1203, Kazım Karabekir Caddesi 8)* have both been catering to travellers for decades. They both look pretty bashed about but offer singles/doubles with bath for US$9/12, marginally less without bath. Should they fail to appeal there are several other cheapies in this street, the **Hotel Fatih** even boasting its own hamam.

Much better than any of these is a long-time favourite, the two-star **Otel Polat** (☎ *218 1623, fax 234 4598, Kazım Karabekir Caddesi 4)*. The Polat has had a makeover and now courts its mainly business clientele with modern decor, minibars and double-glazed windows. For all that you still only get charged US$13/21 for a room with decent bath and breakfast.

Another good choice just round the corner is the renovated **Hotel Sefer** (☎ *218 6714, fax 212 3775, İstasyon Caddesi)*. Comfortable, though certainly not fancy, it charges US$15/25, including breakfast, for a reasonably modern room with bath and TV. The ground-floor restaurant is a plus but likely to be busy with tour groups in high season.

Further afield, another excellent choice is the spotlessly clean and well-regarded **Yeni Otel Çınar** (☎ *212 1050, fax 233 8963, Ayazpaşa Caddesi 18)*, which charges about the same as the Hitit and Örnek and yet offers lots more comfort. To find it, look for the Gürpınar Sineması (cinema) in the bazaar. The street opposite leads to the Çınar.

The nearby **Otel Arı** (☎ *218 3141, Ayazpaşa Caddesi 22)* is presentable enough, with rooms for US$5 a head. Your room may have a sink, or shower, or toilet, or a combination of these; in winter hot water is available on request. The hotel is right next to the Ayazpaşa Camii. From Gürcü Kapı, walk uphill along the street to the left of the Türk Ticaret Bankası (Türkbank on the sign) and when it widens into a square go left towards all the 'Avukat' signs.

If you'd rather be right in the swing of things, the **Otel Dede** (☎ *218 2591, Cumhuriyet Caddesi 8)* offers comfortable rooms with bath but, unusually, tries to charge more than the official prices for so-called 'luxe' facilities which are nothing of the sort. If you can persuade the proprietor to settle for the usual US$11/12.50 it's a good choice. If not, go elsewhere.

Places to Stay – Mid-Range
Erzurum also has a couple of comfortable mid-range hotels but as yet no hotels in the luxury class.

The three-star **Hotel Dilaver** (☎ *235 0068, fax 218 1148, Aşağı Mumcu Caddesi, Pelit Meydanı)* is Erzurum's most comfortable city-centre hotel, with good rooms for US$70/100/130 a single/double/triple, including breakfast. You get modern decor and fittings, TV, air-con, a minibar and bathroom. The top-floor restaurant offers splendid views over Erzurum. At the time of writing there were plans to add a sauna and hamam, which might push prices up a bit.

Just off Cumhuriyet Caddesi, opposite the Yakutiye Medresesi and right in the heart of the dining-out district, **Kral Otel** (☎ *218 7783, fax 218 6973, Erzincankapı 18)* was in the middle of a complete refit at the time of writing. By 2001 it was intended that it would be a three- or four-star hotel with all the necessary luxuries. The omens were certainly good, with the new rooms boasting attractive decor even before the furniture was installed.

Places to Eat
As with hotel prices, meal prices in Erzurum are generally low. For the best choice of places to eat just stroll down Cumhuriyet Caddesi and take your pick along with half

of Erzurum. Prices drop a little in the backstreets but the choice won't be as extensive.

Salon Çağın on the southern side of Cumhuriyet Caddesi, just west of the Yakutiye Medresesi, is clean, bright and cheery with tasty food. On Sunday come for the house speciality, *mantı* (Turkish ravioli, US$2). If you can face it, they'll even do you *işkembe çorbası* (tripe soup) for breakfast.

Across the street is **Salon Asya**, very popular with students and boasting a large variety of kebaps, including İskender for US$2.50. **Dönerci Hacıbey**, opposite the Yakutiye Medresesi, is nearly as good: clean, bright and welcoming to female diners. *The* place for *döner kebap* (spit-roasted meat) used to be **Dönerci Canbaba** where huge vertical spits of lamb twirl all day long, but on a recent visit the kebap there was barely edible.

Just opposite the Akçay Otel is **Mulenruj Kebap Salonu** *(Kamil Ağa Sokak),* or Moulin Rouge, which is decorated with a fine 3-D model of a hydroelectric power plant! Döner kebap, along with *kuru fasulye* (beans in tomato sauce), *pilav* (rice) and a soft drink comes to about US$3.50.

Moving further away from the centre, near the Çifte Minareli Medrese and Ulu Cami, try **Sultan Sekisi Şark Sofrası** *(Ebuishak Sokak 1),* Sultan's Bench Oriental Dinner Table, in the narrow street across Cumhuriyet Caddesi from the Çifte Minareli Medrese. Low Ottoman-style tables, kilims on the walls, traditional Turkish dishes and decent prices make it well worth a try – plenty of locals certainly seem to think so anyway. A *kiremit tavuk* (tile-baked chicken) and soft drink costs just US$2.50.

Üçler Kebap Salonu *(Osmanpaşa Sokak No 2)* also off Cumhuriyet Caddesi near the Ulu Cami, serves *kuşbaşı* lamb kebaps (marinated in salt, oil and chilli for several days) for US$1.50 as well as the usual range of *pides* (Turkish pizza, US$1). There's an unusually attractive *aile salonu* (family room) at the back.

If you're staying in Kazım Karabekir Caddesi, look out for the **Meram Lokantası** where fresh trout with a cold drink makes a nice change from kebap for just US$3.50.

The **Vatan Lokantası**, opposite the Hotel Polat, has a good selection of *hazır yemek* (ready food, mostly stews) at lunch. Full meals can be had for around US$3.

For more than 70 years, Erzurum's best restaurant has been the **Güzelyurt Restorant** *(☎ 218 1514),* directly facing the Yakutiye Medresesi across Cumhuriyet Caddesi. Its shrouded windows give it the look of a Soviet-style Mafia bolthole from the outside, but inside the soft lighting, quiet music and experienced black-clad waiters ensure that this is the place where Westernised businessmen come to down a meal with a beer after a hard day's toil. Try the house speciality, *mantarlı güveç* – a delicious casserole of lamb, pimientos, onions, tomatoes, mushrooms and cheese, big enough for two people if you've already had several appetisers. The bill could rise as high as US$20 per person if you go heavy on the alcohol but you can get by on much less.

Several cafes and pastry shops on Cumhuriyet Caddesi are useful for a quick bite or breakfast. Best is **Kılıçoğlu Baklavaları**, two doors west of the Salon Çağın. Bright and modern, it sells excellent milk puddings and cakes with coffee to wash them down. **Patisserie Zirve**, further west from the Salon Çağın, is popular with courting couples who commandeer its upstairs room, ostensibly for coffee and pastries.

Shopping

Erzurum's market areas are scattered throughout the old part of the city and it's easy to get lost in the narrow, winding streets. Start your wanderings at the Lala Mustafa Paşa Camii, then walk north along Adnan Menderes Caddesi, the street next to the mosque, until you see the covered Rüstem Paşa Çarşısı on your right. Built between 1540 and 1550 this two-storey *han* (caravanserai) now serves as a centre for the manufacture and sale of prayer beads *(tesbihler)* made from the local black amber *(oltutaşı),* and other jewellery.

Along Kavaflar Çarşısı Sokak you'll find many tinsmiths selling handmade cookers, heaters and samovars – much prized in a town renowned for its snow.

EASTERN ANATOLIA

Getting There & Away

As eastern Turkey's main city, Erzurum is well served by all modes of transport.

Air Turkish Airlines (☎ 234 1516, fax 233 1070, Kazım Karabekir Caddesi) has two daily flights to Ankara, with connections to Antalya, İstanbul and İzmir. There's another branch on Cumhuriyet Caddesi from where buses to the airport depart two hours before each flight (US$1.75).

Bus The otogar, 2.5km from the centre along the airport road, handles most of Erzurum's intercity traffic. It has a post office, barber, *emanetçi* (left luggage room), shops and a restaurant.

Details of some daily services from Erzurum's otogar are listed in the table below.

The Gölbaşı Semt Garajı, about 1km north-east of Gürcü Kapı through the backstreets, handles minibuses to towns to the north and east of Erzurum, including Ardanuç, Ardeşen, Arhavi, Çayeli, Fındıklı, Hopa, Pazar, Rize, Şavşat, Şelale, Tortum and Yusufeli. The Gölbaşı Semt Garajı can be difficult to find unless you take a taxi. Look for the Hotel Ersin and a Petrol Ofisi station; it's behind the Petrol Ofisi station.

For Iran (if you already have your visa), take a bus to Doğubayazıt from where you can catch a minibus to the Iranian frontier.

Train The train station, Erzurum Garı, is at the northern end of İstasyon Caddesi, 600m

north of Gürcü Kapı and over 1km from Cumhuriyet Caddesi. You can walk from the station to most hotels. City buses depart from the station forecourt every 30 minutes and circulate through the city.

Erzurum has good rail connections with İstanbul and Ankara on the *Doğu Ekspresi* via Kayseri, Sivas, Divriği and Erzincan.

Getting Around

A taxi to or from the airport, 10km from town, costs around US$6. A taxi trip within the city costs US$2 to US$4.

City bus No 2 passes the otogar and will take you into town for US$0.30; a taxi costs about US$2.50.

AROUND ERZURUM
Palandöken Ski Resort
☎ 442

From December to mid-May you can ski at the Palandöken Kayak Tesisleri on the outskirts of Erzurum, 5km south-west of the centre. The Dedeman Palandöken Ski Centre offers seven ski lifts (including two for beginners) and 28km of ski runs on three levels. The slopes are at their liveliest during the April winter festival.

If you want to stay overnight, the *Dedeman* (☎ 316 2414, fax 316 3607) has all the luxuries for US$90/110 a single/double with breakfast, US$10 per person more with breakfast and dinner. On a budget you'll have to stay in Erzurum and make a day trip of it. Other luxury hotels on the

Services from Erzurum's Otogar

destination	fare (US$)	time (hr)	distance (km)	daily services
Ankara	20	12	925	several buses
Artvin	8.50	4	215	several buses
Diyarbakır	14	8	485	several buses
Doğubayazıt	7	4	285	5 buses
İstanbul	24–30	16	1275	several buses
Kars	7	3½	205	several buses
Sivas	13	6	485	several buses
Tortum	2	1	53	several dolmuşes
Trabzon	9	6	325	several buses
Yusufeli	4	3	129	several dolmuşes
Van	9	6	410	several buses

slopes include the *Tour Inn Palan Hotel* (☎ 317 0707, fax 317 0200) and the *Kardelen* (☎ 316 1686, fax 315 6155).

Minibuses run to Palandöken during the ski season. You may be lucky and find one on a summer weekend as well.

Pasinler (Hasankale)
☎ 442

Some 38km east of Erzurum is Pasinler. The hillside above it crowned by the **Hasankale fortress**. Much of the triple-walled fortress, reached by a block-paved street on the western side of the highway, is in good repair (some restored). It dates from the 1330s when the İlkhanid emir Hasan had it built. Extensive repairs were made later by the Akkoyunlu leader Uzun Hasan.

The village is conservative in the eastern way, with fiery-eyed, white-bearded men and many women completely enveloped by burlap chadors. Watch out for shops selling *hasankale lavaşı,* the village's special metre-long thin loaves of bread.

Pasinler is famous locally for its **kaplıcalar** (hot springs). From the main intersection next to the *belediye* (town hall), cross the railway line, turn left and continue 800m to a bridge leading to the Kale Otel. On either side of the bridge stand bathhouses for men and women. Those for women are open from 10.30 am to 6 pm, those for men are open longer. To use them costs about US$0.30 and it's a great experience.

Lovers of hot springs might like to stay at the nearby *Kral Otel* (☎ 661 4994, fax 661 4992) which charges US$9/18 a single/double for quiet, newly decorated rooms with shower. There's a good ground-floor restaurant where a sizeable meal including alcohol should cost less than US$10. But the hotel's biggest assets are the private cabins at the back with their own plunge pools and massage areas (although whether everyone will think the newly added and uncurtained toilets are an improvement is debatable). To rent a small cabin for an hour costs US$3.50; a larger one costs US$5. Men can also take advantage of a full-size swimming pool. Since the last half-hourly shuttle bus to Pasinler from Erzurum (US$0.75) goes at 10 pm in summer, there's little to stop you staying here instead of in Erzurum itself.

Sadly, as so often in Turkey, these assets stand amid what looks like a building site. Near the baths is a small amusement park with a boating pool and an exhibition steam train, put here no doubt to lure Erzurumlus out to Pasinler on weekends.

GEORGIAN VALLEYS

The mountainous country north of Erzurum towards Artvin was once part of the medieval Kingdom of Georgia, and has numerous churches and castles to show for it. The trouble you take to see this region will be amply rewarded. The mountain scenery is at times spectacular, and the churches, which mix many characteristics of Armenian, Seljuk and Persian styles, are interesting and seldom visited. If you happen to be passing in mid-June, the orchards of cherries and apricots should be in bloom – a special treat. Late September and early October can also be fine times to visit (if the rains hold off), when the trees will have autumnal colouring.

Getting Around

The small mountain villages in these valleys are a delight to explore, but public transport to and from most of them consists of a single minibus which heads down to Erzurum early in the morning for the market, returning in the afternoon. Hiring a car, although relatively expensive, is the best way to explore this region and needn't be too costly if you get together a group.

A taxi for a 12-hour excursion around the churches from Erzurum will cost about US$100, so hiring a car or using Yusufeli as a base is more sensible. You can see quite a bit in a one-day excursion, but even more if you spend the night in Yusufeli. Another day allows you to make the beautiful drive from Yusufeli to Kars.

Most of the villages can rustle up a glass of tea but food is a much taller order. There are a few restaurants along the main highway from Erzurum to Yusufeli and plenty of children hawk fruit by the roadside. Otherwise, unless you're especially fond of dry biscuits, stock up on picnic foods before setting out.

EASTERN ANATOLIA

If you have time for only one or two churches, head for İşhan or Öşk Vank first.

Bağbaşı (Haho)

About 25km north of Tortum is a turn-off on the left (west), near a humpback bridge, to the village called Haho by the Georgians. Go 7.5km up the unpaved road through orchards and fields to the village and ask at the teahouse for the church key *(kilise anahtarı)*; a guide will probably accompany you for the last 600m up the road to the church which dates from the 10th century. There he'll show you several reliefs reminiscent of those at Akdamar.

Probably because the church is now in use as a mosque, it's not signposted as a monument from the highway. No doubt for the same reason, some restoration work has taken place here.

Öşk Vank

Another 15.5km north of the Bağbaşı turn-off, in a wide valley with the river to the left (west) of the highway, is the road to Öşk Vank, 7km off the highway and up into the mountains. In winter, you must ford the river and wind up the road to the village, where you can't miss the big, impressive monastery, built in the 10th century. Most of the roof is gone, but there are still traces of paintings, inscriptions and fine reliefs, both on the outside and on the columns inside. The *Coşkun Çay Evi* to the right of the church serves tea.

Tortum Gölü

West of Öşk Vank, the highway skirts the western shore of Tortum Gölü (Tortum Lake), which was formed by a landslide about three centuries ago. The lake is a considerable distance from Tortum village.

The 48m Tortum Şelalesi (Waterfall), in the grounds of the Türkiye Elektrik Kurumu (TEK), is worth seeing in winter when there's plenty of water. In summer, the meagre flow of water is diverted to the hydroelectricity plant. The lake makes a beautiful picnic spot, but if you arrive alone the guard at the gate to the TEK grounds may demand a US$6 admission fee. Ac-

companied by a Turk you should have no problem getting in for free.

A few kilometres west of the lake at Çamlıyamaç is a lookout across the valley and the mountains to the Tortum Çayı river gorge cut through the banded rock. Children from the green oasis below will no doubt be on hand to sell you whatever fruit is in season in an area famous for its orchards.

İşhan

Heading north from the lake, take the road on the right marked for Olur and go 6km (exactly 50km from the Vank road) through dramatic scenery to a road on the left for İşhan, marked by a sign reading 'İşhan Kilisesi'. This village is another 6km up a steep, muddy road carved out of the mountainside and probably impassable in bad weather.

The mountain village is spectacularly sited, and the **Church of the Mother of God**, 100m past the village and down the hill, is wonderful. The front faces an open space, while the back nestles into the hillside. The church was built in the 8th century and enlarged in the 11th. There are some traces of fresco inside (vanishing fast – 25 years ago whole walls were covered in them), an arcade of horseshoe-shaped arches in the apse and several reliefs on the exterior, including one of a lion battling a snake.

There are several other churches and castles east of İşhan along the Olur road. For more details, see the Yusufeli to Kars section later in this chapter. Return to the Olur road, go back the 6km to the highway and then north towards Artvin. In the 8.5km between the Olur and Yusufeli roads, the highway passes through a dramatic gorge, wild and scenic, with striking bands of colour in the tortured rock of the canyon walls. The Yusufeli turn-off is at a place called Su Kavuşumu (Water Confluence), where the waters of the Tortum Çayı and the Oltu Çayı join the Çoruh River. From here, it's 10km up the Çoruh Valley to the town.

YUSUFELİ
☎ 466 • pop 6400 • elevation 1050m
The swift Barhal Çayı rushes noisily through Yusufeli on its way to the Çoruh River

nearby, and in recent years the town has become a popular base for white-water rafting and trekking groups.

A short stroll reveals everything Yusufeli has to offer: Halim Paşa Caddesi, the main street; the belediye facing the main market street next to the river; the three banks with ATMs (İş, Ziraat and Halk); and the few small hotels and restaurants. The town hospital *(devlet hastanesi)* is on the road into the village.

Unfortunately plans for a new dam just outside Yusufeli have blighted tourism development. Should they come to fruition, it looks as if the rafting will be no more.

Things To See & Do

Several hotels in town can arrange **rafting trips** for around US$18 for five hours; ask at the Barhal or Çiçek Palas Hotels for starters. Rafting is best in May and June; by August the volume of water is insufficient.

Mountain guides Özkan Şahin (☎ 811 2187) and Fatih Şahin (☎ 811 2150, also contactable through Celal Düz at the Çiçek Palas Oteli), will lead you on customised **treks** up into the Kaçkar Dağları.

Yusufeli also makes a convenient base for visiting the churches at Barhal and Dörtkilise. At the time of writing there were limited dolmuş services to these villages. Hopefully one day the drivers will wise up and offer day tours to these and other Georgian churches.

Places to Stay

Cross the footbridge from the town centre and follow the signs to find *Akın Camping* and *Greenpeace Camping*, both very simple and cheap.

Yusufeli's pensions are of the most basic type although hardy trekkers and rafters probably don't head here in search of luxury. You can expect to pay about US$5 a head for a bed in an uninspiring waterless room. Only in May and June are you likely to have problems finding somewhere to stay.

Best of a poor choice is probably the *Hotel Barhal* (☎ 811 3151), by the rickety suspension bridge over the river, which has a few rooms with showers. The bare white

rooms at the nearby *Çiçek Palas Oteli* (☎ 811 2393, fax 811 3393) are not bad, and one or two also have baths.

Otherwise there's not much difference between the *Genç Palas* (☎ 811 2102), the *Hotel Çoruh* (☎ 811 2155) and the *Keleş*, all grouped together near the footbridge across the river. They're all perfectly alright and the Çoruh even has some rooms with river views, but none of them is in anyway outstanding.

Places to Eat

Yusufeli's best is the *Mavi Köşk Et Restaurant*, entered via an inconspicuous stairway opposite the Halkbank. You'll pay about US$4 to US$7 for a meal with a drink here, a bit less at the riverside *Çınar Restaurant* under the Hotel Barhal. In season these places are probably fun. Out of season they're dishearteningly empty.

For cheaper fare there's the *Yılmaz Pide*, in an alley opposite the Hotel Barhal, or the rather good *Abzet Lokantası* more or less across from the bus stop. Near the Abzet is the simple *Yıldız Pastanesi* where you can get a coffee and cake for afters.

On the far side of the river near the footbridge, the neighbouring *Mahzen Fıçı Bira* and *Çorçun Yeri*, are very pleasantly placed for a nightcap. *Fıçı bira* (draught beer) is a strong point, as are the balconies right over the river.

Getting There & Away

Dolmuşes depart from Erzurum's Gölbaşı Semt Garajı several times daily for Yusufeli (US$4, 130km) and other towns and villages in the Georgian valleys.

There's at least one bus a day to and from Hopa (US$5) and to and from Artvin (US$2.50).

AROUND YUSUFELİ
Barhal (Altıparmak)
☎ 466 • elevation 1300m

About 28km north-west of Yusufeli, high in the mountains over an unpaved road, Barhal (officially called Altıparmak) preserves a fine 10th-century **Georgian church** long used as the village mosque. The church and

EASTERN ANATOLIA

the village's mountain setting are well worth the bumpy drive. One dolmuş a day does the two-hour run from Yusufeli, departing at 2 pm and returning in the morning. Having to stay in Barhal is no hardship as the handful of pensions here are far more inviting than those in Yusufeli itself.

Best of them is Mehmet Karahan's *Barhal Köyevi* (☎ 826 2071), or Village House, where for US$12 a head you get half board in an old wooden chalet set high up in the hills beside the church; a chairlift is there to help you get up to the house. Rooms are very simple with beds on the floor, but on a balmy summer's night you can drag them out onto the wide terrace and sleep beneath the stars. Food here is a definite plus – fresh village honey and cream to slap on the bread at breakfast time.

Mehmet arranges treks of between two and four days across the mountains to Çamlıhemşin with horses to carry your baggage. One horse, costing US$25, can porter for two trekkers. Other costs are negotiable.

It's wise to phone ahead to make sure there's space at the Barhal Köyevi – if it's full you can stay at the *Marsis Village House* (☎ 826 2026) for US$10 for half board. There's a kitchen here if you'd rather cook for yourself.

A final possibility is the *Barhal Pansiyonu* (☎ 826 2031) which has extremely simple, rather cramped rooms but a terrace with a view of the river. Half board costs US$10

Dörtkilise
☎ 466

Dörtkilise (Four Churches), about 13km south-west of Yusufeli, has another ruined 10th-century **Georgian church** and monastery. It's similar to, but older and larger than, the one at Barhal, and it takes less time and effort to see it. On the way there you'll pass the shell of another church perched like an eyrie on top of a sheer rock. If you don't have a car, take a dolmuş towards Kılıçkaya or Köprügören and get out at Tekkale, then hike 6km to Dörtkilise, bearing in mind that there is no sign for the church, which is high up amid the vegetation on the left-hand side

of the road. If you do have a car, the road is pretty rough from Tekkale onwards.

At Tekkale, *Cemil's Pension* (☎ 811 2908) is another inviting place to stay, a big wooden chalet with terrace right beside the river. A bed in a simple room costs US$10, including breakfast; to sleep on the terrace costs US$8. Evening meals are also available. Owner Cemil Albayrak can arrange treks into the surrounding countryside, prices negotiable depending on the size of the group. There's a trout farm attached to the pension and at the time of writing a kitchen and more showers for guests were being added.

YUSUFELİ TO KARS
With your own vehicle, the 3½-hour, 210km drive between Yusufeli and Kars can be one of the most enjoyable in Turkey. The natural beauty and dramatic scenery is completely unspoiled, and there's virtually no traffic.

The scenic drive up the valley of the Oltu Çayı from Yusufeli to Olur is along a good paved road. The aptly named Taşlıköy (Stony Village), 22km east of the İşhan turn-off, illustrates the harshness of life in this remote, if beautiful, backwater: low stone houses with earthen roofs are built half into the earth to escape the rigours of the winter cold.

Just north-east of the Olur road, look over the bridge over the Gölbaşı to see a ruined Georgian **castle** perched on a rock spur, one of many in the region.

Continue south to Yolboyu, the junction with roads east to Bana (Penek) and Göle, and south to Oltu. At Yolboyu, **twin castles** on opposite sides of the stream guard this fertile valley, the eastern gateway to the mountainous region.

There's an even grander **citadel** at Oltu, south-west of Bana and 36km south of the Olur castle.

Bana (Penek), 11km east of Yolboyu, has a fine 7th-century **Georgian church** set in a riverside meadow 1km south-east of the road across the Penek Çayı. Though the church is worth a visit, access is difficult and only for the truly devoted Georgian-church visitor.

From the Bana church it's 7km north-east to the Şenkaya turn-off and another 3km to the village of Akşir. About 17km past Akşir in a particularly lush valley is Değirmenlidere village, a collection of low **stone houses** with wooden gateways – an eerie sight when unoccupied – which serve as summer quarters for herders.

At the upper end of Değirmenlidere, the road emerges from the pine-fringed mountain valleys and the countryside widens out into a vast rolling steppe. The road surface deteriorates markedly soon after, the potholes slowing your speed. It doesn't improve until 30km short of Kars.

ARTVİN

☎ 466 • pop 20,000 • elevation 600m

Perched on a hill above the road linking Hopa and Kars is Artvin, capital of the province bearing the same name. Given the town's spectacular mountain setting, it should be a much nicer place to spend a few days than it actually is. In fact Artvin is terribly two-faced, putting on a show of small-town respectability by daylight that rapidly gives way to something raunchier as the sun goes down. Artvin has been dubbed 'one large brothel'. There's a nightlife here to equal Trabzon's, but not of a kind to suit everyone.

The real pleasure of a visit to Artvin lies in getting there. You can approach from Erzurum, Yusufeli, Ardahan or Hopa (on the Black Sea coast). The ride to Artvin via any of these routes is wonderfully scenic. As you approach the town you will notice ruined medieval castles guarding the steep mountain passes. Sit on the right-hand side of the bus coming up from Hopa to get the best views, and remember that any liquid-filled containers in your luggage will expand and leak as you ascend into the mountains. Keep them with you and open them periodically to adjust the pressure.

Over the last weekend of June, the Kafkasör Yaylası, a pasture 7km from Artvin, becomes the scene of the annual Kafkasör Kültür ve Sanat Festivalı (Caucasus Culture and Arts Festival), with *boğa güreşleri* (bull wrestling matches) as the main attraction. It's the one time of year

when you should take care to book a hotel room ahead of arrival.

Orientation & Information

Artvin is perched on a high hill which snakes its way upwards above a bend in the Çoruh River. It's little more than one steep street (İnönü Caddesi) and is easily negotiated on foot, except for the trip to and from the otogar which lies in the valley below.

İnönü Caddesi is lined with banks and government offices: the *valilik* (provincial government headquarters, also called the *hükümet konağı*) and the belediye. Most hotels are within a block or two of the valilik.

Artvin's otogar is in Köprübaşı, the riverside district at the foot of the hill. Artvin minibuses (US$0.30) shuttle passengers between the town centre and the otogar at Köprübaşı. Alternatively, a taxi up will cost you about US$4.

Places to Stay

As in Trabzon, most of the cheap hotels have long since abandoned the unequal battle to make money out of tourism in favour of the easier pickings from prostitution. At the time of writing the following hotels seemed to be sticking to tourists, but this is subject to change.

Artvin's best hotel is the *Karahan Otel* (☎ 212 1802, fax 212 2420, İnönü Caddesi 16), with its entrance up a flight of stairs beside the Merkez Cami. The rooms are big and pleasingly modern in appearance, with TVs and baths. At busy times you might get charged the official rate of US$40/50 a single/double, but at other times you'll probably be charged less than half that.

Newer and more modern than the Karahan is the *Çağdaş Turistik Otel* (☎ 212 3333, İnönü Caddesi 27/2), also up a flight of stairs. Rooms here are very inviting with excellent baths and the US$27 per room price tag is reasonable for a couple. However, almost uniquely in Turkey, single travellers are not granted any discount.

A couple of cheaper places also welcome travellers. The *Otel Uğrak* (☎ 212 6505, Hamam Sokak), across İnönü Caddesi from the valilik and down a few steps behind the

PTT and Türk Telekom, has clean, simple waterless rooms for US$5.50/7.50. Some rooms have mountain views. The Şehir Hamamı is only a few metres away, guaranteeing a good bath. It's basically for men but women can use it later in the day if they make a prior appointment.

The *Kaçkar Oteli* (☎ 212 3397, Hamam Sokak 5) is beginning to show its age and the rooms are pretty simple, although a few have mountain views. A single costs US$10, a double US$13.50, definitely negotiable.

Otherwise, places like the *Şafak, Konak* and *Trabzon* are cheap and that's the best that can be said for them. Only stay if you don't mind nocturnal goings-on.

Kafkasör Tatil Köyü Dağ Evleri (☎ 212 5013), or Caucasus Holiday Village Mountain Chalets, are simple lodgings near the Kafkasör meadow. Ask about them at the Karahan Otel.

Places to Eat

The Artvin eating-out scene seems to be deteriorating into a drinking-out scene. *Efkar Restaurant* (İnönü Caddesi), at the foot of the street where it turns to descend the slope, boasts 'million dollar views' from its terrace and would probably make a good place for a nightcap, as would the *Nazar Restoran* downstairs. Sadly though, modern construction work is rapidly robbing Artvin of what used to be a matchless panorama.

Hanedan Restaurant (İnönü Caddesi) has a few tables by the window but once again the view is deteriorating rapidly, as is the menu. On a recent visit only the bar was busy and there were no less than four tele-visions in the dining area – but only three hot dishes on offer in the kitchen!

For cheaper fare, stroll along İnönü Caddesi and size up the assorted small kebapçıs and pidecis. *Saray Pide Salonu*, to the left of the Kaçkar Oteli, has good, fresh, cheap pide and fine valley views. Other promising choices include the *G. Antep 27 Adana İskender Salonu*, the *Birlik Pide ve Lahmacun* and the *Çınar Lokantası*, all offering meals for about US$3 a head.

For tea, pastries and light meals, try the two *Köşk Pastanesis*, across the street from one another midway along İnönü Caddesi, near the big *Aile Çay Bahçesi*. Above one branch is the Televole Internet Cafe. The *Karahan Otel* restaurant is one of Artvin's best but it's not cheap: a set dinner costs US$12.

Getting There & Away

The roads from Artvin to Hopa and Erzurum are fairly good, smooth and fast, but the one from Ardahan is not.

A few minibuses for Yusufeli, Hopa and Rize depart from Artvin in the morning and early afternoon, circulating through the upper town looking for passengers before descending to Köprübaşı and the otogar. Artvin Expres and As Turizm have ticket offices on İnönü Caddesi, across from the valilik, as well as at the otogar.

Details of some daily services from Artvin are listed in the table below. Some buses coming from Erzurum or Ardahan and heading on to Hopa don't go into the otogar but drop you at the roadside at the bottom of the hill. Dolmuşes from here take time to fill

Services from Artvin's Otogar

destination	fare	time	distance	daily services
Ardahan	7	2½	115	several minibuses
Erzurum	7.50	4	215	several buses and dolmuşes
Hopa	2	1½	70	frequent dolmuşes
Kars	8	5	270	2 buses
Samsun	15	8	577	1 or 2 buses
Tortum	6	2½	91	several dolmuşes
Trabzon	8	4½	255	frequent buses
Yusufeli	2.50	1¼	75	several dolmuşes

up, and the taxis waiting will charge about US$4 to run you to the top.

ARTVİN TO KARS

The most direct route between Artvin and Kars, a distance of 205km, is via the old Georgian town of Şavşat. The road deteriorates east of Şavşat, so plan on taking more time for the journey than the distance alone might indicate, although at the time of writing work on upgrading the road had already begun. The southern road via Ardanuç is little more than a track; go via Şavşat. Both roads meet at Ardahan, then go on via Gölebert and Susuz to Kars.

If you have your own vehicle, start early from Artvin (or Kars) and plan to make an excursion to one of the Georgian churches within easy reach of the main road. It's a good idea to fill your petrol tank before setting out on this journey. Take some water and snacks with you as well.

Ardanuç, on the southern route, boasts a large **Bagratid Fortress**. The village of Bulanık is 14km further on, and the 10th-century **Church of Yeni Rabat** is a few kilometres off the main road.

On the road to Şavşat just after passing the Ardanuç turn-off, look for a stone bridge and a sign to Hamamlı. This village, just over 6km off the main road, boasts the fine 10th-century Georgian **Church of Dolishane** (now a mosque). Back on the main road, another 12km brings you to Pırnallı village and the trail head for the 30- to 45-minute hike up to the 9th-century Georgian **Monastery & Church of Porta**.

Another **fortress** guards the western approach to Şavşat, a depressing modern town. From here you can make an excursion north via the Veliköy road for 10km to Cevizli to see the 10th-century monastery **Church of Tbeti**, in ruins but in a beautiful setting.

East of Şavşat the road skirts the **Karagöl Sahara Milli Parkı**, a national park with spectacular mountain scenery. You'll pass several villages inhabited only in summer by farmers and their animals. With your own car, plan to stop at one of the small restaurants specifically sited to soak up the views.

Ardahan, when you finally reach it, is the sort of town you'll be glad you weren't born in. Still, it does have a few basic hotels and restaurants as well as banks with ATMs. Be warned that minibuses to Ardahan arrive in a different piece of waste ground to those heading on for Kars and Posof – take a metered taxi between the two to avoid being overcharged by so-called 'helpers'.

From Ardahan all the way to Kars there is a good tarmacked road with fine views of empty pastoral countryside, framed with mountains and dotted with poverty-stricken villages. About 15km after Ardahan a turning on the left leads 70km up into the mountains to Posof. Provided you have already obtained a visa (see the Land section in the main Getting There & Away chapter for more details on crossing into Georgia) you could cross into Georgia here, thereby reducing the length of the journey to Tflis (Tbilisi; seven hours). It would be interesting to hear from any readers who have done this.

ERZURUM TO KARS

The highway and the train line follow the broad flood plain of the Aras River from Pasinler 43km east to Horasan. In Köprüköy just before Horasan you may spot the **Çoban Köprü**, a 16th-century stone bridge designed, it is said, by the great Sinan.

At Karakurt, the road leaves the river valley to climb into the mountains through pine forests, passing one fertile mountain pasture after another on its way to **Sarıkamış**. You might come to Sarıkamış, 152km east of Erzurum, for its small ski resort. Otherwise a huge army base and a stone monument on the eastern outskirts are poignant reminders of a military disaster. In December 1914, during the early days of WWI, the Ottoman Third Army was encamped for the winter at Sarıkamış, defending this approach to Anatolia against an equal force of Russian troops. The egomaniacal Enver Paşa, effective head of the Ottoman war effort, ordered his troops to attack and push eastwards – a disastrous tactic in midwinter. (Mustafa Kemal, Atatürk, was astounded and appalled when he heard of the order.) The Ottomans lost 75,000 troops to cold, hunger and casualties. The Russians counterattacked and took Erzurum.

You're unlikely to want to stay but if you do the only reasonably comfortable place to do so is the *Turistik Hotel Sarıkamış* (*☎ 474-413 4176, Halk Caddesi 64*), in the centre of town and marked by prominent signs. Although the hotel is hardly fancy, the lobby is colourfully decorated with local carpets and animal skins, and the rooms are well kept and fairly cheerful. The dining room is quite serviceable. Singles/doubles with bath cost US$7/14, including breakfast. Alternatively, *Çelik Palas*, near where the buses stop, is as basic as they come.

KARS
☎ 474 • pop 87,100 • elevation 1768m

East of Sarıkamış, the highway climbs out of the lush mountain valleys and away from the evergreen forests to vast rolling steppes pasturing castle and sheep, with mountains soaring in the distance. Not surprisingly, Kars, a lonely agricultural and garrison town, has a suitably frontier air about it. The locals are said to be descended from the Karsaks, a Turkish tribe who came from the Caucasus in the 2nd century BC and gave their name to the town.

How you'll feel about Kars probably depends on what kind of weather you see it in. When the sun shines the fine pastel-coloured stone buildings look almost chirpy, giving the town the look of a Little Russia in Turkey. But when it rains the impoverished backstreets and muddy old bus terminal hardly encourage you to linger.

The main reason for coming to Kars is usually to visit Ani but you can easily while away half a day on the other sites around the castle.

History

Dominated by a stark medieval fortress, Kars was a pawn in the imperial land-grabbing game played by Turkey and Russia during the 19th century. The Russians captured Kars in 1878, installed a garrison, and held it until 1920 and the Turkish War of Independence, when the republican forces retook it. One of the town's large

Namık Kemal – A Turkish Polymath

Kars' most famous resident was Namık Kemal (1840–88) who played a significant role in the development of modern Turkey. Born in Tekirdağ, the son of the Sultan's court astronomer, he became a government translator. An interest in European society and philosophy led him to translate the works of Rousseau and Montesquieu, and then to expound a similar political philosophy in plays, essays, articles and poems.

Kemal advocated Turkey's adoption of European political, technical, economic and social advances, but he did so in the context of devout Islam. He reinterpreted European progress for an Islamic context, adapted it to Islamic traditions, and made it more acceptable to traditional Muslims. Kemal's calls for 'freedom and fatherland' got him into trouble with the sultan. He died in internal exile on Chios, but his ideas were eagerly absorbed by the Young Turks and by Mustafa Kemal (Atatürk).

mosques was obviously built as a Russian Orthodox church and many of the sturdier stone buildings along the main streets date back to the Russian occupation.

Orientation & Information

The Russians obviously had great plans for Kars, which they laid out on a spacious grid plan for which today's visitors can be grateful. Most banks (and ATMs), hotels and restaurants are in and around Gazi Ahmet Muhtar Paşa, Atatürk, Faik Bey and Küçük Kazım Bey Caddesis. Although the new otogar is 2km from the centre, off the Artvin-Ardahan road on the south-eastern outskirts of the town, almost everything else except the train station and the museum is within walking distance. Dolmuşes run from the otogar.

Kars' tourist office (☎ 223 2300, fax 223 8452) is on the 1st floor of the Milli Eğitim Müd Hizmet Binası on Atatürk Caddesi. You'll need to come here to get a permit to visit Ani – see the Ani section later in this chapter for more details.

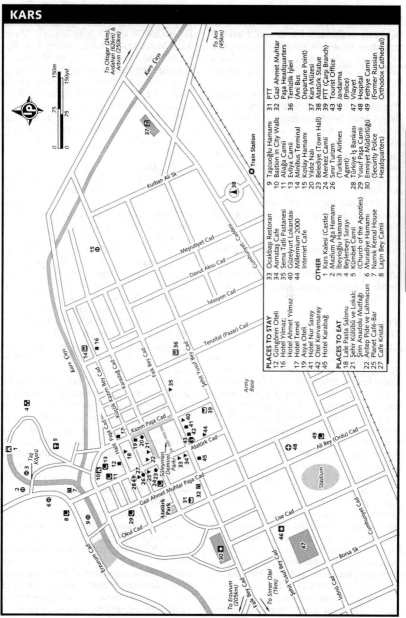

KARS

To Otogar (2km),
Ardahan (62km) &
Artvin (250km)

To Ani
(45km)

Kars Çayı

Train Station

Kurban Ali Sk

Meşrutiyet Cad

Davut Aksu Cad

Cumhuriyet Caddesi

Istasyon Cad

Tenzifat (Pazar) Cad

Şehit Yusuf Bey Cad

Kars Çayı

Falik Bey Cad

Karabağ Cad

Küçük Kazım Bey Cad

Halit Paşa Cad

Kazım Paşa Cad

Taş Köprü

Army
Base

Atatürk Cad

Ali Bey (Ordu) Cad

Süleyman
Demirel
Parkı

Gazi Ahmet Muhtar Paşa Cad

Atatürk
Park

Stadium

Lise Cad

Okul Cad

Borsa Sk

Cumhuriyet Cad

İnönü Cad

Şehit Yusuf Bey Cad

Falik Bey Cad

Erzurum Cad

To Erzurum
(205km)

To Simer Otel
(1km)

PLACES TO STAY
12 Güngören Oteli
16 Hotel Yılmaz;
    Hotel Ahmet Yılmaz
17 Hotel Temel
19 Asya Oteli
41 Hotel Nur Saray
42 Otel Kervansaray
45 Hotel Karabağ

PLACES TO EAT
18 Lale Pasta Salonu
21 Şehir Kulübü ve Lokali;
    Şirin Anadolu Mutfağı
22 Antep Pide ve Lahmacun
25 Planet Café-Bar
27 Cafe Kristal

33 Ocakbaş Restoran
34 Asmataş Cafe
35 Sema Tatlı Pastanesi
40 Güzelyurt Lokantası
44 Millemnium 2000
    Internet Cafe

OTHER
1 Kars Kalesi (Castle)
2 Mazlum Ağa Hamamı
3 Beylerbeyi Sarayı
5 Kümbet Camii
    (Church of the Apostles)
6 Muradiye Hamamı
7 Namık Kemal House
8 Laçin Bey Camii

9 Taşçuoğlu Hamamı
10 Bastion in City Walls
11 Allağa Camii
13 Evliya Camii
14 Minibus Terminal
15 Kızılay Hamamı
20 Yıldız Nalı
23 Belediye (Town Hall)
24 Merkez Camii
26 Sınır Turizm
    (Turkish Airlines
    Agent)
28 Türkiye İş Bankası
29 Yusuf Paşa Camii
30 Emniyet Müdürlüğü
    (Security Police
    Headquarters)

31 PTT
32 Gazi Ahmet Muhtar
    Paşa Headquarters
36 Temizlik İşleri
    (Ani Bus
    Departure Point)
37 Kars Müzesi
38 Atatürk Statue
39 PTT (Çarşı Branch)
43 Tourist Office
46 Jandarma
    (Police)
47 Vilayet
48 Hospital
49 Fethiye Camii
    (Former Russian
    Orthodox Cathedral)

0   75   150m
0   75   150yd

Kars Müzesi

The museum could hardly be more inconveniently positioned, but as you'll have to come here to buy a ticket for Ani it's as well to plan on looking around. Opening hours are from 8.30 am to 5.30 pm daily; admission costs US$1.75.

There are exhibits from the Old Bronze Age, the Roman and Greek periods, and the Seljuk and Ottoman times. Photographs show excavations at Ani and the ruins of some of the Armenian churches in Kars province. Look out for a pair of carved doors from the town's main Orthodox church (now a mosque) and a Russian church bell from the time of Tsar Nicholas II (1894–1917).

Upstairs the ethnographic section displays costumes, saddlebags, jewellery, samovars and a carpet loom.

Behind the museum is the railway coach in which representatives of Russia's Bolshevik government and the fledgling Turkish Republic signed the protocol ending the Russian occupation and annexation of Kars in 1920.

Kars Kalesi

There has probably been a fortress at this strategic spot since earliest times, but records show that one was built by the Saltuk Turks in 1152 and torn down by Tamerlane in 1386. It was rebuilt for the Ottoman sultan Murat III by his grand vizier Lala Mustafa Paşa in 1579. Further repairs were made in 1616 and 1636, and the entire complex was rebuilt yet again in 1855.

The kale was the scene of bitter fighting during and after WWI. When the Russian armies withdrew in 1920, control of Kars was left in the hands of the Armenian forces, which had allied themselves with Russia during the war. Civilians, whether Christian or Muslim, suffered oppression and worse when under the control of irregular troops of the opposing religion. Just as Christian Armenians were slaughtered in some parts of eastern Turkey, so Muslim Turks and Kurds were slaughtered around Kars until the republican armies took the kale.

Kars castle is open during daylight hours (free). Take the road which passes the Church of the Apostles and the ruined Beylerbeyı Sarayı. The huge sign dominating the kale is a quote from Atatürk: 'Vatan Sana Minettardır' (Your Country is Grateful to You), referring to the armed forces.

Inside the kale, besides the ubiquitous boys asking for handouts, you'll find the tomb of Kahraman Celal Baba, the Kale Camii, a 19th-century cannon, and the İç Kale (Castle Keep) which is off limits. In fine weather, the views over the town amply reward the climb.

Old Kars

Along the river banks below the kale huddle assorted crumbling reminders of Kars' ancient past. One of the more attractive – and intact – structures is the 15th-century Taş Köprü (Stone Bridge). It was repaired in 1579 along with everything else in town, but was later ruined by an earthquake. In 1725 it was rebuilt by the local Karaoğulları emirs. Namık Kemal (see the boxed text earlier in this section) was born in a house near the bridge in 1840.

Renamed the Drum-Dome Mosque (Kümbet Camii), the nearby Church of the Apostles was built between 932 and 937 by the Bagratid King Abas. It was repaired extensively in 1579, when the Ottomans rebuilt much of the city, and the porches were added in the 19th century. The relief carvings on the drum are of the apostles. The church is locked and slowly surrendering to weeds, so for now the only way to see the interior is to peek through the doors on the river side.

Walking up the hill beside the church you'll see the ruins of the Ulu Cami and the Beylerbeyı Sarayı nestling beneath the castle.

Gazi Ahmet Muhtar Paşa Headquarters

The best example of a traditional Kars house is the Gazi Ahmet Muhtar Paşa Headquarters on the corner of Faik Bey and Gazi Ahmet Muhtar Paşa Caddesis. This stone house was used as an HQ by Gazi Ahmet Muhtar Paşa, commander of the Ottoman forces during the Russian war in 1877. Later it was a school, then for a while the tourist office. It's currently off limits to visitors.

Hamams

Near the Taş Köprü are several old hamams, some of them ruined, others still in use despite their almost equally ruined external appearance. Although a couple of them are theoretically open to visitors, their standards of cleanliness are hardly inviting. Most people will feel more comfortable using the modern Kızılay Hamamı at Faik Bey Caddesi 143. It's open for women from noon to 5 pm and for men until midnight, daily, for around US$3.50 for the full works.

Places to Stay – Budget

Although Kars still has a few very basic, not to say seedy, hotels, others are quickly upgrading to higher standards (and prices).

Best value for money is the *Güngören Oteli* (☎ 212 5630, fax 223 4821, Halit Paşa Caddesi, Millet Sokak 4) where spacious rooms have baths with tub and shower, and there's an adjoining hamam and *ocakbaşı* (open grill) restaurant. Singles/doubles are US$15/25.

The longtime owner of the Hotel Yılmaz, near the bus station, died in 1997 and upon his death two factions in his family went to war over his estate, which included the hotel. *(Yılmaz* means 'He doesn't give in'.) The Solomonic settlement was to divide the hotel right down the middle. At the time of writing both were undergoing building work, making it hard to decide which was the better. If you want to make the decision the *Hotel Yılmaz* (☎ 212 5174, fax 212 5176, Küçük Kazım Bey Caddesi 146)* occupies the right side of the building and the *Hotel Ahmet Yılmaz* (☎ 212 4215, fax 223 5216, Küçük Kazım Bey Caddesi 148)* the left.

The *Asya Oteli* (☎ 223 2299, Küçük Kazım Bey Caddesi 50)* is a real penny-pinchers' choice, run-down but quiet. Beds in waterless rooms go for US$5 each.

Similarly basic is the *Otel Kervansaray* (☎ 223 1990, Faik Bey Caddesi 124)*. Basic and beat-up, its double rooms come waterless or with sink for US$7, or with shower (but no toilet) for US$11; you can haggle for discounts if it's not busy. Rooms at the back are quieter. Next door to the Kervansaray, the *Hotel Nur Saray* (☎ 223 1364, Faik Bey

Caddesi 208)* is even more basic but charges a mere US$6/10 for waterless rooms.

Places to Stay – Mid-Range

The three-star *Hotel Karabağ* (☎ 212 3480, fax 223 3089, Faik Bey Caddesi 142)* has comfortable modern singles/doubles with bath, minibar, TV and (supposedly) air-con for US$40/60; rooms at the front may be noisy. The restaurant is the most genteel in town and there's an American bar with swirling disco ball.

Groups tend to favour the similarly priced *Anıhan Motel* (☎ 212 3517, 223 7404)*, but its location 2km south of central Kars detracts from its usefulness unless you have a car.

At the time of writing the popular *Hotel Temel* (☎ 223 1376, fax 223 1323, Kazım Paşa Caddesi 4/A)* was undergoing a complete upgrade to become a three-star hotel. Its prices are likely to rise accordingly.

Places to Stay – Top End

At the time of writing the four-star *Simer Otel* (☎ 212 1068, Eski Erzurum Yolu)* was nearing completion but had yet to open its doors. It was shaping up to be a fine modern hotel, roughly 1km west of the centre.

Places to Eat

Kars is noted for its excellent honey. If your heart sinks at the thought of one more little packet of butter and jam for breakfast, look out for the *Lale Pasta Salonu* (Halit Paşa Caddesi)*, near the Güngören Oteli. Here, you can breakfast on Kars honey and butter spread on half a loaf of bread, washed down with a large glass of tea or hot, sweet milk. Several *shops* near the Temel and Güngören hotels also sell Kars honey and the local *kaşar peyniri* (a mild yellow cheese). Even if you're not normally a keen picnicker a glimpse in the windows along Kazım Paşa Caddesi or Halit Paşa Caddesi is likely to set your mind racing to sandwich-making.

Until recently eating out in Kars was not a particularly exciting prospect, but suddenly things are looking up with the opening of a couple of excellent new restaurants and cafes. Best of the lot is *Şirin Anadolu Mutfağı*

(Karadağ Caddesi 55) where a bowl of piping hot soup with a kebap to follow is likely to cost around US$4 in a big, bright dining room. Afterwards you can have a coffee in the upstairs cafe, which is deservedly popular with local students of both sexes.

Just doors away is the *Şehir Külübü ve Lokalı* where a three-course meal with Efes beer will probably cost US$6 to US$9. Its grungy corridor and gawping waiters hardly make for a woman-friendly environment.

Another promising newcomer offering burgers, sandwiches and chips alongside the usual Turkish dishes is the big *Planet Cafe-Bar (Atatürk Caddesi)*. Here you can sip cocktails in a brightly lit bar with decor that wouldn't look out of place on İstiklal Caddesi in İstanbul, or eat more intimately in a candle-lit upstairs restaurant.

Also on Atatürk Caddesi is the older *Cafe Kristal* that serves a wide range of ready meals including *piti*, a local meat and chickpea stew for US$1.75. Just up the street, *Antep Pide ve Lahmacun* is more traditional but does at least make an effort with its decor.

Güzelyurt Lokantası (Faik Bey Caddesi), a few doors down from the Otel Kervansaray, is open all day but in the evenings tends to attract men who are more interested in drinking than eating. Check prices before ordering as bills have a habit of mounting up apparently by themselves.

For ocakbaşı dining, try the restaurant at the *Hotel Güngören* or the brand-new *Ocakbaşı Restoran (Atatürk Caddesi)*, which is popular with lunching business types in suits.

The two branches of *Sema Tatlı Pastanesi (Faik Bey Caddesi 23)* near the Kars Şehir Sineması (cinema) are good for light meals and pastries.

At *Asmataş Cafe (Atatürk Caddesi)* you can have coffee and a sandwich in a grotto-like room with paisley tablecloths. It's popular with Kars' student population. Across the road is the *Millennium 2000 Internet Cafe*, with a pleasing ordinary cafe downstairs and the computers tucked away above.

Shopping

Kars used to be a good place to pick up a locally made Kars carpet, coarse woven with simple but bold patterns and colours, using undyed local yarns retaining the natural colour of the fleece. Unfortunately the troubles of the last 16 years have driven most of the dealers to the west and, in a reversal of the usual situation, if you want to buy a Kars carpet in Kars, it'll be you hunting down the carpet seller rather than the other way round.

At Yıldız Halı at Kazım Paşa Caddesi 191 you can inspect both old and new Kars carpets, the newer versions priced by the metre.

Getting There & Away

Air Turkish Airlines runs a daily nonstop flight to and from Ankara, with connections for İstanbul. The ticket agency is Sınır Turizm (☎ 212 3838, fax 212 3841), Atatürk Caddesi 80, next to Cafe Kristal. There's no special bus to get you to the airport though.

Bus Kars' otogar is 2km from the centre, and dolmuşes shuttle back and forth to the town centre. Unless you're in for the long-haul back to Ankara or İstanbul you may never need to go to the main otogar since *servis* minibuses ferry people from the town-centre bus offices.

The major local bus company, Doğu Kars, has a ticket office on Faik Bey Caddesi, between Atatürk and Kazım Paşa Caddesis, near the Otel Kervansaray. The table lists some useful daily services. For almost all westbound trips you'll need to take a minibus to Erzurum, then board a full-size bus for the onward journey. For details of transport to Ani, see the Ani section.

If you're heading for Doğubayazıt be warned that there are few direct buses from Kars to Doğubayazıt. The usual way to get there is to take one bus to Iğdır, then another to Doğubayazıt. The wait in Iğdır varies from minutes to hours which doesn't stop people from selling you premium-priced 'direct' tickets to Doğubayazıt. The ticket may indeed take you all the way to Doğubayazıt, but chances are when you reach Iğdır it will stop like all the rest and you'll have to change.

If you're heading for Georgia, you'll need to take a minibus to Posof. Should the

Services from Kars' Otogar

destination	fare (US$)	time (hr)	distance (km)	daily services
Akyaka	1.75	1	71	a few minibuses
Ankara	17	16	1100	a few buses
Ardahan	3	1	62	several minibuses
Artvin	5	5	270	a few buses
Erzurum	6	3½	205	few minibuses
Iğdır	4.50	2½	206	a few buses
Posof	5	2½	142	a few minibuses
Trabzon	12	9	525	a few direct buses, or change at Erzurum or Artvin

border with Armenia eventually reopen to travellers, you'll need to get a minibus to Akyaka. Minibuses leave from the old otogar opposite the two Hotel Yılmazes.

Train One might hope that the train station, Kars garı, would be a 19th-century Russian architectural extravagance, but unfortunately it's a crumbling, characterless modern structure. A statue of Atatürk greets you as you approach, and a valiant old steam locomotive, mounted in front of the station, evokes a more romantic age of rail travel.

The *Doğu Ekspresi* connects Kars with Erzurum, Ankara and İstanbul. Readers have reported waits of several days for a booking. The comparable bus journey costs more but takes much less time.

ANİ

The ruined city at Ani, 45km east of Kars, is well worth the trouble of getting to. Its great walls, over a kilometre in length, rise to challenge you as you drive across the wheat-covered plains and into the Turkish village of Ocaklı Köyü. Within the walls stands a medieval ghost town set in grassy fields overlooking the deep gorge cut by the Arpa Çayı, which forms the boundary between the Turkish and Armenian republics.

During the Soviet period, Ani was within the 700m no-man's-land imposed by Moscow on the Turkish border. Visits to the ruins were governed by the strict terms of a protocol agreed between Moscow and Ankara. Things are much more relaxed now – photography, note-taking and picnics are permit-

ted – but remnants of the past linger on in the hoops you must jump through before you'll be allowed to visit the site.

History

Anahid, the Persian equivalent of the Greek goddess Aphrodite, was worshipped by the Urartians and has left her name on this great city as Ani.

On an important east-west trade route and well served by its natural defences, Ani was selected by King Ashot III (952–77) as the site of his new capital in 961, when he moved here from Kars. His successors Smbat II (976–89) and Gagik I (990–1020) reigned over Ani's continued prosperity but after Gagik, internecine feuds and Byzantine encroachment weakened the Armenian state.

The Byzantines took over the city in 1045, then in 1064 came the Great Seljuks from Persia, then the Kingdom of Georgia and for a time local Kurdish emirs. The struggle for the city went on until the Mongols arrived in 1239 and cleared everybody else out. The nomadic Mongols had no use for city life, so they cared little when the great earthquake of 1319 toppled so much of Ani. The depredations of Tamerlane soon after were the last blow: trade routes shifted, Ani lost what revenues it had managed to retain, and the city died. The earthquake-damaged hulks of its great buildings have been slowly crumbling away ever since.

Information

Despite the ending of the Cold War you must still get permission before you can visit

Ani. The excuse given is that the ruins stand on the Armenian border. However, even if that is the case there is no reason why permit and ticket could not be dealt with in one place, thereby saving you the time wasted in visiting three separate buildings.

That said, the procedure for getting permission usually takes no more than 30 minutes (local taxi drivers are well-versed in where to go), and is pretty much of a formality; you should have little trouble getting it by yourself, even if you speak no Turkish.

Start by filling in a form at Kars tourist office. Then take it to be stamped at the Emniyet Müdürlüğü (ehm-nee-**yeht** mew-dewr-lew, Security Directorate), two and a half blocks west on Faik Bey Caddesi. Then trek out to Kars Museum to buy a ticket for Ani (US$2.50; no tickets are sold at Ani itself). Ani is open from 8.30 am to 5 pm. Allow yourself at least 2½ hours at the site, and preferably three or four.

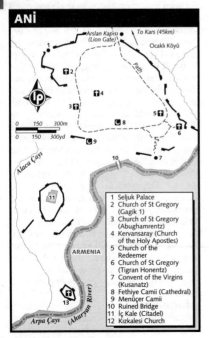

ANİ

Arslan Kapısı (Lion Gate)   To Kars (45km)
Ocaklı Köyü
Path
0 150 300m
0 150 300yd
Alaca Çayı
ARMENIA
Arpa Çayı (Ahuryan River)

1 Seljuk Palace
2 Church of St Gregory (Gagik 1)
3 Church of St Gregory (Abughamrentz)
4 Kervansaray (Church of the Holy Apostles)
5 Church of the Redeemer
6 Church of St Gregory (Tigran Honentz)
7 Convent of the Virgins (Kusanatz)
8 Fethiye Camii (Cathedral)
9 Menüçer Camii
10 Ruined Bridge
11 İç Kale (Citadel)
12 Kızkalesi Church

On the way to Ani you will be stopped at a military checkpoint where your paperwork will be inspected.

The Ruins

Ocaklı Köyü, in the lee of the great walls, is a typical dirt-poor Kurdish-Turkish village of stone houses with earthen roofs topped by TV aerials. Despite its proximity to one of eastern Turkey's biggest tourist drawcards, the village has obtained little benefit from tourism and if you wander round you'll still smell the distinctive aroma of burning *tezek*, cakes of dried dung used for fuel. The modern *'rest facilities'* (restaurant, toilets, shops) opposite the main gate may or may not be open and serving, although their reputation is not of the best. Village children will volunteer to guide you in exchange for tourist treats: coins, sweets, empty plastic water bottles, pens and cigarettes.

Enter the ruined city through the **Arslan Kapısı**, a gate supposedly named after Alp Arslan, the Seljuk sultan who conquered Ani in 1064, but probably also suggested by the lion in relief on the inner wall.

Your first view of Ani is stunning: wrecks of great stone buildings adrift on a sea of undulating grass, landmarks in a ghost city of nearly 100,000 people which once rivalled Constantinople in power and glory. Use your imagination to reconstruct the one- and two-storey buildings that would have crowded the city's streets, with the great churches looming above them. Today birdsong is almost the only sound carried on the constant breeze, and the tangy scent of mint rises from underfoot as you walk.

The shepherds of Ocaklı Köyü pasture their flocks on the lush grass which grows atop the sprawling field of rubble from Ani's collapsed buildings. During your explorations, you're sure to be approached by someone wanting to sell you *eski para* (old coins) or perhaps a bit of coloured tile unearthed in the ruins.

Follow the path to the left and tour the churches in clockwise order.

Church of the Redeemer This church dates from 1034–36, but only half of the ruined structure remains, the other half having been destroyed by lightning in 1957.

Church of St Gregory (Tigran Honentz) Beyond the Redeemer church, down by the walls separating Ani from the gorge of the Arpa Çayı and easy to miss, is the Church of St Gregory the Illuminator, called the Resimli Kilise (Church with Pictures) in Turkish. Named after the apostle to the Armenians, it was built by a pious nobleman named Tigran Honentz in 1215, and though exposure and vandalism have done great damage to the interior, it is still in better condition than most other buildings here. Look for the long Armenian inscription carved on the exterior walls, as well as the fast-fading frescoes depicting scenes from the Bible and Armenian church history.

Convent of the Virgins Follow the paths south-west and down into the Arpa Çayı gorge to visit the Convent of the Virgins (Kusanatz), enclosed by a defensive wall. Scant ruins of a bridge across the river lie to the west.

Fethiye Camii Up on the plateau again, the cathedral (Fethiye Camii) is the largest and most impressive of the churches. Ani cathedral was begun by King Smbat II in 987, and finished under Gagik I in 1010. Trdat Mendet, the cathedral's architect, also oversaw repairs to the dome of Sancta Sophia in Constantinople, brought down in the earthquake of 989. Ani became the seat of the Armenian pontiff. As the grandest religious edifice in the city, it was transformed into a mosque whenever Muslims held Ani, but reverted to a church when the Christians took over. The cathedral demonstrates how Armenian ecclesiastical architecture emphasised height above all else: the churches were not long or wide so much as high – reaching towards heaven. In the case of Ani's cathedral, heaven comes right in – the spacious dome fell down centuries ago.

Menüçer Camii The Menüçer Camii is the square building with the tall octagonal minaret. Claimed as the first mosque built

by the Seljuk Turks in Anatolia (1072), six vaults remain, each different, as was the Seljuk style. Several other vaults have fallen into ruin. This odd but interesting blend of Armenian and Seljuk design probably resulted from the Seljuks employing Armenian architects, engineers and stonemasons in the work. The structure next to the mosque may have been a Seljuk medrese or palace. Some people climb the minaret, although it's debatable how wise this is.

İç Kale (Citadel) Across the rolling grass, south-west of the mosque and beyond the ruined walls, rises the İç Kale (the keep), which holds within its extensive ruins half a ruined church. Beyond the İç Kale on a pinnacle of rock in a bend of the Arpa Çayı is the small church called the **Kızkalesi** (Maiden's Castle).

Church of St Gregory (Abughamrentz) On the western side of the city, this church dates from the mid-1000s and was built to plans by the same architect as the Church of the Redeemer.

Kervansaray The Church of the Holy Apostles dates from 1031, but the Seljuks added a gateway after their conquest of the city in 1064 and used the building as a caravanserai, hence its name.

Church of St Gregory (Gagik I) North-west from the caravanserai, the gigantic Church of St Gregory (Gagik I) was begun in 998 to plans by the same architect as Ani's cathedral. Its ambitious dome, like that of Constantinople's Sancta Sophia, collapsed shortly after being finished, and the rest of the building is now also badly ruined.

Seljuk Palace To the north-west of the Church of St Gregory (Gagik I) is a Seljuk palace, built into the city's defensive walls and recently restored.

Getting There & Away
Transport to Ani has always been a problem but the decline in tourism to the east has made a bad situation even worse.

EASTERN ANATOLIA

The cheapest transport (US$1.25) is the municipal bus to Ocaklı which makes one run daily from Kars to Ani at 1 pm, departing from the Temizlik İşleri building on Pazar Caddesi, between Faik Bey and Şehit Yusuf Bey Caddesis. Unfortunately, this is of little use since there is no return service until the next morning and you're not allowed to stay overnight at the site.

The tourist office in Kars attempts to organise taxi dolmuşes to the site for US$6 or US$7 per person, but if there are no other tourists around you may have to pay the full fare of US$40 return plus waiting time; the drive takes around 50 minutes. If you do, consider how much you'll enjoy having Ani all to yourself. Make sure that your driver understands that you want a minimum of 2½ hours (*iki buçuk saat*, ee-**kee** boochook sah-aht) and preferably three hours (*üç saat*, **ewch** sah-aht) at the site.

KARS TO IĞDIR & DOĞUBAYAZIT

To reach Doğubayazıt and Mt Ararat, go south via Kağızman, Tuzluca and Iğdır, a distance of 240km. The road is badly potholed as far as Tuzluca, then improves considerably after that.

North of Kağızman, above Çamuşlu Köyü, the villagers can show you 12,000-year-old *kaya resimleri*, or **rock carvings**. You'll also get a look at authentic village life. At Tuzluca, there are **salt caves** to visit.

From Tuzluca the road to Iğdır passes near the Armenian frontier, and is closed between dusk and sunrise. The army patrols the area to prevent border violations and smuggling, and if you're on that road at night they'll assume you're doing one or the other.

Maps indicate several ruined Armenian churches along this route. However, the authorities are not keen for you to explore them and they are not signposted with the usual tourist signs, making them hard to find. For some, you need advance permission, which is likely to be slow in coming. You can try approaching the Ministry of Culture in Ankara, but don't hold your breath.

In **Iğdır** there are two decent two-star hotels: the *Parlar Oteli* (☎ 476-227 7199,

İrfan Caddesi 14); and the even better *Otel K Yıldırım* (☎ 476-227 9844, fax 227 7429, Hürriyet Caddesi 48)* in Bağlar Mahallesi beside a Fiat dealer. Both charge around US$10 per person. Coming in from the north you'll pass the cheaper *Otel Öztürk* (☎ 476-227 0099, Evrenpaşa Caddesi 172)*.

From Iğdır it's possible to take a bus east to **Dilucu** and from there cross into the Azerbaijani enclave of **Nakhitchevan**, provided you have already obtained a visa. This is cut off from the rest of Azerbaijan by Armenia and although you could in theory cross overland, for security reasons most people fly to Baku.

Despite taking its name from the Turkish name for Mt Ararat (Ağrı Dağı), the town of **Ağrı** 100km west of the snowcapped peak, is a strong contender for the title of drabbest town in Turkey. There's an otogar on the western outskirts with taxis waiting to ferry passengers into town. Once there, however, there's nothing to hold you bar the few very modest emergency-only hotels, the *Otel Can* and *Otel Salman*, within a block of the main crossroads in the town centre. You'd do better to head on to Doğubayazıt in the east or Erzurum in the west.

DOĞUBAYAZIT
☎ 472 • pop 36,000 • elevation 1950m

Doğubayazıt (doh-**oo**-bay-yah-zuht) is a dusty frontier town crawling with soldiers but with a range of bare, jagged mountains towering above it and a table-flat expanse of wheat fields and grazing land stretching in front of it. Despite its relative isolation, Doğubayazıt has two great drawcards: Mt Ararat (Ağrı Dağı, 5137m), a soaring volcano capped with ice and often shrouded in dark clouds; and İshak Paşa Sarayı, a beautiful fortress-palace-mosque complex perched on a terrace 5km east of town (it's tempting to conclude that not a single building of note has been erected in Doğubayazıt since the demise of İshak).

It's only 35km between Doğubayazıt and the Iranian frontier, making the town the main kicking-off point for the overland trail through Iran and Pakistan to India and China.

Orientation & Information

Doğubayazıt is small and easily negotiated on foot. Its markets sometimes offer tempting bargains on goods smuggled in from neighbouring Iran.

Despite its relative importance, Doğubayazıt has no official tourist office. Instead, various travel agencies about town will be able to help with your queries. Mefser Tur, opposite the Hotel Ararat, is particularly useful if you're heading on into Iran. None of the banks are enthusiastic about changing money, whether cash or travellers cheques, but most have ATMs. The Omega Internet Cafe is upstairs at the junction of Belediye and Meryemana Caddesis.

İshak Paşa Sarayı

İshak Paşa Sarayı was begun in 1685 by Çolak Abdi Paşa and completed in 1784 by his son, a Kurdish chieftain named İshak (Isaac). The architecture is an amalgam of Seljuk, Ottoman, Georgian, Persian and Armenian styles. A grand main entrance leads to a large courtyard. The magnificent gold-plated doors that once hung here were removed by the Russians and now grace the Hermitage Museum in St Petersburg.

Recent restoration has put a new roof and external walls around the 366-room fortress-like palace, which was once equipped with such unheard-of luxuries as central heating, sewerage and running water. You can visit the mosque (which was used for prayers until the 1980s) and assorted rooms, including a hamam, the beautiful dining room of the harem, the kitchen and a squat toilet with claims to one of the finest views in the world. Note especially the little tomb with fine relief work in a corner of the courtyard.

The palace is 6km uphill east of town. At weekends dolmuşes often pass nearby; otherwise a taxi driver will want about US$5 for a return trip, waiting time included. Walking back down is pleasant although women in particular might feel rather isolated. It's open from 8 am to 5.30 pm (closing slightly earlier in winter). Admission to the site costs US$4. It's well worth coming here at sunset for the spectacular views over the surrounding rocky landscape.

Fortress, Mosque & City Ruins

Across the valley from the palace are a mosque, a tomb and the ruins of a fortress. The fortress foundations may date from

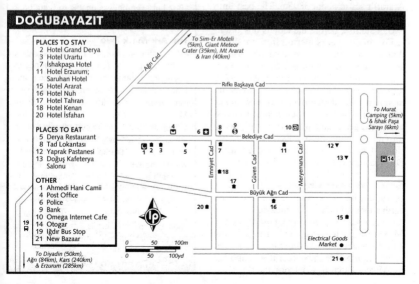

DOĞUBAYAZIT

PLACES TO STAY
2 Hotel Grand Derya
3 Hotel Urartu
7 İshakpaşa Hotel
11 Hotel Erzurum;
    Saruhan Hotel
15 Hotel Ararat
16 Hotel Nuh
17 Hotel Tahran
18 Hotel Kenan
20 Hotel İsfahan

PLACES TO EAT
5 Derya Restaurant
8 Tad Lokantası
12 Yaprak Pastanesi
13 Doğuş Kafeterya
    Salonu

OTHER
1 Ahmedi Hani Camii
4 Post Office
6 Police
9 Bank
10 Omega Internet Cafe
14 Otogar
19 Iğdır Bus Stop
21 New Bazaar

To Sim-Er Moteli (5km), Giant Meteor Crater (35km), Mt Ararat & Iran (40km)

To Murat Camping (5km) & Ishak Paşa Sarayı (6km)

Ağrı Cad
Rıfkı Başkaya Cad
Belediye Cad
Emniyet Cad
Güven Cad
Meryemana Cad
Büyük Ağrı Cad

Electrical Goods Market

0   50   100m
0   50   100yd

To Diyadin (50km), Ağrı (84km), Kars (240km) & Erzurum (285km)

Urartian times (from the 13th to 7th centuries BC), though the walls will have been rebuilt over and over again by whoever needed to control the mountain pass.

The mosque is thought to date from the reign of Ottoman sultan Selim I (1512–20), who defeated the Persians decisively near Çaldıran in 1514, thus adding all of eastern Anatolia to his burgeoning empire. He went on from here to conquer Syria and Palestine.

Nearby stands an 18th-century striped tomb containing the grave of the popular Kurdish writer Ahmedi Hani.

The ruined foundations you see rising in low relief from the dusty plain are of **Eski Beyazıt**. The old city of Eski Beyazıt was probably founded in Urartian times circa 800 BC. Modern Doğubayazit is still a relative newcomer, the villagers only having moved from the hills to the plain in 1937.

Mt Ararat (Ağrı Dağı)

The twin peaks of Mt Ararat have figured in legends since time began, most notably as the supposed resting place of Noah's Ark (see the boxed text in this section). The left-hand peak, called Büyük Ağrı (Great Ararat), is 5137m high, while Küçük Ağrı (Little Ararat) rises to about 3895m. The best time to view the mountain is within an hour or two of sunrise, before the clouds obscure it.

For many years permission to climb Ararat was routinely refused because of security concerns. As life in the east slowly returns to normal, permission is likely to be granted again, but even in good times the mountain was dangerous: severe weather, ferocious sheepdogs, rock and ice slides, and smugglers and outlaws could easily turn an adventure into a disaster. An experienced guide is essential. Ask about in Doğubayazit for the latest information.

Giant Meteor Crater

In 1920 a bit of celestial refuse arrived on earth about 35km from Doğubayazıt. To find the vast crater it formed (supposedly 60m x 35m, making it the second largest in the world), head out towards the Iranian border. About 4km before the border it's signposted as 'Meteor Çukuru' (Meteor Crater).

The Search for Noah's Ark

The story of Noah's Ark, as related in Genesis, is one of the best known of all Bible stories. Deciding the world he had created was corrupt, God instructed Noah to build an Ark and fill it with one male and one female of each living animal. A great flood then swept the earth but, after 40 days, the Ark carried Noah and his family to safety. Afterwards the human and animal occupants of the Ark repopulated the world. A similar story also appears in the pre-biblical Sumerian *Epic of Gilgamesh*.

In folk memory it has long been believed that the Ark came to rest on Mt Ararat in eastern Turkey.

The Ark Mark One

Over the years several people reported seeing a boat shape high up on the mountainside, and in 1955 an expedition brought back what was presumed to be a piece of wood from the Ark, found in a frozen lake. Later, radio-carbon dating indicated that the wood dated from only AD 450–750. The most famous Ararat Ark-hunting expedition of all was organised by ex-US astronaut James Irwin in 1982 but even he was unable to bring back wholly convincing evidence.

The Ark Mark Two

After Irwin's expedition, the political situation in the east put Mt Ararat out of bounds to Ark-seekers. Rather conveniently, then, another expedition in 1985 organised by American David Fusold 'discovered' the Ark on Musa Dağı, near the village of Üzengili, east of Doğubayazıt. The site custodian will point out an elongated oval shape in stone that is supposed to be the boat. He has a sheaf of papers, including a French report setting out at length the 'proof' that this is the true Ark. For those sceptics who are sure that the biblical Ark was wooden, it points out that the meaning of the Hebrew word usually translated as 'cypress wood' is actually uncertain. Whether that convinces you or not, probably depends on your level of cynicism.

Diyadin Hot Springs

At Diyadin you can wonder at a spouting rock formation in the sulphur springs said to resemble the two Ararats, and explore a river which flows into a cave. Afterwards you can bathe in one of the local swimming pools. Not all are very clean so it's best to make inquiries first. If you tip the guardian about US$3 you can get a pool to yourself. Security concerns may make it advisable to visit Diyadin on a guided tour. Ask about in town and one of the guides may be able to help.

Places to Stay – Budget

Camping Just before you reach İshak Paşa Sarayı, you'll come to *Murat Camping* on the left-hand side of the road, where you can pitch a tent for about US$1. There's a tea garden here, and you're within easy walking distance of the palace. Some people pitch tents uphill beyond the palace and the mosque. Alternatively there's *Paraçut Camping* further up or *İsfahan Camping* down on the plain.

Hotels Doğubayazıt has plenty of cheap hotels but some are very basic and women travelling alone may not feel comfortable in them. On the main street is *Hotel Erzurum* (☎ 312 5080, Belediye Caddesi) where spartan waterless rooms go for US$3.50 a head. *Saruhan Hotel* (☎ 311 3097) charges the same and, in exchange for very basic accommodation, offers good views of Mt Ararat or İshak Paşa Sarayı.

The tidy *Hotel Tahran* (☎ 311 2223, Büyük Ağrı Caddesi 124), up the street from the big Hotel İsfahan, hosts devout Muslims who delight in simple but clean singles/doubles with shower for US$5/9.

An excellent choice is *Hotel Ararat* (☎ 312 8889, Belediye Caddesi), across from the otogar and offering cheerful, clean rooms with bath, some with decent views of Mt Ararat, for US$12/20 including breakfast.

The nominally two-star *İshakpaşa Hotel* (☎ 312 7036, fax 312 7644, Büyük Ağrı Caddesi) has 21 rooms on four floors, each with shower and balcony. There's a restaurant and bar, and rooms cost US$9/14. The *Hotel Kenan* (☎ 312 7869, fax 312 7571, Emniyet Caddesi 39) also claims to be two-star but offers only simple rooms with dodgy wiring for US$7/12. There's a licensed restaurant right next door.

The *Hotel Urartu* (☎ 312 7295, 311 2450, PTT Karşısı) looks pricier than it actually is. Pleasant modern rooms with bath and TV cost US$14/25, including breakfast.

Places to Stay – Mid-Range

The two-star *Hotel İsfahan* (☎ 215 5289, fax 215 2044, Isa Geçit Caddesi 26) has five floors of rooms with showers for US$20/30/40 a single/double/triple. The decor is in need of an update but the rooms are comfortable enough and there's a car park and wheelchair ramp.

The three-star *Hotel Grand Derya* (☎ 312 7531, fax 312 7833, Belediye Caddesi), right beside the Ahmedi Hani Camii, offers comfortable rooms for US$25/42 a single/double.

The three-star *Hotel Nuh* (☎ 312 7232, fax 312 6910, Büyük Ağrı Caddesi 65) is better inside than its rather run-down exterior suggests. There's a private car park, a lift and constant hot water; and the rooms, some of which have views of Mt Ararat and the palace, are clean and comfortable for US$30/55.

Tour groups are often taken to the three-star *Sim-Er Moteli* (☎ 215 5601, fax 215 3413, İran Transit Yolu), 5km east of town on the highway to Iran.

Places to Eat

Belediye Caddesi has three or four kebapçıs, including the excellent *Tad Lokantası* which does döner sandwiches for US$1.50. The same people run *Doğuş Kafeterya Salonu* near the otogar which makes good fresh pide as well as more substantial meals. Also popular is the *Derya Restaurant* near the post office, which offers lots of cheap stews.

Yaprak Pastanesi (Belediye Caddesi) offers afternoon tea and pastry for about US$1.50. You can hardly miss the displays of cakes and biscuits in the windows.

For full meals with drinks, try the top hotels.

EASTERN ANATOLIA

Services from Doğubayazıt

destination	fare (US$)	time (hr)	distance (km)	daily services
Ankara	24	16	1210	a few buses
Erzurum	5	4	285	a few buses
Iğdır	2	¾	51	hourly dolmuşes
Kars	5	3	240	a few buses
Van (via Çaldıran)	3.50	2½	185	several dolmuşes

Getting There & Away

At the time of writing, minibuses (US$1.50) to the Iranian border were leaving from outside the petrol station near the junction of Ağrı and Büyük Ağrı Caddesis. For more information on crossing into Iran, see the Land section in the main Getting There & Away chapter at the front of this guide.

Bus services from Doğubayazıt are relatively limited and mostly go via Erzurum or Iğdır. The table above lists details of some daily services.

South-Eastern Anatolia

Turkey's south-eastern region shares some characteristics with the north-east: its history is involved and eventful, its landscapes dramatic and its tourist traffic much lighter than along the congested Aegean and Mediterranean coasts. Other than this, the regions are dramatically different.

South-eastern Anatolia is mostly hot and dry, with elevations ranging from Şanlıurfa's 518m to Van's 1727m. The people are mostly Kurds who depend on farming for their livelihood. Since 1992 the region has been changing slowly as the vast South-East Anatolia Project (Güneydoğu Anadolu Projesi, GAP) began to take effect (see the boxed text 'South-East Anatolia Project' in the Şanlıurfa section later in this chapter). Eventually it is intended that water will be brought even to towns like Mardin, which now seem almost impossibly dry and dusty.

This is the part of Turkey that was most affected by the troubles of the last 16 years (for more discussion of the Kurdish troubles, see the History section of the Facts about Turkey chapter). Since the capture of the Kurdistan Workers Party (PKK) leader Abdullah Öcalan in 1999, the situation has eased considerably and the atmosphere is now much more hopeful than hitherto was the case. Nonetheless it remains wise to check on the latest situation before setting out, and to come prepared for minor security hassles (for more discussion of the safety issue, see the boxed text 'Is it Safe to Travel in South-East Turkey?' on the facing page).

This section assumes you're travelling east from Kayseri or Sivas to Kahramanmaraş and Gaziantep, or to Malatya, with a side trip to Elazığ and Harput. It then looks at the various ways of visiting Nemrut Dağı and Şanlıurfa. After that it assumes you will travel east to Diyarbakır and Mardin and thence to Lake Van (Van Gölü) and Van.

KAHRAMANMARAŞ

☎ 344 • pop 230,000 • elevation 568m

Kahramanmaraş (also known as Maraş) is famous throughout Turkey for its ice cream, which is so thick you need a knife and fork to cut it. The city's lengthy name was given to it in 1973 in honour of its role during the War of Independence. The populace put up such fierce resistance to French rule during WWI that parliament added Kahraman (Heroic) to its traditional name half a century later.

Wars and earthquakes have destroyed much of the old city, and today's Maraş is a modern city set where the agricultural plain meets the slopes of Ahır Dağı (Stable Mountain, 2301m). It's a farming centre with vast, rich crops of cotton, peppers and potatoes in the surrounding countryside. Copper working is also important and the outskirts are filled with textile factories. There are no major sights but if you need to stop for a meal or for the night you can while away a few hours pleasantly enough.

History

Marqasi was the capital of a principality which sprang up after the collapse of the Hittite Empire based at Boğazkale/Hattuşa in 1200 BC. Destroyed by King Sargon of Assyria in the 8th century BC, it rose again under the Romans, who called it Germaniceia. The Byzantines used its citadel as an eastern defence-point against Arab invasion, but the Arabs took it in AD 637 anyway. The Byzantines reclaimed it in later centuries, but while they were dealing with the Seljuk invasion up north, control of Germaniceia passed to an Armenian strongman named Philaterus in 1070. He briefly ruled over a large kingdom until it was conquered by the crusaders and returned to Byzantine control.

A succession of Kurdish, Seljuk and Turkoman emirs and sultans governed the city until it was conquered by the Ottoman sultan Selim in 1515. Maraş had a significant Armenian population until the War of Independence, after which many fled to neighbouring Syria or abroad.

Is It Safe to Travel in South-Eastern Turkey?

For most of the 1980s and '90s south-eastern Turkey was torn apart by the struggle between the Kurdistan Workers Party (PKK) and the Turkish army. During the course of that struggle tourists in the south-east were kidnapped and bombs were set off in İstanbul and tourist resorts. Western governments reacted by warning their citizens against travelling in south-eastern Turkey. The ultimate low point was reached in 1999 after the capture of PKK leader Abdullah Öcalan, when Western embassies stepped up their warnings to travellers, insurance companies withdrew cover for people travelling in the east, and tourism to Turkey effectively collapsed.

In 2000 a page seemed to have been turned at last. The PKK announced a cease-fire, emergency rule was lifted from some of the south-eastern provinces, and a more positive mood was discernible, not least because Turkey's enthusiasm for membership of the European Union will more or less force the government to change its approach to the Kurds.

So is it safe to travel in the south-east now? In the course of researching this guidebook I have travelled around south-eastern Turkey twice in the last three years. While no-one can ever give any cast-iron guarantees, I was in no doubt that the situation had eased dramatically this time round. There are still regular police and army ID checks once you travel east of Diyarbakır but they are, for the most part, fairly speedy and not too intrusive. I was stopped once by a plain-clothes police officer in Elazığ but was otherwise left to my own devices.

Bus transport still stops early in the day south and east of Diyarbakır but in towns like Batman where, two years ago, no-one ventured onto the streets after 5 pm, life seems to be returning to normal.

There are still a few peripheral hot spots. If you stray into Tunceli, Hakkari or Şırnak you are still likely to be given an enforced police escort throughout your stay. But, at the time of writing, there were no particularly valid reasons for tourists to visit those places anyway.

Before venturing east, you should of course check the latest advice on travelling in the area from one of the following sources of information (before you leave home) or from your embassy in Ankara.

Australian Department of Foreign Affairs & Trade (☎ 1300-555 135)
British Foreign Office (☎ 020-7238 4503)
Canadian Dept of Foreign Affairs & International Trade (☎ 1800-267 8376)
New Zealand Dept of Foreign Affairs & Trade (☎ 4-494 4500)
US Dept of State (☎ 202-647 5225)

Pat Yale

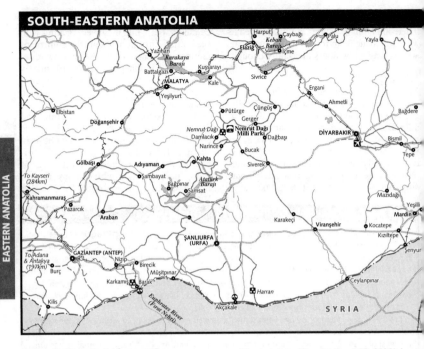

SOUTH-EASTERN ANATOLIA

Orientation & Information

The city's otogar is 100m west of the main highway on Azerbeycan Bulvarı. This major thoroughfare continues west for 400m to the archaeology museum, and beyond it another 900m to Kıbrıs Meydanı (Cyprus Square), with its statue of Atatürk, in the heart of the business district. Many hotels are near Kıbrıs Meydanı, or along the 400m stretch of Atatürk Bulvarı which goes west from Kıbrıs Meydanı to the Ulu Cami, an ancient building which marks the city's traditional centre. East of Kıbrıs Meydanı is Trabzon Caddesi dominated by the purple and mustard coloured Özel İdare İş Merkezi building, a handy, if rather unlikely, landmark.

There are no hotels near the otogar or near the train station which is at the foot of Cumhuriyet Caddesi, just east of the main highway, 2km north-east of Kıbrıs Meydanı.

To get to the centre from the otogar take a dolmuş along Azerbeycan Bulvarı to Kıbrıs Meydanı (US$0.25).

The tourist office (☎/fax 212 6590) is at Trabzon Caddesi, Dedezade Sokak, Özgür Apt, No 6 (2nd floor).

Things to See & Do

The **Kahramanmaraş Müzesi**, 400m uphill from the otogar on Azerbeycan Bulvarı, is open from 8 am to 5 pm daily except Monday. Admission costs US$1.75. Exhibits include dinosaur bones found locally and a dozen fine Hittite stelae covered in lively reliefs. An Assyrian border marker is covered in cuneiform inscriptions. Other exhibits cover every period from the Old Bronze and Hittite to Ottoman. The ethnographic section is rich in textiles, costumes of gold cloth, inlaid woodwork and beautiful local kilims.

The **Ulu (Acemli) Cami**, on Atatürk Bulvarı, was built in Syrian style in 1502. Note especially its tall and unusual minaret, which has survived the depredations of earthquakes and invaders relatively intact. Across the

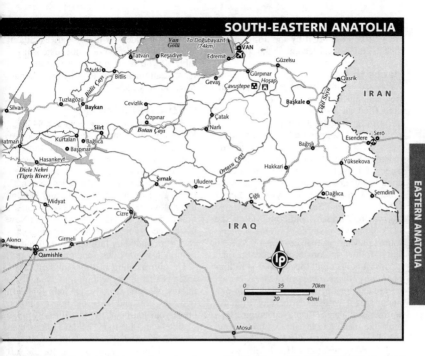

SOUTH-EASTERN ANATOLIA

park to the south-west is the recently restored tomb of the founders. The **Çukur Hamamı** Turkish bath is nearby as well.

A few steps to the north is the **Taş Medrese**, a religious seminary dating from the 14th century. The **Taş Han** was the city's caravanserai.

The **citadel** (kale) to the south has been repeatedly rebuilt and repaired over the centuries. Inside the walls a pleasant tea garden overlooks fine views of the city.

Parallel with Atatürk Caddesi, to the north, is Kahramanmaraş's lively **bazaar**. Poke around here and you'll find men making saddles, beating vast copper vats and manufacturing buckets out of old tyres.

Places to Stay

Because it's an agricultural trading centre, Kahramanmaraş has several comfortable two-star hotels right in the centre, off Kıbrıs Meydanı, although prices are pretty steep for what you get.

Hotel Çavuşoğlu (☎ 225 3524, fax 214 2303, Şeyhadil Caddesi 50), uphill from Kıbrıs Meydanı, has clean simple singles/doubles with light decor for US$20/29 (subject to discount) with bath, including breakfast. Across the road the crumbling *Otel Celtik Palas* is only for those on the very tightest budgets.

Round the corner is the better value *Otel Büyük Maraş* (☎ 223 3500, fax 212 8894, Milli Egemenlik Caddesi 7). Rooms with bath are US$29/42, including breakfast.

Otel Kazancı (☎ 223 4462, fax 212 6942), signposted uphill from Kıbrıs Meydanı, is central, yet fairly quiet, but charges a surprisingly high US$40/70 for a room with bath and breakfast.

Right next to the Yaşar Pastanesi is the two-star *Hotel Belli* (☎ 223 4900, fax 214 8282, Trabzon Caddesi 2). Spacious rooms are clean and comfortable and some have hamam basins and scoops in their bathrooms, a nice touch. Rooms cost US$33/50, including breakfast. Anyone worried about fire will be comforted by the array of fire buckets and shovels decorating the corridors.

Places to Eat

Maraş is noted for several culinary specialities, among them *saç kavurma*, pieces of lamb fried on a convex steel griddle; and *külbastı*, grilled lamb chops with *çemen* (cumin), red pepper and garlic. Finding these in the local restaurants isn't easy and you may have to fall back on the familiar range of kebaps. The bazaar has several small restaurants serving lunch to the local traders. A good place to try is *Öz Lezzet Kebap ve Döner Salonu (Kösker Çarşısı 24)*, where Turkish handicrafts adorn the walls alongside pictures of alpine scenery. Soup, salad and a kebap costs just US$1. To find it, follow the sounds of copper beating.

Most famous of all local dishes is Kahramanmaraş *dövme dondurma* (Maraş beaten ice cream), made with so much glue-like binder that it withstands the city's intense summer heat, can be displayed hanging on a hook like meat, and is eaten with knife and fork. For a sample, try the *Yaşar Pastanesi (☎ 225 0808)*, next to the Hotel Belli, where you can tuck into ice cream (US$1.25) and baklava beneath photos of such notables as former prime ministers Çiller, Demirel, Özal and Erbakan doing likewise. It's worth coming here just for the decoration that puts many formal Turkish museums in the shade.

Getting There & Away

Maraş shares the traffic which crisscrosses the region from Kayseri to Gaziantep and Adana to Malatya. Most bus services originate elsewhere, and may or may not have onward seats. There are hourly dolmuşes to

Gaziantep (US$2, one hour, 80km) from Şeyhadil Caddesi or the otogar. Details of some other daily services are listed in the table. If you're driving, note that the road from Kahramanmaraş to Adıyaman is narrow and very slow.

GAZİANTEP (ANTEP)

☎ 342 • pop 702,000 • elevation 843m

Known in Ottoman times as Aintab, the city of Gaziantep got its modern name from the heroism displayed by its citizens during the War of Independence. More recently Gaziantep has been one of the cities to benefit from the problems of the 1980s and '90s, as the professionals, the skilled workers and the rich fled west to this haven of safety. Now it's the economic powerhouse of the southeast, surrounded by farmland and ringed by light industry (textiles, food processing etc).

Despite its long history, modern Gaziantep is a large city with just a few sights to interest visitors: namely, the kale (citadel), two museums and some old houses. If you break your journey here, you'll find a range of hotels and far more baklava shops than you can imagine. The region is also known for excellent grapes and olives, for the soft Arabic 'pizza' called *lahmacun* and for pistachio nuts. This is the *şam fıstığı* (pistachio) capital of Turkey, growing, shelling, packing and shipping hundreds of tonnes each year.

History

Archaeologists sifting through the dirt which forms the artificial hill beneath the kale have found prehistoric artefacts dating from Neolithic times (7000–5000 BC), but the town's history really begins when small Proto-Hittite, or Hatti, city-states grew up between 2500 and 1900 BC.

Services from Kahramanmaraş' Otogar

destination	fare (US$)	time (hr)	distance (km)	daily services
Adana	5	3½	190	frequent buses
Adıyaman	5	3	164	several buses
Antakya	4	4	185	frequent buses
Kayseri	7.50	4½	291	several buses
Malatya	6	4½	226	several buses

Hittites and Assyrians battled for this region until it was taken by Sargon II, King of Assyria, in 717 BC. The Assyrians ruled for almost a century before being overcome by the Cimmerians, a Crimean people driven from their traditional lands by the Scythians. The Cimmerians swept through Anatolia destroying almost everything that lay in their path, setting an example that would be followed by numerous uncreative hordes who showed up later.

The Cimmerians cleared out and the Persians took over from 612 to 333 BC, only to be followed by Alexander the Great, the Romans and the Byzantines. The Arabs conquered the town in AD 638 and held it until the Seljuk Turks swept in from the east in the 1070s.

With the crusades, Gaziantep's history perked up a bit but the crusaders didn't stay long before the Seljuks took over again. Aintab remained a city of Seljuk culture, ruled by petty Turkish lords until the coming of the Ottomans under Selim the Grim in 1516.

During the Ottoman period, Aintab had a sizeable Christian population, especially Armenians. You'll see Armenian churches,

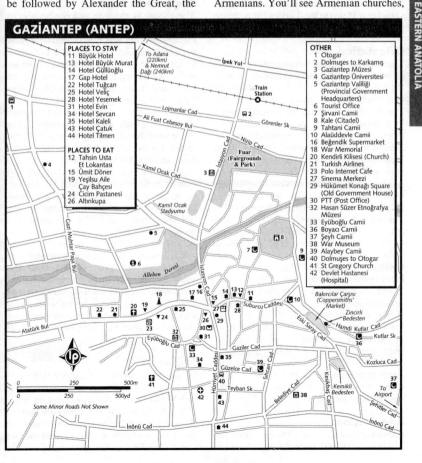

GAZİANTEP (ANTEP)

PLACES TO STAY
11 Büyük Hotel
13 Hotel Büyük Murat
14 Hotel Güllüoğlu
17 Gap Hotel
22 Hotel Tuğcan
25 Hotel Veliç
28 Hotel Yesemek
31 Hotel Evin
34 Hotel Sevcan
35 Hotel Kaleli
43 Hotel Çatuk
44 Hotel Tilmen

PLACES TO EAT
12 Tahsin Usta Et Lokantası
15 Ümit Döner
19 Yeşilsu Aile Çay Bahçesi
24 Cicim Pastanesi
26 Altınkupa

OTHER
1 Otogar
2 Dolmuşes to Karkamış
3 Gaziantep Müzesi
4 Gaziantep Üniversitesi
5 Gaziantep Valiliği (Provincial Government Headquarters)
6 Tourist Office
7 Şirvani Camii
8 Kale (Citadel)
9 Tahtani Camii
10 Alaüddevle Camii
16 Beğendik Supermarket
18 War Memorial
20 Kendirli Kilisesi (Church)
21 Turkish Airlines
23 Polo Internet Cafe
27 Sinema Merkezi
29 Hükümet Konağı Square (Old Government House)
30 PTT (Post Office)
32 Hasan Süzer Etnografya Müzesi
33 Eyüboğlu Camii
36 Boyacı Camii
37 Şeyh Camii
38 War Museum
39 Alaybey Camii
40 Dolmuşes to Otogar
41 St Gregory Church
42 Devlet Hastanesi (Hospital)

To Adana (220km) & Nemrut Dağı (240km)
İpek Yol
Train Station
Lojmanlar Cad
Ali Fuat Cebesoy Bul
Görenler Sk
Nizip Cad
İstasyon Cad
Fuar (Fairgrounds & Park)
Kamil Ocak Cad
Kamil Ocak Stadyumu
Gazi Muhtar Paşa Bul
Alleben Deresi
Atatürk Bul
Eyüboğlu Cad
Gaziler Cad
Hürriyet Cad
Güzelce Cad
Teyban Sk
Sırçan Cad
Belediye Cad
Keskikaş Cad
İnönü Cad
Suburcu Caddesi
Bakırcılar Çarşısı (Coppersmiths' Market)
Eski Saray Cad
Zincirli Bedesten
Hamdi Kutlar Cad
Kutlar Sk
Kozluca Cad
Kemikli Bedesten
To Airport
Şehitler Cad
İnönü Cad

0 — 250 — 500m
0 — 250 — 500yd
Some Minor Roads Not Shown

community buildings and mansions scattered throughout the city's historical core.

In 1920, as the victorious allies sought to carve up the Ottoman territories, Aintab was attacked and besieged by French forces intent on adding Turkish lands to their holdings in Syria and Lebanon. Aintab's nationalist defenders held out for 10 months, at a cost of 600 lives, before finally surrendering on 8 February 1921. Their tenacious defence kept the French forces busy and allowed the embattled nationalist army to fight on other fronts. In recognition, Turkey's Grand National Assembly added Gazi (War Hero) to the Turkicised Antep to yield the city's new name: Gaziantep.

Orientation

The centre of this sprawling and fast-growing city is the intersection of Atatürk Bulvarı/Suburcu Caddesi and Hürriyet/İstasyon Caddesis, former site of the *hükümet konağı* (government house) and marked by a large equestrian statue of Atatürk. Although the provincial government is now housed in a modern building to the north, locals (and, more importantly, dolmuş drivers) still call the place Hükümet Konağı.

The *devlet hastanesi* or state hospital, another useful landmark, is a few blocks past Hükümet Konağı on Hürriyet Caddesi.

Most hotels, banks with ATMs, and many restaurants are within a block or two of the main intersection. The museum is 500m away. The kale, on the high hill topped by the mosque with twin minarets, lurks behind the bazaar area.

The otogar is 1.5km from the main intersection, accessible by frequent minibus (US$0.30) and less frequent city buses; to get to the otogar, take a bus or dolmuş from just south of the central Hotel Kaleli. The train station is a short walk east of the otogar. Walk from the station to the first large intersection to catch the 'Devlet Hastanesi' minibus into the centre. A taxi to the centre costs about US$3.25.

Information

Gaziantep's tourist office (☎ 230 5969, fax 234 0603), 100. Yıl Atatürk Kültür Parkı İçi,

is behind the new Gaziantep *valiliği* (provincial government headquarters) near the fairgrounds. To find it from the centre, walk north along İstasyon Caddesi until you reach the big circular Beğendik department store on the left. Cross the stream beside it and follow the path into the park on the left until you see a pinkish building standing on its own.

Should the worst come to the worst while you're in the east, it's worth knowing that Gaziantep has a good, modern hospital close to the otogar on Ali Fuat Cebesoy Bulvarı.

The Kale District

The citadel is thought to have been constructed by the emperor Justinian in the 6th century AD, but was rebuilt extensively by the Seljuks in the 12th and 13th centuries. Don't go through what appears to be an enormous stone gateway but is actually the fosse (dry moat), straddled in ancient times by a drawbridge high above. Around to the right of the fosse you will come to a small mosque, opposite which is a ramp leading to the citadel doors. If they're open, proceed across the wooden bridge that spans the fosse and leads into the kale.

At the foot of the kale is an interesting quarter with a fruit and vegetable market, workshops where you can watch men beating copper into coffeepots and shiny bowls, old stone houses and little neighbourhood mosques. Trucks for hire are gathered at one side of the kale, heirs to the ancient carters and teamsters who may have gathered here in centuries past. You can walk back into town through a partially covered **bazaar** area, looking out for saddlemakers and other artisans at work. If you're unlucky you'll stumble upon the old stone building housing the city's meat market, not a place to explore if you're even slightly squeamish.

Museums

Gaziantep is about to become the beneficiary of the rescue dig undertaken at the rich Roman site of Belkis-Zeugma in 2000, just before the new Birecik Dam flooded the site for ever. At the time of writing the many fine mosaics recovered from the site stood in pallets in the grounds of the old museum but a new annexe is to be built to house them. It's probably best to anticipate a delay of a few years though.

In the meantime, **Gaziantep Müzesi**, next to the stadium on İstasyon Caddesi, holds something from every period of the province's history: from mastodon bones to Hittite figurines and pottery, Roman mosaics and funeral stones complete with portraits of husband and wife. Unusually it also devotes space to 'nostalgia' with a few cases containing old cameras, radios, children's toys and postcards. In theory there's even wheelchair access, although the gradient of the ramps looks alarmingly steep.

Follow the signs on narrow Hanifioğlu Sokak for the **Hasan Süzer Etnografya Müzesi**, a two-century-old Gaziantep stone house restored to house a museum of local ethnography.

A central *hayat* (courtyard) patterned with light and dark stone provides light and access to the rooms. Those on the ground floor were for service; those on the first floor made up the *selamlık*, for male family members and their visitors; and those on the second floor made up the *haremlik*, for female family members and their visitors. Many of the rooms have been decorated according to their historical function: kitchen, hamam and reception rooms (with nighttime bedding stored in the cupboards). Several rooms now hold local historical exhibits, including one showing Gaziantep's role in the War of Independence, through photographs, documents and artefacts.

On the top floor, one room holds life-size wax figures of the museum's benefactor, Mr Süzer, currently owner of Pera Palas Hotel in İstanbul, and his parents.

The Mesk Odası, a room set apart for the men's games, now holds an exhibit of a *tandır* (charcoal brazier or oven) set under a stone table covered with a *yorgan*, or cotton-filled quilt. This was the traditional way in which humble country families generated winter warmth: occupants put their legs under the quilt to keep warm, and talked or played games on the quilted table above.

Several rooms also feature striking examples of *sedef* furniture (inlaid with mother-of-pearl), a Gaziantep speciality. Don't miss the two-storey Cappadocia-style cellar carved from the rock beneath the house, with a deep well and huge jars to store wine.

Both museums are open from 8 am to noon and 1.30 to 5.30 pm daily except Monday. Admission costs US$1.75.

Places to Stay – Budget

If you're on a tight budget head straight for Kayacık Sokak, a dingy lane of card rooms, beer halls and billiard saloons just west of the hükümet konağı. Bypass the inappropriately named *Gül Palas* (Rose Palace) and the two-star *Hotel Uğurlu* (☎ 220 9690) to reach *Hotel Evin* (☎ 231 3492), which offers simple singles/doubles for US$7/10.

Places to Stay – Mid-Range

Two hotels close together charge US$12/19 for rooms with bath and there's not much to choose between them. *Hotel Güllüoğlu* (☎ 232 4363, Suburcu Caddesi 1/B) has rather cramped rooms but comes attached to a renowned baklavacı (see Places to Eat following). Just to the east *Hotel Büyük Murat* (☎ 231 8449, fax 231 1658) offers slightly more space for the same price. Some quieter rooms at the back have the added bonus of fine castle views.

The two-star *Hotel Veliç* (☎ 221 2212, fax 221 2210, Atatürk Bulvarı 23) charges US$20/30 for pleasant modern rooms, including breakfast.

The two-star *Hotel Çatuk* (☎ 231 9480, fax 233 0043, Hürriyet Caddesi 27), just across from the hospital, has smallish, air-con rooms for US$17/28, including breakfast. If you could wangle a discount this might make a good choice.

The three-star *Hotel Kaleli* (☎ 230 9690, fax 230 1597, Hürriyet Caddesi), between the main intersection and the hospital, has rather old-fashioned but spacious rooms for US$28/37; those at the front have bathtubs, those at the back have small showers. The rooftop restaurant is among the city's best.

The three-star *Gap Hotel* (☎ 220 3974, fax 234 2102, Atatürk Bulvarı 10) is central and fancy, with a huge statue of a Kangal sheepdog adorning its marble-paved lobby.

Spacious rooms cost US$50/80 (breakfast included), but the decor is somewhat frenetic. There's a car park and 1st-floor nightclub.

Places to Stay – Top End

These days every new hotel that opens in Gaziantep seems to be aimed at the big spenders. The best place to stay has to be the five-star **Hotel Tuğcan** (☎ 220 4323, fax 220 3242, Atatürk Bulvarı 34), about 400m west of Hükümet Konağı. Rooms with all mod cons cost US$150/170, and there's a swimming pool, sauna and restaurant. Luckily, discounts are not hard to obtain when it's quiet.

More or less opposite Hotel Kaleli is the glistening four-star **Hotel Sevcan** (☎ 220 6686, fax 220 8237, Göz Hastanesi Sokak 16) with modern rooms, some with bath, for US$110/160.

Hotel Tilmen (☎ 220 2081, fax 220 2091, İnönü Caddesi 168) offers big modern rooms with inviting bathrooms for US$90/ 120. The tiled lobby and bar are very attractive.

Two other three-star options are the **Büyük Hotel** (☎ 220 8550, fax 232 4053, Karagöz Caddesi 20) and **Hotel Yesemek** (☎ 220 8888, İsmail Say Sokak 4).

Places to Eat

Along Suburcu Caddesi and Atatürk Bulvarı, banks are interspersed with an incredible number of shops selling baklava, pastries, cakes and other Turkish sweets. Most famous is **Güllüoğlu**, attached to the hotel of the same name. Its fame grew because of its şam fıstıklı baklava (baklava with pistachios), but the shop serves many other varieties as well, including kaymaklı (with clotted cream).

Otherwise, try the **Cicim Pastanesi** (Atatürk Bulvarı), south of the Hotel Veliç, which has a little fountain in the centre. The nearby **Liman** and **Kenem** pastanesis are similar. Afterwards you can take tea in the pleasant Yeşilsu Aile Çay Bahçesi opposite.

For pre-baklava courses, there are many small kebapçıs and restaurants on and off Suburcu Caddesi. A modern choice is **Tahsin Usta Et Lokantası** (closed Sunday), serving a variety of south-eastern kebaps but specialising in oven-baked lahmacun and pide. The dining room is airy and bright. Alcohol-free dinners cost US$2 to US$3. If you're just after a good, quick döner, **Ümit Döner** (İstasyon Caddesi) fits the bill perfectly for about US$3.

For a more formal dinner with drinks, try the rooftop restaurant at **Hotel Kaleli** on Hürriyet Caddesi. Prices are not at all bad; a full meal with drinks costs only about US$7 to US$10 per person.

On the corner of Suburcu and Hürriyet Caddesis is a shopping complex containing several licensed restaurants, the best of which is the upstairs **Altınkupa** with Turkish-style şantöz (chanteuse) entertainment some nights.

Along the western reaches of Atatürk Caddesi you'll find a few **cafes** where young men congregate to eat burgers and play billiards in more appealing surroundings than the old-fashioned teahouses.

Entertainment

Right in Hükümet Konağı is the **Sinema Merkezi**, a state-of-the-art multiplex cinema with computerised seating, showing the latest Hollywood blockbusters with Turkish subtitles. The cafe here sells cappuccino and the sort of boiled sweets you associate with cinema visits at home. Tickets cost US$3.50.

Getting There & Away

Air Turkish Airlines (☎ 230 1563, fax 230 1565), Atatürk Bulvarı 30/B, near Hotel Tuğcan, operates twice daily nonstop flights between Gaziantep's Oğzeli airport (20km from the centre) and Ankara and İstanbul. An airport bus departs from outside the office 1½ hours before flights and costs US$3.

Bus The otogar is 2km from the town centre and too overcrowded to cope with all its bus traffic comfortably. Details of some daily services are listed in the table opposite. Dolmuşes to Karkamış leave from outside the train station (US$2, 1½ hours).

Train The Toros Ekspresi connects Gaziantep with İstanbul (US$13). It leaves İs-

Services from Gaziantep's Otogar

destination	fare (US$)	time (hr)	distance (km)	daily services
Adana	5	4	220	several buses
Ankara	17	10	705	frequent buses
Antakya	5	4	200	frequent minibuses
Diyarbakır	10	5	330	frequent buses
İstanbul	18–26	14	1136	several buses
Kahramanmaraş	2	1	80	frequent buses & minibuses
Kahta (for Nemrut Dağı)	8	4	210	several buses
Mardin	12	5½	330	several buses
Şanlıurfa	5	2½	145	frequent buses

tanbul on Tuesday, Thursday and Sunday at 8.55 am and reaches Gaziantep at 11.45 am the following day, stopping in Eskişehir (Enveriye), Afyon, Konya and Adana along the way. There are also local trains to Nusaybin (for Syria), leaving daily at 7 am, but the journey is so slow you'd be better off taking a bus.

AROUND GAZİANTEP
Yesemek Open-Air Museum
If you're heading south from Gaziantep to Antakya you might want to stop to visit the Yesemek Open-Air Museum 23km southeast of İslahiye. Here you'll find a vast quarry with 300 Hittite stones and statues in various states of completion lying in the fields.

Karkamış
At Nizip, east of Gaziantep, a turn-off heads south for the site of Karkamış (Carchemish), a neo-Hittite city which flourished around 850 BC, about the time Akhenaten occupied the throne of Egypt. Though Karkamış assumed the role of Hittite capital after the fall of Hattuşa, you won't be able to approach the ruins now because of a minefield. If you do want to see it, hourly dolmuşes leave from outside the train station in Gaziantep.

Birecik
Even further east of Gaziantep, is Birecik, where you cross the Euphrates River (Fırat Nehri). The town has a ruined fortress, rebuilt and used by the crusaders. Birecik used to be the only nesting place of the eastern bald ibis, a bird species that hovers on the brink of extinction.

MALATYA
☎ 422 • pop 395,500 • elevation 964m

Malatya is a bustling modern town grown large and rich on agriculture. This is the kayısı (apricot) capital of Turkey, and after the late-June harvest thousands of tonnes of the luscious fruit are shipped throughout the world. Almost as good are Malatya's cherries, which are harvested from early to mid-June. Malatya citizens celebrate the end of harvest with a July apricot festival.

Malatya offers an alternative way of approaching Nemrut Dağı. Otherwise its claim to fame is as the birthplace of İsmet İnönü (Atatürk's right-hand man and successor) and Mehmet Ali Ağca (who shot Pope John Paul II).

Little remains of the Ottoman city although there are some old wooden houses in Sinema Caddesi. With the exception of one privately restored building, they're in a miserable state of disrepair.

History
Malatya has stood at the crossroads of major trade routes since Neolithic times. There was an early Assyrian settlement here, and a Hittite one also. After the fall of the Hittite Empire, various city-states emerged, among them Milidia (or Maldia), a name preserved for more than 3000 years and now pronounced Malatya.

The Assyrians and Persians conquered the city alternately, and later the kings of Cappadocia and Pontus did the same. In 66 BC Pompey defeated Mithridates and took the town, then known as Melita. The Byzantines, Sassanids, Arabs and Danışmend emirs held it for a time until the coming of the Seljuks in 1105. Then came the Ottomans (1399), the armies of Tamerlane (1401), Mamluks, Dülkadır emirs and Ottomans again (1515).

When the forces of Egypt's Mohammed Ali invaded Anatolia in 1839, the Ottoman forces garrisoned Malatya, leaving it in ruins on their departure. Later the residents who had fled the war returned and established a new city on the present site.

Orientation & Information

Malatya stretches for many kilometres along İnönü/Atatürk Caddesi, the main drag. Hotels, restaurants, banks and other services are near the main square with its ugly statue of İnönü. The Belediye Parkı, on the northern side of İnönü Caddesi, is a convenient landmark.

The otogar is 4km west of the centre, just off the main highway, Turgut Özal Bulvarı, the westward continuation of Buhara Bul-

varı. The train station is also on the outskirts, 2km west of the centre. City buses and dolmuşes marked 'Vilayet' operate between the station and the centre.

The helpful tourist office (☎ 323 3025) is on the ground floor of the *vilayet* (provincial government headquarters). It's open Monday to Friday. There's an Internet Cafe on the 1st floor of the otogar, so you can pick up your email while you wait for your bus.

Old Malatya (Battalgazi)

About 11km north at Battalgazi are the remains of old Malatya, the walled city inhabited from early times until the 19th century.

As you come into the village from the west you'll see the ruins of the old **city walls** with their 95 towers on the right. They've lost all their facing stone to other building projects, and apricot orchards now fill what were once city blocks, but it's easy to see that this was once a great city. The village of Battalgazi has grown up in and around the ruins.

The **Ulu Cami** (1224), also on the right as you come in on the bus (look for the broken brick minaret), is a Seljuk building dating from the reign of Alaettin Keykubat I, with

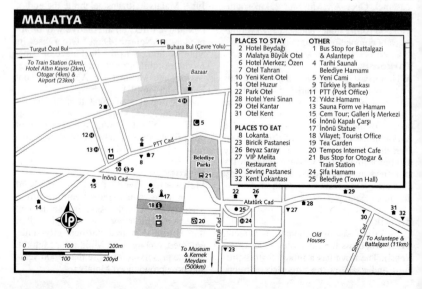

MALATYA

PLACES TO STAY	OTHER
2 Hotel Beydağı	1 Bus Stop for Battalgazi
3 Malatya Büyük Otel	& Aslantepe
6 Hotel Merkez; Özen	4 Tarihi Saunalı
7 Otel Tahran	Belediye Hamamı
10 Yeni Kent Otel	5 Yeni Cami
14 Otel Huzur	9 Türkiye İş Bankası
22 Park Otel	11 PTT (Post Office)
28 Hotel Yeni Sinan	12 Yıldız Hamamı
29 Otel Kantar	13 Sauna Form ve Hamam
31 Otel Kent	15 Cem Tour; Galleri İş Merkezi
	16 İnönü Kapalı Çarşı
PLACES TO EAT	17 İnönü Statue
8 Lokanta	18 Vilayet; Tourist Office
23 Biricik Pastanesi	19 Tea Garden
26 Beyaz Saray	20 Tempos Internet Cafe
27 VIP Melita	21 Bus Stop for Otogar &
Restaurant	Train Station
30 Sevinç Pastanesi	24 Şifa Hamamı
32 Kent Lokantası	25 Belediye (Town Hall)

Turgut Özal Bul — Buhara Bul (Çevre Yolu)

To Train Station (2km),
Hotel Altın Kayısı (2km),
Otogar (4km) &
Airport (23km)

Bazaar

PTT Cad

Belediye
Parkı

İnönü Cad

Atatürk Cad

Fuzuli Cad

Sinema Cad

Old
Houses

To Aslantepe &
Battalgazi (11km)

To Museum
& Kernek
Meydanı
(500km)

0   100   200m
0   100   200yd

a fine eyvan with Arabic inscription. Beside it are the ruins of the **Sahabiye-i-Kubra Medrese**, with another broken brick minaret.

The **Silahtar Mustafa Paşa Hanı** on the main square is an Ottoman caravanserai dating from the 17th century. Although it has been restored, it's now virtually abandoned and peaceful enjoyment of it is likely to be undermined by persistent small boys in hot pursuit.

Buses to Battalgazi (US$0.25) leave from the northern side of Buhara Bulvarı at the junction with Turgut Temeli Caddesi. This is also where you'd catch a Bahçebaşı bus to the Hittite site at **Aslantepe**, although the scant remains are of specialist interest only.

Malatya Müzesi

Malatya's museum is about 750m from the town centre. Walk down Fuzuli Caddesi and cross over the main road to find the museum, up a few steps to the left of the big tea-garden-cum-funfair in Kernek Meydanı.

The dimly lit collection covers everything from the Palaeolithic, Chalcolithic and Old Bronze Age through to Roman and Byzantine times. It also contains finds from the excavations at Aslantepe and from the Lower Euphrates Project, a rescue mission conducted in the Euphrates valley before the Keban Barajı (Keban Dam) flooded it in the 1960s. The ethnography section upstairs contains some fine carpets and embroidery.

The museum is open from 8 am to 5.30 pm daily except Monday; admission costs US$1.75.

Bazaar

Malatya has a particularly vibrant bazaar which sprawls north from PTT Caddesi and the Malatya Büyük Otel. The large covered area is fascinating provided you're not too squeamish or concerned about fish rights, and there's an even livelier metal-working area – watch out for welders in the middle of the road. You can pick up some fine baskets or packeted *mercimek çorbası* (lentil soup).

Hamams

The men-only Tarihi Saunalı Belediye Hamamı faces the Malatya Büyük Otel. The

modern Sauna Form ve Hamam and the Yıldız Hamamı are on a side street near the PTT. The small Şifa Hamamı, tucked away behind the belediye, is open to women on Friday and Saturday afternoons only. A simple bath costs US$2, more if you opt for a wash and massage.

Places to Stay – Budget

Malatya is doing so well that cheap hotels are being squeezed out. The fact that the former Mercan Palas Oteli in PTT Caddesi is now a bank says everything about the situation. Meanwhile the quieter hotels tend to be the older ones with the least inviting rooms along PTT Caddesi. The better rooms are mainly in the hotels along Atatürk Caddesi, where you'll need one at the back to escape the traffic noise.

For rock-bottom budgets, *Otel Tahran* (☎ *324 3615, PTT Caddesi)* offers basic singles/doubles with sinks for US$5/9, but at the time of writing it was undergoing restoration which could mean a price rise. The nearby *Hotel Merkez* and the *Özen* are considerably less appealing but very cheap.

Noisier but more cheerful is *Park Otel* (☎ *321 1691, Atatürk Caddesi 17)*, across from the belediye. Rooms with shower are US$8.50/10.

A good choice would be the welcoming *Otel Kantar* (☎ *321 1510, Atatürk Caddesi 21)*, where clean if simple rooms cost US$7.50/12.50 with shower, less if you forgo bath and TV. There's a pleasant restaurant attached, with outdoor as well as indoor seating.

Places to Stay – Mid-Range

Perhaps the best deal in town is the two-star *Malatya Büyük Otel* (☎ *321 1400, fax 321 5367)*, a block north of the Belediye Parkı, which looks more expensive than it actually is. All rooms have baths (with lashings of hot water) and some have TVs, and rates can go as low as US$17/21 a single/double, including breakfast, when it's quiet. Despite its position in the bazaar, this is likely to be one of the quieter places to stay – except for the morning call to prayer from the Yeni Cami across the road.

One block away is the newer *Hotel Bey-dağı* (☎ 322 4611, fax 323 2258) with a large restaurant on the ground floor. Pleasingly modern rooms cost US$20/27, with bath and breakfast; one big family room with a balcony is especially good value. Expect street noise though.

The other star-rated hotels are on Atatürk Caddesi, east of the vilayet. The one-star *Hotel Yeni Sinan* (☎ 321 2907) has nine floors, a lift and a bar, and charges US$15/25, including breakfast. Most readers enjoy staying in the clean, modern rooms with TV, minibar and big bathroom, though one complained of street noise.

A bit further east on the opposite side of the road is the one-star *Otel Kent* (☎ 321 2175, fax 312 3529, Atatürk Caddesi 43) which charges US$17/25, including breakfast, subject to haggling when it's quiet. Rooms are fairly basic but clean, and those on the top floor at the back have pleasant views. The same people also own *Yeni Kent Otel* (☎ 321 1053, fax 324 9243, PTT Caddesi 33) where newer rooms justify higher prices: US$20/25. The decor is pleasingly modern, but ask for a room on the PTT (front) side to escape street noise. Breakfasts here are big enough to suit an apricot trader's stomach…and include apricots, of course!

Heading west, the new *Otel Huzur* (☎ 323 5928, Nasuhi Caddesi 6) is another good choice on a relatively quiet side street with very reasonably priced rooms for US$12/20 with bath.

Places to Stay – Top End

The four-star *Hotel Altın Kayısı* (☎ 211 4444, fax 211 4443), or 'Golden Apricot', is at the top of İstasyon Caddesi where it meets Buhara Bulvarı. Externally it's nothing to write home about, but inside the rooms are big and modern, with TVs, fridges, air-con and apricot-decorated curtains and bedcovers. There's a restaurant and bar, and plenty of parking space. The rather remote situation also ensures it's quieter than other choices in the town centre. Posted prices for singles/doubles are a hefty US$80/120 but when it's quiet they drop dramatically.

Places to Eat

Next to the Otel Tahran is *Lokanta (PTT Caddesi 29)*, clean, white and very popular with Malatya's business community. The food is good and moderately priced; no alcohol is served.

Near the Park Otel, the popular *Beyaz Saray (Atatürk Caddesi)* serves excellent İskender kebap for around US$2. There's a choice of ready meals as well. A few doors uphill from the Otel Kent is the even more popular *Kent Lokantası (Atatürk Caddesi 137)*. Its İskender kebap leaves something to be desired but the soups and stews are excellent. Meals cost between US$3 and US$6.

Malatya's best restaurant is just off Atatürk Caddesi on the first floor of the Turfanda İş Hanı. *VIP Melita Restaurant* (☎ 322 5412) offers a tempting trolley of cold mezes and some beautifully cooked kebaps and other dishes. Despite its size it fills up with courting couples and businessmen any night of the week, and there's music to accompany the delicious food. Of course it depends on what you choose to eat but you can have a very good two-course meal with soft drink for less than US$7.

Malatya positively creaks with tempting cake shops. One such place is *Sevinç Pastanesi (Atatürk Caddesi)*, virtually opposite the Otel Kantar, where gleaming showcases are stuffed with all sorts of sweet treats. Another is the *Biricik Pastanesi (Fuzuli Caddesi)*, which does Paris-quality coffee and cake for nothing like Paris-level prices. It's well placed for a stop on the way to or from the museum.

Atatürk Caddesi is lined with *dried-fruit shops* selling baskets of apricots and other dried fruits, as well as nuts and snacks, both sweet and salty. More dried-fruit shops can be found in the bazaar and at the otogar.

Malatya also has several very pleasant *tea gardens*. A good one can be found behind the vilayet, although the one in Kernek Meydanı in front of the museum is even better, backed as it is by an artificial waterfall.

Getting There & Away

Air Turkish Airlines (☎ 324 8001), Kanal Boyu Caddesi 10, Orduevi Karşısı, has one

Services from Malatya's Otogar

destination	fare (US$)	time (hr)	distance (km)	daily services
Adana	12	8	425	a few buses
Adıyaman	5	3	190	frequent buses
Ankara	20	11	685	frequent buses
Diyarbakır	7	4	260	a few buses
Gaziantep	7	4	250	a few buses
Elazığ	3.50	1¾	101	a few buses
İstanbul	25	18	1130	a few buses
Kayseri	12	4	354	several buses
Sivas	7	5	235	several buses

nonstop flight daily between Malatya's Erhaç airport and Ankara, with connections to İstanbul and İzmir. There is also a daily nonstop flight to İstanbul. The airport bus costs US$1.50 and leaves from the Turkish Airlines office 1½ hours before the flight departure time.

Bus Malatya's gorgeous otogar, or MAŞTİ, is 4km out on the western outskirts. Some through buses (eg, to Van) will drop you on the highway to pick up a dolmuş (US$0.25) into the town centre. Buses to the otogar leave from opposite the vilayet but you have to check with the drivers to be sure of which one to take. A taxi to the otogar costs about US$7. Some daily bus services to major destinations are listed in the table above.

Train Malatya's train station can be reached by dolmuş (US$0.25) or by 'İstasyon' city buses from opposite the vilayet. The city is served daily by express train from İstanbul's Haydarpaşa train station (US$11) and Ankara (US$7) via Kayseri (US$3) and Sivas (US$5). There are also daily trains to Elazığ (US$5) and to Diyarbakır (US$2). The 1st-class-only *mavi tren* to Ankara (US$9.50) also passes through Malatya.

ELAZIĞ
☎ 424 • pop 250,000 • elevation 1200m

A new town founded in the 19th century, Elazığ is a farming centre and university town, which lost much of its importance when the lake created by the Keban Barajı cut it off from main roads to the north and east. Viticulture is important; Tekel, the government spirits company, raises its big dark-red *öküzgözü* (ox-eye) grapes in the region.

If you need to stay for the night, plan to spend some time seeing the Urartian treasures in the archaeological museum and the ruins of ancient, earthquake-ruined Harput, 5km to the north-east.

Although on a map, Elazığ looks a long way from the south-eastern corner of Turkey it was one of the areas worst affected by the troubles of the 1980s and '90s. Security in and around the town remains tight.

Orientation & Information
The town centre is Cumhuriyet Meydanı at the intersection of Bosna-Herzek Bulvarı (shown as İstasyon Caddesi on old maps) and Gazi and Hürriyet Caddesis, near the İzzet Paşa Camii; turn left along Gazi Caddesi for Fırat Üniversitesi and right along Hürriyet Caddesi for the hotels, Harput and the banks.

The belediye and PTT are in Cumhuriyet Meydanı, while the helpful tourist office (☎ 212 3301) is at Bosna-Herzek Bulvarı 35, in the library building, İl Halk Kütüphanesi.

Elazığ Arkeoloji ve Etnografya Müzesi
In the 1960s the building of the Keban Barajı north-west of Elazığ caused the flooding of the valleys to the north. Before the new lake was created, a rescue dig excavated some of the most likely archaeological sites; the artefacts uncovered are

displayed in the Arkeoloji ve Etnografya Müzesi (Archaeology & Ethnography Museum) on the campus of Fırat Üniversitesi (Euphrates University) on the outskirts of the city. Among the most valuable finds were Early Bronze Age royal seals, gold jewellery and a cuneiform inscription from the time of Menua, King of Urartu.

You may have to hunt around for someone to open the museum and sell you a ticket for US$1.75. Given that this is a university museum it's a shame that the labelling is so perfunctory, both in Turkish and in English. Upstairs, carpets to make a Kayseri salesman weep with envy languish unlabelled and poorly lit.

To get to the museum take a bus marked 'Üniversite' (US$0.25) from Hürriyet Caddesi and ask the driver where to get off. The campus is vast so don't try and walk it.

Places to Stay & Eat

There's a handy cluster of places to stay in Hürriyet Caddesi, although they all suffer from street noise. Try **Hotel Divan** (☎ 218 1103) or **Hotel Çınar** (☎ 218 1811), both of which have singles/doubles for US$10/19, slightly less without bath. If they're full the **Turistik Otel** (☎ 218 1772) across the road is similar.

If you can afford a bit more, the nearby two-star **Beritan Hotel** (☎ 218 4484, fax 212 7970, Hürriyet Caddesi 24) has comfortable rooms with bath for US$25/38 (ignore the ludicrous posted prices of US$70/100!).

If you're just passing through, it's worth noting that the **Kafeterya** in the otogar serves better than average food.

Getting There & Away

Daily Turkish Airlines flights connect Elazığ with Ankara, and there are at least two non-stop flights from İstanbul each week. The Turkish Airlines office (☎ 218 1576, fax 218 3730) is at Vali Fahribey Caddesi 39.

Elazığ's spacious otogar is 3km east of the centre. If there's no *servis* bus, dolmuşes will ferry you into the centre for less than US$0.20; a taxi costs more like US$4.50.

There are fairly frequent services to and from Diyarbakır (US$5, two hours, 151km),

Erzurum (US$20, seven hours, 324km) and Malatya (US$3.50, 1¾ hours, 101km).

HARPUT

Harput was an important staging post on the Silk Road to and from China and India, but its importance evaporated after it was ruined by earthquakes in the 19th century. Today it's a pleasant enough place to while away a few hours on a side trip out of Elazığ.

The main attraction is the huge and photogenic **castle** astride a rocky outcrop. The Urartians built the first castle on this site way back in the 8th or 9th century BC, but what you see today are the remains of the castle built by Turks in the 11th century. It's a shame there's no custodian to protect tourists from unwanted attention and fend off the graffiti artists whose handiwork is already defacing the newly restored main gateway.

Besides the castle, you can also visit the **Ulu Cami**, dating from the 1100s and thus one of the oldest in Anatolia, the **Meryem Ana Kilisesi** (Church of the Virgin Mary), and the Seljuk **Arap Baba Türbesi**. There's also a poky little museum optimistically asking a US$1.25 entrance fee, and assorted other ruins scattered about. Pick up a plan at Elazığ tourist office before you go.

Frequent minibuses (US$0.30) run to Harput from Harput Caddesi in Elazığ.

ADIYAMAN

☎ 416 • elevation 669m

The provincial capital of Adıyaman is one of the main tour centres for visiting Nemrut Dağı. It's a booming oil town with canyons of faceless high-rises stretched along several kilometres of highway D360, known locally as Atatürk Bulvarı. The museum is interesting; otherwise there is little reason for visitors to linger.

The tourist office (☎ 216 1008, fax 216 3840), Atatürk Bulvarı 184, is next to the PTT.

The **museum** on Atatürk Bulvarı is well worth a look since it houses finds from the various archaeological sites drowned by the creation of the Atatürk Barajı, most importantly Samsat. It's open from 8 am to noon and 1.30 to 5.30 pm daily except Monday. Admission costs US$1.75. Otherwise Adıyaman has few specific sights other than the **Ulu Cami**, dating from the 14th century, which is buried in the shopping streets to the south of the museum.

You're unlikely to want to stay in Adıyaman, where the hotels are mostly strung out along the busy main thoroughfare, when there are much nicer options either on Nemrut Dağı or even in nearby Kahta. That said, the *Hotel Serdaroğlu (☎ 216 4841, fax 216 1554)*, near the junction of Atatürk Bulvarı and Turgut Reis Caddesi and handy for the museum, is a decent hotel with singles/doubles for US$12/24, including breakfast. Rooms are reasonably modern and there's a pleasant lobby with TV and a ground-floor *restaurant*.

The new airport has twice-weekly flights to Ankara, with connections to İstanbul, İzmir, Antalya, Bodrum, Samsun and Trabzon. For reservations call ☎ 216 1436, fax 216 1440.

Adıyaman is served by frequent buses, and dolmuşes run between Kahta and Adıyaman (US$0.85, 30 minutes, 35km) throughout the day.

KAHTA
☎ 416 • postcode 02400 • pop 75,000

Kahta is a depressing base from which to explore the wonders of Nemrut Dağı. It says everything about priorities that the most prominent piece of sculpture in town is a mock-up oil pump decked out in fairy lights. Tourists have been coming to Kahta for well over 10 years but not one cent of their money seems to have been ploughed back into the infrastructure; pavements are cracked and higgledy-piggledy, there's rubbish everywhere and every child seems to stick out their hand for *para* (money) as soon as a tourist comes into view.

That said, the new hotels that have opened in the last few years are perfectly comfortable and the vast lake formed by the Atatürk Barajı laps at the edges of Kahta, a good place to come for a meal especially if you have your own wheels.

Mahmut Arslan at the tourist office (☎/fax 725 5007), on Mustafa Kemal Caddesi near the Pension Kommagene, speaks good English and is a mine of useful local information.

A good time to visit would be in late June when the **International Kahta Kommagene**

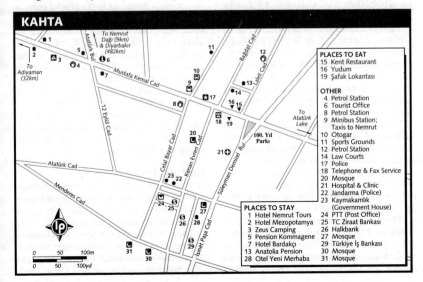

KAHTA

To Nemrut
Dağı (9km)
& Diyarbakır
(482km)

To
Adıyaman
(32km)

Mustafa Kemal Cad

Bağdat Cad

Lalebit Cad

Atatürk Bul

12 Eylül Cad

Celal Bayar Cad

Kenan Evren Cad

Süleyman Demirel Bul

Atatürk Cad

Menderes Cad

İsmet Paşa Cad

To
Atatürk
Lake

100. Yıl
Parkı

0   50   100m
0   50   100yd

PLACES TO EAT
15 Kent Restaurant
16 Yudum
19 Şafak Lokantası

OTHER
4 Petrol Station
6 Tourist Office
8 Petrol Station
9 Minibus Station;
   Taxis to Nemrut
10 Otogar
11 Sports Grounds
12 Petrol Station
14 Law Courts
17 Police
18 Telephone & Fax Service
20 Mosque
21 Hospital & Clinic
22 Jandarma (Police)
23 Kaymakamlık
   (Government House)
24 PTT (Post Office)
25 TC Ziraat Bankası
26 Halkbank
27 Mosque
29 Türkiye İş Bankası
30 Mosque
31 Mosque

PLACES TO STAY
1 Hotel Nemrut Tours
2 Hotel Mezopotamya
3 Zeus Camping
5 Pension Kommagene
7 Hotel Bardakçı
13 Anatolia Pension
28 Otel Yeni Merhaba

EASTERN ANATOLIA

Festival takes place, with music, folk dancing and all sorts of fun and games. On the other hand all the hotels will be filled with tour groups, so it's wise to phone ahead at this time.

Places to Stay

The cheapest backpacker accommodation in Kahta is at *Anatolia Pension* (☎ 725 6483, Adliye Karşısı), where extremely basic single/double rooms cost US$5/8.50. Breakfast is served in the tea garden in front.

At the junction with the Nemrut Dağı road is the pleasant *Pension Kommagene* (☎ 725 5548, fax 725 7614), which has Turkish carpets dotted about to lend atmosphere. The comfortable rooms on the 2nd floor cost US$12/18 with bath, slightly less if you forgo breakfast in the pleasant courtyard. Self-caterers can use the restaurant kitchen, and you can camp in the grounds for US$9 a van or US$6 a tent.

Many tour groups stay at *Hotel Nemrut Tours* (☎ 725 6881, fax 725 6880, Mustafa Kemal Caddesi), on the main road on the western outskirts of Kahta. Although rooms on the 2nd floor are decent enough (with air-con), some of those on the 1st floor leave a lot to be desired, so if you don't like the first room you're shown, ask to see another. The food in the restaurant is surprisingly good and the atmosphere can be fun, especially when a local *saz* (a traditional stringed instrument) player drops by. Individual travellers are likely to be charged US$15/25 a room. At the time of writing more upmarket rooms were about to open in a newly built annexe.

Immediately across the road is the two-star *Hotel Mezopotamya* (☎ 725 5112, Mustafa Kemal Caddesi 18) with cheerful, air-con rooms for US$9 per person. Beside it, *Zeus Camping* (☎ 725 5695, fax 725 5696) charges US$9 for a van and tent, although until nearby building work is finished it's not particularly inviting.

The three-star *Hotel Bardakçı* (☎ 725 8060, fax 725 5385, Mustafa Kemal Caddesi 24), opposite the tourist office, also boasts air-con and a variety of rooms, some more attractively decorated than others. Singles/

doubles cost US$25/45, and the downstairs lobby is a good place to relax over a drink.

The three-star *Otel Yeni Merhaba* (☎/fax 725 7111, Çarşı Caddesi) is lost down a backstreet but boasts comfortable rooms with air-con for US$55/70.

Places to Eat

Kahta's choice of places to eat is pretty uninspiring. In the town centre, the best of a bad bunch is the spacious *Yudum* (Mustafa Kemal Caddesi), upstairs near the police station. A fairly standard range of kebaps are at least well cooked and presented. A few doors east the smaller *Kent Restaurant* has been open for years and still turns out decent, cheap food at low prices. Across the road is the friendly *Şafak Lokantası* which serves kebaps beneath hand-painted murals. At any of these places, two plates of food and a soft drink costs about US$3.50.

With a car you may prefer to drive along Baraj Yolu, the continuation of Mustafa Kemal Caddesi, to the lake where there are several restaurants to choose from. Nicest (not least because the building is actually finished) is the *Akropolian* (☎ 725 5132), the first you'll come to. Here you can dine on a terrace overlooking the lake or indoors if the weather is bad. A plate of mezes, salad and fish will come to about US$4. They bake wonderful loaves of bread a metre long here, and you can also sample *şalgam*, a bitter but refreshing drink made from root vegetables, garlic and lettuce. Dolmuşes pass this way, or you can phone and ask to be picked up in town.

Closer to the small ferry is *Neşetin Yeri* (☎ 725 7675) which serves a range of kebaps, including an appetising plate of mixed kebaps for about US$3.

Getting There & Away

Kahta's small otogar is in the centre of town with the dolmuş and taxi stands right beside it. The table opposite lists some useful bus and dolmuş services.

The road east to Diyarbakır was flooded by the lake formed behind the Atatürk Barajı and buses from Kahta now travel to Diyarbakır via Adıyaman and the south of

Services from Kahta's Otogar

destination	fare (US$)	time (hr)	distance (km)	daily services
Adana	10	6	532	a few buses
Adıyaman	0.85	½	32	frequent dolmuşes
Ankara	17	12	807	a few buses
İstanbul	25	20	1352	3 or 4 buses
Kayseri	13	7	487	2 buses
Malatya	5	3½	225	a few buses, or change at Adıyaman
Şanlıurfa	3.50	1	106	frequent dolmuşes

the lake (US$6, five hours). A more interesting way to travel is to take one of the five daily dolmuşes to Siverek which are timed to meet the ferries across the lake. In Siverek you may have to wait an hour or so for a connection to Diyarbakır (US$5, four hours) but the bazaar is enough fun to fill in the time.

NEMRUT DAĞI MİLLİ PARKI

Nemrut Dağı (**nehm**-root dah-uh), not to be confused with the mountain of the same name on the shores of Lake Van, in the Anti-Taurus Range rises to a height of 2150m between the provincial capital of Malatya to the north and Kahta in Adıyaman province to the south.

Nobody knew anything about Nemrut Dağı until 1881, when an Ottoman geologist was astounded to come across this remote mountain-top covered in statues. Archaeological work didn't begin until 1953, when the American School of Oriental Research undertook the project.

The summit was formed when a megalomaniac pre-Roman local king cut two ledges in the rock, filled them with colossal statues of himself and the gods (his relatives), then ordered an artificial mountain peak of crushed rock 50m high to be piled between them. The king's tomb and those of three female relatives may well lie beneath those tonnes of rock. Nobody knows for sure.

Earthquakes have toppled the heads from most of the statues. At the time of writing many of the colossal bodies sit silently in rows with the 2m-high heads watching from the ground. But vandals have damaged some of them and work was to begin on replacing

the heads on the bodies. Anticipate some disruption at the site for the next few years.

Nemrut Dağı is one of Turkey's World Heritage Sites, and deservedly so. Not surprisingly, you'll see tour operators enthusiastically touting it as the Eighth Wonder of the World!

History

From 250 BC onwards, this region straddled the border between the Seleucid Empire (which followed the empire of Alexander the Great in Anatolia) and the Parthian Empire to the east, also occupying a part of Alexander's lands. A small but strategic area, rich, fertile and covered in forests, it had a history of independent thinking ever since the time of King Samos (circa 150 BC).

Under the Seleucid Empire, the governor of Commagene declared his kingdom's independence. In 80 BC, with the Seleucids in disarray and Roman power spreading into Anatolia, a Roman ally named Mithridates I Callinicus proclaimed himself king and set up his capital at Arsameia, near the modern village of Kahta Kalesi. Mithridates prided himself on his royal ancestry, tracing his forebears back to Seleucus I Nicator, founder of the Seleucid Empire to the west, and to Darius the Great, king of ancient Persia to the east. Thus he saw himself as heir to both glorious traditions. He married a Parthian princess.

Mithridates died in 64 BC and was succeeded by his son Antiochus I Epiphanes (64–38 BC) who consolidated the security of his kingdom by immediately signing a non-aggression treaty with Rome, turning his kingdom into a Roman buffer against attack

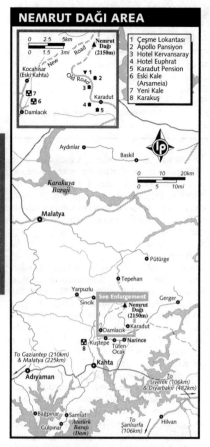

NEMRUT DAĞI AREA

1 Çeşme Lokantası
2 Apollo Pansiyon
3 Hotel Kervansaray
4 Hotel Euphrat
5 Karadut Pension
6 Eski Kale (Arsameia)
7 Yeni Kale
8 Karakuş

Rome or by puppet kings until AD 72, when Emperor Vespasian incorporated it into Roman Asia. The great days of Commagene were thus limited to the 26-year reign of Antiochus.

In the late 1980s the economy and topography of this area were greatly affected by two developments: the filling of the vast lake behind the GAP project's Atatürk Dam, and the discovery of oil near Kahta. You'll see the nodding-donkey rigs in the fields around Kahta, although it's Adıyaman, the provincial capital, which has benefited most from the influx of money for building and development.

Orientation & Information

Nemrut Dağı Milli Parkı lies between the villages of Sincik to the west, Tepehan to the north, Gerger to the east and Eski Kahta to the south. In turn these villages are sandwiched between Adıyaman, Kahta and Malatya, with the sprawling Atatürk Barajı to the south and the Malatya Dağları to the north.

Visiting Nemrut Dağı is one of the rare occasions when there's no substitute for bringing your own car which frees you to explore all the lesser sites along the way, stop to appreciate the views when the mood moves you and call in at the various hotels and restaurants along the way. However, most people take tours, organised either in Kahta or Malatya, or, increasingly, from Şanlıurfa or Cappadocia. If you do decide to organise a tour locally it's probably best to opt for the greater comfort of travelling by minibus; a taxi may be cheaper but the driver is unlikely to be able to offer any guidance.

Plan to visit Nemrut between late May and mid-October, and preferably in July or August; the road to the summit becomes impassable in snow. Remember that at any time of year, even in high summer, it will be chilly and windy up on top of the mountain. This is especially true at sunrise, the coldest time of the day. Take warm clothing (gloves, socks, a thick jumper/sweater or jacket and scarf) on your trek to the top, no matter when you go. Turks in the know will be found on the summit swaddled in their hotel blankets.

from the Parthians. His good relations with both sides allowed him to grow rich and revel in delusions of grandeur. As heir to both traditions, he saw himself as equal to the great god-kings of the past. It was Antiochus who ordered the building of the fabulous temples and funerary mound on top of Nemrut.

Antiochus must have come to believe himself immortal, for in the third decade of his reign he sided with the Parthians in a squabble with Rome, and in 38 BC the Romans deposed him. From then on, Commagene was alternately ruled directly from

There are a couple of accommodation options on the mountain, at the village of Karadut, and further up the mountain, about 8km from the summit. If you can stay on the mountain it's well worth it since the stunning views and peaceful setting make up for any lack of mod cons. Remember that on the mountain it will be cold at night even in August so make sure you bring warm clothing and check that adequate blankets are provided.

Karakuş

Highway D360, marked for Nemrut Dağı Milli Parkı (9km) and Sincik (36km), begins in Kahta next to the Pension Kommagene. Along the way this once agricultural landscape has become a busy oilfield with nodding pumps, storage tanks and earth-moving equipment. More than 100 local oil wells produce around 60% of Turkey's petrol.

You enter Nemrut Dağı Milli Parkı at Karakuş, 10km from Kahta, via a road to the left off the highway. Like that on Nemrut, the Karakuş mound is artificial, created to hold the graves of royal ladies of Commagene. An eagle tops one of the columns ringing the site. The summit of Nemrut is clearly, if distantly visible, from Karakuş; it's the highest point on the horizon to the north-east.

Highway D360 descends into the river valley to cross it. Stay on this road marked for Cendere and Kahta Kalesi to see the other sites and for the quickest ascent of the mountain.

Cendere & Kahta Kalesi

About 19km from Kahta and 5km before Kahta Kalesi, the road crosses a Roman bridge built at Cendere in honour of Emperor Septimius Severus, his wife and sons, long after Commagene had become part of Roman Asia. Of the four original columns (two at either end), three are still standing. Some historians think that the missing column was removed by one of the sons, Caracalla, when he murdered the other son, Geta, in 212. Unfortunately a heavy petrol truck caused the collapse of the original bridge which has had to be reconstructed.

As you leave the bridge, a sign points to the right for Nemrut Dağı and Gerger; the road to the left is for Kahta Kalesi.

You approach Kahta Kalesi along the valley of a stream called the Kahta Çayı. Opposite the village are the ruins of a 14th-century Mamluk castle, now called Yeni Kale (New Fortress), with some Arabic inscriptions – although originally a Turkic people, the Mamluks were assimilated into Egyptian society. You can climb up to look at the castle but only if you're reasonably fit and wearing appropriate shoes.

Several decades ago the only way to reach the summit of Nemrut Dağı was to walk and it's still possible to engage a guide in Kahta Kalesi to lead you up a trail to the summit.

Eski Kale (Arsameia)

About 1km further along the main road, a road to the left takes you the 2km to Eski Kale, the ancient Commagene capital of Arsameia. Admission costs US$1.75. Walk up the path from the car park and you'll come to a large stele with a figure (possibly female) on it. Further along are two more stelae, a monumental staircase and, behind them, an opening in the rock leading down to a cistern.

Another path leads from the first path to a striking and undamaged stone relief which portrays the founder of Commagene, Mithridates I Callinicus, shaking hands with the god Heracles. Next to it is a long inscription in Greek and to the right is a tunnel descending 158m through the rock. Bring a torch (flashlight) with you if you want to descend the steps to the room at the bottom.

Above the relief on the level top of the hill are the foundations of Mithridates' capital city and a spectacular view, the perfect spot for a picnic.

A new 8km road now makes it possible to drive straight from Arsemeia to Nemrut Dağı.

Eski Kale to Karadut

About 3km up from Eski Kale is Damlacık. The next settlements are Kuştepe (7km), then Tüten Ocak (3km). After Narince the road becomes rougher and steeper. Another 7km east of Narince is a turn-off to the left marked for Nemrut, which you want to take; to continue straight on would take you to the village of Gerger. North of Karadut, the last half-hour's travel (12km) to the summit is on a steep, fairly rough road paved with black basalt blocks.

The Summit

By the time you climb the final ridge to the summit you're well above the tree line. Admission to the archaeological site costs US$2.50.

Beyond the building you must hike 500m (15 or 20 minutes) over the broken rock of the stone pyramid to the western temple. Sometimes donkeys are on hand to carry you, but this is not much help since staying on the donkey is almost as difficult as negotiating the rocks on your own. Make sure you're wearing sensible shoes.

Antiochus I Epiphanes ordered the construction of a hierothesium, or combined tomb and temple here:

I, great King Antiochus, have ordered the construction of these temples, the ceremonial road, and the thrones of the gods, on a foundation which will never be demolished...I have done this to prove my faith in the gods. At the end of my life I will enter my eternal rest here, and my spirit will join that of Zeus-Ahura Mazda in heaven.

As you approach, the first thing you see is the western temple with the conical funerary mound of fist-sized stones behind it.

At the western temple, Antiochus and his fellow gods sit in state, although their bodies have partly tumbled down along with their heads. But at the eastern temple the bodies are largely intact, except for the fallen heads, which seem more badly weathered than the western heads. On the backs of the eastern statues are inscriptions in Greek.

Both terraces have similar plans, with the syncretistic gods, the 'ancestors' of Antiochus, seated. From left to right they are Apollo, the sun god (Mithra to the Persians; Helios or Hermes to the Greeks); Fortuna, or Tyche; in the centre Zeus-Ahura Mazda; then King Antiochus; and on the far right is Heracles, also known as Ares or Artagnes. The seated figures are several metres high, their heads alone about 2m tall.

Low walls at the sides of each temple once held carved reliefs showing processions of ancient Persian and Greek royalty, Antiochus' 'predecessors'. Statues of eagles represent Zeus.

The flat space next to the eastern temple, with an 'H' at its centre, is a helipad to save the rich and important the hassle of walking. It stands on the site of an ancient altar. Look down and you'll see a white building with 'Müze' written on its door – this actually serves cups of çay (tea)!

Places to Stay & Eat

The village of Karadut, 5km up the mountain from the turn-off to Nemrut, has a few small eateries and Mehmet Çınar's *Karadut Pension* (☎ 416-737 2169) where beds in simple rooms cost US$7. Meals are also offered. You can camp in the grounds and soak up the wonderful views for US$3.50. This is a great place to stay if you would like to experience life in a tiny mountain village.

North of Karadut is the big *Hotel Euphrat* (☎ 416-737 2175, fax 737 2179), 8km from the summit, which charges US$30/44 for singles/doubles with breakfast and dinner. A little further up, the *Hotel Kervansaray* (☎ 416-737 2190) has a shady garden with swimming pool and charges US$20/35 for half board. Both must have been designed by the same architect, and their tin roofs are a bit of an eyesore, but the views are magnificent, and most people rate the food highly. Unfortunately we have received information from a reader about a problem with security at the Kervansaray. Continuing up the mountain the most basic place is *Apollo Pansiyon* (☎ 416-737 2041), on the right, a converted village house with a garden *restaurant*. Bed and breakfast here costs just US$7.50, with another US$3.50 for dinner.

Finally there's the *Çesme Lokantası* (☎ 416-737 2032) which has a few dormitory-style beds for US$12.50 in an annexe behind the restaurant.

At the summit itself, just up from the car park, is a *cafe* for snacks and hot tea, soft drinks and souvenirs. The staff run a basic *pension*, described by one reader as 'two cement boxes', for US$5 to US$7 per person.

About 3km from the summit in the valley below is the *Güneş Hotel*, of use mostly to those coming up from Malatya (see the Organised Tours subsection following for more details).

Getting There & Away

Taxi & Dolmuş From Kahta, taxi drivers charge about US$25 to run you up to the summit but you shouldn't expect anything in the way of guidance.

One dolmuş a day leaves Kahta at about 3 pm to go up the mountain as far as the Çeşme Lokantası, about 6km from the summit, stopping at Karadut village (US$1.50) on the way. From Karadut, a passing minibus may charge US$2 or more; to rent an entire minibus for a trip to the summit and back to Karadut costs about US$13.

Car To ascend the southern slopes of Nemrut from Kahta, you can either drive along the old road via Narince or take the shorter new route via Karakuş, Cendere, Eski Kahta and Arsameia. Make sure you have fuel for at least 200km or 250km of normal driving. Though the trip to the summit and back is only about 110km by the old road (70km by the new road), much of that will be driven in low gear, which uses more fuel.

Whichever way you go, you might want to pack a bottle of water and some dried fruit, biscuits or nuts as the return journey can take between four and six hours and services along the way are limited. Plan on spending up to two hours driving from Kahta to the summit and back, then add a good two or three hours for sightseeing at the various sites.

Alternatively, you can approach the summit from Malatya (110km one way); unlike the road from Kahta, the Malatya road is paved all the way to the summit. However, by taking this route you miss seeing other sites like Arsameia along the Kahta to Nemrut road. Also, be warned that if you are driving yourself, the road is extremely steep and very rough – certainly not for novices.

Organised Tours The main tour centres are Adıyaman, Kahta and Malatya, but there are also tours from Şanlıurfa and Cappadocia.

From Kahta Kahta has always had a reputation as a rip-off town and you still need to be wary of what's on offer. Always check exactly what you will be seeing in addition to the heads themselves and how long you'll be away. Agencies in Kahta offer two sorts of minibus tour. The short tour (US$35 per group, five hours, 106km) takes you from Kahta to the summit and back again, allowing about an hour for sightseeing. The long tour (US$45 per group, eight hours, 140km) takes you to the summit, and on the trip down stops at Arsameia, Cendere and Karakuş.

Although it may be more enjoyable to go up the mountain in the middle of the day when it's warmer and you can enjoy the scenery in both directions, most tours are timed to capture the drama of sunrise or sunset; without your own transport or enough people to make your own arrangements you're likely to travel either up or down in darkness.

From Malatya Malatya tourist office organises hassle-free minibus tours to Nemrut Dağı from April to mid-October. They leave at noon from outside the vilayet, although if you wait in the tea garden at the rear the driver will come and find you there.

It's a four-hour ride through dramatic scenery to the summit. The last 30km of road is unpaved but goes right to the summit, unlike the road from Kahta. After enjoying the sunset for two hours, you descend to the Güneş Hotel, a forlorn little place in the village of Büyüköz, slated for restoration at some unspecified date in the near future. Here you have dinner and stay the night before taking the minibus back up to the summit for sunrise. After breakfast at the Güneş you return to Malatya for around 10 am.

The per person cost of US$30 includes transport, dinner, bed and breakfast, and you pay another US$2.50 for admission to the national park. In theory there are tours every day but if you turn up alone you have to be prepared to pay substantially more. Some readers have negotiated a transport-only fare, and taken a sleeping bag and food to the summit with them. If you want to do this, remember that the mornings are freezing cold even in July.

If you prefer to descend via Kahta, hike across the summit to the car park and cafe building, and ask around for a minibus with an empty seat; or hitch a ride with someone going down to Kahta.

Cem Tour (☎ 322 6666, fax 322 8444) on the first floor of the Galleri İş Merkezi in Malatya also offers two- (US$120) and three-day (US$170) tours to Nemrut provided there are at least four people. These take in Şanlıurfa and the Atatürk Dam as well but are quite pricey compared with trips out of Cappadocia.

From Şanlıurfa Two-day tours to Nemrut (US$40/50 depending on accommodation) are also available from Harran-Nemrut Tours in Şanlıurfa (see that section for details). Some of these tours take you to the Atatürk Barajı along the way.

From Cappadocia Several companies in Cappadocia offer minibus tours to Nemrut, despite the distance of almost 600km. Two-day tours cost about US$125 and involve many hours of breakneck driving. If time allows, it's better to opt for a three-day tour (costing about US$150) which allows the journey to be broken into more manageable chunks and also allows you to see the other ancient sites around Nemrut.

Ötüken Voyage (☎ 384-271 2757) opposite the otogar in Göreme has been offering good three-day tours to Nemrut for several years, with regular Tuesday and Friday departures. Tours take in the Karatay Han near Kayseri, and ice cream and a visit to the bazaar in Kahramanmaraş, before arriving in Kahta. On the second day you visit Nemrut Dağı for sunrise and then take in the sights at Arsameia, Cendere and Karakuş. Afterwards you continue to Harran, before stop-

ping for the night in Şanlıurfa. On the last day you drive back to Göreme via Gaziantep, following the road through Adana and over the Taurus Mountains to Niğde.

Neşe Tour (☎ 384-271 2525) in Göreme offers similar tours departing on Wednesday and Saturday. Other companies in Göreme offer similar packages but it's worth checking exactly where you'll be stopping.

ŞANLIURFA (URFA)
☎ 414 • pop 295,000 • elevation 518m

The great pilgrimage town of Şanlıurfa, the Prophets' City, is a strange mixture of old and new, serene and raucous. In the shadow of a mighty medieval fortress, grey-bearded men and women cloaked in black chadors toss food into a pool full of sacred carp or gather at a cave said to be the birthplace of the patriarch Abraham. In the cool darkness of the covered bazaar, shopkeepers sit on low platforms in front of their stores, as was the custom in Ottoman times. Amid the hubbub of Turkish you'll also hear Kurdish and Arabic. But out on the highway the traffic is noisy and unruly and the high-rises as unappealing as anywhere else in Turkey.

Of all the towns in the south-east, Urfa has the most to offer tourists. Not only are there several specific sights worth stopping for but much of the town is architecturally interesting. Although people are keen to practise their English on you, the level of hassle rarely becomes irksome. You could easily spend four or five days here without getting bored, but to get the best out of Urfa allow at least one night and a full day. If you want to make an excursion south to Harran, the biblical town of beehive houses near the Syrian frontier, and to the surrounding archaeological sites, you'll need at least another day. To see the Atatürk Barajı, out on the road to Adıyaman, allow another half day.

History
Urfa has been sizzling in the sun for a long time. It's thought that a fortress stood on the hill now occupied by the kale more than 3500 years ago. Its people built a powerful state – called Hurri (Cave) by the Babylonians – simply because they knew what a

Urfa's Favourite Son

You won't be in Turkey for long before you hear the dulcet tones of İbrahim Tatlıses, the moustached Kurd from Şanlıurfa who was supposedly discovered while singing to himself over a glass of tea during a break from his labouring work, and whose tapes and CDs far outsell everybody else's.

Since his chance discovery Tatlıses has gone from strength to strength as the best-known exponent of the style of music known as *arabesk*. His success has brought him phenomenal wealth which he has ploughed into ventures as varied as the Tatlıses Lahmacun chain of fast-food shops, hotels and his own bus company.

But his career has been no more free of controversy than that of the late lamented Frank Sinatra. Some years ago he was accused of assaulting his partner, and photos of her battered face wound up on the walls of Turkey's first refuge for battered women.

EASTERN ANATOLIA

chariot was and how to use it in battle when few of their neighbours had heard of such a thing. Although the Hurrites allied themselves with the Egyptian Pharaohs, the Hittites finally got the better of them around 1370 BC. After the fall of Hattuşa, Urfa came under the domination of Carchemish.

The alliance with Egypt produced an interesting cultural exchange. After Amenhotep IV (Akhenaten) popularised the worship of the sun as the unique and only god, a similar worship of Shemesh (the sun) was taken up here. Sun worship was not just a religious belief but a political posture. Thus Urfa defied the cultural, political and religious influence of the nearby Hittites by adopting the customs of the Egyptians, who were a safe distance away.

After a period of Assyrian rule, Alexander the Great came through. He and his Macedonian mates named the town Edessa, after a former capital of Macedonia, and it remained the capital of a Seleucid province until 132 BC when the local Aramaean population set up an independent kingdom and renamed the town Orhai. Though Orhai

maintained a precarious independence for four centuries, bowing only slightly to the Armenians and Parthians, it finally succumbed to the Romans, as did everywhere hereabouts. However the Romans didn't get it easily. Emperor Valerian was badly defeated here in AD 260 and subsequent Roman rulers had a hard time over the centuries keeping the Persians out.

Edessa pursued its contrary history (witness the sun worship) by adopting Christianity at a very early time (circa AD 200), before it became the official religion of the conquerors. The religion was so new that for Edessan Christians the liturgical language was Aramaic, the language of Jesus, and not the Greek on which the church's greatness was built. Edessa, having pursued Christianity on its own from earliest times, had its own patriarch. It revelled in the Nestorian Monophysite heresies as yet another way to thumb its nose at its faraway rulers, whose armies so often trooped through and flattened everything.

Edessa was at the outer edge of the Roman Empire near the frontier with Persia, and as the two great empires clashed, it was batted back and forth from one to the other. In AD 533 the two empires signed a Treaty of Endless Peace that lasted seven years. The Romans and Persians kept at it until the Arabs swept in and cleared them all out in AD 637. Edessa enjoyed three centuries of peace under the Arabs, after which everything went to blazes again.

Turks, Arabs, Armenians and Byzantines battled for the city from 944 until 1098, when the First Crusade under Count Baldwin of Boulogne arrived to set up the Latin County of Edessa. This odd European feudal state lasted until 1144 when it was conquered by a Seljuk Turkish emir. The 'loss' of Edessa infuriated the pope, who called for the Second Crusade, which never set foot near it and accomplished little except to discredit itself. But the Latin county made its mark in history by giving Europeans a look at Eastern architecture. Some of what they saw turned up later in the Gothic style.

The Seljuk Turkish emir, from the Zengi family, was succeeded by Saladin, then by

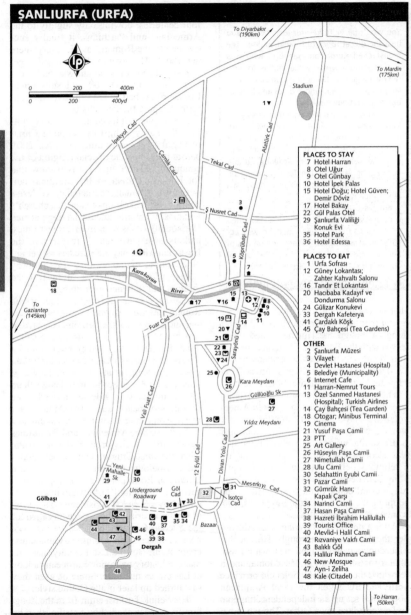

ŞANLIURFA (URFA)

EASTERN ANATOLIA

To Diyarbakır (190km)

To Mardin (175km)

Stadium

İpekyol Cad

Çamlık Cad

Tekal Cad

Atatürk Cad

Ş Nusret Cad

Köprübaşı Cad

1 ▼

2 🏛

3

4 ✚

5

6 ▣

7

13

15

17 🏛 ▼16

Karakoyun River

To Gaziantep (145km)

18 🏛

Fuar Cad

Sarayönü Cad

Vali Fuat Cad

12 Eylül Cad

Divan Yolu Cad

19 🏠
20 ▼
21 ●
22 🏛
23 ▼
24 ▼
25 ●
26 ●

Kara Meydanı

Güllüoğlu Sk

27 ●

28 ●

Yıldız Meydanı

Meserkıyı Cad

Yeni Mahalle Sk

29 ●

30 ●

Gölbaşı

Underground Roadway

41 ▼

42 ▼
43
44 ▼

47

46 ●
45 ▼
39 38
40 37

Göl Cad

36 🏛 ▼33

32

31 ●

İsotçu Cad

Bazaar

35 34

Dergah

48

To Harran (50km)

PLACES TO STAY
- 7 Hotel Harran
- 8 Otel Uğur
- 9 Otel Günbay
- 10 Hotel İpek Palas
- 15 Hotel Doğu; Hotel Güven; Demir Döviz
- 17 Hotel Bakay
- 22 Gül Palas Otel
- 29 Şanlıurfa Valiliği Konuk Evi
- 35 Hotel Park
- 36 Hotel Edessa

PLACES TO EAT
- 1 Urfa Sofrası
- 12 Güney Lokantası; Zahter Kahvaltı Salonu
- 16 Tandır Et Lokantası
- 20 Hacıbaba Kadayıf ve Dondurma Salonu
- 24 Gülizar Konukevi
- 33 Dergah Kafeterya
- 41 Çardaklı Köşk
- 45 Çay Bahçesi (Tea Gardens)

OTHER
- 2 Şanlıurfa Müzesi
- 3 Vilayet
- 4 Devlet Hastanesi (Hospital)
- 5 Belediye (Municipality)
- 6 Internet Cafe
- 11 Harran-Nemrut Tours
- 13 Özel Sanmed Hastanesi (Hospital); Turkish Airlines
- 14 Çay Bahçesi (Tea Garden)
- 18 Otogar; Minibus Terminal
- 19 Cinema
- 21 Yusuf Paşa Camii
- 23 PTT
- 25 Art Gallery
- 26 Hüseyin Paşa Camii
- 27 Nimetullah Camii
- 28 Ulu Cami
- 30 Selahattin Eyubi Camii
- 31 Pazar Camii
- 32 Gümrük Hanı; Kapalı Çarşı
- 34 Narinci Camii
- 37 Hasan Paşa Camii
- 38 Hazreti İbrahim Halilullah
- 39 Tourist Office
- 40 Mevlid-i Halil Camii
- 42 Rızvaniye Vakfı Camii
- 43 Balıklı Göl
- 44 Halilur Rahman Camii
- 46 New Mosque
- 47 Ayn-i Zeliha
- 48 Kale (Citadel)

0   200   400m
0   200   400yd

South-East Anatolia Project

The character of the landscape all around Urfa is changing as the South-East Anatolia Project (Güney-Doğu Anadolu Projesi), better known simply as GAP or Güneydoğu, comes on line, bringing irrigation waters to large arid regions and generating enormous amounts of hydroelectricity for industry. Parched valleys have become fish-filled lakes and dusty villages are becoming booming market towns, factory cities or lakeside resorts.

The scale of the project is awe-inspiring, affecting eight provinces and two huge rivers, the Tigris and Euphrates. By the year 2005 when completion is envisioned, 22 dams and 19 hydroelectric power plants will have been built and 3 million hectares of land will have been brought under irrigation. There will be new employment opportunities for 1.8 million people; per capita income in the region is expected to double.

The Atatürk Barajı (Atatürk Dam), keystone of the project, is capable of generating 8.9 billion kilowatt-hours of electricity annually from the runoff of the vast lake (817 sq km, 162m deep) which its construction created. At 26km the Urfa Irrigation Tunnel is the longest such tunnel in the world.

Such a huge, hope-generating project can also generate sizeable problems, especially ecological ones. The change from dry agriculture to wet has already caused an explosion of disease. Incidence of malaria has increased tenfold, and it is feared that diarrhoea and dysentery, already on the rise, will follow suit.

The project has also generated political problems, as Syria and Iraq, the countries downriver for whom the waters of the Tigris and Euphrates are also vital, complain bitterly that Turkey is using or keeping a larger share of the water than it should.

the Mamluks. The Ottomans, under Selim the Grim, conquered most of this region in the early 16th century, but Edessa did not become Urfa until 1637 when the Ottomans finally took over.

As for its modern sobriquet, Urfa became Şanlıurfa (Glorious Urfa) a little over a decade ago. Since 1973, when Heroic Antep (Gaziantep) was given its special name, the citizens of Urfa had been chafing under a relative loss of dignity. Now their city is 'Glorious', the inhabitants can look the citizens of 'Heroic' Antep straight in the eye.

Orientation

Except for inside the bazaar, it's fairly easy to find your way around Urfa. You'll see the fortress (kale) to the right (south) as you enter the town along the highway from Gaziantep. The otogar is next to the highway by a stream bed which is usually dry. If you take a taxi to the centre, ask for the belediye in order to reach most hotels and Harran-Nemrut Tours; or for the Dergah, also called Gölbaşı, for the mosques, pools and bazaar. The Dergah is 1.5km from the otogar.

Along different stretches the city's main thoroughfare is called Atatürk, Köprübaşı, Sarayönü and Divan Yolu Caddesis.

Information

At the time of writing the tourist office (☎ 215 2467, fax 216 0170) was a booth in the Dergah rose garden. However, you may find it more helpful to head for Harran-Nemrut Tours (☎ 0542-761 3065), just behind the Özel Sanmed Hastanesi, off Köprübaşı Caddesi, where Özcan Arslan, a local teacher, runs tours to local sites and can fill you in on what's what around the city.

Demir Döviz, on Sarayönü Caddesi between Hotel Güven and Hotel Doğu, and several other banks and exchange offices can change your money. US dollars and deutschmarks are the preferred currencies.

Gölbaşı

Legend had it that Abraham, who is a great Islamic prophet, was in old Urfa destroying pagan gods one day when Nimrod, the local Assyrian king, took offence at this rash behaviour. Nimrod had Abraham immolated on a funeral pyre, but God turned the fire into water and the burning coals into fish. Abraham himself was hurled into the air but landed safely in a bed of roses.

The beautiful Gölbaşı area of Urfa is a symbolic recreation of this story. Two rectangular pools of water (Balıklı Göl and Ayn-i Zeliha) are filled with supposedly sacred carp while the whole area west of the Hasan Paşa Cami is a gorgeous rose garden. Local legend has it that anyone catching the carp will go blind so these must be the most pampered fish in Turkey. You can buy fish food from vendors at the poolside (US$0.15). Most of the time they're so well nourished they can barely muster a feeding frenzy.

Gölbaşı is an extraordinarily picturesque quarter with the castle rising up on its rock as a backdrop. On the northern side of Balıklı Göl is the **Rızvaniye Vakfı Camii** and **Medresesi**, while at the western end is the **Halilur Rahman Camii**, a 17th-century building on the site where Abraham fell to the ground, replacing an earlier Byzantine church. The two pools are fed by a spring at the base of Damlacık hill, on which the kale is built.

After feeding the fish, take a seat at a shady table in one of the tea gardens and have a cool drink or bracing glass of çay to ward off the heat of the day.

Whoever was responsible for the large shop and hotel complex to the north of the area deserves lots of Brownie points for achieving what very few Turkish town planners manage: a development which not only doesn't damage its surroundings, but actually enhances them.

Dergah

Immediately to the south-east of the pools and the park is the Dergah complex of mosques and parks surrounding the **Hazreti İbrahim'in Doğum Mağarası** (Prophet Abraham's Birth Cave) in which, legend has it, the Prophet Abraham was born. This is still a place of pilgrimage and prayer with separate entrances for men and women. A large new Ottoman-style mosque stands to the west of the cave.

Next door is a complex of mosques and medreses called **Hazreti İbrahim Halilullah** (Prophet Abraham, Friend of God), built and rebuilt over the centuries as an active place of pilgrimage. To the east, on Göl Caddesi, is the **Hasan Paşa Camii**, an Ottoman work. The **Mevlid-i Halil Camii** holds the tomb of a saint named Dede Osman.

All of these places are open to visitors, but as they are places of worship and this is a conservative city, you should be neatly and modestly dressed, and should behave quietly and decorously, although you may be surprised at some of the sights you see inside.

Fortress

Depending upon where you go for your information, the fortress on Damlacık hill was built either during Hellenistic times or by the Byzantines or during the crusades or by the Turks. No doubt all are true, as fortresses are normally built and rebuilt over the centuries. In any case, it's vast, looks magnificent when floodlit and can be reached up a flight of stairs which then cascade back down again via a tunnel cut through the rock. On the top, the most interesting things are the pair of columns that local legend has dubbed the Throne of Nemrut after the supposed founder of Urfa, the biblical King Nimrod (Genesis 10: 8-10). Really, you come up here for the spectacular views down over Urfa, which are worth the US$1.75 entrance fee to see.

Bazaar

Urfa's bazaar spreads itself out east of the Hasan Paşa Camii. It's a jumble of streets, some covered, some open, selling everything from sheepskins and pigeons to jeans and handmade shoes. Although there are specific highlights to look for, the best idea is just to dive in and take your time exploring. Don't worry too much about getting lost – someone will soon point you in the right direction and the main roads are rarely far away.

One of the most interesting areas is the old **bedesten**, an ancient caravanserai. Here you'll find carpets and second-hand kilims on sale for very reasonable prices, as well as the silk scarves local women wear tied around their foreheads. Hidden away in the heart of the bedesten is the **Gümrük Hanı**, or customs depot, with a delightful tea garden shaded with plane trees in its courtyard. Here men sit sipping çay and playing cards until summoned by the loudspeaker to attend the mosque upstairs.

To the left (south) of the caravanserai courtyard is the **Kapalı Çarşı**, or Covered Bazaar, barely changed over the centuries, except for what's on sale.

Buried in the lanes of the bazaar are several ancient **hamams**, generally open for men from 9 am to 1 pm, for women from 1 to 6 pm, and then for men again in the evening. These are cheap places to while away a few hours but so busy that it takes a bit of confidence to plunge into them.

Mosques

Urfa's Syrian-style **Ulu Cami** on Divan Yolu Caddesi dates from the period 1170–75. Its 13 eyvans open onto a spacious forecourt with a tall tower topped by a clock with Ottoman numerals.

At Kara Meydanı, the square midway between the belediye and Dergah, is the **Hüseyin Paşa Camii**, a late-Ottoman work built in 1849.

In Vali Fuat Caddesi, which leads up from behind Gölbaşı to the Konuk Evi, you'll see the enormous, beautifully restored **Selahattin Eyubi Camii**, once a church and liberally adorned with Arabic inscriptions.

Old Houses

Delve down Urfa's backstreets and you'll find many examples of the city's distinctive stone houses with protruding bays supported on stone corbels. Although many of these houses are falling into decay (and some are far too large for modern families), a few have been restored, most notably the house of Hacı Hafızlar, opposite the Hüseyin Paşa Camii, which has been turned into an **art gallery**. The art is often pretty awful but the courtyards and fine carved stonework are a joy to behold.

You can also wander into the **Şurkav**, a local government building immediately behind the Hotel Edessa, where two courtyards are draped with greenery and you can see carvings, similar to those in Harran castle, of dogs wearing chains.

Şanlıurfa Müzesi

Up the hill to the west of the vilayet building, off Atatürk Caddesi, is Şanlıurfa's museum.

The gardens contain various sculptures, and on the porch as you enter are several mosaics, the most interesting showing assorted wild animals. Inside, noteworthy artefacts include Neolithic implements, Assyrian, Babylonian and Hittite relief stones and other objects from Byzantine, Seljuk and Ottoman times. A downstairs room displays finds from Kurban Höyük, one of the ancient sites that has disappeared beneath the great lake of the Atatürk Dam.

Upstairs, the ethnology section contains some incredibly intricate wooden doors and window shutters from old Urfa houses. There are also fine examples of local calligraphy and statues salvaged from Christian churches as well as the more standard rugs and embroidery.

The museum is open from 8.30 am to noon and 1.30 to 5.30 pm daily except Monday. Admission costs US$1.75.

Prophet Job's Site

Otherwise known as Eyüp Peygamber Makamı, Prophet Job's Site is marked by signs off the road to Harran; you can visit free at any time. Eyüp (Job), standard-bearer of the Prophet Mohammed, passed through Urfa with the Arab armies riding into Anatolia to attack Constantinople. Local legend holds that he became ill here, but was cured (or at least made to feel a bit better) by drinking water from a spring on the outskirts of town. The spring is now in a grotto next to a mosque within a walled grove of evergreens.

Places to Stay – Budget

With few foreign tourists passing through, most Urfa hotels cater for visiting pilgrims and businessmen. Maybe it's the heat but the city seems to boast an unusually large number of surly receptionists. The hotel in which one of the authors of this book once stood open-mouthed while the receptionist head-butted a youth is, not surprisingly, no more, but many of the men staffing the front desks here seem to think no more is required of them than to grunt at their guests.

Most hotels are near the belediye. A good place to start looking is Köprübaşı Caddesi behind the Özel Sanmed Hastanesi, which

EASTERN ANATOLIA

has a line-up of hotels that should, in normal times, amount to a real backpackers enclave.

The *Hotel İpek Palas* (☎ *215 1546)* has decent singles/doubles from US$12/20 but is one of those places which will only give single travellers its smallest, shoddiest room unless they're prepared to pay full double prices. A few doors along and up some steps, the very basic *Otel Günbay* (☎ *313 9797)* is cheap as they come, with waterless rooms at US$5/9. Finally, there's *Otel Uğur* (☎ *313 1340)*, up a perilous flight of steps at the end of Köprübaşı Caddesi, opposite the Hotel Harran, where very basic rooms cost US$5/9.

Out on the main road *Hotel Güven* (☎ *215 1700, fax 215 1941, Sarayönü Caddesi 133)* has pleasant enough rooms for US$17/25, with shower, but the welcome may depend on who's staffing the desk. The nearby *Hotel Doğu* (☎ *212 1528)* is cheaper at US$9/14 a room but much more basic.

Around the corner is the *Hotel Bakay* (☎ *215 2689, fax 215 1156, Fuar Caddesi)* where air-con rooms complete with TV and balcony cost US$14/20. Readers have enjoyed staying here although you must expect some traffic noise.

Heading down towards the bazaar you'll find *Hotel Park* (☎ *216 0500, Göl Caddesi 4)*. Waterless rooms here are clean but as basic as they come for US$5 per person. The owner, Mustafa Arslan, speaks English.

One last possibility off Sarayönü Caddesi with big but very basic rooms is the *Gül Palas* (☎ *215 7201, Beyaz Sokak 15/A)*. Rooms cost US$5/9 but they're really only used to male visitors.

Places to Stay – Mid-Range

The best place to stay in Urfa is not actually the highest priced although it only has six rooms and tends to get booked up. *Şanlıurfa Valiliği Konuk Evi* (☎ *215 9377, fax 215 3045, Vali Fuat Caddesi)* is a delightful 19th-century stone building near the Selahattin Eyubi Camii which was turned into the provincial government's guesthouse in 1991. Staff wear Ottoman costume, corridors are pleasantly carpeted and filled with huge pieces of wooden furniture and the

central courtyard with fountain offers a delightful cafe, so it's slightly disappointing to find the bedrooms furnished in more or less standard Turkish hotel style. Still, the views from the roof more than make up for that and the prices, at US$32/50 a single/double, are surprisingly reasonable (but expected to rise soon).

Places to Stay – Top End

Urfa's best hotel is well-positioned in the new shopping mall overlooking the rose garden by the Dergah. *Hotel Edessa* (☎ *215 9911, fax 215 5589, Balıklı Göl Mevkii)* has bright, modern rooms with every comfort: TV, air-con, minibar, comfy armchairs and bathroom with a range of toiletries. Secretarial and email services are available and there's a choice of places to eat. For all this luxury you pay a steep US$140/160.

By far the most comfortable rooms in Urfa are at the four-star *Hotel Harran* (☎ *313 2860, fax 313 4918, Atatürk Bulvarı)*, directly opposite the belediye. Unusually, although the lobby looks just as old-fashioned as ever, the rooms have been completely made over in shades of pink and boast air-con, baths, TVs and refrigerators. The inviting *restaurant* looks straight onto an even more inviting swimming pool and serves good food. Rates are US$60/86 a room. Be sure to ask for a back room to escape the traffic noise.

Places to Eat

Urfa's culinary specialities include *çiğ köfte* (minced uncooked mutton), a sure-fire recipe for gastrointestinal disaster in this hot climate; *içli köfte* (a deep-fried croquette with a mutton filling); and Urfa kebap (skewered chunks of lamb or minced lamb meatballs broiled on charcoal and served with tomatoes, sliced onions and hot peppers). If you find baklava too sweet, you may enjoy Urfa's *peynirli kadayıf*, cheese-filled shredded wheat doused in honey, which you'll see on sale on round metal plates.

It pays to be a bit careful what you eat here because the heat makes food poisoning more likely. Make sure whatever you choose is hot and freshly cooked.

Güney Lokantası (Köprübaşı Caddesi) is a popular choice because it's close to many of the cheap hotels. It sells a full range of stews, vegetable dishes, pilavs and soups, and a simple meal should cost around US$3.

Next door is *Zahter Kahvaltı Salonu* where a breakfast of honey and fresh cream mixed together and spread on flat bread, washed down with a large glass of çay, costs around US$1.

If you don't mind splashing out for the surroundings, a good place to sample içli köfte is *Urfa Sofrası (Atatürk Caddesi)*, opposite the stadium. A blowout meal of soup, kebap, cooked meat and lahmacun with soft drink and coffee will come to around US$6.

The food is as good and the bill will probably come to about the same at *Tandır Et Lokantası (Fuar Caddesi)*, within easy walking distance of Köprübaşı.

In the evenings little *stalls* are set up all along Köprübaşı and Sarayönü Caddesis and men sit chopping salads on wooden boards and wrapping skewered pieces of *ciğer* (liver) in flaps of bread as they're handed out fresh from the grill.

You can sample peynirli kadayıf at *Hacıbaba Kadayıf ve Dondurma Salonu (Sarayönü Caddesi)* next to the Yusuf Paşa Camii. A fair-sized portion costs about US$1.

Perhaps the most pleasant place for an inexpensive meal is in the park at Gölbaşı. The various *çay bahçesis* all serve simple grills. Perhaps the nicest is the one behind the Ayn-i Zeliha where you can watch families boating round the fountain as you eat. A *domatesli kebap* (köfte grilled with chunks of tomato and served with chopped scallions, grilled hot peppers and huge flaps of flat village bread) with a tankard of cool *ayran* (yogurt drink) should cost around US$4.

Tucked away in the backstreet behind the main post office is the lovely *Gülizar Konukevi (☎ 215 0505, İrfaniye Sokak 22)*, a restaurant set up in a wonderful old Urfa house where you dine on floor cushions in a series of rooms set around a courtyard. If there are a few of you and you phone ahead they can prepare a feast of local dishes, like *şıllık*, a type of walnut pancake. Otherwise the menu is standard kebabs at fairly standard prices.

The *Çardaklı Kösk (☎ 217 1080, Tünel Çıkışı 1)* is also in an old house but one that has been so restored it feels almost new. Once again you dine on cushions in what were the rooms around the courtyard, but the menu here rarely strays from the standard kebabs.

If you feel like enjoying a beer, *Büfe 33*, more or less opposite Hotel İpek Palas, sells canned Efes Pilsen. The restaurant at *Hotel Harran* also serves alcohol. Dinner here can be good and not too outrageously priced (assume about US$8 per person for a full meal) but pick a night when it's busy since the empty dining room can seem very soulless.

Getting There & Away

Air Turkish Airlines (☎ 215 3344, fax 216 3245) at Kaliru Turizm Seyahat Acentesi, Sarayönü Caddesi 74/A, Köprübaşı, has daily nonstop flights to and from Ankara with connections to İstanbul and İzmir. There are also two weekly nonstop flights to İstanbul. Service buses to the airport stop outside the office.

Bus The gloomy otogar has a run-of-the-mill restaurant and a left-luggage depot. On the main highway serving the south-east, it receives plenty of traffic, but most buses are passing through, so you must take whatever seats are available. Buses to the otogar can be caught on Atatürk Bulvarı (US$0.30). If you don't have much luggage it's quicker to walk, but assuming you're heavily laden note that the circuitous route favoured by the dolmuş takes 20 minutes. A taxi should cost around US$3. Details of some daily services are listed in the table on the following page.

Minibuses to Akçakale, Birecik and Adıyaman (US$3, 1½ hours) leave from the minibus terminal immediately beside the otogar.

Train The nearest station to Urfa is at Akçakale on the Syrian frontier, 50km south of the town, from where buses head north to Urfa (US$1.50).

Services from Şanlıurfa's Otogar

destination	fare (US$)	time (hr)	distance (km)	daily services
Adana	10	6	365	several buses
Ankara	20	13	850	several buses
Diyarbakır	7	3	190	frequent buses
Erzurum	23	12	665	a few buses
Gaziantep	5	2½	145	frequent buses
İstanbul	29	24	1290	a few buses
Malatya	9	7	395	a few buses
Mardin	9	3	175	several buses
Van	14	9	585	a few buses

EASTERN ANATOLIA

HARRAN
☎ 414 • pop 6900

And Terah took Abram his son, and Lot the son of Haran his son's son, and Sarai his daughter-in-law, his son Abram's wife; and they went forth with them from Ur of the Chaldees, to go into the land of Canaan; and they came unto Harran, and dwelt there.
Genesis 11:31

This is what the Bible has to say about Harran's most famous resident, who stayed here for a few years back in 1900 BC. It seems certain that Harran is one of the oldest continuously inhabited spots on earth. Its ruined walls and Ulu Cami, crumbling fortress and beehive houses give it a feeling of deep antiquity.

Of Harran's ancient monuments the most impressive is the kale which looms over the modern village. However, most people are more interested in the lifestyle of the local inhabitants even though most have long since abandoned the beehive houses to their livestock in favour of more conventional dwellings. Traditionally they lived by farming and smuggling, but the coming of the Atatürk Barajı looks set to change all that as cotton fields sprout all over what was once desert. Many seemingly poor villagers are actually quite comfortably off, with huge TVs and ghetto blasters in their houses.

On arrival in Harran you are officially expected to buy a ticket (US$1.75) but there may not be anyone in the booth to collect the money. If anyone in the castle tries to charge you, insist on being given the official ticket.

History
Besides being the place of Abraham's sojourn, Harran is famous as a centre of worship of Sin, god of the moon. Worship of the sun, moon and planets was popular in Harran and at neighbouring Soğmatar, from about 800 BC until AD 830, although Harran's temple to the moon god was destroyed by the Byzantine emperor Theodosius in AD 382. Battles between Arabs and Byzantines occupied the townsfolk until the coming of the crusaders. The fortress, which some say was built on the ruins of the moon god's temple, was restored when the crusaders approached. The crusaders won and maintained it for a while before they too moved on.

Beehive Houses
Harran is famous for its beehive houses, the design of which may date back to the 3rd century BC, although the present examples were mostly constructed within the last 200 years. It's thought that the design evolved partly in response to the lack of wood for making roofs and partly because the ruins provided a ready source of reusable bricks. Locals will tell you that the houses stay relatively cool in summer and warm in winter. Although the Harran houses are unique in Turkey, similar buildings can be found in northern Syria and in Apulia in Italy.

The **Harran Kültür Evi**, within walking distance of the kale and the Ulu Cami, is set up to allow visitors to see inside one of the houses and then to sip cold drinks in the garden afterwards (make sure you pay the exact money or you'll be told the caretaker has no change). Some villagers will also let you look around their compounds although they usually expect to be paid for doing so.

Kale

On the far (east) side of the hill, the **kale** stands in the midst of the beehive houses. As soon as you arrive, children will crowd around you demanding coins, sweets, cigarettes, ballpoint pens and 'presents'. Some people find their attentions charming, most find their omnipresence detracts from the enjoyment of Harran.

Although a castle probably already existed on the site from Hittite times, what you see now dates mainly from after 1059 when the Fatimids took over and restored it. Originally there were four multiangular corner towers but only two remain. Once there were also 150 rooms here, but many of these have caved in or are slowly filling up with silt. Make sure you see the **Eastern Gate** adorned with carvings of chained dogs. If you've acquired a 'guide' they may also point out extremely worn carvings of angels and assorted inscriptions.

Young men who'd like to guide you wait in the shaded tent that serves as a cafeteria on the summit of the kale. They'll probably want around US$6 for their services.

Walls & Mosque

The approach road is lined with crumbling stone **walls**, once 4km long and studded with 187 towers and four gates; of these only the restored **Aleppo Gate** remains.

Of the ruins inside the village other than the kale, the **Ulu Cami**, built in the 8th century by Marwan II, last of the Umayyad caliphs, is most prominent – you'll recognise it by its tall, square and very un-Turkish minaret. It's said to be the oldest mosque in Anatolia. Near here stood the first Islamic university (although the precise site has not been discovered), and on the hillside above it you'll see the low-level ruins of ancient Harran dating back some 5000 years.

Places to Stay

Although most people visit from Urfa, Harran now has its own hotel on the approach road as you come into town. The *Bazda Motel* (☎ 441 3590, fax 441 2145) has been designed to mimic the beehive houses and rooms are surprisingly big, airy and modern. Beds cost a very reasonable US$20 a head.

Getting There & Away

Getting to Harran is relatively straightforward. The cheapest way is to catch an Akçakale bus south from Urfa and ask to be dropped off at the road junction 10km west of Harran. Here you can wait for whatever transport may appear, bearing in mind that some drivers will expect payment for giving you a lift and that there's little shelter against the boiling sun of high summer.

You may well decide that it's worth paying just a bit more to go on a tour organised by Özcan Arslan at Harran-Nemrut Tours (☎ 0542-761 3065) off Köprübaşı Caddesi, Şanlıurfa. Provided there are at least four people, tours depart at 9 am and 4 pm daily and cost US$10 per person. You'll spend two hours in Harran and be back in Urfa by 1 or 8 pm depending on which tour you take.

If you're driving to Harran, leave Urfa by the Akçakale road at the south-eastern end of town and go 37km to a turn-off to the left (east). From there, it's another 10km to Harran. As you approach you'll see a *jandarma* (police) post, a small restaurant, a camping ground and a souvenir shop.

AROUND HARRAN

To get to the sites beyond Harran without your own transport is virtually impossible unless you have limitless time. Even with your own car the roads are rough and poorly signed, and it would be easy to go astray amid the dusty tracks. The longer Harran tours offered by Özcan Arslan (see the Getting There & Away section in Harran earlier) are therefore particularly well worth considering. For US$20 per person (for four people) you are taken to Harran, Han el Ba'rur, Şuayb City and Soğmatar, with a chance to take tea with villagers and see the astonishing transformation wrought on the local scenery by the GAP Project – field upon field of cotton where once there was just desert. In high summer tours leave at 6 am and return at 6 pm.

Han el Ba'rur Caravanserai

About 20km east of Harran are the remains of the Seljuk Han el Ba'rur Caravanserai, built in 1128 to service the local trade caravans. Although some restoration work has been done here, there are not enough visitors to justify any services (or tickets for that matter).

Şuayb City

Another 25km north-east of the caravanserai are the extensive remains of Şuayb City, where hefty stone walls and lintels survive above a network of subterranean rooms. One of these contains a mosque on the site of the supposed home of the prophet Jethro. Once again, don't expect to find any services, although villagers will probably be happy to show you around and point out the more accessible cave rooms. It's a good idea to bring a torch (flashlight) and to wear sturdy shoes.

Soğmatar

About 15km north of Şuayb is the isolated, poverty-stricken village of Soğmatar with, at its heart, a cave-temple, the Pagnon Cave, probably constructed around AD 150–200 for the cult of the local moon god, Sin. Lifesize figures are carved onto the walls on three sides and, although they're extremely worn, two appear to wear crescent headdresses. Inscriptions on the wall are in ancient Syrian.

Soğmatar is surrounded by bare rocks and ledges and on one of these ledges there was once an open-air temple to the sun and moon gods whose effigies can be seen carved into the side. On the top of the rock are assorted inscriptions. Standing on the summit you can see remains of other temples, thought to be linked to other planets, on the surrounding hills.

Most striking of Soğmatar's other ruins is a circular structure on another rocky ledge, with rooms cut underneath it that look as if they may once have been tombs. This is thought to have been a temple to Venus.

Once again there are no services – not even the most basic shop – at Soğmatar, although villagers will no doubt be happy to point out the sites.

DİYARBAKIR

☎ 412 • pop two million • elevation 660m

The tourist office may try hard with its talk of the Watermelon Festival, but for most people Diyarbakır, on the banks of the Tigris River (Dicle Nehri), is best known as the town that, throughout the 1980s and '90s, was the centre of the Kurdish resistance movement (see History in the Facts about Turkey chapter for more details about the Kurds). To make matters worse it was also the focal point for the shadowy Hezbollah (same name, same mentality but completely separate from the Lebanese group Hezbollah) who did their utmost to drive out the few remaining Christians. Behind the grim basalt walls political parties appeared and disappeared, terrible things happened to anyone who stepped out of line, and those with any sense kept their mouths shut and their heads down. Not surprisingly, most travellers gave Diyarbakır a wide berth.

Fortunately, since the last edition of this book came out the situation seems to have improved considerably. Gone is the rather sullen, oppressed atmosphere of just two years ago. Life may still be hard for the many people who fled here from the surrounding villages to escape the antics of the Kurdistan Workers Party (PKK) and the Turkish army, only to find themselves jobless, but these days the security apparatus is nowhere near as conspicuous, and the atmosphere nothing like as desperate. It's still wise to avoid getting drawn into political conversations with strangers, but these days your worst problem is likely to be shaking off the ubiquitous street children who can make your life a misery.

Diyarbakır may be further west than Van but it's here, rather than there, that you begin to feel you've reached the Orient. The women in their cumbersome chadors or colourful Kurdish headscarves, the men with their big beards and baggy pants, the narrow alleys and the Arab-style mosques with black and white bands of stone all add up to an air of exoticism. As you stroll in the bazaar in early evening, the sights, sounds, smells and sheer pressure of human bodies seem a foretaste of teeming Pakistan.

In summer it's scorching hot here, something to bear in mind when choosing a room.

History

Considering that Mesopotamia, the land between the Tigris and Euphrates Valleys, saw the dawn of the world's first great empires, it's no surprise that Diyarbakır's history begins with the Hurrian Kingdom of Mitanni circa 1500 BC, and proceeds through domination by the civilisations of Urartu (900 BC), Assyria (1356–612 BC), Persia (600–330 BC) and Alexander the Great and his successors the Seleucids.

The Romans took over in AD 115, but because of its strategic position the city changed hands numerous times until it was conquered by the Arabs in AD 639. Until then it had been known as Amida, but the Arabs settled it with the tribe of Beni Bakr, who named their new home Diyar Bakr, the Realm of Bakr.

The next few centuries were troubled ones as the city was occupied in turn by obscure Hamdanids, Buweyhids and Marwanids. In 1085 a Seljuk Turkish dynasty, the Cüheyroğulları, took over, only to be overthrown by Syrian Seljuks, Artukids and Ayyubids.

In 1259 the Mongol emperor Hulagu Khan restored the city to the Seljuks. They, in turn, lost it to the Mardin Artukids. In 1394 Tamerlane conquered Diyarbakır and gave it to Akkoyunlu Kara Yülük Osman Bey. The Akkoyunlu (White Sheep Turkoman) ruler formed a pact with the Venetian Empire against the Ottomans, but was defeated by Mehmet the Conqueror (Mehmet Fatih) in 1473. After 1497, the Safavid Dynasty founded by Shah Ismail took over Iran, putting an end to more than a century of Turkoman rule in this area.

The Ottomans came and conquered in 1515, but even then, Diyarbakır was not to know lasting peace. Because it stands right in the way of invading armies from Anatolia, Persia and Syria, it suffered many more tribulations. It's to be hoped that at long last peace may be coming the way of the people of this troubled city.

Orientation

Old Diyarbakır has a standard Roman town plan, with a circle of walls pierced by four gates at the north, south, east and west. From the gates, avenues travel to a central crossroads. Parts of the walls have since been razed and new gates opened to ease traffic circulation. Within the walls the city is a maze of narrow, twisting, mostly unmarked alleys. It's virtually impossible to find your way around this labyrinth without the help of a guide. Local boys will press their services upon you, and you may have to use them to find the mosques, museums and churches hidden within the maze, which may, in any case, be closed when you find them. Be sure to agree on a price in advance. If you decide you need a more formal guide ask in the Hasan Paşa Hanı or at the Demir Otel and expect to pay up to US$50 a day.

The train station is at the western end of İstasyon Caddesi which heads east to the Urfa Kapısı (Edessa Gate), the city's western gate. Inside the walls, the continuation of İstasyon Caddesi is called Melek Ahmet Caddesi or sometimes Urfa Caddesi. To get to the centre from the train station (about 1.5km), walk out of the front door, go to the first big street and wait on the left (northeast) corner on the far side for a dolmuş going to the Dağ Kapısı (Mountain Gate), also called Harput Kapısı.

The otogar is north-west of the city where Elazığ Caddesi (also called Ziya Gökalp Bulvarı) intersects the highway. From the otogar take a dolmuş 3.5km along Elazığ Caddesi to the centre and you'll pass the Turistik Oteli just before penetrating the walls at the Dağ Kapısı. From this gate, Gazi Caddesi leads to the centre. Don't let people tell you that there are no dolmuşes and that you must take a taxi; if you do the US$0.25 fare will rocket to around US$6.

New Diyarbakır sprawls to the west of the old city but you'll have no reason to go there unless you're desperate for an Internet cafe.

Information

The tourist office (☎ 221 2173, fax 224 1189) is inside the Dağ Kapısı but has little useful information.

EASTERN ANATOLIA

EASTERN ANATOLIA

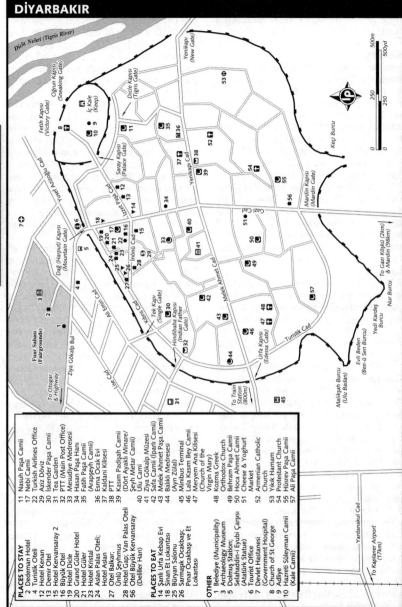

DİYARBAKIR

PLACES TO STAY
1 Nasuh Paşa Camii
2 Dedemen Hotel
4 Turistik Oteli
12 Hotel Kenan
13 Demir Otel
15 Hotel Kervansaray 2
16 Büyük Otel
19 Hotel Dicle
20 Grand Güler Hotel
21 Hotel Güler
23 Hotel Kristal
24 Aslan Palas Oteli;
     Hotel Aslan
27 Otel Balkar;
     Ünlü Şeyhmus
28 Hotel Gap; Van Palas Oteli
56 Otel Büyük Kervansaray
     (Deliller Han)

PLACES TO EAT
14 Şanlı Urfa Kebap Evi
18 Sinan Et Lokantası
25 Büryan Salonu
26 Sarmaşık Ocakbaşı;
     Pınar Ocakbaşı ve Et
     Lokantası

11 Nasuh Paşa Camii
17 Nebi Camii
22 Turkish Airlines Office
29 Aziz Döviz
30 İskender Paşa Camii
31 Tea Garden
32 PTT (Main Post Office)
33 Mesudiye Medresesi
35 Fatih Paşa Camii
     (Arapşeyh Camii)
36 Esma Ocak Evi
37 Kaldani Kilisesi
38 PTT
39 Kasım Padişah Camii
     (Dört Ayaklı Minare/
     Şeyh Metar Camii)
40 Ulu Cami
41 Ziya Gökalp Müzesi
42 Safa Camii (İparli Camii)
43 Melek Ahmet Paşa Camii
44 Balıklı Medresesi
     (Ayn Zülal)
45 Minibus Terminal
46 Lala Kasım Bey Camii
47 Meryem Ana Kilisesi
     (Church of the
     Virgin Mary)

48 Kozma Greek
     Orthodox Church
49 Behram Paşa Camii
50 Hoca Ahmet Camii
51 Cheese & Yoghurt
     Market
52 Armenian Catholic
     Church
53 Yıkık Hamam
54 Protestant Church
55 Hüsrev Paşa Camii
57 Ali Paşa Camii

OTHER
1 Belediye (Municipality)
3 Archaeology Museum
5 Dolmuş Station;
     Selahaddin-i Eyubi Çarşısı
     (Atatürk Statue)
6 Tourist Office
7 Devlet Hastanesi
     (Government Hospital)
8 Church of St George
9 Adliye
10 Hazreti Süleyman Camii
     (Kale Camii)

Most banks have branches with ATMs on İnönü Caddesi. At the time of writing you needed to go into the new city of Diyarbakır to find an Internet Cafe. This may well have changed by the time you read this. If not, it might be better to wait until you get to Van or Şanlıurfa to check your email.

City Walls & Gates

Diyarbakır's single most conspicuous attraction is its great circuit of basalt walls, probably dating back to Roman times, although the present walls date from early Byzantine times (AD 330–500). At almost 6km in length these walls are said to be second in extent only to the Great Wall of China, although a more obvious parallel might be the walls of Derry/Londonderry in Northern Ireland. They make a striking sight whether you're walking along the top or the bottom.

The massive black walls are intercut with 72 bastions and towers, many of them clustered around the İç Kale (citadel or keep) on the north-eastern corner, with fine views of the Tigris. There were four main gates originally: Harput Kapısı (north), Mardin Kapısı (south), Yenikapı (east) and Urfa Kapısı (west).

The most interesting stretch of the walls in terms of inscriptions and decoration is heading west (away from the river) from the İç Kale to Mardin Kapısı. Start at the Mardin Kapısı near the Deliller Han, a stone caravanserai now the Otel Büyük Kervansaray. Climb up to the top of the walls, walk along and you'll pass the Yedi Kardeş Burcu (Tower of Seven Brothers) and Malikşah Burcu (Tower of Malikşah, also called Ulu Badan). This bird's-eye vantage point allows you to see a lot of Diyarbakır's street life below. You must descend at Urfa Kapısı but you can climb up again on the opposite side of İstasyon Caddesi.

At the time of writing several stretches of the wall were under restoration. Unfortunately, you must be careful when walking on and along the walls as there have been reports of attempted robberies. Try to go in a group, although until tourism to Diyarbakır picks up this may be easier said than done.

Mosques

Of Diyarbakır's many mosques, the most interesting is the austere **Ulu Cami**, built in 1091 by Malik Şah, an early Seljuk sultan, and extensively restored in 1155 after a fire. It's rectangular in plan – Arab-style, rather than Ottoman – with a huge courtyard where, unusually, representatives of all four rites of Sunni Islam (Hanifi, Maliki, Shafii and Hanbali) meet to pray together every Friday.

Across the courtyard from the Ulu Cami is the **Mesudiye Medresesi**, now used as a polyclinic, which has revolving columns on either side of its mihrab. Across Gazi Caddesi from these buildings is **Hasan Paşa Hanı**, a 16th-century caravanserai, occupied by carpet sellers and souvenir vendors.

Alternating black and white stone banding is a characteristic of Diyarbakır's mosques, many of which date from the time of the Akkoyunlu dynasty. One of these is the **Nebi Camii** (1530) at the main intersection of Gazi and İzzet Paşa/İnönü Caddesis, which has a detached minaret.

The spectacular **Behram Paşa Camii** (1572), in a residential area deep in the maze of narrow streets, is Diyarbakır's largest mosque. The **Safa Camii** (1532) is more Persian in style, with a highly decorated minaret with blue tiles incorporated in its design.

The **Kasım Padişah Camii** (1512) is also famous for its minaret, but its engineering is even more interesting – the tower stands on four slender pillars about 2m high, lending it the name Dört Ayaklı Minare or Four-Legged Minaret.

The 12th-century **Hazreti Süleyman Camii** beside the İç Kale is particularly revered because it houses the tombs of heroes of past Islamic wars. Local people flock here on Thursdays to pay their respects.

Note that most of these mosques have more than one name. The alternative names are shown on the map key.

Gazi Köşkü

The Gazi Köşkü, traditionally known as the Seman Köşkü, dates from the time of the 15th-century Akkoyunlu Turkoman dynasty and is an example of the sort of Diyarbakır house which its wealthier citizens would retire to in high summer. It was given to Atatürk by the city in 1937.

The house is actually quite small and simple but dramatically striped and with a courtyard through which runs a stream used to cool drinks in the days before refrigeration. The furnishings are pretty prosaic compared with those in the museums inside the city walls, but there's a fine tea-set specially designed with the insignia of Atatürk's CHP party on it. It's open whenever the caretaker can be found, and you should leave him a tip for showing you round.

To get there, leave the city by the Mardin Kapısı. It's a pleasant, if isolated, 2.5km downhill walk towards a landmark bridge over the Tigris, or you can take a taxi for about US$7 including waiting time. From this side of the city you get fine, unimpeded views of Diyarbakır's dramatic walls.

Arkeoloji Müzesi

Diyarbakır's Arkeoloji Müzesi (Archaeology Museum) is near the Fuar Sahası (Fairgrounds) off Ziya Gökalp Bulvarı; to get there, leave the old city through the Dağ Kapısı and turn right shortly after the Turistik Oteli. Besides the usual archaeological and classical finds and the obligatory ethnological rooms, it has collections showing the accomplishments of the Karakoyunlu and Akkoyunlu, powerful tribal dynasties who ruled much of eastern Anatolia and Iran between 1378 and 1502.

It's open from 8.30 am to noon and from 1.30 to 5 pm daily except Monday; admission costs US$1.75.

Diyarbakır House Museums

Old Diyarbakır houses were made of black basalt and decorated with *cis* or *kehal* stone stencilling. They were divided into summer and winter quarters and the centre of the summer house was always the eyvan, an arched room opening onto the courtyard with a fountain in the centre. In summer the family moved high wooden platforms called *tahtlar* (thrones) into the courtyard for sleeping, making it possible to catch any breeze.

The traditional Islamic division into selamlık (the men's rooms) and haremlik (the women's) was supplemented by a room called the *mabeyn* (interval) which joined the two. A *serdap* (larder) filled the basement while the upper floors were known as *çardaklar* (shelters).

The best way to see one of these old houses is to visit one of the museums inside the city walls. The poet Cahit Sıtkı Tarancı (1910–56), for example, was born in a two-storey black basalt house near the Ulu Cami which now houses the **Cahit Sıtkı Tarancı Museum**. The house was built in 1820 and although only the haremlik and the traditional courtyard survive, it's well worth visiting. It contains some of the poet's personal effects and furnishings, exhibits on his life and work, and standard ethnographic displays. The museum is open from 8 am to 5 pm daily except Monday; admission costs US$1.75.

The **Ziya Gökalp Müzesi** commemorates sociologist Ziya Gökalp (1876–1924), a formative influence on the Turkish movement. His house in the Tacettin district is open from 8 am to noon and 1.30 to 5 pm daily except Monday; admission costs US$1.75. The beautiful old house is of more general interest than the specialist exhibits dealing with his life and work.

The beautiful grey-and-white-striped **Esma Ocak Evi**, not far from the Dört Ayaklı Minare, used to belong to a female writer. It's only open on Saturday and Sunday and you'll need to bang hard on the door to alert the caretaker, who will expect a tip for showing you the gracefully furnished living rooms.

Churches

The population of Diyarbakır once included many Christians including Armenians and Chaldeans but most of them are long gone, with only their churches left as reminders. The **Kaldani Kilisesi** (Chaldean Church), off Yenikapı Caddesi, was, until recently, used by Christians of the Syrian rite (in communion with the Roman Catholic church) although the main building has long been in ruins.

The wonderful **Meryem Ana Kilisesi**, the Church of the Virgin Mary, is still used by Orthodox Syrian Christians (Jacobites or Monophysites, who refused to accept the doctrines laid down at the Council of Chalcedon in AD 451 – for more details, see the boxed text 'One Nature or Two?' in the Mardin section, following). It's surrounded by a high basalt wall, inside which three families live. The church is beautifully maintained, although only about 15 families still attend services. You will have to hammer on the door as the custodian lives two courtyards away and may not hear you.

Other churches have found new uses: one near the Dört Ayaklı Camii as a PTT, another inside the İç Kale as a prison. The Ulu Cami itself was once a Syrian church.

Places to Stay – Budget

Kıbrıs Caddesi is Diyarbakır's answer to Akbıyık Caddesi in İstanbul with a range of hotels in all price brackets interspersed with restaurants, and with a cinema and bars just across the way. It's the first place to start looking for a room. In summer, avoid rooms just beneath the roof or those that get full late-afternoon sun. It goes without saying that few of these places, especially at the bottom end of the price range, are used to lone female guests.

As you turn down Kıbrıs Caddesi from the Dağ Kapısı you'll see the **Hotel Dicle** (☎ 223 5326, Kıbrıs Caddesi 3) on the left. It can be noisy but is otherwise fine with singles/doubles for US$9/15. West of it, the **Aslan Palas Oteli** (☎ 221 1227, Kıbrıs Caddesi 21) charges just US$6/9 for very basic rooms; right next door the **Hotel Aslan** (☎ 224 7096) charges US$14/20 for more comfort.

Down a quiet alley off Kıbrıs Caddesi, **Hotel Güler** (☎/fax 224 0294, Yoğurtçu Sokak 7) has always offered good value for money but at the time of writing it was being renovated which could mean prices rise from the current US$14 per person. If so, try the **Hotel Kristal** (☎ 224 0297, fax 224 0187, Yoğurtçu Sokak 10), directly across the street, which charges US$17 per person.

Keep walking for the **Otel Balkar** (☎ 228 1233, fax 224 6936, Kıbrıs Caddesi 38), an

excellent choice, offering smart, modern rooms with TV, air-con and minibar for US$20/30.

If you'd rather get away from Kıbrıs Caddesi there are a couple of real cheapies one street back in İnönü Caddesi. **Hotel Gap** (☎ 223 6419) charges just US$5 per person for extremely basic rooms, but with a pleasant downstairs courtyard. The **Van Palas Oteli** next door is similar.

The **Hotel Kenan** (☎ 221 6614, Hz. Süleyman Caddesi 20), near the Demir Otel, offers clean if basic rooms for US$7/12. Avoid those with glass panels onto the corridor. The **Hotel Kervansaray 2** (☎ 221 4966, fax 223 5933, İnönü Caddesi 13) is a very poor relative of its sister hotel; dreary rooms cost US$14/20.

Places to Stay – Mid-Range

Still on Kıbrıs Caddesi, the new **Grand Güler Hotel** (☎ 229 2221, fax 224 4509) is a good choice with clean, modern, air-con singles/doubles, with TV and bath for US$30/45.

The three-star **Turistik Oteli** (☎ 224 7550, fax 224 4274, Ziya Gökalp Bulvarı 7), a block north-west of the Dağ Kapısı, has been welcoming guests since 1953. Rooms are rather small but spotlessly maintained for US$45/75. There's a swimming pool at the back and guarded parking.

The **Demir Otel** (☎ 228 8800, fax 228 8809, İzzet Paşa Caddesi 8) claims to be four-star but although the rooms are satisfactory, they're often cramped and facilities are limited. Rooms cost US$40/60, including breakfast.

Much better is the nearby **Büyük Otel** (☎ 228 1295, fax 221 2444, İnönü Caddesi 4) with clean, modern rooms with bath for US$25/35. Some have fine views over the old town, as does the roof terrace and restaurant.

Places to Stay – Top End

Without doubt the most atmospheric place to stay is **Otel Büyük Kervansaray** (☎ 228 9606, fax 223 9522, Gazi Caddesi) in the 16th-century Deliller Han, a converted caravanserai inside the Mardin Kapısı. The rooms are small but cosy, with air-con and TV. There's a swimming pool in the rear courtyard. Singles/doubles cost a very reasonable US$50/75, including breakfast, but don't let that seduce you into drinking in the delightful courtyard – there's a 500% mark-up on a drink! Fixed dinner menus in the restaurant, converted out of a camel stable, are US$25, steep by Turkish standards.

If you absolutely must have luxury, Diyarbakır's best is the *Dedeman Hotel* (☎ 299 0000, fax 224 7353, Elazığ Caddesi, Belediye Saray Yanı), an ugly high-rise in the most dismal surroundings, convenient only for the Arkeoloji Müzesi. Rooms cost US$120/155.

Places to Eat

A stroll along Kıbrıs Caddesi reveals plenty of small, cheap places to eat, often featuring goat's head soup. One of the best places is the *Sarmaşık Ocakbaşı* which has a selection of dishes, but specialises in ocakbaşı (grills) – you can sit right beside the grill, watch the chef, and eat as he hands you the skewers. A *şiş kebap* (roast skewered lamb) dinner costs about US$3 to US$5. Also popular is the long-lived *Büryan Salonu* nearby. To wind up your meal drop in on the *Ünlü Şeyhmus* pastry shop and enjoy a portion of baklava and chewy Maraş-style ice cream for US$1.25.

In the evenings men set up *kebap stands* at the Dağ Kapısı end of Kıbrıs Caddesi. Those with sensitive stomachs should probably walk past quickly but the smells are nigh on irresistible.

Near the Demir Otel, *Şanlı Urfa Kebap Evi* (İzzet Paşa Caddesi 4) doesn't look much, but descend to the basement at lunch time and you'll find the locals lapping up bowls of ayran and tucking into roast peppers and delicious köfte, always a good sign. You won't pay more than US$3 for your meal.

Another fine place to eat is the *Sinan Et Lokantası*, not far from Dağ Kapısı. Sitting on its vine-shaded terrace, sipping a cold Efes beer and watching the street-life below is one of the most pleasant ways to wind up a long day's sightseeing. The *Pınar Ocakbaşı ve Et Lokantası* (Kıbrıs Caddesi) also has an airy terrace, though its unprotected edge is dangerous for children.

For other places where you can drink with your meal, cut across the Selahaddin-i Eyubi Çarşısı (the litter-covered modern precinct across from the Dağ Kapısı) and you'll see a line-up of licensed restaurants. For after-dinner drinks, turn down any side street to find Diyarbakır's gazinos. If you decide to do this, it's advisable to be a bit careful what you talk about and who you befriend.

Getting There & Away

Air Turkish Airlines (☎ 228 8401, fax 228 8403), İnönü Caddesi 8, next to the Büyük Hotel, serves the city's Kaplaner airport with daily nonstop flights to and from Ankara and İstanbul. A taxi to the airport costs about US$4.

Bus Many bus companies have ticket offices in town on Kıbrıs or İnönü Caddesis or

Services from Diyarbakır's Otogar

destination	fare (US$)	time (hr)	distance (km)	daily services
Adana	12	8	550	several buses
Ankara	18	13	945	several buses
Batman	2.50	1½	85	frequent dolmuşes
Erzurum	13	8	485	several buses
Kahta (Nemrut Dağı)	6	3	192	several buses
Malatya	5	5	260	frequent buses
Şanlıurfa	5	3	190	frequent buses
Sivas	9	10	500	several buses
Van	9	7	410	several buses

in other spots near the Dağ Kapısı. Free *servis* minibuses will ferry you to the otogar. There's a separate minibus terminal outside Urfa Kapısı, with services to Mardin, Elazığ, Malatya and Siverek (to get to Kahta without going right round the lake via Adıyaman). Other local buses leave from the Selahaddin-i Eyubi Çarşısı, the precinct across from the Dağ Kapısı; come here for dolmuşes to the otogar (US$0.25). Details of some daily services on the main routes are listed in the table on the previous page.

Train Train services to the south-east are neither speedy nor reliable. You're better off taking a bus. The *Güney Ekspresi* departs İstanbul (Haydarpaşa) on Tuesday, Thursday Friday or Sunday at 8.05 pm, stopping in Ankara, Kayseri, Sivas and Malatya and Elazığ Junction, before continuing on to Diyarbakır and Kurtalan (east of Diyarbakır).

MARDİN
☎ 482 • pop 62,000 • elevation 1325m
About 175km east of Şanlıurfa and 100km south of Diyarbakır, Mardin is a beautiful ancient town crowned with a castle and an immense radar dome, overlooking the vast, roasted plains of Mesopotamia to Syria.

In another time and another place travellers would flock to Mardin to explore streets of honey-coloured stone houses that trip down the side of the hillside giving it something of the feel of old Jerusalem. Unfortunately, after the Gulf War tourism to Mardin virtually dried up and even now as you stroll in the wonderful bazaar every eye will be upon you.

Once the town was home to a large Christian community and there are still a few Syrian Christian families to keep the church alive. On the outskirts is the monastery of Deyrul Zafaran where Aramaic, the language of Jesus, is still the liturgical tongue.

Mardin is not well equipped with hotels; if you value your comfort it might be better to stick with a day trip from Diyarbakır, although to do so would be to miss out on Mardin's particular beauty.

History
As with Diyarbakır, Mardin's history is one of disputes between rival armies over dozens and dozens of centuries, though in recent years the only dispute that anyone really cared about was the one between the PKK and the government. A castle has stood on this hill from time immemorial and the Turkish army still finds the site useful.

Assyrian Christians settled here during the 5th century. The Arabs occupied Mardin between 640 and 1104. After that, it had a succession of Seljuk Turkish, Kurdish, Mongol and Persian overlords, until the Ottomans under Sultan Selim the Grim took it in 1517.

Orientation & Information
Perched on a hillside, Mardin has one long main street, Birinci Caddesi (1st Street), running for about 2km from the Belediye Garajı at the western end of town and then forking suddenly, after the main square, Cumhuriyet Alanı. The left fork leads on to Konak, a small square with the hükümet konağı and military buildings at the eastern end; the right fork drops steeply to the area where the bus companies have their offices.

Everything you'll need is along or just off Birinci Caddesi (a one-way street), and dolmuşes and city buses run along it to save you the effort of walking. If you're driving your own car, you can park in Cumhuriyet Alanı.

The tourist office (☎ 212 7406, fax 212 5845) is at Cumhuriyet Alanı 515.

Things to See & Do
Mardin's most obvious attraction is its rambling **bazaar** which parallels Birinci Caddesi one block down the hill. Here donkeys are still the main form of transport and you'll see them decked out in all the finery you sometimes see on sale in carpet shops. Look out also for saddle repairers who seem to be able to restore even the shabbiest examples.

Strolling through the bazaar, look out for the secluded **Ulu Cami**, an 11th-century Iraqi Seljuk structure, which suffered badly during the Kurdish rebellion of 1832.

Mardin Müzesi may be prominently positioned on Cumhuriyet Meydanı but unless you come in a group you are unlikely to gain admittance. Still, you can admire the building, second only in beauty to what must surely be Turkey's most gorgeous **post office**, housed in a carefully restored 17th-century caravanserai with carvings like frills around the windows and teardrops in stone dripping down the walls.

Heading east from the main square, look for steps on the left (north) which lead to the **Sultan İsa Medresesi**, dating from 1385 and the town's prime architectural attraction, with an imposing recessed doorway.

The **Kasım Paşa Medresesi**, below the main street near the western end of town, was built in the 15th century.

Look out, too, for the 14th-century **Latifiye Camii** and for the **Kırklar Kilisesi** (Forty Martyrs' church) though you'll probably find both locked.

One Nature or Two?

In the 6th century AD, Jacobus Baradeus, bishop of Edessa (Urfa), had a difference of opinion with the patriarch in Constantinople over the divine nature of Christ.

The patriarch, and official doctrine, held that Christ had two natures, being both fully divine and fully human. The bishop held that He had only one (mono) nature (physis), that of being divine. Branded a Monophysite heretic and excommunicated, the bishop promptly founded a church of his own, which came to be called the Jacobite (or Syrian Orthodox) church after its founder.

At the same time and for the same reason, the Armenian Orthodox Church, the Coptic Church in Egypt and the Ethiopian Church were established as independent churches.

In the case of the Jacobites, control from Constantinople soon ceased to be a problem, as the Arabs swept in and took control, allowing the Monophysites to practise their religion as they chose.

Today the monks living in the Tür Abdin monasteries of Mardin and Midyat are successors to the man who was prepared to brave excommunication over this fine difference of theological opinion.

Places to Stay

Mardin has just three hotels, none of them ideal. For any semblance of comfort you must head for the three-star *Otel Bilen* (☎ 212 5568, fax 212 2575), 1.5km out on the outskirts near the highway, where spacious if darkly decorated rooms with TV and baths cost US$20/33 a single/double. To get into the centre, cross the highway and flag down any dolmuş.

In the lovely old town centre there's the poor old *Hotel Bayraktar* (☎ 212 1338), on the main street facing Cumhuriyet Alanı. It would be hard to imagine a hotel that looked more sorry for itself, but if you pick one of the rooms at the back the stunning view down onto the bazaar and out over the plains might just make up for the abject state of the wiring, plumbing and furniture. Rooms cost US$7/9.

Tucked away up some stairs on the left as you head along the main street is the tiny *Otel Başak* (☎ 212 6246, Birinci Caddesi 360), where very simple rooms are at least clean and fan-equipped. Beds cost US$9 a head.

Places to Eat

Mardin has some interesting local specialities, some of which reflect the influence of Syria. At the *Pınay Kafeterya* upstairs in the shopping block immediately in front of the Hotel Bayraktar, and at the *Turistik Et Lokantası* on its other side, you can sample *sembusek* (a folded pide sandwich) and *kaburga dolması* (lamb and rice with almonds). Down in the bazaar area look out for lokantas serving *etli pilav*, a rice and lamb dish.

In the *pastry shop* near the Hotel Bayraktar you can also try *taş kadayıf*, a sticky sweet stuffed with walnuts.

East along Birinci Caddesi are several *tea gardens*, the best of them with a fine view of the beautiful PTT across the road.

Getting There & Away

There is now an airport 20km south of Mardin but at the time of writing there were only two flights a week to Ankara so its usefulness to visitors was strictly limited.

For reservations call ☎ 213 0315, fax 212 2575. An airport bus leaves from the THY office right beside the Otel Bilen (US$2).

Minibuses run every hour between Mardin's Belediye Garajı and the minibus terminal just outside Diyarbakır's Urfa Kapısı (US$2.50). The journey takes around 1½ hours.

Most other buses leave from just east of Cumhuriyet Meydanı, at the bottom of the hill east of the centre. Several daily buses connect Mardin with Urfa (US$8.50, three hours) but, heading west, they're often already full when they arrive in Mardin; you'd be well advised to book a ticket as soon as you arrive.

Minibuses to Midyat (US$2.50, one hour) and Nusaybin (the Syrian border; US$1.75) also leave from this area. From around 4 pm services start to dry up so you're best off making an early start.

Organised Tours While the situation around Mardin/Midyat remains uncertain you might prefer to travel in an escorted group. It's worth inquiring at Harran-Nemrut Tours in Urfa (for details see Information in that section) since Özcan Aslan occasionally organises two-day tours taking in Harran and the Deyrul Zafaran and Morgabriel monasteries. Tours cost US$50 per person but require a minimum of six people.

AROUND MARDİN
Deyrul Zafaran

About 6km along a good but narrow road in the rocky hills east of the town stands the monastery of Mar Hanania, called Deyrul Zafaran (Saffron Monastery in Arabic), supposedly because saffron crocuses were used in the mortar. The monastery was once the seat of the Syrian Orthodox patriarchate, and although this has now moved to Damascus, it still has the modest trappings due to the patriarch and continues to act as the local orphanage.

In AD 495 the first monastery was built on a site previously dedicated to the worship of the sun. Destroyed by the Persians in 607, it was rebuilt, only to be looted by Tamerlane six centuries later.

Shortly after you enter the walled enclosure via a portal bearing a Syriac (a dialect of Aramaic) inscription, one of the orphans will volunteer their services as a guide. First they'll show you the **original sanctuary**, an eerie underground chamber with a ceiling of huge, closely fitted stones held up as if by magic, without the aid of mortar. This room was allegedly used by sun worshippers, who viewed their god rising through a window at the eastern end. A niche on the southern wall is said to have been for sacrifices.

The guide then leads you through a pair of 300-year-old doors to the **tombs** of the patriarchs and metropolitans who have served here.

In the chapel, the **patriarch's throne** to the left of the altar bears the names of all the patriarchs who have served the monastery since it was refounded in 792. To the right of the altar is the **throne of the metropolitan**. The present **stone altar** replaces a wooden one that burnt down about half a century ago. The walls may be fairly plain but are adorned with wonderful paintings and wall hangings. Services are held in Aramaic.

In the next rooms you'll see **litters** used to transport the church dignitaries and a **baptismal font**. In a small side room is a 300-year-old **wooden throne**. The floor **mosaic** is about 1500 years old.

A flight of stairs leads to a suite of very simple guest rooms for travellers and those coming for meditation. The patriarch's small, simple bedroom and parlour are also up here.

As you leave, take a moment to enjoy the fine view of the mountains. Other monasteries, now in ruins, once stood further up the slope. Some of Deyrul Zafaran's water comes from near these ruins, through underground channels excavated many centuries ago. At the end of the tour, be ready to tip the guide.

You can visit the monastery between 8.30 and 11.30 am and between 1.30 and 3.30 pm any day. There's no public transport so you must take a taxi. Hopeful drivers wait outside the bus company offices in Mardin and will ask US$9 to run you there and back and wait while you look round.

Midyat

About 65km east of Mardin is Midyat, a sprawling settlement, part prosaic modern Turkey, part gorgeous old town with wonderfully carved old houses to make up for the absence of a hillside setting to match Mardin's. Dolmuşes from Mardin will drop you off at a crossroads, with the old town tucked away behind a row of jewellery shops in front of you. It's a rabbit warren of a place, its alleyways lined with **honey-coloured houses** whose demure doorways open onto huge courtyards surrounded by intricately carved walls, windows and recesses. The **church** is kept locked and the key is unlikely to be available.

Midyat has the small, basic *Otel Yuvam* (☎ 462 2531, *Dörtyol Caddesi 1*), where waterless doubles with fan are US$9. It's beside the roundabout in new Midyat where the Mardin dolmuşes first stop.

Morgabriel

About 18km east of Midyat, Morgabriel (Deyrul Umur) Monastery rises like a mirage from its desert-like surroundings. Though much restored, the monastery dates back to the 5th century and has some fine floor and ceiling mosaics. Morgabriel is home to the archbishop of Tür Abdin (the surrounding plateau), although these days he presides over a much diminished flock. Fortunately, life for the residents seems to be looking up and there should be no problem about visiting. Who knows – any day now it may even be possible for those in need of a retreat to pass the night in the lovely new guesthouse.

To get to the monastery take a dolmuş heading east along the Cizre road and ask to be dropped at the signposted road junction, from where it's a 2.5km uphill walk to the gate. At the time of writing there were no official yellow taxis in Midyat although *özel* (special) private taxis will probably run you out and back for around US$17, an hour's waiting time included. Ask around.

BATMAN & HASANKEYF

☎ 488 • pop 213,000

For most people finding a place called Batman on the map sets the pulse racing. It's a disappointment, then, to discover that the Turkish Batman is a dreary modern town, transformed from a tiny village to a sprawl after oil was discovered in the Batı Raman mountains in 1948; the curious name appears to be nothing more than an abbreviation of the mountain. Still, Batman has all the facilities a traveller could want: banks, hotels, restaurants and – or so it's claimed – no less than 40 Internet cafes.

You come to Batman not for the town itself, but as a base for visiting nearby Hasankeyf, a gorgeous honey-coloured village clinging to the rocks of a gorge above the Tigris River, a sort of Cappadocia in miniature where some of the 5,000 inhabitants still live a troglodyte lifestyle. Not for much longer though. Despite its beauty and venerable history, Hasankeyf is slated to vanish forever beneath the waters of Turkey's latest dam. That this should be is hard enough to believe. That the British government should still (at the time of writing) be considering underwriting this piece of environmental vandalism is nothing short of scandalous.

Things to See

As you arrive in Hasankeyf you'll see on the right-hand side of the road the conical **Zeynel Bey Türbesi**, isolated in a field near the river. This turquoise-tiled tomb was built in the mid-15th century for Zeynel, son of the Akkoyunlu governor, and it's a rare survival from this period.

A modern bridge now spans the Tigris but as you cross you'll see, to the right, the broken arches of the **Eski Köprüsü** (Old Bridge), their size giving some idea of the importance of Hasankeyf in the period immediately before the arrival of the Ottomans.

Across the bridge a sign to the right points to the **Kale** (Castle) and **Mağaralar** (Caves). As you walk along the road you'll see on the right the **El-Risk Cami**, dating from 1409 and sporting a beautiful, slender minaret similar to those in Şanlıurfa and Mardin. Just past the mosque, the road forks. The right fork leads down to the banks of the river with a great wall of rock soaring up on the left. The left fork cuts through a rocky defile, the rock faces pitted with caves. Slippery stone steps lead up on the right to the castle.

You quickly come to the finely decorated main gate to the castle, built in the 14th century on a site that had probably been occupied since Byzantine times. Beyond the gate are caves, which youthful guides will describe as shops and houses. Eventually you pass through a more ruined second gate and emerge on top of the rock, facing the ruins of the **Small Palace** and with superb views down over the river.

Continue along the top of the rock, passing the remains of a small mosque on the right, and then cut in past the **Big Palace** and climb up to the substantial remains of the **Ulu Cami**.

Although there are a couple of cafes on the way up, it's a tough walk so it's wise to come equipped with hat and water.

Places to Stay & Eat

At the time of writing there were no hotels in Hasankeyf although if you ask at the *Oğretmenevi* they may be able to accommodate you. Batman has hotels to suit all budgets (particularly those of oil men). A reliable choice in the town centre is the *Altınbaşak (☎ 213 9153, Cumhuriyet Caddesi 25),* where comfortable, spacious singles/ doubles with bath cost US$12.50/21.

Batman also has the usual range of kebapçıs and other places to eat. But few things could be more pleasurable than lunching in Hasankeyf where a series of *çardaks* (leafy-roofed shelters) have been set up along the foreshore. Tables stand right in the river so while you tuck into your fish you can soak your lower limbs in the icy clear water of the Tigris. There's no alcohol and it's probably wise to check the price of fish before ordering, but a normal meal of grilled meat with salad and a cold drink is unlikely to come to more than US$3.

Getting There & Away

There are regular dolmuşes to Batman from Diyarbakır (US$2.50, 1½ hours), or you can pick up a minibus to Batman from Ziyaret on the main Diyarbakır to Tatvan road (US$2, 1½ hours). Frequent minibuses run from Batman to Midyat and Nusaybin, transiting Hasankeyf (US$0.85, 40 minutes).

BİTLİS
☎ 434

About 345km east of Diyarbakır is Bitlis, an interesting but dusty and somewhat chaotic old town squeezed into the narrow valley of a stream. A **castle** dominates the town, and two ancient bridges span the stream. The **Ulu Cami** was built in 1126, while the **Şerefiye Camii** and **Saraf Han** (a caravanserai) date from the 16th century. The town was the capital of a semi-autonomous Kurdish principality in late Ottoman times.

Up the hill at the eastern side of the town, on the left (northern) side of the road, is an old caravanserai, the **Pabsin Hanı,** built by the Seljuks in the 13th century.

On the way to Bitlis, about 88km east of Diyarbakır, is the town of Silvan from where it's another 22km to Malabadi. Just east of here is the Batman Suyu, a stream spanned by a beautifully restored humpback **stone bridge** built by the Artukid Turks in 1146 and thought to have the longest span (37m) of any such bridge in existence.

TATVAN
☎ 434 • pop 54,000

About 26km from Bitlis is Tatvan, the western port for Lake Van steamers. Several kilometres long and just a few blocks wide, Tatvan is not much to look at but its setting on the shores of Lake Van (backed by bare mountains streaked with snow) is magnificent. Most people pass through Tatvan on their way to Van but it's well worth stopping to visit spectacular Nemrut Dağı (see The North Shore section later in this chapter) to the north. Fortunately everything you'll need (hotels, restaurants, the PTT and the bus company offices) huddles together in the town centre. The tourist office (☎ 827 6301, fax 827 6300) is at Zirağı Caddesi No 6, beside the Tatvan Kardelen hotel.

Places to Stay

Unfortunately Tatvan is going the way of many smaller Turkish towns where good medium-priced accommodation is vanishing as the better hotels upgrade and the older ones are left to disintegrate.

Right next to the belediye, the three-star **Tatvan Kardelen** (*☎/fax 827 9500*) offers spacious rooms, some of them with bathtubs and decent views. Nice reading lights, shame about the tepid water. Few travellers in transit would want to pay the posted prices of US$39/60 a single/double. Barter hard and they'll probably cave in.

Otherwise, a few basic places cater for budget travellers; among the better ones are the lakeside **Hotel Üstün** (*☎ 827 9014, Hal Caddesi 23*), where beds cost US$7 a head, and the cheery **Akgün Otel** (*☎ 827 2373, Hal Caddesi 51*), charging US$9.50 a head. **Hotel Altlar** (*☎ 827 4096, fax 827 4098, Cumhuriyet Caddesi 164*) has beds for US$10 per person, including breakfast, in presentable rooms with comfy-looking beds.

Getting There & Away

At the time of writing the *Vangölü Ekspresi* was still not running east of Elazığ because of security worries. Should the situation change Tatvan's train station is about 2km north-east of the centre along the road to Ahlat and Adilcevaz.

Without the need to fit in with the trains, the Turkish Maritime Lines ferry from Tatvan to Van crosses the lake to a schedule known only to its captain; unless you've got endless time for hanging about, forget it and take the bus round the southern shore of the lake (US$3.50, two hours, 156km).

VAN GÖLÜ

By far the most conspicuous feature on the map of south-eastern Turkey is Lake Van (Van Gölü), which was formed when the Nemrut Dağı volcano north of Tatvan (not the one with the statues) blocked its natural outflow. The water level is now maintained by evaporation, which results in a high mineral concentration and extreme alkalinity: clothes washed in the lake come clean without soap.

The water at the eastern extremity of the lake near Van itself is polluted, but the beaches at Gevaş and Edremit are good for

The Van Monster

Lake Van is too vast not to have spawned a powerful mythology, and one of the most enduring of the myths tells of a Van Gölü Canavarı (Lake Van Monster).

Rumours of the existence of this Nessie lookalike first surfaced in the 1960s when a newspaper article referred to an otter-like animal, perhaps 2m long, spotted swimming in the lake. Since then, of course, the stories have got wilder. Sometimes the monster is said to resemble a horse; at other times it's more like a dinosaur. But the list of sightings gets longer and there have been some tentative – and unsuccessful – attempts to track the beast to its lair.

In the meantime, Van is dining out on its famous phantom, with shops about town selling Canavar Salam (Monster Salami). The beast has also acquired a range of fantastic nicknames, among them Barış (Peace), Van Gülü (the Rose of Van) and Suların Kralı (King of the Waters). These days even Van's footballers call themselves the Canavarlar (Monsters) and wear a blue and white strip in Vannie's honour.

MICK WELDON

a swim. Don't go in if you have sunburn or open cuts or sores as the alkaline water will burn them intensely.

The South Shore

Travelling south around the lake from Tatvan to Van, the scenery is beautiful, but there's little reason to stop except at a point 8km west of Gevaş, where the 10th century Church of the Holy Cross at Akdamar is a glorious must.

Akdamar Akdamar Kilisesi, or the Church of the Holy Cross, is one of the marvels of Armenian architecture. It's perched on an island 3km out in the lake, and motorboats ferry sightseers back and forth.

In AD 921 Gagik Artzruni, King of Vaspurkan, built a palace, church and monastery on the island. Little remains of the palace and monastery, but the church walls are in superb condition and the wonderful relief carvings are among the masterworks of Armenian art.

If you're familiar with biblical stories, you'll immediately recognise Adam and Eve, Jonah and the Whale, David and Goliath, Abraham about to sacrifice Isaac, Daniel in the Lions' Den, Samson etc. The frescoes inside the church are rapidly vanishing, but their vagueness and frailty seem in keeping with the shaded, partly ruined interior.

North of Akdamar another even more isolated and forgotten 11th-century Armenian church stands on the island of **Çarpanak**.

Gevaş Like Ahlat, Gevaş has a cemetery full of tombstones dating back to the 14th to 17th centuries. Most notable is the polygonal **Halime Hatun Türbesi**, built in 1358 for a female member of the Karakoyunlu dynasty.

Edremit About 15km before you reach Van you'll pass through Edremit, a small lakeside settlement with the feel of a seaside resort: all Lilos, beach balls and ice cream.

Places to Stay & Eat Although there are several basic camping grounds at Edremit, by far the best bet is to head straight for the *Akdamar Camping ve Restaurant* (☎ 432-622 2525), immediately opposite the ferry departure point for Akdamar island. Not only is the camp site here raised up, with fine views of the lake, but you'll be in the best position to see when other would-be visitors to Akdamar arrive. The restaurant has a terrace with lake views and an indoor

area in case of bad weather. A meal of meat stew with peppers and tomatoes, rice and salad will cost about US$3.50. To pitch a tent costs US$1 a head.

Getting There & Away Dolmuşes run the 44km from near Beş Yol in Van to Akdamar harbour for US$1.25. If no direct transport is available, take a dolmuş to Gevaş for US$0.90 and get out when it cuts inland from the lake. If it's not too hot you could walk the remaining 8km along the lakeshore to the boat dock.

Alternatively, agree a price all the way to Akdamar before you board the dolmuş in Van. In Gevaş itself drivers are likely to demand US$3 for the onward journey.

Boats to the island run as and when traffic warrants it; except at the height of the season, your best bet is to come on Saturday or Sunday when Vanlıs head to Akdamar to picnic. Provided others are there to share the cost a return ticket for the 20-minute voyage and admission to the island costs US$4.50.

Getting to Çarpanak is harder; the boatmen are likely to want US$150 before they'll consider the voyage.

The North Shore

If anything the journey around the north shore of Lake Van from Tatvan to Van, with first Nemrut Dağı and then Suphan Dağı looming beside the road, is more beautiful than going around the south shore. The road is rough in parts, however, so aim to get a seat as far forward in the bus as possible. Security checks become more frequent once you pass Erciş.

Nemrut Dağı (Mt Nemrut) The Nemrut Dağı rising to the north of Tatvan should not be confused with the more famous one near Kahta (with the giant heads on top). This Nemrut Dağı (3050m) is an inactive volcano with five crater lakes on its summit. It was outflow from the Nemrut volcano that dammed Lake Van, causing it to spread to its present vast area of 3750 sq km.

A trip up Mt Nemrut is an unforgettable experience, not least for the fine views back over Lake Van. On the summit the scenery is almost completely unspoilt. In spring and early summer the lower slopes of the mountain are a sea of sweet-smelling wild flowers. Midweek, the only company you're likely to have is the shepherds with their flocks (and dogs) and the hoopoes, nuthatches, skylarks and other birds.

Dolmuşes run up the mountain whenever enough picnicking Tatvalis are interested (mainly weekends). Alone, you may have to hire a taxi from Tatvan for a flat US$35 return including waiting time. The taxi driver will be able to point out a natural hot water bath, a *buz mağarası* (ice cave) in which a bottle of water will freeze in half an hour, the curious 'chimneys' of steam, said to be good for rheumatism, and the various different lakes.

With your own transport, leave Tatvan by the road around the lake and then turn left towards Bitlis and then immediately right following a sign saying 'Nemrut 13km'. The road is rough but should be passable in an ordinary car except in wet weather. At the time of writing there were no facilities of any kind on the mountain.

Ahlat Continue north by car or dolmuş along the lake shore for 42km and you'll come to the small town of Ahlat, famous for its Seljuk Turkish tombs and graveyard.

Founded during the reign of Caliph Omar (AD 581–644), Ahlat became a Seljuk stronghold in the 1060s. When the Seljuk sultan Alp Arslan rode out to meet the Byzantine emperor Romanus Diogenes in battle on the field of Manzikert (see the following Malazgirt section), Ahlat was his base.

Later, Ahlat had an extraordinarily eventful history even for Anatolia, with emir defeating prince and king driving out emir, hence perhaps the fame of its cemeteries.

The fortress on the shore was built during the reign of Süleyman the Magnificent.

Just west of Ahlat you'll see the overgrown 13th-century polygonal **Usta Şakirt Kümbeti** to the right (south) of the highway, in the midst of a field near some houses and a new mosque.

Across the highway is a little museum, and beyond it a unique **Seljuk cemetery** (Selçuk Mezarlığı), with stele-like headstones of lichen-covered grey or red volcanic tuff with intricate web patterns and bands of Kufic lettering. It's thought that Ahlat stonemasons were employed on other great stoneworking projects, such as the decoration of the great mosque at Divriği, near Sivas.

Over the centuries earthquakes, wind and water have set the stones at all angles, so they stand out like broken teeth. Each and every one has a rook as sentinel, and tortoises cruise amid the ruins.

On the north-western side of the graveyard is the beautiful and unusual **Bayındır Kümbeti ve Camii** (Bayındır Kümbet and Mosque, 1477), with a colonnaded porch and its own small prayer room.

The **museum** has a few archaeological bits and bobs which barely justify even the small entry fee. However, it does provide a place to leave your bags while you look around the cemetery, provided you arrive during opening hours (9 am to noon and 1 to 5 pm daily except Monday).

Continue walking towards Ahlat and you will come to a sign on the left pointing to the **Çifte Kümbet** (Twin Tomb), clearly visible across the field.

Malazgirt About 60km north of Ahlat is Malazgirt (Manzikert), where, on 26 August 1071, the Seljuk Turkish sultan Alp Arslan and his armies decisively defeated the Byzantine emperor Romanus Diogenes in battle, throwing Anatolia open to Turkish migration and conquest.

The Seljuks went on to establish the Sultanate of Rum with its capital at Konya, and other nomadic Turkish tribes followed them out of central Asia and Iran. Eventually a band of Turkish warriors following a leader named Osman arrived to found the state that would become the vast Ottoman Empire. It all started here, in 1071, when the heir of the Caesars was defeated by a Turkish emir.

Adilcevaz About 25km east of Ahlat is the town of Adilcevaz, once a Urartian town but now dominated by a great Seljuk Turkish fortress, the **Kef Kalesi**, and the even greater bulk of **Süphan Dağı** (4434m).

Meltwater from the year-round snow-fields on Süphan Dağı flows down to Adilcevaz, making its surroundings lush and fertile. As you enter the town along the shore, the highway passes the nice little **Tuğrul Bey Camii**, built in the 13th century and still used for daily prayer. Now that life in the south-east is slowly returning to normal, it is once again possible to climb Süphan Dağı in summer.

Erciş If you continue around the lake for another 64km, you'll pass through Erciş, a forgettable modern town covering settlements that date back to Urartian times. At this point the roads diverge and you can head south for Van (98km) or north for Doğubayazıt (137km).

Getting There & Away The big bus companies take the shortest route from Tatvan to Van which goes south of Lake Van. If you want to travel around the north shore you'll probably have to break your journey into sections. Regular dolmuşes run from opposite the PTT in Tatvan to Ahlat (US$1.25, 45 minutes, 40km). From Ahlat to Adilcevaz takes just half an hour and costs US$0.75. From Adilcevaz to Erciş takes one hour and costs US$1.75. Buses that run between Erciş and Van charge US$2.75 and take 1¼ hours. Most travel in the morning.

VAN
☎ 432 • pop 400,000 • elevation 1727m

Almost 100km from Tatvan across vast Lake Van lies Van, once the eastern railhead on the line to Iran, and now a sprawling modern town doing its best to put a troubled past behind it.

Lake Van aside, Van's main claim to fame is Van Kalesi (Van Castle or the Rock of Van), which boasts several long cuneiform inscriptions from the days when Van was the Urartian capital. The town is also home to a unique breed of white cat with one blue and one yellow eye. These days such cats fetch so high a price tag that their owners tend to keep them locked up indoors; the nearest you're likely to come to seeing them are the fluffy photographs adorning every carpet

shop window and the faintly absurd statue of mother cat and kitten on the road out towards the lake. The Van cat is said to be adapted to swimming in the lake – as is a more recent addition to the local fauna, the Van Canavarı, a virtual monster which looks set to give Scotland's Nessie a run for her money (see the boxed text, 'The Van Monster' earlier).

A day trip to the south-east takes you past the ancient Urartian city at Çavuştepe and the craggy mountain fortress of Hoşap. Beyond them lies troubled Hakkari, deep in the alpine scenery of the Cilo Dağı mountains and likely to be unsuitable for tourism for some years to come.

History
The Kingdom of Urartu, the biblical Ararat, flourished from the 13th to the 7th centuries BC. Its capital, Tushpa, was near present-day Van. The Urartians were traders and farmers, highly advanced in the art of metalwork and stone masonry. They borrowed much of their culture, including cuneiform writing, from the neighbouring Assyrians with whom they were more or less permanently at war. The powerful Assyrians never subdued the Urartians, but when several waves of Cimmerians, Scythians and Medes swept into Urartu and joined in the battle, the kingdom met its downfall.

Later the region was resettled by a people whom the Persians called Armenians. By the 6th century BC it was governed by Persian and Mede satraps.

The history of the Armenians is one of repeated subjugation to other peoples as they occupied a strategic crossroads at the nexus of the three great empires of Syria, Persia and Anatolia. Tigranes the Great succeeded in gaining control of the kingdom from its Parthian overlords in 95 BC, but his short-lived kingdom was soon crushed in the clash of armies from Rome and Parthia.

In the 8th century AD, the Arab armies flooded through from the south, forcing the Armenian prince to take refuge on Akdamar Island. Unable to fend off the Arabs, he agreed to pay tribute to the caliph. When the Arabs retreated, the Byzantines and Persians took their place, and overlordship of

Armenia seesawed between them as one or the other gained military advantage.

After defeating the Byzantines in 1071 at Manzikert, north of Lake Van, the Seljuk Turks marched in to found the Sultanate of Rum and were followed by a flood of Turkoman nomads. Domination of eastern Anatolia by the powerful Karakoyunlu and Akkoyunlu Turkish emirs followed and continued until the coming of the Ottomans in 1468.

During WWI, Armenian guerrilla bands intent on founding an independent Armenian state collaborated with the Russians to defeat the Ottoman armies in the east. From then on the Armenians, formerly loyal subjects of the sultan, were viewed as traitors by the Turks. Bitter fighting between Turkish and Kurdish forces on the one side and Armenian and Russian on the other brought devastation to the entire region and to Van.

The Ottomans destroyed the old city of Van (near Van Kalesi) before the Russians occupied it in 1915. Ottoman forces counterattacked but were unable to drive the invaders out, and Van remained under Russian occupation until the armistice of 1917. After the founding of the Turkish

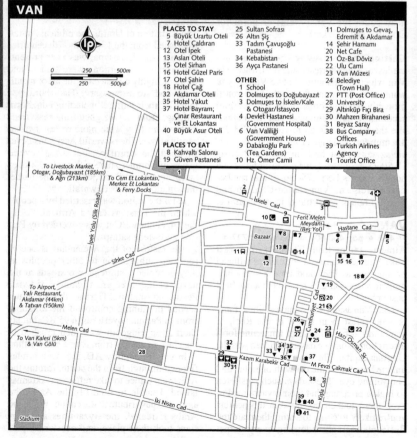

VAN

PLACES TO STAY
5 Büyük Urartu Oteli
7 Hotel Çaldıran
12 Otel İpek
13 Aslan Oteli
15 Otel Sirhan
16 Hotel Güzel Paris
17 Otel Şahin
18 Hotel Çağ
32 Akdamar Oteli
35 Hotel Yakut
37 Hotel Bayram;
    Çınar Restaurant
    ve Et Lokantası
40 Büyük Asur Oteli

PLACES TO EAT
8 Kahvaltı Salonu
19 Güven Pastanesi
25 Sultan Sofrası
26 Altın Şiş
33 Tadım Çavuşoğlu
    Pastanesi
34 Kebabistan
36 Ayça Pastanesi

OTHER
1 School
2 Dolmuşes to Doğubayazıt
3 Dolmuşes to İskele/Kale
    & Otogar/İstasyon
4 Devlet Hastanesi
    (Government Hospital)
6 Van Valiliği
    (Government House)
9 Dabakoğlu Park
    (Tea Gardens)
10 Hz. Ömer Camii

11 Dolmuşes to Gevaş,
    Edremit & Akdamar
14 Şehir Hamamı
20 Net Cafe
21 Öz-Ba Döviz
22 Ulu Cami
23 Van Müzesi
24 Belediye
    (Town Hall)
27 PTT (Post Office)
28 University
29 Altınküp Fıçı Bira
30 Mahzen Birahanesi
31 Beyaz Saray
38 Bus Company
    Offices
39 Turkish Airlines
    Agency
41 Tourist Office

To Livestock Market, Otogar, Doğubayazıt (185km) & Ağrı (213km)

To Cem Et Lokantası, Merkez Et Lokantası & Ferry Docks

İpek Yolu (Silk Road)

İskele Cad

Ferit Melen Meydanı (Beş Yol)

Hastane Cad

Bazaar

Sihke Cad

To Airport, Yalı Restaurant, Akdamar (44km) & Tatvan (150km)

Melen Cad

To Van Kalesi (5km) & Van Gölü

Cumhuriyet Cad

Hacı Osman Sk

Kazım Karabekir Cad

M Fevzi Çakmak Cad

Kışla Cad

İki Nisan Cad

Stadium

0   250   500m
0   250   500yd

Republic, a new planned city of Van was built 4km east of the old site.

Orientation & Information

Although its present-day appearance hardly matches up to the exotic images conjured up by its history, the highway passing between the town and the lake was once the ancient Silk Road (İpek Yolu). The city's otogar is on the north-western outskirts, just off the Silk Road, and most bus companies operate *servis* buses to get you there from the town centre.

In the city itself, the main commercial street is Cumhuriyet Caddesi, where you'll find banks with ATMs, hotels and restaurants. At the northern end of Cumhuriyet Caddesi, where it meets four other streets, is Ferit Melen Meydanı, otherwise known as Beş Yol (Five Roads). Here you'll find several dolmuş and bus stops. An imposing landmark around which many hotels are gathered is the barracks-like Van valiliği (provincial government building).

The main train station is north-west of the centre near the otogar, with another station, İskele İstasyonu, several kilometres to the north-west on the shore. At the time of writing no passenger trains were servicing Van.

Van's best known tourist sight, Van Kalesi, is about 5km west of the centre. Every day, except Sunday, you can also drop in on the livestock market which takes place from early in the morning just north of the otogar.

The tourist office (☎ 216 2018, fax 216 3675) is at the southern end of Cumhuriyet Caddesi at No 127, but no-one there speaks English and the most they can rustle up is a street plan.

There are several Internet cafes in and around Kazım Karabekir Caddesi, but perhaps the best is the Net Cafe upstairs at Cumhuriyet Caddesi Örnek İşhanı 71/1.

Van Müzesi

The ground floor of Van's museum displays Urartian exhibits including jewellery, some with amber and coloured glass, cylindrical seals and pots from the Old Bronze Age (circa 5000 BC). In the inner courtyard you'll find rock carvings from the Trişin Plateau, 120km away, where thousands of prehistoric carvings of bison, reindeer and other beasts have been found.

The ethnographic exhibits upstairs include local Kurdish and Turkoman kilims and a carpeted sitting area, such as is found in village houses. The Genocide Section is a piece of one-sided propaganda displaying the contents of graves left from the massacres of Turks and Kurds by Armenians at Çavuşoğlu and Zeve. Many would think it was long past time to re-consign these skulls and bones to the ground.

The museum is open from 8 am to noon and 1.30 to 5.30 pm daily except Monday. Admission costs US$1.75.

Van Kalesi

From across the surrounding plain, Van Kalesi (Van Castle or Rock of Van) dominates the view of the city. It's a wonderful place to come for a picnic but you should allow plenty of time and bring a drink with you in summer. It's also important to visit in the middle of the day when other people are around and to make sure you're back on the main road by sunset.

On the northern side of the rock is the **tomb** of Abdurrahman Gazi, a Muslim holy man, frequently visited by pilgrims including infertile women who are thought to be helped by coming here.

A stairway from the car park at the north-western corner leads to the top of the rock, where you can see the fortifications, including the **Sardur Burcu** (Sardur Tower, 840–830 BC) with several cuneiform inscriptions in Assyrian praising the Urartian King Sardur I.

On the southern side a narrow walkway with an iron railing leads to several rock-cut **funeral chambers**, including that of King Argishti I (786–764 BC). Before reaching it you pass a lengthy **cuneiform inscription** that recounts the high points of his reign.

If you look to the south of the rock you'll see a flat space broken up by the grass-covered foundations of numerous buildings. Although this was the site of Tushpa, an Urartian city which flourished almost 3000 years ago, the foundations you see are those of the **old city** of Van, destroyed during the upheavals of WWI and the futile struggle to carve out an Armenian republic here. It's well worth walking around the base of the rock afterwards to inspect these ruins, preferably taking someone with you.

Of the Seljuk **Ulu Cami** only a broken brick minaret remains, but the **Hüsrev Paşa Külliyesi**, dating back to 1567, has been restored and you may be able to get inside to see the fine brick dome and fragmentary murals; if not, you can still inspect the delicate kümbet or tomb attached. The nearby **Kaya Çelebi Camii** (1662) has a similarly striped minaret but is still in use and likely to be locked except at prayer times.

To get to Van Kalesi take a 'Kale' dolmuş from Beş Yol (US$0.15). These are frequent at weekends but if there's nothing direct, take an 'İskele' dolmuş and get out at the road junction leading to Van Kalesi (stick with this main road since along the minor roads you may come across stone-throwing children). Even the direct Kale dolmuşes drop you 500m short of the ticket office and women in particular are likely to be hassled if they walk this last stretch on their own.

On a cool day you can easily walk the 5km to the site in less than an hour. Once there go right around the base of Van Kalesi to the entrance; however tempting it may look, if you scramble up the side of the Rock you'll end up stranded outside the walls.

Van Kalesi is open from 9 am to 6 pm daily. Admission costs US$1.75.

Places to Stay – Budget

Van has plenty of good cheap hotels. Those in the bazaar to the west of Cumhuriyet Caddesi tend to be cheapest; those to the east are slightly more expensive, but also cleaner and more comfortable.

Among the better choices in the bazaar area are *Otel İpek* (☎ 216 3033, *Cumhuriyet Caddesi 1, Sokak 3*), with clean if uninspiring rooms with bath for US$5 per person; and the more basic *Aslan Oteli* (☎ 216 2469) where a kilim-draped lobby leads to more respectable rooms for US$4.50 a head. The Şehir Hamamı is opposite.

Two short blocks down towards the lake from Beş Yol, and therefore handy for the dolmuşes, *Hotel Çaldıran* (☎ 216 2718, *Sihke Caddesi, Sokak 176*) charges US$7/10 for basic singles/doubles.

Near the Van valiliği, *Hotel Güzel Paris* (☎ 216 3739, fax 216 7897, *İrfanbaştuğ Caddesi*) offers big, comfortable rooms with shower in an excellent location for US$15/23. Also good value is the nearby two-star *Otel Şahin* (☎ 216 3062, fax 216 3064, *İrfanbaştuğ Caddesi 30*), which charges US$10/19 for clean, pleasant rooms with bath and breakfast.

Tucked away behind the main shopping street, *Hotel Çağ* (☎/fax 214 5713, *Hastane 2 Caddesi*) has pleasant enough rooms with a random selection of furnishings for US$10/15 a room. Some are dimly lit so if you want to read in bed be sure to check first.

Perhaps the best choice is the two-star *Büyük Asur Oteli* (☎ 216 8792, fax 216 9461, *Cumhuriyet Caddesi, Turizm Sokak 5*), which has a restaurant, lift and 48 rooms with metal bed frames and well-sprung mattresses. Posted prices are US$18/25 a room with shower and plenty of hot water. The lobby has a Turkish corner with big floor cushions. The manager, Remzi Bozbay, speaks English and is a great source of local information. He can also organise tours to Doğubayazıt, Kars, Hoşap Castle and other local attractions.

Nearby *Hotel Bayram* (☎ 216 1136, fax 214 7120, *Cumhuriyet Caddesi 1/A*) is a good choice, with clean, fairly modern rooms with shower and huge sink; some rooms are much larger than others so it's worth looking at several. Rooms cost US$15/20 with breakfast.

We've had reports of single women travellers feeling uncomfortable at the prominently positioned *Hotel Beşkardeş*.

Places to Stay – Mid-Range

The best hotel in town is the four-star *Büyük Urartu Oteli* (☎ 212 0660, fax 212 1610, *Cumhuriyet Caddesi 60*), across from the hospital. Big, comfortable rooms, with bath and TV, are priced at US$70/100 a single/double, subject to a certain amount of discussion when it's quiet. Decor is pleasantly modern and some of the rooms have bathtubs. There's a covered swimming pool, bliss after a hot day's sightseeing.

Hardly in the same league as the Urartu is the three-star *Otel Sirhan* (☎ 214 3463, fax 216 2867, Cumhuriyet Caddesi), on the southern side of the Van valiliği. Rooms cost US$30/45, including breakfast. The popular 1st-floor restaurant-cum-nightclub pumps up the volume until midnight, which might be something to bear in mind if you are after an early night.

The *Hotel Yakut* (☎ 214 2832, fax 216 6351, Posta Caddesi 8) charges US$30/50/70 for cheerful singles/doubles/triples with modern baths and TV. Its central position is an asset.

The newer *Akdamar Oteli* (☎ 214 9923, fax 212 0868, Kazım Karabekir Caddesi) charges US$50/60 for pleasing, modern rooms with bath and TV, although for lone travellers it's overpriced.

Places to Eat

Van specialities include *otlu peynir* (cheese mixed with a tangy herb) and *Kürt köftesi* (Kurdish köfte, also called *kurutlu köfte* – a meatless mixture of bulgur wheat and onions flavoured with mint, formed into balls and cooked). Kürt köftesi can sometimes be found in restaurants, and some of the hotels serve otlu peynir for breakfast; if yours doesn't, head straight for the *Kahvaltı Salonu*, opposite the Hz. Omer Cami, which offers two choices of cheese with honey for breakfast as well as other Turkish breakfast staples like *sucuk ve yumurta* (garlic sausage fried up with eggs).

Facing the post office is the fantastically popular *Sultan Sofrası* (Cumhuriyet Caddesi), open 24 hours a day and serving soups, stews and spit-roasted chicken to an enthusiastic student clientele. Across the road is the *Altın Şiş* kebap shop with a selection of cheap kebaps, including good döner (US$2) at lunch time.

Right beside Hotel Bayram the *Çınar Restaurant ve Et Lokantası* serves up reliable soups and grilled meats in a pleasant upstairs dining room.

Tadım (Kazım Karabekir Caddesi) offers a routine choice of kebaps and stews; turn down the lane beside it for *Kebabistan* which serves pide on one side of the road and has an ocakbaşı on the other. There are a few outside tables for summer evenings. The rest of the lane is filled with teahouses and on a summer's evening you can hardly move for men sipping tea and clicking backgammon pieces.

If you're prepared to take a dolmuş west along İskele Caddesi for about 1km you'll come to the *Cem Et Lokantası* (☎ 212 1193) beside the Türk Petrol station. Here the main draw is a buffet table spread with a vast choice of cold mezes for a set US$3, no matter how high you pile your plate. You may need to watch the final bill for fiddling though. Further down the road is the *Merkez Et Lokantası*, concentrating on grilled meats and deservedly popular.

On a sunny summer evening another possibility is to head out along Lake Van in your own car or by Gevaş dolmuş. Edremit, 11km to the south-west, has several small lakeside restaurants serving fish, and pleasant tea gardens. Even closer to Van you'll find the *Yalı Restaurant* with tables right beside the lake for watching the sunset.

Van has a good selection of *pastanes* (pastry shops) for cakes and sweet snacks at US$1 per portion. *Ayça Pastanesi* (Kazım Karabekir Caddesi), just west of Cumhuriyet Caddesi, is cosy, as is the *Çavuşoğlu Pastanesi*, near Tadım. But best of all is the *Güven Pastanesi* (Cumhuriyet Caddesi), just north of the Vakıfbank, which has floor cushions at the back and tables placed so you can soak up the sun at the front.

For alcoholic drinks with dinner the restaurant in the *Büyük Urartu Oteli* is a good bet. Alternatively, try *Beyaz Saray* (see Entertainment, following).

Entertainment

There's precious little nightlife in Van. For a beer, try *Altınküp Fıçı Bira* (Kazım Karabekir Caddesi 53), meaning 'Golden Mug Draught Beer', or the nearby *Mahzen Birahanesi* (Kazım Karabekir Caddesi 37), downstairs at the rear of the street. Both are

EASTERN ANATOLIA

exclusively male hang-outs – and even some men might find their atmosphere oppressive. For something more comfortable try the *Beyaz Saray* (☎ 214 8233), upstairs at Kazım Karabekır Caddesi, Akdamar Oteli Karşışı. This is a gazino serving food and drink, with a floorshow that encompasses singers and a belly dancer. Watch the prices, which can mount up quickly – especially if you feel obliged to tip the belly-dancer the seemingly standard US$6.

Getting There & Away

Air Turkish Airlines (☎ 215 5354, fax 215 5353), Cumhuriyet Caddesi 196, in the Enver Perihanoğlu İş Merkezi building, has two daily flights to/from Ankara, and another to/from İstanbul; the Ankara flight has connections for Antalya, İstanbul and İzmir.

Bus Many bus companies, including Van Gölü, VanTur and Van Seyahat, have ticket offices at the intersection of Cumhuriyet and Kazım Karabekir Caddesis. They customarily provide *servis* minibuses to shuttle passengers to and from the otogar. Details of some services are listed in the table below.

Train At the time of writing the *Vangölü Ekspresi* from İstanbul and Ankara was terminating at Elazığ; only freight trains were using Van train station. Should the situation change, you can get to the station by dolmuş from near Beş Yol (US$0.25).

Ferry With no connecting passenger train service to keep it to schedule, the ferry across Lake Van from Tatvan to Van leaves only when there's enough freight to justify it. 'İskele' dolmuşes ply up and down the main road to the harbour (US$0.25) but unless you're a glutton for punishment, stick with the buses.

Getting Around

There are no airport buses; a taxi for the 6km ride to the airport will cost about US$5.

For dolmuşes to Van Kalesi and the ferry dock (İskele), go to the dolmuş terminal near Beş Yol at the northern end of Cumhuriyet Caddesi. Dolmuşes to the waterfall at Muradiye (US$2, one hour) and Doğubayazıt leave from a few streets further west. For dolmuşes to Edremit, Gevaş and Akdamar you need to cut inland a few blocks from Beş Yol.

AROUND VAN
Çavuştepe & Hoşap

A day excursion south-east of Van along the road to Başkale and Hakkari takes you to the Urartian site at Çavuştepe, 25km from Van, and the Kurdish castle at Hoşap (Güzelsu), another 33km further along.

Hoşap Castle perches photogenically on top of a rocky outcrop with the village of Güzelsu and a stream beneath it. On the left-hand side of the road before the village

destination	fare (US$)	time (hr)	distance (km)	daily services
Ağrı	7	4	213	frequent buses
Ankara	25	22	1250	frequent buses
Diyarbakır	10	7	410	several buses
Doğubayazıt (via Çaldıran)	4	2½	185	frequent morning dolmuşes
Erciş	2.50	1¼	95	a few buses
Erzurum	10	6	410	several buses
Hakkari	4.50	4	205	several morning buses
Malatya	12	10	500	several buses
Şanlıurfa	12	9	585	a few buses
Tatvan	5	2	150	frequent buses
Trabzon	17	15	733	few direct buses, most via Erzurum

Services from Van's Otogar

is a badly ruined caravanserai or medrese. Cross the bridge into the village and follow the signs around the far side of the hill to reach the castle entrance.

Built in 1643 by a local Kurdish chieftain, the castle has a very impressive entrance gateway in a round tower. The guardian will quickly spot you and rush up to sell you a ticket (US$1.75). You then enter the fortress via a passage cut through the rock. Many of its hundreds of rooms are still clearly visible and the view is stunning. Across the valley are the remains of badly eroded mud-brick defensive walls, looking disconcertingly like a dinosaur's spine. Soft drinks and simple meals are available in the village.

The narrow hill on the left side of the highway at Çavuştepe was once crowned with the fortress-palace Sarduri-Hinili, home of the kings of Urartu, built between 764 and 735 BC by King Sardur II, son of Argisti. Climb the hill to the car park where there's a guardian to collect the US$1.75 entrance fee and perhaps show you what there is to see. No drinks or refreshments are available.

Climb the rocky hill to the temple ruins, marked by a gate of black basalt blocks polished to a high gloss. A few of the blocks on the left side of the doorway are inscribed in cuneiform. As you walk around, notice the cisterns for water and, at the far end where the palace once stood, the royal Urartian loo.

To get to these sites, catch a bus heading to Başkale (US$5) and say you want to get out at Hoşap. After seeing the castle, catch a bus back to Çavuştepe, 500m off the highway, and then catch a third bus back to Van. Pack a lunch and water, and plan to be gone for most of the day as buses are scarce.

HAKKARİ

☎ 438 • pop 90,000 • elevation 1700m

Tucked away in Turkey's far south-eastern corner, Hakkari is ringed with mountains, and in good times this was a place to which people came for climbing holidays. At the time of writing, however, it was hard to recommend that anyone should go there. With the Iraqi border just a five-hour walk away and the Iranian border just seven hours walk

away, it's first port of call for refugees who continue to find their away into Turkey, not to mention being a transit point for smugglers. Not surprisingly the police and army view foreign visitors with suspicion and at the time of writing you were not allowed to go anywhere without a police escort. Partly this is for your own protection but no doubt it's also to prevent you seeing anything they would prefer you didn't.

Hakkari is 210km south of Van via a twisting road that gets more and more spectacular as you travel along it. Although there are daily buses from Van, the journey takes four hours because of the frequent checkpoints; at some of these your baggage may be searched. The road bypasses Çavuştepe, whips through Hoşap, skirts the Zernik Barajı and, after 112km, arrives at Başkale, notable only for its altitude (2450m).

About 48km further along at Yeni Köprü a road forks left for Yüksekova and Esendere, an alternative base for climbs into the mountains in better times. Esendere is also a border crossing for Iran. If you cross here you'll arrive at the tiny border post of Serö, from where you can take a shared taxi to the town of Orumiyeh.

After one final checkpoint you arrive in Hakkari. If things have not changed since the time of writing, you will be escorted from the bus to a hotel by security officers. Hakkari has two hotels: the grungy *Otel Ümit* and the nominally three-star *Şenler Oteli* (☎ *211 5512, fax 211 3809*). It's a seller's market so even the Ümit charges US$9 per person and will try to get away with more even though your shower and toilet are unlikely to function. The better Şenler charges the same price, but is often full with builders hard at work expanding Hakkari to take the people who have fled from surrounding villages for the comparative safety of the town. The Ümit is home to many refugee families whose stories and circumstances make a mockery of any idea of visiting Hakkari as a tourist.

When you want to eat, the security officers will lead you to *Çiçek Kebap Salonu* near the Ümit which serves everything from çorba (soup) at breakfast time to pide in the evening. They will accompany you on a circuit around the town and will ensure that you don't take any photographs, even of the mountains.

Climbing in the mountains was out of the question at the time of writing.

NORTH FROM VAN

If you're bound for Doğubayazıt from Van, you have a choice of routes. Some buses still take the long way round via Erciş, Patnos and Ağrı, but the minibuses all travel via Muradiye, Çaldıran and Ortadirek, a considerably shorter 185km run and one well worth taking for the spectacular pastoral scenery along the way. Keep your passport handy for the army checkpoints and bear in mind that the road officially closes at 5 pm, partly for security reasons and partly so that the army can keep an eye out for smugglers.

If you want a break of journey along the way, the Muradiye Şelalesi (waterfall) is still reasonably picturesque despite a couple of half-built concrete blocks doing their best to mar the view.

Language

Turkish is the dominant language in the Turkic language group which also includes such less-than-famous tongues as Kirghiz, Kazakh and Azerbaijani. Once thought to be related to Finnish and Hungarian, the Turkic languages are now seen as comprising their own unique language group. You can find people who speak Turkish, in one form or another, from Belgrade all the way to Xinjiang in China.

In 1928, Atatürk did away with the Arabic alphabet and adopted a Latin-based alphabet much better suited to easy learning and correct pronunciation. He also instituted a language reform to purge Turkish of obscure Arabic and Persian borrowings, in order to rationalise and simplify it. The result is a logical, systematic and expressive language which has only one irregular noun (*su*, 'water'), one irregular verb (*etmek*, 'to be') and no genders. It's so logical, in fact, that Turkish grammar formed the basis for the development of Esperanto, an artificial international language.

Grammar

Word order and verb formation in Turkish are very different from what you'll find in Indo-European languages like English. This makes it somewhat difficult to learn at first, despite its elegant simplicity. A few hints will help you comprehend road and shop signs, schedules and menus.

Suffixes

A Turkish word consists of a root and one or more suffixes added to it. While English has only a few suffixes (-'s for possessive, -s/-es for plural), Turkish has loads of them. Not only that, these suffixes are subject to an unusual system of 'vowel harmony' whereby most of the vowel sounds within individual words are made in a similar manner. What this means is that the suffix might be *-lar* when attached to one word, but *-ler* when attached to another; the suffix retains the same meaning, though. In some cases these suffixes are preceded by a 'buffer letter', a 'y' or an 'n'.

Here are some of the noun suffixes you'll encounter most frequently:

-a, -e	'to'
-dan, -den	'from'
-dır, -dir	emphatic (ignore it!)
-dur, -dür	
-(s)ı, -(s)i	object-nouns (ignore it!)
-(s)u, -(s)ü	
-(n)ın, -(n)in	possessive
-lar, -ler	plural
-lı, -li,	'with'
-lu, -lü	
-sız, -siz,	'without'
-suz, -süz	

Here are some of the common verb suffixes:

-ar, -er, -ır, -ir,	simple present tense
-ur, -ür	
-acak, -ecek,	future tense
-acağ-, -eceğ	
-dı, -di, -du, -dü	simple past tense
-ıyor-, -iyor-	continuous (like English '-ing', eg, '... is eating')
-mak, -mek	infinitive ending

Nouns

Suffixes can be added to nouns to modify them. The two you'll come across most frequently are *-ler* and *-lar*, which form the plural: *otel* (hotel), *oteller* (hotels); *araba* (car), *arabalar* (cars).

Other suffixes modify in other ways: *ev* (house), *Ahmet*, but *Ahmet'in evi* (Ahmet's house). Similarly with *İstanbul* and *banka*: it's *İstanbul Bankası* when the two are used together. You may see *-i, -ı, -u* or *-ü, -si, -sı, -su* or *-sü* added to any noun. A *cami* is a mosque; but the *cami* built by Mehmet Pasha is the *Mehmet Paşa Camii*, with a double 'i'. Ask for a *bira* and the waiter will bring you a bottle of whatever type is available; ask for an *Efes Birası* and that's the brand you'll get.

Yet other suffixes on nouns tell you about direction: *-a* or *-e* means 'to': *otobüs* (bus), *otobüse* (to the bus) and *Bodrum'a* (to Bodrum). The suffix *-dan* or *-den* means 'from': *Ankara'dan* (from Ankara), *köprüden*, (from the bridge). Stress is on these final syllables *(-a* or *-dan)* whenever they are used.

Verbs

Verbs consist of a root plus any number of modifying suffixes. Verbs can be so complex that they constitute whole sentences in themselves, although this is rare. The standard example for blowing your mind is *Afyonkarahisarlılaştıramadıklarımızdanmısınız?* (Aren't you one of those people whom we tried, unsuccessfully, to make resemble the citizens of Afyonkarahisar?). Luckily it's not the sort of word you see every day!

The infinitive verb form is with *-mak* or *-mek*, as in *gitmek* (to go) or *almak* (to take). The stress in the infinitive is always on the last syllable ('geet-MEHK', 'ahl-MAHK').

The simple present form is with *-r*, as in *gider* (he/she/it goes), *giderim* (I go). The suffix *-iyor* has a similar meaning: *gidiyorum* (I'm going). For the future, there's *-ecek* or *-acak*, as in *alacak* (ah-lah-JAHK), he will take (it).

Word Order

The nouns and adjectives usually come first, then the verb; the final suffix on the verb is the subject of the sentence:

I'll go to Istanbul.	*İstanbul'a gideceğim.*
I want to buy (take) a carpet.	*Halı almak istiyorum.* (lit: 'Carpet to buy want I')

Pronunciation

Once you learn a few basic rules, you'll find Turkish pronunciation quite simple to master. Despite oddities such as the soft 'g' (ğ) and undotted 'i' (ı), it's a phonetically consistent language – there's generally a clear one-letter/one-sound relationship.

It's important to remember that each letter is pronounced; vowels don't combine to form diphthongs and consonants don't

combine to form other sounds (such as 'th', 'gh' or 'sh' in English). Watch out for this. Your eye will keep seeing familiar English double-letter sounds in Turkish – where they don't exist. It therefore follows that **h** in Turkish is always pronounced as a separate letter; in English, we're used to pronouncing it only when it occurs before a vowel, but in Turkish it can appear in the middle or at the end of a word as well. *Always* pronounce it; your Turkish friend Ahmet is 'ahh-meht' not 'aa-meht', and the word *rehber* (guide) is pronounced 'rehh-behr' not 're-behr'.

Here are some of the letters in Turkish which may cause initial confusion:

A, a	as in 'art' or 'bar'
â	a faint 'y' sound in the preceding consonant
E, e	as in 'fell' or as the first vowel in 'ever'
İ, i	a short 'i', as in 'hit' or 'sit'
I, ı	a neutral vowel; as the 'a' in 'ago'
O, o	between the 'o' in 'hot' and the 'aw' in 'awe'
Ö, ö	as the 'e' in 'her' said with pursed lips
U, u	as the 'oo' in 'moo'
Ü, ü	an exaggerated rounded-lip 'yoo'
C, c	as the 'j' in 'jet'
Ç, ç	as the 'ch' in 'church'
G, g	always hard as in 'get' (not as in 'gentle')
ğ	silent; lengthens preceding vowel
H, h	always pronounced; a weak 'h' as in 'half'
J, j	as the 'z' in 'azure'
S, s	always as in 'stress' (not as in 'ease')
Ş, ş	as the 'sh' in 'show'
V, v	soft, almost like a 'w'
W, w	same as Turkish 'v' (only found in foreign words)

Greetings & Civilities

Hello.	*Merhaba.*
Good morning/ Good day.	*Günaydın.*
Good evening.	*İyi akşamlar.*

Good night.	*İyi geceler.*
Goodbye. (said by one departing)	*Allaha ısmarladık.*
Goodbye. (said by one staying)	*Güle güle.*
Stay happy. (alternative for 'goodbye')	*Hoşça kalın.*
How are you?	*Nasılsınız?*
I'm fine, thank you.	*İyiyim, teşekkür ederim.*
Very well.	*Çok iyiyim.*
What's your name?	*İsminiz ne?*
My name is ...	*İsmim ...*

Useful Words & Phrases

Yes.	*Evet.*
No.	*Hayır.*
Please.	*Lütfen.*
Thanks.	*Teşekkürler.*
Thank you very much.	*Çok teşekkür ederim.*
You're welcome.	*Bir şey değil.*
Pardon me.	*Affedersiniz.*
Help yourself.	*Buyurun(uz).*
What?	*Ne?*
How?	*Nasıl?*
Who?	*Kim?*
Why?	*Niçin, neden?*
How many lira?	*Kaç lira?*
large	*büyük*
medium	*orta*
small	*küçük*
not ...	*... değil*
and	*ve*
or	*veya*
good	*iyi*
bad	*fenah*
beautiful	*güzel*

Language Difficulties

Do you speak English?	*İnglizce konuşuyor-musunuz?*
Do you understand?	*Anlıyormusunuz?*
I understand.	*Anlıyorum.*
I don't understand.	*Anlamıyorum.*
Please write it down.	*Lütfen yazınız.*
How do you say ...?	*... nasıl söylüyorsun?*

What does ... mean?	*... ne demek?*

Countries

Where are you from?	*Nerelisiniz?*
Australia	*Avustralya*
Austria	*Avusturya*
Belgium	*Belçika*
Canada	*Kanada*
Denmark	*Danimarka*
France	*Fransa*
Germany	*Almanya*
Greece	*Yunanistan*
India	*Hindistan*
Israel	*İsrail*
Italy	*Italya*
Japan	*Japonya*
Netherlands	*Holanda*
New Zealand	*Yeni Zelanda*
Norway	*Norveç*
South Africa	*Güney Afrika*
Sweden	*İsveç*
Switzerland	*İsviçre*
UK	*İngiltere*
USA	*Amerika*

Getting Around

Where is a/the ...?	*... nerede?*
airport	*havaalanı*
bus station	*otogar*
dock	*iskele*
left luggage office	*emanetçi*
railway station	*gar/istasyon*
When does it ...?	*Ne zaman ...?*
leave	*kalkar*
arrive	*gelir*
aeroplane	*uçak*
flight	*uçuş*
gate	*kapı*
bus	*otobüs/araba*
direct (bus)	*direk(t)*
indirect (bus)	*aktarmalı*
train	*tren*
couchette	*kuşet*
sleeping car	*yataklı vagon*

dining car	*yemekli vagon*
no-smoking car	*sigara içilmeyen vagon*
ship	*gemi*
boat	*tekne/motor*
ferry	*feribot*
cabin	*kamara*
berth	*yatak*
class	*mevki/sınıf*
ticket	*bilet*
a ticket to (...)	*(...'a) bir bilet*
timetable	*tarife*
reserved seat	*numaralı yer*
1st class	*birinci sınıf*
2nd class	*ikinci sınıf*
one-way	*gidiş*
return	*gidiş-dönüş*
student (ticket)	*öğrenci (bileti)*
full fare (ticket)	*tam (bileti)*
early	*erken*
late	*geç*
fast	*çabuk*
slow	*yavaş*
next	*gelecek*
last	*son*
daily	*hergün*
car	*araba*
diesel (fuel)	*mazot, motorin*
highway	*otoyol*
motor oil	*motor yağı*
petrol (gasoline)	*benzin*
regular/super (fuel)	*normal/süper*
map	*harita*
street/avenue	*sokak/cadde(si)*
left	*sol*
right	*sağ*
straight on	*doğru*
here	*burada*
there	*şurada*
over there	*orada*
near	*yakın*
far	*uzak*

Accommodation

Where is ...?	*... nerede?*
Where is a clean, cheap hotel?	*Ucuz, temiz bir otel nerede?*

Signs

Giriş	**Entrance**
Çikiş	**Exit**
Açık/Kapali	**Open/Closed**
Danişma	**Information**
Boş Oda Var	**Rooms Available**
Dolu	**Full/No Vacancies**
Polis/Emniyet	**Police**
Polis Karakolu/ Emniyet Müdürlüğü	**Police Station**
Yasak(tir)	**Prohibited**
Tuvalet	**Toilets**

Do you have any rooms available?	*Odanızvar mı?*
I'd like a room ...	*Bir ... oda istiyorum.*
with one bed	*tek yataklı*
with two beds	*iki yataklı*
with a double bed	*geniş yatak*
with a shower	*duşlu*
What does it cost for (three) nights?	*Kaç lira (üç) gece için?*
Is a hot shower included?	*Sıcak duş dahıl mi?*
Does it include breakfast?	*Kahvaltı dahil mi?*
Is there a cheaper room?	*Daha ucuzu var mı?*
May I see the room?	*Odayı görebilir miyim?*
It's too small.	*Çok küçük.*
It's very noisy.	*Çok gürültülü.*
It's fine. I'll take it.	*İyi, tutuyorum.*
Where's the toilet?	*Tuvalet nerede?*
air-conditioning	*klima*
bath	*banyo*
cold water	*soğuk su*
hot water	*sıcak su*
light(s)	*ışık(lar)*
light bulb	*ampül*
shower	*duş*
soap	*sabun*
toilet paper	*tuvalet kağıdı*
towel	*havlu*

Around Town

Where is (a/the) ...?	... *nerede?*
customs	*gümrük*
exchange	*kambiyo*
post office (PTT)	*postane/postahane*
poste restante	*postrestant*
restaurant	*lokanta*
toilet	*tuvalet*
Turkish bath	*hamam*

Is there a local Internet cafe?	*Civarda Internet cafe var mı?*
I want to look at my email.	*E-mailime bakmak istiyorum.*

open	*açık*
closed	*kapalı*
(by) air mail	*uçakla* or *uçak ile*
cash	*efektif*
cheque	*çek*
commission	*komisyon*

Highway Signs

Girilmez	**No Entry**
Gişeler	**Toll Booths**
Katotopark	**Parking Garage**
Otoyol	**Motorway/ Expressway**
Paralı Geçiş	**Toll Highway**
Park Alanı	**Rest Stop**
Park Yeri	**Car Park/ Parking Lot**
Servis Alanı	**Service Area**
Şehir Merkezi	**City Centre**
Tırmanma Şeridi	**Overtaking/ Passing Lane**
Ücret Ödeme	**Toll Collection**
Ücretli Geçiş	**Toll Highway**
Yağışta Kaygan Yol	**Slippery When Wet**
Yavaşla	**Slow Down**

Note Motorway signs are green with white lettering; town signs are blue with white lettering; village signs are white with black lettering. Yellow signs with black lettering mark sights of touristic interest. Yellow signs with blue lettering mark village development projects.

dollars	*dolar*
exchange rate	*kur*
foreign currency	*döviz*
identification	*kimlik*
postage stamp	*pul*
telephone token	*jeton*
working hours	*çalışma saatleri*

Shopping

Where is (a) ...?	.... *nerede?*
bookshop	*bir kitapçı*
covered bazaar	*kapalı çarşı*
market/shopping district	*çarşı*
newsagent	*haber ajansı*
shop	*dükkan*

I want to buy ...	... *satın almak istiyorum.*
Do you have ...?	... *var mı?*
We don't have ...	... *yok.*
Give me ...	... *bana verin.*
I want ...	... *istiyorum.*
Which?	*Hangi?*
this one	*bunu*
How much/many?	*Kaç/Kaç tane?*
this much	*bu kadar*
It's (very) cheap.	*(Çok) ucuz.*
It's (very) expensive.	*(Çok) pahalı.*
I'll give you ...	... *vereceğim.*

price	*fiyat*
service charge	*servis ücreti*
tax	*vergi*

Food

restaurant	*lokanta*
pastry shop	*pastane*
'oven' (bakery)	*fırın*
Turkish pizza shop	*pideci*
köfte restaurant	*köfteci*
kebap restaurant	*kebapçı*
snack shop	*büfe*

alcohol served	*içkili*
no alcohol served	*içkisiz*
breakfast	*kahvahltı*
lunch	*öğle yemeği*
supper	*akşam yemeği*

portion/serving	*porsyon*
fork	*çatal*
knife	*bıçak*
spoon	*kaşık*
plate	*tabak*
glass	*bardak*
bill/cheque	*hesap*
service charge	*servis ücreti*
tip	*bahşiş*

Health

I'm ill.	*Hastayım.*
Please call a doctor.	*Cankurtaran çağırın.*
Please call an ambulance.	*Doktor/Hekim çağırın.*

Where's the nearest ...?	*En yakın ... nerede?*
doctor	*doktor*
hospital	*hastane*
chemist/pharmacy	*eczane*
dentist	*diş hekimi*

diarrhoea	*ishalim*
fever	*ateşim*
handicapped	*özürlü/sakat*
headache	*ibaş ağrısı*
nausea	*mide bulantısı*
stomachache	*mide ağrısı*

condom	*kondom*
medicine	*ilaç*
mosquito repellent	*sivrisineğe karşı ilaç*
sanitary pad	*hijenik kadın bağı*
tampon	*tampon*

Time, Date & Numbers

What time is it?	*Saat kaç?*
It's (8) o'clock.	*Saat (sekiz).*
It's half past three.	*Saat üç buçuk.* ('hour three-one half')
At what time?	*Saat kaçta?*
When?	*Ne zaman?*
day	*gün*
week	*hafta*
month	*ay*
year	*sene/yıl*

Sunday	*Pazar*
Monday	*Pazartesi*
Tuesday	*Salı*

Emergencies

Help!	*İmdat!*
It's an emergency.	*Acil durum.*
I'm ill.	*Rahatsızım.*
Call the police!	*Polisi çağırın!*
Find a doctor!	*Doktoru arayın!*
(There's a) fire!	*Yangın var!*
There's been an accident.	*Bir kaza oldu.*
Go away!	*Gidin!* (polite) *Git!* (informal)
I've been raped/ assaulted.	*Tecavüze/Saldırıya uğradım.*
I've been robbed.	*Soyuldum.*
I'm lost.	*Kayboldum.*
Where are the toilets?	*Tuvalet nerede?*

Wednesday	*Çarşamba*
Thursday	*Perşembe*
Friday	*Cuma*
Saturday	*Cumartesi*

January	*Ocak*
February	*Şubat*
March	*Mart*
April	*Nisan*
May	*Mayıs*
June	*Haziran*
July	*Temmuz*
August	*Ağustos*
September	*Eylül*
October	*Ekim*
November	*Kasım*
December	*Aralık*

0	*sıfır*
1	*bir*
2	*iki*
3	*üç*
4	*dört*
5	*beş*
6	*altı*
7	*yedi*
8	*sekiz*
9	*dokuz*
10	*on*
11	*on bir*
12	*on iki*
13	*on üç*

20	*yirmi*
30	*otuz*
40	*kırk*
50	*elli*
60	*altmış*
70	*yetmiş*
80	*seksen*
90	*doksan*
100	*yüz*
200	*iki yüz*
1000	*bin*
2000	*iki bin*
10,000	*on bin*

one million   *milyon*

-½ (*yarım*) – used alone, as in 'I want half'
-½ (*buçuk*) – always used with a whole number, eg, '1½', *bir buçuk*
    Ordinal numbers consist of the number plus the suffix *-inci, -ıncı, -uncu* or *-üncü*, depending upon 'vowel harmony'.

first	*birinci*
second	*ikinci*
sixth	*altıncı*
13th	*onüçüncü*

Glossary

Here, with definitions, are some unfamiliar words and abbreviations you may find in the text and maps of this guide.

acropolis – hilltop citadel and temples of a Graeco-Roman city
ada(sı) – island
adliye (sarayı) – court (house)
agora – open space for commerce and politics in a Graeco-Roman city
aile salonu – family room; dining room for couples, families and single women in a Turkish restaurant
Allah korusun – 'God protect me'; a common exclamation, often seen in cars, taxis and buses
altegeçidi – pedestrian subway
Anatolia – the Asian part of Turkey; also called *Asia Minor*
apse – semicircular recess for the altar in a church
arabesk – Arabic-style Turkish music
arasta – row of shops near a mosque, the rent from which supports the mosque
Asia Minor – see *Anatolia*

bahçe(si) – garden
banliyö – suburb(an)
basilica – form of architecture used for early Christian churches
bedesten – vaulted, fireproof market enclosure where valuable goods are kept
bekçi – guardian, caretaker
belediye (sarayı) – municipality, town (hall)
bey – 'Mr'; follows the name
birahane – beer hall
bouleuterion – place of assemby, council meeting-place in a Graeco-Roman city
büfe – snack bar
bulvarı – often abbreviated to 'bul'; boulevard or avenue

caddesi – often abbreviated to 'cad'; street
cami(i) – mosque
capital – the top of a column
caravanserai – large fortified way-station for (trade) caravans

çarşı(sı) – market, bazaar
çay bahçesi – tea garden
çayı – stream
çeşme – spring, fountain
cicim – embroidered mat
Cilician Gates – a pass in the Taurus Mountains in southern Turkey; known as Gülek Boğaz in Turkish

dağ(ı) – mountain
Damsız girilmez – sign seen on many Turkish nightclubs meaning that men unaccompanied by a woman will not be admitted
DDY – Devlet Demiryolları (Turkish State Railways)
deniz – sea
deniz otobüsü – literally 'sea bus'; hydrofoil or catamaran
Denizyolları – Turkish Maritime Lines
dere(si) – stream
dervish – member of a mystic Muslim brotherhood
dolmuş – shared taxi; can be a minibus or sedan
döner kebap – meat roasted on a revolving vertical spit
döviz (burosu) – currency exchange (office)

eczane – chemist/pharmacy
emanet(çi) – left-luggage (baggage check) office
eski – old (thing, not person)
ev pansiyonu – private home that rents rooms to travellers
eyvan – vaulted hall opening into a central court in a *medrese* or mosque
ezan – the Muslim call to prayer

feribot – ferry
faience – glazed tilework

GAP – South-East Anatolia Project, a mammoth hydroelectric and irrigation project
gazino – Turkish nightclub, not a gambling den
geçenek – aisle

geçit, -di – (mountain) pass
gişe – ticket booth
göl(ü) – lake
gözleme – Turkish pancake
gulet – traditional Turkish yacht

hamam(ı) – Turkish bath
han(ı) – inn or caravanserai
hanım – polite form of address for a woman; goes after the name
harabe(ler) – ruin(s)
harem – family/women's quarters of a residence; see also *selamlık*
hazır yemek – 'ready food'; food prepared and kept hot on a steam table
heykel – statue
hisar(ı) – fortress or citadel
Hittites – nation of people in Anatolia during the 2nd millennium BC; founded an empire based at Hattuşa (Boğazkale)
hükümet konağı – government house, provincial government headquarters

ilkokul – primary school
imam – prayer leader, Muslim cleric
imaret(i) – soup kitchen for the poor, usually attached to a *medrese*
işhanı – office building
iskele(si) – jetty, quay

jandarma – gendarme, paramilitary police force/officer

kale(si) – fortress, citadel
kapı(sı) – door, gate
kaplıca – thermal spring or baths
Karagöz – shadow-puppet theatre
KDV – katma değer vergisi, Turkey's value-added tax
kebapçı – place selling kebaps
kervansaray(ı) – Turkish for *caravanserai*
kilim – napless woven rug
kilise(si) – church
köfte – Turkish meatballs
köfteci – *köfte* maker
konak, konağı – mansion, government headquarters
köprü (sü) – bridge
köşk(ü) – pavilion, villa
köy(ü) – village
kule(si) – tower

külliye(si) – mosque complex including seminary, hospital, soup kitchen etc
kümbet – vault, cupola, dome; tomb topped by this
küşet(li) – (train carriage containing) couchette(s), shelf-like beds

liman(ı) – harbour
lise – high school
lokanta – restaurant

mağara(sı) – cave
mahalle(si) – neighbourhood, district of a city
Maşallah – 'Wonder of God'; said in admiration or to avert the evil eye
medrese(si) – Islamic theological seminary or school, attached to a mosque
mescit, -di – prayer room, small mosque
Mevlâna – also known as Celaleddin Rumi, a great mystic and poet (1207–73), founder of the Mevlevi whirling *dervish* order
meydan(ı) – public square, open place
meyhane – wine shop, tavern
mihrab – niche in a mosque indicating the direction of Mecca
mimber – pulpit in a mosque
minare(si) – minaret, tower from which Muslims are called to prayer
müezzin – cantor who sings the *ezan*, or call to prayer
müze(si) – museum

nargileh – traditional water pipe (for smoking)
narthex – enclosed porch or vestibule at the entrance to a church
nave – middle aisle of a church
necropolis – city of the dead, cemetery

ocakbaşı – grill
oda(sı) – room
odeon – odeum, small classical theatre for musical performances
ortaokul – secondary school
otogar – bus station
otoyol – motorway, limited-access divided highway
Ottoman – of or pertaining to the Ottoman Empire which lasted from the end of the 13th century to the end of WWI; the height

of Ottoman glory was under Sultan Süleyman the Magnificent (1520–66)

pansiyon – pension, B&B, guesthouse
pastane – also pastahane; pastry shop (patisserie)
pazar(ı) – weekly market, bazaar
peron – gate (at the otogar or train station)
pide – Turkish pizza
pideci – *pide* maker
PTT – Posta, Telefon, Telegraf, the national post, telephone and telegraph office; although the term PTT is still widely used, the telephone network is now controlled by private companies

Ramazan – Islamic holy month of fasting

şadırvan – fountain where Muslims perform ritual ablutions
saray(ı) – palace
sarcophagus – a stone or marble coffin or tomb, especially one with inscription
sebil – public fountain or water kiosk
şehir – city; municipal
selamlık – public/male quarters of a residence (see also *harem*)
Seljuk – of or pertaining to the Seljuk Turks, the first Turkish state to rule Anatolia from the 11th to 13th centuries
sema – *dervish* ceremony
serander – granary
servis – a shuttle minibus service to and from the otogar

şiş kebap – roast skewered meat
sokak, sokağı – often abbreviated to 'sk'; street or lane
Sufi – Muslim mystic, member of a mystic (*dervish*) brotherhood

tabhane – hostel for travellers (archaic term)
TC – Türkiye Cumhuriyeti (Turkish Republic); designates an official office or organisation
TCDD – Turkish State Railways; see also *DDY*
Tekel – government alcoholic beverage and tobacco company
tekke(si) – *dervish* lodge
TEM – Trans-European Motorway
tersane – shipyard
THY – Türk Hava Yolları, Turkish Airlines
TML – Turkish Maritime Lines, Denizyolları
TRT – Türkiye Radyo ve Televizyon, Turkish broadcasting corporation
tuff – soft stone laid down as volcanic ash
tuğra – sultan's monogram, imperial signature
türbe(si) – tomb, grave, mausoleum

vezir – vizier (minister) in the *Ottoman* government
vilayet, valilik, valiliği – provincial government headquarters

yalı – waterside residence
yol(u) – road, way
yüzyıl – century

Acknowledgments

THANKS

Thanks to the many travellers who took the time and trouble to write to us with helpful hints, useful advice and interesting anecdotes about their experiences in Turkey. They include:

Paul Adrian, Ovezmurad Agayev, Mark Alexander, Denise Alnes, Fern & Morey Anderson, Fiona Anderson, Matt Anderson, Richard Anderson, Angela Archer, Glenn Arendts, Walt Bachman, Don & Joan Bailey, Eszter Balazs, Daniel Bampton, Bron Barnacle, Lance Bartholomeusz, Daphne Bell, Stewart & David Bell, Kristen Berger, George Biro, Therese Bismire, F Blackwood, Mick Blair, Lindsay Bligh, Carolyn Bloomfield, Hetty Boelens, Sally Bothroyd, Carl Bowden, Claire Bowern, Alan Bowtell, Fred Brace, Phil Bradshaw, John & Louise Brekelmans, Ian Brown, Karl Buchanan, Jack Buckley, Sevda Bulet, M Burnett, Patrick & Tamsin Bynne, M J Byrne, Kevin Callaghan, Corinne Campbell, John Campbell, Tanya Campbell, Jonathon Carapetis, Joe Carter, Amy Castro, Burak Catakoolu, Gary Chapman, Lorenzo Cimarra, Quent Coe, Anthony & Sue Cook, Phil & Denise Copeland, Shellie Corman, Katerina Cosgrove, Helen Coutts, G Cozens, Richard Crampton, Lindsay & Ann Crawford, Bob Creed, M Creighton Scott, Michelle & Chris, Jackson Cresp, Bob Cromwell, Brian Cruickshank, C Danby, Mark David Bell, Des De Silva, Lucy Donovan, Annette Doornbosch, Mark Doupe, Ellen Doyle, D Drengubiak, Tracey Duigan, Hakan Durak, Cindy Dyball, Dyan Eastman, Sharon Ede, Ellen Edmonds-Williams, Ayshe Ege, Colin & Dianne Elliott, Nalan Erem, Stephen Ferguson, Nancy Fingerhood, Ian Finlay, Dawn Finlayson, Anthony Finocchiaro, Hugh Finsten, Ayelet & Ari Fleischer, Paul Ford, Emiko & John Foster, M Foster, Richard Freed, Micheal S Freedus, Jim & Ann Gage, Shirley Galvin, J Gates, Kathryn Gauci, Michele Genovese, Mark Gilchrist, Carolyn Girvin, Elizabeth Godfrey, Sally Goldin, Elizabeth Goldring, G S Goodman, Michael Gore, Jan Grant, Vincent & Mary Gray, David & Jane Greenwood, James Guest, Paul Hagman, Tarnya Hall, Barbara Hani, Zac Hanscom, Peggy Hanson, Carol & Chris Harman, J Harris, Karl Heinz Girnan, Brian Heyton, Nancy Higbie, Lindsay Hill, Erik Hoogcarspel, Petr Horeni, Mike Inkson, Mohammed Ally Islam, Tracy Johnstone, Robert Jones, Sandor Judit, P Kae Forbes, Norman Kan, J Keith Mercer, Judith Kiddlo, Gail & Peter Kirby, Tracey & Ian Kirkland, Helaine Knickerbocker, Krystye Knox, Bobbi Kraham, Baylor Lancaster, Jane Lane, Jeri Lang, Lois Lemehens, Mabelle Lernoud, Rob Leutheuser, Brian & Carol Little, Elizabeth & David Luke, Jim Lum, Natalie Lysenbo, Vivian Mackereth, Bronwyn Magdulski, Linda Main, J Mall, Sarah Mankawa, Jo Mann, Mary Maskell, P Mattinson, Matthew Mattiske, Cathryn Mayers, Penny McAllum, June & Ian McCormack, Tim McLaughlin, Marianthe McLiesh, Simon McPherson, Helen Meistrich, Bob Meller, Steven Merel, Aschi Meyer, Stuart Michael, Jan Miller, Justine Miller, Henry Mitrani, Judy Moore, C & S Murphy, Maureen Murphy, Kay Murray, Martyn Mursa, Paul Myers, Nick Nasev, Maya Naunton, Carol Nelson, Scott Nelson, Debby Nicholls, Zoe Nielsen, Annette Novotka, Douglas Oles, Pavlina Otmar, Brent Ower Caldwell, Isobel Palson, Robert Patterson, Ben Peacock, Rebecca Pearce, Frank Pears, Scott Penhaligon, W D Pennycook, Michelle Plozza, Jane Poirrier, Darren Pratt, John Preston, Gail & Colin Priest, C Reyner, Clive Richards, Michael & Annamaria Roberts, Betty Robinson, Terry Robinson, Michael Rowell, Linda & Chester Rowland, Nathalie Roy, Ian Russell, Jay Russian, Tara & Bruce Ryan, Albert Salinas, Joanne & Bert Schnitzer, Elizabeth Schweizer, Cameron Scott, Ian & Jan Scott, Sarah & Heinz Seeberg, Russ Siddall, Katie Sigelman, Sheila Sim, Sheri Slike, Anne Smith, Jean Smith, Lynda Smith, Tracey Smith, Micheal Spiro, Melody & Fred Squires, Carolyn Squirrell, Charles Stanford, Anne Stanley, Ken Steele, Joan Stokes, Pauline Symonds, Nina Ta, Bobbie Taba, Polly Tafrate, Kyla Talmi, Robert Taylor, A Templeton, Andrew Ten Seldam, Daniel Theil, G Thomas, Karen Thompson, Priscilla Thorley, Katrina Turner, John & Peggy Tyler, Bernard van Cuylenburg, George Vasilev, Kari Vaughan, Ilse

Van Barne Veld, Karen Visser, Jo Vrachnas, Hilton & Carmen Ward, Owen & Angela Warner, Tom Weingarten, Sico van der Werf, Paul Werny, Colin Whitaker, Saly Whitney, G Whittle, Trevor Williams, Tracy Witham, Eric & Jenny Wong, Gill Wood, Rhona Woodbury, Louise Woollett, Julian Wright, Kim Yaged, Michael Yeoh, Matthew Yovich, Bob Zhang

LONELY PLANET

You already know that Lonely Planet produces more than this one guidebook, but you might not be aware of the other products we have on this region. Here is a selection of titles that you may want to check out as well:

Middle East
ISBN 0 86442 701 8
US$24.95 • UK£14.99 • 180FF

World Food Turkey
ISBN 1 86450 027 1
US$11.99 • UK£6.99 • 89FF

Turkish phrasebook
ISBN 0 86442 436 1
US$6.95 • UK£4.50 • 50FF

Greece
ISBN 0 86442 682 8
US$19.95 • UK£12.99 • 160FF

Iran
ISBN 0 86442 756 5
US$21.99 • UK£13.99 • 169FF

Syria
ISBN 0 86442 747 6
US$17.95 • UK£11.99 • 140FF

Europe on a shoestring
ISBN 1 86450 150 2
US$24.99 • UK£14.99 • 179FF

Mediterranean Europe
ISBN 1 86450 154 5
US$27.99 • UK£15.99 • 189FF

Istanbul
ISBN 0 86442 585 6
US$14.95 • UK£8.99 • 110FF

Istanbul City Map
ISBN 1 86450 080 8
US$5.95 • UK£3.99 • 39FF

**Istanbul to Cairo
on a shoestring**
ISBN 0 86442 749 2
US$16.95 • UK£10.99 • 130FF

Istanbul to Kathmandu
ISBN 1 86450 214 2
US$21.99 • UK£13.99 • 159FF

**Available wherever books
are sold**

LONELY PLANET

ON THE ROAD

Travel Guides explore cities, regions and countries, and supply information on transport, restaurants and accommodation, covering all budgets. They come with reliable, easy-to-use maps, practical advice, cultural and historical facts and a rundown on attractions both on and off the beaten track. There are over 200 titles in this classic series, covering nearly every country in the world.

 Lonely Planet Upgrades extend the shelf life of existing travel guides by detailing any changes that may affect travel in a region since a book has been published. Upgrades can be downloaded for free from **www.lonelyplanet.com/upgrades**

For travellers with more time than money, **Shoestring** guides offer dependable, first-hand information with hundreds of detailed maps, plus insider tips for stretching money as far as possible. Covering entire continents in most cases, the six-volume shoestring guides are known around the world as 'backpackers' bibles'.

For the discerning short-term visitor, **Condensed** guides highlight the best a destination has to offer in a full-colour, pocket-sized format designed for quick access. They include everything from top sights and walking tours to opinionated reviews of where to eat, stay, shop and have fun.

CitySync lets travellers use their Palm™ or Visor™ hand-held computers to guide them through a city with handy tips on transport, history, cultural life, major sights, and shopping and entertainment options. It can also quickly search and sort hundreds of reviews of hotels, restaurants and attractions, and pinpoint their location on scrollable street maps. CitySync can be downloaded from **www.citysync.com**

MAPS & ATLASES

Lonely Planet's **City Maps** feature downtown and metropolitan maps, as well as transit routes and walking tours. The maps come complete with an index of streets, a listing of sights and a plastic coat for extra durability.

Road Atlases are an essential navigation tool for serious travellers. Cross-referenced with the guidebooks, they also feature distance and climate charts and a complete site index.

LONELY PLANET

ESSENTIALS

Read This First books help new travellers to hit the road with confidence. These invaluable predeparture guides give step-by-step advice on preparing for a trip, budgeting, arranging a visa, planning an itinerary and staying safe while still getting off the beaten track.

Healthy Travel pocket guides offer a regional rundown on disease hot spots and practical advice on predeparture health measures, staying well on the road and what to do in emergencies. The guides come with a user-friendly design and helpful diagrams and tables.

Lonely Planet's **Phrasebooks** cover the essential words and phrases travellers need when they're strangers in a strange land. They come in a pocket-sized format with colour tabs for quick reference, extensive vocabulary lists, easy-to-follow pronunciation keys and two-way dictionaries.

Miffed by blurry photos of the Taj Mahal? Tired of the classic 'top of the head cut off' shot? **Travel Photography: A Guide to Taking Better Pictures** will help you turn ordinary holiday snaps into striking images and give you the know-how to capture every scene, from frenetic festivals to peaceful beach sunrises.

Lonely Planet's **Travel Journal** is a lightweight but sturdy travel diary for jotting down all those on-the-road observations and significant travel moments. It comes with a handy time-zone wheel, world maps and useful travel information.

Lonely Planet's eKno is an all-in-one communication service developed especially for travellers. It offers low-cost international calls and free email and voicemail so that you can keep in touch while on the road. Check it out on **www.ekno.lonelyplanet.com**

FOOD & RESTAURANT GUIDES

Lonely Planet's **Out to Eat** guides recommend the brightest and best places to eat and drink in top international cities. These gourmet companions are arranged by neighbourhood, packed with dependable maps, garnished with scene-setting photos and served with quirky features.

For people who live to eat, drink and travel, **World Food** guides explore the culinary culture of each country. Entertaining and adventurous, each guide is packed with detail on staples and specialities, regional cuisine and local markets, as well as sumptuous recipes, comprehensive culinary dictionaries and lavish photos good enough to eat.

LONELY PLANET

OUTDOOR GUIDES

For those who believe the best way to see the world is on foot, Lonely Planet's **Walking Guides** detail everything from family strolls to difficult treks, with 'when to go and how to do it' advice supplemented by reliable maps and essential travel information.

Cycling Guides map a destination's best bike tours, long and short, in day-by-day detail. They contain all the information a cyclist needs, including advice on bike maintenance, places to eat and stay, innovative maps with detailed cues to the rides, and elevation charts.

The **Watching Wildlife** series is perfect for travellers who want authoritative information but don't want to tote a heavy field guide. Packed with advice on where, when and how to view a region's wildlife, each title features photos of over 300 species and contains engaging comments on the local flora and fauna.

With underwater colour photos throughout, **Pisces Books** explore the world's best diving and snorkelling areas. Each book contains listings of diving services and dive resorts, detailed information on depth, visibility and difficulty of dives, and a roundup of the marine life you're likely to see through your mask.

LONELY PLANET

OFF THE ROAD

Journeys, the travel literature series written by renowned travel authors, capture the spirit of a place or illuminate a culture with a journalist's attention to detail and a novelist's flair for words. These are tales to soak up while you're actually on the road or dip into as an at-home armchair indulgence.

The new range of lavishly illustrated **Pictorial** books is just the ticket for both travellers and dreamers. Off-beat tales and vivid photographs bring the adventure of travel to your doorstep long before the journey begins and long after it is over.

Lonely Planet **Videos** encourage the same independent, tough-minded approach as the guidebooks. Currently airing throughout the world, this award-winning series features innovative footage and an original soundtrack.

Yes, we know, work is tough, so do a little bit of deskside dreaming with the spiral-bound Lonely Planet **Diary**, the tearaway page-a-day **Day-to-Day Calendar** or a Lonely Planet **Wall Calendar**, filled with great photos from around the world.

TRAVELLERS NETWORK

Lonely Planet Online. Lonely Planet's award-winning Web site has insider information on hundreds of destinations, from Amsterdam to Zimbabwe, complete with interactive maps and relevant links. The site also offers the latest travel news, recent reports from travellers on the road, guidebook upgrades, a travel links site, an online book-buying option and a lively traveller's bulletin board. It can be viewed at **www.lonelyplanet.com** or AOL keyword: lp.

Planet Talk is a quarterly print newsletter, full of gossip, advice, anecdotes and author articles. It provides an antidote to the being-at-home blues and lets you plan and dream for the next trip. Contact the nearest Lonely Planet office for your free copy.

Comet, the free Lonely Planet newsletter, comes via email once a month. It's loaded with travel news, advice, dispatches from authors, travel competitions and letters from readers. To subscribe, click on the Comet subscription link on the front page of the Web site.

LONELY PLANET

Guides by Region

onely Planet is known worldwide for publishing practical, reliable and .no-nonsense travel information in our guides and on our Web site. The Lonely Planet list covers just about every accessible part of the world. Currently there are 16 series: Travel guides, Shoestring guides, Condensed guides, Phrasebooks, Read This First, Healthy Travel, Walking guides, Cycling guides, Watching Wildlife guides, Pisces Diving & Snorkeling guides, City Maps, Road Atlases, Out to Eat, World Food, Journeys travel literature and Pictorials.

AFRICA Africa on a shoestring • Cairo • Cairo City Map • Cape Town • Cape Town City Map • East Africa • Egypt • Egyptian Arabic phrasebook • Ethiopia, Eritrea & Djibouti • Ethiopian (Amharic) phrasebook • The Gambia & Senegal • Healthy Travel Africa • Kenya • Malawi • Morocco • Moroccan Arabic phrasebook • Mozambique • Read This First: Africa • South Africa, Lesotho & Swaziland • Southern Africa • Southern Africa Road Atlas • Swahili phrasebook • Tanzania, Zanzibar & Pemba • Trekking in East Africa • Tunisia • Watching Wildlife East Africa • Watching Wildlife Southern Africa • West Africa • World Food Morocco • Zimbabwe, Botswana & Namibia
Travel Literature: Mali Blues: Traveling to an African Beat • The Rainbird: A Central African Journey • Songs to an African Sunset: A Zimbabwean Story

AUSTRALIA & THE PACIFIC Auckland • Australia • Australian phrasebook • Australia Road Atlas • Bushwalking in Australia •Cycling New Zealand • Fiji • Fijian phrasebook • Healthy Travel Australia, NZ and the Pacific • Islands of Australia's Great Barrier Reef • Melbourne • Melbourne City Map • Micronesia • New Caledonia • New South Wales & the ACT • New Zealand • Northern Territory • Outback Australia • Out to Eat – Melbourne • Out to Eat – Sydney • Papua New Guinea • Pidgin phrasebook • Queensland • Rarotonga & the Cook Islands • Samoa • Solomon Islands • South Australia • South Pacific • South Pacific phrasebook • Sydney • Sydney City Map • Sydney Condensed • Tahiti & French Polynesia • Tasmania • Tonga • Tramping in New Zealand • Vanuatu • Victoria • Walking in Australia • Watching Wildlife Australia • Western Australia
Travel Literature: Islands in the Clouds: Travels in the Highlands of New Guinea • Kiwi Tracks: A New Zealand Journey • Sean & David's Long Drive

CENTRAL AMERICA & THE CARIBBEAN Bahamas, Turks & Caicos • Baja California • Bermuda • Central America on a shoestring • Costa Rica • Costa Rica Spanish phrasebook • Cuba • Dominican Republic & Haiti • Eastern Caribbean • Guatemala • Guatemala, Belize & Yucatán: La Ruta Maya • Healthy Travel Central & South America • Jamaica • Mexico • Mexico City • Panama • Puerto Rico • Read This First: Central & South America • World Food Mexico • Yucatán
Travel Literature: Green Dreams: Travels in Central America

EUROPE Amsterdam • Amsterdam City Map • Amsterdam Condensed • Andalucía • Austria • Baltic States phrasebook • Barcelona • Barcelona City Map • Berlin • Berlin City Map • Britain • British phrasebook • Brussels, Bruges & Antwerp • Brussels City Map • Budapest • Budapest City Map • Canary Islands • Central Europe • Central Europe phrasebook • Corfu & the Ionians • Corsica • Crete • Crete Condensed • Croatia • Cycling Britain • Cycling France • Cyprus • Czech & Slovak Republics • Denmark • Dublin • Dublin City Map • Eastern Europe • Eastern Europe phrasebook • Edinburgh • Estonia, Latvia & Lithuania • Europe on a shoestring • Finland • Florence • France • Frankfurt Condensed • French phrasebook • Georgia, Armenia & Azerbaijan • Germany • German phrasebook • Greece • Greek Islands • Greek phrasebook • Hungary • Iceland, Greenland & the Faroe Islands • Ireland • Istanbul • Italian phrasebook • Italy • Krakow • Lisbon • The Loire • London • London City Map • London Condensed • Madrid • Malta • Mediterranean Europe • Mediterranean Europe phrasebook • Moscow • Mozambique • Munich • the Netherlands • Norway • Out to Eat – London • Paris • Paris City Map • Paris Condensed • Poland • Portugal • Portuguese phrasebook • Prague • Prague City Map • Provence & the Côte d'Azur • Read This First: Europe • Romania & Moldova • Rome • Rome City Map • Russia, Ukraine & Belarus • Russian phrasebook • Scandinavian & Baltic Europe • Scandinavian Europe phrasebook • Scotland • Sicily • Slovenia • South-West France • Spain • Spanish phrasebook • St Petersburg • St Petersburg City Map • Sweden • Switzerland • Trekking in Spain • Tuscany • Ukrainian phrasebook • Venice • Vienna • Walking in Britain • Walking in France • Walking in Ireland • Walking in Italy • Walking in Spain • Walking in Switzerland • Western Europe • Western Europe phrasebook • World Food France • World Food Ireland • World Food Italy • World Food Spain
Travel Literature: Love and War in the Apennines • The Olive Grove: Travels in Greece • On the Shores of the Mediterranean • Round Ireland in Low Gear • A Small Place in Italy • After Yugoslavia

LONELY PLANET

Mail Order

onely Planet products are distributed worldwide. They are also available by mail order from Lonely Planet, so if you have difficulty finding a title please write to us. North and South American residents should write to 150 Linden St, Oakland, CA 94607, USA; European and African residents should write to 10a Spring Place, London NW5 3BH, UK; and residents of other countries to Locked Bag 1, Footscray, Victoria 3011, Australia.

INDIAN SUBCONTINENT Bangladesh • Bengali phrasebook • Bhutan • Delhi • Goa • Healthy Travel Asia & India • Hindi & Urdu phrasebook • India • Indian Himalaya • Karakoram Highway • Kerala • Mumbai (Bombay) • Nepal • Nepali phrasebook • Pakistan • Rajasthan • Read This First: Asia & India • South India • Sri Lanka • Sri Lanka phrasebook • Tibet • Tibetan phrasebook • Trekking in the Indian Himalaya • Trekking in the Karakoram & Hindukush • Trekking in the Nepal Himalaya
Travel Literature: The Age of Kali: Indian Travels and Encounters • Hello Goodnight: A Life of Goa • In Rajasthan • A Season in Heaven: True Tales from the Road to Kathmandu • Shopping for Buddhas • A Short Walk in the Hindu Kush • Slowly Down the Ganges

ISLANDS OF THE INDIAN OCEAN Madagascar & Comoros • Maldives • Mauritius, Réunion & Seychelles

MIDDLE EAST & CENTRAL ASIA Bahrain, Kuwait & Qatar • Central Asia • Central Asia phrasebook • Dubai • Hebrew phrasebook • Iran • Israel & the Palestinian Territories • Istanbul • Istanbul City Map • Istanbul to Cairo on a shoestring • Jerusalem • Jerusalem City Map • Jordan • Lebanon • Middle East • Oman & the United Arab Emirates • Syria • Turkey • Turkish phrasebook • World Food Turkey • Yemen
Travel Literature: Black on Black: Iran Revisited • The Gates of Damascus • Kingdom of the Film Stars: Journey into Jordan

NORTH AMERICA Alaska • Boston • Boston City Map • California & Nevada • California Condensed • Canada • Chicago • Chicago City Map • Deep South • Florida • Great Lakes • Hawaii • Hiking in Alaska • Hiking in the USA • Honolulu • Las Vegas • Los Angeles • Los Angeles City Map • Louisiana & The Deep South • Miami • Miami City Map • New England • New Orleans • New York City • New York City City Map • New York City Condensed • New York, New Jersey & Pennsylvania • Oahu • Out to Eat – San Francisco • Pacific Northwest • Puerto Rico • Rocky Mountains • San Francisco • San Francisco City Map • Seattle • Southwest • Texas • USA • USA phrasebook • Vancouver • Virginia & the Capital Region • Washington DC • Washington, DC City Map • World Food Deep South, USA • World Food New Orleans
Travel Literature: Caught Inside: A Surfer's Year on the California Coast • Drive Thru America

NORTH-EAST ASIA Beijing • Beijing City Map • Cantonese phrasebook • China • Hiking in Japan • Hong Kong • Hong Kong City Map • Hong Kong Condensed • Hong Kong, Macau & Guangzhou • Japan • Japanese phrasebook • Korea • Korean phrasebook • Kyoto • Mandarin phrasebook • Mongolia • Mongolian phrasebook • Seoul • Shanghai • South-West China • Taiwan • Tokyo
Travel Literature: In Xanadu: A Quest • Lost Japan

SOUTH AMERICA Argentina, Uruguay & Paraguay • Bolivia • Brazil • Brazilian phrasebook • Buenos Aires • Chile & Easter Island • Colombia • Ecuador & the Galapagos Islands • Healthy Travel Central & South America • Latin American Spanish phrasebook • Peru • Quechua phrasebook • Read This First: Central & South America • Rio de Janeiro • Rio de Janeiro City Map • Santiago • South America on a shoestring • Santiago • Trekking in the Patagonian Andes • Venezuela
Travel Literature: Full Circle: A South American Journey

SOUTH-EAST ASIA Bali & Lombok • Bangkok • Bangkok City Map • Burmese phrasebook • Cambodia • Hanoi • Healthy Travel Asia & India • Hill Tribes phrasebook • Ho Chi Minh City • Indonesia • Indonesian phrasebook • Indonesia's Eastern Islands • Jakarta • Java • Lao phrasebook • Laos • Malay phrasebook • Malaysia, Singapore & Brunei • Myanmar (Burma) • Philippines • Pilipino (Tagalog) phrasebook • Read This First: Asia & India • Singapore • Singapore City Map • South-East Asia on a shoestring • South-East Asia phrasebook • Thailand • Thailand's Islands & Beaches • Thailand, Vietnam, Laos & Cambodia Road Atlas • Thai phrasebook • Vietnam • Vietnamese phrasebook • World Food Thailand • World Food Vietnam

ALSO AVAILABLE: Antarctica • The Arctic • The Blue Man: Tales of Travel, Love and Coffee • Brief Encounters: Stories of Love, Sex & Travel • Chasing Rickshaws • The Last Grain Race • Lonely Planet Unpacked • Not the Only Planet: Science Fiction Travel Stories • Lonely Planet On the Edge • Sacred India • Travel with Children • Travel Photography: A Guide to Taking Better Pictures

Index

Text

A

Abana 575
accommodation 80-1
activities, see individual
    activities
Adana 455-8, **456**
Adilcevaz 676
Adıyaman 644-5
Adrasan 410
Afrodisias 342-4, **343**
Afyon 336-40
Ağrı 626
Ağrı Dağı 628
Ağzıkarahan 534
Ahi brotherhoods 562
Ahlat 676
air travel
    departure tax 93
    to/from Turkey 91-6
    within Turkey 102
Aizanoi 333-4
Ak Han 352
Akbil 173
Akçakale 585
Akçay 226
Akdamar 675
Akkum 258
Akliman 221
Akpınar 358
Aksaray 530-1
Akyaka 364
Akyarlar 300-1
Ala Dağlar Milli Parkı 569
alabaster 39
Alacahöyük 497-8
Alaçatı 257
Alanya 434-40, **435**
Alarahan 440
Alay Hanı 534
Alçıtepe 204
alcohol 86-7
Alevis 511
Alexander the Great 16
Alexandria Troas 220
Alibey Adası 230
Altın Portakal Filim Festivali
    417
Altınkum 257

Altınoluk 226
Amasra 572-4
Amasya 500-5, **501**
Anadolu Hisarı 183
Anadolu Kavağı 184
Anamur 440-3, **441**
Anamurium 440-1
Anavarza 459-60
Anazarbus 459-60
Andriake 406
Ani 623-6, **624**
Anıt Kabir 475-6
Ankara 470-87, **472**, **476**
    accommodation 477-8
    Anıt Kabir 475-6
    Museum of Anatolian
        Civilisations 473
    travel to/from 482-4
Antakya 463-8, **465**
Antakya Arkeoloji Müzesi 464
Antalya 412-22, **413**, **416**
Antalya Müzesi 415
Antep 634-9, **635**
Antioch ad Orontes 464
Antioch-in-Pisidia 360
Antiocheia 342
Antiphellus 400
antiques 40
Anzac battlefields, see Gallipoli
    Peninsula
Anzac Cove 202
Anzac Day 201
archaeological sites, see
    individual entries
Ardahan 617
Ardanuç 617
area codes 57
Arezastis 336
Argonauts, the 583
Armenia
    kingdom of 17
    travel to/from 99
Armenian people 32-3, 677-9
Arsameia 649
Arslankaya 336
Artemision 261
arts, visual 33-4, see also crafts
Artvin 615-17
Arycanda 407
Asclepion 234
Aspendos 426

Aspendos Opera & Ballet
    Festival 417
Assos 223-6
Atakent 448
Atatürk 23, 24-5
Atatürk's mausoleum, see Anıt
    Kabir
Avanos 545-7, **546**
Aya Sofya 126, 132-6, **135**
Ayazinköyü 336
Ayder 598-600
Aydin 340
Aydıncık 443
Aydınlık Beach 282
Ayvacık 220
Ayvalı 552
Ayvalık 226-30, **227**
Azizabat 342

B

Baba Haydar Mağarası 352
Babakale 221
Bağbaşı 612
Balıkesir 326-7
Balıklı Kaplıca 515-16
Ballıca Cave 510
balloon trips 528
Bana 614
Bandırma 326
bargaining 88
Barhal 613-14
Batman 672-3
Bayburt 595
beaches
    Alanya 437
    Antalya 417
    Aydınlık Beach 282
    Bodrum Peninsula 300-4
    Bozcaada 221
    Bozköy 575
    Çeşme 255
    Demre 407
    Dilek Peninsula 281-2
    Eğirdir 356
    Fethiye 385
    Gökçeada 214
    Güllük 290-1
    İztuzu Beach 379, 380
    Kemer 412
    Kızkalesi 450
    Kumluca 575

Bold indicates maps.

beaches continued
Kuşadası 277
Marmaris 366
Ölüdeniz 389
Ortakent Yalısı 295
Pamucak 274
Patara 396
Side 429
Sinop 577
Bebek 178-9
Beçina Fortress 288
beehive houses 660-1
Behramkale 223-6
Belcekız 389, **391**
Beldibi 412
Belen 463
Belevi 275
Belkis-Zeugma 636
Bergama 231-8, **231**
Bey Mountains Coastal
National Park 408
Beydağları Sahil Milli Parkı 408
Beylerbeyi Palace 182-3
Beyşehir 359-60
bicycle travel, see cycling
Binbirkilise 560
bird-watching 449
birds, see wildlife
Birecik 639
Bitez 300
Bitlis 673
Black Sea Coast 570-600,
572-3
Blue Mosque 136-7
Blue Voyage 367
boat charter 367
boat travel
to/from Turkey 100-1
within Turkey 109-10
boat trips 367
Alanya 437
Antalya 417
Ayvalık 227-8
Çeşme 255
Dalyan 378-9
Datça 374
Eğirdir 356
Fethiye 385-6
Foça 239
Kaş 400-2
Köyceğiz 376
Marmaris 366-7
Ölüdeniz 390
Side 431
Üçağız 404
Bodrum 291-300, **293**
Bodrum Peninsula 300-4, **301**

Boğazkale 493-7, **495**
Bolaman 581
books 59-61, see also literature
border crossings 96-7
Bosphorus 175-84, **112**
Asian Shore 180-4
European Shore 176-80
tours 176
Boyabat 493
Boyalık 255
Bozburun 372-3
Bozburun Dağı 427
Bozcaada 221-3, **222**
Bozköy 575
Bozyazı 443
Bulanık 617
Bulgaria, travel to/from 98-9,
194
Burdur 359
Burdur Gölü 359
Burgazada 185
Bursa 311-25, **313**, **316-17**
bus travel
to/from Turkey 97
within Turkey 102-3, 109
business hours 77
Butterfly Valley 392
Büyükada 184
Byzantine Empire 19

C
Çağıllı 407
Calvert, Frank 219
Camel Wrestling Festival 224
Çamlıhemşin 597
Çanakkale 208-13, **210**
Çanakkale Trova
Festivali 209
Çandarlı 238
canoeing
Köprülü Kanyon 427
Cappadocia 527-60, **529**
car travel 105-8
driving licence 52
rental 107-8
road rules 105-6
road safety 106
caravanserais, see hans
Caria, Kingdom of 259, 286
carpets 37-9
buying 88-9, 166
Yahyalı 569
Çarşamba 581
Castle of St Peter 292-4
Çatal Höyük 526-7
Çavdarhisar 333-4
Cave of St Thecla 446

caves
Baba Haydar Mağarası 352
Ballıca Cave 510
Cave of St Thecla 446
Cennet ve Cehennem 448
Karain Cave 424
Çavuşin 544
Çavuşköy 410
Çavuştepe 682-3
Cendere 649
Cennet ve Cehennem 448
ceramics 39
Çeşme 253-7, **254**
Çevlik 468
children, travel with 73
Chimaera, the 408-10
Chios, travel to/from 257
Chora Church 144-5
Christianity 18
Chunuk Bair 203
churches, Georgian
Bana 614
Barhal 613
Church of Dolishane 617
Church of Porta 617
Church of Tbeti 617
Dörtkilise 614
churches, rock-cut
Çavuşin 544
Göreme 537-9
Ihlara 531-3
Soğanlı 556
Zelve 544
cicims 39
cinema 42
Çırağan Palace 177
Çıralı 409-10
climate 27-8
Commagene 17-18
Constantinople 113-14
consulates 52
copperware 40
Çorlu 195
Çorum 498-500
costs 55
courses 80
crafts 37-41
Croesus, King 252
cruises, see boat trips
crusades 20
cultural considerations 42-4,
49
mosque etiquette 43-4
currency, see money
customs regulations 53-4
Cybele 266
cycling 79-80, 108

Cyprus 23
  travel to/from 101, 422,
    444-5, 454

D

Dalaman 382-3
Dalyan 377-82, **378**
Damsa Gölü 552
Daphne 468
Daraçya Peninsula 371-6
Dardanelles 198
Datça 373-5
Datça Peninsula, see Reşadiye
  Peninsula
Davras Dağı 358-9
Değirmenlidere 615
Demre 405-7
Deniz Müzesi 176-7
Denizli 345-6
Derinkuyu 555
dervishes, see whirling
  dervishes
Deyrul Umur Monastery, see
  Morgabriel
Deyrul Zafaran 671
diarrhoea 67-8
Didyma 284
Dikili 230-1
Dilek Milli Parkı 281
Dilek Peninsula 281-2
disabled travellers 73
diving, see scuba diving
Divriği 516-17
Diyadin 629
Diyarbakır 662-9, **664**
Doğubayazıt 626-30, **627**
Dolmabahçe Palace 146-7
dolmuş travel 103-4, 109
Dörtkilise 614
drinks 86-7
driving, see car travel
Düden Falls 423
Dumlupınar, Battle of 338

E

Eceabat 207-8
economy 30
Ecumenical Council 307
Edirne 186-95, **188**
Edremit 226, 675
education 33
Eğirdir 354-8
Eğirdir Gölü 354

Egyptian Bazaar, see Mısır
  Çarşısı
Elaiussa-Sebaste 451
Elazığ 643-4
electricity 62
embassies 52
emergencies 76
  İstanbul 126
Emir Han 315
Emir Sultan Camii 313-14
Endymion 285
environmental issues
  28, 49
Ephesus 266-74, **270**
Ephesus Festival 268
Ephesus Müzesi 261
Erciş 677
Erciyes Dağı 535, 568-9
Erythrae 257
Erzincan 603
Erzurum 604-10, **605**
Erzurum Congress 604
Eski Gümüşler Monastery
  558-9
Eski Kale 649
Eskihisar 364
Eskişehir 327-9
Espiye 585
etiquette, see cultural
  considerations
Eumenes II 17, 231
Euromos 288-9
events 77-9, see also festivals
  and Islam, holidays

F

faience, see tiles
Fairy Chimneys, Valley of the
  545
Fatih Camii 144
fauna, see wildlife
fax services 58
ferry travel, see boat travel
festivals 77-9
  Altın Portakal Filim Festivali
    417
  Aspendos Opera & Ballet
    Festival 417
  Camel Wrestling Festival
    224
  Çanakkale Trova Festivali
    209
  Ephesus Festival 268
  Hacıbektaş Festival 560, 561
  International Black Sea
    Giresun Aksu Festival 583

International Faience &
  Ceramics Congress 330
International İstanbul Music
  Festival 151
International İstanbul
  Theatre Festival 151
International İzmir Festival
  246
International Kahta Komma-
  gene Festival 645
İstanbul International Film
  Festival 151
Karagöz Festival 312
Kaş Lycia Festival 402
Kırkpınar Oiled Wrestling
  Festival 192
Marmaris Yacht Festival 367
Mesir Şenlikleri (Manisa)
  241
Mevlâna Festival 523-4
Pamukkale Festival 349
Turkoman Folkloric Song &
  Dance Festival 447
Fethiye 384-9, **386-7**
films 61, see also cinema
Finike 407
flora 28-9
Foça 238-40
food 81-6
  glossary 82
  vegetarian 84-5
frescoes, see also mosaics
  Eski Gümüşler Monastery
    558
  Göreme Open-Air Museum
    537

G

Galata Tower 151
Gallipoli National Historic Park
  200-5
Gallipoli Peninsula 196-208,
  197
  history 197-9
  organised tours 199-200
GAP 28, 655
gay & lesbian travellers 73
Gaziantep 634-9, **635**
Gazlıgöl 336
Gelibolu 205-7, see also
  Gallipoli Peninsula
geography 27
Georgia, travel to/from 99,
  617
Georgian churches, see
  churches, Georgian

Bold indicates maps.

Georgian Valleys 611-12
Gevaş 675
Gideros 575
Giresun 582-5
Göcek 383-4
Gökçeada 213-15, **214**
Göklıman 407
Gökova 364
Göksu Delta 449
Gökyurt 527
Golden Fleece 583
Golden Horn 143-4
Gölköy 303-4
Gordian Knot 486
Gordion 485-7
Göreme 537-44, **538**
Göreme National Park
    539-40
Göreme Open-Air Museum
    537-9
government 29-30
Göynük 412
Göynüş Vadisi 336
Greece, travel to/from 98,
    100-1, 194, 196
Güllük 290-1
Gülpınar 221
Gülşehir 560
Gümbet 300
Gümüşhane 595
Gümüşlük 302-3
Güzelçamlı 282
Güzelyurt 533-4

H
Hacıbektaş 560-1
    festival 560, 561
Haho 612
Hakkari 683-4
hamams 320-1
Han el Ba'rur Caravanserai 662
hans *between pages 560 & 561*
    Ağzıkarahan 534
    Ak Han 352
    Alarahan 440
    Alay Hanı 534
    Emir Han 315
    Han el Ba'rur Caravanserai
        662
    Karatay Han 568
    Koza Han 315
    Mama Hatun Kervansarayı
        604
    Şarapsa Hanı 440
    Sarıhan 547-8
    Sultan Han 568

Sultanhanı 527
    Tepesidelik Hanı 534
Harbiye 468
Harput 644
Harran 660-1
Hasankale 611
Hasankeyf 672-3
Hatay 463-8, **465**
Hattuşa 493-7, **495**
Havsa 195
health 63-72
    diarrhoea 67-8
    immunisations 63-4
    malaria 69-70
    medical services 66
Hellespont 198
Hemşin people 571
Herakleia 285-6
Heybeliada 184
Hierapolis 347-9, **348**
Hierapolis-Castabala 461-2
hiking 79
    Barhal 614
    Davras Dağı 358
    Göreme National Park
        539-40
    Ihlara Gorge 532
    Kaçkar Dağları 597-8, 613
    Köprülü Kanyon 427
    Kuyucuk Dağları 427
    Lycian Way 411
    Pigeon Valley 536
    Yusufeli 613
Hippodrome 137-8
Hisarönü, *see* Reşadiye
    Peninsula
history 15-27
hitching 108-9
Hittite sites 493-7
    Alacahöyük 497-8
    Hattuşa 494-6
    Yazılıkaya 496-7
Hittites 15, 493-4
Hoca, Nasreddin 36
holidays 77-9
Hopa 600
Hoşap 682-3
hot springs, *see also* thermal
    baths
    Ayder 598-600
    Balıklı Kaplıca 515-16
    Diyadin 629
    Ihlara 532
    Kestanbol Kaplıcaları 221
    Pasinler 611
    Sultaniye Kaplıcaları 380
hotels, *see* accommodation

I
Iasos 289
İçel 451-4, **452**
İçmeler 371
İçmeler Köyü 282
Iğdır 626
Ihlara 531-3
Ihlara Gorge 532, **531**
Ihlara Vadisi 532
Ilıca 255
immunisations 63-4
İncekum 440
İncesu 569
İnebolu 575
International Black Sea Giresun
    Aksu Festival 583
International Faience &
    Ceramics Congress 330
International İstanbul Music
    Festival 151
International İstanbul Theatre
    Festival 151
International İzmir Festival 246
International Kahta Komma-
    gene Festival 645
Internet
    access 58-9
    resources 59
Ionia 15, 259
İpsala 196
Iran, travel to/from 99, 683
İshak Paşa Sarayı 627
İşhan 612
İskenderun 462-3
Islam 19, 44-5
    holidays 77-8
islands
    Alibey Adası 230
    Bozcaada 221-3, **222**
    Gökçeada 213-15, **214**
    Karaada 295
    Kekova 402
    Princes' Islands 184-5
Isparta 352-3
Issos 462
İstanbul 111-85, **112**, **116-23**
    accommodation 151-7
    Aya Sofya 126, 132-6, **135**
    Beyoğlu 145-51, **118-19**
    Blue Mosque 136-7
    emergencies 126
    entertainment 162-6
    festivals 151
    food 157-62
    Golden Horn 143-4
    hamams 165-6
    history 113-15

information 124-6
İstiklal Caddesi 147-50, **118-19**
Kapalı Çarşı 140-2, **141**
Mısır Çarşısı 143-4
museums 137, 138, 139-40, 150
Old İstanbul 126-43
orientation 115-24
shopping 166-7
Taksim Square 146, **118-19**
travel to/from 167-72
travel within 172-5
İstanbul International Film Festival 151
Italy, travel to/from 100
itineraries 46-7
İzmir 241-52, **243**
İznik 307-11
İztuzu Beach 379, 380

J
Janissaries 130
Jersey Tiger butterfly 392
jewellery 40-1
Julius Caesar 510

K
Kabatepe 202
Kaçkar Dağları 597-8
Kaçkar Mountains, see Kaçkar Dağları
Kadıkalesi 302
Kadirli 460
Kahramanmaraş 630-4
Kahta 645-7, **645**
Kahta Kalesi 649
Kaleköy 214, 405, 505
Kalkan 397-9, **398**
Kangal sheepdogs 515
Kaniş-Karum 568
Kanlıca 183
Kanytelis 451
Kapadokya, see Cappadocia
Kapalı Çarşı (İstanbul) 140-2, **141**
Kapıkayalar 336
Kapıkule 194
Kapısuyu 575
Kaputaş 399
Karaada 295
Karacasu 342
Karadut 650

Karağöl Milli Parkı 617
Karagöz 312
Karagöz Festival 312
Karain Cave 424
Karakuş 649
Karaman 559-60
Karatay Han 568
Karatepe-Aslantaş Milli Parkı 461
Karatepe-Aslantaş Müzesi 461
Karatay Han 568
Karkamış 639
Karmylassos 393
Kars 618-23, **619**
Kaş 400-4, **401**
Kaş Lycia Festival 402
Kasaba 493
Kastamonu 491-3
Kastellorizo 400
Kaunos 379-80
Kavaklı Burun 282
Kayaköy 393
kaymak 336
Kaymaklı 554
Kaymaklı Manastiri 589
Kayseri 562-7, **563**
Kekova 402
Kemal, Mustafa, see Atatürk
Kemal, Namık 618
Kemer 412
Kemerhisar 559
Keramos 290
Kestanbol Kaplıcaları 221
Keşan 196
kilims 39
Kilistra 527
Kilitbahir 208
Kilyos 180
Kınalıada 185
Kipi 196
Kırkpınar Oiled Wrestling Festival 192
Kırşehir 562
Kıyıkışlacık 289
Kızıl Adalar, see Princes' Islands
Kızkalesi 450-1
Knidos 375-6
Konya 517-26, **518**
Kop Geçidi 595
Kop Pass 595
Köprülü Kanyon 426-8
Kos, travel to/from 299-300
Kovada Gölü Milli Parkı 359
Köyceğiz 376-7
Koza Han 315
Kozlubel 329
Kültepe 568

Kum Limanı 204
Kümbet 336
Kumluca 407, 575
Kurban Bayramı 78
Kurdish people 26, 31-2
Kurşunlu Şelalesi 425
Kurucaşile 575
Kuş Gölü 326
Kuşadası 275-81, **276**
Kuşcenneti Milli Parkı 326
Kütahya 329-33, **330**
Kuyucuk Dağları 427
Kuzu Limanı 213
Kyaneai 405

L
Labranda 289-90
Lake District 352-60
Lake Van 674-7
lakes
    Burdur Gölü 359
    Damsa Gölü 552
    Eğirdir Gölü 354
    Kovada Gölü 359
    Kuş Gölü 326
    Lake Van 674-7
    Salda Gölü 424
    Tortum Gölü 612
    Yedi Kuğular Gölü 505
Laodicea 351-2
Laodikya, see Laodicea
language 685-92
Latmos 285-6
laundry 63
Laz people 571
leather 41
legal matters 77
Lesvos, travel to/from 229
Letoön 395
Limyra 407
literature 36, 42, see also books
Lone Pine 202
Lüleburgaz 195
Lycian Way 411
Lycians 385
Lydians 15-16
Lystra 527

M
magazines 61
malaria 69-70
Malatya 639-43, **640**
Malazgirt 676
Mama Hatun Kervansarayı 604
Mamure Kalesi 441
Manavgat 434

Bold indicates maps.

Manavgat River 434
Manisa 240-1
maps 48
Maraş, see Kahramanmaraş
Mardin 669-71
Marmaris 364-71, **365**
Marmaris Yacht Festival 367
Mary's House 266
Mausoleum of Halicarnassus 294-5
Mausolus, King 291, 292
Mazıköy 555
measures, see weights & measures
medical services 66
meerschaum 41, 328, 329
Meis Adası 400
Mersin 451-4, **452**
Meryemana 266
Mesir Şenlikleri (Manisa) 241
Mevlâna 150
Mevlâna Festival 523-4
Mevlâna Museum 519-20
Meydancık Kalesi 443
Midas, King 486
Midas Şehri 334-6
Midnight Express 194
Midyat 672
Milas 286-8, **287**
Miletus 283-4, **283**
Mısır Çarşısı 143-4
money 54-7
    ATMs 55
    bargaining 56
    costs 55
    tipping 56
monk seals 239
Monophysites 670
Morgabriel 672
mosaics
    Antakya Arkeoloji Müzesi 464
    Aya Sofya 136
    Chora Church 145
mosques, see individual entries
    etiquette 43-4
motorcycle travel 108
Mt Ararat 628
Mt Argeus, see Erciyes Dağı
Mt Nemrut, see Nemrut Dağı
mountains
    Bozburun Dağı 427
    Davras Dağı 358-9
    Erciyes Dağı 568-9
    ʼucuk Dağları 427
    kar Dağları 597-8
    ʼrarat 628
    rut Dağı 647-52, 675

Muğla 361-3
Museum of Anatolian Civilisations 473
Museum of Underwater Archaeology 292-4
music 34-6
Mustafapaşa 552-6
Myra, see Demre

N
Nakhitchevan 626
Narlıkuyu 448
Nazilli 341-2
Neandria 221
Nemrut Dağı 647-52, 675
Nemrut Dağı Milli Parkı 647-52, **648**
Nevşehir 534-5
newspapers 61
Nicaea, see İznik
Niğde 557-8, **557**
Nightingale, Florence 181
Niksar 509
Noah's Ark 628
Nyssa 341

O
oiled wrestling 191, 192
Olimpos 408-10
Ölüdeniz 389-92, **391**
opium 336
Ordu 582
Ören 290
Orhaniye 371-2
Orontes River 464
Ortahisar 548
Ortakent 300
Ortakent Yalısı 295
Ortaköy 178
Öşk Vank 612
Osman Paşa, Gazi 21
Osmaniye 460-1
Ottoman Empire 20-2
Ottoman houses
    Afyon 338
    Amasya 503
    Safranbolu 487-9
    Tokat 507-8
Özkonak 548
Özlüce 554

P
Pagnon Cave 662
Palaeokastron, see Balıkesir
Palandöken 610-11

Pamphylia 426
Pamucak 274
Pamukkale 346-51, **349**
Pamukkale Festival 349
Paşabahçe 183
Pasinler 611
Patara 395-7
Patrica Nature Reserve 230
Payas 462
Pazarkule 194
pensions, see accommodation
Pergamum 231-8, **233**, **235**
Perge 425, **425**
Peristrema 531-3
Perşembe 581
Phaselis 411
Phocaea 239
photography & video 62
Phrygians 15-16, 335
Pigeon Valley 536
Pınara 394
plants, see flora
Polatlı 485-7
police 75
politics 29-30
pollution, air 76
Pontus 17
population 30-3
postal services 57
pottery 545
Priene 282-3, **282**
Princes' Islands 184-5
Prophet Job's Site 657

R
radio 61-2
rafting
    Köprülü Kanyon 427
    Yusufeli 613
Ramazan 77
Republic, Turkish 22-3
Reşadiye Peninsula 371-6
Research Institute for Mediterranean Civilisations 417
Rhodes, travel to/from 299-300, 370, 422
Rize 595-7
Rock of Van 679-80
Romans 17-18
Rumeli Hisarı 178-9
Rüstem Paşa Camii 144
Russia, travel to/from 101

S
safety considerations 74-6, 631
Safranbolu 487-91, **488**

Sagalassos 353-4
St John Basilica 261
St Nicholas 406
St Paul 18, 224, 266, 268, 454
Saklıkent Gorge 394
Salda Gölü 424
Salihli 252-3
Samandağ 468
Samsun 578-80
Şanlıurfa 652-9, **654**
Santa Claus 406
Şarapsa Hanı 440
Sarayiçi 191
Sarayık Koyü 505
Sardis 252-3
Sarıhan 547-8
Sarıkamış 617
Sarıyer 179-80
Saros 196
Sarp 600
Sart, see Sardis
Şavşat 617
scams 75
Schliemann, Heinrich 216
scooter travel 372
scuba diving
    Gümüşlük 302
    Fethiye 386
    Marmaris 367
Seddülbahir 204
Şeker Bayramı 77-8
Selçuk 259-66, **262**
Seleucia, see Silifke
Seleucia ad Piera 468
Seleukeia 434
Selge 426-8
Selime 532
Selimiye 371-2
Seljuk architecture
    Afyon 338
    Divriği 516-17
    Kayseri 564-5
    Konya 520-2
    Sivas 511-13
Seljuks 19-20
senior travellers 73
    cards 52
Senpiyer Kilisesi 465
Şenyuva 597-8
Sepetçi Köyü 329
Seraglio, see Topkapı Palace
Seven Churches of the
    Revelation 18, 351
Şeytan Sofrası 228

shadow puppets 312
shopping 88-90
Side 429-33, **432**
Sidyma 394-5
Sığacık 258
Silifke 445-8, **446**
Sille 527
Sillyon 425-6
Simena 405
Sinop 575-8, **576**
Şirince 274-5
Sivas 510-15, **512**
skiing 79
    Erciyes Dağı 568-9
    Palandöken 610-11
    Sarıkamış 617
    Uludağ 325
Smyrna 242
Softa Kalesi 443
Soğanlı 556
Soğmatar 662
Söke 285
Sokullu Mehmet Paşa
    Kervansaray 462
South-East Anatolia Project 28,
    655
spectator sports 87-8
Stratonikea 364
Şuayb City 662
suede 41
Süleyman the Magnificent 20-1
Süleymaniye Camii 142
Sultan Ahmet Camii, see Blue
    Mosque
Sultan Han 568
Sultan Marshes Bird Paradise
    556-7
Sultan Sazlığı Kuş Cenneti, see
    Sultan Marshes Bird Paradise
Sultanhanı 527
Sultaniye Kaplıcaları 380
Sunken Cistern 138-9
sumaks 39
Sumela Monastery 593-4
Sungurlu 497
Susanoğlu 448
Syria, travel to/from 99

T
Tarabya 179
Tarsus 454-5
Taşlıköy 614
Taşucu 443-5
Tatvan 673-4
tavla boards 40
taxes 89-90

taxi travel 109-10, see also
    dolmuş travel
tea plantations 595
Tea Research Institute 596
Teimiussa, see Üçağız
Tekirdağ 195-6
Tekirova 410
telephone services 57-8
television 61-2
Telmessos 384-5
Temple of Apollo 284
Teos 258
Tepesidelik Hanı 534
Tercan 603
Termal 306-7
Termessos 423-4, **423**
Tevfikiye 219-220
thermal baths, see also hot
    springs
    Bursa 319
    Termal 306-7
Thrace 186-215, **187**
Tigris River 662, 672
tiles 39, between pages 304 &
    305
    Kütahya 331
time 62, see also business hours
tipping 56
Tirebolu 585
Titüs ve Vespasiyanüs Tüneli 468
Tlos 393-4
toilets 63
Tokat 505-9, **506**
Topkapı Palace 127-34, **128**
Toprakkale 462
Tortum Gölü 612
tourist offices 49-50
tours 110
Trabzon 585-93, **586**
train travel
    to/from Turkey 97
    within Turkey 104-5
travertine pools 348
treehouses
    Butterfly Valley 392
    Olimpos 409-10
trekking, see hiking
Trojan War 217
Troy 216-20, **218**
Turgutreis 301-2
Turhal 509
Turkish delight 159
Turkish people 30-1
Turkoman Folkloric Song &
    Dance Festival 447
turtles 379, 380
Tuzluca 626

Bold indicates maps.

U

Üçağız 402, 404-5
Uçhisar 535-7
Uğurlu 214
Uludağ 325
underground cities 548, 554-5
Ünye 581
Urartians 15-16
Urartu 677-9
Urfa 652-9
Ürgüp 548-52, **549**
Üsküdar 181-2
Uzun Yol 534
Uzuncaburç 449-50
Uzungöl 595
Uzunköprü 196

V

Valley of the Fairy Chimneys 545
Van 677-82, **678**
Van Castle 679-80
Van Gölü 674-7
Van Kalesi 679-80
video, see photography & video
  video systems 62
visas 50

W

walking, see hiking
War of Independence 22

water sports 79
weights & measures 62
whirling dervishes 150, 520,
  523
white-water rafting, see rafting
wildlife 28-9
windsurfing 257, 258
wineries 550
wooden houses between pages
  488 & 489
women travellers 72-3
work 80
World Heritage Sites
  Divriği 516-17
  Göreme Open-Air Museum
    537-9
  Hattuşa 493-7, **495**
  Nemrut Dağı 647-52, **648**
  Pamukkale 346-51, **349**
  Safranbolu 487-91, **488**

X

Xanthos 395

Y

yacht cruising 79, see also boat
  trips
yacht marina
  Kalkan 397
  Marmaris 365

Yahşi Yalısı 300
Yahyalı 569
Yalıkavak 303
Yalova 305-6
Yalvaç 360
Yassıçal 505
Yassıhöyük 485
Yazılıkaya 334, 496-7
Yedi Kuğular Gölü 505
Yedigöller 569
Yeni Foça 240
Yeni Kale 649
Yerebatan Sarnıçı, see Sunken
  Cistern
Yesemek Open-Air museum
  639
Yeşil Cami 314
Yılankale 459
Yıldız Palace 177-8
Yolboyu 614
Yörük Köyü 491
Yozgat 498
Yusufeli 612-13

Z

Zelve 544
Zigana Geçidi 595
Zigana Pass 595
Zından Mağarası 359
Zile 509

Boxed Text & Special Sections

Akbil 173
Alevis, The 511
Antiques 40
Anzac Day 201
Army Days 31
Atatürk 24-5
Battle of Dumlupınar,
  The 338
Blue Voyage, A 367
Çanakkale 211
Cappadocia *between pages
  528 & 529*
Cappadocia from
  the Air 528
Caravanserais & Hans *between
  pages 560 & 561*
Commissions – A Colossal
  Rip-off 56
Cream from Contented Cows
  336
Daraçya Peninsula by Scooter
  372
Dream Pipes 328
Ephesus – A Walking Tour
  266-74, **270**
Florence Nightingale 181
Fluid Balance 65
Food & Drinks Glossary 82-3
Frank Calvert, Discoverer of
  Troy 219
Future for the Kurds?, A 26
Gazi Osman Paşa 21
Going Underground 554-5
Göksu Delta, The 449

Golden Touch & Gordian Knot
  486
Hacı Bektaş Veli & the Bektaşi
  Sect 561
Hamam Experience, The 320-1
He Came, He Saw,
  He Conquered 510
Hellespont, The 198
Highlights of Turkey 46
Hittites, The 494
Is it Safe to Travel in South-
  Eastern Turkey? 631
İskender Kebap 84
Janissaries, The 130
Karagöz 312
Kekova Boat Trips 402
Kısmet & Kader 105
Kütahya Tilework 331
Laz & Hemşin Peoples, The 571
Life in the Cage 132
Lycian Way 411
Lycians, The 385
Maşallah 144
Mevlâna & the Whirling
  Dervishes 520
Midnight Express 194
Namık Kemal – A Turkish
  Polymath 618
Nasreddin Hoca, Storyteller
  Supreme 36
Natasha Syndrome, The 590
Oiled Wrestling 192
Old Pera Wineshops 163
On Foot 174

One Nature or Two? 670
Pergamum: Acropolis &
  Asclepion 231-8, **233**, **235**
Phrygians, The 335
Political Headgear 42
Sacrifice at the Bridge 445
St Paul in Ephesus 268
Santa Claus 406
Search for Noah's Ark,
  The 628
Seed of a Myth? 583
South-East Anatolia
  Project 655
Sublime Porte, The 139
Top of the Turkish Pops 35
Topkapı Palace Museum
  127-34, **128**
Traditional Patterns 38
Turkey's Wooden Houses
  between pages 488 & 489
Turkish Arts & Crafts
  37-41
Turkish Delight 159
Turkish Tiles *between pages
  304 & 305*
Turkish Knockout, The 74
Turtle Alert 379
Urfa's Favourite Son 653
Van Monster, The 674
Visas for Neighbouring
  Countries 50-1
Warning 345, 543
Whirling to Ecstasy 523
Yörük Markets, The 356

MAP LEGEND

CITY ROUTES

Freeway .... Freeway	===== ...... Unsealed Road
Highway .... Primary Road	——→—— ... One Way Street
Road ..... Secondary Road	.... Pedestrian Street
Street .... Street	⊔⊔⊔⊔⊔⊔ ...... Stepped Street
Lane .... Lane	⊃ ═ ═ ......Tunnel
.... On/Off Ramp	.... Footbridge

REGIONAL ROUTES

══════ ....Tollway, Freeway
════ .... Primary Road
════ ...... Secondary Road
════ .... Minor Road

BOUNDARIES

—·—·—·— .... International
—··—··—·· .... State
⊥⊥⊥⊥⊥ .... Cliff
▬▬▬▬ .... Fortified Wall

HYDROGRAPHY

.... River, Creek	◠ ◠ ...Dry Lake; Salt Lake
........................Canal	◉ ↝ ...... Spring; Rapids
.... Lake	◐ ⊣⊢ ◄ .... Waterfalls

TRANSPORT ROUTES & STATIONS

⊢⊢⊢⊢─O─ ....Train	─────⊟ .... Ferry
⊢ + + + ⊢ ·..Underground Train	─────· ....Walking Trail
═══─Ⓜ─ .... Metro	·········· ....Walking Tour
▬▬▬▬ ....Tramway	▨▨▨▨ .... Path
⊪──⊪──⊪──⊪·. Cable Car, Chairlift	▬▬▬ ....Pier or Jetty

AREA FEATURES

▬▬▬ .... Building	▨▨▨ .... Market	⣿⣿ .... Beach	▨▨▨▨ .... Campus
▨ ❈ .... Park, Gardens	◠ .... Sports Ground	+ + + ... Cemetery	⌐⌐ .... Plaza

POPULATION SYMBOLS

◎ **CAPITAL** .... National Capital	● **CITY** .... City	● Village ....Village
◉ **CAPITAL** .... State Capital	● **Town** ....Town	▬▬▬ .... Urban Area

MAP SYMBOLS

● ....Place to Stay	▼ ....Place to Eat	● .... Point of Interest
✚ ⊠ ..... Airfield; Airport	ᗡ .... Dolmuş/Bus Stop	⚲ .... Monument	⬛ ....Post Office
⬛ .. Archaeological Site	◖ .... Embassy	◖ .... Mosque	⬛ ....Pub or Bar
◉ ....Bank	☨ .... Fountain	▲ .... Mountain	▨ .... Shopping Centre
◍ ......Border Crossing	⊓ .... Gate	⊞ .... Museum	▨ ...... Swimming Pool
⬛ ......Cafe; Teahouse	◑ .... Hammam	⬛ .... National Park	◙ .... Synagogue
⬛ .... Camping Area	⬛ ....Historic House	⬛ Otogar (Bus Station)	⬛ ....Taxi Rank
⬛ .... Castle	⊕ .... Hospital	ⓟ .... Parking	◉ ....Telephone
⌂ .... Cave	⬛ .... Internet Cafe	● .... Petrol Station	⬛ .... Temple (Classical)
▬ ⬛ ....Church	◕ .. Islamic Monument	◎ .... Picnic Area	◉ ..Tourist Information
⬛ ⬛ ......Cinema; Theatre	☗ ☀ Lighthouse; Lookout	⬛ .... Police Station	⬛ ....Transport

Note: not all symbols displayed above appear in this book

LONELY PLANET OFFICES

Australia
Locked Bag 1, Footscray, Victoria 3011
☎ 03 9689 4666 fax 03 9689 6833
email: talk2us@lonelyplanet.com.au

UK
10a Spring Place, London NW5 3BH
☎ 020 7428 4800 fax 020 7428 4828
email: go@lonelyplanet.co.uk

USA
150 Linden St, Oakland, CA 94607
☎ 510 893 8555 TOLL FREE: 800 275 8555
fax 510 893 8572
email: info@lonelyplanet.com

France
1 rue du Dahomey, 75011 Paris
☎ 01 55 25 33 00 fax 01 55 25 33 01
email: bip@lonelyplanet.fr
www.lonelyplanet.fr

World Wide Web: www.lonelyplanet.com or AOL keyword: lp
Lonely Planet Images: lpi@lonelyplanet.com.au